A
HISTORY OF
MODERN GERMANY

1840-1945

A
HISTORY OF
MODERN GERMANY
1840-1945

B Y

H A J O H O L B O R N

Princeton University Press
Princeton, New Jersey

Published by Princeton University Press, 41 William Street,
Princeton, New Jersey 08540
In the United Kingdom: Princeton University Press,
Guildford, Surrey
Copyright © 1969 by Hajo Holborn
All rights reserved
First Princeton Paperback printing, 1982

LCC 82-0126
ISBN 0-691-05359-6
ISBN 0-691-00797-7

Printed in the United States of America by
Princeton University Press, Princeton, New Jersey

Reprinted by arrangement with Alfred A. Knopf, Inc.

TO ANNEMARIE

Foreword

T HE PRESENT VOLUME deals with the history of Germany in the period of nationalism and imperialism, from the abortive attempt of popular forces to found a liberal national state and Bismarck's German unification through the Prussian military monarchy to the expansionist programs of the age of William II and Hitler's world conquest. The volume is the third and last one in a series that narrates and analyzes the history of Germany since the end of the Middle Ages. I have ended my book with the catastrophe of 1945, instead of going on to the present. Although the surviving Germany has not broken all her ties with the older German history, the chasm created by the disaster of 1945 has been profound. The loss of one quarter of the territories belonging to the Germany of 1937 and, most of all, the division of Germany into two separate political and social entities together with the radical changes of the European and world scene under which the post-1945 Germany lives have greatly altered conditions, and her brief history cannot be treated as a mere projection of the history of earlier epochs. Moreover in the absence of the intimate sources which we possess for the times before 1945 no historian can claim the opinions which he may form to be critical historical judgments. A selective bibliography of modern German history, prepared by the author, is contained in *A Guide to Historical Literature*, published under the auspices of the American Historical Association by G. F. Howe and others, New York, 1961, pp. 549–66.

I have greatly appreciated the help that I have always received from the members of the College Department of Alfred A. Knopf, Inc. My deepest thanks are due to my wife, Annemarie, who not only took many technical chores from me but was throughout my wisest critic and counselor.

HAJO HOLBORN

New Haven, Connecticut
June 8, 1968

Contents

PART II

The Age of Imperialism, 1871–1945

Contents

Maps

BY THEODORE R. MILLER

PART
I

Liberalism *and* Nationalism 1840–1871

CHAPTER 1

Social and Political Movements, 1830–48

THE DECLINE OF SPECULATIVE IDEALISM, the rise of science, and the spread of positivist and naturalist philosophies that characterized the second third of the nineteenth century in Germany were strongly conditioned by the experience of the social and economic changes taking place in this period. Metternich and the statesmen of the Germanic Confederation had succeeded in subduing the political movements that threatened monarchical government in the wake of the French Revolution. But the political ideas of the French Revolution had been only one aspect of the broad process of social transformation from feudalism to a bourgeois society, and this transformation was not brought to a standstill by the political victories of the rulers of the restoration.

In England feudalism had been waning long before the French Revolution, and the Industrial Revolution had begun its course during the second half of the eighteenth century. In her advanced state of social development England had been relatively immune to direct political influences from France. During the twenty-odd years of war with France after 1792 even ultraconservative political forces could gain strength within England. But, from the 1820's on, the momentum of continuing social change and new economic needs led to the great liberal reform of England's society, economy, and constitution. Although the era of reform was tumultuous, revolution was avoided even in 1848, when the new liberal order was still incomplete and untested. But in the eyes of the British people the reforms accomplished by then augured well for the future of political and social freedom. As in the past, the British parliament seemed an adequate agency for the achievement of national progress. The continental revolutions of 1848–49 had no repercussions in England.

Although in France the continuity of political forms was definitely broken by the Revolution, not only Napoleon but also Louis XVIII accepted the social changes that the Revolution had imposed. In the subsequent revolutions of 1830 and 1848 the new propertied classes asserted their strength against attempts both at social reaction and at radical social subversion. The French bourgeoisie preserved its power in the midst of the transitoriness of French political institutions. This spectacle was the more impressive since the development of modern capitalism proceeded in France more slowly and modestly than in England.

✑ *Economic and Social Forces*

THE ECONOMIC AND SOCIAL FORCES that determined the forward course of English and French history in the first half of the nineteenth century had no counterparts in Germany. The German economy did not experience a very considerable expansion between 1815 and 1848. Even disregarding the years immediately prior to the revolution of 1848, years of special hardship and misfortune, we are driven to conclude that the German people as a whole were economically hardly better off in 1845 than they had been in 1800. To be sure, the losses caused by the Napoleonic wars were made up in the decade after 1815, and production continued to increase thereafter. But economic growth kept barely ahead of the rising population. Between 1815 and 1845 the population of Germany (excluding Austria) grew from 25 to 34.5 million. The German governments were alarmed, and Malthus' predictions about the dire consequences of a multiplying population prompted some of them, chiefly in southern and central Germany, to issue laws making marriages contingent on a means test. These rather ineffective laws, some of which were abolished only after 1867, were signs of prevailing doubts about the chances for an expansion of the economy, and optimism was certainly ill-founded as long as Germany lacked the capital required for any large-scale development.

✑ *Weakening of the Guilds*

BUT EVEN IN GERMANY, where the political restoration seemed to have reestablished the dominant position of the old classes, and economic activity developed at a halting pace, important social and economic shifts occurred. Enlightened despotism had already started undermining some of the institutions that had served as typical forms of organization of economic life for centuries. The support that absolute rulers had given to manufacturers at the expense of the old guilds may serve as an example. But in the period following the French Revolution the governments had gone much further in breaking down the traditional forms of economy by freeing the individual from his corporate ties. In the Rhineland the new French laws concerning landholding and industrial freedom had been fully introduced under French rule, and the German states belonging to the Rhenish Confederation had emulated the French legislation to a greater or lesser extent, while the Stein-Hardenberg reforms in Prussia had created similar conditions.[1] In a number of German states the political reaction after 1815 stopped the movement toward industrial freedom. Hamburg, Mecklenburg, Oldenburg, Hanover, and Hesse-Kassel retained the direction of industrial production by guilds till the middle of the century. But in the rest of Germany progress toward the abolition of guild control started much earlier.

Neither Prussia nor Bavaria ever attempted to revoke the French legislation in the provinces on the left bank of the Rhine that they had acquired in 1815. For Bavaria itself the government in 1825 issued a law that did not abolish guilds but placed them under government direction, thus making a liberal admission policy possible. Prussia was divided into three areas of different industrial laws: the Rhine province and Westphalia, where, as has been mentioned, French laws continued; the eastern provinces as far as they had belonged to Prussia between 1807–14, in which the Stein-Hardenberg reforms became law; and finally the newly acquired eastern provinces, where guild control remained the rule after 1815. In 1845, a single Prussian code leaving only minor functions to the guilds superseded the different practices of the three areas. In many other German states, beginning with Nassau in 1819, the general trend over the whole period ran in the direction of liberal industrial legislation. The preconditions for a new system of production based on factories were thus evolving in most of Germany, and at the same time the guilds were driven on the defensive.

✎ *Agriculture*

IN THE AGRARIAN SECTOR of German society the stage was also prepared for capitalistic enterprise. Here the variety of conditions was enormous. It can be said that as a result of the agrarian reforms in the preceding period the serfdom of peasants had been generally abolished, and individual peasant ownership of land had become the rule. This was, of course, the main entering wedge of individualistic capitalistic enterprise into German agriculture. But the actual realization of the reforms of the early years of the century was only slowly achieved during the years 1815–48. Moreover, many manorial dues and services had not been touched by the agrarian reform legislation in most German states. Nowhere did the emancipation of the peasants improve their economic situation. The

[1] See the author's *A History of Modern Germany: 1648–1840* (New York: Alfred A. Knopf; 1964), pp. 386–7, 395 ff.

transformation of feudal dues and services into money rents was always executed in a manner advantageous to the landowning class.

In the Germany east of the Elbe, as has already been seen,[2] the liberation of the peasants led to the displacement of a substantial section of the East German agrarian population. A large group of landless workers came into being, many of whom eventually drifted into the towns. But even in western and southern Germany, where the agrarian reforms had dealt with servitudes less harsh than those prevailing in the east, the new financial obligations proved onerous and spoiled the joy over any newly gained freedom. Conditions were particularly grim in some parts of the southwest and the Rhineland, where the continuous division of peasant farms had created districts of "dwarf economy." Peasants found even a plough unnecessary for the cultivation of their tiny patches. Only the development of industrial job openings in nearby towns could eventually relieve the poverty of these peasants.

The big landowners alone could take advantage of the opportunities for capitalistic development, which were greatly enhanced by the new agronomic methods learned from England and were subsequently improved by the new German biochemistry. Still, even these opportunities were not immediately available. Grain exports from East Germany to England had been large before Napoleon's Continental System ended this trade. The years 1816–17 were years of disastrous crop failure. The ensuing inflation of agrarian commodity prices produced a large expansion in soil cultivation. The bumper crop of 1818 brought a catastrophic price collapse, which lasted for almost a decade. The calamity would not have been so great if grain exports had fully revived after 1815, but the English corn tariff blocked their full resurrection. Only at the end of the 1830's did the situation of the agrarian producer begin to improve, chiefly on account of the growth of the German market. The abolition of the English corn duties in 1846 finally ushered in the quarter-century of greatest prosperity for German agriculture, between 1850 and 1875.

The checkered history of German agriculture in the first half of the century was full of threats even to the big landowners. Many of them absorbed additional peasant land during the agrarian crisis, and the payments received from those peasants whom the agrarian reform legislation enabled to liquidate dues and services made it possible for the landowners to improve their agricultural equipment, or to start industrial activities, such as sugar refining, brick manufacture, sawmills, or alcohol distilling, on their estates. Yet land prices and mortgages were exaggerated, while anticipated profits were miscalculated, and many failures resulted. One third of the *Junker* estates came into the possession of bourgeois families. Small wonder that not even the noblemen found the liberal economic

[2] See the author's *A History of Modern Germany: 1648–1840*, pp. 408 ff.

system an unmixed blessing and called for protection through legal permission to turn their estates into entailed trusts. On balance, however, the expansion of modern capitalistic methods gave the enterprising and industrious big landowner considerable opportunity for profit. The large groups of East German peasants who were either uprooted or at least made less secure experienced a complete loss of social status. Even in those parts of Germany where this was not true because peasants dominated agriculture, as in Schleswig, western Holstein, or Hanover, they suffered economic hardships due to population pressure. The large-scale emigration of Germans to overseas countries, from the beginning practically confined to North America, began after 1815.[3] But more important was the movement in all parts of Germany from the countryside to the towns and cities.

Internal Migration

WE HAVE no precise knowledge of the character of this movement. Existing statistics are based on a rather meaningless historical distinction between towns and villages, which made one third of the Prussian "towns" consist of places with less than 2,000 inhabitants. Moreover, in this period German towns and villages were not strictly distinguished by the economic pursuits of their inhabitants. Many handicrafts and industries were carried on in the countryside, while even in relatively large towns the number of *Ackerbürger*—"farming burghers"—was not small. Still, some idea of the extent of the internal migration can be gleaned from the fact that whereas in 1815 four out of five Germans lived in rural communities, the ratio was close to two out of three in 1850.

This picture gains greater distinctness when we look at the growth of the most prominent cities. Most notable was the growth of Berlin. In 1815 the Prussian capital had a population of 191,500. It had risen to 231,000 by 1831 and grew at an accelerated rate thereafter to 322,626 in 1840, to 380,103 in 1845, and 403,586 on the eve of the revolution in 1847. (In the

---

[3] The year 1816-17 saw a great wave of German emigration, in which 20,000 Germans went to the United States and probably a number not much smaller to Russia and the Habsburg Empire. Later on the migration to Russia and to European countries became unimportant compared to the overseas migration. After 1820, 85 to 90 per cent of all German emigrants went to the United States. Although United States immigration statistics, which started in 1820, hardly registered all German immigrants, they give a good idea of the growth of German migration. According to them, 7,729 Germans entered the United States in 1820-30; 152,454 in 1831-40; 434,626 in 1841-50. Most of them departed from French and Dutch ports. In the 1850's Bremen and Hamburg begin to predominate. The bulk of the German immigrants came from Württemberg, Baden, and the Palatinate while the number of immigrants from the Rhineland and northwestern Germany was steadily increasing. Emigration from northeastern Germany remained small in the first half of the nineteenth century. About German immigration after 1850 see pp. 122-3, 637-8.

early 1850's Berlin replaced Vienna as the largest German city.) Other German cities showed a similar, if relatively smaller, growth. Hamburg had slightly over 100,000 inhabitants in 1815, 160,000 in 1842; Breslau 76,800 (1817), 114,000 (1850); Königsberg 63,800 (1819), 76,000 (1850); Danzig 52,800 (1817), 66,800 (1846); Cologne, 52,900 (1816), 97,000 (1850); Leipzig 33,800 (1815), 60,000 (1846); Munich 30,000 (1800), 110,000 (1850); Magdeburg 34,600 (1816), 44,700 (1840); Frankfurt 48,000 (1800), 65,000 (1850); Bremen 36,000 (1813), 53,000 (1848); Nürnberg 25,000 (1806), 47,000 (1847).

✎ Decline of the Craft Guilds

TOGETHER WITH THE GROWTH of cities and towns the conditions of the craft guilds were changing. The new industrial freedom enabled many journeymen to settle down as masters, and their number continued to increase after 1815. On the other hand, few of the masters employed journeymen, and even by 1840 the total number of journeymen in Germany was not much larger than that of the masters. Sluggish business by itself would have depressed the situation of artisans, but the rise of the modern industrial system caused even greater hardship. In some crafts the masters had ceased long ago to produce directly for the customer. For example, this had been the case in the linen or cloth industries, but it began to extend to many new fields, such as furniture and garment manufacture. The first big German store selling ready-made dresses opened its doors in Berlin in 1842, at a time when some German governments still suppressed the sale of finished garments to the public. But while the new garment industries continued to rely on the work of individual tailors and only controlled output and prices, other handicrafts were totally replaced by factory production. Many journeymen were forced into factory jobs, others were deprived of work altogether.

The bane of eighteenth-century town life, the existence of a large class of indigent people and beggars, what Karl Marx called the *Lumpenproletariat*, became a still more serious problem in Germany during the new century. Even the masters who managed to survive in the old crafts earned a dwindling livelihood. They were still spoken of as members of the *Mittelstand*, that is, the medium estate of society. But actually they no longer formed the backbone of society. They tended to belong to the lower strata of the middle groups and became true *Kleinbürger*, petty bourgeois.

✍ Growth of Factories

THE GROWTH of the modern factory system, so closely connected with the rise of technology, was slow in Germany in the twenty-five years after 1815. Only with the arrival of the railroad age after 1840 did it begin to gather speed and momentum. Practically all the factories that the governments had created in the period of mercantilism fell victim to the adversities of the war years of 1806–15. The acceptance of the ideas of Adam Smith excluded any determined effort to rebuild industries owned and managed by the state. Only in mining did direct state activity remain considerable. The effects on industrial activities of Napoleon's policies had not been altogether negative. The German territories on the left bank of the Rhine had benefited from the French annexation, which opened to them the opportunities that a rich national market offered. In this French period the region around Aachen and Eschweiler as well as the Saar district began to lay the foundations for their modern industrial development. The German territories on the right bank of the Rhine that belonged to the Rhenish Confederation were economically separated from France by a moderate tariff, but the Continental System protected them against British competition.[4] The industries of the grand duchy of Berg, which included the major part of the modern Ruhr district, derived substantial gains from these circumstances, and the Rhineland both west and east of the Rhine was able to preserve its improved level of production after 1815, when English imports flooded continental markets.

The Continental System had, however, raised havoc with the economy of central and eastern Germany. Here, too, the exclusion of British products had increased the opportunities of one or the other industry, but this was only a temporary growth, and with the exception of mining in Upper Silesia all industries suffered profoundly from the restoration of English competition in 1815. Some industries, such as the silk and the wool-cloth manufacture of Brandenburg, begun and nurtured with such care by Frederick William and Frederick the Great, were practically destroyed. They had relied to a large extent on export to foreign markets which had fallen into British hands. Furthermore, the introduction of high Russian tariffs in 1820 also interfered with German exports to Poland and Russia, and a good many Silesian weavers saw no other way of survival but migration and settlement in Poland. Not even the German home market was secure. Since English production methods were vastly superior, British textile goods successfully invaded Germany and placed the very existence of German textile industries in jeopardy.

The adjustment to the new conditions after 1815 was slow and painful.

[4] See the author's *A History of Modern Germany: 1648–1840*, p. 383.

At first it led to the growing dependence of artisans on commercial entrepreneurs. These might have reorganized production by a change-over from the domestic system to the machine-driven factory system. But capital was scarce and machines were expensive, since they had to be imported, often together with an engineer who could instruct Germans in their maintenance. Still, the number of machines increased over the years. Cotton-spinning, which lacked a continuous tradition in Germany, was practically never carried on by handlooms and in private domestic production. But in wool and linen the transition was extremely slow. In 1837 Prussia had only 421 steam engines of 7,507 h.p.; in 1846, 1,139 of 21,176 h.p. In the latter year all of Saxony possessed 197 steam engines with 2,446 h.p.; Berlin in 1849, 113 with 1,265 h.p. Yet these were still few and puny. In Prussia less than half of the machines were used in mining, nearly a quarter in metal and machine industries. Except for textile manufacture, mining was the chief economic activity in which capitalist organization began its progress at the expense of the customary corporate forms of handicraft production. In the 1840's the machine in-dustry assumed a growing significance.

∽ The Arrival of the Railroad Age

THE DEVELOPMENT of machine-building was boosted by the coming of the railroad age. One may see a prelude to it in the importation of steamboats for use on German rivers after 1815, when for the first time an English steamboat had ventured up the Rhine to Cologne. In these years the Rhine became again the great waterway of Germany, after the French administration had swept away all the artificial impediments and restric-tions by which rapacious princes had choked the river traffic. Mainz and Cologne had claimed absolute staple rights, which meant that all goods had to be unloaded. From Strasbourg to the Netherlands, ships paid tolls at thirty-two stations. The Congress of Vienna had provided for freedom of navigation on the common German rivers but had left the execution to the riparian states. Conventions governing the navigation on the Elbe and Weser were concluded in 1821. The river states failed to grant other states freedom of navigation and reserved many of their own sovereign rights, which, among other things, prohibited common planning for river regulation and improvement.

The negotiations of a Rhine convention proved very difficult, since the Netherlands attempted to make the most of their control of the Rhine estuary. In the Rhine Navigation Act of 1831 the Netherlands retained the right to levy duties, but all restrictions on navigation were removed, and the new steamship companies, of which the first had been founded in Cologne in 1826, were able to expand their activities. Passenger traffic predominated in the successful business of these companies in the 1830's, but in the next decade freight barge traffic flourished, due to the tugs of the new towage companies. The rise of these capitalist and competitive companies destroyed the work of the old boatmen's guilds along all the German rivers. It was a classic example of the displacement of an old craft by the machine age.

The lively expansion of river navigation, which was greatest on the Rhine, was halted by the growth of railroads prior to the middle of the century. The inland waterways of Germany were to achieve substantial increases in transportation again only late in the century. Railroad-building was originally delayed by the resistance of the German governments. The first German railroad of 1835, not much more than a suburban line extending for a length of eight miles between Nürnberg and Fürth, was initiated by a group of merchants of the former imperial city in order to demonstrate the feasibility of railroads. The technical and financial success of this enterprise contributed to the ultimate victory of the champions of the railroad. But the pleas of farsighted advocates for building according to a national plan remained unfulfilled. Provincial interests and ideas were decisive in the early period of railroad-building. Nevertheless, before long the nation was joined by iron links. The first German railroad line of major consequence was the line from Dresden to Leipzig, built 1837–39 and extended to Magdeburg in the following year. By that time an almost feverish building activity had started in various parts of Germany. A Berlin-Potsdam railroad was completed in 1838, Berlin-Anhalt in 1841, Berlin-Stettin in 1842, Berlin-Frankfurt on the Oder in 1842, while Berlin-Hamburg followed in 1846. The line between Cologne and Aachen, completed in 1838, was particularly important, since it could be connected with Antwerp (five years later), thereby breaking the Dutch monopoly over the Rhineland's access to the sea. The connection between the Rhine and Weser was only created in 1847, and in the following year the link was established that made it possible to go by train from Berlin to Cologne. In 1847 both German port cities, Hamburg and Bremen, were connected with Hanover and thus gained easy access to a wide hinterland.

The Germany east of the Oder saw no railroad-building in the 1840's. Only the Oder valley itself was opened for railroad traffic. In southern Germany the upper Rhine railroad was begun in 1843, and by 1847 Frankfurt and Basel were connected. Smaller lines, such as Munich-Augsburg or Bamberg-Nürnberg, came into being in Bavaria during these same years. By 1848, the then existing German railroads radiated from a number of regional centers, such as Berlin, Leipzig, Hanover, Hamburg, Cologne, Frankfurt, and Munich. Only in the subsequent twenty to twenty-five years were these lines fully knit together. But the achievement of the 1840's was truly remarkable; it placed Germany ahead of France in railroad-building.

This was especially impressive since the majority of the railroads were built by private financiers. Prussia favored private companies, although it was later forced to construct state railroads as well because no private capital could be found for the building of railroads in East Germany. In Bavaria the development was the opposite. Here the government in the beginning was determined to maintain strict state ownership but in a later period left the building of most East Bavarian lines to private interests. Baden from the outset followed the example that Belgium had set by the creation of her national rail system. Still, as late as 1870, only somewhat more than half of the German railroads were state-owned.

About 800 million marks had been invested in German railroads by 1851. Obviously the greater portion of the capital came from foreign sources. Most of the equipment, particularly engines and rails, had to come originally from abroad, primarily from England, but also from Belgium and the United States. Yet the influence of railroad-building on the German economy was tremendous. It created work for many people. Incidentally, never before had such large numbers of people been massed together for industrial purposes, and railroad construction greatly stimulated the building of hard-surface roads as well. But most important was the upsurge in the production of coal, iron, and machines. Most of the big machine factories of modern Germany originated in this period. In 1837 August Borsig opened a workshop in Berlin. Using an American model, he produced his first railroad engine four years later. By 1848 he could fill almost the whole demand of the Prussian railroads. At the same time, Josef Anton Maffei founded his factory in Munich and Emil Kessler the machine works in Karlsruhe and Esslingen. In 1848 the first engine, the "Dragon," left the Henschel works in Kassel. By the middle of the 1850's German industries not only totally supplied German railroads but also began to export.

✍ *The Prussian Customs Union*

THE PRUSSIAN CUSTOMS UNION of 1834 assumed a new significance in the railroad age. The railroad planners usually underrated the possibilities of an expanded freight traffic. A young Prussian army major, Helmuth von Moltke, who invested his small savings in the Berlin-Hamburg Railroad Company, was one of the few to emphasize this aspect in public, as, no doubt, he meditated on the potential use of railroads in warfare. The results of such military study, however, were to be applied only twenty years later in Moltke's conduct of the wars of German unification. What the railroads immediately did was to turn the area of the German Customs Union into a common market. The wide and greatly intensified exchange of goods quickened industrial production. It was, for example, of fundamental importance that coal, so far mined in Germany for local use, became available everywhere. Only in conjunction with the railroads did the customs union become a powerful, dynamic influence on German economic life.

The railroad industry played its part in displacing such old trades as the guilds of livery and coachmen and the business of many innkeepers. Most important, however, in the long run, was the impact of the railroad industry on the basic organization of large-scale economic enterprise. The capital required for railroad construction could be mobilized only through the creation of stock companies, and this led to entirely new forms of banking and finance.

✍ *Banking and Finance*

THE BANKING BUSINESS in Germany, with the exception of some state-controlled banks of issue in Prussia, Saxony, Bavaria, and Hamburg, was still exclusively in the hands of private bankers. Almost all banks were very small firms, and often merchants carried on banking as a sideline. Money exchange and deposits, together with personal credit, formed the main lines of activity. As late as 1860, the merchants of Hamburg and Bremen found it detrimental to their reputation to discount bills of exchange with bankers. Larger banking developed early in the century only in connection with the management of the fortunes of princes or of state loans. Prior to 1815 the firm of Simon Moritz von Bethmann in Frankfurt had placed most of the many Austrian loans. It remained one of the most prominent German houses in the period thereafter, when the Rothschilds rose to greater fame and power. Amschel Meyer Rothschild, who died in 1812, had started his career in the fashion of an eighteenth-century *Hofjude*,[5] managing the financial properties of the landgrave of Hesse. By sending his sons to London, Paris, Naples, and Vienna he had been able to conduct the big financial operations required by the wartime needs of the various states. During the Wars of Liberation the Rothschilds lent their services chiefly to the allied states and subsequently backed the restoration of the monarchies. But well into the 1850's they concentrated on public finance and neglected industrial investment.

The financing of railroads called for a type of bank that would form new capital by collecting small savings and deposits and would make such capital available for investment. The classic model for this type of bank, in its turn organized as a stock company, was the *Crédit Mobilier* of Paris, founded by the Pereire brothers. In Germany, the first bank company

[5] See the author's *A History of Modern Germany: 1648–1840*, p. 287.

combining the deposit and industrial investment business was the *Schaaff-hausensche Bankverein* of Cologne, established by Gustav Mevissen in 1848. In the years after 1851 some larger establishments followed. But the decisive role that the railroads played in the growth of industrial and banking companies can be seen in the fact that as late as 1870 half of all the issues traded at the Berlin stock exchange were railroad stocks.

✍ *Economic Crisis*

THE RAILROAD DEVELOPMENT of the 1840's was proof of the existence of an active and bold entrepreneurial spirit. It contributed much to the transformation of the methods of business organization and production, although for the time being it failed to make Germany a prosperous country. Just at the moment when German industries began to become capable of producing the major part of railroad equipment at home, and when ways for assuming a large share of the financing of railroads from German sources were being developed, the economic crisis of 1846–47 worsened the situation of the masses. The German crisis of these years was not the result of an international business cycle, since Germany was not yet part of a world economy. The severe crisis that the English economy went through in 1847 as a result of industrial overexpansion had little effect on Germany. Only ten years later a world-wide economic crisis engulfed Germany for largely identical reasons.

The German crisis of the late 1840's did not even originate in the industrial sector, but started, as in all preceding centuries, with the misfortunes of agriculture. A blight destroyed the potato crop of 1845 all over northern Europe, and in 1846 both the potato and grain crops were largely ruined by weather conditions. The customs union, normally a heavy exporter of grain, was compelled to import large amounts of grain in 1846–47, but distribution proved difficult, particularly in regions hit hardest by famine, such as East Prussia and Upper Silesia, which lacked proper communications. In addition the cost proved forbidding. The general shortage drove the price of staple foods up by 50 per cent. The distress suffered by the poor in rural districts was grave, but the privations of the urban poor were even more serious. The crisis made it impossible for many peasants to keep up their compensatory payments for liberation from feudal dues or for mortgages. The flight from the countryside to the cities increased, only to swell the number of the unemployed, which was growing at the same time on account of the journeymen who were losing their jobs in the depression. In 1846 the number of emigrants to the New World jumped to 93,000 and in the following year went beyond 100,000 for the first time.

Yet compared to the masses of suffering people this emigration was

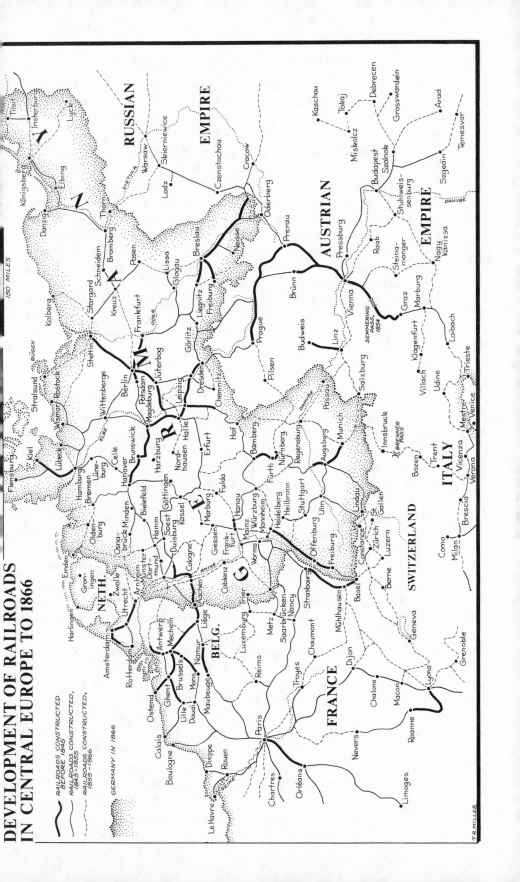

DEVELOPMENT OF RAILROADS
IN CENTRAL EUROPE TO 1866

150 MILES

RAILROADS CONSTRUCTED
BEFORE 1845

RAILROADS CONSTRUCTED,
1845–1855

RAILROADS CONSTRUCTED,
1855–1866

GERMANY IN 1866

RUSSIAN EMPIRE

AUSTRIAN EMPIRE

FRANCE

SWITZERLAND

ITALY

BELG.

NETH.

T. R. MILLER

small. Crime spread in city and country, and a spirit of violence added embitterment to the popular riots, which became more frequent than before. The most ominous event was the "potato revolution" in Berlin. On April 21, 1847, the mob plundered the food stands on the public market squares, and fighting with troops developed, which lasted for three days. These events confirm the observation that can be made with regard to the earlier period as well, namely, that the spirit of revolt ripened among the impoverished artisans and jobless journeymen sooner than among any other group. The most serious outbreak of violence in the 1840's, made famous half a century later by Gerhard Hauptmann's play, *The Weavers*, was the revolt of the Silesian weavers of the Eulengebirge. A few thousand strong, they burned and looted the houses of their hated employers. There is no doubt that the weavers were inhumanly exploited, but the old linen industry operating as domestic industry, with the individual families working at handlooms, was actually moribund because it could not compete with modern mechanical cotton manufacture.

✎ Industrial Development

THE MODERN or, as in the case of mining, modernized industries developed steadily and maintained their employment even during the depression of the late 1840's. The chief regions of industrial development were the Rhineland and Saxony, but in addition to the Upper Silesian mining district a number of individual cities became industrial centers—Berlin, the most important, and, on a smaller scale, Nürnberg, Mannheim, Esslingen (near Stuttgart), and Magdeburg. It is impossible to determine how many factory workers existed in Germany by the end of the 1840's. Their number has been estimated at 4 per cent of the population or one third of the nonagricultural labor force. But these figures are probably greatly exaggerated, since the official statistics counted as factories many establishments that had not outgrown the size and character of handicraft shops. Even the modern factories were small. Machine-building plants in Prussia and Saxony employing 250 workers then belonged to the large firms. Alfred Krupp (1812–87), whose father started the family business in 1819, employed only 140 workers in 1846. In 1840, the average Prussian mine employed about forty miners.

Even in the centers of the new industrialism the industrial proletariat was small. Working conditions were bad, often outrageous. Unhygienic rooms, high exposure to accidents, endless hours of work, and, worst of all, personal insecurity under the arbitrary regime of tyrannic entrepreneurs were common features of this early industrialism. Women and children were employed as widely as possible to keep labor costs low.

The truck system, under which workers were paid in commodities the value of which was stipulated by the employer, was widespread. Concern about the physical fitness of army recruits was a factor in causing the Prussian government to issue in 1839 the first piece of social legislation. The employment of children under nine years of age was forbidden, and children under sixteen were permitted to work no more than ten hours a day. The regulations of 1839 also envisaged some health supervision for industrial workers. But since no proper methods for enforcing these rules were created, it is doubtful whether they were of great practical consequence outside the state mines.

✍ Workers and Artisans

IN GERMANY, the incipient industrialization produced about the same misery and moral devastation as in England. However, the fact that industrialization proceeded at a slower pace and affected a smaller segment of society than in England allowed the German situation to appear in a slightly better light. Not everything was bad in the development of industry. It should not be forgotten that the lot of the agrarian workers and of most artisans was hardly any better than that of the industrial workers. On the contrary, among the latter were groups that enjoyed higher wages and steadier work than the artisans. Conditions were worst in those fields where the new industries developed on the ruins of broken-down handicraft production, as many branches of the textile industries did. Political restlessness was not found so much among the German factory workers, a class still relatively small and lacking in a common consciousness, as among the impoverished German artisans.

The distinction between artisans and factory workers should not be drawn too sharply, but it can be said without reservation that nowhere in Germany in 1848 was popular revolutionary action originally started by the workers of the modern factories. Not even Marx and Engels claimed that the German revolution of 1848–49 was a proletarian revolution, but they always spoke of it rather contemptuously as a result of the petty bourgeoisie. The *Communist Manifesto* of February, 1848, did not cause the slightest ripple in Germany, because the sentiment of the artisans never ran in the direction of Marxist socialism. As a matter of fact, the thinking of the artisans, whether profitably employed, unemployed, or driven into factory work, in all these years tended to be conservative and even reactionary. Quite naturally they saw in the decline of the guild system and in the growth of mechanical production the real bane of the time. They demanded from the governments the restriction of industrial freedom and the restoration of the corporate privileges of the guilds. No doubt there was a difference between masters and journeymen, insofar as the latter wanted to see the paternalistic power of the masters reduced, but even journeymen and apprentices were strict believers in the guild system and opponents of industrial freedom.

Since they expected that the old governments would assist them in their plight and restore the old corporate order, the artisans and workers were not attracted by ideas of political and constitutional change. These were the ideas of the champions and beneficiaries of industrial freedom, the manufacturers, bankers, lawyers, and other members of the upper middle classes. The workers had their eyes on concrete material advantages, such as better wages, job opportunities, and job security. In the 1840's a very small fringe of the workers, characteristically mostly artisans, turned toward violent communist ideas. Migratory journeymen came in contact with modern socialist ideas in Paris. Among them was Wilhelm Weitling (1808–71), a tailor from Magdeburg, who absorbed the socialism of Fourier and preached by word and writing a Christian communism reminiscent of the radical religious sects of the sixteenth century. But communism or socialism—the words were then still used synonymously—appealed only to a negligible minority.

Yet, disinclined as the workers seemed over many years to cooperate with the liberals in their demands for the reform of government, the continually negative response of the autocratic governments to the petitions of the guilds finally drove the masses into an attitude of hostility against the existing authorities. The economic crisis after 1845, when the governments failed so conspicuously to mitigate misery and starvation and when at the same time the liberal agitation among the bourgeoisie assumed a more radical note, changed the mood of the masses. On the eve of the revolution of 1848 they were united with the liberals in a deep distrust of rule by princes, soldiers, and bureaucrats. Although an identity of political aims and interests was not thereby established, common political action for a change of national conditions became at least temporarily possible.

✍ *The Rise of Capitalists*

THE ECONOMIC DEVELOPMENTS of the period before 1848 made possible the rise of a group of capitalists in German society. It would probably be wrong to speak of them in this period as a new class, for most of them were still anchored in the traditional social structure. In East Prussia capitalist enterprise grew up almost entirely on the basis of an agrarian economy linked to an international market. Prussian *Junkers* played the dominant role in the exploitation of these opportunities, and few of them were willing to part with their old class, even though they might somewhat deviate in their political ideas from the old country squires. In

Upper Silesia it was largely the nobility that directed the industrialization of the district, practically as a mere extension of the management of their old estates. In most of Germany the rebuilding of merchants' fortunes was achieved chiefly by the traditional methods of trading. Bold capitalistic ventures were frowned upon even in those places that were in closest contact with the economic and political conditions of England and America.

Hamburg and, even more so, Bremen could rebuild and advance their commercial position after 1815 to a large extent by beginning trade with America. Still excluded from trading in the British Empire, the Hanseatic cities became the managers of trade between Germany and the United States. The trade treaty of 1827 between the United States and Hamburg and Bremen served for almost a century as the legal framework for the commercial relations of the two nations. But in this early period the exchange of goods was limited chiefly to the importation of raw materials, such as cotton and tobacco. The dearth of German industrial products capable of competing on the American market would have made westbound voyages unprofitable if German shippers could not have carried the human cargo of emigrants. The economic activities of the two cities in this age could still be carried on without requiring any radical changes of traditional business methods or political organization. Both Hamburg and Bremen were still completely ruled by merchant aristocracies cultivating a patrician conservatism in political and economic affairs. Their republicanism as well as their connection with world trade, which were unusual in Germany, tended to strengthen their localism. However, there were signs in the 1840's of new trends of thought. The younger generation nurtured bolder projects in foreign trade and was more conscious of the cities' dependence on the future of Germany as a whole. The resilience shown by Hamburg in the repair of the terrible losses that it suffered by the fire of 1842, when one fifth of the city was left in ashes, betrayed some of the latent sources of future development.

With the growth of industries in western Germany their founders acquired social prominence. The members of this first generation of German industrialists came from all classes and occupations. Former merchants were strongly represented in the textile industries, whereas in the machine industries and all those industries dependent on new inventions, former artisans were numerous. It has already been mentioned that even with regard to size most of the new factories were not yet much more than overgrown artisans' shops. Some of the old suspicion of the artisan against the merchant as the clever profiteer from the honest work of the craftsman lingered on. Even in much later years Alfred Krupp shunned the financiers. Among the leading Rhenish businessmen of this period the capitalistic motive was often strongly tempered by other sentiments.

Friedrich Harkort (1793–1880), who in 1819 founded his factory on the Ruhr, which combined iron production and machine manufacture and was later connected with many other enterprises, such as railroads and steamship lines, was almost more a patriotic industrial educator than a capitalist entrepreneur. In the tradition of Baron Stein, this Westphalian propagated initiative and self-reliance of free citizens as the lifeblood of a healthy community. A feeling of nationalism was also present in Harkort. An admirer of English political institutions, he resented the commercial and industrial monopoly of contemporary England. While he could start his own industries only with the help of English engineers and foremen, he longed for the day when German industries would be fully independent of English industries. Gustav Mevissen (1815–99), one of the foremost founders of the modern Rhenish economy in industry and finance, began his career strongly influenced by Saint-Simonism and temporarily cooperated with Karl Marx on the editorial board of the *Rheinische Zeitung*. Others of the leading Rhenish merchants, such as David Hansemann (1790–1864) in Aachen, Ludolf Camphausen (1803–90) in Cologne, Hermann Beckerath (1808–74) in Krefeld, or August von der Heydt (1801–74) in Elberfeld, were less reserved in their conviction that the untrammeled pursuit of capitalistic enterprise would in the end produce only benefits to all social classes.

On a national scale the rising group of capitalists and industrialists was small and far from homogeneous. The problems with which they struggled were quite different in the various regions of Germany, and it was only natural that they failed to formulate strong common political beliefs. Prior to the late 1840's they were not even inclined to work out the rational framework of a national economic policy, as their reaction to the activities of Friedrich List (1789–1846) demonstrated.

✑ *Friedrich List*

FRIEDRICH LIST was born in the imperial city of Reutlingen, which was incorporated into Württemberg during the Napoleonic period, and burgher pride as well as love of Germany accompanied him throughout his life. After a few years as a professor in Tübingen, he aroused the anger of the Württemberg government through his advocacy of customs legislation by the Germanic Confederation. Deprived of his academic post and eventually jailed as a "demagogue," he was "pardoned" in 1825 on condition of emigrating to America. He was active in the United States as a journalist and businessman, but though not unsuccessful, he was driven back by nostalgia. Protected by the title of United States consul, he came to Leipzig in 1832 and began at once a lively agitation for his economic ideas, which had been confirmed by his American experiences.

A true son of eighteenth-century Enlightenment, List remained animated by humanitarian and cosmopolitan ideals. But he was also a pupil of romanticism in his historical thinking and a precursor of the later nineteenth century in his admiring recognition of material success. Given to politics rather than to systematic scholarship, he nevertheless had fruitful general insights into the nature of economic life. Though he shared with Adam Smith the hope that the evolution of economic forces would and should lead to a harmonious world economy, he did not think that the simple adoption of free trade could lead to this ideal state. In the present circumstances, he argued, it would lead to English world domination, since the advanced state of the English economy would overwhelm all other less developed economies. Only national economies that had reached an equal state of development could enter upon free competition. List designed not only a theory of the evolutionary stages through which economics would pass but also a theory of the conditions which promote the healthy growth of the "productive forces" of an economy. For List the aim was the achievement of an equilibrium of agrarian, commercial, and industrial productivity, and the way to this goal was the education of the people as well as the creation of incentives that state policy could provide by the imposition of a protective or—as List preferred to say—"educational" tariff. He pointed out that English commerce and industry had been nursed by the Navigation Act in the past and that English agriculture was still protected by duties on grain.

List insisted that the component entities of a future world economy were the economies of nations. Their internal unity demanded the abolition of all domestic barriers, but their foreign economic policy was a function of the historical stage that they had reached in their evolution. List's most important and mature work bore the title of *The National System of Political Economy* (1840). It reflected his experiences in the United States, where the speedy growth of a national economy was promoted by the complete absence of internal restrictions and the simultaneous protection against English competition. America had also given List a sense of the large dimensions of modern economic structures. The Prussian Customs Union appeared too small to exist safely among the British Empire and a growing United States and Russia. List wanted to see all of Germany and the whole Habsburg Empire brought into an economic union. He called this metamorphosis of the old German Empire *Mitteleuropa*.

Such were the general ideas which the fiery Swabian propagated through speeches and publications. At the same time, he tried to persuade the German business world that railroads, as he learned in America, were the most powerful agents in the promotion of industry. He drafted a well-designed plan for a national German railroad system and took a hand in organizing a company that was to finance the chief Saxon line, thought to be central in this system. This line was actually built, although List was excluded from its direction. But all his other projects came to naught. Despondent over the hostile reaction to his ideas, List died by his own hand in 1846.

It was not so surprising that List's practical proposals met with defeat in these years, for he challenged many of the dominant economic forces in Germany. But it was revealing that his conception of the nation as an economic unit did not elicit from any of these groups any comparable attempt to formulate an alternative program of a national economic policy. As it happened, the Prussian Customs Union introduced moderate import duties on iron and textiles in 1844. Yet even more important was the abolishment of the English corn tariff, in the year of List's death, which settled for a long time the ascendancy of economic liberalism in Germany. List's ideas, however, were to come to life again after the political unification of Germany had been achieved.

✑ *Political Movements*

AFTER 1846 the new capitalist elements of German society moved somewhat closer together, but they were united by their defensive attitude toward bureaucratic supervision and intrusiveness rather than by a clear and positive political program. Prior to 1850 the formulation of general political ideas was almost exclusively the work of intellectuals, whose activities centered mostly around the universities. Although these universities were state institutions, the continuous exchange of students and professors among them made them in practice national establishments. The suppression of academic freedom that the Karlsbad Decrees[6] had inaugurated caused much resentment in university circles, but radical opposition did not survive except in small students' groups. Professors, as state appointees, were dependent upon the state; so also were the students, most of whom wished to enter the civil service or make a career in the professions, which were strictly supervised by the governments.

Freelance writers, however, did not have to rely on income from government sources, and the growth of newspapers in Germany provided an outlet for an increasing number of intellectuals who were excluded from the civil service or the old professions. It was not surprising that among the literati and journalists Jewish graduates were particularly numerous, since even in the states where they had been given equal civil rights, Jews were still not admitted to public offices, including teaching posts, unless

[6] See the author's *A History of Modern Germany: 1648–1840*, pp. 466–8.

they converted to Christianity. Press and publishing were under the closest governmental supervision, and it was easy to run afoul of censorship. On this count, the division of Germany proved a blessing, since the censorship was very differently handled in the different states. Moreover, in such conditions readers learn to understand even muted innuendoes or remote analogies, and while the censorship was relentless in suppressing or coloring German news, it interfered little with reports of events in foreign countries.

✎ *Western European Influences*

GERMAN READERS followed the political events and debates of Western Europe with deep interest. From the observation of the advanced social and economic development of England and France the Germans hoped to gain some knowledge of the potential consequences of the new economy, which existed in Germany only in embryonic form. The rise of liberalism in Western Europe gave the opposition elements in Germany encouragement and ideas in their attempts to overcome German absolutism. Although it is true that the models presented by England, France, and Belgium were too variegated to produce a uniform reaction in Germany, German liberal and democratic thought could not have sprung up as fast as it did between 1830 and 1848 without these examples. The year 1830 marked the decisive beginning of an opposition movement in Germany. The revolutions in France, Belgium, and Poland created a threat to the whole international and internal order of Europe as it had been established by the Congress of Vienna. But the danger of a general war passed by. The regime of Louis Philippe was recognized by the great powers and so was the new kingdom of Belgium. The principle of the sovereignty of the people was vindicated by these events, and liberalism gained great victories, though in both France and Belgium the revolutions ushered in merely the rule of the high bourgeoisie. England followed the liberal trend by the Reform Bill of 1832.

The similarity of social and political conditions helped to cement Anglo-French cooperation in international affairs. Diverging interests and the eruption of antagonistic popular sentiment still caused occasional friction between the two Western nations, but the Concert of Europe thereafter remained divided into a Western and an Eastern group, a situation that was bound to lend encouragement to the internal opposition in the Eastern world. Still, for the time being the three Eastern monarchies were able to weather the shock of the revolutions of 1830 without any noticeable diminution of their external and internal power. Russia reconquered Poland in months of bloody fighting and declared that by its revolt the Polish nation had forfeited all rights of special political institutions which the Congress of Vienna had promised the unhappy Poles. Both Prussia and Austria gave at least indirect assistance to Russia's war in Poland by holding armies ready in their own Polish territories in order to guard against the extension of the revolt beyond Russian Poland. In the meantime Austrian troops quelled revolts that had flared up in Italy. Yet neither Austria nor Prussia was faced with unrest in its German lands.

⌒ Repercussions of Revolutions of 1830

IN SOME of the lesser German states, however, the foreign revolutions caused strong repercussions. In Brunswick indignant citizens drove the ruling Duke Karl, a mad and brutal tyrant, out of the land, and the princes of the Germanic Confederation felt sufficiently embarrassed by this rascally confrère to forget the inviolability of the legitimate order. Karl's younger brother William became duke and gave the small state a constitution. In Hesse-Kassel an angry popular movement demanded the end of the despotic and corrupt regime of the degenerate Elector William. A liberal constitution, the work of a professor at the Hessian university of Marburg, Sylvester Jordan, was adopted, and the heir to the throne made a co-regent. Unfortunately, the troubles of the country were far from over. Prince Frederick William was as repulsive a character as his father. As soon as the general climate in Germany favored the reactionary forces again, the government began to disregard and undermine the constitution, and the Hessian people continued to suffer under the lawlessness of their rulers.

Rumblings among the populace induced the governments of Saxony and Hanover, the two largest North German states aside from Prussia, to reform their constitutions. Minister Bernhard von Lindenau prevailed upon the senescent King Anton of Saxony to accept his nephew Frederick August (King Frederick August II, 1836–54) as co-regent. The old estates agreed to the new constitution of September 1831, and in the following decade the able Saxon bureaucracy initiated many administrative reforms. Although the Saxon constitution, like those of Brunswick and Hesse-Kassel, was more or less identical with the South German constitutions of 1814–20, it signified politically a greater departure from existing conditions. For the southern states entered upon the constitutional age after certain more basic reforms, such as equality before the law, equal taxation, or a single financial administration of the state, had already been introduced by the legislation of the French period. In contrast, many institutions and practices of the feudal past had still to be cleared away when the North German constitutions were introduced.

Hanover, in spite of its connection with Great Britain, had institutions as old-fashioned as those in Saxony. Only the aftermath of the French Revolution terminated the rule of the Hanoverian nobility, which was dominant not only in the country itself but also in the German Chancellery in London, on which the king of England depended for his information. Now William IV appointed the duke of Cambridge as viceroy, and together with the old estates the constitution of 1833 was worked out. The Hanover constitution was the most modest of all the German constitutions, but considering the somewhat delayed social and political development of the German northwest, it could have been the right beginning for a steady evolution of public life. Yet almost from the start the future was under a cloud, since Duke Ernst August of Cumberland, heir to the throne, indicated his displeasure with the new policy.

The introduction of constitutions in the most important of the northern German states apart from Prussia brought the popular movement of the north and south of Germany closer together. But even within the southern states the differences of aims and methods were great. The most active agitation centered in the southwest. Swiss democratic newspapers were easily circulated, and the influence of neighboring France was great. The Diet of Baden of 1831 had a liberal majority, and the government had to make a good many concessions, among which a liberal censorship law was the most popular measure. In Bavaria, however, King Ludwig I was unwilling to compromise. As a matter of fact, after 1830 he showed increasing animosity against the constitution as a shackle on monarchical power. Popular feeling against the antiliberal policy of the Bavarian government was welling up most strongly in the remote western Bavarian province, the Palatinate of the left bank of the Rhine, which had been French for practically twenty years and continued to like the internal reforms of the French period. No doubt, the Palatines gladly saw the French prefects go, but they were not happy to see Bavarian instead of indigenous officials appointed. Oppressive taxation was maintained, in spite of the depressed condition of the economy, which was choked by all-around trade barriers.

✑ *The Hambach Meeting*

THE PALATINATE became the breeding ground of political radicalism. The contacts with France were close, particularly with the democratic groups of Alsace. When in the winter of 1831–32 thousands of Polish soldiers, together with many hundreds of the Polish gentry and intelligentsia, fled to Central and Western Europe, they were enthusiastically greeted as fighters for freedom by most German liberals, but particularly so in the Palatinate. The radical movement formed the Patriotic Press Association, which was composed of democratic journalists and managed to spread the idea of such an association to other parts of Germany, even to the Germans residing in Paris. This group hatched the plan of a celebration greater than many others held at that time, when political meetings of the people were forbidden. The celebration, intended as a national demonstration, was declared to be in celebration of the anniversary of the Bavarian constitution. The plan succeeded beyond the boldest expectations of its authors, among whom J. A. G. Wirth (1798–1848) and Philipp Siebenpfeiffer (1789–1846) were the chief leaders. At least 25,000 to 30,000 people from the Palatinate, Baden, Hesse, Nassau, and Alsace as well as small numbers from more distant provinces came together at Hambach on May 26–27, 1832. It was an amazing assembly in an age of limited transportation. For the first time in German history women were invited to a political meeting and participated in large numbers. The use of black, red, and gold colors of the students' unions as emblems of the gathering crowd made them the colors of the popular movement in Germany.

Very radical speeches were made in Hambach against the German princes and the German nobility. But the idea of national unity dominated all other arguments. The German princes were accused of being responsible for the division and the ensuing weakness of Germany. They were declared guilty, too, of abusing German national power in order to increase the suppression of nations in Europe. The realization of the sovereignty of the people would restore a healthy Germany and also replace the existing "league of princes" by a peaceful "league of nations." While Siebenpfeiffer counted chiefly on the cooperation of France, Germany, and Poland, Wirth emphasized that each nation must win its national freedom by its own efforts. He took strong exception to any consideration of French assistance in the establishment of German democracy, because it would necessitate the further loss of Rhenish territory, a crime to which no German should become an accessory. Wirth ended his speech with a salute to the "united free states of Germany" and to a "confederate republican Europe."

Strong as the democratic note sounded in all the declarations of Hambach, the prominence given to the expression of national sentiment left no room for the discussion of concrete grievances which the people felt against the governments of the states. Many believed that freedom had to be won in the states. The members of the South German parliaments were not impressed by the Hambach events. The intellectual leader of the Baden liberals, Carl Rotteck (1775–1840), went so far as to state "I prefer liberty without national unity to unity without liberty." But the leaders of the May Day celebration at Hambach also failed to reach any agreement on an action program. The prevailing opinion assumed that moral appeals would suffice for the eventual achievement of democracy. Not everybody, however, was so easily comforted, and it was quite obvious that the reactionary governments were preparing to suppress the popular movement through the German Confederation.

✍ *The Frankfurt* Putsch

THE HAMBACH CELEBRATION had a strange aftermath in the Frankfurt *Putsch* of April 3, 1833. It originated with groups of the students' unions, which had revived after the French July Revolution. The hope of starting a general revolution in Germany by the seizure of the guard house in Frankfurt, the seat of the Germanic Confederation, was childish, and the plot, in which a few dozen students were involved, failed miserably. It may be noted as a sidelight that some of these students made notable careers in Germany and America in their later years.

✍ *The Cause of Reaction*

THE AUSTRIAN AND PRUSSIAN GOVERNMENTS had been deliberating since 1831 on how to suppress the liberal and democratic movements—called by Metternich simply "the party of subversion." In June 1832 the Germanic Confederation decreed strict limitations on the authority of the existing parliaments and on freedom of the press. After the Frankfurt *Putsch* the confederation established again, as in 1819,[7] a confederate "central office of investigation," and a wave of repression and vindictive court actions was set in motion. The constitutional governments could now hide behind the will of the confederation and abrogate laws which they disliked as being too liberal. But, with the exception of one monarch, the governments of the small states did not dare annul these constitutions nor amend them in a drastic manner. They were content to hold liberalism at bay by the assertion of their monarchical supremacy. Still, the liberal movement was growing stronger by proselytizing new members. The Germanic Confederation became forever identified with the cause of reaction.

The only state in which the constitution was openly abolished was Hanover. The death of King William IV of England in 1837 that brought Victoria to the British throne made her die-hard uncle the duke of Cumberland, King Ernst August of Hanover. An ultraroyalist who considered even the old duke of Wellington a deviationist, Ernst August was surrounded by a reputation for scandal. A London newspaper once wrote that the duke had committed every crime in his life except suicide. Ernst August refused to recognize the Hanover constitution of

[7] See the author's *A History of Modern Germany: 1648–1840*, p. 466.

1833 and released the civil servants from their oath to the constitution. Seven eminent members of the Göttingen faculty, the historians Friedrich Christoph Dahlmann (1785–1860) and Georg Gottfried Gervinus (1805–71), the Grimm brothers (1785–1863; 1786–1859), the orientalist Heinrich Ewald (1803–74), the jurist Wilhelm Eduard Albrecht (1800–76), and the physicist Wilhelm Weber (1804–91), declared that they felt still bound by the oath. They were at once deposed; Dahlmann, Jacob Grimm, and Gervinus were forced to leave Hanover within three days. Few of these professors had ever before participated in any political action and, if they did, had proved themselves moderates. The deed of the "Göttingen Seven" was essentially an act of conscience and aroused the sympathies not only of the liberals but also of fair-minded conservatives. "Göttingen associations" sprang up all over Germany and took up subscriptions for paying the victimized scholars their salaries until after some years they found academic posts in other German states.

Yet the "Göttingen Seven" were a small minority even among their colleagues. The nobility and a subservient Hanover bureaucracy supported the king. Although in the mayor of Osnabrück, J. K. B. Stüve, the opposition possessed a brave and able spokesman, it could have found a common line of resistance only if the Germanic Confederation had declared the action of Ernst August a violation of the Federal Act. When the confederation refused to act in the matter, open opposition fizzled out in Hanover. In 1840, the Hanover estates bowed to the dictation of the Guelf king. On this occasion even the future succession of Ernst August's blind son was accepted.

✍ *The Young Germany School*

THE OUTWARD DEFEAT of all efforts to gain a wider participation of the people in government strengthened the admiration of foreign political institutions in many circles. The profound disappointment at the practical and moral state of German politics aggravated the crisis of the waning faith in the spiritual and intellectual ideas that had animated the preceding generations. It was in the years of renewed reaction after the Hambach festival that the writers of the so-called Young Germany School, with their radical and acid criticism of every aspect of German civilization, exercised a great influence. The Diet of the Confederation branded these writers as subversive characters, and they had to take refuge abroad or be exposed to constant vexations from the police and the courts. From Paris, Ludwig Börne (1786–1837) and Heinrich Heine (1799–1856) described the superiority of French over German life. They were by no means blind to the shortcomings of the bourgeois monarchy of Louis Philippe, and both were in their hearts fervent German patriots. As German Jews who had seen the French administration grant full equality to the Jews, both were favorably predisposed toward France. But the France which they observed in the 1830's was the France of Victor Hugo, Balzac, Berlioz, and Delacroix, a country in full cultural bloom and also a country in which artists, writers, and scholars took a prominent part in public life. It was such an intellectual leadership at which the German exiles aimed.

Ludwig Börne added a new bitterness to all political debate in Germany with his revolutionary democratic radicalism. Still, his new literary style was perhaps a more lasting contribution to German politics than his doctrinaire opinions. In place of the ponderous academic style that dominated even political writings and speeches, Börne created an easy conversational prose which was not without false glitter but appealed to large groups. Without it the infant German political newspaper press could not have grown to real strength.

Heinrich Heine developed journalistic polemic into a fine art. He was an incomparably richer personality than Börne or any other Young German. Much of the impasse that German life had reached was symbolized in his thought and life. He felt the dangers emanating from the collapse of religion, German idealism, and indeed any single philosophy of life more intensely than any of his contemporaries. He also saw that the effect of these losses would be more devastating upon a people not used to determining its own social forms. Heine was anxious to tear down the artificial façades of German life, but his own vision did not reach far enough beyond the aesthetic realm to enable him to offer clear solutions. He was to some extent influenced by the sensualism of the school of Saint-Simon and advocated a humanist reconciliation of body and spirit, which Judaism and Christianity had unnaturally separated. Still, there was too much self-irony in him to pose as a priest or prophet. Yet this extremely sophisticated man possessed also a sense of the simple feelings of the heart and a mastery of the melodic elements of the German language that gave his lyric poems the character of classic German folk songs.

The writings of the other members of the Young Germany group have been mostly forgotten. None of them was an original literary or poetic talent, but the novels of a Karl Gutzkow (1811–78) or a Heinrich Laube (1806–84) carried the critique of the traditional forms of social and individual life to a large public and made all the problems of the common man, particularly of the burgher, legitimate problems of literature. Filled as these writings were with romantic and philosophical matters, now mostly stale and shallow, they made their numerous readers conscious of a rapidly changing world, in which politics held a central place.

✌ *Frederick William IV of Prussia*

WITH THE GROWING ECONOMIC ACTIVITY, as has been mentioned before, the 1840's brought a new wave of political demonstrations. The succession of Frederick William IV to the Prussian throne in 1840 raised popular hope for a reform of his father's military-bureaucratic regime. Frederick William III was personally responsible for the fact that despite his repeated public promises, made in the years 1811–20, nothing was done to create a general representation in Prussia. He left to his son a written statement, often called his political testament, in which he warned him against the introduction of Prussian general estates, and in case of the need for new taxes he recommended the formation of a small committee composed equally of representatives of the provincial estates and of members of the council of state who were appointed by the king.[8] This "political testament" of Frederick William III gave Czar Nicholas I, Frederick William IV's brother-in-law, as well as his brother Prince William, heir apparent to the Prussian throne, and, of course, Metternich, a welcome means for keeping the new Prussian king from making any move in constitutional matters. But the Rhenish and East Prussian estates reminded him at once of the unfulfilled promises of his father.

By a number of acts Frederick William IV, in the first years of his reign, tried to close wounds left by the policies of past decades. He ended the acute conflict with the Roman Catholic Church.[9] He was instrumental in having the Central Investigation Agency of the Germanic Confederation adjourned *sine die*. The king granted a generous amnesty to the imprisoned "demagogues" and liberalized Prussian censorship. In Bonn, Ernst Moritz Arndt was allowed to resume his teaching, and the leader of the "Göttingen Seven," F. J. Dahlmann, was made a professor. The Grimm brothers were invited to Berlin as members of the Prussian academy. All these actions were expressions of the convictions of Frederick William IV and not merely opportunistic gestures to restore good feeling. Insofar as they indicated the king's aversion to a policy of violent suppression, they could be called liberal acts, and understandably they swelled the expectations of the liberals for a while. But a deep and unbridgeable gulf separated Frederick William IV from the liberal movements of the age.

Frederick William IV, born in 1795, developed a lively German national sentiment under the influence of the patriotic revival during the wars of liberation. His was a conservative and romantic national sentiment absorbed in the company of the members of the so-called "Christian-

---

[8] See the author's *A History of Modern Germany: 1648–1840*, p. 456.
[9] See the author's *A History of Modern Germany: 1648–1840*, pp. 508–9.

Germanic" circle.[10] It centered around a nostalgic admiration of the Middle Ages as the high time of German history. In concurrence with the church, the Holy Empire had represented the divine order on earth. This national ideal was actually identical with the universal Christian principle. Christian universalism assured unity and peace, while it tolerated and even stimulated the growth of a variety of nations and a wealth of local and regional life.

In this light the Germanic Confederation, a fraternal association of sovereign princes under the chairmanship of the former imperial dynasty of Austria, embodied the most essential national traditions. Frederick William IV felt, however, that its common institutions needed strengthening if the confederation was to serve effectively as the keystone of European peace. He wanted to create a unified German defense organization and nationally integrated economic policies. In order to satisfy the popular longing for national unity, Frederick William IV wanted to induce Austria to renew the imperial Roman crown, and he was prepared to sacrifice the position of strength that Prussia had acquired in Germany through the customs union by expanding it into an all-German institution under the control of the confederation. Prussia was to receive recognition of her special role in Germany by the appointment of her kings as hereditary marshals of all the military forces of a revived Roman empire.

Frederick William IV was the only successor of Frederick the Great who took up residence in Sans Souci, the palace of his famous ancestor, but by subordinating Prussian aspirations to Austrian supremacy for the benefit of German national unity, he acted in complete disregard of Frederician traditions. This contrast extended far beyond foreign politics. Frederick William IV felt diametrically opposed to the rationalism of the Enlightenment and judged the state of Frederick the Great to have been inhumanly mechanistic. In his eyes, even the regime of Frederick William III was bureaucratic and despotic. Constitutionalism, liberalism, and democracy were to Frederick William IV products of the same irreligious rationalism. In order to gain new life, the state had to be directed again toward its universal purpose. This was the king's mission, and in its realization he could expect from his subjects loyalty and obedience. Monarchy was not despotism, and freedom of expression should, therefore, be allowed. The king also might consult with representatives of the historical estates, but he could not be bound by the decisions of a parliament that was artificially created by abstract rational principles.

Frederick William IV failed to see that his Christian philosophy would in practice become just another form of absolutism and that its pious unctuousness and condescending paternalism might be even more offen-

---

[10] See the author's *A History of Modern Germany: 1648–1840*, p. 494.

sive than a despotism unsentimentally asserting its power. Moreover, certain personal traits of the king contributed to an early opposition. Frederick William had great gifts. His love of peace and of the works of peace was sincere. He was genuinely interested in the arts and sciences. Yet though he had artistic tastes, a broad education, and oratorical talent, he did not possess an original mind. His self-consciousness made him wary of taking advice and very sensitive to criticism, particularly if it came from people whom he thought he had won by persuasion or benefaction. His restlessness and sentimental exaltation were probably signs of a psychopathological disposition, but it was only in his last years that he succumbed to mental illness.

✑ Church Policy

FREDERICK WILLIAM'S INTENTION to allow free expression did not mix well with his fervent desire to promote the cause of religion. J. A. F. Eichhorn, whom he appointed minister of education and church affairs as successor to Baron Altenstein, soon alienated the universities. Professors were again dismissed, among them Hoffmann von Fallersleben, the author of what was to become the German national hymn ("*Deutschland über alles* . . ."). But the Eichhorn era became notorious chiefly for its propagation of orthodoxy. Lack of toleration unnecessarily inflamed the movement of the "Illuminati" (*Lichtfreunde*), which started in the province of Saxony, where the theological rationalism of the eighteenth century was surviving in considerable strength.[11] The rationalistic ministers forced to leave the official church gathered free congregations around them in central and eastern Germany. The movement was not only a protest against orthodox doctrine but also against the authoritarian church government by the state. The Illuminati, who found it difficult to agree on common religious principles, increasingly turned to the cultivation of common political ideals. The outbreak of the revolution drew their main strength into political channels, and what remained after the revolution could easily be snuffed out by the political reaction.

✑ The "German Catholic" Movement

SIMULTANEOUSLY WITH THE PROTESTANT ILLUMINATI a movement sprang up in the Roman Catholic Church. It was led by an Upper Silesian priest, Johannes Ronge, who had been suspended by the church on account of a radical newspaper article. Ronge protested against the hierarchical direction of the church and promised to free the church from its Roman bondage. The movement, which adopted the name "German

[11] See the author's *A History of Modern Germany: 1648–1840*, p. 485.

Catholic," at first aroused many hopes. To some people it seemed a way to overcome the religious division either by a midway meeting of Catholicism and Protestantism or by the eventual absorption of the Catholics into the Protestant churches. Actually "German Catholicism" never attracted many followers outside of Silesia and Saxony. The latter had few Catholics to begin with, while Silesia's contribution to the cause was also small. Ronge was a political rather than a religious figure, and no prominent leader of the church joined him. The movement might not have arisen if the lay activities within the church had been developed in the eastern as much as in the western provinces.[12] The Roman Catholic Church gained in respect by demonstrating how little it had to fear from such political threats.

✌ *The "United Diet"*

POPULAR AGITATION GREW during the 1840's on all fronts, but the central problem remained the question of whether Prussia would move or could be moved closer to a policy of liberal reform. After years of vacillation in which he drifted toward an authoritarian bureaucratic regime Frederick William IV decided to implement the promise of his father for the establishment of general estates. On February 3, 1847, he announced the convention of a "United Diet," which was to be composed of the members of the estates of the eight Prussian provinces. However, the diet was weakened in its authority by a privileged curia of lords and even more by the definition of its rights. The king reserved the power to determine the agenda of the assembly and indicated that it would be chiefly concerned with new taxes and loans, though no assurance was given that the United Diet would become the only organ of the state to deal with these matters. Not even regular meetings were promised.

In opening the United Diet in April 1847, the Prussian king called it the realization of "Germanic" estates and emphatically expressed his determination to resist the "un-German" craze for constitutions. No paper document should force itself as a "second providence" between God and Prussia. Whatever such declamations might have meant, it was clear that the king wished to continue as the providential authority in all major political affairs. He overestimated his power and missed the still existing chance for strengthening his throne. The provincial estates were by no means a true popular representation, but they enjoyed the high esteem of the majority of the people. Besides, while the provincial estates, particularly the Rhenish and East Prussian estates, had vented their dissatisfaction with governmental policies loudly, they were not in a revolutionary mood. If the Prussian government had assured the United Diet of a regu-

[12] See the author's *A History of Modern Germany: 1648–1840*, pp. 506–8.

lar participation in legislation, the diet would have loyally cooperated with the government. In all probability, the revolution of 1848–49 would not have deprived Prussia of her freedom of action.

For the first time in modern German history the United Diet brought together political figures from a variety of distant parts of Germany. It also saw for the first time members of the nobility cooperate in a major political effort with members of the bourgeoisie. Even the reactionary German governments were impressed with how well and effectively the opposition handled itself, in contrast to the ministers, whose lack of candor and political logic was apparent. The tone of the debates was largely determined by the Westphalian Baron Georg von Vincke (1811–75), the son of the first high-president of Westphalia, who had been a close friend and follower of Stein.[13] With him in the limelight were the Rhenish merchants David Hansemann, Ludolf Camphausen, and Hermann Beckerath. Still, defenders of the royalist cause were not missing. While the future king, Prince William, made himself unduly unpopular by acting as an overbearing champion of dynastic absolutism, a young Brandenburg-Pomeranian *Junker*, Otto von Bismarck (1815–98), aroused attention by the reckless challenges which he threw into the face of the liberal majority.

The debates ranged far. The anomalous position of the army as standing outside the general laws and yet demanding general recognition of its ways from civil society received an airing. The extension of Hardenberg's Jewish emancipation laws to the provinces Prussia acquired in 1815 led to extensive discussions of the basis of citizenship, which the king wanted to confine to Christian members, though he was ready to grant Jews some rights as a special nationality. But the chief political struggle hinged on the financial laws that the government presented to the United Diet and that actually had been a major reason for convening it. Foremost was the wish of the government to have the diet assist in financing the railroad that was to connect East Prussia with Berlin. The government had embarked on preparatory work, since private capital had refused the building of the expensive line.

Hansemann pointed out quite correctly that the Prussian government was ill-advised in withdrawing capital from the economy for a war chest instead of using it for productive purposes. But the crucial question was the backing of governmental expenditures by representation of the people. The United Diet refused to underwrite a guarantee of state loans for the eastern railroad as long as it was not itself assured of a permanent existence. Since its demand for regular meetings was turned down, it rejected by a large majority any state loans. The United Diet was adjourned in July. Frederick William IV was disappointed but not worried.

---

[13] See the author's *A History of Modern Germany: 1648–1840*, p. 400.

He did not think that the people could defeat a monarch and grossly underrated the effect that the crystallization of an inimical public opinion through an organ like the United Diet was bound to have on the German nation. Prompted by the revolution in Paris, the Prussian government granted permission for the United Diet to meet periodically. But this concession of early March 1848 fell far short of the popular demands that had grown in the meantime and that were no longer concerned exclusively with Prussia. The liberal movement that suddenly enveloped all of Germany aimed at a modern constitution and a national state.

✑ *1848: Liberal Leaders*

IT WAS ASTONISHING how in the spring of 1848 the political agitation which so far had been carried on in relatively small groups seemed to gain the elemental support of the masses. Almost overnight the liberals became the spokesmen for the whole nation, whereas a while before they had been representatives of special social and regional segments of German society. Under the reactionary conditions of the Germanic Confederation political party organizations had not developed on the state, let alone on the national, level. In the absence of any national political institutions, common political programs were particularly important. The unusual emphasis on theoretical discussion that characterized the liberal movement in Germany was explained as much by these political circumstances as by the fact that the liberals were mostly scholars and moreover the heirs of the philosophical age of German history. The question at the beginning of the year 1848 was whether the political thinkers of Germany had prepared a theoretical framework that could hold together the bursting revolutionary energies of the people and channel them toward constructive political action.

✑ *Dualists and Moderates*

ACTUALLY THERE WERE STRONG DIVISIONS among the German liberals both with regard to their ultimate ideals and to the methods of realizing these ideals. In the early constitutional life of Baden, a school of liberalism grew up that had as its recognized heads two professors at the university of Freiburg, Karl von Rotteck (1775–1840) and Karl Theodor Welcker (1790–1868). Rotteck, who spent his whole life in his native Breisgau, had grown up as an Austrian subject. Nurtured by the philosophies of the Josephine Enlightenment, he had advanced through the French Enlightenment, Kant, Rousseau, the post-Napoleonic French writers, and Guizot. Rotteck was not capable of creating an original political philosophy out of these ingredients, but he gave southwestern German liberalism a doctrine suitable to German conditions. Though doctrinaire in many respects, he did not forget historical forces altogether. As a matter of fact, the old idea of the "dualistic" state of the preabsolute age, of which more than mere memories lived on in Breisgau and neighboring Württemberg, was transformed by him into a theory of liberalism. Though he believed that democracy was the most natural, and indeed the original, form of the state, he recognized that under modern conditions the existence of an independent, or monarchical, power was justified. The ideal was a mixed state, in which a popular representation asserted and defended the freedom of the individual against the unlimited exercise of governmental authority. Rotteck saw, so to speak, a continuous war over boundaries going on between two political powers that were irreconcilable, for the state had no unity. He refused to harmonize monarchical government by theories such as that of the organic nature of the state or of the nation. The rights of the individual were to be extended and made more secure against encroachments of monarchical government, but popular representation was not to take the place of government. Rotteck denied the right of revolution and accepted the existing constitutional order. In this setting radical demands were expressions of philosophical conviction rather than attempts at popular control of the state.

Rotteck's political theories have often been called the German version of Louis Philippe's *juste milieu,* and thereby the contrast of the political situation of France and Germany was thrown into bold relief. There was no unbridgeable "dualism" in France. The monarchy of Louis Philippe was only the façade of the high bourgeoisie rule, of the *gouvernement censitaire* which had come to power after a revolution. Rotteck's "dualistic" construction of the state reflected the sentiment of the upper strata of the German middle class, who wished to safeguard their private sphere and voice their public aspirations but knew that they did not command the social strength to remold the state after their own image.

Rotteck, a brave and honest person, was probably the most popular intellectual leader in Germany between 1820 and 1840. The decree of the Germanic Confederation of 1832 that forbade him and Welcker to teach made both men martyrs of the liberal cause. Together they began to publish the *Political Dictionary* (*Staatslexikon,* 1834; 2d ed., 1845–48) that served liberal burghers for a generation as the chief foundation of all political wisdom. K. T. Welcker was the less original of the two men, but his practical political activities were of great consequence. Welcker took as his ideal of government the British constitution, which he, like practically all German political writers, interpreted in the manner of Montesquieu. This predilection for British models was almost general among the liberals of North Germany. But the distinction between the southwestern and northern German liberals went much deeper. It lay in a different

attitude toward reality. Rotteck built his state on abstract-rational principles, whereas the North German liberals respected the given historical
institutions. The "dualists" and the "moderates" were in agreement in
their general intent that politics should serve the realization of ethical
principles, but the "moderates" believed that this could best be achieved
by developing the historic political institutions. The moderate liberals
were deeply influenced by the new historical thought of a Hegel or a
Ranke and by the contemporary empirical sciences.

Hesse was a sort of middle ground between north and south, but the
most prominent liberal leader and the chief author of the Hesse-Kassel
constitution of 1831, Sylvester Jordan (1792–1867), a South Tyrolean by
birth, must be counted among the "dualists." The most important work
of the moderate school, appearing almost simultaneously with the Rot-
teck-Welcker *Political Dictionary*, was from the pen of F. C. Dahlmann.
Born in Wismar, the port town of Mecklenburg, which in 1785 was still
under Swedish rule, Dahlmann had first participated in the political
struggle between the Holstein nobility and the Danish crown and later, as
professor in Göttingen, in the drafting of the Hanover constitution of
1833. In 1835 he published his *Politics, Reduced to the Ground and
Measure of Existing Conditions*. He rejected the "shallow" liberalism of
Baden which constructed the state on rationalistic principles. The state
was to him a primordial institution of human life, like the family. The
state, he argued in an almost Hegelian manner, was closer to the divine
order than anything on earth and therefore could demand compliance
with its regulations of all secular affairs. But the state had to grant enough
freedom to the individual to fulfill in his own moral and spiritual life
those absolute commandments which the state by its nature could not
realize. To this extent the individual had a right to be represented. Constitutional laws ought at least not be changed without popular consent, and
in a good state all legislation required the participation of the people. But
sovereignty rested in the princes, and a right of resistance could not be
tolerated. Even under despotism the individual could do nothing but
retire "to the realm in which everyone was a legitimate king," his own
soul, and set a model of the good state in his own family.

For Dahlmann the state was the chief agent of human destiny, and it
was the concretely existing state that he had in mind. All subjective rights
had to be adjusted to the variety of historical states and social classes. In
1835 Dahlmann was quite willing to see the proper organization of German national life in the Germanic Confederation. With regard to the
individual states he subscribed not only to the principle of hereditary
monarchy but also to a house of peers and a second house composed of
corporate as well as individual members. A state that was grounded on
traditional political and social institutions would form a community capa-

ble of channeling individual forces and of thus achieving the highest vitality and ethical perfection. As the fundamental instrument of social and political integration the constitution was sacrosanct in Dahlmann's eyes, and this conviction prompted his protest against the coup of King Ernst August in 1837. Even after his expulsion from Göttingen he refused to demand more than the restoration of the moderate Hanover constitution.

Dahlmann, whose *Politics* was the most important systematic statement of moderate or "classic" German liberalism in the first half of the century, displayed the pattern for all future moderate liberalism in Germany. The respect for historic institutions as embodying the seeds of a transcendent ideal and the simultaneous belief that progress toward the ideal state required the preservation of a strong governmental authority remained characteristic of this school of German liberalism. It showed a strong imprint of Protestant traditions and often enough, beginning with Dahlmann, this moderate liberalism was presented as the political philosophy of Protestantism, although for these liberals the state had totally absorbed the church. Yet the scope of the hoped-for transformation of the existing political and social institutions became much broader in the 1840's. The Rhenish liberals, such as Camphausen, Mevissen, and Hansemann, wanted the active assistance of the state in promoting the interests of modern industry and commerce. But they, too, were loyal supporters of the existing political and social order and recommended their programs of economic development as the means for strengthening the power of the state, since the combination of "property and knowledge" was to provide a strong foundation for the state.

✐ Radicals

THE "RADICALS" stood beside the "dualists" and "moderates" as a third group of German liberalism. Most of the intellectuals of the Young-Germany and the Young-Hegelian schools belonged to this group. Radicalism first showed considerable popular strength in the Palatinate at the time of the Hambach festival of 1832. In the 1840's the radical movement spread into Baden, where it found two colorful political leaders in Gustav von Struve (1805–70) and Friedrich Hecker (1811–81), both lawyers in Mannheim. The radicals shared with the other German liberals a strong ethical approach to politics, and like the dualists they constructed their ideals of freedom on the basis of natural law. Yet, fundamentally, it was not the more sweeping nature of their political demands that distinguished the radicals from the dualists and, of course, even more so from the moderates but their belief that the ideal was capable of full realization through political action.

Still, German radicals remained rather vague about the character of their ideal democratic state and equally vague about the type of action that was recommended for its actual achievement. They preached the right of resistance but at times saw in Frederick William IV a leader for reform or, as Struve did, placed their trust in the South German parliaments. In Struve's case it was particularly clear that only the reactionary policies of the Baden government drove him into full republicanism. In the full sense, however, this did not happen before the revolution of March 1848. It remained characteristic of the Pre-March (*Vormärz*), as the Germans liked to call the period before 1848, that no clear distinction existed between the various progressive groups. The radicals were still radical liberals, and not democrats, and none of the groups presented a clear-cut program of political action.

German liberals of every shade agreed on demands for some guarantees against the absolutist exercise of governmental authority. Some form of constitutionalism was generally considered necessary along with an extension of local self-government. Certain specific claims of reform were also universally heard: freedom of speech and of the press, freedom of association, an independent judiciary, public trial by jury, and civil equality, which meant the abolition of the political privileges of the nobility and of the social bonds of the peasants. But the concrete form of the state, whether republic or monarchy, and if monarchy, the distribution of powers between crown and popular representation, remained rather nebulous. No clear political lines were developed with regard to the formation of representative organs. Corporate representation and representation by general election were seldom sharply divided, and little attention was paid to the franchise.

✎ Rechtsstaat

GERMAN LIBERALISM had not as yet come down from the realm of political philosophy into the field of political theory. How anxiously German liberalism avoided the unequivocal assertion of democratic rights was shown by the general adoption of the concept of *Rechtsstaat*, which occurred in the 1840's. Ever since, this concept has remained a cherished political ideal in Germany. The term *Rechtsstaat*, "law-state," which may be translated as "government founded on law," became popular as the opposite to the arbitrary "police state." But this broad meaning was not necessarily incompatible with absolutism. Enlightened despotism had already aimed at the exclusion of capricious acts of government and demanded that the authority of the state should be exercised only in conformity with general laws applicable to all citizens. From the eighteenth century on, this ideal had champions in the Prussian bureaucracy.

Adam Müller[14] employed the very term *Rechtsstaat* in his romantic philosophy of state for essentially absolutist purposes, and Hegel's philosophy construed the omnipotent state as an agent of law. The chief representative of a conservative political philosophy, Friedrich Julius Stahl (1802–61), during the Pre-March period was already evolving his doctrine of the *Rechtsstaat*, which, as finally enunciated in 1856, became the most influential interpretation of the concept in the subsequent history of Germany. "It means," said Stahl, "not the aim and content of the state but only the form and method of realizing them." The liberal theory of the *Rechtsstaat*, which Robert von Mohl (1799–1875), a professor in Tübingen and Heidelberg, developed after 1829 contended that law was to determine not only the forms of government action but also the purpose of the state, which he described as the realization of the freedom of its citizens. Although Mohl insisted on some form of participation of the individual in the government, the relationship between the rights of the individual and the sovereignty of the monarchical state was very flexible. Mohl's conception of *Rechtsstaat* was not a forceful program for the establishment of a liberal state.

✍ *Relationship with France*

THE WEAK and indefinite character of German political theory manifested itself also in all attempts at formulating a new national sentiment. German national consciousness grew steadily after 1830, and even faster after 1840. New roads, railroads, and enlarged trade as well as wider intellectual intercourse greatly contributed to an awareness of national affairs. The example set by the political life of France and England was a continuous influence in this direction. At the same time, national sentiment fed also on the distrust of foreign intentions. The memories of the Napoleonic age were not forgotten. During the whole half century after 1815 Frenchmen were deeply interested in Germany, and German ideas were eagerly absorbed. Equally, the Germans studied France. But even those Germans who saw in the political institutions of France an immediate model for Germany were afraid of political collaboration with France. This distrust was caused by the demand for the "natural frontiers" that was still raised in French public discussions.

Already the speakers of the Hambach festival had taken great pains to express fierce opposition to any bartering away of Rhenish territory to France. When in 1840 French diplomacy actually looked for gains in the Rhineland, a storm of resentment broke loose in Germany. Adolphe Thiers' attempt to recoup French prestige, damaged in the Egyptian

---

[14] See the author's *A History of Modern Germany: 1648–1840*, p. 351; on Hegel, p. 513; on Stahl, p. 517.

crisis, by a diversion toward the Rhineland was a brief episode in European diplomatic history. The monarchy of Louis Philippe was far from wishing war, and Thiers was quickly replaced by Guizot. But the incident caused a most formidable outburst of national feeling in Germany. At that time the political Rhine songs, such as *The Watch on the Rhine,* were written. For the next century they helped to fan hostility against France among the German people. But while the songs were demonstrations of a noisy and assertive patriotism, they were originally not expressions of a blind chauvinism. No agitation over the question of Alsace existed in Germany. Still, the passionate form of this early German nationalism indicated that many Germans began to feel resentful over the minor role that Germany played in Europe.

✍ Nationalism

POLITICAL OBSERVERS, among them the Russian czar, were startled that the declared internal foes of the existing German governments seemed to be the most fervent nationalists, and it is true that national sentiment had permeated German political radicalism. The pure intellectuals had no use for any agency between the absolute ideal and the individual, and they also disliked the emotional elements in nationalism. But every popular political movement needs the appeal of a concrete group ideal. Karl Marx, who became an internationalist in his Young-Hegelian years, found it in a social class, the proletariat. It should also not be overlooked that Marx considered national revolutions as the proper means for wrecking the evil internationalism of monarchs and that he favored in particular German national unification. Since imperial Russia was judged to be the mainstay of the monarchical international, Marx and still more so Engels could even at times indulge in a strong nationalist anti-Russian language.

The majority of the German radicals of the Pre-March period refused to identify their political aspirations with a social class. Instead, the idea of nationhood served as the rallying cry for a movement aimed at the overthrow of the regime of the despotic German princes and princelings. The people had common rights and common interests which could be realized only in a national state. "Let us strive fraternally for unity, law, and liberty with heart and hand" read a characteristic line in *Deutschland über alles.* The national state was not to be sought for its own sake but was to come as the fulfillment of the moral faith of the people. To instill a consciousness of the innate national virtues and of common freedom in the people was, therefore, of more immediate concern than to define the political institutions of a future national state. For the time being the cultural bond of language seemed adequate for establishing an ideal community.

While Rotteck remained opposed to nationalism to his death in 1840, other South German constitutionalists discovered in nationalism the way to a synthesis of the power of sovereign governments and the popular demand for freedom and justice. National policies also helped to bring the various liberal groups closer together. The Swabian Paul Pfizer (1801–67) opened this discussion in his *Correspondence between Two Germans* of 1831–32. He granted the radicals that a constitutional system was an inevitable demand of the age and that it could achieve its full liberalizing results only by turning a culturally united people into a political nation. But he also pointed out that the drive for freedom would become meaningless if the future national state did not have the necessary power to maintain itself on an equal footing among the European nations. Spirit by itself would not do; force was required as well. This force Pfizer found in the Prussian state. The idea of a special mission of Prussia on behalf of the German nation had some antecedents among the leaders of the Prussian reform period and still survived with some members of the Prussian bureaucracy, which was busy in these very years building the German Customs Union. Pfizer was the first writer who publicly propagated a closer union of the German states under Prussia's protectorate or, as he put it, under Prussian "hegemony."

Pfizer recognized that no closer union was possible as long as two great powers were members of the confederation. He resolved the dilemma by excluding Austria from a future German federal state, since Austria, with her far-flung interests in the Danube region and Italy, was unlikely ever to identify herself completely with the German nation. A *grossdeutsch*, "Great German," solution of the problem of national unification, which would have included all the land belonging to the Germanic Confederation in a federal state, was declared impossible, and the *kleindeutsch*, "Little German" or Prussian, solution was advocated as the only realistic method of superseding the confederation by a national state. Pfizer was convinced that national unity had to come before freedom and not, as the radicals thought, freedom before unity. He was inclined to forgive gladly some of the threatening aspects of Prussian military armor. As a matter of fact, since he wanted a powerful state as a guarantor of German unity, he even liked the Prussian army. Moreover, being convinced that liberalism was the logical outcome of contemporary history, he wondered whether an absolutist Prussia, after establishing German unity, would not be compelled to adopt a new constitution in order to strengthen the new German state.

At the same time, as a prerequisite of an acceptance of Prussian hegemony, Pfizer expected clear signs of a liberal policy, for example, the grant of freedom of the press. He was uncertain whether Prussia should introduce a general representation beyond the existing provincial estates.

He was right in assuming that a federal state which included two great powers could not exist, but was it possible to federate one big state with a number of small states? And would not the weight of Prussia grow even further if she became a constitutional state? The South German theorist hoped, therefore, that Prussia for a while might accept national German estates and forgo the introduction of a central Prussian parliament. This came, however, close to demanding the dissolution of the Prussian state into its provinces at the very time when the massed power of this monarchy was supposed to achieve the great work of German unification. Pfizer was the first thinker to grapple with the difficulty of the problem of Prusso-German relations within a German federal state, which was to be one of the key problems of German politics till 1933, but he was unable to offer a viable solution. When in 1832 Prussia joined with Austria in the suppression of the liberal movement through the Germanic Confederation, Pfizer lost hope that Prussia could be brought together with the constitutional states of Germany in the near future. Pfizer was representative of all the southwestern constitutionalists insofar as national unity was for him essentially a means for the achievement of constitutional freedom, but the national idea received concrete meaning through the concept of a federal state and the discussion of the problems of power which its realization might pose. In the same year of 1831 in which Pfizer's *Correspondence* appeared, another southwestern liberal, K. T. Welcker, introduced a resolution in the Baden parliament demanding the creation of a national parliament besides the Diet of the Germanic Confederation.

The moderate liberals of northern Germany trailed behind in embracing national ideas. Their emphasis on history tied them more closely to the traditional German states. But they were drawn increasingly into the national agitation of the 1840's. Their ideal of a federal state tended to be less critical of the monarchical and military side of Prussia than that of the South Germans. The Prussian historian, Johann Gustav Droysen (1808–84), in his *Alexander the Great,* raised the vision that the military monarchy of the north would have to abolish the independence of the small German states as Macedonia had brought an end to the division of Greece into small republics. The Rhenish liberals on their part put a great deal of trust in the unifying force of a growing economy.

In 1847 the signs increased that the liberals of the various parts of Germany were trying to cooperate in order to advance the national cause. Friedrich Bassermann and Karl Mathy founded a newspaper in Mannheim, the *Deutsche Zeitung,* designed to promote German unification in a constitutional state. G. G. Gervinus acted as editor, while articles came from many regions and from many people, among them J. G. Droysen, then professor in Kiel. When, on February 12, 1848, Friedrich

Bassermann (1811–55) made a motion in the Baden parliament for popular representation within the Germanic Confederation, the echo in Germany was loud. Two weeks later the revolution in Paris made the German princes also lose the heart to resist the popular demand for freedom and unity.

CHAPTER 2

The Revolution of 1848–49

WHILE SOCIAL GRIEVANCES and popular demands for political changes were intensified in the "hungry" years after 1845, external events contributed to the growing distrust of the ruling governments.

Poland: Insurrections

IN 1846, fresh insurrections in Poland induced the three Eastern powers to abolish the freedom of the city of Cracow, because it had become a center for the revolutionary activities of the Polish nationalists. With the incorporation of this city into Austria the three conservative powers themselves changed an important piece of the settlement of Vienna, which they were always wont to declare sacrosanct.

The Schleswig-Holstein Succession

THE POLISH INSURGENTS found much sympathy among German liberals, but events in Denmark and Schleswig-Holstein made an even more profound impression on all Germany. In July 1846, King Christian VIII of Denmark (1839–48) issued an "open letter" that threatened to change the legal status of the German duchies. Their legal status was not easy to define, since it derived from a very distant and different age. The two duchies had first come to the Danish crown in 1460, and after his election by the estates the Danish king had sworn that neither duchy should ever be divided and that the two duchies should be held together. This pledge was soon disregarded, and only in 1773 did the two duchies receive a single ruler. Thereafter, the Danish king was sovereign duke of Schleswig, but as duke of Holstein he recognized the feudal overlordship of the emperor. As duke of Holstein the king of Denmark had become a member of the Germanic Confederation in 1814.

The Danish monarchs had been absolutist rulers in the eighteenth century, and the estates of the duchies had not been convened after 1717.

Still, the rather wealthy German nobility of the duchies had played an eminent role at the royal court of Copenhagen, and German culture was greatly cherished in Denmark, especially in the age of Klopstock and Schiller. But the growth of an indigenous national Danish movement around the turn of the century had undermined the position of the German nobility in the Copenhagen government and loosened the cultural ties between Denmark and Germany. In these circumstances the German noblemen became anxious to defend the autonomy of the two duchies and their relations with Germany, but only after 1830 did the Danish government grant the establishment of estates in each of the duchies. These assemblies of notables, which had no actual power, served as centers around which a developing German popular movement could crystallize.

Unification of all the territories under the Danish crown became the aim of the Danish national and liberal movement that broke forth with great strength. The Danish nationalists looked for a centralized Danish state constitutionally governed by one monarch. They wished in particular to see Schleswig, which did not belong to the Germanic Confederation and contained considerable Danish elements, fully integrated into the monarchy. Altogether, about one third of the population of Schleswig understood Danish, and about one fourth, chiefly concentrated in the north, spoke it. Still, it became the aim of the Danish nationalists to turn all of the land as far south as the Eider, the little river dividing Schleswig from Holstein, into a Danish province. The "Eider-Danes" were spurred on in their activities by imminent dynastic complications. The ruling King Christian VIII had an heir, but the latter was without male issue. In the case of his death the Danish throne would fall to the descendant of a princess of the royal house, while under the Salic law of Germany, that disallowed female claims, a member of the German princely family of Augustenburg would inherit the duchies of Schleswig and Holstein.

The open letter of Christian VIII of July 1846 tried to preclude any separation of the duchies from Denmark. It announced the validity of the Danish law of inheritance in Schleswig, and, though admitting some doubts about the applicability of this law to Holstein, stressed the lasting connection of the two duchies. The letter aroused the German sentiment in the duchies. The lively agitation, in which J. G. Droysen and other professors of Kiel University were prominent, was not confined to the duchies but was directed toward German public opinion in general. Even the Diet of the Germanic Confederation, to which the Holstein estates appealed, took note of the national excitement, though perhaps chiefly on account of the dynastic issues which were involved. The diet expressed the pious hope that in a final settlement the Danish king would not disregard existing rights. The response from Copenhagen was not reassuring, and when Christian VIII died in January 1848, his successor Frederick VII announced at once the introduction of a constitution of Great Denmark. Without abolishing the estates of the duchies, it created a common parliament, and there could be no question that this parliament would completely enfeeble the politically weak estates and block the accession of the Augustenburg family of Schleswig. The popular reaction in Schleswig-Holstein was passionately hostile, and it found warm support in all of Germany. But conflicts in this region of Europe, which contained the key to the Baltic Sea, were also bound to put England and Russia on the alert.

✍ *Switzerland: Civil War*

OTHER STIRRING EVENTS occurred in Switzerland, which in this period had a greater influence on German politics than at any other time. The Swiss had generously given refuge to many German radicals and political fugitives since the years of the Karlsbad Decrees, and Swiss democracy enjoyed high prestige, particularly in the southwest. From 1845 on, however, conflict had been brewing in Switzerland. The radical liberals were bent upon strengthening the power of the central government and thereby also suppressing the allegedly reactionary forces in the Catholic cantons, which in the fall of 1845 formed a special federation. The neutrality of the Swiss Confederation had been placed under an international guarantee by the Vienna Congress. Metternich saw in this a welcome chance to intervene in conjunction with Russia and Prussia and inflict a serious blow to European liberalism. But with Palmerston's connivance the majority of cantons ordered the dissolution of the special federation and enforced this order in an ably conducted three weeks' war against the Catholic cantons, before foreign powers could intervene. The way was open for the transformation of the Swiss Confederation into a federal state.

✍ *European Revolutions of 1848*

THIS LIBERAL VICTORY in the face of the predominance of the conservative powers on the Continent had an electrifying impact on liberals everywhere. Italy was most immediately affected. In early 1848, insurrections occurred in Sicily and Naples. On February 24, a rising of the people of Paris drove Louis Philippe from the French throne and led to the proclamation of the (second) republic. The news of the revolution in Paris set the final spark to popular demonstrations for reform in Germany. They began in the last days of February in Baden. Public meetings held in Mannheim, Heidelberg, and Offenburg were the first assemblies attended by members of all classes of the population in modern German history. With their demands for freedom of the press, trial by jury, introduction of constitutions in all German states, and the convention of a national parliament they struck the keynote of the general movement which in the following weeks engulfed all of Germany.

✐ Revolutions in Germany

THE EVENTS of Paris filled the hearts of the German princes with deep fear. None of them was prepared to put up more than temporary resistance to the aroused people. As a matter of fact, the majority became rather obsequious. The Baden government was the first one to surrender. The liberal Karl Mathy became prime minister, and another leader of the opposition, Karl Theodor Welcker, minister to the Federal Diet. Other states followed suit: Württemberg's liberal cabinet included Paul Pfizer as one of its members; in Hesse-Darmstadt Heinrich von Gagern, soon to be transferred to a greater stage, was made chief of the government. The evil elector of Hesse-Kassel had to bow; the stubborn King Ernst August of Hanover had to accept Johann Stüve as a minister and to see all the results of his coup of 1837 undone. In Saxony, too, a liberal cabinet was formed as well as a revision of the constitution promised, and the small states of Germany followed these examples. Bavaria had its own type of revolution, caused by the resentment of the ordinary Munich burghers against Lola Montez, a Spanish dancer of Irish-Creole extraction, who not only ruled the private affections of King Ludwig I but also was meddling in Bavarian politics. This farcical affair ended with the expulsion of the adventuress and the abdication of Ludwig I in favor of his son Maximilian II (1848–64).

The little thrones of Germany had been shaken earlier by the July revolution of 1830, but before long political reaction held sway again, because the two great German powers, Austria and Prussia, had not felt the impact of this revolution at all. It was decisive that in 1848 the revolutionary flames did envelop these two German states. Whereas the political revolution in the other German states had been bloodless, the demise of the old regimes in Austria and Prussia was accompanied by violence.

✐ Austria

AT FIRST METTERNICH had underrated the approaching dangers, but when the crisis occurred, he was inclined to assign a finality to the events, which, as the course of the Austrian revolution was to show, they did not possess. All during his career Metternich had defended his political system as the last barrier against the all-destructive "social revolution." He saw no way of accommodation to the forces that raised their heads in March 1848. On March 13, the resistance that he recommended led to serious street fighting.

But the decision was no longer in the hands of the Austrian chancellor. Since 1835, when the half-witted Ferdinand had been proclaimed emperor, Austria had been officially ruled by the so-called "state conference," a council of regency composed of members of the imperial family, the chancellor, and another minister. A desire to protect the dynastic interests by sacrificing Metternich, who had been the symbol of the existing regime, prevailed in this group. Metternich took his leave with dignity. It was bitterly ironic that he had to look for a refuge in liberal England, which he reached by a devious route through countries in revolutionary upheaval. For almost forty years this Rhenish nobleman had governed Austria. He had led her from deep humiliation in 1809 to a towering position in Europe. In particular, he had restored Austria to a position of power in Germany, such as she had not occupied for more than a century. This achievement was not the result of a diplomacy of guile, as the enemies of Metternich now asserted, but of a principled policy. Metternich's statecraft also had successfully protected Germany from foreign wars. Welfare and peace for Europe were natural objectives of his diplomacy, because he felt a deep loyalty to Europe as an organic whole. Yet Metternich was quite incapable of seeing the political and social forces which appeared in the wake of the French Revolution as anything more than aberrations from the timeless norms of a well-ordered society. He lacked the mind that would have tried to find a useful outlet for some of these modern energies. This debonair son of eighteenth-century aristocracy had basically no other answer to the pressures and tensions which the new national and social movements created than the call for the police. German popular sentiment grew indifferent or even hostile. The nationalities of the Danube region, which in their infancy might have been molded, proved less tractable when they revolted in 1848 against the bureaucratic absolutism of Vienna.

Even members of the high nobility cooperated in the removal of Metternich, and it seemed that the revolutionary movement in the Austrian capital could be held in moderate channels. A civil guard and an academic legion of students assumed control of the city, but it was the upper and petty bourgeoisie, still united, that determined the character of the movement. The monarchy as such was not questioned nor even a radical change in the composition of the cabinet demanded. The government immediately promised freedom of the press and the convocation of delegates from the provincial estates for the framing of a constitution. But developments quickly took a more radical course. The peasants as well as the workers raised their own social demands in the midst of grave economic difficulties, which were enhanced by the ruinous condition of the Austrian state finances.

✍ National Revolutions

EVEN GRAVER was the revolution of the nationalities against Vienna. The Magyars had to be granted a government and a parliament of their own. The Czechs achieved the promise of a popular representation and special administration in Bohemia. In Croatia a national movement gathered. All of Venetia and Lombardy rose in arms against Austrian domination. The dissolution of the Habsburg Empire seemed imminent. While by the end of July Austria ceased to be a factor in European politics, the revolution in Vienna incapacitated the Habsburg Empire as well.

✍ Prussia

WITH AUSTRIA shaken to its very foundations, the eyes of Germany turned of necessity toward Prussia. Most Germans were afraid that the revolution in France would lead to a renunciation of the Vienna settlement by the French and to an invasion of the Rhineland. This was not just a German prejudice strengthened by the events of the year 1840. Apprehension was felt also in London. Actually, the peaceful Lamartine, not Thiers nor the bellicose Jacobins, emerged as the director of the French foreign policy. Still, not even Lamartine dared give unequivocal recognition of the frontiers of 1815. England no doubt would not have objected to the assumption of Prussian leadership in Germany during the spring of 1848. It was unfortunate that Anglo-Prussian relations were soon to be beclouded by the military intervention of Prussia in Schleswig-Holstein.

Internal developments in Germany in early March also appeared to place the Prussian government in the position of a supreme arbitrator. The international situation was only one of the reasons inducing the governments of the German small and middle states to look to Prussia. There were early warnings that the masses would press the economic and social claims whose fulfillment they were expecting from the revolution. Therefore, the establishment of a strong government was highly desirable, perhaps imperative. It was clear that Prussia would have to become a liberal state and devote itself to the cause of national unification, possibly, as some hoped, to the extent of not even creating a general Prussian parliament but of placing her provinces individually under a central national authority headed by the Prussian king as German emperor.

The Diet of Frankfurt changed its composition, with new representatives being appointed by the "March cabinets" in various German capitals, and even the old members changed their tune. The Prussian minister Count Dönhoff, presiding in the absence of his Austrian colleague, took it upon himself to deviate from his official instructions and to lead the diet toward a determined national policy. The diet adopted the black, red, and gold emblem and, historically quite mistakenly, declared the symbol for which it had sent hundreds of people to jail to be the colors of the old Empire. But hereby the diet implicitly propagated the idea of a German emperor. On March 10, it requested the governments to send seventeen men of their trust—one for each curial vote of the council—to Frankfurt to help frame a constitution. The Prussian envoy implored his king to act while the revolution could still be channeled through traditional organs.

But Frederick William IV could not be moved by these arguments. Ambition for expanding the Prussian state was but weakly developed in this successor to the throne of Frederick the Great. Yet he was in the Prussian tradition, insofar as he was intensely conscious of his royal prerogatives. The divine-right theory and other religious symbolism with which he surrounded the royal authority did not hide a stark absolutism. Frederick William IV was not tempted by the opportunities to advance Prussian power at the expense of Austria or other German states; moreover, he was willing to employ Prussian might for the unselfish service of general German aims—but not to share authority with representative organs. This offended his conception of monarchical dignity.

Early in 1848 Frederick William IV had revived his plans for a reform of the Germanic Confederation and sent his intimate friend, General Joseph von Radowitz (1797–1853), to Vienna. The plans which Radowitz presented to a diffident Austrian cabinet were just another version of the earlier reform project of Frederick William IV,[1] and the negotiations produced only agreement to call a congress of German princes in Dresden. Ironically, Metternich arrived in Dresden on the appointed day, though as a political fugitive. Radowitz was still in Vienna when the revolution struck, and before he reached Berlin, Frederick William had fallen from his pedestal.

Unemployment, scarcity, and misery were great in the Prussian towns and cities, as elsewhere in Germany, when the year 1848 began. But hunger riots like those in the preceding year did not flare up again. Public discussion of political discontent was well-nigh impossible. It was remarkable that the town councils often made themselves mouthpieces for popular demands, and in Cologne and Königsberg the drafting of popular petitions led to demonstrations which were, however, at once suppressed.

[1] See p. 31.

Berlin was quiet and remained so even after the arrival of the news of the revolutions in Paris and South Germany. But obviously expectations that a new chapter of history was about to open were widely held. Still, there was confidence that the king would take the initiative, and if Frederick William IV had acted before the middle of March, he would have remained master of developments in Germany.

The king made himself believe that events as they had happened in other German capitals could not possibly happen in Berlin. Yet the government moved additional regiments into a city that already had an unduly big army garrison. At this critical juncture, when the majority of the population showed such notable trust in the generosity of the king, it was inconsiderate and unwise to lay bare the physical foundation on which his absolute power rested. The troops on their part during these days displayed such a reckless contempt of all civil and political rights of the people that they became the chief target of any criticism of the existing order. Frederick William IV in the meantime felt no need to change his political attitude. He agreed to reconvene the United Diet but only on a distant date. He considered the reform of the Germanic Confederation to be the exclusive right of the German sovereigns. Any possible danger from France he proposed to meet with Russian support. The idea of seeing a Russian army moved to the Elbe caused horror among the Germans, particularly in the eastern provinces.

None of the moves of the Prussian king actually met the early hopes of the people, and as the days slipped by the unrest grew in Berlin. The beer gardens before the Brandenburg Gate became centers of public discussions which developed into bigger and noisier demonstrations and which on March 13 and on the days following were dissolved by troops with appalling brutality. Even the most harmless burghers deeply resented the conduct of the soldiers. On March 16, as news of the events in Vienna spread in Berlin, tension rose. Frederick William IV became convinced that concessions were inevitable. A change of cabinet was prepared, and royal proclamations were drafted which lifted censorship, called together the United Diet, demanded a reform of the Germanic Confederation, and indicated the need for constitutions in all German states. The proclamations left quite a few uncertainties, and the pretense that they constituted a voluntary gift of the king to his people was no longer very creditable when they were issued after a day's delay, on March 18.

✍ *March 18 in Berlin*

BUT THE PUBLICATION of the proclamations met with a favorable popular reaction, and many people went to the square at the royal palace in order to give the king an ovation. During these demonstrations, however, a change in the temper of the mob occurred. Apparently the confidence in the reliability of governmental promises had suffered by the events of the last few weeks, and the presence of the unusually strong military guards raised the demand for an immediate guarantee of a liberal course. Shouts for a withdrawal of the troops went up among the masses. The decision to adopt a liberal policy had been strongly fought over in the councils of the king. Concessions to popular opinion had been opposed by the military leaders. Prince William, the brother of the king, had been the chief advocate of the suppression of all popular movements by military force. In the afternoon of March 18, the officers recommended clearing the squares around the royal palace, and the king gave in. As the troops, with their customary disregard of popular sentiment, proceeded to push people back, two shots were unintentionally fired by two soldiers. Outcries of treason were heard, and the bitter hatred of the soldiers that had developed during the preceding days turned into wild determination. Barricades went up in all the streets of the vicinity, people began to arm, and within an hour they opened fire on the soldiers. Grim and passionate fighting went on through the evening and night.

The number of active fighters was probably not greater than a few thousand because of the scarcity of arms, but the enthusiastic assistance given by the population to the revolutionaries came from wide circles. The largest group among the insurgents were members of the craft guilds, but there were a good number of merchants and students on their side. The revolutionaries were not only short of weapons, but they also lacked military experience and leadership. It was a general uprising without any general plan. Therefore, the regular troops were able to make steady progress in occupying a substantial section of the center of the city. No fraternization took place. On the contrary, the anger of the soldiers grew in the fighting. The many prisoners were treated cruelly. Yet in spite of the relative success of the operations, the commander, General Karl von Prittwitz, felt that he could not conquer the whole city block by block but would have to lay siege to Berlin from without. In this case a large part of the city might have been wrecked.

Frederick William IV was thrown into despondency. He was not a martial man, and the reports of General von Prittwitz were not altogether reassuring, nor was the news from the provinces. On Sunday morning, March 19, to the dismay of the officers, he issued a tearful proclamation to his dear Berlin subjects, declaring them the victims of evil and foreign manipulators but offering them forgiveness and the withdrawal of the troops if they would put down the barricades. This proclamation, with its mixture of sentimentality and paternal condescension, did not appease anybody. The king eventually ordered the retreat of all troops to the royal palace. In the confusion, much inaccurate information was passed, and some commands were not executed. These circumstances, together with the indignation of the officers over the king's defeatist attitude, led to the withdrawal of the troops to their barracks and thereafter from the city. The guard of the royal arsenal was removed, and only a few companies of soldiers remained in the palace.

✎ *Frederick William Accepts Constitutional Government*

PERHAPS THE MILITARY ENTOURAGE of the king expected the royal family to leave Berlin, but if Frederick William ever contemplated such action, it became impossible by the influx of the mob into the courtyard of the palace, to which they carried the bodies of the killed civilians, their wounds bared. The royal couple was made to view the macabre show, and the king had to pay his respects to those killed by his army. It was, indeed, a deep humiliation of the military monarchy of Prussia. A civil guard, supplied with arms from army stores, was formed, and the city and palace were placed under its protection. The king now accepted the constitutional form of government, agreed to the convention of a parliament elected by the people, and invited the leader of the liberal opposition of the United Diet, the Rhenish merchant Ludolf Camphausen, to form a government. The United Diet met only briefly to draft an election law for the promised Prussian parliament. In view of its strong admixture of conservative elements, it granted a surprisingly liberal suffrage, although it defined the function of the assembly as "the negotiation of an agreement with regard to a constitution of the Prussian state," thus legally protecting some of the sovereign powers of the king, and at the same time assigned to the future constituent assembly only those limited legislative rights that the United Diet possessed. These stringent provisions were to prove an Achilles heel of the Prussian parliament.

✎ *National Policy of the Prussian King*

THE NEW CONSTITUTIONAL POLICY of the king was accompanied by a new foreign policy, for which Baron Heinrich von Arnim-Suckow was largely responsible. On March 21 Frederick William rode through the streets of Berlin decorated with black, red, and gold signs. In the declaration of this day he assumed the role of the leader in the establishment of a united Germany. "From now on Prussia will merge into Germany!" He objected to a public acclamation as emperor of Germany and tried to make it clear that he had no intention of deposing German princes and that he assumed the task of leading Germany toward freedom and unity only temporarily. In the pursuit of the new policy the Prussian government became the protector of the rights of the duchies of Schleswig-

Holstein. On March 24 a provisional government of the duchies had been formed by indigenous liberal leaders in reply to the publicly announced intention of the Danish government to incorporate Schleswig into the Danish state. The provisional government in Kiel as well as the duke of Augustenburg appealed for help and were reassured by Prussia. The relatively friendly attitude of the Prussian government toward the aspirations of the Poles in Posen, though from the beginning not free of ambiguities, was at least a manifestation of the Prussian intention to conduct a policy without, or possibly even against, Russia.

An unprepared and leaderless popular uprising had routed military autocracy in Prussia overnight. Prince William, the stalwart champion of the old order, was sent posthaste from Berlin on an indifferent diplomatic mission to London. Frederick William IV attempted to adjust himself to the role of a constitutional ruler. He was impressed by the elation of the German people in this spring of revolution and not unaffected by the warm applause he received from wide groups of the people once he had granted liberal concessions. But by temper and conviction Frederick William was ill-suited to become a constitutional ruler. Even after the formation of the government he issued orders over the heads of the ministers to all governmental agencies, and he doubtless was never fully oblivious of the fact that the army was still at his call.

⌂ Reactions in Germany

THE IMPRESSION which the revolutionary events in Prussia made in Germany was not very favorable. Until March 17 the power in the hands of the Prussian king was deemed to be great, and his personal reputation was untarnished. If he had declared himself in favor of a united and free Germany in these days and boldly reached for the German crown, the people would have followed him, and, except for Austria, the German princes would have submitted to his leadership. After March 18 he was tainted with the blood of the victims of the Berlin revolution, while his new policy was considered the result of his defeat by the revolution and thus open to suspicion. It was also not difficult to discover some hedging in the declamations of Frederick William IV, even after March 19, and certainly signs of a desire to make Berlin the directing center of the national movement. What did the statement that "from now on Prussia will merge into Germany" really mean if Prussia was to have her own parliament? The princes, who before March 19 had seen in Prussia a strong bulwark against the revolution and might have agreed to subordinating themselves to Prussia, now argued that Frederick William IV was under the influence of the street. Prussia was still distrusted as being either too liberal or not sufficiently liberal, or because it seemed too strong or too weak. This last opinion was shared by the radicals and the princes. The Berlin revolution following the Vienna events convinced many radicals that monarchy could be overthrown in Germany altogether. Thus the radicals turned into democrats.

✑ The Preparliament

THE DUBIOUS POPULAR REACTION to Frederick William's gestures made the original center of the revolution, the German southwest, decisive for the progress of the national movement. The Heidelberg meeting of March 5, which was the first meeting to demand the election of a German parliament, had appointed a "committee of seven" to prepare the convocation of a nationally more representative congress than the Heidelberg meeting had been. This assembly was to prepare the elections for a national parliament. The seven had sent out invitations to all present and former members of German legislative bodies, and even a good many representatives from city councils were included. About 500 people convened in Frankfurt. It was the first relatively representative national assembly of Germany created by democratic initiative, though not by democratic election. The regional distribution was very uneven. Most glaring was the weak representation of Austria, with only two members, and naturally the southwest was disproportionately strong, though the representatives from Prussia, Saxony, and Bavaria were numerous enough to give the "Preparliament" (*Vorparlament*) national resonance.

With great jubilation the members of the Preparliament were welcomed in Frankfurt. The radicals, under the leadership of Struve and Hecker, tried at once to make the assembly an organ for carrying the revolution forward. They wanted to keep the assembly in session until a freely elected parliament could convene. They urged the election of an executive committee, which would actually have been a kind of provisional national government. This committee was at once to be charged with the preparation of a truly revolutionary legislative program. Struve demanded the abolition of hereditary monarchy, an elected president, and a federal constitution "after the model of the North American republics" and in addition offered a long list of further constitutional and social objectives.

The majority of the representatives had not come in order to pour oil on the fire of revolution but rather to prepare the codification of the liberal concessions made so far by the governments. They were not unaware of the fact that the national state had not been created as yet and that national unity required the existence of a strong popular movement. Therefore, they brandished the principle of the sovereignty of the people but equally their loyalty to the monarchical principle. It was true that the Preparliament had no proper democratic basis, because it was not elected by the people, but by its early adjournment a political force was removed just at the time when the conservative powers in Germany had not yet recovered from the shock of the March revolution. As a concession to the radicals the Preparliament appointed a committee of fifty which was supposed to supervise the Diet of the Germanic Confederation. But to place the diet clearly under the control of the committee of fifty seemed too daring. The diet had already changed its composition, insofar as a good many reactionary envoys had been replaced by liberal men, and the committee of the seventeen "trustees" had been added.[2] The Preparliament insisted that the diet should revoke every discriminatory antiliberal law and that every member of the diet who had voted for such prohibitive legislation should resign. The frightened diet, eager to save its existence, quickly obeyed. It also sanctioned what remained the most important act of the Preparliament, a law of election for a national parliament.

The election law was taken by many as providing for universal suffrage, though actually it did not do so. It gave the vote to every male "independent" citizen who had reached majority, and even though it recommended direct elections, they were not required. As a matter of fact, only in a few states were direct elections held, and the restrictive clause of "independence" of citizens was in various ways exploited for withholding the franchise from the poor urban population. Yet at the time of election the number of voters was much smaller than the number of enfranchised citizens, since, lower-class people in particular, failed to show up at the polls. In this political indifference a cleavage of the popular movement appeared which in the early March revolutions had been covered up by the enthusiastic opposition to a common enemy.

Revolution in Germany had been the result not of the agitation of liberal intellectuals but of the explosion of the social tensions which had resulted from disintegration of the social order, recently accelerated by the economic crisis. The bulk of the discontented masses, the guildsmen and peasants, who by their appearance on the street and in the meetings or on the barricades of Berlin had decided the success of the revolution, had been rather traditional in their political and economic outlook. Only years of vain expectation for help from the existing governments had convinced them that they could not achieve relief from absolutist rulers. Thus they came to agree with the liberals in demanding limitations of autocracy and participation of the people in government. Only at the very beginning of the revolution was the social movement of these classes

[2] See p. 51.

in full accord with the political liberalism of the German bourgeoisie. It was an unforgettable experience for many Germans to see the vast majority of the people fraternally united in a great national effort that blotted out state and class lines.

✍ *The Peasantry*

A FESTIVE SPIRIT prevailed in this unusual spring, unusual also on account of its weather. March was as warm and pleasant as May. The heady wine of revolutionary patriotism also produced a national pride that at times had Jacobin overtones. Yet the social unrest of the peasants and the artisans was little concerned with the constitutional aims of liberalism. They wanted immediate satisfaction of their social and economic needs. Even in the early weeks of March, peasants' uprisings of serious dimensions occurred in the very regions which had been the scene of the peasants' wars of 1525. Just as three centuries before, they started in the Black Forest and went north to the Odenwald and Franconia, from there to Hesse, Nassau, the Rhineland, Thuringia, and Saxony. The center of the storm was in the small principalities and on the domains of noble magnates. The peasants attacked and occasionally looted the castles of their landlords, often forcing them to renounce property rights and burning records of indebtedness or manorial duties. They began to use the forests of the noblemen for getting timber or for hunting.

In the Germany east of the Elbe the social unrest of the peasants was not so widespread, though Silesia, Mecklenburg, and Schleswig-Holstein saw outbreaks of violence. Bismarck's later reports have often led to the belief that the Prussian peasants were peaceful and even antirevolutionary in the spring of 1848. But there is ample evidence, including contemporary statements of the young Bismarck, indicating grave concern about the attitude of the East Elbian peasants. Among the Prussian *Junkers* many were convinced that it was wise to tread softly and to make some concessions as long as they would not jeopardize the basic political and economic order as it had grown in the eastern countryside during the last fifty years. Among the nobility of the south and west voices recommending the liquidation of the remaining feudal duties and dues were raised. Still, the noblemen were not inclined simply to renounce their financially valuable rights, and in this attitude they found the support of the liberal bourgeoisie, which hated anything that was likely to undermine the security of property. Before long the new liberal March ministries used the chief tools of the old autocracy to defend their social ideals. Soon soldiers marched and put down the agrarian revolts in southern Germany. By the middle of April the revolts ended, and naturally enough the peasantry, still the largest segment of the German people, became from then on a less active element of the movement directed toward the creation of constitutional rights and national unity.

✑ *Journeymen and Masters*

IN THE TOWNS AND CITIES the most revolutionary elements were the downtrodden journeymen and poor masters. The industrial workers proved unamenable to the revolutionary doctrines of Marx and Engels in 1848-49. The only socialist movement to make visible progress was the one led by Stephan Born in Berlin and that was reformist rather than revolutionary. Formation of trade unions, the improvement of working conditions and wages, as well as suffrage for the workers were the chief aims of this social-democratic group. But the mass of the manual workers consisted of artisans who expected neither revolutionary nor reformist socialism from the governments. They wanted work and a decent liveli-hood, and they saw the way to it chiefly in the abolition, or at least drastic curtailment, of economic freedom. The restoration of the guild system protected against the competition of factories and foreign countries was their chief political demand.

Simultaneously with the peasant riots of March, a wave of acts of destruction was perpetrated by journeymen against factories and other institutions of the modern industrialism. In the Rhineland and in Saxony numerous attempts were made to destroy machines that threatened to replace the work of the artisans. Thus the cutlers of Solingen, for example, destroyed one of the iron foundries in the neighborhood. Most pathetic was the vengeance of the jobless boatmen of the Rhine and Danube against the steamships and that of the displaced wagoners of Nassau against the Taunus railroad. Soldiers had to be employed to end these disorders.

The guildsmen continued to press for the relief of their grievances. Since they felt that the old and new parliaments did not give them enough attention, they debated their problems in a number of regional and national congresses. They all wanted a protectionist economy and in general did not show much interest in the political aims of liberalism. The March ministries on their part did not produce more than minor pallia-tives for dealing with the miserable situation of the masses. The most important practical economic program was presented to the Prussian United Diet in April by the liberal minister Camphausen. By launching a substantial credit expansion, this Rhenish merchant departed from the traditional fiscal policies of the Prussian treasury. The measures taken by him were quite effective in speeding up economic recovery, but since in the beginning they chiefly benefited industry and banks, not only the petty bourgeoisie but also the agrarian *Junkers* looked askance at the demonstration of the new power of financial capitalism.

✍ *The Specter of Communism*

AFTER THE DEFEAT of their republican plans by the Preparliament, Struve and Hecker hoped to advance their cause by a revolutionary coup. On April 12, they issued from Constance the proclamation of a provisional government and at the head of small battalions of poorly armed insurgents started a march through South Baden in the hope that the common people would rise and join them. But the revolt caused only temporary confusion and was easily dispersed by South German troops. By late April, the enthusiasm for political action that had been great in March was ebbing among large groups of the population. Moreover, divisions had appeared which were to determine the further course of the revolution.

For the time being the moderate liberals were on top. Everywhere in Germany the old authorities had compromised with them or, as in the southwest, had ceded their power to them. The German liberals, though bent on the limitation of monarchical power, did not question the institution of monarchy as such. They wished to preserve the continuity of historical development and were afraid of jettisoning the monarchy, because they saw in it an element of stability that would contribute to keeping the popular movement from turning into a general social revolution. If Karl Marx erred in assuming that a proletarian revolution was imminent, he was quite right when, in the introductory sentences of the *Communist Manifesto,* he spoke of the terror that the "specter of communism" was working in the hearts of the bourgeoisie. The social revolts of March and April frightened the German liberals and made them even more determined to adhere to the monarchy as well as to restrict popular participation. They opposed universal suffrage and also made sure that the poor were excluded from the civil guards. Yet hard as many of the moderate liberals tried to forget that their own political influence was the result of the revolution, they could not renounce the principle of the sovereignty of the people if they wanted to achieve constitutional government and national unification against the resistance of the monarchical forces, and the cooperation of the whole popular movement, both liberal and democratic, was required in this struggle. The position of the liberals was bound to weaken to the extent to which the political movement of the people was slackening or splitting into parts. If, in addition, the old powers succeeded in convincing important social groups that the liberals were not the champions of their interests and ideals, and in organizing these groups for conservative ends, the liberals would lose all political stature.

↝ *The German Constituent National Assembly*

SIGNS OF SUCH DANGERS could already be discovered when on May 18, 1848, the "German Constituent National Assembly" convened in St. Paul's Church of Frankfurt. About 800 delegates had been elected, of whom, however, not many more than 500 were present at any time. The parliament has often been called a "parliament of professors," but although it contained 49 university professors, it was chiefly composed of lawyers within and without the government service. With three quarters of its members composed of university graduates, the assembly was mainly a representation of the educated middle class, which in Germany centered largely around the civil service and for its moral inspiration liked to look to the professors. Four guild masters and one lone peasant, but not a single worker, were the only representatives of the lower classes. Practically all of the approximately 140 members from agriculture, business, industry, and finance belonged to the well-to-do class.

It was the first and only time in German history that freely elected members from so many German lands joined in a political gathering. Representatives came from all the states and provinces belonging to the Germanic Confederation. Most Austrians arrived late, and the Czechs of Bohemia and Moravia refused to participate in elections for a German parliament. Schleswig and the Prussian provinces of East and West Prussia, however, were represented, since through the initiative of the Preparliament they had been incorporated into the confederation on April 1, 1848. The large assembly proved to be rather unwieldy. The number of people with parliamentary or political experience was small, and in the absence of any German political parties no organization existed which could have imposed easily accepted rules on this crowd of individualists. Their delight in making speeches was irrepressible. Parliamentary procedures remained cumbersome, though the intellectual level of the debates was impressive. Real political parties with an organized membership in the country did not develop in these years. But within the assembly, groups came into existence which eventually imposed voting discipline on their members and adopted all the tactics customary in the interparty game.

The issues over which such division occurred were those that had already occupied the Preparliament. Soon after the opening of the National Assembly the radicals renewed their attempt to declare the parliament the supreme political authority. They wished to assert the sovereignty of the people by subordinating all state governments, including state parliaments, to the National Assembly, which for that purpose was to create an executive arm. But the majority of the assembly was not willing to embark on such a revolutionary course. Only a declaration that the projected national constitution would ultimately supersede conflicting provisions of state constitutions was passed with a large majority. The radicals split on this occasion. Many voted with the majority of the assembly, because they saw the democratic principle preserved and considered it necessary to maintain political cooperation with the liberals. Two groups developed: a moderate one, under Robert Blum and Karl Vogt, and a more radical one under Wilhelm Zimmermann, Arnold Ruge, Lorenz Brentano, Ludwig Simon, and others. Since all political groups in Frankfurt were named after their meeting places, usually hotels, the former was known as the *Deutsche Hof*, the latter as the *Donnersberg*, though it called itself "the democratic party."

On the other side of the parliament was the *Café Milani*, composed of the rightists, among whom General von Radowitz, the Silesian Prince Felix Lichnowsky, Ernst von Lassaulx, and the leader of the United Diet of 1847, Baron von Vincke, were the most eminent. None of them was a diehard, and all were convinced that a reform of the confederation and of the autocratic state governments was necessary. In Vincke this was a matter of genuine faith, while the debonair Lichnowsky was too shrewd to misjudge realities. Radowitz sadly but bravely parted with many deeply held ideas which the revolution had shown to be hollow. None of the Prussian ultras, such as the Gerlachs or Otto von Bismarck, had come to Frankfurt. But the conservatives of the *Café Milani* were somewhat reluctant members of the assembly, to which they denied the right to assume any executive functions or even to create a constitution except through negotiation with the governments.

In the middle between the conservatives and the radicals was the liberal majority of the assembly, which was slower than the two minority groups in getting organized. Two major groups developed, often named the right and left center. The right-center liberals, on the whole men who would have liked nothing better than to make a constitution in negotiation with the government, assembled in the *Casino*. They wanted unity and constitutional guarantees, but at the same time protection against the social revolution. The *Casino* party, which found a continuation in the so-called Gotha group of the 1850's and the National Liberal party of the Second Empire, was studded with professors, in particular professors of law and history. But it also contained the industrialists, among them Mevissen and Beckerath. The *Casino* group included the chief champions of German unification under Prussian leadership. The left-center liberals, who met at the *Württembergische Hof*, were generally united by belief in the sovereignty of the people and the exclusive right of the National Assembly to create the constitution. While staid North Germans largely set the tone in the *Casino*, delegates from the southwest, among them a good many younger people, predominated in the *Württembergische Hof*.

Here debates were long and heated, and unity was not always easily achieved.

On May 19 the parliament elected Heinrich von Gagern (1799–1880) as its president. Growing up under the influence of patriotic fervor that had animated the students' unions after the war of liberation, this descendant of a family of imperial knights had become a convinced constitutionalist. In March 1848 he had become minister in Hesse–Darmstadt. Gagern was chivalrous and idealistic, but he was no original political thinker, and as a political tactician he was lacking in versatility and a quick grasp of changing political situations. Although Eduard Simson (1810–99), who succeeded him in December, was a more accomplished chairman at the debates of the assembly, Gagern was the most representative political figure of the Frankfurt parliament. The parliament was rich in talented, knowledgeable, and idealistic men but failed to produce statesmen who combined the capacity for leadership of the masses with an unfailing judgment of political realities.

✍ *"Central Authority" and "Imperial Regent"*

THE PROBLEM of how to organize popular support for the policies of the parliament did not even concern the majority of the assembly very much. Most members trusted that the power of ideas would gain the acclamation of the people and the assent of the princes in the end. In this spirit the majority was inclined to straddle real political issues rather than to meet them squarely. Thus the assembly proceeded to create a "central authority" in place of the despised Diet of the Germanic Confederation. On June 29 it elected Archduke John, the youngest brother of Emperor Francis, "imperial regent." Archduke John had acquired the reputation of being a liberal by some of his actions, among which his marriage to the daughter of a postmaster appealed most to the popular fancy. The archduke appointed a government of the Empire under the liberal Prince Karl von Leiningen, with the Austrian Anton von Schmerling as foreign minister and the Prussian general Eduard von Peucker as war minister.

Heinrich von Gagern, who was most responsible for the creation of this quasi-government, characterized the act as a demonstration of the sovereignty of the nation, but he quickly added that the assembly should win the cooperation of the state governments as well. The choice of a prince satisfied the monarchical sentiment, while the selection of an Austrian archduke avoided a challenge of Austria's leadership in Germany. The real problem, however, was the entirely unclarified position of the "central authority." Its recognition by the German governments meant practically only its acceptance as an agency provisionally taking the place of the diet. Thus it was no more than a gesture that the diet turned over the powers it held under the Federal Act of 1814 to the imperial regent. Quite apart from the fact that this made it possible later to say that the confederation had never ceased to exist, the powers of the diet were those of a confederate rather than a federal agency. When on July 16 the Frankfurt government demanded the outward recognition of its authority by the various German armies, Prussia, Austria, Hanover, and Bavaria refused any impairment of their control over their own military forces. Therefore, the new government in all its actions remained dependent on the good will of the individual German governments.

The establishment of the imperial regency might have been a practical intermediary step toward a German federal state if the Frankfurt Assembly had moved fast in presenting a German constitution while neither Austria nor Prussia was capable of acting with determination. But during the spring and summer of 1848 the Frankfurt parliament proved unable to produce such a constitution. A first blueprint of a federal German state had actually been already published before the opening of the assembly by the committee of the seventeen trustees. This draft of a constitution, chiefly the work of J. C. Dahlmann, envisaged a hereditary German monarchy with a two-chamber parliament. The German princes were to be members of the upper chamber. Foreign policy, military affairs, and general economic legislation were to come under federal jurisdiction. The draft of the seventeen aroused much criticism, not only among the state governments, as was to be expected, but also among the members of the Frankfurt parliament. Although the draft carefully avoided promoting the Prussian king as German emperor, it was obvious that it envisaged a Prussian solution of the German problem. The assembly was not ready to commit itself on this and similar far-reaching issues. Thus the draft never reached the floor of the house, nor did the parliament turn immediately to the organizational problems of a German federal state. Instead it plunged into months of discussion of "the fundamental rights of the German people."

✎ Fundamental Rights

IT WAS understandable that the Frankfurt parliament wished to advance the freedoms of the individual citizen and make them secure against violations by the autocracy of the princes and their bureaucrats, from which all classes except the nobility had severely suffered. In demanding such freedoms the majority of the assembly was united, and therefore the debates were a suitable method for acquainting the diffuse membership with one another. The fifty articles that were the result of these debates and were promulgated as German law on December 28, 1848, even before the constitution was ready, aimed at the complete abolition of all feudal forms and institutions still in existence in Germany and at the same time at the destruction of absolutism. Equality before the law and the abrogation of all class privileges, including political rights based on landed property, were proclaimed. In addition, freedom of association, assembly, the press, scholarly teaching and publication were guaranteed. At last, the right of habeas corpus was asserted in Germany, as was the separation of the judiciary from the executive.

However, these "fundamental rights" had as their objective not only the establishment of a liberal and constitutional order but also the creation of a national state. The freedoms and principles embodied in the catalog of fundamental rights were to determine the constitutions of the thirty-eight German states, and the individual German, who was to receive complete freedom of migration and settlement, was to enjoy the same civil and political rights everywhere in Germany. But the proclamation of such rights of national citizenship could not bring into existence a German national state as long as no government had been created that could subordinate the individual German states to its will, and in October when the Frankfurt Assembly began its deliberations on a German constitution, the general political conditions had changed so much as to make this task extremely difficult.

✍ The Test: Schleswig-Holstein

Yet during the summer of the fateful year of 1848 the Frankfurt parliament and its central authority experienced the limitations of their own power vis-à-vis the individual German states and simultaneously vis-à-vis the great European powers. The Schleswig-Holstein question became the acid test of the strength of the Frankfurt parliament. The formation of a provisional government of Schleswig-Holstein had taken place just at the time when Frederick William IV had declared that Prussia would merge into Germany. The Prussian foreign minister, Baron Heinrich von Arnim, saw in a policy of strong support of the Schleswig-Holstein people a good means for the expression of Prussia's devotion to the national German cause and for winning the sympathies of the German people. Prussia recognized the provisional government and, on behalf of the Germanic Confederation, moved a Prussian army, augmented by some forces from Hanover and other North German states, under the command of General von Wrangel into the duchies. The troops made rapid progress on the mainland and soon invaded even Jutland.

But these Prussian actions alarmed both England and Russia. Both powers had a natural interest in Denmark as the gatekeeper of the Baltic. To the czar the people of Schleswig-Holstein were mere rebels, and he was willing to rally to the defense of the monarchical principle. In England there existed some groups who disliked the whole German national movement, because they were afraid that it might unsettle the international order of Europe. Disraeli, one of the leading Tories, spoke with contempt of that "dreamy and dangerous nonsense called German nationality." Many Englishmen also worried lest the inclusion of the North German maritime region, which had been outside the German Customs Union, in a German federal state might pose a threat to British trade with the Continent. Actually the British government of John Russell, in which Palmerston was foreign secretary, was not much affected by these considerations. Palmerston and his colleagues would have accepted the establishment of a *kleindeutsch* Empire under Prussian leadership, which from a commercial point of view would have been preferable to a unified Central Europe including the Germanic Confederation and the whole Habsburg Empire. Yet the major motive of British policy was Palmerston's belief that a Prusso-German state of moderately liberal complexion in the center of the Continent would be the best guarantee of the European order between an autocratic Russia and a chaotically democratic France.

The British government would not have objected if Prussia had taken the initiative in leading the German unification movement. As a matter of fact, at the time of the risings in Baden in April 1848 when republicanism seemed to undermine social stability, it might even have welcomed such an initiative. The British cabinet frowned upon any attempt to change the frontiers of 1815 by revolutionary methods. In this attitude, no doubt, it had the support of the whole people. England, watching the general upheaval on the Continent, which, some feared, might also engulf her, quite instinctively fell back on the defense of the international *status quo*. But Palmerston was willing to make some adjustments to new developments, particularly to the expressed wishes of a national group, provided they could be achieved through diplomatic negotiations. Palmerston warned against the use of troops in the duchies and offered his services as a mediator. In May he proposed the joining to the confederation of both Schleswig and Holstein under the duke of Augustenburg after the death of the Danish king. But the predominantly Danish-populated northern sections of Schleswig as defined by linguistic maps were to be annexed by Denmark. Baron Arnim was sensible enough to accept this British plan for Prussia on May 19, but he was not able to carry through this policy, because opposition arose in Germany which played into the hands of the Danish nationalists.

This opposition came from the Frankfurt parliament and the provisional Schleswig-Holstein government. The latter declared the partition of Schleswig intolerable, while in Frankfurt a passionate chorus of voices condemning the weak policy of Prussia was heard. The left was particularly wild in chauvinistic outcries, but none of the members of the right center presented a constructive policy nor showed the courage to throw himself against the nationalist flood. The absence of any reason in diplomatic affairs among the democratic and liberal members of the assembly must be largely traced back to the complete lack of any practical contact with foreign relations, but it also showed to what extent the Germans had lost a feeling of responsibility for the European community of nations. Obviously, a united Germany was bound to have tremendous power in Europe, and the confidence of the other European nations was sorely needed if they were to accept German unification. Such trust could not be acquired by marching against a small neighbor and raising exaggerated claims against her. The German attitude turned international sympathies toward Denmark—especially, of course, in Sweden, but also in England—with the result that the general attitude toward the national aims of the Frankfurt parliament became unfriendly.

The anti-Danish sentiment of the German democrats and liberals was accompanied by a lively agitation for the building of a German navy. The naval superiority of Denmark had proved a considerable handicap in the Schleswig-Holstein campaign, and the Danes were quite successful in their blockade operations in the Baltic. But the fervor which the propaganda aroused throughout Germany showed that the individual German longed not only for personal freedom but also for the freedom to assert his strength in the world through a powerful national state.

✐ The Armistice of Malmö

IN THE END Frederick William took the worst possible course. In his innermost heart he always tended to agree with his brother-in-law the czar in judging the provisional government of Schleswig-Holstein a collection of rebels, and he had justified the Prussian occupation of the duchies with the necessity of keeping the popular movement under control. When Sweden intervened and Russia threatened a rupture of relations, he decided to extricate himself from the political impasse without paying much attention to the Frankfurt parliament. His penchant for dynastic diplomacy and his Russian-inspired fear of identifying himself with British policy led him to conclude an armistice under Swedish auspices, thereby forgoing some of the guarantees for a fair peace settlement that he might have gained through English mediation. The armistice of Malmö of August 26 sacrificed the provisional government of Schleswig-Holstein and placed the duchies under the administration of a mixed commission on which the Danes prevailed, while the ultimate political settlement remained open.

∽ *Impotence of National Assembly*

THE ARMISTICE OF MALMÖ met with profound popular resentment all over Germany. Its conclusion without the approval of the Frankfurt authorities was a challenge to the position of the national parliament. On September 5 the assembly passed a resolution presented by Dahlmann, the moderate liberal historian, which forbade any implementation of the armistice of Malmö. The government of Prince Leiningen resigned, and Dahlmann attempted to form a cabinet, but he could have found a majority only by allying himself with the radical left, which he was loath to do. On September 16 the assembly reversed its earlier vote and approved of the armistice with slight reservations. Some of the foremost champions of the Schleswig-Holstein cause, among them J. G. Droysen and Georg Waitz, were arguing now for the acceptance of the armistice, and even Dahlmann voted with them in the end. Not only was the lack of political judgment and determination among the intellectual leaders of the right center revealed by this action but also the actual political impotence of the parliament. It bowed to the will of the Prussian government. The anger of the democratic left was great and was shared by the masses, who felt betrayed by the meek surrender of the parliamentary majority after all the nationalist speech-making that had gone before. The Frankfurt parliament and the central authority saw themselves exposed to tumultuous street demonstrations and had to call for protection by Prussian and Hessian soldiers. These troops quelled the popular uprisings on September 18, but two rightist members of the parliament, General Hans von Auerswald and Prince Felix Lichnowsky, were cruelly murdered by mob action. A few days later Struve started an armed revolt in southern Baden with the avowed aim of setting up a German republic, but this attempt was easily suppressed.

∽ *Turning Point in the Revolution*

THE SEPTEMBER EVENTS constituted a turning point in the history of the German revolution. The conflict between democrats and liberals became so embittered as to make any constructive cooperation between the two groups impossible in the future. The red flags which had appeared in Frankfurt and the attacks on private property in the Baden revolt frightened the German burghers and drove many of them into the arms of the reaction. When, in early October, the Frankfurt parliament began its work on the federal constitution, the discussion with the house and the flagging popular support already made it unlikely that the constitution could be imposed on the German state governments by the sovereign will of the representatives of the nation. It was obvious that the Frankfurt parliament would eventually have to seek a compromise with these monarchical governments through negotiations.

✍ *Austria's Recovery*

AUSTRIA AND PRUSSIA, the two great governments that counted more than all the others, had recovered a great deal of the strength which they had lost in March. The Austrian empire had been on the brink of complete dissolution. The revolution had not only opened the gates for the political and social reform of the empire but also for the defection of the nationalities from the imperial government. Hungary asserted her autonomy at once. The Lombardo-Venetian kingdom was soon engulfed in the national struggle of the Italian people, for which the ruler of Piedmont-Sardinia, King Charles Albert, risked his army. The Czechs and Slovaks, while demanding recognition of special national rights, were afraid that the transformation of the Germanic Confederation into a German federal state as promoted by the Frankfurt parliament would make the realization of a Czech state impossible. From the outset the Czechs refused to participate in the work of Frankfurt. It was at this moment that Franz Palacký, the leader of the Czech national movement, made his famous statement that if Austria did not exist, it would have to be invented.

Yet this did not mean that Palacký had anything to say in favor of the Austria of Metternich. In contrast to a Great German Empire, the Habsburg Empire offered the opportunity for advancing the position of the Slavs. As a demonstration against the first German National Assembly in Frankfurt, the Czechs convened the first Pan-Slav congress in Prague in June 1848. Although voices were heard expressing hope that a reconciliation between the Russians and Poles would soon produce fraternal cooperation between all the Slavs, the problems of the Slavs within the Habsburg Empire dominated the debates of the congress. Czechs and Yugoslavs combined to demand the transformation of the Habsburg Empire into a federal state in which the Slav nationalities would play an equal role with the Germans and Magyars. Austro-Slavism prevailed over Pan-Slavism, and it was one of the tragic events in the history of Germany and Europe that the movement was not used to give some satisfaction to the aspirations of the West Slavs and South Slavs.

Since late May, Prague and Bohemia had been ruled by their provincial governor. He had formed a governmental council in which German conservatives and Czech moderates, among them Palacký, cooperated. But the Czech workers were disappointed at the lack of more drastic social and political reform, and, as the people of Berlin had done on March 18, they sensed, not incorrectly, that the new order could not be called secure as long as the old powers exercised complete control over the armed forces. On Whitsunday, June 13, friction between the populace and the soldiers led to open revolution. Prince Alfred Windischgrätz, the fearless military commander, did not hesitate to fight the rebellion, and made himself master of the city. All dreams of a separate constitution for Bohemia came to an end, and the Pan-Slav congress was dispersed. The consequences of the bombardment and reoccupation of the Bohemian capital were far-reaching. It was the first open victory of a military counterrevolution. Two weeks later General Cavaignac, on a much larger scale, fought the bloody battles that broke the power of the revolution in Paris.

Meanwhile, the Austrian army under Field Marshal Count Joseph Radetzky was already beginning to regain control of Venetia. In July Radetzky broke into Lombardy and defeated King Charles Albert of Piedmont at Custozza on the 25th of the month. On August 6 the Austrians occupied Milan again, and Piedmont was saved from invasion largely through the intercession of British diplomacy. In general Britain proved more persistent than France in her support of political reforms in Italy. Although all the French governments showed sympathy with the national movement, none ever went beyond mere gestures, in spite of the fact that the forced withdrawal of Austria from Italy would have seriously shaken the Vienna settlement of 1815, so much resented by the French. But in the face of her internal troubles France was not prepared to take risks which might have brought on a general European war. Thus Austria could restore her position in Italy for the time being. These events strengthened the hand of the imperial court, which had withdrawn from revolutionary Vienna to Innsbruck, the capital of the loyal Tyrol.

The imperial court had left Vienna on May 17, when it became clear that the government had lost control of the city to the democratic movement. The imperial ministers of this period were benevolent administrators without political gifts. The actual power was in the hands of a committee of Viennese citizens who relied on the national guard and on the academic legion. Whereas in the beginning the moderates had considerable influence and the workers were excluded from full political participation, conflicts with the government and a worsening economic situation tended to drive the movement toward greater radicalism. No political leader of any stature appeared, however, either among the liberals or the radicals. Few if any Viennese seemed to realize how isolated the city really was. While the political developments in Vienna in the summer of 1848 showed a certain similarity with those of the great French Revolution, no Vienna committee of public safety could hope to rule the Habsburg Empire in the way Paris could dominate France. For one thing, the political mood of Vienna was out of tune with that of the Austrian countryside. In addition, the nationalities wanted to gain freedom from Vienna while on the other side they were resentful of the strong sympathies which the Viennese felt for the Great German cause. From March till October the black, red, and gold flag was flown on St. Stephen's Cathedral.

✐ *The* Reichstag

ON JULY 22, an all-Austrian parliament (*Reichstag*) convened in Vienna. All Habsburg lands except the Lombardo-Venetian kingdom and Hungary proper were represented. Almost half of the members were Slavs; there were also Ruthenians, Rumanians, and Italians from the Trentino, Trieste, and Dalmatia. The Germans were in the minority. The *Reichstag* mirrored not only the variety of the nationalities which lived in the Habsburg Empire but also the vast differences in their stages of cultural development. In contrast to the Frankfurt Assembly, the Vienna parliament was composed of members of all social classes, particularly of peasants and small landowners. The latter showed little interest in constitutional questions, and many of them went home after agrarian reform legislation had been passed. The security committee of Vienna looked askance at the imperial parliament, which in their eyes was a strange and primitive group, and moreover one dominated by non-Germans.

✐ *The October Revolution*

FOR A WHILE a somewhat calmer air prevailed in Vienna. The imperial court returned to the capital on August 12, but although the upper classes were obviously tired of the revolution and became politically less active, this only strengthened the influence of the radical left in the revolutionary committee, which was still the real power in Vienna. Republican and also socialist tendencies grew stronger, and serious riots occurred when the government curtailed the workers' dole. The decision of the government to open war against the Hungarian revolution brought on the final crisis. The imperial government supported Banus Jelačić in his fight for Croatian independence from Budapest. He was to spearhead the attack, for which imperial troops were made ready, among them German troops in Vienna. The heroic fight of the Hungarian revolutionaries under Ludwig Kossuth was much admired by the Viennese democrats. It was also clear that once the imperial government succeeded in subduing Hungary, the democratic movement in Austria would be doomed. When on October 6 a battalion of German grenadiers was to leave Vienna for Hungary, the soldiers mutinied under mob pressure. The court fled again, this time only as far as Olmütz. The wild mob found little resistance. The minister of war, Count Latour, was massacred in bestial fashion, the armory was forced, and the people were armed.

The revolutionary regime which established itself did not represent the majority of the population, which it held down by terroristic methods. The October revolution developed a radical social character, in some respects foreshadowing the Paris Commune. But it failed to produce any outstanding leaders who were able to give it a clear direction and to devise a feasible policy of defense. A delegation of the left of the Frankfurt parliament, among them Robert Blum and Julius Froebel, could do no more than boost the popular morale. A Hungarian army attempted to make its way to Vienna, but was forced back by Jelačić. Thereafter Vienna's fate was sealed. With his army, chiefly composed of Czech, Slovak, and Polish troops, and supported by Jelačić's Croatian hordes from the south, Prince Windischgrätz reconquered the city in bloody fighting between October 26–31, and cruel vengeance was wreaked on many revolutionaries as well as on many innocent people. Prince Windischgrätz specifically authorized the execution of Robert Blum, disregarding Blum's immunity as a member of the Frankfurt parliament.

This action, which aroused a wave of popular indignation in Germany, had the prior approval of the general's brother-in-law, Prince Felix Schwarzenberg (1800–52), who in these days emerged as the leading Austrian minister. These two Bohemian magnates wished to teach the Frankfurt parliament a lesson. Their minds were set on the full restoration of the Habsburg Empire and equally of Austria's position in Germany. While they used chiefly Slav forces to subdue the German element in Austria, they were sincerely convinced that they served a German cause, insofar as their policy would preserve the prevailing influence of the Germans in all of Central Europe. Schwarzenberg, by his upbringing as officer and diplomat, was a statesman of high stature. The scion of a famous old family, he did not display any showiness of manner, but he combined a determined will, strong and supple as steel, with a cool, realistic grasp of people and events. Undoubtedly he would have been a serious opponent of Bismarck if an early death, in 1852, had not put an end to his career.

Schwarzenberg devoted himself with great zeal to rebuilding the Habsburg monarchy. The time had not yet come for dropping all liberal trappings. The Austrian parliament, which the government had adjourned and banned from Vienna, was reopened late in November in the small Moravian town of Kremsier. Here Schwarzenberg professed his belief in the unity of the Habsburg Empire as a vital need of Germany and of Europe, but he posed at the same time as a champion of constitutionalism and liberalism. Although Schwarzenberg intended to carry through a number of reforms in the social and economic field and had added to his cabinet some liberal figures such as Alexander von Bach (1813–93) and Karl von Bruck (1798–1860), he remained essentially a Josephinian autocrat. He persuaded the imbecile Emperor Ferdinand to resign in favor of the eighteen-year-old Archduke Francis, who ascended the throne on December 2, 1848. For sixty-eight years Emperor Francis Joseph was to serve as the symbol of the unity of the Habsburg Empire. By the end of 1848 Schwarzenberg had laid a powerful foundation for the reconstruction of this empire. He had also made it clear that the Austrian government was strongly opposed to the work of the Frankfurt parliament. Still, Italy was not yet fully pacified, and, most serious, a fierce war with Hungary was imminent. Therefore Austria could not as yet bring her full weight to bear on German affairs, and theoretically at least, Prussian policy enjoyed considerable freedom of action.

✍ *Prussia's Recovery*

EVENTS IN PRUSSIA had, however, produced conditions which made it doubtful whether she was willing to take the initiative in Germany. On May 22, four days after the opening of the Frankfurt parliament, the Prussian National Assembly convened in Berlin. In the elections of the two representative bodies, which were held simultaneously, the voters had usually sent the intellectual leaders to Frankfurt and the representatives of local interests to Berlin. Thus the Berlin parliament had fewer members from among the intellectuals and more from the lower classes, particularly peasants and artisans. No workers could be found in the Berlin assembly and almost no conservative *Junkers*. The party divisions were not very different from those in Frankfurt, and the liberal center was decisive. The left center, however, was somewhat stronger than in Frankfurt, and in the Westphalian Franz Benedict Waldeck (1802–70) and the East Prussian Johann Jacoby (1805–77) it had most impressive advocates of popular rights. The leader of the right-center liberals, Hans Viktor von Unruh (1806–86), who became president of the assembly in October, did not have as wide an appeal.

Officially the assembly had been called in order to cooperate and agree with the government on a Prussian constitution, but the majority was inclined to consider the assembly as a constituent convention. The government of Ludolf Camphausen presented a draft constitution which, though with serious omissions, followed the Belgian constitution. This draft was hardly used by the committee of the assembly, which prepared its own draft, the "*charte* Waldeck," so called because Waldeck had his democratic convictions written into it. But before the new draft reached the plenary assembly, in October, a series of conflicts developed between the assembly and the government. The March revolution had been ostensibly victorious; otherwise no parliament would have come into existence, nor would a civic guard have taken over the protection of the city from the royal guards. The burghers of Berlin were now even allowed to smoke in public on *Unter den Linden*. But no liberal could fail to feel that the old powers, if momentarily frightened, were still very strong. The old bureaucracy still held full sway over the administration, and the army, though momentarily conspicuous by its absence in Berlin, was firmly in the hands of an officers corps that knew only loyalty to the king and did not care to cover up its disdain for the revolutionary achievements.

Small wonder then that the liberals looked for assurances from government circles with regard to their willingness to cooperate with the popular forces in a constitutional manner. It was also natural that such demands were directed particularly at the political attitude of the Prussian officers. Many liberals, not only of the left but also of the right center, saw in these guarantees the only way to stave off a new revolutionary outbreak, which everybody in the assembly, with the exception of the right, wished to see avoided. But the Prussian cabinets never acted as representatives of the parliamentary majority; at best they served as brokers between the king and the assembly. For months Berlin remained in a state of fruitless revolutionary agitation. This unrest worsened the economic situation, and street mobs demonstrated against the unproductive assembly.

It is not true that the Prussian National Assembly fell under the spell of the radicalism of the street. The parliamentary majority stubbornly pursued its aim of transforming the Prussian military monarchy into a liberal and constitutional state. Largely frustrated in its efforts by the resistance of the old powers, the majority of the assembly was threatened with political isolation. Its protective force, the civil guards, went into action against radical outbreaks, but while this deepened the break between the revolutionary elements of the city and the parliament, it did not satisfy the burghers. The civic guards were inadequate to keep complete order in Berlin, and not even the creation of a special constabulary, following the English model, sufficed. Many people wished for the return of the military garrison as well as of the court and society, whose patronage was missed by many a merchant and artisan. By the fall of 1848 the unity and fervor that the popular movement had displayed in March was broken up. Even those groups that had remained politically active worked at cross-purposes.

✎ *The* Kamarilla

FREDERICK WILLIAM IV spent most of the summer of 1848 at Potsdam, close to his guard troops and surrounded by what the people called the *Kamarilla*, the circle of his ultraconservative personal friends and advisors, among whom General Leopold von Gerlach, Captain Edwin von Manteuffel, Baron Senfft von Pilsach, and H. H. von Kleist-Retzow were most prominent. All these Prussian *Junkers* were men of deep and honest, if narrow, convictions. They worked hard to instill new courage in the king, whose wavering they deplored. Actually, Frederick William IV, though temporarily confounded, had not changed his ideas of royal government. It was most important in these circumstances that the men of the *Kamarilla* succeed in organizing political support in the country with the help of their friends and *Junker* cousins. Among them the young Otto von Bismarck began to play a noticeable role. They decided to fight democracy with its own tools. From the members of the *Kamarilla* and other old-Prussian *Junkers*, as well as from the Russian ambassador in Berlin, funds were contributed for the founding of the *Neue Preussische Zeitung*, commonly called the *Kreuzzeitung*, because in its masthead it showed the iron cross, the war decoration of the War of Liberation, together with the slogan of the period "With God for king and fatherland." The *Kreuzzeitung* first appeared in 1848 under the able editorship of Hermann Wagener; it preached against German nationalism, liberalism, and democracy as steps that inevitably would lead to communism and anarchy. The preservation of the traditional institutions and policies of the Prussian monarchy, including friendship with Russia, was the task of statesmanship. Until the days of Hitler the *Kreuzzeitung* remained the sonorous and uninhibited voice of die-hard Prussian conservatism.

✎ *The* Junker *Parliament*

THE JULY debates of the Prussian National Assembly on the abolition of manorial rights alarmed the *Junkers* and drove them to form party-like organizations. "The association for the protection of the interests of landed property" was formed and held general meetings in Berlin on August 16–18. The public dubbed this first conservative national convention the "*Junker* parliament." The ideological proclamations were somewhat muffled by materialistic agrarian concerns, on which common policies and tactics were formulated. While the *Junkers* as a class thus entered the political arena, they were active in mobilizing wide popular support, which they found chiefly among their own peasants, the small people of the rural towns, and the disenchanted artisans of the cities. The

Protestant churches proved staunch supporters in these reactionary efforts. All over the Prussian provinces patriotic Prussian or pastoral associations sprouted.

✎ Dissolution of the Prussian National Assembly

THE CABINET that had been appointed in March had fallen after the middle of June. It had received its political character by the membership of the two leaders of Rhenish liberalism, Ludolf Camphausen and David Hansemann. The succeeding government, in which Rudolf von Auerswald took Camphausen's place as prime minister, was still largely under the influence of Hansemann and other liberals. But when the Auerswald-Hansemann cabinet failed to defeat attempts of the assembly to extend its control over the army, Frederick William prepared for a showdown. General Friedrich von Wrangel was made commander of the military forces in all the districts around Berlin, and about 50,000 men were assembled in a wide circle around the capital. On September 22 the king selected another general, Ernst von Pfuel, as prime minister of a cabinet composed largely of bureaucrats. It seemed to be a government intended for conflict. But General von Pfuel was a liberal officer of the Scharnhorst-Boyen tradition, though unfortunately too old to maintain himself for long under the trying conditions. He calmed the opposition by liberal concessions, such as the grant of a habeas corpus act and the abolition of the hunting rights of the landlords. The debates on the draft constitution by the plenum in October aroused the indignation of Frederick William IV. The majority abolished noble ranks and titles as well as all decorations. What hurt the king most was the dropping by the assembly of the formula "king by the grace of God." The divine-right theory of monarchy was the tenet of faith dearest to his heart. Actually the resolutions of the assembly were not final, since the draft constitution was still to be negotiated with the government. But now the king was ready to impose his will. The conquest of Vienna by the army of Prince Windischgrätz had made him confident.

On November 2 the king appointed Count Frederick William Brandenburg prime minister. This handsome Hohenzollern, son of King Frederick William II and his morganatic wife, Countess Sophie Dönhoff, had been corps commander in Silesia and had stoutly defended royal authority and military privileges during the revolution. He was not a man of great political gifts, but his name was a political hallmark. The chief political brain of the cabinet was the minister of the interior, Baron Otto von Manteuffel, a shrewd and experienced bureaucrat. On November 9 Count Brandenburg proclaimed the removal of the Prussian National Assembly from Berlin to the provincial town of Brandenburg. The pressure brought on the free deliberations of the assembly by street demonstrations was given as reason for this change of scene. Protesting against the illegal action of the government, the assembly assumed an attitude of passive resistance but finally called for a general tax strike of the people.

On November 10 General von Wrangel rode into the city with 13,000 soldiers. The troops were not enthusiastically welcomed by the population, although there was no open defiance. Whatever preparations for revolts were being made quickly petered out when, on November 12, a state of siege was declared over all of Prussia. Only in the Rhineland and in Silesia did unrest occur, but this was soon suppressed. It proved simple to keep the assembly from further meetings in Berlin. The members of the left at first refused to attend sessions in Brandenburg. When they appeared there, they were excluded from the assembly by strange maneuvers of the right. The government dissolved the badly discredited National Assembly on December 5 and simultaneously imposed a constitution.

Only with great difficulty had the ministers persuaded the king that even in victory he ought to adhere to his promises to grant a modern constitution. Flushed by the delight over the success of his soldiers, Frederick William IV saw no need for a new parliament, and he hoped that he might return to his romantic schemes of representation by estates at a later date. His conservative ministers reminded him that no reconciliation between the monarchy and the people could be expected if the king went back on his word. Moreover, the ministers wanted Prussia to play a role in Germany and were quite correctly convinced that only a Prussian monarchy which showed itself open to new ideas would be able to hold the sympathies of the rest of Germany. But at the same time the ministers intended to preserve the power of the crown. They preferred to talk about monarchical-constitutional instead of constitutional government.

✑ The Imposed Constitution

THE IMPOSED Prussian constitution of December 5, 1848, impressed the liberals in Prussia and abroad, while to many royalists it seemed almost a surrender. The document was a revised version of the proposal that the government had presented to the Prussian National Assembly as a basis for its constitutional debates.[3] As has been mentioned before, the draft of May 1848 followed the general scheme of the Belgian constitution of 1830 except in the definition of monarchical authority, which was given a more independent position, as in the French *Charte* of 1814. The Prussian constitution of December 5, 1848, went even further in this direction, though adopting some of the constitutional demands of the opposition.

[3] See p. 73.

✑ Civil Rights

IN ITS FIRST section, the Prussian constitution of 1848 very generously granted civil rights, such as equality before the law, freedom of person, of migration, of religion, of expression, of assembly, and of association. The Evangelical and Roman Catholic Churches were promised independence from all state interference. The constitution stated that the legislative power would be exercised jointly by the king and two chambers. The first chamber was to be elected by men over thirty years of age, but through the introduction of a high property qualification only the members of the middle and upper classes were enfranchised. Still, the formulation of a first chamber without reference to birth and rank was resented by Frederick William IV and the nobility. The second chamber, in their eyes, was equally bad, because it rested on universal and direct suffrage. According to article 99, the chambers possessed as their most important right that of approving the annual budget.

✑ Reassertion of Divine Right

THE ENDOWMENT of citizens with broad freedoms and the participation of liberally organized chambers in legislation, together with provisions for an independent judiciary and the development of free self-government on the local level, shone forth as the democratic elements of the Prussian constitution of 1848. But it carefully avoided repeating the key principle of the Belgian constitution, that all state power derives from the people. On the contrary, it highlighted the divine-right character of the monarchy and gave the king the exclusive control of the executive. Appointments of ministers, officials, and officers remained the sole privilege of the king, who also received special emergency powers, including the possible suspension of civil rights. Large exemptions were granted to the vast crown domains, in order to make the royal house fully independent financially. The true anchor of royal supremacy, however, was the army, which was treated as a separate establishment within the state.

✑ Liberal Legislative Acts

IN ORDER to strengthen the appearance of its liberal intentions the Prussian government of Count Brandenburg and Baron Manteuffel in the next weeks issued a number of liberal legislative acts, such as a provisional alleviation of manorial services, abolition of patrimonial jurisdiction on the landed estates, a revision of the court trial system, and the ending of the stamp on newspapers. This policy contributed to the generally favorable reception of the imposed constitution and made people overlook its "cloven hoof." The constitution was expressly called provisional and open to debate with the chambers to be elected. These elections resulted in a moderate conservative majority, even for the second chamber, and thereby the way was opened for further revision in a reactionary direction. When the second chamber, however, urged the Prussian government to lift the state of siege and to accept the German constitution which the Frankfurt National Assembly had completed, the government dissolved the chamber in early May 1849.

✑ Three-Class Suffrage

ON MAY 30, Manteuffel imposed a new election law for the second chamber. It still theoretically left every male Prussian beyond the age of twenty-five enfranchised, but it divided the voters into three classes according to the amount of direct taxes. The total revenue of a community or district was divided into three parts, and beginning with the biggest taxpayers the people were distributed into classes. There would be few in the first class of voters, who together paid the first third of the sum total; the second class had more, though not necessarily very many, members, while the third class comprised the mass of the people paying small or no taxes. Each class elected the same number of electors, who thereafter as a body would choose one deputy to the Prussian *Landtag* (Diet) through open ballot.

The three-class electoral law was an outright plutocratic system and as such somewhat surprising in still precapitalistic Prussia. Its political effect was to favor the big landowners. The chamber elected with the new suffrage was completely dominated by a conservative majority, and the royalist revision of the constitution of 1848 proceeded smoothly thereafter. Among the major changes was the transformation of the elected first chamber into a "House of Lords," the second chamber henceforth being called "House of Deputies." Of great and fateful consequences was the rewording of the original article 108, which had been of a merely transitional nature. It stated that the existing taxes and duties should continue being levied by the government. But the article could be misinterpreted as overriding the necessity for the approval of the budget by the diet. Attempts to recast and clarify this article proved unsuccessful. On the other hand, an article was inserted exempting the army from taking an oath to the constitution. The monarchy with its absolutist tools—the army, the bureaucracy, and the ruling *Junker* class—emerged victorious from the revolution. Still rather reluctantly, Frederick William IV finally took the oath to the imposed constitution of January 31, 1850, which, except for minor changes, remained the fundamental order of Prussia until the monarchy collapsed in 1918.

✧ The Constituent National Assembly: New Problems

THE REVIVAL of monarchical authority in Austria and Prussia during October and November 1848 had created a new situation for the Constituent National Assembly at Frankfurt. On October 19, 1848, at its one-hundredth meeting, the assembly turned to discussion of the constitution. The first three articles of the draft which the constitutional committee presented to the house posed the most crucial problem for any attempt to found a German national state. The committee proposed to confine the new state to the lands of the Germanic Confederation and in addition required that no part of the new Empire could form a single state together with non-Germanic territories. "If a German land and a non-German land have the same head of state, the relations between the two lands must be regulated by the principles of mere personal union." This clause applied chiefly to the Habsburg Empire. It demanded the relative separation of the German provinces of Austria, among which not only the old Austrian duchies but also Bohemia and Moravia were counted, from the rest of the Habsburg monarchy. The proposal found surprisingly little opposition in the assembly. Only a minority of the Austrian delegation and some South German and Rhenish Catholics voted against the articles.

But the vote was taken before the subjugation of Vienna by the Austrian reaction. Even at this moment, however, it was doubtful whether the Austrians were fully aware of the implications of including German Austria in a German national state. The vast majority of the Germans in Austria probably wished not only to retain the ties that bound Austria to Germany but even to strengthen them. But few Austrians liked to lose the opportunities and connections which the Danubian Empire had created. A clear political program which would have resolved this conflict of sentiments could not be found. Prince Schwarzenberg did not have to be afraid of the feelings of the German Austrians with regard to what was called the Great German problem, the more so since he claimed that his own policy was directed toward some sort of Great Germany as well.

✧ Schwarzenberg's Policies

FROM THE VERY beginning the outlines of Schwarzenberg's policies were clearly fixed in his mind. He was first and foremost a believer in the Habsburg Empire. The restoration of the dynastic control over all historic Habsburg possessions was his immediate aim. Next came the introduction of greater centralization of the administration in order to make the imperial government secure against any future insurrections of democratic or national movements. A restored Habsburg Empire was then to assume its leading position in Germany as well. But with the creation of a centralized Habsburg Empire not only the German lands, as in the past, but rather the total Habsburg monarchy would have to be accepted into the Germanic Confederation. Such a program was in every respect the opposite to the liberal and national aims of the German revolution. No federal state was possible under it, but only a confederation, though possibly one with slightly increased jurisdiction. No constitution granting popular rights and representation could come into being. Last but not least, a confederation joining the whole Habsburg Empire to Germany would have contained more than twenty-five million non-German people or one third of the total population. In terms of national unification the type of confederation that Schwarzenberg envisaged was a retrogression. As a matter of fact, it was not a Great Germany but a Great Austria that the prince wished to establish.

✍ Great Germany or Great Austria

HERE SCHWARZENBERG'S plans clashed not only with the national hopes of the German people but also with the interests of a conservative Prussia. The accession of the whole Habsburg Empire would have changed the balance of power within the confederation to the detriment of Prussia. Prussia had always demanded that Austria should respect her special influence in northern Germany; the Prussian government had urged a better military organization for the Germanic Confederation as well as an independent command function for the Prussian king. This was the minimum that even the reactionary Prussians were expecting from Austria. Schwarzenberg offered a plan which would have subordinated the small German states to the major ones. No doubt the removal of the midget states from the high political councils of Germany would have been rather beneficial, but it would have narrowed Prussia's role in the confederation. Schwarzenberg suggested that the small states be placed in individual groups under the five kingdoms, Prussia, Saxony, Hanover, Bavaria, and Württemberg. Since the latter four would inevitably look toward Austria for the protection of their sovereignty, Prussia would have been isolated at just the moment when the extension of the area of the confederation might have made her liable to assist Austria in the defense of her Italian possessions or her southern Danubian countries.

Schwarzenberg was careful not to unveil his whole program at once. For a long time to come, Austria could not hope to intervene in Germany except by propagandist words and gestures or by diplomacy. Still, the execution of Robert Blum had given the world a warning of the contempt felt by the new Austrian rulers for the Frankfurt Assembly. Schwarzenberg's declaration before the All-Austrian Assembly of Kremsier, on November 27, placed on record his absolute determination to build a unified Habsburg state. In this announcement many members of the Frankfurt Assembly saw quite correctly a definitely negative reply to the question that the assembly had laid before Austria with articles 2 and 3 of its draft constitution. The attitude of the Austrian government undermined the position of the Austrian Anton von Schmerling (1805–93), who had led the Frankfurt ministry since the September revolts. Heinrich von Gagern became the new prime minister; Eduard Simson (1810–99), a Prussian, followed him as president of the National Assembly. But other members were not yet convinced that in the future the Frankfurt Assembly would be dependent on the cooperation of Prussia. They still wished to—and consequently did—discover in the policies of the Schwarzenberg cabinet possibilities of keeping Austria and Germany together or even of restoring Austria's presidential role.

✑ Grossdeutsch *vs.* Kleindeutsch

A REALIGNMENT of parties took place in the Frankfurt Assembly during December 1848. Schmerling organized the forces which were willing to defend the Austrian cause. They consisted largely of conservative Catholics, many of whom were moved by anti-Prussian feeling rather than by any strong attachment to Vienna. These *grossdeutsch* groups fought against the champions of a *kleindeutsch* solution, which envisioned the establishment of a federal state under Prussian leadership with the exclusion of Austria. The *grossdeutsch* group found parliamentary support on the left side of the house. The democrats, placing freedom above unity, still believed that they could impose a free constitution on all the German princes.

✑ *Prussian Policies*

IT WAS amazing that the center groups of the Frankfurt Assembly could believe that Prussia would be ready to accept the leadership of a *kleindeutsch* federal state. But in these months there was more than one Prussian policy. As seen from Frankfurt, the hopeful attitude of Ludolf Camphausen carried great weight. After his resignation as prime minister in July, this Rhenish liberal had become the representative of the Prussian government in Frankfurt. He was confident that he would bring the Prussian government and the Frankfurt Assembly together. He felt that the constitution that the assembly would produce should be accepted only as a basis of discussion by the German governments, who then could pull out its sharpest democratic teeth. In this way he expected to overcome Frederick William IV's resistance to the sovereignty of the people. On the other hand, he trusted that in the end the National Assembly would agree to revisions, provided the king would identify himself with the struggle for national unification.

On these broad assumptions Camphausen encouraged the champions of the *kleindeutsch* solution to move forward. Actually, the Brandenburg-Manteuffel cabinet, preoccupied with internal Prussian affairs, liked to listen to Camphausen's advice on German affairs. The great gains which Prussia might make appealed even to these conservative Prussians, but at the same time they were afraid of the risks involved in an active foreign policy that was bound to bring Prussia into conflict with Austria. Moreover, they had to compromise with the king and, worse than that, were not even aware of some of the negotiations which the king conducted behind their backs. Frederick William IV had recovered his haughty pride and was anxious to act autocratically. In his view the time had arrived when the Austrian and Prussian governments should agree on a common solution of the German problem and, together with the major German princes, impose it as law. When he learned, however, in what direction Schwarzenberg's ideas were moving, he became unsure.

✍ *Constitution of the German Empire*

THE FRANKFURT National Assembly completed the first reading of a constitution of the German Empire in the last days of January 1849. At that time the constitution placed at the head of the new Empire an emperor to be chosen from among the German ruling princes. Whether this emperor would be elected for a limited number of years, for his life, or as a hereditary ruler had not been decided by the assembly as yet. The emperor represented Germany internationally, held the command over the army, and was charged with the executive power. He was expected to reside at the seat of the government, which was not named in the constitution, though presumably the assembly would have chosen Frankfurt, and certainly not Berlin. He was to receive a civil list from the diet (*Reichstag*).

To this diet the emperor was closely tied. The imperial ministers were responsible to the diet, which consisted of two houses, the House of States and the People's House. The House of States was composed of 176 members, half of them appointed by the state governments, the other half elected by the state parliaments. Although the Frankfurt parliamentarians had taken the American Constitution as their model, they rejected the construction of the United States Senate. The size of the thirty-odd German states was too different for equal representation, and through the double form of membership the monarchical nature of these states was expressed. The People's House was a national parliament elected for a three-year period. It enjoyed predominant power in all financial matters. The members of both houses were not bound by instructions of their voters or state governments. They had the right of impeachment.

The authority of the Empire extended over all foreign affairs, the navy, and most army affairs. The Empire was to form a single customs union; it had supervision over all trade and commerce, transportation, and communication. It was to establish full unity of currency and to inaugurate national codes of civil, commercial, and criminal law, as well as court procedure. For its financial sustenance it was to depend on customs duties. If they proved inadequate, the states were to make so-called "matricular" contributions, that is, direct payments according to a quota system. The authority of the Empire was great, though not unlimited. Although the Empire could introduce new national institutions and directive laws by way of simple legislation, constitutional changes required a two-thirds majority of both houses. The emperor's approval of all legislative acts was required, but he possessed only a suspensive veto. This could be overridden if the two houses passed the rejected law in three successive sessions. A supreme court, in contrast to the American Supreme Court, was confined to political problems and to guarding the constitution.

The events in Austria forced the Frankfurt Assembly to reach its final decisions. On March 4, Schwarzenberg dissolved the *Reichstag* of Kremsier and imposed a hastily drafted liberal constitution. This constitution, which was never put into operation and actually was withdrawn entirely in 1851, was an absolute denial of all the constructive plans for a federal organization of the Habsburg Empire that the assembly at Kremsier had brought forth. Thereby all chances for a *grossdeutsch* solution of the German problem were destroyed. Schwarzenberg officially presented to the ministry in Frankfurt the demand to admit the whole of the Habsburg Empire to a Germanic Confederation that was to have no People's House but only a House of States to be composed of members of the individual state diets.

In this new situation those members of the *grossdeutsch* groups in the Frankfurt Assembly whose opposition to a German national state under Prussian leadership was motivated largely by fear that such a state would be neither national nor constitutional joined the *kleindeutsch* parties of the center. But they extracted a high price. They not only expunged from the draft constitution some provisions designed to give the states influence within the central government but also lessened the power of the emperor. All plans to give the emperor an absolute veto, if not on all legislation at least on constitutional changes, were abandoned. The projected government became more centralistic and more parliamentarian. But the most important concession that the democrats wrested from the right-center liberals was a new election law. The constitutional committee had proposed to give a vote, and for that matter only a public vote, to "independent" men over twenty-five years of age. It was understood that this system would have excluded all journeymen, factory workers, farmhands, and homeworkers from active participation in elections. There can be no doubt that the majority of the National Assembly was in favor of such a limited suffrage. But the liberals of the right center needed the votes of the democrats for the election of the Prussian king as hereditary "emperor of the Germans," and they fulfilled the condition of the democrats by passing with them an election law which granted universal, equal, and secret suffrage. In addition, the democrats received from Heinrich von Gagern and eighty other liberals written declarations that they would not support any substantial alterations of the constitution as finally passed by the assembly if such amendments were demanded by the governments. This constituted a final effort to assert the sovereignty of the Constituent Assembly.

∾ *Frederick William Elected Emperor*

THE DIVISION between liberals and democrats, which to such a large extent had been responsible for the early ebb of the revolutionary fervor, was overcome by a common desire to achieve national unification. Yet it was not a political alliance of consequence, only a parliamentary deal to which the partners assented with a bad conscience. It opened the way for the final acceptance of the German constitution. On March 28, 1849, the assembly elected Frederick William IV emperor. Two hundred and ninety delegates voted, and two hundred and forty-eight abstained. The church bells of the old imperial city were ringing, and cannons were booming on this seemingly great historic day.

∾ *Frederick William's Refusal*

ACCOMPANIED BY A DELEGATION of members, Eduard Simson, president of the assembly, went to Berlin. On April 3, they offered the imperial crown to the Prussian king. Many forces had been working on him in the preceding days. With the exception of the ultraconservatives, including the *Kamarilla*, everybody in Berlin, even the king's brother Prince William, favored some form of cooperation with the Frankfurt Assembly. The conservatives wished only to make certain reservations. This was also the position that the Prussian cabinet adopted. The king was to decline the imperial title but declare his willingness to become the head of the federal state, provided that the other German princes gave their approval. The right of a future revision of the constitution by the princes was to be reserved.

In his formal reply to the delegation Frederick William did not say clearly yes or no. But he was emphatic in his assertion of the supreme right of the princes to define the constitution, and he stressed that he would act only in accordance with them. A few days later he expressed his intimate feelings quite succinctly in a private letter, in which he stated his determination to have no truck with the principle of popular sovereignty and complained that the Frankfurt delegates, through the offer of an imperial crown, had wished to put on him a "dog collar" that would make him "a serf of the revolution of 1848." The delegates judged correctly that the king did not wish to cooperate with the Frankfurt National Assembly at all. This was soon borne out. For when twenty-eight German governments, beginning with Baden, declared their collective approval of the election of a hereditary Prussian emperor and their general assent to the Frankfurt constitution, Frederick William IV changed his line again. The situation was most auspicious for Prussia. Obviously the small states would not have gone as far as they did if popular pressure had not driven them. While the four kingdoms hung back, the Frankfurt constitution aroused particular enthusiasm among the people of Hanover and in the Bavarian Palatinate and Franconia. If, together with the twenty-eight princes and the Frankfurt Assembly, the Prussian king had taken the initiative in the German question, German unification would have been within reach. But now Frederick William IV objected to the fact that the twenty-eight princes had accepted not only Prussian leadership but also the horrible Frankfurt constitution. On April 21 the Prussian government announced that it could not accept the Frankfurt constitution without changes and thereby assumed the odium for the final break with the National Assembly. Bavaria, Saxony, and Hanover quickly identified themselves with the Prussian declaration. Ludolf Camphausen, seeing all his hopes coming to naught, left the Prussian government.

✎ *Dissolution of the National Assembly*

MEANWHILE THE NATIONAL ASSEMBLY had considered the possibilities of making the constitution effective. In the first days of May the Frankfurt ministry had sent the constitution formally to all states with the request to recognize it as the law of the nation. This move was an anti-Prussian gesture, though merely a gesture as long as the majority was not ready to appeal to the people to resist those governments that refused to conform to the constitution. In this case the assembly itself would have turned into a revolutionary convention. But the largest single group of the assembly, the moderate liberals, did not wish to fight except by "moral" means, nor even to give their moral support to those who were ready to mount the barricades. These men of property, law, and order were unfit for revolutionary activities. Heinrich von Gagern and his political friends looked for a possible compromise with Berlin to the last. When the Prussian government followed the Austrian example and declared the mandates of the Prussian delegates ended, they went home. The delegates who remained as a rump parliament, about 136 in number, were practically all South German democrats. Since Frankfurt refused to play host to an assembly of dubious legal standing, they finally went to Stuttgart. The rump parliament called for the election of the first German *Reichstag* on August 15 and decided to hold the assembly together till that date. But on June 18 it was forcefully dispersed by Württemberg soldiers.

For a while the rump parliament served at least as a symbol of continued resistance of the national lawmakers against the political reaction. As such it was significant in the revolutions that broke out in many places during May 1849. Undoubtedly they would have become more serious if the moderate liberals had supported them and the majority of the assembly had given them some central direction from Frankfurt. But even then it is probable that the governments would have crushed all insurrections. Still, in this struggle a greater unity of purpose might have been formed among all the groups of the German middle classes, and this could not have failed to gain a decisive influence on German political life. As it was, the German princes could quote at the time of the Prussian coup of November 1848: "*Gegen Demokraten/helfen nur Soldaten.*" (Only soldiers can put democrats in their place.)

✌ The Central March Association

EVER SINCE the political reaction had raised its head in October and November, determined radicals had banded together, first locally, and eventually nationally. Late in November, the Central March Association (*Zentralmärzverein*) had come into existence with a central executive, provincial committees, and about a thousand local organizations with a membership estimated at half a million. Information, propaganda, and also arms were distributed through the association. Its aim was a people's state, which originally was not considered incompatible with monarchical institutions. Only the turning of the monarchical governments against the national state brought republican ideas to the fore. The movement also had strong social overtones. Carried forward chiefly by journeymen, petty bourgeois, and small peasants, it did not turn socialist, although persons like Friedrich Engels in the Rhineland or Mikhail Bakunin in Dresden attempted to win the ideological leadership. Although the red flag made its appearance, it was not the banner of communism but of those who, in contrast to the majority of the black, red, and gold liberals, were willing to fight for the achievements of the revolution in Germany. At a moment when the survival of the new national constitution became the dominant issue, the international ideals of Marx and Engels had no appeal.

✌ Popular Uprisings

EVERYWHERE THIS ISSUE was the cause for popular uprisings. They broke out in Saxony, where the king had dissolved the chambers which urged him to accept the Frankfurt constitution. His flight from Dresden led to the formation of a revolutionary committee of public safety. For four days the revolutionaries fought with bitter determination against Saxon troops and Prussian battalions sent on the request of the Saxon king. The young conductor of the royal opera, Richard Wagner, was active in these days in organizing popular resistance; the state architect, Gottfried Semper (1803–79) advised on the building of barricades. But Dresden and Saxony were brought to heel, and the political reaction was even more thorough than in Prussia.

In the Rhineland, too, unrest flared up. In Elberfeld-Barmen, Hamm, Iserlohn, Düsseldorf, Solingen, and other places people armed and demonstrated. But although some units of the national guard fraternized with the insurgents, the movements lacked coordination and capable leadership even on the local level. Nowhere did they arouse strong popular passions. The declaration of military law enabled regular Prussian troops to restore order without much shooting. In Württemberg developments were stormier, but the government succeeded in regaining control without outside assistance.

In the Bavarian Palatinate, on the left bank of the Rhine, and in Baden, revolutionary governments temporarily replaced the established authorities. The grand duke of Baden fled and, at least for a time, sought refuge in French Alsace. He called for Prussian help, as did the Munich government, the latter with great reluctance, because it feared the extension of Prussian military power to southern Germany. Of the few Bavarian soldiers stationed in the Palatinate, still fewer joined the democrats, whereas in Baden practically the whole army, with the exception of most of the officers, joined the revolutionaries. The senior and general officers were particularly difficult to replace. In the Polish revolutionary Ludwig von Mieroslawski a young and highly competent commander was won, but his tactical ability could not make up for the shortcomings of the army in training, equipment, and numbers. There may have been altogether 45,000 men—regular troops, free corps, and people's guard—with some arms in Baden. A foreign legion of revolutionaries from all over Europe was formed. Even armed amazons appeared, for example Robert Blum's daughter in her black velvet dress on horseback, carrying a red flag with the inscription, "Vengeance for Robert Blum." Mieroslawski had about 20,000 men in his army, but he judged that only one third to one half of them were efficient in combat.

Large and vastly superior Prussian forces, augmented by Hessian and Mecklenburg troops, were placed under the command of Prince William of Prussia to subdue the revolution in southwestern Germany. While the Palatinate was occupied without very serious fighting, the Baden army was able to offer stronger resistance. In the first major test of arms at Waghäusel, north of Heidelberg, the Baden soldiers fought with extraordinary bravery. In spite of that they were beaten, although Mieroslawski managed an orderly retreat and lost little of his army's equipment. With the Prussian army always in a position to overwhelm the insurgents by its sheer weight of numbers in frontal attacks or outflanking maneuvers, the odds were too uneven. Before the middle of July the whole of Baden was conquered. Only in Rastatt, a fortress of the confederation, 6,000 men held out until July 23. Among them was the young Carl Schurz, who at the time of the capitulation avoided capture by an adventurous escape. Special military courts composed of Prussian officers, though announcing their verdicts in the name of the grand duke of Baden, handed out draconic punishments for the leaders and many participants in the Baden revolution. This severity embittered the population, and the high figure of emigration was proof of its sentiments. But even the restored government of Baden complained about the bills for the cost of the war and the Prussian occupation of the state, which was to last two and a half years.

Prussia's Postrevolution Policies

THUS ENDED THE REVOLUTION of the German people of 1848–49. Frederick William IV, who had played such a crucial role in wrecking it, felt that the moment had arrived for him, in conjunction with the other German sovereigns, to advance the national union of Germany. After the resignation of Camphausen, Count Brandenburg and Baron Manteuffel would have preferred to discontinue an active Prussian policy with regard to a reform of the Germanic Confederation, with the possible exception of gaining official Prussian leadership of the small North German states. But for Frederick William IV the idea of a German nationhood had greater appeal than for most of the Prussian *Junkers,* provided it was not the result of popular sovereignty. He brought his personal friend, Joseph Maria von Radowitz (1797–1853), back to Berlin as an advisor to himself and the cabinet in German affairs.

✍ *Joseph von Radowitz*

RADOWITZ, GRANDSON of a Croatian officer who in the Seven Years' War had become a prisoner and then decided to stay in North Germany, was an eminent officer and military teacher. As a youth he had attended French military schools and as a Westphalian lieutenant had fought in the battle of Leipzig under Napoleon. In 1823 he had come to Prussia, where his brilliant mind and universal education had brought him the quick recognition of his military superiors. But more important was the growth of a close friendship with the crown prince, with whom Radowitz cultivated common political ideals. After ascending the throne, Frederick William had used his counsel and services in many political questions. On the eve of the revolution, as we have mentioned,[4] he had sent him to Vienna for the negotiation of a reform program for the Germanic Confederation. Radowitz had begun as a champion of the conservative German-Christian ideals but later had grown beyond them. He had a keener eye than his royal friend for the historical trends of the age. He recognized the significance of the social problem and of the national idea for the future of the modern state, and he felt that a conservative order could not survive unless it solved the social problem and made concessions to constitutionalism.

Radowitz was a devout Roman Catholic. As a member of the Frankfurt Assembly he had acted as the chairman of the informal association of Catholic delegates and had been largely responsible for the new freedom which the Frankfurt constitution extended to the churches. But when he voted for the Prussian king, the German Catholics viewed him with suspicion. Also among the conservative Prussian *Junkers* his Catholicism and German patriotism made him distrusted. Although he had married into the old Prussian aristocracy, he was still not considered rooted in the Prussian tradition. His own political authority, therefore, rested almost exclusively on the personal support of the king, and there were limits beyond which Radowitz could not hope to move this wavering sentimentalist. Bismarck's characterization of Radowitz as the man who tailored the costumes for the medieval fancies of Frederick William was entirely unjust. More than any other person of the king's entourage he strove to acquaint him with some of the new forces of the age. But it is true that he

---

[4] See p. 5.

himself was far from perceiving all of them and that by conviction and temperament he was not prepared to deal with all of them effectively. His judgment on international affairs was unsure, largely because he underrated the element of power in them, and in his own policies his strong belief in the sanctity of law kept him from playing his trump cards in time.

ᴄᴂ Radowitz's German Program

IN MANY of its parts the program for which Radowitz gained the king's assent was not novel. It proposed the erection of a larger and a smaller union. The former was to become a confederation, the latter a federal state. The large union was to combine the whole of the former Germanic Confederation, to which the non-Germanic possessions of Austria were to be added. This new confederation was to be directed by a directory in Regensburg in which Austria, Prussia, and all the other German states together were each to have two votes. Forming a Central European Customs Union was contemplated, as well as adopting common commercial policies. Radowitz not only wanted to turn the consular representation of all member states over to it but also hoped that it would serve as an organ for the formulation of a common foreign policy.

The "small union" was to be a federal state composed of all the German states except the German and non-German lands of the Habsburg Empire. It was to receive the title of a German Empire. The Frankfurt constitution was used as a model, but only after its democratic and centralist features had been struck out. The executive power was vested not in a hereditary emperor but in the crown of Prussia as the head of the Empire, supported in legislation by a college of six princes. The head of the Empire received absolute veto power over all legislation. The two chambers were given equal rights, even with regard to money bills. But universal, direct, and secret suffrage was replaced for the second chamber by a plutocratic system and indirect elections. All these changes were intended to strengthen the monarchical principle and in addition to give the states a greater share in the government of the Empire. Also by the financial dependence of the Empire on the states their influence was considerably strengthened. The Empire was to rely on matricular contributions of the states and beyond that on loans. Of more immediate importance, however, was the declaration that membership in the new union would be entirely voluntary. A state that refused to join would simply remain a member of the larger confederation. Once it could be seen how many governments wanted to join the federal state and accept its draft constitution, its parliament should be convened and should pass on the constitution. Thereafter, with the appointment of federal ministers and the organization of its high agencies, the new organization was to begin its existence.

This plan, to create a German federal state under Prussian leadership through the cooperation of allied German princes, while exploiting the popular national movement only for limited support, was a memorable step in the direction of the Bismarckian policy of the 1860's. Radowitz's draft had some serious weaknesses. It was not to be expected that Austria would agree to her exclusion from Germany, nor could it be assumed that the medium-sized German states would subordinate themselves to a central authority unless fear of revolution would make them accept the protection of Prussia. On the other side, Prussian monarchists could argue that Prussia, with only one out of six votes in the council of princes and less than a quarter of the seats in the house of states, might find herself overruled by the small states, in spite of the exclusive executive power of the Prussian king.

The Potsdam Conferences

ON THE INVITATION of the Prussian government the major German states held conferences in Potsdam in May 1849. Bavaria reserved her decision, but Hanover and Saxony, on May 26, 1849, concluded an alliance for one year, in which the members were to work together for the establishment of a German union under the constitution proposed by Radowitz. Still, Hanover and Saxony accepted the alliance only because they were afraid of popular unrest. Moreover, they made strong reservations, stipulating that they would enter only a union of all German states and would insist on some changes of the constitution. The smaller states joined the Three Kings' Alliance more readily. By the end of the summer, all the German states, with the exception of Bavaria, Württemberg, and a few insignificant lands, had joined the alliance. In June, about a hundred and fifty members of the right-center groups of the Frankfurt Assembly convened in Gotha and announced their approval of the projected union.

Chances of Radowitz's Policy

IF IN THE SUMMER of 1849 Prussia had demanded from her allies the immediate convention of the new *Reichstag* and the subsequent establishment of the union, she would most probably have been successful. It would have been necessary to back up her demand with the mobilization of the whole Prussian army under the pretext that the continuing revolutionary situation called for this measure. Austria was still occupied with war and revolution in Hungary and Italy. As a matter of fact, the Hungarian events took a grave turn, and this induced the Austrian government in May to request Russian assistance. Czar Nicholas sent an army of more than 120,000 soldiers into Hungary. But it was not before August 13 that the Magyars surrendered at Vilagos. Two weeks later fighting in Italy came to an end with the capitulation of the Venetian republic of Daniele Manin. Thus neither Austria nor Russia could have reacted strongly against a Prussian *fait accompli* in Germany, and it is doubtful whether Russia would have intervened even at a later date, especially since Russian support of Austria against Prussia would have affected England and France.

In the early phase of the revolution of 1848 the czar's sympathies had been with Prussia rather than Austria. While the Schleswig-Holstein question had caused a much more critical attitude toward Prussia, the arrival of Schwarzenberg and his resolute reactionary policy had raised Russia's esteem of Austria. Yet in 1849 Nicholas still saw the best solution in the cooperation of Austria and Prussia, which he tried to promote. However, the Schleswig-Holstein problems produced renewed friction. The Danes denounced the Malmö armistice in February, and the Frankfurt government sent a German army under the command of the Prussian General von Prittwitz against them. The progress of the German troops was impressive, and even Prussia hesitated to come to terms with Denmark. Russia brought the strongest diplomatic pressure on Berlin and sent a naval squadron into Danish waters. As in the year before, Britain and France also made it clear that they would not tolerate the inclusion of the two duchies into a nationally reorganized Germany. Frederick William always felt ill at ease in supporting rebels against their legitimate rulers. Radowitz urged the liquidation of the Schleswig-Holstein war, because the diplomatic isolation of Prussia in Europe would make any Prussian initiative in Germany impossible. In this he was right, but by now a Prussian retreat had become much more costly. Whereas in 1848 relatively satisfactory prospects of a future accession of the duchies to Germany might have been achieved through diplomatic negotiations, particularly if the Germans had been willing to cede the Danish North Schleswig, the new armistice of July 10, 1849, did not contain specific assurances about the future of these duchies, although future German claims were not entirely blocked.

The willingness of the Prussian government to compromise on the Schleswig-Holstein issues eased relations with both Russia and the Western powers. Palmerston expressed himself as favoring an integration of Germany under Prussian leadership. France, too, was not hostile to Prussian progress. She was alarmed at Schwarzenberg's plans for a Central European Confederation and, more specifically, at the Austrian policy and warfare in Italy. Drouyn d l'Huis and his successor, the great historian Alexis de Tocqueville, the two French foreign ministers during the summer of 1849, were inclined to see in the national consolidation of Germany a development which would strengthen Europe against Russia. What doubts the two Western governments entertained about Prussian policies were concerned with the seriousness of Prussian intentions and with the capacity of the government of Frederick William IV for translating such intentions into practical and determined policies.

These doubts were well founded. Prussia continued to negotiate with the reluctant German kingdoms, to which she herself had given new confidence by the armed suppression of the revolution in the Bavarian Palatinate and Baden. Meanwhile Austria could turn her attention to Germany again. Prussia was persuaded to assist in recognizing the continued existence of the old Germanic Confederation. Schwarzenberg most generously—so it seemed—suggested that for the time being Austria and Prussia together should assume its central authority. This authority, no doubt, had great international significance and could not be allowed to expire, after the Frankfurt Assembly, its ministry, and its regent, Archduke John, had fallen. On September 30, Austria and Prussia agreed on an interim arrangement under which together they would assume, till May 1, 1850, the rights and duties of the regent, to whom the Federal Diet had turned over its authority in April 1848.[5]

⟿ *Radowitz Fails*

RADOWITZ'S POLITICAL FORTUNES were sinking fast. He contributed substantially to the acceptance of the Prussian constitution of January 31, 1850, by Frederick William IV. But when it came to convening a German parliament in order to give popular support to what by now was called, more modestly, a union rather than a German Reich, he saw himself everywhere surrounded by opposition. Hanover and Saxony announced that as long as all German states had not signed the Three Kings' Alliance, there should be no attempt to activate the union. The two kingdoms withdrew from the alliance when elections were held in February 1850. Participation in these elections was unusually small. The democrats urged abstention, since the three-class system would not produce a true popular representation. The parliament that assembled in Erfurt on March 20, 1850, was dominated by the moderate liberals, next to whom a strong group of Prussian conservatives—among them Friedrich Julius Stahl, Ludwig von Gerlach, and Otto von Bismarck—made their weight felt. Their influence reached beyond the parliament into the Prussian cabinet and court. Frederick William IV had already begun to drag his feet, as the conflict with Austria became ever more imminent. He

5 See p. 63.

insisted on a conservative revision of the draft constitution. The Erfurt Assembly complied, but when it concluded its work on April 29, the king did not appoint ministers of the union but sent the revised constitution to the individual German governments for reconsideration. It seemed that he wished for their defection in order to get an excuse for dropping the whole enterprise. When the princes met in Berlin in May, only twelve declared that they were prepared to accept the revised constitution without further changes. As a consequence, the establishment of the union was left until such time when an agreement between the governments might be reached.

✑ Resurrection of the Germanic Confederation

In the meantime, however, Prince Schwarzenberg had gone on the offensive. He would have been ready to allow Prussia to gain the leadership in northern Germany, but the Prussian king and Radowitz declined to adopt plans for the mere aggrandizement of Prussia in place of their projected national reform. At first Schwarzenberg used the four German kingdoms to oppose the Prussian policy, but in May 1850 he considered the time ripe for showing his hand. He invited the German states to Frankfurt, and although Prussia and her closest allies did not attend, declared the conference a revival of the plenary council of the Federal Diet of the Germanic Confederation. A race for the favor of the czar was started by Prussia and Austria. The latter fared decidedly better in this competition, and again the Schleswig-Holstein questions were largely responsible for the czar's attitude.

The armistice of July 10, 1849, had created only a provisional order whereby the duchies remained occupied by Danish and Prussian troops and were administered by a mixed commission. The negotiations for a final settlement proved difficult. The czar demanded that Prussia not only should withdraw all support from the "rebels" but also should actively assist the Danish king in the restoration of his rule. Prussia's hesitation irritated Nicholas I, and the policy of the Erfurt union, with its national representation, seemed to him a further straying from the straight path of conservative principle which he wished his brother-in-law Frederick William IV to walk. On July 2, 1850, the Prussian government signed a treaty with Denmark which left the duchies to their fate. But the treaty did not close this tragic chapter. The Schleswig-Holstein army fought on alone and was beaten by the Danes in the battle of Idstedt on July 24-25. Schleswig had to be left to the Danes, but Holstein was defended by the Schleswig-Holstein troops. As duke of Holstein, the king of Denmark requested the intervention of the Germanic Confederation against his revolutionary subjects, and Nicholas I urged strongly that the confederation act at once. The czar's prompting worked into Schwarzenberg's hands. Prussia still had not recognized the restoration of the Federal Diet in Frankfurt, but now Schwarzenberg went further by reestablishing, in addition to the plenary council, the select council and proclaiming it, even in the absence of Prusssia, competent to deal with the Holstein question.

Still another request for federal intervention was accepted by the Federal Diet. For a long time Hesse-Kassel, more than any other state, had suffered under the arbitrary despotism of her wretched rulers. Now, when the revolutionary tide was ebbing, Elector Frederick William I wished to rid himself of the limitations which a liberal parliament and membership in the German union had placed on his sovereignty. His minister Daniel von Hassenpflug dissolved the liberal chamber and confronted the new chamber with the peremptory demand to approve the continuation of all existing taxation, while withholding from it the budget estimates. When under these conditions the chamber refused to pass direct taxes, it was dissolved and taxes were imposed by decree. Mindful of their oath to the constitution, state officials and judges declined to enforce the unconstitutional ordinances, and subsequently all the officers of the Hessian army resigned their commissions. The elector placed the land in a state of siege and went to Frankfurt.

On September 21, the Federal Diet made its support of the elector known. The Federal Diet was supposed to be a guarantor of the rights of the German people and of lawful procedures as much as of the monarchical principle. But at this moment Austrian policy had only one aim, that of demonstrating the usefulness of the Germanic Confederation as an instrument for the preservation of the sovereignty of the individual German princes. The defection of the elector of Hesse from the Prussian-inspired German union was particularly likely to frustrate this Prussian scheme, since Prussia had very special interests and rights in Hesse-Kassel. This state formed the most convenient bridge between the separated western and eastern sections of the Prussian monarchy, and Prussia possessed the right to use two Hessian roads for the movement of troops.

Prussia declared the plans for a federal execution illegal. But Russia, though anxious to see a war avoided, supported Austria. A Russian minister was accredited in Frankfurt to express Russian recognition of the Federal Diet. Schwarzenberg received a secret promise that Russia would consider Prussian opposition to a federal intervention in Holstein a *casus belli* and would lend her moral support in the Hessian question. Earlier the czar had given his consent to Schwarzenberg's plans for the creation of a Central European Federation. On October 11, an alliance was concluded between Austria, Bavaria, and Württemberg. At the end of the month, Bavarian troops moved from the south and Prussian units from

the north into Hesse-Kassel. Count Brandenburg had been sent to Warsaw on October 15, in order to defend Prussian policies before Czar
Nicholas. Prussian aims by now had become very modest. The Prussian
government still insisted that the Federal Diet should be reinstituted after
the German states, in free conferences, had agreed on a reform of the
Germanic Confederation. Prussia demanded to become a presidential
power of the confederation together with Austria and to have the
executive entrusted to Austria and Prussia. She agreed that popular representation could not be built into the diet. While admitting that the constitution of the union could presently not be realized, the right of voluntary
association of states within the confederation was to be maintained. On
the other hand, the whole Habsburg Empire was to be accepted into the
confederation. Mixed Austro-Prussian commissions were to settle the
pending troubles over Holstein and Hesse.

Schwarzenberg, who arrived with his monarch for a state visit in Warsaw and on this occasion conferred also with Count Brandenburg, was not
willing to grant Prussia the satisfaction of posing as the champion of
German unification. He insisted on the open revocation of the constitution of the German union. Nor was the Austrian prime minister prepared
to give Prussia equal status with Austria in the confederation. The only
concession he made was the acceptance of diplomatic conferences for the
discussion of a reform of the confederation, and this would have implied
a delay in Prussia's recognition of the Federal Diet. But Count Brandenburg had lost all faith in the union, which had always appealed to him
only as a means for strengthening Prussia rather than as a decisive step
toward national German unification. He was easily persuaded that the
assurance of free conferences, at which he hoped Prussia would gain
further concessions from Austria, was worth the renunciation of the
union.

✑ The "Punctation" of Olmütz

RETURNING TO BERLIN, Brandenburg advocated a conciliatory policy, in
contrast to Radowitz, who wished to cling to his program and proposed
to answer Austrian troop movements by the mobilization of the Prussian
army. The possibility of war particularly frightened Baron Otto von
Manteuffel, who, probably quite correctly, argued that Prussia could not
hope to win a war unless she allied herself with the liberal forces in
Germany, which in this case were likely to gain the upper hand within
Prussia as well. This ideological argument had an effect also on the king.
On November 3, he accepted the resignation of Radowitz. On the same
day, Count Brandenburg fell seriously ill. He died on November 6, and
Manteuffel became Prussian prime minister. Although a critical period

followed, Prussia's retreat from practically all her former positions had opened the road to a settlement. The final result was achieved by an Austrian ultimatum. On November 29, 1850, Manteuffel and Schwarzenberg signed an Austro-Prussian "punctation" at Olmütz. Prussia received small concessions in the Hessian question. In Holstein the old order was to be restored through Austrian and Prussian commissars acting under the authority of the Germanic Confederation. Austria consented to free conferences for the discussion of the reform of the confederation, to be held in Dresden and not in Frankfurt or Vienna, since Prussia had publicly abandoned her union project. But Schwarzenberg and Manteuffel did not agree on a common reform program to be presented to the German states, and it was difficult to believe that in the absence of a prior agreement between the two great powers the conferences would yield positive results. Actually, the conferences, which took place between December 1850 and March 1851, proved to be useless wrangling. Austria denied Prussia equal status, whereupon Prussia in return refused the admission of the whole Habsburg Empire to the confederation. Schwarzenberg had to give up the idea of "the empire of seventy millions" in Central Europe, the more so since France and England protested vigorously in Vienna against this scheme, and even Czar Nicholas now found it inopportune. In these circumstances the simple return to the old system of 1814 was the only answer. In the summer of 1851 the Federal Diet resumed its activities in Frankfurt.

CHAPTER 3

The Age of Reaction

T HE TRANSFORMATION of the authoritarian into a popular state and the achievement of German national unification had been the chief aims of the revolution of 1848–49. Both aims had proved unattainable. The revolutionary tide, which in March 1848 had engulfed all of Germany, quickly receded and dissolved. In the spring of 1848 the revolutionary movement seemed to have succeeded not only in winning great visible concessions but also in shaking the faith of the ruling class in the moral foundations of the old political order. But as soon as the governments had indicated their willingness to compromise, the popular movement had begun to lose its inner unity. Diversities of social and political objectives came to light which sapped the power of the revolutionary movement and made the eventual victory of the counter-revolution possible.

ᨅ Why the Revolution Failed

THE CAUSES of the failure of the German revolution lay deep in the historical structure of German political and social life, which the recent growth of new economic and ideological forces had somewhat disarranged, but not basically altered. Originally social discontent had fired the revolution. Without the peasants' riots and, most of all, the fighting of artisans and workers, a revolution in Germany would not have taken place, nor would the "March governments" and the parliamentary assemblies of Frankfurt, Berlin, and Vienna have come into existence. But these mass risings momentarily lifted the higher middle classes to a leading position. As the elections clearly showed, respect for education and self-acquired wealth was still quite general in Germany. In these circumstances it was natural that the political liberalism these groups had preached seemed the political panacea to almost all revolutionary elements, although the implications of the liberal program were hardly understood by the masses.

✐ *Absence of a Common Front*

IN THIS AGE the peasants as a class had no far-reaching political conceptions. They were preoccupied with their immediate needs, with liberation from the feudal burdens that still rested on land and people. Since even the conservatives were prepared to liquidate these obligations, the peasants in most parts of Germany soon fell back into political inertia. For the political course of the revolution, this development probably was chiefly important through its effect on the armies, which were primarily composed of peasants' sons. If unrest had continued in the countryside, the Prussian army would have become more susceptible to revolutionary propaganda. As it was, the Prussian army remained a reliable instrument in the hands of the king.

But even the urban middle classes pulled in different directions. The artisans, threatened in their livelihood by the growing population as well as by the beginning of machine production, did not want legislation that would assist in the transition to modern industrial organization; on the contrary, they asked for the protection or even restoration of the old guild system. The development of the political attitude of the artisan class, in itself already divided by the contrast between masters and journeymen, was not everywhere identical. But substantial forces within this social sector learned within a year that for the leaders of liberalism political and economic freedom went together and that corporate institutions were considered evil by them. Thus they became inclined to make their peace with the conservative governments, which for their part were not slow to see their political chance.

At the very minimum, a common front of the urban middle classes would have been required in order to produce the pressure needed for making the German governments bow to the popular will. Speculating for a moment on what issues a great revolutionary leader might have been able to exploit in order to maintain the revolutionary momentum, one would have to think of such measures as the abolition of all feudal burdens without indemnification of the old lords, or even of a revolutionary land distribution. Yet, while such policies might have kept the revolutionary spirit among the peasants alive, only a declaration such as everybody's right to work could have mobilized sufficient support in the towns. Such a declaration would not have satisfied the masters of the craft guilds, although it might have won over the journeymen; but it certainly would have appealed to the factory workers and might have given them a more significant part in the revolution than they actually played.

∽ Sanctity of Property

SUCH SPECULATIONS, however, are helpful only insofar as they throw the existing conditions into bolder relief. The sanctity of property was too essential to the liberal credo to allow liberal groups to consider a revolutionary land reform, or even the abolition of feudal obligations without compensation. The adoption of the right-to-work principle was equally incompatible with liberal thought. To use one or the other policy as a temporary tactical device, the way Bismarck fifteen years later employed revolutionary principles in order to advance a conservative cause, was not in the nature of the German liberals of 1848. Moreover, so far as the liberals, and particularly the moderate liberals, were disposed to make tactical compromises, they were rather inclined to deal with the old powers. From the onset, the German bourgeoisie, including the petty bourgeois groups, was obsessed by fear lest the revolution might lead to a repetition of the terror of the great French Revolution or to communism. This fear made them hesitate from the beginning to press home the early advantages gained from the old authorities. Nowhere did the "March governments" truly subject the monarchs to their own will. The liberals were content with half-concessions, because they saw in the old state institutions a guarantee against chaos. Soon they employed the police powers of the states quite vigorously against social disturbances and carefully kept the members of the lower classes out of the civic guards.

∽ Class Distinctions

ALTHOUGH EVERYBODY WISHED for the creation of a national community comprising all classes, class distinctions went too deep to be readily bridged. The tradition of a graded social order was ingrained in the German middle classes as much as in the nobility. Not only the rich but also the educated people recoiled from contacts with the masses. Higher education gave its representatives little sense of social reality; rather it endowed them with an aristocratic individualism. One month after the outbreak of the revolution we hear the radical David Friedrich Strauss complain that he had lived more happily under the old police state. Then he had been able to devote himself exclusively to "free theory," without consideration of its practical application. And he concludes that "the principle of equality is as hostile to spiritual as to material preeminence," a statement to be repeated in endless variations by generations of educated Germans.

✌ *Too Many Arenas*

THE CENTRIFUGAL TENDENCIES among the middle classes frustrated a sustained common effort for the achievement of a liberal order. Doubtless the fight was further complicated by the necessity of its being waged in many arenas. In France, Paris always served as the stage of ultimate decisions. The course of revolutions hereby assumed a singular dramatic quality. In contrast, the events in Germany were broken up into occurrences in Vienna, Berlin, Frankfurt, and lesser state capitals. In these circumstances, it was difficult to marshal all forces toward common goals. In France, national unity was a possession largely inherited from the *ancien régime*. In Germany, it was an unfulfilled dream over and above the struggle for liberal and democratic institutions. To what extent national ideals appealed to the peasant population is questionable. They exerted some influence in the southwest, in Schleswig-Holstein, and in some other frontier regions. In southern Bavaria, in Brandenburg, and Pomerania, the peasants were not aroused by national slogans, and they looked exclusively to their state governments for redress of their grievances. But national sentiment of various forms pervaded the middle classes and was harbored by some conservative circles as well as by proletarian groups. For Marx and Engels, a unified German republic was a necessary step in the organization of an international working class movement.

✌ *Popularity of Nationalism*

NATIONALISM BECAME a most popular force in the revolution, because it was a means of overcoming many of the centrifugal tendencies which stemmed from the social and regional sectionalism of the German people. The national ideal brought about the great political compromise between liberals and democrats that created a majority in the Frankfurt Assembly for the acceptance of the constitution of March 28, 1849. Similarly, the *grossdeutsch* opposition was composed of representatives of different constitutional programs. Nowhere in Germany did nationalism become completely divorced from the desire for governmental reform. As a matter of fact, any progress toward national unification was bound to bring a measure of new freedom through liberation from the bureaucratic supervision of the small states. But under existing German conditions the ideal of national unity easily overshadowed the ideal of freedom, particularly among those who yearned to see Germany assume an independent position in international affairs.

In January 1849 the historian Dahlmann, the chief champion of the cause of Schleswig-Holstein against Denmark, said in Frankfurt: "The winning of power alone will fully satisfy the seething desire for freedom;

for it is not only freedom that the Germans have in mind, but they are primarily craving for power, which has been denied to them until now." In this statement Dahlmann revealed more than his own feelings or those of the moderate liberals, his close political friends. Even among the German radicals the desire for national power often seemed to outweigh the passion for internal reform. It is not altogether surprising that a people in a state of revolutionary exaltation becomes overbearing toward those who disturb its plans from the outside. The turning of the Jacobins to conquest is an early example of such a reaction. The danger was even greater in Germany, where the existing order was closely related to international forces. What now usually was called the Holy Alliance, that is, the cooperation of the Russian czar, the Austrian Emperor, and the Prussian King, had been a supporting element of the conservative regimes in Germany. The oral threats of war which were made against Russia should not be taken as proof of a congenital German obsession with war, the more so since the popular excitement died down rather quickly.

◌ *Attitude Toward Other Nations*

MORE SERIOUS was the apparent proclivity of the majority of the German liberals and democrats to slight the rights of the small nations and nationalities at the very moment when the German revolution proclaimed national self-determination as the basis of all law. It should not be forgotten, however, how novel many of the national problems were in 1848. For example, the growth of a national consciousness among the Czechs had started from small beginnings only thirty years earlier, and there was nobody in Europe who would have thought the grant of statehood to the Czechs sensible. Let us mention that the Frankfurt National Assembly, on May 31, passed a resolution giving foreign nationalities the right to use their language in church, schools, and law courts, and that this protection of minorities was embodied in the fundamental rights of the constitution. But when it came to the cession of territories inhabited by people of foreign nationality, most liberals and democrats balked. They did not wish to give up Trieste or Trentino, in spite of their undisputed Italian character, and they objected to the separation from Germany of the predominantly Danish parts of North Schleswig. The explanations offered for such an attitude were mostly references to the higher claims which Germany as a great nation could assert.

With regard to the Polish problem, the German excuses assumed shrill chauvinist tones, worst of all in the speech of the East Prussian democrat Wilhelm Jordan, with its appeal to "national egotism," "the right of the stronger," "the right of conquest," and "the preponderance of the German race over most Slav races," coupled with a denial of the applicability of rules of law to the fate of nations. It was the recklessness of the language of this advocate of German national superiority that was ominous for the future rather than the frustration of any reform in the government of the Polish provinces of Prussia, for which Frederick William IV and the Prussian army were chiefly responsible.

The Polish national movement in Germany centered in the grand duchy of Posen (Poznania), which, in 1815, was promised far-reaching privileges and the preservation of its Polish civilization. But after the Polish revolution of 1830 these rights were abolished, and for a decade the Prussian government adopted moderate policies of Germanization. Frederick William IV, conscious of the strength of national culture, gave the Polish language a new freedom after 1840, but this more liberal regime was soon used for conspiratorial activities. The revolts that sprang from them in 1846, when Austria annexed Cracow, were easily suppressed, and the Prussian government, unlike the Russian and Austrian governments, did not use the gallows and shooting squads in dealing with the Polish risings of that year. The Polish national movement was deeply divided. As late as 1830 it was almost exclusively led by numerous Polish noblemen, but thereafter democratic ideas spread. They inspired expectations of social revolution among the uneducated and downtrodden Polish peasants. No Polish middle class that might have acted as a mediating force had come into existence as yet. The restoration of the Poland of 1772 in 1848 would probably have led to the destruction of the whole Polish upper class and to leaderless chaos.

But the cause of Polish freedom was dear to all the liberals. A wave of enthusiastic popular support for the restoration of Poland swept through Germany in the spring of 1848, and demands for war against Russia were raised. Heinrich von Arnim, the Prussian foreign minister, was inclined to follow the popular sentiment, and armed Polish emigrants were allowed to enter the province of Posen. Frederick William IV was by no means willing to war against the czar, but he had permitted the creation of a Polish national committee. This soon refused all cooperation with the Germans, who constituted more than one third of the population. Even worse, violent riots broke out against Germans and Jews. The weak Prussian garrisons were powerless. The Germans of Posen and the eastern Prussian provinces were alarmed and requested help. At the same time any plans for a Russian war were smothered, partly by Frederick William IV, partly by British diplomatic pressure. All those to whom the grant of freedom to the Poles was only an anti-Russian move lost interest in the Polish question. The Prussian government proceeded to disarm the Poles in Posen, and the Frankfurt Assembly decided that the largest part of the province should be considered German and should send representatives to Frankfurt. Only an area containing about two fifths of the Poles of the province was recognized as Polish. With a few exceptions, such as Robert Blum, nobody rose in the assembly to point out that the majority was betraying the very ideals on which it proposed to build a German national state.

✍ *The Political Reaction*

THE POLITICAL REACTION in Germany had already begun in 1849. Originally it had largely taken the form of prosecution of individual persons. In Prussia, political trials through which the government tried to defame the leaders of the revolution were particularly vexing. But in order to make Prussia appear liberal in the eyes of Germany at the time when an active policy for the creation of a German union was pursued, liberal reforms of state institutions were still being enacted. The most important lasting reform was the adoption of the Prussian constitution of January 31, 1850, which we have discussed before.[1] Earlier reform legislation, which had introduced a liberal court organization, with trial by jury as its chief innovation, and had abolished the patrimonial jurisdiction of the owners of the landed estates, was followed by a law abolishing the exemption of the *Junker* estates from the land tax and by another law speeding up the liquidation of the feudal burdens of the peasants. On March 11, 1850, two most far-reaching laws on local, county, district, and provincial government were issued. For the first time a municipal order was created not only for individual provinces but also for the whole Prussian state. The new order was largely conceived in terms of French administrative law, which so far had left a strong imprint only on the Rhineland. Town and countryside were treated equally. The organization of the village administration, though simpler than that of the towns and cities, followed the same principles. The most drastic political consequence was the absorption of the *Junker* estates by the village and the ensuing abolition of the police powers of the agrarian *Junkers.* Local self-government of the rural and urban municipalities found its extension on the county and provincial level. The old county estates and provincial diets, which were dominated by the nobility, were replaced by new representative bodies, which disregarded birth. Still, in practice, the new organs did not look very different from the older ones, since the suffrage was dependent on property. The municipal councils were elected by the three-class suffrage. The councils elected the members of the county councils, and these in turn the delegates to the provincial diets. The additional condition, that one half of the membership of all these representative organs was to consist of landed proprietors, strengthened still further the influence of the *Junkers* as the largest group of big landowners.

[1] See pp. 77–80.

After the collapse of the Prussian policy aiming at the establishment of a German union, the reactionary forces within Prussia could not be stopped any longer. The king would have liked to get rid of the constitution. But his prime minister, Otto von Manteuffel, kept him from breaking his oath. Moreover, it could not be denied that after the introduction of the three-class suffrage, parliament had become a serviceable instrument in the hands of the political reaction. The government used every means at its disposal to influence the elections. All state officials were supposed to work actively for the election of conservative representatives. The county councillors (*Landräte*) in particular, as the officials closest to the grass roots, were used extensively as managers, and often enough as candidates, for elections. The Prussian House of Representatives of 1855 contained seventy county councillors.

❧ The New House of Lords

KING FREDERICK WILLIAM IV insisted on at least one major change of the constitution of January 1850 and received full authority from both chambers in May 1853. Article 65 of the constitution had created a first chamber consisting of ninety members who were elected by a class of high taxpayers and thirty members elected by the councils of the large cities. On October 12, 1854, Frederick William replaced the first chamber by a House of Lords (*Herrenhaus*) consisting of ninety members elected by the old agrarian nobility, representing about 10 per cent of the *Junker* estates, about thirty members elected by the larger cities, and one representative from each of the six Prussian universities. The plutocratically-composed first chamber would have given the high bourgeoisie at least some influence beside the *Junkers*. But the House of Lords, which to Frederick William IV seemed to be the equivalent of the English House of Lords, was actually controlled by the agrarian nobility, who through it had veto power on all Prussian legislation. To the very last days of the monarchy, in November 1918, the Prussian *Junkers* never hesitated to exploit their advantages. The king retained the right to appoint any number of members, thereby coercing the house into submission. But the monarchical government of Prussia rarely made use of this right. On the whole, the House of Lords was too valuable an institution for the conservative system to be unduly impaired in its authority by the royal government.

❧ Reaction and Self-Government

WHEREAS THE HOUSE OF LORDS originated chiefly from the initiative of Frederick William IV, the fight against the law on self-government, of

March 11, 1850, was opened by the *Junkers*. The execution of this law was inhibited at once. Finally, on May 24, 1853, the law was rescinded, together with article 105 of the constitution, which it was intended to implement. The Prussian gentry stormed against the abolition of the division of town and countryside and equally against the suppression of the provincial differences, since these measures implied the loss of many of its privileges. As a result, the *Junkers* achieved the restoration of the old pre-1848 county estates and provincial diets. Separate laws for the regulation of local government in the eastern and western provinces were drafted. This meant the continued independence of the *Junker* estates in the east and the further exercise of the police power by their owners. Yet the *Junkers* did not receive seignorial jurisdiction back, nor were they able to block the liquidation of the feudal obligations of the peasants. On the other hand, the nobility won permission to establish entailed estates (*Fideikommisse*), which the constitution had expressly forbidden.

The *Junkers* did not gain a decisive influence on the organization of the eastern cities nor of the western cities and municipalities. In all these the bureaucracy held its own. The three city statutes (for the six eastern provinces, of 1853; for Westphalia, of March 1856; and for the Rhineland, of May 1856) did not differ from each other very much. The Rhineland retained a system more akin to the French *maire* system, whereas the other provinces followed a somewhat more collegiate organization. These statutes of 1853–56 were essentially revisions of the law of 1850, introducing restrictions on self-government similar to those that the law of 1831 had introduced after the July revolution. They strengthened the independence of the city officials from the elected city council, while subjecting the whole city administration to a very rigid supervision by the state bureaucracy. All policy functions were reserved to the state. In the larger cities royal presidents of police were appointed; in the smaller cities the mayor became chief of police. In this capacity, however, the mayor was not considered the representative of the self-government of the town but was commissioned by the state and consequently bound by the orders of the district governor. At least the statutes of 1853–56 made no attempt to restore the old corporate divisions among the city residents. A special law was issued for the rural communities of the Rhineland. This was a half-hearted attempt to impose on the west the division of town and countryside as it existed in the east. In practice it amounted to little more than a gesture, since the Prussian bureaucracy realized that the urbanization of the Rhenish countryside could not be undone. The three city statutes and the Rhenish communal order of 1853–56 remained in force until 1918. It may be added that in the three provinces that Prussia acquired in 1866—Schleswig-Holstein, Hanover, and Hesse-Nassau—analogous laws were enacted.

✐ Diverse Character of Reaction

THE POLITICAL REACTION in Prussia after 1850, which determined the character of the last seventy years of the Prussian monarchy to a large degree, was not a well-coordinated movement. At no other time of Prussian history did the *Junkers* exercise so great an influence on the building of the fundamental institutions and general policies of the monarchy. But even in the reign of such a confused, if stubborn, ruler as Frederick William IV, Prussia did not lose her character as a bureaucratic absolute state. Even at this moment of their greatest power, after the defeat of the revolution and before the formation of a modern bourgeoisie, the East Elbian *Junkers* failed to formulate a program that would have set new goals for the policy of Prussia. They were too much preoccupied with defending the past as well as their own regional and social interests to integrate the new social forces into the state. A threat made by Bismarck in 1852 shows the dismal hypocrisy of the eastern agrarians. He bluntly denied "that the true Prussian people" could be found in the cities. "If the cities ever were to revolt again," he said, this people "would know how to make them obey, even though it had to erase them from the earth."

✐ Purge of the Liberals

AS A RESULT of the reaction the bureaucracy was purged of most of its liberal elements. The high-presidents of the provinces, the district governors, and the county councillors were declared removable as political officers at the discretion of the government. Although the judges could not be dismissed, they could now be transferred to other posts. But even a conservative bureaucracy, owing to its contacts with the problems of all classes and provinces, hesitated to hand over the government to the *Junkers* altogether. Baron Otto von Manteuffel, Prussian prime minister from 1850 to 1858, wanted to suppress liberalism but was not inclined to identify the monarchical government of Prussia with the interests and ideas of a small group. Although he did not dispute the claim of the nobility that it constituted the highest class in the state, he felt that the state of Frederick the Great ought to demand the subordination of all the classes under the crown. But Manteuffel's absolutism did not enjoy reliable support from the king, who leaned toward the romantic conceptions of his personal entourage, the *Kamarilla*, which, particularly with General Leopold von Gerlach and his brother, Court President Ludwig von Gerlach, included men of high religious idealism who were no mere courtiers anxious to please the monarch. Ludwig von Gerlach was to prove the sincerity of his convictions twenty years later when he turned against Bismarck.

✎ *The Role of the Churches*

BUT THE IDEAL of the Christian state which animated the political activities of the Gerlachs and was academically represented by Friedrich Julius Stahl was too easily exploited by the ruling groups as a convenient ideology and gave rise to mere bigotry. To the new classes of a nascent industrial society the doctrines about divinely ordained class differences had a hollow ring. It did not help to bring the Protestant Church into politics, since this only tended to confirm the reputation of the church as a propagandistic tool of the conservative government.

✎ *The Protestants*

THE REVOLUTION had opened a new chapter in the history of the churches. The Prussian constitution of 1850 had proclaimed the freedom of church from state. With this promise the Roman Catholic Church received exactly what it wanted, and, as we shall see later,[2] put it to immediate use. But the Prussian Church of the Evangelical Union was a state church and did not possess the organs to live independently, even if the state continued to provide the external means. The specter of a parliamentary government composed of irreligious liberals that was raised in the early months of the revolution produced some commotion among Protestant church leaders. But the introduction of a presbyterial and synodal constitution also aroused fear lest the church might become swamped with irreverent laymen. The Protestant ministers saw their authority and with it the right creed endangered. The rapid recovery of the conservative powers relieved the Protestant churchmen of making decisions. The formula that freedom from the state would be realized if the episcopal office of the king was understood to be an exclusively ecclesiastic function unrelated to his state duties was gladly accepted. As a consequence, the Evangelical High Council (*Evangelischer Oberkirchenrat*) was established in July 1850 and was made independent of the state cabinet. But actually a great deal of the external church administration remained with the ministry of church affairs and education as well as with the district government, and the direct influence of the king on the church through the High Council became even stronger.

During the 1850's the church government was conducted in a narrow orthodox-Lutheran way that imperiled not only liberal religious thinking but also the union with the Reformed groups. Simultaneously Karl Otto von Raumer, the Prussian minister of education, tried to extend religious orthodoxy to education. While the universities were not seriously bothered, the public schools were greatly affected. In 1854 religious teaching

[2] See p. 259.

was made the major subject in the grade schools, and the churches received supervisory authority over the schools. Reading the classic German writers was forbidden in the teachers' colleges.

✐ Police State Methods

NATURALLY this system produced not only supervision of the thinking of the people but also the inevitable reaction, faked conformity. In public life the situation was equally bad due to the policies of Count Ferdinand von Westphalen (1799–1876), who held the key position of minister of interior in the Manteuffel cabinet. Strangely enough, although he was the brother-in-law of Karl Marx, he was the chief confidant of the *Kamarilla* among the ministers. The organization of an intense spy apparatus shadowing both friends and foes was his work. Even Prince William, heir to the throne, came under surveillance after he had criticized Prussian policy during the Crimean War. The police did not hesitate to use forged documents in order to bring opponents of the government to trial, and political as well as press offenses were now withdrawn from jury trial. Even then, however, the Prussian judges stood up well to the methods of the police state. It is unnecessary to describe other corollaries of these methods, such as censorship and suppression of all forms of political association insofar as they went beyond strictly local activities.

There was no better critic of the results of the workings of the Prussian reaction than Manteuffel, the man who officially presided over its operations. But he locked away the memoranda in which he set down his worries and dark forebodings. A dyed-in-the-wool monarchist and a bureaucratic administrator of modest political inventiveness, he suffered the whims and vacillations of Frederick William IV. But he would have lacked allies if he had openly fought the *Kamarilla*. In the eyes of the opposition that arose in these years he was not only the front man of the Prussian reaction at home but also the man of Olmütz, and as such responsible for the international humiliation of Prussia. Manteuffel did not take any pride in the Olmütz agreement except that he felt with some justification that he had saved Prussia from greater disasters.

✐ The Wochenblatt Party

THE OPPOSITION which developed in the parliament and at the court came from conservative quarters. Some of its ideas were inspired by Radowitz, who before his early death, in 1853, had come forward as a public advocate of a conservative constitutionalism and federalism. The leader of the new group was Moritz August von Bethmann-Hollweg (1795–1877) in Bonn, who was driven into opposition when the Manteuffel-Westphalen cabinet called together the provincial estates which the Prussian constitution had abolished. The group known originally as "party of Bethmann-Hollweg," later as the "*Wochenblatt* party," after its organ the *Berliner Wochenblatt* (*Berlin Weekly*), was composed of a number of noblemen, a good many of them active diplomats, and high state officials. The fact that some members of the former imperial aristocracy also belonged to this political coterie was of some consequence, since they interested some of the small ruling princes in the ideas of a liberal conservatism. In Count Robert von der Goltz (1817–69) the *Wochenblatt* party had its most prolific political brain and most active operator in Prussia.

The *Wochenblatt* party never addressed itself to the people. It wanted to achieve its aims by convincing the king that strict adherence to the constitution and a foreign policy in accordance with Prussian interests and unhampered by ideological prejudices would afford the greatest advantages. The majority of this group lived in the western provinces. They disliked both the agrarian feudalism and the Russophile attitude of the eastern *Junkers* and on their part wished a rapprochement with the Western nations. Under Frederick William IV the party had no practical success, although its ideas had a leavening effect on the thinking of the younger conservatives and also attracted Prince William, the brother and heir presumptive of the king.

✑ Prince William

PRINCE WILLIAM, in these years military commander of the western provinces, though a conservative, was not a reactionary. All through his life he believed that small Prussia could maintain her place among the European powers only through a strong army and that her strength and effectiveness depended on the preservation of the exclusive royal control of the army and the state executive. In this respect an inflexible absolutist, he was not averse to making concessions to demands for popular participation in legislation and for guarantees of the lawful exercise of the executive power. Although, in contrast to his brother, he was a Prussian first and a German second, he saw in the assumption of the national leadership by Prussia a welcome opportunity for strengthening Prussia. Radowitz's plan of a German union had his approval. But he took the events of Olmütz as a degrading defeat and became resentful of Czar Nicholas, who in his opinion was chiefly to blame for the Prussian misfortune. This experience made him receptive to the criticism of the *Wochenblatt* party, whose members in addition enjoyed much support from his wife Augusta, daughter of the liberal Grand Duke Karl Friedrich of Weimar. On domestic policies, too, Prince William was in agreement with them. He considered the constitution adequate for the preservation of the monarchical prerogatives and disapproved of the efforts of the ruling circles to bypass and undermine the constitution, as well as of the use of arbitrary police methods and of attempts to interfere with religion and thought.

✌ *Spirit of the Prussian Army*

BUT WHILE Prince William thus began leaning toward more liberal political ideas, his closest ties remained with the officers' corps of the army. As second son he had been given an exclusively military education and had devoted himself with praiseworthy diligence to an army life. He did not possess a gift for high strategy, but he was a competent, if slightly pedantic, officer. Small wonder that he was deeply affected by the army spirit. It can be said that the gulf that separated the military from the civilians was one of the foremost reasons for the outbreak of the revolution of 1848, as it was again seventy years later. The Prussian army was also the true conqueror of the revolution and the guarantor of the restored autocracy. The self-confidence of the army and the tension between the army and the people had grown through these events. "Like two entirely different nations and races," a conservative observer wrote in 1854, "civilians and military were facing each other." The officers wished to draw upon the lessons of the revolution, and this meant to them the exclusion of all those forces that had proved susceptible to liberal influences within the military establishment. The misgivings which the regular army had always harbored with regard to the national guard became more violent after the revolution, and it is true that a few units of the national guard had fraternized with revolutionary groups. Criticism could also be leveled against the national guard on purely technical military grounds. The desire to reduce the role of the national guard grew among the regular officers during the 1850's, and Prince William shared their feelings. The plan of an army reorganization with which William entered upon his reign in 1859 was to show that military thinking was the dominant trait of his character.

✌ *The Old Order Is Restored*

THE POLITICAL reaction killed the liberal gains of the revolution practically all over Germany. In North Germany, as in Prussia, this reaction took a feudal-conservative line, while in South Germany it followed more of a bureaucratic-absolutist course. Saxony restored her constitution of 1831, which gave the agrarian nobility the decisive influence on the legislation of this most highly industrialized German state. Hanover also saw a return to her old constitution of 1831 in the modified and more reactionary form of 1837–40. Prussia, Saxony, and Hanover settled the constitutional conflict in Mecklenburg, where the liberal constitution of 1849 had abolished an essentially medieval system that literally divided the administration between the duke and the nobility. The "hereditary compromise" of 1775 which had codified the old relations was fully restored as the fundamental law of the land. Actually, Mecklenburg was to live under these conditions until 1918.

Württemberg removed the new institutions by governmental action, and the same happened in Baden under the protection of Prussian arms. Bavaria constituted an exception. Her prime minister, Ludwig von der Pfordten (1811–80), even continued for a while to implement some basic liberal legislation. Subsequently the government adopted a strong conservative policy, but in view of the liberal parliamentary opposition it refrained from abolishing basic laws or institutions. The avoidance of a break in the legal continuity by arbitrary governmental action in this period contributed in the following era to a greater willingness of the people to defend the autonomy of Bavaria even within a national German state.

The elector of Hesse-Kassel, as we have mentioned before, had invoked the assistance of the Diet of the Germanic Confederation in 1850 in order to rid himself of the liberal constitution of 1831. The confederation issued a new constitution, which, however, did not satisfy the elector and his minister Hans Daniel Hassenpflug (1794–1862), and even less the population. The ensuing conflicts lasted to the end of the state in 1866 and ruined popular allegiance to the dynasty, which for at least a century had exploited its people in the most shameless manner. The ruler of Hesse-Kassel could not have undertaken his fight against popular rights without the active help of the Germanic Confederation. The small states waited willingly or unwillingly for the initiative of the Diet of the Confederation. The restored Federal Diet officially declared void the fundamental rights of the Frankfurt constitution, which a good many states had adopted, and in August 1852, on a joint motion of Austria and Prussia, established a commission, popularly known as the "reaction commission," which was to remove obnoxious liberal ideas from all German state constitutions. The activities of this commission led to the restoration of dynastic supremacy in all the midget states, supported either by aristocratic estates or by representative bodies elected by the rich. The four existing city states of Germany—Frankfurt, Hamburg, Bremen, and Lübeck—deserve special mention. Frankfurt returned to her old oligarchic constitution, but the three Hanseatic cities managed to retain the elements of modern constitutionalism, although the Bremen constitution of 1854 and the Hamburg constitution of 1860 possessed a strong plutocratic character.

✍ Significance of the Reaction

GERMAN HISTORIANS have usually described the age of reaction as an unpleasant but brief interlude between the German revolution of 1848–49 and the period of national unification of the 1860's. Such an appraisal fails to grasp the significance of the age of reaction in modern German history. During the decade after 1849 the authoritarian powers succeeded in consolidating their regained strength through the creation of political institutions most of which lasted to the end of the German monarchies in 1918. It is true that the transformation of German society, which gathered momentum under the impact of industrialization, in due course necessitated a broadening of the social basis of government. It is equally true that the breakdown of the alliance of Russia, Austria, and Prussia, at the time of the Crimean War, made the adoption of new foreign policies both possible and inevitable. Yet Bismarck, who made these historic adjustments, only modified the authoritarian institutions without fundamentally changing their nature.

✍ The Victims: German Democrats

THE POLITICAL reaction of the 1850's had a great impact on the further development of the popular forces in Germany. The foremost victims of the counterrevolution were the German democrats. Practically all their leaders and a large number of their followers were forced into exile. Most of them went to the United States, where they found a friendly reception and made a notable contribution to the consolidation of American democracy at a crucial juncture of the country's history. While their connection with the political life of Germany practically ceased, a few returned to their native country and made their peace with Bismarck. The German radicals who found a refuge in Switzerland remained in closer contact with Germany, but most of them were professors and teachers who seldom concerned themselves with the immediate practical issues of the political movement. The loss of the most activist and vocal elements of German radicalism was an important factor in, though not the cause of, the enfeeblement of any radical or democratic movement among the German middle classes.

The popular prestige of the democratic cause had suffered seriously by the abortive fights and revolts that had been launched in its name in 1848–49. No political party in Germany before 1918 outside of Württemberg used the word "democratic" for self-description. Occasionally the label "people's party" appeared as a tame substitute. Actually, the radical leaders who remained in Germany limited their political aims and concentrated their political activities on more narrowly circumscribed social groups. Therefore the formation of an active radical movement that would have appealed to the broad masses became impossible just at the moment when the class of factory workers assumed greater stature. In England the workers continued to accept the radical ideas of the middle class as consonant with their own political aspirations well into the twentieth century. By the time the political labor movement made itself independent of the old political parties, it did not abandon its adherence to liberal constitutionalism. Such an evolutionary development of the working class movement, which avoided the rupture of political continuity within the national community, could not take place in Germany due to the absence of a strong radical movement among the German middle classes.

Only in the wider perspective of the experiences of the popular movement during the revolution can the development of the political left in Germany be understood. All the various liberal and democratic groups came to realize that the expiration of the common spirit of the March revolution had been largely caused by the predominance of group interests over the political programs that the Frankfurt National Assembly had offered. We have seen that belief in the great systems of German idealistic philosophy had already been breaking down in the 1840's. The revolution brought a temporary revival of idealistic thought which proved valuable by supplying not only the intellectual framework for broad general programs but also the moral justification for the many personal acts of unselfish dedication that were seen in these years. Carl Schurz, in his *Memoirs*, wrote: "What should make the spring of 1848 particularly memorable to the German people is the enthusiastic willingness to make sacrifices for the great cause which, with rare uniqueness, generally permeated practically all social classes at that time." But this idealistic spirit broke under the impact of divergent social forces.

The failure of the revolution opened the dikes to a flood of frank materialistic thinking. Simultaneously most Germans turned with grim determination from politics to work, and the astonishing expansion of business and industry in the 1850's gave economic and social issues a widely heralded significance.

✑ *Hermann Schulze-Delitzsch*

THE POLITICAL leaders, trying to draw upon the lessons of the revolution and to set their future course, acknowledged social factors as conditioning elements of their political programs. On the left, Hermann Schulze-Delitzsch (1808–83) demonstrated this transition most clearly. During the revolution he had fought for his democratic ideals without reference to special class conditions. He loyally kept to his ideal of freedom and justice, which the ideal state was to accept and protect. In theory, he also continued to conceive of all classes as subordinate organs of society. But he felt bitter disappointment at the attitude of the upper middle classes and believed strongly that the realization of true constitutionalism could be the work only of the masses, who for this warm-hearted son of a small Prussian town in the industrial province of Saxony consisted of the artisans and workers. Now he argued that before the political questions could be solved, a solution had to be found for the economic problems, for this was vital for the development of the individual toward freedom.

✎ *The* Genossenschaften

THIS BELIEF made him the founder of self-help associations of artisans and tradesmen in the towns for the organization of credit and the common purchase of raw materials and wares. He also founded consumers' cooperatives. Their voluntary nature and the total exclusion of any state assistance were the main principles of all these cooperatives (*Genossenschaften*), which Schulze-Delitzsch originally founded as tiny local agencies. Within the next decades they developed into a flourishing national movement, closely paralleled in the cooperatives which Friedrich Wilhelm Raiffeisen (1818–88), a Rhenish village mayor, began to build for the rural population after 1849. They, too, eventually spread from small beginnings into a far-flung network of national associations.

Schulze-Delitzsch started the organization of his cooperatives in the hope that they would also contribute to an improvement of the lot of the workers. But whereas consumers' cooperatives were useful for workers, cooperative credit and purchase associations were practical only for producers and people owning some, if small, capital and tools of their trade. They did not meet the situation of the worker, who owned no property and had nothing to sell but his labor. Although the idea of the cooperatives probably had a stimulating effect on the incipient German trade union movement, this consideration did not enter Schulze-Delitzsch's scheme, for he distrusted the trend among the working class movement to call for state intervention. The distinction between artisans and workers that originally had been loosely drawn hardened with the appearance of a socialist movement. In contrast to most of his political friends, Schulze-Delitzsch was in favor of universal and equal suffrage, but he argued that, lacking the time and education for devoting themselves to politics, the

workers ought to trust the middle class in political affairs. While maintaining his ideal of liberty and equality, he considered the establishment
of a free economy with the help of the middle class a prerequisite for the
achievement of the ideal state.

But it was not the only prerequisite. Schulze-Delitzsch was convinced
that only a united nation could attain freedom, and he approached the
goal of national unity with the same practical resoluteness that he displayed in dealing with the economy. Events and circumstances had proved
to him that national unification depended on Prussian leadership and had
to be won against Austria, and he had furthermore been persuaded that
power was needed in this struggle for unification. But nationalism and a
free cooperative system of economy were for him only means to an end,
the realization of freedom. As in the early sixties Schulze-Delitzsch broke
with the socialists because they endangered this ideal, he later refused to
accept Bismarck's constitution for the same reason. Yet the political
movement he had launched found its support chiefly among the lower
middle classes and was led by men who had to win material benefits for
them through parliamentary tactics. Eugen Richter (1838–1906), the
foremost leader of the left liberals in the next generation, did not possess a
belief in a political ideal transcending economic and national issues. To
him the uppermost ideal was economic freedom, which he defended
acrimoniously against the paternalism and protectionism of the conservative government as well as against the Social-Democratic movement of
the German working class.

✑ Realpolitik

RETURNING TO THE 1850's, we find the vast majority of the liberals
looking at social realities with fresh eyes. Those standing farther to the
right of the liberal movement saw in the rise of a bourgeois class and its
ever-increasing command of the resources and the wealth of the nation an
assurance of the ultimate victory of the liberal ideas. This thought was
forcefully expressed in a widely read book which brought the new term
Realpolitik into circulation. Its author was August Ludwig von Rochau
(1810–73), who as a young student had participated in the Frankfurt
Putsch of 1833 and subsequently had spent ten years as an exile in France.
When, in 1853, he published his *Principles of Realpolitik, Applied to the
Political Conditions of Germany*, he was far removed from his youthful
activist radicalism, although he still liked to impress people with his radical formulations. "To rule means to exercise power, and only he who
possesses power can exercise it. This direct connection of power and rule
forms the fundamental truth of all politics and the key to all history." But
for Rochau the state was merely the sum total of the social forces, and a

government that did not represent the class of "wealth, opinion, and intelligence" was not built on power. However, since these attributes were in the process of changing from the landed aristocracy to the owners of mobile capital, it was inevitable that the "young" social groups would become the ruling class and make their ideas prevail. *Realpolitik,* which in later popular usage assumed many different meanings, in the parlance of Rochau stood for the acceptance of the facts of social reality as the supreme and objective causes of all political life. Ideas are only subjective convictions. Their truth matters less than the strength with which they are held and with which they affect public opinion. Because in the long run the government cannot rule the state against public opinion, ideas are the "bridges" to political power for one class after another.

Rochau's theory of *Realpolitik* was a strange concoction of French sociology and a perverted Hegelian philosophy. But it made an impression in Germany, among others on the young Heinrich von Treitschke (1834–96), and it was symptomatic of the new attitude of moderate liberalism. While the speculative construction of an ideal state was abandoned, the existing historic state was accepted and the only demand raised was to broaden its social basis by the representation of the new bourgeoisie. The expected growth of the power of the state rather than the progress of the liberty of its citizens served as the chief justification for the admission of the bourgeoisie to political influence. Thus German liberalism became ever more ready to compromise with the traditional state authorities, although the reactionary course steered by the German governments during the 1850's kept liberalism in opposition.

✎ *Johann Gustav Droysen*

AN INTELLECTUAL adjustment to the existing political forces could be made not only from a positivistic or materialistic position but also in an idealistic vein. The historian Johann Gustav Droysen (1808–84), one of the fathers of the Frankfurt constitution, revised his political ideas in a direction that appealed to many of his political friends, particularly in the universities. He, too, was convinced that in 1848–49 ideas had been defeated by interests, and in the rise of the new economic forces he saw the danger of the coming rule of a mechanistic authority that would bury all free spiritual life. Against this peril he wanted to mobilize the enlivening force of nationalism, which he wanted to wed to his native Prussia. Prussia had the power to defeat the obstacles to German unity, and she also had the inner freedom to do what the time demanded, since more than any other state the Prussian state embodied the Protestant spirit that had set the world on the road toward freedom.

Droysen deplored the fact that the Prussia of Frederick William IV was betraying the ideal Prussian heritage, but he expected her to resume her historic mission once a "strong-willed" personality took the helm again. Devoting the rest of his life to historical research he tried to demonstrate in voluminous writings that for four centuries the state of the Hohenzollern had been the German state representing the national principle in German history. Droysen's interpretation made the election of the Prussian king as German emperor by the Frankfurt Assembly as well as the exclusion of Austria the logical outcome of German history and attempted to build up hope that what had miscarried in 1849 would be accomplished in the future by men able to act heroically.

∽ *The* Kleindeutsch *Historians*

DROYSEN WAS the founder of what became known as the *kleindeutsch* or Prussian school of political historiography, which found its most eminent representatives in Heinrich von Sybel (1817–95), Ludwig Häusser (1818–67), and Heinrich von Treitschke. These men called themselves political historians not only because their interests centered around the political events of the past but also because they wanted history to influence the politics of the present. Leopold von Ranke (1795–1886)[3] pointed out that he who wants to make history bear on politics must be sure that his history is objective; otherwise history will not influence politics but rather politics history. The political historians of the mid-century did not produce objective history, and the statesman can learn more from Ranke's works. But the *kleindeutsch* historians were superior to many of their academic colleagues, and even more to many of their successors, by not letting historical research degenerate into a positivist study of unrelated specialties but by insisting that the task of historiography is not merely the description but also the understanding and interpretation of significant developments. In their intent these political historians were still closer to the universal aspirations of the German idealism of the early nineteenth century than most of the other contemporary intellectual leaders.

∽ *Specialization of Scholarship*

THE 1850's were a time when the specialization of German scholarship began to advance more rapidly. Although this specialization was inevitable in the further growth of modern studies, it happened at the very moment when the unifying direction which philosophy had provided in the preceding half-century was practically discarded. In all departments

---

[3] See the author's *A History of Modern Germany: 1648–1840*, pp. 523–7.

research proceeded on strictly empiricist and positivist lines. But whereas in France and England positivism and empiricism retained the tradition of an optimistic trust in the progress of humanity, the corresponding German schools, as a rule, were without any such belief. In this respect the destructive results of German idealistic philosophy, particularly that of Hegel, survived the breakdown of faith in idealism. The contempt in which Hegel was held in Germany in this period even by the relatively most philosophical minds should logically have led to a revival of the theory of natural law, which had been so completely submerged by Hegel. But this did not happen, although much Western European thinking was absorbed in Germany at this time. Whether the disillusionment with the aftermath of the revolution can be made responsible for this refusal to adopt the confidence of Western positivism in the rational faculties of man, as Ernst Troeltsch has suggested, cannot be decided in any exact way. The movement of the *Illuminati (Lichtfreunde)*,[4] which had cultivated an enlightened rationalism together with progressive political ideas, quickly dispersed after 1849. On the whole, Western positivism did not strengthen the liberal ideals in Germany but rather moderated, or even deflated, them. Now man was seen as bound by his empirical circumstances.

✐ *Rise of the Natural Sciences*

SUCH VIEWS found wider credence as a result of the rapid rise of the natural sciences.[5] The German scientists of this period found themselves in greater conflict with the philosophical tradition of their country than did their French and English counterparts. From Descartes to Hume, Western European philosophy had grown in close connection with evolving modern science. In Germany, the philosophical movement had led to Hegel's and Schelling's teleological philosophy of nature, which now appeared as mere mythology. Some of the leading German scientists, such as Justus Liebig (1803–73), Hermann Helmholtz (1821–94), and Emil DuBois-Reymond (1818–96), warned against the arbitrary application of scientific principles, especially the law of mechanic causality, to problems of inner life. But these warnings were not able to stem the flood of materialistic thinking that broke over Germany. Jacob Moleschott (1822–93) taught that thought is produced by phosphate in the brain. In 1855, Ludwig Büchner (1824–99), with his *Energy and Matter*, published the key book of German materialism, which was widely distributed in many editions beyond the turn of the century. Matter was declared to be the source of all spiritual and intellectual energy. Büchner's crude ideas did

---

[4] See p. 32.
[5] See the author's *A History of Modern Germany: 1648–1840*, pp. 527–31.

not have a very pronounced influence on academic circles. The fact that they found such an enormous popular audience was a clear sign that the universities had ceased being the chief centers for the formation of the national spirit, as it was an unmistakable indication that ever larger numbers of people, mostly Protestants, no longer looked to the church for answers to their human problems.

✐ *Interest in Schopenhauer*

ALONGSIDE WITH positivism and materialism the philosophy of Arthur Schopenhauer (1788–1860)[6] suddenly began to exercise a powerful fascination. His great work, *The World as Will and Idea*, which he published in 1819, had not caused a ripple for twenty-five years, and in the Berlin of Hegel and Schleiermacher the young *Docent* had lectured to a total of nine students in twelve years. But the old man, living in outward comfort in Frankfurt, could see the beginnings of his fame. From the 1850's until the end of the century there were few educated Germans who in their younger years had not been deeply moved by Schopenhauer. Beginning in the 1890's Friedrich Nietzsche, who himself started philosophizing under Schopenhauer's influence, vied with him for the faith of the young, and eventually he pushed him into the shadow. When we are inquiring into what attracted the attention of such a wide audience in the 1850's, we are less concerned here with the effects of Schopenhauer's philosophy on the most articulate leading spirits, starting with Richard Wagner (1813–83) and Jacob Burckhardt (1818–97) in this very period and still strong in Thomas Mann (1875–1955).

Only from a generation that had lost its faith in Christian doctrines, or at least in the compatibility of faith and reason, which German idealism had still wished to restore, could Schopenhauer find a response. With its assumption of the will as the underlying driving power of life as well as of individuation, his philosophy, while deposing the absolutes of reason, offered a causal explanation of life. At the same time, by showing that the nature of the individual is at best only partly remediable, this philosophy gave a certain sanction to all the private appetites of the individual, particularly to the sexual problem. The average reader was not desirous of nirvana, nor was there in this "Victorian" age any widespread advocacy of immoralism. But the love affairs of the individual received a philosophical significance such as not even romanticism had bestowed on them.

The view that the generation of 1850 embraced this pessimism in despondency over the loss of the revolution is not tenable. It was not

---

[6] See the author's *A History of Modern Germany: 1648–1840*, pp. 343–5.

Schopenhauer's general pessimism that the members of this generation cherished most. On the contrary, they applied all their energies to the practical tasks of this world. But they no longer conceived of their activities as direct contributions to the political future of the country. Politics was now considered the domain of the government, while the prudent citizen would concentrate on his private job in the economic or cultural life of the nation. Such an attitude went well with Schopenhauer's teaching that the state, though only a necessary evil, deserves gratitude for protecting property and allowing the individual to devote himself to the true human problems. In Schopenhauer's opinion the idea of progress was preposterous nonsense, and he called the democrats of 1848 the "sovereign canaille." He felt that the misery of man could never be helped by political change, and for that reason he had no interest in history. Only in philosophy and art could man's nature and destiny be recognized and a way to his salvation be found. This reduction of human life to the private sphere, in disregard of the individual's participation in the political and social process, made Schopenhauer's philosophy particularly timely to the German middle classes of the 1850's.

✑ Economic Conditions

THIS DECADE saw the decisive breakthrough of modern capitalistic enterprise in Germany. The spurt of new capitalistic enterprise which had been witnessed in the 1840's was followed after 1852 by a massive expansion of economic production. Werner Sombart has called the 1850's the period in which "modern capitalism was definitely made the basis of the national economy." Between 1849 and 1858 the percentage of the agrarian population in Prussia declined from 51.2 to 45.4 per cent, an illustration of the general effect which the increase of commerce and industry had on the occupational life of the German people. The growth of the German population from 35.4 million in 1850 to 37.8 million in 1860 began to swell the towns and cities rather than the countryside. But the development of industry did not keep pace with the actual population growth. Between 1850 and 1859 close to one million Germans migrated overseas, mostly again to the United States.[7]

The huge wave of German emigration, which reached its climax in 1853–54, was not a political movement. Perhaps 10,000 to 20,000 German immigrants to the United States could be called political exiles, people who fled Germany because they were persecuted on account of their political activities during the revolution or because they refused to live under the conditions of political reaction. It is probable, too, that political resentment was a contributing factor in the emigration of many of those

---

[7] For the German emigration before 1850 see p. 7.

who left Germany for the New World. Not only the political refugees but also the masses of the immigrant Germans embraced American democratic ideals with remarkable alacrity. But the major cause of the emigration was economic and social. The majority of these people were farmers and artisans from southwestern Germany (Württemberg, Baden, Palatinate, Hesse-Darmstadt, and Hesse-Kassel), the Rhineland, and northwestern Germany (Hanover, Oldenburg, Schleswig-Holstein, and Mecklenburg), all of them regions in which agrarian overpopulation had become particularly pressing. In some cases the local communities helped to finance the emigration of the poor as being less expensive than lifelong relief. But though occasionally groups of indigent Germans were dropped on the threshold of the United States, the German immigrants as a rule arrived in the new country with some savings of their own, and most of them without great difficulties were settled as farmers in the new midwestern states. The artisans were easily absorbed into the growing American industries, although many suffered severe reverses in the economic crisis of 1857.

The large emigration of the 1850's eased conditions in Germany, because employment and nominal wages improved after 1850, and after 1852 many additional jobs were created. The new boom that swept the world was caused chiefly by the discovery and production of gold in California and Australia. Due to large American imports from Europe, the precious metal quickly found its way there. In England the new capital was used as early as 1850 for large investment activities, while on the Continent the gold was merely hoarded. Only the stabilization of the political conditions, finally symbolized by the establishment of the Second Empire, engendered confidence in new business ventures after 1852. In the stormy upsurge of industrial development in Germany, railroad construction still constituted the strongest element. The length of the German railroad lines roughly doubled between 1850 and 1860 (3,639 to 6,891 miles); at the end of the decade what had been started rather arbitrarily as a group of regional transportation systems had become a national network through the opening of a number of east-west and north-south trunklines. The simultaneous extension of turnpikes and roads created a historically unheard of capacity for moving men and commodities on a national scale.

∽ Industrial Production

THE RAILROADS provided the greatest stimulus to the coal, iron, steel, and machine industries. Broadly speaking, production in all these fields tripled in this period. The discovery of large iron-ore resources in the Ruhr region set into full motion the fabulous development of the Ruhr district as the chief center of German coal and mining production with all its auxiliary and derivative industries. Altogether the output of capital and consumer goods more than doubled in Germany during this period. Great strides, for example, were made in the textile industries. Historically, however, the new organization of economic enterprise was more important than the quantitative increase in German national production.

✍ *Finance*

THE DEMAND for capital required new methods of financing. All financial resources had to be mobilized in order to make investments on the modern scale. Normally, neither the private entrepreneur nor the private banker was in a position to give the capital needed for the grandiose projects now to be undertaken. More "democratic" methods for the mobilization of funds were required. The decade saw the definitive establishment of the stock company as the typical form of organization of large-scale industrial enterprises. Between 1837 and 1848, six stock companies with a capital of 43.99 million marks had been founded in Bavaria, while between 1849 and 1858 forty-four companies with a capital of over 145 million marks came into being. Fifty-nine coal and mining companies with a capital of 70.69 million taler were founded in Prussia in 1852–57, compared to fourteen with a capital of 23.29 million taler in 1834–51. In the single year of 1856 the Prussian government sanctioned railroad, turnpike, coal, iron, and other industrial companies worth 116 million taler.

The enormous expansion of business activities called for new financial institutions. For the increase of the money supply German capitalists had to go outside of Prussia, since the Prussian government followed a policy of tight restriction of money. The German petty states around Prussia, however, were easily persuaded to establish banks of issue. Only nine of them existed in 1851, while by 1857 twenty-nine were counted. For raising the capital needed in the industrial development and for issuing commercial and industrial obligations, bonds, and shares, the model of the *Crédit Mobilier*, the great French bank founded as a stock company in 1852, was emulated in Germany. Thus under the leadership of Gustav Mevissen the Bank for Commerce and Industry of Darmstadt (*Darmstädter Bank*) was founded in 1853. David Hansemann, whom the political reaction in Prussia removed from the directorship of the Prussian state bank, organized the *Diskonto Gesellschaft*, which was to become the largest German banking company for many decades. In 1855 Austria followed with its "privileged credit institute for commerce and industry," the Austrian *Creditanstalt*.

To this investment boom of 1852–56 foreign capital from England, France, and Belgium still contributed to a considerable extent. French capital, for example, helped in the reorganization of the *Diskonto Gesellschaft*. There were at least nineteen English mining companies in the Rhineland, among them the prosperous Shamrock and Hibernia mines of W. T. Mulvany, a most successful Irish entrepreneur. But German industries gradually were outgrowing the patronage of foreign financiers as well as the tutorship of foreign engineers and foremen. At the same time Germany was drawn into the modern world economy. The international trade of the states united in the customs union practically doubled between 1850 and 1857, almost exactly equaling the growth of world trade during these years. Fuller participation in world trade also stimulated the development of German shipping. The first regular service between Germany and the United States was established by the Hamburg-Amerika line in 1847. Ten years later the North-German Lloyd was founded in Bremen. Still, the development of shipping did not keep pace with that of domestic industries. Particularly slow was the transition from sailing vessels to steamships. As late as 1870 the German mercantile navy owned a steam tonnage of only 82,000 tons out of a total of 982,000, compared to the British figures of 1,113,000 tons out of 5,691,000.

✑ Employment

THE BOOM OF THE FIFTIES created new conditions of employment. Immediately after the revolution the wages of workers rose considerably. But these gains were soon wiped out by the rise of prices which characterized the years till 1857. Certain workers' groups, for example the coal miners, managed to win and hold wages that constituted an improvement in purchasing power even under the stress of the general price inflation. But the general wage level declined in relation to the cost of living after 1852. Moreover, the expansion of industrial production was not produced by a simple augmentation of the national labor force but largely by the introduction of machines. The tripling of iron-ore output between 1848 and 1857 was achieved with a working force increased by only 40 per cent. In other branches, such as mechanical weaving, machines may even have driven workers from employment. In these circumstances the situation of the growing working class remained insecure.

✑ A New Moneyed Class

THE RAPID ENLARGEMENT of industrial production at a time of relatively low cost of production and high prices brought high profits to the financier and industrialist. The early and middle fifties were years in which substantial fortunes could be amassed. Compared to England and France the number of wealthy people still remained small in Germany, but the nucleus of a rich bourgeoisie was laid, around which a class of well-to-do people came into being. The growth of a sizable group of financially independent people was a novel chapter in the history of the German burgher class and did not fail to strengthen the social pride of its members. Industry and finance became the special domain of the German third estate. The *Junkers* were not shy of acquiring industrial shares or gaining profits by lending their names for publicizing new financial projects, but they refused to enter upon commercial and industrial careers, which is somewhat startling, since they themselves managed their estates more and more on the basis of strict capitalistic calculation. With the final separation of peasant and noble land and with the beckoning of a profitable market, German agriculture became more highly rationalized. More scientific methods were adopted, and greater capital investment was made to increase production. Although the feudal lords thus became capitalistic entrepreneurs, the Prussian *Junkers* looked disdainfully upon the new masters of industry and finance. Blue-blooded nobility, in their opinion, would only prosper on green pastures and wither among black smokestacks. To be sure, some of the great Upper Silesian landowners early discovered that there was greater profit in digging coal and minerals than in digging potatoes on their estates, and these men built some of the largest German industrial enterprises. But these were exceptional cases; as a class, the Prussian *Junkers* remained aloof from the new industrialism. Even the *Junkers* without landed possessions, members of families which had lost their estates, or second or third sons of landowning *Junkers*, were seldom found in industry or commerce. They looked to the army or the civil service as sources of a livelihood that conferred higher social status.

✑ *Germany: Part of the World Economy*

THE AWAKENING of new economic forces and activities, together with closer contact with international trade and finance, drew Germany into the whirlpool of a fluctuating world economy for the first time. What economic crises she had suffered before had been caused by natural adversities, such as poor harvests, or by political events, such as the ravages of war or the closing of foreign markets. The economic depression after 1845 was still the result of crop failures, though in 1847 a temporary British stock exchange panic brought down a few German banking firms. But the world economic crisis of 1857 hit Germany with elemental force. The investment boom had ended on the Continent as early as the end of 1856. The crash in the United States in October 1857 also shook the English economy to its very foundations and thereafter created chaos all over Europe. The German losses, though considerable, did not prove crippling in the end. The bulk of the industrial and financial establishments founded in the preceding years survived the storm, although much wealth and profit had to be written off. Even Hamburg, which was most deeply enmeshed in the world economy and, due to the collapse of commodity prices and the capital market, was threatened with the ruin of all its major firms, was restored to normal through a loan given by the Austrian government. The full recovery of the German economy took some years, since the Italian war of 1859 injected new problems and uncertainties. The sixties then became times of slow but steady growth. It has been asserted that the effect of the economic crisis of 1857 on the German liberals was similar to that of the loss of the revolution of 1848–49. Having gained fresh confidence after the political defeat by demonstrating the value of individual initiative in economic enterprise, they found themselves suddenly frustrated by the depression and forced to call for help from the government. Our historical sources are not adequate to prove such a thesis, but there can be no question that the troubles of the years of 1857 and thereafter dampened the optimism of those who considered free economic activity not only a welcome release from the rigid practices of the reactionary state but also the means by which the state would eventually be reformed in accordance with liberal ideas. Moreover, the conduct of business affairs proved exacting and left little time for political activity.

The Government's Attitude Toward Capitalism

IN FRANCE as well as in Austria the new absolutism that had defeated the political liberalism of 1848–49 endeavored to win the adherence of the upper bourgeoisie by the support of capitalistic development. It was the time in which both Paris and Vienna recklessly sacrificed much of their medieval past. The rebuilding of Paris by Baron Haussmann found its counterpart in the removal of the walls of old Vienna and the construction of the opulent "ring streets" around the city as showpieces of the modern bourgeois culture. In Prussia the backing of capitalistic enterprise took less ostentatious forms. The conservative government actually tried to strengthen the position of the artisans by legislation favorable to the guilds. It also intervened for the benefit of the workers through various measures, of which the progressive law of 1853, forbidding the labor of children under the age of twelve and imposing relatively strict rules on juvenile employment in general, was the most important one. This law was decried by the liberals as an infringement of liberty, while the capitalists complained about many bureaucratic obstacles which were raised against their activities.

Yet the Prussian government was far from any determined opposition to the new industrial capitalism. The benefits which accrued to the state treasury were most welcome, and there was no desire to alienate businessmen. Even such a hardy *Junker* as Bismarck recommended in 1851 that the Prussian government should champion the advancement of German material welfare as the cause most likely to win the sympathies of the majority of the Germans, who, he judged, were more concerned with material things than the noblemen were. In an active economic policy he also saw the best means to enhance the relative power of Prussia vis-à-vis Austria. The growing economic strength of Prussia was, indeed, a most important factor in her stand against the overbearing policies of the Austria of Prince Schwarzenberg.

✛ Zollverein

THE CUSTOMS UNION TREATIES which Prussia had concluded with the central and southern German states were going to expire late in 1853. Baron Karl Ludwig von Bruck was anxious to have the Prussian *Zollverein* superseded by a customs union that would combine the whole Habsburg Empire, Prussia, and all of the countries of the Germanic Confederation. Schwarzenberg would have liked to wrest the direction of German economic policy from Prussia altogether and to transfer it to the Frankfurt agencies of the Germanic Confederation, which after Olmütz seemed safely under Austrian control. But Schwarzenberg's death in December 1851 removed his great political energy from the pursuit of the ambitious project, and a year later Bruck saw himself forced to return to his private business in Trieste. His chief difficulty had lain in the neglected state of Austrian economic legislation. The defeat of the Hungarian revolution in 1850 had enabled Bruck to unify the Habsburg Empire economically by the abolition of the customs line between Hungary and Austria. He also had made progress in the liberalization of Austria's foreign economic policies through the exclusion of crude prohibitive methods. But Austrian industries still depended on a protective tariff, and a merger with the Prussian *Zollverein* would have required the introduction in Germany of protective duties on industrial goods. The South German states had always chafed under the relatively liberal economic policy of the customs union, and it seemed for a while that they would not renew their ties with the *Zollverein* but form an association with the Habsburg Empire instead.

The Prussian government prepared for such a contingency by closing the gap that still existed in northern Germany, where Hanover, Oldenburg, and some petty northwestern states, the so-called Tax Union, had maintained a separate customs system. The Prussian Customs Union distributed its revenue according to the population of its member states, and this was advantageous for the less industrialized states like those of South Germany. As a matter of fact, the possible loss of the income from membership in the *Zollverein* was eventually the major reason that induced the South German states to renew the *Zollverein* treaties. Prussia went one step further by offering Hanover exceptionally profitable financial arrangements and actually gained her accession to the *Zollverein*. Only Mecklenburg, Schleswig-Holstein, and the three free cities of Hamburg, Bremen, and Lübeck remained outside the Prusso-German Customs Union after 1854. With northwestern Germany joined to the *Zollverein* the western and eastern provinces of Prussia gained easy communications with one another and also direct access to the North Sea.

Rudolf Delbrück (1817–1903), a young official in the Prussian ministry of commerce, was largely responsible for securing the independence of Prussian economic policy. The trade treaty which he negotiated with Austria in 1853 granted some preferential treatment to Austria and promised new discussions of a Central European customs union for 1860. It looked like a first move in the direction of Bruck's plans. Actually, however, the Austro-Prussian trade treaty was only the shield behind which Prussia moved closer to Western Europe. The extension of the *Zollverein* to the northwest of Germany and the preservation of relatively liberal principles in foreign economic policy seemed to offer the chance of taking advantage of the opportunities which had opened through the liberalization of British trade policies by such measures as the abolition of corn duties and of the navigation act.

It is curious to see how the momentum of material interests forced upon the Prussian government a course of action quite opposite to its general policies, which aimed at conservative restoration, which in turn implied the maintenance of close relations with monarchical Russia and Austria. Internally, too, the growth of industrial capitalism to some extent undid the reactionary and coercive policies that Prussia followed after the defeat of the revolution.

✍ *Diplomatic Aftermath of the Crimean War*

WHILE THE RENEWAL of the *Zollverein* already was a sign that Austria could not hope to exploit the diplomatic defeat of Prussia at Olmütz to the extent of reducing her to a minor European power, the developments connected with the Crimean War freed Prussia from the immediate threat of an overbearing Austrian policy and accorded her a greater role in European affairs. The attempt of Russia to extend her influence over the Balkans and the Turkish empire in general met not only with Anglo-French resistance but also with Austrian obstruction. The Austrian policy seemed to the Russians perfidious, particularly in view of the assistance that Nicholas I had given to the restoration of Habsburg power during the years 1848–50. The diplomatic history of the Crimean War does not reveal great wisdom in the diplomacy of any of the European nations. But the Austrian policy, largely controlled by Schwarzenberg's successor, Count Karl Ferdinand von Buol-Schauenstein (1797–1865), had the most far-reaching results. It brought to an end the friendship of the two empires, which was never fully restored, although in the following sixty years periods of diplomatic cooperation recurred. Immediately after the war Russian animosity led even to a Franco-Russian *rapprochement*, which prepared the ground for Napoleon III's intervention in Italy in 1859.

Prussian foreign policy during the Near Eastern crisis was timid and confused. Frederick William IV resisted strong pressures which urged the formation of a common front with the Western powers against Russia. The members of the *Wochenblatt* party were most active in advocating such a course, and in Prince William they won an important ally. On the other hand, the king's desire not to lose contact with Austria led to difficult situations and made it impossible for Prussia to exploit the chance for an extension of Prussian influence. Right then the small German states resented the Austrian leadership that threatened to drag them into perilous European adventures, and they expected Prussia to protect them against these dangers. But undecided as Prussian policy was in the years of the Crimean War, Russia did not forget that Prussia had been the only power which had not taken a hostile attitude against her. Czar Nicholas I died early in 1855, deeply offended by the ingratitude of the young Austrian emperor, whom he had favored over and above his Prussian brother-in-law since 1848. His son and successor, Alexander II (1855–81), though less at home in Germany than his father, looked on Prussia with sympathy. Chancellor Count Charles von Nesselrode, for decades the chief diplomatic advisor, resigned, and Prince Alexander Gorčacov became Russian foreign minister. He entertained a strong aversion to Austria and liking for France, but it was Alexander who determined foreign policy, and the czar was far from seeing in an alliance with the country of revolutions and of Napoleon, a country which moreover harbored plans for the restoration of Poland, a satisfactory guarantee of Russian security.

Thus Prussia became the chief beneficiary of the diplomatic aftermath of the Crimean War, although Frederick William IV deplored the collapse of the "Holy Alliance" of the three conservative monarchies. In 1857 he suffered a number of strokes and was mentally incapacitated. His brother William acted in 1857 as his deputy and in 1858 was made regent of Prussia. Only then did he begin to introduce changes. Otto von Manteuffel was dismissed, and a "New Era" opened.

CHAPTER 4

The Constitutional Conflict
in Prussia and the Early Years
of the Bismarck Ministry

S IN 1840 the accession of Frederick William IV to the Prussian throne had aroused keen expectations for the opening of a new chapter of German history in which the monarch would seek close contact with the popular political trends, so the assumption of the regency by his brother William in 1858 awakened similar hopes. In both cases the public misjudged the personalities and political intentions of the new Prussian rulers. In some ways the younger of the two brothers, who at the age of sixty-one was called upon to direct the fortunes of the Prussian state, was closer in nature to his father Frederick William III than his elder brother. The man who was to become King William I in 1861 and German emperor ten years later possessed none of his brother's exuberant imagination or artistic interests. His was a rather ordinary military mind and a consciousness centering around the Prussian state rather than around Germany. William I did have both the simplicity and personal modesty of his father, qualities which, however, were coupled with an exalted pride in the monarchical office.

Prince William had been deeply hurt by what seemed to him the humiliation of Prussia through the policies of Austria and Russia at Olmütz, and he was prepared to defend the autonomy of Prussian policy with greater determination than his brother had done. In particular, he wanted to have Prussia's military contribution to the security of the Germanic Confederation recognized by some form of Prussian command over the non-Austrian confederate forces. In internal affairs, William objected to the disorderly management of the government created by the continuous interference of the court *Kamarilla* with the work of the state ministers. He also objected to the police and spy methods of the government, especially its invasion of the religious field. While William himself was a devout orthodox Protestant, he disliked the imposition of religious views by the state.

✍ The New Era

AFTER WILLIAM had assumed the regency in October 1858, he dismissed the cabinet of Otto von Manteuffel and Count Westphalen. The new prime minister, Prince Karl Anton of Hohenzollern, was a South German grandee of a slightly liberal bent. Most of the other ministers were regular Prussian conservatives. But the ministerial appointments of Rudolf von Auerswald, the Prussian prime minister of 1848,[1] and of Moritz von Bethmann-Hollweg gave the new cabinet a definitely liberal complexion in the eyes of the general public. Actually, William did not intend at all to adopt a liberal course. By selecting men from more than one political camp he rather wished to emphasize the independence of the royal government from political parties. The preservation of royal authority vis-à-vis the parliament was one of the chief tenets of William's political faith. He fully revealed his conception of kingship in a coronation ceremony, held in Königsberg after the death of his brother, when he himself took the crown from the altar of the church and placed it on his head.

✍ The Election of 1858

THE PEOPLE took the appointment of the new cabinet of 1858 as the beginning of a liberal era, and since the government stopped influencing elections through its officials, many persons must have felt that the election of liberals was not displeasing to it. The elections for the lower house of the Prussian diet of December 1858 were stimulated by these new expectations. Even the democrats, who since 1849 had advocated abstention from voting under the three-class system of elections, participated. But the increase in the number of voters was not great, least of all in the third class. What the elections brought to light was the transformation of Prussian society as a result of the Industrial Revolution. The new rich and well-to-do packed the first and second class of voters in many constituencies. The victory of liberalism was astounding. The liberal groups gained a strong majority of 210 seats in the House of Representatives, while the conservatives kept only 59 out of their former 236 seats. For a time the liberals were relatively united, if not about their ultimate aims at least about their immediate tactics. They agreed that reforms should not be pushed too quickly and radically in order to get the prince-regent used to liberal policies. Yet the defeat of all the small reform measures by the House of Lords in 1859 aroused dissatisfaction and, in combination with the growing acuteness of the issue of national unification, led to a more active policy of the liberals.

[1] See p. 76.

✍ *Impact of the Italian War*

IT WAS THE ITALIAN WAR of 1859 that revived national hopes all over Central Europe. By promising the Sardinia-Piedmont of Cavour military assistance for driving the Austrians out of Italy, Napoleon III wanted to wreck one of the main pillars of the Vienna peace settlement, and Russia, which had assured Napoleon of her neutrality in an Italian war, was willing, in contrast to her policy in 1848–50, to tolerate the destruction of the old order. The appearance of the French army in northern Italy and its victorious progress in Lombardy alarmed the German governments as well as the leaders of public opinion. A tremendous outpouring of political articles and pamphlets was the immediate result. The overwhelming sentiment was in favor of full national support for Austria. In reaching this conclusion not all groups were motivated by anti-French feelings. The majority of the German Catholics saw in Austria the natural ruling power of Germany, which ought not to be weakened, and the Italian national movement also threatened the temporal position of the Holy See. But suspicion of France was entirely dominant in the non-Catholic segments of the German people. Leopold von Gerlach, for example, saw in Napoleon III only the heir of the French Revolution, against whom the principles of the Holy Alliance had to be defended.

Such an attitude of mere conservative principle, however, had become a rare exception in Germany. Most conservatives, liberals, and democrats argued that Napoleon, after gaining Italian successes, would direct his efforts toward the conquest of the Rhineland. The fact that Lombardy and Venetia did not belong to the Germanic Confederation, whose members, consequently, were under no obligation to come to the help of Austria, was in this view rather irrelevant, since it was necessary, as the slogan ran, to defend the Rhine on the Po. Even Friedrich Engels, with the approval of Karl Marx, wrote that all of Germany ought to fight Napoleon, in whom they recognized the head of the European counter-revolution. In contrast, Ferdinand Lassalle (1825–64), who a few years later was to become the founder of the first political German working-class movement, found the greater danger in a victory of reactionary Austria and was convinced that the regime of Napoleon III was bound to collapse on account of its inner contradictions. Thus he advocated that Prussia should exploit Austria's distress in order to establish a Great German nation.

Lassalle's unashamed realism was not too far from the attitude of another "coming" man, Otto von Bismarck. When William assumed the regency with the intention of improving Austro-Prussian relations, the Brandenburg *Junker*, who as Prussian minister at the Diet of the Germanic Confederation had pressed the Prussian demands for practical equality with Austria with utmost vigor, had been sent into an "honorable exile" to the Prussian embassy in St. Petersburg. Bismarck wished that Prussia would use her army for forcing Austria to admit Prussian leadership in the major part of Germany. Yet the decision lay in the hands of Prussia's ruler. While a good many of the governments of the smaller German states added their voices to the general public clamor for armed intervention on the Austrian side, their military forces were too small and ill-prepared to take the field by themselves against France. And since Austria had no considerable force left which it could contribute to a confederate German army on the Rhine, the small German states could make their weight felt only in conjunction with the Prussian army.

✑ The Peace of Villafranca

THE PRUSSIAN PRINCE-REGENT was essentially willing to bring armed assistance to Austria. The memories of the War of Liberation from Napoleon, in which he had participated as a brave youngster, never faded from his mind, nor did he wish to see Prussia accused of lacking a sense of national responsibility. But on this occasion he wanted to have Austria acknowledge the great role that Prussia deserved in German and European affairs. Therefore, he demanded the command of all the German forces on the Rhine. Although Austria was reluctant to give Prussia the opportunity of posing as the leader in a great national effort, the Franco-Italian victory of Magenta on June 4, 1859, made her accept the Prussian condition. But Prussia announced on June 14 that she would first make an attempt at armed mediation. Ten days later Austria suffered her second major defeat at Solferino. When the Prussian prince-regent had mobilized the whole Prussian army and was about to begin his mediation, Francis Joseph and Napoleon III met and concluded the peace of Villafranca. Austria ceded Lombardy to France, which meant in practice to Sardinia-Piedmont, while she retained Venetia and was promised the restoration of the Habsburg princes in Tuscany and Modena. In all probability the conditions were not worse than those Austria might have received if the Prussian mediation had taken its course. For this appraisal it is irrelevant that in November 1859 when Austrian, French, and Piedmontese diplomats convened in Zurich to seal the provisions of Villafranca in a final peace, the Italian nationalists had already started the movement that was to remove all Habsburg influence from Central Italy.

Francis Joseph and his advisors accepted Napoleon's proposals largely because they did not want to give Prussia the chance of gaining a leading position in Germany at the expense of Austria. In public they even pinned the blame for the deplorable outcome of the war on Prussia and on that basis attempted to solidify Austrian predominance in Germany again. But there were signs of serious weaknesses which foreshadowed the grave problems that Austria had to meet during the subsequent decade. Austria's finances, never strong, had suffered badly from the mobilization of the army during the Crimean War. Hardly had Baron Bruck succeeded in restoring a balance when the Italian war ruined his work completely. Moreover, a continuation of the war would have brought on revolutionary movements in Hungary. Napoleon had encouraged the formation of a legion of Hungarian revolutionaries in Italy. And the dismal course of the war had not only inflamed the national tensions within the Habsburg Empire but also evoked new demands for a liberal system of government.

Napoleon's reasons for making peace with Austria were equally complex. The threat of a Franco-German war that the Prussian mobilization posed was undoubtedly the chief cause for his direct approach to Austria, which disappointed the expectations he had raised with Cavour and the Italian nationalists. Also, he was not unimpressed by the restiveness shown by French Catholics over his Italian policy and the consequences which it was likely to have with regard to the church states. Looking beyond the year 1859 it can be said that Napoleon III passed the zenith of his career after Magenta and Solferino. The Italian national movement could not be halted halfway. Within the next few years all of Italy, with the exception of Rome and Venetia, fell to the new kingdom of Italy, and it was British rather than French diplomatic support that contributed to these achievements. On the other hand, the annexation of Savoy and Nice, which Napoleon extracted as a prize from Italy, awakened British suspicions with regard to the reckless goals and methods of his policies. His colonial enterprises in the Levant and Mexico during the early sixties hardened British animosity to such an extent as to make England look rather with indifference upon the fall of the French empire in 1870.

◢ *Results of the War*

WHILE IN RETROSPECT it is possible to discover in the events of 1859 the seeds of developments which would eventually work into the hands of an ambitious Prussian policy, their immediate results were highly embarrassing to the Prussian government and most of all to the prince-regent, who had intended to demonstrate the high rank of Prussia among the European powers and to live up to the promise he had made when he took over the regency, that Prussia would make "moral conquests" in Germany. Instead he had antagonized both Austria and France, while not gaining any sympathy in Germany. Altogether, events had shown the impotence of the smallest of the great powers of Europe.

The peace of Villafranca was a bitter lesson for William, which made him less self-confident with regard to his personal capacity for conducting foreign policy. But this lesson strengthened his determination to act in the field in which he felt thoroughly competent. A reform of the army organization, he was sure, would in the end win for Prussia the respect which she deserved. In General Albrecht von Roon (1803–79) he found the man who was willing to make the ideas of the monarch his own and to fight for their practical realization without thinking of compromise. With the appointment of Roon as minister of war, in December 1859, the reform of the army became the central objective of the regent's policy, and Roon's entry into the cabinet was to prove the beginning of the end of a liberal New Era in Prussia.

✍· Reorganization of the Army

THE ORGANIZATION of the Prussian army, which fundamentally rested on Boyen's law of 1814,[2] was in need of reform. But the form which the reform plans took in the thinking of the Prussian monarch and his loyal paladin, as well as the political methods by which they proposed to realize their program, were from the outset deeply colored by strong political convictions. The army law of 1814 breathed the spirit of the Prussian reformers, who had tried to close the gulf between government and people, as well as between civilians and soldiers, as it had existed in eighteenth-century Prussia. Boyen's organization of the army aimed at spreading military experience among the people. But universal military service was not used by him to extend the control of the regular army over all of society. As a matter of fact, after a three-year period in the army the individual draftee stayed for only two more years in the army reserve, which was designed to bring up the regular regiments to full strength in case of war. After these five years the reservists changed over to the national guard, which was divided into two levies. The individual belonged to either for a period of seven years. The regiments of the first levy of the national guard, comprising men of the age of twenty-five to thirty-two, were in wartime placed in the field army, where each brigade consisted of one regular and one national guard regiment, while the second levy, of men of thirty-two to thirty-nine, served as fortress garrisons and noncombat troops.

National guard and regular army were largely separated in peacetime. Up to the rank of captain, the guard had its own officers. They were selected from among the only group that enjoyed the privilege of serving one instead of three years in the army, a privilege Boyen had given to those who had acquired a secondary school education. These so-called "one-year volunteers" were likely to attain a respected place within their

[2] See the author's *A History of Modern Germany: 1648–1840*, pp. 454–5.

local communities in later life. Therefore, they formed the natural link with those people whom the Prussian reformers had wished to entrust with the chief responsibility for local self-administration. Not the highest technical military perfection, but rather the deep-rooted morale that stemmed from the love of the home and community, was to animate the national guard, and it was this patriotism that the guard was to infuse into both the army and the nation in war.

Boyen's system had certain weaknesses from the beginning. Because of financial limitations there were always men who could not be drafted into the regular army but were immediately assigned to the national guard, in which they received only a very superficial military training. With the growth of the population, the number of these "national guard recruits" increased. This process was only temporarily stopped when, in the 1820's, the period of service in the regular army was lowered from three to two and a half and, in the 1830's, to two years. Finally, close to one half of the first levy of the national guard was composed of "recruits."

But equally serious was the poor training of the national guard officers. The regular army showed little interest in the "one-year volunteers," and their preparation for officer's duty remained highly deficient. The difficulties of both the recruits and the officers of the national guard were not inherent in Boyen's system of organization; they could have been largely remedied if the Prussian army and government had really wanted to make the system effective. In the listless period between 1819 and 1848, however, the energy was lacking for tackling these problems, and according to the prevailing reactionary sentiment it was not even deplorable that the national guard did not live up to the expectations of its founders. Moreover, the separation of the national guard from the regular army offered the old regulars in the army the opportunity to make the army fully their own again. In the years of reaction the officers' corps quickly regained the old caste character. The bulk of the Prussian officers' corps was still composed of *Junkers*. In 1859, two thirds of all the lieutenants, three quarters of the senior officers, nine tenths of the generals were noblemen. Their actual influence in the army was even greater, since the bourgeois element was largely concentrated in the technical branches. Numerous were the officers, mostly sons of indigent *Junker* families, who were graduates of the army cadet institutes, which Scharnhorst had vainly tried to abolish. From early boyhood these officers were isolated from civilian society.

Around the middle of the nineteenth century the Prussian officers' corps contained more generally educated people than in the days of Frederick the Great. But the enthusiasm had evaporated with which men such as Scharnhorst and Boyen had embraced the new humane ideas of their age and had acted upon them even against the strongest opposition. The succeeding generation, while finding enrichment of their personal life in broader intellectual experiences, was not in a mood to question social and political traditions, and it applied its education to the study of the realities of life. Friedrich Meinecke has judged that the transition from the idealistic to the realistic age, and with it from a universally minded man to the modern *Fachmensch*, that is, the person living essentially for the compartmental interests of his profession, occurred first among the military class.

✑ *Albrecht von Roon*

ALBRECHT VON ROON was a perfect model of the officer of the period following the Wars of Liberation. He had wide intellectual interests and much knowledge, but his heart was exclusively in the army, for which, and in which, he had grown up after he had entered the cadet institute. The excellence of the Prussian army lay for him in its *esprit de corps*, which set it apart from the civil society. Roon believed that whereas soldiers could well serve as models of discipline to civilians, people who were preoccupied with their homes and private occupations would never acquire the superior skill nor the true spirit of military men. Thus the national guard was declared an ill-conceived institution and its vaunted contribution to the liberation of 1813–15 was branded as largely legendary. Roon asserted that a well-trained army would always respond to the challenge of war with a heightened morale and would not require the peculiar patriotic fervor which animated citizen-soldiers who were convinced that they were fighting for a just cause in defense of home and country. In Roon's opinion this motivation for the bravery of citizen-soldiers placed the government under the unbearable handicap of having to conduct its policies with a view to the popular reaction.

Roon's thinking was diametrically opposed to that of the Prussian reformers. While the latter had aimed at the identification of the military and national spirit, Roon wanted to set the army apart from civil society. He preferred an army limited in numbers, provided it was highly trained, to Boyen's scheme for the mobilization of the whole people in a national emergency. But the attitude of Roon also expressed a sharp distinction in political beliefs. The Prussian reformers of 1813 had intended to revitalize the defeated monarchy of Frederick the Great by stimulating the political initiative of its citizens and giving them a share in the direction of public affairs. Roon and the prince-regent, representatives of an age of revived governmental authority, were by now considering the duties which the reformers had imposed, such as universal military service, as natural tributes owed to the government and not requiring in return a readjustment of the political order. The revolution of 1848–49 had shown them that the survival of this order depended upon the exclusive royal control of the army. Judging on the basis of a few rare incidents, when national guardsmen had fraternized with democrats, Prince William and Roon saw in the national guard the liberal wedge that might destroy the army as the pillar of royal power.

In drafting the military reform plans which Roon prepared and the prince-regent made his own, political convictions were inseparably intertwined with professional miltary considerations. Although it should not be denied that the Prussian army organization could stand an overhauling, it could have been achieved in different forms and in agreement with the liberal forces. The most radical note was injected into the conflict by General Edwin von Manteuffel (1809–85). Though a member of Frederich William IV's *Kamarilla*, he had maintained himself at the court of Berlin. Since 1858 chief of the personnel division of the war ministry, he urged the prince-regent to exercise the royal command of the army not through the war ministry, which owed information to the parliament, but through an independent agency, a "royal military cabinet." This cabinet, which was to function to the last days of the Prussian monarchy in 1918, was created with Manteuffel as its chief in 1859. All army appointments were thereby withdrawn from the ministry of war, and the king also issued direct orders to the troops. As chief of the military cabinet, Edwin von Manteuffel was in a position to exhort the king to defend his royal prerogatives to the utmost. He could even assume the role of a self-appointed spokesman of the officer corps by slyly intimating that Prussian officers might not approve of a monarch who wavered.

✑ Army Bill of 1860

SUCH WAS THE POLITICAL SETTING in which the army bill of 1860 was born. It proposed the removal of the first levy of the national guard from the field army. In order to maintain the numerical strength of the field army, the number of infantry battalions was to be almost doubled, the artillery increased by 25 per cent, and a large number of new cavalry regiments to be formed. This expansion of army cadres called for a great expansion of the officer corps and of the number of noncommissioned officers. It also required the drafting of an annual contingent of 63,000 recruits instead of the 40,000 customarily called up since 1815. The last provision, no doubt, was the strongest feature of the whole program; with an increase of the Prussian population from 11 to 18 million after 1815, universal military service actually had become unreal, while an ever-larger number of recruits had been assigned directly to the national guard, which thereby lost in military quality. But the aim of Roon's reform was not the adjustment of Boyen's army organization to new conditions but the creation of a novel system. His army bill demanded that every draftee serve for three years (or, in the cavalry, four years) in the regular army and remain in the reserve for another four or five years. This meant that the two youngest annual age groups in the national guard were taken away from it and, beyond this, that the national guard was excluded from the field army, since henceforth the regular army was brought to war strength by the reserves, while the reduced first levy of the national guard remained outside. It was logical that the government showed even less interest in the second levy of the national guard.

The proposed new army was expensive, not only on account of the large increase of professionals and the increase in drafted men but also because of the long period of service. Not even the majority of the Prussian generals, and for that matter even Roon himself, were convinced that three years were needed to turn out a good soldier. But this was one of the ideas by which the prince-regent was obsessed. He argued that only the third year would imbue a man forever with that disciplined military spirit which he wished to see spread over the whole community. Most of the officers knew that in a system of compulsory military service the average individual would be ready to learn the military skills but would grow restless if kept with the colors for an extra year beyond the period necessary for training. Yet Roon had to fight for the three-year period, on which the prince-regent stubbornly insisted.

The army bill was received with understandable suspicion in the Prussian diet. The national guard was a popular institution among German liberals and particularly among the upper bourgeoisie, which was strongly represented in the officers' corps of the national guard. Moreover, the political feelings of these groups were most clearly reflected by the moderate liberals, or "old-liberals," who dominated the Prussian parliament. Still, the parliamentary majority was not unaware of the weaknesses of the military system, and since its members wished to see Prussia conduct a strong policy in German national affairs, they showed themselves prepared to accept a rather radical reorganization, as well as a drastic increase of the annual draft. The offer made by the majority envisaged that at least one third of the field army should consist of national guard elements, but these were to be trained and organized in such a manner as to become virtually indistinguishable from the reserves of the regular army which Roon wanted. The majority assented to an annual draft of 60,000 men, but it refused the three-year period of active service. It was convinced that the third year was unnecessary and would require an exaggerated expansion of the professionals in the army together with great outlays for buildings.

The majority of the house was willing to grant the government large additional funds for military purposes, though it tried to pare down somewhat the steep demand for a 25 per cent increase in the state budget. In all probability, however, the government would have had no real difficulty in winning parliamentary approval for a program that would have given it substantially the additional military strength it wished. In the war ministry it was felt at an early stage that the concession of a two-year instead of three-year service would save the whole army bill. But the regent and Roon, eagerly backed by all reactionary forces, did not wish to make any gesture of compromise, although a military establishment approved by the representatives of the people would have guaranteed a much easier relationship between the army and the people. The reorganization of the army had actually already been begun by the government when the Prussian troops were demobilized after the war crisis of 1859. Prince-regent William believed that article 46 of the Prussian constitution, which gave the king the supreme command of the armed forces, should include the right to organize the military forces of Prussia as he deemed best. Manteuffel, who was prepared to see the whole constitution go by the board, and Roon encouraged him to declare any concrete work of the parliament on the organization of the Prussian defense system as an impertinent intrusion on his royal prerogatives. Parliament then would have only the right—or the duty—to vote the funds needed. The army bill was withdrawn and the parliament instead was requested to make a provisional appropriation of 9 million taler to be placed at the free disposal of the government to cover military expenditures for the budget year ending July 1, 1861.

The leaders of the liberal majority, of whom Georg von Vincke at this moment was the most prominent parliamentarian, felt relieved that they had gained time by voting only for a provisional money bill. But they fooled themselves if they assumed that they still retained the power to get their conception of a reformed military system realized. As a matter of fact, the government appointed commanders of the new regiments even before the parliament voted the "provisional" money bill; it interpreted its passing as clear evidence of the desire of the liberals for a face-saving device and thereafter felt few qualms in quickly going ahead with the establishment of an army such as the original government bill had proposed. The decision of the Prussian liberals to pass the "provisional" bill proved one of the most fateful events in German history. It made Prussia an absolute and militaristic state for more than another half-century.

∽ A Fateful Hour for Liberalism

It was, indeed, a fateful hour for German liberalism. Even then the right wing of the moderate liberals would have preferred simply to accept the government's military program in order to preserve their influence on the government of the New Era. But it is most doubtful whether the liberals had any influence in the sense that they could have hoped to remodel the Prussian state by courting the benevolence of the prince-regent. Prince William always considered the ministers royal servants rather than the representatives of the popular will. Even if the liberal majority had submitted to the wishes of William in the military reorganization, it would not have had the slightest assurance of having its aims supported by the government in other fields. At this very moment when the government demanded the support of parliament for its military plans, it made no efforts to overcome the opposition of the House of Lords to some pending liberal legislation in other fields. But by passing the finance bill the Prussian liberals failed to take a stand and thus jeopardized their future political position. If they asserted that they had only approved a provisional measure and would be free to impose a military system at variance with the one proposed by the government, they overlooked the fact that by their action they had minimized their chances for achieving their major aims. These chances were whittled down even further when a year later they passed a "provisional" money bill again. At this time the many new regiments had received from William their regimental colors with much display, and William, on his full accession to the throne after the death of his brother on January 2, 1861, had paraded the divine-right character of the Prussian monarchy by his demonstrative coronation.

The opposition of the liberals to the army bill had not been an opposition to a strong Prussian army but merely to an army that would become the praetorian guard of the dynasty. They wished for an army rooted in the people and they believed that only such an army would live up to the highest aspirations of the nation, which they saw in the struggle for German unification. The Italian war of 1859 and the subsequent formation of the kingdom of Italy had aroused a deep desire for the early achievement of German unity. A flood of political pamphlets showed a passionate interest in the national question, and with the New Era the belief in Prussia as the natural leader toward German unification had gained much ground. In January 1858 a monthly periodical appeared, significantly called *Preussische Jahrbücher* (*Prussian Annals*), in which a group of the most eminent German historians reviewed the problems of past and contemporary history in the light of a Prussian solution of German unification. Rudolf Haym (1821–1901) was the first editor of the organ, in which the young Heinrich von Treitschke began his political writing career and to which Theodor Mommsen (1817–1903) and Wilhelm Dilthey (1834–1911) also contributed.

Public Demonstrations

DEMONSTRATIONS ON a national scale multiplied. Scholars and professional men used their annual congresses for such purposes. The national mass meetings of German rifle clubs and glee clubs were even louder displays of patriotism. Educated and ordinary people, so rarely united in common action in Germany, combined in 1859 to make the centenary of the birth of Friedrich Schiller a memorable celebration all over the country. In addition, national organizations designed to bring steady pressure on the governments began to be formed. In line with the new "realistic" attitudes of the postrevolutionary age and with the interests of the new bourgeoisie, which had grown up in the wake of the industrial expansion of the 1850's, economic demands first found such representation in the Congress of German Economists. It came into being in 1858 on the initiative of small businessmen hard hit by the economic crisis of 1857 but soon became predominantly an organ of all those interested in free trade and an economic policy of laissez faire. These groups were stronger in North Germany than in the South, and their natural objective was to modify the policies of the *Zollverein* through the Prussian government, which was not entirely unresponsive to such economic aims, provided they could be divorced from the constitutional demands of liberalism. Rudolf von Delbrück, who was just rising to the virtual directorship of Prussian economic policy, was a convinced free-trader. But cooperation with the official Prussian government made the leaders of the Congress forget political principles for the sake of economic concessions. Future events were to prove that among certain sections of the German bourgeoisie the political ideals of liberalism could easily pale before their preoccupation with their social pursuits.

The National Union

A DIRECT attempt to create a liberal organization on a nationwide basis for political ends was the National Union (*Nationalverein*) founded in September 1859 under the influence of the Italian events and chiefly by the initiative of northwestern and southwestern liberals and democrats. Schulze-Delitzsch represented the left, people like Victor von Unruh and A. L. von Rochau, the editor of the union's weekly, the right, while Rudolf von Bennigsen (1824–1902) from Hanover tried to steer a middle course. The National Union wanted to awaken the whole people to the urgency of German national unification. It declared that the Frankfurt constitution of 1849 had been the true expression of the people's desire for a national state and had shown the right way to achieve it. It was remarkable that the democrats now openly accepted the *kleindeutsch* solution of the German problem and, more than that, saw in the Prussian monarchy the right instrument for achieving German unity. Among the German democrats who had not gone into exile hardly any republican hopes had survived, though they wished to realize the fundamental rights which the Frankfurt constitution of 1849 and the Prussian constitution of 1850 contained.

ᘒ An Era of Conflict

As THE New Era turned into the era of conflict, the tension between democrats and moderates was considerably enhanced. For the moderates the National Union was an instrument for organizing middle-class pressure upon the Prussian government to adopt a national German policy, while the democrats tended to expect national unity and constitutional government as the result of a wide popular movement. When the events in Prussia after 1860 showed the Prussian government growing less amenable to liberal counsels, the democrats gained in influence in the National Union. But the propagation of the idea of German unification through Prussian leadership appeared utopian unless the Prussian government was reformed beforehand. Therefore, the political efforts of the liberals were concentrated on parliamentary activities. The National Union reached at times a membership of over 20,000, but the intensity of its propaganda declined fast after 1864.

The National Union might have made itself into a large movement of the people if it had not only appealed to the masses for the support of its political aims but had also given their social demands at least some room in its program. But in this regard liberals and democrats were quite united. Both believed that political leadership belonged to people "of education and property," and they considered laissez faire the natural concomitant of such a philosophy. For the first time since the revolution of 1848–49 the early sixties saw political group movements among German workers. In October 1862 a labor meeting in Leipzig demanded that the National Union arrange for the payment of dues in such a manner as to make it possible for workers to join the union. The executive committee discussed this request at great length. It knew that the labor groups also wanted the union to sponsor a national workers' congress and to open agitation for the introduction of universal suffrage in Prussia. The committee was fearful of compromising its middle-class ideals and middle-class leadership. In February 1863 it rejected the request with the rather condescending statement that the workers should consider themselves spiritual members and "honorary members by birth" of the union.

৩ *The Progressive Party*

WHEN KING WILLIAM I opened the 1861 session of parliament, little in the way of internal liberal reforms was offered by the Prussian government. The atmosphere was laden with bitter feelings. Georg von Vincke, the leader of the moderate liberals, once more succeeded in organizing a majority, which, on May 31, 1861, granted 7.3 million taler to defray the cost of the expanded army. The funds were passed as an extraordinary grant with the proviso that they were to be normalized in the following year by a law on the army organization. This time, however, the left wing of the moderate liberals rejected the spineless tactics of Vincke. Two noblemen from East Prussia, Leopold von Hoverbeck (1822–75) and Max von Forckenbeck (1821–92), led the opposition that constituted itself in June 1861 as the German Progressive party (*Fortschrittspartei*), the first modern national party in Germany. It was a controversy over political tactics rather than goals that separated the Progressives from the old liberals. The Progressives, affirming their loyalty to the king, did not intend to conquer the state; they denied being opposed in principle to the present government but demanded the full realization of the constitution, especially in the administration of justice, local self-government, freedom of the press, economic liberty, separation of church and state, and, most of all, recognition of the rights of the legislature. They also strongly demanded the continuation of the national guard, the acceptance of two-year military service, and an active Prussian policy with regard to German unification.

The Progressives, no doubt, represented different shades of opinion. Some, like Schultze-Delitzsch, Benedikt Waldeck, Rudolf Virchow, Leopold von Hoverbeck, from the beginning placed a somewhat greater emphasis on the budget rights of the parliament, whereas Karl Twesten (1820–70), Eduard Lasker (1829–84), Max von Forckenbeck, and Theodor Mommsen originally were more inclined to look for a negotiated solution of the issue of army reform. But they were all united in their ardent belief in lawful government or, as they put it, the *Rechtsstaat*. They were fully conscious that in their endeavor to determine the moral principles of public life under the monarchy they were claiming for the bourgeoisie the place in the state which it deserved on the ground of its contributions to the physical and cultural strength of the nation. They also felt that in fighting absolutism they were at the same time defending the monarchy against the encroachment of the nobility.

In the elections of December 1861 the German Progressive party achieved a great victory. While the conservatives retained only fifteen of their fifty-seven seats, the Progressives won more than one hundred seats. The old moderate liberals lost considerable support, although ninety-five of their complexion, known after their leader as the "Grabow group," entered the new parliament. Another fifty liberals, the "Bockum-Dolffs group," took their place in the left center between the Grabow group and the Progressives. This Bockum-Dolffs group, in which Rhenish liberalism was strongly represented, held a pivotal position in the parliament during 1862, since the Grabow group was willing to cooperate with it, while being disinclined to collaborate with the Progressives. A further moderating force was thereby introduced into the new parliament, which, however, was distinctly further to the left than the parliament of the New Era.

✎ Conservative Reaction

THE PRUSSIAN conservatives were alarmed by the outcome of the election, which they viewed as a sign of imminent revolution. The wily General Edwin von Manteuffel saw in it the coming chance for getting rid of the constitution. But even the less sanguine Albrecht von Roon brought strong pressure on William I not to make any concessions to the liberal trend in the country nor to listen to the more liberal-minded members of the cabinet. These loyal vassals of the absolute monarchy were bold enough to spike their advice with threats that the king might lose the support of the officers and the army if he were to compromise on the royal control of all army affairs. It did not take much persuading to convince William I to stick to his position. When in March 1862 the parliament heard again that the government refused to accept the two-year military service, it declined to pass the money bill for the army unless the government would present an itemized budget. As a result of this move the parliamentary majority hoped to see the replacement of the cabinet by a more liberal one. Instead, the king decided to dissolve the parliament and accept the resignation of those ministers who counseled moderation.

✎ Crisis

THE NEW CABINET, under the official leadership of Prince Hohenlohe-Ingelfingen, was formed largely under the influence of Roon, who believed that once the conservative cause was properly presented and brought home to the people, the common man would rally around the monarch. In practice this meant the greatest possible use of government pressure in the election, which took place in April–May 1862 and proved to be a disastrous defeat for the government. The conservatives went down to 10 seats, while the liberals won 284 of the 325 seats. The 135 Progressives, together with 96 members of the Bockum-Dolffs group, held an overwhelming majority in the new House of Representatives. They were determined not to tolerate any further delay in achieving an army law on a strictly constitutional basis. But even now the moderate elements were clearly leading. If the government had conceded to them the two-year instead of the three-year military service, the army reform bill, together with the necessary finance bills, would have found a majority in parliament.

As a matter of fact the new cabinet, and, for a moment at least, even Roon, was inclined to make this concession. It was William I who insisted that the three-year period should be kept and that in general the army reform bill should not be made a matter of bargaining with incompetent representatives of the people. Not only his monarchical pride but also his professional military judgment resented the intrusion of what he considered the prejudiced layman's opinion. It should be mentioned on the side, however, that in spite of what happened as a result of William I's stubborn opinions, the Prussian serviceman never served for more than a two-and-one-half year period at the utmost before 1870, since the government did not have the funds for implementing a three-year service. The often-heard assertion that the military judgment of William I created the foundation for the Prussian victories in 1866 and 1870–71 is quite erroneous. On the other hand, whatever his personal prejudices were—and they were strongly reinforced at this moment by members of his military entourage—they were the opinions of a sincere person. In September 1862 a great majority in the parliament refused to pass the first financial measures for William's army. As a consequence the majority of the cabinet recommended a compromise with this majority. William I, however, stood firmly on the governmental bill and, short of its passage, threatened to resign.

William called his son, Crown Prince Frederick William, and told him of his intention. Through his marriage to a daughter of Queen Victoria of England, the crown prince had come into close contact with English political life and thereby had gained a liberal political outlook. But he was neither yearning for power nor was he attracted by the prospect of ascending the throne in the aftermath of a complete defeat of all monarchical authority, as the abdication of his father would have signalized. The refusal of the crown prince to assume the reins of government contributed to William's willingness to explore political possibilities which he had been reluctant to exploit before. He had been critical of Bismarck. The latter's strong anti-Austrian tendencies had induced him to move Bismarck from his position as Prussian representative at the Frankfurt diet to the cold banks of the Neva as Prussian ambassador in St. Petersburg. Although William held no doubts about the *Junker*'s profound loyalty to the dynasty, he was suspicious of what seemed to him

Bismarck's irregular political notions, such as his ideas about possible cooperation with France, as well as of his unduly strong language, which had made him hated among all the liberals. But when William's conflict with the liberals grew more embittered and his foreign policy remained without practical results, Bismarck came under consideration as a cabinet minister. William had sent him in the spring of 1862 as ambassador to Paris, and only at the height of the crisis was he willing to try out Bismarck.

On September 22, 1862, Bismarck met the king, who was practically ready to abdicate, and declared his readiness to defend the army bill and royal supremacy even against a hostile parliament. He succeeded in building up the morale of the king and in gaining his confidence. William appointed him prime minister and foreign minister. He himself and Germany had found their master.

∽ Otto von Bismarck

OTTO VON BISMARCK was born in 1815, the son of an old *Junker* family which had resided on the eastern bank of the Elbe for centuries. Most of his early boyhood was spent on the Pomeranian estates of the Bismarcks. If Frederick the Great liked to describe the nobility of Brandenburg as inclined to a pleasurable life, Bismarck's father lived up to this pattern, at least to the extent of being a warm-hearted and unambitious man, a rustic squire not given to any intellectual effort or state service. The mother came from a burgher family, which for generations was a dynasty of university professors, though her father, A. L. Mencken (1752–1801), had become a Prussian diplomat and risen to considerable influence as the enlightened secretary of the royal cabinet under three kings. The attractive, strong-willed, if nervous, mother, who was early afflicted by physical suffering, was given to all the higher things of life. She liked the social and political activities of the court of Berlin and was much concerned with intellectual questions. She wanted her sons to become truly educated men who made government their career. Otto von Bismarck inherited his drive for power, high intelligence, and sensitivity but also a streak of coldness from his mother and her family. From the earthy Bismarck clan he received not only his titanic build but also his zest for life and indomitable courage.

During Bismarck's adolescence the relationship with his mother cooled; he would have wished to receive less advice and more love. He preferred the natural warmth of his father and the unartificial rural world, in which the totality of the human personality could develop. A *Junker* by blood, he became one by conviction as well. As a student in Göttingen and Berlin he conducted himself very much as the young nobleman. Although there was much in his mother's thinking and even more in the teaching of his humanist school teachers that might have led him in a liberal direction, even as a student he showed himself a conservative Prussian patriot and rather unreceptive to the German national ideas which were widespread among the students of the age.

Bismarck also had already broken loose from the faith that his mother and school teachers had tried to implant in him. His mother, in a feminine fashion, held on to the thoughts of her father's rationalistic deism, while his teachers were the students of German idealism, which had attempted to find a synthesis of Christian religion and reason on a new level. But the young Bismarck found both forms of faith unsatisfactory. His skeptical mind developed the critical consequences of rationalism to the extreme conclusion of denying religion, while at the same time he refused to view the world rationalistically. What he took from idealism and romanticism was the belief in the individual and his right to follow the beckoning of his inner self. The highest measure of self-expression and self-fulfillment seemed not only justified but even required.

Such a Byronic philosophy cannot be adduced to explain the excesses of Bismarck's student years, with his extreme conviviality, his exaggerated pugnaciousness in dueling, and his passionate love affairs. In all these events the freedom of an exuberant youth prevailed. But his decision, after two years in apprenticed government service, to resign and turn to the private life of a country squire by assuming the management of one of the family's estates was reached with greater clairvoyance. Two years spent in government service as a junior assistant convinced him that he would be unable to stand the routine work and, even less, to subordinate himself to bureaucratic superiors. "I want to make music as I think good or none at all." He became an efficient manager of his Pomeranian estates without gaining the personal satisfaction for which he longed. His inner restlessness found expression in his prankishness and boisterousness as well as in his bold arguments. At this time his neighbors talked of him as the "mad *Junker*." But it was also a period of wide reading in literature, where Shakespeare captivated him most, in history, and in some philosophers.

But philosophy meant little to a mind that could not abstract from the concreteness of nature and human life. In the contact with the pietistic circles,[3] which flourished at that time in many manors of the Pomeranian nobility, Bismarck acquired a faith that stopped the corroding consequences of his extreme subjectivism and served to integrate the conflicting qualities of his soul. We do not question the honesty of this development if we stress the fact that it was the deep admiration for one of the young ladies of the pietistic circle, her sudden death, and the love for one

[3] Cf. the author's *A History of Modern Germany: 1648-1840*, p. 494.

of her friends that enhanced his receptiveness to the thinking and feeling of the group around Adolf von Thadden-Trieglaff (1796–1882). Thus he found not only a wife but also a faith in a personal God. Such "submission to a strong power," as he called it, disciplined his excessive subjectivism, and his marriage to Johanna von Puttkamer gave his human affections a firm center.

Still, Bismarck did not become a Pietist. He cared little for special Christian doctrine or dogma and never cultivated any group worship, nor did he wish to be "edified by mouth of ministers." Bismarck's religion remained highly voluntaristic and subjective, and though it provided him with a heightened sense of moral responsibility, it failed to dampen his pugnacious character. The man who lay awake whole nights "hating," who could perhaps forget but not forgive, had experienced only a limited vision of Christianity. And just as he managed to keep much of his personal life unaffected by Christian sentiment, he held that there was no Christian politics. His pietistic friends often distrusted the state church, because in their eyes it tended to suppress genuine individual religiousness and because they suspected the ministers of this church of having been led astray by the philosophies of the universities. But these Pietists believed that in their conventicles pure Christians would grow and in public life would act on Christian principles.

Bismarck did not have any use for the associative function of religion, and his doubts about ministers arose from the fear that they might easily turn into power-seeking men. He accepted the state church, since he recognized in the state the major agent of history and did not wish to see the church, through priests and ministers, become an independent force. The church, therefore, was not to advise on public affairs, nor could the individual Christian apply Christian principles to his political activities. The world and its orders were created by God, and the course of history was directed by Him. To replace the divinely sanctioned historic authorities by man-made institutions, as the French Revolution and its children, the liberals and democrats, proposed, was presumptuous. Such an attempt was also hopeless, because history had proved that after great chaos and suffering an authoritarian order would return. But since the plan of God was unknown to man, there were no universal Christian principles which a statesman could apply to politics.

In 1847 Bismarck could still say that the realization of Christian religion was the task of the state. But such pietistic thoughts were soon completely suppressed. In his later life Bismarck occasionally admitted that at fleeting moments the statesman might see in concrete historical happenings an adumbration of divine intent. Yet such experiences could not provide him with political directions, and he had to act on a lower level of reality. This sinful world was characterized by a continuous struggle between the selfish ambitions of men, parties, and nations. The statesman, however, was able to fasten his eyes on the highest super-individual forces of political life, the states, and would then recognize their major and lasting interests, which could help him to chart his course of action. Bismarck actually took the *raison d'état* as the guiding star of his policy. Yet it must be stressed that this disregard of unequivocal rules of action, often called Bismarck's *Realpolitik*, was by no means identical with opportunism. Bismarck held strong convictions about the ultimate goals of statecraft on which he was never willing to compromise, since for him they were not only expressions of his own nature but also religious commandments.

✑ *Bismarck's Goals of Statecraft*

THE PRESERVATION of the dominant position of the crown in the government of Prussia was one of these absolute aims. Bismarck did not favor monarchical autocracy, since it would have jeopardized the privileges of the nobility and thereby deprived monarchy of its strongest natural support. Moreover, Bismarck believed that public criticism would make for better government and give all classes a sense of participation in the affairs of state. But he considered it imperative that the royal power should remain free to formulate the basic policies of state. Command of the army and exclusive control of the formulation of foreign policy were the mainstays of royal power, which thereby gained superiority over any representative popular organs.

While this was Bismarck's ideal for his native Prussian state, he was opposed to having Prussia submerged into a German national state. He shared the conservative national sentiment which resented any foreign influence on German affairs, while it saw the German national character expressed in the existence of a variety of individual states. German nationalism, as preached by liberal professors and parliamentarians, was to him as much a product of the revolution as liberalism was. Bismarck was not devoid of a German national sentiment, but in his opinion German history was characterized by the growth of a plurality of states. Among the existing states the Prussian monarchy was the best administered and, through its military strength, contributed most to the international security of Germany as a whole. Therein lay Prussia's claim for the leading position in Germany. But Bismarck fiercely resented the attempt of the Frankfurt National Assembly of 1848–49 to achieve German unification by liberal and democratic means. It meant little to him that the Frankfurt Assembly had offered the imperial crown to the Prussian king, for he would have become fully dependent on a parliament; and Prussia herself, if not dissolved into her component parts, would have been subordinated to a popular national government.

Only on condition that the Prussian monarchy would preserve its traditional character was Bismarck willing to accept a reform of the Germanic Confederation. No doubt, he early contemplated the enhancement of power which might accrue to Prussia if she gained direct leadership in Germany, or at least in North Germany. It became clear to Bismarck that such gains could be won only on European battlefields. But it was not his purpose to jeopardize the fundamental order of Europe. Whatever turned out to be the ultimate political consequences of the founding of the new German Empire, Bismarck never intended to cripple the European state system by the destruction of any of its constituent members. If he wanted to bring about a shift in the balance of power in Europe in favor of Prussia, or of a Germany led by Prussia, this was to be achieved within the framework of the traditional family of European states. Bismarck was no democratic nationalist and, therefore, no believer in national self-determination. He was prepared to make the continuation of the multi-national Habsburg Empire possible by leaving millions of Germans outside of the new German Empire, as he also avoided any move that might have aroused the suspicion of czarist Russia that Germany, by adopting a policy based on the freedom of nations and nationalities, might endanger her domination of the Baltic and Polish peoples.

Bismarck's political conservatism, for which he found ultimate sanction in his Christian faith, established a number of fixed goals for all his policies and thereby kept these from becoming a mere drive for the expansion of power. Bismarck also accepted a certain Christian restraint as binding on the conduct of the individual statesman. The exercise of power was not in order to achieve personal ends but rather to preserve the natural order of the world and to serve the state. While genuine Lutheran ideas were reflected in this conception of service, by excluding religion from the formulation of concrete policies Bismarck was far from Luther's original ideas.[4] It is true that for Luther the political world was not the arena for the realization of the kingdom of God, and he had insisted that, like the practitioner of any skilled occupation, a political ruler needed special knowledge and experience. But Luther was far from accepting anything like the *raison d'état* as compatible with good government. Whereas Luther did not believe that the state as such was a Christian institution, he considered it the duty of every individual Christian to assert in political life a special moral attitude derived from his Christian faith. Luther justified war only in self-defense and advised

---

[4] See the author's *A History of Modern Germany: The Reformation* (New York: Alfred A. Knopf; 1959), pp. 187 ff.

Christian princes to suffer an occasional injustice and forget about their own "reputation" rather than go to a war that was bound to bring untold suffering to their people. To be sure, Bismarck never faced war light-heartedly and repeatedly condemned preventive wars, but he accepted war as inherent in the nature of the world and consequently as a proper means for accomplishing his own political aims. Also, he ruled out wars for the prestige, but not for the honor, of the state.

✍ *The Role of Religion in Politics*

HIS EARLY POLITICAL FRIENDS, the Gerlach brothers, and even more Fried-rich Julius Stahl, were closer to Luther's original teachings than Bismarck. With regard to practical politics, Christian religion, in Bismarck's thinking, had the function of denigrating liberalism and democracy while permitting recourse to the use of power as the chief arbiter of political conflicts. Several years before Bismarck, William E. Gladstone began his political career in England as a conservative. Like the Gerlachs in Prussia, Gladstone believed that the state needed "sanctifying principles" and demanded the closest relations between church and state. The church, in Gladstone's view, was not an institution subordinated to the state but had its own mission. When he turned to liberalism, Christian ideas remained regulative forces of Gladstone's political thinking. He found a synthesis of a religious and a liberal political faith that set a model for many liberals of the next generation in England and America. Woodrow Wilson, in particular, may be called a Gladstonean. Bismarck, who always considered Gladstone his worst ideological and political opponent, denied the possibility of such a synthesis. Although he linked Christian religion to conservative politics, he established a dichotomy between the inner life of the individual, which was ruled by Christian ideals, and his political activity, which had to conform to the interests of the state. The success of Bismarck's statecraft was to induce the majority of the devout members of the German Protestant churches to adopt his political ethics after 1871, while many of those Germans who were not bound by the teachings of the churches were simply to disregard the Christian elements of his thought.

✍ *Bismarck's Early Ultraconservatism*

WELL INTO THE 1850's Bismarck's fundamental political ideas remained greatly influenced by the thought of his pietistic friends and by the members of the *Kamarilla* of Frederick William IV. When he entered the political arena for the first time as a member of the United Diet of 1847, he appeared as a diehard who fought for the class privileges of the *Junk-*

ers. The revolution of 1848 threw him into distress, because he saw King
Frederick William IV surrender to forces that he felt could have been
conquered by the army and the loyal population outside of the big cities.
Soon he became active in building up support for the regeneration of a
conservative Prussia. He played an important role in the formation of the
Conservative party and of the first antirevolutionary government of
November 1848 in Prussia. In the first Prussian parliament elected under
the constitution imposed by this government Bismarck appeared as a
noisy representative of the ultraconservatives. While his royalism made
him wholeheartedly approve of Frederick William IV's refusal of the
crown offered by the Frankfurt Assembly, it was too exclusively Prussian
to allow him to become a supporter of the policies of Radowitz, which in
many respects were akin to the policies he himself was to bring to success
fifteen years later.

In 1849–50 Bismarck still saw in Radowitz's German Union an attempt
to use Prussia for alien aims. To him German unification smelled of
liberalism as well as romanticism. Bismarck sensed that Prussian policy
could not hope to achieve German unification unless Prussia was willing
to go to war. For this the hour was not propitious nor Frederick William
prepared. Therefore, Bismarck welcomed the Olmütz agreement, considered by many Prussians, among them William I, a humiliating defeat, as
a sensible solution of an unnecessary crisis. But the speech with which he
defended the Olmütz settlement had a ring not entirely consonant with
the sentiments of the old Prussian conservatives. "The only healthy foundation of a great state," he said on this occasion, "is political egotism and
not romanticism, and it is beneath the dignity of a great state to fight for
a cause that is outside of its own interests."

✑ Bismarck as Minister in Frankfurt

THE CHAMPION of the prerevolutionary order of Germany seemed to
Frederick William IV the right person to represent Prussia at the Diet of
the restored Germanic Confederation. From 1851–59 Bismarck was Prussian minister in Frankfurt. He learned much in this city, which was not
only the political marketplace of the German states but also host to a
good many embassies from European states. In addition, it was one of the
centers of European high finance and the home of a prosperous bourgeoisie. Bismarck's horizon broadened, and he began to see the peculiari-
ties of his native Prussia in a clearer light than before. But these new
experiences made him still more eager to assert the power of the Prussian
state in Germany and Europe.

Bismarck had believed in the Germanic Confederation as an organ for
insuring the conservative stability of the German states. But he had as-

sumed that the confederation rested essentially upon the cooperation of Austria and Prussia, a cooperation requiring mutual respect for the fundamental interests of the two major German powers. He found, however, that Austria asserted its predominance in the confederation in a form that offended his Prussian pride. His reaction to the Austrian policies, and even more to the Austrian representatives in Frankfurt, was not altogether fair, but it is true that the revolution of 1848–49 had changed the relations of the two major powers. In the years between 1815 and 1848 the possibility of a German unification under Prussian leadership had seemed remote, and Metternich had been able to maintain a trusting cooperation between Austria and Prussia. But the revolution of 1848–49 had not only revealed the magnetic power that Prussia possessed in the national movement of the German people but, in the policy of Radowitz, also shown what ambitions existed in the conservative circles of the Prussian monarchy. Thus Austria was driven by necessity to strengthen her ties with the smaller German states, which meant in particular Bavaria, Württemberg, Saxony, Baden, and Hesse-Darmstadt, and, together with them, to try to strengthen the authority of the Diet of the Germanic Confederation.

Whereas Bismarck was willing to accept the confederation as "an insurance company against revolution and war," he resented any attempt to increase the power of the diet over the German states, since the acceptance of majority decisions would have clipped the wings of Prussia forever. Prussia was to retain the opportunity for gaining additional strength unhampered by the confederation. Thus Bismarck contributed greatly to the defeat of the Austrian schemes for a Central European Customs Union and to the renewal of the enlarged Prussian-German Customs Union in 1854.[5] The need for an independent Prussian policy appeared to Bismarck even more urgent when the "Holy Alliance" broke up during the Crimean War. The breach between Austria and Russia was likely to bring Russia and France more closely together and threatened to isolate Prussia. It was in the Prussian interest to find an understanding with France as the natural enemy of the Habsburg Empire. Such an understanding at the same time would deprive the small German states of any foreign support and force them into the arms of Prussia.

✑ The Need for Freedom from Principle

THE PROBLEM OF RELATIONS with Napoleon III forced Bismarck to announce his opposition to any foreign policy motivated by the belief in unalterable principles. Leopold von Gerlach, whose lieutenant Bismarck had been in the fight against the revolution of 1848–49 and whose influ-

[5] See p. 129.

ence with Frederick William IV had been instrumental in securing his diplomatic appointment, now heard from Bismarck that the attitude of the old school of Prussian conservatives in foreign affairs was untenable. Gerlach demanded that Prussian policy should always take a stand against everything that originated from the French Revolution and consequently also against Napoleon III, who based his regime on the sovereignty of the people. Only firm adherence to the principle of legitimacy and not "fluctuating conceptions of interests" could give Prussian policy continuity and moral prestige. Bismarck, while emphasizing his royalism in Prussian politics, denied that principles could be applied to foreign policies in such a radical manner. To him the struggle between legitimacy and revolution did not show any clear fronts, since to some extent most modern governments were tainted by the use of revolutionary means, even though the passing of time had made such events of the past forgotten. Bismarck also stressed that, much in contrast to republicanism or English liberalism, Bonapartism was not an export article. But his chief argument was the contention that no principle should be allowed to interfere with one's absolute devotion to one's own state. Patriotism called for subordination of all principles and subjective sentiments to the interests of the state, and not even the king could subordinate the interests of state to "his own feeling of love and hatred against foreigners." In a somewhat different perspective he expressed later the need for freedom from principle in the conduct of foreign policy by stating that, "You cannot play chess if from the beginning sixteen out of the sixty-four squares are forbidden to you."

Thereby Bismarck's separation from the political thought of the "Christian-Germanic circle" was consciously and openly established. Behind it lay his growing conviction that a co-dominion of Austria and Prussia through the confederation was impossible, because the latter would rather help Austria to keep Prussia in check. Very early he began to face up to the possibility of an eventual war against the old imperial power, and he did not hesitate to warn his Austrian colleagues, whose life in Frankfurt he made miserable. No issue was too small for him to be used for fighting Austrian policy in Germany and for demonstrating the futility of the Diet of Frankfurt as an organ for the formulation of a common German policy. The weak government of Frederick William IV and his prime minister, Otto von Manteuffel, not only gave Bismarck much freedom in the diplomatic tactics which he employed in Frankfurt but also allowed him to participate in the deliberations and cabals of the Berlin court and government. Bismarck knew that neither the king nor his prime minister would ever fight Austria, but he could at least contribute to thwarting close cooperation between Prussia and Austria.

✑ *Bismarck in St. Petersburg*

THE REGENCY OF WILLIAM I deprived Bismarck of his post in Frankfurt, which he had come to consider the politically most important Prussian legation from which in the future it would be easy to acquire a portfolio in the Berlin government. But the liberal slant of the New Era made it desirable to have a Prussian representative of liberal bent in Frankfurt. Bismarck was sent as envoy to St. Petersburg. He was dismayed at his removal from the center of political decisions just when the Italian war of 1859 created the situation for which he had always hoped. If at this moment he had been the director of Prussian policy, he would have intervened against Austria with or without an alliance with France and would have replaced the confederation by a federal state that would have united most, if not all, of non-Austrian Germany under Prussian leadership. With other men in control who were not even very amenable to his counsels, Bismarck could only implore them from St. Petersburg to steer a neutral course. He was terrified to see the prince-regent about to embark on a policy that might have saved Austria, but the peace of Villafranca stopped the Prussian move that Bismarck had considered suicidal.

The years 1859–62 in St. Petersburg were useful, however, because they gave Bismarck an understanding of the working of the Russian court and government and at least a glimpse of the Russian people and their civilization. He noted the decline of German influence in a society increasingly permeated by Slav nationalism and recognized that the liberation of the peasants just launched in these years would be only the beginning of social and political changes extending far into the future. The establishment of personal relations with Czar Alexander II and with the chancellor, Prince Gorčacov, as well as with other Russian political figures proved of inestimable value in Bismarck's later career. Developments in Berlin led to his recall from St. Petersburg in the spring of 1862, but King William hesitated to appoint him minister and instead sent him as ambassador to Paris. After a few summer months in France he was called back to Berlin, where he won his appointment as prime minister.

✑ *Prime Minister*

BISMARCK WAS BURNING to assume power, and the moment seemed favorable for getting the king into his hands. William had never quite lived down Bismarck's support of the Olmütz agreement and the subsequent regime of Otto von Manteuffel. William's wife, Augusta, a princess of the liberal Weimar dynasty, had kept his distrust of Bismarck alive, and in later years she was often trying to counteract Bismarck's policies with the king. William was also most suspicious of Bismarck's sympathies with Franco-Prussian cooperation. It is also probably right to assume that the conscientiously plodding king was fearful of this imperious man who, with his bold speech, his sharp wit, and cunning, did not fit into any of the customary molds. Still, Bismarck was bound to accept certain political conditions. He promised the king to uphold the army bill, including the three-year-service provision, and to govern even without an approved budget. He also could hardly have any doubts that the king would never allow him to make a deal with Napoleon.

Bismarck did not believe in the necessity of the three-year service, and it is revealing of his political nature that he did not hide his own opinion from others. As a matter of fact, he disclosed it to the moderate liberals, whom he approached in order to find out about a possible compromise between government and parties. He wanted them to accept the government program on his assurance that he would do his utmost to persuade the king within two years to agree to a two-year period of military service. But the majority of the Prussian parliament no longer had any trust in mere promises of the government. The more radical wing of the Progressive party gained ascendancy over the moderates and demanded parliamentary control not only of military expenditures but also of the formation and organization of the army. Voices were raised demanding the replacement of the army by a citizens' militia.

On the other side, such royalists as Edwin von Manteuffel had their way against Bismarck and Roon. Even the decision on the actual peacetime strength of the army and the number of draftees as well as the whole organization was declared to be within the "personal regime of the king"; otherwise, as General von Manteuffel put it, the army would think that "the law and no longer the king was its lord." The struggle thereby became truly one over a parliamentary versus a royal army. Bismarck's place in this conflict was, of course, never in doubt. To preserve the Prussian army as an instrument that would guarantee the ultimate independence of the crown from popular forces was to him an article of faith. But he did not believe in absolutism as the ideal and strongest form of government. Provided the superiority of the royal power was assured, he was willing to accept certain constitutional limitations in exchange for the cooperation of a popular representation. In this respect Bismarck differed strongly from the rabid reactionary sentiment of Edwin von Manteuffel and other military and civilian ultras at the court and in the Conservative party.

✐ Prime Minister vs. Parliament

BUT FOR THE FIRST YEARS this difference rarely appeared in public. With all his energies Bismarck threw himself into the fight against the parliamentary majority. In excited debates he countered the attacks of the embittered deputies by his sarcastic wit, his gibes, and his stubborn insistence on royalist principles. He adopted an unusual theory, which others had already implanted in the king, for justifying his policy. This theory contended that article 109 of the Prussian constitution of 1850 authorized the government to manage the state finances on the basis of former tax grants in case agreement on the budget had not been reached by the government and the other two organs of the state, the House of Representatives and the House of Lords. It was a wild theory that made a farce of any power of the popular representation over the budget, and article 99 actually stated very clearly the obligation of the government to seek an agreement on the budget with the parliament. But the parliamentary majority had no constitutional means for making a correct interpretation of the constitution prevail over the trumped-up official theory. The constitution, as might be expected, did not provide for any judicial review. If the majority wanted to fight the government in earnest, it had only the choice of organizing a tax strike of the people. But whether such a call would have met with a general popular response is doubtful, and in any event none of the parties and groups represented in the Prussian parliament ever seriously contemplated a step that might easily have led to open revolution. Not even the more radical members were prepared to face the consequences that might have brought into play again those revolutionary elements that in the opinion of the Progresssives had been largely responsible for the miscarriage of German liberalism in 1848–49. Beyond arousing general moral indignation the majority did not intend to go.

The Progressives even failed to organize the popular support that they undoubtedly possessed in these years. They were still a party of notables relying in elections largely on the social prestige which they enjoyed in their local constituencies. The democrats of 1848 had at least theoretically demanded universal suffrage. The Progressives, fifteen years later, were well satisfied with the three-class system which produced overwhelming liberal majorities in parliament. But popular participation in elections, which even in the first class of voters was not overly impressive, was exceedingly poor in the second and third classes. In the election of 1863, close to 1.1 million eligible voters existed, of whom only 30.9 per cent cast a ballot. In class I, 57 per cent, in class II, 44 per cent, and in class III, 27.3 per cent voted. In this election the liberals, polling 52.8 per cent, elected 73.4 per cent of the deputies, whereas the conservatives, with a popular vote of 30.5 per cent, elected only 10.3 per cent of the deputies. Naturally, the conservatives, including Bismarck, argued that the election results did not represent a true picture of the political sentiment of the people.

All available indications, however, tend to prove that in these years the conservative vote would not have gained in relative strength under universal suffrage. The conservatives might have won a fuller representation in parliament if the election through single constituencies had been abolished. But it is true that the three-class system deterred many eligible voters from going to the polls and particularly the mass of the people. It is revealing that the participation in elections was weakest in the Rhineland, the province with the politically most conscious population. If the Progressives had championed universal suffrage, they would have gained more active popular support, but it might have required political leaders more ambitious for mass appeal than the staid generation of German liberals produced.

✑ Army and Bureaucracy

IN HIS UNCONSTITUTIONAL POLICIES Bismarck could rely on the backing of the army and of the bureaucracy. There were some officers with liberal sympathies, as there were liberal *Junkers*, particularly in East Prussia. But the army was an absolutely obedient instrument in the hands of a conservative government. The bureaucracy was shot through with liberal elements. The number of civil servants who were liberal members of parliament was rather large, and many others were active as liberal speakers in the towns. The relatively greatest number of liberals was found among the judges. Bismarck, who had left the civil service because he refused to subordinate himself to superiors, was determined not to tolerate views deviating from the governmental policy and soon began to apply various forms of coercion. But as a whole even the Prussian bureaucracy was a secure executive organ of the government. Liberal officials discharged their duties in line with superior orders. The acts which came closest to sabotage were the lenient decisions of judges in cases of liberals getting into conflict with ordinances of the government. In general, Bismarck could only complain that a good many officials failed to support the government when acting as private citizens.

✑ The "Most Miserable" Suffrage

IN ADDITION TO THE PRESSURE brought upon officials through dismissals, refusal of promotions, or transfer to minor jobs Bismarck attempted to muzzle the press through ordinances. But actually the parliamentary elections which were held in 1863 and in which the government used every means at its disposal to influence and intimidate the electorate brought only an insignificant increase of conservative representation. Bismarck looked for the reasons for such failure to the three-class system of election. This "most miserable" suffrage, he argued, gave the liberal bourgeoisie disproportionate power. Napoleon III had demonstrated that universal suffrage could be successfully used for building up an absolutist regime. Through the organs of the state and the churches, the common people—and this meant chiefly the peasants—could be mobilized for the support of an authoritarian system. But perhaps even the rising class of industrial workers, with its hostility toward the bourgeoisie, could be employed against the liberals, though this might imply concessions in the direction of state socialism. Bismarck did not hesitate to explore such possibilities with the foremost German socialist, Ferdinand Lassalle (1825–64).

Yet from the beginning Bismarck was convinced that the key to victory was not to be found in elections and parliamentary debates but in German and European politics as well as in economic policies that would satisfy the well-to-do. As early as 1851 he had written to Leopold von Gerlach that Prussia should take the initiative in matters of German material welfare, since they were most important to the majority of Germans. Impressed by what he had seen in his years at Frankfurt, he moved away from the socioeconomic thinking of his older conservative friends. No longer did the craft guilds appear to him as a natural basis for Christian education and conduct, nor did he see any point in the protection of a corporate structure of society against industrial freedom.

↭ *Unification Used to Defeat Liberalism*

THE WILLINGNESS to adjust the economic policies of the state to the needs and wishes of the politically strongest classes remained one of the basic traits of Bismarck's twenty-eight years of rule. But in the early years the intention to take the wind out of the sails of a political opposition through economic concessions was completely subordinated to the greater device of using the national unification of Germany to defeat liberalism. "We are a conceited nation," he wrote in 1857, "and we are even resentful if we cannot boast; we allow much to a government which makes us important externally and in return stand a great deal of abuse even with regard to our purse." He was at least right in that the demand for a powerful national state was as strong as the wish for constitutional freedom and that among the moderate liberals nationalism had clearly become the most desired aim. What had made the army bill of William I and Roon so unattractive to the parliamentary majority was the lack of any purposeful national policy of the government. As the bill was stubbornly defended by the government, it seemed chiefly meant to preserve absolutism.

✑ *"Iron and Blood"*

IN THE BUDGET COMMISSION of the Prussian parliament, where Bismarck for the first time explained some of his ministerial duties, he emphasized the task of an active foreign policy, though with strong invectives against the liberals. Said he: "Germany does not look at Prussia's liberalism but at her power—Prussia must keep her power together for the auspicious moment, which already has been missed a few times; the Prussian boundaries are not favorable for the formation of a healthy state. The great questions of the age are not settled by speeches and majority votes—this was the error of 1848–49—but by iron and blood." This was a rather incautious and infelicitous formulation of his intentions. It did not sound well in the ears of Prussian conservatives who believed in monarchical solidarity. If the young Heinrich von Treitschke called the statement of the "shallow *Junker*" "mean" and "ridiculous," he expressed the sentiment prevailing among German liberals.

✑ *Austria: Aftermath of the Italian War*

MEANWHILE BISMARCK DEMANDED from Austria the unreserved recognition of Prussia's equality within the Germanic Confederation and of her leading role in North Germany. But Austria was not inclined to give up any of her rights and prerogatives in Germany. She emerged from the Italian war of 1859 with her finances ruined and with an internal system of government that now became clearly untenable. The bureaucratic absolutism and centralism which Schwarzenberg had imposed was undermined by the flood of nationalism. Through the imperial diploma of October 1860 a constitution was granted which restored much of the autonomy of the historic lands, while creating an Imperial Council (*Reichsrat*), whose membership was partly elected by the diets of the lands, partly appointed by the emperor. The *Reichsrat* was to "collaborate" in the legislation, though only in a few cases its "consent" was needed. The October diploma satisfied neither the Magyars, who wanted the restoration of their constitution of 1848, nor the southern Slavs, who wished for a kingdom of their own, nor the Germans, who resented being demoted from their position of leadership within the Empire.

✍ Reorganization of the Empire

EMPEROR FRANCIS JOSEPH appointed Baron Anton von Schmerling, who had been a member of the Frankfurt government in 1848, minister of state. Liberal, centralist, and German-national ideas were combined in Schmerling, and they were reflected in the February patent of 1861 that drastically changed the recently imposed order. The organs of the central government were strengthened. The *Reichsrat* was composed of a House of Lords and a House of Deputies elected by the land diets. Matters concerning the western half of the Empire were reserved for deliberation of a "small *Reichsrat*," a first concession to an Austro-Hungarian dualism. The actual power of the *Reichsrat* was ill-defined; the ministers were not responsible to it; and a competing organ, the state council, was established, which was a representative of the high bureaucracy and, though in theory only an advisory body, was able to wield considerable influence. The constitution promulgated by the February patent favored the Germans and liberals. The Hungarians never appeared in the *Reichsrat*, and the Czechs and Poles withdrew from the "small *Reichsrat*" in 1863. In June 1865 the emperor decided to find a compromise with the Hungarians, the politically strongest nationality. Count Richard Belcredi superseded Schmerling; the February patent was suspended; and before the year had ended, the emperor had publicly promised the Magyars to accept a compromise on a dualistic basis if they, in turn, would accept a revision of the constitution.

The reorganization of the Habsburg Empire was a tortuous process, and one may question the liberal nature of some of these reform moves. Yet the new Austrian policies were naturally appraised against the background of the Schwarzenberg-Bach era of Austria, and they were also compared with the reactionary regime of Prussia. Austrian policy gained a fresh appeal in Germany not only among the dynastic governments, which were used to looking toward Austria for the protection of their sovereignty, but also among the democratic elements of South Germany. In these circumstances the Austrian government felt strong enough to take the initiative for a reform of the Germanic Confederation. This happened at a time when questions of economic policy brought additional conflicts in Austro-Prussian relations.

✍ Trade Policies

WITH THE ANGLO-FRENCH trade treaty of 1860, the so-called Cobden treaty, liberal principles had achieved their highest triumph in European interstate relations. Subsequent negotiations between Paris and Berlin led to an agreement of 1862 that embodied similar provisions for the free exchange of goods and adopted the most-favored-nation clause. This agreement, called by a prominent Austrian economist an Austrian "Villafranca" in trade relations, was protested by the Austrian government as precluding any possibility for the formation of a Central-European Customs Union. When attempts at such a union had broken down in 1853,[6] fresh negotiations had been promised for 1860. But the Prussian government did not wish the inclusion of Austria in the customs union. When Bavaria and Württemberg, which desired protection for their small industries, joined Austria in her objections to the Franco-Prussian trade agreement, the Prussian government declared the acceptance of this treaty a prerequisite for the renewal of the Prusso-German Customs Union but agreed not to ratify the French trade agreement till the members of the customs union had formally acceded to it.

✍ *Austro-Prussian Conflict*

BISMARCK CONTINUED this policy of his predecessors which suited his aims of excluding Austria from Germany. He also liked to demonstrate what Prussia was able to do in support of the growing commercial and industrial forces in Germany. Practically all of them desired access to the rich French market and thought little of the economy of the Danube lands. Saxony, in these years the most active political collaborator of Austria, was, next to Prussia, the most highly industrialized German state and, regarding trade policies, felt in accord with Prussia. Even for the South German states the advantages of belonging to the Prussian Customs Union outweighed the economic difficulties resulting from free trade. Whatever doubts existed were assuaged by the fiscal profits derived from the Prussian Customs Union. Since the revenue from duties was split according to population rather than actual volume of trade, all states except Prussia and Saxony received a disproportionately large financial income. In 1864, at the time when Prussia and Austria were seemingly closely united in fighting Denmark, the trade treaty between Prussia and France was ratified, and in 1865 the Prusso-German Customs Union was renewed for the last time.

The full political implications of these economic developments were probably only dimly known to the public in these years, while the strictly political events in the Austro-Prussian conflict attracted the major attention. The limitations of any Austrian policy aiming at the strengthening of the Germanic Confederation could never be overcome. The multinational Habsburg Empire was unable to contemplate even a relative subordination under a central German government. Nor was it possible to have only the German lands of Austria join in a German federal state,

[6] See p. 129.

since the German element constituted the strongest force of unity within the Habsburg Empire. The Austria of 1862 could not agree to the creation of a federal German state nor even offer anything substantial for strengthening the confederate ties of Germany.

Together with the small German kingdoms, among which Saxony, under her prime minister, Baron Friedrich Ferdinand von Beust (1809–86), was especially active, Austria proposed in 1862 a convention of delegates from the parliaments of the member states of the Germanic Confederation for the discussion and drafting of a common code of trial procedure and commercial law. Bismarck furiously attacked the proposal as incompatible with the Federal Act of 1814, and he branded it as an Austrian attempt to bring pressure on Prussia. He actually succeeded in defeating the motion at the Diet of Frankfurt in January 1863 because some of the smaller states became frightened at his threatening language. But it aroused laughter in Germany when the reactionary Prussian statesman denied in Frankfurt that delegates elected by the individual state parliaments were an organ through which the nation could exercise influence on its common affairs and claimed that only a representation directly elected by the people could assume such a function.

✍ *The Polish Revolt of 1863*

IN THE SAME MONTH serious national revolts against the Russian regime and its strong-handed methods broke out in Russian Poland. They caused grave trouble in Russia, the more so since within the Russian government advocates of a policy of sheer repression were struggling with advocates of attempts at reconciliation. Bismarck was alarmed lest the more liberal forces might win out and an autonomous Poland become the base of a national Polish movement demanding the restoration of the Poland of 1772. Even the remote possibility of a Polish revival evoked the strongest passions in Bismarck, who feared that the loss of Danzig, West Prussia, and Posen would cut the "best sinews" of the Prussian monarchy. In a frivolous form he expressed his fierce hostility to the Poles in a letter to his sister in 1861: "Hit the Poles so hard that they despair of their life; I have full sympathy with their condition, but if we want to survive, we can only exterminate them; the wolf, too, cannot help having been created by God as he is, but people shoot him for it if they can."

✍ *The Alvensleben Convention*

THE WISH TO PERSUADE Czar Alexander II to accept a firm anti-Polish policy led to the immediate mobilization of the army in the four eastern provinces of Prussia and to the dispatch of General Gustav von Alvensleben to St. Petersburg. Alvensleben impressed the czar by arguing the reliability of the traditional cooperation between Prussia and Russia and negotiated with the somewhat reluctant Russian chancellor a convention with regard to the collaboration of the military commanders on both the Russian and the Prussian side of the Polish frontier. The convention, signed on February 8, 1863, with Bismarck's approval, contained the provision that on the request of the military or police authorities of either party their troops could be empowered to assist each other and if necessary could cross the frontier in the pursuit of retreating insurgents.

The Alvensleben Convention drew criticism from all sides. The German liberals sympathized with the revolutionary Poles, though with less enthusiasm than in 1848. They criticized the despicable reactionary policy of Bismarck that made Prussia a subservient bailiff of Russian czardom. But more unpleasant for Bismarck was the indignation caused by the convention in France and Britain. Public opinion in both countries was strongly in favor of the Poles. Napoleon, who had originally been bothered by the recrudescence of the Polish problem as interfering with close Franco-Russian relations, discovered in the convention, which could be labeled a Prussian intervention, an opportunity for linking the Polish problem with pressure against the Rhine frontier. He approached Austria while trying in the first place to induce England to launch, together with France, a strong protest against the convention as an act that might justify the intervention of other powers in Poland. The English government, however, was not so easily led down a path that might end in tying England to France in a new Crimean war. Napoleon was viewed with grave suspicion after the annexation of Savoy and Nice in the wake of the Italian war. It was guessed that Napoleon ultimately intended to fish in the Rhine rather than in the Vistula.

The English government of Lord John Russell and Palmerston deplored Bismarck's internal and foreign policies, although it considered the existence of a strong Prussia as a bulwark against Russia and France of highest importance for England. Austria was considered too weak to defend Central Europe. While internally threatened by the conflict of nationalities, Austria had even refused to forestall the enmity of Italy by selling Venetia to the new kingdom. Prussia, it was thought in London, would not always, and possibly not even for long, be ruled by Bismarck and William I. The marriage of Queen Victoria's daughter Victoria to the liberal Prussian Crown Prince Frederick William in 1858 had given rise to the hope that Prussia might some day join the liberal camp. Queen Victoria herself did not tire of admonishing her ministers to beware of Napoleon's trickery and to refrain from any duly harsh action against Prussia.

The basic English attitude was one of the fortunate circumstances that

Bismarck was able to exploit at that time and during the following years. He was quick to announce that the Alvensleben Convention had not become practical and had not even been ratified, and he thereby blocked a common diplomatic action of England and France in Berlin. France, now in addition involved in her attempt to win a position of strength in Mexico, could not intervene alone in Poland. From Austria, which after all could not feel unconcerned about her Polish possessions, Napoleon did not receive any encouragement either. During the spring and summer of 1863 England and France directed a war of notes against Russia, demanding the realization of the political and civil rights which the Treaty of Vienna of 1815 had granted to Poland. But while these efforts helped to vent and deflate British excitement, they poisoned the relations between Alexander II and Napoleon III forever. Whereas England could merely drop the issue in August 1863, Napoleon, due to his internal position, remained in need of some success in his foreign policy. In November he proposed to the principal powers of Europe a congress that was to discuss all questions threatening to disturb the peace of Europe, and he indicated in public that he expected a revision of the Vienna Treaty from such a congress. The European powers saw in Napoleon's plan of a congress a scheme that was likely to accentuate the existing conflicts and might even become the prelude to war. The English government blocked the realization of Napoleon's objective, thereby inflicting a grievous defeat on the ambitious French emperor. This event marked the final rupture of the Anglo-French alliance of the Crimean War, which had been tottering for some time.

Bismarck had no part in bringing on the collapse of the major groupings among the European powers in 1863. The end of close relations between France and Russia as well as between France and Britain was not his doing, and it is even doubtful whether the risks which he took with the Alvensleben Convention noticeably changed the course of great events. But unquestionably the Prusso-Russian friendship emerged strengthened from the Polish crisis.

✧ *Austrian Plans Thwarted*

BISMARCK WAS NOT ABLE, as he seems to have wished in the early months of his ministry, to fan the Prusso-Austrian conflict into a full war crisis. For the time being he had to be satisfied with thwarting Austrian initiatives in the reform of the Germanic Confederation. We mentioned that the first Austrian attempt was foiled in January 1863.[7] But the Schmerling cabinet used the summer, when, owing to his policies vis-à-vis the Polish revolution, Bismarck's prestige had fallen even lower, to prepare a

[7] See p. 165.

comprehensive program of reform, which was to be propagated by an assembly of all the German princes. The Austrian draft proposed the creation of a "directory" of five members, consisting of Austria, Prussia, and Bavaria as permanent members and two states elected by the other German states. In addition there was to be a council of all princes as the chief legislative body and at its side a representation of delegates from the state parliaments, meeting every third year. The small council of the confederation was to be transformed by the grant to Austria and Prussia of three votes instead of the customary one vote, thus raising the total vote from seventeen to twenty-one. A High Court of the Confederation was to be added to the confederate institutions.

The Austrian plan thus envisaged a closer integration of the Germanic Confederation. But this integration would have been achieved largely at the expense of Prussia. For Prussia would have found herself in a minority in all the council decisions, since Austria was bound to enjoy the support of the small states. The Austrian draft, if adopted, in all probability would have made it impossible for the German states to refuse military assistance, as happened during the Italian war of 1859. The Austrian cabinet realized that its project would use the German waters to drive the Habsburg mill and that it would not be simple to gain Prussia's assent to it. Therefore, the plan was sprung on King William I by Emperor Francis Joseph at short notice. Bismarck succeeded, however, in convincing William not to attend the congress of German princes in Frankfurt. But when ten days later, under seemingly general popular acclaim, practically all the princes assembled in Frankfurt and dispatched the king of Saxony to invite King William, who sojourned at a spa in the neighborhood, Bismarck had to struggle hard to keep William from joining his princely cousins.

By keeping William from attending the Frankfurt meeting Bismarck actually torpedoed the Austrian scheme. The Austrian threat that Prussian opposition might lead to a union of the other German states under Austrian leadership was ill-conceived, because a majority of the small German states, while favoring Austria's predominance, was not prepared to accept the exclusion of Prussia from the Germanic Confederation. The Frankfurt congress gave the Austrian plan its endorsement, though with the fatal proviso that the princes were bound by it only till Prussia would make her attitude known. Bismarck announced that Prussia would not agree to a directory but would insist on the alternation of the presidency between Austria and Prussia. He also demanded a veto with regard to the use of military power and reiterated the claim for a German parliament directly elected by all the Germans and representing the actual size of the population of each state.

The Austrian reform proposal might have produced the end of all cooperation between the two major German powers. But actually the Austrians did not have the nerve to follow through the policy which they had begun. Napoleon's initiative for a European congress with its implications of French assistance to Italian demands for Venetia and the flaring up of Polish revolutionary activities in Austrian Galicia made the conservative Austrian foreign minister, Count J. B. Rechberg (1806-99), hesitate. But the chief reason for abandoning the anti-Prussian policy in Germany in favor of close cooperation with Prussia was the reappearance of the Schleswig-Holstein problem. Although earlier the Austrian government had scorned the Prussian demand for a dualistic regime, it now agreed for all practical purposes to a common Austro-Prussian management of this crucial national issue.

✍ Schleswig-Holstein

THE DISTURBANCES OVER SCHLESWIG-HOLSTEIN,[8] which had contributed so greatly to the defeat of the national movement in 1848-49, had been settled by the great powers through the London Treaty of May 8, 1852, which recognized Prince Christian of Glücksburg as heir to the Danish throne. But Prussia had insisted that the contender, who under Germanic law held valid claims to the succession in the duchies of Holstein and Schleswig, should voluntarily renounce his rights. Bismarck, then Prussian minister at the Diet of Frankfurt, had conducted the negotiations with Duke Christian of Augustenburg, who had publicly promised that he and his family would not obstruct the succession of the Glücksburg line in all the possessions of the Danish crown. The Danish king, Frederick VII, on his part had proclaimed that the two duchies within the monarchy would receive their own administration and representation. These promises made in 1852 were not kept, and even the reactionary Diet of the Germanic Confederation had found fault with Danish policies and finally threatened military execution; this, however, applied only to Holstein, since Schleswig had remained outside of the confederation.

On November 13, 1863, the Danish parliament passed a new constitution which incorporated Schleswig into the Danish kingdom. Two days later, Frederick VII died without having signed the constitution. The prince of Glücksburg, as Christian IX, ascended the Danish throne. The excited nationalist sentiment of the cabinet and the Danish people moved him, against his better judgment, to sanction the new constitution. The London Treaty of 1852 was thus clearly violated. To German liberalism this event seemed to remove the international obstacles to Schleswig-Holstein's union with Germany. Frederick, son of the duke of Augustenburg and a political liberal, appeared an ideal German ruler. Prince Fred-

[8] See p. 45.

erick declared that the surrender of the Augustenburg claims by his father could not bind him, and he proclaimed himself Duke Frederick VIII of Schleswig-Holstein. The sentiment of most of the small German states tended to support the self-styled duke by the full use of the power of the Germanic Confederation. In a vote of the Diet of Frankfurt on December 7, they came close to having such a policy officially adopted. The diet decided to send confederate troops into Holstein, but Prussia and Austria insisted that this action was not intended as a challenge to the dynastic rights of King Christian IX.

Bismarck chose to deal with the Schleswig-Holstein issue as an international rather than a Germanic problem. In conformity with the London Treaty, he recognized the succession of King Christian in Denmark and in the duchies but demanded from the Danish government the fulfillment of the other provisions of the treaty as well. This made it difficult from the beginning for the signatories of the treaty, particularly for England and Russia, to interfere with Prussian policy. Moreover, on this basis Bismarck was able to win the cooperation of Austria, which had an interest in the preservation of the existing international law of Europe and had to beware of joining in a policy of national self-determination. On the other hand, Austria was worried that, in the case of her abstention, Prussia in the eyes of Germany would earn all the laurels of a defender of Germany against Danish nationalism.

∾ *War with Denmark*

ON JANUARY 16, 1864, the Austrian and Prussian governments presented an ultimatum in Copenhagen, demanding the cancellation of the constitution of November 1863 within forty-eight hours. The Danish government rejected this ultimatum. On January 21 an army, composed of an Austrian corps and a Prussian corps and guard division, entered Holstein, already occupied by Saxon and Hanoverian units. In early February the army also occupied Schleswig. Its commander, the eighty-year-old Field Marshal von Wrangel, was not a competent strategist and allowed the main Danish forces to entrench themselves on the Düppel peninsula as well as on the neighboring island of Alsen. Not until April 18 were the Prussian troops able to storm the Düppel fortifications and force the Danish army to withdraw to Alsen.

Britain and Russia had tried in vain to forestall the outbreak of war. Both powers wished to preserve a strong Danish state and for that reason to uphold the London Treaty. But the British government was divided. Palmerston's original statements seemed to promise British assistance to Denmark. Actually, he raised false hopes among the Danes, for the English were by no means prepared to get involved in a war for Denmark, at least not as long as the sea passages to the Baltic were not directly threatened. They also realized that Prussia and Austria could not be stopped in Schleswig-Holstein by naval demonstrations. Only a French mobilization could have had real effect. But after the treatment that Napoleon had suffered from the British in connection with Poland in the year before, he was extremely wary. In view of the Austro-Prussian alliance and the popularity of the struggle for a German Schleswig-Holstein, Napoleon did not wish to challenge Germany without firm pledges of support from England, which would have implied toleration of French territorial gains in the Rhineland. Yet the very thought of such Napoleonic schemes that might have jeopardized Belgium was distasteful to the British statesmen, and although they tried to intimidate Bismarck by pointing to the likelihood of French intervention, they did nothing to restore the Anglo-French alliance. Napoleon, on his part, judged that Bismarck's activist policy would sufficiently trouble the waters of European politics to allow him in due course to make a good catch. Bismarck did his best to impress on Napoleon his willingness to cooperate with France in the future.

Russia, like England, was interested in the integrity of Denmark. But, in contrast to the British government, Czar Alexander was anxious to keep Bismarck in power. His fall, it was thought in St. Petersburg, would be followed by a victory of liberalism in Germany, and this was bound to have an infectious influence on all revolutionary national movements, in Poland, Rumania, Hungary, and Italy. In addition, Bismarck should not be pressed too hard, because this might drive him into the arms of Napoleon, who probably was venal for a small *pourboire*. Bismarck's attitude during the Polish crisis was not forgotten, and his acceptance of the London Treaty in the face of strong liberal objections was appreciated. The Russian government was inclined to admit that Bismarck needed at least some moderate success in order to maintain himself in office against the internal opposition in Germany.

The European powers were deeply divided in the motives, methods, and aims of their policies. Therein lay Bismarck's opportunity to move step by step closer to his ultimate aim, the Prussian annexation of the two duchies. He had gained the cooperation of Austria for intervention in Schleswig-Holstein on the basis of the London Treaty. After the common occupation of Holstein and Schleswig, he prevailed on Austria to accept a convention by which Prussia and Austria renounced the London Treaty, although they assented to a conference of the European powers in order to reach an agreement on new bases for the constitutional position of the duchies within the Danish monarchy. However, Austria failed to reach a clear understanding on what should really be done with the duchies, while she accepted the Prussian proposal to bring the war to a conclusion by the invasion of Danish Jutland. At the London conference, which took place from April 25 to June 25, 1864, Bismarck still proposed the personal union of the duchies and Denmark under King Christian IX as well as actual political separation of Schleswig-Holstein from Denmark.

Actually, this was for Bismarck only a tactical starting point. He anticipated the defeat of his proposal, because he counted on the disagreement among the European nations and the stubbornness of the Danish government, as he was convinced of the inability of the powers to frame and impose any settlement. His capacity for diplomatic maneuvering in these months was extraordinary, and he overcame the moments of great danger when the resistance of England, Russia, and France appeared to coalesce. Russia and Austria blocked Napoleon's suggestion of a plebiscite and a partition of Schleswig according to nationalities, while Bismarck opposed the candidacy of the Augustenburg prince, which Austria began to champion at the later stage of the London conference.

By straying so far away from the London Treaty of 1852 while failing to reach any new solution, the conference made any return to that treaty impossible. When the conference adjourned, Austria and Prussia were practically at liberty to settle the conflict by themselves. Austrian and Prussian troops occupied all of Jutland. On June 28, 1864, Prussian troops, in a well-conducted landing operation, took Alsen, the chief island off the coast of Schleswig. Danish resistance ebbed, and the hopes for help from England finally faded. In a preliminary peace of August 1, later codified in the Vienna Peace treaty of October 30, King Christian IX gave up all his claims for Schleswig-Holstein in favor of the emperor of Austria and the king of Prussia.

The achievement of the separation of the duchies from Denmark, an objective passionately, though vainly, sought by the German liberals in 1848–49, did not fail to make an impression on many German liberals and tended to moderate the opposition to the Prussian government of some of them. But Bismarck's resistance to the liberal duke of Augustenburg caused new disappointment. For Bismarck, though he was never oblivious of the popular reaction, there remained the major question of how to reach an agreement with Austria on the final disposition of the duchies. The alliance with Austria had proved immensely valuable in staving off all foreign intervention. It was questionable, however, whether it would keep an ambitious Prussian policy from reaching its goal in Germany. Thus the end of the Danish war immediately opened a period of new tests and trials.

CHAPTER 5

The Founding of the New German Empire, 1865–71

✍ Reform of Germanic Confederation

AFTER THE SUCCESSFUL CONCLUSION of the Danish war Bismarck could place his cards on the table and present his demand for the annexation of Schleswig-Holstein by Prussia, which had been his ideal aim from the beginning of the war crisis. But even now the annexation was treated by Bismarck as part of a broad policy that embraced the reform of the Germanic Confederation. The reform could be achieved either by war against Austria or, possibly, by the cooperation of Austria and Prussia as it had existed during the Danish war. As a matter of fact, this collaboration in 1864 had been most advantageous for Bismarck. It had separated Austria from the small German states and stymied the Germanic Confederation. Bismarck was eager to explore the possibilities of a continuation of the Austro-Prussian alliance, which in the future would have to lead to the virtual division of Germany between the two major German powers and to mutual support in European affairs.

Such a program was discussed in conversations held at Schönbrunn on August 20–24, 1864, between the two monarchs, as well as Bismarck and the Austrian foreign minister, Count Johann von Rechberg. Rechberg wanted to commit Prussia to a military alliance for safeguarding and reconquering Austria's position in North and Central Italy. In return Austria was to give Schleswig-Holstein to Prussia and to respect Prussia's predominance in North Germany. Presumably, the small states of the north could have been tied together by military alliances and economic unions and thus have been subordinated to Prussia.

This program was completely reactionary. It would have been hostile to both the German and Italian national movements and would have found its logical conclusion in the reconstruction of the old alliance of the three eastern monarchies. It would also have meant war with Napoleon's France over Italy. The other possible way of reforming the Germanic

THE GERMANIC CONFEDERATION,
1866

KINGDOM OF PRUSSIA, 1866

NORTH GERMAN STATES AND THE CITY OF
FRANKFURT ACQUIRED BY PRUSSIA AS A RESULT
OF THE AUSTRO-PRUSSIAN WAR, 1866

NORTH
GERMAN
CONFEDERATION,
1866

SOUTH GERMAN STATES, 1866

AUSTRIA,
WITHIN THE CONFEDERATION, 1815-1866

POSSESSIONS OF AUSTRIA
OUTSIDE THE CONFEDERATION, 1815-1859 and 1866

BOUNDARY OF THE
GERMANIC CONFEDERATION,
1866

DENMARK

SCHLESWIG

Flensburg

Schleswig

Kiel

Rostock

HOLSTEIN

Wismar

Lübeck

MECKLENBURG-
SCHWERIN

Emden

Hamburg

OLDEN-
BURG

Bremen

Groningen

NETHERLANDS

Amsterdam

Utrecht

Rotterdam

Hanover

PROVINCES

U

Magdeburg

Osnabrück

Purmont

LIPPE

BRUNSWICK

ANHALT

Münster

WESTPHALIA

R

Göttingen

OF SAXONY

Lei

Calais

Ghent

Wesel

Düsseldorf

Kassel

WALDECK

Gotha

Weimar

THURINGIAN
STATES

Brussels

BELGIUM

Cologne

P

Aachen

HESSE-KASSEL

HESSE

Lille

Liége

RHINE PROVINCE

Plauen

Arras

Namur

NASSAU

Frankfurt

Ege

LUXEMBOURG

Mainz

MAIN

Sedan

Würzburg

Bamberg

Reims

PALATINATE
(BAV.)

Heidelberg

Nürnberg

Verdun

Metz

LORRAINE

Regensburg

Stuttgart

WÜRTTEM-
BERG

DANUBE

Strasbourg

BAVARIA

Ulm

Augsburg

FRANCE

ALSACE

BADEN

Freiburg

Munich

Salzbur

Mühlhausen

Besançon

Basel

Zürich

NEUENBURG

Berne

SWITZERLAND

Innsbruck

SAL

TYROL

Geneva

Sitten

Bozen

SAVOY
(TO FRANCE, 1860)

RHINE

Trent

Ud

LOMBARDY
(TO PIEDMONT, 1859)

VENETIA
(TO ITALY, 1866)

KINGDOM

Milan

Verona

Venice

Turin

OF

Mantua

PO

SARDINIA-
PIEDMONT

ITALY

PARMA

MODENA

T R MILLER

Confederation while simultaneously expanding Prussian power was the transformation of the confederation in the direction of a federal German or North German state under Prussian leadership. This would have necessitated war against Austria, in which case some collaboration with German liberalism by the advocacy of a national representation of the German people and, in the foreign field, the avoidance of an open challenge to France was called for. It was characteristic of Bismarck that he probed carefully into the political currents and to the last kept various avenues open.

The Schönbrunn conversations did not lead to any decisions. In Schleswig-Holstein the Austro-Prussian condominium continued. But Austrian policy began to shift. Count Rechberg, the chief champion of a conservative alliance with Prussia, had to resign, because the Prussian government failed to make him any concessions in the negotiations over the customs union. Count Alexander Mensdorff-Pouilly (1813–71), a cavalry general of good intentions, though with little diplomatic experience, became Austrian foreign minister. Under him the forces bent on preservation of the Austrian rule over Germany gained in influence. The Austrian government began to press again for the recognition of the duke of Augustenburg. On February 22, 1865, Bismarck announced the conditions under which Prussia might be willing to assent to the creation of a duchy under the Augustenburg prince within the Germanic Confederation. His demands, which included among other things the incorporation of the Schleswig-Holstein troops into the Prussian army, would have made the duke a Prussian vassal rather than a confederate prince. Other small rulers of Germany shuddered, wondering whether Bismarck intended to set a model for the Prussian control of her German neighbors in the future. Some of them felt that in these circumstances the outright annexation of Schleswig-Holstein by Prussia might be preferable.

Austria rejected the Prussian conditions, and growing friction developed between the two occupying powers in Schleswig-Holstein. While Austrian administrators favored the Augustenburg cause, the Prussians displayed their determination to absorb Schleswig-Holstein. The relations between Berlin and Vienna rapidly deteriorated. In a Prussian crown council of May 29 King William showed his inclination to choose war, and Moltke stated the army sentiment in favor of a policy of strength. But Bismarck advised against a policy that would make war inevitable, although he admitted that in the long run it might be unavoidable, while an equally propitious moment in European politics was not likely to recur. In all probability Bismarck believed that the risk of war should no longer be taken merely for the acquisition of Schleswig-Holstein. Austria's hold on Schleswig-Holstein was bound to grow weaker in any event. Schleswig-Holstein ought to be made the occasion, but not the prize, of a showdown with Austria. If a war were to be fought, it should bring the decision on the future leadership of Germany. But for this ultimate objective the ground did not seem sufficiently prepared.

✑ *Gastein Convention*

THUS BISMARCK ONCE MORE fell back on negotiations with Austria. In order to settle all conflicts, he offered the partition of Schleswig-Holstein. This was a great concession, since it would have delayed a Prussian acquisition of Holstein for years. The chief gain to be found in a partition would have lain in Austria's final consent to the exclusion of the Germanic Confederation from all the decisions affecting Schleswig-Holstein. Within the Austrian government, Count Mensdorff would have preferred war to a doubtful compromise, even though Austria was in dire financial straits and was forced to cut her military budget. Emperor Francis Joseph felt the necessity of finally settling the revolutionary situation in Hungary. Thus, in July 1865, he replaced Prime Minister Schmerling with Count Richard Belcredi (1823–1902), who was supposed to find a solution to the constitutional problem of Hungary through negotiations with the moderate Magyars. Count Mensdorff remained foreign minister in the Belcredi cabinet but was overruled by the emperor in his Prussian policy. Yet the emperor was not prepared to accept the division of Schleswig-Holstein as suggested by Bismarck and thought it less embarrassing to propose only the separation of the joint administration. Bismarck quickly accepted this lame bid, by which Austria actually sacrificed one of the chief advantages that Bismarck had offered, the renunciation of such sovereign rights in Holstein as Prussia had acquired through the peace treaty with Denmark. Whereas, under the terms of the Bismarckian draft convention, Austria could have ceded Holstein to the duke of Augustenburg, Prussia now retained her sovereign rights in both duchies and in the final convention, which was signed at Gastein on August 14, 1865, only agreed to the factual separation of the joint administration. The convention made it possible at any moment to reopen all the political issues over which Prussia and Austria had wrangled.

The Gastein convention caused great indignation in Germany. This resentment was largely directed against Austria, because she had failed to uphold the Augustenburg cause and had abandoned the principle of the indivisibility of the duchies. In its desire to regain lost ground the Austrian administration of Holstein tolerated renewed popular agitation for the duke of Augustenburg in January 1866. Bismarck at once accused Austria of a breach of the Gastein Convention and threatened to assume full freedom of action. This time Austria decided not to retreat, while a Prussian crown council, on February 28, resolved not to shy away from war, though it did not wish to seek it. But this reservation only expressed Prussia's intention to prepare for the imminent war by winning allies.

✑ Prusso-Italian Alliance

ITALY WAS ANXIOUS to go to war in order to win Venetia. She wished to gain this province by her own exertions rather than as a gift from a protector such as Napoleon. If the Italians entertained any doubts about an alliance with Prussia, they were caused by the suspicion that Prussia might leave Italy in the lurch if Austria in the course of the war ceded Schleswig-Holstein to Prussia. Bismarck assured the Italian government that the Schleswig-Holstein question had become only incidental to the German problem. Italy was persuaded to conclude an alliance by which she promised to go to war if and when Prussia opened war against Austria after the breakdown of negotiations on the reform of the Germanic Confederation. Napoleon assisted in dispersing the last Italian misgivings about Prussian intentions. The Prusso-Italian Alliance of April 8, 1866, was limited to three months and contained a provision against the conclusion of a separate peace before the coveted territorial conquests had been accomplished.

✑ Napoleon III and the German Question

NAPOLEON THUS HELPED to plant a time bomb, because he wished for an Austro-Prussian war. Bismarck always judged quite correctly that Napoleon III possessed none of the qualities of his great uncle and, in particular, was not a military conqueror but rather a calculating bourgeois statesman who carefully counted his risks and commitments. The general aim of Napoleon's foreign policy was the destruction of the Vienna settlement of 1815, which had been built on the defeat of the first French empire and thereafter had been maintained largely by the conservative solidarity of the three eastern monarchies. Napoleon's propagation of national self-determination was intended to undermine the foundations of the Vienna system. His support of the Italian national movement had led to a drastic weakening of Austria's key position. With the annexation of Savoy and Nice, France had made some palpable gains, which, however, were not overly impressive and were bought at a very high price. The French annexations not only adversely affected Franco-Italian friendship but also aroused grave misgivings among the European great powers.

The German problems presented Napoleon with the most serious challenge. To be sure, the breakup of the Germanic Confederation, an integral and crucial organization instituted by the Congress of Vienna, might not have been deplored in France, especially if the confederation were to split into three, or at least two, groups of German states. But even then Napoleon would have wished to gain some token success in order to strengthen his prestige within France. Bismarck took the view that Napoleon would be cautious in the knowledge of how sensitive the British were to changes that might have a bearing on the security of the Rhineland and Lowlands. Bismarck expected Napoleon to be satisfied with a minor territorial adjustment, such as the restoration of the frontiers of 1814, which would have meant the acquisition of Landau and of parts of the Saar district. There were moments prior to the end of the Austro-Prussian war of 1866 when Bismarck seems to have felt that some such concession to Napoleon might become inevitable, and he left him under the impression that eventually Prussia might be accommodating, although Bismarck knew that William I was absolutely opposed to the yielding of any German territory.

But if Germany was to be united under the leadership of a single state that could draw on all the resources of the country, the French reaction was bound to be a much stronger one. The rise of a national state as powerful as, and possibly more powerful than, France constituted a major shift of the European balance of power and was likely to arouse French demands for greater compensations. Napoleon, whose foreign policies had met with growing criticism in France and whose basis of internal power had become less secure, might then be driven into bolder ventures than he would normally have thought prudent.

Bismarck did not think it necessary to buy French neutrality by a treaty which he could have secured only by offering territorial gains to Napoleon. He was satisfied with seeing Napoleon take a generally benevolent, though noncommittal, attitude toward an active Prussian policy. Austria was driven into closer dealings with the French emperor. On June 12, 1866, she concluded a secret treaty in which she promised to cede Venetia after a victorious war in Germany. It showed the despair of a diplomatically isolated Austria as well as the unbending pride of her emperor that he lent his hand to this transaction, which compelled him to have an Austrian army fight a campaign for the defense of Venetia that had been surrendered by him beforehand. For Francis Joseph knew that the treaty would not keep Italy from making war. Only the neutrality of France was secured, and in the case of an Austrian victory France approved of a territorial aggrandizement of Austria as long as this would not upset the European balance.

In an oral exchange of ideas between France and Austria, the latter gave her assent to the enlargement of Saxony, Württemberg, and Bavaria through the annexation of small German states and to the formation of a new German state comprising the Rhineland. The Rhenish state, according to Austrian plans, was apparently to be a member state of the Germanic Confederation and to be given to one of the Habsburg branches recently deposed in Italy. Although this exchange of ideas was not necessarily binding, great potential national dangers were created through these Franco-Austrian compacts. Napoleon's motives and objectives in these diplomatic actions remain mystifying. Obviously he was eager to be able to act as mediator or arbiter in the coming war. There are signs that he expected a long war and most probably a stalemate, which to him meant an Austrian rather than a Prussian victory. In this case the treaty with Austria of June 12, 1866, may have seemed to him a good protective device for insuring the chance of French intervention.

✑ *The Approaching War*

MEANWHILE BISMARCK HAD BEGUN to broaden the Schleswig-Holstein issue into both a struggle for the reform of the Germanic Confederation and a struggle between Austria and Prussia for the leadership in Germany. On April 9, the day after the conclusion of the alliance with Italy, by which Prussia had broken the Federal Act of 1814 in a flagrant way, Prussia made a motion at the Diet of Frankfurt calling for a convention of a German parliament to discuss a reform of the German constitution. As in 1863 Bismarck proposed to have this parliament elected by universal suffrage. At this moment he wanted chiefly to put pressure on the governments of the German states. But neither by threats nor by blandishments did he succeed in turning any of the medium-sized German states into allies of Prussia. However, by playing up to Bavarian ambitions he was able to widen the differences that existed between Bavaria and Austria. In Ludwig von der Pfordten (1811–80) Bavaria had a prime minister who thought it possible to win for his state an intermediary position between Austria and Prussia as well as a leading role in South Germany. He agreed to an expansion of Prussian power in North Germany, although he refused to follow Bismarck in a policy directed toward the total exclusion of Austria from German affairs. By conducting a Bavarian policy independent of Austria, Pfordten unwittingly facilitated Bismarck's efforts at isolating Austria.

While as early as March 1866 war preparations were begun by Austria and Prussia, attempts were made by European and German diplomats to mediate between the two governments. But even if they had possessed a common policy, the German governments were too weak to exercise any influence. The European powers were unable to develop a joint policy, and Napoleon actually wanted to see Austria and Prussia go to war. Whereas Austria was resigned to war, Bismarck wanted it and was only maneuvering to put the blame for its outbreak on Vienna. On June 1, Austria turned to the Diet of the Germanic Confederation and requested its intervention in the settlement of the Schleswig-Holstein conflict. Thereupon Bismarck accused Austria of violating the treaty of alliance of January 14, 1864, and of the subsequent Gastein Convention, by which Prussia and Austria had agreed to settle the Schleswig-Holstein question only by mutual understanding, which, incidentally, Prussia had continuously tried to thwart.

✎ Diplomatic Struggle in Frankfurt

ON JUNE 9, Prussian troops, under the command of General Edwin von Manteuffel, moved from Schleswig into Holstein. Bismarck's hope that this invasion would lead to open hostilities did not materialize, since the Austrian forces were able to withdraw without an exchange of shots. But diplomatic relations were severed, and at the Diet of Frankfurt Austria made a motion for the mobilization of all non-Prussian armed forces. On June 10, Bismarck presented to all the German governments a plan for the formation of a new German constitution in case of the collapse of the Germanic Confederation. He proposed the exclusion of Austria and of the Netherlandish territories—i.e., Luxembourg—from the confederation. The reapportioning of votes in the Federal Diet and, at the same time, the creation of a national popular representation, elected by the franchise of 1849, were suggested. The latter's authority, however, would be limited; it would not even receive control of the budget. While military and naval affairs as well as economic policy were declared matters of federal concern, the military and naval forces of North Germany were to come under Prussian, those of South Germany under Bavarian, command.

Bismarck's program of reform contained some of the basic ideas on which the future constitution of the North German Confederation of 1867 and of the Empire of 1871 were going to be built. The role offered to Bavaria and the narrow definition of federal powers and of parliament betray tactical adjustments to the political circumstances of the moment, and in addition show that Bismarck was anxious to gain contact with the popular national movement. With his proposal of a national parliament he did not offer much, since its power was narrowly circumscribed, while the proposed universal suffrage was intended to and, as the liberals agreed, likely to produce a more conservative parliament than the Prussian parliament elected by the three-class system had been. But in contrast to Austria, which fought for the mere preservation of a confederate system that was disliked by most Germans, Bismarck held out the hope for greater German unity. In conversations with some of the liberal leaders he intimated his interest in some compromise that might settle the constitutional conflict in Prussia. Yet Bismarck's credit had fallen too low among the liberal parliamentarians to make his words appear trustworthy. Actually Bismarck again dissolved the Prussian parliament in May 1866 without having reached an agreement on the budget. The date of elections was set for July 3.

✑ *Outbreak of War*

ON JUNE 14, 1866, the Federal Diet reached its decision on the Austrian move. Bavaria prevailed in changing the Austrian resolution ordering the mobilization of all non-Prussian forces into one ordering the mobilization of all non-Prussian and non-Austrian forces. The Bavarian minister, Pfordten, still entertained some hopes that the confederation might mediate between the two major German powers. The amended resolution was passed by a majority of nine to six. The Prussian representative declared the Federal Act thereby broken and consequently void. The legal argument was hardly convincing, quite apart from the earlier violation of the constitution by the Prussian alliance with Italy. The Prussian announcement, which at the same time invited the German states to form a new federation on the basis of the Prussian program of June 10, was essentially a declaration of war. Bavaria, Württemberg, Saxony, Hanover, Hesse-Darmstadt, Hesse-Kassel, Nassau, Frankfurt, and some petty states sided with Austria, while the Thuringian states, except for Saxony-Meiningen, as well as Oldenburg, the two Mecklenburgs, Anhalt, Hamburg, Bremen, and Lübeck voted with Prussia. Baden abstained from voting but was compelled to join forces with the other South German states later on, when the rump diet proclaimed the federal action against Prussia.

It was of great importance for the course of the war that Bavaria and the other South German states did not enter into direct military cooperation with Austria. If the Bavarian army had joined forces with the Austrian army in Bohemia—as the Saxon army did—the Prussian armies entering Bohemia on June 21 would have met superior forces. But alone the South German armies fought a losing campaign against relatively small Prussian forces under the command of General Edwin von Manteuffel in the area of the Main valley. Even before this Franconian campaign the Hanoverian army had been completely vanquished. On June 27, the bravely fighting army had inflicted an unpleasant setback on Prussian forces under the command of General Vogel von Falckenstein at Langensalza. But hesitation among the enemy allowed the Prussians to regroup and encircle the Hanoverian army, which had to capitulate on June 29. The blind King George V was permitted to go abroad, while the soldiers were disarmed and sent home. The fighting in Germany demonstrated the military and political impotence of the small states.

In Italy the Austrian army again proved its superiority over Italian troops. The Italian attempt to invade Venetia was frustrated by Archduke Albrecht in the battle of Custozza on June 24. Only after Sadowa, when the Austrians were forced to withdraw troops from Italy, were the Italians in a position to occupy Venetia to the Isonzo. Their fleet, however, suffered defeat at the hands of the Austrians under Admiral Wilhelm Tegethoff in the battle of Lissa on July 20.

✍ *The Bohemian Campaign*

THE MEETING of the main Prussian and Austrian armies was the crucial test of the war. Austria possessed a fine army of great experience and high morale. Her artillery and cavalry were probably superior to that of Prussia. But her infantry was equipped with old-fashioned guns and still used outdated shock tactics, which made it even more vulnerable to the modern needle-guns of the Prussian infantry. The Prussian army was composed of younger men as a result of the reorganization of the preceding years. They did not serve for three years, which had seemed to King William I an issue essential enough to justify the constitutional conflict. Financial reasons had forced the war ministry to dismiss the soldiers as a rule after two-and-a-half years of service.

The railroad system of North Germany, far more highly developed than that of the Habsburg empire, was one of Prussia's greatest assets. It allowed the speedy mobilization and concentration of all the Prussian army corps from East Prussia to the Rhineland and proved highly advantageous in all subsequent operations.

Altogether the factors that tended to favor Prussia were not so overwhelming as to make a Prussian victory, or at least a quick and complete Prussian victory, inevitable. It was the ability of the two opposing commanders that determined decisively the course of the war. Archduke Albrecht was the best army commander of the Habsburg empire, but the emperor wished to employ him in Italy, where victories were easier to reap. Ludwig von Benedek (1804–81), who had spent his whole military life in Italy, was appointed commander of the northern army. Though a competent and fearless officer, he was, as he himself knew best, unsuited for the high command, particularly in conditions entirely novel to him. Over his protestations he was put in a place where he would have to rely on advisors, among whom Major General Gedeon Krismanic, a man learned in eighteenth century theory of war rather than in the principles of modern warfare, became predominant.

In Prussia the war of 1866 witnessed the transformation of a military institution into a new state institution. In the fifty years after 1815 the Prussian general staff, as organized by Scharnhorst, had existed without any publicity. It had not been inactive, however, and had not only trained a corps of efficient staff officers but also developed strategic ideas which drew their peculiar strength from the teachings of Clausewitz. Yet as an agency designed for the actual conduct of war the general staff had found little notice outside of, and even within, the army in half a century of peace. Practically all the time it had been a subordinate section of the war ministry. It was the minister of war who represented the army with king and country, although under Edwin von Manteuffel the personnel chief of the army had virtually removed himself from the authority of the minister of war. The chief of the general staff was never consulted by Roon on questions of the Prussian army reform.

✍ Moltke

WILLIAM I HAD APPOINTED Helmuth von Moltke (1800–91) chief-of-staff in 1857. Apparently he had come to like Moltke, who had served as aide-de-camp to his son in the two preceding years. But even in the early phase of the Danish war Moltke's advice was hardly taken, and he was left ill-informed about the course of operations. Only when the blunders of the senile Field Marshal Wrangel had become intolerable was Moltke sent to Schleswig in order to act as chief-of-staff of Wrangel and his successor, Prince Frederick Charles. Moltke's preparation and direction of the landing on the island of Alsen aroused admiration. From 1865 on, Moltke was regularly invited to the crown councils and, with Manteuffel removed from Berlin, became the speaker of the army in the deliberations on the coming war with Austria. On June 2, 1866, William I authorized him to issue orders in his name directly to all the army commanders, bypassing the minister of war. Although the royal order created a high command only for the duration of the war, Moltke's success as commander was to make it the beginning of a permanent institution.

The man who at the age of sixty-five was made the actual supreme commander of the Prussian army was descended from a poor Mecklenburg *Junker* family. His father had become a Danish officer, and the son received his education in the Danish cadet institute, from where he entered the Danish army as a lieutenant in 1819. Two years later, Moltke chose to transfer to the Prussian army. His youth was grim, a school of Spartan asceticism as well as of highest self-discipline and modesty, from which the life of an impecunious junior officer in Prussia brought little relief. The hardships of Moltke's early years made him shy among people. Since by nature he cared less for ruling men than for mastering the world by observation and thought, he gave the appearance of a scholar as much as of a soldier. The education which he acquired through tireless study comprised languages and literature, history, geography, and economics. His private letters and published writings were to make him one of the most eminent masters of German prose. But his humanist inclinations were directed toward a clear and precise understanding of reality which shunned mere speculation. His whole personal education and intellectual endeavor were propelled by the hope that the complete understanding of reality coupled with iron self-discipline might at some crucial moment allow him to be of decisive service to army and state. The power of persuasion through knowledge and sharp logical thinking seemed to him a better instrument for action than fighting for personal influence.

Except for five years as a lieutenant, Moltke did not serve with the troops. From 1828 on he was always in staff or teaching positions, or both, when he acted as aide-de-camp to Prussian princes. From 1835–39 he was lent to the Turkish army as a military instructor and experienced the defeat of the Turks in their war against Mehmet Ali at Nisib. The general who assumed command of the Prussian army in early June 1866 had never commanded a company in his life and was to exercise his influence only through strategic orders to army commanders, an event without historical precedent. So far every great commander had directed campaigns not only by marching orders and general battle instructions but also by the personal inspiration that he gave his soldiers before and during battle. Undoubtedly, the conditions of modern war called for a new type of commander; it was not possible for the new national armies any longer to troop around a single commander, especially since roads and railroads extended the space of operations. Loyalty and discipline had to be inculcated in the troops in peacetime, and the maintenance of morale as well as the tactics of battle had to be placed in the hands of commanders of smaller units. Moltke directed all the Prussian operations by telegraph from Berlin and did not arrive in the Bohemian theater of war until four days before the battle of Sadowa.

Moltke's achievement was the clear recognition of the changed conditions of war. His method of separate marches of the individual armies, though in such a way as to make their concentration on the battlefield possible, exploited modern communications to the best advantage. It also enabled Moltke to conduct operations against the flank and the rear of the enemy, a method likely to produce decisive results. In an age of great firepower the defensive was strong, and frontal attacks were not very promising. However, the true greatness of Moltke's leadership lay in the flexibility of all his planning. He made a virtue out of necessity by adjusting his plans not only, as any commander must do, to the actions and reactions of the enemy but also to the tactical gains and blunders of the field commanders. Moltke remained unruffled by this "friction of war."

His capacity for finding *ad hoc* solutions for any new situation, while steadfastly pursuing his ultimate strategic objectives, was proof of his undoctrinaire attitude, which rested on an unusual understanding of human motives and actions. His own major decisions were often of extraordinary boldness, although they were never built on a blind trust in fortune but on a shrewd estimate of the likely countermove of the enemy.

Bismarck's judgment that Moltke was cold and a "mere general-staff person" failed to grasp the latter's true nature, which was actually grounded on very rich inner experiences no less than on a very broad education. But Bismarck never came to know Moltke except as the apparently cool planner of campaigns and battles and in addition as the champion of a specific army point of view on the conduct of war. Clausewitz's teaching that war was an act of politics and that the proper conduct of war required the subordination of strategy to policy was not understood by Moltke. He asserted that once war had begun, the military leader should not be molested by political impositions of the statesman in order to achieve full victory, by which Moltke meant chiefly the annihilation of the armies of the enemy. Only after the achievement of military victory was the statesman to resume the direction of state policy. This unrealistic conception implied a division of powers between the army and the government, which in World War I was to become one of the chief reasons for the German defeat. But the man whose policies had enabled the Prussian army to win its victories in 1864, 1866, and 1870–71 was not willing to have the army chiefs ruin his work. Bismarck forcefully opposed Moltke's demands, and by now his influence with the king had become strong enough to make William I decide in his favor in political matters. Moltke on his part, not seeking personal political power, accepted the decisions of the king. Thus the conflicts that arose between Bismarck and Moltke remained without serious political consequences.

✍ *Battle of Sadowa*

AGAINST THE HESITANT DEFENSIVE TACTICS of Benedek and Krismanic, Moltke's swift strategy was completely successful. On July 3, 1866, the tenth day after the opening of hostilities, the Austrian army suffered a shattering defeat at Sadowa. But Moltke did not see the fulfillment of all his hopes. His conception of the battle as one of encirclement was not realized nor the gains won which might have been derived from a quick and energetic pursuit of the beaten Austrian army. Yet it was one of the most decisive battles in European history. With one quarter of the army lost and the remaining forces retreating toward Vienna, the Austrian government was willing to give up the struggle for Germany and Italy. It was impossible for Austria to fight a war of utmost resistance, since she could not rely on some of the non-German nationalities. Bismarck had taken up contacts with the revolutionary movement of Hungary before the war, and he now instigated the organization of a Hungarian legion. Moreover, both Prussians and Italians encouraged the Serbians and southern Slavs to rise.

✑ *Peace Settlement*

BUT BISMARCK was not eager to dissolve the Habsburg empire by fomenting national revolutions. Only in a desperate situation would he have activated such forces. Still, the victory of Sadowa created grave political problems. French public opinion reacted violently against the emerging German national state under Prussian leadership, and Napoleon was compelled to assert the French prestige in the settlement of the war. Although France was badly prepared to intervene with military means, this possibility could not be altogether excluded. Austria hurried to request Napoleon's mediation and ceded Venetia to him on July 5. Bismarck was therefore forced to negotiate with the French government. He threatened that any active intervention of France would be countered by Prussian acceptance of the Frankfurt constitution of 1849, which would allow him to rally the liberal movements of North and South Germany for an all-out national war against foreign intervention. But this threat, which was repeated when the Russian czar raised objections to Bismarck's policy, again did not express Bismarck's real intentions. The constitutional order that he hoped to create in Germany was decidedly less liberal than the Frankfurt constitution and also envisaged a much stronger position for Prussia within the future federal state. In order to achieve such a solution Bismarck was actually prepared to confine the new union to North Germany for the time being.

Napoleon, obviously apprehensive of challenging German national sentiment by raising demands for territorial concessions to France, declared his willingness to leave Bismarck a free hand in North Germany. The Prussian ambassador in Paris, Robert von der Goltz, arrived at an agreement that provided for the replacement of the Germanic Confederation by a North German Confederation under Prussian leadership and for the right of the South German states to form a southern federation. Schleswig-Holstein was to become Prussian, except for North Schleswig, where a plebiscite was to settle which districts were to go to Denmark. Finally Napoleon assented to Prussian annexations comprising about four million people but insisted upon the survival of the Saxon kingdom.

✍ *Peace of Nicolsburg*

ON THIS BASIS Bismarck could reach agreement with Austria on a preliminary peace that was signed at Nicolsburg on July 26. Austria withdrew from Germany paying a small war indemnity, although she did not have to make any territorial concessions. Bismarck also respected Austria's wish for the preservation of Saxony, her most loyal ally. Bismarck had to overcome King William's strong objections to his attempt not only to make peace with Austria speedily before the European powers might intervene but also in a form that would allow him in the future to reestablish cooperation with Austria in international affairs. William I wanted to inflict penalties in the form of territorial cessions from almost everyone who had fought against Prussia. Only reluctantly did the king give in to the arguments which Bismarck presented with passionate vigor in stormy meetings.

Bismarck warned the king not to alienate the feelings of the South German states, which he considered immediate allies against France and future members of a German federal state. For that reason he did not wish to take land from them. In North Germany, where he wished annexations in order to undo the separation of the eastern and western half of Prussia, which the Congress of Vienna had created, he wanted the total annexation of Hanover, Hesse-Kassel, Nassau, and Frankfurt, since the forced cession of some of their territories would turn them into resentful and unreliable members of the North German Confederation. William I found the deposition of legitimate princely dynasties, among them the Guelf, the oldest of Germany, incompatible with monarchical principles. But Bismarck finally had his way.

✍ *Foreign Pressures*

NEW DANGERS TO BISMARCK'S POLICY arose after the Nicolsburg peace, when Napoleon suddenly presented demands for territorial compensations. They were originally confined to the frontiers of 1814 but were soon expanded into claims for Mainz and the Bavarian Palatinate. Bismarck's reply that these extravagant demands were like conditions imposed after a victorious war led to a quick French retreat. Bismarck, however, who personally might have been inclined to make minor concessions to Napoleon if they had secured friendly relations between France and Prussia, was no longer in a position to discuss even minor changes of frontiers, since after the Prussian victory over Austria William I had become completely adamant in his refusal of any cession of German territory to France. A little later Napoleon tried to win the active support of Prussia for a French annexation of Luxembourg and

Belgium, but no such commitment was given by Bismarck.

The French demands for compensation, first presented on the day of the signing of the preliminary peace at Nicolsburg, might have become even more embarrassing if other powers had intervened. On July 27, the day after the signing of the Nicolsburg treaty, Russia proposed a European congress for the settlement of the war. The idea was rejected by England, where the Prussian victory over Austria was almost generally applauded. But the czar was greatly alarmed by the revolutionary methods of Bismarck's policy. The appeals to Czech nationalism, which had been issued by the Prussian commanders in Bohemia, the support of the Hungarian revolutionaries, the proposal of a German parliament, and last but not least the deposition of old dynasties caused great apprehension about Bismarck's ultimate aims and the reaction that his policy might have on the internal political life of Russia. Bismarck sent General Edwin von Manteuffel to St. Petersburg in order to allay the feelings of the czar. He made it clear to the Russians that any interference with Bismarck's policies would drive the latter into even closer cooperation with nationalism and liberalism. But at the same time Bismarck transmitted through Manteuffel the offer of Prussian assistance in Russia's endeavor to revise the Paris treaty of 1856 and especially to abolish the clause which forbade the building of a Russian navy in the Black Sea. Although the Manteuffel mission did not quiet all the misgivings of the Russians about the developments in Central Europe, with England keeping aloof and without the chance of finding a common ideological and political line with the France of Napoleon III, Bismarck's assurances of good will had a soothing effect.

✍ Treaties with South German States

THE FRENCH PRESSURE made Bismarck doubly anxious to secure an arrangement with the South German states for German defense. Between August 13 and 22 he concluded treaties of alliance with Württemberg, Baden, and Bavaria, by which the signatories guaranteed each other's integrity and in case of war promised to place all their military forces under the command of the king of Prussia. With these alliances one provision of the final Austrian peace treaty that was signed in Prague on August 23, 1866, was compromised beforehand. The article that stipulated the international independence of a future South German confederation was considered by Bismarck both unrealistic and obnoxious; unrealistic, because he correctly believed that no such confederation would ever come into existence, since Württemberg and Baden would not subordinate themselves to Bavaria; obnoxious, because he intended not only to use the South German resources for national defense but also for continuing the Prusso-German Customs Union. Moreover, there was one South

German state, Hesse-Darmstadt, that consisted of two separate sections, one of which, Upper Hesse, lay north of the Main and became part of the North German Confederation, while Rhine-Hesse remained outside.

While Bismarck did his best to undermine any rigid division between North and South Germany, he was well satisfied with confining the building of a federal state to North Germany. With the tremendous superiority that Prussia possessed in the north, particularly after swallowing Schleswig-Holstein, Hanover, Hesse-Kassel, Nassau, and Frankfurt, the new constitution could anchor Prussian leadership more firmly and could be made more centralistic and less liberal than would have been possible if the southern states had been included at once, in which case concessions would have become inevitable. While the South German governments would have asked for comprehensive state rights, the strong Catholic as well as the democratic groups of the people would have insisted on a more liberal constitutional order than Bismarck was prepared to offer.

ᗡ The End of the Constitutional Conflict

YET BISMARCK REALIZED that the time had come to settle the constitutional conflict. Many Prussian conservatives, among them probably the majority of the Prussian officers, felt that the battle of Sadowa had decided the constitutional conflict as well as the future of Germany. They expected that after achieving these tremendous successes for the national cause the royal government would be at liberty to rule without the constitution, which after all the king had granted by his own volition only in 1850, or to revise the constitution in an absolutist direction. Bismarck agreed that Sadowa had brought to a head the decision in his struggle with liberalism, as had been his hope when he unloosed the war against Austria. Since he was convinced that not only Austria but also German liberalism had been defeated on the Bohemian battlefields, he wished to end the struggle, though only on his own terms. He even felt strong enough to make some concessions to the parliamentary opposition. He was convinced that peace between the government and parliament was needed for the integration of the annexed German states into Prussia no less than for making Prussia appear strong in the eyes of foreign powers. Moreover, the alliance with German liberalism was to give him the strength to combat the particularist forces as represented by the German princes as well as by some popular movements even within Prussia herself.

For these reasons Bismarck presented to the Prussian parliament the so-called indemnity bill, by which parliament was requested to grant indemnity to the government for having conducted its administration without a budget approved by the parliament. Although no excuse was made for these practices of the past nor any assurances given about the future, the bill represented the recognition of the budget rights of the parliament and as such was a gesture of reconciliation. William I found it extremely difficult to approve of this move of his minister, while most Prussian conservatives, who saw in the bill an act of defeatism, reacted with fierce indignation.

The Prussian parliament had been dissolved on May 9, 1866, when war became imminent. On June 25, with the people impressed with the early military successes, electors had been chosen, while the final elections were held on July 3, the day of Sadowa. The shift of political sentiment was astounding. Although the popular participation in the election was not noticeably higher than in the earlier elections of the 1860's and again only 27 per cent of the voters in the third class went to the polls, the Progressives and the liberals of the left center were reduced from 253 to 148 seats, whereas the Conservatives captured 142 instead of the former 38 seats. The opposition to war credits that most liberal candidates proclaimed was not liked by the electorate, and Bismarck's policies had thrown the liberal leaders into great confusion. Within the liberal opposition some groups were interested in a national German policy of Prussia rather than in democratic rights, while another group was most willing to cooperate with the government, provided the cause of free trade and industry was advanced. The latter group, best represented by Otto Michaelis, was encouraged by the liberal economic policies that Rudolph von Delbrück had been allowed to conduct in Bismarck's ministry; the former groups had been wavering in their attitude toward the Prussian government ever since the Danish war. The Austrian war showed that the majority of the German liberals cherished unity more than liberty, although there were characteristic differences in approach, which in the future were to lead to new divisions within German liberalism. Beside those who, like Heinrich von Treitschke, now embraced the ideal of German unity as the practical fulfillment of their political dreams stood others who decided to support Bismarck, because they believed that liberal aims could be more easily realized within a national state. The contrast of the two views was manifested most clearly in the thinking of the two foremost leaders of liberalism in Hanover. Whereas Johannes Miquel showed little regret about the restrictions that Bismarck imposed on liberal rights, Rudolf von Bennigsen (1824–1902) recognized the defeat of liberalism. He admitted that the German nation could hardly expect to get parliamentarianism and all freedoms granted by the grace of the Prussian crown and of the "German Richelieu," but he believed that a strong liberal party supporting Bismarck's German and foreign policies could hope to wrest important liberal concessions as compensation from the government.

Thus the majority of the German liberals were ready to use the indemnity bill as the bridge that led from opposition to collaboration. On September 3, the Prussian parliament voted the indemnity bill 230 to 75. The liberals voting for the government, among them half of the Progressives and two-thirds of the Bockum-Dolffs group, were fully aware that they were the vanquished of the constitutional conflict and that the influence of the parliament would be limited. Bismarck had not failed, in particular, to remind the parliament of its negligible role in military affairs by requesting the unconditional grant of a war chest. On the other hand, he promised improvements in Prussia's internal conditions by the fulfillment of certain promises contained in the constitution. However, Bismarck announced the participation of a North German *Reichstag* in the making of a German constitution.

✧ *The National Liberal Party*

AFTER THE CLOSE of the session of the Prussian parliament two dozen former Progressives, among them Karl Twesten, Edward Lasker, and Max von Forckenbeck, issued a declaration affirming their intention to support the foreign policy of the government while continuing to assume at home "the duties of a vigilant and loyal opposition." At the time of the convention of the North German *Reichstag*, in February 1867, this incipient "national party" merged with the National Liberal party which Rudolf von Bennigsen had founded with identical aims in Hanover during the winter and which had begun to organize in other states. The new National Liberal party, of which Bennigsen became chairman, had its greatest strength in the non-Prussian states and in the states presently annexed by Prussia. Socially this national and moderately liberal party drew its major support from among the upper bourgeoisie, the industrialists, the merchants, and the academically educated people.

In the parliamentary debates of 1866–67 the Progressive party survived, however. Benedikt Waldeck, Rudolf Virchow, Theodor Mommsen, Hermann Schulze-Delitzsch, and Leopold von Hoverbeck continued to present the unadulterated ideals of the years of constitutional conflict. Although the Progressive party did poorly in the elections for the North German *Reichstag*, it gained a larger following later on, particularly among the lower middle classes.

✧ *The Conservative Camp*

THE EVENTS OF 1866 not only led to a new orientation of the liberal parties but also caused great commotion among the Conservatives. As early as May 1866, Ludwig von Gerlach, who twenty years earlier had assisted in drawing Bismarck into politics, had protested against Bismarck's policy, which to this old member of the Christian-Germanic circle of Frederick William IV seemed to violate all political morality. In a pamphlet he now expressed himself forcefully against the lawlessness of the Prussian annexations. But although some Conservatives were uneasy about the deposition of German princes, the majority were narrow Prussian royalists who worried little about the exclusion of Austria from traditional Germany or about the fate of other German states; rather, they were bitterly disappointed that Bismarck, instead of exploiting the military victories for destroying the constitution, moved even closer to an understanding with liberalism. They could not very well go into open opposition, yet they clearly showed their disappointment, and they might have succeeded in obstructing the parliamentary cooperation with the National Liberals on which the success of the new internal order largely depended.

In these circumstances it was important that a group of Conservatives seceded from the old party and formed the "Free Conservative Union," which after 1871 became the German *Reich* party. This new party was composed largely of rich Silesian and Rhenish noblemen who often enough combined industrial with agrarian interests. They were joined by a good many former high government officials and diplomats. Altogether they represented a more open-minded and versatile element than the *Junkers* who composed the Conservative membership of the parliament. It may be questionable whether the Free Conservatives constituted a political party in the strict sense, because they did not have a strongly organized following. They were, however, an exceedingly influential group of notables. They proclaimed their full support of the national objectives, for which in their opinion the development of constitutional institutions was needed. In this they were far from showing any inclination to modify the authoritarian structure of the German state and society in any important respect. They only were less dogmatic and parochial than the old conservatives, and, most of all, they believed in Bismarck. Count Bethusy-Huc (1829–93) and Wilhelm von Kardorff (1828–1907) were the outstanding early leaders of the group, who not only helped to shield Bismarck against the criticism of the Prussian ultras but also mediated between the government and the German National Liberals.

In contrast to the old Conservatives, the Free Conservatives could more naturally offer a political home to the conservatives from non-Prussian lands. Still, before 1871 few non-Prussian conservatives entered into a free political collaboration with Bismarck. Count Georg von Münster (1820–1902), the son of Count Münster who had restored the kingdom of Hanover by his diplomatic endeavors at the Congress of Vienna, was one among relatively few aristocrats who placed his national ideals above his regional attachments. Later he was to become a distinguished ambassador of the new German Empire. In Hanover the conservative elements, consisting of most of the nobility, the Catholics, and large elements of the Lutheran peasantry, felt a particularly strong resentment against the Prussian annexation, which there as everywhere else was imposed without any consultation with the people. This particularist movement in Hanover was to retain considerable strength until the days of the Weimar Republic. The incorporation of Hesse-Kassel into Prussia was accomplished with little opposition. The frivolous regime of the Hessian rulers had cut the moral roots of popular loyalty. But originally even here an attempt was made to build a popular movement in favor of the former dynasty. In all the states that became members of the North German Confederation, whether we look at Saxony, which entered under duress, or at Mecklenburg, which had old and close ties with Prussia, the nobility supported the governments in defending the preservation of state rights.

↜ *The North German Confederation*

FOR THESE REASONS Bismarck could not help wishing that the liberal movement would not ebb too much. He needed the liberal groups in order to frighten the princes into making those concessions that he considered necessary for the foundation of a strong confederation. In the negotiations with the governments on a treaty establishing the new confederation he did not hesitate to threaten that he might move the Acheron, which meant that he would make the new constitution with the liberals even if this meant that thrones would topple. But soon he said just the opposite, warning that if the parliament pushed its demands for the control of the government too far, he would ground the confederation exclusively on agreements with the German princes. It was the arcanum of Bismarck's constitutional policy that he extracted from the princes the surrender of a part of their sovereignty to the confederation by using the pressure of popular liberalism and nationalism while, by his alliance with the princes, checkmating any move of the liberals to undermine the primacy of monarchical government. This system of balances and counterbalances was employed by Bismarck in a masterly fashion in the making of the constitution, and since it was institutionalized by the confederation, it was to dominate German political life for the next half-century.

On August 18, 1866, Prussia had concluded a treaty of federation with the North German states which had fought on her side. In addition to a mutual guarantee of their territorial integrity the signatories had agreed to bring into existence a new constitution in accordance with the Prussian proposition to the Federal Diet of June 10, 1866. The governments together were to convene a parliament, elected by universal suffrage, in order to reach agreement on the final constitution. Saxony and Hesse-Darmstadt, for her territories north of the Main, as well as two petty Thuringian principalities declared their accession to the federation in the peace treaties which they signed with Prussia a little later.

Bismarck, who spent the months of October and November at the Baltic Sea trying to recover from illness and exhaustion, had various Prussian ministries work on the technical chapters of the future constitution. But even from a distance he sketched the outlines of the future constitution in written directives. After his return to Berlin in early December he concentrated on the preparation of the final draft that was presented to a conference of German governments on December 15. Except for some small details this draft entirely reflected Bismarck's conceptions. As far as possible he had insisted that every commitment to firm constitutional principles should be avoided. In one of his directives he even recommended that the confederation be given the outward form of a federation of states, though in practice it should achieve the nature of a federal state, "through elastic, unpretentious, though far-reaching expressions" in the constitution. It is doubtful whether such a squaring of the circle has ever been successful. But for the same reason of playing down the greatness of the step to be taken in the integration of the German states, Bismarck clung closely to existing institutions and traditional practices. As he expressed it: "The more we continue the old forms, the more likely we are to score, whereas the endeavor to have a full-fledged Minerva spring from the head of the presidium will bury the matter in the sand of professorial controversies."

Thus the draft of December 15 proposed as the chief organ of the new confederation an institution that looked like a touched-up version of the Diet of Frankfurt. However, Bismarck did not renew the select council of the Federal Diet[1] but chose the plenary council, in which every state had at least one vote while Austria and the four kingdoms had four votes. Bismarck did not change the distribution of votes, with the single exception of adding the thirteen votes of the states annexed by Prussia to the four votes which Prussia had held before. Considering that Prussia comprised four fifths of North Germany, a vote of seventeen in a group of forty-three seemed modest indeed, but actually, by the exclusion of Austria, the position of all the small states was automatically changed. So far they had derived their major strength from the tensions and jealousies prevailing between the two major powers. Once these tensions had been dissolved, the small states of North Germany could not stand up to Prussian leadership. The petty states, such as Anhalt, Lippe, Waldeck, Reuss, were seldom able even to make themselves felt by a minor dissent. Prussia was certain to command the additional five votes needed for a majority.

[1] See the author's *A History of Modern Germany: 1648–1840*, pp. 445–6.

All decisions of the new Federal Council, as Bismarck renamed the former Federal Diet that had become so unpopular, were taken by simple majority. Only changes of the constitution required a two-thirds majority. And here the seventeen Prussian votes were sufficient to block any undesirable move.

The authority of the presiding state was greatly enhanced. Whereas in the Germanic Confederation the presidency of the Austrian ministry was confined to chairing the meetings of the diet, the "presidium" of the North German Confederation was to receive far-reaching powers of its own. It represented the confederation internationally, had the right to declare war and make peace, exercised the command of all armed forces, and had the duty to supervise, if necessary to enforce, the execution of the decisions of the confederation in the member states.

The new confederation was given exclusive control not only of defense and of foreign policy, including foreign economic policy, but also of internal economic policy, such as freedom of trade, freedom of migration and settlement, railroads, navigation, post and telegraph, as well as of legislation in the field of commercial law. Thus the new Federal Council was to receive wide powers, which in Bismarck's draft were to be shared with a popular representation only to a very small extent. The draft provided for a parliament elected by universal, though nonsecret, suffrage, which in Bismarck's opinion would allow the government to influence the elections very greatly. This parliament was given little authority. First of all, it would not confront any agency responsible to it, such as a federal cabinet or a federal chancellor. To be sure, a federal chancellor was provided in the draft constitution, but he was only the presiding officer of the Federal Council. The parliament would actually face the whole Federal Council, the amorphous group of twenty-odd state delegates. Moreover, the parliament was to have only very limited rights with regard to the budget. Military expenditure was now declared to be within the jurisdiction of the confederation. It was not to be covered by annual appropriations, however, but by a permanent scheme anchored in the constitution. The army of the confederation was to consist of 1 per cent of the population, and for each soldier an annual allowance of 225 taler was envisaged to be paid by the confederation. The presidium of the confederation was authorized to collect from the member states annual contributions, the amount of which was arrived at by multiplying 225 taler with 1 per cent of the population figure of the individual states. This constitutional arrangement meant that the military budget would not have to depend on parliamentary approval, whether state or federal parliament. In addition, since military expenditures accounted for more than nine tenths of the federal budget, it would have left the national parliament with little power. According to the draft it was to review the percentage of population figures every tenth year, otherwise it could only debate legislation presented by the Federal Council. It was to be expected that without the power of the purse, debates were not likely to change legislation that could be declared to be the result of difficult compromises between twenty-two governments.

✍ The Constituent Assembly

THE DISCUSSION OF THE BISMARCKIAN DRAFT by the German state governments after December 15 produced many proposals for changes. The Prussian representatives deigned to ponder only a few of them, while Bismarck accepted even fewer. With the threat that he could make a constitution with the parliament alone, Bismarck compelled the representatives of the state governments to accept a draft constitution essentially in accordance with his original ideas. It was presented to the North German *Reichstag* on March 4, 1867. No single party had a majority in this parliament of 297 deputies, while no majority for the government could be won without the National Liberals, who had elected 79 members. About 40 other unattached moderate liberals could be counted on, while the Progressives got only 19 seats. On the right side, there were 59 Conservatives and 40 Free Conservatives. The rest of the membership consisted of a large variety of particularists.

The National Liberals, though largely dependent on the Free Conservatives, made a brave and skillful stand during the *Reichstag* session and wrested very important concessions from Bismarck. These changes were concerned with the position of the *Reichstag*. The immunity of its members from any legal prosecution, the right to present petitions to the Federal Council or chancellor, and the limitation of the government's right to adjourn sessions of the *Reichstag* or delay its reelection after a dissolution strengthened the significance of the parliament. Of considerable consequence was the modification of universal suffrage, which the liberals correctly suspected to be a device of the government for manipulating the popular vote. They intended to defeat this aim by adding the secrecy of the vote. Bismarck most reluctantly accepted the secret vote and also gave in on the eligibility of governmental officials, whom he had wished to exclude from the parliament, remembering the role which state officials, and particularly judges, had played in the Prussian parliament during the constitutional conflict. But he refused to accept any remuneration for deputies, hoping vainly to stop the growth of a class of professional politicians.

The majority of the North German *Reichstag* compelled Bismarck to grant a very considerable extension of its right over the budget. The draft constitution had envisaged that the *Reichstag* was to approve nonmilitary expenditures for a three-year period but would have nothing to say about revenue. Revenue was to come from duties and post and telegraph charges as well as from common indirect taxes. Beyond this the presidium was empowered to demand from the states so-called "matricular contributions," i.e., direct payments determined by the population figure of the individual states. The *Reichstag* declared such "matricular contributions" acceptable only as a transitional measure and gave the confederation authority to levy not only indirect but also direct taxes. In addition, it was now stated that all revenues and expenditures of the confederation would have to be presented in the form of an annual budget law to the *Reichstag.* One very important exception was made, however. By special law the military expenditure as proposed by Bismarck was approved until the end of 1871. The parliamentary majority conceived of this law as a temporary measure, but it will be seen that Bismarck entertained different ideas. He felt less hesitation in seeing the competency of the confederation extended to further fields of legislation, such as right of citizenship, criminal law, right of civil and criminal procedure, public health control, building of roads and waterways, and supervision of railroads.

But the greatest single issue was discussed in the debates on the character of the presidium. The liberals understandably took exception to its anonymous character. As a matter of fact, Bismarck did not intend to create any federal agencies but envisaged only the appointment of an under-secretary in the Prussian foreign office, who, as federal chancellor, was to preside over the meetings of the Federal Council and was to receive his instructions from the Prussian foreign minister. The last Prussian diplomatic representative at the Diet of Frankfurt, Karl Friedrich von Savigny, was slated for the post. The liberals on their part aimed at the establishment of a full cabinet responsible to parliament. Undoubtedly, to them it was the first step in the direction of parliamentary government, but for the same reason Bismarck fought their demand with the utmost determination, arguing that such a ministry was incompatible with a federal state. Although stated in such general terms this was not true, it was correct to say that a ministry responsible to parliament would have affected the position of the Federal Council.

Bismarck agreed, however, to a compromise proposal, made by Bennigsen. Accordingly article 17 of the constitution read: "The official publication of federal laws as well as the supervision of their execution is the obligation of the presidium. The directives and orders of the federal presidium are issued in the name of the Confederation and require for their validity the countersignature of the federal chancellor, who thereby assumes responsibility." To the liberals this article of the constitution meant at least a stepping stone toward parliamentary government. But the latter was not to come about in the North German Confederation and the subsequent Empire. Bismarck and his successors still interpreted "responsibility of the chancellor" merely as an obligation to inform the parliament about legislation and not even necessarily about policies which were the prerogative of the presidium, such as the conduct of international affairs or the exercise of the command of the armed forces. It was not construed as requiring the confidence of a parliamentary majority for the chancellor. Yet the Bennigsen amendment raised the significance of the *Reichstag* insofar as it made it the forum for regular debates on all questions concerning national life. It also created the beginnings of a distinct German federal government. Whereas under the terms of the Bismarckian draft constitution the preparation as well as the execution of federal laws would have been in the hands of the state governments, now at least the supervision of the execution of federal laws required a federal office. In these circumstances Bismarck's original idea of running federal affairs under the auspices of the Prussian foreign office became unfeasible. Bismarck himself had to assume the federal chancellorship, in addition to his office of Prussian prime minister, and to develop an agency in charge of federal administration.

In this form the constitution was passed by the North German *Reichstag* and subsequently adopted by all the state parliaments. On July 1, 1867, the constitution went into effect and remained in force for half a century, since the changes made in 1871, when the South German states joined the confederation, were of minor significance. The concessions made by Bismarck to the North German *Reichstag* and to the National Liberal party were far-reaching. Although he succeeded in his major objectives—the establishment of Prussia's predominance and the exclusion of parliamentary government—in spite of later arguments the confederation was a federal state. Changes of the constitution required common action of the Federal Council and *Reichstag*. Moreover, the confederation possessed what German constitutional lawyers called by the curious name *Kompetenz-Kompetenz*, i.e., the authority or competency to extend the competency of federal legislation to new fields.

✍ Customs Union

BISMARCK'S ACCEPTANCE OF SO MANY of the National Liberal wishes was due to the threatening foreign situation. At the time of the parliamentary debates, the European crisis over Luxembourg reached its height, and Bismarck was anxious to avoid the appearance of a Germany weakened by internal rifts. Moreover, he sensed that the compromise with North German liberalism, as embodied in the final constitution, would be the minimum needed in order to win over South German liberalism. It was in these months after Sadowa that Bismarck underwent the transformation from an exclusively Prussian into a German statesman. The alliances with the southern states were clear proof of his intention to include them eventually in a German union. He took a further step in this direction when, in the summer of 1867, he renewed the customs union. He insisted on a reorganization in close analogy to the North German Confederation. In the new Federal Customs Council, Prussia held seventeen votes, Saxony four votes, Mecklenburg and Brunswick two votes each, as was the case in the Federal Council of the Confederation. The only difference was that the South German states which were members of the customs union also received a pluralistic vote—Bavaria six, Württemberg four, Baden and Hesse-Darmstadt two votes each. But the right of veto that formerly belonged to every member was abolished; instead, the Federal Customs Council reached decisions by simple majority vote. In addition, a customs parliament was created. It consisted of the members of the North German *Reichstag*, to whom eighty-three specially elected representatives from the southern states were added. The Bavarian and the Württemberg governments accepted this plan most reluctantly, because they rightly suspected that Bismarck intended to use popular representation as a means to bring pressure on them. Such intentions, however, were frustrated by the outcome of the elections. Whereas in Baden and Hesse-Darmstadt mostly National Liberals were elected, the particularists won out in Bavaria and Württemburg. But the frame was set which helped in the accomplishment of the unification of all the German states outside of Austria a few years later. As a result of the annexation of Schleswig-Holstein by Prussia, the area of the customs union after 1867 comprised also this strategic land that linked the Baltic with the North Sea. And now even Mecklenburg and Lübeck joined the customs union. Only the two major German port cities, Hamburg and Bremen, still stayed out expecting to derive greater advantages from the progress of free trade in the world than from participation in the customs union.

✧ *The North German Confederation after 1867*

BISMARCK FELT UNCERTAIN of how soon the full political unification of Germany might occur. Often he was inclined to assign such an event to a remote future, but we see him again and again probe into the internal and foreign developments lest an opportunity for action might slip out of his hands. In the meantime he steadily worked on the strengthening of the internal conditions of the North German Confederation. Obviously he was at times worried that he might have opened the gates to liberalism too far and that the liberal flood might wash away the ramparts of monarchy, especially the full control of the army by the king. By 1870 serious friction had arisen over what form the military budget that was to replace the provisional arrangements of 1867 was to take in the future. But on the other hand Bismarck wanted to broaden the popular support of the government and for that reason did not even wish to suppress parliamentary criticism. On the contrary, often this appeared to him desirable in order to bring not only the German princes to a broader understanding of contemporary needs but also his own—the Prussian—king.

"Discontent among the lower classes may produce a serious illness for which we have remedies, but discontent among the educated minority leads to a chronic disease, the diagnosis of which is difficult and the cure protracted," Bismarck wrote in 1895. It is doubtful whether he really knew of a good cure for the discontent of the lower classes, and when he talked of the "educated classes" he was not thinking of the professors and their following, whom he disliked, but of the new capitalist merchants and industrialists. And while he was unwilling to grant them any responsible participation in the direction of state policy, he was ready to fulfill most of their social and economic demands. Whereas the reactionary governments in 1848-49 and all through the 1850's had supported the traditional guilds in an attempt to wean the mass of the artisan class away from the support of liberalism,[2] Bismarck recognized the social claims of modern capitalism at the expense of the artisans and handicraft workers in order to make the capitalists compromise on their political ideals. His policy was successful, as the class support of the National Liberal and Free Conservative parties or, negatively, the social composition of the Progressive party proved.

Among the legislation introduced in the years after 1867 the one making industrial freedom the law of the land was the most symbolic. How strongly Bismarck felt about the freedom of industry was shown by the fact that he introduced it by provisional decree on July 8, 1868, when parliamentary debates and committees delayed the passage of the law presented by the government. Industrial freedom thereby became practically general in all of Germany, since some German states had already initiated such legislation in the early 1860's. The introduction of industrial freedom was accompanied by a host of other measures promoting the unhindered development of the capitalistic and industrial economy. Freedom of movement for the people, freedom to found economic and commercial companies as well as coalitions of workers, a unified order of bills of exchange, a North German code of commercial law and the establishment of a court of appeal in commercial matters, a unified patent and copyright law, finally even a North German code of criminal law were among the most important steps taken in the liberation of the economy from precapitalistic shackles that had existed before 1870.

Transportation and communication were greatly improved by the re-

[2] See p. 100.

moval of tolls from waterways and roads and the building of a federal postal and telegraph service. The latter work was accomplished by Heinrich von Stephan, a man of extraordinary gifts for practical administration, which he again proved a decade later in the organization of the World Postal Union. The consular service was at once placed under the confederation, and the foreign service followed in 1870. The adoption of a common flag also served the purpose of making the confederation appear as a unified state abroad. Bismarck rejected, however, the flag that for the last half-century had flown wherever Germans demonstrated for German unity and popular freedom. The black, red, and gold colors of the students' movement, of liberalism, and of 1848–49 were, in the eyes of Bismarck and his king, tainted by revolutionary and Great German memories. The Prussian black and white and the Hanseatic red and white flags, as the ones most often displayed on German vessels, were combined into the new German black, white, and red tricolor. For the benefit of William I Bismarck could explain the tricolor also as a synthesis of the Prussian and Brandenburg colors.

The reforms of the early years of the North Germanic Confederation opened the gates for a free capitalistic growth in Germany. Whereas this freedom was welcomed by the industrialists and the entrepreneurial class, it caused hardships among the artisans and small merchants. The political division of German liberalism into the Progressive and National Liberal parties—the latter representing largely the industrial interests—received from this economic policy its social significance. There was also a widening of personal freedom, such as the abolition of governmental obstacles to marriage and the declaration of equality for people of every religious faith, from which all classes benefited.

Reforms were carried forward also in the political realm, though not on the federal level. The annexation of Hanover, Schleswig-Holstein, Hesse-Kassel, Nassau, and Frankfurt was executed in dictatorial fashion by the Prussian bureaucracy. The Prussian administrators not only introduced the Prussian tax system and military service but also started to apply all other Prussian laws. After 1815 the Rhineland had kept its French law code, but the new Prussian provinces annexed in 1866 were deprived of most of their traditional German institutions to the dismay not only of the conservative and particularist elements but also of the National Liberal forces.

๛ Prussia and the Annexed Provinces

BISMARCK WAS too preoccupied with the North German constitution and foreign affairs to pay much attention to the execution of the annexations. Actually, he was not in favor of an exaggerated centralization and coordination. When the simple seizure of the large state properties of Hanover and Hesse-Kassel by the Prussian treasury in July 1867 aroused vigorous protests from the population, the Prussian government for the first time held conferences with prominent leaders of the people of the new provinces. As a result important concessions were made with regard to the future administration of these territories. Hanover received a provincial diet, which to some extent continued the diet of the former kingdom, but the provincial diet was made more representative than its predecessor, which had suffered from the predominance of the nobility. However, the authority of the provincial diet did not go very far. Assistance to agriculture, the building of roads, and the administration of institutions for the mentally ill as well as the blind and deaf were its major tasks, which, however, were assigned to it not merely for deliberation but also for decision and execution. Moreover, the diet could create provincial agencies and supervise their operations. The Prussian state made a fixed annual appropriation of the provincial self-administration. Hanover also saved some of her peculiar forms of local administration. Similar arrangements were made for Hesse-Kassel and Nassau.

These plans for a modicum of self-administration in the new provinces met with the strong opposition of the Prussian conservatives. Formerly the East German *Junkers* had demanded the strengthening of provincial institutions as a safeguard against the centralism of the Prussian ministries or, since 1848, of a parliament in Berlin. Bismarck's attitude stemmed partly from this tradition. But the Prussian conservatives of the late 1860's saw in a reform of the agencies of provincial self-administration a threat to their privileged position in the eastern provinces. Particularly in the local and county administrations were they anxious to defend their rights. It was characteristic of the Prussian *Junkers* that these fears served as a catalyst for their dislike of the West Elbian Germans and the liberal concessions made to them by Bismarck. The new legislation for Hanover and Hesse was passed by the Prussian parliament, in which the Free Conservatives and National Liberals meanwhile had enhanced their membership by the addition of representatives from the new provinces. But the fight was bitter, and as a result the government delayed further action, although other Prussian provinces, such as the Rhineland, Saxony, and Silesia, began to clamor for similar reforms. Instead, in 1869 it presented a law on the reform of the county (*Kreis*) administration which, however, had not been passed when the parliamentary session closed. Only in 1872 was a law concerning the reorganization of the county administration adopted and three years later a general law on provincial self-administration issued.

In these years the debates revived on whether it would be desirable to build up the Prussian provinces into states and abolish the Prussian parliament and government in favor of the North German government. Yet Bismarck was not inclined to consider the dissolution of the Prussian state, as some of the liberals of 1848–49 had done. On the contrary, in his opinion the Prussian monarchy was to serve as a centralizing power not only in the Prussian provinces but also in the rest of Germany. He was not unaware of the difficulties which the simultaneous existence of a parliament of four fifths of North Germany—the Prussian parliament— and a North German parliament might engender. But he thought that friction between these parliaments would work to the detriment of par- liamentarism and that the Prussian government would always lend suffi- cient support to a federal German government. The reforms of the Prus- sian provincial administration were not intended to go beyond the modest scope on which they were planned in these years. Prussia still remained a rather highly centralized state, and with the preservation of the social and political privileges of the *Junkers* this centralization gave the old eastern provinces a dominant political influence in Prussia. But after 1866 six of her twelve provinces were located west of the Elbe, and they were far richer in population and industry than the eastern half of the monarchy. Although their influence could be kept within bounds, it could not be disregarded. Particularly in the economic and social life western interests and habits began to transform the character of the old Prussian state.

The integration of the new Prussian provinces into Prussia progressed rapidly after 1866 because the national sentiment of the populations con- cerned was stronger than their local loyalties. In these circumstances even the small gestures of the Prussian government in the direction of a mod- ernization of local and provincial government sufficed to satisfy the great majority of the people in the new provinces. In view of the preponder- ance of Prussia in the new North German Confederation, the integration of Hanover, Hesse, Nassau, Frankfurt, and Schleswig-Holstein solved many problems of the establishment of this new confederation. Among the member states Saxony was the most important one. Austria, Russia, and France had made great efforts to safeguard at least some semblance of sovereign statehood for Saxony. Thus Saxony did not, as happened in 1815, lose any of her territories, nor was her king deprived of all his command functions over the Saxon army. King Johann, one of the most highly educated princes of his age, accepted the verdict of the war and loyally worked for the success of the North German Confederation. The intensely industrialized land was connected with surrounding Prussia by a thousand threads, and no popular resentment between Prussians and Sax- ons survived the war of 1866.

✑ The National Movement in South Germany

THE RELATIONS between the North and South German states remained uncertain. As an immediate result of the war public opinion in the south seemed to demand close cooperation or even federation with the north. The French threat of intervention galvanized national sentiment in South Germany, while Austria's reputation suffered on account of her close dependence on Napoleon III. But the first wave of high national feeling began to ebb and disperse in the subsequent period when the particularist forces rallied and won fresh popular support. The North German constitution, with its narrow circumscription of parliamentary powers, met with the strong disapproval of the democratic elements of South Germany and was also a disappointment to the liberals. Moreover, the introduction of Prussian military organization, as necessitated by the military alliances with Prussia, and its high cost gave the movement against "Prussification" its concrete targets. In the south one gibed that the new North German constitution actually contained only three articles, all of them imperatives: namely, first, pay taxes; second, serve in the army; third, keep your mouth shut.

Popular sentiment in favor of an early entry into the new confederation was relatively strongest in the southwest. The second chamber of Hesse-Darmstadt voted for such an accession in June 1867, but the first chamber rejected the move. The real political power in Darmstadt rested in the hands of the prime minister, Baron K. F. R. Dalwigk zu Lichtenfels (1802–80), the last active German statesman in whom the patriotism of the old German empire was still alive, although under the changed conditions of the age it could only take the form of radical Great German and particularist policies. Dalwigk was inclined to do anything in order to stave off the absorption of Hesse-Darmstadt by the new confederation or, still better, to undo the Bismarckian successes. To this end he was willing even to cooperate with France. Yet he was unable to turn back the wheels of history. Hesse-Darmstadt was already a member of the North German Confederation as far as Upper Hesse was concerned, the part of the grand duchy located north of the Main river. In April 1867 Hesse-Darmstadt concluded a military convention and alliance with Prussia. But Dalwigk's activities stymied the popular national movement in Hesse-Darmstadt and also kept Baden from direct contact with Prussia, which it eagerly sought.

Like Crown Prince Frederick William of Prussia, Grand Duke Frederick I of Baden (1826–1907; Grand Duke since 1856), brother-in-law of William I, had formed his political ideas under the influence of Prince Consort Albert of England. He wished to be a constitutional monarch and also to satisfy the popular demand for a national state. Together with Karl Mathy (1806–68) and subsequently with Julius Jolly (1823–91), whom he appointed prime ministers, he prepared the way for Baden's entry into the North German Confederation. Since Bismarck refused in 1867 to receive Baden into the confederation unless Hesse-Darmstadt joined the move, and he later preferred to wait until all of South Germany could be brought in, the Baden government tried to keep pace with the legislation of the North German Confederation and to speed the reorganization of the Baden army along the Prussian model.

Württemberg's dynasty was not ready to subordinate itself to the trend toward German unification and found encouragement in the strong anti-Prussian attitude of wide circles of the Swabian people. The most vocal groups were represented in the democratic German People's party, which championed Swiss civil and military institutions as conforming better to the Swabian character than those of the Prussian military monarchy with its rigid class divisions. This sentiment was a world apart from the attitude of the proud and headstrong Queen Olga, the sister of Czar Alexander, who simply refused to give up any sovereignty. Although King Karl largely shared her views, he had been shocked by the poor showing of his army and he recognized that irrespective of whether Württemberg remained independent or joined the new confederation, military reforms were urgently needed. In foreign affairs, too, he was more cautious than the queen. Although he retained his foreign minister, the versatile Baron Friedrich von Varnbüler (1809–89), he dismissed two of the other ministers most responsible for the anti-Prussian course of Württemberg policy prior to 1866, namely the president of the privy council, Baron Konstantin von Neurath, and Julius von Hardegg (1810–75), the minister of war. In all military matters thereafter he took the advice of a major from Mecklenburg, the energetic Albert von Suckow (1828–93), who, first as an aide to the new minister of war, and from 1870 as minister, effected the reorganization of the Württemberg army along Prussian lines. But with the exception of these military reforms, which, at least in the eyes of the king, had a very ambiguous political meaning, no progress toward German unification was made between 1866 and 1870.

The key to the future policies of the South German states lay in Bavaria, though this largest South German state could by no means give any orders to the others. The idea of the formation of a South German Confederation that had been written into the Peace of Prague proved utterly unrealistic as soon as the Bavarian government attempted to implement it. South Germany had no other unity but the common desire of the individual South German states to preserve their autonomy. None of the three other South German states was willing to grant Bavaria any political superiority. The young King Ludwig II (1845–86), who had come to the throne in 1864 entirely unprepared for governing, was not in a position to steer a firm course. In these years he was strongly under the influence of Richard Wagner, whom he had drawn to Munich. His enthusiasm for modern opera and his indulgence in the building of fantastic castles kept Ludwig II preoccupied. Signs of mental illness, which ultimately were to lead to insanity, were already apparent in him before 1870.

In the last days of 1866 Ludwig II appointed Prince Chlodwig von Hohenlohe-Schillingsfürst (1819–1901) prime minister. This Franconian magnate, a liberal Catholic, had spoken on the eve of the Austro-Prussian war for Bavaria's cooperation with Prussia. He believed that the unification of Germany was inevitable and expected that Bavaria's accession could be facilitated if Austria could again be brought closer to Germany, preferably in the form of a permanent alliance. But Austria was not in a mood to accept her defeat of 1866 as final. Emperor Francis Joseph had appointed Baron F. F. Beust (1809–86) Austrian prime minister, who as Saxon prime minister had led Saxony on the side of Austria into the war against Prussia. This choice clearly indicated that the emperor's hopes for a reversal of the decision of Sadowa were still alive. Under Beust, in the so-called *Ausgleich* (compromise), the Hungarians received practical autonomy within the Habsburg empire that now assumed the name of Austria-Hungary. Only in foreign policy and defense were common institutions maintained. In the end the *Ausgleich*, which was concluded in the expectation that it would enable the Habsburg empire to resume an active foreign policy in Germany, was to contribute to Austria's final acceptance of her separation from Germany. The Magyars were opposed to seeing Austria involved in German affairs, and as their influence on the conduct of Vienna's foreign policy increased, all ideas about a renewal of the struggle over Germany dropped to the background. But prior to 1871 Austrian policy was not prepared to enter into a relationship with Germany that would have implied the recognition of the conditions created by the Prussian military victories of 1866.

Prince Hohenlohe's policies neither stood much of a chance of realization nor even were able to stop a revival of strong particularist feelings. As mentioned before,[3] the elections for the customs parliament in 1868 already showed the tide of anti-Prussian sentiment growing. The Bavarian election for the second chamber in 1869 brought a rally in the "party of Bavarian patriots" that gained a majority over the nationally minded groups. The Bavarian particularists had their chief support in the nobility and in the Roman Catholic clergy and its popular following, particularly in the part of Bavaria south of the Danube. Since Hohenlohe aroused the enmity of these circles by his internal policies as well, he had to resign in February 1870 and was followed by the Bavarian minister in Vienna,

[3] See p. 200.

Count Otto Bray-Steinburg (1807–99), a firm believer in Bavarian statehood and Austro-Bavarian cooperation.

The standstill of the national movement in South Germany after 1867 was of deep concern to Bismarck. There can be no doubt that he wished to include the South German states in the confederation, but he did not intend to buy their support by constitutional concessions that would have jeopardized the predominance of royal power that he had established in the north and that had been a major reason for his willingness to leave the South German states outside of the confederation of 1866. Thus he could say that the full unification of Germany might take another generation. Yet he was also aware that the accession of South Germany in all probability would cause a grave international crisis, which on the other hand would make it easier to overcome the resistance felt in many southern quarters against union with the north.

✒ Relations with France

IT HAS OFTEN BEEN ASSERTED that Bismarck hoped or even attempted to start a war with France from 1866 on, but this is not true. Although he recognized the fear and resentment that the German unification movement caused in France, he also realized that Napoleon III was driven to oppose it more by the exigencies of his weakening internal position than by personal conviction. Bismarck considered it not impossible that the French might eventually accept German unification. As late as 1869, when the Second Empire became a constitutional monarchy, Bismarck expressed the hope that this would contribute to such a development. He was conscious of the grave risks of a Franco-German war. Yet after the Austrian war Bismarck was unwilling to make concessions that might have assuaged French feelings, particularly concessions that would have exposed him to the slightest criticism from the German nationalists. This was already apparent in the first big Franco-Prussian crisis, following the Austro-Prussian war. We have seen[4] that Napoleon tried to win some German territory after Sadowa and that Bismarck evaded his importunities. In order to make up for the loss of prestige that he had suffered as a consequence of Sadowa and presently by his Mexican adventures, Napoleon turned to Belgium and Luxembourg as possible objects of French expansion. Bismarck had actually encouraged him in this direction. Obviously the acquisition of Belgium would have brought France into direct conflict with England, and consequently Napoleon finally chose Luxembourg as his object of annexation.

[4] See p. 188.

✑ Luxembourg Crisis

THE POSITION OF LUXEMBOURG was highly complex. It had been a member of the Germanic Confederation, and the city of Luxembourg had been a confederate fortress, with Prussia maintaining a garrison there. Luxembourg was also a member of the German Customs Union. But the king of the Netherlands was the grand duke of Luxembourg, and the Treaty of Prague had stipulated that the possessions of the Netherlands were not to be included in the North German Confederation. Thus the status of Luxembourg had become most precarious. If Napoleon had taken possession of Luxembourg immediately after the Treaty of Prague, nothing probably would have happened. But by the spring of 1867 German nationalist feeling had risen, and Bismarck, having established the North German Confederation, was intent on taking a stronger position. Napoleon negotiated with King William III of the Netherlands about the sale of Luxembourg. The latter would have liked to take French money and to get rid of the embarrassments resulting from the personal union of Luxembourg and the Netherlands, but he did not dare create a *fait accompli* without the knowledge of the Prussian government. Over the objections of the French he consulted Berlin. Thereby Bismarck found himself in a situation that demanded from him an active and open cooperation in the alienation of a land considered by the Germans a part of Germany. He now decided to place himself on the side of German national sentiment. He needed its support just in these weeks for the completion of the North German constitution and the consolidation of the military alliances with the South German states. On April 3, 1867, he advised the Dutch king not to go through with the sale, since in view of the public agitation war was practically inevitable if Luxembourg were ceded to France.

Napoleon could not bow to this challenge, and for over two weeks war seemed imminent. But Napoleon was aware of the unprepared state of the French army, while Bismarck did not overlook the fact that a war over a country declared by him ineligible for the North German Confederation could not easily be justified. He rejected Moltke's argument that war with France was inevitable before long and that it should be fought now while Germany enjoyed military superiority. After the North German constitution had been finally passed, he accepted a Russian compromise proposal that, at a diplomatic conference of the great powers held in London in early May 1867, became the final settlement. Under its terms the Prussian garrison was withdrawn from Luxembourg, whose fortifications were dismantled. The independence of the grand duchy was placed under a rather loosely formulated common guarantee of the great powers. Luxembourg remained a member of the Prusso-German Customs Union.

On balance, the final outcome of the Luxembourg crisis was a thinly veiled diplomatic defeat of Napoleon. The French emperor turned immediately to a reform of the army, which received new arms during the next years. At the same time, he attempted to build up alliances with which to enforce Prussia's respect for the separate existence of the South German states. Austria and Italy were to be activated for these aims. But Italy had no good reason to help in obstructing German national unification unless such policy would have completed her own national union. Apart from claims that Italy still held against Austria, her chief desire was that of winning Rome. This demand, however, Napoleon could not fulfill, because it would have meant the loss of support for his regime by the clerical groups. But Napoleon did not find even an alliance with Austria to be an easy matter. For Austria, an alliance with France was not the right means to win popular sympathies in Germany, not even among many South German particularists and, for that matter, not even among the Germans in Austria. The Hungarians, on their part, did not want to see the Danube monarchy involved in the problems of the Rhine and wished for French support against Russia in the Balkans. The secret tripartite treaty that in May 1869 had reached a final draft stage was never signed. The emperors merely exchanged personal letters which were not of a binding nature, although Napoleon apparently thereafter believed that he could count on Austria.

It is highly doubtful that Bismarck saw in these efforts a grave threat to the North German Confederation. Prusso-Russian relations had developed very favorably in 1867–68, largely owing to Austro-Russian conflicts over Balkan problems. Bismarck did not accept the Russian proposal of a bilateral alliance in March 1868 but reached an informal understanding with the czar about mutual support in case either of them were attacked by two powers. But the lively diplomatic exchange between France, Austria, and Italy threw a shadow over the Continent that encouraged all the forces opposed to Prussia, or at least to any further progress of German unification under Prussian leadership. Obviously the South German particularists found added confidence in the pulling together of the three powers, although even in the case of the Bavarian clericals the participation of antipapal Italy caused some confusion. This effect of the French diplomatic activity induced Bismarck to lay his own political mines against France. Events in Spain offered such an opportunity.

✐ The Spanish Throne Candidacy

IN 1868 THE CONSERVATIVE GROUPS in Spain, under the leadership of the army, had driven the dissolute Queen Isabella into exile. Thereafter a search for a suitable candidate for the Spanish throne had begun, and the

Spaniards finally had become most interested in Prince Leopold of Hohenzollern-Sigmaringen. When its cousins had risen in the late Middle Ages to become Franconian and Brandenburg rulers, the Sigmaringen line of the Hohenzollern had remained in Swabia. Its members had remained Roman Catholics and built up a small principality that was even accepted into Napoleon's Rhenish Confederation and subsequently into the Germanic Confederation. In 1849, however, the ruling Prince Karl Anton had turned over the government of his territory to Prussia. Thereafter the Sigmaringen Hohenzollern were counted as members of the royal Prussian house. Prince Karl Anton was Prussian prime minister during the New Era, while his sons, Leopold and Charles, served as officers in the Prussian army.

Leopold's younger brother, Prince Charles, had become the ruler of Rumania with Napoleon's approval and assistance. Through his mother, a Murat, Leopold was a distant relative of Napoleon, and he was married to a Portuguese princess. These qualities made the Spanish supporters of his candidacy hope that it would eventually not be opposed by Napoleon. But the simplest method of probing the French emperor's attitude, consultation, was deliberately avoided. It is true, however, that after the introduction of constitutional forms of government French policy in such matters was no longer in the hands of Napoleon. With the establishment of the *empire libérale* French public opinion exercised a much greater influence on governmental action.

The first official contacts between the Spanish government of Marshal Prim and Prince Leopold of Hohenzollern-Sigmaringen occurred in February. By this time Bismarck had already been very active in bringing about the acceptance of the throne by the prince. But in spite of Bismarck's pleading King William refused to favor the project, let alone to direct Prince Leopold to proceed with the negotiations, while the latter made his acceptance conditional on such specific orders. Bismarck, however, let Marshal Prim know that this refusal should not be considered final and sent out missions who were to bring back reports that would convince Prince Leopold that Spain's internal conditions would not offer serious obstacles to a new monarchical regime. In June the Spaniards approached Prince Leopold again and on June 19, 1870, he accepted in principle. The determined attitude of the prince induced King William to approve his candidacy.

Bismarck was admittedly responsible for bringing about the renewed Spanish offer as well as its acceptance. No adequate evidence has been produced that he initiated these actions in order to start a fire that would end in war between France and Prussia. But the Spanish candidacy was a move designed to harass Napoleon, and Bismarck was fully aware that it would engender great political tension. With a Hohenzollern on the Spanish throne, he expected that in times of international crisis at least some French military forces would be tied down at the Pyrenees. Obviously Bismarck foresaw that the French would resist the establishment of a Hohenzollern prince in Madrid, but apparently he expected to defeat any French countermove by keeping his own activities a complete secret and by declaring King William's approval of Prince Leopold's candidacy as merely a personal affair of the family head. Since the election by the Spanish Cortes would be the first announcement of the transaction, the French would be forced to challenge the right of the Spanish nation to order its internal affairs according to its own wishes. Bismarck seems to have hoped that the French would be compelled to abandon any ideas of intervention in Spain. Whether he expected that such a setback would lead to serious internal convulsions in France cannot be clearly proven but only surmised.

On July 2 the Spanish cabinet announced the candidacy of Prince Leopold and an early convention of the Cortes for his election. The news caused great irritation in France. Since Bismarck's direct contacts with Spain had not remained unknown, the French government and public at once suspected a Prussian plot against the security of France's southern frontier. The statement of the Prussian foreign office—that the Prussian government had nothing to do with the candidacy and that King William had given his permission not as king but only as the head of the house of Hohenzollern—could only be taken as a rather brazen form of evasion and added fuel to the French agitation. The French chamber fanned the national excitement, and on July 5 the French foreign minister, the Duke of Gramont, expressed in threatening language the opposition of France to the establishment of a German prince "on the throne of Charles V."

Since in the absence of Bismarck from Berlin the French government could not hope to get any satisfaction from negotiations with Berlin, it sent its ambassador, Count Benedetti, to Bad Ems, where King William was taking the waters. Between July 9 and 13 William I had four meetings with the French ambassador. William most readily admitted that he had approved of the prince's actions and that he could not reverse his attitude, whereas he would not raise any objections if the prince were to change his mind voluntarily. Actually, the king was frightened lest the matter of the Spanish throne candidacy that he had never particularly liked might become the cause of war. Since Prince Leopold, vacationing in Switzerland, was out of reach, William I persuaded Leopold's father, Prince Karl Anton, to renounce the candidacy of his son. On July 12, Karl Anton informed both Madrid and Paris of his son's resignation. Naturally Paris remained somewhat skeptical whether this announcement fully expressed Prince Leopold's intentions. But at the same time the

French government wished to exploit the apparent Prussian retreat for a demonstration of French superior strength. Benedetti was instructed to request from William I a statement that he not only approved of Leopold's resignation but also would not tolerate any future candidacy of the prince.

When Benedetti approached William I in Ems on July 13 with this demand, the king declared his willingness to express his approval of the prince's resignation but refused to assume a guarantee for the future. However, he indicated in the conversation, which was conducted on both sides in a polite manner, that he might wish to see the ambassador once more after receiving word from Karl Anton concerning the prince's resignation, about which so far he had only read in the papers. After the communication from Sigmaringen was received, the king informed Benedetti through his aide that he approved the resignation but having nothing else to add saw no point in another meeting. The king was far from any intention to cold-shoulder the French diplomat, with whom he exchanged friendly words at the railroad station when he left Ems on the next day. The afternoon message of July 13 was partly motivated by the information about Bismarck's attitude that had reached the king after his morning's meeting with Benedetti.

Bismarck was sojourning at his Pomeranian estate of Varzin when the news of Leopold's candidacy broke in Madrid. He was greatly irritated by the threatening language that the Duke of Gramont used in the French chamber debate. He wanted to avoid anything that might make it look as if Prussia were retreating under French pressure. Obviously he was especially afraid of the impression made by such an event on the South German states, in which the particularist forces lately had made great progress. As all his moves showed in these days, Bismarck was determined to meet the French threat without giving ground, even if this meant war. But William I ruined Bismarck's policy through his conversations with Count Benedetti and by his entreaties with the Sigmaringen Hohenzollern to abandon the Spanish candidacy. Bismarck decided to go to Ems in order to make his policy prevail. If he failed to convince the king, he intended to resign. Upon his arrival in Berlin, however, he learned of Prince Leopold's resignation and decided against proceeding to Ems, since he felt that he had lost his fight.

✑ *The Ems Dispatch*

BUT BISMARCK WAS NOT THE MAN to resign fast. Through the minister of the interior, Count Eulenburg, the king was informed about the chancellor's angry reactions to the developments in Ems and Sigmaringen. Count Eulenburg saw the king shortly after William's meeting with Benedetti, and his report had a certain influence on the king's decision not to see Benedetti again. The member of the foreign office in the king's entourage wrote a dispatch to Bismarck reporting the events of the day precisely and correctly. The telegram added that the king left it to Bismarck's discretion whether or not "Benedetti's new demand and its rejection" should be at once communicated to the Prussian ambassadors and to the press.

When this "Ems dispatch" of July 13, 1870, arrived, Bismarck had dinner with Moltke and Roon. They were depressed by the king's conciliatory attitude that seemed to have helped the French to a diplomatic triumph. But the communication that Bismarck drafted for the press and the Prussian foreign minister restored the mood of the party by its challenging tone. He took advantage of the importunity of the French demand that the king should promise not to permit a Hohenzollern candidacy in the future. By leaving out all other exchanges between the king and Benedetti and only reporting that the king had "thereupon" declined to see the ambassador again and had subsequently informed him through his military aide that he had nothing further to tell him, the impression was created that the offensive French diplomacy had brought Franco-Prussian relations close to a rupture. Bismarck's press release was a grave misrepresentation of the actual events. On the other hand, French policy had aimed at cornering Bismarck and humbling Prussia under the threat of war.

After intensive deliberations the French government had decided that the results of Benedetti's conversations with William I were substantial enough to allow them the announcement to the chamber that as in 1866, when it stopped Prussia on the Main river, the French Empire had again demonstrated that it exercised a dominant influence on the Continent. But the gauntlet thrown down by Bismarck made such a declaration impossible. In the eyes of the world acceptance of peace would have appeared as the acceptance of an insult and would have greatly weakened Napoleon's position within France. He had particular reasons to be concerned about the attitude of the army. While the plebiscite held in the spring of 1870 to approve the constitutional changes establishing the *empire libérale* had given Napoleon strong endorsement, the many dissenting votes from among the army had been disconcerting. On the other hand, the French government felt powerful with regard to both the military strength of the army and its international relations. It counted not only on Austria but also on the neutrality of the South German states, for it thought that the Spanish issue would give the South German governments a perfect excuse for declaring the defensive alliances of 1866–67 inapplicable. These considerations induced the French government to declare war on Prussia.

∽ Declaration of War

THERE CANNOT be any doubt that on that evening of July 13, 1870, Bismarck knew that his press release would precipitate this French reaction. Actually, he wanted this result, since he judged that a serious diplomatic setback would gravely impair the chances of the ultimate consummation of German unification. The trend toward this goal had been lessening for some time. Nothing could galvanize the national movement in South Germany more effectively than a threat or a slight from France.

Bismarck's political judgment proved absolutely right. When the Bavarian government of Count Bray made a lame attempt to evade the obligations of the alliance with Prussia, it was quickly shown that such a policy could not be conducted in the face of the passionate anti-French sentiment of the people. Bismarck was also correct in his appraisal of the international situation. He rightly assumed not only that the South Germans would fight on the side of Prussia but also that Austria-Hungary would stay out of the war on account of both divided counsel at home and Russia's attitude. Moreover, he accurately guessed that the general international reaction to the diplomatic events would be favorable to Prussia. The Prussian king had shown great patience with French impetuosity, and only the impertinence of the French in demanding a promise of the Prussian king for the future had brought on the break in Franco-German relations. But there were other influences as well. The British resented Napoleon's imperialistic activities both in the western hemisphere and in the Levant and had always liked the idea of German unification under Protestant Prussian auspices.

Thus on the French as well as on the Prussian side international and national reasons caused the bloodiest European war of the nineteenth century, a war that was to lead to German national unification but at the some time create unresolved tensions from which Europe never recovered. When on July 19, 1870, the French declared war, they were not aware of the speed of the German military mobilization. They were misled by the long delay in the opening of hostilities in 1866. This, however, had been caused not by technical difficulties but by the protracted political struggle between Bismarck and William I. The French armies were still assembling in the interior of France when the German armies were taking the offensive from the Saar district and the Palatinate. The French army that had been tested in the Crimean and Italian wars of the 1850's was practically a professional army. On the average, every soldier in the army of the Second Empire had served for seven years, whereas the Prussian soldiers had spent no more than two and a half years in military service. Still, in numbers the German troops were greatly superior to the French army. The French used outmoded cavalry tactics, and their artillery was still fighting Krupp's breech-loading guns with muzzle-loading. But in their *mitrailleuses* they possessed an early machine-gun, and their infantry was equipped with the *chassepôt* rifle that was vastly better than the Prussian needle gun.

✍ *War Against the French Empire*

ON BALANCE it must be said that numbers and strategy decided the first part of the Franco-Prussian war. Although Moltke's authority was now more readily accepted than in 1866, some actions taken by individual army commanders frustrated his original strategic plan that had envisaged a decisive general battle of the Sadowa type to be fought in the very first weeks of the campaign. But the early successes of the German armies were of some consequence. They were gained against the army of Mac-Mahon in northern Alsace and in Lorraine against the strongest French army, originally commanded by Napoleon but soon turned over to François Achille Bazaine. These early German victories thwarted any chance of a French offensive into Germany and thereby contributed to Austria-Hungary's decision to stay neutral. In addition, the frontier battles confounded the confidence of the French military leaders. Mac-Mahon's army had not even reached full readiness when it was bruised by the army of the Prussian crown prince. MacMahon took his army back to Châlons in order to build up its strength.

Bazaine's army fell back toward Metz followed by the Germans, who took the bold step of crossing the Moselle south of Metz, thereby threatening Bazaine's lines of communication with the interior of France. On August 16–18, murderous battles were fought with reversed fronts—the Germans facing east—at Mars-la-Tour and Vionville on the 16th and at St. Privat and Gravelotte on the 18th. For a long time the outcome of the bitter fighting hung in the balance. King William's temporary interference in the command as well as the pigheadedness of one of the army commanders led to critical moments. The decision fell on August 18, when Crown Prince Albert of Saxony succeeded in moving his Saxon army corps into the northern flank of the French lines. The French were forced to retreat to the fortress of Metz, to which large German troops under the command of Prince Frederick Charles of Prussia laid siege.

Two German armies under the command of the crown prince of Prussia and the crown prince of Saxony marched toward the Champagne, where they expected to meet MacMahon in battle. But in the meantime MacMahon had turned north with the intention of bypassing the German armies and reaching Metz from the northwest, thus lifting the German siege. The Germans discovered MacMahon's operations in time to follow him north. While the French were hampered in their opportunities for maneuver by the Belgian frontier, Moltke was able to force MacMahon to accept battle at Sedan on September 1, 1870. The Germans threw an iron ring around the old fortress town, and, in spite of the brave fighting of the French troops, the encirclement was not broken. On September 2 MacMahon's army and with it Emperor Napoleon had to surrender. To the vast majority of the German people this brilliant victory seemed a full justification of the Prussian military system and of Prussian leadership, under which Germans from every part of the nation had fought. This national union, it was now generally argued, had finally succeeded in avenging the indignities which Louis XIV and the two Napoleons had inflicted upon Germany in the past.

✑ *War Against the French Republic*

THERE WAS great patriotic rejoicing in all of Germany. Popular pressure on the governments increased for the completion of German national unification in an empire that would include the southern German states. But national pride demanded also external satisfaction in the form of the return of Alsace to Germany. Bismarck, and even more so Moltke, were convinced that as a result of the war Germany's frontier on the upper Rhine should be moved westward. However, the republican "government of national defense" that was formed in Paris on September 4 under General Trochu, with Léon Gambetta and Jules Favre as ministers of the interior and of foreign affairs, rejected any such concessions, and on this issue had the support of the whole French nation. Thus the war continued for five more months after the debacle of the second French empire.

Since the French imperial army had been largely professional in character, only a relatively small segment of the manpower of France had been mobilized. Yet the American Civil War seemed to have demonstrated that great armies could be created without a large officer corps and other professionals. Actually, the provisional French government succeeded in conscripting 600,000 men, whose military quality, however, was very uneven. Their arms and equipment—much of it hurriedly bought in England and in the United States—were of motley character. Still, as these French armies sprang up in the southern and western provinces, they posed a serious threat to the Germans in France. The Prussian army reform of William I and Roon, with its neglect of the training of the national guard and of the formation of a large pool of reserve officers, had not provided for an easy wartime expansion of the Prussian army. The army of 1870 consisted of young conscripts intensively trained by a professional officer corps predominantly composed of noblemen. Therefore, it was difficult to strengthen the German field forces greatly.

The German armies which had fought at Sedan arrived near Paris on September 19 but were not sufficiently strong to lay the great French metropolis under an effective siege. The fall of Metz and the capture of Marshal Bazaine's army on October 3 freed the troops of Prince Frederick Charles. Soon, however, some of these troops had to be detailed for fighting in the provinces. Moltke saw no way of conquering Paris quickly. Storming the city would have meant ghastly losses without the guarantee of victory. A bombardment of the city that Bismarck demanded was unlikely to produce results as long as the German army had few siege guns, while many weeks were needed in order to bring a substantial number of them from Germany. In these circumstances the starving of the French metropolis proved to be the chief weapon. Bismarck was greatly alarmed by the slowness of the military operations and by the danger of growing national resistance in France. In this respect, too, the generals seemed to Bismarck lacking in determination. Occasionally he demanded the use of terroristic methods as the best means to keep Frenchmen from following a handful of ambitious political hotheads. It was a strange misreading of the patriotism of the French people and their leaders.

Actually, Bismarck was only too willing to respect French national pride and the rules of humanity, provided he could find a French government prepared to accept an early peace that would include the cession of territories on the Rhine. For a while he pondered the possibility of using Napoleon III or Marshal Bazaine for this end. But these vague ideas led nowhere and left Bismarck with the continuing fear of a war of indefinite duration that might give the great neutral powers the chance to intervene and to bring the question of a Franco-German peace settlement before their forum. Therefore he redoubled his efforts to gain influence on the military planning of the war. But here he found himself the captive of his own previous policies. In the Prussian constitutional conflict he had vigorously defended the exclusive command authority of the king in all army affairs. As a consequence, he himself, as the Prussian prime minister and federal chancellor, had no power over the army.

✍ *Conflict Between Moltke and Bismarck*

MOLTKE CONSIDERED himself to be the guardian of the Prussian army tradition and the exclusive military advisor of the king and the prime minister, the king's highest political councillor. Moltke claimed that for the conduct of war military objectives must prevail over political considerations. He admitted that the decision on when to begin a war belonged to the statesman and that the latter would have to conclude the peace, but only after the success or failure of the war had been settled by the military. Moltke defined success as the achievement of the highest aim that the existing military means permitted. In the case of the present war with France this meant the capture of all French armed forces and the complete occupation of France. He judged that an absolute defeat of France was within reach and that only such an absolute defeat would remove future French threats to Germany.

Moltke, who had learned most of his strategy from Clausewitz, had failed to grasp firmly the latter's fundamental teaching that war is an act of politics and that military strategy should at all times remain subordinate to the aims of policy. By conceiving of war as a duel of two armies fought in a professional fashion Moltke saw no need for close political consultation, let alone the statesman's direction of the war. He did not recognize that by demanding a free hand for the achievement of total victory he imposed on the state a policy that was difficult to conduct and, even if successful, unlikely to have lasting results. Moltke had to admit that total victory could not be gained quickly. But in these circumstances would the European powers look on impassively or might they not intervene? On the other hand, assuming that the German armies would accomplish the complete occupation of France after the disposal of all the French armed forces, with whom was Germany to conclude a peace? And after such a humiliation would not the French nation concentrate all its energies on the reversal of its political fortunes?

Although Bismarck at times carried his criticism of the military operations into matters which were not germane to statesmanship, his demand for the subordination of the military command to the general policy of the state was well justified. Although conflicts between military and civilian leaders over war policies have happened under any system of government, they were most difficult to resolve in a monarchy that rested so largely on the army. Naturally the king would be inclined to side with the generals, particularly at times when by great victories the army seemed to have proved its excellence in action. The struggle between Bismarck and Moltke in 1870–71 was a warning of a structural weakness in Bismarck's state that forty-five years later contributed greatly to its downfall.

Yet in 1870–71 the statesman's will power proved far superior to that of the military commander. Moltke's calm genius did not desire personal power, while his sense of duty made it impossible for him to rebel against a decision made by the king. William I was deeply torn by the conflicting advice he received, but it was difficult for him to resist the passionate pleading of his prime minister, who had safely guided him through many a frightening political crisis. Thus in the middle of January 1871 Bismarck could even assume the negotiations over the surrender of Paris. In contrast to Moltke, who wished to impose a tough "capitulation" on the enemy, the chancellor concluded a "convention" that tried hard to avoid anything that looked like retribution. The city of Paris was not even occupied by German troops during the suspension of hostilities that was signed on January 28, 1871. It was Bismarck's chief desire to promote the formation of a French government willing to conclude a peace. The convention of January 28 had provided for early general elections of a French national assembly that could represent France in peace negotiations with Germany. On February 13 the national assembly convened in Bordeaux and appointed a provisional government headed by Adolphe Thiers. A week later Adolphe Thiers and Jules Favre arrived in Versailles in order to open the discussion of a preliminary peace treaty.

✑ *Peace Negotiations*

THE NEW FRENCH GOVERNMENT found itself completely isolated on the international plane. All over Europe popular sympathies were with France, particularly after the fall of the French Empire, and no single government, including Russia, approved of the German war aims. But the age of the Concert of Europe was over. The Franco-German frontier, which the Congress of Vienna had considered of fundamental importance for the maintenance of the peace of Europe, was now left to the dictate of a single power. The Austrian prime minister, Count Beust, had been busy after the battle of Sedan trying to build up a front of neutral powers which might mediate between France and Germany for the conclusion of an armistice and subsequent peace. Russia, however, refused to participate in such moves. Instead, the Russian government, encouraged by Bismarck, decided to free itself of the most resented obligation that the peace of Paris of 1856 had imposed on Russia. On November 9, 1870, it renounced the so-called "Pontus clause" that forbade Russia the maintenance of naval forces on the Black Sea. This breach of international law caused profound resentment in England not only against Russia but also against Germany, which, with good reason, was suspected of being an accomplice. But England was not inclined to go to war. Even if allied with Austria, where temporarily at least bellicose elements seemed in the ascendancy, she considered the chances of a war against Russia rather dim. The British government eventually was gratified that Russia accepted Bismarck's suggestion to have the Pontus clause formally annulled by a conference of the signatories of the Paris treaty. Such a conference convened in London in January 1871. France's hope to gain admission to it and to plead her own case before the powers of Europe was frustrated by Russia and Prussia. The French representatives were admitted only in March, that is, after the signing of the preliminary peace treaty between Germany and France.

In the negotiations between Bismarck on the one side and Adolphe Thiers and Jules Favre on the other held in Versailles in the last week of February the German chancellor presented as the German demands the cession of Alsace with Strasbourg and of a group of German-speaking districts of Lorraine as well as the big fortress of Metz in the midst of a large French-speaking region. Besides, Bismarck demanded the cession of the fortress of Belfort, which dominated the Burgundian gate between the mountains of the Vosges and the Swiss Jura, and the payment of an indemnity of 6 billion French francs ($1.2 billion).

There was more doubt and less self-assurance in Bismarck's approach to the settlement with France than he had shown in his peacemaking with Austria. In 1866 he had been determined to achieve a peace that would assure reconciliation and future cooperation with Austria. In 1870–71, too, we can see him endeavoring to avoid a victor's peace. Further conditions that Moltke would have liked to impose, such as limitations on the strength of the French army or the dismantling of the system of French fortifications, were not accepted by Bismarck. Still, the peace that France had to sign blocked the restoration of friendly relations between France and Germany for the foreseeable future, and Bismarck was fully aware of the grave consequences.

✍ *Annexation of Alsace-Lorraine*

BISMARCK WAS NOT DISPLEASED with the general popular outcry for the annexation of Alsace-Lorraine which he had first elicited and then helped to fan. Through police measures he did his best to quiet the voices, particularly of German socialists and democrats, raised in warning against annexations. Yet Bismarck did not share the motivations and expectations which prompted an excited public opinion to urge the recovery of the old German lands. The German nationalists who now set the tone insisted on the acquisition of Alsace-Lorraine because their inhabitants were German by race and language. The argument that the people of Alsace and Lorraine were happy and loyal French citizens was easily swept aside. Once Alsace-Lorraine had been brought back to Germany, it was reasoned, the hearts of the Alsatians would soon begin to beat in the same rhythm as those of the Germans now united in a single national state. It had also become fashionable in Germany to think of the French as a physically and morally decadent nation. Heinrich von Treitschke hysterically concluded: "The domination of a German tribe by Frenchmen has always been an unhealthy condition; today it is a crime against the reason of history, a subjugation of free men by half-educated barbarians," and "We Germans who know Germany know better what is good for the Alsatians than these unfortunate people themselves, who, warped by their French life, have remained without honest knowledge of the new Germany. We want to give them back their own self against their will." This was the language of a nationalism in which a vulgarized Hegelian philosophy was mixed with an ill-applied Darwinism.

Bismarck did not believe in national self-determination. He was also skeptical whether the inhabitants of this Upper-Rhenish region, which from the days of the first Napoleon France had developed into one of the most prosperous regions of the Continent, could easily be turned into contented German subjects. In 1871 Alsace was a more fully modernized land than Baden on the opposite bank of the Rhine or for that matter any province of Germany. Moreover, Alsatians played an important role in the public and cultural life of France. Obviously, Bismarck was conscious of these facts. His decision to change the frontiers of 1815 was based on strategic considerations. The annexation of Strasbourg and of Alsace appeared to him necessary in order to enhance the security of southern Germany and make any French pressure on the South German states impossible.

This intention might have been satisfied by the annexation of the German-speaking regions on the left bank of the Rhine. Although in view of the evident attitude of the Alsatians this move would not have been a fulfillment of national self-determination, it would have been taken by the world as an indication that Germany wanted to complete her national unification rather than gain a position of permanent strategic superiority over France. Actually Bismarck hesitated to go beyond the annexation of the German-speaking districts, but, having won his feud with the army in political matters, he was inclined to give more weight to Moltke's military recommendations. He himself was convinced that the French would in any event, and most certainly after the cession of Alsace, try to undo the results of the present war. In this case the acquisition of a strong military frontier seemed an overriding consideration. Moltke assigned great significance to the possession of Belfort and an even more crucial importance to Metz. Somewhat reluctantly, Bismarck accepted the accession of Belfort and Metz in his original peace program, but he took half a step back when he dropped the demand for Belfort in his negotiations with Thiers and Favre. Even in his later life Bismarck was never quite convinced that the seizure of Metz had been a wise decision. At the time, he, too, was affected by the bellicose nationalism that both the German and French people had shown during the war. The peace that he concluded failed to attempt to exorcise the evil spirit of this nationalism and thus contributed markedly to its further spread in the coming age.

The preliminary peace treaty, signed on February 26, contained a further concession. The French war indemnity was lowered from 6 to 5 billion francs ($1 billion). The timetable of French payments, which was to be synchronized with the withdrawal of German troops from France, as well as the exact delineation and the methods of surrender of the ceded territories were left to future negotiations. These problems were finally settled in the peace treaty of Frankfurt, which Bismarck and Jules Favre drafted in the first days of May 1871. In the final treaty France received a stronger military frontier around Belfort than had been contemplated in the preliminary peace, while Germany got some additional districts which happened to be rich in iron mines.

✺ *National Unification of Germany*

A NEW GERMANY had already come into being before the negotiations over the French peace treaties had started. The prompt succor of the South German states at the time of the outbreak of the war as well as the early victories of armies combining troops from all German states had brought an upsurge of popular demands for the completion of national unification. The shift of sentiment was particularly startling among the democrats of South Germany, whose Great German sympathies suddenly faded and who placed their democratic ideals second to their wishes for national unification, even if this meant the acceptance of Prussian leadership. But also the liberals in North and South Germany redoubled their national agitation. Their position was strongest in Baden. Grand Duke Frederick I, William I's brother-in-law, and his liberal government had sought admission to the North German Confederation as early as 1867, and Frederick was most active in 1870–71 in his endeavor not only to join Baden with northern Germany but also to assist Bismarck in overcoming the obstacles that were raised against the speedy achievement of the union of all the German states.

The opposition centered around the South German courts and, at least in the case of Bavaria, had considerable popular support. In Bavaria the liberal and national movements were strong only in the cities and in the Protestant regions of Central Franconia and the Rhenish Palatinate, while the rural areas, particularly those of the historic Bavaria, still cultivated their separate character and found their political representation in the clerical party. In Württemberg King Karl and even more Queen Olga disliked the diminution of sovereignty that a German federal state would entail. But they had little popular backing for such a policy. The grand duke of Hesse-Darmstadt, who, prior to 1870, had not hesitated to recommend himself to the French as an ally, was the most resentful of all the German princes, and he comforted himself with the thought that the new order would not last very long. But with one half of his country, Upper Hesse, already included in the North German Confederation and with the people strongly in favor of national union, he had no other choice left.

Bismarck was most anxious to accomplish the founding of a German federal state without further delay. He wished to take advantage of the high tide of national enthusiasm in order to win general cooperation. In the creation of such a state he also saw an immediate strengthening of Germany's international position. He refused to reopen the problems which had been settled in 1866–67 and to dissolve the North German Confederation in order to found a new German state. Such a procedure would have been time consuming and politically risky. It would have demanded negotiations with many governments and would also have given the political parties a chance to launch lengthy debates. A good many Prussian conservatives were worried that if expanded into a German parliament by the accession of the South Germans, the North German parliament would assume a rather democratic complexion. Therefore, they proposed the creation of an upper chamber composed of the German princes and governments. This idea had its champions among the South German governments as well, and also in Saxony. With the joining of the South German states the Saxon government hoped for the construction of a federal state in which the medium-sized states would exercise greater influence than Saxony possessed in the North German Confederation.

But Bismarck categorically rejected any talk about a new constitution and insisted that only an expansion of the North German Confederation was under consideration. He was careful, however, to avoid the appearance of dictating to the South German states. Quite wisely he argued that if they were to become loyal and contented members of the new federal state, they should be under the impression of having joined on their own volition. But the South German governments knew well that Prussia had the power of enjoining the accession of the South German states at a later date. The Prusso-German Customs Union had to be renewed in 1876, and it would have been easy for the Prussian government to deny the renewal of the customs union to a state by then outside of the German federal state. Not even Bavaria could have faced such an economic isolation, particularly since the Rhenish Palatinate was physically separated from Bavaria. Moreover, membership in the customs union had always been financially profitable.

ᴗᴏ *The November Treaties*

THE BAVARIAN PRIME MINISTER, Count Bray-Steinburg, was not in favor of German unification, and he was fully aware of how sensitive King Ludwig was to any loss of independence. Even during these weeks the king removed himself from regular meetings with his ministers, who were not quite united among themselves. In spite of his misgivings, Count Bray-

Steinburg felt it imperative to take the initiative in the unification issue. But his expectations as to the concessions that Bismarck would make in answer to such a move were highly unrealistic. Bray-Steinburg still did not give up the idea of gaining something like equality for Bavaria. The project of a separate South German federation related by loose ties to the North German Confederation was broached again. Prior to 1870 Bismarck might have accepted the offer of such loose ties between Bavaria and the North, but times and conditions had changed, and Bismarck was absolutely opposed to anything that might have led to a new dualism after the Austro-Prussian dualism had just been buried. For the same reason he declined a little later such proposals as Bavarian participation in the direction of foreign policy or the alternation of the office of emperor between the Prussian and Bavarian kings.

The rulers of both Bavaria and Württemberg strangely misread the signs of the time when they thought it possible to use the occasion for grabbing territories, as the princes of the Rhenish Confederation had done under Napoleon's auspices. Bavaria wanted a corridor through North Baden connecting the Rhenish Palatinate with Bavaria proper. Württemberg coveted the Prussian Hohenzollern. They suggested that in exchange Prussia and Baden should take some Alsatian territories. While there was no good reason why the grand duke of Baden or the Prussian king should give away lands and people well satisfied under their rule, there were even less grounds for carving up Alsace for the benefit of two South German states. Alsace-Lorraine had been won as the result of the common military efforts of all the German states. Bismarck had made up his mind that Alsace-Lorraine was to become a *Reichsland* or federal territory.

In these circumstances the two South German kingdoms could only bargain with Bismarck for a maximum of exemptions and special rights. Since Bavaria was convinced that more was due to her than to any other state, she did not coordinate her diplomatic steps with Württemberg, let alone with the other South German states. Bismarck on his part found it most practical to conduct separate negotiations with each state, although, from late October on, representatives of all these states were present in Versailles. The treaties with Baden and Hesse-Darmstadt were signed on November 15, and also the treaty with Württemberg was ready, when a court intrigue delayed the signing. Thus the treaty with Bavaria, though the most difficult one to achieve, was concluded on November 23, two days ahead of the treaty with Württemberg.

∾ *The Constitution of 1871*

THE CHIEF IMPACT of the November treaties on the North German constitution of 1867 was the strengthening of the federal elements at the expense of certain unitarian arrangements. Whereas under the constitution of 1867 the president was empowered to declare war, the constitution of 1871 required the approval of the Federal Council "unless there is an attack upon the federal lands or coasts." Still more important, the authority of the president to supervise the execution of federal laws and to initiate action against recalcitrant member states was made dependent on the consent of the Federal Council. And in the new Federal Council the position of Prussia was considerably weakened. Fifteen new votes were added to the forty-three of the North German council. Any change of constitution, it was furthermore stipulated, could be defeated by fourteen votes. This gave the three kingdoms—Bavaria with six votes, Württemberg and Saxony with four each—a veto if they agreed among themselves, and the same applied to the South German states, with Baden and Hesse-Darmstadt taking the place of Saxony in that case. It is true, however, that Prussia, with her seventeen votes out of a total of fifty-eight, retained an absolute veto on any constitutional amendment.

The federative character of the new confederation was particularly emphasized by the departure from the principle of equality of all member states and the grant of a number of special rights to individual states. Some of them were rather meaningless from the beginning, such as the provision that the Bavarian representative should act as chairman of the Federal Council in case Prussia was unable to preside, or that Bavarian diplomats would substitute for an absent chief of a German diplomatic mission. The important changes lay in the grant of the so-called *Reservatrechte*, i.e., reserved rights. All the South German states were exempted from the federal beer and liquor tax. Bavaria and Württemberg retained their separate railroad, post, and telegraph administration.

In military affairs all the South German states, as before them the North German ones, were committed to accept the Prussian army organization, including length of military service. The annual strength of the army was a matter of federal legislation. But within these limitations Württemberg and Bavaria received special privileges. Although Württemberg's army corps became a part of the Prussian army and its commander, though not its officers, was appointed by the emperor, the army administration was left to a Württemberg war ministry. In Bavaria the command of the two Bavarian army corps remained in peacetime with the Bavarian king, whereas in wartime they came automatically under the command of the emperor, to whom they took an oath expressing this obligation. Even in peacetime, however, the emperor had the right of inspecting the Bavarian troops as to their readiness for war. But Bavaria retained not only her own ministry of war but also her own general staff. A peculiar institution was introduced by Bismarck in order to satisfy Bavaria's demand for participation in the conduct of foreign policy. A foreign affairs committee of the Federal Council was created over which Bavaria was to preside and on which Saxony and Württemberg were permanently represented together with two annually elected states.

The *Reservatrechte* appeared to be a retreat from the building of a strong unitarian government. Actually, however, it did not prove to be of serious consequence. The foreign affairs committee of the Federal Council never gained any influence on the direction of German foreign policy. It was convened only once under Bismarck, in order to receive some confidential information on the Austrian alliance of 1879, and rarely met under his successors. Of all the other special rights only the exemption of the South German states from the beer and liquor tax proved of practical significance, since it raised the position of the individual states in the organization of the federal tax system.[5] Bismarck was right when he judged that these concessions would not stop the integration of all the German states into a single state, while the South German states would join more willingly once they had been assured that the new order would not mean the complete loss of their historic identity. During the negotiations there were even indications that the South German states might find it useful for their own political purposes to extend the scope of the legislative authority of the federal government. The Württemberg government, afraid that it would be incapable of getting a satisfactory regulation of the right of association and of the press from its liberal diet, successfully urged an amendment to the constitution of 1867 through which these subjects were made matters of federal legislation.

✑ Proclamation of the Emperor

YET BISMARCK KNEW of an even better method for insuring German unity. It had been the fondest dream of the national movement to restore a German *Reich* under a *Kaiser*. The Frankfurt National Assembly had vainly attempted to fulfill this dream. In Bismarck's opinion the moment had now arrived when the names *Kaiser* and *Reich* would give his federal state a firm anchorage in the sentimental thinking of the vast majority of the German people and thereby provide a strong momentum for the further growth of German unity. He knew, however, that William I disliked the title that, without giving him any additional power, would only obscure his title of king of Prussia, of which he was inordinately proud. The title of emperor brought to William memories of the revo-

[5] See p. 226.

lution of 1848–49, and if it had been offered to him by the parliament, he would not even have considered it at all. The creation of an emperor through vote of parliament was unfeasible for the additional reason that it would have given the impression that Prussia wanted to coerce the German princes into subordination with the help of democratic forces. Only the offer of the imperial crown by the German princes could sway William I, and the king of Bavaria, as the foremost German prince, seemed the logical figure. Ludwig II, with whom Bismarck negotiated through the king's chief equerry, Count Holstein, was persuaded to write a letter to William I, inviting him to assume the imperial dignity, while at the same time he urged the other German princes to express their consent. Ludwig's letter was actually drafted by Bismarck, who simultaneously accommodated the unhappy king in his desire to indulge in his building mania without being hampered by the Bavarian parliament. In a weird secret deal Bismarck pledged the annual payment of a sum of 300,000 marks to the king. It was actually paid, with Count Holstein acting as secret courier, up to the time of Ludwig II's death in 1886. Apparently Bismarck took the money from the so-called Guelf fund, the great properties of the royal Hanoverian family, which he had sequestered, because George V refused to drop his claims to the throne. Bismarck used the revenues of the great Guelf fortunes for his own secret operations.

There remained the acceptance of the treaties with the South German states by the North German parliament and the South German diets. The National Liberals and Progressives of the North German parliament and even a good many Prussian Conservatives were greatly alarmed by the *Reservatrechte*. But they did not dare block the passage of the treaties and the new constitution, since this would have brought upon them the opprobrium of having been responsible for the failure of the completion of national unification. Although the Bavarian diet would have preferred to reject the November treaty that was considered by the majority an ignominious surrender to Prussia, even in Munich popular pressure was too strong, and the treaty was finally passed with a majority of two votes.

On December 18, 1870, a delegation of the North German parliament appeared before William I in Versailles. It was headed by Eduard Simson, the leader of the group of members of the Frankfurt Assembly that had offered a German crown to Frederick William IV in 1849. Then the crown had been intended to be the gift of the people; this time it was offered by the princes, and the deputies came as suppliants begging the king to accept it. This event symbolized the decline of the power of the democratic and liberal forces in Germany.

To the last moment William I struggled against the assumption of the imperial dignity. When Bismarck told him that in order not to offend the princes he would not be able to call himself "emperor of Germany" or "emperor of the Germans" but only "German emperor," the title seemed to him completely meaningless. Tension between the king and the chancellor reached great heights in the days just before the proclamation. In these days the king suffered, in addition, from the feud between Bismarck and Moltke over the methods for ending the war with France.[6]

On January 18, 1871, the one hundred and seventieth anniversary of the coronation of the first Prussian king, William I was proclaimed German emperor in the hall of mirrors of the Versailles palace. With the massed regimental colors of German troops as a backdrop, surrounded by princes and generals, William I received the acclaim of a large gathering of officers representing all the units of the German army around Paris. *Exercitus facit imperatorem*, the army creates the emperor, the Romans used to say, and the martial show of this day, thereafter annually celebrated in Germany as the birthday of the new *Reich*, could almost appear as a reenactment of ancient events. But while the proclamation ceremony was no election by the legions, it was at least a demonstration that the *Reich*, as the Prussian monarchy before, would give the military element the rank of an elite of the nation. The army guaranteed the actual independence of the crown from the popular will. In the hour of victory over France the majority of the German people had come to accept, or at least condone, the privileged position of the army in state and society.

[6] See p. 218.

The Age of Imperialism, 1871–1945

CHAPTER 6

Bismarck and the Consolidation of the German Empire, 1871–90

∽ Germany and Europe

EVER SINCE A SYSTEM of European powers had come into existence around 1500, the European balance of power had presupposed a division of the Germanic world. Thus, the founding of the modern German Empire was a dramatic change deeply felt all over Europe. It inevitably caused misgivings among the old powers and stimulated their endeavor to build up their strength in order to maintain their stature. The competition among the nations of Europe had become more intense just at a time when the population growth accelerated and the capacity for economic production multiplied. But even in these developments Germany soon took the lead. The population of the German states, later united in the German Empire, had overtaken that of France after the middle of the 1860's; the loss of one and a half million Alsace-Lorraine people to Germany considerably widened the margin, and in the next forty years Germany added 50 per cent to her population, whereas the French population grew only by 10 per cent. The German economy had become as strong as the French by 1870. Here, too, the acquisition of the Alsatian industries and the large French indemnities benefited Germany. Twenty-five years later German industries had almost caught up with those of Great Britain, and before 1914 Germany had become the greatest European industrial nation. Thus it was the new Germany rather than any other country that set the pace for the enormous transformation of European life in the four decades after 1871.

∽ Foreign Reactions to Unification

THE NATIONAL UNIFICATION of Italy and Germany spurred the national movements elsewhere. In the Habsburg empire the Slav nationalities grew increasingly restive under a governmental system that from 1867 on consisted of two centralistic states, each dominated by a single nationality which was a minority among the Slav and other nationalities. Russian popular reaction to the founding of the German Empire was hostile. This anti-German sentiment fanned the Pan-Slav movement into supporting any anti-German activity either within Central Europe or, as in the case of the groups of French people bent on revenge, in Western Europe. The czarist government was still far from identifying itself with the Pan-Slavist aims, although it went as far as adopting a policy of Russification of the foreign nationalities within the Russian empire. This policy particularly undermined the position of the small minority of German and largely aristocratic families which formed the ruling class of the Baltic provinces. From these families an unusually large number of high Russian government officials had been drafted, but after 1871 the number of Germans in court and government positions declined.

Many people suspected that Bismarck would wish to add further lands to the new German Empire. In England fears were expressed that the German-Swiss or the Dutch territories might become objects of a policy of further aggrandizement. But such notions never crossed Bismarck's mind. Nor did he ever contemplate the acquisition of the Baltic provinces of Russia or of the German parts of the Habsburg empire. Although many ties of personal friendship linked him with the Baltic barons, he absolutely refused to raise his voice in St. Petersburg against the policy of Russification conducted by the czarist government in the Baltic provinces. On the contrary, he assured the Russians that Germany was completely disinterested in the fate of the Baltic Germans. His attitude toward the Germans in the Habsburg empire was similar. He once went so far as to remark that if the Austrian provinces would try to force their way into Germany, "he would be capable of opening war—against them!" Bismarck did not want the Austrians in his Empire, because they would greatly strengthen the Roman-Catholic element and necessitate a loosening of the union of the states. In his opinion, the place of the Austrians was where history and geography had put them, in the Danubian world, where they had built an empire that was a necessary pillar of the European order. But southeastern Europe could not be organized along national lines. Bismarck always admonished the Austrians to remain loyal to the Habsburg dynasty and benevolent to the other nationalities.

✍ Bismarck's Foreign Policy

BISMARCK'S FOREIGN POLICY between 1862 and 1871 had aimed at the expansion of Prussian power and had not eschewed bold measures and the risk of war. In the following nineteen years, 1871–90, his fundamental

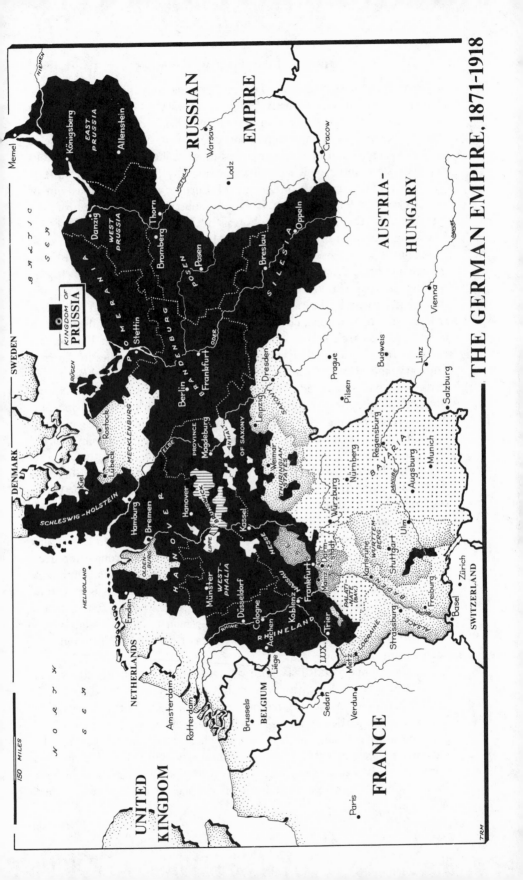

THE GERMAN EMPIRE, 1871-1918

objective was the stabilization of the achievements of the first nine years. Bismarck believed that the early years had given the Germans everything they could hope for and the maximum of what the powers of Europe would tolerate. He had weakened the position of Austria and France as well as enhanced that of Prussia but had most deliberately avoided wrecking the system under which Europe was ruled by five major powers. The continuity of the international order of Europe was a conscious aim of Bismarckian diplomacy, since it would contribute to the security of Germany. In this sense Bismarck was not only a German but also a European statesman in the tradition of Metternich, as he liked to state his rejection of all Great German and Pan-German designs with the Metternichian phrase that "Germany was saturated."

After 1871 Bismarck counted on the lasting enmity of the French and their desire to undo the results of the Franco-German war. It was clear that France had no chance for revenge unless she found allies against Germany. Bismarck favored the survival of the republic in France, because he felt that a republic would be less likely to find allies in Austria-Hungary and Russia. Count Harry Arnim, the German ambassador in Paris, who had supported a monarchical revival and refused to execute Bismarck's policy, experienced the most terrible wrath of the chancellor. The German occupation forces were withdrawn from France in 1873, when Thiers' government managed to pay the full war indemnity earlier than expected.

Yet the danger that France might find allies could be reduced only by winning friends for Germany, preferably as permanent allies. "When there are five, try to be *à trois*." With this remark Bismarck described his desire to enter into an alliance with two of the great European powers. In his view they could be only Russia and Austria-Hungary. Russia had saved Prussia in 1806 and ever thereafter had been its strong supporter. To be sure, she had enabled Austria to triumph over Prussia at Olmütz in 1850, but, then, Prussia had been at fault in 1848–49. Russia's attitude toward Prussia's policy between 1862 and 1871 had been essential to the German successes. For William I, Russo-German relations rested largely on the kinship and friendship of the two dynasties, to which he attached a deep sentimental value.

Bismarck looked at Russia with a much cooler head. He knew that Russia had derived great profits from her relations with Prussia, while in her interventions in the internal and external affairs of the country she had often disregarded Prussia's best interests. He was also aware of the growing anti-German sentiment and of the inclination of the Pan-Slav movement to see in France Russia's natural ally. He believed, quite correctly, that Russian foreign policy was made by the czar, but the very fact that Pan-Slav propaganda went on unchecked made him apprehensive about the future. On the other hand, an alliance of the two monarchies still seemed the best means of making the czar assert his authority against the Pan-Slav movement.

Yet to build German foreign policy on a bilateral alliance with Russia seemed impossible to Bismarck, because it would make Germany wholly dependent on Russian whims. Most immediately, it would encourage Russian expansion in the direction of the Near East, and since Austria-Hungary would oppose this, it would lead to an Austro-Russian war. And Bismarck was as unwilling to tolerate a Russian invasion of Central Europe as Metternich had been. He was prepared to allow Russia considerable gains in the Balkans, as a matter of fact much greater gains than Austria-Hungary thought should be allowed, although he did not want to see the Habsburg monarchy weakened within its frontiers of 1866.

The growing influence of the Magyars in the Habsburg empire after 1867 helped the early *rapprochement* of Germany and Austria-Hungary. The Hungarians were opposed to any renewal of the fight for Austrian leadership of Germany and desired Austro-Hungarian policy to concentrate on guarding against any harmful schemes that Russian diplomacy might advance. Cooperation with the new German Empire was the key to such a policy, since it could be expected to exercise at least a restraining influence on the Russian government.

However, among the Germans of the Habsburg empire the separation from Germany in 1866 was forgotten remarkably soon. Actually, the contacts of the average Austrian with Germany had been rather tenuous in the half-century prior to 1866, and Bismarck had been wise in leaving Austria her historic boundaries.

In December 1871 the Hungarian Count Gyula Andrassy (1823–90) succeeded Count Beust as foreign minister. The following September the three emperors met in Berlin in a demonstration of monarchical solidarity, which in 1873 was reinforced by military conventions. But the Three Emperors' Convention, concluded in order to safeguard and if necessary enforce the European peace "against all disturbances from whatever side they might come," was essentially a personal pledge of the three monarchs to consult with each other. It was not a guarantee pact and in particular did not imply a recognition of the German annexation of Alsace-Lorraine. Yet the cornerstone was laid for a diplomatic relationship that for reasons of foreign as well as domestic politics Bismarck considered the most effective bulwark of German security.

✑ *War Crisis of 1875*

IN MAY 1875, however, Bismarck received an unpleasant jolt. Two months earlier the French chamber had passed an army law that was intended to enable France in case of war to send a stronger army into action. The Prussian military leaders were alarmed, and Bismarck, though definitely opposed to a preventive war, instigated a press storm threatening dire consequences for France. An article under the headline "Is War in Sight?" proved most sensational, and since Count Moltke and members of the foreign office were reported to have expressed themselves in a similar vein, alarm over Germany's intentions spread. The French foreign minister, Decazes, appealed to England and Russia to protect France and the peace. The British government suggested a collective diplomatic action in Berlin and offered its good services for the solution of the Franco-German differences. At the same time Czar Alexander II passed through Berlin and was easily persuaded that Germany had no intentions of going to war. His chancellor, Prince Gorčacov, when leaving the German capital, issued a statement to the effect that the maintenance of peace was assured.

For the first time Russia and France were coming together in an unfriendly action, and simultaneously the incidents made Russia and England, the two bitter antagonists in world politics, forget their dissension. It was a warning of the three powers to Germany that they were not prepared to allow her to weaken France still more or to enhance her own dominant position. For Bismarck it was especially unpleasant to be reminded by the monarchical Russia that she thought of France as a natural counterweight to Germany. Although the "War-in-Sight" crisis passed by quickly, for a moment it brightly illustrated the limitations and potential dangers of Germany's place in Europe.

↶ Near Eastern Crisis

IN THE LATE SUMMER of 1875 revolts against Turkish rule broke out in Bosnia, followed in May 1876 by similar uprisings in Bulgaria, and by the opening of war against the Porte on the part of Serbia and Montenegro. By the stormy Pan-Slav agitation, which this time reached the highest ranks of Russian society, Alexander II was slowly inveigled into contemplating, and eventually making, war on Turkey. At first he tried to get from the German government a definitive pledge that it would maintain an attitude of benevolent neutrality if it came to a war between Russia and Austria-Hungary. The czar argued that in the light of his own policy vis-à-vis the Franco-German war this request was well justified.

The attempt to draw Germany entirely over to the Russian side was firmly if gently repulsed by Bismarck. He declared the existence of a strong and independent Austria-Hungary a major German interest. The neutrality that he offered Russia covered only Russian actions in the Near East. In contrast to Russia and Austria-Hungary, he could not find there any German interest calling for a political engagement or, as he phrased it in a speech before the German parliament, any interest "worth the healthy bones of a single Pomeranian musketeer."

⌒ *Russo-Turkish War*

BEFORE GOING TO WAR in April 1877 Russia had to come to terms with Austria-Hungary. She allayed Austria-Hungary's fears that from a Turkish defeat one or two sizable Slav states might originate in the Balkans which would inevitably attract the Slavs within the Habsburg empire. As one means of averting such a development Austria-Hungary was to have the right to occupy and administer Bosnia and Herzegovina. After initial delays and adversities, the Russian military campaign led to full victory over the Turks. The Russians decided against occupying Constantinople, but on March 3, 1878, imposed the peace treaty of San Stefano that broke the agreements with Austria-Hungary as well as promises to Britain. This was done although Britain, through the dispatch of a fleet to the Marmara sea, had already indicated that she would not tolerate Russia's intention to keep actual control of the Balkans and with it the guiding direction of Turkish affairs.

British and Austrian protests forced the Russians to agree to a review of the peace treaty of San Stefano by a conference of the great powers of Europe. Russia and Austria-Hungary, subsequently joined by the other powers, agreed to hold the congress in Berlin. Bismarck hesitated. He was gravely worried that since Germany was the only nation without any direct interests in the Near East, he would be made responsible for all disappointments that one or the other state was bound to suffer. They could blame their failure to realize their aims on the German refusal of support. Bismarck was equally concerned with the enmities that might result if he appeared in the role of arbiter of Europe. Publicly he called himself "an honest broker," and in this capacity he convened the congress after Russia and England, in direct negotiations, had reached substantial agreement on some of the fundamental problems of the forthcoming congress. Bismarck's step was ultimately motivated by the fear that, in the case of a war of England and Austria-Hungary against Russia, Germany could not hope to maintain neutrality, particularly since France was likely to exploit the events by reasserting herself. But a German option for either Russia or Austria-Hungary would have made Germany fight in a cause in which she had nothing to gain and which would have left her dependent on either Russia or England even after the war. Bismarck accepted the idea of a congress because he wished to preserve the diplomatic freedom that Germany had acquired.

✑ Congress of Berlin

THE CONGRESS OF BERLIN lasted from June 13 to July 13, 1878. It was the first time in German history that a great international conference was held in the Prussian capital, and the selection of the meeting place as well as of the congress president was clear evidence of the eminent position among nations that Germany had acquired through Bismarck. More important than this gain in power and prestige was the fact that Berlin was chosen because the Bismarckian policy was now recognized as devoted to peace, and Bismarck's conduct of the congress confirmed this general judgment. As a matter of fact, without the existence of the German Empire, which had arisen in the center of the Continent and aroused apprehension among its neighbors, Europe would have experienced a repetition of the Crimean War.

Lord Salisbury, then British foreign secretary, had the impression that in the discussions of the congress Bismarck leaned more toward the Russian than the English side, and it is true that he made himself the solicitor of Russian interests as far as this was compatible with his chairmanship and the ultimate success of the congress. Nevertheless, the results of the congress were bound to appear to the Russian public as a terrific setback. The changes of the San Stefano treaty with regard to Bulgaria were especially galling. Whereas the peace had planned the creation of a Great Bulgaria with access to the Aegean sea and including areas in the western Balkans, the congress created a much smaller Bulgaria and left even half of this country, the province of East Rumelia south of the Balkan mountains, under Turkish suzerainty. While Russia was thus forced to give up most of her military gains, Austria-Hungary was allowed to occupy Bosnia and Herzegovina without any effort.

✑ Alliance with Austria-Hungary

IN VIEW OF THE FACT that Russia would not have been in a position to defend the gains of her Turkish war if England and Austria-Hungary had struck, even under the terms of the Berlin treaty she won a great deal. But the Russian government was unwilling to accept any blame for San Stefano and seemed satisfied that the newspapers heaped all their criticism on Germany. Finally it even made official recriminations and threatened dire consequences in its diplomatic exchange with Germany. Bismarck quickly decided to seek a firm alliance with Austria-Hungary. When opening negotiations with Count Andrassy he proposed a general alliance that would be further strengthened by some federative institutions. Bismarck spoke of it as the revival of the Germanic Confederation in forms adjusted to the new age. In addition to a joint defense system he thought of common economic policies.

Count Andrassy did not show any interest in a federation, nor was he inclined to conclude a general alliance which would have been applicable to a Franco-German war. Bismarck agreed to an alliance that committed the signatories to mutual assistance in case of a Russian attack on either of them. In case of an attack by another power the allies were at least to maintain benevolent neutrality. The alliance was concluded for a five-year period, and its text was not published. However, whereas Bismarck reached agreement with Andrassy rather easily and quickly, he had to struggle fiercely to win William I's approval of his policy. William's feelings were outraged by the idea of a secret alliance directed against his nephew the czar, who at a meeting on September 4 had succeeded in restoring William's trust in the friendly and peaceful nature of his intentions. William lived entirely in the tradition of the dynastic friendship of the two courts. For weeks Bismarck tried in vain to convince the king of the compelling need for the Austrian alliance. When the king finally gave Bismarck permission to sign the alliance, he still was not convinced that this was the right course, but he knew that Bismarck could not be absent from the helm.

The Austro-German Alliance was signed on October 7, 1879, and lasted until 1918. This event has often been called Bismarck's option for Austria. But this characterization can be misleading. The Austro-German Alliance thereafter was for Bismarck the most important instrument for making central Europe secure against Russian inroads, and since a French attempt at revenge was unlikely unless undertaken with Russia, the alliance also served to strengthen Germany against France. But Bismarck continued to believe that it was absolutely imperative to do everything possible to maintain close relations with Russia. He dreaded war with Russia. It was difficult to beat Russia, and even if she were defeated, her millions of people as well as her vast territory would allow her an early comeback. In addition, a war with Russia would endanger the monarchical principle and undoubtedly reopen the Polish question. As long as Germany managed to secure Russia's cooperation, she could disregard any French threat and would automatically become the full leader within the dual alliance. If Germany had only one ally, she would be compelled to honor its wishes, and Bismarck still did not wish to be drawn into Balkan questions.

✍ *Three Emperors' League*

ACTUALLY BISMARCK expected that the alliance with Austria-Hungary would sober Russia and induce her to seek a reconciliation and the restoration of the Three Emperors' League. This expectation proved correct. The news of the negotiations between Bismarck and Andrassy in Vienna sufficed to bring a Russian diplomatic emissary to Berlin who was authorized to conduct conversations on the reconstruction of the Three Emperors' League. An agreement was delayed by the hesitancy of the Austrian government to enter into a written understanding with Russia. But on June 18, 1881, the Three Emperors' Alliance was formally signed. The agreement was more specific than that of 1873. Under the treaty of 1881 the three powers pledged themselves to maintain benevolent neutrality if one of them was at war with a fourth power. In addition it contained the coordination of their policies with regard to Turkey and the Balkans. The significance of the treaty was enhanced by the approval of Alexander III, who had succeeded his assassinated father to the throne. Although he was much more an outspoken Russian nationalist than Alexander II had been, he trusted Bismarck. The alliance was concluded for a three-year period and was renewed on the same terms in 1884.

The Three Emperors' Alliance initiated the years of the greatest foreign security for Germany. Yet Bismarck was skeptical about the future of the alliance. As early as 1880 he admitted that the Russian power was no longer fully integrated. "A treaty with the emperor . . . today commits only one part of the Russian power; the other remains refractory and makes a policy of its own." Even in this period of renewed friendship between the courts of Berlin and St. Petersburg a good many unpleasant incidents occurred. The real crux of the Three Emperors' Alliance, however, remained the Austro-Russian frictions over the Balkans. In 1881 Austria-Hungary concluded an alliance with Prince Milan of Serbia that made her the protector of the principality. Since 1879 she had also occupied Bosnia and Herzegovina. At the same time Russian officers organized the government and administration of Bulgaria. Bismarck tried in vain to induce Russia and Austria-Hungary to come to a permanent agreement on a division of the Balkans into spheres of interest. He argued that Austria had no reason to fear a Russian seizure of the Turkish Straits, since in such an overextended position Russia would be forced to come to terms with Austria-Hungary. But he failed to convince the Austrian statesmen.

ᵡ *Triple Alliance*

THE CONGRESS OF BERLIN had shown the Italians the power of the new Germany and the hopelessness of the *irredenta* movement. Bismarck had given the nod to the French wish to acquire Tunisia. The French foreign minister, Waddington, was not a man of revenge, and Bismarck felt that colonial activities would turn French eyes away from the Vosges. In 1881 the French declared Tunisia a protectorate. The Italians were greatly dismayed, since they had hoped to acquire Tunisia because it was closest to Italy and seemed ideally suited for the settlement of Italians. Thus Italy aimed at overcoming her diplomatic isolation when she approached Germany. Bismarck, however, made close relations dependent on an understanding between Italy and Austria-Hungary. The Italian alliance to him was subsidiary to the Austro-German Alliance, and it seemed useful that in case of a conflict Austria would not have to fear Italian attacks. Italy could also give some support to Germany in a war with France.

The Triple Alliance of May 20, 1882, was turned into a defensive alliance against France. The treaty did not fail to stress the strengthening of the existing political and social order through the monarchical principle, but its chief articles committed Germany and Austria-Hungary to assisting Italy with all their forces if she were attacked by France without direct provocation, while Italy was to give military support to Germany in case of unprovoked French aggression. If one or two members of the alliance were attacked and at war with two or more great powers, all the members were bound to mutual support. The Triple Alliance was concluded for five years. Prior to World War I it was regularly renewed, but the shifting balance of power in Europe enabled Italy to achieve important changes in the alliance. In 1883 Germany acceded to a friendship and alliance treaty of Austria-Hungary and Rumania. This treaty committed the two great powers to come to the assistance of Rumania if she were attacked by Russia, while Rumania was to come to the assistance of Austria-Hungary if Russian aggression were directed against neighboring provinces of the Habsburg empire.

ᵡ *Bismarck and England*

ALL THESE ALLIANCES left England on the outside. But England was never forgotten in Bismarck's planning. He fully appreciated her enormous power and saw no conflict of interest between Britain and Germany. Although in theory Germany might have become an ally of both Russia and England, the hostile Anglo-Russian relationship made this impossible. Bismarck gave German-Russian relations precedence over Anglo-German ones, because he wanted to avoid a war with Russia and believed that the monarchical solidarity could be used for the stabilization of the friendship between the two governments. England doubtlessly would have liked to see the German-Russian friendship lapse, but she was not in a mood to accept firm treaty ties with Germany or with Germany and Austria-Hungary. During the crisis of 1879 the British government publicly welcomed the conclusion of the Austro-German alliance, but Bismarck's diplomatic inquiry in London as to what Britain might be willing to do if Germany were involved in a war with Russia brought no promises of active British support. Britain had no need to bind herself by rigid commitments, whereas a Germany that had lost her ties with Russia and tried to lean on Britain would become in large measure dependent on her. Besides, Bismarck feared that the parliamentary system with its changing party governments would make steady cooperation difficult and uncertain.

✑ Colonial Acquisitions

THESE FACTORS, however, did not hinder Bismarck's careful cultivation of friendly diplomatic relations with England. This was facilitated by the absence of any concrete German demands on England apart from Germany's wish for the recovery of the tiny island of Heligoland in front of the estuaries of the Elbe and Weser rivers. Bismarck did not raise this issue in the 1870's and in the 1880's he did not press it. But when in 1883 the British government obstructed German colonial projects, he did not hesitate to make life uncomfortable for them. The motives of Bismarck's sudden entry into the colonial race lay almost exclusively in domestic politics, the wish to please the merchants.[1] The state of foreign affairs in the years 1883–85 explains why he felt strong enough to acquire colonies at this moment. The German alliances made him confident that he could risk the temporary displeasure of England, especially since, beginning in 1882, strong tensions between France and England had developed over the English occupation of Egypt. England was faced with a very difficult task in Egypt, which was considerably aggravated in the following years by the revolts in the Sudan. Germany as well as France could make themselves obnoxious to the English government of Egypt, since they were represented on the council of the international debt administration, on which the public finances of the country depended.

In the same years France, just having taken Tunisia, launched colonial expeditions in Indo-China involving her in heavy fighting. The cabinet of Jules Ferry was resolved to subordinate the anti-German sentiment to an active colonial expansionism. It was prepared to cooperate with Germany in the colonial field. This cooperation, sometimes called the Franco-

[1] On additional colonial acquisitions, see p. 307.

German "colonial marriage," reached its climax at the Congo Conference of Berlin in December-February 1884–85, where, in settling the controversial problems of Central Africa, the two nations put some limits to the British monopoly in the colonial realm. England's diplomatic isolation and her own imperial preoccupations, which in 1885 were further increased by a Russian threat against Afghanistan, forced the English government to tolerate Germany's colonial acquisitions. The chief opposition actually came from the Cape Colony and from Australia, which the London government had to assuage.

The request of the Bremen merchant Adolf Lüderitz for the protection of the territories he had acquired at the bay of Angra Pequena in South-West Africa became the occasion for the opening of the Anglo-German duel. Bismarck, angered by the long delay of an English reply to his inquiry about English rights in this region, declared on April 24, 1884, a German protectorate over what became German South-West Africa. English protests were rejected. By June 1884 the English government recognized the German colony after stiff negotiations, for which Bismarck sent his son Count Herbert Bismarck to London. Each subsequent German acquisition, however, brought similar British resistance.

In July 1884 Togo and the Cameroons were made German colonies. Here, at the Gulf of Guinea, the Hamburg merchant Adolf Woermann (1847–1911), had been active since 1882 acquiring property and setting up commercial stations. The origins of another colony, however, must be attributed to a man who speculated on the future. Carl Peters (1856-1918), an adventurous pastor's son, founded in 1884 a "society for German colonization" and in the fall of that year began on his own to induce some African chieftains on the East African coast opposite Zanzibar to accept the protection of his society. In February 1885 Peters received from the Empire a patent of protection, which was to lead to the largest of all German colonies, German East Africa (Tanganyika). Starting with a more solid group and with the promise of future government support behind him, Adolf von Hansemann, the head of the biggest German bank, had launched the New Guinea Company with territorial acquisitions in northeastern New Guinea. These territories, too, under the name of *Kaiser-Wilhelms-Land* and the *Bismarck-Archipelago*, became German protectorates in May 1885.

It was Bismarck's continental European diplomacy that largely enabled him to win the German colonies overseas. But he was fully conscious of the unique world constellation under which this happened. Firm or even tough as his and his son's language and diplomatic methods had been, he avoided any conflict over truly vital British interests. He pointed out that Germany's acquisition of colonies was actually proof of her desire to live in friendship with England, since in any war German colonies would be at the mercy of the British navy. Although this argument may have been a little specious, Bismarck never planned to build a navy and was fully aware of Germany's need for friendly or at least normal relations with England. Therefore, he was anxious to terminate all friction as soon as possible. In March 1885 Count Herbert Bismarck reached a settlement of practically all the serious differences in London. It was just in time to enable Bismarck to face the revival of tensions on the Continent, the absence of which had made it possible for him to pursue colonial objectives.

✑ *The Bulgarian Crisis*

ON MARCH 30, 1885, the government of Jules Ferry was defeated in the French chamber as a result of reverses suffered by the French troops in Indo-China. French patriotic sentiment soon reverted from colonial ambitions to the old demand for the revenge of 1870–1, which found a leader in General Boulanger, minister of war from January 1886 till May 1887. One of the causes of the rising hopes of the French chauvinists, and naturally the source of greatest worry for Bismarck, was the deterioration of relations between the eastern monarchies. Again the disturbing developments originated in the Balkans. On Czar Alexander II's suggestion the Bulgarians had elected the czarina's nephew, Alexander Battenberg, prince. Prince Alexander, however, could not help deviating from the Russian political line and tried to ally himself with the indigenous nationalism of Bulgaria, whereupon Alexander III's suspicious and finally hostile attitude brought him into open conflict with Russia.

In 1885 popular uprisings in East Rumelia had brought about the practical unification of Bulgaria, the very aim that Russia had striven to realize and the Congress of Berlin had prohibited. But the czar did not wish Prince Alexander to enjoy such successes. On the other side, England, which in 1878 had been chiefly responsible for the division of Bulgaria, had come to believe that the growth of national states in the Balkans would not simply result in an extension of Russian influence, since the young nations would assert their national independence equally against Russia.

Austria-Hungary had saved Serbia from the dire consequences of the disastrous defeat she suffered in the war she had begun in November 1885 against Bulgaria to secure compensation for the gains the latter had made through the accession of East Rumelia. Austria-Hungary's active role in Balkan politics was further extended when, in November 1886, the Austrian foreign minister, Count Kálnoky, under Hungarian pressure, declared that Austria-Hungary could not tolerate a Russian protectorate over Bulgaria. This declaration followed the resignation of Alexander

Battenberg that had been forced by Russia. In the summer of 1887 the Bulgarian parliament elected Prince Ferdinand of Coburg ruler of Bulgaria. Austria-Hungary recognized the former Austrian officer at once, whereas Russia balked. The Austro-Russian enmity flared up again, and the Three Emperors' Alliance broke down. However, Russian resentment was directed not only against Austria-Hungary, but even more furiously against Germany. There was acute danger that the anti-German agitation in Russia and France would coalesce and lead to a two-front war.

Bismarck met the grave crisis by a series of diplomatic moves which fulfilled his ideal that he had once described as the creation of "a universal political situation in which all the powers except France need us and by their mutual relations are kept as much as possible from forming coalitions against us." He warned Austria-Hungary that he considered Russia's influence preponderant in Bulgaria and that Germany would not fight on the side of Austria-Hungary if the latter were to get involved in a war with Russia over Bulgaria. The Austro-German Alliance committed Germany to go to war in support of Austria-Hungary's independence but not of her expansionist ambitions. It was not easy to make the Vienna government understand Bismarck's position, especially since his policies were disputed even in Berlin. The deputy-chief of the general staff, Count Alfred von Waldersee (1832–1904), who succeeded Count Moltke in 1888, believed he discerned a huge buildup of Russian military forces and advocated a preventive war against Russia. Through the German military attaché in Vienna he spread these ideas also in the Austrian military circles. Bismarck eventually stopped these political activities of the military men. He did not discover, however, that Friedrich von Holstein (1837–1909), councillor in his foreign office, secretly used his position to give the Austrians information designed to deepen the gulf between Austria-Hungary and Russia.

∽ Triple Alliance Renewed

WHILE BISMARCK GAVE the Austrian alliance a narrow interpretation, he did not wish to weaken the defensive strength of the Habsburg empire. Therefore, after some hesitation, he renewed the Triple Alliance in 1887, although the Italians raised their price. Italy expressed her dissatisfaction with the alliance, because it had not given her a stronger voice in the councils of nations nor improved her prospects of sharing in their colonial exploits. The alliance treaty of 1882 was renewed on February 20, 1887, for another five years, but simultaneously two separate treaties, between Germany and Italy and between Austria-Hungary and Italy, were signed. In the former treaty the signatories agreed that they would use their influence to oppose any changes on the Ottomanic coasts and the islands of the Adriatic and Aegean seas. Germany promised to come to the assistance of Italy if the latter were to go to war against France in case of further French expansion in North Africa, i.e., Tripolitania and Morocco. The treaty even hinted that in case of a Franco-Italian war Germany would try to help Italy regain Nice and Savoy. A subsequent military convention envisaged the use of Italian troops also north of the Alps in a joint German-Italian war with France.

These new arrangements with Italy constituted a departure from the strictly defensive and conservative nature of all the earlier Bismarckian treaties. Bismarck justified the new commitments by saying that, irrespective of the existence of a special treaty, Germany would be compelled to protect Italy in case of a Franco-Italian war and that it remained the aim of his general policy to maintain the *status quo*. But the treaty showed the strong bargaining position that Italy had gained. This was also reflected in the simultaneous Austro-Italian treaty, in which the two governments agreed that no changes in the Balkans and the adjacent islands should be made without prior agreement between Italy and Austria-Hungary. It was this treaty that allowed Italy to stay neutral in 1914.

✧ "The Mediterranean Entente"

YET BISMARCK FOUND the chief support of Austria-Hungary against Russia not in Italy, but in England. England's conflicts with France over Egypt continued, while Russia's threat to the Turkish Straits inflamed hostility against her. Bismarck's stern refusal to have the Austro-German Alliance serve as a defense of the eastern Balkans and the straits against Russian penetration forced England to accept an explicit responsibility for the preservation of the *status quo* in cooperation with continental powers. Under Bismarck's prodding, Lord Salisbury reached a secret understanding with Italy. By an exchange of notes, on February 12, 1887, the two powers agreed to maintain the *status quo* in the Mediterranean, Adriatic, Aegean, and Black seas. Italy promised England her support in Egypt, while England reciprocated in Tripolitania. Austria-Hungary joined the understanding on March 24, 1887.

The "Mediterranean Entente" was further strengthened before the year was over, but only after Bismarck had given Salisbury a reassuring interpretation of the present and future German policy. Salisbury expressed his uneasiness about the political inclinations of the German emperor's grandson, Prince William, who, owing to the fatal illness of Crown Prince Frederick William, was likely soon to ascend the throne. In a masterful letter Bismarck explained that any ruler would have to conduct German policy in strict accordance with Germany's vital interests. These demanded abstention from direct involvement in Near Eastern conflicts, on the one hand, and the active defense of Austria-Hungary against Russian aggression as well as of Italy and England against French aggression, on the other. The chancellor also showed the British government the text of the Austro-German Alliance. Thus, having received Bismarck's moral encouragement, Salisbury, in December 1887, transformed the Mediterranean Entente into a triple alliance which guaranteed the integrity and independence of the Turkish Empire and the Turkish control of the Dardanelles.

✍ *Reinsurance Treaty*

AT THE TIME of the conclusion of the Mediterranean Entente Bismarck had already succeeded in restoring a "wire" between Berlin and St. Petersburg. On June 18, 1887, the so-called Reinsurance Treaty had been signed in Berlin. Under its terms Germany and Russia promised each other benevolent neutrality in case one of them were at war with a third power, except if Russia or Germany were to start a war against Austria-Hungary or France. Germany recognized Russia's historical rights in the Balkans, especially her "preponderant and decisive" influence in Bulgaria and East Rumelia, and both powers agreed not to tolerate any territorial changes in the Balkans made without their prior assent. Whereas a special article of the secret treaty reaffirmed the existing rules of international law concerning the straits, a "very secret supplementary protocol" contained Germany's promise of benevolent neutrality as well as moral and diplomatic support if the czar himself found it necessary to take over the defense of the straits in order "to keep the key of his empire in his hand." Germany also promised to continue to assist Russia in restoring a legal and orderly government in Bulgaria.

The Reinsurance Treaty was intended to thwart a possible Franco-Russian alliance, which in 1887–88 would most probably have led to war. It was at the same time a bold attempt to retain something of the mediating role between Austria-Hungary and Russia that Germany had played within the Three Emperors' Alliance. In spite of the broken link between Vienna and St. Petersburg both governments remained allies of Germany. Moreover, the system of alliances built by Bismarck in 1887 gave Germany some freedom between Britain and Russia. But Germany's advantageous diplomatic position rested on precarious ground. The individual agreements contained conflicting provisions. Whereas the Mediterranean Entente that Bismarck had at least morally promoted protected the straits against Russia, the Reinsurance Treaty encouraged Russian schemes for the conquest of the straits. The Austro-Italian treaty signed in 1887 in conjunction with the renewal of the Triple Alliance between Germany, Austria-Hungary, and Italy made decisions on Balkan affairs matters of joint deliberation among the contracting members, while in the Reinsurance Treaty Germany, on her own, assigned Bulgaria to Russian tutelage.

∾ *The Zenith of Bismarck's Diplomacy*

BISMARCK'S DIPLOMACY reached a high degree of finesse. He himself was not without apprehension that in case of war some of the commitments accepted by the German government might prove embarrassing. But he was convinced that by the careful balance and counterbalance of the diverse interests and power thrusts war could be avoided. Bismarck's aim was German national security, which he identified with European peace. And actually peace was preserved. After the spring of 1888 the international tensions diminished. Bismarck had refused to commit Germany to the Reinsurance Treaty, as the Russians had proposed, for a five-year period but had insisted on three years. He said that he did not wish the Russians to believe that Germany felt dependent on Russia. Apparently he also wished to observe for a while the development of the European situation and, most of all, the czar's capacity for standing up to the anti-German nationalist agitation. The last meeting with Alexander III in October 1889, while convincing the czar that close Russo-German relations were largely contingent on Bismarck's continuation in office, must have persuaded the latter that it was still worthwhile extending the Reinsurance Treaty. He was ready to renew it in March 1890, when William II forced him to resign.

How long the Reinsurance Treaty might have lasted if Bismarck had remained chancellor is doubtful. The treaty was a dynastic instrument in an age in which even absolute rulers did not like to stray very far from the opinions and sentiments of the classes of the people supporting the monarchy. Of this Bismarck was not unaware. But the growth of the economic forces, which were equally apt to undermine the freedom of the monarchical decisions, was not correctly appraised by him. In retaliation for Russian antiforeign legislation in Poland, which interfered with the property rights of many Germans living there, Bismarck, in November of 1887, blocked the German financial market for Russian government loans by having the Federal Central Bank refuse to accept Russian bonds as collateral security for loans. Thereupon the Russian government turned to Paris. In the winter of 1888 a sizable French loan was issued, the first of many loans with which France supported the czarist regime until 1917. This financial aid contributed greatly not only to the early formation of the Franco-Russian alliance but also to its subsequent solidification.

In January 1889 Bismarck cautiously explored the possibility of a secret or public alliance with England for a joint defense against French aggression. Such a treaty, he reasoned with Lord Salisbury, would preclude any chance of war in Europe. This step has been interpreted as a turning away from Russia toward a western orientation. But although England now loomed larger in Bismarck's speculations than in earlier years as a result, at least partly, of his greater skepticism of Russia, the exchange with Lord Salisbury had also the limited aim of making the isolation of France complete, because a France kept at bay by Germany and England could no longer be a potentially strong ally of Russia. Lord Salisbury was not willing to follow through Bismarck's suggestion. England, though at times annoyed by French policies, did not anticipate war with France and saw no cogent reason to accept a commitment with regard to a possible Franco-German conflict.

In the conduct of his foreign policy after 1871 Bismarck showed his greatest political craftsmanship. His uncanny genius for making conflicting state interests serve the stability of peace was unique. His greatest single achievement, little understood by his German contemporaries and even less by his successors, was his growing success in convincing Europe that the existence of a big power in the center of the Continent could strengthen the foundations of the international order of Europe. It is true, however, that Bismarck's diplomacy did nothing to arrest the continuous increase of armaments. Actually, in spite of the alliances, Bismarck felt it imperative to expand the German army in 1873, 1880, and, most drastically, in 1887, while France and Russia particularly were building up their armies. The beginnings of the modern arms race created if not fear at least uneasiness and injected suspicion into the relations of governments.

∽ Bismarck's Domestic Policies

WHEN WE TURN from Bismarck's diplomacy to the internal history of the new Empire, however, the results of his policies appear doubtful. His imperious temper, disciplined in his dealings with independent powers, flared up with unbridled passion in domestic politics. Here policy was to him, to vary Clausewitz's famous dictum, the continuation of war with different means. And whereas Bismarck always kept an ear to the ground in international affairs, he discerned only vaguely the great social changes which industrialization worked in Germany. The social reality that Bismarck observed was the aristocratic society of courts and governments on the one hand and the villagers and farmhands of his estates on the other. He knew little about the new bourgeoisie and even less about the new industrial workers' class. The image of the ideal society that determined his political actions was still essentially a projection of the German world of the 1850's. His domestic policy was as conservative as his foreign policy, but much less adaptable to changing conditions and more combative in execution.

The general objective of Bismarck's internal policy was the strengthening of the Empire by the development of its institutions and the mobilization of universal popular support. In the early years after the founding of the Empire, Bismarck believed that the strongest divisive forces were found among the princes and state governments and therefore an extension of federal power and the full use of the legislative authority of the federal (*Reich*) government was required. Thus he sought the cooperation of the parliament, in which the National Liberal party was dominant. After the accession of 30 South German votes it commanded altogether 155 votes and, either in combination with the Free Conservative party to its right or the Progressive party to its left, was able to form a majority, which called for 200 votes. Even then the relations between Bismarck and the National Liberals were uneasy. Bismarck was prepared to grant the liberals individual freedom in economic activities and also concessions with regard to a unitarian organization of the Empire, but he was violently opposed to any attempt to broaden the political influence of the parliament and the parties.

✍ Free Trade

No LEGISLATION was needed in order to promote free trade. On this principle the government and the liberals had been in agreement for some time. The last consequences of the liberal economic policy were reached when in 1873 it was decided to abolish gradually the import duties on iron. The last duties were to be dropped by 1877. Great progress was made with the unification of the German currency. The thirty-three various state currencies were abolished and replaced by the German mark in December 1871. The French war indemnity facilitated the transition and made it possible to base the new currency on gold. In 1875 a central federal bank, the *Reichsbank*, was founded that received a near monopoly for issuing money bills. The state banks of Bavaria, Württemberg, Saxony, and Baden retained the right of issue, though only of small amounts. Another act of unification, the standardization of weights and measures, had been passed by the North-Germanic parliament in 1868 and was extended to the rest of Germany.

In the last years of the Germanic Confederation a beginning had already been made to create a common German commercial law. In 1870 the North German Confederation had added a code of criminal law. The German constitution of 1871 expanded the federal authority to include legislation on legal procedure, but a constitutional amendment of 1873 broadened this to include all civil and criminal law. In 1877 a law on the organization of courts and codes of criminal and civil procedure were promulgated. Thereafter local, district, and state or provincial courts throughout Germany were of an identical type and used identical rules of procedure. When in 1879 the new organization of the judiciary became effective, a federal supreme court (*Reichsgericht*) in Leipzig was established as highest court of appeal. The codification of civil law took many years. The first draft of such a code was presented for public discussion in 1888. It aroused much criticism, because it was almost exclusively based on Roman law and couched in unduly technical language. A new commission was appointed that by 1896 produced an improved, if still predominantly "Roman," draft that was approved with minor changes by the Federal Council and the German parliament. The civil code went into effect on January 1, 1900.

In launching the unification of laws during the 1870's the government and the liberal majority of parliament worked together reasonably well. However, serious conflicts arose whenever matters came under discussion which touched directly on the discretionary authority of the government. Thus, in 1874, the liberals had to sacrifice some of their cherished principles in order to get a press law at all. But the politically most important concession they were forced to make concerned the military appropriations.

✍ The Military Budget

THE NORTH GERMAN CONSTITUTION of 1867 had stated that until the end of 1871 the standing army was to consist of 1 per cent of the population. Thereafter the figure was to be fixed by legislation. The individual states were made responsible for recruiting as many soldiers as corresponded to the size of their population as well as for the payment of 225 taler per soldier. In 1871 this temporary arrangement was extended for another three years. Only in 1874 did the government present a military law. The draft law laid down the figure of 401,659 men as the permanent strength of the army. This would have made the right of parliament to approve the budget practically meaningless, especially since about four fifths of all federal expenditure was spent on the army. Although few liberals of any shade would have liked to forgo the right of budget approval, the National Liberals and even some of the Progressives shied away from renewing the conflict of a decade ago. The army was still immensely popular after its recent victories, and the government, through its controlled press organs, endeavored to build up pressure on the parliamentarians. The liberals would probably have considered it a fair compromise if each parliament had voted the military budget once; since the parliament was elected for three years, this would have meant a triennial military budget.

But Bismarck was unwilling to satisfy the liberals. He did not make a stand for a law of unlimited duration, since he was aware that such a law would have made the army independent not only of parliament but also of the government. Instead, he offered the National Liberal leaders a septennial law (*Septennat*), an arrangement that flouted any reference to parliamentary sessions. All National Liberals and even a handful of Progressives voted for the septennial law. This vote was a reaffirmation of the defeat that the liberals had suffered at Bismarck's hands in the Prussian constitutional conflict, and the loss of the full right of budget approval blocked the growth of a parliamentary system in Germany.

Many liberals comforted themselves with the thought that Bismarck would not rule forever. William I's great age seemed to make an early succession of Crown Prince Frederick William likely, and with his well-known preference for the British governmental system it was assumed that he would inaugurate a liberal era. Meanwhile many liberals were satisfied with measuring progress in this direction by mere inches.

✍ Self-Government in Prussia

COOPERATION WITH BISMARCK in federal legislation appeared to be a prerequisite for cooperation in Prussian affairs as well, and here the liberals hoped to gain important concessions that would start the transformation of this autocratic state into a modern state or at least undo the harm wrought by the reaction of the 1850's and open the road to the spread of self-government. They also wanted to persist in their fight against the Catholic Church, in which they were united with the government and with which we shall have to deal shortly.

The development of self-government had already been a concern after the founding of the North German Confederation.[2] At that time the most urgent problem had been the integration of the newly acquired provinces into Prussia, but it was generally assumed that the grant of some amount of self-government to the new provinces would necessitate a reform of the local and provincial administration in the old provinces as well. Count Friedrich Eulenburg (1815-81), the minister of interior in the period of the constitutional conflict, had become amenable to more liberal ideas after 1867 and had aimed at making the achievement of reform a historic monument to himself. A shrewd tactician at the court, in government, and in parliament, he managed to outmaneuver even Bismarck, who, being a *Junker*, found Eulenburg's reform of the local ad-

[2] See pp. 203-4.

ministration too bureaucratic and Eulenburg himself too liberal a Prussian minister.

Although the law on the administrative organization of the rural counties (*Kreisordnung*) of 1872 was not a historic monument to its chief author, it was at least a landmark of the final demise of feudalism in the bulwarks of the Prussian nobility. The hereditary representation of noble families on the county's diet was abolished, as was the selection of the chief of the county administration, the county councillor (*Landrat*), from the indigenous nobility. Although the new order still left the manorial estates separated from the villages, it took the police power away from the individual estate owner. Instead, police districts, composed of estates and villages, were created, and an honorary officer was appointed by the provincial high-president. In practice this change was not very far-reaching, since this district officer as a rule was chosen from among the landed property owners of the district. More important was the right given to the villages to elect their own administrative boards, consisting of the village mayor and two selectmen.

On the county level the diet was remodeled. Yet while, as mentioned above, the hereditary lifetime membership of the *Junkers* was abolished, more than one half of the seats were given to the landowners. The remaining half were elected by the people of the towns and the small peasants. The county diet, meeting under the chairmanship of the county councillor, elected a county committee that, again under the chairmanship of the county councillor, administered the county. Self-government and bureaucratic state government were thus joined, though in a form that gave the state government the lion's share. With greater administrative tasks given to the counties, the character of the county councillor changed. Formerly, indigenous *Junkers* had held the office practically for life and had considered themselves as much the advocates of the local interests as the representatives of the king. From this time on a law-trained state official was to be appointed, who considered his post as a station in a career leading to higher office, for which he had to recommend himself by keeping his county in line with the policies of the central government.

The interests of the *Junkers*, however, did not suffer under the new system. The representation in the county diets was heavily weighted in favor of the landed proprietors, among whom the *Junkers*, who still inspired awe among the small peasants, set the tone. The liberal elements in the towns thereby were well contained. Only towns with a population of up to 25,000 belonged to the rural counties (*Landkreise*), and in most of them liberalism was not very strong. Towns and cities with a larger population formed counties by themselves (*Stadtkreise*). Under these conditions the rural counties of the eastern provinces remained the strongholds of a conservative Prussia, and the contrast between country and city, so characteristic of the absolute and mercantilistic Prussia of the eighteenth century, lived on in the age of capitalism. The opposition of the Conservative party to the law on the organization of the rural counties was shortsighted. The final passage of the bill was forced by the government against the Conservative majority of the House of Lords by the royal appointment to the house of twenty-four new members, mostly generals and high state officials.

∽ *Provincial Government*

THE SATISFACTION evinced by the liberals over the new law was rather ill-founded, and the subsequent legislation on provincial self-government actually found a divided reaction among the liberals. The provincial organization law (*Provinzialordnung*) of 1875 provided for little self-government. If, as would have been logical, the organization of the counties had been followed on the provincial level, the Prussian monarchy would have become decentralized to some extent. But decentralization was stubbornly opposed by the state bureaucracy with the support of the Conservative party. Only lesser political administrative tasks were handed over to the provincial self-government. Thus the highway administration, welfare institutions, such as asylums and poorhouses, as well as, from the 1880's on, the new social insurance institutes, soil amelioration, vocational agricultural schools, conservation of natural and historical monuments were matters assigned to a provincial agency of the self-governing type.

The provincial diet was no longer composed of estates. Its members were elected by the county diets and by the city magistrates and councils. The composition of the county diets assured a conservative majority also in the provincial diets. The provincial diet elected a land director, who after confirmation by the king became the head of the provincial self-government. He was supported by a provincial committee and empowered to appoint his own executive assistants and officials. The provincial self-government was linked with the state government only in a very loose fashion through a provincial council, consisting of the high-president of the province, another appointed state official, and five elected lay members. But the function of this council was strictly limited to the supervision of the provincial self-government. It could not act as a supervisory, nor even as an advisory, agency of the general provincial government, which remained authoritarian. In some respects the latter, if not more authoritarian, became at least more centralistic. The high-president of the province, who originally had been sent out from Berlin in order to act as an intermediary between the province and the central government,[3] as the governing head of the province, became the mere executive of the central government.

Within its narrow limits the law on the provincial organization produced self-governing bodies that successfully solved the tasks entrusted to their care. They even proved a stimulus to regional sentiment and pride. The provinces vied with each other in building the institutes of self-government. But neither the new organization of the rural counties nor that of the provinces modified the authoritarian character of the Prussian government substantially. In some of the small German states, which reformed their local and municipal government in the same years, self-government was carried further than in Prussia, where to the end of the monarchy the principles of the laws of 1872 and 1875 remained essentially unchanged.

✍ City Government

IN 1876 COUNT EULENBURG presented a draft law intended to liberalize the self-government of the cities, but since the amendments voted by the liberals in the Prussian second chamber were rejected by the House of Lords, the law failed. No new attempt to modernize municipal self-government was undertaken under the Prussian monarchy. Yet even the existing self-government of the cities was more far-reaching than that of the rural counties and provinces introduced in 1872–75. In the cities all the functions of the local administration, with the important exception of the police, were in the hands of organs of the municipal self-government. In this realm, which in an age of rapid urbanization was growing in importance, liberalism was still able to play a prominent role in public administration.

But the liberals' hopes of making decisive gains in the direction of parliamentary participation in the national government proved vain. Since the expansion of the activities of the federal government was increasing the need for central administrative agencies, the liberals urged repeatedly the creation of a cabinet of federal ministers. But Bismarck argued that a federal cabinet would dethrone the Federal Council from its dominant place. He also saw in the establishment of a ministerial cabinet a step toward parliamentary government. When in 1877 he decided to lighten the burden of his office, he proposed the appointment of deputies who would be placed in charge of departments, but these "secretaries of state" remained subordinate to the chancellor, who was free to execute governmental business in any department. In addition to the existing departments, the foreign office, the admiralty, and the department of justice, a

[3] See the author's *A History of Modern Germany: 1648–1840,* p. 400.

treasury department and department of the interior were created. While the establishment of these departments avoided the dangers that Bismarck sensed in a cabinet of federal ministers, it strengthened the unitarian character of the Empire. Henceforth most of the legislation presented to the Federal Council was drafted by the federal departments rather than the Prussian ministries. Moreover, it became customary to make some of the secretaries of state Prussian ministers without portfolio as well as to select the majority of the Prussian representatives on the Federal Council from among the federal officialdom. The membership of the federal secretaries in the Prussian cabinet gave the chancellor support in the coordination of federal and Prussian policies.

✑ Liberalism vs. Catholicism

AT THE TIME when the law on the chancellor's deputies was issued, the political cooperation between Bismarck and the liberal parties, as it had existed after 1866, had actually already ended. From 1866 on this cooperation had expressed itself in the broad legislation designed for the realization of a liberal economic and social order. Starting in 1872 they also joined in a common fight against the Roman Catholic Church. In 1864 Pope Pius IX, through the encyclical *Quanta Cura* with its *Syllabus*, had denounced practically all liberal principles and thereby aroused the anger of the European liberals. When Pius IX called a general church council in order to promulgate the dogma of papal infallibility, suspicions were aroused not only among liberals but also among some conservative governments, who feared that an infallible pope might reassert medieval claims to the superiority of the church over the state.

On July 18, 1870, the Vatican council announced the dogma of papal infallibility. The pope's primacy over the bishops was affirmed and his *ex cathedra* decisions in matters of faith and morals declared to be infallible. As far as doctrine was concerned, the resolutions of the Vatican council were the logical conclusions of a development already clearly foreshadowed in the final outcome of the Council of Trent.[4] The primacy of the pope over the bishops had occasionally been challenged until the second half of the eighteenth century.[5] But these episcopalian tendencies had chiefly depended on the aristocratic character of the high clergy, and they disappeared when the French Revolution uprooted feudalism. Actually, the exercise of papal primacy had suffered chiefly from the control of the states over the churches that sometimes, as in the case of Emperor Joseph II, assumed extreme forms. Thereafter Napoleon had shown what frightful damage the modern secular state was able to inflict on the

[4] See the author's *A History of Modern Germany: The Reformation*, pp. 270 ff.
[5] See the author's *A History of Modern Germany: 1648–1840*, p. 301.

church. Faced with the growth of state power and of irreligious forces, the church, in the half-century after 1815, had looked for strength in greater unity under the papacy. This strong trend helped to create the climate in which the Vatican council reached its decisions.

The liberals believed that the individual ought to give his loyalty only to the national state. They found it inconceivable that devout Catholics should accept the definition of their basic political principles from an ecclesiastical and, still less, from a supranational authority. North of the Alps the Catholics were stigmatized as "ultramontanes," and this label, when used by the liberals, strongly connoted lack of patriotism. Thus the German Catholics faced much enmity just at the time when, through the exclusion of Austria in 1866, they became a minority. The Prussian annexation of Schleswig-Holstein, Hanover, Hesse-Nassau, and Frankfurt strengthened the Protestant majority within Prussia, since, except for a part of the Frankfurt population and some small Hanoverian districts, no Catholics lived in the new provinces. The non-Prussian member states of the North German Confederation were likewise solidly Protestant. Although the accession of South Germany considerably increased the number of Catholics, there were twice as many Protestants as Catholics even in the Empire.

✍ *The Center Party*

As EARLY AS THE SPRING of 1870 a group of Catholics had felt the need for the organization of a political party able to defend the interests of the Catholic Church in the North German and Prussian legislatures. In the Frankfurt Assembly the Catholic members had temporarily banded together when the articles of the constitution concerning state-church relations came under discussion, and the same had happened again in the first Prussian parliament. In 1852 the suspicions aroused by the church policies of the reactionary Prussian government had induced the Catholic members of the Prussian legislature to form a distinct "Catholic faction," later on called the Center party, because its representatives took their seats in the center of the house. But when, after 1859, friction between the state and the Catholic Church ceased and the general political problems of the Prussian constitutional conflict became dominant, a regrouping of the parliamentary factions took place. The original Center party was not even revived after 1866.

The men who founded the new Center party in 1870, most of whom were from Silesia, Westphalia, and the Rhineland, named it the "Center, a constitutional party." They wanted to emphasize the most cherished gain of all the earlier political activities by the German Catholics. Both the Frankfurt constitution of 1849 and the Prussian constitution of 1850 had guaranteed the freedom of the churches. The extension of such a guarantee to the new German Empire became the immediate aim of the Center party. Because of the exclusion of Austria from the Empire, the relative subordination of the states to a federal authority, and the growing secularism of popular liberalism and nationalism, a constitutional guarantee of the freedom of its external and internal life appeared essential to the leaders and members of the church, who were keenly aware of their minority position.

During the Franco-Prussian war Bishop Ketteler of Mainz had written to Bismarck strongly recommending the insertion in the new federal constitution of an article guaranteeing the freedom of the churches. But Bismarck, as we have seen,[6] was most anxious to avoid any changes in the constitution of 1867, which had declared state-church relations as well as education to be exclusively under the jurisdiction of the individual states. Bismarck, therefore, was irritated by the Catholic demands, which were renewed by the Center faction in the German parliament, and was antagonized by the further request to intervene for the protection of the secular rule of the pope over Rome and the church states, which the Italians had abolished after the withdrawal of the French garrison from Rome during the Franco-German war. His fighting instincts were aroused by the appearance of a strong party that seemed to him not only to challenge his untrammeled leadership but also to form the spearhead of a powerful opposition to his solution of the problem of German unification.

Actually the Center party was not founded as a mere opposition party. Apart from the political representation of the interests of the church the original program of the party postulated an easing of the tax burden, the decentralization of the state administrations, and, most of all, the cultivation of state rights against centralistic tendencies. Although in the advocacy of the latter ideals one could sense something of the anti-Prussian feeling of the former Great German Catholicism, it was rather surprising to see how fully the members of the Center party had accepted the new political conditions created by Bismarck. It is true, however, that at the same time the Center party was willing to cooperate with groups unalterably opposed to the Bismarckian order.

In the elections of the fall of 1870 the Center party succeeded in electing fifty members to the Prussian parliament. In the spring of 1871 fifty-seven deputies of the Center party entered the *Reichstag*, making it the second largest party. Its political weight was greatly enhanced by the collaboration with the small group of conservative Protestant Hanoverians, who rejected the Prussian annexation of Hanover and demanded

[6] See p. 224.

the restoration of the kingdom of Hanover under its old dynasty. The close relationship between this so-called Guelf party and the Center party was highlighted by the rise of Ludwig Windthorst (1812–91) to the leadership of the Center party. A former minister of justice in Hanover, he retained his loyalty to the Guelf dynasty. His genuine Catholic faith was at the bottom of his political activities, to which, together with personal unselfishness, he brought brilliant forensic skill and an uncanny talent for parliamentary tactics. He became the most formidable opponent of Bismarck on the rostrum of the *Reichstag*.

The Center party also maintained close relations with the "party of Bavarian patriots," a radical particularist group whose members displayed a raucous anti-Prussianism. Even more objectionable in Bismarck's eyes was the close connection between the Center party and the Poles. The Polish faction of around fifteen delegates naturally felt attracted by the Catholic party, especially its opposition to the liberal program of the exclusive control of the state over the schools. The Poles wished to see the ecclesiastic supervision of schools retained in Germany, since it protected the native tongue in Catholic regions with foreign nationalities. The Alsatian deputies, who joined the *Reichstag* in 1874, also cooperated closely with the Center as the party most sympathetic to their regional needs.

✑ Church Legislation

IN THE FORMATION of the Center party and its affiliations Bismarck saw the rise of a powerful *Fronde* against the Prusso-German monarchy that would stifle or reverse the evolution of a healthy popular support for the national community. The possibility of collusion between these inimical internal forces with an Austria and France dominated by clerical party governments added to Bismarck's concern. His first actions, however, were caused by his concern over the growth of the Polish national movement in the eastern provinces of Prussia, which was receiving help from the Catholic clergy and even from agencies of the Prussian government. In July 1871 Bismarck had the so-called Catholic section of the Prussian ministry of ecclesiastical affairs and education dissolved. In his judgment this section, instituted by Frederick William IV as an instrument of peacemaking between the Prussian state and the Roman Catholic Church, had become a tool of the church within the Prussian government.

More important in principle was the abolition of the supervision of the schools by the churches. This removed not only the Catholic priest but also the Protestant minister from all participation in school administra-

tion. The order of March 1872 meant the acceptance of the liberal program of state schools, a break with the tradition of the Christian state that
the old Prussian Conservatives, among them the incumbent minister of
ecclesiastical affairs and education, Heinrich von Mühler (1813–74),
greatly deplored. Bismarck essentially shared the liberal view of the desirability of the separation of church and state, although his distrust of
priests as likely to meddle in politics made him inclined to seek a maximum of state control over the churches. The liberals themselves tended to
forget the only policy that could logically be derived from liberal principles. Instead of being satisfied with the realization of the separation of
church and state, the majority of them dreamed that the Roman Catholic
Church, through forceful measures, could be remolded to fit national and
free thinking. Therefore, they welcomed and supported every step taken
by the state in order to force the church to adapt itself to the secular
national style. For this generation of German liberals the struggle with
the Catholic Church actually was a fight for the spread of a modern
culture, a *Kulturkampf*, as Rudolf Virchow, the eminent scientist and liberal deputy, called it in early 1873.

Bismarck hesitated to attack the church. Originally he had sought to
win the help of the Vatican against the Center party. Yet in December
1871 he acceded to Bavarian wishes to have the "pulpit paragraph" added
to the criminal code. This paragraph made the public discussion of matters of state by clerics "in a manner endangering public peace" a
criminal offense. The law concerning the order of the Society of Jesus,
issued in July 1872, was again initiated by Bavaria. It suppressed all centers of the order in Germany and made it possible to limit the stay of
individual Jesuits in Germany as well as to ban non-German Jesuits
altogether. The myths current about the influence of the Jesuits in past
history explain the ready acceptance of this blatantly discriminatory law
by the parliament, although a few liberals raised their voices against such
a flagrant violation of liberal principles.

ᴄᴏ *Falk and the May Laws*

THE WAR against the church was opened in full earnest only in 1873. It
was carried on chiefly in Prussia, and although Baden and Hesse conducted a parallel *Kulturkampf*, the struggle did not reach the federal level
except in a few instances. Adalbert Falk (1827–1900), who became Prussian minister of ecclesiastical affairs and education in 1872, was the protagonist of an aggressive policy. An able jurist, Falk preferred to use
legislative methods to achieve his ends. Bismarck, however, soon disliked
Falk's legalism and would have preferred to use largely administrative

measures for undermining the position of the clergy. But Bismarck was by no means less hostile to the church than Falk; on the contrary, he added great harshness to the actions of the government.

The struggle with the church reached its full force with the passing of the Prussian "May laws" of 1873. The first law made the appointment of any priest or minister dependent on his regular attendance at a German high school and subsequent study at a German university. In addition, candidates for ecclesiastical positions had to pass an examination in philosophy, history, and German literature before a state board. The aim was to minimize all training by church schools in order to imbue the servants of the church with the ideals of the nation as understood by the government. The law demanded from the church authorities information about all the appointments and gave the state a veto against them.

Another law abolished the papal jurisdiction over the Catholic Church in Prussia. The disciplinary authority of the church was transferred to German agencies. The clergy was made responsible for keeping the state government informed of church penalties. At the same time the law established a royal court to which church penalties could be appealed by individual church members or by the state government. Two other laws forbade the publication of church penalties and made separation from the church easier.

The German bishops, supported by the Roman Catholic clergy and laymen, refused to recognize the legal validity of the May legislation because the church had not even been consulted. Only a small group of Catholic magnates and high government officials, dubbed "State-Catholics," expressed satisfaction with the laws. Soon the government rained fines and penalties on the bishops and priests. By 1876 all the Prussian bishops were imprisoned or had been driven to take refuge abroad; of 4,600 Catholic parishes 1,400 were without a priest by 1877. The opposition of the Catholics spurred the Prussian government to pass laws designed to deflate the position of the church in public life and to drive a wedge between hierarchy and laymen. The "expatriation law" of May 4, 1874, gave the government the power to confine to certain places of residence or even to ban from the Empire those clerics who, though deprived of their position, continued to practice their priestly function. This law was followed by one concerning the administration of vacant bishoprics. If a bishop were deposed by court decision and the chapter refused to elect a successor, the state could appoint a commissar for the administration of the properties of the diocese. The right to appoint local priests was to devolve on local patrons or, where they did not exist, on a meeting of parish members convened for this purpose by the mayor or county councillor.

The attempt to mobilize the parishes against the hierarchy was carried still further a year later by a law that ordered the election of parish boards or vestries which were to administer the property and finances of the parish. Fresh passion was aroused when on February 5, 1875, a papal encyclical declared the whole ecclesiastic legislation of Prussia invalid and threatened those who obeyed it with excommunication. The Prussian government countered this denunciation by issuing a law of April 22 that stopped all financial support of the church through state funds until the bishops would accept the state laws. And five weeks later a law excluded all the monastic orders, except those devoted exclusively to hospital work, from Prussia. The radicalism and spitefulness of the legislation of 1875 no less than its actual execution may already have been signs that the Prussian government no longer felt so sure that it would be easy to break the will of the Roman Catholic Church in Germany.

As a matter of fact, there was no visible loss of determination among the clergy, while the Catholic laymen intensified their support of the hierarchy and clergy. The expectation of a good many liberals that large groups of Catholics would oppose the decrees of the Vatican council and therefore leave the church proved fallacious. Although some prominent Catholic scholars, foremost among them Ignaz von Döllinger (1799–1890), rejected papal infallibility, they did not win a considerable following for open opposition against the Roman Church even in the academic world, while among the people their voices found only a faint echo. Although much favored by the government, their so-called "Old-Catholic Church" had never more than a few thousand members.

Only those laws that separated state and church could be defended from a liberal point of view. Full state control over schools was a liberal ideal. It was also logical to introduce the obligatory civil marriage law and entrust civil agencies with the keeping of vital statistics, as was done in Prussia in 1874 and the following year in the Empire. But all the other measures constituted shocking violations of liberal principles. German liberalism showed no loyalty to the ideas of lawful procedure or of political and cultural freedom which had formerly been its lifeblood. With few exceptions the German liberals were hypnotized by the national state, which they wished to imbue with a uniform pattern of culture. They were unable to recognize that the *Kulturkampf* was bound to undermine the belief in the *Rechtsstaat* (government by law) and to divide the German people profoundly.

✎ *Results of the* Kulturkampf

AT THE SAME TIME the *Kulturkampf* showed the limitations of Bismarck's statesmanship. The battle he had opened with the aim of destroying the

Center party quickly turned into a fight against the church. The attack against the church and the fierce attempts to intervene in its internal life rallied the Catholic people to its defense. While the many Catholic lay associations that had sprung up after 1848[7] were the centers of the resistance to the governmental policies and practices, it was inevitable that the German Catholics became most anxious to strengthen their political representation. The new Center party gained support in all regions and social classes of Catholic Germany. In the federal elections of 1874 the party doubled its popular vote and became the second largest party in the federal parliament. This was not a merely temporary success. Although the relative strength of the parliamentary representation of the Center party fluctuated, its actual vote remained more stable than that of any other German party for the next sixty years, during which time it was usually impossible to form a parliamentary majority without the Center party.

Thus Bismarck's policy ended in a dismal failure. He always argued that the fight of the state against the church miscarried because, as he put it in his memoirs, "honest if clumsy Prussian policemen with spurs and dangling sabres could not catch up with smooth and light-footed priests moving through back doors and bedrooms." These remarks prove that he failed completely to see what was actually involved in the church struggle. It was not the Machiavellism of the priests but the fervent faith of the German Catholics in their church that defeated the Prussian government. Bismarck was unable to recognize in churches anything but institutions for the control of people. While this made him suspicious even of the Protestant churches, it deprived him of any understanding of the religious foundation of the Roman Catholic Church.

In his memoirs Bismarck expressed the view that the state gained from the *Kulturkampf*, particularly by the control of the schools, to which we may add the only other measure that survived the years of struggle, namely civil marriage. But these gains could have been won without opening war against the Catholic Church, as was demonstrated in Austria in these years. The *Kulturkampf* created deep and lasting mistrust of the government among the German Catholics. They could not easily forget that they had been branded by Bismarck as "enemies of the Empire," or that their church had been exposed to humiliations and persecutions aiming at its total subjugation. The majority of the German Catholics felt the absolute need to organize as a separate camp in every field of life, and especially in politics. Thus the division of the nation along denominational lines was deepened again. The wounds that the state-church struggle inflicted on the German Catholics did not make them secessionists, nor did Great German ideals revive among them. But they bitterly re-

[7] See the author's *A History of Modern Germany: 1648–1840*, pp. 507–8.

sented the fact that Protestants and liberals should judge them unreliable Germans on account of their faith. In Alsace-Lorraine and in the Polish provinces of Prussia the *Kulturkampf* heightened the aversion to Germany.

✆ Conservative Party

ALTHOUGH THE ATTACK was directed against the Roman Catholic Church, the legislation tended to limit the public influence of the Protestant churches as well. This added to the hostility with which the Prussian Conservatives viewed Bismarck's policies. For the time being they were losing strength at the polls, but they remained powerful in the Prussian House of Lords and had many channels through which they were able to present their views at the royal court. This criticism of his old cronies greatly irritated Bismarck, while he was annoyed that the parliamentary weakness of the Conservative party made him so dependent on the liberal groups.

Only in 1876 was an attempt to reorganize the Conservative party successful. A German Conservative party was founded, whose name indicated that these conservatives proposed not to question the Bismarckian constitution any longer. The emphasis of the party program was shifted to economic objectives. The party was now able to attract votes also in the new Prussian provinces and outside of Prussia, as well as in the agrarian sectors of the German society in general. In the elections of 1877 the Conservatives practically doubled their vote and together with the Free Conservatives could muster a parliamentary representation of 79 deputies. The same elections showed that liberalism was weakening. The National Liberal party lost twenty-four seats. Although, with 128 seats, it still remained the strongest single party, it was no longer in a position to form a majority with the Progressives. For some time the National Liberal party had been suffering from serious internal tensions. It had on the whole supported Bismarck over many years and extracted from him some political concessions. But whether these concessions were of such consequence as to justify the disregard of liberal principles that the party had practiced for national reasons had been a serious problem to many of its members. Now with the rear guard of the Progressive party lost, the bargaining power of the National Liberal party vis-à-vis the government was gravely diminished.

✆ Bismarck's Reforms

BISMARCK on his part still had to find a parliamentary majority for the new policies which slowly took shape in his mind during 1876–78. He wanted to reform the finances of the Empire and reestablish the aims of German economic policy with a view to stabilizing not only the political institutions which he had created but also the social order which he considered necessary for sustaining these institutions. The economic developments after 1871 had created novel problems. A tremendous burst of economic expansion had followed the Franco-German war only to end in the terrific crash of 1873 that wiped out the major part of these gains. For a number of years the economy limped along, and when it started growing, did so sporadically and on a small scale. Still, the "founders' years" of 1871–73 had laid the base for the growth of big industries and cities, as well as of a proletariat. After 1873 the depression naturally raised questions about the causes of the crash and its aftermath, and liberal economic policies came under fire.

The amended act on stock companies of 1869, which had practically abolished the requirement of governmental permission for the founding of industrial corporations, was especially criticized. Equally the free-trade policy of the government was opposed by certain agrarian and industrial groups. Actually the transition to a full free-trade policy had not been launched before 1862, and the last import duties were abolished by Rudolf Delbrück, the director of German economic policies, only in the years after the big crash. The first counteragitation was directed against the lifting of the last duties on iron in 1877. It centered in the Central Association of German Industrialists founded by Wilhelm von Kardorff (1828–1907) in 1875. The big landowners of East Germany on their part felt the pinch of the large imports of American and Russian grain that made grain prices topple. All through the century, the *Junkers*, as exporters of grain, had been champions of a liberal trade policy. But, from the 1870's on, Germany needed more foodstuffs than her agriculture could produce. Therefore, the loss of foreign markets became inconsequential for the agrarian producers, whereas the exclusion of cheaper foreign competition from the German market seemed vital for the survival of the large estates in East Germany. Thus from both the agrarian and the industrial sectors of the German economy powerful interests rose up against liberal trade policies, while at the same time even the economic institutions that liberalism had introduced were being questioned. By 1878 more than half of the members of the *Reichstag*, among them not only Conservatives but also most of the Center members and a group of National Liberals, favored a tariff.

As early as 1876 Rudolf Delbrück sensed that Bismarck was moving away from economic liberalism and resigned. In 1877 Bismarck approached the leader of the National Liberals, Rudolf von Bennigsen, and discussed with him taxes and tariff. In addition, he offered him the vice-chancellorship and a Prussian ministry. Bismarck certainly did not intend to introduce parliamentary government, against which he fought all his life. Rather, he wanted to make sure that the right wing of the National Liberal party would support his forthcoming legislative program. Bennigsen, however, saw in Bismarck's offer the intention of giving the parties a greater role in government. Being fully aware of the internal political tensions within his own party and anxious not to be politically isolated in the cabinet, he demanded the simultaneous appointment of two other National Liberals, both belonging to the left wing of the party, whereupon Bismarck discontinued the conversations.

✑ *Election of Leo XIII*

AT THE BEGINNING of 1878 Pope Pius IX died. In these years the Roman Church had political difficulties not only with Germany but also with the Habsburg monarchy, while in France the clericals had just lost their hold on the government. In Leo XIII the conclave elected a pope who was expected to resolve some of the international frictions and conflicts. Bismarck apparently at once recognized in this event an opportunity for ending the *Kulturkampf* and achieving some cooperation between the government and the Center party. But he had still to contend with the pivotal role of the National Liberal party in any parliamentary vote on a government bill, when suddenly some unexpected events gave him the chance to remove it from this position.

✑ *Rise of Socialism*

THE RISE of a German socialist party after 1871 had alarmed the chancellor. The Paris Commune of 1871 and the nihilist movement in Russia had made him extremely apprehensive of revolutionary socialism, and although he did not believe in an exclusively negative approach, he was convinced that as a first step the socialist movement of the workers should be suppressed by any means. On May 11, 1878, a vain attempt on the life of William I was made. Although the perpetrator of the crime, Max Hödel, a desolate character, was never shown to have had any contact with the Social Democratic party, this did not keep Bismarck from presenting to the *Reichstag* a law banning the party. The hastily drafted law met with the disapproval of all parties except the Conservatives. But only a few days later a second attempt by a vain individual, Dr. Karl Nobiling, who wounded the old emperor seriously, gave Bismarck the chance to dissolve the *Reichstag*. Although Nobiling, who committed suicide, was not a Social Democrat either, the elections were conducted as if socialism were an immediate threat to the very foundations of the Empire. The government campaign was successful. Even during the elections the National Liberals were compelled to promise the excited electorate an antisocialist law, but naturally they lost face by this turnabout. Instead of their former 127 seats only 98 were returned. The Progressives also suffered losses, while the Center party held its own. The winners of the elections were the Conservatives and Free Conservatives. Together they commanded 115 votes in the new *Reichstag* and were now in a position to form a majority with either the National Liberal or the Center party.

ᴄ⋅ Cooperation with Liberals Ends

THIS WAS THE END of the "liberal" period that had begun in 1867. It had been liberal in the sense that the National Liberals had cooperated with Bismarck in building up the basic institutions of the national state. In this process they had been able to realize their major social and economic ideas, though little of their ultimate political aims. Their influence helped to make the Empire more unitarian than Bismarck, starting from a more federative conception, had originally intended. But Bismarck frustrated any progress toward the liberal ideal of parliamentary government, and his aversion to any kind of parliamentary influence did not diminish over the years. The further limitation of the power of parliament was also one of the objectives of his new program of economic and financial policies of 1878–79.

ᴄ⋅ Economic Reforms

THE LAW against the Social Democratic party was passed by a Conservative–National Liberal majority in October 1878, and during the following winter Bismarck announced his new economic program, which after long and acrimonious debates was finally passed by the *Reichstag* in July 1879. Bismarck proposed to make indirect taxes and import duties the mainstay of federal finance. While he asserted that indirect levies were more easily borne by the population than direct taxes, his preference was also motivated by the fact that indirect levies weakened parliament's right of the purse. Although the *Reichstag* cut the proposed indirect taxes very sharply, it was soon apparent that the tariff would have a solid majority. The most problematic item was the tariff on grain. It was an unpopular, and probably an unjust, measure to raise the price of bread for the common people. But Bismarck insisted that all national production should be protected and indicated that for him the grant of duties on iron was dependent on simultaneous grain duties. The latter were set rather low at ten marks per ton but were raised as early as 1885 to thirty and in 1887 to fifty marks. The new tariff that was passed on July 12, 1879, provided for import duties of 5 to 10 per cent according to the value of goods.

The passage of the tariff was preceded by a decision of equal political significance. The National Liberal party, through Bennigsen, offered the chancellor its parliamentary support for his bills, provided he would agree to having the *Reichstag* annually pass on the salt tax and coffee duties in order to safeguard the budget rights of the parliament. The revenue collected from duties and indirect taxes would go to the federal government, which then could give up the "matricular" contributions from the states. The Center party, though as eager as the National Liberals to defend the budget rights of the parliament, wished to preserve the power of the individual states. For this reason it resisted the abolition of the "matricular" contributions that seemed to chain the federal government to the states. A difficult formula was worked out, which, after its author, became known as the "Franckenstein clause." Under this clause the revenue from customs duties and the tobacco tax that exceeded 130 million marks had to be turned over to the individual states in proportion to their population. Since the sum of 130 million marks was quite inadequate for covering the federal expenditure, the "matricular" contributions were to be continued; their actual size, as before, was to be fixed annually by the *Reichstag*, which thus exercised its influence over the budget.

There could be no doubt that this proposition of the Center was technically difficult and, most of all, that it stopped the tide which in the preceding twelve years had run in the direction of concentrating growing strength in the hands of the federal government. Just the same, Bismarck accepted the cooperation of the Center, in spite of strong opposition from members of the Prussian cabinet. He knew that the left wing of the National Liberal party was opposed to his protectionist program. In the parliamentary debates he had done his utmost to attack the eminent leaders of the left wing by invective, satire, and calumny in the hope of splitting the party. Actually, these attempts merely led to the separation of a small segment of its right wing from the National Liberal party. The bulk of the party still held together in 1879, though tottering from the blows that Bismarck inflicted on its members. But, in any event, he wanted a clearly conservative majority and felt that the Center party was better suited to his purposes. He was no longer afraid that the strengthening, or at least stabilization, of the influence of the states in federal politics was undesirable, since the political solidarity of the emperor and the German princes would put the *Reichstag* in its place. It was obvious that the acceptance of assistance from the Center party would necessitate rather far-reaching concessions to the Roman Catholic Church. But since the enthronement of Pope Leo XIII Bismarck was confident that the *Kulturkampf* could be ended by diplomatic negotiations with the Vatican.

Thus Bismarck agreed to the Franckenstein clause and parted company with the National Liberals. Thereby a weak system of federal finance was created. Although federal revenue was increased, it proved inadequate as early as 1881, when higher military expenditure had to be covered. When the *Reichstag* refused to grant the federal government additional taxes, it was driven to borrowing. This method of financing the federal budget was used at an increasing rate in the following decades. The fact that this development was not altogether unforeseeable proves that through financial reform Bismarck wanted to achieve not only an improvement of the federal treasury but also broad political gains.

∽ *Bismarck and the Center Party*

SOME OF THESE GAINS did not accrue as easily as he had expected. The Vatican was not in a position to bargain on most of the Prussian church legislation, nor was it inclined to see the Center party weakened, or even crippled, as Bismarck wished. The retreat from the punitive Prussian church legislation was slow, especially since Bismarck still had to contend with the unabated antichurch sentiment of the German liberals. His relations with the Center party remained tense. The fiercest parliamentary battles between the ebullient chancellor and the wiry Ludwig Windthorst took place in the mid-eighties. Windthorst succeeded in making the Prussian government withdraw most of the *Kulturkampf* legislation. He also managed to defeat Bismarck's endeavor to split the Center party, even when in 1886–87 the Vatican sided with Bismarck and disavowed some of the demands that Windthorst had made. The year 1887 marked the definite end of the *Kulturkampf*. The concession that the pope made concerned the obligation of the church to inform the state of all permanent church appointments and the right of the state to disapprove under certain conditions. Otherwise, of the *Kulturkampf* legislation, only the scrapping of the articles of the Prussian constitution guaranteeing freedom of the churches, the exclusive state supervision of schools, the pulpit paragraph, the obligatory civil marriage, and, for the time being, a modified anti-Jesuit law were retained; everything else was repudiated. The bishop sees were filled, church seminaries and monastic centers reopened, and an independent church life revived.

Still, the Center party survived in undiminished strength. While it was supported by Catholic members of every social class, noblemen as well as workers, it derived its numerically strongest backing from country and small-town people. Peasants, artisans, and small tradesmen, with their traditionalistic outlook, desired help from the government for the preservation of the forms of their economic activities and their social status, which were imperiled by the explosive growth of an industrial society.

Therefore, the Center party was prepared to oppose liberalism and push legislation for the economic and social protection of the lower middle classes and of the workers. The conservative social philosophy of the Catholic Church also favored a protectionist policy which, from 1879 on, made the Center party support most of the economic policies of the government. But the party remained firm in its defense of the existing parliamentary institutions. Although it did not demand full parliamentary government, it insisted on the right of the federal and state parliaments to pass the budget and criticize governmental policies. The *Kulturkampf* had taught the lesson that only through parliamentary institutions could Catholic political action be made effective.

✍ Liberal Parties

BISMARCK'S DECISION to end the cooperation with the National Liberal party was eventually to lead to its split. Ever since the Industrial Revolution had gathered momentum, German liberalism had been changing in character.[8] No doubt, the experience of a common national market as well as of common economic crises had strengthened the consciousness of interdependence and of the need for further internal integration in view of international competition. But while the national ideal was thus strengthened, it became at the same time more materialistic, and these material interests tended to divide German liberalism. The moderate liberals had always been inclined to cooperate with a government that conducted a national policy and in return for this support had expected the grant of personal freedom. By 1879 they felt that most of their hopes had been fulfilled. A national state had been created, and its government, though not divesting itself of its authoritarian powers, had given to the people individual freedom. In view of the threat of a proletarian revolution the survival of this freedom depended on the government, as did a healthy state of the national economy. As the moderates had formerly compromised on political freedom in exchange for political nationalism, they were now prepared to compromise in exchange for social nationalism.

On the other side of the liberal spectrum were the Progressives. They continued the political attitude they had chosen during the Prussian constitutional conflict of the 1860's. They demanded strict constitutional guarantees of individual liberties and stressed the budget rights of the parliaments. They had been opposed to all paternalism and became bitter foes of the new protectionism. Free trade became the central tenet of their creed together with a belief in restricting government activities and holding budgets low.

[8] See p. 115.

In between the moderates and Progressives was a group of men who were uneasily trying to strike a balance between the liberal ideal and practical effectiveness. In 1866, together with the moderate liberals, they had formed the National Liberal party, and their contributions to the fundamental institutions of the Empire, such as Ludwig Bamberger's leading role in the legislative establishment of the currency and banking system, were outstanding. Their desire to use their ideas for the practical reform of national life made them willing for a while to put aside their ultimate constitutional objectives. Yet they were not only conscience stricken but also sufficiently astute to realize that Bismarck's political methods maneuvered the liberals into a situation where they would have to bury their high ideals. In this group at least a few felt some anguish over the *Kulturkampf*, while the antisocialist law of 1878 aroused even more serious concern and the economic reforms of 1879 real horror. Bennigsen's argument that a difference of opinion regarding free trade and protectionism should not be cause for a division of the National Liberal party did not prevail for long. In 1880 individual members began to leave the party, to be followed by the "secession" of 1881, when a large group of National Liberals formed the "Liberal Association."

Bismarck had done his utmost to encourage the representatives of material interests to come forward and press their claims. He thought that it would be easier for the government to deal with social groups than with political parties. Actually, his policy of fragmentizing the parties by stirring up conflicts of interest achieved the division of the National Liberal party. But it was not just the left wing that seceded in 1881. Such eminent leaders as Max von Forckenbeck, lord mayor of Berlin, and the champion of national unification in Bavaria, Baron Franz von Stauffenberg, together with such accomplished parliamentarians as Eduard Lasker, Ludwig Bamberger, and Heinrich Rickert formed the core of the Liberal Association.

The elections of 1881 proved the Liberal Association to be as strong as the National Liberal party. The elections evinced sharp popular dissatisfaction with the new economic policies of the government. The Conservatives suffered considerable losses, whereas the Progressives became the second largest party after the Center. In 1884 the Liberal Association and the Progressive party merged into the German Liberal party (*Deutsch-Freisinnige Partei*). This fusion was undertaken in order to have a liberal party on which the crown prince could lean when ascending the throne, an event that in view of the emperor's age seemed fast approaching. Yet the elections of 1884 were disappointing. The German Liberal party retained only 67 of the former 105 seats of the Liberal Association and the Progressive party and never grew beyond this level again. On the contrary, over the next thirty years it was smaller than the National Liberal party. The coalition of the Liberal Association with the members of the old Progressive party was an uneasy one, and as early as 1893 secessionist tendencies reappeared. While the commercial and banking interests remained opposed to protectionism and saw their political representation in the German Liberal party, it, nevertheless, derived its mass support chiefly from the lower middle class, whose hero was Eugen Richter (1838–1906). He practically ruled the party, as he had ruled the Progressive party from 1875 on. Free trade and resistance to any intervention of the government or extension of its activity were his main concerns. His minute knowledge of the budget made him a formidable critic, much feared by the members of the government. But since purity of liberal doctrine rated higher with Richter than practical political achievements, the German Liberal party remained strictly oppositional not only to the government but also to the other parties, particularly to the Social Democratic party on its left.

After the secession the National Liberal party for all practical purposes became a governmental party, ready to cement the alliance between heavy industry and large-scale agriculture that Bismarck's tariff of 1879 had brought into existence. In 1884 the National Liberals drafted a new program in Heidelberg. It clearly indicated that henceforth they would seek influence with the government by supporting it rather than trying to mold it according to their wishes through parliamentary debate or battle. Although national patriotism served as the justification for this further retreat from liberalism, it was actually in response to the material gifts which the government dispensed and the protection which it offered against the working-class movement that the National Liberal transformation took place. The National Liberal party became the party of the upper bourgeoisie in Protestant Germany. Except for certain groups which continued the free-trade tradition and kept close to the German Liberal party, practically all the non-Catholic industrialists voted National Liberal, as did the majority of the free professions—lawyers, doctors, high school teachers, and university professors.

The split of the great National Liberal party of 1866 in 1880–81 had been caused by a conflict of political and economic views and was hardened by the social division of the German bourgeoisie. This division was to last to the end of the Weimar Republic. Bismarck did not set into motion this growth of a social differentiation of the German middle classes on the basis of economic interests, but by proposing his protectionist policy he threw an apple of discord between the diverging groups and made their final separation inevitable.

Yet the political situation that followed Bismarck's destruction of the old National Liberal party did not fulfill his hopes. The ground swell of popular dissatisfaction with Bismarck's economic and financial policies drastically weakened the Conservatives in the election of 1881, while leaving the strength of the Center unimpaired. But as has been mentioned before, the Center in these years was still in a largely oppositional mood, and in order to form a governmental majority even some undependable votes, from among the Guelfs, Poles, or Alsatians, were required. The election results of 1884 were not very different. Only in 1887 did Bismarck succeed in getting a *Reichstag* with an ideal majority. The international crisis and the danger of a war with Russia and France enabled him to whip up national sentiment. The National Liberals agreed with the Conservatives on an election *Kartell*, that is, they agreed not to oppose each other in constituencies that were safely in the hands of one or the other party. With the *Kartell* majority Bismarck was able to have another seven-year army bill passed that provided for large military increments. But the elections of February 1890 reversed the whole party constellation again.

ᢒ *Domestic Policies after 1880*

BISMARCK WAS greatly embittered by the parliamentary conditions in the early 1880's. Even less than before did he hide his contempt of parties and parliamentarians. He was incapable of feeling any respect for the honest convictions of those who differed from him, and his harangues poisoned the political life of the nation. He now declared that he would prefer to have laws passed by practical men, and in 1880 he introduced in Prussia an economic council, composed of representatives of industry, agriculture, commerce, and the trades, which he tried to turn into a German economic council in 1881. His experience with the Prussian economic council was not very encouraging, however, and Bismarck dropped the project when the *Reichstag* cut off the funds for this potential rival. The *Reichstag* also withstood the chancellor's attempt to introduce biennial instead of annual budgets. But all through the 1880's he entertained in the back of his mind ideas about a possible change of the constitution that would diminish the power of parliament. He advanced the spurious theory that the Empire had been brought into life by an act of federation of the German princes and, therefore, could also be dissolved by these princes, who then could agree on a new constitution. In this way Bismarck hoped to get rid of the universal suffrage in federal elections. These ideas remained projects to be applied only in a great emergency. After the elections of 1890 Bismarck apparently thought such an emergency close at hand, but his dismissal in March 1890 kept him from making a final decision.

All through the last decade of his reign we see Bismarck anxious to bolster the position of the states and of their chief organ, the Federal Council. And strengthening the states meant at the same time strengthening Prussia, where, in contrast to the Empire, it was possible to exclude all liberalism. The policy changes of 1879 had induced the last three members of the Prussian cabinet who could be identified with liberal policies to resign their offices. Among them was Falk, who as minister of education and ecclesiastical affairs was replaced by Robert von Puttkamer (1828–1900), a conservative Pomeranian *Junker*. He began the settlement of the state-church conflict, but more important was his subsequent management of the ministry of interior from 1881 to 1888. Puttkamer weeded out all liberals on all levels of Prussian internal administration and saw to it that nobody who was not a strict conservative monarchist would receive an appointment to a political post. The candidates were usually chosen from among the members of the elegant dueling fraternities and, if possible, were supposed to hold a reserve officer's commission in the army. There was more than a sprinkling of *Junkers* in the body of Prussian interior administrators, and they were dominant on the higher rungs of the official ladder.

Puttkamer also expected these officials to be active on behalf of Conservative candidates during elections, and they undoubtedly helped the trend developing in Prussia during the 1880's. Whereas before that time the universal, direct, and secret suffrage in the Empire and the three-class, indirect, and open suffrage in Prussia had produced parallel results, these began to differ markedly from 1887 on. The plutocratic franchise in Prussia vastly improved the chances of the National Liberals over the German Liberals and practically suppressed the Social Democratic vote. In the Prussian parliament the Conservatives could always form a majority with either the National Liberals or the Center party, and the moves of any other majority that the Conservatives disliked could be foiled by the House of Lords, which was forever a Conservative stronghold. The contrast between the Empire and Prussia was thus sharpened, and in view of the place that Prussia occupied in the Empire the state of her politics could not fail to act as a break on most federal policies.

When Bismarck adopted universal suffrage for the new Empire in 1867 and 1871, he was under the influence of the constitutional conflict, when the Prussian three-class franchise had produced liberal majorities. He had assumed that universal suffrage would bring the common people to the polls, who being still essentially royalist in sentiment could be maintained in this mood by proper governmental manipulation. This view was quite mistaken. In an expanding urban and industrial society universal suffrage, far from serving as the shield of the traditionalist forces, was bound to become the weapon of the rising masses. But not even Bismarck himself put his theory to a real practical test, since the conflict between him and the Conservatives in the early years of the Empire made it rather inexpedient for the government to help the Conservative party.

✑ The Jewish Question

YET THE METHODS adopted by the Conservatives themselves for gaining mass appeal deserve close attention, since they were ominous premonitions of future events in German history. Some Conservatives saw in the anti-Semitism then rampant the ready means for undermining Bismarck's position. In 1875 the *Kreuzzeitung*, the conservative newspaper that Bismarck had helped to found during the revolution of 1848–49, published a series of articles on the financial and economic policies of the new Empire. The policies of the National Liberal era were declared to be managed by Jews for the benefit of Jews, and Bismarck was seen as being under the influence of his banker Gerson Bleichröder and made chiefly responsible for these policies. Although the new German Conservative party of 1876 avoided the direct use of anti-Semitism, many of its members were in sympathy with the Christian-Social party that the court chaplain Adolf Stöcker launched in 1878. In this movement anti-Semitism in Germany was based on Christian principles for the last time. But before discussing Stöcker's political activities we must look at the development of the Jewish emancipation during the nineteenth century.

We have seen[9] how the Enlightenment and mercantilism began to lift the bondage in which the Jews had been held since the later Middle Ages. The French Revolution proclaimed the equality of the Jews, and Napoleon carried this principle into the Rhineland and the kingdom of Westphalia. Although the German princes of the Rhenish Confederation did not follow this example, a Prussian edict of 1812, the work of Wilhelm von Humboldt and Karl August von Hardenberg, gave the Jews in Prussia equality as citizens. But the reaction after 1815 undid many of the advances made in Germany in the preceding twenty years. In Prussia, also, the law of 1812 was whittled down. Not before the revolution of 1848–49 was the trend reversed. The National Assembly of Frankfurt accepted the equality of the Jews as one of the fundamental constitutional rights.

Although the constitution failed, practically nowhere was there a complete return to the former legal status of the Jews, and the full emancipation that came about in North Germany in 1869 and in all of Germany after 1871 did not meet with any opposition in the legislative bodies of the Empire or the states. Nevertheless, a popular opposition existed, and

---

[9] See the author's *A History of Modern Germany: 1648–1840*, pp. 285–8, 320–1, 446–7.

the German Jews were ill-prepared to face this unexpected hatred. A tremendous change had been taking place in the three generations of German Jews between 1780 and 1870. The Jews of 1780 had been out-casts not only from the political but also from the cultural life of the nation. With no access to schools their ghettos became cultural ghettos as well, from which very few could rise by their own exertions. Moses Mendelssohn had been the first shining model of a German Jew who became not only a thoroughly educated man but also a creative thinker. The generation that followed him showed an insatiable quest for learning and education, and its members found manna in the classic German litera-ture and philosophy of the early nineteenth century. Their influence went beyond Germany to the Israelite congregations of Poland, Galicia, and Hungary, which turned to German civilization. The impact on the Jews of the new German education was so strong that little survived of the old Jewish religion. The German sermon and German hymns domi-nated worship in the Jewish congregations. By 1870 the old Jewish ortho-doxy had completely vanished. The great majority of the Jews belonged to liberal, the rest to neo-orthodox, congregations.

Many Jews, however, had given up their ties with Judaism altogether and joined one of the Christian churches, in most cases a Protestant one. Often this was done for worldly preferment, to get rid of the handicaps which the state imposed on the private and public life of members of the Jewish community. And many felt that what little remained of specific content in Jewish religion could not justify the humiliations suffered by them. Karl Marx even saw in Judaism an evil reactionary force. But there were, particularly in the age of romanticism, a good many Jews who embraced Christianity with deep conviction and contributed to the Chris-tian values of their age. The composer Felix Mendelssohn-Bartholdy[10] and the conservative political thinker Friedrich Julius Stahl[11] are exam-ples. Intermarriage between Jews and gentiles frequently occurred even in the beginning and the middle of the century and increased steadily after 1875.

The cultural assimilation of the German Jews was accomplished within little more than a half-century in spite of far-reaching legal discrimina-tion. But although the Jews were not a homogeneous social group, they were not too widely spread among the classes and occupations of German society. For many centuries they had been deprived of the right of hold-ing land; consequently there were no Jewish peasants and farmers. Their exclusion from the craft guilds explains the absence of Jewish artisans except in a few specialized vocations, such as diamond cutting, which they had been allowed to enter by the princes. The lack of a tradition in

[10] See the author's *A History of Modern Germany: 1648–1840*, p. 485.
[11] *Ibid.*, p. 517.

the crafts may also have been a cause for the relatively weak representation of Jews in the modern industries. Only in industries where they
had played a role as financiers in earlier days, such as the various branches
of the textile industry, did they become in larger numbers builders of
modern industrial firms.

Commerce and finance were still the major pursuit of the mass of
German Jews. They were found as lowly peddlers, as cattle and grain
dealers, storekeepers, retail and wholesale merchants, and finally as bankers. However, the relative influence of the Jews on finance declined after
1871. None of the big industrial fortunes that came into being were in
Jewish hands, and the modern big banks which financed the German
industrialization were not decisively directed by Jewish interests.

Jewish university graduates naturally desired to be admitted to governmental service and teaching positions like other graduates. But the governments blocked the entrance to these offices to all nonconverted Jews,
and even after 1871 these policies were not greatly relaxed. Although
Jews were appointed university professors if the universities pressed hard
enough, there were few Jews among the high school or grade school
teachers. Short of emigration, which many Jews chose, these university
graduates had no other choice but the professions. Before long the law
and medical professions and especially journalism absorbed many of the
university-trained Jews, who constituted a much larger percentage of the
membership of these professions than corresponded to the total percentage of Jews in Germany.

The great majority of the Jews belonged to the middle classes, and
while many Jews were poor, few belonged to the proletariat. On the
other hand, the number of those who became members of the upper
bourgeoisie and acquired considerable fortunes was not small. Although
only few Jews took an active interest in politics, with very few exceptions they understandably sympathized with liberalism, which had begun
the Jewish emancipation, and tended to see in the Progressive and German Liberal parties the best champions of full social and political equality. In view of the social composition of the German Jewry, adherence to
free trade created another bond with these parties. Likewise, the politically active Jews were mostly connected with the two parties. Since few
could or did become parliamentarians, most of them had to content themselves with practicing journalism, and the left-liberal papers, such as the
Berliner Tageblatt, *Vossische Zeitung*, or *Frankfurter Zeitung*, gained
many readers outside the left-liberal sections of the people. With the
arrival of the Social Democratic party on the scene some young Jewish
intellectuals joined the working class movement and became functionaries
of the Social Democratic party and the trade unions. They were individuals who by their criticism of the existing regime were driven away not

only from liberalism but also from the Jewish community, which seemed to them moribund.

The assimilation of the Jews during the nineteenth century seemed to prove those Germans right who had predicted that the Jewish problem would quickly disappear once the Jews were given equality and freedom of opportunity. But in reality they never received full equality, nor did their assimilation remain altogether unquestioned even by many of those who welcomed it in principle. While Wilhelm von Humboldt was confident that the Jews would rise to the level of other German citizens, he felt that they would not become full equals unless they gave up the isolation of their congregations as well as the poverty of their religion. He hoped to promote such a development by not allowing any union or federation of the Jewish congregations, and actually the Jewish congregations in Prussia and Germany were never to have a common representation.

Whereas Humboldt was kindly disposed toward the Jews, the German governments of the period of 1819–59 used membership in the Jewish congregations as a weapon of renewed discrimination, and the internal reform of these congregations made no difference in these practices. In spite of the numerous conversions the membership of the congregations between 1816 and 1871 grew from 300,000 to 403,000, which constituted 1.25 per cent of the population. Religious or philosophical convictions, love of their ancient customs, pride of family, and a sense of honor that made it appear improper to convert and derive personal advantages from this action were among the major motives for remaining in the Jewish congregations. This continuation of religious Jewish communities was considered to be a sign of incomplete Germanization even by the many non-Jewish liberals who were Christians only in name. The claim of the Jews to be recognized unconditionally as full Germans of Jewish faith was widely accepted only with strong mental reservations. If feelings of political partisanship were aroused, anti-Jewish hostility easily expressed itself. Although Heinrich von Treitschke stated his belief in the ultimate assimilation of the Jews, the criticism leveled by many left-liberal Jews against the political conditions in the Bismarckian Empire made him resentful, and he added fuel to the anti-Jewish sentiment by threatening the Jews in 1879 with the ire of the German people.

✍ Growth of Anti-Semitism

AT THAT TIME Germany was rife with anti-Jewish agitation. It had broken loose after the crash of 1873 had ended the two years of speculative fever that for the first time, in addition to the upper bourgeoisie and nobility, had drawn the lower middle class in large numbers into the stock exchange. The losses suffered, whether in invested money or in unrealized income in the subsequent depression, convinced many small storekeepers, artisans, and peasants who had felt threatened by the new industries or trading methods of the utter depravity of modern liberalism. And it did not prove difficult to persuade them that the Jews were responsible for the destruction of a healthy economy. The first strong appeal to these sentiments came from a journalist, Wilhelm Marr, who in 1873 published *The Victory of Judaism over Teutonism*, a pamphlet that reached twelve editions in six years. Marr, who introduced the term "anti-Semitism" in Germany, denied that the Jewish problem was a religious issue. The Jews, he wrote, were a race that had shown itself capable of preserving its identity for over 1,800 years. In the nineteenth century they had become a world power and turned Germany into a "New Palestine" chiefly through their influence on the government and control of the press. Marr was pessimistic about the outcome of the struggle between Germans and Jews but admitted that a desperate last counter-attack of Europe or an explosion of the wrath of the German people was still possible.

In the following year a series of articles by Otto Glagau appeared in one of the most widely read weeklies and shortly thereafter was published as a book as well, under the title *The Stock Exchange and Founding Swindle in Berlin*. More concretely than Marr, Glagau described how unlimited capitalism destroys the middle class and kills idealism. The Jews were spearheading capitalism, while Manchester liberalism had given them the opportunity to concentrate on trading with the products of the work and intellectual achievements of others. This alien race operating through the stock exchange was sucking the marrow out of the bones of the German people.

Marr and Glagau were the most effective journalists among a host of anti-Semitic propagandists. It was significant that anti-Semitism appeared in a politically radical garb. According to the two writers, the hated Jews had become powerful because the governments had protected them. Marr and Glagau also made some efforts to appeal to the socialist workers, not, however, by approving their socialist aims but by praising them for their rightful indignation at existing social conditions. On the other side, both writers found grave faults with the Conservatives.

ᔭ Christian-Social Workers Party

BUT A GOOD MANY Conservatives believed that the groups which proved receptive to the anti-Semitic agitation, possibly even the working class population, could be won over to the Conservative cause. From 1878 on, the court chaplain, Adolf Stöcker (1835–1909), had launched a political campaign in the industrial districts of Berlin. Stöcker, the son of a subaltern government official, grew up respecting the traditional order in Prussia, which to him was further elevated by the Prussian unification of Germany. As chairman of the Berlin city mission he had seen the misery of the workers and the growing hold that the Social Democratic party gained over them. National patriotism, Conservative loyalty, and a Christian social consciousness, which did not always blend very well in his personality, were the major motives for his political activities. He judged that the workers would not turn patriotic or Christian unless their social needs were met. His Christian-Social Workers Party, for which he attempted to win the masses with great eloquence, demanded far-reaching social reforms on the basis of Christian faith and love of king and fatherland.

To his contemporaries it was a startling scene to see a Prussian court chaplain holding mass meetings in proletarian districts and criticizing capitalism. But it was quickly shown that the gulf between Christian conservatism and the working class movement in Germany had become unbridgeable. Only a few years earlier Disraeli in England had been very successful in gaining mass support for the Conservative party. But this Tory democracy was the fruit of the many contributions that the Tories had made since the 1830's not only to social improvement but also to the spread of political freedom that guaranteed this social advancement. Even the British working class considered the British parliament, and with it the old political parties, useful instruments of progress. But the Conservative party in Prussia and the Protestant churches had no comparable record, and it was obvious that the monarchical government, with the backing of all the Conservative forces, had always blocked every attempt at giving the parliament a respected position.

In the elections of 1878 Stöcker's Christian-Social Workers party suffered a disastrous defeat. Thereafter the character of the party changed. After 1881 the party ceased calling itself a "workers' party," and although demands for the reform of labor conditions were not dropped, the party concentrated from then on largely on the lower middle classes. In order to attract them Stöcker peppered his progapanda and program with violent anti-Semitism. He managed, though not through the Berlin vote, to gain a seat in both the federal and Prussian parliaments, where he joined the Conservative party. But the Christian-Social party failed to rally substantial groups of voters. Bismarck, who was not a pronounced anti-Semite and even considered anti-Semitism subversive if it was linked with belligerent anti-capitalism, gave Stöcker some indirect support in the election of 1881, because he hoped that the latter would take votes away from the Progressives. When this hope proved vain, he lost interest in Stöcker and even fought him when the prospective heir to the throne, Prince William, got mixed up with the movement.

Anti-Semitism and Social Classes

IT WAS DOUBTFUL, however, how much such a movement was likely to gain from the patronage of the government. To the discontented and restless members of the lower middle class Stöcker was too conservative and too Christian. Their mood demanded radical polemics against the ruling classes, and their anti-Semitism was no longer confined to religious Jews, as was true in Stöcker's case. The first anti-Semitic deputy of the Reichstag, who after his election in 1887 refused to join the Conservative party, was a man who conducted his campaign chiefly by railing at *Junkers* and Jews. The small Hessian peasants who gave him their votes felt blocked by the large *Junker* estates and exploited by the Jewish tradesmen. It was this racist anti-Semitism blended with a measure of social radicalism that proved more catching than Stöcker's Christian-Social action.

While the upper middle classes continued to find their political representation in the National Liberal and Conservative parties, anti-Semitic feeling in this period made great progress even among them. Thus Richard Wagner and his Bayreuth circle flaunted anti-Semitism, and it was an important element in the writings of Paul Lagarde (1827–91), which for many educated Germans of this and of a later period constituted a major source of their nationalist sentiments. In 1881 the League of German Students (*Verein Deutscher Studenten*) was founded which was to propagate anti-Semitism and nationalism in the German universities.

But the attempt to transform the Conservative party, that "small and mighty party" as it was called, into a mass party was unsuccessful. As in the past, the Conservatives derived their strength chiefly from the political and social privileges they had been granted by the state. Bismarck was eager to broaden the social basis of the ruling class. He proposed to ennoble those industrialists and financiers whose wealth seemed sufficiently solid, while successful businessmen, lawyers, and doctors received titles that gave them seemingly equal rank with upper government officials. This assimilation of influential members of the bourgeoisie, by German historians not very felicitously called the "refeudalization of German society," undoubtedly strengthened the conservative character of German public life.

∽ Socialist Movement

ADOLF STÖCKER'S actions were the last significant attempt by an orthodox Protestant to win the adherence of the German working class to the church and the existing monarchical order. As we indicated before, the response of the workers was almost completely negative. With the exception of those Catholic workers who joined the Christian trade unions and a very small segment of the working class population that entered the Hirsch-Duncker trade unions, which were close to the Progressive party, the workers found their representation in the socialist movement.

∽ Ferdinand Lassalle

THE FIRST Socialist organization was the General German Workers' Association, founded in Leipzig in 1863 under the influence of Ferdinand Lassalle (1825–64). The son of a Breslau merchant, the highly gifted Lassalle had worked with Marx during the revolution of 1848–49 trying to launch a socialist movement in the Rhineland. But only in the years of the New Era and the constitutional conflict was he able to carry his message directly to the workers.

Although Lassalle was not uninfluenced by Marx, his political ideas tended in a different direction. According to Lassalle, the working class could never be freed from impoverishment under the conditions of the existing economic system, and it was an iron law that workers would never receive higher wages than would allow them the barest sustenance. Only by making the workers owners of the means of production could a change be accomplished, and to this end he proposed the founding of "workers' production cooperatives." The capital needed for such cooperatives was large and could only come from the state. But since a state dominated by a parliament elected through a three-class suffrage was not likely to grant such funds, the adoption of universal suffrage was an absolute prerequisite for the liberation of the working class. Lassalle was willing to accept universal suffrage even as the gift of a reactionary government. Bismarck held several conversations with Lassalle, in whom he saw a helpful left ally against the liberals. In 1866 Bismarck imposed universal suffrage, though, as we have seen, with expectations very different from those of Lassalle.

Lassalle headed the German socialist movement only for a short time. He was killed in a duel in 1864. But he left his mark on the movement. The emphasis placed on the struggle for the mass vote as well as the reliance on the state as the agency for fundamental reforms that remained characteristic of German socialism stemmed largely from Lassalle. He was succeeded as leader of the General German Workers' Association by a young Frankfurt lawyer, Johann Baptist von Schweitzer (1833–75). Even more than Lassalle, Schweitzer was inclined to deal with Bismarck, whose German policy he supported, and did not allow Marx and Engels any influence on his planning. His association, therefore, did not become the channel for the infiltration of Marxist ideas into the German working class.

Karl Marx

KARL MARX at that time was the German secretary of the First International, which was founded in 1864. It brought together disparate groups such as French Proudhonists, followers of the Russian anarchist Bakunin, and English trade unionists. The International was incapable of agreeing on a systematic program, although its congresses formulated a few of the goals that became standard objectives of socialist parties the world over. Among them were the legal protection of juvenile labor, the abolition of indirect taxation, the nationalization of mines, railroads, and forests, as well as an end to standing armies. Marxism reached Germany through Wilhelm Liebknecht (1826–1900), the loyal emissary whom its founder sent to Germany. Liebknecht came from a scholarly family and had in his veins some of Martin Luther's blood. Even as a very young man he had been a radical democrat with some communist notions. During the Revolution of 1848–49 he eagerly participated in the fighting in Baden. Later he found a refuge in London, where he was in close contact with Karl Marx. Liebknecht was not a profound theoretical thinker; his gifts were of a more practical nature. He was a passionate believer in democratic rights and a fearless man of action.

Social Democratic Workers' Party

AS A FERVENT anti-Prussian and Great German democrat Liebknecht was unable to cooperate with Schweitzer. Thus he turned from Berlin to Leipzig, where in August Bebel (1840–1913) he found a congenial political friend. Bebel was the son of a Prussian noncommissioned officer and the stepson of a prison warden. Early orphaned, he was apprenticed to a wood carver and after the usual *Wanderjahre* found a job in Leipzig in 1860. Soon he was lured into political activity with the workers' associations that were under the aegis of the Progressive party. He read Lassalle in order to fight against him at political meetings. But the socialist virus proved irresistible. Under Liebknecht's influence he adopted many Marxian ideas, and his Federation of Workers' Associations became socialist. In 1868 Bebel and Liebknecht induced a workers' convention in Nürnberg to adopt a declaration in favor of the International. It was the last convention that combined democratic and socialist groups. But the latter were no longer willing to be held back by the democratic groups, which had their main strength in Southwest Germany. At a workers' congress held in Eisenach in 1869, Bebel's Federation of Workers, together with dissenting Lassalleans and some other socialists, founded the Social Democratic Workers' party. Later on the party called itself the Social Democratic party (SPD).

The Eisenach program of the new party contained some Marxian and Lassallean ideas as well as a series of general democratic demands, most of which had become law in democratic Swiss cantons such as Zurich. Obviously the Social Democratic Workers' party wanted to appeal to the South German democrats. But although Marx was already casting his shadow over the scene, even Bebel and Liebknecht were not accomplished students of his works. While serving a prison term in 1869, Bebel for the first time read the first volume of Marx's *Capital*, published in 1867, and again, later on, such involuntary leisure gave him the opportunity for further study. Bebel and Liebknecht opposed the Franco-Prussian war from its beginning, while the followers of Lassalle voted the war credits. Marx and Engels actually welcomed the German unification, because they judged quite correctly that the German labor movement would gain much greater strength on a national plane than in a loosely federated Germany. But the continuation of the war after the demise of the French Empire and the exaction of Alsace-Lorraine united all the German socialists in opposition against the government.

Once the division between *kleindeutsch* and *grossdeutsch* had been settled by events and with the government harassing all socialists, the merger of the various socialist groups made rapid progress. In 1875 a conference in Gotha accepted the full union on the basis of a program that, while displaying the growing impact of Marxian thought, made strong concessions to Lassalle and was heavily weighted toward more democratic reform measures. The party was to work "with every legal means for the free state and a socialist society." This implied a radical change of the existing social order and was interpreted by contemporaries as the clarion call of revolution. But, as Karl Marx and Friedrich Engels pointed out, the state was never clearly described as a class state, and in crucial places the program spoke of the liberation of labor rather than of the laborers. Although social betterment was declared to be possible only as the task of the working class facing the hostile mass of all other classes, the program still seemed to envisage in Lassallean fashion the assistance of the state in building production cooperatives. As immediate objectives the program listed universal suffrage, freedom of association, civil liberties, direct democracy as exemplified by popular referenda and plebiscites, and social reforms, such as the limitation of working hours and the improvement of working conditions for women and children.

Not without good reason Engels called this program "incoherent" and wrote to Bebel that only the fact that it had achieved the union of the German working class and was taken everywhere as a blueprint of revolution would keep him and Marx from denouncing the program publicly. To be sure, Bebel himself, who in May 1871 had spoken in the *Reichstag* of the Paris Commune as the vanguard battle of the great war that the European proletariat would conduct in a few decades against all governments, believed in a future revolution, but his preoccupation was the organization of a socialist party, for which the vagueness of the program even offered some advantages. There is some indication that in these early years many non-Socialists were members of the party.

ᔉ *The Antisocialist Law*

THE FOUNDING of the Social Democratic Workers' party was the beginning of a steady growth of the organized working class movement. Whereas in 1871 Bebel had been the only Socialist in the federal parliament and in 1874 the Socialists had won nine seats, the new party got twelve seats in 1877, while the growth of the popular vote, reaching 9 per cent of the total national vote in 1877, was considerably greater than that of its actual parliamentary representation. But the strength of the party was no immediate threat to the existing social and political order, in spite of all the dissonant noise that the Socialist representatives made. Bismarck's antisocialist law of 1878 saw the party unprepared for such a blow, although, as it turned out, the organization had gained sufficient cohesion to survive the persecution. This antisocialist law of 1878 constituted, however, a milder form of suppression than that adopted by the French government after the Paris Commune in 1871, when about 38,000 Communards were arrested, 20,000 executed, and 7,500 deported to New Caledonia. The German law did not employ such terror. Under its terms all social democratic, socialist, and communist associations, meetings, and publications could be forbidden or dissolved. The law provided that professional Socialist agitators, if found guilty of its violation, could be banned from certain towns or districts. In "imperiled" districts the government also received the power to lift the right of assembly and free political expression and to expel persons who seemed to endanger the public peace. Innkeepers, printers, and book dealers were threatened with the loss of their license if they came in conflict with the law.

The antisocialist law achieved the complete destruction of the existing Social Democratic party institutions, which included prosperous newspaper and publishing firms. The police actions also took a heavy toll among the trade unions, although their connection with the Social Democratic party was rather tenuous. During the twelve years in which the law was in force 900 persons were expelled from their homes and about 1,500 imprisoned. But these actions, which aroused great bitterness, did not succeed in stamping out the Social Democratic movement. In the election of 1881 the Social Democratic vote fell off by 25 per cent. Many of those who had merely wanted to register their protest dropped out, and many Social Democratic workers joined the great masses of overseas emigrants in these years. But by 1884 the strengthening underground organization produced a vote considerably larger than that of 1878, while in 1890 the vote had more than tripled. The loyalty of the Social Democratic workers to their movement no less than the shrewdness and courage with which they built illegal organizations showed a greater political maturity than could have been expected from a downtrodden class that was just entering the political arena. Glee clubs, bowling and gymnastic clubs, hiking groups, and similar social associations served as fronts for the forbidden political formations. Many a meeting was held at dawn in a quarry or sandpit outside a city in order to escape the watchful eye of the police, while small groups in backrooms or backyards of inns explored together the venerated writs of Marx and other socialist authors. A strong sense of solidarity developed among these men working and living together in danger. It was no empty gesture that they addressed each other as "comrades." Through the party the individual worker acquired a feeling of belonging. Although he was told that he was only an anonymous member of the proletariat, it was this class that was to inherit the earth, and a man who acquired the consciousness of the process of history was marching in the vanguard of his class.

Great as the initiative of the rank and file of the party was, it depended for its coherence on a strong central leadership. The sentiment among the followers that only a united party would be strong enough to survive the persecution by the state and ultimately be able to go on the offensive gave its leaders great power over the movement. The escaped and exiled leaders directed the movement largely from Switzerland. Here the party organ, the *Sozialdemokrat*, was issued, which, thanks to the devotion of the German party workers—in this case chiefly the railroad workers— was distributed on a fairly large scale. No change occurred when in 1888 the Swiss government gave in to the demands of the German government and expelled the editors. Thereafter the *Sozialdemokrat* appeared in London.

The first party congress after the antisocialist law had gone into force had been held in Wyden, Switzerland, in 1880. It was decided to expunge the words "with every legal means" from the statement of the Gotha program that the party would work for a free state. The party congress did not wish to propagate revolution with this action, but only to endorse

Social Democratic agitation and organization. But radical groups appeared which rejected parliamentary methods and wanted to conduct the fight against the government by anarchical means. The party chiefs, however, excluded all such elements from party membership. In their opinion the adoption of revolutionary tactics would have brought on the breakup of all mass organizations and also have made it impossible to lift the antisocialist law in the foreseeable future.

The years of 1878–90 were the heroic years of the Social Democratic movement in Germany. In these years a unified party came into existence that contained a large body of tested members always ready to work for it. In contrast to the old parties, it was not a mere contraption for winning elections. Its function was the infusion of communal ideals into its members, something neither state nor church was capable of doing any longer. The party became a state within the state. It broke all sentimental ties not only with the institutions of the monarchical state but also with the other parties. A high wall was erected between the party of the proletariat and the "bourgeois" parties. Thus the years of oppression following the issuance of the antisocialist law deepened and hardened the chasm between the working class and the existing state and society.

Violent suppression, however, was not Bismarck's only answer to the rise of the Social Democratic party. While his fear of social revolution was genuine and was heightened by the Paris Commune and the nihilist movement in Russia, he never doubted that the working class had legitimate grievances, some of which at least were curable by governmental intervention. The predominance of liberal economic thought not only in the liberal but also in the conservative parties made it impossible to act in the 1870's, and Bismarck himself was still undecided about the proper methods.

✑ Academic Thought on Social Reform

Meanwhile the discussion of social problems in academic circles became livelier. For years the only writer trying to solve the needs of the working class had been the philosopher Friedrich Albert Lange (1828–75), author of the classic *History of Materialism*. In 1865 he had published his *Labor Question*, in which he went a long way toward trying to meet the demands of the workers. The economist Lujo Brentano (1844–1931), who was just starting out on his long and brilliant academic career, saw the best solution in the stimulation of free labor unions, whose operations he had intensively studied in England. In 1872 he convened at Eisenach a conference of scholars interested in social problems, who founded the Association for Social Policy (*Verein für Sozialpolitik*). The association comprised both liberals and conservatives as long as they were in favor of some form of government activity for the regulation of social problems. Professors, government officials, journalists, businessmen, and parliamentarians thereafter joined at annual meetings for the discussion of the acute problems of social policy and legislation, and the association was responsible for many solid studies of the socioeconomic reality which so far had been little explored.

Although the association did not propagate one-sided solutions, and representatives of the Social Democratic party were conspicuous by their absence, it was quickly accused of being the Trojan horse of socialism. Because professors predominated in the association, the public dubbed its members *Kathedersozialisten,* i.e., socialists of the academic chair. Heinrich von Treitschke even spoke of them as "the patrons of socialism." While the prejudices behind such polemics could not be stamped out where, as among many industrialists and employers, they were the result of selfish interests, they were more tractable as far as they were merely the uncritical carry-over of traditional thinking. Although the political influence of the association should not be overrated, it contributed greatly to a better understanding of social and economic problems among the educated and politically interested people, who were principally found in the civil service of the states and the Empire.

✑ *Social Policies of the Center Party*

OF MORE immediate political consequence was the positive attitude that the Center party as a whole took with regard to governmental action for the solution of the labor problem. Originally such leaders of German Catholicism as Bishop Baron von Ketteler had seen in the problem chiefly a spiritual crisis, but at least from the sixties on the need for the reform of material and economic conditions was clearly recognized. These men tended to see the remedy particularly in labor protection, that is, in such measures as the legal limitation of working hours, as well as the improvement of working conditions of women and children, and factory inspection.

Bismarck welcomed the positive attitude of the Center party toward social action and occasionally expressed satisfaction with the *Kathedersozialisten,* but the social legislation that he proposed used little of the ideas of these movements. Bismarck liked to call his social legislation applied Christianity, as he did in particular in the imperial message to the *Reichstag* of November 17, 1881, that opened the decisive debates on his program. But the rational aim of his social policy, in which incidentally the churches were to have no part, was directed toward the strengthening of the state. By bestowing visible and palpable material benefits on the workers he expected them to become willing supporters of the existing order. What tariffs had done with the grain and iron producers, state insurance was to do with the workers.

⟋ *Bismarck's Social Legislation*

BISMARCK'S SOCIAL LEGISLATION was strictly confined to obligatory workers' insurance against the main threats to their working capacity, namely sickness, accident, incapacity, and old age. Three laws were accordingly presented for the creation, under federal auspices, of an accident insurance system, to be followed by one for health insurance, and to be crowned by a system of disability and old-age insurance. In the parliamentary struggles the relatively easiest to achieve was health insurance, for which in the health funds of the miners' and craft guilds a beginning existed. Moreover Bismarck was least interested in health insurance, which was unlikely to produce a class of recipients of state benefits, and as a consequence was willing to agree to a decentralized organization and the participation of its members in its administration. The law of 1883 introduced health insurance for a large segment of wage earners. As a rule the health service was set up on a local basis and the cost divided between employers and workers—one third to be paid by the employers and two thirds by the workers. The minimum payments for medical treatment and sick pay up to thirteen weeks were legally fixed. The individual local health bureaus were administered by a committee elected by the members, and here the workers won majority representation on account of their large financial contribution. It was the first chance for the Social Democrats to gain a small foothold in public administration.

The government had to present three draft laws before a law on accident insurance was passed in 1884. Bismarck had finally to drop his wish to make a federal contribution to this insurance, which was important to him as a demonstration of the government's willingness to free the less fortunate citizens from hardship. But the National Liberals saw in this law an unbearable expression of state socialism, while the Center party was afraid of the expansion of federal power that might result from it. The whole cost was underwritten by the employers. Bismarck, who, as will be remembered, toyed with the idea of replacing the parliament by a council of corporations in these years, got his way by having the organization of employers in occupational corporations made responsible for the administration of the accident insurance. As supervisory agencies rather centralistic and bureaucratic insurance offices on the federal and, in a few cases, on the state level were instituted. The accident insurance took over cases from the fourteenth week onward. It paid for medical treatment and a pension of up to two thirds of the earned wages in case of full disability. The law was extended in 1886 to include workers in agriculture.

The third major law, introducing old-age and disability insurance, was not passed until 1889. In addition to industrial workers, it made from the outset agrarian laborers, artisans, and servants eligible for its benefits. But the old-age pensions were payable only after the seventieth year, an age relatively few people reached in this period of low life expectancy. This time the principle that the government would make a contribution to each pension was accepted, while employers and employees divided the remaining cost. In each Prussian province and German state supervisory offices were established, in which the bureaucratic-authoritarian element dominated.

Although the German social legislation was to a considerable extent the work of ministerial councillors, Bismarck impressed his personal stamp on it and was responsible for getting it adopted. As a novel type of state activity Bismarck's social legislation subsequently acquired significance far beyond Germany. However, by 1889 Bismarck himself had lost interest in social legislation, which had not stopped the growth of the Social Democratic party. Actually, it was not surprising that the social legislation of the years 1883–89 made no impression on the German workers. In their eyes a government that discriminated against the working class through the antisocialist law could not be credited with humane designs in offering the insurance laws. The practical value of these laws could only appear after they had been operative for a number of years. Moreover, the laws did not deal with those problems that were central to the workers in their wretched circumstances. More than anything else they wanted improved working conditions and higher wages.

These improvements could have been achieved only through labor protection and through the grant of full freedom to labor unions. But Bismarck stubbornly refused any legislation on working hours, woman and child labor, factory inspection, as well as any revision of governmental policy with regard to labor unions. All the recommendations and supplications of his councillors were met with the stock answers of Manchester liberalism and the assertion of the need for the untrammeled leadership of the entrepreneur. The actual situation of the urban proletariat and modern factory worker was entirely unknown to him. He was a country squire who knew his servants, peasants, and farmhands and judged the social conditions of industrial workers by those of the workers in his sawmills. When he realized that the social legislation did not reverse the rising tide of the Social Democratic party, he was prepared to fight the movement with more violent means than the antisocialist law. But his forced resignation in 1890 removed him as an active opponent of the Social Democratic party.

It can be argued that Bismarck's insurance laws helped in later years to produce a friendlier attitude of the workers to the state, and it is certainly true that the very substantial health program removed much misery from the worker's life. His participation in the administration of the local health bureaus was also a beginning of his occasional cooperation with nonsocialist groups. But compared to its general failure as a political device for separating the workers from the Social Democratic party, these delayed and modest results of Bismarck's social legislation carry little weight. The outlawing of all working class organizations under the antisocialist law would have frustrated the effect of even more far-reaching social programs than the insurance laws offered. Although the German Empire had enough soldiers and police to maintain the existing order against powerful and potentially revolutionary opposition, the breach between the working class and the other social classes created grave tensions. The ruling classes became more assertive and authoritarian in language, while the mood of the Social Democrats became more hostile.

∽ *Opposition of Foreign Nationalities*

IN ADDITION to these social conflicts the new Empire was beset by the opposition of its foreign nationalities. No good purpose was served by the retention of the Danes of North Schleswig. Although in article V of the Austro-Prussian Treaty of Prague, which ended the war of 1866, Prussia had promised to hold a plebiscite in North Schleswig, this article was never executed. Instead, when Germany and Austria-Hungary concluded their alliance of 1879, agreement was reached to drop the article. Bismarck asserted that William I did not like to give up land conquered by war, and he was also aware of the opposition to a cession of North Schleswig among the Germans of Schleswig-Holstein. After 1871 he probably had the additional fear that such a plebiscite would raise demands for a plebiscite in Alsace-Lorraine. The North Schleswig question made a reconciliation with Denmark impossible and strained German relations with Scandinavia and the Netherlands, which as small Germanic countries took a lively interest in Germany's treatment of Denmark. The Danes of North Schleswig, determined to defend their own nationality, were an embarrassment for the Prussian government.

On a much broader front the Prussian administration suffered defeat at the hands of the Poles. Prussia's policy toward the Poles had gone through many conflicting stages. Bismarck saw the best chance for controlling the Poles in depriving them of their national leadership, which in his opinion was provided by the Polish clergy and nobility. The launching of the *Kulturkampf* was to a large extent motivated by the situation in the Polish provinces, but the fight against the church proved a complete failure. Rather, the latter strengthened its hold over the people. It was especially unwise that the Prussian administration simultaneously raised the language issue. In the upper high school classes instruction in religion had to be conducted uniformly in German from 1872 on, and in the following year the teaching of the German language was introduced even in the Polish village schools. This made the Polish peasant afraid of Germanization, which Bismarck actually did not plan.

He wished, however, that the Germans should hold their own against the Poles, whose large population increase alarmed him. In 1886 he had close to 30,000 Polish resident noncitizens expelled from Prussia, creating great hardships among those who had to give up their jobs and businesses so suddenly. His action also displeased the Russian and Austrian governments, who had to find room for the homeless. In April 1886 the land-settlement law was passed, which created a fund to be used by the Prussian government to buy estates of the Polish nobility that fell under foreclosure and transfer them to German ownership. Bismarck thereby wanted to undermine the position of the Polish nobility. But the results of the law were limited even in this direction. Moreover, a Polish middle class was developing, which became the chief champion of the Polish national idea and found increasing support among the awakening peasants, most of whom had not shown a very active interest in politics before the *Kulturkampf*.

✐ Alsace-Lorraine

WHILE IN THE EASTERN BORDERLANDS the Poles continued their hostile opposition to the Prusso-German Empire with growing strength, the people in the new borderlands of the west remained in their hearts aloof from the German state. The three French *départements* on the Rhine and the Moselle were not annexed singly or together by one or more of the German states nor formed into an additional member state of the German Empire, but were made into a *Reichsland*—a federal province under the direct rule of the federal government. This was a most anomalous situation. In 1874 the people of Alsace-Lorraine were given the right to elect deputies for the *Reichstag*, but, since the land had no state government, it was not represented on the Federal Council, the chief federal government organ. In 1876 a "land committee" (*Landesausschuss*) was brought into existence for land legislation. It could not be called a parliament, since it was elected by the county and district diets. Moreover, land laws still were initiated and had to be passed by the Federal Council, on which Alsace-Lorraine remained unrepresented, since the emperor, who was the sovereign ruler of the *Reichsland,* could not appoint members who would strengthen the Prussian vote in the council.

Alsace-Lorraine, therefore, was a country that did not have the rights of a state of the Empire, and in these circumstances the impression that it was a German province acquired by conquest against the will of its inhabitants could not be eradicated. Emigration from Alsace-Lorraine into France was very great. Between 1871 and 1914 over 400,000 people left the country that originally had a population of 1.2 million. Alsatians played a prominent role in the life of the Third Republic.

In 1874 the people of Alsace-Lorraine participated for the first time in the elections for the federal parliament and elected only opponents of the Empire. These Alsatian deputies issued a formal declaration protesting the annexation. By this time the German administration had already committed grave blunders. The government of Alsace-Lorraine was in these years conducted chiefly from Berlin, while a high-president, Eduard von Möller, resided in Strasbourg as the chief executive. Although, as we have seen, the major part of the *Kulturkampf* legislation was Prussian rather than federal, not only the federal laws but also many of the Prussian measures were introduced in Alsace-Lorraine. The results were disastrous in a land in which more than three quarters of the population were Roman Catholic. But even the Protestants were alienated by stricter state control of their church, which had a largely Calvinist tradition.

Many industrialists, though probably the social group most highly imbued with French thought and manners in Alsace, for the sake of their large enterprises wished for a relationship with the new German rulers that would keep the heated political agitation in check. For this reason they demanded autonomy within the Empire. A reorganization of the administration of Alsace-Lorraine in 1879 was a step in this direction. A governor was appointed who represented the emperor and assumed the functions so far exercised by the chancellor in the government of the *Reichsland.* But the anomalous and inferior status of Alsace-Lorraine was only slightly changed. The Federal Council, on which Alsace-Lorraine remained unrepresented, was the upper house that could block any action of the land committee, while, unlike the ruler of one of the German states, the governor was not representing his state but rather the emperor. Moreover, the governor had the authority to assume dictatorial powers in case the internal security was threatened.

The first governor was Field Marshal Edwin von Manteuffel. This archconservative politician of the period of the Prussian constitutional conflict had earned his well-deserved laurels as military commander in 1866 and 1871. He had also proved himself an efficient administrator in Schleswig in 1865–66 and as the commander-in-chief of the German occupation forces in France during the years 1871–73. In the latter capacity he had gained great respect in France on account of his chivalrous humaneness. Although bigotry, self-esteem, and partisanship made him easily lose touch with the political realities, he was a highly educated man who made every effort to win over the notables of the province. But he was mistaken in the belief that this policy by itself could turn the tide of the prevailing anti-German sentiment. His friendly relations with the bishops of Strasbourg and Metz did not deliver the popular Catholic vote to the German administration. As a matter of fact, the bishops did not control their clergy in political matters, and it was the lower clergy that was stubbornly opposed to Germany and whipped up resistance to the German administration in the towns and villages. Likewise, the courting of the upper bourgeoisie was of little avail as long as there was not at least some indigenous administration. Actually the administrative services from the governor down to the office clerk and gendarme were composed of Germans. In addition, the Alsatians were constantly annoyed by the large military forces garrisoned in their land. The domineering attitude of their officers was not only offensive to the Alsatian people but also often enough embarrassing to the German civil administration.

The elections of 1881, which sent only Alsatian protestors to Berlin, made the failure of the Manteuffel mission apparent. He himself became unsure of his political course and more inclined occasionally to use coercive measures, which could not possibly produce any better results. When the field marshal died in 1885, Bismarck selected a man as governor who even more than Manteuffel was given to methods of diplomatic persuasion. Prince Chlodwig von Hohenlohe (1819-1901), a member of one of the great aristocratic families of South Germany, had been a most effective German ambassador to France before coming to Strasbourg. Though prudent and conscientious, he had no new political conception for solving the problem of Alsace-Lorraine nor the strength to defend his moderate views against interference from Berlin. Against his better judgment he accepted in 1888 the introduction of passport requirements for Frenchmen visiting Alsace-Lorraine, which were intended to reduce the contacts with France to a minimum. It was a clearly discriminatory law that caused bitter resentment among the people.

✍ *The Empire after 1890*

BISMARCK'S SUCCESSORS resolved the problems of the foreign nationalities as little as they relieved the general tensions that existed within Germany. Fundamentally the structure of state and society that Bismarck had built remained unchanged to the end of the Empire in 1918. The hard core of the Empire was the Prussian military monarchy, with which the German bourgeoisie had made its peace. The latter accepted the supremacy of an authoritarian government that had fulfilled the burgher's fondest dream, the realization of national unification. The bourgeoisie also received most of the rights and institutions that the liberals had championed short of participation in the government. Nevertheless, it should have been a warning to the bourgeoisie that the equality before the law was ill-protected if the Prussian royal government could issue laws that discriminated against whole sections of the population, going as far as expelling Germans from the country of their birth, as in the case of the *Kulturkampf* and antisocialist legislation. That the opposition to such actions was so lamentably weak among the bourgeoisie was a sign of the strength of bourgeois class interest. Strong-handed measures of the government against the threat of social revolution were widely welcomed as a defense of order and property, and the lack of participation in the direction of governmental policy was easily forgotten as long as the government honored the material interests of the bourgeoisie. In this respect John Maynard Keynes rightly remarked that Bismarck's Empire was founded on "iron and grain" rather than on "iron and blood." It should be added, however, that the government had eventually to distribute smaller gifts to other social groups as well. The enormous expansion of economic productivity that took place after 1890 allowed such policies.

❧ Duration of the Bismarckian System

THE PSEUDO-CONSTITUTIONAL SYSTEM that Bismarck created even worked in the hands of his inferior successors. Only two eventualities could have broken its hold. The first, never realized, would have meant that substantial groups of the bourgeoisie had made common cause with the Social Democratic movement. The second was a decisive defeat of the army that would jeopardize the whole nation. Then all the internal tensions that had remained unresolved were bound to have an explosive effect. This actually happened, and twenty-eight years after Bismarck had left the helm, his Empire collapsed.

CHAPTER 7

Germany Under William II

BISMARCK'S POSITION as the actual ruler of Germany was based on the fact that William I gave him his full confidence. Although military matters remained the domain of the emperor, in all political questions the chancellor's opinions prevailed. For many years the advanced age of William I gave rise to expectations that Crown Prince Frederick William would soon succeed to the throne and that this event would terminate the reign of Bismarck. The crown prince, married to Queen Victoria's daughter, Princess Victoria, was a believer in liberal and constitutional methods of government. Unquestionably, he would have tried to translate his ideas into practice, for he was an earnest and devoted man. But a liberal reform of Prussia would have been a far more difficult task than the one the crown prince's brother-in-law, Grand Duke Frederick I, had accomplished in Baden. Bismarck actually had done his utmost to entrench the conservative forces in Prussia more securely and to weaken liberalism.

✒ Succession of William II, 1888

YET WHEN WILLIAM I died in March 1888 at the age of 91, his son, now Emperor Frederick III, stood on the threshold of death. Cancer of the throat had struck him the year before. He had lost his faculty of speech, and although he bore his pains bravely and calmly, he was practically incapacitated by his sufferings. Bismarck remained in full control of the government. The emperor's illness allowed him to keep Frederick III in isolation. The only change in the internal government was the dismissal of the reactionary Prussian minister of interior, Puttkamer. On June 15, 1888, Prince William succeeded his father to the throne. He was twenty-nine years of age, almost as young as Frederick the Great had been at the time of his accession. William liked to emulate his great ancestor, but he possessed none of Frederick's high gifts, such as cool political judgment, fearlessness, diligence, and tenacity, not to mention Frederick's military genius or his love of arts and letters.

William II's education suffered from the competing and contradictory influences that his parents, William I, and Bismarck exercised. Besides, he was not very teachable. His parents succeeded in having him attend a regular Prussian high school and what little systematic knowledge he later possessed he derived almost exclusively from these years, although as emperor he gave vociferous expression to his resentment of the discipline of his schooling. The school failed totally to give him a more liberal outlook, and at Bonn University he did not even expose himself to further study but spent his time in the company of an aristocratic student fraternity. His personal style, however, was chiefly stamped by the years spent as a young officer with the Potsdam guard regiments. Here he found the grandeur and splendor that made his heart swell. At the same time this military life had enough variety not to become boring, and it did not demand strenuous intellectual efforts. The applause and flattery which the future heir to the throne received from the guard officers built up his ego. He had opinions on every problem, although he never took the time to study any of them carefully. In 1886 his father called him "unexperienced, immature, and presumptuous." For a while Prince William worked in the interior administration, but he showed little interest in the instruction he received.

William II's political ideas were formed by his military surroundings. The strictest royalism was the only political conviction permitted in these circles. It went together with the contempt for constitutions and the low estimate of the military men for civilian statesmanship. William's tutor, Georg Hinzpeter, had already planted the divine-right theory of monarchy in his mind, and in the Prussian military world this antiquated theory seemed quite proper and realistic. In this William was greatly encouraged by Bismarck's applause. Bismarck was glad to see William turn away from the ideas of his parents and did his best to influence him in this direction. Although he was somewhat surprised and obviously worried by William's ideas about German federalism as well as the possible solution of the social problems, and some friction developed over these problems, he was relieved when the reign of Frederick III was so quickly superseded by the rule of William II. But he did not realize that the young emperor would not be satisfied with the modest role that William I had played. Apparently he was not even aware of the need for keeping in close contact with the monarch, for in 1888–89 he stayed many months away from Berlin on his estate. Meanwhile the ambitious chief-of-staff of the army, Count Alfred Waldersee (1832–1904), and the wily Friedrich von Holstein, councillor in the foreign office, insinuated doubts about the superior political wisdom of the chancellor.

The first clash between emperor and chancellor occurred over the labor problem. In May 1889 the miners of the Ruhr district staged a general strike that aroused sympathy with the workers among the public.

William II intervened on their behalf and subsequently decided on a demonstration of monarchical benevolence toward the working class. He accepted the advice of his friends to make himself the champion of labor protection that everybody interested in an active social policy, with the exception of Bismarck, favored. The sensible program of the emperor, which was enacted in 1891, proposed to abolish Sunday work and limit the working hours of women and children. At a crown council on January 24, 1890, Bismarck criticized the emperor's plans sharply, while William II passionately protested against the intention of the chancellor under certain conditions to conduct the fight against the Social Democrats with violent means.

Bismarck had proposed to the Reichstag that the antisocialist law, which since 1878 had to be renewed every two and a half years, be transformed into a permanent law. The parliament was dominated by the "cartel," as the cooperation of the Conservative and National Liberal parties was called. But the National Liberals were not prepared to agree to a permanent law unless the provision that allowed the government to expel socialists from their place of domicile was dropped, and the Conservatives declared their opposition to an emasculated law. Actually the antisocialist law fell through. But this meant the breakdown of the cartel, which had always been considered by Bismarck the ideal parliamentary majority.

Still worse things happened in the elections of February 1890. In 1887 the Germans had gone to the polls impressed by the grave international situation and had elected a parliament ready to grant military credits. But the international crisis had passed by 1890, and the dissatisfaction with Bismarck's internal policies welled up again. The cartel parties were reduced from 220 to 135 seats. The National Liberals lost half of their seats to the Progressive party. The Social Democratic vote doubled, although the 35 seats they received failed to reflect these gains. This defeat impaired Bismarck's position just at the moment when a safe majority could have strengthened his hand vis-à-vis the emperor. Public sentiment, too, was not alarmed in the light of rumors about the chancellor's imminent retirement.

Bismarck himself saw events in a different light. He proposed to take to the new parliament the labor protection laws of William II but in addition suggested the presentation of an increased military budget and of a new antisocialist law containing the expulsion provision. He felt sure that at least this law would be rejected, and he hinted that after repeated dissolutions of the parliament universal suffrage might be abolished. He argued that the Empire had been founded by the federation of the German princes, and that it could be dissolved and refounded by them with a new constitution. It was a reckless theory that showed Bismarck's utter contempt for any form of constitutionalism. After all, the Empire had been an eternal federation of states, and its constitution had been confirmed by all state parliaments after they had gained the approval not only of the state governments but also of a German parliament.

Bismarck's program of action was a remodeled version of the program which he had espoused in 1862, when he assumed the direction of Prussian policy. As it had helped him then to make William I accept his political leadership, he now hoped to take William II under his wing in a new war against the parliament and possibly even against an uprising of the Social Democratic movement that he apparently expected once the antisocialist law had expired. But during the Prussian constitutional conflict of 1862–66 the achievement of German national unity was the means by which an ultimate reconciliation with the liberals was to be brought about. In contrast, the program of 1890 was entirely repressive and without an aim beyond the period of conflict. After some hesitation William II declined to follow Bismarck on a road likely to lead to a bloody civil war. The emperor on his part believed that the workers could be won over through such measures as he had proposed in his message on labor protection. Suprisingly, Bismarck accepted the emperor's decision and through a meeting with Windthorst began to explore the possibilities of a parliamentary majority, but the move toward the Center party alienated the cartel parties (National Liberals and Conservatives). His attempt to keep firm control over the Prussian ministers and hinder the free consultation between the emperor and individual ministers opened the final angry conflict between chancellor and emperor. William II's recriminations of Bismarck, in which even the latter's conduct of foreign policy figured, were sad demonstrations of the emperor's lack of judgment and personal tact. He gave Bismarck the chance to place the blame for his dismissal on him. The power that Bismarck had preserved and augmented in the hands of the Prussian monarchs struck him down. On March 18, 1890, he accepted his dismissal.

✍ *Bismarck's Dismissal*

IT IS STRANGE that this event did not cause the profoundest commotion in Germany, but rather was taken with relative calm. The ministers, government officials, and diplomats felt almost relieved to have lost a frightfully imperious chief, and the reaction of the parliamentarians of the right was similar, while those parties that Bismarck had called *Reichsfeinde* (enemies of the Empire) looked on coldly. In the country at large many conservatives and liberals of the older generation had retained reservations with regard to Bismarck and his work, and this was true even among his strong supporters. They were aware of Bismarck's passionate desire for personal power, his inability to treat honest opponents in a chivalrous manner and to tolerate independent men at his side in the government. In addition, they knew that Germany had become less principled and more materialistic under the influence of his political practices. But for the generation that had grown up in the years of German unification Bismarck had become the idol of German greatness. To the students who lustily celebrated his seventieth birthday anniversary in 1885 the iron chancellor was the incarnation of Teutonic courage, strength, and, not entirely to be forgotten, wisdom. But while this Bismarck enthusiasm produced innumerable Bismarck statues and memorials in cities and towns during the next twenty-five years, it was not apt to produce opposition against the monarchy which Bismarck had taught his followers to respect. The defeat of the monarchy in World War I created a new situation. Thereafter the Bismarck cult proved stronger than the monarchical sentiment among the enemies of the Weimar republic, and the counterrevolution clamored for a political genius or leader rather than for the return of a king-emperor.

William II thought of himself as the true successor of Bismarck. He intended to conduct a "personal regime" and considered his ministers mere assistants. But although his bustling activities gave the public the impression that he actually governed, this was not entirely true. He did not have the diligence and persistence required for such a personal regime. His restlessness, manifesting itself particularly in continuous travels, left him not too much time for attending to the study of matters of state and even less for following out a policy over a long period of time. His interventions in the normal course of government were intermittent and capricious. The ministers had to spend a great deal of time trying to keep the emperor from actions or gestures that they considered blunders, or, once they had happened, trying to repair the damage. William's frequent public speeches were a special source of embarrassment. The shallow pompousness, the immodest exaltation of his office and person, as well as the militant nationalism of these speeches had the most detrimental consequences and aroused hostility against Germany abroad. Although they were applauded by many members of the German ruling classes, as the years wore on they were increasingly resented by the educated groups.

✍ Caprivi's Chancellorship

AFTER BISMARCK'S RESIGNATION General Leo von Caprivi (1831–99) was made chancellor and Prussian prime minister. Bismarck himself had called him well suited for high office. Expecting internal tensions early in the year he had wanted a soldier in command. William II appointed Caprivi rather in the expectation that a general was likely to follow the direction of his commander-in-chief. Caprivi was a fine officer who had shown great administrative skill when he was chief of the admiralty from 1883 to 1887. Politics had no attraction for him, and he agreed to serve as chancellor most reluctantly. He was an honest man of great modesty and sober judgment, though of little political imagination.

Since Count Herbert von Bismarck (1849–1904) refused to continue as foreign secretary, Baron Adolf Marschall von Bieberstein (1842–1912), the representative of Baden at the Federal Council, was chosen for his post. Marschall was a lawyer without any preparation in foreign affairs. His surprising appointment actually made the ambitious Baron Friedrich von Holstein the principal director of German foreign policy, which he remained till 1906. Holstein had endeared himself to the Bismarck family by many acts of personal loyalty, but in the last years had secretly worked against Bismarck. He had attempted, as we have mentioned, to counteract the chancellor's foreign policies by giving the Austrian government secret information and had undermined Bismarck's position with William II by supplying Count Waldersee with intelligence that let Bismarck's diplomacy appear in a doubtful light. Holstein remained an operator behind the scenes, from where he spun his personal intrigues and directed German foreign policy. His intrigues were directed against those by whom—rightly or wrongly—he felt offended and those who seemed actual or potential competitors for influence. As early as 1891 he had a hand in the removal of Count Waldersee from Berlin. William II's friendship with Moltke's successor as chief-of-staff suddenly ended, and he sent Waldersee as corps commander into the province. The new chief-of-staff, Count Alfred Schlieffen (1833–1913), was devoted exclusively to military matters and was on good terms with Holstein. Although in the direction of German foreign policy Holstein displayed shrewdness in details, he showed little wisdom in the appreciation of the great trends of world politics, especially of the motives and aims of British policy.

✑ The New Foreign Policy

ALTHOUGH BISMARCK'S foreign policy had played only a minor part in the events that led to his downfall, the effects of his resignation were greatest in the diplomatic field. In the last days of Bismarck's chancellorship the Russians had expressed the desire to renew the Reinsurance Treaty of 1887. But Bismarck's successors declined to sign such a treaty. Bismarck was as poor an educator as Frederick the Great had been. While he had done much to lift the stature of the German diplomat, none of the eminent German ambassadors had been acquainted by him with the total aims of his foreign policy, and none of them had raised any objections when one of the essential components of the Bismarckian system was thrown away. To be sure, the Reinsurance Treaty was open to some doubt, chiefly because in certain circumstances it conflicted with the German alliances with Austria and Rumania. But just in these years the danger that these circumstances would arise was minimal. Actually the Russians had no intention, as the Germans suspected, to move towards the straits. The Russian government was about to begin the building of the Trans-Siberian railroad, and for the next fifteen years the Far Eastern problems were more important to it than the Near Eastern ones. From the German point of view it would have been desirable in the case of a renewal of the treaty to drop the most secret protocol concerning a Russian seizure of the straits and preferably also the second article, by which Germany had recognized the predominant position of Russia in Bulgaria.

But Caprivi and Marschall, advised by the German diplomats, informed the Russian ambassador that, while the new government intended to continue the cultivation of Russia's friendship, it could not make far-reaching treaty commitments. The Russians, who from the outset had not insisted on the renewal of the most secret protocol, came back two months later and proposed to remove article 2 as well. But now the *Wilhelmstrasse* argued that the existence of a German-Russian treaty as such was politically detrimental. The Russians believed that the German government had adopted a new foreign policy, and this impression was strengthened by the conclusion of the Heligoland-Zanzibar treaty. This Anglo-German treaty had been negotiated since 1889 with the aim of settling the last colonial conflicts and giving Germany possession of the small, though strategic, island of Heligoland. In exchange Germany ceded Zanzibar and other islands before the coast of German East Africa (Tanganyika) and limited the further expansion of this colony. Although the treaty met with some sharp criticism in both countries, in general its conclusion afforded an opportunity for the expression of mutual friendliness, and in the early 1890's German policy wished to draw Britain close to the Triple Alliance.

The actions of Bismarck's successors greatly speeded up the coming of the Franco-Russian Alliance. In 1892 a Franco-Russian military convention was signed to be followed by the formal alliance of 1893. If the German government had seriously wished to halt the Franco-Russian *rapprochement*, it should not only have renewed the Reinsurance Treaty but also have opened to the Russian government the German financial markets, from which it had been banned by Bismarck in 1887. Instead, Caprivi even started a tariff war against Russia in 1893. After the conclusion of the Franco-Russian Alliance Germany did not hold the fulcrum of the European balance of power any longer. With the Franco-Russian Alliance and the Triple Alliance facing each other on the Continent, England gained great freedom of action, whereas Germany had less leeway.

The full implications of this turn of events were hidden from the contemporary observers. The growing involvement of Russia in the Far East made the Franco-Russian Alliance far less menacing than it had appeared at first. As a matter of fact, Russia's preoccupation with Asia made French statesmen occasionally wonder whether they had not been overbold in concluding an alliance that might expose France to great dangers without giving her any assurance of active Russian assistance. England was equally preoccupied not only in the Far East but also in Africa. In the Far East England opposed Russia, while in Southeast Asia and Africa conflicts with France developed. Actually during the whole last decade of the nineteenth century England found herself more often in trouble with Russia and France than with Germany or the Triple Alliance.

Anglo-German relations were initially very friendly under the influence of the Heligoland-Zanzibar treaty, and Caprivi as well as the able German ambassador in London, Count Paul Hatzfeldt (1831-1901), hoped that Britain might in due course be persuaded to join the Triple Alliance. But the last government of Gladstone discouraged such suggestions, and in 1893 Holstein recommended that the value of German support be demonstrated to the British through its withdrawal. The emperor was particularly sensitive and erratic with regard to Anglo-German relations. This grandson of Queen Victoria had great admiration for England and things English, although it was somewhat superficial and eclectic. The British constitution for example was not to his liking, but he respected the British as colonizers and ocean rulers. For these reasons they seemed to him truly modern men worthy of emulation. It was a love unfortunately shot through with unruly jealousy, and whenever England refused to play the German game, William II turned spiteful. His love-hatred of England was shared by many Germans of the ruling classes, especially the upper bourgeoisie, and in their ranks were the people who clamored loudest for a German "world policy."

Beginning in 1893 a number of threatening incidents occurred. England was warned that Germany would change her policies in British-occupied Egypt if she did not show herself accommodating to German interests in Turkey. Together with France Germany forced Britain in 1894 to withdraw from a treaty she had concluded with the Congo State in order to be able to build the railroad from the Cape to Cairo as an exclusively British enterprise. Germany also displayed a strong proclivity for assuming a protective attitude toward the Boer republics which resisted the policies of Cecil Rhodes aimed at their integration with the English population in South Africa. A little later Rhodes sent a party of irregulars, under Dr. Jameson, into the Transvaal in order to start a revolution, which, however, was thoroughly defeated by the Boers. On January 3, 1896, William II dispatched a telegram to President Paul Krüger congratulating him on having been able to restore peace and the independence of his country "without having to appeal to friendly powers for assistance." The telegram was proposed and drafted by Marschall in order to stave off even worse actions of the emperor such as the declaration of a German protectorate over the Transvaal, the rupture of diplomatic relations, and similar proposals that would have brought Germany and England to the brink of war. The English understandably felt insulted by the Krüger telegram.

The pressure tactics against England were accompanied by a heightened cooperation with Russia from the end of 1894 on. Alexander III's death brought Nicholas II to the Russian throne. William II had been on friendly personal terms with his cousin and hoped to influence Russian policy through the new czar, of whose intellectual gifts he had a low opinion. But the czar's ministers usually had no difficulty in finding the cloven hoof in the political schemes with which Willy tried to beguile Nicky. Still, the accession of Nicholas II as well as Caprivi's replacement by Prince Chlodwig von Hohenlohe (1819–1901) as German chancellor eased Russo-German relations. Whereas Caprivi was regarded by the Russians in the light of his discontinuation of the Reinsurance Treaty, Hohenlohe was closer to the Bismarckian school.

The Sino-Japanese War of 1894–95 and its aftermath gave Germany her first opportunity for cooperation with Russia. Germany seized it not without ulterior motives. The quick collapse of all Chinese resistance in the Korean War and the stern conditions which the Japanese imposed on China in the peace of Shimonoseki raised the specter of China's complete dissolution and her possible partition among the powers. William II and his naval and diplomatic advisors felt that, in case the other powers should occupy territories in China, Germany, too, should secure a naval station. Admiral Tirpitz, then commander of the German cruiser squadron in the Far East, had recommended Tsingtao on the Shantung peninsula as a suitable port. Russia was alarmed by the great Japanese successes and in particular found the seizure of the Liaotung peninsula that controlled the whole coast of Manchuria intolerable. William II tried to fan this Russian hostility against Japan. He visualized a Japan that, making herself master of the teeming millions of China, would lead the Asiatic world against the Christian West. He and the czar together would have to defend the heritage of Christianity against the "yellow peril."

Whether the czar was much impressed by his cousin's pompous utterances is not known, but he was pleased to see Germany join Russia and France in a protest in Tokyo against the provision of the peace of Shimonoseki that gave Japan the Liaotung peninsula. Japan yielded to the protest of the three powers. She felt most resentful over the German protest, which had been unduly stringent, although Germany seemed to have no political interests of her own in the Far East and the Japanese liked to see in Germany the model for their Westernization. But Germany's cooperation with Russia after Shimonoseki brought Russian acquiescence in her acquisition of Tsingtao. The murder of two German missionaries in 1897 gave Germany the opportunity to gain from the Chinese government a ninety-nine year concession of the Kiaochow territory on the Shantung peninsula. In 1898 Germany bought the Caroline and Mariana islands in the Pacific from Spain, and in the following year received two of the Samoa islands, after the Anglo-American-German condominium had been dissolved. The years 1897–99 witnessed the relatively greatest successes of German world politics, made possible, however, by continuing the methods of Bismarckian continental policy.

✐ Building the German Navy

To THE GERMAN POLICY MAKERS and to the German public in general a new political age seemed to have dawned. The advent of Japan among the great powers and the active intervention of the United States in world affairs through and after the war with Spain appeared to usher in an epoch in which the old European system of states would be superseded by a system of world powers. What this would imply, nobody could say with certainty, but at least people felt sure that a nation without colonies and naval forces would not be counted among the future world powers. William II was obsessed with the desire to build up Germany's *Seegeltung*, i.e., a respected naval posture. In Admiral Alfred von Tirpitz (1849-1930) he found the political and technical architect of the new navy. Nobody among his German contemporaries matched in will power this wily man with the long forked beard. He knew how to maintain the enthusiastic support of the emperor and at the same time had a great talent for the manipulation of public opinion. The German Navy League, founded at his instigation in 1898, was the loudest propaganda organization, but he used many other publicity devices and was not squeamish in making the industrialists, who derived the greatest profits from the naval building, contribute to the public and private drives for a larger and larger navy. In contrast to the army bills, Tirpitz's naval bills were passed by the German parliament without great difficulty.

Yet the resolute secretary of the navy had a highly limited understanding of foreign nations. Bismarck once defined statecraft as the knowledge of what the other statesman would do in any given circumstances. Tirpitz did not possess this imaginative ability. He relied on the false clichés which were current in Germany, such as the decadence of the French or the storekeeper spirit of the English. Moreover his judgment on naval strategy was not unfailing. The first naval bill that he presented in 1898 projected a navy of 19 battleships, 12 heavy cruisers, and 30 light cruisers. It meant the strengthening of the existing navy by 7 battleships, 2 heavy cruisers, and 7 light cruisers. This first bill could well be defended. The German navy was weaker than the French, and the Franco-Russian Alliance had posed new problems in the defense of the German coasts. However, the opening in 1895 of the Kiel canal connecting the Baltic sea and the North sea had made up for some of these difficulties.

But even in 1898 Tirpitz had his eyes on a more distant goal. It was the British naval supremacy that he intended to challenge. The Spanish-American War and above all the anti-British sentiment evoked in Germany by the Boer War made him present a new naval bill before two years had passed. This naval bill of 1900 doubled the estimates of the first bill. By 1917 the German navy was to consist of 38 battleships, 8 heavy cruisers, and 24 light cruisers. For service overseas an additional 8 heavy cruisers and 15 light cruisers were provided. Naturally, there was to be an adequate number of destroyers and small craft. It was now openly stated that Germany intended to build a navy strong enough to impress on the strongest naval power the "risk" it would incur in going to war against her. Though likely to be defeated, the German navy would be able to send so many British ships to the bottom as to make England's naval power inferior to that of countries like France or the United States. Although the risk theory contained a morsel of truth, it could be largely invalidated once England became the ally of all the other major naval powers, as she practically did before 1914.

It was a foolhardy assumption that England would ever tolerate the rise of German naval power to a point where it could seriously jeopardize the British command of the sea, on which the independence and prosperity of the British isles depended. Mahan, the great American thinker on naval strategy, wrote in 1902 that it was the dilemma of England "that she cannot help commanding the approaches to Germany by the very means essential to her own existence as a state of the first order." This fact rightly or wrongly was galling to a man who on the basis of his observation of the sharp competition between English and German merchants in the Far East had reached the conclusion that England might one day choose to destroy German foreign trade and colonial enterprise. Yet why this same England, suspected of such evil designs, should watch impassively the building up of German naval strength was one of the mysteries of Tirpitz's mind. If at times he hoped to be able to steal a march on the British and somehow expected the English people would not be willing to pay the growing cost of additional naval armament, all these were fatuous reasons.

Moreover, the theoretical justification that Tirpitz gave for his naval laws was completely mistaken. In order to break the stranglehold of the

British navy over German communications with the world at large, it would have been necessary to defeat the British navy in a decisive battle. But an inferior navy stood no chance of such a victory. As a matter of fact, the German fleet could not even force the British fleet to accept a major battle. Tirpitz and his officers believed that in a war the British would send their battle fleet into the bight of Heligoland, where, through minefields and an island-based artillery, the German fleet would gain in power. To the bewilderment of the German naval strategists this proved to be a vain expectation. When in World War I the British operated the blockade from the northern entry into the North sea, the German fleet was not even able to strike at them, because it was not built for such a wide range of operations, particularly not its destroyers.

✍ Anglo-German Relations

THE NAVAL LAW of 1898 did not arouse any fear in England and even the law of 1900 only caused apprehension after the first ships had come from the dockyards with great regularity. In the years around the turn of the century England's major concern was the hostility that she met in the colonial field. In Asia the growing expansion of Russia and in Africa France's aspirations caused her worries. And everywhere England was alone in defending her interests. No longer was her isolation a splendid one, as Lord Salisbury had called it. In March 1898 Joseph Chamberlain, the minister of colonies, assisted by Arthur Balfour, the head of the treasury, approached the German ambassador in London, Count Hatzfeldt, with the suggestion of an Anglo-German alliance, which they said would have to be confirmed by the British parliament. This proposal was received with grave suspicions in Berlin. Since 1897 Bernhard von Bülow had been foreign secretary, but Holstein's opinions still carried the greatest weight. While an alliance without parliamentary ratification seemed worthless to them, in view of the anti-German sentiment in England and the anti-British feeling in Germany they doubted that a majority would vote for this alliance. But if it was rejected by the British parliament, Germany would be badly compromised in Russian eyes and might even be exposed to severe Franco-Russian pressure. The German government was confident that Germany's position in the world was secure, whereas it would be hazardous to attempt the conclusion of an English alliance. Therefore Count Hatzfeldt was instructed to negotiate in a dilatory fashion. This ended the conversations at once, since Chamberlain needed a strong positive response if he was to convince the cabinet and especially the prime minister, Lord Salisbury, of the desirability of a British alliance with Germany.

The inconclusive character of these negotiations did not keep William

II from claiming in a letter to Nicholas II that the British government had offered him an alliance. Simultaneously he was asking Nicholas what he would be ready to offer if the German emperor turned down the English bid. It is hard to believe that William II was so naïve as to think that Nicholas II would drop the French alliance when faced with such trumped-up arguments. The czar replied in kind by not offering anything and declaring with seeming unconcern that a little while earlier he had been similarly approached by England. The imperial cousins vied in dupery, but actually William II was more gullible. Although Nicholas' remark about England was rather a hoax, it succeeded in making the German government even more suspicious of British policy.

Yet in 1898 the German and British governments reached an agreement on the virtual partition of the Portuguese colonies in Africa if Portugal were to prove financially incapable of administering them. The treaty, however, was so hypothetical as to be practically meaningless. It was of greater significance that the German government remained strictly neutral when the Boer War began in October 1899. German public opinion even more than that of other Continental nations grew highly agitated over the British war policy in South Africa. The popular hostility against England was by now steadily fed by influential organizations in Germany. Besides the older Colonial League, the Navy League was just starting its implicitly anti-British propaganda. But the most damaging work was done by the Pan-German League, which had its roots in two organizations. The one was founded by the colonialist Carl Peters in 1890 in protest against the Heligoland treaty, which was declared to be a shameful surrender of vital German interests to England. The other association had been launched in 1891 by the young Alfred Hugenberg (1865–1951) for the cultivation of German national ideals. The Pan-German League, into which the two groups merged in 1894, had these functions: to promote nationalist sentiments and fight all movements opposed to an integral nationalism within Germany; to spread German national ideas among Germans living in foreign countries and support these Germans in their struggle to preserve their identity; and, finally, to further an active policy advancing German interests in Europe and overseas.

The membership of the Pan-German League was composed of relatively few Conservatives, a considerable number of Free Conservatives, but mostly of National Liberals and anti-Semites. The strongest social groups represented in the league were the industrialists, the merchants, and the professional men, among whom the numerically strongest single group were the high school and university professors. The latter gave the league its chief influence on broad sections of the middle classes, particularly on the students. The actual number of full members was only a few ten-thousands. Although the league throughout the period prior to

World War I was in opposition to the official German policy as being lukewarm and timid and almost never had any direct contacts with the German foreign office, some of the ideas propagated by it proved catching even among diplomats and also with William II. Moreover, while, as during the Boer War, the government might conduct a policy very different from the one desired by the Pan-German League, it shied away from open disapproval of the Pan-German propaganda.

In the fall of 1898 Chamberlain and Bülow had agreed to prepare the public for closer Anglo-German cooperation. In his speech at Leicester of November 29, 1899, in which he suggested that the best guarantee for world peace would lie in an alliance of the three great Germanic nations, England, Germany, and the United States, Chamberlain lived up to his promise. But in view of the hostile reception of this speech Bülow failed to reply, and at the same time Tirpitz was able to prepare his naval program.

↶ Boxer Rebellion

IN THE SUMMER of 1900 dangerous antiforeign uprisings, known as the Boxer Rebellion, broke out in China. Siege was laid to the embassy section of Peking, and the German minister was murdered, while the rest of the diplomatic corps lived in fear for their lives. The troops that were landed from the foreign naval vessels in Chinese waters had difficulties in fighting their way to Peking. The great powers sent more troops from their Asiatic possessions. William II, outraged by the murder of the German minister, originally wanted to send a full division and was most eager that a German general should serve as the commander of all the international forces. He nominated Field Marshal Count Waldersee for this post. Reluctantly the other powers accepted the international command. In doing so they disregarded the disgusting exhortation that William II had given the German soldiers on their departure. "If you meet the enemy you ought to know: no pardon will be given, no prisoners will be taken. As a thousand years ago the Huns under their king Attila made a name for themselves that lets them even now appear mighty in tradition, so may the name German be impressed by you on China in such a manner that never again a Chinese will dare to look askance at a German." The hysterical outburst of the emperor was to cost Germany dearly during World War I. Count Waldersee arrived in China too late to perform any major military feat. The embassies, in Peking in particular, had been relieved six weeks before he landed.

The Boxer Rebellion and the subsequent intervention of the European powers raised again the possibility of the further extension of foreign influence in China. Russia was suspected of harboring new expansionist notions, and the German policy makers did not cherish the prospect of such Russian inroads that might eventually block European trade with most of China. Although open opposition to Russia appeared unwise, Germany concluded an agreement with England, known as the Yangtse agreement, by which the two governments proclaimed the principle of the open door in China. They disavowed any intent to win territorial advantages from the existing turmoil and agreed on consultation if any other power should make such gains.

✍ New Attempts at Anglo-German Alliance

THE CONCURRENCE of English and German policy in the Far East prepared the ground for the resumption of the conversations on an Anglo-German alliance. In January 1901 Chamberlain again expressed the hope for an intimate understanding between England and Germany and warned that if this proved unattainable, England would have to turn to the Franco-Russian Alliance. At first Holstein did not wish to negotiate at all. He considered Germany to be in a strong position, while England was at loggerheads with both France and Russia. He judged that England's conflicts with the two powers would grow in intensity and that she would come to appreciate the true value of the German friendship. Since British and Russian interests could never be reconciled, or, as Holstein put it, "whale and bear could never come together," England would eventually be forced to offer a high price for German assistance.

It was largely due to the unauthorized initiative of the councillor at the German embassy in London, Baron von Eckardtstein, who often substituted for the ailing ambassador Count Hatzfeldt, that diplomatic talks continued. Holstein and Bülow, who since 1900 had been federal chancellor, insisted that the alliance should not be an Anglo-German one, but one between England and the Triple Alliance. The defensive alliance, which was to be ratified by the British parliament, was to become operative in case of an attack of two or more powers against either partner. Holstein and Bülow argued that Russia and France might go to war against Austria-Hungary, in which case Germany would have to come to the latter's assistance. If the English alliance were confined to Germany, she would have no claim to English assistance, since she would be going to war without having been attacked. The German diplomats saw behind the offer of an Anglo-German alliance the sinister intention of the English statesmen to promote, or at least to tolerate, a war between the Triple Alliance and the Franco-Russian Alliance so that the Continental powers would weaken each other. Another German fear was the expectation that, by not assuming any treaty obligations vis-à-vis Austria-

Hungary, England wanted to keep the way open for a direct understanding with Russia on Balkan and Near Eastern affairs.

The fact that England's willingness to accede to the Triple Alliance was made the acid test of her intentions was the chief cause for the failure of the Anglo-German conversations. While Salisbury remained in the background of the negotiations, Chamberlain was joined by the foreign secretary, Lord Lansdowne, who must have received from the prime minister general permission to enter upon these talks. But the German demand for a British alliance with the Triple Alliance met with the disapproval of all the members of the British cabinet who participated in the conversations. Salisbury believed that the Habsburg empire would collapse after Emperor Francis Joseph's death. He also felt that the Austro-German policy of preserving the Turkish empire was unrealistic. Salisbury was less sanguine than Lansdowne and Chamberlain about the reception that even a bilateral Anglo-German alliance would find in the British parliament. He would have preferred special agreements on concrete issues, an approach of the type that led three years later to the Anglo-French Entente. If the German statesmen had not insisted on an alliance between England and the Triple Alliance, it would have been possible to conclude an Anglo-German alliance or at the very least to lay the foundation for close cooperation between England and Germany.

None of the policy makers in Berlin was willing to consider a major change of foreign policy. They were firmly convinced that Germany could well afford to continue the so-called "policy of the free hand." It was William II who at rare moments became worried. "After all I cannot continually alternate between the Russians and British. I would eventually fall between two stools," he said in February 1901. But he was not the man to hold on to a single thought and persevere in its realization. The emperor's temporary inclination to seek an English alliance induced Bülow to give him little information on the actual course of the negotiations. Bülow and Holstein rejected the warnings of the old German ambassador in London, Count Hatzfeldt, and of his designated successor, Count Wolff-Metternich (1859–1938). Both warned that the British statesmen were not bluffing in hinting that they would be able to compose England's conflicts with France and Russia, while on the other side a German threat to combine with Russia would not carry conviction in view of the Franco-Russian alliance. Count Wolff-Metternich also very forcefully argued that Britain could not possibly intend to set the Continent on fire just at a moment when, as a consequence of the Boer War, she was unable to influence the outcome of the warfare and for example might have to tolerate a Russian seizure of the straits. But even in less extraordinary circumstances England was not apt to conduct an incendiary foreign policy that would jeopardize the basis of her commercial position.

Bülow and Holstein remained unimpressed by this good counsel. Although it may not have been easy to anticipate the future Anglo-Russian *rapprochement,* and it may be said that only the subsequent German policy made it inevitable, as early as 1901 there were certain straws in the wind. For one thing, the possibility of an Anglo-French understanding had been clearly discernible ever since the French had retreated in 1898 after Fashoda. The German foreign office also failed to appraise correctly the weakness of the Habsburg empire that just around the turn of the century was increasing at an alarming pace. To be sure, Germany had no reason to give up the alliance with Austria-Hungary, but it was unwise to make it the exclusive instrument of German security, which it had not been even in the days of Bismarck. It was equally obvious that Italy was not a wholehearted member of the Triple Alliance, since it did not provide sufficiently strong assistance for the achievement of Italy's acquisitive aims in the colonial field. Moreover, Italy could never afford to remain an active member of the Triple Alliance in case England became hostile to the grouping.

Thus an Anglo-German alliance would have strengthened the Triple Alliance, although in the case of a grave crisis of the Habsburg empire or that of serious Balkan developments, it would have allowed England to come to terms with Russia. But this would not have meant that England could have changed over to an Anglo-Russian alliance. Only in alliance with a major Continental power would she have been able to achieve Russian adherence to a compromise agreement over the Balkans. In addition, if Britain was unwilling to accept definite commitments with regard to southeastern Europe and the Near East, Germany, too, was free to negotiate with Russia over these matters. And the route from Berlin to St. Petersburg was possibly shorter than the one from London to St. Petersburg.

✐ Bagdad Railroad

THERE WAS still another political project that the German political leaders ought to have taken into consideration in connection with a possible Anglo-German alliance. In 1888 a German bank, the *Deutsche Bank,* had received from the Turkish government the concession for building a railroad from Constantinople to Ankara. This so-called Anatolian railroad was envisioned from the beginning as the first section of a line eventually to run to Bagdad and the Persian Gulf. Bismarck, in accordance with his general policy of denying any political interest of Germany in the Near East, had told the German bankers that the German government would not be able to protect their venture in politically adverse circumstances. Undoubtedly he would not have let German economic enterprises in Turkey interfere with his general foreign policy.

But this attitude changed under William II, who saw in the Turkish empire a potential political ally of Germany and at the same time a field for German economic expansion. When the emperor visited Palestine in 1898, he made a speech heard around the world, in which he called himself the protector of the 300 million Mohammedans, most of whom, incidentally, lived in India or Asiatic Russia. The directors of the *Deutsche Bank*, who might have preferred to finance the Bagdad railroad on an international basis, were urged by the government to undertake the building of the line to Bagdad and Basra. In 1898–99, the *Deutsche Bank* received the concession for the erection of the port of Haidar Pasha, the starting point of the Anatolian and Bagdad railroad on the Bosporus, and late in 1899 it also received in principle the concession for the construction of the Bagdad-Basra line. Russia viewed this German penetration of Turkey with grave misgivings. She expected from the German activities a considerable strengthening of the Turkish empire and, with good reason, distrusted Germany's declarations that her interests were exclusively commercial.

Germany's active policy in Turkey was bound to antagonize Russia and was politically feasible only if Germany was sure of English support. The "policy of the free hand," which Bülow and Holstein still considered adequate in 1901, was incompatible with the creation of strong German interests. Since the Bagdad railroad established a land route from the Mediterranean to the Persian gulf parallel to the seaway to India via Suez, even the British did not like Germany's exclusive control of the enterprise. Yet these differences were not fundamental and actually later were rather easily solved by the German concession to leave the last section of the line from Bagdad to Basra in English hands. If the Anglo-German conversations in 1901 had led to general cooperation, English capital would have participated in the Bagdad company, as the German bankers had always wished.

Whereas Germany could have avoided growing Russian hostility only by abstaining from an active policy in Turkey and gained an alliance with Russia only by giving up the Austrian one, close Anglo-German cooperation merely demanded a reasonable limitation on German naval building. It is true that this would have made it impossible to achieve full equality with England, the goal so fiercely or lightheartedly desired by wide circles of the German people. Bülow and Holstein constantly referred to the fact that German public opinion would not approve of an Anglo-German alliance and that even an alliance of England and the Triple Alliance would be found barely acceptable. Bismarck had always justified the suppression of any parliamentary control of foreign policy by the exposed position of Germany in the center of Europe that made it imperative to conduct German foreign policy without regard to the fluctuations of party opinion. This became the stock phrase in defense of the German pseudoconstitutionalism. But whereas Bismarck had not hesitated to conduct an unpopular foreign policy, Bülow shied away from boldly facing German public opinion. He himself had greatly contributed to its anti-British bias at the time of the naval laws of 1898 and 1900. His participation in the naval legislation was proof of his own animosity against England, and this could be sensed again during the Anglo-German conversations of 1901 in the deep suspicion with which Bülow and Holstein viewed the British proposals. The dislike of liberal England and the wish not to lose all contacts with Russia showed that the traditions of the Holy Alliance were not fully dead among Prussian Conservatives. As we mentioned before, the chief champions of the German navy were the National Liberals and the Free Conservatives. The Conservatives voted for naval bills in order to get their grain tariffs. But they were army people and Bismarckians to the extent that they wanted to continue friendly German-Russian relations. An Anglo-German alliance actually would have required a realignment of the internal forces of Germany as well.

Bülow obviously did not feel that an alliance with England could easily be fitted into the policy which German conditions seemed to dictate and which appeared normal to him. The Germans were swelling with pride right then over the tremendous strides they were taking in these years toward industrial and commercial prominence among the nations of the world. In his rash and easygoing optimism Bülow thought the policy of the free hand was amply justified, and he dismissed all British suggestions of an Anglo-French and Anglo-Russian understanding as bluff. But English statesmen were in bitter earnest. In 1902 Lansdowne concluded an alliance with Japan that shifted to the latter the burden of stopping further Russian encroachments on China. And in 1904 England and France reached a settlement of all their colonial conflicts. The most important arrangement of this entente was their accommodation in North Africa. In return for French recognition of British interests in Egypt the British recognized the French drive for the control of Morocco and, in a secret article, even promised to shield the penetration of the country by the French against the opposition of a third power. By 1907 Germany's naval policy on the one side and her policy in Turkey on the other had brought England and Russia together as well. Thereafter Germany and Austria-Hungary were isolated among the great powers.

✐ *Caprivi's Domestic Policies*

IN THE SEVENTEEN YEARS that saw this decline of Germany's political position in the world, her internal government suffered from the unsteady course steered by William II and his ministers. Caprivi, Bismarck's successor, undoubtedly was one of the finest officers in the Prussian army. Without any personal ambitions, he was able to look at problems realistically and ready to act upon his conclusions with courage. He felt that the pugnaciousness of his great predecessor had done great harm to the relations between government and parties and that Bismarck's domineering temper had driven men of independent mind from the civil service. But Caprivi occupied a position that demanded extraordinary political skill, which this trusting officer had not acquired in his military career. It proved impossible to raise the level of the ministers and secretaries of state. Only servile people, by fawning on William II, could hope for office and the extension of their influence, and once a Prussian minister possessed the personal confidence of the emperor it was very difficult to restrain him from following his own policies. Caprivi often struggled in vain to integrate the policies of the Prussian cabinet and to coordinate Prussian and German policies.

Caprivi took a more moderate attitude toward the parties than Bismarck. The Center party greatly benefited from this change. The concessions gained in the form of further cancellation of some *Kulturkampf* measures were by themselves of minor significance. More important was the fact that its improved relations with the government made the Center party forget the bitter sentiments that the *Kulturkampf* had aroused among its followers. The party also adjusted itself to the social climate of the new age of the rising masses. The agrarian agitation of the 1890's as well as the working class movement convinced the Center party that it had to take as firm a stand in economic and social questions as it had taken before in the matter of church-state relations. The founding of the People's Association for the Catholic Germany (*Volksverein für das katholische Deutschland*) in 1890 constituted the successful attempt to set up a brain center and propaganda organization for making the popular basis of the Center party secure. The Center party kept its practically complete hold on the farm vote in the Catholic districts. It also continued to command the loyalty of the lower middle class, such as the craftsmen and the storekeepers, who in Protestant Germany were often lured into the anti-Semitic movement. In addition, the Center party, through its Christian trade unions, made inroads into the industrial workers' vote. Pope Leo XIII's bull *Rerum novarum* of 1891 gave this broad social policy both a strong momentum and theoretical justification.

In practice, this led the German Center party to a predominantly conservative policy in the sense that the social classes of an agrarian and small-town society were to be preserved by paternal or, as we would say today, welfare measures of the state. But the rising class of industrial workers was at least recognized, and the leaders of the Christian trade unions soon realized that if they wanted to improve the lot of the workers and win their allegiance, they would have to fight the employers instead of expecting, as the very small liberal Hirsch-Duncker unions did, that they could be won over by mere persuasion. It occasionally happened that the Christian trade unions proved tougher bargainers than the Social Democratic free trade unions.

The social composition of the leader group of the Center party underwent a change. The originally rather large number of noblemen decreased, while the influence of members of the upper educated bourgeoisie prevailed. In 1891 Ludwig Windthorst died, and Ernst Lieber (1838–1902) followed him as chairman. Lieber, who did not possess the cunning of Bismarck's great parliamentary opponent, continued Windthorst's policy of cooperating with the government and in return extracting concessions to the Center's political program. While the Center party was far from aiming at parliamentary government, it jealously guarded the right of the parliament to pass the budget.

Besides being more tolerant toward political parties in general than Bismarck had been, Caprivi also mitigated the Prussian policies against the Guelfs and the Poles. A major complaint of the Hanoverian legitimists had been the seizure of the large assets of the Guelf family. Bismarck had used the income of the "Guelf fund" for his secret operations, particularly in connection with the German and foreign press. Caprivi restored the assets to the Guelf dynasty in 1892, thereby simultaneously ending a good many malpractices in the government's press relations. Even more courageous was his decision to discontinue the execution of the law of 1886 through which Bismarck had intended to strengthen the German element in Posen and West Prussia.[1] In these years, when the Poles saw with bitter disappointment their old protector France ally herself with Russia, it might have been advisable to adopt new Polish policies altogether.

∾ *Reform of Foreign Economic Policy*

ONE OF THE URGENT MAJOR problems Caprivi found was the need for reform of German foreign economic policy. Since the introduction of tariffs in 1879 Germany had followed an autonomous economic policy confining treaty relations to the most-favored nation clause. But other nations had gone protectionist, too, and international trade was threatened

[1] Cf. p. 294.

by chaotic conditions. Exports, however, had become an ever-growing need for Germany. Trade treaties were negotiated and concluded for a twelve-year period with Austria-Hungary and Italy in 1892, and with Switzerland, Belgium, and Rumania in the year thereafter. In order to gain lower tariffs for the export of German industrial products Germany had to bring down her agrarian import duties. The grain duties were lowered from 50 to 35 marks per ton. The Central European system of trade treaties stabilized commercial relations in a large market and created the conditions for a great expansion of German exports. In 1894, after a short but violent customs war with Russia, a similar German-Russian trade treaty was signed. The treaty was symptomatic of the shift of German foreign policy from England to Russia that, as we have seen, was characteristic of the mid-nineties. But the trade war of 1893 had had its lasting effects by contributing to the formalization of the Franco-Russian alliance.

The trade treaties were fought by the Conservatives as undermining the economic and social position of the agrarian classes. This was certainly not Caprivi's intention, who during his years at the chancellery tolerated the grant of many gifts to the *Junkers,* but in view of the extraordinary growth of the population he saw in the expansion of German exports the only method of avoiding the export of men. And actually German emigration in the years 1890–95 was very large. It was an unfortunate coincidence that in these same years the prices of agrarian products declined in the most alarming fashion. Whereas in 1891 the price of a ton of rye was 208 marks in Danzig, it dropped to 110 marks in 1894. The tremendous expansion of grain production in North and South America and India, together with the cheap maritime freight rates, wrecked the whole price structure of grain products.

The collapse of the market was a terrible blow to all agrarian producers. In February 1893 the Federation of Agriculturists (*Bund der Landwirte*) was founded and quickly attracted almost a quarter of a million members. Its proclaimed aim was to get protection and support from the government through tariffs, credits, low taxes, and so on. To this end the public was to be informed through the press and meetings, and agrarian candidates were to be backed in parliamentary elections. The federation was originally not a strictly Conservative organization, and among its founders were members from other political parties. But very rapidly it came under the exclusive leadership of the Conservatives, who made the federation an organ for reaching social groups which had not been attracted by a Conservative-monarchist ideology. Many farmers who so far had placed their faith in liberalism and looked to liberal cooperatives for the furtherance of their economic interests turned to the federation. The fact that it gave the Conservatives a relatively broad social base made the federation soon determine the tone and the policies of the Conservative party. The same party that claimed to defend the monarchy as being above parties and classes thus became an unashamed champion of narrow economic interests.

⌒ *Army Bill and 1893 Elections*

THE NEW BALANCE of internal forces was revealed in connection with the army bill that Caprivi presented in 1892. Caprivi intended to strengthen the army in order to counter the Franco-Russian Alliance. He planned to achieve this aim by increasing the size of the army and even more by rejuvenating it through a larger draft of the young people, who, as a result of the population growth, were now available in greater numbers. Caprivi conceded that army service should be limited to two instead of three years. In addition, he no longer insisted on the passing of the army bill for a seven-year period. Henceforth five years were to be the norm, in accordance with the life span of the individual parliaments.

Only the Conservatives, the National Liberals, and the Poles supported the army bill. With the exception of a few of its members the Center party was opposed to it, and as a consequence the German Liberal party, with its seventy deputies, held the balance. If they had voted for the government bill, they might have deepened the rift between the Center party and a government that normally tended to conduct conservative policies supported by the Conservatives and Centrists. Considering the history of military legislation, the concessions that Caprivi offered the parliament might have justified the support of the German Liberal party. But Eugen Richter was a man of rigid principles and unfit for exploiting tactical opportunities. He ruled that the increase in army estimates would create an unbearable financial burden for the people. Some of the liberals, in fact most of those who had seceded from the National Liberal party in 1880 and joined with the Progressives in founding the German Liberal (*Deutsch-Freisinnige*) party of 1884, chose to vote for the army bill, whereupon Eugen Richter excluded them from the party. In 1893 they formed the Liberal Union (*Freisinnige Vereinigung*).[2] The German Liberal party now called itself the Liberal People's party (*Freisinnige Volkspartei*).

When after the failure of the army bill Caprivi dissolved the *Reichstag* and ordered new elections for 1893, it was the German Liberal party and the Liberal Union that suffered the greatest losses. Whereas the Center party did not lose much and the Conservatives gained little, these two liberal parties lost heavily. Only twenty-four deputies of these two liberal parties were returned, while the Liberal Union did not elect more than

[2] See p. 273.

thirteen members. The reason for this defeat of liberalism at the polls lay chiefly in the widespread dissatisfaction with the economic policies of the government. In 1893 the liberals lost most of the votes of the small farmers. The agitation of the League of Agriculturists drove them into the arms of the Conservatives or anti-Semites. Except for southwestern Germany and a belt from East Friesland to Schleswig-Holstein along the coast of the North sea the liberal farm vote was practically lost.

But the elections of June 1893 also cut deeply into the support which the Liberal People's party and the Liberal Union had received from the urban population. The losses to the Social Democratic party probably were not considerable, since the Liberals had never had a large following among the industrial workers. More important must have been the shift of many lower middle-class people to the anti-Semites, who received sixteen seats and for the first time were able to form a real party in the German parliament. Yet the rise of an independent anti-Semitic movement did not last very long. The party strength declined in the following elections, and to the end of the monarchy anti-Semitism remained a peripheral phenomenon of German party life, although as an ideology and sentiment it was kept very much alive by the German right. At its convention of 1892 the Conservative party had formally adopted anti-Semitism into its program.

The passing of the military bill of 1893 by a slim majority of the *Reichstag* did not restore Caprivi's political position, which had been steadily deteriorating since 1892. In order to pass the social legislation that the emperor had announced in 1890 and to promote internal peace the chancellor had greatly relied on the Center party. His belief that Christian religion was the best defense against the further spread of socialism induced him in 1892 to accept a school bill that the Prussian minister of education, Count Zedlitz-Trützschler (1837–1914), presented to the Prussian parliament, where it was welcomed by the Center and the Conservative parties. The law proposed the segregation of schools along denominational lines, the grant to the individual churches of authority to certify the teachers of religion in the schools, and the unrestricted permission for the founding of private schools. The law ran into the bitter opposition of the Liberal People's party and the Liberal Union who for once were joined by the National Liberals. In the universities loud protests arose against the anticipated control of the intellectual life by clerical forces. William II became frightened and demanded a revision of the proposed law. Zedlitz-Trützschler resigned, and under his successor, Robert Bosse (1832–1901), the Prussian government dropped all plans for school legislation.

It was a serious defeat for Caprivi, who had identified himself with Zedlitz-Trützschler's law and chose to resign as Prussian prime minister.

But a chancellor who was not Prussian prime minister at the same time had only limited power and was easily vulnerable if the Prussian premier had political ambitions of his own, as was the case with Count Botho von Eulenburg, the former Prussian minister of the interior and as such the initiator of the antisocialist law of 1878. He presented himself as the statesman who would satisfy the demands of the agrarians for a reform of economic policies as well as those of the industrialists for a strong antisocialist policy. In Baron Stumm-Halberg (1836–1901), the most prominent Saar industrialist and a Free Conservative politician who won the ear of William II, this policy had an effective champion. The paternal regime that the "uncrowned king of the Saar" practiced in his iron factories and mines, under which the workers had to forswear all oppositional ideas as well as special social rights, seemed to William the model for the management of labor relations.

William II, deeply disappointed that the workers had not turned monarchist when he had promised to carry forward social reforms, had quickly grown tired of such reforms. As early as 1890 Adolf Stöcker had to give up his office as court chaplain, at the emperor's request. The assassination of President Carnot of France by an anarchist in 1894 made William inclined again to adopt coercive measures against the Social Democratic party. "Religion, decency, and order" were to be restored "against the parties of subversion." But a bill against subversion (*Umsturzvorlage*) containing drastic punitive provisions against various forms of associations and public statements failed to find a parliamentary majority. As in 1890, though this time by Bismarck's successors, plans for the forceful revision of the German constitution were discussed within the government, but William II was too timid to stage a *coup d'état*. He dismissed both the moderate Caprivi and the more venturesome Eulenburg, who had believed that his hour had come.

∽ Chancellor Hohenlohe

THE EMPEROR prevailed on Prince Chlodwig Hohenlohe (1819–1901) to become German chancellor and Prussian prime minister. This Bavarian magnate, a liberal Catholic, who had had a long and distinguished career in politics and diplomacy,[3] was by then a year older than Bismarck had been at the time of his retirement. Never a man of bold and independent action, he was a conciliatory diplomatist rather than a statesman, and age had made him even more cautious and reticent than before. He exercised little leadership and only a moderating influence on William II and some of the excesses of the reactionary forces in Prussia. Yet even in these endeavors he was never entirely successful.

[3] See pp. 207 and 296.

Hohenlohe had particular difficulties in controlling the Prussian scene, where just in these years the Conservatives began to assert their power quite recklessly. While the House of Lords was their exclusive domain, the Prussian system of suffrage, though slightly revised under Caprivi, gave them a position in the House of Representatives that enabled them to form a majority with either the Center or the National Liberal party. The Conservatives pressed their advantage even against the king. Although the theory that the Prussian ministers, as servants of the king, were not in need of the confidence of a parliamentary majority was outwardly maintained, it proved impossible to keep ministers who did not enjoy the support of the Conservative party. The royal prerogatives so staunchly defended by Bismarck were undermined, and Prussia had virtually a parliamentary government that served as the active champion of the reactionary interests of the country. The stagnation of Prussian politics bore heavily on the chancellor's conduct of German affairs. The frictions between the federal government and the *Reichstag* increased, and in order to avoid dangerous clashes between the Prussian and German government, legislation in the Empire either had to be heavily weighted toward the Conservative right or to be suppressed altogether.

The ablest among the Prussian ministers in the Caprivi-Hohenlohe period was Johannes Miquel (1828–1901). He was an unusual figure among the Prussian ministers insofar as he had not reached his station through the bureaucratic career as was customary in Germany, but through his service in parliament. Together with Rudolf von Bennigsen he had been one of the foremost leaders of the National Liberals in the Bismarckian era, and had led them to the practically unreserved acceptance of the pseudoconstitutionalism of the new empire. After he had become Prussian minister of finance in 1890, his reform of the Prussian tax system gave the Prussian monarchy the solid financial basis on which it rested in the last quarter-century of its existence. But only by granting extraordinary exemptions to agrarian proprietors and by dropping the simultaneous proposal of an inheritance tax was it possible for him to introduce a graded modern income tax. In spite of his great ability and merit as well as of the continuing favor of William II, Miquel became, in 1897, the victim of the dissatisfaction of his die-hard colleagues, although as minister he had supported the Conservative course in all these years.

The power of the Conservatives was glaringly exposed when, in 1899, they defeated the bill for the building of the *Mittelland* canal which had the strong support of William II. This canal was intended to connect the Rhenish industrial district with the Elbe. The eastern agriculturists, afraid that the canal would open the gates to the import of cheap agricultural products to Central Germany, fought the project with all their might. Even most of the government officials who were members of parliament placed their loyalty to their class above their loyalty to the king. Although Hohenlohe wanted to dissolve the Prussian parliament, the members of the Prussian cabinet were divided in their attitude, and William II shied away from a test of strength.

Hohenlohe's chancellorship was characterized by such leniency toward Conservative obstruction at the expense of coordinated and constructive policies. In foreign affairs these were the years in which Germany sought new links with Russia again. To Hohenlohe, who had been a prominent member of Bismarck's foreign office and whose wife owned large Russian estates, this move appeared as a turning back to the Bismarckian tradition, while actually, under the changed conditions, it could not solve the fundamental problems of German security. Hohenlohe, though with meager results, also attempted to assuage Bismarck, the angry Titan, who after his dismissal was conducting, through newspapers and public speeches, a continuous and at times furious campaign of polemics against William II and his helpers.

In the domestic field social legislation came to a complete halt, while the relations between the government and the Social Democratic party worsened. These years of social inactivity popularly became known as the "era Stumm," and the official policies in social questions were indeed formulated under the influence of the industrialists among whom Baron Stumm was the most ebullient. William II made threatening speeches against the Social Democrats whom, on account of their international ideals, he dubbed "fellows without a fatherland" (*vaterlandslose Gesellen*). Thus the very years in which Germany experienced an amazing expansion of her economy and national income became years of growing social tensions. In the fall of 1898 the emperor announced that the government would present a law that would make it a felony to attempt to interfere with workers willing to work during a strike. Although the so-called "penitentiary bill" (*Zuchthausvorlage*) that the new secretary of the interior, Count Posadowsky-Wehner (1845–1932), presented, was somewhat milder than the emperor's irresponsible speech, its punitive measures still appeared excessive, and it was defeated by the *Reichstag*. The federal elections of 1898 saw a further rise of the Social Democratic vote on the one hand and Conservative losses on the other.

✑ *Chancellor von Bülow*

IN 1897 Count Bernhard von Bülow (1849–1929), the son of Bismarck's trusted foreign secretary, Bernhard E. von Bülow, had become foreign secretary. He succeeded Baron Marschall von Bieberstein, who went as ambassador to Constantinople, where during the next decade he became the foremost protagonist of the extension of German influence in Turkey. Bülow had been brought to Berlin in the expectation that he would replace the aging Prince Hohenlohe before long, and in 1900 he followed Hohenlohe as chancellor. His rise in the foreign service, although not as meteoric as that of Herbert von Bismarck, had been rapid. In the twenty years prior to 1897 he had served in most of the major capitals of Europe, with the exception of London. His marriage to an Italian lady made him consider Italy practically his second home, and he had a cosmopolitan air about him. This man of the great world had an extraordinary gift for disposing of routine business, and in his hands even the serious conflicts of parties and nations lost much of their gravity. In speeches and conversations, always studded with amusing quips and rich literary quotations which seemed to reflect a broad education, he managed to spread good feelings. Many German contemporaries were cheered by his sovereign management of the government. Moreover, his optimism about the internal and external strength of Germany and her great future was avidly accepted by a generation which believed that Germany's stunning rise as one of the three economic powers of the world would be followed by her acquisition of corresponding political position. Irrespective of whether Bülow was judged to be a new Bismarck or not, he was considered the ideal statesman who would lead in modern world politics as Bismarck had done in the Continental politics of his age.

Yet behind the brilliant appearance stood a man of shallow character and narrow vision. His education had given him polish without firm ideals, and his diplomatic talents were not matched by a capacity for critical assessment of long-range political trends. Bülow was a courtier rather than a statesman, driven chiefly by his desire to enjoy the glamor of power and the company of the mighty. He hated not only his enemies but also all those who seemed to detract in the least from his achievements and glory. He did not consider the use of calumny beneath his dignity, nor was truthfulness a categorical imperative to him. If Bülow made it his chief task to hold the personal confidence of the emperor, this was inevitable within the framework of the Bismarckian constitution. Only with the support of the monarch could the chancellor hope to exercise full control over all the civilian branches of the Prusso-German government, and only if he possessed the emperor's trust could he expect to steer the latter and keep him from imprudent actions. The wiles of the courtier were useful means in the establishment of a relationship of this type, particularly in the case of such a self-centered personality as William II. But the friendship between the sovereign and his chancellor would have had to meet its test in the latter's ability to win the emperor's approval for policies that, though unpalatable to him, were required by the national security and welfare. Thus Bismarck had wrestled with William I again and again.

Yet Bülow unblushingly employed any amount of flattery and should not have been surprised that William II's embarrassing acts of public showmanship continued. And while building up William II's swollen ego even more, Bülow failed completely to acquaint him with the dangers with which a responsible German policy would have to cope. No doubt Bülow himself underrated these dangers and did not recognize the serious mistakes which the German government had committed after Bismarck's dismissal. As a matter of fact, at least till 1906 Baron Holstein remained the chief architect of German foreign policy, and Bülow readily accepted the cues which the eccentric councillor gave him. What Bülow and Holstein had in common, and what in William II appeared in its most exaggerated form, was their obliviousness to the perils with which a new state in the heart of the Continent was inevitably surrounded. Whereas Bismarck had been constantly awake to existing or potential dangers, his heirs took the empire for granted and its power for a safe possession. Therefore they were not afraid to expose Germany to the serious risks that were involved in the so-called German "world policy."

From time to time Bülow felt misgivings about the German naval policy, but except in the last year of his chancellorship he never seriously argued the case with the emperor, since he knew that William II was unalterably committed to Tirpitz's program, which also enjoyed the overwhelming support of German public opinion. Although he knew that the building of the navy made Germany vulnerable, he was not disturbed by this grave liability in the conduct of foreign policy. Bülow accepted the responsibility for the German foreign policy, which, as we have seen, produced in response the Anglo-French Entente of April 12, 1904. While the emperor was momentarily alarmed, Bülow publicly stated that he could not discern any adverse development. The Russo-Japanese War, which had started in February 1904, seemed to offer opportunities to demonstrate the importance not only of the Anglo-French Entente but also of the Franco-Russian Alliance. Russia's involvement in the war against Japan, which was protected by an alliance with England, left France isolated. The outbreak of the Russian March revolution in 1905 encouraged Holstein and Bülow to bring home to France the extent of her weakness. Against his originally strong objections, William II, who thought the moment favorable for achieving an understanding with both Russia and France, was induced during a Mediterranean cruise to land at Tangier for a meeting with the sultan of Morocco. By treating the sultan as a full sovereign the German government challenged the validity of the Anglo-French agreement on Morocco and insisted that the international Madrid convention of 1880 which had defined the status of Morocco could not be abrogated by the arbitrary fiat of two powers.

Holstein apparently was aiming at war with France, although we cannot prove this point beyond any doubt. It was also in these months that the chief of the general staff, Count Alfred von Schlieffen (1833–1913), prepared the "classic" version of his war plan that envisaged the annihilation of the French army by a bold campaign through Belgium and Holland. Schlieffen, who kept out of politics, did not urge the government to make war on France. But Holstein knew from him that the army was confident of its ability to conduct a successful lightning war against her. Bülow was not prepared to go to extremes but wanted to employ the utmost pressure in order to break up the Anglo-French Entente and win colonial concessions from France. Neither did William II think of war against France. During the summer of 1905 he met his cousin Czar Nicholas II in Bjoerkoe at the Finnish coast. With no Russian or German minister present he lured the czar into the signing of a Russo-German Alliance. William II, triumphant over his tremendous achievement, was completely shaken when Bülow declared the treaty inadequate because of its restriction to Europe. Obviously the chancellor saw the meaningless character of the compact, which was incompatible with the Franco-Russian Alliance. The Russian ministers, too, refused to take the treaty seriously, and before long the czar had to confess to its uselessness.

✍ *The First Morocco Crisis, 1905–6*

YET THE GERMAN DIPLOMACY succeeded in frightening the French government. Under German pressure, Prime Minister Rouvier went so far as to drop his foreign minister Delcassé, the French builder of the entente. If at this moment the German foreign office had agreed to negotiate with Rouvier a bilateral colonial agreement, in the opinion of shrewd contemporary observers, it would not only have received worthwhile colonial concessions but would also have impeded the transformation of the Anglo-French Entente, originally not much more than a settlement of colonial differences, into a close political association even in European affairs. But Bülow and Holstein demanded the convening of a European conference, where they expected to demonstrate before the whole world the futility of any English aid for France. Although in July 1905 the French government agreed to this conference, which met in the Spanish sea resort of Algeciras, near Gibraltar, in January 1906, diplomatic negotiations between Berlin and Paris failed to produce a compromise that might have avoided Germany's isolation.

Thus, supported only by Austria-Hungary, Germany faced a front of powers who were strongly opposed to her colonial ambitions. It was particularly embarrassing to see the fragility of the Triple Alliance revealed before the world. Italy, already hatching her own plans for North African conquest, kept close to Britain and France. Compared to her major diplomatic defeat, the concessions that Germany received with regard to the legal status of foreigners in Morocco were negligible. It was logical that in these days William II accepted one of the letters of resignation that Holstein periodically submitted in order to prove his indispensability. Yet the jolted schemer was to take his revenge on those whom he held responsible for his dismissal.

The gravest consequences of the first Moroccan crisis were not immediately apparent. The British government had recognized from the beginning that a successful German challenge of the Anglo-French agreement would profoundly discredit British diplomacy. Moreover it saw that if France were standing alone, she was bound to succumb in the case of a German military aggression. France's submission to Germany, possibly accompanied by a Russo-German alliance, would have cut off England's political influence on the Continent or might even have arrayed the Continental powers against her. Therefore, the British foreign secretary Lansdowne did his utmost to assure the French government of British support. But mere diplomatic support and, in the case of war, even the use of the British navy could not have saved France. Thus Lansdowne took the unusual step of hinting at the possibility of direct military intervention on the Continent.

Rouvier felt that England did not possess the military forces needed for this purpose, and for this reason had decided to sacrifice Delcassé and to negotiate with the Germans. The rebuff he received from them led to the renewal of the Anglo-French discussions on the assistance that England would provide if Germany went to war. The foreign secretary in the new Liberal government, Sir Edward Grey, while refusing any firm commitment, readily agreed to conversations of the British and French general staffs with a view to drafting technical plans for making such assistance effective.

Thereby the beginning was made for making the Anglo-French Entente into an instrument not only of close cooperation in all political questions but also of common defense. The technical staff agreements reached between 1906 and 1914 tended to turn into mutual moral obligations. With the passing of the danger of war after the conference of Algeciras the contacts between the two general staffs were not intensified for some years. But in this period the military establishment of Britain was thoroughly modernized, and the reforms of Lord Haldane created a British expeditionary force that had not existed in 1905–6. The political experiences of these years also were a strong stimulus for bringing the negotiations with Russia on a settlement of the Middle Eastern questions to a positive conclusion in 1907.

Thereafter the international situation of Germany was exceedingly precarious. While the "policy of the free hand" had become a daydream of the past, loud complaints were heard about the "encirclement" of Germany, for which chiefly England was blamed. Germany's principal ally, Austria-Hungary, was convulsed by the bitter strife of the various nationalities within her boundaries which had serious international implications. In the Austrian half the struggle between Germans and Czechs exploded again in 1908, and soon the Vienna government ruled only by emergency decrees. Although in Hungary the parliament continued to function, it did so only because the non-Magyar nationalities were inadequately represented and the Magyars conducted a determined policy of Magyarization. The suppression of the Slavs of Istria, Croatia, Dalmatia, and Bosnia made them susceptible to the appeal of Great Serbian nationalism that aimed at the union of all southern Slavs under Serbian leadership. As a first step the Serbian nationalists hoped to win Bosnia, which, with the approval of the great powers, had been occupied, though not annexed, by Austria-Hungary in 1878.

It is doubtful whether at this late hour, when the possession of a national state was taken by every nationality to be a natural human right, a cure could have been found for the ills of the Habsburg empire. Theoretically most promising appeared the proposal to transform the dual into a tri-partite monarchy by creating, alongside Austria and Hungary, a southern Slav realm, consisting of Croatia, Dalmatia, and Bosnia. The program of "trialism," which the heir to the throne, Archduke Francis Ferdinand, espoused, still would not have solved the Czech problem, and it is difficult to see how "trialism" could have been realized against Magyar resistance. Without the abolition of the privileges of the Magyar nobility this end could not have been achieved, and it is unlikely that a Habsburg ruler would have turned into the protagonist of civil war and social revolution. Still, the program of trialism worried the Serbian nationalists.

✍ *Annexation of Bosnia and Herzegovina*

THE TURKISH REVOLUTION of 1908 caused a recrudescence of all the various and conflicting aspirations on the Balkan peninsula. Bulgaria finally won her independence from Turkey and thereby increased the old jealousy of Serbia. But the latter felt directly threatened and thwarted in her highest national hopes when in October 1908 Austria-Hungary declared Bosnia and Herzegovina annexed. At the same time this annexation was a blow to the prestige of Serbia's protector, Russia. The Austrian foreign minister, Baron von Aehrenthal, had played a hard and fast game against his Russian colleague, Isvolski. The latter had visited Vienna, Paris, and London in order to gain the approval of the powers for a change of the international status of the Turkish straits that would permit the passage of

Russian warships. Aehrenthal had declared his approval, provided Russia would not object to the annexation of Bosnia and Herzegovina by Austria. While Isvolski had accepted this condition in principle, he felt duped when Austria-Hungary announced the annexation, although the British refusal to consider a change of the status of the straits had blocked any Russian action.

The German government, too, was angry at Aehrenthal because he had failed to inform Berlin of his intentions and the annexation seemed to ruin the friendly relations between Germany and Turkey. But since the loss of allied Austria-Hungary was even more frightening to contemplate, Bülow felt compelled to throw Germany's full support behind the Habsburg empire, to which he declared Germany would remain loyal in any adversity. After the experiences of Algeciras he even refused Grey's proposal to normalize Austria-Hungary's unilateral abrogation of the Congress act of Berlin through an international conference. This, he believed, would humiliate Austria and thereby directly reflect on the prestige of Germany. Most of all, Bülow reminded the Russian government in no uncertain terms that Germany's great military might would be used to protect her ally.

Russia had to give in. Her army was still disorganized and poorly armed. The German alliance with Austria-Hungary had won a full success that was rounded out by the restoration of amiable relations with the Young-Turk government, which accepted the Bosnian annexation in return for financial compensation. But Russia's defeat made both her government and her officers' corps anxious to build up a big and fully modernized army, as was done after 1909, while her incapability of defending Serbian national interests in 1908 made her more sensitive to Serbian wishes than before. The most immediate result of the Bosnian crisis with its open threats of war was Europe's growing concern about a possible general catastrophe. Even Bülow believed that it would not be wise to repeat a test of strength of this type. He had also grown apprehensive during the crisis on account of the hostile attitude shown by England. The passing of a new German naval bill in 1908 had provoked heated accusations in England and raised demands for an agreement on the limitation of the naval race. Although Bülow convinced himself of the need for moderating the pace of German naval building, his internal position had become too weak to give him a chance against Tirpitz and the emperor. When he resigned in July 1909, the problem was left to his successor.

✍ *Government and Parties*

WHEREAS none of Germany's fundamental internal questions was solved under Bülow's regime, he was quite successful in making his supremacy effective in both the federal and Prussian governments. The coordination of the two governments rested on the reconciliation of the Conservatives as well as the cooperation of the government with identical majorities in the Prussian and German parliaments. The Conservative party was appeased by the new trade treaties, concluded in 1901–3, which raised the duties on grain from 35 marks to 50 marks again. The rising tide of the Social Democratic movement, which in the elections of 1903 received almost a quarter of the national vote and a fifth of the seats in the *Reichstag*, did not annoy Bülow unduly. Both in the Prussian and federal parliaments he at first relied on the support of what was popularly called the "black-blue bloc," which meant the coalition of the Conservatives and the Center party, a grouping that by itself did not form a majority in the *Reichstag*, where it had to be supplemented by the accession of the National Liberal party and other forces.

Bülow accepted the consequences of a policy aiming at the creation of a working parliamentary majority that tended to strengthen the influence of the parliament. Legislation had to be discussed with the leaders of the majority parties, and ministers had to be appointed or dismissed according to their ability to get along with the majority. While under the existing conditions such practices did not lead to a noticeable liberalization of the government, they weakened the authority of the monarch. The official theory that the ministers were nothing but the men enjoying the king's trust became a fiction.

The government considered its dependence on the Center party burdensome and did not receive the demands for fuller representation of Catholics in public administration and universities too well. In addition, the Center was very exacting in the examination of the budget, extending its meticulous review even to the military expenditure. Bülow grew anxious to find an opportunity for showing the Center party that it was not indispensable and thereby to demonstrate that the German government stood above parties. Such an occasion arose when in December 1906 the Center, together with the Social Democratic party, refused to pass supplementary funds to cover expenses incurred in fighting native revolts in the German colony of South-West Africa, while the Conservatives and all the liberal parties voted for the bill. Bülow dissolved the *Reichstag*, accusing the Center of hostility to German colonial activity and of letting down the German soldier during a war. With flimsy pretexts a nationalist electioneering slogan was fabricated against the Center and Social Democratic parties. In January 1907 Bülow tried to get a new progovernmental majority together by announcing that "a union of the conservative with the liberal spirit" was demanded by the times. Yet the elections of 1907 did not shake the "Center tower," and the party even raised its strength from 101 to 103 seats. The Social Democrats, however, while gaining a slightly larger popular vote than in 1903, lost 38 of their 81 seats. Chiefly as a result of the unusually large participation of qualified voters, which the patriotic excitement produced, the Conservative and liberal parties won practically half of the seats, and with the addition of some independent members, the "Bülow bloc" held a majority.

The attitude of the Liberal People's party was novel. Eugen Richter's death allowed new forces, which had been stirring for some time, to overcome the policy of negative opposition that the party had practiced during the last decades. They maintained that the retreat from all responsibility deprived liberalism of its full influence on German public life, and that a party claiming a national role would have to assume some of the burdens of government. Thereby, the party largely adopted the ideas of the Liberal Union that in 1893 had split off from the German Liberal party, and it was logical that the members of the Union returned in 1909 to the fold. Together with the German Liberal party and the German People's party[4] they constituted the Progressive People's party (*Fortschrittliche Volkspartei*) in March 1910.

The new turn of German left-liberalism was to some extent the expression of the strong national sentiment that animated the generation which entered public life in the 1890's. Even those who were opposed to the authoritarian structure of the Bismarckian Empire and regarded its ruling classes with skepticism believed that the Empire had to fulfill the great historic mission of securing for the German civilization an equal place beside the world civilizations. To this end, however, it was thought necessary that the classes which truly represented the new industrial society, that is, the bourgeoisie and the working class, would have a full share in Germany's political life. The brilliant sociologist Max Weber (1864–1920) defined in 1895 the German situation in this sense, while at the same time pointing out that whereas the rule of an economically declining class, such as the *Junkers*, was undesirable, the German bourgeoisie had proved politically inept and the leaders of the working class movement immature.

◆ Naumann's National Social Association

IN THE SAME YEAR and chiefly under Max Weber's personal influence Friedrich Naumann (1860–1919) founded his National Social Association. Naumann, who as a young Protestant minister had worked with Adolf

[4] See p. 320.

Stöcker, had come to the conclusion that only in a dynamic progressive policy could the solution of the social question be found. The worker was entitled to demand the rights that would make him an equal citizen and as such could be expected to support a strong foreign policy. Naumann hoped that the monarch could be convinced that the mobilization of the popular forces, including the workers, would strengthen the roots of the monarchy as well as add to the national power. But his attempt to found a political party on this program was in vain and was given up by him after the elections of 1903.

Naumann's program was essentially an appeal to the liberal and Social Democratic parties for more concerted action. A man of imagination, wide knowledge, and artistic sense, Friedrich Naumann, through his speeches and publications, attracted large audiences and, with some of his ideas, exerted considerable influence on educated liberals. While the need for greater independent activity of the liberal parties as well as for a greater willingness on the part of the government to take the parties into its confidence was widely recognized, its justification was seen not only in internal peace but also in the necessity for a powerful international policy. The young National Liberal Gustav Stresemann (1878–1929), just starting out on his political career, was impressed by Naumann's advocacy of a greater role for the parliament. On the other hand, even most of the Progressives were wary of actively backing the introduction of equal suffrage in Prussia. This measure, however, was absolutely crucial if the Social Democratic party was to be given equal opportunity. While the three-class vote in Prussia deprived the Progressives of their true weight in the Prussian parliament, it made their position in the municipal councils unusually strong, and all the liberals cherished their leadership in the administration of the modern German cities.

✒ *William II's* Daily Telegraph *Interview*

FOR A MOMENT it seemed that the "Bülow bloc" would lead to some constitutional reform. On October 28, 1908, the London *Daily Telegraph* published an amazing interview with William II, in which the emperor posed as a staunch friend of England. In order to prove his point he made the fantastic assertion that he had given the British staff the war plan that had enabled the army to bring the Boer War to a successful conclusion. This article that contained a good many other tactless statements aroused a storm of angry criticism in the German press. For a considerable time the organs of liberal public opinion had criticized and lampooned William II and poured ridicule on his autocratic fits, bombastic oratory, and mania for travel. This time the indignation, shared by people of all parties, went deeper than before. It dawned on many people that the ship of state might founder if William II was allowed to continue to hold the helm.

The interview actually had been seen by the chancellor and the German foreign office beforehand, and it has remained a riddle whether Bülow was just negligent or wanted to embarrass William II. In the *Reichstag* debates of November 10–11 all the parties, including the Conservatives, found fault with the emperor. Bülow on his part refused to accept the responsibility for the emperor's interview but promised to induce him "in the future to observe also in his private conversations the prudence indispensable both for a unified policy and the authority of the crown." It was a clear condemnation of William II's "personal regime," without much of an attempt to plead mitigating circumstances. The emperor was confounded and signed a declaration in which he promised to respect his constitutional responsibilities, approved the chancellor's *Reichstag* speech, and assured Bülow of his confidence. William II's sense of grandeur was badly shaken, and in his depression he thought of resigning. He actually became more careful in his public utterances, though hardly less impulsive and demanding in his dealings with his ministers, at least after he had got rid of Bülow, "that scoundrel" as he now called him before his intimate friends.

Bülow's victory over the emperor was a Pyrrhic one. To be sure, the *Reichstag* had gained some significance, and voices were heard demanding greater constitutional powers for the parliament. Yet nothing came of this, and what Bülow needed most immediately in order to keep the emperor at bay was the support of a solid majority in the *Reichstag*. The Bülow bloc, however, was a temporary parliamentary configuration rather than a working alliance and quickly fell apart. In the summer of 1909 the government presented a bill for the reform of the federal finances. Owing to the limited sources of federal revenue and the growing expenditure, including the cost of naval building, the federal debt had passed beyond the sum of 4 billion marks, and a gap of one-half billion marks in the annual budget had to be closed. The government saw no other solution but to depart from the principle that the Reich should live on indirect taxes. While leaving the income and capital tax to the states, the bill of 1909 proposed a moderate federal inheritance tax. The Conservatives, Poles, and the Center party defeated the bill, whereupon Bülow, with a sharp statement against the Conservatives, resigned. Since he well knew that he did not possess the confidence of the emperor, he preferred to appear as the political victim of the parliamentary struggle with the Conservatives. He left the political scene expecting that he would return later.

∽ *Chancellor Bethmann-Hollweg*

WILLIAM II felt relieved and selected as his fourth chancellor the secretary of the interior, Theobald von Bethmann-Hollweg (1856–1921). The latter had made his entire career in the Prussian interior administration, in which he had rapidly risen to high offices. He was an earnest and most conscientious man, who brought to his duties an orderly, if not original, educated mind that was inclined to judge its experiences in wider perspectives. He was not a reactionary but knew that reforms of German political life were needed, nor was he unaware of Germany's precarious international position. Still, the urgency and radical nature of the needed reorientation of German domestic and foreign policies were not recognized by Bethmann-Hollweg. Without much knowledge of foreign nations he overrated the power of the Empire considerably. He believed in the superiority of the German army and the professional excellence of its leaders as well as in the indestructible character of the German monarchy.

Moreover, Bethmann-Hollweg lacked many of the human qualities that would have been desirable for a statesman in his place. He was not a fighter, but rather a mediator using reasonable persuasion. Reserving his final opinion, he liked to listen to various factions and people. This quality exposed him to the fate of many men who are able to understand differing points of view. Many people, believing to have found him sympathetic to their views, were greatly disappointed when his final actions were quite at variance with what they had expected from him. Thereby, he acquired the reputation of being easily swayed by the entrenched powers, and it is true that he tried to avoid head-on collisions, usually in the hope that in due course the conflicts could somehow be harmonized. But these tactics made him appear overly cautious and weak, and his moderate talent for public speaking could not overcome this impression.

∽ *British-German Naval Rivalry*

BETHMANN-HOLLWEG MADE Alfred von Kiderlen Wächter (1852–1912) his foreign secretary. Kiderlen, though a shrewd man, was fond of strong words and gestures. The Anglo-German tension, as already mentioned, had reached an alarming state in 1908, and in the hostile attitude of British diplomacy during the Bosnian crisis Germany had felt the serious agitation in England. In 1904 the latter had turned to the building of a new type of battleship, much bigger and more heavily armored and armed than the existing battleships, which as a consequence lost much of their value. The British admiralty expected that the German shipyards would not be capable of producing this so-called Dreadnought type. But as early as 1907 Germany put her first modern battleship into service. The new German naval bill that the *Reichstag* passed in 1908 limited the time of service of a battleship from 25 to 20 years and determined the annual building program for the years 1908–17. For the period of 1908–11 the new law proposed the building of 4, and for the years thereafter 2, big battleships annually, while the British had scheduled 20 altogether for 1908–11. Considering the world-wide nature of British commitments, the ratio of 20 to 16 left only a tenuous British superiority that no Englishman was willing to accept. Since the Liberal government was already concerned about its finances on account of the social legislation then under discussion, a considerable expansion of the navy could have been achieved only by a drastic rise in taxation. Before making a final decision on this issue, the English ministers approached the German government in order to find out whether it was willing to cut back its naval building program or at least spread it over a longer period of time in such a way as to make real savings for England possible.

The diplomatic conversations that were intermittently held in 1908–11 remained without positive results. Tirpitz, with the strong backing of William II, was not willing to limit the naval building program at all. Although at times Tirpitz was prepared to reschedule the launching of the projected battleships, he would do so only on condition that England would accept a fixed power ratio, and he was foolish enough originally to consider the ratio of 4 to 3 realistic. The British government was not interested in an agreement that, while failing to bring financial relief, would have placed it under a binding limitation. As early as the spring of 1909 it decided to build 8 Dreadnoughts at once and to aim at a 3 to 2 ratio of naval strength. Thereafter it might have accepted some agreement on this basis, provided Germany at the very minimum would have given the assurance that she would not expand her naval building beyond the law of 1908. But not even this much was Tirpitz prepared to do.

For Bethmann-Hollweg and Kiderlen-Wächter the negotiations on the naval problem were only part of the larger design to pry England loose from her ententes with Russia and France. But this policy, as the wise and perspicacious German ambassador in London, Count Wolff-Metternich, continuously warned, was hopeless as long as the German government was not prepared to make substantial concessions in the naval race. The chancellor himself was convinced that the naval law of 1908 could not be touched not only because the emperor and Tirpitz were immovable but also because the *Reichstag* and the German people would not tolerate any departure from it. Still, he hoped that the emperor would change his attitude if the British could be brought to conclude a political agreement in which they would promise to remain neutral in case Germany should be involved in an unprovoked two-front war. Actually, William II would have found in such an English treaty the best reward for his naval policy, through which he intended to compel the British to be friends.

But it was impossible for any self-respecting British government to make this far-reaching concession as a first move for the opening of serious negotiations over a possible limitation of naval building. Such a step would have appeared as giving in to threats. In addition, Sir Edward Grey was anxious not to arouse French and Russian fears about the reliability of British policy. In his view, a German concession with regard to naval armaments had to precede any talks about an Anglo-German *rapprochement*. However, he was not averse to the attempt to settle causes of secondary political friction between Germany and Britain, such as the altercations over the Bagdad railroad and Germany's unfulfilled desire to reach an understanding on the future of the Portuguese and Belgian colonies which she coveted in the hope of creating an integrated German Central-Africa.

Bethmann-Hollweg failed to recognize the absolutely crucial importance of the naval race. The issue was moreover brought home to every Englishman, because it entailed a steep rise of taxes in addition to those caused by Lloyd George's social reforms. The internal struggles over the British budget were so serious as to lead to constitutional conflicts, which ended in the diminution of the position of the House of Lords. Like most other Germans, the chancellor laid the growing political antagonism to British fears of being outdone by a prospering Germany. Although the rise of Germany's industrial and commercial power was, indeed, watched with some concern, it was chiefly because any political threat on her part would thereby become more formidable. Their trade rivalry did not keep England from seeking closer political relations with Germany in the first years of the century, when England also improved her relations with the United States, the other rising giant. The agitation for a protective system for the British empire carried on in the same years was decisively defeated by the victory of the Liberal party at the polls in 1905–6. This victory at the same time ended a decade of English history in which jingoism, though never dominant, had been a notable influence, and in Edwardian England the pacifist groups were gaining in strength. In Germany the development was exactly the opposite. While the growth of the Social Democratic party showed pacifism spreading among the masses, this trend was of no avail, and the nationalism of the German bourgeoisie grew ever shriller and less rational.

↶ "Panther's *Leap to Agadir*"

NEW INTERNATIONAL COMPLICATIONS arose when in April 1911 the French sent troops to Fez, the capital of Morocco. The German government intimated in Paris that it would not necessarily object to the further French penetration of Morocco provided the German iron interests in West Morocco would not be interfered with and France would cede parts of the French Congo to Germany. In order to put pressure behind his demands, Kiderlen-Wächter had a German gunboat, the *Panther*, sent to West Morocco. It anchored on July 1 off Agadir in order to protect German interests. This so-called *"Panther's* leap to Agadir" alarmed the world, particularly the British government, which saw in it a direct war threat. The British cabinet authorized the chief-of-staff, General Henry Wilson, to go to Paris and conclude conventions for the transportation and deployment of a British expeditionary force of 170,000 men that was to be mobilized simultaneously with the French army and to be under French command. Lloyd George announced that Britain had a vital stake in these matters and would not tolerate the disregard of her position in the councils of Europe. The closing words of this speech, that Britain would not accept "peace at that price," since it "would be a humiliation intolerable for a great country like ours to endure" sounded like a war clarion.

Kiderlen-Wächter's position in his negotiations with France had weakened, and he was unable to secure more than a few useful concessions for the benefit of the German firms in Morocco and the ceding of a strip of French colonial territory that gave German Cameroons a small corridor to the Congo. The German public, that after Agadir had dreamed of a German acquisition of West Morocco, was deeply disappointed by these extremely meager results, and Kiderlen-Wächter became the target of acrimonious and venomous attacks.

Tirpitz, however, saw in the open English animosity a welcome opportunity for the further increase of the German naval building. He quickly went to work to prepare a plan that was to be presented to the *Reichstag* in the fall of 1912. Bethmann-Hollweg thought that in view of the existing strength of the French army and the fast-growing military might of Russia Germany's army should be expanded and feared the disastrous consequences of a new navy bill. With the utmost vigor and courage Count Wolff-Metternich implored his government to desist from this bill, but the mischievous and dilettantish German naval attaché, Captain Wilhelm Karl Widenmann, a lackey of Tirpitz, kept William II in line by his reports that the British were already weakening and that the naval arming of Germany was certain to force them at a not too distant moment to accept Germany as an equal partner in world affairs.

Although the British were far from waxing soft toward Germany, the recognition of the gravity of the international situation came as a distinct shock to them. The public reaction to the Agadir crisis revealed the unwillingness of the British people to face war in support of French colonial expansion. The timely publication of the secret articles of the Anglo-French Entente of 1904 by the English writer Edmund Morel showed the British entanglement in the French penetration of Morocco. In connection with these events a lively public discussion arose on whether all secret diplomacy was evil and ought to be abolished through public or parliamentary control. Woodrow Wilson, who was to raise the demand for open diplomacy before the world six years later, listened keenly to this English debate. In these circumstances the British government agreed to make another attempt at direct negotiations with Germany on the naval problem. Albert Ballin (1857–1918), the director of the largest German shipping firm, together with circles of the City of London, established the first contacts that, in early February 1912, led to the mission of Lord Haldane, the British secretary of war, to Berlin.

Although the English government had been forewarned, Tirpitz's new navy bill had not been made public. Now in Berlin Haldane was given the full text and was simultaneously told that the impending bill was not negotiable. Even with regard to a slower pace of building Tirpitz turned out to be unwilling to make more than insignificant concessions. William II's sincere assurances that Germany hoped to live in political accord with England made little impression under these conditions. Bethmann-Hollweg in this case fought harder than at any other time of his political career and, in his conversations with Haldane and subsequent negotiations with London, tried to find the basis for Anglo-German cooperation that would allow him to persuade the emperor, if not to drop, at least to modify the naval bill. But it was senseless to expect that a period of Anglo-German political amity could be initiated just at the moment when Germany increased her naval threat against England. Consequently, Bethmann-Hollweg got nowhere, and Count Wolff-Metternich was recalled from his London post. With the emperor's prompting Tirpitz presented his naval bill to the *Reichstag*, which passed it with blind patriotism.

Thus the British government felt compelled to reach an agreement with France whereby the British battleship squadron was withdrawn from the Mediterranean and joined to the home fleet, while the chief French naval forces were transferred from Atlantic to Mediterranean ports. By enabling Britain to maintain an imposing superiority over the German navy in the North sea, France could henceforth expect that in case of war Britain would protect her Atlantic coast against German naval attacks. Through the military and naval agreements of 1911–12 the Anglo-French Entente virtually assumed the character of an alliance.

Sir Edward Grey was most anxious to avoid a clash of the two armed camps facing each other in Europe, although he remained determined to preserve close political cooperation with France and Russia. Anglo-Russian relations were repeatedly strained, and even after 1912 a constructive German statesmanship might have found opportunities for a drastic improvement of Anglo-German relations. For such a policy, however, concessions with regard to the German naval building program would have been an absolute prerequisite. But William II and Tirpitz continued to hamstring any German initiative. Moreover Bethmann-Hollweg became less concerned about the political position of England. Grey's policy to meet some of Germany's colonial ambitions in order to forestall the explosion of the Anglo-German antagonism into war kindled Bethmann-Hollweg's hope that England after all was not completely committed to the Triple Entente and might at least stay aside if Germany and Austria-Hungary were to become the victims of an unprovoked attack by Russia and France.

This idle hope induced Bethmann-Hollweg on his part to be conciliatory in negotiating with London. Two Anglo-German treaty drafts were ready for formal signature by the two governments just prior to the outbreak of World War I. The first one dealt with the rather academic issue of the future of the Portuguese colonies, while the second settled all the points of friction that had arisen in connection with the Bagdad railroad and related business interests in Turkey. In order to make a fully satisfactory compromise possible, Germany made very considerable concessions with regard to her own commercial share in Turkey.

∽ *European Politics after 1911* ∾

IT WAS a very encouraging sign that the Balkan troubles, which in 1911 had begun to overshadow the political scene of Europe, led to acts of fruitful cooperation between Germany and England for the preservation of peace among the great powers. Italy's war against Turkey for the conquest of Tripolitania in 1911 set the stage for the war of Serbia, Bulgaria, and Greece that broke out in the spring of 1912 and led to the complete military victory of the Balkan allies over Turkey in the fall of the year. At various moments there was the danger that the Balkan fire might envelop the whole house of Europe, and it was chiefly the mediating policy of England and Germany that confined the flames. While England's calm attitude kept France and Russia from irresponsible moves, Germany prevailed on Austria-Hungary to desist from a preventive war against Serbia, for which the Serbian demand for an access to the Adriatic could have served as an excuse. At the ambassadorial conferences which on Grey's suggestion were opened in London in December 1912 Germany's support of English diplomacy contributed greatly to a Balkan settlement that ended the crisis.

What this settlement could not end, however, was the restless striving of the Balkan nations after the complete realization of their unification within national states, particularly the movement toward a greater Serbia that posed a strong threat to the existence of the multinational Habsburg monarchy. But it was even more ominous that the successful work of the diplomats in avoiding war among the great powers did not quiet the national fears and passions that had brought the nations so close to the abyss. On the contrary, in some of the key countries nationalist forces became even more vociferous and powerful.

Russia's hatred of Austria-Hungary was again intensified by the latter's success in limiting Serbia's expansion. In France and Germany the second Morocco crisis resulted in a recrudescence of acute mutual hostility. The election of Raymond Poincaré (1860–1934) as president of the republic in 1912 ushered in a period of high national sentiment and of great efforts to strengthen the military buildup of France. In Germany also, in spite of the growth of the Social Democratic movement, nationalist feelings rose to a high pitch. The Moroccan and Bosnian crises had revealed the political isolation of Germany and Austria-Hungary. Only German military superiority, it was generally argued, could contain the encirclement of the Central Powers, popularly ascribed to the sheer envy of the satiated nations toward a young aspiring giant. Yet the feeling that this superiority by itself would never suffice to make Germany a world power of an equal rank with Great Britain, Russia, and the United States made an increasing number of people suspect or at least fear that one day her encirclement would have to be broken by force. And in view of Russia's colossal arming a good many hoped that such an opportunity might offer itself soon. The Pan-German League stepped up its agitation in these years, and it is symptomatic of the reception which these ideas found among the German public that such a pamphlet as General Friedrich von Bernhardi's *Germany and the Next War* went through six editions in 1912–13.

In this pamphlet Bernhardi (1849–1930) declared that Germany faced the choice between an ascendancy to world power and a decline. In order to survive and rise she would have to conduct an aggressive foreign policy, which for its support needed the maximum mobilization of the physical and psychological energies of the German people. This implied great armaments on land and on sea as well as the indoctrination of the people with the belief in the historic world mission of Germany as opposed to its common belief in peace and law. Law, according to Bernhardi, is merely an arbitrary fiction of the human intellect and has no supranational validity. Treaties do not have to be respected unless they conform to the interests of the partners. Preventive war, consequently, is permissible provided it offers a chance of success. Although Bernhardi did not believe that Germany had such a chance right then, he admonished his readers to be prepared for an offensive war. He saw its goals in the complete destruction of France's political power in order "that she can never block our way again," the founding of a Central European Federation under German leadership, the acquisition of colonies, and the predominant political influence on other foreign markets. At the same time, he offered this program as the expression of a German cultural mission, whereby he exploited Germany's cultural past from Goethe, Schiller, and E. M. Arndt to Nietzsche and Treitschke only for the purpose of demonstrating the need for German world power. Not Germany's foreign enemies but the German nationalists began to build up those catalogs in which practically every eminent German writer and philosopher figures as a champion of German world power.

Bernhardi's book did not reflect the official thinking of the German government or of the general staff. Apparently, though being on the inactive list, he was even reprimanded for his bold publication by the army chiefs. Yet the book was by no means the escapade of a daring cavalryman; rather, it mirrored opinions widely current among leading social groups, such as the industrialists, bankers, and professors, as well as government and army circles. Colonel Ludendorff, who in these years already played a prominent role in the general staff, certainly shared Bernhardi's views.

✍ The Army Bill of 1912

THESE SOCIAL GROUPS exerted the popular pressure that induced the government in 1912 to propose a large increase of the army. There had been no considerable expansion of German land forces since Caprivi's army bill of 1893, which had attempted to improve Germany's military posture in view of the Franco-Russian Alliance. At the turn of the century, the combined strength of the Franco-Russian armies had surpassed that of the German army. Still, both the Conservative Prussian ministers of war of the years 1896–1909 proved impervious to the repeated urging of the chief-of-staff, Count Schlieffen, to provide him with more troops for the implementation of his projected war plans. In 1912, Germany actually drafted only 52 per cent of the manpower that was available under the compulsory service law, compared to 70 per cent in France.

The ministers of war were afraid of demanding substantially larger funds for the army. They knew the limitations of federal revenue and how much of it was absorbed by the building of the navy. In 1908 the naval budget amounted to almost one half of that of the army, and neither Count Schlieffen nor the war ministers ever dared oppose the emperor's naval predilections, although in their correct opinion the navy contributed little to the defense of Germany. But also their Conservative convictions made these generals shy away from a large expansion of the army. It had already become difficult to find an adequate number of officers who came from the right families and represented the traditional type of Prussian officer with his blind loyalty to the king and feudal code of honor, and the competition with the navy, which, incidentally, was somewhat less exclusive, had tightened the situation even more. The enlargement of the army would have made it necessary to draw increasing numbers of officers from among the smaller middle classes. Equally, the noncommissioned officers, who came largely from politically safe peasant stock, would have had to be augmented by less reliable urban elements. Irrespective of the vaunted claim that the army was the nation in arms, the Prussian war ministry wanted it to be the army of the king. Naturally, the ministers mostly advanced different arguments. They questioned, for example, the possibility of usefully employing millions of soldiers on the battlefield; equally fatuous was their boast that the quality of the German army would make up for the quantity of the enemies' forces. In their patriotic self-conceit they forgot that without her stronger battalions Germany could not have won her great victories of 1870. On the other hand, it was difficult to contradict them when they claimed that any strong increase of the German army would be countered by equal or even larger increases of the Russian and French forces.

Whereas in the years of the Russo-Japanese War and the first Russian revolution the Russian army had actually ceased to be a threat to Germany, the building of a huge Russian army that, as we have mentioned before,[5] began in earnest in 1909, created a grave danger. The Russian army was aiming at a strength of 1.5 million men by 1914 and 2 million by 1916. But in Germany great popular agitation, most effectively directed by the newly founded and quickly growing Defense League (*Wehrverein*), was needed before the war ministry was finally spurred into action. While the army bill of 1912 resulted only in the modest addition of 29,000 men, public dissatisfaction and the determined prompting of the general staff, for which Colonel Ludendorff was chiefly responsible, induced the government in 1913 to demand the enlargement of the army by 117,000 men and 19,000 officers. The *Reichstag* passed this bill and accepted the proposal of the government to finance the measure by a special capital levy.

The unusually large increase in the numbers of officers was intended for the organization of substantial groups of reserves who, in the case of war mobilization, were not immediately needed for bringing the units of the standing army up to war strength, a provision that contributed to the superiority of men and arms with which the German armies broke into Belgium and France in August 1914. Otherwise, the military balance among the powers remained unchanged. Still, during the *Reichstag* de-

[5] See p. 330.

bates the French announced the adoption of a three-year instead of the two-year military service and thereby at once gained 160,000 trained soldiers, in contrast to the 72,000 additional men that the German army was able to draft in 1913–14. While the German army with 750,000 men remained stronger than the French, even together with the Austro-Hungarian army of 450,000 men it was considerably smaller than the Russian army.

The task of defending Germany with an army of this size against France and Russia was staggering. Earlier the elder Moltke had wrestled with the problem of the two-front war after 1871. Once the French had completed the line of modern fortresses from Verdun to Belfort, Moltke thought it impossible, from then on, to win a total victory over the French quickly, even by using all the available military forces of Germany. Moreover, the long war against the French Republic had taught him that modern national wars could not easily be decided by the destruction of the mobile forces. Therefore Moltke considered it unfeasible to seek an early decision in the west before turning Germany's total might against Russia. He proposed to divide the German army and with one half of it to await the attack of the French in strongly fortified Alsace-Lorraine, while joining the other half with the Austro-Hungarian army for offensive operations against Russia. Although Germany's long and open eastern frontier could not be protected defensively, Moltke did not wish to invade the interior of Russia. He only wanted to conquer Poland, thus gaining a shorter eastern front along which the armies of the Central Powers could remain on the defensive.

Moltke considered Germany's military power insufficient for imposing a victor's peace on either France or Russia. Since he saw no desirable acquisitive aims in the east or west, he was satisfied with such military results as would make it possible for the diplomats to restore peace on the basis of the *status quo ante*. What worried him was the length of any future war, and in his last parliamentary speech he warned the Germans that it might well develop into a seven or thirty years' war.

∾ Schlieffen's Strategy

COUNT ALFRED VON SCHLIEFFEN, who was Prussian chief-of-staff from 1891 to 1906, considered himself a true student of Moltke, with whom he had many qualities in common, such as a broad education, the absence of showmanship, the concentration on military affairs, and the simultaneous avoidance of a role in politics. An indefatigable worker who put his disciples through a hard school, he was a wonderful teacher, whose brilliant intelligence and personal unpretentiousness brought his students completely under his spell. Schlieffen set a style which the best officers of the German army down to the Hitler period tried to emulate. But in contrast to Moltke's sober appraisal and calm acceptance of reality, there was in Schlieffen a strong belief that the brain that understands reality can then subject it to its will. Whereas Napoleon had planned only the first moves of a campaign beforehand and had made his battle plans on the eve or morning of the battle, Moltke had planned the opening of the campaigns and the initial battles in one piece. But Moltke was too keenly aware of the unpredictable nature of war to make plans for more than the first phase of a campaign. Schlieffen, however, undertook to plan a whole campaign. Though no gambler, he had great confidence in the power of human reason to see through what Clausewitz called the "fog of war." With his boldness of thought he reexamined the problem of the two-front war. He was convinced that modern civilization could not stand the terrific strain of modern war, and he was particularly apprehensive that the sociopolitical structure of the German monarchy would not emerge unchanged from a long, costly, and destructive trial. Therefore Schlieffen sought a strategic solution that would decide the war speedily.

While Schlieffen agreed with the elder Moltke that no early strategic decision could be achieved in the east, he reached the conclusion that it would be possible for the German army to defeat the French decisively and within a few weeks if its main forces were used at the beginning of the war for a strategic operation that implied the disregard of Belgian neutrality. In the expectation that Russia's mobilization would be relatively slow Schlieffen wanted to leave at the eastern front in the initial phase of the war only weak forces which would fall back while fighting a delaying defensive to the line of the Vistula. Meanwhile only one third of the German army in the west was to be deployed facing the fortified French frontier. Its task lay not in the offensive but in holding the major part of the French army in Lorraine. Two thirds of the German army was supposed to move through Belgium into northern France and envelop the French left wing, finally encircling the enemy. After the total victory over France the German army would be able to deal with the Russian armies.

Schlieffen developed this grandiose conception from 1891 on. In 1897 he drafted the first complete plan of operations which reached its classic form in the plan of 1905. As Gerhard Ritter has conclusively shown, the military risks of this "Schlieffen plan" were great. Since few roads led from Germany into Belgium, Schlieffen intended to use the roads of Dutch Limburg and thereby violate the neutrality of the Netherlands as well. Yet even provided the Belgian fortress of Liège could be taken quickly and the German army rapidly advance and spread into northern France, its lines of supply, while still remaining few in number, would grow longer and become more vulnerable. The detaching of troops for sealing off Antwerp and other smaller fortresses as well as for occupation duties and the losses from fighting were bound to weaken the strength of the front troops available for the crucial battles. For its successful implementation the Schlieffen plan demanded a numerical superiority of the German army as it had existed in 1905. But since that time the French army had grown considerably stronger, and the military situation in the east had changed.

Schlieffen's firm intention to seek victory first in the west consciously disregarded the fate of the Austro-Hungarian army. He thought very little of the military value of the army of Germany's only ally and reasoned that Austria-Hungary's survival would be decided at Paris and not in Galicia. But if the Austro-Hungarian army was left alone to meet the main thrust of the Russian army, it was likely to be badly maimed and to lose its capacity for future offensive action. Moreover, the demoralization of the Austro-Hungarian army, which was still the strongest bond that held the Habsburg monarchy together, could not fail to have a profound impact on the fragile internal conditions of this empire.

But the gravest consequences of the Schlieffen plan lay in its international implications. By violating the neutrality of Belgium, Luxembourg, and possibly even of the Netherlands, Germany would commit an act of aggression against peaceful small countries and display a reckless contempt for international law. None of the justifications which Schlieffen advanced can be accepted. He argued that without a German march into Belgium the French would move in and threaten the German positions in Lorraine. But while such a move could have been easily countered, the French had good military and political reasons for respecting the Belgian neutrality and actually never made any preparations for entering Belgium. The German general staff also spread the word that the Belgians were conniving with France and England, thereby compromising their neutrality. This was, however, nothing but a baseless assertion. The probability that a German invasion of Belgium would bring England into the war entered Schlieffen's discussion solely under the aspect of how much the British expeditionary force would add to the strength of the French army, and he judged that its addition as well as that of the Belgian army would be of only minor military significance.

In May 1900 Schlieffen informed the foreign office that the general staff intended "in the case of a two-front war not to be limited in its operations by existing international treaties." Holstein replied that if the chief-of-staff considered this necessary "it became the duty of diplomacy to face up to such a measure and prepare for it in a suitable manner." It never occurred to the civil government that such a war plan, with its grave political implications, at the very minimum called for a thorough discussion by a crown council on which both the political and military leaders would be represented. But such was the awe in which Bismarck's successors held the military that no council on war plans was ever convoked before 1914. If the chancellor, after gaining full knowledge of the plan of operations which the chief-of-staff recommended, had come to agree with him, it would have been his obligation to conduct an armaments policy that would have enhanced the chances of success of this plan. This would have called for a better understanding of the overall needs of the national defense problem by the war ministry and the navy office. In any event, no chancellor should have conducted the foreign policy of the Empire without a clear appreciation of the problems of German security. Bethmann-Hollweg, while being somewhat worried about the slight margin of success that the Schlieffen plan offered, still believed that if need be Germany could risk the two-front war even though the German military plans contained the grave danger that the intervention of England would turn this two-front into a three-front war.

✐ *Moltke as Schlieffen's Successor*

HELMUTH VON MOLTKE (1848–1916), a nephew of the elder Moltke, became Schlieffen's successor in 1906 against his own expressed wish, because William II thought it a good idea to have a Moltke head the general staff. A sensitive and conscientious man, the younger Moltke had little of his predecessor's brilliance. In reviewing the war plans he essentially adopted the Schlieffen plan, though with certain changes. While not weakening the right wing of the army numerically, he strengthened the left wing and center of the front with the new military units that became available at that time. This modification has often been called a watering down of the Schlieffen plan and the cause of its failure in 1914. But the different ratio of strength between the two wings, which Moltke introduced with the full concurrence of his chief of operations, Colonel Ludendorff, was inevitable, since the French army had grown much stronger and was correctly expected to launch vigorous offensives. In the east Moltke left fewer troops than Schlieffen had provided for in 1905. On the other hand, in 1912 he rejected the retired chief's last advice, not to leave any troops in the east, since in view of the acceleration of the Russian mobilization this move would have laid open northern Germany as far as Berlin and have paralyzed Austrian warfare completely. Although this decision was undoubtedly right, Moltke's attempts to gain additional forces for the passage through Belgium from increased German arming had, as we have seen, only meager results.

Politically Moltke was somewhat more circumspect than Schlieffen. He at once abolished the idea of violating the neutrality of the Netherlands by marching through Dutch Limburg and argued that the Netherlands ought to be preserved as Germany's "windpipe" in the case of a British blockade. However, respect for the neutrality of the Netherlands would render the entry into Belgium more difficult and seem to make it imperative to move into the country and capture Liège before the Belgians could mobilize. But such a violation of Belgian neutrality itself caused Moltke deep worries. He was convinced that it would call forth British intervention. In order to prevent it, he suggested that the Belgians be guaranteed the full restoration of their sovereignty and boundaries. Still, he could not persuade himself that Britain's entrance into the war would thus be avoided, since she could not tolerate the German entrenchment at the coast of Flanders or the full defeat of France that would end the European balance of power. But although Moltke feared the addition of the British expeditionary force of 132,000 men and that of 150,000 Belgian soldiers to the enemy's side, he did not give up the Schlieffen plan, because in contrast to the ideas of his great uncle it still seemed to offer the only chance of a quick German victory and, we may add, a decisive one that would unhinge the European balance-of-power and enable Germany to overcome any future threat of encirclement. From 1913 on, the German general staff discontinued the annual preparation of a plan of deployment for the eventuality that the army would have to fight Russia alone.

Moltke adopted the Schlieffen plan with a heavy heart. At times his appalled assistants heard him quote the German adage: "Many dogs are the hare's death." He firmly stated that the plan should be valid only for the original deployment and the direction of the first operations, but not for the total campaign. He obviously hoped that a French offensive in Lorraine might give the opportunity for a German victory of major significance. But just because of his inner doubts he insisted that once the hour had come the plan should be executed with precision and without delay. And this tied the German chancellor's hands still further. Henceforth from the moment the Russians mobilized their army, Germany had to declare war on Russia in order to be able to break off relations with the latter's ally, France, and thereby gain the excuse for presenting an ultimatum to Brussels demanding the unopposed passage of the German army. In other words, since the strategic planning was exclusively concentrated on a general war, the German government was forced at a certain point of a crisis to assume the responsibility for opening a general European war, irrespective of whether or not all the diplomatic means for settling, or at least localizing, the conflict had been exhausted.

The German public had no knowledge of the technical intricacies of the German military situation. It sensed the danger of war and was both alarmed and offended by Germany's encirclement, which outside the

Social Democratic party few people wished to see countered by concessions, least of all in the field of armaments. The desire to stiffen the official policy in the pursuit of the German ambitions in the world might have enabled the government to win even larger funds than those readily granted by parliament for the naval bill of 1912 and the army bills of 1912–13. The excitement of the public over Germany's international position was something of a new awakening of the bourgeoisie to political consciousness, although the critical attitude did not go very deep. The general direction of the official foreign policy met with approval, and the question raised was rather whether it was executed with sufficient energy.

✐ *Elections of 1912*

YET UNEASINESS EXISTED with regard to the internal conditions. The breakdown of the Bülow bloc had driven the left liberals into opposition. In the federal elections of 1912, the Progressive party made arrangements with the Social Democratic party that enabled the latter to cash in more fully on its big popular vote. Since under the existing election law deputies had to win a majority vote in the individual constituencies, the Social Democratic candidates had often lost out in the runoff elections owing to the attitude of the Progressives who had refused to cooperate with them. Nobody expected the tremendous growth of the Social Democratic party. Its popular vote rose from 28.9 to 34.8 per cent, its seats from 10.8 to 27.7 per cent or from 43 to 110 seats. Thereby it became the strongest German party, which it remained until 1932. The foremost losers of 1912 were the Conservatives and anti-Semites, who received only 68 instead of the 109 seats they had occupied in the parliament of 1907. In relative losses they were followed by the National Liberals, who lost 12 of their 56 seats, and by the Progressives, who lost 8 of their 50. But even the Center party sent only 90 instead of 104 deputies to the *Reichstag*. Considering the continued presence of the Polish and Alsatian members of parliament, the new *Reichstag* made it difficult for the government to legislate at all. In addition, the coordination of the federal and Prussian governments, which was required for any active imperial policy, was lagging. Bethmann-Hollweg fell back on the old Bismarckian theory that the imperial and royal governments were above the parties and rested exclusively on the will and consent of the monarch. But this theory had grown somewhat threadbare, particularly after Bülow's handling of the *Daily Telegraph* affair of 1908. As a matter of fact, Bethmann-Hollweg on his part carefully tried to avoid any head-on collision with the *Reichstag* by not presenting bills which he considered certain to be defeated, and by quietly accepting the failure of a good many items of legislation.

On the other side, the circumstances seemed favorable for allowing the

Reichstag formally to assume a bigger place in the political life of Germany. But with the exception of the Social Democrats no party wanted to go so far as to demand parliamentary government. For such a challenge, which would have meant the reopening of the constitutional conflict of the 1860's, this time on the federal level, the position of the government appeared much too strong, particularly on account of its control of Prussia. In addition, the parties were not at all ready to bury their mutual enmities. In order to bring real pressure on the government, the cooperation of the Social Democrats with the Center, the Progressives, and the National Liberals would have been needed. But the Social Democrats were distrusted by the bourgeois parties not only on account of their socialist aims but also because of their pacifism. It was characteristic of this cleavage that the left-liberal humoristic organ, *Simplicissimus*, which castigated the sins and idiocies of William II's personal regime as well as the role of the *Junkers* in state and army with bold superior wit, played up to the nationalist sentiments of its readers through its cartoons of the malevolent anti-German nations. For a coalition "from Bebel to Bassermann" (the leader of the National Liberals) the time was not yet ripe.

The four parties agreed, however, in May 1912 on new rules of parliamentary procedure. From now on, in the question period resolutions were to be admitted expressing agreement or disagreement of the house with the chancellor's policy in regard to the debated matter. A constitutional amendment could not very well be introduced by a revision of the rules of parliamentary procedure, and the move was not intended to establish parliamentary government. Still, it was the attempt of a substantial majority to give the *Reichstag* a stronger and more independent voice. Undoubtedly, the new policy of the parliament made the position of the government somewhat more precarious than it had been before, but at the same time it exposed the actual impotence of the *Reichstag*. When after a debate on the Saverne affair, which we shall discuss a little later, the *Reichstag* expressed its lack of confidence in the chancellor by a vote of 293 against 54, Bethmann-Hollweg again emphasized the monarchical prerogative in appointing his cabinet. Philipp Scheidemann, one of the Social Democratic leaders, could jeer at a system that did not allow a statesman who had lost his authority to resign but made him wait until he was dismissed by the grace of His Majesty. And Matthias Erzberger, a member of the Center party, reminded Bethmann-Hollweg of the precedent that Prince Bülow had set. But these rhetorical tilts, while greatly embarrassing to the chancellor, could not unseat him. The Prussian bastion of royalism was unconquerable for the opposition. It also continued to throw its shadow over the internal developments in the Empire during the last years before the First World War.

✑ *Nationality Problem in Alsace-Lorraine and Polish Districts*

THE PROBLEMS OF NON-GERMAN NATIONALITIES remained another source of German vulnerability. Little change had occurred in the German administration of Alsace-Lorraine as well as in the reaction of the people of this "imperial land" to German rule. Around the turn of the century minor vexations of the people had been removed, and their agitation had somewhat calmed down, not because the hope for a return to France had been abandoned but because on both sides of the frontier its fulfillment appeared to be more distant. But the revival of the *revanche* sentiment in France during and after the second Moroccan crisis created new restlessness in Alsace-Lorraine.

With great difficulty Bethmann-Hollweg achieved the introduction of a new constitution for Alsace-Lorraine, which, though not giving the province equal statehood, would at least, in the words of the chancellor, enable the Alsatians to develop their individuality. Through this constitution of 1911 Alsace-Lorraine received two chambers, the first to be composed in equal parts of members appointed by the emperor, and of representatives of the churches, the city governments, and professional corporations, the second chamber of deputies elected by universal and secret popular ballot. The universal suffrage was granted by the *Reichstag* against much Prussian opposition. The other federal states objected to giving Alsace-Lorraine votes in the Federal Council. Since the representatives of Alsace-Lorraine would receive their instructions from the governor, who was appointed by the emperor, the German states feared a further increase of Prussian influence in the Federal Council. Nevertheless, Alsace-Lorraine received three votes in the council, though with the anomalous proviso that they would not be counted if in combination with them Prussia was found in a majority.

The constitution of Alsace-Lorraine of 1911 probably went as far toward an equalization of the status of the land as was possible under the Bismarckian constitution. But it remained a constitution imposed through German federal legislation rather than one drafted by the Alsatians themselves. Moreover, the bicameral system still left the actual government in the hands of the governor. The civilian government of the heavily garrisoned country was made more difficult by the attitude of the troops toward the population, which they considered unruly and hostile. An incident of November 1913 revealed this tension between army and people and at the same time showed that the officers did not feel bound by the law of the land. The colonel of the regiment stationed in Saverne had twenty-eight demonstrating civilians arrested and held, a right reserved to the courts and to the police. With no good reason he asserted that the police had failed to protect the soldiers against the townspeople. The

Alsatians demanded satisfaction, but the crown prince sent a congratulatory message to the colonel, who, together with other inculpated officers, was soon cleared by accommodating courts. Even before this happened, Bethmann-Hollweg, seconded by the Prussian minister of war, had defended the officers before the *Reichstag*. Thus on the eve of World War I Alsace-Lorraine was seething with discontent.

The conditions in the Polish districts of the Prussian monarchy were equally unsatisfactory. The attempt to strengthen the position of the Germans in the Polish provinces that had been inaugurated under Bismarck by the colonization law of 1886 had been largely a failure. This law set funds aside with which large Polish estates could be bought and used for the settlement of German farmers. But the sums placed at the disposal of the royal colonization committee tended to drive the land prices up and thus to limit the size of the land purchases. Worse than that, money paid to Polish landlords enabled them to reinvest in land. It is true that through the partition of large estates the number of German farm settlements was increased. But the number of Polish settlers multiplied even faster. With the growth of a Polish middle class, capital became available for a systematic Polish settlement policy. While the total population of the German Empire between 1871 and 1914 grew from 40 to 67 millions, the eastern provinces of Prussia did not add to their population, whereas in the nationally mixed provinces of Posen and West Prussia the Poles steadily increased their relative strength.

There was a twofold movement of Germans from and within the east. The former consisted in the emigration overseas and to West Germany, the latter in the transfer of people from the countryside to the towns and cities of the Eastern provinces. The shortage of farmhands became a grave handicap on the big estates and led to the large-scale importation of seasonal farm workers from Russian and Austrian Poland. Since this labor was cheaper than that of German farm workers, even the *Junkers* were eager to employ Polish farmhands and prevailed upon the Prussian government to keep the frontiers open.

Caprivi had relaxed Bismarck's stern anti-Polish course. He had been skeptical about its success, and the conflicts with Russia in the years after 1890 made it seem desirable to him to appease the Poles. This slackening of governmental anti-Polish efforts aroused resentment chiefly among Conservatives and National Liberals and gave three wealthy landowners in Posen the opportunity for founding in 1894 the "Association for the Advancement of the German Nationality in the Eastern Marches." Although the association, which spread over Germany, never grew very large and did not have a numerically impressive membership even in the eastern provinces, it was very vociferous and its propaganda reached wide circles through other patriotic associations and universities, which were largely willing to rely on it for their ideas on East German political questions. The association also had a substantial following among the Prussian bureaucracy. Its leaders did not agitate for the expulsion of the Poles and, in deference to the East German landowners, always took a softer position than the government on the issue of Polish seasonal labor. Their chief tenets were the predominance of German landownership and the supremacy of the German language. To achieve these ends they agitated for the adoption of laws which increased the unequal status of the Poles within the Prussian state.

The failure of the colonization law of 1886 induced the association to advocate the expropriation of the large Polish landholdings. Though it did not propose expropriation without compensation, its demand was a serious violation of existing property rights. Perhaps even more enraging to the Poles was the fight for the exclusion of the Polish language from the public scene. The association's slogan that "nationality follows language" was patently wrong, as a glance at the Alsatians or at the Masurians should have taught. If the Poles had been an illiterate people, the suppression of the Polish language or at least the simultaneous use of German might have become possible. But while even this cannot be proved, the Poles in all their classes had become a literate nation with a literature and a press of its own, who in the persecution of its language saw an attack against its most personal possession.

The noisy activities of the East Marches association poisoned the relations between Germans and Poles in the borderlands and, in the rest of Germany, also contributed to the continuation of the widespread attitude of arrogant superiority. But at least some voices were heard that warned against the radical suppression of the Polish language and even urged Germans to learn it. When the new law of associations of 1908[6] was presented to the *Reichstag*, the parliament compelled the government to drop the old provision which banned all public meetings not conducted in German. The government conceded that in districts at least 60 per cent Polish the use of the Polish language would be allowed. Although this illogical ruling of the final law discriminated against the Poles and gave them reason to complain, it showed that the Center party and the parties to the left disagreed with the chauvinistic policies under which the Poles suffered.

The Poles saw in the East Marches association the agency that inspired the Polish policies of the Prussian government. This was not fully correct. Although a good many government officials were closely allied with the association, Hohenlohe never cared about the Polish question. His successor, Bülow, however, needed no prodding. Ever since 1874–76 the Polish language had been banned from all the schools both as an

[6] See p. 362.

instrument and as a subject of instruction. Only the teaching of religion could still employ Polish, but it was left to the discretion of the district superintendents to order the teaching of religion in German if they found the children adequately prepared for it. Thus step by step even in religious instruction, Polish had been removed from the high schools and grade schools by German officials, and this resulted in the outbreak of school strikes of serious proportions. To combat them, Chancellor Bülow did not object to using all the coercive powers of the state, thereby inflaming Polish feelings to a high degree. Bülow also took the initiative in expanding the scope and stringency of the colonization law in the early years of his chancellorship. In 1908 he had the Prussian parliament pass a law that authorized the government to expropriate big Polish estates for the settlement of German farmers. It was noteworthy that the bill was passed only by a small majority in the House of Lords, where it was denounced by the large landowners as a Marxist attack on property.

Under Bethmann-Hollweg the expropriation law was used only once in 1912. The Austrian government complained that it caused disaffection among the Poles of the Habsburg empire, and Bethmann-Hollweg apparently saw the hopelessness of waging the German-Polish struggle through such measures. He failed, however, to take an open stand and thus left the expropriation law as an effective issue for Polish agitation. After 1919 the law even served the Poles as an excuse for their expropriation of German holdings.

The failure of the imperial government to overcome the hostility of the Poles and the people of Alsace-Lorraine left an open wound, which, however, in peacetime did not seriously sap the vitality of the German nation. But the disaffection with the existing authoritarian state that by 1912 had become rife among one third of the German people was a cause of weakness and made many fearful about the future of the Empire.

✍ *Social Democratic Party*

AS WE HAVE SEEN,[7] the persecution of the Social Democratic party by the state in the years 1878–90, far from suppressing the movement, did not even succeed in halting its further spread. The government was able to interfere only with its effective organization. For keeping its members united, ideology thus became even more important than would have been the case if the organization could have grown unimpeded by hostile governmental intervention. In the 1880's the *Sozialdemocrat*, edited by the exiled Eduard Bernstein in Zurich and later in London, served as a beacon of theoretical enlightenment. Then, with the lifting of the antisocialist law in 1890, both ideology and organization could systematically

[7] See pp. 287–9.

be rebuilt. In 1891 the party adopted in Erfurt a new program consisting of a general theoretical part and another one dealing with immediate practical aims.

The theoretical section stated the theory of the class struggle as the great theme of history and described capitalism as a necessary transitional form of economy that intensified the productive forces while simultaneously it abused them for the dehumanization of society. The Erfurt program went on to predict the collapse of capitalism as a result of the impoverishment of the masses and of the concentration of capital in the hands of the few.. The Marxian doctrines thus became the shibboleth of German socialism, and although even in the version of the Erfurt program they lent themselves to varying interpretations, they served as the chief tenets of faith for the indoctrination of the party followers.

As such they performed an important social and political function that decisively molded the character of the next generations of German workers. The individual worker was taught to regard himself as a member of a class that, though locked in a deadly struggle with bourgeois capitalism, was destined to preside over a happier future of mankind. From this belief sprang a strong ideal of solidarity with one's fellow workers together with a sense of pride that the working class was elected to realize full human freedom and justice. On the other hand, even under the capitalistic system that deprived the worker of his true deserts, productive work had a meaning beyond the earning of one's upkeep, since it maintained the dynamics of capitalistic development on which the eventual arrival of socialism depended. In this respect Marxism, by producing laborers willing to work, and to work well, made a direct contribution to the success of German industrialism. In general Marxism endowed the German worker with remarkable self-discipline and reasoning ability. Knowing that certain objective forces were underlying all the political developments, he did not react to the events of the day or to provocations with spontaneous outbursts of personal passion. Rather, he was willing to wait until his leaders would tell him that the historic moment for action had arrived.

Yet did the Social Democratic leaders know when this would happen? Historical materialism contained no clear criteria. It was both a theory that explained the course of history deterministically in terms of economic forces and a theory of revolution that called for the self-willed action of men. The two aspects were never fully reconciled by Marx or for that matter by the Erfurt program. Therefore it was quite possible to think of the coming revolutionary crisis as a still more or less distant event and to concentrate upon political and social aims which would advance the position of the working class within the existing society. The second part of the Erfurt program contained such a program of immediate action. It consisted without exception of democratic goals, such as proportional representation, the franchise for women, the replacement of the army by a militia system, the total secularization of education, and the eight-hour day for workers. The pursuit of these ends became the almost exclusive preoccupation of the practical policy of the party, which it tried to advance through propaganda, ballots, and parliamentary debates.

Bismarck's grant of universal suffrage for the *Reichstag* elections, although made for very different political purposes, proved to have the potent effect of keeping the socialist movement on a democratic keel. The elections were an impressive means of registering before the world the irreversible growth of the movement, and the success of 1912 raised the hope that the *Reichstag* might in the not too distant future be dominated by a Social Democratic majority. Actually the influence of the Social Democratic party on the legislation of the federal parliament was not very great so long as all other parties refused to have any dealings with it, and the *Reichstag* served mainly as the most powerful sounding board beyond the party's own membership.

Being a party that wanted to create not only a new state but also a new civilization required a new type of organization. It was not enough that the individual member, through his ballot and contributions to the campaign fund, would become active only during an election campaign, but he had to work at all times winning new members and making the policies of the party understood by his friends and neighbors. To this end he had to be immunized against the ideals of the bourgeoisie and to be assisted in improving his own socialist education not only in economic and political matters but in cultural matters as well. The political party was soon surrounded by a network of affiliated associations, such as youth organizations, sports clubs, dramatic and literary associations, glee clubs, and organizations for the spread of atheism. It was fitting to say that in his work and leisure the Social Democratic worker was organized "from the cradle to the grave." The genuine idealism behind these activities was proved by the fact that they all stemmed from the initiative of the members themselves and were maintained by their small contributions, which, in view of their meager wages, constituted real sacrifices. In addition, they made it possible for the party to build up a powerful daily press.

Within all these organizations and institutions of the party democratic practices prevailed and were important for keeping the members engaged and active. On the other hand, the freedom of the local party organizations was limited by the control exercised by the central party committee. The local organizations, which in the illegal period before 1890 had enjoyed considerable independence, accepted this control only reluctantly, while some of them even refused to subordinate themselves and formed the nucleus of a small syndicalist movement that survived in Germany until 1933. Yet the vast majority of all the local cells and clubs that existed at the time of the lifting of the antisocialist law complied with the demands of centralization, which seemed the logical expression of the solidarity of the working class and of the need for united action against the bourgeoisie. It was inevitable that with the rapid growth of the party a corps of functionaries arose who had to be paid for giving all their time to the manifold party business. With few exceptions they came from the working class and remained modest and simple in their conduct of life. But their petty-bourgeois existence lifted them somewhat above the proletarian level of the ordinary members of the party. They were not readily willing to jeopardize the institutions of the party on which their own jobs depended for revolutionary adventures. To a greater extent than the party rank and file these party secretaries and editors of party journals were inclined to accept the orders and directives of the national and state chairmen, whose influence on the appointment and, through the apportionment of funds, on the work of the functionaries was very great.

↬ Trade Unionism

ON THE WHOLE it can be said that the growth of this party apparatus contributed to the ability of the national leaders to maintain their moderate course against the strong pressures that arose from time to time in various places. But the most decisive force that steered the party into the reformist direction were the trade unions. The modern German trade unions developed sporadically at the time of the revolution of 1848-49, but little of this movement survived in the political reaction of the 1850's. Their growth began with the spread of industrialism and the beginnings of a political working class movement in the decade thereafter. The interdependence of the trade union movement with the Socialist party existed from the beginning in the close relation or even identity of their leaders and was reflected in the reaction of the workers. The Hirsch-Duncker trade associations, which the liberals founded in the same years,[8] with their program to settle all labor conflicts through peaceful negotiations and without strikes, attracted only a few members and remained forever a small group.

The great majority of the workers who banded together in the trade unions believed that they could improve their lot only through fighting and that as a cumulative result of such militancy a reform of the existing social order could be achieved. For this reason they thought of themselves as socialists. It is surprising that almost from the beginning these trade

[8] See p. 284.

unions tended to go beyond the local level and form national organizations. Thus in the fifteen years before 1878 about thirty central socialist trade unions came into being. These unions of printers, carpenters, masons, shoemakers, and so on, were organized along the lines of special crafts. They were the activists among the skilled workers. It has been estimated that their number did not surpass the 50,000 mark.

Although the antisocialist law was directed against the Social Democratic party and not necessarily against the socialist trade unions, the police treated the latter mostly as party organizations. All the central unions were dissolved. Some local unions continued or survived in disguised form and, in 1890, became the nuclei of the new, so-called "free," trade union movement. The tradition of building centralized trade unions along occupational lines was resumed and made the norm by the first general congress of German trade unions in Halberstadt in 1892. The principles of organization were identical for all unions. The organization rose from the representative in the individual factory or firm over the local and district administration to the central one. While the paid and unpaid members of the administration of the local unions were elected by a meeting of all members, the salaried members had to be confirmed by the central administration, which also appointed the paid officers of the district committee that was elected by delegates from the local unions. The central administration was elected by a general convention of delegates from all the member unions.

The power of the national chiefs of the trade unions was imposing. They received all the money collected from the members and decided how much of it might be retained by the local and district organizations for their own purposes. Although the opening of a strike required a qualified majority of all the local union members, it was the prerogative of the central administration to call the beginning and the end of the strike. The advantage of this procedure was that it made it possible to use the united strength of a national union against local employers. On the other hand, the policy-making national chairman, relying on the apparatus of local and district functionaries, sometimes lost contact with the sentiment of the masses. Soon a strike against individual enterprises became difficult, because the employers on their part formed national federations for mutual support.

The individual trade unions, among which those of the miners and metal workers became the largest, were sovereign in their policies. However, they maintained the "General Commission of German Trade Unions"—later named General German Trade Union Federation—in order to coordinate the policies of the individual national unions. In 1891 Karl Legien (1861–1920), the son of a working man, had suggested the founding of the commission, whose chairmanship he held to the time of his death. In this capacity he was not only the coordinator but also the chief initiator of the general policies of the free German trade union movement that grew from a membership of ca. 300,000 in 1892 to 2.5 million in 1924. An important organizational shift occurred with the greatly increasing employment of unskilled laborers by the big industries. While some of the older trade unions, such as the metal and wood workers, admitted them to membership, others preserved their character as craft associations, but formed auxiliary unions for the unskilled laborers. In addition, a special factory workers' federation was created. This expansion and the actual participation of unskilled labor in all the conflicts over the improvement of working conditions went far to avoid a cleavage between skilled and unskilled labor that might have split and weakened the whole working class movement in Germany.

Even after 1890 the trade unions were not legally recognized and remained exposed to continuous police chicanery. Any local police commissioner could declare a trade union a political association and thereby automatically have all its meetings subjected to prior certification and supervision. Still, the growth of the trade unions was not stopped, and since many industries began to recognize their constructive function in the building of a rational industrial system, they soon showed considerable successes. Although labor conflicts and strikes were rather frequent before 1914, there were also an ever-increasing number of collective agreements on wages. By 1914 the wages and hours of about two million workers were covered by wage scales negotiated between the industrial employers and the trade unions. These wage scales had no legal force, and their practical interpretation and application by the employers was not always fair. But in many industries the road had been opened toward a partnership of the workers in the industrial process.

These achievements of the German trade unions were considerable and explain the loyalty of their members. To the millions of German workers the alleviation of their working and living conditions was of greater immediate importance than the struggle for more distant political ends. This might have been very different if the trade unions had been blocked or if serious unemployment had struck the workers more often. But between 1890 and 1914 the average unemployment of the workers organized in the trade unions ranged between 3 and 3½ per cent, with two weeks as the average duration of unemployment.

∽ *Social Democratic Party and the Trade Unions*

WHEN THE SOCIAL DEMOCRATIC PARTY was reconstituted in the early 1890's, many of its radical members wished it to have no dealings with the trade unions as the agents of a mere social reformism that was incompatible with the ultimate revolutionary aims of the party. Therefore, they did not object to the complete independence of the free trade unions from the party. But it was unrealistic to expect an actual separation. The active members of the trade unions simultaneously belonged to the party, and their general membership provided the largest bloc of Social Democratic voters at the elections. If the Social Democratic party had intended to become nothing but a political vanguard of revolution that disregarded the demands of the masses clamoring for an early improvement of their living conditions, it could not have become a mass party but, like the Bolshevik party of Russia, would have remained a small militant elite of workers and intellectuals. But to the German Marxists the ideal society of the future was a democratic one and the democratic organization of the whole proletarian class was the necessary preparation for the realization of the classless society.

Thus the Social Democratic party found it impossible to rebuff the trade unionists. It became the accepted practice of the Social Democrats to back the demands of the free trade unions in the municipal, state, and federal parliaments, and even to give them a voice in the councils of the party. The trade unionists tended to strengthen the trend toward reformist objectives that had already become strong in the party. Moreover, the development of the capitalist economy seemed to indicate that the great crisis that Karl Marx had predicted was not close at hand.

Eduard Bernstein (1850–1932), who had edited the central organ of the party from Zurich and London during the time of the antisocialist law, even went one step further. In his *The Presuppositions of Socialism and the Tasks of Social Democracy* of 1898 he denied the validity of Marx's theory of the impoverishment of the proletariat and the approaching final crisis of capitalism. He argued that, in contrast to Marx's prophecy, the conditions of the workers had visibly improved and no collapse of capitalism could be anticipated. But if pressed with energy, further reforms could be achieved by party and trade unions even under the existing economic system. Bernstein stated that in reality the Social Democratic movement was following a reformist rather than a revolutionary course of action and that it would profit from clearly acknowledging the new situation.

Bernstein's views, which were influenced by his observations of the English trade unionist socialism and the Fabian theory of gradualism, caused a storm of protest in the party. August Bebel was quite incensed. For him there was no conflict between the present policy of practical reforms to which all his actions were devoted and the expectation of the wonderful dénouement which he carried in his heart. The cold scientific theory of the ultimate crisis of capitalism, for which he had found some proof in the twenty years of relative stagnation of the capitalist development after 1873 and in the concentration of large-scale capital in the hands of a few, was for him the indispensable source of his ardent faith. And this was true for most German Social Democrats of his generation and the following one. Although their practical politics were little influenced by Marxian doctrine, they clung to the enthusiastic hope that it infused. The Austrian-born Karl Kautsky (1854–1938) became the official interpreter of the party doctrine. He managed to combine the justification of the general policies of the party with the proof of the unimpaired validity of Marxian teachings in the midst of a rapidly changing world.

✍ *Social Democratic Cooperation with the Government*

WHILE EDUARD BERNSTEIN's "revisionism" was denounced, though not completely banned, by the majority of the party congresses of 1899 and 1903, the actual practices of the party continued to be reformist or revisionist. As a matter of fact, practical revisionism gathered growing momentum. The South German Social Democrats were the first to give up strictly negative parliamentary tactics. They repeatedly voted with the liberals for the government budget in order to secure legislative concessions and made election alliances with the Progressives. A "great bloc" of National Liberals, Progressives and Social Democrats opposed the Center party and supported the government's liberal course in Baden after 1906. The South German Social Democrats even horrified their North German comrades by allowing members of the party who had been elected vice-presidents of their land parliaments to participate in the customary New Year's reception at the court dressed in tailcoats! Although the national party congresses voted against budget approval, election alliances with other parties, and "courtiers," these votes did not keep the leader of the Bavarian party, the fearless and homely Georg von Vollmar (1850–1922), from persisting in his policies, and the Baden members were equally stubborn.

The less pronounced class differentiation, the stronger liberal tradition of the middle classes, and the more civil attitude of the princes in South Germany played a decisive part in this cooperation of Social Democrats with other parties within the constitutional framework of the existing state. But even the national party began to move away from its self-imposed isolation. After the turn of the century the beneficial impact of the social legislation of the years of 1887–1891 was more clearly felt. Count Posadowsky-Wehner (1845–1932), who had started his tenure as secretary of interior rather unhappily by advocating the passage of the "penitentiary bill" of 1898, became the active champion of further social legislation, although the various laws passed under his guidance remained confined to the extension and implementation of workers' protection and insurance and did not tackle the recognition of the trade unions as equal social partners in industry. The more liberal revision of the law of associations of 1908 restated in paragraph 153 the authority of the government to treat the trade unions as political associations. The same law featured a provision that, though of general significance in the development of German political life, was particularly welcome to the trade unions and the Social Democratic party. Whereas the old law had forbidden the admission of "female persons" to political associations, women were now allowed to join such organizations.

The period of active social legislation ended in 1912, when Posadowsky-Wehner's successor, Clemens von Delbrück (1856-1921), under the influence of an approaching economic recession, declared a general standstill since a further extension of social legislation might prove a severe handicap for German enterprise. But the debates on social legislation between 1890 and 1911 contributed greatly to winning the Social Democratic party over to positive cooperation in parliament. The opposition to election alliances with other parties quieted down, and the new attitude paid handsome dividends in the elections of 1912.

The most amazing step taken by the Social Democrats was their approval of the finance bill in connection with the passing of the great army bill of 1913. The large army increases of that year were passed by a majority composed of the Conservatives, the liberal parties, and the Center, with the Social Democratic party opposed. But whereas the Conservatives balked at financing the considerable new expenditure by a special property levy, as the government proposed, the Social Democrats gave their assent to this tax measure. The taxation of property had been a coveted goal of socialist policy, and the Social Democrats were glad to have a chance for getting at least the principle supported by a majority. Still, their pivotal role in making the big army bill of 1913 possible was an astounding departure from their staunch opposition to militarism.

Until this time the Social Democrats had always vociferously fought against militarism. With this not clearly definable polemic term they had aimed in the first place at the domineering role of the military in the internal government of the state as the chief obstacle to any form of democratization, but it was also used to denounce the danger of highly professionalized armies as promoters of an international war. The cure was seen in the adoption of a militia system that would abolish the officers' caste, which made the army the chief tool of a class-bound authoritarian monarchy and the potential spearhead of aggressive war. But even from a merely technical point of view a militia was suitable only for a defensive war. Consequently, the Social Democrats regularly voted against the military budget and railed against the abuses and cruelties of the existing army. They also fiercely opposed Germany's policy of naval building and her colonial ambitions as useless and possibly dangerous national policies. Naturally, they were in favor of international disarmament, for which imperial Germany had nothing but contempt.

Yet the Social Democratic party never spoke out against the defense of the nation. On the contrary, the duty of every citizen, including the Social Democratic worker, to defend the fatherland was often emphatically stated and, particularly with regard to Russia, was reinforced by the ideological argument that the Social Democratic movement could not possibly tolerate the victory of czardom. In his last speech in the *Reichstag*, in which he criticized the army bill of 1913, August Bebel pointed out that in the case of Russian aggression every man would be needed and that the Social Democratic program of a militia alone envisaged the training of every German citizen. But as mentioned before, it was the Social Democratic vote that, though in an oblique manner, made the increase of the traditional German army possible.

The Social Democratic attitude toward war was, however, blurred by the activities of the Second International, in which the German party was by far the strongest member. The growing international tension after 1905 and the impression made by the first Russian revolution had led to lively debates on whether the Socialist International had sufficient power to protect the peoples against the catastrophe of war. At the congress of the International held in Stuttgart in 1912 it was resolved that in case the ruling classes were to start a war, the workers would be called upon to turn their arms against their own governments. Although the right of national defense against aggression was not condemned by this declaration, many people expected thereafter that the socialist parties of the world would cooperate in the forceful resistance to an international war.

Altogether it was true that the Social Democratic party came to feel that in a revolution the German worker had to lose far more than "his chains." Though ostracized in many respects by the state and the ruling classes, the Social Democrats had the organizations which they themselves had built up and which by no means only the functionaries but also the membership did not wish to see lightly jeopardized by doubtful revolutionary actions. In addition, they had made very considerable social gains through the social legislation of the state and the improvement of wages won chiefly by the trade unions. The majority of the German workers, though certainly dissatisfied with the existing political and social conditions, were not in a revolutionary mood but were willing to follow their leaders in their reformist course even when at times they wished them to conduct their policies in a more radical manner.

There were significant and portentous countermovements to this prevailing trend. After 1905 a party left wing arose led by the bold Karl Liebknecht (1871–1919), the son of Wilhelm Liebknecht, by the theoretically gifted and intrepid Rosa Luxemburg (1870–1919), and by the writer Franz Mehring (1846–1919). In contrast to Karl Kautsky, who expected the strife of the imperialist powers for colonies eventually to end peacefully in a cartel-like agreement among the powers, these leaders saw in imperialism the last dialectic stage of capitalism and the approach of world revolution. They accused Bebel of being a "party-centrist," that is, a man who, though actually following the policies of the non-Marxian reformist right wing, tried to hold the support of the left wing by professing a Marxist faith. They wished to stir up the revolutionary temper of the masses by preparing them for a general strike for high political gains.

◊ Suffrage Problems

JUST AT THAT TIME the issue of the suffrage engendered considerable excitement among the party followers in various German states. In 1896 Saxony had adopted the Prussian three-class system in the place of a rather liberal suffrage, and in 1905 the Saxon government contemplated further changes. In Lübeck equal suffrage was abolished in 1904, while Hamburg tightened in 1905 her three-class system still further to the detriment of the low-income groups. Hesse, too, was agitated by the problems of franchise. In November meetings for suffrage reform, which led to big mass demonstrations, were held in Saxony, and the movement carried over into Hamburg, Hesse, and Prussia. It subsided not only because the governments remained firm but also on account of the strong pressure that the trade unions brought to bear on the party against the use of the mass strike for political ends.

Still, the national leadership was not always able to stem the mass demonstrations originating among the local party organizations, particularly at times when labor trouble heightened the social tension. Thus in April 1910, when a suffrage bill was under debate in the Prussian parliament, a wave of mass demonstrations spread through the country. But the movement ebbed again, and the party chiefs succeeded in channeling the energies of the party members into the preparation of the federal parliamentary elections of 1912. Thus the socialist left wing of the party failed to make much headway in the years before the First World War.

The suffrage issue, however, remained very much alive. It was quite clear that even if the Social Democrats should some day acquire a majority in the *Reichstag*, they would be far from controlling the imperial government, which still could hope to maintain its relative independence from the *Reichstag* as long as it could count on the power of the unreformed Prussian monarchy. As the decisive first step the reform of Prussia called for the introduction of universal suffrage, which was bound to produce a party constellation roughly identical with that of the *Reichstag*. It would have revealed at once that the peculiar character of existing Prussian politics did not reflect the will or sentiment of the Prussian people but was the result of the political manipulations of entrenched social minorities. The Prussian franchise was resented not only by the workers but also by the middle classes, whose members found themselves pushed in large numbers into the third class of voters. While education counted for nothing, even a man of means might find himself in the third instead of the second class if he moved from one side of the street to the other, since the division of the election districts was utterly silly. As a consequence, many monarchists abstained from participating in elections.

Bethmann-Hollweg, who was convinced that the three-class system was an affront not only to the Social Democrats but also to intelligent government supporters, presented a new election law to the Prussian diet in 1910. It did not provide for the introduction of universal and equal suffrage and, by the proposal of plural votes for certain groups, still discriminated against the left. But the chancellor withdrew the bill when it became clear that the Conservative party, with the support of the House of Lords, would have let only a farcical law pass. When in 1912 the Social Democratic Party made its tremendous gains in the *Reichstag* elections, the rightists declared that the Prussian system would have to be preserved as "the last bulwark against the red flood." Bethmann-Hollweg, however, who through his reform bill had indicated that he considered at least a moderate assimilation of Prussian to federal conditions inevitable, was accused by the Prussian diehards of weakening the position of Prussia within the Empire. For this reason, on January 10, 1914, the House of Lords passed a vote of nonconfidence against the prime minister-chancellor. Seven Social Democratic members had entered the Prussian House of Representatives, and the Prussian elections brought their number to ten. Unable to influence legislation, they merely made blasphemous speeches against hallowed Prussian institutions. But these public demonstrations of the Social Democrats and the reaction of the government and the Conservatives made the question of preservation or reform of the Prussian franchise the major issue of German internal politics.

✍ The Empire in 1913

THE TWENTY-FIFTH ANNIVERSARY of William II's ascension to the throne in 1913 was celebrated with a torrent of official laudatory speeches, all of which competed in describing the magnificent achievements that Germany owed to his rule. Actually, there was no justification for such praise. Except for her alliance with Austria-Hungary, Germany was politically isolated, and as much as any other person William II, by his speeches and actions, had contributed to this perilous situation. In addition, the German Empire was fast approaching an acute constitutional crisis, for which again the emperor's "personal regime" carried much responsibility. Finally, Germany suffered from the deep split between the working class and the rest of the people, a split that William II alternately had tried to heal and had hardened. It was unfortunate that an eccentric poseur could assume the royal power that Bismarck had regained for the Prussian monarch. Nevertheless, William II's personality was not the truly decisive factor in the development of Germany during these twenty-five years. The emperor might have proved pliable, if a strong *Fronde* among the nobility or a powerful opposition among the bourgeoisie had arisen. As a matter of fact, among his advisors and friends there were quite a few who knew his frightful shortcomings and entertained grave doubts about the general course of German policy. But they remained voices in the wilderness, since the Prussian *Junker* class saw in an authoritarian monarchy the indispensable shield of their class privileges and since the German upper bourgeoisie was equally convinced that its interests were best protected by such a strong monarchy. The national idea, which half a century earlier this bourgeoisie had championed as a means for the realization of freedom, had become largely, and for some exclusively, the lever for higher rank among the nations of the world. William II's colonial and naval policies were most heartily supported by the German bourgeoisie. In their general direction the German policies of this period expressed the sentiments of the ruling classes, which, blinded by Germany's rapidly rising economic strength, were unaware of the harsh realities of political life that strong as well as weak powers must meet responsibly.

CHAPTER 8

Economic and Social Life in the Empire

THE GERMAN EMPIRE of Bismarck and William II awed the world not only with its military might but also with its phenomenal economic growth. By 1900 Germany had become the biggest industrial power of Europe.

✍ *Population Growth*

ONE OF THE BASES of Germany's industrialization was the continuous increase of her population. Although after 1875 the relative birth rate was beginning to decline, first slowly, then, after the turn of the century, more drastically, with the annual arrival of over two million babies the years of 1900–5 registered the highest absolute birth rate in German history. The decline of the relative and, after 1905, absolute birth rate, however, did not retard the steady population growth. Better hygiene, medical care, and social conditions enhanced the life expectancy of the individual. Whereas in 1871 one fourth of all infants died in their first year, their number had decreased to one fifth in 1900, and further progress was made thereafter. The average life span of the individual, which had been 37 years in the decade after 1871, exceeded 42 in the last decade of the century and had reached 50 by 1910.

The total population figures are 40.9 million in 1870, 45.3 million in 1880, 49.5 million in 1890, 65 million in 1910, and 67.8 million in 1914. The population growth would have been even more rapid if German emigration had not been so great in the first twenty-five years of the Empire's existence. In the years 1871–75 almost 400,000 people emigrated; in 1875–80, 231,000; in 1880–85, 857,000; in 1885–90, 485,000; and in 1890–95, 402,500. As in the past, the German emigrants went mostly to the United States. The great majority came from rural districts, and in contrast to the earlier emigration, which had largely originated in the southwest and west, northern Germany, particularly Pomerania, Brandenburg,

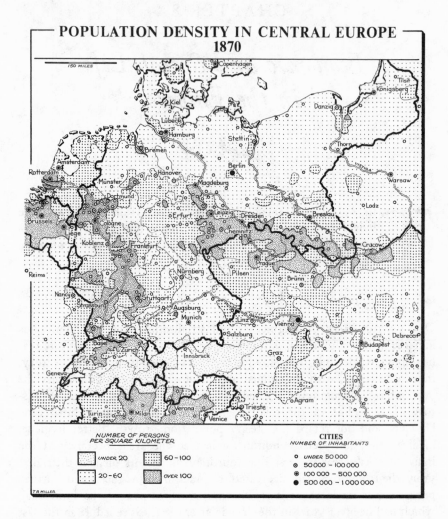

POPULATION DENSITY IN CENTRAL EUROPE
1870

NUMBER OF PERSONS
PER SQUARE KILOMETER

☐ UNDER 20   ▦ 60–100

▨ 20–60   ▓ OVER 100

CITIES
NUMBER OF INHABITANTS

○ UNDER 50 000
◉ 50 000 – 100 000
◉ 100 000 – 500 000
● 500 000 – 1 000 000

Hanover, and Schleswig-Holstein, was strongly represented in these twenty-five years.

After 1895 German emigration suddenly ebbed. Until 1914 the annual rate remained between 20,000 and 30,000. In addition, there was a substantial wave of remigration in the decade after 1895 when almost 150,000 Germans, most of them people who had gone to America after 1880, returned. By 1895 the German economy had grown strong enough to absorb the increasing population, and the prosperity of the years before World War I made emigration unattractive.

But compared to internal migrations in the period from 1871 to 1914 the German overseas migration was small. A census taken in 1907 shows that about half of the population had stayed at the place of their birth or

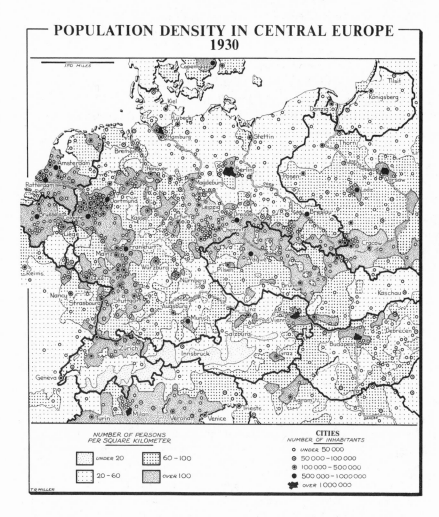

POPULATION DENSITY IN CENTRAL EUROPE
1930

NUMBER OF PERSONS
PER SQUARE KILOMETER

UNDER 20
20 – 60
60 – 100
OVER 100

CITIES
NUMBER OF INHABITANTS

○ UNDER 50 000
◎ 50 000 – 100 000
◉ 100 000 – 500 000
● 500 000 – 1 000 000
⬤ OVER 1 000 000

had returned there. One third lived in places within the state or, as in Prussia, within the province of their birth. About 16 per cent had moved to distant parts. In general the movement was away from the villages to the cities and industrial regions. East Prussia had the most mobile population. Only one third of all the East Prussians remained at their birthplaces, two fifths moved to other places within the province, while about one quarter left the province. In other eastern provinces, in West Prussia, Posen, and Pomerania, the situation was not much different. In contrast, from Silesia only 15 per cent migrated to other parts of Germany, many of them to Berlin, a sure sign that the Upper Silesian industries and the growing city of Breslau absorbed many people. The highly industrialized state of Saxony kept all but 8 per cent of its people, while the number of

people leaving the Rhineland was even smaller and of those leaving Westphalia, only slightly higher. The migration from all the southern German
states to the north was very small.

The internal migration swelled the population of the Rhineland and
Westphalia and made the rise of Berlin possible. But the population increase in Saxony was also considerable. In general the Germany west of
the Elbe became decidedly more populous than her eastern parts. The
agriculture of Prussia's eastern provinces even experienced a shortage of
labor. Germany's entire population increase of 24 million between 1871
and 1910 benefited towns and cities only. Whereas 63.9 per cent of all
Germans had lived in communities with less than 2,000 inhabitants in
1871, there were only 39.9 per cent in 1910. In 1871, 4.8 per cent of the
population were found in the eight cities with more than 100,000 inhabitants. In 1910 there were forty-eight such cities, and better than every
fifth German (21.3 per cent) lived in a big city, among which Hamburg
was just then moving toward the million mark, while Berlin with 2.1
million (and together with its suburbs 3.7 million) approached the size of
Paris. The number of cities with a population of 20,000–100,000 had risen
from 75 to 223 or in national percentages from 7.7 to 13.4.

Behind these changes effected through migration and urbanization was
the force of industrialization. We do not have exact occupational statistics
except for the years of 1882, 1895, and 1907. In 1882, when industrialization had already gone a long way, 42.5 per cent of the German people
were still making their living in agriculture, forestry, and fishery, whereas
only 35.5 per cent were active in industry, mining, and building. By 1895
the latter occupations had already surpassed the former ones, and by 1907
the relation had become more than reversed with 42.8 per cent of the
population working in industry and only 28.6 per cent in agriculture. In
the same period the number of people employed in commerce and transportation rose from 10 to 13.4 per cent. Since agricultural employment
remained practically at the same level, it must be assumed that almost all
the new millions of people were absorbed by the new industries and
commerce.

✍ Agricultural Modernization

WHILE GERMANY became an ever more highly industrialized country,
agriculture was not stagnant. The steadily rising prices for agricultural
products had been a strong incentive for the expansion of production in
the two decades after 1850. German agriculture was transformed by the
increasing adoption of more businesslike and scientific methods. The
three-course rotation system, under which one third of the soil was left
fallow each year and which had required communal management, was

replaced by free crop rotation, made possible by the use of chemical manure. The agricultural chemistry initiated by Justus von Liebig increased the yield of crops. Chilean saltpeter, which had been used since the early fifties, was replaced later on by potash found in great quantity in Anhalt in 1857 when deeper salt mines were drilled. After the turn of the century the potash resources of Alsace were opened, which not only benefited Germany's agriculture but also gave her a virtual world monopoly. The German steel industry became another producer of fertilizer when it adopted the Thomas method of production that left by-products usable for this purpose.

New methods of cultivation, among which deeper plowing was the most important single reform, were propagated through agricultural exhibitions and schools. The application of science and strict business methods went furthest on the big estates. How far and how quickly this attitude spread among the peasants is questionable, although the preponderant role of the peasants who operated large farms in the great expansion of cattle raising shows that they were aware of the opportunities which the market offered.

With growing production German agriculture might have been able to provide bread for her ever-larger population. But the demand for higher-quality food, in the form of both finer flour and more meat, which meant the diversion of grain to cattle feeding, necessitated the import of foreign grain in the years after 1871. Yet this development coincided with the appearance of a flood of cheap American grain that threatened the prosperity of German agriculture. After the Civil War the American farmers had begun to produce for the world market on a large scale. Their farms, acquired at a minimal price, imposed very small financial burdens. The virgin soil of the American Midwest brought high yields, and the perfection of the railroad system provided the corn states with access to the eastern ports. Navigation was just reaching a new stage. With the shift from sailing to steamships and from wooden to iron vessels the safety and carrying capacity of ocean transportation were enormously enhanced, while freight rates dropped.

The American grain, to which imports from Argentine and Russia were later added, ruined grain prices. At the end of the century freight rates between Chicago-New York and Hamburg fell so low that German grain transported at a distance of more than 240 miles inland could not compete with the imported grain. We have seen that the German government came to the rescue of the German grain producers, who had powerful champions in the East Elbian *Junkers*.[1] Whether this high protectionism was an unmixed blessing for German agriculture may be doubted. It might have been better if grain production had been limited

[1] See p. 267.

in favor of cattle raising, dairy farming and the production of high-quality foods, as was done in Denmark and the Netherlands. As late as 1902 about 60 per cent of the cultivated land was used for grain. But even the high grain tariff could not maintain the prices of the 1860's, when a ton of wheat sold for 205 marks, whereas in the last years before World War I it fetched only 187 marks. And these were relatively good years, for in 1902 the ton sold for only 130 marks, of which more than half, 75 marks, represented the tariff.

The development of the world production of grain since the 1870's showed that the expectation of steadily rising prices which had inflated land values was fallacious. As a consequence, the debt burden of German agriculture proved uncomfortably high. In 1902 the overall agrarian indebtedness in Prussia equaled one quarter of the value of the agricultural properties, but the figure was actually as high as 37.9 per cent in the six eastern provinces but only 17.6 per cent in the western six. The peasants had been forced to seek credit from private sources until the 1860's. This was an expensive practice, often laying them open to usury from which they also frequently suffered when selling their products. The creation of special credit institutes for the rural economy and the growth of saving banks improved the availability of credit. Peasants' associations and co-operatives for production and sales eventually enabled the farmers to gain higher profits on their products. The big landowners, on the other hand, had had their own credit institutes since early in the century. Their relative indebtedness was on the average much higher than that of the peasants, because they had made heavy investments in the modernization of their estates. Although a lowering of the interest rate on mortgages brought some relief, a satisfactory solution for the indebtedness of agriculture was not found before World War I. The hyperinflation of the post-War years completely wiped out all agrarian debts. But the great economic crisis of the years after 1929 revealed again the sensitivity of German agriculture to the movements of the world market which had been only superficially overcome by the protectionist policies after 1879.

The rise of the productivity of German agriculture during the nineteenth century was remarkable. Between 1815 and 1878 the yield of wheat increased by 50 per cent, while that of rye, barley, and oats doubled. In the following twenty-five years rye production rose by another 50 per cent and that of the other grains by about one third. Altogether German agricultural production more than doubled and maybe even tripled in the nineteenth century. The potato crops contributed to this increase. By 1913 Germany harvested one third of the world's potatoes. It has been rightly said that without potatoes the growing proletariat could not have been fed, but they were also used in the modern food industries and distilleries. A close link between agriculture and industry existed from the beginning in the cultivation of sugar beets, which after the middle of the century freed Germany from the need for importing cane sugar. Beet sugar even became a strong competitor on the world market. This, in 1902, led to the Brussels sugar convention, the first "global" economic plan.

✑ Land Ownership

CHANGES IN LAND DISTRIBUTION were insignificant. Almost three fourths of the agricultural land consisted of medium-sized and big farms; slightly more than one fifth were large estates, and the rest were tiny farms. But the regional differences were considerable. In so-called East Elbia the big estates were predominant. In East and West Prussia as well as in Brandenburg estates of more than 200 hectares (1 hectare = 2.4710 acres) occupied about three tenths of the land, in Silesia two fifths, in Posen and Pomerania about one half, and in Mecklenburg as much as 56 per cent. In the Prussian province of Saxony only a little less than one fifth of the agrarian area was taken over by large estates. Thus it formed the transition to the peasant country of northwestern Germany. In Brunswick, Hanover, Westphalia, Oldenburg, and Schleswig-Holstein the large peasant farms accounted for from two fifths to two thirds of the total acreage. The kingdoms of Saxony and Bavaria also had peasant economies, although the prevailing type of farm was smaller than in the northwest. In the west and southwest the small and even diminutive farm was most strongly represented. In Württemberg, Hesse, and in the Rhineland one third of the land was owned by peasants with farms of less than 5 hectares, in Baden more than two fifths. In the Rhineland and in the three southern states close to one half of the land was in the possession of peasants with farms of from 5 to 20 hectares, which as a rule could be worked by the peasant and his family. Thus these peasants with small holdings had little opportunity to add to their inadequate living through work for landowners and peasants with large farms. But with the high degree of urbanization and industrialization of western and southwestern Germany they found jobs in industry, while the ownership of farmsteads kept them out of a proletarian existence. The revisionism of the South German Social Democrats found support in this group.

✑ Problems of Farm Labor

IN NORTHWESTERN GERMANY, as in many parts of southern and central Germany, the big farmers and the relatively few big estate owners could solve their labor problems by the part-time or seasonal employment of small farmers. The relations among the various groups of farmers were rather harmonious in these parts. Yet the situation on the large East Elbian estates was different. The agrarian reforms of 1808–16 had left on these estates only daily wage earners. While their actual wages were not much more than pocket money, as a rule they received housing, some garden land, and payments in kind. Thus they were completely dependent on their landlords and did not have a chance to become peasants. Many came to accept only temporary work contracts, which would allow them to work at harvest time in the sugar cultures of Saxony or Silesia and give them other escapes from the monotonous life on the eastern estates. Here, however, the introduction of machines and the intensification of agriculture created a strong demand for seasonal labor. The big landowners began to hire migrant workers from Russian Poland and Austrian Galicia in growing numbers. Bismarck had them expelled in 1886 and the frontiers closed, because he was afraid that their influx would further strengthen the Poles in Prussia.[2]

Under pressure from the politically powerful landowners the government soon lifted the ban. Whereas in 1890 only about 17,000 Polish seasonal workers entered Germany, by 1902 their number approached 300,000, and it continued to mount thereafter. Thus, 62 per cent of the seasonal workers in Mecklenburg were foreign labor in 1906, as compared to 30 per cent in 1902. The immigration of these workers, who were cheap and submissive, caused a deterioration of the position of the German agricultural workers with the result that an even larger number left the eastern rural districts and went to the cities and industries in the west. The agricultural structure of East Germany thus began to imperil the position of the Germans vis-à-vis the Poles. The efforts made by the Prussian government between 1886 and 1914 to create peasant farms in the eastern provinces[3] did not have any appreciable effect on their social organization or on the precarious balance of Germans and Poles.

∽ *The Development of Industry*

WHEREAS THE INDUSTRIALIZATION of England in the late eighteenth and the first decades of the nineteenth century began with the stormy expansion of her textile production, made possible by the introduction of machines and the factory system, and entered upon a second period of accelerating growth in the railroad age after 1830, the industrialization of Germany gained its initial momentum from railroad-building, which, as we have seen, started in 1840. The German textile production could not hope to compete with the British industry, which was far superior due to

[2] See p. 294.
[3] See pp. 352–4.

its higher mechanization and great markets. Thus the transition to machine production was slow in the German textile industry, which achieved its full modern stature only in the last third of the century.

✑ *Railroads and Coal Mining*

WE NEED not point out that the creation of a network of communications moving raw materials to the factory and distributing finished goods was the absolute prerequisite of big industrial production. The railroads became the dynamic element that started off the large-scale industrialization and they remained one of the most powerful forces in German economic life. In 1850 Germany possessed 3,638 miles of railroad lines; in 1860, 6,840; in 1870, 11,600; in 1880, 21,165; in 1890, 26,136; in 1900, 31,174; and in 1910, 36,894 miles. What made the railroads immediately important for the structural transformation of the German economy was their tremendous effect on coal mining as well as the iron and machine industries. Previously, little coal had been mined, although the German coal deposits were large. Whereas in 1850 German fuel output had been smaller than that of France or Belgium, in the following decade Germany was outpacing her two western neighbors. By 1871, with 29.4 million tons, she produced more than twice as much coal as France, and her output steadily rose thereafter. In 1913 Germany mined 191.5 million tons of coal, compared to 40.8 in France, although she still remained considerably behind England, which produced 292 million tons. But, in addition, Germany possessed large deposits of lignite (brown coal), a fuel of only limited heating power but easily mined in open pits. Germany raised her lignite production from 8.5 million tons in 1871 to 87.5 million in 1913.

Coal mining created the new industrial districts. First among them was the Ruhr district composed of Rhenish and Westphalian areas grouped around the Rhine and its three tributaries Wupper, Ruhr, and Lippe. Sixty per cent of German coal production in 1913 originated in the Ruhr. Although much smaller in size and output, the Saar with about 10 per cent of the coal production became one of the most important centers of German industry. All except two of the coal mines in the Saar, which were in the possession of Bavaria, were owned by the Prussian state and were built up by the government to high technical efficiency.

The Prussian state also possessed large coal fields in Upper Silesia, but the greatest part of this rich coal region was owned by a group of noblemen who owned large latifundia. These Dukes of Ratibor, Counts Schaffgotsch, Ballestrem, and Henckel von Donnersmarck, and Princes Pless were active in developing coal mining on a large scale. Before the region was linked up by railroads with the rest of Germany and with Austria and Poland, the Upper Silesian coal was not widely marketable. Moreover, the local industries for a long time gained an ample supply of wood from the huge Upper Silesian forests. Thus the full exploitation of the coal resources began in earnest only after 1871. After the turn of the century Upper Silesia contributed over 20 per cent to the total annual coal output in Germany.

There were a number of small coal districts, three, for example, in the state of Saxony, but they were of no more than local significance. The bulk of the lignite was found in Central Germany, chiefly in Anhalt and Lower Lusatia in the province of Saxony. But another district that eventually produced 25 per cent of all German lignite was developed on the left bank of the Rhine in the neighborhood of Cologne.

The growth of coal mining was accompanied by the expansion of iron mining as well as iron and steel production. Until the middle of the nineteenth century the valley of the Sieg river had been the major iron district, and the firms had been mostly small family enterprises. It was in the early fifties that the geologists discovered the "black band" in the Westphalian part of the Ruhr district, which, like the black band in Scotland, seemed to promise rich supplies of both iron ore and coal. But although this find marked the beginning of the modern iron and steel industries of the Ruhr, its iron ore base soon proved inadequate in quantity and quality.

Iron and Steel Production

WITH THE ACQUISITION of Lorraine in 1871 Germany came into possession of rich deposits of high-grade iron ore. This so-called minette ore had a strong phosphoric content, which made it unsuitable for steel production till the Thomas Gilchrist process, by which phosphorus could be extracted, was invented in England. In 1881 the first German blast furnace employing the new method went into operation, and in the following decade, in which the British output of steel rose by only 40 per cent and its output of pig iron remained almost stationary, Germany doubled her steel production and came close to doubling her pig iron output. By 1900 Germany's steel output had surpassed that of Britain, while her pig iron production had almost reached the British figure. In 1910, with 13.1 million tons, Germany produced almost twice as much steel as Britain and almost 50 per cent more pig iron. After 1900 the colossal growth of the iron and steel industry made it increasingly necessary to import iron ore, mostly from Sweden and Spain. In 1910 this imported ore amounted to one fifth of the ore worked in German furnaces.

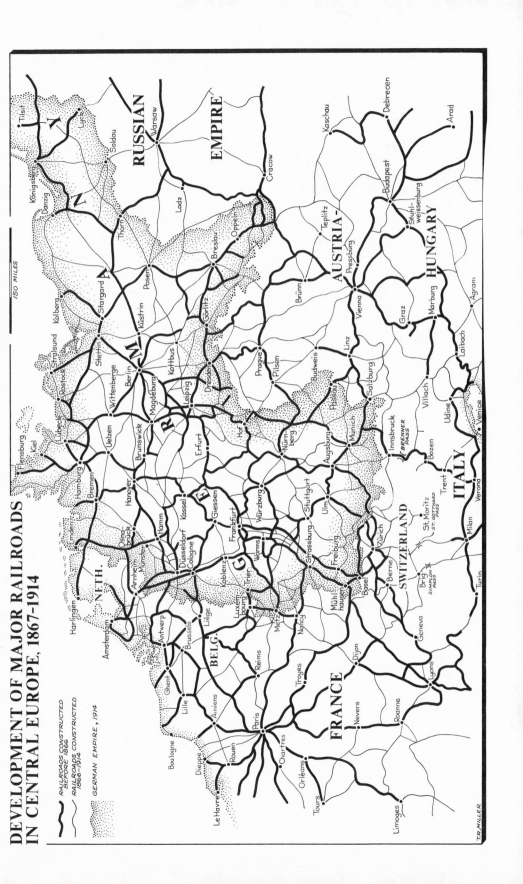

DEVELOPMENT OF MAJOR RAILROADS
IN CENTRAL EUROPE, 1867–1914

RAILROADS CONSTRUCTED
BEFORE 1866

RAILROADS CONSTRUCTED
1866–1914

GERMAN EMPIRE, 1914

150 MILES

T.R.MILLER

RUSSIAN EMPIRE

AUSTRIA-HUNGARY

FRANCE

SWITZERLAND

ITALY

NETH.

BELG.

Tilsit
Luck
Warsaw
Königsberg
Soldau
Danzig
Thorn
Lodz
Cracow
Kolberg
Stralsund
Stargard
Küstrin
Posen
Breslau
Oppeln
Görlitz
Flensburg
Kiel
Lübeck
Rostock
Stettin
Wittenberge
Berlin
Magdeburg
Leipzig
Dresden
Kottbus
Teplitz
Prague
Pilsen
Brünn
Vienna
Pressburg
Budapest
Stuhl-
weissenburg
Kaschau
Debrecen
Arad
Graz
Marburg
Agram
Laibach
Villach
Salzburg
Linz
Budweis
Passau
Munich
Innsbruck
BRENNER
PASS
Bozen
Trent
Udine
Venice
Verona
Milan
Turin
Hamburg
Bremen
Hanover
Uelzen
Brunswick
Erfurt
Hof
Nürn-
berg
Augsburg
Ulm
Stuttgart
Würzburg
Giessen
Frankfurt
Kassel
Hamm
Osna-
brück
Münster
Arnheim
Amsterdam
Harlingen
Emden
Düsseldorf
Cologne
Koblenz
Trier
Luxem-
bourg
Metz
Nancy
Strassburg
Freiburg
Mühl-
hausen
Basel
Zürich
Berne
Brig
SIMPLON
PASS
St. Moritz
ST. GOTTHARD
PASS
Geneva
Lyons
Roanne
Dijon
Nevers
Troyes
Reims
Amiens
Lille
Boulogne
Dieppe
Rouen
Le Havre
Paris
Chartres
Orléans
Tours
Limoges
Antwerp
Brussels
Ghent
Liège
Worms

◈ Metallurgical Industries and Shipbuilding

THE IRON AND STEEL industries formed the basis for the development of vast and many-sided metallurgical industries, which spread far over Germany. Soon every branch of the metal-working industry could be found there and, more than that, substantially contributed to the German export trade. Lancashire spinning machines and American harvesting machines were the only machines that Germany had to import, even in the last years before World War I. A remarkable feat was the founding of a big shipbuilding industry, chiefly in Hamburg, Bremen, Stettin, Elbing, Kiel, and Vegesack. In 1871 Germany possessed 1 million tons of shipping, less than one tenth of which were steamships, and even these not necessarily iron vessels. By 1880, when even a country such as Spain still owned a larger steam tonnage, the number of German steamships had a little more than doubled, and by 1890 they had tripled the 1880 figure and were now practically all steel-built. Obviously the accession of Hamburg and Bremen to the German customs union in 1888 helped the forward thrust of German shipping. In 1900 steam tonnage amounted to 1.348 million; in 1912 it had increased to 2.5 million; and in 1914, with a total tonnage of 3 million, Germany had outstripped all other nations except Britain with her 11.7 million. After 1910 German shipyards had the capacity to turn out 400,000 tons of mercantile shipping annually in addition to the big program of naval building, which naturally greatly contributed to the vast expansion of the shipping industries. After 1912 the Hamburg-Amerika Line, the biggest German shipping firm, built the two largest passenger liners then afloat.

◈ Electrical and Chemical Industries

THE CHEMICAL and electrical industries began their massive growth in the 1880's, although their origins were older. The large salt and potassium resources of Germany, and later also the derivatives of coal and lignite, favored the development of the chemical industries, which, however, could not have achieved their excellence if chemical science in Germany had not risen to such a high level. The heavy chemical industries produced chemicals in bulk, such as fertilizers for agriculture, ammunition, and, for industrial purposes, sulphuric acid, sodium, and chlorine. But it was the light chemical industries that gained for German chemicals a world-wide reputation. In the creation of dyestuffs and pharmaceutical products, Germany was ahead of all other nations before World War I.

The beginnings of electrical engineering go back to the 1840's, when the telegraph was invented, but there was no special electrical industry as yet. The invention of the telephone and its general introduction after

1877 boosted the production of telecommunication equipment tremendously. In 1867 Werner von Siemens invented the first dynamo, which eventually was to make it possible to produce any amount of electrical energy. After more knowledge about the transmission of electricity had become available, Siemens, in 1879, started his experiments with electric traction. In the early 1880's the building of small private power stations was begun, and after 1885 the electrical industry itself provided sectional energy centers for individual cities. In the 1890's the systematic construction of power stations for whole cities was undertaken, often simultaneously with that of trolley systems, both usually built and owned by the municipalities. After the inventions of Oskar von Müller had made the transmission of electric power over long distances possible, big regional overland stations were developed, as a rule by the electrical companies or the states. In the last decade before World War I, the erection of dams and the production of hydroelectric power were started. Within thirty years the German electrical industries grew to gigantic proportions, producing 50 per cent of the world's electrical equipment. By far the greatest part of this production was concentrated in two Berlin combines, the AEG (*Allgemeine Elektrizitäts-Gesellschaft*, founded in 1883 by Emil Rathenau with the support of Werner Siemens as the German Edison Company) and the Siemens works.

✍ *Foreign Trade*

HAND IN HAND with the mighty growth of German industries went the expansion of international trade. Whereas in 1870 Germany ranked behind Britain and France, she had surpassed France by 1890. Between 1872 and 1900 Germany's international trade doubled. Thereafter in less than half that time it more than doubled again, practically reaching the volume of British trade in 1913. The dependence of German industries on foreign raw materials and foodstuffs is shown by the fact that the combined imports of raw materials and foodstuffs were much greater than the export of finished goods. The growing strength and diversification of the German industries could be seen in the diminishing import of semifinished goods, such as yarns in the textile field. Raw cotton and wool were the largest single import items, amounting to about one tenth of the total. Grain came second. The export of finished goods steadily rose from 38 per cent of the total exports in 1873 to 63 per cent in 1913. Machines as well as steel and iron in all forms were the most important exports, but the export of cotton, wool, and silk textiles was also large. In addition, that of coal and sugar was considerable, although British coal sold as far as Berlin and Germany bought the exportable surplus of Austrian lignite.

Russia, delivering 15.5 per cent of all German imports in 1910, and the

United States, with 13.3 per cent, were the chief sources of German imports. Britain and Austria-Hungary, with 8.6 and 8.5 per cent, and France, with 5.7 per cent, came next. Russia's imports from Germany amounted to less than half of what she exported to her, and the United States' imports to about two thirds of its exports. On the other hand, the German trade balance was active with all the European states, particularly England and Austria-Hungary, which absorbed 14.7 and 11 per cent of the German exports. It is noteworthy that Germany's international trade was chiefly European. In 1889 almost 80 per cent of her exports went to European countries, from where also more than 77 per cent of her imports came. In the 1890's a change set in, and by 1912, largely owing to the growing imports from the Americas, India, and Australia, only 56.2 per cent of Germany's imports originated in Europe, although still close to three quarters of her total exports went there.

Beginning in the late 1880's the German trade balance became less favorable. In 1913 the value of her exports was 10,097 billion marks, while the value of imports was 10,770 billion. The deficit was more than covered, however, by income from services to foreigners. Germany's central location made her railroads the carriers of many transit goods. The proceeds from shipping grew, as did German foreign investments from the 1880's on. They took the form of commercial or industrial companies, participation in the ownership of foreign companies, the acquisition of foreign securities, and even the underwriting by German banks of foreign capital issues in Germany. Particularly in the 1880's, the decade in which Germany turned from a debtor into a creditor country, many foreign securities were issued. Thereafter the greatly expanding capital needs of German industry and trade placed limitations on such operations. Although Germany's foreign investments were small compared with those of Britain and even considerably smaller than those of France, they were estimated to have reached a total of 30 billion marks by 1913 while foreign investments in the German economy amounted to 5 billion marks.

↶ Stages of Economic Growth

THE GROWTH of modern German industries was not a steady progress over the decades. The 1860's had been a period of general prosperity and quiet expansion, in which both industry and agriculture participated. The end of the war and the windfall of the indemnity of 5 billion francs, as already mentioned, created a frenzy of financial speculation and investment that drew even the small saver into reckless business ventures. The government used a substantial part of the French indemnity for lowering the public debt through the retirement of state bonds. The money thus freed looked for new investment opportunities, which financing of both the respectable and unscrupulous variety hurried to satisfy. In 1870 a federal law had abolished the special government permission that so far had been required for the founding of any joint-stock company. The new law gave little protection to the shareholders and was widely used in these years by foolhardy or outright fraudulent operators. Legions of companies were founded and the prices at the stock exchange were driven up to fantastic heights. The end of the unhealthy boom period, in Germany called the *Gründerjahre*, came with the worldwide economic crisis of 1873. The warning sounded by the crash of the Vienna stock exchange in May was mostly disregarded in Germany. Here the crash occurred in October 1873. It wrecked the majority of the newly founded companies, ruining thousands of fortunes and lives. This collapse was the beginning of a long depression that lasted till 1895 and was interrupted by moderate business upswings only in 1879–82 and 1886–89. This long depression did not stop the rise in output and trade but rather resulted in a sharp and irregular fall of all prices. On the whole, commodity and stock prices, discount rates, profit margins, and wages remained below the average level of the period of 1849–73. The consumer gained from the low prices, and although nominal wages fell, the real income of workers and employees increased. Since, except for a few years, unemployment was slight, there was a certain improvement in the conditions of the working class and beyond it of the salaried class.

The last five years of the century saw a fabulous prosperity wave, which was largely triggered by electrification. The whole period from 1895–1914 may be called a single prosperity era interrupted by two mild and brief recessions in 1901–2 and 1908–9. Although the Morocco crisis of 1911 and again the outbreak of the Balkan War produced panics at the stock exchange, they failed to halt the growth of national production.

✍ *Banking and Commerce*

WHEN GERMANY had begun the building of her industries, she was a country poor in capital. In the opinion of the leaders of the industrial movement, such as Gustav Mevissen and David Hansemann, only the mobilization of all her financial resources, big and small, could achieve the development of powerful industries. The ideas of Saint Simon and the example of the *Crédit Mobilier* of the Pereires had led them to adopt the joint-stock bank as the best organization for this purpose. We have already mentioned[4] that Mevissen established the *Schaaffhausensche Bankverein* in this manner. In 1851 David Hansemann founded the *Diskonto Gesellschaft*, which in 1853 was followed by the *Darmstädter*

[4] See pp. 13–14.

Bank für Industrie und Handel. In 1856 the *Berliner Handelsgesellschaft,* the *Schlesische Bankverein* in Breslau, and the *Allgemeine Kreditanstalt* in Leipzig came into being. The economic crisis of 1857 stopped the establishment of banks for ten years. Thereafter additional banks were created, of which the *Deutsche Bank* of 1870 and the *Dresdner Bank* of 1872 were the most important ones.

From the outset, the modern German banks were designed as the powerful engines of industrial development. England's industrialization between 1750 and 1850 had been carried through without the organization of joint-stock companies except for railroads and other utilities. Individual proprietorship and partnership were the norm there, while the working capital was provided by credits from local banks. Only after 1856 did joint-stock companies begin to spread in England, particularly in such industries as mining, iron and steel, shipbuilding, and electricity that demanded large capital investments. But the English banks continued to concentrate on the deposit business and short-term credit operations, whereas long-term loans and industrial promotion were left to investment firms. In contrast, the new German joint-stock banks formed in the boom periods of the fifties and early seventies were commercial banks, investment banks, and investment funds all in one, and promotional and speculative activity loomed large in their operations. Deposit banks were unknown in Germany as late as 1870, when the *Deutsche Bank* started a deposit office. Though soon adopted by practically all the German banks, this system was slow in producing great results. Yet, by 1900 the deposits were as large as the capital of the banks and by 1914 greatly exceeded their capital and reserves.

Until World War I, when the war bonds brought about a change, only a small part of the funds of the German banks was held in government securities. A larger part was kept in commercial bills which could be rediscounted with the *Reichsbank* and therefore used as a liquid reserve. It was chiefly in this function that the *Reichsbank* served as the bank of banks and thereby allowed the other banks to employ their major assets for loans—and, for that matter, chiefly long-term loans—and for the promotion of industrial and commercial enterprises. In the 1860's and again in the years after 1873 railroad financing, either in the form of the issue of state bonds or shares of private railroad companies, was the chief occupation of the banks, and even in the 1880's, when all the railroads passed into state ownership, the financing of the transfer through loans to the states formed a substantial part of the banking operations. But industrial development assumed an ever-growing role. Since it required very large capital assets, not only was the banking capital augmented but also bigger institutes were created through the absorption of small and eventually even sizable banks by the big ones. The movement toward the concentration of the banking capital in a few giant companies was continuous, and it accelerated in the 1890's. By 1914 the four big "D-banks" in Berlin (*Deutsche Bank, Diskonto Gesellschaft, Dresdner,* and *Darmstädter Bank*) held a commanding lead in German finance through their own huge capital as well as through the vast number of provincial banks affiliated with them. Even those among the four that originally had been founded in other cities soon moved their headquarters to Berlin. The nature of their business drew them to the seat of the *Reichsbank* and the greatest German stock exchange. During the first decade of the Empire Berlin also became the dominant financial capital of Germany.

The German banks had a free hand in the investment not only of their own capital but also of the sums deposited with them, and actually industrial investment resulted in the employment of the major part of their funds in long-term loans or other long-term business. In order to found new industries or make it possible for a family firm to expand, joint-stock companies would be established by a bank which took over the whole capital issue at a fixed price expecting to dispose of it on the market at a higher one. If the risk of this venture was great, a group of banks was formed. The bank might keep part of the shares in its own portfolio in order to retain control of the company, a procedure that as a rule led to the election of a bank director to the board of the industrial company. The bank would also recommend the purchase of shares to its private customers. Thereby the control of industry through the banks was further strengthened, since they claimed the right to represent their customers at the shareholders' meetings. It was not fortuitous that the term "finance-capitalism" (*Finanzkapitalismus*) was invented in Germany for the description of the advanced stage of capitalistic development.

Naturally the banks were vitally concerned with the prosperity of the industrial firms in which they had invested. In order to enable them to produce profitably, the banks would assist their growth to the ideal size or help them to win control over subsidiary industries. Thus big combines came into being that integrated the divided production of a whole branch of industrial activity, as, for example, coal and iron mining were linked up with the production of semifinished and finished iron and steel. In some cases other metal-using industries were added, such as firms for railroad and engineering equipment, construction firms, and shipyards. Although the formation of combines led to the merger of many companies, probably more often the individual companies were continued and only blocks of shares exchanged in order to insure interdependence. With the help of the banks this vertical integration was carried furthest in the industries requiring the greatest capital supply, such as mining, metallurgy, machine construction, as well as the modern chemical and electrical industries.

◌ Cartelization

ANOTHER MEANS of maintaining the prosperity of German industries was found in cartelization. In England and all the other industrialized countries agreements in restraint of trade were held legally void and consequently unenforceable in the courts. The United States even made them a criminal offense. Only in Germany were cartel agreements treated by law like ordinary contracts. The depression after 1873 brought cartels to the fore, and the protective tariff of 1879 made them easier to operate. Except for products such as potash, of which Germany possessed a virtual world monopoly, German cartels could maintain a high price level only if foreign competition was excluded. The year of 1893 was another turning point. By then vertical integration had reached a stage at which the major industries were no longer apprehensive that cartelization would drive up the prices of their raw materials.

The cartels were of a highly diversified nature. In all cases they were intended to limit competition and stabilize prices. But while many were content to agree on the terms of delivery or fixed production quotas, others fixed minimum prices and divided markets. The most rigid form of cartel, in Germany called a syndicate, fixed production quotas and established a single sales organization. The most important syndicates were those of the Ruhr industries. The Rhenish-Westphalian Coal Syndicate, founded in 1893, comprised 100 members with production shares from 0.10 to 8.75 million tons and produced more than 50 per cent of the German and 95 per cent of the Ruhr coal. At the same time the cartelization of the steel industry was begun and, in 1904, led to the formation of the mighty Steel Works Union. The big Potash Syndicate, dating back to 1881, actually aimed at the exploitation of foreign markets. By 1908 Gustav Schmoller estimated that about 500 cartels existed in Germany. Later developments made it probable that already there were many more, but it should be emphasized that the majority of them were only loose combinations.

Moreover, many firms did not enter cartel arrangements, and those that did often broke away in times of prosperity. Even in the rigidly organized syndicates fighting went on almost continuously, and the renewal of the cartel agreements caused major crises. In 1910 the government stepped in and forced the potash industry to continue its cartel, and in 1915 this happened to the Rhenish-Westphalian Coal Syndicate. But the process of cartelization had a cumulative effect on the economy by narrowing the field of free competition. In addition, the big cartels and syndicates of the basic industries were able to exercise great influence on the national economy, although it is doubtful whether their power was beneficial for the general economy. Emil Kirdorf (1847–1938), the chairman of the Coal Syndicate, stated that "under the protection of the Syndicate the values of the coal industry have immensely risen." While in 1861–88 the price of coal per ton had ranged between 4.7 and 6.6 marks, it climbed to between 7.5 and 12.6 after the founding of the syndicate between 1893–1906. Some of this price rise was undoubtedly justified, among other reasons because it made a higher and stabler wage level possible. Yet the rise of 3 to 6 marks was in all probability an act of exploitation of the monopolistic position that the syndicate had acquired. The complaints of the other industries about the resulting increase in their own production costs, though general, were of no avail.

Cartelization undermined the free market economy which in Germany had seemed to come into existence in the 1860's and early 1870's. German experience with economic liberalism was actually very brief. It should also not be forgotten that, through its ownership of the railroads, mines, domains and forests, the state governments retained a very great direct influence on the economic life of the country. The governments might have used this power to counteract some of the undesirable consequences of cartelization, but the state enterprises were administered in a fiscal spirit rather than for the benefit of the consumer.

Although the big company combines and cartels of heavy industry towered above the German economy, they did not change its organizational structure altogether. Only one-half of one per cent of the business units of Germany in the beginning of the twentieth century were joint-stock companies. As a matter of fact, by then there were many more in Great Britain, though they were of a somewhat different complexion. About 92 to 93 per cent of all German business enterprises were owned by individual proprietors, and not only the consumer industries but also some mining, iron and steel, machine, electrical, and chemical businesses belonged to this category. Yet the large bulk of the individual proprietorships was to be found in commerce and in the crafts.

❧ Business Specialization and Concentration

IN COMMERCE a trend toward specialization and concentration as well as proliferation could be observed. The traditional firms dealing with every sort of merchandise disappeared and were replaced by businesses trading in special goods only. Naturally, many big companies developed, whose sales organizations often extended all over Germany and even to foreign countries. But in the retail field, where specialization went furthest, small stores multiplied at a dangerous rate. Between 1882 and 1907 the number of persons active in such stores doubled, an increase far out of proportion to the population growth. The number of retail and wholesale firms serving 10,000 people rose from 44 in 1861 to 77 in 1895; or in 1895 one out of 39 Germans, as against one out of 83 in 1861, expected to make a living for himself and his family by serving distribution rather than production.

This was a heavy lien on Germany's capitalistic economy. Many people saw in the opening of a retail store the only escape from becoming dependent employees or workers. Nothing except a little capital or small bank credit seemed needed for starting a business, while commercial training, let alone a general education, appeared unnecessary. These assumptions proved utterly fallacious in many cases where these small storekeepers eked out a merely marginal living and frequently became bankrupt. Economically these people were scarcely better off than proletarians or better protected in times of depression. Some of them—for example, the large group of tobacconists, of whom often more than one could be found in a single city block—hardly had to perform any work. But instead of seeking the reasons for their pecuniary hardships in themselves, they were inclined to find them in the lack of help from the government. The German merchant, they clamored, should be shielded against street vendors and peddlers, but most of all against cooperatives as well as chain and department stores. Among these small storekeepers anti-Semitic slogans against competitors found a fertile ground, and chain and department stores in particular were branded as a Jewish invention.

Within these groups of store owners potential social dangers were brewing which, though not grave in the prosperity prior to World War I, were to prove corrosive forces of consequence after the war. It should be noted that the development of big department stores began in Germany only in the 1890's, much later than in France, England, or the United States and that as late as 1914 no German department store was as big as the great houses of Paris and London.

↩ *Alteration of the Craft Guilds*

ANOTHER GROUP with steady grievances were the craftsmen. They had understandable complaints, although it was unreasonable of them to continue their demands for the restoration of the guild system to the end of the nineteenth century. The crafts, formerly the mainstay of all industry, had to bear the brunt of the onslaught of the industrial revolution. Not only did machines wipe out whole crafts, as in the case of the weavers' craft that had disappeared by 1871, or confine them largely to repair work, as in the case of the shoemakers, but the new capitalistic organization of large-scale production also placed the surviving crafts under the domination of the new capitalistic forces, as can be seen most clearly in the tailors' and furniture-makers' crafts. Actually, the absolute number of handicraft workers did not decline in the period between 1871 and 1914, but, due to the tremendous increase in the number of industrial workers, their relative part in production fell off drastically. Moreover, many craftsmen had become dependent on capitalistic industries; bakeries, for example, were often established by the flour-producing companies. But since many crafts were still needed not only for luxury production but also for such large industries as the building trade, artisans were able to earn a living, and often a rather substantial one.

Nowhere in Germany were compulsory craft guilds reintroduced. Instead, the government favored voluntary guilds. Handicraft chambers were created and placed in charge of the examinations of craftsmen. They also provided legal advice and information on new production methods as well as other industrial developments. Eventually only certified masters were permitted to employ apprentices. Around the turn of the century the resentment of the craftsmen and artisans against modern capitalism and industrialism visibly subsided. The survival of a large group of craftsmen and their adjustment to modern conditions, at least in days of prosperity, was an element of great strength for Germany's economy and social life.

✑ *Increase in Personal Incomes*

THE TOTAL real income of Germany rose from 14.67 billion marks in 1871–75 to 34 billion in 1896–1900 and to 48 billion in 1911–13, while the real average income of the individual rose from 352 marks to 603 and 728 marks in the same years. Thus, in spite of the large population growth the average per capita income had doubled. To be sure, these figures tell only a small part of the story. Regional differences were considerable. While Prussia as a whole stayed slightly under the German average, Saxony was substantially above average, and Hamburg and Bremen were high above it. Bavaria and Hesse, on the other hand, lagged behind Prussia. Within Prussia, which produced 60 per cent of the national income, the differences were large. Whereas in West Prussia and Posen the average per capita income was 30 to 40 per cent under the Prussian average, Berlin surpassed it by 60 per cent.

The growth of the national income did not change the income distribution among the great masses of the population to a considerable extent. What actually disappeared was the large bottom layer of society composed of truly destitute people who had experienced daily hunger and starved to death in large numbers in the 1830's and 1840's. Although many people still were in grave need, the lowest income now started at a somewhat higher level, and submarginal livelihoods were no longer a mass phenomenon. The conditions of the people with an income of under 900 marks improved. Whereas in 1892, 70.27 per cent of the population had an income that low, the figure was 62.41 per cent in 1900 and 42.84 per cent in 1910. While that group was tax exempt, the lowest group of Prussian taxpayers, with an income of between 900 and 3,000 marks, increased from 2.1 to 5.5 million between 1892 and 1910. Within this category those with incomes of between 1,200 and 2,100 marks multiplied most, as a result of the proliferation of white collar workers and low-salaried state officials, who, among others, included the grade school teachers as well as the lower-rank railroad and post officials. Among all the taxpayers those with incomes of 900 to 3,000 marks were by far the largest group; by absorbing formerly indigent people and at the same time strengthening its own medium and upper brackets, this group grew from 82 to 89 per cent of the total taxpaying population between 1892 and 1910. Even in 1913 the great mass of the German people lived in modest circumstances, although they could entertain the encouraging notion that hard work was slowly improving their lot.

The greatest change that occurred was the formation of a class of well-to-do and wealthy people. This class was not very large. In 1900, 6.1 per cent of the Prussian population had an income of over 3,000 marks and not quite 1 per cent an income of over 9,500 marks. Again, in the former category a steady expansion and movement toward the higher rungs can be observed. But most spectacular was the emergence of a class of very wealthy people. Werner Sombart estimates that apart from the landed nobility, of which, however, only some sections were rich, not even 1,000 people in all of Germany had an income of, or beyond, 10,000 marks in 1800. It was this group that multiplied most rapidly in the age of industrialization. In 1895, 86,552 people in Prussia were worth between 100,000 and 500,000 marks, with an average of close to 200,000 marks. By 1911, this group comprised 135,843 people. And while 8,375 persons were worth between 500,000 and 1 million marks (on the average 700,000 marks) in 1895, their number had risen to 13,800 by 1911. The number of people with fortunes of between 1 and 2 million marks (on the average 1.5 million marks) grew from 3,429 to 5,916 between 1895 and 1911, and those with 2 million and above from 1,827 to 3,425. Only in this last category did the average wealth rise simultaneously, namely from 4.7 to 5.3 million marks.

✑ Growth of the Bourgeois Class

ALTOGETHER THE AVERAGE GERMAN was not yet as well off as the contemporary Englishman, American, or Frenchman. Yet Germany, which to Voltaire had seemed condemned to eternal poverty, had become one of the five richest countries. Never had she seen so many well-to-do and wealthy people as in the new Empire, particularly after 1895. The rise of these new groups was a sign of greater social mobility than had been the rule in former ages. In the early stages of German industrialization as many as three fifths of the leaders of the new industries had come from the class of small townspeople and laborers, a little less than three tenths had been sons of independent artisans, tradesmen, or lesser state officials, while only slightly over one tenth had come from the higher stratum of society. By 1890, when modern German capitalism had become rather well institutionalized, the lower classes were represented with only one fifth of the industrial leaders, while almost two thirds were of middle-class origin, and close to one eighth came from the upper bourgeoisie and nobility. We may assume that the social rise of the individual at this time ordinarily depended on his attendance at a secondary school and a university or institute of technology. A social rise from the lower classes to the top of the social pyramid occurred as a rule only in the course of at least two generations.

The new bourgeoisie, which, more than any other class, determined the culture of Germany, was not a homogeneous class. Not only the nobility but also the old wealth and the representatives of the higher intellectual professions looked down on the *nouveaux riches* of industry. The latter, on their part, were divided by their different interests, as could be seen most clearly in the conflict over the protective tariff. These divisions help explain Bismarck's defeat of German liberalism in 1866 and 1878. It is true, however, that, even if united, the German bourgeoisie was unlikely to wrest the power from the old Prussian ruling class as long as it did not make an attempt to represent the interests and aspirations of wider groups of society, something the English bourgeoisie managed to accomplish. But the German bourgeoise held itself aloof from the masses. The growth of the socialist movement served it not only as an excuse for the attitude but also as justification for the discontinuation of the struggle for political liberty. An authoritarian government seemed the only safeguard of the existing social order.

Thereby the bourgeoisie at the same time recognized the preeminence of the *Junker* class. Although many members of the upper middle classes, particularly those with a strong intellectual bent, looked with some ridicule at the antiquated style of life and manners of the *Junkers*, the latter were an admired model just the same for most German bourgeois. The wealthy industrialists and merchants usually had no higher aspirations than to acquire a landed estate, preferably an entailed one, and partake in the elegant sports of hunting, horse racing, and the rest. But even the less wealthy hoped to become accepted by the ruling class. By joining exclusive students' dueling fraternities and acquiring officers' commissions in the reserve they expected to gain preferment in the higher civil service.

Thus the *Junker* class retained not only the predominant power in the state but also wielded a great influence on the social behavior of the upper bourgeoisie.

This does not mean, however, that the bourgeoisie did not carry political weight with the government. The latter fully knew that its gilded glamour and might rested largely on the work of the bourgeoisie and therefore was eager to protect and promote the interests of the industrialists, as the tariff and labor policies showed. Undoubtedly the government of William II also believed that its colonial and maritime policies especially served business and industrial circles who were most vociferous in their support of those policies. Still, the government followed its own line. The *Deutsche Bank*, which in 1888 had undertaken to build a railroad from Constantinople to Ankara and on this occasion had been told by Bismarck that it could not expect protection in a crisis from the government, received strong governmental support after 1890 for its growing Turkish enterprises. The government's intention to make Turkey a sphere of German influence frustrated the bank's sensible plan to undertake the biggest project, the Bagdad railroad, in alliance with British and French banks. Likewise, Germany's intervention in Morocco in 1905 had an exclusively political motivation, the breakup of the Anglo-French Entente. The mining interests of the German Mannesmann Company were only belatedly discovered by the German foreign office and used merely as a screen.

✑ *Political Engagement of the Intellectuals*

NEITHER WAS the intellectual community overlooked by the government. The latter quickly dropped its reactionary school bill in the face of vigorous public protests from the educated people. Since in general there was little political opposition in the universities, the government on the whole respected their autonomous rights. Social Democrats, however, were not tolerated. When it was discovered that an unsalaried lecturer of physics was a member of the Social Democratic party, he was removed from the Berlin faculty. This flagrant breach of academic freedom was applauded by the great majority of the professors.

After 1871 the German bourgeoisie turned away from politics more drastically than it had after the breakdown of the revolution of 1848–49. At that time, as we have seen, the active democratic elements were largely driven into emigration, while many liberals gave up their political aspirations and devoted themselves to business and industry. Under the influence of political "realism" those who continued in politics underwent a change in outlook. The defeated liberals of 1848 saw in a powerful national state the chief prerequisite for the realization of a liberal program. For this reason Bismarck's successes of 1866–67 and 1870–71 evoked general jubilation, and many liberals by now were willing gratefully to accept national unity, even though the new Empire did not live up to the ideals of their youth. Some men, such as Heinrich von Treitschke and Johannes Miquel, even went over into the conservative camp. Others, though retaining some critical attitudes, cooperated with Bismarck just the same and after a while were either swept along in the tail of this political comet or, if they realized that Bismarck would not allow them any real participation in the framing of governmental policies, left politics altogether.

A few became absolute critics of the regime. After the failure of the revolution of 1848 the great historian Theodor Mommsen (1817–1903) had poured his disillusionment into the writing of his famous *Roman History*. The unification of Italy through Rome's military might is the central theme of this work and Caesar the towering Roman genius. Mommsen became an active literary supporter of the Bismarckian policy of unification. But after a decade of life in the Prusso-German Empire he began to loathe the new political and social order, the pseudoconstitutionalism that made it impossible for the average man to feel a citizen, and the antagonistic class divisions that militated against the unity of the nation. He scorned the Germans who in their majority not only accepted but even glorified the regime. William II's reign drove Mommsen into profound despair.

No new political philosophy was born. Whereas the German idealistic philosophers, Kant, Fichte, and Hegel, had made the state a major subject of their speculations, German philosophy after 1871 made no important contribution to political thought. The justification of the legal order was left to academic jurisprudence. The leading philosopher of law was Rudolf von Ihering (1818–92). In his chief work, *The Purpose of Law* (1877–84), natural law and all universal ethical norms of law are declared meaningless. The ultimate purpose of law is the preservation of the conditions under which the state is able to live and grow. Justice and law are found only in the positive laws of the individual state, which, as the regulating center of the social process, is their exclusive source. The valid positive law of the sovereign state commands absolute respect. This narrow positivistic definition became the dominant conception of law. It was a theory that failed to create any criteria by which the justice of a law could be tested. The consequences of this emasculation of legal thought were far-reaching and had a devastating influence on the events of the Hitler period.

✑ *Heinrich von Treitschke*

IT FELL to the historians to justify the new political order in historical terms. The most important work was Heinrich von Treitschke's *German History in the 19th Century*, of which the first volume appeared in 1879. Although the *History* remained unfinished, leading only to the eve of the revolution of 1848, its luxuriant literary style made it a book widely read and admired. Treitschke portrayed the movement toward national unification under Prussian leadership as the glorious culmination of German history. Whereas Austria in that period had become alienated and the small German states were acting as obtacles to German unity, Prussia was destined to rise to national leadership, particularly after she enhanced her excellence in arms and administration by adapting the culture of Germany's classic age. From 1874 on, Treitschke regularly gave a lecture course on *Politics* at the university in Berlin. Although he was still under the influence of German idealism to the extent that he assigned moral aims to the state, and was more careful than Ihering not to turn it into a naturalistic phenomenon, his thinking was not determined by natural law or philosophy. The state to him was the highest personality in historical life and needed a maximum power for its self-realization. The one-sided emphasis on power and the facile interpretation of the victories of the mightier states as moral victories opened the gates to lesser writers and agitators for whom the power state became an end in itself.

✑ *Cultural Decline*

ALTHOUGH THE HAPPY FINAL CONSUMMATION of national unification in the wars of 1864, 1866, and 1870–71 was often cited as proof of the superiority of German culture, the period from the founding of the Empire to the early 1890's was a time of low cultural creativity. The unity of style, which had characterized former ages of history, had disappeared in all the European countries by the middle of the century, and nowhere were the artists able to create a style that would have given adequate expression to the industrial epoch. Rather, it was a time of historical styles. Gothic, Renaissance, Baroque, Byzantine, and every other known style of the past were revived at random and were applied to the new industrial buildings as well as to the long streets of residential houses which mushroomed in the new big cities. In this respect the picture in Germany was no worse than in England, though worse than in France, where these architectural excesses were practiced with greater moderation.

Whereas in these years the French impressionists revolutionized the art of painting, freeing it from conventional rules and letting the individual artist choose his *sujets* from nature and social reality, German painting was still given to mythical and historical subjects that were presented in conventional forms. Hans Makart (1840–84), with his sensuous canvases, was admired as the great genius, only soon, and rightly so, to be forgotten completely. Among all the German painters of this period Adolf von Menzel (1815–1905) alone reached out for new realms. A similar sterility prevailed in the field of literature. The one author whose literary standing has endured is Theodor Fontane (1819–98), who, in spite of a deep longing for the continuity of the past, created living symbols of the new bourgeois society and was a sensitive critic of the changing German social scene. The theatrical stage was dominated by shallow French plays and their German imitations. Only the theater of the grand duke of Saxony-Meiningen developed new forms of stagecraft, which for the time being chiefly served the classical drama.

✍ *Johannes Brahms*

IN THE MUSICAL FIELD alone was genius still at work. Johannes Brahms stood in the line of succession to the great classic-romantic masters of instrumental and vocal music. Brahms, born in Hamburg in 1833, lived in Vienna after 1862 but remained in close contact with Germany. His most important works were composed between 1871 and the year of his death in 1897. In spite of the innovations of his music, Brahms lived not only in the musical tradition of Beethoven, Schubert, Mendelssohn, and Schumann but also in the world of the humane literature of their period. He was neither a revolutionary nor a prophet.

✍ *Richard Wagner*

UNLIKE BRAHMS, RICHARD WAGNER (1813–1883) was both a revolutionary and a prophet. His social-revolutionary ideas and active participation in the Dresden revolt of May 1849 forced him into exile in Switzerland, and he did not return to Germany before 1860. Wagner's first operas, such as *Rienzi* (1842), were following the "great opera" style of Rossini and Meyerbeer or, as in the case of the *Flying Dutchman* (1843), the older romantic operas of Carl Maria von Weber. Yet Wagner saw the highest art in the "music drama" that was to combine poetry, music, and, by way of the stage, visual art as well. Only such a *Gesamtkunstwerk*, that is, a work to which all the arts contribute, would have the regenerative power that the stage ought to exercise in the life of a people. He assigned to the theater the role that it had played in classic Greece. As a new Aeschylus he intended to elevate the German people beyond materialism and philistinism and to free it from false morals. The poetic revival of medieval legend and old-Germanic myth seemed to him the best means for conveying his message. *Tannhäuser* (1845) and *Lohengrin* (1848) were the first operas using this legendary style. The year of the revolution was the time of the conception of the central work of his whole career, the *Ring of the Nibelungen*, which consisted of four operas. By 1852 the text had been completed, and by 1857 more than two of the operas. A long interval followed before the remaining two operas of the *Ring* were completed, but during that time *Tristan and Isolde* (1859) and *Die Meistersinger* (1867) were created. Around this time a public drive was begun for funds to build a great national temple where annual festivals of Wagnerian music could be held. Chiefly through the munificence of the Bavarian king the festival theater in Bayreuth was built. There in the setting of a friendly landscape and a quiet town pilgrims from every land could experience the profound purification that the arts provide. In 1874 Wagner finished the last part of the *Ring*, and in August 1876 the first Bayreuth festival was opened in the new house with a four-evening performance of the opera. Wagner, now living in grand style, presided over the ceremonies, which had attracted a distinguished audience.

Wagner made his outward peace with Bismarck's Empire, although he was very critical of the chancellor, who on his part took no interest in the composer. But Wagner's revolutionary temper remained a basic element of his art. According to his views, if life was to be liberated, conventional civilization had to be torn down with all its customs and morals that fetter the deep passions of man. Wagner agreed with Schopenhauer's pessimistic outlook on life. But in contrast to the philosopher, who had seen the way to salvation in the conscious suppression of human desires and in progress toward wishless beatitude, for which art and especially music prepare one, Wagner believed that the intensification of love leads to the elevation of man, a love that spurns all laws and even life itself. Rather than redemption, Wagner sought self-fulfillment, even though this might imply lustful self-destruction.

Big as the success of this great German theatrical genius was, his expectation of being able to regenerate Germany was a presumptuous dream. In a general way Wagner's operas strengthened German nationalism, although the ancient Germanic gods remained a distant myth to the public. This he himself may have sensed when in his last opera, *Parsifal* (1882), he turned to Christian symbolism. Actually Wagner's gods and heroes are modern characters who have a greater affinity to Dostoevsky's novels than to the primordial age. Although Wagner's art contains much false pomposity and even trite matter, it has added new provinces to musical expression and form. In spite of his praise of Germandom, however, Wagner was out of touch with German folk music, which left its marks on the music of his contemporary, Brahms. Wagner's Germandom was highly stylized, and his sensuous music represented the luxuriant traits of the German post-mid-century generation. Although the annual Bayreuth festivals created large congregations of Wagner devotees, they failed to implant a new spirit in the nation.

David Friedrich Strauss

A WIDELY READ BOOK, *The Old and the New Faith* by David Friedrich Strauss, epitomized the prevalent thinking of the bourgeoisie in this period. Strauss, a Swabian, who in 1835 had caused a sensational storm with his *Life of Jesus*,[5] had by now left Hegelian idealism far behind. Positive science had become for him the key to all the mysteries of the universe. Thus in the light of modern science materialism emerges as the only valid philosophy and Darwin as its chief guide. Christianity is a matter for the past, although religion still exists in man's "sentiment of absolute dependence" on the universe, a vestigial pantheism that Strauss left vague. But essentially religion has been replaced by the worship of the arts, particularly of classic German literature and music. With regard to ethics, Strauss offers only conformism to the group. In politics the former people's deputy of 1848 had become an arch-conservative for whom the social question did not exist. The "new faith" of Strauss was the grossest expression of self-contented bourgeois sentiment. It was bare of all ethical incentives, as well as social and political imperatives, and recommended the arts merely as a cultural holiday pursuit.

Ernst Haeckel's Monism

DARWINISM spread fast in Germany. Ernst Haeckel (1834–1919), for more than fifty years professor of zoology at the University of Jena, was its foremost German apostle. His scientific works were important milestones in modern biology. Of his *History of Natural Creation*, published in 1868, Charles Darwin said that he would probably not have completed his *Descent of Man* (1871) if it had not been finished before the publication of Haeckel's book. But Haeckel also used his science for the development of a popular philosophy. Against the dualism of soul and matter in theology or reason and nature in philosophy, he posited his monism. According to this theory, the universe is composed of matter of unchanging quantity. This matter, in turn, contains an unchanging quantity of energy which by transmutations and configurations, changes the small particles of matter into structured forms of any size. Although Haeckel does not deny the existence of souls, psychology is a part of physiology, and not only organic but also inorganic matter has a soul.

Haeckel propagated a new "monistic religion," in which all concepts of

[5] See the author's *A History of Modern Germany, 1648–1840*, pp. 491 and 517.

a transcendental nature, such as a personal God or immortality, were dropped. God is simply identified with the universe. The ideas of the true, the good, and the beautiful are proclaimed to be the inspiring ideals. Science, being the search for truth, thus became part of religion. In ethics Christian love of one's neighbor was taken as the golden rule, although in Haeckel's opinion Christian altruism should be balanced by a heavy dose of self-respect.

In spite of strong disapproval by the churches and sharp criticism by philosophers and scientists, the impact of Haeckel's monism on the general public was considerable. It was greatest in the years after 1893 when he published a number of books for lay readers. One of them, *The World Enigmas*, became the most widely distributed philosophical book in Germany. At the same time a federation of monists was founded for the dissemination of the monistic belief and for gathering the faithful into local congregations. Monism thus became a quasi-religious movement. A good many varieties existed, some leaning toward a full pantheism, others stressing the materialistic aspects of monism. While most of its intellectual leaders and followers were left liberals, monism also appealed to a good many nationalists.

Although monism had started in a university, it did not make many converts among the professors. The leading scientists, such as the physicist Helmholtz or the physiologist DuBois Reymond, warned that science was far from having solved the riddles of life. At the time, the German universities were enjoying an enormous prestige at home and abroad, with students coming to them from practically all countries. The years 1871–1900 saw the height of the influx of Americans, who took from Germany the inspiration for the modern American graduate schools. Although the German universities were doubtlessly productive in all fields of learning and research, they had great shortcomings as educational institutions. Many students went through the universities without acquiring the knowledge that would enable them to make critical judgments on the fundamental questions of their own lives or the general problems of the age. Most of them gained merely the professional training for a specific career and in the conduct of their later lives simply conformed to the prevailing ethical standards of their social group.

✑ Wilhelm Dilthey

THE INFLUENCE of the German universities on the spiritual and political life of the nation was much weaker than in the earlier part of the century.[6] As the sciences amassed an ever-growing knowledge, the departments of study proliferated, and the individual could call only a relatively small

[6] See the author's *A History of Modern Germany, 1648–1840,* pp. 479–84.

field his own. The trend away from philosophical speculation made the mere positivistic pursuit of knowledge supreme. Still, the idealistic tradition was not entirely broken off. Wilhelm Dilthey (1833–1911), since 1882 professor of philosophy in Berlin, demonstrated that the humanistic sciences were applying methods different from those germane to the natural sciences. He became the father of a new type of history of ideas that takes ideas not as rational abstracts but as expressions of the human experience of historical civilizations. Life in its totality was for him the reality with which not only history but also philosophy had to deal. But the greatest problem with which Dilthey's profound and wide-ranging mind was wrestling throughout his life was not brought to a solution. The relativism produced by the modern study of history with its capacity for the understanding of different cultures led to an "anarchy of world-views." This dilemma of historicism Dilthey was unable to resolve.

Among Dilthey's great historical writings those analyzing the classic period of German philosophy and literature gained the widest distribution. Dilthey thus helped to renew the interest in Kant. The return to Kant was championed by two schools. One had its chief representatives at the university of Marburg in Ernst Cohen (1842–1918) and Paul Natorp (1854–1924), the other flourished at the three southwestern universities of Heidelberg, Freiburg, and Strasbourg, with Wilhelm Windelband (1848–1915) and Heinrich Rickert (1863–1936) as its leaders. It was the critical and antimetaphysical Kant who was restored by the German neo-Kantians, whose main concern was epistemology. But the Marburg philosophers also revived Kant's ethics and developed a program of social action, which, however, did not find much public attention. The rigorous discipline of the Kantian or neo-Kantian theory of knowledge, which not only social scientists such as Max Weber and Friedrich Meinecke but also natural scientists of the stature of Max Planck and Albert Einstein adopted, improved the standards of the German sciences, while at the same time it set the academic scholar apart from the general public. The laymen looking for concrete answers to their vital problems turned to the philosophers outside the universities.

ᴄᴏ *Friedrich Nietzsche*

ALONG WITH SCHOPENHAUER, Friedrich Nietzsche (1844–1900) was eagerly read, particularly by the younger generation, from the 1890's on. Born in a Protestant rectory in Saxony, Nietzsche was professor of classics in Basel from 1869 until 1879, when failing health forced him to resign. In the following decade, living the life of a true ascetic and tormented by illness, he wrote his main philosophical works before mental collapse silenced him. Nietzsche had grown up with the ancient Greeks as well as Schopenhauer and originally had been an ardent champion of Richard Wagner, until the latter's turn to Christianity in *Parsifal* killed his enthusiasm. In his *Thoughts out of Season* directed against Strauss' *The Old and the New Faith*, he had castigated the philistine materialism and boastful nationalism of Germany after the founding of the Empire, and the state of human civilization remained the central problem of all his philosophizing. He took pride in being an unsystematic thinker and liked to startle his readers with the paradoxes of his seductive prose.

Nietzsche followed Schopenhauer in the interpretation of life as a process dominated by man's blind urge to reach beyond himself to ever new forms. For Nietzsche, too, there is nothing higher than life itself, no God, no final goal, nor absolute moral law. But in contrast to Schopenhauer, who wished to escape life with its sufferings, Nietzsche drew the opposite conclusion. He sensed still a Christian note in Schopenhauer and argued that if there is no other reality but life, it must have its meaning within itself and be accepted with all its sufferings, its evil, guilt, and fatefulness. Nietzsche, rejecting every belief, carries atheism one step further by asserting that there is no truth and everything is permissible. He called his philosophy nihilism, since "God is dead," that is, dead as an historic power in the consciousness of man.

Nietzsche suffered deeply from the terrifying aspects of the modern age. But he demanded that man, if he belonged to those who wanted to regenerate the world, should love his fate and assert his nature. At this point the probing student of the human condition turned into a prophet. God being dead, man became indeed the measure. But humanity was in decay and had grown meek under the influence of Christian religion, while modern democracy and mass civilization had transformed the individual into a "herd-man." There would always be a herd that had to be ruled. What was needed was to produce the rulers. These "supermen" would be a natural nobility that had proved its mettle by defying the sham values of modern life and who would possess the maximum will to power, which is the true and only essence of life. Their self-assertion is the expression of the "morals of masters" as opposed to the Christian "slave morals" of the herd. What this envisioned superman actually would be like cannot clearly be discovered in Nietzsche's writings. "A Roman Caesar with the soul of Christ," we read in one place, while elsewhere Nietzsche admits that the new master-men would be nothing but "free roaming beasts of prey."

Nietzsche noted that, in history, periods of decadence are followed by periods of regeneration and creation. This "eternal recurrence," he said, was about to happen again. This was no time for "small politics" but for "great politics of long range," in which the future of man would be settled. Although Nietzsche meditated on the rearing and training of the supermen and spoke of slave and master races, he was contemptuous of racialism, particularly anti-Semitism, and he was anything but a German nationalist. His impact on the Germans was quite ambiguous in the beginning. The critique of the shallowness of the German civilization of the last third of the nineteenth century spurred those who, as we shall soon see, endeavored to lead more meaningful lives, while his absolute sincerity removed much pretense and hypocrisy and helped to introduce a greater naturalness in Germany. But his phobia of democracy had the opposite effect on the social level and advanced a belief in the privileges of the elites. Most dangerous, however, was Nietzsche's unbridled subjectivism and rabid irrationalism that considered it possible to create a new image of man through sheer will power. Yet although this subjectivism and irrationalism had followers earlier, they changed the general intellectual climate of Germany drastically only after 1918, when Nietzsche's praise of the will to power and of war as its necessary and proper means was also reechoed many times. That Nietzsche exerted a direct influence on the formation of Hitler's ideas cannot be proved, but there is no doubt that he was a strong power that induced many an intellectual to join the National Socialist movement in the 1920's and greatly contributed to the surrender of the majority of the German intelligentsia to Hitler in 1933.

But in 1890 and the twenty-five years thereafter it was not so much the hostility to reason as a deeper understanding of man and the world shown by the leading writers and artists of the period that can be traced to Nietzsche's influence. The members of the new generation who in the years around 1890 gained an audience displayed an awareness of the many dimensions of life and of the crisis of modern civilization that had been missing in the materialism and facile optimism of the earlier decades. At the same time they did not share Nietzsche's radical nihilism, for they were not prepared to jettison the great values of the West.

∽ Literary Naturalism

THESE NEW intellectual trends found their first expression in literature with the emergence of naturalism. Whereas France had produced Balzac, Flaubert, and Zola, Scandinavia had Björnsen, Jacobsen, Ibsen, and Strindberg, and Russia had Tolstoy and Dostoevsky, naturalism had no old tradition in Germany. Now, mainly inspired by Zola, Ibsen, and the two great Russians, naturalism appeared on the German literary scene. In 1889 the Free Theater (*Freie Bühne*) was founded in Berlin by a group of young theater men and critics, because the existing German theaters cultivated the trashy French play or its German imitations exclusively. The success of this venture was assured with the staging of the play of the young Silesian Gerhard Hauptmann (1862–1945), *Before Sunrise*. This first naturalistic German drama by a genuinely poetic mind was a sensation that was surpassed four years later by another Hauptmann play, *The Weavers*, which dramatized the revolt of the Silesian weavers in 1844.[7] European naturalism aimed at the application of science and sociology to literature. Whether the former aim is in any real sense possible may be doubted, but even the latter was not greatly desired by the German writers. The Prussian censor considered *The Weavers* a revolutionary stage play and suspected the people around the Free Theater to be socialists. Actually, however, Gerhard Hauptmann was not inclined to make writing a mere weapon of active social reform. He almost immediately moved away from pure naturalism toward German neoromanticism.

Thus German literary naturalism existed for only a brief interlude. One of its lasting results was the opening of the German stage for serious contemporary productions and for a revival of the classic drama. Under the leadership of gifted stage directors the theatrical arts achieved a high state of perfection. It was the work of private entrepreneurs rather than of the state theaters that brought on this flowering of the theater. The greatest impact was made by Max Reinhardt (1873–1943), an Austrian who for the major part of his life lived in Berlin.

✎ *Thomas Mann*

THE MODERN German epic novel was created by Thomas Mann (1875–1955). He came from a prominent merchant family of the Hanseatic city of Lübeck, and the story of four generations of such a family formed the subject of his first great—or as many would have it his greatest—novel *Buddenbrooks* (1901). Although Mann's style may be called naturalistic, his philosophy did not derive from science and sociology but rather from Schopenhauer, Wagner, and Nietzsche. The story of the rise and fall of the Buddenbrook family can be read with profit as a chapter in the social history of the German merchant class in the nineteenth century. For Thomas Mann, however, the rise and fall of a family of property was not intended as contemporary social criticism but as the foreground for probing into the problem of human decadence. Through four generations of a patrician family he studies the decline of man's vital energies under the subtle attacks of a growing critical consciousness. The problem of the inimical relationship of life and intellect occupied Mann in subsequent works also, though he never carried it to extreme philosophical solutions. It gave tragic depth to the world that the artist created and superior irony to his narrative. Mann was not a reformer and was free from all servitude to society.

[7] See p. 16.

✍ Regeneration of German Poetry

It was the achievement of Stefan George, Hugo von Hofmannsthal, and Rainer Maria Rilke to restore Germany to the Parnassus of lyric poetry, which since the middle of the century had been occupied almost exclusively by the French and Belgian symbolists. Baudelaire, Mallarmé, Rimbaud, Maeterlinck, Verhaeren, and others had led the movement toward the creation of pure art that was above all social and political reality. According to their views, art has its own laws and through its symbols is bringing imaginary worlds into existence.

✍ Stefan George

Stefan George (1868–1933), the son of Rhenish peasants, spent his early formative years in France, where he had escaped from what seemed to him in Nietzschean terms the empty state of German life. He found his spiritual home in Latin or, ultimately, pagan Greek cultures although, having grown up in an old Catholic tradition, he never threw off the spell that the Platonic elements of medieval thought as well as the ideals of medieval knighthood and saints' cults cast on him. When George came back to Germany, he had not only absorbed the rules of French symbolism but was also well on his way toward the development of the image-laden marble language with which he restored German lyric poetry to an elevated position. To him poetry was the highest form of artistic objectification, for the novel was dead, the stage mere histrionics, and music subjectivist. But it was, in addition, the highest expression of the national spirit, and therefore the poet was not only the true spokesman but also the molder of the nation.

Stefan George had in the 1890's withdrawn from the contemporary scene into an aesthete's isolation. He condemned industrial mass civilization, including modern science, as well as all egalitarian and democratic currents. George's world order was strictly aristocratic and hierarchic. At the same time it was a male society, in which women, being inferior to men, were to be subordinate. George offered his cult of beauty, for which he found a deity in the person of a young deceased friend, as a religion which would regenerate the world. Through a disciplined elite the example of a new humanity was to be set. A group of poets, writers, and worshippers gathered around the "master." George was an exacting leader demanding not only complete devotion to his person and work but also personal conduct that lived up to his high and austere standards. Like a sect, the members of the George circle dressed in a special manner. The esoteric character of the movement was also emphasized by the original type with which the books and magazines of the group were printed and their peculiar spelling.

George attracted some of the noblest young minds desirous of beauty as well as of heroic ideals. But this faith, based on the aesthetic achievement of a poet, failed to come to grips with the realities of the age. The modern mass society could not be cured by simple damnation and the cultivation of an elite style. George saw the first World War approach and welcomed it, because he saw in the war an event that would transform men. Before 1914 George had already moved close to the belief that the salvation of the world from the ills of modern civilization would be the work of Germany, and after the outbreak of the war he took part in the wild invectives against the West in which the German intellectuals indulged. He went as far as to malign French civilization, which had contributed so much to his own personal development.

The war did not purify men but, on the contrary, opened deeper human pitfalls. Still, George saw the danger chiefly in democracy, against which he and his followers propagated the leadership principle and discussed among themselves projects of dictatorship. George thus unwittingly helped to prepare the ground for the arrival of a popular movement that pretended to rejuvenate Germany through its heroic ideals and the establishment of a "leader state." Actually there was a profound difference between George and Hitler. George always thought of Germany as a spiritual rather than biological unit. He despised anti-Semitism, as Nietzsche had done, and envisaged the new man as a highly cultured and even cosmopolitan human being. When in 1933 the Nazis tried to win George's cooperation by offering him great honors, he chose exile in Switzerland. To him, the outrage done by Hitler to all human dignity was unpardonable. The same feeling was also strong in Count Klaus von Stauffenberg, one of his disciples, who in July 1944 directed the attempt at Hitler's life and regime.

✌ *Hugo von Hofmannsthal*

IN THE LITERARY and artistic field the relations between Austria and Germany were close, and one could even say that they grew more intensive after 1866. Foremost among the Austrian poets and writers was Hugo von Hofmannsthal (1874-1929). He was a lyric poet in his younger years but after 1900 turned mostly to writing dramas, essays, and texts of operas. Of the five libretti which he wrote for Richard Strauss (1864-1949), the *Rosenkavalier* may be called one of the few great German comedies. Although Hofmannsthal began as a neoromantic symbolist like George, he had no desire to dominate others, exalt his own self, or become a prophet. Rather, he sought to identify himself with the world from which he was separated through his introspection and reveling in beauty, while at the same time he felt the impact of the world past and present on his being. Melancholy and lethargy seemed originally the inevitable result of this tension. But Hofmannsthal had the strength to free himself from a purely aesthetic creed and face the real world and its moral conflicts. The poet "who could think with the heart" served his age, whose values he knew were dilapidating, as an interpreter of the human condition. The range of Hofmannsthal's vision was extraordinary. He was at home in antiquity as well as in the Catholic Middle Ages. His legend-play, *Everyman*, regularly performed in the cathedral square during the Salzburg festivals, evokes medieval piety. But he was equally familiar with the century of Shakespeare and Calderon as well as with that of Goethe. Hofmannsthal loved his Austria, and the Habsburg empire, by bringing together a number of nationalities, seemed to him a small Europe. He believed in the unity of European culture, which was for him the sum total of the best that all nations have produced. After the collapse of the Austro-Hungarian monarchy he addressed himself more consciously to the wider German audience but he remained loyal to his European ideal, trying to his death to give it reality by adding to the understanding of the European tradition.

✌ *Rainer Maria Rilke*

THE THIRD GREAT POET of the literary revival was Rainer Maria Rilke (1875–1926). Born in Prague, the son of an old and respected German family, Rilke felt homeless in the predominantly Czech city. But this sentiment denoted a more universal martyrdom, namely the experience of the loneliness of the individual in the midst of a soulless modern civilization. Rilke lived the life of the migrant. From Moscow to Paris, from Sweden to Italy, extended the stations of his life and his search for a home, but everywhere he suffered the sense of alienation from actual life and his fellow men. He liked to compare life to the moon, of which we see only one side. Similarly the life of the individual, the meeting of time and eternity in the uniqueness of the self, can only be understood if its invisible dimensions are recognized. The transcendent is part and parcel of the world, although only the imagination of the poet is able to unify the here and the beyond and overcome the limits of space and time. Rilke warns against belittling the earth. It shares its temporal character with men whose possession and friend it is. Through suffering and passion they should reach for its essence in the full awareness of its transcendent origin and aims. Rilke's highly philosophical and spiritual lyrics anticipate what

Martin Heidegger and Karl Jaspers undertook in their existentialist philosophies after World War I. But he remained the poet who believed that verses could create new worlds. In his magnificently pure language he unveiled new provinces of the human heart.

✑ Culture and Society

THOMAS MANN, Stefan George, Hugo von Hofmannsthal, and Rainer Maria Rilke were the towering figures of the literary revival that had stirred since the 1890's. But the creative literary production was larger and richer than can be discussed here. It reached a wide audience, although it is difficult to judge how large the groups were that were deeply affected by the new ideas. There can be no doubt, however, that there existed among the highly educated people in many, and perhaps in most, German cities circles that fully participated in the fresh intellectual and artistic life.

Prosperity and the growing accumulation of fortunes created for the first time in German history a leisure class, members of which devoted their life entirely to cultural pursuits, be it as patrons or collectors or as mere consumers. The arts and literature became more independent of the courts than they had ever been before. While in Berlin William II's immature taste kept all the important modern art away from the state theaters and galleries, Dresden, Munich, and Darmstadt followed a more liberal course. But state policies were of little significance for the progress of modern art. The citizens of Hamburg, Cologne, and Frankfurt excelled in building their art galleries. These cities were also the first to develop an initiative in these years toward the founding of universities.

✑ The Visual Arts

THE GROWTH of a better taste can best be seen in the refinement of the visual arts. The "youth style" (*Jugendstil*), the German counterpart of the *art nouveau* of France, put an end in the 1890's to the emulation of historical styles in architecture and handicrafts. Instead, the "youth style" turned to nature to find new forms. Its results were not felicitous. But the ice was broken, and from the *Jugendstil* evolved the beginnings of modern architecture. The practical uses of modern building materials were carefully studied. It was also stipulated that the function of a building, whether residence, meeting hall, factory, or railroad station, ought to determine its plan, and consequently that the architect would, as it were, have to build from the inside out. This by itself tended to simplify the façade, free it from artificial ornaments, and stress elementary lines and measures. The first important building embodying the norms of such a style was a Berlin factory constructed in 1910 by Peter Behrens (1868–1940). Like Walter Gropius (b. 1883), who founded the *Bauhaus* in 1919, Behrens had originally begun in the *Jugendstil* manner. However, the modern architecture was by no means successful enough with the public to eliminate shoddy and dull building. As a matter of fact, even in the Weimar Republic modern architecture had many enemies, and in 1933 Hitler declared the *Bauhaus* "cultural bolshevism." But obviously modern architecture from the outset had a good deal of support both from industry and private persons. The *Werkbund*, a free association for the promotion of distinctive art and craftsmanship, was the center for public discussion and information.

✑ *Universities and Sciences*

THE GERMAN universities experienced the change in the general outlook on life that characterized the period before World War I in a milder form than literature and the arts. They continued to amass a stupendously expanding knowledge of the empirical world. But the most eminent of the German professors of this period were not insensitive to the dangers posed to scholarship and general education by the growing separation of the departments of knowledge and the absence of clear general philosophical methods. Only with a few examples can we illustrate here some of the essential aspects of the history of the universities of this period.

It was the age in which the natural sciences in Germany reached their richest bloom. In all fields of the natural sciences and medicine a number of German scholars must be counted as leaders of the gigantic progress of knowledge that revolutionized human thinking and, through technology, all human conditions. No period of history had ever witnessed such a rapid and radical transformation of science as the first quarter of the twentieth century, which challenged the principles on which classic science had rested and which had been considered absolute truth.

The experiments of Wilhelm Roentgen (1845–1923) that led to the discovery of the X-ray in 1895 and enabled the Frenchman Henri Becquerel (1852–1908) to discover radioactivity a year later immediately preceded the new theoretical physics. At the same time the development of radiology destroyed one of the basic tenets of traditional chemistry, namely that of the immutability of chemical elements. In 1900 Max Planck (1858–1947) published the first version of his quantum theory, which was incompatible with the fundamental scientific assumption that all the dynamic effects in nature are continuous. Planck's hypothesis in contrast assumed that the emission or absorption of radiation does not take place in a continuous stream but in well-defined intermittent amounts of energy, which he called quantums. The Danish physicist

Niels Bohr (1885–1962), through the construction of his atom model of 1912, brought about the general acceptance of the quantum theory.

Albert Einstein (1879–1955) in 1905 presented his special theory of relativity, which abolished the classic concepts of absolute three-dimensional space and one-dimensional time in favor of a four-dimensional space-time continuum. In 1916 he published his general theory of relativity. In Planck's and Einstein's physics, nature can no longer be envisioned but is only thought and described in abstract mathematical formulas. Most of the new insights into nature, particularly in microphysics, are not gained through sensorial observations. At the same time the phenomenal world is only a small part of the objective world, which remains shrouded in mystery.

Planck and Einstein, friends of very different tempers, shared the strong belief that the disparity of the new and old physical theory was not the sign of a disordered world. "Without the faith that it is in principle possible," wrote Einstein, "to make the reality understandable through our theoretical constructions, without the faith in the inner harmony of our world, there can be no natural science."

But the loss of unitary methods in the natural sciences could not fail to affect the social and humane sciences as well, which in the later nineteenth century had looked up to the natural sciences or even tried to model themselves after them. The result was a greater awareness of the hypothetical character of many too readily accepted concepts and greater caution with regard to a simple positivism. The best work done after 1900 showed a marked gain in circumspection and depth, though they were usually bought at the price of further specialization.

✑ *Historical Scholarship*

THE DEVELOPMENT of historical writing reflects some of these experiences. Although quite a few professors continued Treitschke's nationalistic and propagandizing historiography and found wide academic audiences, the leading historians of this generation, represented in particular by the school of Max Lenz (1850–1932), advocated a return to Ranke's objective history. The name neo-Rankeans, which was applied to them, is not quite appropriate. For these historians followed Ranke exclusively in his role of the student of the great power struggles and not in that of the universal historian who never lost sight of the ideal forces within and behind history.[8] To the neo-Rankeans states were the chief subjects of history. When Karl Lamprecht (1856–1915) attempted to make the history of civilization the central theme of historical study while at the same time proposing that the growth of civilizations was determined by

[8] See the author's *A History of Modern Germany, 1648–1840*, pp. 523–7.

scientific laws, he was practically ostracized by the profession not only because he introduced the methods of natural science to the humanities but also because he questioned the dominant historic role of the state. Although the *Kulturgeschichte* of the Swiss Jakob Burckhardt (1818–97) was widely read in Germany, it found hardly any successors among German historians. Social history, too, was eschewed by them nor were they inclined to take up sociological questions.

✒ Friedrich Meinecke

A NEW WINDOW was opened by Friedrich Meinecke (1862–1954) when in 1907 he published his *Cosmopolitanism and National State*. The book contained studies on the genesis of the German national state from the cosmopolitan age of Kant to the times of Ranke and Bismarck. Meinecke carried over into political history the methods of the history of ideas which Dilthey had applied to philosophy and literature. Thereby he greatly broadened the field of political history. Not only the statesmen but also the thinkers and writers in their capacity as molders of the contemporary mind are actors in the drama of history. Although Meinecke's historiography proceeded from different premises, it contained the key to a full understanding of Ranke. Meinecke's admonition that the historians should "more courageously plunge into philosophy and politics" aimed at lifting historical thought to Ranke's plane. For Ranke had drawn inspiration from philosophy as well as the contemplation of the political events of his times.

When calling for closer contact with politics, Meinecke did not intend to turn the clock back to Treitschke and the Prussian school. Rather, he wanted to learn from the political tensions of the present something about the problems which had been underlying the historical development leading to the contemporary age. Meinecke saw the strain in the relations between Germany's liberal middle classes and the Prussian ruling groups, as well as the hostility of the industrial working class to the existing state. He did not question that the unification of Germany through the Prussian military monarchy was fortunate and that even modern Germany needed Prussia for her defense. But he believed that just as the Prussia of Frederick the Great had been reformed by Stein, Scharnhorst, and Humboldt, the Prussia of Bismarck and Roon was capable of change. In order to close the gap between Prussia and the liberal Germany, Meinecke recalled the universal ideas of the classic and romantic period, which, as he showed, greatly contributed to the formation of the German character. Meinecke's interpretation of modern German history, as he himself was later to recognize, underestimated the gravity of the conflict of social forces and overrated the power of pure ideas in relation to them. But

Meinecke not only extended our organs for discovering historical realities behind the actual events but also gave historical thought renewed practical significance.

✍ *Werner Sombart*

THE SOCIAL PROBLEMS, which in Meinecke's writings appeared only in a highly sublimated form, were more directly attacked by the economists. Just after the turn of the century Werner Sombart (1863–1941), in his *Modern Capitalism,* presented an analytical synthesis of the history of modern European capitalism. It was a work of enormous erudition that showed not only the economic factors but also the human element which had set into motion the process toward the rationalized modern economy. At the same time Sombart described the evolution of modern social institutions that followed from this transformation of the Western world. The book was an attempt to replace the Marxian picture of capitalism with its dogmatic theoretical bias by a concrete historical description. History in Sombart's hands, however, was not a mere chronological narrative, but a critical study of the different forces, material and human, that determined economic and social life. Sombart was no blind defender of capitalism. As a matter of fact, in his early years he had been greatly attracted by the Social Democratic party, although after World War I his advocacy of a "German" socialism made him an intellectual companion of the radical right.

✍ *Max Weber*

THE PROBLEM of modern capitalism was also in the center of the studies of Max Weber (1864–1920), who at the same time was absorbed in the problems of the modern state. While a nervous ailment interfered with his public activities for several years, the circle of friends surrounding him in Heidelberg experienced the influence of his rich, energetic, and fearless personality. Weber, son of a National Liberal deputy of the Bismarck period, had established himself as a scholar in Roman and medieval legal and social history. In 1894 he became a professor of economics in Freiburg, and from there he went to Heidelberg in 1897. But he was also passionately interested in politics. For a short time he had cooperated with the Pan-Germans and Conservatives but was repelled by their lack of selfless national devotion and political wisdom. Weber had then assisted Friedrich Naumann in launching the Christian Social movement.[9] It was his deep conviction that Germany still had to win her place among the great world powers and that only democratization and internal social

[9] See p. 332.

pacification could give her the strength needed for this end. To Weber democratization did not mean abolition of the monarchy, although he early discovered that William II was a dilettante and a fraud who, with his irresponsible public speeches, made Germany hated abroad. In Weber's opinion it was dangerous that an economically declining class, the *Junkers*, was holding the highest power in the state. But he did not detect any capacity for political leadership in the bourgeoisie, which Bismarck had crippled politically, nor among the leaders of the German working class, who were lacking in the will for national power. Yet when World War I broke out, he argued that Germany had to act as a power state and had to accept the risk of war in order to participate in the decision on the future of the globe. He even went so far as to say "we would have had to do so even if we had reason to fear defeat." The ineptitude of the government in the conduct of the war, particularly with regard to war aims and to the unlimited submarine warfare, made him a public champion of parliamentary government from 1917 on, and after the revolution, as we shall see,[10] he contributed to the drafting of the Weimar Constitution. He cannot, however, be called a democrat in the full sense of the term, since constitutional forms were to him only techniques for producing the leadership for a strong national state.

The same man whose heart belonged so wholly to the nation, for which he postulated a great responsibility in world history, banned all value judgments from the scholar's work. Although he admitted that the original choice of the subject of study implied a value judgment, he demanded that thereafter any substantive research had to proceed on a strictly rational and causal basis. Intuitive understanding, he said, has to be checked by empirical tests. The social scientist in his investigations can elucidate the variety of value ideas and the incompatibility of some with other values. He is able to spread light on the scene of present and past social action but unable to "tell anyone what he ought to do, but rather what he can do." The course of action to be chosen is the responsibility of acting man who will reach his decision in accordance with his own conscience and personal view of the world. No absolute hierarchy of values can be established. In this respect Weber was a radical relativist or, as he called it, a polytheist.

This dichotomy between fact and value might have had dangerous nihilistic implications, but at first it had the effect of a fresh wind blowing through stuffy academic classrooms, over which too many pseudo-prophets presided. Max Weber's fearless search for truth and his simultaneous unselfish commitment to great causes never let him appear as a skeptic in the eyes of those who came into contact with him. Weber, like Sombart, had absorbed what seemed to him valid in Marx, but he refused

[10] See pp. 542–3.

to accept the role that the latter had assigned to ideas as mere "superstructures" of economic developments. In his famous treatise on "Protestant Ethics and the Spirit of Capitalism" he showed that the spread of modern capitalism and the rationalistic form it took were decisively caused by Calvinistic ideas. Few historians today will accept this thesis as it was originally presented more than half a century ago. Many other ideas beside Calvinism were actually involved. But Weber raised problems which opened novel vistas of history, and most social scientists will agree that he established an additional causal sequence, at variance, though not necessarily incompatible, with the Marxian interpretation of history.

Weber then turned to studies of the great world religions. They were much broader in scope than his investigations of Calvinism. In studying Confucianism, Hinduism, Buddhism, and Judaism he wanted to learn why only the West had brought forth a rational economy and, more than that, a rational civilization, for what applied to economy applied equally to state, science, and art. Weber actually wrote comparative studies of civilizations. The focus had shifted from that of the Calvinist studies: He was concerned not only with the part played by religion but also with the impact of the material conditions on the formation of the social teachings of the different religions and on art and science.

Max Weber intended to present the sum total of his sociological thought in a large book on *Economics and Society*, the completion of which his early death prevented. In the extensive fragment posthumously published he gave an account of the theoretical concepts of his sociological methods, followed by an analysis of economic and political action. Weber's new political science divided the forms of government in accordance with the principles that legitimized the monopoly of the use of violence. He distinguished three forms of legitimacy: the patriarchal monarchy invoking the eternal tradition and operating through a ruler who is surrounded by officeholders bound to him as a person; regimes based on rationalistic legal rules in which bureaucracy wields major power; rule by a man of real or imputed extraordinary gifts or charisma. The charismatic leader, a prophet or hero, will act in a revolutionary fashion, disregarding tradition, neglecting law, and using as officials loyal followers and believers. In due course these new institutions become routine and bureaucratized. Weber was convinced that in politics as in all other fields of life the drift towards rationalization was ineluctable. Modern scholarship was working toward the same end, thereby not only liberating man from superstition and illusions but also drying up the life-spending force of religious and philosophical creation.

ᢌ The "Unpolitical" Germans

THE LITERARY, artistic, and intellectual life of the twenty to twenty-five years before the first World War was rich in high achievements. But they failed to set the tone for German society as a whole. The period of William II was dominated by cheap pomposity and a crass materialism that was dressed up as idealism with the help of nationalistic ideas. Even the great mass of the educated people preferred to read Paul de Lagarde (1827–1891) or Julius Langbehn (1851–1907), who preached Germanic racism and superiority, than the serious writers and thinkers, let alone the scholars, who endeavored to solve the social and political problems arising from the industrialization of Germany. Outside of the socialist camp practically all these scholars thought of solutions within the framework of the existing constitutional order. Even those who like Max Weber were convinced of the necessity for a reform of the Bismarckian constitution did not see how it could be achieved in view of the great power of the monarchy, which, in the midst of an unexampled prosperity, enjoyed the full support of the upper and middle classes. This frustration generated political weariness and passivity among people who might have contributed to the conduct of politics or at least to political education.

The great writers and artists of this period even took pride in not mingling in politics, which they shunned as interfering with the sublime world of the spirit. During World War I Thomas Mann, in his *Meditations of a Non-Political Man*, declared that Germans unlike the rest of the West, believed that the spirit of individual men rather than politics was the means of improving the world. In practice this meant the acceptance of the authoritarian state in Germany. The book was published a few weeks before the revolution of November 1918. In subsequent years Thomas Mann established a positive relationship to democracy, but he found few followers among the intellectuals of this generation that still dominated the Weimar Republic.

ᢌ The Youth Movement

EQUALLY NONPOLITICAL was a movement that at the turn of the century arose within the German youth. In 1901 the first group of the *Wandervögel* (Migratory Birds), as its members called themselves, rallied in Steglitz, a middle-class suburb of Berlin. In the following decade the movement spread, first slowly and then more rapidly, into many parts of Germany. But it always attracted only a section of the German youth. It is estimated that at no time did it have more than 60,000 members, who came chiefly from the urban communities of Protestant Germany. In the Catholic regions the church-directed youth organizations impeded the growth of a religiously neutral movement. Thus South Germany, the Rhineland, and Upper Silesia were not strongly represented, nor was relatively little-urbanized East Germany.

The movement was a protest against the straitlaced life of the Victorian family and the intellectualism of the secondary schools. Both were unduly restraining the imaginative gifts and the autonomous development of the teenagers. They wanted to have some time of their own to cultivate their friendships, get away from the apartment life in cities, train their bodies, and dream their own dreams. What was novel was their rejection of the forms and rituals of the academic fraternities, after which the associations of high school students had been modeled until that time. The *Wandervögel* disliked the false aristocratic pretensions of the fraternities and wished to be close to the people. It is true, however, that they never succeeded in breaking the class barriers. The Social Democratic party in 1904 started its own youth organizations, which were managed by older men, whereas the *Wandervögel* groups were led by older high school pupils or young university students.

In simple dress, carrying their provisions and cooking utensils in a rucksack, these youngsters went out into the country to discover nature again. Their long marches were eased by songs accompanied by guitars. Food was prepared over campfires, which also served as the background for a revival of folk dancing. The folk songs the *Wandervögel* collected were their best cultural contribution, but otherwise their art was poor and conventional. At a national convention on the Hohe Meissner mountain in 1913 the members adopted a pledge to shape their own lives "at their own initiative, on their own responsibility, and with deep sincerity." This formula left room for a good many interpretations, as actually the movement was composed of a large variety of groups. What they had in common was the will to rid themselves of the shams of a materialistic culture and restore honesty and warmth to human relations. In certain respects the youth movement exerted an influence far beyond its own ranks. It helped to cleanse the life of the German middle classes of many useless social conventions and endowed it with a greater naturalness.

It was not to be expected that these young people would be able to formulate a program of social and political action of their own. Essentially they were interested in their own education. Like their fathers they regarded the existing political and social order as permanent. They did not challenge parental authority as such nor the prevailing moral code. The admission of girls to the *Wandervögel* groups was blocked by the majority, and most girls were organized in special groups. Like their basic moral attitudes these youngsters took their political ideas largely from their fathers, except that the sons would altogether prefer the more romantic notions. Lagarde and Langbehn with their cultural pessimism and praise of Germanic values impressed them deeply. The youth movement as such did not identify itself with a single political program and even avoided noisy patriotism. But the escape from the city was at the same time a flight from the modern age. The movement was a poor school for hard and sober thinking about the present. World War I and the revolution eventually demanded political decisions, and the reconstituted youth movement had to find new ways.

✍ *Expressionism*

AFTER 1905 a new group of writers and painters appeared who broke not only with naturalism and impressionism but also with symbolism and neoromanticism. Although expressionism had its parallels in the other European countries, before and during World War I it reached its greatest intensity in Germany. These young artists all lived in the consciousness of a radical world crisis which they met as political activists. They felt that the existing world rested on illusions, which must be exploded in order to make room for a better world. The expressionists were anticapitalist and antimilitarist and were committed to socialism and pacifism. In their opinion the artist, too, had failed to tear off the mask that hid the true image of man. To be sure, symbolism had revealed other realities behind reality, but it had aesthetically stylized them and not uncovered the demonic forces. This ultimate reality the expressionists tried to lay bare by means which went beyond logic, conventional language, or perspective. Dadaism, cubism, and surrealism were extreme forms of expressionism.

In retrospect the early expressionists seem like petrels before the impending storm. Many of them were killed in the war or died in its aftermath, and only a few, such as Gottfried Benn (1886–1958) and Berthold Brecht (1898–1958), were granted long productive lives.

CHAPTER 9

The First World War and the
Revolution of 1918–19

✍ Assassination of Habsburg Heir

ON JUNE 28, 1914, the student Gavrilo Princip, a Serbian by race and an
Austro-Hungarian by nationality, killed Archduke Francis Ferdinand of
Austria and his wife in the Bosnian capital of Sarajevo. There was good
reason to suspect that the assassin of the heir to the Habsburg throne had
been abetted by persons or agencies of the Serbian government, although
even during Princip's trial no direct evidence could be found. After half a
century all we can document today is the fact that some lesser official
persons were implicated, whereas it has remained highly controversial
whether high-ranking members of the Serbian government were involved.

However, there was no question that the bloody deed was the result of
the fierce Great Serbian nationalism that propagated the inclusion of the
Yugoslav provinces in the Serbian state. The least the Vienna government would have had to demand in these circumstances was that the
Serbian government should actively support the inquiries into the crime
and give firm assurances that in the future it would desist from encouraging the propaganda directed against the integrity of the Habsburg empire.
Yet although such a policy would not have led to war, it is highly doubtful whether it could have stopped the collusion between Serbian national
ambitions and the revolutionary elements of the south Slav provinces of
Austria-Hungary.

✍ Germany's Reaction

BARON FRANZ CONRAD VON HÖTZENDORF (1852–1925), the chief of staff of
the Austro-Hungarian army, urged that the opportunity should be used
to make war on Serbia and destroy her capacity for serving as a center of
the drive for Yugoslav unity. The Hungarian prime minister, Count
Stefan Tisza (1861–1918), objected to this course of action by emphasiz-

ing the strength of Russia, and he probably also feared that a war might bring even more Yugoslav people into the Habsburg empire and increase the difficulties of the ruling Magyar minority. The foreign minister, Count Leopold Berchtold (1863–1942), was hesitant on account of the international repercussions. Emperor Francis Joseph leaned toward Baron Conrad's recommendations, but all the Austro-Hungarian statesmen agreed that their ultimate decision had to be made dependent on Germany's attitude.

It was of decisive importance that the German government, represented by the emperor, the chancellor, and the acting foreign secretary, urged the Vienna government to go to war against Serbia and gave the strongest assurances that Germany would protect Austria-Hungary if "her intervention would lead to the great war." This German "blank check" tipped the scales in the Austro-Hungarian cabinet. On July 7 it accepted the hard course, although, on Berchtold's initiative, Serbia was not to be invaded without first being presented with an ultimatum containing unacceptable demands. All these plans had the full approval of the German government. As a matter of fact, the German pressure for determined Austrian action was so insistent during the following weeks that the statesmen in Vienna came to believe that they would lose Germany's support if they took a more moderate line.

Germany's determination to push Austria-Hungary into forceful action was the result of both fear and calculated audacity. The Germans, and particularly the emperor, were profoundly shocked by the assassination of Francis Ferdinand and saw in it a sign of the imminent disintegration of the Habsburg monarchy and the loss of its position as a great power. Germany then would be isolated in Europe and be completely surrounded by hostile nations. The subjugation of Serbia would restore the shaky structure of the dual monarchy by removing the Yugoslav cancer. At the same time the destruction of the chief Russian bastion in the Balkans would enable the Central Powers to tighten their alliance with Rumania and draw Bulgaria, and perhaps also Greece, closer to their camp. Germany's policies in Turkey would thereby win a much improved base.

The German policy makers believed that the moment was unusually opportune for making such gains, and William II, at least in the beginning, was convinced that the czar would not protect regicides. What the Germans and Austrians failed to realize, however, was that even if clear proof of a connection between the Serbian government and the crime of Sarajevo had been established, the world would have judged the extinction of the Serbian national state an excessive penalty. The belief that in spite of the progress of the Russian armaments the military superiority was still in hands of the Central Powers was the main cause of the

WORLD WAR I IN EUROPE

FINLAND

Helsingfors

KRONSTADT

Petrograd
(ST. PETERSBURG)

Reval   Narva

ESTONIA

Pskov

LATVIA

Riga

LITHUANIA

emel

Kaunas

Vilna

Suwalki

Grodno

NIEMEN

BATTLELINE
FEB., 1915

saw

Brest-
Litovsk

WHITE
RUSSIA

Minsk

Pinsk

PRIPET

MARSHES

PRIPET

EASTERN FRONT
AT ARMISTICE OF
BREST-LITOVSK
DEC.,1917

BRUSILOV'S
COUNTER THRUST
JULY & AUG.
1917

Lemberg

GALICIA

rlice

Tarnopol

Czernowitz

Debrecen

TRANSYLVANIA

Hermannstadt

owa

RUMANIA

Bucharest

A

Nish

DANUBE

Varna

Sofia

BULGARIA

Uskub

Strumitza

GREECE

Salonika

GALLIPOLI

AEGEAN
SEA

DARDANELLES

R   U   S   S   I   A   N

Vitebsk

Orscha

Minsk

Gomel

Kiev

RUSSIAN
FRONT

U   K   R

EXTREME LIMITS OF
GERMAN OCCUPATION
SUMMER, 1918

Orel

DON

E   M   P   I   R   E

Kharkov

Poltava

A   I   N   E

DONETZ

Kursk

Rostov

DNIESTER

PRUTH

BESSARABIA

Jassy

DNIESTER

Odessa

SEA
OF
AZOV

Galatz

CRIMEA

Sevastopol

Constantsa

B   L   A   C   K   S   E   A

Sinope

(OTT.
EMP.)

Constantinople

HALYS

Angora

OTTOMAN   EMPIRE

German boldness. The German statesmen started from the vague hope that Bülow's policy in the Bosnian crisis of 1908 could be successfully repeated. But although the Russians were still lagging behind in arms, their army had grown very formidable, and the risk contained in a German challenge had by now become very grave. Whatever hopes the German statesmen might have entertained in the early days of July 1914 were quickly dispersed by the actual Russian reactions. But, convinced of Germany's military might, the German leaders, both civilian and military, were willing to accept war with Russia and France. As to the awful calamity of a war among the great powers, they comforted themselves by arguing that since the war between "Germans and Slavs" was bound to come before long, it was better to have it happen then, when Germany was definitely stronger than would be the case two or three years later.

If the Germans considered the moment favorable for a test of strength with Russia and France, they based their judgment on their estimate of British policy. Bethmann-Hollweg in particular, who during the whole crisis proved himself in full command of German policy, was strongly convinced that Anglo-German relations, as the colonial agreements of May 1914 showed, had become very friendly. The chancellor believed that England would remain neutral, provided Russia would appear as the aggressor. Therefore the German policy during the July crisis was entirely bent on placing the responsibility for transforming a local conflict into a general war upon Russia. To this end the German government declared that it knew nothing about the contents of the imminent Austro-Hungarian ultimatum and that it viewed the conflict between Austria-Hungary and Serbia as a local one, in which none of the powers ought to intervene.

These German declarations appeared to the other powers too clever to be trusted or shared. It was obvious that the Vienna government would not dare follow a policy of uninhibited force without having at least Germany's moral support, and nobody felt that the German government was so naïve as to assume that an issue that might involve Austro-Hungarian domination of the Balkans and thereby a drastic change in the European balance of power could seriously be considered a local affair. It did not make any difference that Austria-Hungary denied any intention to annex Serbian territory; the well-founded fear that she intended to crush Serbian independence was the crucial point. Thus from the beginning the German policy made a bad impression on England, and the British foreign office quickly surmised that the events were moving toward a general test of strength among the great powers. It should have been obvious even to a mediocre diplomat that Britain could not disinterest herself and, at the very minimum, would never tolerate that the position of France as a great power be seriously impaired. But though earnestly warned from the outset by Prince Lichnowsky (1860–1928), the German ambassador in London, Bethmann-Hollweg was impervious to such advice.

✒ *Austro-Hungarian Ultimatum*

WITH THE PRESENTATION of the Austro-Hungarian ultimatum in Belgrade, on July 23, the international crisis reached its acute stage. The reason for the long delay of this step had been the wish of the Vienna government to find out what results the investigation of the Sarajevo crime would produce and to make it impossible for the Russian and French governments to formulate a common policy at once. President Poincaré and the French Premier Viviani had been on a state visit in St. Petersburg from July 20 to 23. And although Poincaré had warned against any unnecessary provocation of Germany, he had assured the Russians most emphatically that France would fight on the side of Russia if a general war should occur.

While in her reply to the Austro-Hungarian ultimatum on July 25 Serbia went rather far in accepting the Austrian demands, she refused to comply with those that openly impinged on Serbian sovereignty, and she mobilized her army. The Austro-Hungarian minister at once left the Serbian capital, and on the following day Emperor Francis Joseph ordered the mobilization of eight army corps—almost one half of the Austro-Hungarian army. On July 28 the Habsburg monarchy declared war on Serbia. The German government was highly satisfied with these Austrian actions. It wished to create a *fait accompli* in order to be able thereafter to accuse Russia of transforming a local conflict into a general war. The various attempts of English Foreign Minister Sir Edward Grey to bring the Austro-Serbian conflict before a conference of Britain, Germany, France, and Italy or to induce the German government to press for moderation in Vienna were consistently sabotaged. In order not to antagonize Britain completely, Vienna was informed of the British endeavors but at the same time discouraged from paying any attention to them, while London was told that the German government had become active in Vienna in the direction of Grey's proposals. Nor did this German policy change when, on July 28, William II, after reading the Serbian reply of July 25 to the Austrian ultimatum, commented that hereby every cause of war had been removed, that the few Serbian reservations were negotiable, and all that was needed was a guarantee of the fulfillment of the Serbian promises which Austria could secure by the "temporary occupation of a part of Serbia." Thus he arrived at the same conclusion as Grey, namely, that Austria-Hungary should halt in Belgrade.

✍ *British Policy*

BETHMANN-HOLLWEG and the foreign secretary, Gottlieb von Jagow (1863–1935), obsessed with the idea that the Austro-Serbian conflict could be localized and England kept neutral by pinning the blame for the outbreak of a general war on Russia, received a rude shock on the night of July 29–30. On July 29 the Russians had announced the partial mobilization of their army as an answer to the Austrian mobilization against Serbia. At this point General von Moltke gave the chancellor a strong and detailed warning against the inescapable automatism of this mobilization. He argued that the partial mobilization of Russia would necessarily have to be answered by the total mobilization of Austria-Hungary; in an ineluctable sequence the total mobilization of Russia and Germany would have to follow, and this at once would raise the problem of France, earmarked as the first victim of the German strategy. Until that time the German military leaders had abstained from forcing the hands of the German diplomats. If they shared the latter's responsibility, it was due to the fact that through their appraisal of Germany's military superiority they had emboldened the civilian government in its political decisions. But under the existing war plans the moment was approaching when military necessity was to supersede diplomatic convenience.

The running out of time and ill-founded reports about the attitude of King George V induced Bethmann-Hollweg to approach the British government directly in order to win its neutrality. He told the British ambassador, Sir William Goschen (1847–1924), in a conversation late at night on July 29 that, provided England would remain neutral, Germany would be willing to forgo territorial annexations at the expense of France, even after a victorious war. He also informed him that Germany would respect the neutrality of the Netherlands if the other powers did likewise, and that the integrity of Belgium would be restored after the war, provided Belgium would not side with Germany's enemies. It was, indeed, understandable that the ambassador had difficulty in suppressing his amazement while listening to the chancellor's entreaties. Grey called it an "infamous" offer and drew the conclusion that Germany, while intending to go to war, had hesitated so far only out of fear that England would come to the assistance of Belgium and France. In these circumstances it was probably a good thing that Bethmann-Hollweg did not prevail on the emperor and Tirpitz to propose an Anglo-German naval convention to the British. As it was, they were at least not offered a bribe for staying neutral in the coming conflict.

The British reply came with unexpected suddenness. After midnight the chancellor received a report from the German ambassador in London that made the whole policy that until now he had so eagerly and stubbornly conducted collapse like "a house of cards." Prince Lichnowsky related that Grey once more had urged the acceptance of his proposal of a four-power mediation as well as German-British mediation in Vienna, St. Petersburg, and Belgrade. However, Grey had added that Britain would not be able to stay aside the moment France was drawn into the war. It must have been an agonizing hour that followed Bethmann-Hollweg's reading of the report of the man whose advance warnings were now irrefutably proved correct. The chancellor decided to change his course. He passed the London report on to Vienna with the recommendation to accept the British offer of mediation, though he failed to put strong pressure behind his advice. At this point nothing probably would have impressed the Vienna government except a clear threat that under the terms of the defensive dual alliance Germany might not recognize the obligation to come to Austria-Hungary's assistance.

✑ Last Days of Crisis

ACTUALLY, Austria-Hungary, having been urged by Germany for a long time to move fast and forcefully against Serbia, was at this very moment pressed to announce her total mobilization. The only sharp criticism that had reached Vienna from her German ally concerned Austria's sluggishness in contributing to the German policy of burdening Russia with the guilt for a general war and her unwillingness to keep Italy from joining the entente by the immediate cession of the Trentino. Thus it was not surprising that the Austro-Hungarian government refused to agree to the British mediation proposal. Moreover, the German chancellor himself, impressed by reassuring information about the English attitude, countermanded his recommendation on the following night, of July 30–31, before he had heard about the Austrian decision.

Though momentarily confounded in the early morning hours of July 30, Bethmann-Hollweg was unwilling or incapable of revising his policy. Later in the morning of the same day he confessed to the members of the Prussian cabinet that the chances for English neutrality were nil but added that, as long as Russia's guilt could be demonstrated, the German government did not have to fear any opposition or direct counteraction to war by the Social Democrats. Whereas up to this day Bethmann-Hollweg had declared it imperative to stamp Russia the aggressor in order to secure the neutrality of England in the coming conflict, this motive was suddenly suppressed in favor of internal gains. Apparently he had already become practically resigned to the inevitability of war and was fast losing control over events to the military men. The emperor and the generals were alarmed when they learned that Russia's partial mobilization actually involved more troops than the whole Austro-Hungarian army comprised. General von Moltke strongly urged Baron Conrad to initiate the total mobilization of the Austro-Hungarian army against Russia, a measure on which the Vienna government had decided the night before, though with the proviso that it should not be announced before August 1 nor start before August 4. On the evening of July 30 Moltke and the Prussian minister of war, General Erich von Falkenhayn (1861–1922), persuaded the chancellor to proclaim on the following day a "state of imminent war danger," which was in fact a preparatory step toward general mobilization.

✍ *Russian and German Mobilization*

ON THE MORNING of that July 31 strong forebodings were felt in Berlin that the Russians might have already begun their total mobilization, and shortly before noon the formal confirmation of this event was received. The Russian foreign minister, Sasonov, had persuaded the czar on the previous day to sign this order. Sasonov was discouraged by the failure of all his approaches to Austria and was worried that, as in 1908, Russia might be caught off guard. In view of the way the Russian army was organized, a partial mobilization, on which the czar had originally insisted, was technically extremely difficult. Still, the total mobilization, to which the czar agreed with the greatest reluctance, was not meant as a break-off of negotiations. Yet before the czar's letter to William II containing the assurance that the Russian army would not engage in hostilities as long as negotiations on Serbia were going on had arrived in Berlin, a German ultimatum was on its way to St. Petersburg demanding that within twelve hours Russia should declare her willingness to cancel all her mobilization orders.

This German ultimatum had been sent off shortly after the proclamation of the "state of imminent war danger" in the expectation that it would be rejected. For how could Russia have accepted the German demands, thereby admitting defeat in Serbia? Rather, the ultimatum was to serve as the justification of German mobilization. But for Moltke it implied even more: it was to supply the basis for the declaration of war on Russia. Moltke knew that in view of the relative slowness of her mobilization Russia could well afford to negotiate for a while, but he felt that Germany had everything to lose if she did not attack Belgium and France at once, before the full weight of Russia's military power had come into play. Therefore he insisted on the immediate declaration of war on Russia, and the chancellor sided with him. The declaration was drafted in the evening of July 31 and sent to the German ambassador in St. Petersburg for delivery to the Russian government at 5 P.M., irrespective of whether by that time the Russians would have rejected the German ultimatum or not have sent a reply at all. At the same hour William II had already signed the order for total mobilization.

Whereas, so far, Bethmann-Hollweg had considered a declaration of war by Russia a necessary prerequisite for nailing her down as the aggressor, his assent to Moltke's pleading showed that by now he was satisfied to accept her total mobilization as ample proof of her aggressiveness. He was right in assuming that German public opinion would follow his lead. It was an interesting sidelight that the German declaration of war was issued without the approval of the Federal Council as required by the German constitution. Only after the event was this approval given. But both the chancellor and the chief of staff had overlooked what an easy pretext the declaration of war would give to Italy and Rumania for ridding themselves of all their obligations under the terms of their defensive alliances with the Central Powers and how unfortunate would be the reaction to Germany's step in the whole world.

General von Falkenhayn, the Prussian minister of war, noticed this mistake and on the morning of August 1 persuaded both Moltke and Bethmann-Hollweg to hold back the German declaration of war, only to learn from the foreign office later on that the telegram had already gone to St. Petersburg. Falkenhayn, no doubt, could point out that under the existing war plans the German army in East Prussia was not supposed to cross the Russian frontiers and that before the launching of the great offensive in the west 8 to 10 days were needed for assembling the German troops on the left bank of the Rhine. It is true, however, that Moltke did not believe that he could wait that long. He considered the capture of Liège absolutely essential for the success of the German offensive and in 1913 had accepted a plan, conceived by Colonel Ludendorff, who soon was to win greater laurels, that envisaged the seizure of the fortress through a surprise attack by a small German force before the Belgians would have had time to block their frontiers. It may remain an open question whether this operation, which Ludendorff himself executed with great bravery, though with only doubtful success, on the third day of mobilization, was really essential, but once accomplished it left little time for further negotiations.

The difficulties involved in trying to maintain any political freedom while being committed to the Schlieffen plan were again starkly revealed when on the evening of August 1 the British seemed to suggest that they might stay neutral if Germany would desist from any westward drive. The emperor and chancellor clung to this last straw, and even Tirpitz, fearing for his navy, recommended that the British proposal not be rejected outright. Moltke, however, was seriously shaken when William II, in his childish ignorance of military matters, told him to deploy the mass of the German army eastward, and, on Moltke's rejoinder that in the absence of any prior plan this was impossible, snarled at him that his uncle would have given a different reply. Moltke's nerves had become frayed. More, perhaps, than anybody in the German government he visualized the catastrophe that war would mean to European civilization, while the fate of Germany, which he felt entrusted to himself, made him stick to every detail of the existing war plan. He was greatly disturbed when it was decided to delay the occupation of Luxembourg and to inform England that no German troops would cross the French frontier before the evening of August 3, although the concentration of the army in the west continued. Yet within a few hours the hope for English neutrality turned out to be a mere mirage and the military had their way.

Presumably as a consequence of the bad impression that Germany's admittedly precipitous declaration of war on Russia presented to the world Moltke and Falkenhayn suddenly insisted that no declaration of war should be made on France. They angrily accused the chancellor and foreign secretary of legal pedantry and asserted that popular pressure would force the French government to take the initiative. This was a totally false assumption. The French could not be provoked into hostile action, let alone into an invasion of Belgium, for they were fully conscious of the advantages they could expect to derive from having the Germans clearly marked as aggressors. An honest declaration of war by Germany would not have changed the situation but would at least have demonstrated her willingness not to disregard the proprieties of international law unnecessarily. The altercation between the civilian and military leaders was an ominous prelude to many similar incidents during the coming war. Since the emperor sided with Moltke and Falkenhayn, the German ultimatum to Belgium was presented in Brussels on August 2 before Germany was at war with France.

✍ Invasion of Belgium and France

IN STERN LANGUAGE the ultimatum demanded from the Belgian government that it should tolerate the passage of German troops, which Germany considered necessary for her self-defense and survival. If she did not resist, Belgium was assured not only that her integrity would be restored but also that she would receive French annexations. But in case she refused to accept the German demands, the Belgians would be treated as enemies. Since the Belgians could neither be bought nor intimidated, it was as enemies and aggressors that the Germans entered Belgium on August 4.

On August 3 the German military and civilian leaders had reached a compromise on the issue of a German declaration of war against France. The military agreed to it on condition that the declaration lay the blame for the outbreak of the war on France. They offered proof that France had already opened hostilities, by means of reports on French infringements on German territory, which were then used by the foreign office as justification for the break of diplomatic relations and the beginning of the war with France. Actually, the cited incidents were either quite negligible or, as in the case of the alleged bombings of the railroad line between Nürnberg and Ingolstadt, were immediately shown to be wild rumors. To a critical neutral observer the German declaration of war was bound to appear as a mass of subterfuges and lies.

The German invasion of Belgium removed the last uncertainties about England's attitude. That she could not wish to see France defeated and Germany rule the Continent was clear to every politically thinking Englishman. But even the majority of those people who had still expected that England could guard her position independently were confounded by Germany's violation of the Belgian neutrality of which England was a guarantor. Only a hard core of convinced pacifists, who were represented by two members in the cabinet, resigned themselves to a forlorn opposition to the war. But it was Liberal opinion in particular galvanized into action that lent the British war policy its crusading drive. When on August 4 Grey directed an ultimatum to Germany to stop the military aggression against Belgium, he had his country behind him. Bethmann-Hollweg's remark to the British ambassador, that Britain would not go to war for a scrap of paper, revealed the abyss that had opened between English and German thinking. For England the guaranteed Belgian neutrality was the symbol of the legitimate order of Europe on which her own security also rested.

✍ Origins of World War I

The origins of World War I, in Woodrow Wilson's words, reach far back into history. For a century Europe had managed to avoid a general war. None of the European wars of the century after the Congress of Vienna had involved the survival of the system of relatively independent great powers, between which a good number of small states could peacefully live. In all war crises the abstention of some of the great powers was an important element in the eventual restoration of the fundamental structure of the European system. Although shifts of power had occurred, the greatest in connection with the wars of Italian and German unification, they did not destroy the European system. But the division of the great powers of Europe into permanent camps made it likely that every future conflagration would envelop all of Europe. Moreover, the political situation became more inflammable by the growth of a nationalism that left no room for the recognition of a common responsibility for

European peace. And this modern integral nationalism was a divisive force not only in Europe but also in the internal politics of individual states. The Austro-Hungarian government largely acted the way it did because it could not afford to lose the support of the German and Magyar nationalities on which the power of the monarchy rested. Similarly, Russian policy was mainly determined by the nationalism of the Russian upper classes. The czar would have put off the mobilization of the Russian army if he had not been told that in this case the nationalist elements would turn to the side of the revolutionaries.

Similarly, for the appraisal of the German policy during the July crisis the internal political conditions have to be taken into account. The alarming rise of the antimonarchical opposition as manifested by the elections of 1912 made the government more dependent on the right, which had criticized the lame official policy that had led to the isolation and encirclement of Germany. To be sure, the fear that the further debilitation of the Habsburg monarchy would gravely affect Germany's security was the dominant motive for her support of Austria-Hungary, but that it took the extreme form of readiness for war with Russia and France was also caused by the wish of the government not to arouse fresh criticism of its policy among the German nationalists. It was even hoped that the anti-Russian character of this policy would rally the Social Democratic opposition to the support of the imperial government.

Thus the policies of all the powers in July 1914 were determined by the forces which over a long period had steadily increased the internal and external tensions and heightened the danger of a general war. The gravest problem was the struggle of the nationalities in the Habsburg empire; it undermined the strength of one of the five main pillars on which the relative stability of the European order had depended during the nineteenth century. The collapse of the position of the Turkish empire in Europe and the ensuing rise of the Christian nations of the Balkans intensified the threat to European peace in southeastern Europe. While these were the underlying historic causes of the first World War, it is painful to observe how little the diplomats proved able to rise above the situation, which it should not have been impossible to diagnose correctly in 1914. The heedlessness of the Austro-Hungarian statesmen was astounding, and Russian policy did not show any circumspection either. Still, a heavy responsibility for the outbreak of the war rested with the German government.

Although Germany's policy under William II contributed to the strains on the European system probably more than that of any other power, she had always rejected the use of war. Undoubtedly, William II liked to rattle the sword, but he had always shied away from the idea of a real test. As late as 1912–13 the German government fully cooperated with Britain in keeping the Balkan conflicts from enveloping the major powers of Europe. In July 1914 the German government initially did not expect that Austria-Hungary's firm action against Serbia was likely to lead to a general war, although it was not unaware that it entailed very serious risks. When it quickly became evident that these risks were real and implied war with Russia and France, Bethmann-Hollweg, convinced of Germany's superiority and counting on the neutrality of England, accepted them unflinchingly. Doubts about the British attitude, which caused a brief wavering in the chancellor's policy of unlimited support for Austria's war policy against Serbia, were brief and ineffective. Moreover they came too late to change the course of events, because Russia's mobilization gave the German military leaders the excuse for insisting on the early opening of war against Russia, Belgium, and France. During the whole crisis prior to August 4, 1914, not a single constructive move was made by Germany to stave off the impending disaster.

The shortcomings of the German governmental system were glaringly exposed in the exaggerated part that the army played in the final political decisions. It was serious enough that the "Schlieffen plan" hung like a millstone around the neck of the government, saddling Germany with the guilt of violating Belgian neutrality in the case of war. But the army made things even worse by its insistence on the precipitate declaration of war on Russia as well as by the deplorable form of the ultimatum presented to Belgium and the declaration of war on France, for which the general staff was largely to blame. The utter lack of perceptiveness in appraising the reactions of world opinion shown by the German generals added to the strength that Germany's enemies were able to marshal in the following years.

It is true, however, that the civilian government, particularly the chancellor and the members of the foreign office, did not display a much better grasp of the imponderables of international politics. As a matter of fact, they even failed to deal competently with the ponderable political factors. In October 1916 Bethmann-Hollweg rightly traced the mistakes of German policy to the exaggerated view most Germans, impressed by Germany's amazing growth during the preceding twenty years, took of their nation's strength. And he hinted that this involved not only a faulty judgment on the ratio of power among nations but also a failure to appreciate the sentiments of foreign nations. The German government of 1914 reflected both the lack of political realism and the isolation of national thinking which dominated the ruling and the educated classes of the country.

✐ *National Unity*

IN ALL THE BELLIGERENT COUNTRIES the outbreak of World War I led to national unity among classes and parties. National loyalties proved to be far stronger than any supernational or universal ideals. Even parties which had been locked in bitter battle with their national governments were ready to turn from opposition to cooperation in the defense of the national state against foreign danger. And to every nation the beginning war was a war of defense. In the days after July 25 the German Social Democratic party held large street demonstrations against war. But by July 30 it had become clear that war was imminent and that if the Social Democratic party was going to oppose the war, it could do so only illegally, since together with the proclamation of the "state of imminent war danger," a "state of siege" would be declared which would give the military commanders unlimited power to suppress any move likely to interfere with the untrammeled conduct of the war. Obviously all the party organizations would be destroyed, and, to a much larger extent than in the years of Bismarck's antisocialist law, the Socialist leaders would lose the means of influencing the masses. In addition, far from evincing any inclination to revolt against the government, the great majority of the German workers appeared to share in the general patriotic reaction.

Never in its history had the party denied that the working class ought to participate fully in the defense of its country. Marx and Engels had impressed on their German followers the particular obligation not only of keeping czarist Russia from overrunning Central Europe but also of using a war with Russia for overthrowing the eastern autocracy. It could be followed from such premises that the position that the Social Democratic party had built up in Germany should not be lightly abandoned by an attempted sabotage of the German war effort. Out of the mixture of these considerations, but chiefly driven by the feeling that the working class movement could not possibly be steered into a conflict with its own people, the great majority of the Social Democratic leaders decided to support the German war effort. On July 30 the executive committee of the party had sent Hermann Müller, the foreign policy expert of the party, to Paris and Brussels chiefly in order to explore the possibilities of a common opposition of German and French socialists against the war. But Müller's mission was a futile gesture, since he could not commit the German party to any definite course of action. The French socialists on their part, even if Jean Jaurès had not been felled by an assassin on July 31, would not have been able to start a substantial antiwar movement after the German invasion of Belgium and the declaration of war on France.

The leaders of the German trade unions were the first Social Democrats who resolved to cooperate with the government during the war. After receiving informal assurances that the government would not take any repressive action against the unions, provided they would not impede the war effort, the trade unions, on August 2, called off all labor strikes then in progress. On the following day the party's delegation in the *Reichstag* held its caucus in preparation for the meeting of the federal parliament of August 4. One quarter of the members of this delegation were trade union officials, who presumably formed the bulk of the group of twenty to thirty men who were ready to break the party discipline if the delegation's decision ran against them. But this concern proved unnecessary. The great majority were in favor of supporting the government and taking its place beside the other parties in the national war effort. Only fourteen members, among them one of the two party chairmen, Hugo Haase (1863–1919), fought against this course, but being isolated in the party caucus they agreed to maintain the outward party unity. Haase even agreed to act as the speaker for the party at the parliament's session.

The Social Democratic statement, mentioning the endeavors of all the socialist parties against the imperialist policies that led to war, emphasized that theirs was not a vote for or against war but a decision in favor of the defense of the country threatened by hostile invasions. "In the hour of peril we shall not leave the fatherland in the lurch." This ringing declaration was followed by the rather tame pronouncement that the party called for the conclusion of a peace, "which makes friendship with the neighboring peoples possible, as soon as the aim of security will be achieved and the adversaries will be inclined to make peace." Actually this pronouncement, with the vague term "security," replaced an original paragraph in which the party warned that it would oppose any attempt to turn the war into one of conquest. But Conservative parliamentarians angrily objected to this warning and threatened to take issue with it from the floor, thus treating the public to the spectacle of German disunity. The Social Democrats thereafter substituted the cited version, thereby sacrificing practically the last political reservation they had intended to uphold. But the urge for national unity swept even valid political considerations aside.

On August 4 William II addressed the members of the *Reichstag* describing the war as imposed by Germany's enemies. He appealed for the utmost cooperation of the members of all classes, parties, and churches and affirmed: "I do not know parties any longer, I know only Germans." It was a promise that the government would not treat any of the parties as being outside the pale, as it had done particularly with the Social Democratic party. Therefore it was logical to conclude from the imperial speech that the government would put an end to any discrimination based on disabilities which existed on account of religion and social status. In the afternoon Bethmann-Hollweg presented to the *Reichstag* a description of the origins of the war, without, however, giving a clear picture of the actual sequence of events, and quickly rushed to the conclusion that Germany was the mere victim of plotting enemies. Neither the chancellor's speech nor the highly selective white book of documents concerning the origins of the war published by the foreign office on the eve of the *Reichstag* meeting contained more than the most cursory reference to the crucial exchanges which had taken place between Berlin and Vienna since July 5. But practically everybody in Germany was convinced of the guilt of the other side and was prepared to forgo any discussion of details.

Nor was any exception taken to the chancellor's statements regarding Germany's violation of Belgian neutrality. Though frankly admitting that the German invasion was a breach of international law, he clumsily added that the Germans had been forced to anticipate a French march into Belgium. He promised, however, that once Germany had reached her military objective she would make reparations to Belgium for the present "injustice." This announcement was a last desperate attempt to keep England from entering the war and was well received by the *Reichstag*. After the British entrance into the war Bethmann-Hollweg's admission of Germany's guilt, as we shall see, was to draw much criticism. The parliamentary session that followed the chancellor's speech passed unanimously a credit of 5 billion marks (ca. $1.2 billion). It was on this occasion that Hugo Haase read the Social Democratic declaration in support of the war effort, which was greeted with lively applause. In addition a law was passed that empowered the Federal Council to pass laws and ordinances regulating the German economy. Although the *Reichstag* reserved the right of later review, an enormous authority was thus granted the government in addition to the dictatorial powers it had acquired by the proclamation of the "state of siege." The latter law, issued in 1869, gave the government, under the suspension of a good many civil rights, the power to take all measures considered necessary for the internal security of the Empire, including the full control of all associations and meetings and the complete censorship of all publications. The law of 1851 had laid the exercise of this power in the hands of the military commanders of the corps areas into which Germany was divided.

It was amazing that the *Reichstag* was willing to leave this tremendous authority to a government that, as we have seen, had not enjoyed high respect in any party, without at least setting up a permanent committee through which the parties could, if not criticize, at least advise the government. Understandably the Conservatives did not feel the need for such an institution. They had enough channels through which they could communicate their opinions to the government, and with the growing role of the military in wartime their influence was likely to increase. But not only the Social Democrats but also the Progressives and the Center, and perhaps even the National Liberals, had an interest in formal parliamentary links. But all parties were anxious to avoid the impression that they intended to carry forward the struggle for greater control of the government by parliament. *Burgfriede,* that is, the internal peace kept by the defenders of a castle under siege, became the general watchword. In its practical application to the Germany of 1914 it meant a complete truce among the political parties as well as between the parties and the government.

There was great popular rejoicing in Germany over the unity of the people. Many felt that through the establishment of this popular unity the founding of the Empire by Bismarck had only now been brought to its ultimate conclusion. Actually the internal differences among classes and parties were not overcome but only adjourned in view of a common foreign danger, and as long as this harmony would not be used to settle the basic internal conflicts through mutual political concessions, it was likely to vanish. Naturally such solutions could not be found overnight, and it is not surprising that no fundamental changes were seriously contemplated at a moment when everybody thought of the war as another nineteenth-century war of relatively short duration.

✍ *Offensive in the West*

THE GERMAN MILITARY MOBILIZATION in August 1914 worked like clockwork, and the great operation against France began with impressive successes. After Liège had finally fallen on August 7, the advance of the strong German armies through Belgium was rapid. On August 18 the armies that were expected to achieve the encirclement of the enemy were ready to start the decisive stage of their campaign—the first, second, and third armies approaching from opposite a line running from Brussels through Namur to Givet, the fourth and fifth armies from opposite a line extending from Givet to Verdun. The French, as had been expected, had broken into Upper Alsace, but beginning on August 20 troops of the sixth and seventh armies, under the command of Crown Prince Rupprecht of Bavaria, drove the French army, which had crossed the frontier, from Lorraine. However, the German advance came to a standstill at the French frontier fortifications. The French had planned their chief offensive thrust against the center of the German front north of Metz, which they suspected to be weak. But the German fourth and fifth armies defeated the French offensive on August 22–25 in hard fighting at Neufchâteau and Longwy.

In the same days the northern German armies advanced steadily toward and into northern France. On August 22–23 they defeated the French at Namur and the English at Mons. Thus by August 25, when the fortress of Namur capitulated, the German armies everywhere along the front had shown themselves masters on the battlefields. Impressed by the continuous victory reports, Moltke believed that the final success of the campaign was now within reach. He did not hesitate to order two army corps on the right wing dispatched to East Prussia, from where grim reports had been received. Nor did he cancel this order when on August 27 the first encouraging news from East Prussia arrived. The German northern wing was further weakened by the detachment of troops for the surveillance of Antwerp as well as the siege of Maubeuge and other forts. The five northern German armies comprised only forty of the original fifty-two divisions. Still, fighting successfully, they persisted in their progress, wheeling toward the south. But it became clear that the German armies were no longer strong enough to envelop Paris from the west. On August 30 the first army, in order not to lose contact with the other armies to its left, directed its march in pursuit of the retreating French toward Paris, and on September 2 toward points east of the city.

On the same day Moltke issued the order that the five northern German armies should press the French armies to the southeast, while the sixth and seventh armies were to launch a breakthrough over the upper Moselle between Épinal and Toul. His ultimate aim was the complete encirclement of the French army. But the breakthrough over the Moselle was not likely to be successful in view of the French fortifications, and Moltke would have done better to shift as many forces as possible from the two southern to the five northern armies. By September 4 the latter were assembled along a southward-looking front of 125 miles, reaching from Meaux, 25 miles east of Paris, to a point southwest of Verdun. But the western German flank was now open to French attacks. The French commander, General Joffre, while bringing up additional troops, waited until September 6, when with fifty-two divisions he opened a general offensive against the whole German front held by forty divisions. A new French army, the sixth, under General Maunoury, attempted to outflank the right wing of the German lines formed by the German first army.

✍ Battle of the Marne

WITH REMARKABLE SPEED the first army, which had already crossed the Marne, turned around and engaged the French sixth army in a fierce battle that after three days of fighting practically established German superiority. But by swinging north the first army had opened a gap thirty miles wide between itself and the second German army to the left, a gap that was only superficially screened by cavalry. The British cautiously advanced between the two armies. Thus the German positions became somewhat precarious, although it will probably forever remain controversial whether they were seriously endangered. Moltke had directed the whole campaign from headquarters that were too far behind the fast moving German front lines and did not allow him a clear picture of the events. Until the first days of September he had given undue weight to the optimistic reports of the armies, whose speedy progress was no doubt gratifying. But in spite of heavy French casualties the number of French and English prisoners of war was relatively small, and the retreat of the Allied forces was on the whole an orderly one. In addition, Joffre was able to bring reserves up from the south and managed to shift troops from the Lorraine front to his left wing. Not only had Moltke, as mentioned before, taken two army corps from his right wing and sent them to the Russian front, but he conspicuously failed to transfer troops from Lorraine to his exposed right wing.

After September 4 Moltke began to become deeply worried about the military situation and sent a member of his staff, Lieutenant Colonel Hentsch (1869–1918), to the front. His ill-informed description of the conditions of the first army, together with reports about the flanking movement of the British, induced the commander of the second army to retreat on September 8. The commander and the chief of staff of the first army most reluctantly bowed to Hentsch's entreaties and ordered the retreat of their army from the Marne. When in the evening of September 9 Foch's ninth army began to attack, the retreat of the Germans was already fully under way. But the next days grew critical. The rest of the northern front had actually held its own against the French offensive. Yet Moltke, who had finally come to the front himself, concerned about a possible French breakthrough between the second and third armies, ordered the withdrawal of the northeastern German armies as well. By September 15 the German lines had been stabilized again. In the nick of time it proved possible to close the gap between the first and second armies with troops that had just brought the siege of Maubeuge to a successful conclusion and with others that at long last arrived from Lorraine. General von Moltke, who apparently in his innermost heart had never fully believed in the Schlieffen plan, at the moment of its ultimate failure suffered a nervous and physical breakdown. On September 14 he was replaced by General Erich von Falkenhayn.

Many German military writers have taken the view that the battle of the Marne was lost by Moltke's fumbling. While this is correct with regard to the operations between September 4 and 15, it does not follow that the Schlieffen plan would ever have succeeded in its supreme aim, the virtual annihilation of the French army through encirclement. Even if the German troops had not retreated, they could not have gained that strategically decisive victory. Their own casualties had been heavy, and after five weeks of continuous marching they were approaching the limit of their endurance. The numerical superiority of the French was growing, and the Germans could not have afforded to push much farther to the south with the big fortress of Paris in the rear. Thus, the Schlieffen plan had been a failure.

✐ The Russian Front

MEANWHILE THE BALANCE SHEET of fighting along the Russian front, too, showed no decisive strategic victory. The Russians intended to direct their first major thrust against Austria-Hungary and postpone their big offensive against Berlin to the time when their Asiatic divisions would be fully assembled. But the Russian commander in chief, Grand Duke Nicholas, in order to relieve the French, sent the substantial might of twenty-eight divisions to invade East Prussia from the east and south. The German commander, General von Prittwitz-Gaffron, temporarily thought of withdrawing behind the Vistula, and this momentary hesitation cost him his command. On August 23, 1914, Colonel-General Paul von Hindenburg (1847–1934), who was called into service from retirement, assumed command, and Colonel Erich Ludendorff (1854–1937) was appointed his chief of staff.

The new men decided to attack at once. Leaving only a small shielding force in front of the eastern Russian Njemen army, they led 166,000 men against the 200,000 men of the southern Narew army. From August 26 to 31 they directed in a truly masterly fashion the battle of Tannenberg, which from the outset was conceived as a battle of encirclement. Here, in the smaller dimensions of terrain and army size, Schlieffen's ideal was for once realized. Ninety-two thousand Russians were made prisoners of war, and altogether three fifths of the Narew army were annihilated, while the German losses were only moderate. The battle of the Masurian lakes of September 9–10 fought against the Njemen army did not produce equally great results, since the main body of the Russian army withdrew when threatened by a German flanking movement. By mid-September East Prussia was again fully in German hands.

Yet by then disaster had struck at the Austro-Russian front. No formal military convention had ever been concluded between Germany and Austria-Hungary, nor had the two allies worked out a common war plan. The Austrians were not even given general information on the Schlieffen plan, since the German general staff was rightly afraid that secrets were not too well kept in Vienna. All Count Conrad, the Austrian chief of staff, knew was that the Germans intended to concentrate most of their forces in the west for a big offensive against France and would not intervene in the eastern war until they had defeated the French. Moltke had indicated to Count Conrad as an approximate date the sixtieth day of mobilization. When Conrad urged that the Germans should assist him to the extent of using ten divisions to open an offensive against the Narew line in order to tie down one Russian army, while the Austrians would engage the Russians in Galicia, he had received a rather indefinite promise from Moltke. As a matter of fact, the feasibility of such an offensive depended largely on the Russian buildup in East Prussia and Poland. Besides, the moving of large masses of German troops to the eastern theater of war hinged upon the defeat of France, which did not occur. Only a limited number of German troops could be transferred to the east after the end of September 1914. But by then the Austro-Hungarian army found itself in dire straits.

Count Conrad von Hötzendorf was a soldier of high professional accomplishment and lively imagination. But his patriotism and courage often made him exalt the military capacity of the Habsburg empire and underrate the stubborn realities of the outside world. Thus for many precious days he tenaciously stuck to the belief that he could strike down Serbia before Russia would intervene. For that reason he had mobilized one half of the Austro-Hungarian army on July 25 and continued their deployment at the southern frontier even after it had become clear that Rumania would not fight on the side of the Central Powers and that Russia was building up vastly superior armies opposite Galicia. The mobilization of the other half of the Austro-Hungarian army destined for Galicia started late, while the transfer of the divisions moving south was delayed. Moreover, since the majority of the troops by then had been committed to operations against Serbia, only two of the five armies were immediately redirected to the east. Soon the necessity became inevitable of the withdrawal of a third army that arrived only in parts before the beaten Austro-Hungarian armies flooded back toward the Carpathians.

In spite of the loss of time in the beginning of August, Conrad decided on the offensive in the east. Although he felt with some bitterness that the Austro-Hungarian army was now condemned to act as a mere rear guard for Germany and to fight a war with the western powers in which Austria-Hungary had no direct concern, he was eager to win laurels with his army before the Germans would turn to the east. Assuming that the Russians were still in the assembly stage, he attacked but after initial successes suffered a serious setback in the first battle of Lemberg (Lwov) of August 29–31. Actually the Russians had mounted their offensive simultaneously with the Austrian assault, and with their considerable numerical superiority they inflicted upon their enemy a most grievous defeat in the second battle of Lemberg of September 5–13. The Austro-Hungarian army lost 300,000 in dead, wounded, and prisoners. The loss of officers was particularly grave, and no future Austrian army attained the excellence of the army of 1914. As a consequence of the Russian victory the Austrians had to retire to the high passes of the Carpathian mountains, leaving East Galicia and Bukovina in Russian hands.

✍ Falkenhayn, Chief of Staff

ALTHOUGH, together with the German victories in East Prussia, the Austrian sacrifice had made it impossible for Grand Duke Nicholas to stage his projected offensive against Berlin, the battle of the Marne and the Austrian defeat in Galicia placed enormous burdens on the new German chief of staff. Unlike his predecessor, Falkenhayn was not easily deterred by big tasks. For some time he even remained minister of war. But his willingness to make decisions was not matched by an incisive and bold mind. Not sure enough of his best insights to act upon them with the utmost determination, he fell back on more conventional military solutions, to which he then clung with cold tenacity. Whereas later in the Rumanian campaign of 1917 Falkenhayn proved to be an eminent field commander, he did not possess the gifts needed by a supreme commander.

After the battle of the Marne both sides tried to regain mobility by outflanking the enemy from the north. There began a race toward the sea, but even along this extended front the two armies dug in at once. Attempts to smash the new lines by frontal attacks proved extremely costly and futile. The greatest battle of these weeks was fought at the Yser from October 17 to 30. Here the German high command hurled into battle new divisions consisting largely of war volunteers who had undergone no more than two months of military training and were led by old, second-rate officers. The bravery of these troops, born out of high idealistic patriotism, was extraordinary, but at the same time they suffered grievous losses. Large numbers of the finest young men, out of whose ranks the future officers, let alone future peacetime leaders, would have come, fell on the fields of Flanders in vain. When victory seemed at hand, the Belgians opened their dikes and flooded large sections of the coastal region. Although Falkenhayn continued the attack at Ypres, he became convinced by November 3 that a decisive victory could not be won in the west but should be sought in the east.

On the eastern front, after the battle of Lemberg and the liberation of East Prussia, the major German forces had been shifted to the south and linked up with the Austrian lines in West Galicia and southern Poland. In October the Austrian and German armies advanced to the Vistula as far as Warsaw and Ivangorod. But in the last days of the month the buildup of overwhelming Russian strength forced their rapid, if orderly, retreat from Poland. The Russian forces were able to occupy southern Poland, and they approached Upper Silesia. In a bold and well-executed maneuver Hindenburg transferred the bulk of his troops to the north, to Posen and West Prussia, from where he planned to strike against the lightly protected northern flank and rear of the Russian armies. Provided he received additional troops from the west, Hindenburg felt confident that the forty-five Russian corps could be completely annihilated. Falkenhayn agreed that by now the decision had to be sought in the east and promised the German eastern command six army corps, which were to give the intended blow the necessary momentum.

But the great opportunity was missed. Falkenhayn was afraid that a limited local tactical withdrawal, which would have made the immediate dispatch of the troops to the east possible, might be interpreted as German weakness. He even wished to remove the threat that in his opinion the British position at Ypres posed to the German defensive lines. Thus he launched the costly reserves into the bloody battle of Ypres, in which nothing was achieved and only the most cruel losses were suffered. When on November 18 Falkenhayn broke off the battle, all he could do was slowly pull out his fatigued troops and send them piecemeal to the east, where the moment for decisive action had long since passed. In Poland, merely local successes could be won. Visibly shaken, Falkenhayn reached the conclusion that Germany could not hope to achieve a real decision as long as her army had to fight simultaneously against England, France, and Russia. He requested the chancellor to make a separate peace with one of these powers, a request, as we shall see later, difficult to fulfill. From then on Falkenhayn thought that Germany's enemies could at best be exhausted by a war of attrition.

The War in 1915

AFTER FOUR MONTHS of fighting, a precarious balance had been reached. In spite of tremendous efforts and so far unheard-of sacrifices the strategic stalemate was not broken for almost four years and then only by the intervention of the United States, a non-European power. At the beginning of the year 1915 ninety German divisions faced 108.5 Allied divisions in the west, while in the east 33 German divisions and 45.5 Austro-Hungarian divisions opposed 93.5 Russian divisions. It was perhaps understandable that Falkenhayn hesitated to give up large forces to the east, a step that would have permitted the great offensive proposed by Hindenburg and Conrad. Rolling up both the northern and southern Russian flanks the two men wished to push far into the rear of the Russian army for the final annihilation of Russia's military power. The German armies in France carried an enormous burden. Already the offensives which the Allies had begun in the winter battle of the Champagne late in December 1914, and resumed in February and March 1915, employed heavy arms to a much larger extent than had been done at the beginning of the war, and with each new offensive the use of matériel multiplied many times until 1918. Although the German troops suffered great losses in the Champagne, they inflicted even more serious ones on the French. Here as well as against the heavy attacks which the British started in March in Artois, the German armies, with only insignificant concessions of terrain, stood their ground.

More fully convinced that the western front could be held against an enemy superior in numbers and arms, Falkenhayn was willing to send as many divisions to the east as in his opinion were needed to break the offensive strength of the Russians. Hindenburg had succeeded in freeing East Prussia from the newly invading Russians. In the winter battle of the Masurian lakes of February 7–27, which was won by the German soldiers even more against the climate than against the enemy, another Russian army was annihilated, but an advance beyond the frontier proved impossible. In the last week of January, Austrian and German troops tackled the extremely difficult and slow task of dislodging the Russians from the passes and ridges of the Carpathians, from where they were in a position to pour into the Hungarian plains. After some progress had been made in weeks of fighting, the exhaustion of the troops in April brought a standstill that made the future look uncertain.

In order to relieve the critical situation of the Carpathian front the German-Austrian offensive was opened in Western Galicia. A new German army was formed under Field Marshal August von Mackensen (1849–1945) with Colonel Hans von Seeckt (1866–1936) as chief of staff. In conjunction with the Austrian army it broke the Russian front between Tarnow and Gorlice on May 2–5, and after the neighboring armies to the north and south had joined in the offensive, the whole Carpathian front was shattered. A long series of victories and advances followed throughout the summer. At the end of September all of Poland and Lithuania as well as half of Latvia had been conquered and Galicia, except for a small strip of East Galicia, liberated. The front ran from the Gulf of Riga along the Düna river to Dünaburg and from there straight south to Pinsk, Dubno, and the confluence of the Sereth and Dniester rivers about thirty-five miles from the Rumanian frontier. The Russian losses were estimated at more than two million men. Both in the army and among the people the confidence in the Russian leadership was badly shaken, and the czar was persuaded to assume the high command in place of Grand Duke Nicholas. But strong Russian armies still remained in the field, and Falkenhayn was overoptimistic in assuming that Russia's capacity for effective military cooperation with the Western allies had been definitely crippled.

✍ Italy, Bulgaria, and Turkey in the War

WHILE ALL THESE MILITARY GAINS in the east had been made, fighting, though not of maximum intensity, had not only continued in France but a new front had to be held in Italy. In the secret treaty of London of April 26, 1915, the Allied powers had paid an extraordinary price in order to gain Italy's entry into the war. These excessive promises of future territorial gains were to become some of the worst encumbrances for the creation of sound peace conditions after the war. On the other hand, Italy's participation in the war failed to tip the balance, as the Allies had hoped. The Austrians contained the four offensives which the Italians launched along the Isonzo river from June to December 1915. The Croatian troops fought their national enemies, the Italians, with greater determination than the Slav enemies of the Austro-Hungarian government.

The stability of the western and Italian fronts as well as the great advance in the east encouraged Falkenhayn to undertake the subjugation of Serbia. The alliance concluded between the Central Powers and Bulgaria on September 6 secured Bulgarian cooperation. The campaign against the bravely and desperately fighting enemy began under the command of Field Marshal von Mackensen on October 6, 1915. Late in November the remaining third of the Serbian army, about 140,000 men, made its way through the Albanian mountains to the Adriatic, where it was interned on the neutralized island of Corfu. The landing of an Anglo-French army under General Sarrail in Salonika failed to bring help in time, and it was prevented by the Bulgarian army from uniting with the Serbians in Central Serbia. After the conquest of Serbia Baron Conrad wanted the Germans to move against Sarrail's army, and Austro-Hungarian troops against Montenegro and Albania. Falkenhayn, though not altogether opposed to the offensive against Salonika, became annoyed when Conrad launched operations against Montenegro and Albania on his own and broke off relations with him. After the Austrians had occupied Montenegro and the greater part of Albania, the war on the Balkans became one of attrition. The Bulgarians faced the Anglo-French army along the Macedonian frontier of Serbia and Greece.

Bulgaria's accession to the Central Powers and the conquest of Serbia established a firm bridge to Turkey. On August 2, 1914, Germany had concluded an alliance with Turkey, and in October 1914 the latter had joined in the war. The main link between Russia and her Western allies was thus blocked. Since Russian industries were inadequate to provide the large Russian armies with all the implements of modern warfare, the cutting of the main supply line from the west weakened the military value of the east-west alliance. Winston Churchill's idea of gaining control of the Straits was good strategy, and the execution of such a plan was by no means utopian. The Gallipoli expedition started as a combined Anglo-French enterprise in February 1915 with naval bombardments and in April was followed by the landing of troops. But the job that would have required the closest coordination between the Allies as well as between armies and navies was badly bungled and finally had to be abandoned at the turn of the year. Thus Russia's isolation was not broken.

✍ *Battle of Verdun*

WHILE THE SERBIAN CAMPAIGN was proceeding, the French and British again resumed their spring offensives in the Champagne and in Artois on a much larger scale on September 25, 1915. In spite of a 5 to 3 ratio of strength and a lavish artillery buildup no breakthrough was achieved, and, with only a minimal gain of terrain, the Allies suffered dreadful losses. It was another frightful demonstration of the great superiority of the defense over the offensive at this stage of military history. Yet Falkenhayn reached the conclusion that he would have to adopt similar tactics if he wanted to overcome the stalemate in the west, where, according to his judgment, after Russia's power had been reduced, the next major decision would have to be sought. In order to undermine England's ability to support her French ally he demanded the opening of unlimited submarine warfare against her. Simultaneously, in an effort to make France willing to talk peace, the German army was to force the latter to expend her last reserves in men and arms. The emperor, assenting to the chancellor, rejected the unlimited submarine warfare while accepting Falkenhayn's project of a Verdun offensive.

Verdun was chosen because the strong fortress was the cornerstone on which the whole French front was anchored. To be sure, a defender might readily leave open field positions to an attacking enemy, who then might have to go through all the long and costly stages of such an attack against the defender entrenched only a mile to the rear. But in Verdun every inch would have to be defended by every means at France's disposal. On the other hand, the greater strength that a fortress possessed compared to field positions could be minimized by heavy guns.

The Germans unleashed their attack on February 21, 1916. The early German successes, particularly the capture of Fort Douaumont of ghastly fame, caused a temporary crisis in the French defense, but the German progress was very quickly stalled, and the fighting became a grim endurance test on a narrow battlefield transformed by rain into a grenade-pocketed quagmire. Hecatomb after hecatomb fell to the ground. The heroism of the German and French front soldiers in the "hell of Verdun" was superhuman and defied the dreadful effects of the massed weapons of destruction which modern man had invented. Falkenhayn refused to end the macabre battle, because he insisted that France would have to be bled white at Verdun. Thus he waited till July before giving the order to go on the defensive.

It was high time to bring the offensive to a close, since in the last week of June the British and French, using fifty-two divisions, started an offensive on a front of less than thirty miles north and south of the Somme river. Never before had such a concentration of manpower and firepower, for the first time accompanied by systematic air bombing of the rear, been seen or such enormous losses been suffered. But again the German lines did not snap. After two months of gruesome battle twelve miles of the German front had been pressed back less than six miles. However, grave concern was felt in German headquarters because many of the German western reserves had gone to the east, where a near catastrophe had occurred in June.

✍ *Rumania's Entrance into the War*

THE RUSSIANS under General Brusilov had launched a forceful offensive in Volhynia against the two Austro-Hungarian armies holding the southern end of the eastern front. While some signs of defection among the non-German and non-Magyar nationals of the Habsburg empire had already been noticeable before in the Carpathian fighting during the winter, some troops, chiefly Czech units, this time refused to put up a fight at all. Wide gaps were torn into the Austrian lines, and the Russians occupied the Bukovina with its capital Czernowitz on June 16, 1916. Hurriedly twelve Austrian divisions had to be brought from the Italian front, where Baron Conrad was just conducting a promising offensive. But twenty additional German divisions were needed for stabilizing the front. In terms of prisoners of war, General A. Brusilov, with 200,000, won the greatest victory of the whole war. The most important consequence of the Russian success was the encouragement that the Rumanians derived from it for entering the war on the Allied side. On August 27, 1916, Rumania, having been promised by the Allies the acquisition of the Bukovina and Transylvania, declared war on Austria-Hungary.

✍ *Supreme Command of Hindenburg and Ludendorff*

THE EVENT shook William II's confidence in Falkenhayn, whom he had upheld against the criticism of the chancellor and most army leaders. Falkenhayn's imperiousness was resented by the army commanders, all of whom were older than the chief of staff. Hindenburg and Ludendorff opposed him passionately because he failed to support the total victory in the east that in their opinion was the only way to a successful ending of the war. The Verdun offensive, however, had ruined the belief in Falkenhayn's leadership also among the German commanders in the west. Bethmann-Hollweg on his part had felt that for the active conduct of its policy the government needed the backing of the people, who after the military liberation of East Prussia in the fall of 1914 idolized Hindenburg and admired Ludendorff. To the public the two men assumed the front of the stage, putting everybody else, including the emperor, in the shade.

It was not surprising that William II was afraid of the two generals. To appoint as supreme commanders the men in whom soldiers of all ranks and people of all classes rested their trust meant the virtual resignation from his rulership, of which, after the outbreak of hostilities, little had been left. The war had depressed the emperor, who looked with apprehension into the future, although again and again military successes would fire his boldest expectations. But he felt that he did not possess the capacity to assume the active role in the direction of the war that his grandfather had played in 1870–71, nor did he understand that under the conditions of the German constitution it would have been his obligation to see to it that the chancellor had an adequate voice in the formulation of German policies. Falkenhayn had at least given William II the feeling of having a part in the major decisions. But when on August 29, 1916, the emperor appointed Hindenburg chief of staff and Ludendorff quartermaster general (the traditional title of the deputy chief in the Prussian army), he well knew that from then on his assent would be a mere formality.

The change in the Supreme Command of the German army was generally acclaimed, and the way in which during the next few months the immediate crisis created by Rumania's belligerency was overcome strengthened the boundless popular confidence in the leadership of the two men in whom the people saw something like a reincarnation of William I and the elder Moltke. In a campaign that was a masterpiece of military skill, Rumania was thoroughly defeated by German, Austro-Hungarian, and Bulgarian troops. The major credit for this success must go to Falkenhayn, who led one of the two armies which forced their way into Rumania from Transylvania, and to Field Marshal von Mackensen, who managed to cross the Danube with his army from Bulgaria. On December 6 Bucarest was occupied. Thereafter only Moldavia remained in Rumanian hands. Meanwhile during September the battle at the Somme had been revived with frightful fury. Although the Allies were stopped, their superiority not only in numbers but even more in weapons became a matter of growing German concern. Their air support outdid anything the German army was able to match. In late September the Allies employed tanks for the first time. The potentialities of this new weapon, however, were not recognized by German military leaders.

✑ *Naval Warfare*

IN TWO YEARS of bitter fighting the Central Powers had failed to win a decision in the war, in spite of a good many brilliant military victories and the conquest of much enemy territory. Although no foreign armies had gained a foothold in Germany, she had been cut off from the world and was under a siege that became ever more oppressive as the war continued. The outbreak of the war had revealed the futility of Tirpitz's big battle fleet. The German naval vessels abroad were swept from the seas in the first months of the war. Only two modern cruisers in the Mediterranean were able to escape to Constantinople, where their presence was of greatest importance for the blocking of the Turkish straits. The German colonies were equally lost. Japan entered the war in order to win possession of the German colony at Kiaochow Bay, while Britain and some of her dominions began to occupy the German colonies in Africa. But compared with the blockade that the British navy opened against Germany, the capture of the German colonies was of little consequence for the outcome of the struggle. And by closing the remote exits of the North sea the British fleet remained outside striking distance of the German battle fleet. Short of a direct attack on the English east coast, which was not promising since the British fleet could have cut the lines of retreat, the German navy was not even able to force the British to accept battle.

Tirpitz, who was in favor of seeking a major naval battle, to his dismay was not in command of naval operations. These were in the hands of the naval chief of staff and the commander in chief of the battle fleet, whose advice the emperor had heeded more than that of the builder of the German navy since the outbreak of the war. It was decided to save the German fleet for the time when, after the defeat of France and Russia, England would have reason to fear a naval fight. Apart from small brushes, only one major naval engagement took place, and that was in the waters off Jutland on May 31, 1916. Here the main forces of the two navies were locked in battle. The German fleet displayed better armor and gunnery, and the British lost almost twice as much tonnage as the Germans. Still, the German fleet could not prevail against the vastly superior British fleet, and it was fortunate for it that Admiral Jellicoe was satisfied with forcing it to retreat instead of aiming at its full annihilation, which, if costly, would have been possible. In any event, the battle of Jutland did not produce any strategic result, and Admiral Scheer (1863-1928), the commander of the fleet, admitted that the German battle fleet was incapable of defeating Britain.

But Scheer now joined the chorus of naval officers who asserted that the German navy would be able to defeat the British blockade and make Britain ready to discuss peace terms if it was allowed to unloosen its submarines against British seaborne trade. The international law of warfare on the seas was not a well-defined code, and the recent development of submarines had added new problems. Depending on her navy's capacity for throttling the enemy's economic life, Britain already had shown in former wars her disregard for the freedom of the seas and the rights of neutrals. It was for this reason that she had not signed the London Convention on naval warfare of 1909, an international attempt radically to restrict the methods of maritime war for the benefit of neutrals.

On November 3, 1914, England declared the whole North sea a war zone, thereby interfering with the navigation of neutral nations. She also extended to ever greater lengths the list of goods liable to seizure because they could be used for warfare. The announcement of grain rationing by the German government in December, 1914, made England declare grain a war contraband, and in the course of 1915 new categories were constantly added. Moreover, England insisted that the neutrals should not reexport such goods to Germany and began to license neutral imports. These were all legally doubtful practices which caused strong protests from the neutrals, particularly from the United States, although not even she was ready to contemplate a rupture of relations. Thus the British blockade grew ever more effective, eventually reducing German imports of foodstuffs and strategic raw materials to a mere trickle.

As a countermeasure Tirpitz and his school of admirals proposed what could only be termed terror methods against England, namely the bombing of English cities from the air and the torpedoing of merchant vessels by German submarines. The Zeppelin attacks on England, which began in January 1915, must be called acts of plain stupidity. Germany had few Zeppelins, and they could not carry a sufficient bomb load to damage the British war production even remotely. In addition, they were highly vulnerable, and it was not too difficult to develop a defense against them. With their indiscriminate bombing of civilians the Zeppelin attacks caused a general outcry against German "frightfulness" and spurred the popular war effort. England was still far from mobilizing all her enormous resources, and it was only in 1916 that obligatory military service was introduced.

But the launching of submarine warfare without regard for the customary rules of maritime war, which did not permit the sinking of merchant ships without prior warning, visit, and search, as well as caring for the lives of passengers and crews, was equally brutal. It was also an inconsequential effort as long as Germany possessed only twenty-one small submarines. On February 4, 1915, Germany declared that two weeks later her submarines would begin to destroy every enemy merchant ship in the waters around the British Isles. She warned the neutrals against providing Allied vessels with crews, passengers, or goods and put them on guard against dangers that might befall their own ships entering the war zone, since their identity might easily be mistaken. The declaration of unrestricted submarine warfare was an attempt to cut the trade and commerce of all the neutral powers with England and her allies. It went beyond the British efforts to keep the neutrals from acting as import and production agents for Germany and dealt with the crews of Allied and neutral merchant vessels as if they were members of the enemy's fighting forces. This method, involving not only trading but also human rights, sparked passionate opposition among the neutrals, particularly in a nation as proudly conscious of its strength as the United States.

The exchange of diplomatic notes was still proceeding when the sinking of the British liner Lusitania on May 7, 1915, with a loss of 1,200 lives, among them 139 Americans, caused an outbreak of popular anti-German feeling in America which made the danger of war acute. The circumspection of the American government overcame the crisis, though only after the German government had promised to give up unrestricted submarine warfare. Bethmann-Hollweg achieved this decision in bitter struggles with the chiefs of the German navy, who thereafter angrily confined all submarine operations against merchant vessels to the Mediterranean.

But Tirpitz, supported by the chief of the naval staff, Holtzendorff (1853–1919), continued his advocacy of unrestricted submarine warfare, irrespective of the fact that it was likely to bring the United States into the war. He did not hesitate to mobilize public support for his naval ideas by turning to the political parties and prominent figures of German big business and industry. Tirpitz, who had always shown an unusual talent for the manipulation of public opinion, by employing it now for undermining the position of the chancellor, proved that his nationalism was outweighing his monarchist loyalty. The admirals saw their chances improve when at the turn of 1915–16 General von Falkenhayn accepted their pleas and, as mentioned before, demanded the resumption of unrestricted submarine warfare as a parallel action to the projected Verdun offensive. Once more, however, the chancellor succeeded in convincing the emperor of the extreme dangers of this course. Tirpitz resigned from his office. But the fight was not fully won by the chancellor, and he gave in when, on Falkenhayn's urging, it was decided in April 1916 to step up the submarine war to the extent that submarine commanders would be allowed to torpedo armed enemy merchant ships without warning.

This action was bound to produce new troubles. The sinking of the unarmed French channel boat, Sussex, in April 1916, which resulted in the loss of eighty lives, among them a good many Americans, evoked an

American ultimatum. Although the German government had to beat a retreat, Bethmann-Hollweg made a dangerous concession to his internal foes by promising them to prepare the ground for the eventual adoption of unrestricted submarine warfare. In its reply to the American ultimatum the German government reserved the right to resume unrestricted submarine warfare unless American pressure would lead to a modification of the British blockade practices. Actually the chancellor did not believe that England would budge under such a pressure but rather thought that a rebuff of England would make it difficult for the United States to go to war against Germany. Naturally, the American government refused to make the protection of the rights of American citizens dependent on other than the inherent reasons of the case. Yet Bethmann-Hollweg's opposition to unrestricted submarine warfare had already become less persuasive when Hindenburg and Ludendorff, after assuming command of the German army, renewed their demand for its final adoption. The two generals knew that as long as they were not given greatly increased forces the war could not be won by the army. Therefore even after the successful conclusion of the Rumanian campaign they abstained from planning any large offensive operations for 1917. They concentrated on programs that would yield additional soldiers and arms or, as in the case of submarine war, promised to bring a victorious end of the war in sight. For although Hindenburg and Ludendorff admitted the temporary impasse of the fighting on land, they believed that the war would lead to the decisive defeat of Germany's enemies and a peace that would establish her preponderance in Europe forever.

∽ German Imperialist War Aims

IN THE FIRST DAYS of August 1914 the German people had gone to war deeply convinced that it was fighting a war forced upon Germany by the enemy powers, against which she had not entertained any ideas of conquest. In their original declarations both the emperor and the chancellor had emphatically stressed the defensive nature of the war. But once it had started, the attitude of large groups, presumably even the majority of the people, changed quickly. For decades the Germans had been told that Germany was destined to become a world power but could not hope to survive as a great nation unless she faced up boldly to this destiny. The regime of William II had always found its strongest popular support for its naval and colonial policies. It was not surprising that the advocates of German imperialism saw in the war the final test of Germany's rise to the rank of a world power. And, with nationalist instincts aroused, the agitation of the chauvinists found an eager popular response. The question was whether Germany could hope to make any annexations without gaining total victory over the grand alliance of great powers arrayed against her, a victory unlikely to be achieved by military means only. Military operations would have to be matched by policies that aimed at breaking the hostile ring. But any program of annexations was tying the hands of German diplomacy and thus constituted an outright danger for the direction of German war strategy and policy. Yet there was an outpouring of popular demand for acquisitions in Western and Eastern Europe as well as in Africa and other parts of the world. All these schemes rested on the assumption that military victory would be complete, and nowhere was an effort made to pay proper attention to the rightful interests of the other European nations.

The most active group of propagandists was composed of university professors, among them chiefly economists and historians. The German professors, as will be remembered, had played a prominent role in the formation of a national sentiment in the age of German unification. Yet although in the writings and speeches of a good many of them chauvinistic overtones could be discerned, even Heinrich von Treitschke, the least inhibited advocate of power politics of that generation, was still very much aware of the greatness of Europe's multinational tradition, which he wished to see preserved. In contrast, the German professors of 1914 had forgotten their obligation to the European cultural tradition and with their appeal to popular vanity and passion tended to disregard their foremost duty, the spread of knowledge.

The professors agitating for annexations failed to notice that actually they were becoming largely the front men of more powerful people who identified the national interest with the aggrandizement of their own business. The leaders of industry and banking used their great influence with the government and their wealth for organizing systematic private and public campaigns in order to win wide popular support for a "*Siegfriede*," a peace dictated after military victory. And most of the politically inexperienced and irresponsible industrialists saw the ideal war and peace aims in the fantastic program of the Pan-German League.

But the German government itself was convinced that it would achieve total military victory and was determined to exploit the defeat of the enemy by making Germany a world power. As early as September 9, 1914, Chancellor von Bethmann-Hollweg, in the expectation of early peace negotiations with France, drew up a program of war aims that within limits remained basic to his policies till the end of his chancellorship in 1917 and also to the policies of his successors until final defeat became certain a year later. The chancellor defined as the supreme goal of German war policy "the security of the German Empire in the West and in the East for any foreseeable future. To this end France has to be weakened in such a way that she cannot revive as a great power, while Russia has to be removed as much as possible from the German frontier and her domination over the non-Russian vassal peoples has to be broken." In order to achieve these results he declared his willingness to demand the cession of Belfort, of the fortified territory west of the Vosges, and of the coast from Dunkirk to Boulogne, if the military and naval authorities demanded these conquests, which of course they promptly did. He himself insisted from the outset on the German acquisition of the iron mines of the Briey basin in French Lorraine and on French reparations in rates so high as to make it impossible for France to spend considerable funds on armaments during the next eighteen to twenty years. In addition, the chancellor intended to impose a trade treaty that would make France dependent on Germany, exclude English trade, and give German companies an equal status with indigenous firms in France.

In Belgium the chancellor wanted to annex Liège, Verviers, and possibly even Antwerp. But most of all Belgium was to become a "vassal state" and an "economic province" of Germany and would have to accept German garrisons in her militarily important ports. In order to avoid the domestically insoluble difficulties of annexation, a Belgian state was to survive; it was even intended that Belgium should receive Dunkirk, Calais, and Boulogne. Luxembourg was to become a member state of the German Empire. The extension of German power to the west was expected to lay the foundation for an economic federation and customs union of Central Europe. France, Belgium, the Netherlands, Denmark, Austria-Hungary, Poland, and possibly Italy, Sweden, and Norway should be the members of the bloc expected to stabilize German economic predominance in Central Europe.

It should be noted that this program disregarded Bethmann-Hollweg's promise to restore Belgium. In addition the German chancellor now proposed to force most of the other European neutrals into a Central European system dominated by Germany. In the September 1914 document Eastern European and colonial war aims were not extensively treated, because with the expected imminent victory in the West there seemed to be no time to go into everything. Yet the broad principles were already stated. In Central Africa the building of an integrated empire reaching from the Atlantic to the Indian Ocean was envisaged. Belgian, French, and Portuguese territories were to form the bulk of this black Germany. The above-mentioned inclusion of Poland in the projected German Central Europe showed that the German government wished to throw Russia far back to the east and deprive her of all her non-Russian possessions. Immediately after the outbreak of the war various schemes had been put into operation fomenting national revolts and revolutions in all the non-Russian parts of the Russian empire.

The chancellor himself committed the German government to a peace program of far-reaching annexations. He was determined to break up the Triple Entente once and for all, and in order to achieve this goal he was prepared to replace any form of the balance of power or a concert of powers in Europe by the German domination of the Continent. What apparent reluctance there was in his attitude stemmed from domestic rather than international considerations. Still, much as his program conformed to that of the industrialists and even the Pan-Germans, he was obviously inclined to place a limit on direct annexations and rather to seek the extension of German rule by indirect methods, such as satellite governments and stiff economic controls. He seems to have had some feeling that Germany would not be capable of absorbing large groups of foreign nationalities. But this concern did not keep him from approving annexations large enough to be incompatible with the essentially national structure of the German empire. And still worse, he could even be driven to accept most sinister projects. As early as 1914 the chancellor was convinced that chiefly for military reasons Prussia's eastern frontier ought to be changed irrespective of what happened to the main part of Russian Poland. He accepted the recommendations made by the "experts" appointed by him, who suggested that Germany should take a "frontier strip" of Poland, which was defined as the Poland north of the Narew river, a region twice as large as Alsace-Lorraine. In order not to add too many Poles to the recalcitrant Polish minority in Prussia, but on the contrary to make this "strip" a barrier between the Prussian Poles and a new Polish state to the east, it was proposed to "free" the frontier strip of Poles and Jews by resettling them in the Polish state while populating the strip with Germans. It was the first time in modern European history that the uprooting and transplantation of populations was recommended as a feasible method for the solution of nationality conflicts.

Whereas it is probable that Bethmann-Hollweg would not necessarily have insisted on winning every single item on the list of expansionist war aims, he was convinced that Germany had to make sweeping gains in order to achieve preponderance in Europe. When just before the end of the Marne battle the American government offered to mediate between France and Germany if the latter was willing to accept the territorial *status quo ante* in Europe and be satisfied with receiving French colonies and reparations, Bethmann-Hollweg replied that the acceptance of American mediation would not be understood by the German people. After the defeat of France, England and Russia would have to be beaten. The war had been forced upon the German people, who had made great sacrifices and demanded "guarantees of security." This slogan of guarantees of future security justified by the Allied war guilt became the stock phrase with which the chancellor covered up his program of annexations.

Considerations of domestic politics had a part in the chancellor's annexationist program. The policy of annexations was popular in Germany. Only the Social Democratic party opposed it in all its official statements, although it did little to make this opposition effective. As a matter of fact, even a good many Social Democrats did not find fault with annexations, particularly those in the east. The most passionate champions of the *Siegfriede* were the National Liberals, although the Conservatives and the great majority of the Center were not too far behind. Yet in both the Conservative and Center parties some individuals were highly skeptical, although they did not express themselves in public. On balance, the Progressives, though favoring annexations, were less extravagant in their expectations. Strong pressure for far-reaching and even fantastic conquests came from some of the rulers of the German states. They felt that the national enthusiasm weakened the position of the German states and dynasties and desired to win the limelight by riding the crest of the nationalistic tide. King Ludwig III urged that Alsace be turned over to Bavaria and that Berlin be compensated by the Prussian annexation of Belgium. A Belgium in German hands was needed, he asserted, to give South German industries an outlet to the ocean. It was a sign of the confusion of minds caused by the events that as prudent and able a man as Crown Prince Rupprecht of Bavaria (1869–1955) agreed with his father. However, the crown prince, who from 1914 to 1918 served as army group commander at the western front, was to free himself from his illusions.

It would have been extremely difficult for Bethmann-Hollweg, even if he had been so inclined, to take a stand against annexations. But he made it impossible for himself to exercise even a moderating influence on the hotheaded debate of war aims by withholding from the German people a reasonably clear picture of the military situation. The German Supreme Command under Falkenhayn had drawn up a report on the Marne battle for the press. The chancellor, however, prohibited its publication as likely to harm Germany's prestige in Italy and Rumania, which were edging toward war on the Allied side. But it was no secret to them that the German war plans had gone awry. The limitations of the chancellor's thinking were revealed in his endeavor to shroud the fateful events in secrecy. He feared that the authority of the government would suffer by the admission of the failure of the great military campaign, and he knew quite well that popular criticism of the army was likely to reflect on the whole governmental system. Yet an uninformed German public was able to indulge in high hopes for full victory without restraint. The layman is always inclined to take the occupation of enemy territory as a sure sign of victory. The German front in France, though immobilized since September 1914, still looked good on the map, and Hindenburg's victories in East Prussia, followed in 1915 by the capture of vast territories in the east, made the hearts of the patriotic burghers beat faster. Thus the chancellor's censorship of military news contributed substantially to the rising recklessness of the chauvinistic agitation. At the same time the preservation of the myth of the never-failing excellence of German military leadership tended to weaken the chancellor's role in determining the course of German war policies.

∞ *Peace Feelers*

AS EARLY AS NOVEMBER 18, 1914, Falkenhayn, who, dejected by the failure of the battle of Ypres and the ensuing stalemate at the western front, had taken counsel with Tirpitz, informed Bethmann-Hollweg that it had become impossible for Germany to defeat the Triple Entente and that it was necessary to split off either Russia or France. The general actually believed that if Russia were removed, France, too, was likely to make peace. He proposed to offer both countries peace more or less on the basis of the *status quo ante* and thereafter to concentrate on the war against Germany's chief enemy, England. Bethmann-Hollweg told him that there was no diplomatic method for inducing the czar to make peace as long as the Russian army was unbeaten and that only strong German military successes would sufficiently impress the czar to come to terms. However, he expressed his willingness to extend peace feelers once the German military plans in the east had borne some fruit.

Russia, no doubt, offered better chances than the other Allied countries for separate peace negotiations, and it is true that such negotiations presupposed the concentration of German military efforts in the east. But even in the case of great Russian reverses it was unlikely that negotiations would develop unless, from the beginning, Russia was offered a peace on the basis of the *status quo ante*. Yet the chancellor always hoped to retain at least the "frontier strip" of Poland and in addition to secure important trade concessions. These reservations of the German government were a definite handicap to all the approaches which were made to the czar in 1915, although nobody can say that they were the chief reason for their failure. After all, the czar could be expected to take such an extraordinary step only if driven to extremes, and great as the German military successes were in 1915, they fell short of convincing him that the war was lost. Moreover, to allow the Germans to defeat France and England would ultimately have left Russia at the mercy of Germany, irrespective of the terms of an earlier Russo-German peace.

Although there were no decisive German victories over Russia in 1915, the czar's refusal to enter into separate peace negotiations in early August 1915 induced Bethmann-Hollweg to return to his original program of reducing Russia to the lands she owned before the conquests of Peter the Great; after the occupation of Poland he declared in public that Germany would not be satisfied with the restoration of the *status quo ante* and hinted at the separation of Poland, Lithuania, and Courland from Russia.

The German government had only temporarily cut down its eastern program in order to achieve its western aims through a separate peace with Russia. The German military administration of Belgium in the meantime had tried to lay the groundwork for the future domination of the country by Germany. The greatest possible encouragement was given to the Flemish movement with a view eventually to creating a Belgium weakened by a division into two autonomous states, one of which would voluntarily rely on Germany. German business interests also became very active in an attempt to gain a dominant influence in Belgian economic life. After 1917, however, it was found that the two major German policies for the imposition of permanent controls on the Belgian kingdom, namely, the political division along lines of nationality and economic penetration, were not really compatible. German official historians had been busy proving with some documents picked from the Belgian ministry of foreign affairs that Belgium had violated her neutrality before 1914; this was to lead to the conclusion that Germany had had a right to disregard Belgian neutrality. But nobody outside of Germany was impressed by such fabrications. The chancellor's demands for "guarantees" that in the future Belgium would not serve as an invasion gate to Germany could be taken by the Allies and neutrals as a demonstration of bad faith. The negotiations with the Belgian king, which were conducted by middlemen between November 1915 and February 1916, were from the outset doomed by the official German attitude. Similarly, contacts made later in 1916 with French politicians did not lead anywhere, because the German government considered the cession of the Longwy-Briey basin, to which Falkenhayn still added Belfort, an absolute prerequisite.

The German rule over Belgium, irrespective of whether it would include the direct possession of the coast of Flanders, as the German admirals wished, or would be exercised indirectly, was particularly demanded by those who saw England as the chief enemy. And popular hatred of England had grown in Germany by leaps and bounds, as in general the agitation for annexations had gained in intensity only after the government had forbidden the public discussion of war aims in November 1914. The social groups which championed programs of annexations had organized war committees of various kinds. The most important agencies were the national economic associations, such as the big Federation of Industrialists and the League of Agriculturists, which combined with the prewar nationalist organizations, such as the Pan-German League, the Navy, Defense, and Colonial Leagues. These organizations, in the first place the Pan-German League, provided ideas for the memoranda which were being written and widely circulated. When in the spring of 1915 rumors were heard that the government was trying to make a separate peace with Russia, the organizations were spurred into the highest activity. At this time the practice began of presenting petitions to the government, the parliament, and even to the Supreme Army Command and was to continue for the rest of the war.

But the same media were used by the feuding factions in the government. It was of greatest consequence that Tirpitz had made known his thesis that England could be totally defeated by submarine warfare. This was eagerly taken up by the annexationists, and thus war strategies became mixed up with the discussion of war aims. The annexationists grew hostile toward Bethmann-Hollweg, who, on account of his ban on the public discussion of war aims and personal vagueness about peace terms, was suspected of being an opponent of annexations, and his opposition to the opening of unlimited submarine warfare made him even more distrusted. The chancellor was driven to express his expectations of German war gains more strongly in public, but since he wanted to keep his program somewhat flexible, depending on unforeseeable military and political developments, he still did not satisfy the boiling nationalistic mood of the majority of the German people. His conflicts with the heads of the army and navy as well as the pressures of public opinion made it, however, unlikely that he would ever drastically curb his hopes for large German acquisitions.

When in January 1916 Colonel House, the representative of President Wilson, told Bethmann-Hollweg that the British government might consider peace on condition that Germany would evacuate northern France, Belgium, and Poland, he replied that the restoration of Belgium and the return of Poland to Russia were no longer negotiable. Everywhere in Germany great doubts were entertained about the American president, who was declared to be a strong Anglophile. But the deterioration of the military situation prompted the German government to urge Wilson to undertake the mediation between the belligerents. However, it did not wish Wilson to do more than bring the belligerents to the peace table, where, for no good reason, the Germans hoped to divide the Allies. They were afraid that a general peace congress with the participation of the United States and other neutrals would compel Germany to forgo her wishes for the control of Belgium and other gains. It was unfortunate that the new Supreme Command of the German army directed the attention of the world to the Belgian problem. Ludendorff insisted upon forcing 400,000 Belgian workers into jobs in Germany, a violation of international law that caused indignation not only in England and France but also in Germany. It was not surprising that the American government directed to Berlin repeated inquiries about German intentions vis-à-vis Belgium. These American moves made the German government apprehensive that Wilson might intend to take part in the formulation of the future peace. The Germans did not wish to leave to Wilson the role of peacemaker. Thus on December 5 they decided rather abruptly to have the Central Powers issue to the enemy powers an invitation for the opening of peace negotiations, which was sent out on December 12, six days before Woodrow Wilson made public his declaration. But although the Germans in the months before had begged and even pressed Wilson to act as mediator, henceforth they cared little about American sentiments. A change in personalities underlined the turnabout of German policy. To keep in line with the Hindenburg-Ludendorff command, Jagow was replaced as foreign secretary by the under-secretary, Arthur Zimmermann. In contrast to Jagow, who saw the war chiefly as a struggle between Slavdom and Germandom, Zimmermann (1864–1940) wanted Germany to expand in all directions, and whereas Jagow felt some scruples about international laws, his robust East Prussian successor brought to diplomacy the boisterous manners of the German student dueling fraternities.

✍ Wilson's Mediation Attempt

THE GERMAN PEACE OFFER displayed the strongest confidence in a German victory, a confidence that the capture of Bucarest on December 6 made more credible. But the offer was really nothing but a bid to enter at once into peace negotiations, without any specification of peace terms. The three announced aims of the Central Powers, "existence, honor, and freedom of development of their peoples" were meaningless and could cover up any program of annexations. The Allies declared the peace offer of the Germans to be a mere political device for confusing their enemies and gaining the sympathies of the neutrals. On December 18 President Wilson issued his call to all belligerents to state their war and peace aims in order to determine whether a basis for peace could be found. Since all of them in their public statements had assured the world that they were fighting for defensive ends only, Wilson expressed the hope that a compromise might be closer at hand than was realized. Thereupon the German government declared its willingness to partake in peace discussions at a neutral place, without, however, divulging its war aims. Actually the German government did not intend to pay any serious attention to the American move. On January 9, 1917, a few days after the negative reply of the Allies to the German peace offer of December 12, the German leaders reached the fateful decision to open unrestricted submarine warfare on February 1.

On January 10, 1917, the Allies answered Wilson's inquiry about war aims. They were rather embarrassed by the American request. In early December Lloyd George, the champion of a knockout victory, had formed a government of national union. The British and French knew that they could not win their war aims without hard fighting, for which they prepared vigorously. Therefore they refused to enter into peace negotiations. As nations which had taken up arms in defense of international law and the independence of nations they would not agree to being judged as being morally on the same level as the Germans, but they stated their war aims. These included the restoration of Belgium, Serbia, and Montenegro, the evacuation of the occupied territories of France and Russia as well as reparations for damages. In addition the Allies demanded the restitution of territories seized in the past by force or against the will of their inhabitants—which chiefly meant Alsace-Lorraine—,the liberation of Italians, Slavs, Rumanians, and Czechoslovaks from foreign domination, and the exclusion of the Ottoman empire from Europe. These war aims amounted to the partition of Austria-Hungary, which Germany had wanted to preserve as a great power when she went to war in August 1914, as well as of the Ottoman empire, which had played a major part in all her colonial plans and dreams. And beyond this isolation the loss of Alsace-Lorraine and possibly of the provinces of West Prussia and Posen, at which the Allied note hinted, would have weakened Germany's position directly.

The Allied war aims were stated as if they were merely the application of the principle of national self-determination. In reality the governments of the Triple Entente had disregarded this principle in a number of instances. The secret treaty of London of April 26, 1915, by which Italy was brought into the war, promised her not only the Italian Trentino but also the German South Tyrol, and among the many other gifts were parts of Istria and Dalmatia, which seriously impaired the "liberation of the Slavs" that was proposed in the Allied note to Wilson. French aims, too, went beyond the boundaries of nationality, as the secret negotiations with Russia indicated, which, in February 1917, two weeks before the Russian March revolution, led to an agreement that allowed France to sever the Rhineland from Germany, while Russia was at liberty to settle the German frontiers in the east. Whether this agreement had much practical value may be doubted, since in all probability England would not have tolerated its execution.

The announced Allied war aims program offered no basis for peace negotiations. Only an Allied victory could lead to its realization. Wilson clearly criticized the Allies when in his speech of January 22, 1917, before the United States Senate he declared that only a "peace without victory" had a chance to last, but he came closer to the Allied aims by emphasizing that national self-determination ought to serve as a fundamental principle in establishing a secure international order. It would have been of vital interest to Germany to keep the American government disposed to resume mediation in the future. If Germany had announced her willingness to make peace in the west, it is doubtful whether in the face of military adversity or stalemate the British and French peoples would have sustained the war effort for such formidable aims as proclaimed in the note of January 10. As a matter of fact, the spring offensives launched by the British and French armies caused horrendous losses without producing any strategic results. The French army cracked under the strain, and widespread mutinies occurred. Surprisingly, the army regained its confidence, although slowly, but its morale would perhaps not have been restored if America's entrance into the war had not by then raised the belief in ultimate victory. The Russian March revolution was another blow that might have given the British and French governments pause and induced them to revise their war aims, particularly if Germany had been able to make peace with a liberal Russian government.

Such a Russo-German peace would not have been easy to achieve, since the ties of the Russian liberals with the Western European nations were even closer than those of czarist Russia had been. Moreover, Ludendorff had not only ruined whatever chances that might have existed for reaching a peace with czarist Russia but also gravely prejudiced possible negotiations with the Russian liberals. Eager to find more soldiers he had insisted that the German and Austrian governments should proclaim a separate kingdom of Poland on November 5, 1916. Separated from Russia, it was to be connected with the two allied Central Powers. The Poles were not to participate in the establishment of this state, the frontiers of which were to be defined later. For the time being German and Austrian military government was to continue without change. It was naïve to assume that in these circumstances the Poles would gladly join a Polish army. Instead of the hoped-for three divisions, only 370 Poles, among them 350 Jews, volunteered. Behind this Polish policy lay the hope that Germany might exploit national self-determination as a means of weakening her enemies without giving up her controls over the occupied countries. The extension of German power that was so passionately desired by the ruling classes was exclusively envisioned as German domination. As such it was decried not only by the Allies but also by the European neutrals, whose reaction was entirely disregarded in Germany. Furthermore, it was questionable whether direct or indirect annexations would really strengthen the existing political and social order, as the opponents of internal reform asserted. Alsace-Lorraine and the Polish provinces of Prussia had created serious problems, which would have been dangerously aggravated by the further extension of German rule over foreign nationals. In addition, annexations would have left the European peoples imbued with profound hatred of Germany. For internal and external reasons the German Empire would inevitably have become a more highly militarized state than the Empire had been in 1914, and the internal tensions would have been greatly increased.

✑ *Unlimited Submarine Warfare*

PRODDED BY PRESIDENT WILSON, the German government confidentially gave him a toned-down version of its peace program on January 31, 1917, while simultaneously informing him that on the following day Germany would resume unrestricted submarine warfare. Thereupon the United States broke off diplomatic relations without opening war immediately. Germany's refusal to discuss temporary protective measures for neutral shipping or at least to avoid the sinking of American ships going to England brought on the American declaration of war on April 6, 1917. The Russian March revolution and the eclipse of czardom made it both easier and more urgent for the United States to enter the war on the side of the Allies. The last remaining emotional hurdles were swept aside by the publication of a dispatch that the German foreign secretary, Zimmermann, had sent to Mexico and that the British intercepted, deciphered, and presented to the American government. In this fatuous dispatch Zimmermann offered Mexico an alliance in case of an American-German war and suggested to her the recovery of New Mexico, Arizona, and Texas, which had been ceded to the United States in 1848.

In the spring of 1916 Bethmann-Hollweg had successfully resisted Falkenhayn's demands to adopt unrestricted submarine warfare, which the chief of the naval staff, Admiral von Holtzendorff, declared to be a reliable weapon for forcing England to capitulate. But the heads of the military services had gone on to agitate for this submarine warfare and even made use of the press. When Hindenburg and Ludendorff took over the supreme command, popular demand had reached a feverish pitch. The two generals postponed pressing for the opening of unrestricted submarine warfare till the end of the Rumanian campaign, when they expected to have the necessary troops for guarding the Dutch frontier in case the Netherlands gave up her neutrality. As soon as the Rumanian campaign drew to its close, Hindenburg and Ludendorff joined forces with Holtzendorff and Scheer, the commander of the fleet, to overcome the resistance of the chancellor. The latter was further isolated by the lack of any parliamentary support. On October 7, 1916, the Center party had recommended that he should accept the opinion of the Supreme Command in this matter. By the end of the year Bethmann-Hollweg hoped that the German and American peace initiatives would at least persuade the United States to stay out of the European war, even if Germany conducted unrestricted submarine warfare. As we have seen, the German diplomatic moves were clumsy and not likely to achieve the desired aim. But the military men cut short all these diplomatic actions. They declared that there was no time left to wait for the Allied reply to Wilson's peace note. A day before its publication, on January 9, 1917, the decision on Germany's "Sicilian expedition" was taken.

Karl Helfferich, now vice-chancellor and secretary of interior, was the chief critic of the case that the chief of the naval staff made for the submarine strategy. Although he did not question the capacity of the 100 or so boats to send 600,000 tons of shipping per month to the bottom of the sea, he rightly denied that this would starve England into submission. In its appraisal of the economic realities involved, the navy's presentation was utterly dilettantish. It also bared one of the worst failings of this and subsequent German generations, the gross underestimation of the moral fiber of other nations. But while these German leaders had no idea of what England was able to take, they realized even less what mighty punches the United States was capable of throwing. In place of logical proof, Admiral von Holtzendorff boldly offered his "word of honor" that no American soldier would ever set foot on France, thus implying that the big American navy could be disregarded altogether. Hindenburg and Ludendorff on their part thought that the United States would not be able to raise and organize large fighting forces beyond the existing small American army. The economic and financial reserves of the United States meant nothing to them, although Helfferich, an outstanding economist who had been the director of the biggest German bank, tried hard to make them see the implications of America's entrance into the war. But hubris and ignorance prevailed in the councils of government. The chancellor, though largely relying on Helfferich's judgment, was already half committed to consent to the unrestricted submarine warfare if the German "peace offer" would not elicit a positive response from the Allies, and he gave up his opposition at the meeting of the crown council on January 9, 1917. Out of a sense of patriotic duty he decided to stay in office because he wanted to avoid giving the enemies the impression of a split within the German government and provoking serious criticism among Germany's allies. Bulgaria was particularly sensitive to seeing the United States join in the war. Austria-Hungary, which had suffered severe losses, was shaking in her foundations. With the death of the old Emperor Francis Joseph on November 21, 1916, the greatest living symbol of the unity of the empire had been removed. The young Emperor Charles was convinced that Austria-Hungary was unable to fight much longer and was anxiously exploring the possibilities of peace.

The chancellor's authority, never very strong with the parties and the people, was greatly impaired by his submission to the military leaders. Even those who in the summer of 1917 began to realize that the unrestricted submarine war had been a colossal blunder and could not bring victory to Germany did not think that Bethmann-Hollweg was capable of leading the country. And the problems which he faced in internal politics had grown even more critical since the fall of 1914.

✑ German War Economy

THE WAR WHICH COUNT SCHLIEFFEN had hoped could be won by the armies and arms available at the time of its outbreak became a feverish race between the belligerents in the mobilization of all the resources that could be applied to fighting. Nobody had foreseen that in an age of high industrialization and technology war would press the whole economic and social life of the nations into its service. From the outset Germany was gravely handicapped. Her manpower, food, and resources of raw material were more limited than those of the Allies, and therefore she was compelled to carry the war organization of her society to much greater length than the Allies, who, holding command of the sea, were able to draw on the resources of all the non-European continents as well. For all practical purposes Germany reached the state of total mobilization or total war in 1917, but this condition was not deliberately achieved but rather was the result of individual reactions to rising war pressures. An integration of German social and economic wartime policies was actually never accomplished.

No preparations or plans had been made for the management of Germany's wartime economy. Prior to 1914 she had produced about 80 per cent of her food and might have succeeded in getting along on a tolerable diet if her agricultural production could have been maintained at its prewar level. While it is true that Germany's prewar food deficiencies had been much higher than 20 per cent with regard to such high-grade items as butter, fats, cheese, and eggs, even during the war imports from neutral countries—the Netherlands, Scandinavia, and, till 1916, Rumania—were not cut off. But military service removed a large segment of the working force from the villages and estates, horses were requisitioned by the army, and the supply of fertilizers became inadequate, since nitrogen was diverted to the production of military explosives. In addition, unfavorable weather conditions furthered the decline of German agricultural production. The grain harvest of 1917 was only half that of 1913. The potato crop in 1916 amounted to 25 million tons, compared to 54 million tons in 1913 and 1915, and remained far under normal in 1917 and 1918. The fodder shortage led to a sharp fall in meat production. In June 1917 only 12.8 million pigs were counted in Germany instead of the 25.7 million in 1913.

The government took over the rationing, distribution, and price control first of grain and bread and subsequently of an ever-increasing number of foodstuffs. But these improvised war agencies did not work too well, and a very substantial rise in official prices was not avoided. Moreover the producers succeeded in hiding a large slice of their output and selling it on the black market, where soon astronomical prices were paid. It is assumed that the necessary normal food intake of the average person is 2,250 calories, but as early as 1916 only 1,350 calories were available in rationed food. In the following winter of 1916–17, owing to the potato failure and the shortage of bread, meat, and fat, the mass of the nonagricultural population had to subsist largely on turnips. After this grim "turnip winter" only 1,000 calories were available, an actual starvation diet on which those who could not afford to buy unrationed food at extreme prices were not likely to survive. It is estimated that about three quarters of a million people died of hunger.

The want of food set apart the urban from the rural population and within the cities gave the class struggle a fierce character. Access to the limited supply of free goods and to the black market meant survival, and the poor could not afford these goods, even if they employed the major part of their earnings for the purchase of food. Other essentials of life, too, became scarce and, in spite of rationing, expensive. For wool, cotton, and most of her leather Germany had had to rely on imports. Dresses and shoes were now at a premium, and ill-fed people felt doubly the pinch of the cold winters.

The outbreak of the war in August 1914 had thrown the German economy into confusion. Not only had the export industries had to lay off workers on a large scale, but also vital industries, such as mining and transportation, had been disrupted because the armed forces had called up people without any consideration for the continued operation of needed industries. As early as October and November 1914, shortages of ammunition had developed, and when it became clear that the war would last long, the industries on their own initiative had begun to convert to war production. The farsightedness of Walther Rathenau (1867–1922), the director of the greatest German electrical company, had led in August 1914 to the state control of all strategic raw materials. German scientists succeeded in finding substitutes for some materials in short supply. The most important invention was Professor Fritz Haber's (1868–1934) method for extracting nitrogen from the air.

Once the conversion of German industries had been accomplished in the spring of 1915, it was possible to overcome the serious unemployment that had originated in August 1914, first that of men and thereafter, more slowly, that of women. In order to bring production back to normal the industries had to reclaim from the army a substantial number of their skilled workers, whom they also needed for training their new workers. The latter either came from the industries made idle by the war or were women or youths. By 1918, 28 per cent fewer men and 52 per cent more women were employed than in 1913. Although the wages paid were steadily rising, on the whole they did not keep pace with the rising prices. In 1916 real wages were already over 20 per cent lower than in 1913. However, the differences between the various industries were very great. Whereas in the armament industries real wages probably did not decline at all and a small group of workers of special skills could earn high incomes, workers in the textile and garment industries as well as in a good many trades remained far behind.

At the beginning of the war the government was empowered to permit exemptions from all existing statutory labor protection, and such permissions were freely given. Women entered practically all vocations, even those that overtaxed their strength. By 1918, 37.6 per cent of the working force of a firm like Krupp were women. Disregard of the Sunday rest, and the extension of the workday beyond ten hours imposed crushing burdens on women and juveniles. There was much popular criticism that the juvenile workers had too much money to spend, and it is true that juvenile delinquency increased. But closer inspection reveals that the earnings of the young were essential for the upkeep of families whose fathers served in the army.

War production seemed adequate to the German army leaders until July 1916, when they were rudely awakened by the Somme battle. The production of British and French industries supplemented by American deliveries was prodigious and allowed the Allied command to employ a mass of matériel such as had never before been thrown into battle. Although the morale of the German soldiers withstood the onslaught, deep concern was felt about future "matériel battles." Ludendorff after his appointment as quartermaster general turned his attention immediately to the expansion of German war mobilization. He proposed to the government the introduction of universal obligatory labor service of all those who were not subject to the military draft. Women and juveniles were included in his plan which would have placed the total manpower under state, or rather army, management. The individual worker would have been assigned to a job which he could not have changed by his own volition.

The government raised strong objections to Ludendorff's proposals, which would have deprived the workers of many rights. He was also told that no need existed to draft women, since there was still a large reservoir of women eager for employment for whom working places were not available. Ludendorff's design for forcing the whole society into a military mold was drastically changed by the government and the parliament. Under the law of auxiliary patriotic service (*Vaterländischer Hilfsdienst*) of December 5, 1916, all male Germans from the age of 17 to 60 were obliged to work in the war economy. What was important for the war effort was to be decided by regional boards on which employers and workers were represented. The individual labor draftee was urged to find a war job of his own choice. In case of failure, a local board, composed of a military and civilian officer, two employers, and two workers, was to place him in a job, taking into consideration the social circumstances and the adequacy of wages. A change from one job to another was not allowed except with the permission of the employer, against whose decision recourse could be taken to a committee of three representatives of the employers and three of the workers who met under the chairmanship of a member of the war office. It was supposed to settle each case with the understanding that improved job conditions were a proper cause for change. In addition, in all enterprises with more than fifty workers, the law introduced workers' councils to be elected by all the workers through direct and secret vote, and in enterprises with more than fifty employees it created employees' councils. It was their function to work for a harmonious relationship between the factory workers and white-collar workers as well as between them and the employer. They had the right to bring to the attention of the entrepreneur "requests, wishes and complaints" with regard to working conditions, wages, and welfare arrangements of the enterprise. If there was no agreement on wages and working conditions, an appeal could be taken to the committee of seven just mentioned. Besides, all those entering the auxiliary patriotic service were assured that none of their legal rights of association and public meetings would be curtailed.

The final law constituted a great success for the Social Democratic party and even more for the allied Free Trade Unions. From among the latter all the representatives of labor on the various committees were to be chosen. The public role that the law assigned to the trade unions made it impossible for the government to deny any longer the old demand of the Social Democrats for abolition of the hated article 153 of the law of associations that had enabled the police to declare trade unions political associations and thereby limit their activities.[1] But important as some of the institutions of the auxiliary service law were to become for the social policies of the Weimar Republic, the trade unions, in spite of their loyal

[1] See pp. 287, 358.

cooperation, did not derive the full benefits from the law during the war. Although the government in Berlin was willing to give them a share in the administration of the law, the Conservative officials in the provinces were not disposed to allow Social Democrats to gain in influence. Active resistance, however, came chiefly from the leaders of heavy industry. They took strong exception to the introduction of workers' councils and succeeded in delaying their formation in many cases till the summer of 1918.

The administration of the auxiliary service and war production was placed under a special war office that was under the auspices of the Prussian war ministry. Major General Wilhelm Groener (1867–1939) was made the first chief of this big agency. A Württemberg officer of liberal outlook who rightly enjoyed the reputation of being one of the most gifted members of the general staff, he was not a mere professional army man. His experiences as chief of the railroad section of the general staff and, since 1914, as military director of the German railroad system had given him some insight into the social and political problems posed by the war. And he knew that the question of manpower could not be solved without the trade unions.

✑ Hindenburg Program

BUT MANPOWER WAS ONLY one aspect of war production, for which the new Supreme Command drafted the so-called "Hindenburg program." It envisaged a huge increase in the production of arms and ammunition. The military estimates, however, were made without reference to coal production and the state of transportation. Forty newly built steel furnaces, for example, could not be fired in February 1917, because the railroads were unable to deliver the necessary coal. The order was issued that for the time being only the building of those factories should be carried forward that could be completed in three to four months, and in June the Hindenburg program was further curtailed. Yet even then much effort and scarce material were squandered in building factories which could not possibly be ready in time and on an overproduction of certain arms, such as machine guns and light field guns. An expansion of overall industrial production was limited by the coal shortage, which could have been overcome only if Ludendorff had released from the army all miners as well as a substantial number of skilled workers for the railroad repair shops. As it was, the development of new weapons could not be undertaken, and the lack of tanks was to prove one of the major causes of the ultimate defeat of the German army.

The proliferation of German war production under the Hindenburg program endangered German public finances. It might have been possible to keep the cost of the program down by strict controls. But this would have implied not only the stabilization of wages but also a ceiling on profits through dictation of prices of war deliveries. Doubtless this system would not have been easy to operate, and as long as the rise in prices of vital consumers' goods, growing scarcer as a result of the blockade, proved unmanageable, wage stabilization was probably out of reach and only sliding prices for military hardware would have been realistic. The industrialists gladly made wages the excuse for raising the prices of military production, and there was no question that they raked in tremendous profits. Count von Roedern, secretary of the imperial treasury, remarked in June 1918 that a continuation of the adopted system of war financing would lead "on one side to complete impoverishment, on the other to the accumulation of enormous fortunes."

The German government financed the war almost entirely by loans. This method, inevitable in the beginning and practical in view of the available idle capital, became inadequate and dangerous in later years. The monthly war expenditure, which had risen from ca. 1 billion marks in 1914 to ca. 2 billion in 1915 and the better part of 1916, jumped in October 1916 to 3 billion and steadily increased to reach 4 billion in October 1917 and 4.8 billion in October 1918. By the end of May 1916 a total of 39.78 billion had been spent on the war, of which 36 billion had been covered by four successful governmental war bond drives. But the subsequent five bond drives fell far short of the mounting war expenditure. Of the final war cost of 160 billion only 97 billion were covered by bonds.

As mentioned before, Bismarck's constitution left the empire financially rather weak. The federal finances rested chiefly on revenue from customs duties and indirect taxes, with the states retaining all the other resources. The introduction of a direct federal tax was bound to meet with the resistance of the states. In the *Reichstag* the parties of the right were against any federal property tax while the Social Democrats opposed any levy on consumption. Only with great difficulty did the government in early 1916 prevail on the Federal Council and the *Reichstag* to impose a very modest, one-time tax on capital gains and to introduce some minor indirect taxes. But the government could not bring itself to propose a drastic and permanent tax on war profits and a federal income tax. The hope that the enemies would eventually pay the German war debts made it seem unnecessary to adopt stricter methods of war financing. The huge deficits in 1917–18 were covered by printed money. By October 1918 the mark had fallen to 60 per cent of its prewar value in international trading and would have fallen even lower if the small volume of international commerce had not allowed the government to restrict the amount of German marks traded in neutral exchanges. The currency inflation that began during the war created one of the most perilous mortgages on the German future.

While all social groups suffered in some form from the deprivations of the war, the pressure was hardest on the urban working class. Patriotism ran high in the early period of the war, notwithstanding the serious unemployment of the first half-year. When this unemployment receded in the spring of 1915, the food shortages began and steadily worsened. Eventually, the workers, of whom extraordinary efforts were demanded, profoundly resented the fact that they did not get equal status. Since soon the first consideration of every German was how to survive physically, it was deeply disturbing to realize that food rationing by the government resulted in a near-starvation diet for the workers, while obviously certain groups of the people did distinctly better and did not have to worry much about the famine.

In the factories, progress toward a real partnership of management and workers was slow and uneven. The attitude of the industrialists varied. The consumption industries tended to be more sympathetic than the coal and iron industry, which endeavored to maintain lordly control over its workers. The trade unions were in a difficult position. Since under the *Burgfriede*[2] they had promised to support the war effort, they were forced to back, or at least not openly oppose, many measures of the government and entrepreneurs with which they disagreed. Without strikes the only course left to them was negotiation, and when this was of no avail, they were easily exposed to the suspicion of their members that they always sided with the authorities. The loss of confidence in their leaders was enhanced by the fluctuation of the membership. By December 1916 the free trade unions had lost one and a half of the two and a half million members they had had in 1914. However, the part given to them in the administration of the auxiliary service law caused their membership to increase again by half a million till September 1918. The new members were predominantly workers in the war industries. Another shift in membership originated in the increasing number of women and juvenile workers. These newcomers were ill-attuned to the thinking of the trade union functionaries, who had grown up and been trained in the prewar struggles of the German working class movement. The newly organized members were responsive to radical slogans. Thus the old leaders of the trade unions saw their hold on the masses become more tenuous during the war years, and this in turn did not heighten their stature in the eyes of the government.

[2] See pp. 428–31.

ᗡ *Split of Social Democratic Party*

POLITICAL EQUALITY OF THE WORKERS was not achieved. To be sure, Bethmann-Hollweg believed that the Empire could not conduct a successful war without the genuine support of Germany's largest party. Moreover he felt that the war offered a historic opportunity for closing the chasm that had torn German society apart. Within limits he leaned toward Friedrich Naumann's conception of strengthening the monarchy by providing it with a firm and broad democratic base[3] and was personally inclined to sacrifice some of the old Prussian institutions to this aim. But he knew that the old Prussia was still very much alive and possessed great power, and he thought it impossible to undertake a serious constitutional reform during the war. In the beginning of the war he merely stated that it would result in a "new orientation" of German political life, while limiting his actions to improving the position of the Social Democratic party through administrative measures. All administrative organs were directed to treat Social Democrats on an equal footing with members of any other party. Yet in practice this only applied to those Social Democrats who placed themselves fully behind the government. The military area commanders, who under the law of the "state of siege" exercised dictatorial power, did not tolerate any criticism of the war policies of the government. Thus Social Democratic newspapers could now be sold at the newsstands of the state railroad stations and even be read in soldiers' barracks, but if these papers were critical of war measures of the government or tended to subvert the morale of the people and the army, they were suspended or placed under censorship prior to publication. Likewise, the military commanders did not hesitate to prohibit party meetings —even closed ones—if they expected them to be used for the pronouncement of nonconformist opinions.

The authority wielded by the military, often without good political judgment, constituted a continuous irritant. It forced the Social Democratic party executive, in order to avoid conflicts, to see to it that all party members followed and professed the party line that had been laid down in the resolution to support the defense of the country that had been voted by a majority of the party delegation in the *Reichstag* on August 4, 1914. In the years before the war the party executive had already ruled with a strong hand and suppressed radical trends in the local and regional organizations. This bureaucratic centralism had caused some tension within the party at large as well as within the executive itself. Since the latter was dominated by reformists, its leftist members did not wish to see it wield too much power over the regional and local organizations of the party. And whereas formerly the executive had interfered

[3] See p. 333.

with actions and rarely with opinions and had done so in executing policies voted by the party congress, it now acted without submitting its
policies to a party congress. Thus the dissenting members who had voted
against the war credits in the caucus of the party delegation on August 4,
1914, could claim that they had adhered more closely to resolutions of
former congresses.

The majority of August 4, though enjoying the overwhelming support
of the party rank and file, from the beginning faced strong internal
opposition, which was likely to gain additional force if the sentiment of
the masses should turn against the government. Such a contingency
largely depended upon the measure of success that the party would have
in winning political equality for its members and in holding the government firmly to the course of policy on which the truce between the party
and the government had been founded. In December 1914, on the occasion of the approval of the second war loan, Karl Liebknecht broke away
and voted against the government and his own party. His, however, was a
lonely position. He and a small group of his friends, Rosa Luxemburg,
Franz Mehring, and Clara Zetkin, denied that the war which was imperialistic in origin could lead to anything but capitalistic expansion, and that
meant annexations. It was an idle dream to hope that the war could be
transformed into one of defense. Rather, it had to be opposed as a whole
if its early termination was to be achieved and if it was to be used as a
means of abolishing capitalist rule.

But this was not the attitude of the dissenting minority, the left center
of the party. Although they agreed with the left wing on the imperialist
origins of the war and felt it to be the duty of socialists to fight against
annexations, they did not deny the right of the nation to defend itself.
But just as they demanded a distinctive socialist foreign policy, they
disliked the suspension of the struggle for the realization of political
equality. For a sensitive humanitarian such as Hugo Haase the disregard
of civil rights under the "state of siege" was a shocking experience. The
men of the left center hated to see their principles compromised by cheap
concessions to the government. It was tempting to go into opposition in
order to keep one's escutcheon clean. Yet the solidarity of the Social
Democratic movement was an ideal that they had not only preached but
also lived. The separation of the minority from the majority of the party
was, therefore, delayed, even after the agitation for annexations by the
parties to the right had induced many members of the party to call for a
forceful campaign for a peace of conciliation. The twenty-one members
of the *Reichstag* delegation who voted in the party caucus in March 1915
against the chairmen's plan to pass the annual budget for the first time in
the party's history did not carry their fight to the floor of the house. Yet
when the debate on war aims in December 1915 revealed the govern-

ment's commitment to annexations, twenty members voted against the fourth war loan, while an additional twenty-two left before the balloting. The budget debates in March 1916 led to the open break. Eighteen of the dissenters, excluded from the party caucus, formed the Socialist Collaboration Group under the leadership of Hugo Haase, Wilhelm Dittmann (1874–1954), and Georg Ledebour (1850–1947).

While the majority of the delegation, together with the general commission of the free trade unions, decided to maintain the policy of August 4, 1914, the minority, urging opposition to the government, broadcast its stand to the masses. It was not surprising that the rift could no longer be healed thereafter. The German peace offer and Wilson's peace intervention in December 1916 induced the party opposition to call together a conference of representatives from all over Germany. It was held in Berlin during the first days of January 1917 and issued a manifesto castigating the capitalist governments of both sides for having failed to formulate war aims which might have encouraged the initiation of peace negotiations. Calling national self-determination, disarmament, and international arbitration the chief principles of a sound peace, it challenged the German government to state its war aims in order to make negotiations possible.

The majority immediately excluded the opposition from the party on the ground of the latter's separate organization. In order to form a party of its own, the opposition at Easter held a congress in Gotha, where in 1875 the Lassalleans and Eisenachers had come together and founded the united Social Democratic party. In all declarations the peace issue was dominant and was the strongest reason given for the resumption of the prewar opposition to the government. The continued struggle for internal democratization was seen as a means of bringing strong pressure on the government rather than a striving for the conquest of power in the state. The men who founded the Independent Social Democratic party did not plan for revolution, which seemed to all of them removed to a distant future. The Russian revolution, which had occurred a month earlier, did not, because of its bourgeois character, alert them to the new speed that all social processes had assumed under the violent impact of the war. As their official program they adopted the old Erfurt program, though admitting that it would need reexamination after the war.

The primacy of the peace issue had lessened the significance of many former conflicts. Thus the revisionist Eduard Bernstein as well as the orthodox Karl Kautsky could join the Independent party. The latter offered a roof to the followers of Karl Liebknecht and Rosa Luxemburg as well. The Spartacists, as they were called after their illegally distributed pamphlets, the *Spartacus Letters*, originally constituted a very distinct group within the new party. Their open agitation against the war and national defense and for the violent overthrow of the government was not shared by the regular Independents and for the time being was not reaching a large segment of the masses. Karl Liebknecht had been sent to jail for two years because of "treasonable" speeches he had made on May 1, 1916, and Rosa Luxemburg had been imprisoned by the government later in the year. Still, the Spartacists gained a certain influence on some groups of the Independents, particularly after the Russian November revolution, with their recommendation of "direct action." With the support of strikes, especially the big strike of the armament workers in January 1918, many Independents, leaders as well as followers, turned more radical. In the revolution of 1918–19 the party combined many shades of radicalism and moderation.

✍ *Prussian Franchise Reform*

THE SPLIT of the Social Democratic party was a warning that the masses might get tired of supporting the war effort, and thereby the reconciliation of the Social Democrats with the existing state would also be lost. It was obvious that this could be averted only if the government took the necessary steps for giving the workers political equality. For years the chief demand had been the reform of the Prussian franchise. Bethmann-Hollweg, who as early as 1909 had made a futile attempt to revise it, became convinced in the early months of the war that the reform was needed in the interest of a peaceful internal development. But he felt that it should not be undertaken during the war, and it took him much time to recognize that nothing short of the introduction of universal, equal, and secret suffrage in Prussia would be acceptable to the left. In the speech with which he opened the session of the Prussian parliament in January 1916 William II for the first time mentioned in vague terms the intention of the government to revise the Prussian franchise after the war.

Real pressure on the government to take action in the matter began to be exerted only a year later. It was triggered by the presentation to the Prussian parliament of a bill for the creation of additional entailed noble estates (*Fideikommisse*). The government submitted it on the strong urgings of the Prussian Conservatives, and Bethmann-Hollweg, who suffered under their growing hostility, apparently hoped to appease them through this measure. But the establishment of such large family estates under a system of special privileges for noble families or rich families to be ennobled had always been a thorn in the flesh of German liberals. The revolution of 1848–49 had banned the creation of estates that interfered with the growth of the peasant population. Yet in spite of the Prussian constitution of 1850 the reactionary government had admitted these estates in 1851 again. By 1914 about 12 per cent of the Prussian land had been tied up in this fashion.

Not only the Social Democrats but also the Progressives and National Liberals criticized the government very sharply and called the presentation of the Prussian law a breach of the *Burgfriede*. If the government was risking the internal peace for the benefit of a small group of aristocratic families, it was said, there was no good reason for it to deny that the reform of the Prussian franchise could be solved during the war. As a matter of fact, even outside the Social Democratic party it now was argued that the government ought to settle this issue at once, since by presenting the reactionary bill on entailed estates, its intention to modernize Prussia had become questionable. The provocative language used by the leaders of the Conservatives in the Prussian House of Lords added fresh fuel to the conflict of the parties, and the question was raised whether the *Reichstag* should not settle the Prussian problems. It was fortunate that on March 14 Bethmann-Hollweg convinced the Prussian parliament of his determination to achieve the reform of the Prussian franchise. Had his speech come a day later, his attitude might have appeared to be the result of the collapse of the Russian monarchy, since on March 15 the czar abdicated.

The end of czardom made a profound impression in Germany. It seemed incredible that the mightiest autocracy of the world should have been completely overthrown by a popular uprising. Naturally the Russian revolution also raised hopes for peace, although they were dimmed by the imminent entry of the United States into the war. The events in Russia made it imperative in the eyes of most of the leaders of the nonconservative parties to satisfy the demands of the Social Democrats for equal political treatment. In view of the breaking away of the Independents from the party and of additional hardships, such as the new cut in the bread rations, quick action was required. The hesitation of the government drove the parties to request a greater influence on policy. In ringing phrases Gustav Stresemann, who just then was assuming the leadership of the National Liberal party from the ailing Ernst Bassermann, criticized the political sterility of Germany's government by bureaucrats and expressed high regard for the political achievements of the British and French democratic systems. He urged a strong role for the parliament and argued that a government supported by parliament would enjoy greater respect abroad than an authoritarian one. Stresemann moved that a parliamentary committee be appointed to discuss reforms of the German constitution, and this "constitutional committee" was voted by all the parties except the Conservatives.

Bethmann-Hollweg realized that the government would have to act quickly if it did not wish to lose its leadership completely. But he failed to fight for his conviction that the grant of universal, equal, and direct suffrage in Prussia was inevitable. Meeting strong opposition from among the Prussian ministers and feeling uncertain whether William II could be persuaded to accept equal franchise, the chancellor compromised. In his "Easter message" of April 7, 1917, the emperor promised the Prussian people universal and direct, but not equal suffrage. Also with regard to the reform of the Prussian House of Lords the message was muffled. Yet the promise of reform had at least a temporary impact. It helped the Social Democratic leaders to terminate within a few days the strikes that broke out in the latter half of April as demonstrations against worsening food conditions. But only the grant of the equal vote would have given the German workers the political recognition for which they were longing.

✍ Pressures for Peace

AFTER THE EXPERIENCES of the cruel winter of 1917 everybody dreaded the possibility of a fourth war winter. Although nobody in Germany thought of defeat, there was widespread doubt whether the government was doing its best to bring the war to its conclusion. In the belief that such declarations would bring the belligerents to the peace table, the Social Democratic party had accepted the slogan of the soldiers' council of St. Petersburg that there should be a peace "without annexations and contributions," and Philipp Scheidemann, the Social Democratic leader, had publicized this program all over Germany in many speeches. This attitude of the Social Democrats aroused angry counterattacks from the Conservatives, who by denouncing them as national slackers wanted to discredit Prussian franchise reform as well. War aims and domestic politics became closely intertwined, since the ruling classes believed that the survival of the old order depended on a peace with annexations and contributions. Ludendorff, who did not hide his opposition to the franchise reform, had recently published a pamphlet on the peace problem, distributed in the army, stating that a "German peace" would mean "a free people with only a five billion debt," while a "Scheidemann peace" would make Germany "a wage slave of England with a 170 billion debt."

The Supreme Command tried by every means to strengthen the people's confidence in victory. Its members privately admitted, however, that they could not hope for victory except through the defensive. Ludendorff expected that the capacity of the German army to defeat every Allied offensive, together with the submarine warfare, would lead to a breakdown of French and British morale. Any attempt at holding peace conversations with the Allies before their defeat would be judged as a sign of German weakness and thus prolong the war. In addition, Germany should not deprive herself of the fruits of victory. Large annexations in the east and west were to make her unassailable in case of a future war and would make the monarchical regime immune against the pernicious democratic *Zeitgeist*. Both with regard to international and internal national questions Bethmann-Hollweg seemed to Hindenburg and Ludendorff to lack the unyielding determination that they considered imperative for winning the war. But when in April 1917 Hindenburg and Ludendorff committed the government to a very extravagant program of annexations, the chancellor as well as his deputy Helfferich in their public speeches echoed the firm hope of the Supreme Command for a full and early military victory, while carefully avoiding any official commitment to a peace without annexations and contributions.

The civilian government almost as much as the military chiefs underrated the effect of the blockade and the limitations of German manpower and war production. Not even the rapidly growing weakness of Germany's own allies served as a warning. Bulgaria, which had not overcome the ill effects of the Balkan wars of 1912–13 when joining the Central powers, was overstrained. Turkey, too, was suffering from the extension of the war. But the greatest immediate danger lay in the catastrophic deterioration of the internal conditions of the Habsburg empire.

On November 21, 1916, Emperor Francis Joseph had died. In the sixty-eight years of his reign Austria-Hungary, in spite of great historic losses, had maintained the place of a respected great power. Francis Joseph had become the almost legendary symbol of the unity among her various nationalities, and the performance of the army in the first two and a half years of the war had shown that this unity was still greater than the fierce struggles of the nationalities prior to 1914 seemed to indicate. Yet at the time of the old emperor's death the Austro-Hungarian army, though still containing some fine units, was badly crippled. Serious defections, starting among the Czechs, were becoming frequent, while the manpower resources of the empire were exhausted. Food conditions in the Austrian cities were worse than in Germany, and the resentment of the working class against the wartime absolutism of the government was growing fast.

The young Emperor Charles (1887–1922) was convinced that every effort had to be made to end the war, and the situation of Austria-Hungary seemed to him so desperate as to justify possibly even a separate peace. The negotiations which were conducted between January and April 1917 with France through the empress's brother, who served in the Belgian army, remained without positive results. Count Czernin (1872–1932), the foreign minister, warned the German statesmen that Austria-

Hungary would not be able to survive a fourth war winter. Unless peace was concluded within a few months, a revolution of the people would overthrow the monarchies. Even a bad peace would at least save the social order. Czernin cautioned the Germans that their own conditions were only slightly better than those of Austria and that the tide was running against them.

Yet the Germans considered Czernin a frightened pessimist. Following the line of Ludendorff, Bethmann-Hollweg argued that time was now working for the Central Powers. When Count Czernin came to Germany in May 1917, nobody was willing to discuss with him methods for reaching a negotiated peace. Instead the Germans insisted upon a discussion of the future of the Baltic and Balkan countries as well as of Russian Poland. All of them were to remain under the direct or indirect control of the Central Powers, with Germany claiming the lion's share. Czernin, however, was not interested in annexations but in peace, and he informed Matthias Erzberger (1875–1921), a deputy of the German *Reichstag*, of his grave worries. Erzberger, a member of the Center party, had originally been a school teacher and represented a district of small peasants in South Württemberg. A clever, active, and versatile man, he had gained a reputation and won contacts with the government and with industrialists. During the war he had propagated a program of annexations and agitated for the opening of unrestricted submarine warfare. The government had sent him on occasional missions abroad.

But Erzberger was too soberly judicious not to recognize the shift in the military balance. In fact, in the summer of 1917 the Supreme Command itself began to indicate that the war could not be ended in 1917 and demanded from the government an intensive preparation of the people for the continuation of the war beyond the coming winter. These impressions changed Erzberger's political outlook, and he decided to act. In the first days of July the Social Democrats had urged the government to grant the equal franchise and make a public declaration on its willingness to conclude a peace without annexations and contributions. On July 6 Erzberger made a speech in a closed session of the main committee of the *Reichstag* in which he proved that the assumptions and expectations which had led to the unrestricted submarine warfare were thoroughly mistaken. Although the German submarines had actually sunk more ships than had been considered possible, the Allies had not only British shipping but the whole world tonnage at their disposal. It was clear that the predictions made by the German navy chiefs, that England would be defeated before the harvest, had been utterly erroneous, and it was doubtful whether the submarine war could ever bring decisive results.

This sharp criticism of the government gave the justification for Erzberger's demand that the *Reichstag* should assume the leadership in a policy toward peace negotiations through a public declaration on Germany's purely defensive war aims. Erzberger succeeded in rallying the whole Center party into cooperation with the Progressives and Social Democrats for strengthening the position of the German parliament. The three parties in these days formed an interparty committee in which all the major political issues were discussed and ways sought to have the government execute the proposed policies. Thus a direct line led from July 6, 1917, and the establishment of the interparty committee to the active coalition of the three parties in the Weimar National Assembly of 1919. Even the National Liberals occasionally joined the interparty committee. Stresemann and most other National Liberal *Reichstag* members agreed by now with the parties of the left that the parliament ought to exercise a strong influence on governmental policies. But Stresemann still ardently believed in a peace with annexations, opposed a peace resolution as proposed by Erzberger, and wished to see Bethmann-Hollweg replaced, because he distrusted the chancellor's determination to reach a *Siegfriede*. Erzberger aimed at the removal of Bethmann-Hollweg for the very opposite reason. He felt that the projected peace resolution would make a greater impression at home and abroad if it was accompanied by the resignation of the chancellor who had accepted the unrestricted submarine warfare and the break with the United States.

✑ Bethmann-Hollweg's Resignation

BETHMANN-HOLLWEG PLEADED with the parties not to insist on a peace resolution which would be interpreted as a sign of German weakness. He thought that he could propitiate the majority parties by concessions in constitutional matters. Against strong resistance in the Prussian cabinet and in the face of Hindenburg's and Ludendorff's open disapproval he succeeded on July 11, 1917, in persuading William II to issue a declaration in favor of *equal* suffrage in Prussia. But although the emperor on this occasion assured Bethmann-Hollweg of his confidence, he requested his resignation on the following day when Ludendorff and Hindenburg presented him with an ultimatum threatening their own resignations unless the chancellor was dismissed. The crown prince cooperated in the attack against the chancellor by interviewing the party leaders, who, with the exception of the Progressives and Social Democrats, expressed themselves in favor of a change in the chancellorship.

Still, the most fateful act was that of the two generals. In their endeavor to curb the growing influence of the parliament and to remove the chancellor whom they suspected of collaborating with it they actually ruined the monarchical tradition of Prussia. The selection of his ministers had been the exclusive prerogative of the king-emperor. It was an act of insubordination that the two generals, trusting their reputation in the army and among the people, forced the hapless William II to dismiss the chancellor of his confidence. Like shoguns Hindenburg and Ludendorff assumed a substantial part of the imperial power. Bethmann-Hollweg retired in July 1917 without attempting to make a stand. Although theoretically he might have tried to rally a parliamentary majority, it would have gone against his grain to build his support on the parties of the left. Moreover he believed that Hindenburg and Ludendorff were irreplaceable. Bethmann-Hollweg recommended to the emperor the Bavarian prime minister, Count Georg von Hertling (1843–1919), as his successor, but the latter declined on account of his advanced age. The emperor's entourage eventually suggested Georg Michaelis (1857–1936), a lifelong official of the interior administration who had a good name, since the grain and bread rationing office that he had instituted was the best functioning of all rationing agencies. He was a pietistic and conservative Prussian entirely lacking in vision and a novice in high politics. But it was with the explicit approval of the generals that William II appointed Michaelis to Bismarck's office.

The parliamentary parties were annoyed that they had not been consulted on the appointment. They derived some satisfaction, however, from the drafting of half a dozen parliamentarians for high posts in the federal and Prussian administrations. In the place of the dour Zimmerman the foreign office was taken over by the intelligent and smooth Richard von Kühlmann (1873–1948), who as councillor at the London embassy before the war had endeavored to lay the foundation for an Anglo-German rapprochement. The majority parties of the *Reichstag*, however, were not swayed by Hindenburg and Ludendorff from passing a peace resolution and committing the new chancellor to it. The resolution proclaimed that Germany had gone to war only for the defense of her territorial possessions. "The *Reichstag* strives for a peace of understanding and permanent reconciliation of nations. With such a peace forced cessions of territory and political, economic and financial impositions are incompatible." The resolution was not very clear. It did not condemn all annexations but only "forced" cessions. The separation from the Russian empire of the non-Russian territories already occupied by the Central Powers was not excluded by this phraseology, and the possibility was left open that even in the west, after a German victory in France, some cessions might be negotiated. In accepting the resolution that was passed on July 19, 1917, Michaelis cleverly slipped in the words "[the resolution] as I understand it" and felt certain now that the government was practically free to follow any course of action.

Thus the effect of Erzberger's initiative was small. It failed to change the war and peace aims of the German government and to enhance to any considerable degree the power of the *Reichstag* over the government. Still, the cooperation of the Center, the Progressive, and the Social Democratic parties survived, and the peace resolution had a strong echo in the hearts of the masses, in the army as well as at home in the cities and villages. With this resolution Erzberger had intended to prepare the ground for the peace mediation that he knew Pope Benedict XV was about to undertake. When in August the pope offered to assist in getting the powers together for negotiating a peace more or less on the basis of the *status quo ante*, Michaelis and Kühlmann discussed the German answer to the papal note with the party leaders. With Ebert and Erzberger dissenting, they agreed with the chancellor and foreign secretary that the expression of Germany's readiness for a peace of conciliation should be followed merely by a reference to the peace resolution of the *Reichstag* without a clear statement on Germany's willingness to restore Belgium to full independence. But the chancellor and secretary had already been reminded by the Vatican that such an unequivocal statement was the absolute prerequisite for the success of the mediation, and the first British reaction to the papal note confirmed this judgment. The German government was far from being candid with the leaders of the *Reichstag*, although the very fact that the ministers formally consulted them showed that they recognized the potential power of the parliament.

The question of Belgium was discussed in a crown council on September 11. The emperor now rejected the navy's demand for the retention of the coast of Flanders, though not the old plans for extracting military and economic guarantees that Belgium would not become an exclusive ally of the Western Powers, which meant in reality that Germany would control the Belgian economy and take Liège and the Meuse line. In addition, the emperor approved the diplomatic strategy that Kühlmann proposed. Through neutral diplomatic channels he wished to find out whether the British government would be prepared to enter into the negotiations of a peace that recognized the integrity of Germany and her allies if the German government were to restore Belgian sovereignty. Kühlmann wanted to use the restoration of Belgium as a means of getting palpable concessions. Actually he greatly overrated the inclination of the British government to get into peace conversations on the basis of the *status quo ante*. It would have been more prudent to issue a public statement announcing Germany's readiness to restore an independent Belgium, since this might have activated those popular forces in England that urged peace negotiations. But in its reply to Pope Benedict XV the German government stated that it was not as yet in a position to make definite declarations on Belgium. While the papal mediation thus came to an end, the German diplomatic feelers did not produce any results either, since they were handled clumsily by the neutral diplomat.

Although Michaelis as chancellor subordinated himself completely to Hindenburg's and Ludendorff's wishes, even the two generals were embarrassed by his lack of political dexterity. The majority parties sensed Michaelis' opposition to parliamentarianism, as well as to a peace of conciliation. The chancellor thought that he could strengthen his internal position and weaken the cooperation of the majority parties by an action against the Independent Socialists. He believed that he had sufficient material to prove them guilty of treason and eventually to dissolve the party. On October 9 the chancellor in the *Reichstag* charged the Independent Socialists with responsibility for the mutinies which had occurred in the battle fleet between June and August.

✑ Sailors' Mutiny

LIFE ON THE BIG GERMAN BATTLESHIPS, which were mostly in port, had grown painfully drab and monotonous after three years of war. It was understandable that some resentment developed against the drill and the chores with which the officers tried to fill the endless hours. The relations between officers and the rank and file became strained by the observation of the many privileges which the officers enjoyed, first of all the better food. But the sailors also took offense at the political ideas of the officers, most of whom wanted the war to continue until England would have been totally defeated. In contrast, the majority of the sailors longed for an end of the war. The Russian March revolution excited them, because it seemed to bring the end of the war closer, and they welcomed the peace resolution of the *Reichstag*. Most of the sailors were good patriotic citizens without specific party ties although some were attached to the Center or to the Majority or Independent Socialists. None of these parties was actively trying to carry on propaganda, but by letter and word sailors had occasionally made their complaints known to some *Reichstag* deputies.

The dissatisfaction of the sailors expressed itself first in some protest strikes against the turnip fare served to them, but subsequently a few battleship crews staged demonstrations against the harsh discipline by going on land for a few hours. No violence whatsoever occurred nor were any political demands raised, although there was no doubt that a deep cleavage existed between officers and men in their political sentiment. It was most unfortunate that in the secret court martials, in which the defense was seriously handicapped, the judges thought to discover a scheme of general revolt fostered by the Independent Socialists. Draconic punishment was meted out to many of the leading participants of these demonstrations. Actually the sailors might easily have been brought back to complete obedience by a sensible discussion of the exigencies of the war situation. But while the austere penalties ended the demonstrations of the sailors, they did not quell the mutinous spirit of the battle fleet, which remained smoldering as a latent source of future revolt.

✍ *Count Hertling, Chancellor*

THE ATTACK THAT CHANCELLOR MICHAELIS opened against the Independent Socialist party on October 9 was at once met by sharp and convincing rejoinders by the leaders of the Social Democratic and Independent Socialist parties. Ebert demanded the resignation of the chancellor, who received no support from the Progressives, the Center, or even the National Liberals. It was an indirect and unofficial vote of no-confidence by the majority and led to Michaelis' downfall. Since even the Supreme Command was no longer interested in him, he was replaced in the last days of October by the old Count Hertling. The majority parties insisted this time that the new chancellor should reach an agreement with them on the main issues of German foreign and domestic policy. Hertling accepted their demands for the immediate reform of the Prussian franchise, for liberal changes in the administration of the press censorship and the supervision of public meetings, as well as for a foreign policy in accordance with the peace resolution. The growing strength of the parliament was further indicated by the appointment of two party representatives to high offices. The South German democrat Friedrich von Payer (1847–1931), who was supported by the Progressives and the Social Democrats, was made vice-chancellor, while Robert Friedberg (1851–1920), a left National Liberal, became vice-president of the Prussian cabinet.

Actually the influence of the *Reichstag* was not substantially increased, since under the law on the "state of siege" the decision on censorship and public meetings as well as a great many other powers were left in the hands of Hindenburg and Ludendorff. As things stood, the Prussian diet was not likely to reform the suffrage unless the two generals brought pressure on their political friends in the rightist parties. The war aims were determined by the Supreme Command. Chancellor Count Hertling was in favor of the Prussian suffrage reform and quickly presented a bill to the diet. His ideal was a moderately liberal monarchy of the South German type. On the other hand, he was opposed to parliamentary government through the *Reichstag*, because it would have weakened the rights of the states and the position of the Federal Council. In foreign affairs Hertling avoided any conflict with the Supreme Command, and Payer, the vice-chancellor, proved equally docile. The senescent Hertling was gravely overtaxed by the demands of his office and unable to take many initiatives. Thus he merely tried to keep the army from extending its control over the civilian society still further, without attempting, as his predecessor had done, to break up the cooperation of the majority parties in the *Reichstag*. He was satisfied with keeping them from any new public demonstration similar to the peace resolution. In this respect his very appearance on the political scene as an old former member of the Center party activated its right wing and stalled Erzberger's influence. And Payer kept the Progressives from pressing new demands in public.

✍ *Hindenburg's and Ludendorff's Virtual Dictatorship*

THUS HINDENBURG AND LUDENDORFF were free to impose their will on the German government until their might was broken by military defeat. The common man was not aware of the virtual dictatorship of the two generals, whose military excellence was not questioned. It was a unique event that a whole nation looked up with enthusiastic admiration to two men. Of the two, only Hindenburg won true popularity as the mythical embodiment of extraordinary strength, great practical wisdom, and upright honesty. Ludendorff's personality inspired respect rather than affection, and it was suspected that he more than Hindenburg held the secret of victory, or at least that the two together were needed as heads of the army. Actually Ludendorff was the architect of all of Hindenburg's battles and campaigns. To be sure, the younger Ludendorff had to formulate his plans with greater circumspection in order to convince a senior of more conventional thought, and it is questionable whether he could have built up the same prestige with the soldiers of all ranks that Hindenburg enjoyed. Ludendorff gained more than he was willing to admit later on by having his orders issued over Hindenburg's signature. The intellectual contributions of Hindenburg were small, and he was too phlegmatic to originate plans of his own. General Max Hoffmann, one of his ablest staff officers in the east, early noted that "never had a man become famous with so little intellectual and physical effort of his own" as this "idol of the people." Beginning with his boyhood at the cadet institute, Hindenburg, who came from a *Junker* family that had lost its estate, had spent practically his whole life in the Prussian army. As lieutenant he had fought in the wars of 1866 and 1870–71. Unlike the elder Moltke or Count Schlieffen he had not acquired a broad education nor was he given much to reflective thought. In all his speeches and writings he used the customary ideas and phrases of the monarchist nationalism of the late Bismarckian period. Social problems were alien to him, and he knew little about foreign countries and international politics. But this stolid man of the titanic Bismarckian build impressed people by his human simplicity and directness as well as by his imperturbable calm in the midst of any crisis.

Although Ludendorff was a much brainier type and a true pupil of Schlieffen in his belief that every military task could be solved by the application of will power and reason, he, too, was a narrowly professional soldier. He was a military commander of real distinction, though without great originality. The full tactical potentialities of new weapons, such as planes and tanks, were not recognized by him. Moreover, he was ill-equipped to deal with the problems of economic mobilization, and his disregard of the experts in this field was a sign of his exaggerated self-esteem. In politics, for which he considered himself competent and to which he was passionately committed, he was a simple authoritarian militarist and Pan-Germanist. In contrast to Hindenburg, whom he dragged along in all his major political actions, Ludendorff had no deep sentimental ties to the Prussian monarchical system. It was symptomatic that he refused to be knighted, although his mother belonged to an old Prussian *Junker* family. To him the army had become largely autonomous as the elite of the nation, and the people were to be indoctrinated with a militant nationalistic spirit in order to give full support to the national war effort. In the existing political parties he saw dangerous enemies, with the exception of the Conservatives and the chauvinistic National Liberals, who, however, failed to rally the whole people.

✍ *Fatherland Party*

ADMIRAL VON TIRPITZ AND WOLFGANG KAPP (1858–1922), a rabid Pan-Germanist and prominent East Prussian, attempted to build up a party above all parties. Alarmed by the peace resolution of the *Reichstag* of July 1917, they founded the so-called Fatherland party in September 1917. Asserting boldly that the *Reichstag*, elected before the war, did not represent the true will of the people, they called all patriotic Germans to rally in active support of an energetic government that would not make weak concessions at home and abroad but display an unshakable faith in victory. According to them, constitutional changes during the war would weaken its conduct, while peace declarations, the result of "frayed nerves," would be taken by the enemies as a sign of the collapse of German strength. The Fatherland party demanded a peace commensurate with German sacrifices.

Tirpitz' call "Germany awake, your hour of destiny has arrived!" actually attracted one and a quarter million people, a larger following than the Social Democratic party with its one million members had commanded in 1914. The Fatherland party carried on loud and massive propaganda. It was abetted by the wartime censorship that kept its opponents from expressing themselves with equal force, and the Supreme Command permitted the ideas of the party to be used for the political indoctrination of the troops. Yet, in spite of its impressive showing, the Fatherland party succeeded only in mobilizing the upper classes, while failing to win a mass following outside the bourgeoisie. On the other hand, as a result of its activities the majority parties maintained closer contacts than would have happened without the challenge from the right. In December 1917 the Social Democratic, Christian, and Hirsch-Duncker trade unions formed the People's Federation for Liberty and Fatherland. The philosopher Ernst Troeltsch (1865–1923) and the historian Friedrich Meinecke (1862–1954) were among the leaders of this organization, which attempted to counteract the thunder of the Fatherland party through the propagation of a just peace for all nations and internal reform. The scope of the activities of the People's Federation was more limited than that of the Fatherland party because not the whole Center party was committed to its aims, and the Social Democratic party did not want to subordinate its own propaganda to an interparty group.

✍ *The Bolshevik Revolution*

THE HOPES FOR PEACE with Russia which the March revolution had raised came to naught. On November 7–8, 1917, the Kerenski government was overthrown by the bolsheviks. They also gained control of Moscow, and for the time being the great mass of the soldiers, workers, and peasants accepted them as their rulers. The German government had contributed to these developments. As early as August 1914 it had decided to conduct the war against the British and Russian empires by the widest possible use of revolutionary subversion. Great efforts were made to help the Irish revolutionaries, and extensive operations were carried out from Turkey in order to launch a Pan-Islamic movement that would make the Moslems of Egypt and India rise against their British rulers. Yet none of these projects bore fruit. On the contrary, the British won the active cooperation of Ibn Saud and his Arabic tribes for the destruction of the Turkish empire.

Great results, however, were eventually to accrue from other subversive activities started in the fall of 1914. These originally had aimed at fomenting national separatist movements. Finland, Poland, and Georgia were the immediate targets, and the creation of an independent Ukraine was also envisaged shortly after the outbreak of the war. The close connection between national and social revolution had manifested itself in the Russian revolution of 1905, and, from the spring of 1915 on, the German foreign office proceeded to build up a network of contacts with the revolutionary socialists inside and outside of Russia. These operations were directed by Dr. Alexander Parvus Helphand, a Russo-German revolutionary. Among the German diplomats it was particularly the minister in

Copenhagen, Count Ulrich von Brockdorff-Rantzau (1869-1928), who urged the strongest support for Helphand's subversion of the czarist empire. After the March revolution he recommended that Lenin and other bolsheviks living in Switzerland be permitted to travel back to Russia in order to increase the revolutionary chaos. Actually, Bethmann-Hollweg and Zimmermann (who was still foreign secretary at the time), on the suggestion of the German minister in Berne, had already decided on this course of action, for which they secured Ludendorff's approval. During the next months the German government also provided funds with which the bolsheviks built up their instruments of propaganda.

After traveling in a sealed train through Germany to Sweden, Lenin arrived in Petrograd on April 16, 1917, and was welcomed by the revolutionary workers and soldiers. But during the summer he suffered dangerous setbacks in his rise to power, and even after November 8 the internal position of the bolshevik government remained precarious. But if the new rulers succeeded in ending the war, as they had promised, bolshevism had every prospect of being strengthened, although a bad peace might give the counterrevolution the chance to overpower it. Yet originally the bolsheviks, including Lenin, believed that they possessed the key to success in the international field as well. They were convinced that their program of a peace without annexations and indemnities and with the realization of the right of self-determination would make the masses rise against governments prolonging the war for the sake of gaining foreign possessions— and that it would be possible to incite the German workers in particular to overthrow the militarists who ruled Germany.

The German government was quick to respond to the Russian appeal for peace that was broadcast from Petrograd on November 8. Ludendorff was in a hurry for peace to be concluded in the east. Seeing the Russian army collapse, he had at once decided to try for a victorious ending of the war by mounting a big offensive in the west using the German forces that until now had been tied down in the east. Around the middle of November a good many German divisions were already rolling westward. The Russians were granted a liberal armistice, and the Russian formula, that this armistice should serve the negotiation of a "democratic peace without annexations and contributions," was accepted.

✐ Conference of Brest-Litovsk

THE REPRESENTATIVES of the Central Powers met a Russian delegation at the fortress town of Brest-Litovsk on December 20, 1917. Two days later, Joffe, the leader of the Soviet delegation, presented a set of principles as guideposts for peace negotiations, to which all nations at war were to be invited. These principles excluded forcible annexation of any territories taken during the war and demanded the speedy withdrawal of the occupying armies. Further postulates were the restoration of complete independence to those nationalities who had lost it in the war and the right of nationalities hitherto not independent to choose freely between independence and union with another nation. In regions inhabited by several nationalities the rights of minorities were to be guaranteed. All these tenets were to be applied to colonies as well. On Christmas Day the Central Powers replied through a speech of the Austro-Hungarian foreign minister, Count Czernin. They made two major reservations, that all belligerent powers must bind themselves to the principles agreed upon and that the question of nonindependent national groups had to be solved by each state in accordance with its constitution.

The first reservation was chiefly designed to frighten off the Allies from participating in a conference. By referring to India, Egypt, and Morocco as deserving of national self-determination, this reservation was planned to keep England and France away. The second reservation was to protect Austria-Hungary and Germany against the application of the principle of national self-determination to their nationalities. The reply of the Central Powers contained other qualifications, but it did not seem to deny national self-determination to the nationalities of the Russian empire. This naturally pleased the Soviet delegation while shocking the large section of the German people that demanded extensive annexations. Since the bolsheviks had successfully insisted that the negotiations should be carried on in public, the world heard about them in full detail.

The Russian reaction to the speech of Count Czernin worried the German delegation, which in addition to the new foreign secretary, Richard von Kühlmann, included the representative of the Supreme Command, Major General Max Hoffmann, the chief of staff of the eastern front. Anxious as the Germans were to reach a quick settlement with the bolsheviks and therefore willing to accommodate to the principles which the latter espoused, though only for tactical and propagandistic reasons, the German government had by no means given up its vast program of eastward expansion. In the spring of 1917 it had been decided to disguise the planned annexations by setting up seemingly autonomous states, which, however, were to be forced to grant Germany such far-reaching rights of political, military, and economic control as to leave them puppets in German hands. As a preparatory move in the occupied Courland and Lithuania, "land councils" had been created, which were merely advisory bodies to the German military government. Moreover, in Courland, where the Germans, mostly belonging to the landed gentry and upper class bourgeoisie, formed at best 7 per cent of the people, they constituted a majority in the land council. The Germans planned to maintain that in all these countries the will of the people had found adequate expression and that the official acceptance of the principle of national self-determination did not exclude the separation from Russia of German-dominated Courland and Lithuania, perhaps also of Livonia and Esthonia, which so far had been only partly occupied by German troops.

The members of the German delegation were surprised that the Russians failed to grasp this implication of German policy and decided to warn Joffe before he went home. The delegates had agreed to adjourn the conference for ten days in order to await the reaction of the Allies to the proceedings in Brest-Litovsk. Joffe was profoundly shaken by the information given to him by General Hoffmann and officially stated by Kühlmann at the public session of the conference of December 28. When the Russians left for Petrograd, it seemed uncertain whether they would return. Count Czernin was deeply worried. He wanted peace, any peace. Austria was completely exhausted, her grain reserves would last only for two more months, and the urgently needed bread could only be gotten in the east. He threatened to make a separate peace since the dual alliance did not oblige Austria to fight for German expansionist aims. But the German officers coldly replied that such an Austrian move would merely simplify their military task, because it would enable them to withdraw twenty-five German divisions used to prop up the Austrian forces. When Czernin later had to beg the Germans to send grain, Austrian political influence sank to zero.

Lenin replaced Joffe with Leon Trotsky. Lenin had come to realize that the "capitalist-imperialist" governments of the Central Powers were still in control of the masses and that it would be impossible to postpone the conclusion of peace till a revolution would produce another German government. But he thought it useful to delay the peace and exploit the armistice and peace conference to the utmost for spreading revolutionary propaganda. Trotsky was a master of long-drawn forensic rhetoric and quick rebuttal, and his brilliant intelligence combined with boundless energy made the best of a rather hopeless situation. The government he represented was still struggling for its domestic survival, and there were no armies for fighting the foreign invaders, while the Allies were unable to assist the bolsheviks even if they had wished to do so. But most Allied statesmen were understandably horrified by the bolsheviks and mistakenly believed that the regime of such eccentric brutes could not last very long.

President Wilson, in his great Fourteen-Point speech of January 8, 1918, gave some theoretical help to the bolshevik leaders, and his insistence on the application of national self-determination to Germany, through his demands for the evacuation of the occupied eastern territories and the transfer of the Polish districts of Prussia to an independent Polish national state, at this moment could be taken as a support of the "open diplomacy" practiced by the bolsheviks at Brest-Litovsk. Actually Wilson's speech was the beginning of a drive against the attempt of the bolsheviks to appropriate to themselves the liberal ideas of a new world order that Wilson had proclaimed in early 1917. It was obvious that the bolsheviks were using such ideals as national self-determination chiefly for tactical and propagandistic reasons and were violating them whenever they had the opportunity to do so. The German government in January 1918 saw in Wilson's Fourteen Points only an instrument of Allied political warfare that was detrimental to Germany. Chancellor Count Hertling disparaged the Wilsonian program in a speech before the *Reichstag* on January 24.

The Russians returned to Brest-Litovsk on January 8, and Trotsky prolonged all negotiations by speeches aimed at arousing the masses in the capitalist countries and at denouncing the German acceptance of the principle of national self-determination as sheer hypocrisy. And although Kühlmann showed great skill in defending the German position, Trotsky succeeded in making the Germans appear as representatives of naked power politics. In this he had the involuntary support of General Max Hoffmann, whose threatening outbursts revealed what Kühlmann's suave manners might have left unsaid.

Between the Germans and Austrians the plan was developed to make peace first with the Ukraine. Here in the summer of 1917 a national government had come into being elected by a representative council, called *rada*. On January 7 a Ukrainian delegation had appeared in Brest-Litovsk, and in the course of the month peace terms were negotiated. To the Austrians a peace with the Ukraine meant salvation from starvation. For the Germans, too, it was a "bread-peace," but under the pressure of the tycoons of German industry the Ukraine was viewed as a rich future source of valuable raw materials and a field of German economic enterprise. In order to satisfy the nationalist pride of the Ukrainians, the Austrians were prevailed upon to cede at least one district of their possessions predominately populated by Ukrainians to the new state. The frontiers of this state vis-à-vis what the Germans now liked to call "Great Russia" were generous to the Ukrainians. In return they had to promise to make their supposedly very large surpluses of foodstuffs available to Germany and Austria-Hungary.

Another intermission of the peace conference took place later in January 1918. While the bolsheviks were fighting for their lives in suppressing the just-elected constituent assembly, they fell apart among themselves over the peace issue. Lenin, who urged the signing of the German peace treaty in order to save the revolution in Russia, remained in the minority, and Trotsky's proposal of "no war, no peace" was adopted by the party. This meant the Russian refusal to sign the German peace treaty and the unilateral proclamation of the end of the war. Trotsky believed that the Germans would not dare march more deeply into revolutionary Russia, while in contrast to Lenin he saw a revolution in Germany close at hand. And indeed in Austria-Hungary a serious strike movement was rampant in protest against the food shortages and, even more, the delay in the conclusion of a peace treaty caused by the German demands for annexations. On January 28, 1918, a big strike of 400,000 workers was started in Berlin that spread to many other German cities. It was not instigated by leaders of the Independent Socialist and Social Democratic parties but by delegates elected in the individual factories, who later in the year became known as the "revolutionary foremen." The strikers demanded more food for the working population, the speedy arrangement of a peace without annexations, the democratization of German political institutions, and the lifting of the "state of siege." It was a threatening outbreak of the sentiment of the masses directed particularly against the power of the military men in Germany. The strike was intended as a demonstration and not as the beginning of a revolutionary fight against the government, since its leaders knew only too well that the old authorities were still firmly entrenched. On February 3 the orders were issued to return to work. Ludendorff quickly intervened by having military courts set up and subsequently had thousands of workers drafted into the army and sent to the front.

Trotsky's expectations with regard to the outbreak of revolution in Germany were premature, and he erred if he believed that the bolshevik successes—the capture of Helsingfors (Helsinki) and of Kiev by red troops—would swerve the German government from its course. On February 9 the ministers of the Central Powers signed the peace treaty with the representatives of the Ukraine, who by then had lost practically the whole Ukraine to the bolsheviks and would have to be reinstalled in the country by German armed forces. On the following day Trotsky made his "no war, no peace" declaration which left everybody speechless. But Ludendorff prevailed upon the government to allow him to launch an immediate offensive in the direction of Petrograd. He wished not only to compel the bolsheviks to accept a German peace but also to force them to give up all of Livonia and Esthonia, which meant the whole Baltic coast, since he was to assist the Finns in the formation of an independent Finland. The German troops began their eastward and northeastward drive on February 18, and practically without meeting any resistance moved rather rapidly, causing deep consternation in the bolshevik councils. This time Lenin, after a herculean effort, imposed his will on the Petrograd Soviet. Although in their ultimatum the Germans now demanded that the Russians should not only renounce all interference in Poland, Courland, and Lithuania but also evacuate Livonia and Esthonia, thus cutting them off from both the Baltic and Black seas, the bolsheviks signed the dictated peace on March 3, 1918, in order to save the Soviet Republic.

The Treaty of Brest-Litovsk, which Lenin called the "Treaty of Tilsit," was debated in the *Reichstag*. The Conservatives and the National Liberals found that it did not go far enough, though praising it as a magnificent achievement of German arms. The Centrists and Progressives approved the eastern treaties and found them in accordance with the majority resolution of 1917, although Erzberger expressed the hope that in the Baltic provinces the right of national self-determination might in the future be more strongly demonstrated before the world by a wider vote of the people. The Social Democratic party sharply criticized the treaties, because they had been designed without consultation with the parliament and could not be considered an honest application of the principle of national self-determination. But rather illogically the party abstained from voting, because the treaty had at least brought about peace in the east. Only the Independent Socialists voted against the treaties. With good reason, their leader, Hugo Haase, warned that after the peace of Brest-Litovsk the world would no longer believe in Germany's promises and that it would stiffen the determination of the Allies to continue the war in order not to see naked power politics triumph everywhere in the world.

Germany's Eastern Expansion

LUDENDORFF WAS NOW SUPREME. After the failure of the January strikes he had no reason to fear an opposition majority in the parliament, and actually the majority parties which had voted the peace resolution refused to exercise any influence at this moment. Thus Ludendorff could still extend his program for eastern conquests. Simultaneously with the advance toward Petrograd German troops supported by Austrian units, which the Vienna government sent as a result of strong German pressure, marched into the Ukraine. Here some hard fighting occurred against red guards as well as the Czech legion, and the invaders saw themselves surrounded by a sullen and generally hostile population. On March 1, 1918, Kiev was occupied and later in the month the occupation of the Ukraine was extended eastward to the Don river and Rostow. The services rendered to the rada government by this heavy military investment were used as the excuse for demanding the most far-reaching economic concessions, which were designed to turn the Ukraine into a permanent economic colony. "It is in the East where we may collect the interest on our war bonds," a member of the German government exclaimed.

But conditions in the Ukraine were chaotic, and the rada government, a group of rather young intellectuals with little political experience, failed completely to build up administrative controls. Being moderate socialists, they were hated not only by the bolsheviks but also by the counterrevolutionary big landowners. They felt that their position would become untenable if they made themselves accomplices to all the schemes of present and future exploitation that the Germans were urgently trying to impose. The altercations between the rada and the German command led to the arrest of the former by German troops on April 28, 1918. On the following day a meeting of the landowners' party proclaimed the former Russian general, Pawel Tetrowitsch Skoropadski (1873–1945), "hetman" of the Ukraine. While this government had practically no popular support beyond the big landowners, German soldiers had to enforce its reactionary measures. It proved ready to accept the many schemes devised by the German government and industrialists to exploit the resources of the Ukraine in the future for the benefit of the German economy. Yet the Ukrainian government was unable to deliver the grain, foodstuffs, and industrial raw materials so urgently needed by the Central Powers, and the occupiers had to organize the collection of these goods themselves. The results were modest. The expected huge food surpluses turned out to be of only ordinary size, while a collapsing Ukrainian currency and transportation difficulties limited these operations still further.

In complete disregard of the treaty of Brest-Litovsk the German expansion was carried forward even beyond the Ukraine. German troops occupied the Crimea, which was considered to be part of Russia and, besides a small minority of German settlers, had largely a Tatar population. Ludendorff wanted to make the Crimea a German colony, where he hoped many more Germans could be settled. In addition this German bastion was to protect the lines of communication with the possessions which he wanted to acquire in Transcaucasia. The German foreign office, though agreeing with Ludendorff that the Crimea should not be left in Russian hands and that Germany should seek to build up a strong position in this region, argued that the full separation of the Crimea under German rule would drive the Ukraine into the arms of Russia. The German diplomats therefore pleaded that eventually the Crimea should be linked to the Ukraine.

The Crimea in 1918 served as a stepping stone to Transcaucasia. Since the outbreak of the war German agents had been active in promoting national revolutions in this area with the intention not only of weakening Russia but also of gaining a base of operations against Persia and India. But only after October 1917 did movements get under way aiming at the establishment of autonomous states, possibly united in a Transcaucasian federation. Strong frictions developed between Germany and Turkey over the treatment of Transcaucasia. The Turks, branded by the Germans as "imperialists," used the opportunity to stake out frontiers going far beyond the restoration of those of 1878 that the treaty of Brest-Litovsk envisaged. They were even unwilling to hand over to their German allies at least the economic control of these lands. In May 1918 Germany concluded special agreements with Georgia, while expecting to be able to extend her domination over the other parts of Transcaucasia. The whole region was coveted for its oil, iron, manganese, wool, and other raw materials. In addition, Ludendorff saw in the Georgians good soldiers. Actually it was as late as the middle of September 1918 that German troops moved to the Caspian sea and occupied Baku.

It took the German government a long time to negotiate a peace treaty with the Rumanians, who proved skillful and stubborn in the defense of their national cause. Finally, on May 7, 1918, they were forced by ultimatum to sign the peace treaty of Bucarest together with five economic conventions. But the long delay was also caused by serious conflicts between the Turks and Bulgarians over the peace terms and by differences between Germany and Austria-Hungary. In the end Germany realized practically all her aims. She achieved the domination of Rumania's economic life chiefly through a trade monopoly on oil, the control of the navigation on the Danube as well as of railroad lines, and the establishment of a free port in Constanza on the Black sea. For a number of years Germany was also to direct the Rumanian grain trade.

In 1917 an understanding had been reached that Poland should come under Austro-Hungarian rule, while Rumania was considered a future German preserve. But the Austro-Polish solution had been made dependent on certain conditions. Germany, as has been mentioned before, in the beginning wanted the cession of a "frontier strip" along and beyond the Narew river, a province that was to be built up to a wall between Austrian Poland and the Prussian Polish provinces. In addition, she insisted on securing the predominant influence on Poland's economy. Yet with the growing weakness of the Habsburg empire the German government saw an opportunity of gaining control of Austria-Hungary herself. Clemenceau's disclosure of the peace offers that Emperor Charles had made to the Allies through the Prince of Parma in 1916–17 enabled the Germans to put pressure on the Austrian government, which was forced to promise to accept a close political alliance, a military convention, and a customs union with Germany. But Count Czernin's successor, Baron Burian (1851–1922), made these concessions dependent on the Austro-Polish solution. In the course of July 1918 the German government vainly demanded by ultimatum that Austria-Hungary should yield on the Polish question and afterwards attempted to extract from the Poles recognition of Germany's future domination of their country. With

German power visibly ebbing, however, both Austrians and Poles were able to procrastinate and avoid any final commitment before the end of the war.

Yet as late as August 27 the German government made the bolsheviks sign new treaties, which, though declared to be supplementary to the peace of Brest-Litovsk, actually were imposing additional losses and stringent burdens upon Russia. Before the treaties were concluded, much fighting had taken place in the inner councils of the German government. The former vice-chancellor, Karl Helfferich, who succeeded the first German ambassador to Moscow, Count Mirbach, after the latter's assassination, on July 6, 1918, had strongly pleaded that Germany should end her cooperation with the loathsome bolshevik regime. He argued that since this regime was generally hated, it was bound to fall before long. Only by taking the initiative in overthrowing the bolshevik government could Germany hope to win the sympathies of the other Russian parties and thereby continue her influence on Russia.

Although Helfferich's arguments temporarily swayed William II and even Ludendorff, Admiral Paul von Hintze (1864–1941), who had succeeded Kühlmann in the foreign office in July 1918, convinced everybody except Helfferich that, weak as the bolsheviks were, their internal Russian opponents were powerless to overthrow them and that even if they were to gain the upper hand, they would at once challenge the peace settlement of Brest-Litovsk. The bolsheviks were the best weapon for keeping Russia in a state of chaos, thus allowing Germany not only to tear off as many provinces from the former Russian empire as she wished but also to rule the rest through economic controls. The August treaties forced the Russians formally to cede Livonia and Esthonia, with their frontiers moved far to the east, and also to accept the separation of Georgia. In exchange Germany returned the railroad line Moskow-Rostow-Baku, kept the Turks from occupying Baku, and promised to evacuate the Black sea region. But these concessions had to be paid for by Russia by a tribute of 6 billion marks and deliveries of grain, coal, iron, and oil. In the future Russia was supposed to offer all her surpluses of grain and raw materials to Germany first, and after the war was to serve as an economic colony producing the raw materials for German industries and providing a market for German goods.

Meanwhile the Germans had been busy extending their hold on the Baltic provinces of Russia and tying them forever to the German Empire. A few days after the signing of the treaty of Brest-Litovsk on March 3, 1918, the German-dominated "land council" of Courland passed a resolution to beg William II to accept the ducal crown of Courland. The resolution also expressed the wish that Livonia and Esthonia should be joined with Courland into a single state. Since, even after Brest-Litovsk,

Livonia and Esthonia had still belonged to Russia, the German government did not immediately respond to the last demand, although on March 29 it officially recognized Courland's independence and announced its willingness to conclude such state treaties as would guarantee the close economic and military union of Courland and Germany.

In Livonia and Esthonia the formation of "land councils" and their cooperation with the council of Courland was encouraged. Ludendorff did his best to promote through the local military governors the separate organization of the Baltic region, and he tried to spur on the Berlin government to proclaim the unity and independence of this region. Neither the chancellor, Count Hertling, nor the vice-chancellor, Payer, were opposed to Ludendorff's eastern aims, and the preparations for the conventions which were to chain these countries to Germany were made with a view to achieving these ends. After the signing of the Russo-German treaties of August 27 no further attention was paid to Russia in dealing with the Baltic problems. But in the process of working out the final modalities of appending the Baltic state to Germany the intricate nature of the German constitution caused some delay. Was William II to assume the dignity of a duke in his capacity of German emperor or of king of Prussia? In the latter case it would have been possible to bypass the Federal Council and the *Reichstag*. Thus a group of Prussian ministers was convinced that ultimately the Baltic lands ought to become Prussian provinces. But in the end, in view of Germany's professed adherence to the principle of national self-determination, outright annexation was deemed unfeasible by the chancellor and foreign secretary, and subjoining the Baltic state to Prussia instead of to the German Empire seemed to them likely to offend the feelings of the other German princes and the German people, who saw in the creation of this state the fruit of a common national effort. On September 22 the emperor proclaimed the independence of Livonia and Esthonia, but by November 7, when the "land councils" of the three provinces elected a Baltic regency council in preparation for the establishment of a single state, Germany's military and political might had collapsed. A few days later an Esthonian and a Latvian government came into being.

Whereas in Courland, Livonia, and Esthonia the Germans, while still strong, had found relatively little resistance to their schemes, in Lithuania they met with a national movement not easily cajoled or frightened into cooperation. Besides, it had the advantage of having vocal national committees in some neutral countries. The "land council," the so-called *taryba*, was composed exclusively of Lithuanians and from its inception in September 1917 stubbornly attempted to be recognized as the national representation of the country. But the Germans treated it merely as a consultative body, and their threat to divide the country forced the *taryba* on December 11, 1917, on the eve of the peace conference of Brest-Litovsk, to affirm their desire for a "firm eternal alliance" with Germany that would principally consist of a military, transportation, customs, and currency union. In its official recognition of the independence of Lithuania, in March 1918, the German government made the establishment of a Lithuanian state dependent on the conclusion of such conventions.

Erzberger, who took a special interest in the Catholic Lithuanians and wished to give South Germany a part in the eastern policy of the empire, suggested to the Lithuanians the election of the duke of Urach, a member of the Catholic branch of the Württemberg dynasty, as Lithuanian king. On July 11 the *taryba* proclaimed itself the Lithuanian "state council" and Lithuania a constitutional monarchy and offered the crown to the duke of Urach as King Mindaugas II. The German government, with the general applause of the German press, declared the whole action invalid. But it failed to get from the *taryba* any concessions with respect to the specific conventions of submission, and on October 20, 1918, under the shadow of general defeat, the German chancellor recognized the *taryba* as "state council" with the right to form a government, while stating that Germany would abstain from meddling in the problems of the constitution and the boundaries of the country.

From the first days of August 1914 on, the German government had tried to stir up the Finns against Russia. But all the Finns contacted denied that any revolt was likely to succeed unless it was supported by a Swedish or German army. All that could be done was the formation of a Finnish rifle battalion from among Finnish émigrés. Not even the March revolution of 1917 led to a full separation of Finland from Russia. Although the social-revolutionary forces which were in the ascendancy wished to broaden the autonomy of Finland, they did not want her to cut her ties with Russia. But the elections of October 1917 did not produce a majority of the Finnish socialists. Their chief opponent, Pehr Svinhufvud, became state president, and on December 6 the Finnish parliament proclaimed the country an independent republic. Direct negotiations between Svinhufvud and Lenin, supported by strong German pressure on the Soviets in Brest-Litovsk, resulted on January 4, 1918, in Russia's recognition of Finland's independence, followed by that of Sweden, France, and Germany.

But before the Russian troops had withdrawn, civil war broke out. The socialists, particularly strong in the southern parts, wanted a communist state and for this reason continued their ties with revolutionary Russia. The Russian troops cooperated with the red workers' guards, and in late January Helsinki was taken. Svinhufvud organized resistance in the north, where farmers and middle-class people had started to form defense corps. In the former Russian general, Baron Carl von Mannerheim (1867–

1951), they found an able commander. Mannerheim hoped that Finland would win independence by her own strength and thus avoid future reliance on foreign powers. But this proved impossible. After Sweden's refusal to come to Finland's assistance Svinhufvud turned to Germany for help.

In view of the Brest-Litovsk conference the German government and Supreme Command hesitated to intervene at once. But Trotsky's breakup of the conference in February made it unnecessary to pay further attention to Russian feelings. The Finnish rifle battalion was separated from the Prussian army and sent from Courland, where it had been stationed, to Finland. On March 7, 1918, a group of German-Finnish treaties were signed in Berlin. Finland promised not to conclude any foreign alliances without German permission nor to tolerate foreign military bases, while allowing Germany to build naval bases. In addition Germany secured economic privileges which were bound to give her a dominant influence on the Finnish economy.

Late in March and in early April, 15,000 German soldiers under the command of General Rüdiger von der Goltz (1865–1946) landed in Finland and with their help Mannerheim smashed the red forces in all parts of Finland by the end of April. On October 9, 1918, the Finnish parliament elected Prince Frederick Charles of Hesse, a brother-in-law of William II, king of Finland, but at the end of the war Finland became a republic and was freed of the obligations which the treaties with Germany had imposed upon her.

The tremendous program of Germany's domination of Eurasia all the way from the Oder and Vistula to Vladivostok, by means of a combination of military, political, and economic controls, was pushed with the greatest determination both by the Supreme Command and the civilian government. Ludendorff was more inclined to trample on the political feelings of the Allies, collaborators, and enemies than the civilian government, but in the great aim of breaking up the Russian empire and making its parts submissive to German direction and exploitation, both followed the same policy. Holding sway over such a vast realm Germany then would be the equal of Britain and the United States. In such a result of the war the rulers of Germany saw the best guarantee for the continued stability of the monarchical regime. By gaining world power for Germany and a wealth of resources that would ensure her future prosperity, this regime, it was thought, would not have to be fearful of internal opposition.

It is doubtful whether these assumptions were right. What could perhaps be considered supporting evidence of their correctness was the ready approval that all the parties, with the exception of the two socialist ones, gave to every step taken by the government in the expansion of

German power in the east. They did not even complain that the government had ratified the August treaties with Russia without prior consultation with the *Reichstag*. The parliamentarians in Chancellor Hertling's cabinet, particularly the Progressive Vice-Chancellor von Payer, were most active in persuading the parties to follow the government willingly. Even among the Majority Socialists there were a few prominent members who championed the eastern imperialism.

But in all probability the millions of common people who had fought in the army or suffered at home during the war would not have been willing to return to a Germany of authoritarian rule and exaggerated class division. The Prussian three-class suffrage would not have been tolerated much longer, and the mass of the people would have been likely to demand a thorough reform of German political institutions. Moreover, it was erroneous to believe that the realization of the huge program of conquests would have restored the prewar conditions of the Empire. For holding down the subjected peoples a much larger military establishment would have been needed. A further militarization of German life, however, would undoubtedly have aggravated the social and political tensions in a serious way. At the same time the imposition of Germany's war aims would not only have made millions of people smart under her heel but also have left all the powers outside the German orbit implacable enemies.

The German policies in the east alone would have made this situation inevitable. As it was, as soon as the breakdown of Russian military resistance had raised the hope that Germany might now also bring the war in the west to a successful conclusion, her western war aims concerning Belgium and France and the demands for the acquisition of a big colonial empire in Central Africa had been revived by the German leaders. And while a German victory in France might have forced the latter to cede the iron mines of Lorraine and enabled Germany to rule the Continent, it would not have defeated Britain, let alone the United States. A stable peace could not be won by a conqueror's peace.

✑ Spring Offensive in the West, 1918

THE GERMAN peace aims proved a grave encumbrance to successful military operations. Even before the Russian November revolution Ludendorff had decided to seek a military decision against the French and British armies in the spring of 1918, before the Americans could intervene in force. But only the total collapse of the Russian army as a result of the revolution gave the Supreme Command the chance, through the transfer of German troops from the east to the west, to build up the superiority needed for strategic decisions. However, in order to realize his dreams of an eastern empire Ludendorff eventually left about a million men in the east. It is true that some of these troops were second-rate and unfit for combat at the western front, although in the summer of 1918 half of the eastern divisions were sent to the west. Ludendorff's political passion vitiated his military judgment. In March 1918, 192 German divisions faced 170 Allied ones in France. In actual strength, however, the two sides were practically equal. The German army was weak in transport, and both the British and French air forces were much stronger in numbers than their German counterpart.

Ludendorff knew that the chances for winning a decisive victory over the Anglo-French army were limited and that in case the German offensive failed, the war would be lost. German manpower was running out, and it would be impossible to replace the losses, which were bound to be heavy, while on the Allied side the arrival of the Americans more than made up for all the casualties. But to the idea of choosing the strategic defensive, which would have enabled the Germans to hold out against greatly superior forces, while trying to make a compromise peace, Ludendorff seems not to have given much thought. Actually the defensive conduct of the war might only then have brought a tolerable peace if Germany had publicly renounced all annexationist war aims and declared her willingness to have a general peace congress settle the Eastern European questions in accordance with the principle of national self-determination. Such a peace offensive would have gained in credibility if it had come from a government supported by a parliamentary majority. But all prerequisites were missing for such a policy. In 1918 the majority of the *Reichstag* backed all the eastern annexations, although they were for the Conservatives primarily a means of staving off parliamentary government. For Ludendorff the renunciation of conquest would have meant the admission of defeat. His trust in the quality of the German army and in his own leadership made him confident that even the most difficult objectives could be achieved. Had not the army since the days of Frederick the Great made Prussia-Germany what she was through bold heroic actions?

As the point of attack, and this meant the point of a German breakthrough, Ludendorff selected that section of the Allied front where British and French forces joined hands. The British held a 120-mile-long line that ran in a north-south direction from the sea. The French positions were running west-east from the southern end of this line to Verdun. The German plan was to isolate the British army and by pushing it toward the channel ports bring about its annihilation or forced withdrawal. The first offensive against the southern British front between the Scarpe and Oise, called "Michael," was to be followed by "George," an offensive against the central British positions in Flanders. By that time the British would have moved their reserves south, while during all these operations the

French would presumably be slow to send reserves to the British front. The German plans were no doubt extremely clever, and they were well implemented on the tactical level.

By March 21 seventy-one German divisions were amassed against the twenty-six divisions of the British southern wing. The morale of the German troops was high; they felt that they were to fight the last battle that would bring ultimate victory. After a hellish four-hour cannonade from 2,500 heavy guns, interspersed with the firing of gas shells, the Germans, favored by fog, began their offensive along a line of 42 miles running from opposite Arras to St. Quentin and La Fère. Although the British fought bravely, their front divisions were overwhelmed and suffered huge losses. Also the French to the south were pressed back. Between March 21 and April 5, 30 miles of the Allied front were shattered and the Germans advanced upward 35 miles, toward Amiens. Ludendorff's expectation that the French would be slow in coming to the help of the British was not entirely mistaken, although he lacked the necessary reserves for breaking through the gap that temporarily existed between the British and French fronts. On March 26 General Foch was made the coordinator of the operations of the Allied armies on the western front, and on April 14 was raised to the rank of supreme allied commander.

After March 28 the advance of the Germans slowed down and their losses mounted. When their offensive was stopped short of Amiens, Ludendorff ended it on April 5. While his circumspection and inventiveness had been extraordinary in the preparation of the assaults, he did not show such a sure touch in the strategic direction of the battle operations. But the main reason for the limited success of the offensive was the numerical inadequacy of the forces at his disposal. Still, the results of the battle shook the Allied armies profoundly. The British lost 90,000 men in prisoners and 73,000 in casualties, while the French losses amounted to 77,000 men altogether.

Yet the German losses were equally high, and the next offensive, "George," was turned into "Georgette," that is, could be carried through only with reduced forces against a relatively small, twelve-mile long front between Armentières and La Bassée. But luck favored the early progress of the German offensive that was launched on April 9. For a while the situation of the British seemed desperate and a German breakthrough to the channel ports that would have annihilated half of the British armies appeared a distinct possibility, particularly if the Germans managed to win the few heights of Flanders, south of Ypres, the only natural obstacle on the way to the coast. Although most of their troops were green, the British fought valiantly, as did the Belgians. The French divisions arriving from the south originally disappointed their allies. Kemmel mountain, the major hill of the Flanders heights, was lost by them on April 25, but afterwards, with their organization perfected, they gave an impressive showing. On April 29 Ludendorff broke off the "battle of the Lys" as a failure.

Ludendorff still hoped to be able to win final victory, which he wanted to achieve through the destruction of the British army. But in order to make it impossible for the French to come to the assistance of the British, he intended to attack at the French front, thus forcing the French to move their reserves to the south, while inflicting maximum losses on them. Thereafter the decisive offensive against the British army was to be opened. It took considerable time to prepare this new stroke. On May 27, the Germans stormed the Chemin des Dames, the blood-drenched center of earlier battles, and crossed the Aisne river, and by June 3 they had reached the Marne at Château-Thierry, fifty-six miles from Paris. But by then the force of their offensive had been spent, and the pocket they had gained was too narrow for strategic deployments. In order to broaden the breach, the German Supreme Command decided on a new offensive, in the course of which it hoped to involve a larger number of French reserves.

But this plan meant putting off the offensive against the British in Flanders for a considerable time, since the buildup for the new Marne battle could not be completed before the middle of July. In the early summer the British army that had suffered so terribly was fully rebuilt, and in the first week of June two American divisions had for the first time engaged in major actions at the Marne. They had given a creditable account of themselves, and the morale of their French and British comrades-in-arms was at once greatly bolstered.

On July 15, the new German offensive east and west of Rheims, for which fifty-one divisions had been massed, was opened. But since it had not been kept secret, the enemy was prepared. Whereas the western attack made some headway, the eastern one became a costly failure. On July 18 a big French counteroffensive against the western flank of the bulge was launched. The Germans received only late warnings and had no idea of the great force of the impending blow. Under General Mangin eighteen divisions, with an additional seven reserve divisions, had been assembled in the large forests of Villers-Cotterêt. Their attack was spearheaded by 600 tanks. The breach that the French and American troops tore into the German lines on the first day was considerable, whereas thereafter they advanced at a much slower pace, since the German troops recovered from the surprise and fought back bravely. But the position on the Marne had to be abandoned, and in extricating themselves from their salient the Germans suffered heavy losses, among them 30,000 prisoners and 800 captured guns.

The second battle of the Marne, like the first one of September 1914, was a turning point of the war. The offensive strength of the German army was finally broken. Ludendorff, still reluctant to admit the fundamental change of the military situation, postponed the offensive in Flanders. Actually, it could no longer be undertaken because by now the initiative lay with the Allies. On August 8, 1918, a strong, Allied offensive was mounted at the Somme that took the Germans by surprise. Although the fiercest blows were dealt out by the Canadian corps, the élan of the British, Australian, and French divisions was unflagging, whereas for the first time the morale of some German troops was completely shattered. The Allies took 12,000 prisoners and captured 200 guns. Only on the fourth day was the front stabilized. Ludendorff considered August 8 the "black day of German history." He felt depressed and uneasy about the general military situation, although he still refused to draw the necessary strategic and political conclusions.

✑ Consequences of Military Failure

IN RESTROSPECT it has become very doubtful whether the German offensives of March to July 1918 were the right strategy. Even in the second of these offensives, the battle at the Lys, the German troops had not shown quite the same fighting spirit as in the March offensive. The numerical strength of the individual units was dwindling, while the inadequate replacements consisted either of youngsters who had grown up in the hunger years or older men, among them a good many munitions workers, whom the army had drafted after the January strikes and who wanted to see the war ended. The Supreme Command, moreover, failed to recognize that the fighting strength of the individual German divisions varied enormously, and Ludendorff made the army commanders chiefly responsible for the failure of the four offensives. Although it became clear that the German army could fight at best a strategic defensive, he was unwilling to give up the bulging front positions and take the whole German front back to more easily defensible lines. If Ludendorff objected to this course, it was only partly due to the fact that no strong rear positions had been constructed. Even the relatively strongest defense chain, the "Hindenburg line," was without antitank contrivances. But Ludendorff feared the impression that a retreat would make on the German government and people. And he hoped against hope that the fortunes of war might shift and his expansionist peace program be saved. But this was an idle expectation. Ludendorff's vague ideas that the French or British might become disheartened by the demand for further sacrifices were not justified. Ever since July 18 there had not been the slightest chance of breaking the Allied determination to achieve Germany's full defeat. Although the French were as short of military manpower as the Germans, the British still had a large reservoir of replacements at their command. But in addition there was the steady flow of American troops that gave assurance of ever-growing superiority. Moreover, the co-operation among the allied troops was quite satisfactory.

For a good many months Ludendorff had claimed that, by undermining Allied morale and unity while maintaining the will of the German people to fight on, political warfare should strengthen the military campaign. But the former to him meant nothing but propaganda for his political program. Obviously, however, not even the shrewdest propaganda could have inveigled the Allied governments or people into making peace on Ludendorff's terms. When the foreign secretary, Kühlmann, on June 24, 1918, indicated before the *Reichstag* that the government was moving closer to the peace resolution of the *Reichstag* of July 1917 in order to bring on peace talks with the Allies, Hindenburg and Ludendorff were infuriated, and Kühlmann was dropped by the chancellor and emperor. Admiral von Hintze, a diplomat of Pan-German leanings, became his successor.

Likewise, the trust of the German masses in the government could not be rekindled by words alone. The supply of food and clothing had fallen to a deplorably low state, while the rise in prices ruined many families. Those whose members served at the front worried about these relatives. They knew that the soldiers by now were poorly fed, well-nigh exhausted, and, still worse, had to fight in battles growing ever more murderous. The government had stated that the war would be won by the fall, but clearly the optimistic predictions about the results of the unlimited submarine warfare had been proved utterly fallacious. Not only had Britain not been starved, but the American army had safely arrived in France. After the offensives of the spring of 1918 had not brought a decision, the specter of a long struggle and another war winter, the fifth, with its additional deprivations and hardships, was looming ahead. The victories and peace treaties in the east, too, began to appear in a dubious light. The expected improvement of the food situation as the result of the occupation of the Ukraine did not materialize, and German troops spread farther and farther into the east.

Among Germans the suspicion grew that the war aims of the military were a major obstacle to an early end of the war. The arrogant declarations of the Pan-German League heightened this feeling, since it was well known that they could not be made without the approval of the official censorship. The latter, however, as were so many other functions of the internal government, was in the hands of the generals, who seemed to cow the civilian government completely. The chief of the press office of the government wrote around the middle of August: "Practically nobody believes in any statements of government offices any longer, particularly if they issue encouraging ones." And he pointed out that the censored press also had lost its credibility. Only such actions as would have demonstrated the willingness of the military lords to take the people seriously, instead of treating them as a mass compelled to give the nation every ounce of their strength in blind obedience, could have stopped the growing apathy and opposition. It was a grave omission that the promise of a reform of the Prussian suffrage remained unfulfilled. Of possibly even more serious consequence was the refusal of the government to revise the "state-of-siege" law by transferring such functions as censorship from military to civilian authorities.

At a crown council on August 14 Hindenburg and Ludendorff expressed the opinion that the army could no longer hope "to break" the determination of the enemy but only, through the strategic defensive, "to paralyze" it. While this statement was unduly optimistic, it was an admission of a radical change in the military situation and as such should have alarmed the emperor, chancellor, and foreign secretary. But although the council decided that diplomatic feelers should be undertaken with a view to coming to an understanding with the western Allies, it was held that the right moment for such diplomatic action would arrive only after some military successes had been gained. Thus nothing was done during the next six weeks, in which Germany's adversaries, most of them by now predictable ones, multiplied.

∽ Allied Offensive

THE ALLIES resumed the offensive on August 20 and ever thereafter retained the initiative. Through steady pressure finally exerted along the whole front from Flanders to Lorraine the German lines were continuously forced back by the Allies. The progress of the Allies was slow, however, and their losses were relatively high, though much smaller than during the first half of the year. The chief handicap under which they suffered was the destruction of railroads, roads, and bridges. Their railheads were far back in the rear, and the supplies not only for the armies but also for the civilians had to be carried through desolate country. Foch and Haig, though soberly estimating that the war could not be won before the spring of 1919, were confident of victory, as were their troops.

The superiority of the Allied armies in numbers and matériel had been growing immensely since the spring. By September the German army at the western front had been reduced from three and a half to two and a half million men. Between July 18 and November 11 it suffered 420,000 casualties and lost about 340,000 prisoners of war. By the middle of October the western front consisted of 191 divisions, while the average strength of the battalions had fallen to between 400 and 500, and in the case of 28 divisions to between 200 and 300 men. In these circumstances, reserves were dwindling, and the troops got little rest from combat. The Allied front, where the French units were thinning, though the British maintained the strength of their cadres, was steadily reenforced by the arrival of the American divisions. Whereas in March 1918 about 300,000 American soldiers, with only one combat-ready division, had landed, there were 2,086,000 of them in France at the time of the armistice. As early as late July, 27 American divisions of 28,000 men each were active, and more kept coming.

The outcome of the war could not be in doubt after July 18. But although from August 8 on Ludendorff felt deep concern that one of the enemy's attacks might achieve a major break through the German lines and lead to a catastrophe, only the collapse of the Bulgarian front between September 14 and September 30, 1918, made him admit the urgent need for an end to hostilities. All of Germany's exhausted allies were in imminent danger. But the Austro-Hungarian government implored her in vain to join in a public bid for peace negotiations. The nationalities of the Habsburg empire were increasingly looking for leadership to the national committees set up by the Allies. Although in his Fourteen-Points speech of January 8, 1918, President Wilson had demanded only the "autonomous development" of the nationalities, possibly within the empire, on September 3 the Czech committee was recognized as an Allied government by the United States. While thus the outward breakup of the empire threatened, starvation in the cities heightened social tensions. On September 14, the Austro-Hungarian government made its bid for peace negotiations, which was turned down by the Allies.

◠ Allied Balkan Victories

ON THE SAME DAY the guns were already booming in preparation for the offensive that a bold and ingenious commander of the mixed French, British, Greek, and Serbian forces at the Salonika front had finally been allowed to undertake by the Supreme War Council. Franchet d'Ésperey won a great victory, and quickly the Bulgarians, disheartened by the meager results of their warfare, were completely demoralized. They sued for an armistice that was concluded on September 30. Part of the Bulgarian army was placed in captivity, and the rest disarmed and demobilized, while her transportation system was placed at the disposal of the victors. The roads were now open for the liberation of all of Serbia and Rumania. The brave Serbian troops moved quickly on their northward march, throwing into flight the three German divisions which Ludendorff had moved from the Ukraine. By November 10 the French had crossed the Danube into Rumania, and Hungary sued for an armistice.

The victory at the Graeco-Serbian frontier also sealed the fate of the Turkish empire. The British contingent turned toward Constantinople. It did not have to do any fighting. The Turks just then were decisively beaten in Palestine and Syria, where General Sir Edmund Allenby, in a brilliant campaign begun on September 19, routed the whole army. The Turks signed an armistice on October 30, 1918.

✑ Ludendorff's Confession of Defeat

AFTER AUGUST 8 Ludendorff had been in a highly nervous state. While much of it obviously was the result of sheer physical exhaustion, it was greatly aggravated by the struggle that went on in his mind. Too proud to admit mistakes, let alone defeat, he sharply rebuked the field commanders who suggested the adoption of more cautious tactics because the troops were heavily overtaxed. Although Ludendorff was not in close touch with the conditions at the front, he insisted on the holding of the forward positions, thereby tremendously increasing the risk of an eventual rupture of the German lines. At the same time he was enraged by the lack of support from the civilian government and the country at large. But no government could have engendered an enthusiastic war spirit in the people any longer. Apart from the deprivations from hunger and inflation the reports that soldiers on furlough brought from the front were most disheartening. On the other hand, the replacements sent from home were of doubtful quality. Besides ill-fed and poorly trained lads there were older men, combed from the factories, who were politically conscious. Many among them hated the military caste, which in their opinion was continuing a senseless and hopeless war. The spirit of insubordination touched many units and created fear not only among the commanders but also among those troops that fought on bravely.

The collapse of the Bulgarian front finally convinced Ludendorff that catastrophe might strike the western front as well. Apparently he was less concerned immediately about the danger of an Allied invasion of Hungary than the loss of the last divisions which he had hoped to transfer from the Ukraine to the western front and was now forced to send to Bulgaria. In addition it was clear that Rumania would soon be lost and Germany's whole oil supply cut off. On September 29 he surprised the government with the statement that "the condition of the army demands an immediate armistice in order to avoid a catastrophe." He urged the formation of a government on a broad popular basis and agreed that in order to win an immediate armistice President Wilson should be approached to initiate peace negotiations on the basis of his announced principles.

Ludendorff thus finally conceded military defeat, and he recognized that with the loss of the war the authoritarian character of the German government was doomed. But his attitude toward a democratic government was ambiguous. He had not given up all thought of fighting as yet. In case the enemies should try to impose too stringent conditions, he wanted to resume the battle, and he expected a democratic government to be able to rally all popular forces for heroic resistance. At the same time he made the democratic parties responsible for the defeat. "Let them conclude the peace that now will have to be concluded," he told William II, who agreed.

Once Ludendorff had confessed the hopelessness of the military situation, the fears which he had controlled so far overpowered him and in deep anguish, though in his usual imperious manner, he urged the immediate dispatch of the request for an armistice during the following days.

Suddenly the *Reichstag* was called upon to assume leadership. Since the fall of Bethmann-Hollweg and the rise of Ludendorff to virtual dictatorship it had played only a minor role. The National Liberal and Center parties, except for a few dissenting members, had applauded the policy of eastern annexations. The movement for strengthening the position of the parliament that seemed to have gained great strength in July 1917 was stymied by the appointment of the Hertling government. Not only Count Hertling but also Vice-Chancellor von Payer, one of the leaders of the Progressives, had proved entirely submissive to the policies and wishes of the Supreme Command. In these circumstances, the deliberations on the introduction of parliamentary government still carried on by the interparty committee that the Center, the Progressives, and the Social Democrats had formed in July 1917 had remained purely academic. Only Ludendorff's action opened the way for the introduction of parliamentary government.

Unwilling to accept parliamentary government that was bound to lessen the influence of the states, Count Hertling resigned. On October 2 one of Ludendorff's staff officers reviewed the hopeless military developments before the leaders of the *Reichstag* parties and informed them that the Supreme Command recommended the immediate ending of the war. All of them were completely unprepared for such disastrous news. This was true even in the case of Friedrich Ebert, who, together with most Social Democrats, had for some time distrusted the confidence in victory that the military leaders had displayed. But he fought strongly those in his party who wanted to refuse any cooperation with an obviously bankrupt system. Though admitting that the party was assuming heavy risks, he did not feel that it should withhold its help when the country was threatened with chaos. Ebert's view prevailed, and thereafter the interparty committee agreed on a political program and on the distribution of government posts.

✍ The Government of Prince Max of Baden

THE INTERPARTY COMMITTEE, however, did not propose the appointment of a chancellor from among its own membership. The committee might perhaps most easily have agreed on Payer, but as vice-chancellor the latter had not shown good political instinct or energy. Thus it assented to the choice of Prince Max of Baden (1867–1929), the heir presumptive to the throne of Baden. While Payer remained vice-chancellor, the Centrist Karl Trimborn (1854–1921) became secretary of the interior and the Social Democrat Gustav Bauer (1870–1944) secretary of the new department of labor. In addition the three majority parties nominated some of their most representative leaders secretaries without portfolio. The Center party sent Matthias Erzberger, the author of the peace resolution of 1917, and the more conservative Adolf Groeber (1854–1919) into the government, the Progressives the judicious Conrad Haussmann (1857–1922), while the Social Democratic party delegated its best known orator, Philipp Scheidemann (1865–1939). Whereas most of the government departments kept their conservative professional heads, Dr. Wilhelm Solf (1862–1936), a diplomat and former colonial administrator of liberal outlook, replaced Admiral von Hintze in the foreign office.

Prince Max, who took over his office on October 3, was a highly sensible, cultured, and conscientious gentleman. He had been one of the few prominent Germans who had advocated a conciliatory peace. Although he possessed political judgment, his lack of experience in governmental affairs made him depend a good deal on the advice of his friends. Prince Max came from the most liberal German state, where the dynasty had established fruitful relations with all the political parties. But although Baden had a regime that worked *with* the parties, it did not work *through* them. For the task he had to face in October 1918 Prince Max was not fully prepared. He was no democratic statesman and was somewhat reluctant to do the things which now had to be done. Moreover, he was no Lloyd George who could have rallied the masses. His rhetoric was conventional and pale, and he was unable to impress the people with the image of a new leadership. To most Germans he remained a man who wanted to save too much of the old monarchical regime, if they did not even suspect him of connivance with the military authorities.

Every day after September 29 Ludendorff in a frenzy had demanded that an immediate request for an armistice should be sent to Washington.

Prince Max saw clearly that such an action would be taken abroad as an open confession of total defeat and allow the Allies to impose on Germany any peace they chose. He thought it wise, by first announcing the democratization of Germany, to achieve an improved atmosphere for negotiation. Furthermore he argued quite correctly that the great majority of the German people, fed to this day with official news about the coming victory, would be profoundly shocked by the sudden request for an armistice and peace negotiations. The popular pressure on the government to set an end to the fighting would be overwhelming. The new chancellor asked Hindenburg and Ludendorff whether they were aware that the acceptance of Wilson's Fourteen Points might lead to the loss of German colonies, Alsace-Lorraine, and "Polish-speaking districts of the eastern provinces," to which Hindenburg made the reply that the Supreme Command would consider the cession "of small French-speaking parts of Alsace-Lorraine" but would never cede any territory in the east.

↶ *Armistice Negotiations*

THE LACK OF ANY political good sense in this statement is self-evident. Hindenburg continued, however, to press Prince Max to issue the note to the American government. Reluctantly the chancellor gave in to the entreaties of the Supreme Command, and the request for the opening of peace negotiations as well as the conclusion of an armistice agreement was dispatched in the night of October 3–4.

When on October 2 a critical officer had asked Ludendorff whether if he found himself now in Marshal Foch's place, he would grant an armistice, Ludendorff had replied, "No, certainly not; I would attack even harder." This was exactly the reaction of General Pershing, who wanted to fight on until Berlin was taken and Germany would surrender unconditionally. Foch and Haig naturally never thought of granting an armistice that would allow the German army to rest and recuperate. But in view of the terrible toll that the war had taken of their nations, they were willing to contemplate an armistice, provided it would accomplish those decisive military objectives which the Allied commanders hoped to have achieved by the spring of 1919. To Foch this meant positions on the Rhine and to the British the destruction of Germany's naval power, in addition. The Allied governments approved this concept and left it to Foch and the British admiralty to draft the armistice terms.

The Allied debates over an armistice took some time, and the negotiations over the principles of the peace terms lasted even longer. The Wilsonian peace program as outlined in the Fourteen-Points address and in subsequent speeches had never been officially endorsed by Britain,

France, or Italy. Actually each of the Allies took exception to one point or another. Now with victory in the offing they were doubly reluctant to be tied to a program which they felt was open, at least in part, to different interpretations. Colonel House, who carried on the negotiations in the Supreme War Council in Paris, in the end achieved the consent of the three major allies only by the threat that the United States might proceed with separate peace negotiations. Finally, on November 5 the American government informed the Germans of the willingness of the Allied powers to grant an armistice and prepare a peace treaty.

While the United States and the Allies deliberated on the armistice and peace, Wilson in an exchange of notes with Berlin not only made far-reaching military demands in preparation for the armistice but also raised political issues of great consequence. The first American reply of October 8 demanded a firmer German commitment to the Wilsonian peace program, inquired about the political complexion of the new German government, and declared that the United States could not propose to her allies the conclusion of an armistice agreement before the armies of the Central Powers had evacuated the occupied territories. With Ludendorff's approval Prince Max accepted this condition and also assured Wilson that in future peace negotiations only the practical details for the application of the American principles were to be discussed. Furthermore, he pointed out that his government was supported by a large majority of the German parliament.

The American note of October 14 stressed that no armistice agreement could be concluded that would impair the military superiority over the Germans that the Allies had gained. In addition, it asked for the immediate ending of the illegal unlimited submarine warfare as well as of the devastation wrought by the German army in its retreat from France and Flanders. But the note also stated most emphatically that peace, as President Wilson had said, was dependent on "the destruction of every arbitrary power anywhere that can separately, secretly, and of its single choice disturb the peace of the world," and continued, "The power which has hitherto controlled the German Nation is of the sort here described. It is within the choice of the German Nation to alter it."

The evacuation of the occupied territories and the ending of the unrestricted submarine war seemed to Ludendorff and the navy chiefs gratuitous concessions. Before committing themselves they wanted to know the actual terms of the armistice in full detail. Ludendorff's mood had become more optimistic than it had been in the last days of September. The catastrophe at the western front that he had so strongly feared then had not happened, and he considered it possible to win a better armistice through further fighting. Wisely the cabinet rejected the advice of the military and naval chiefs and in its reply accepted the new American conditions. In the opinion of Prince Max and the other members of the government not only the military situation but also the attitude of the people made an early armistice imperative. Ludendorff declared that although he could not consent, this did not matter, since the Supreme Command did not carry the political responsibility. It was the only time in his career that this dynamic man declared himself politically disinterested. Yet within a few days he wanted to impose his will again upon German policy.

On October 24 the third American note became known to the German government. It said that the President now was willing to take up the conclusion of an armistice agreement with the Allies, but only one that would make it impossible for Germany to resume hostilities. In addition the note talked very bluntly about the inadequacy of the constitutional changes made in Germany during October. It warned that the power of the king of Prussia and of the military was still unbroken and stated that the Allies, though willing to negotiate an armistice, would not discuss peace with them. At once Hindenburg issued an order to the army proclaiming that "Wilson's note demands the military capitulation. . . . For us soldiers this only constitutes the challenge for continued resistance with the utmost effort."

Thus once more the Supreme Command took the initiative in determining German policy. The words "for us soldiers" sounded particularly ominous. They seemed to confirm Wilson's assertion regarding the undiminished influence of the military men. Hindenburg and Ludendorff went to Berlin in order to win the emperor over to their fight of resistance to the last, but he directed them to the government. The latter, however, stood its ground. It pointed out that the people could not be rallied to new great efforts. The sudden demand for an armistice, forced upon the government by the Supreme Command, was generally taken as the admission that the war was lost, and among the masses, suffering under tremendous hardships and deprivations, it had produced an irresistible longing for immediate peace. Prince Max still entertained the secret and mistaken hope that once the people had seen the actual terms of the armistice, they might be responsive to an appeal for a last stand. But, first of all, the actual terms had to be secured.

The government was opposed to breaking off the negotiations for additional reasons. It was afraid that such an action would embitter the Allies and thereby make Germany's position extremely difficult. In contrast to Hindenburg and Ludendorff, who now expressed the opinion that military resistance could be carried on successfully for some time to come, the government was skeptical about these chances. It momentarily expected the collapse of Austria-Hungary and was understandably worried about the dangers at Germany's southern frontiers. But there was good cause for concern even about the western front, although the catastrophe against which Ludendorff had warned earlier in the month had so far not materialized. The cabinet now insisted that other army commanders should also be heard, a request profoundly resented by Ludendorff. An idea that he now endorsed, although he had called it useless earlier in the month, had been rejected by the government. On October 7 Walther Rathenau had issued in the press a proclamation for a general armed rising of the people comparable to the *levée en masse* of 1793. But the call-up of every citizen for the defense of France in 1793 had happened before the average Frenchman had been affected by warfare, and in 1814 or 1815 there had been no talk about *levée en masse* in France any longer. Crown Prince Rupprecht of Bavaria rightly stated that after four years of war in which practically every able-bodied man had been drafted any additional levy would cripple war production and thereby make more than temporary resistance impossible.

On the morning of October 26 Hindenburg and Ludendorff were received by William II. Ludendorff sharply criticized the policy of the government. When the emperor pointed out that the urgent demand of the Supreme Command for an armistice four weeks earlier had shaken the confidence of the people and justified the present policy, Ludendorff in an agitated and disrespectful manner requested to be relieved of further service in his present or any other army post. William II consented, but when Hindenburg made the same request, prevailed on him, by appealing to his patriotism, to stay in office. Hindenburg's monarchistic loyalty made him amenable to the emperor's wishes, whereas Ludendorff was driven by his imperious temper and radical nationalism. He now felt let down also by Hindenburg, "the man I made great." The break between the two soldiers occurred before they left the palace and was never healed.

✑ Constitutional Amendments

WITH THE DISMISSAL of Ludendorff the new constitutional order in Germany had stood its first major test. In his place Wilhelm Groener was appointed quartermaster general. The new constitutional order was formally perfected on October 28, when the law amending the Bismarckian constitution went into force. Henceforth, the chancellor needed the confidence of the *Reichstag*. The position of the secretaries of state was raised so that they became ministers of state in all but name. The declaration of war as well as the conclusion of peace and other international treaties depended on the consent of both the Federal Council and parliament. The appointment, promotion, and dismissal of officers in the army and navy by the emperor required the countersignature of the chancellor.

The ministers of war were made responsible to the Federal Council and parliament.

Thus the monarchical power was limited to a level comparable to that of the English monarchy. At long last the German parliament had gained control of foreign and military affairs. It also had gained ascendancy over the Federal Council, the organ of the state governments. In Prussia, too, changes were begun. Prompted by the Supreme Command the Prussian Conservative party abandoned its opposition to the introduction in Prussia of a suffrage identical with that of the *Reichstag*. The Prussian House of Lords passed the bill on October 24. But before the House of Representatives could act, it was dissolved by the November revolution.

✍ The Coming of the Revolution

YET CONSTITUTIONAL REFORMS by themselves were no longer sufficient to satisfy the masses of the people, who demanded an alleviation of their painful conditions. While the loss of kin affected everyone, the urban population was starving and the farmers, in many cases the wives of farmers serving in the army, were distressed by the decreasing yield of their farms and the growing intervention of government agencies in their operations. The prospect of facing a fifth war winter, after the ever-worsening hardships of the previous ones, was terrifying. Once the government had announced that the war could not be won—for the unexpected request for an armistice was given just this meaning—the urge for an early or even immediate end of the war became irresistible. And the demand for peace was further enhanced by the news about the imminent collapse of Germany's allies, particularly Austria-Hungary.

Despite the request for an armistice, peace did not seem to come closer during October. The new government, and for that matter all the parties except the Independent Socialists, admonished the people to continue fighting until an armistice had been arranged. The *Reichstag* held a meeting on October 5 in order to listen to the first speech of the new chancellor, and thereafter it did not convene till October 22, when it passed the amendments to the constitution. It adjourned four days later. Actually it should have been in permanent session to focus attention on the parliamentary character of the new government and to work on the implementation of the new order, which to the common people did not look so novel after all. The "state-of-siege" law was not lifted, and generals continued to censor the press, restrict meetings, and even arrest people. Nothing changed within the armed forces. What would have been the best symbol of a new relationship between officers and men, equal food rations, was not introduced.

It seemed doubtful whether Erzberger and Scheidemann, who were known to the masses as advocates of an early peace, determined the course of the government or whether it was still in the hands of the military men. Prince Max, scion of one of the ruling dynasties, was not considered to be strong enough to resist the generals and admirals, who continued advocating war to the last soldier. The profound popular resentment that was building up against the officers' corps extended to the emperor, the kings, and the other ruling princes as well, who had always conducted themselves as heads of the military establishments before and above their duties to their states. Their reputations had suffered badly during the war. The services they had performed since 1914 appeared rather insignificant, if not outright superfluous. The centralization of command during the war had minimized the influence of the princes on the federal government, while the weight of Prussia had increased. The impression that the king of Bavaria was incapable of representing Bavarian wishes in Berlin was to cost him his throne even before William II had lost his. The emperor's prestige had been steadily declining. In the eyes of the people he had not contributed anything to the glorious victories of the early war years, for which others, in the first place Hindenburg, were given credit. Now, in the twilight of defeat, he had even less to stand on. It was too late for him to address workers in the Krupp factory in September. His words had assumed a hollow ring.

Although it was not Wilson who undermined the monarchy in Germany, he aggravated its crisis by stating in his notes that the "military autocrats" and the "king of Prussia" could not be accepted as partners in peacemaking. The majority of the German people undoubtedly were in favor of preserving the monarchy, although it is difficult to estimate how many merely clung to the monarchy because they feared the unknown consequences of its fall. In the Weimar Republic the movement for the restoration of the monarchy was never able to muster powerful popular support. Antimonarchical sentiment had its strongest hold on the socialist workers, although it had spread to other groups as well. When the long wait for the armistice and Wilson's notes gave rise to the dark suspicion that William II was the cause of delay, impatience grew, and distrust of the officers was intensified among the soldiers. The number of deserters increased; they were mostly soldiers who refused to go up to the front. The rail centers in the rear of the army swarmed with many tens of thousands of military strikers. The emperor took the worst possible step. He left Berlin on October 29 and went to the military headquarters in Spa. At once rumors spread that, together with the generals, the emperor planned a move against the government.

∽ *Naval Revolt*

ON THE DAY when William II left Berlin looking for protection with the army, the navy, the proudest achievement of his reign, revolted. With the submarine warfare against mercantile vessels called off a few days earlier, the German battle fleet had been allowed to resume offensive operations. The admirals felt it to be their duty to use the fleet in support of the hard-pressed army. They intended to undertake a sally toward the channel in order to cut the communications between England and Flanders. This move was to draw the British fleet south, and in the small passages through the mine fields the German submarines were to inflict heavy losses on it. The ensuing main battle would then be fought under more auspicious conditions than the battle of Jutland. This plan was strategically sound, although it was questionable whether its execution would have brought the German army relief commensurate with the punishment that the German navy was bound to suffer. Moreover it was doubtful whether such an operation made much sense at the moment when the government had accepted all of Wilson's conditions and momentarily could expect the presentation of an armistice. The navy command did not discuss its plans with the government.

Yet the chief problem to which the naval commanders had not given attention was that of the morale of the German battle fleet. Already the mutinies of 1917 had shown that the sailors had become restless. The stern retribution meted out to them had turned their dissatisfaction into sullen resentment against the officers. The boredom of their repetitious activities, many of them useless motions invented only to keep the sailors occupied, disgruntled the men who in many cases had been in the navy for six or seven years. Finally the armistice request seemed to open prospects of peace. But the officers were contemptuous of the new government and glibly talked about fighting to the last man. When the whole battle fleet was assembled in the North sea, word was passed on among the sailors that the officers wanted to attack the coast of England and sabotage the peace negotiations.

On October 29 and 30 the crews of some battleships refused to execute orders, and they extinguished the fire in the engines. The fleet returned to its home ports. After about 600 sailors had been imprisoned in Kiel, demands for their liberation led to a general uprising on November 4. The naval authorities gave in easily with the result that by afternoon the city was in the hands of the sailors, who elected a soldiers' council, and of the dockyard workers, who elected a workers' council. The ships flew red flags. Only the commander of the battleship *König* defended the imperial flag to the death. The whole officers corps, which a few days before had been ready for heroic action, lost its faith in view of the breakdown of military discipline.

The revolt of the sailors was not the work of any special group, and no leaders emerged after its success. Beyond the liberation of their comrades the sailors presented only demands for a moderate reform of the relationship between officers and men. They readily accepted Gustav Noske (1868–1946), the military expert of the Social Democratic party, whom the government sent as governor to Kiel. The revolt was not directed against the majority parties, since on the contrary the sailors felt that they were defending the peace policy of the government. Therefore Noske succeeded in restoring order, though not the authority of the officers. What had happened in Kiel was repeated in Wilhelmshaven and all the naval bases, and soon the radical elements attempted to carry their active revolt against military authority to the big inland centers, of which they won Hamburg, Brunswick, and Hanover. Everywhere the troops went over to their side. In Brunswick the grand duke, son-in-law of William II, abdicated. From Hanover the revolutionary movement spread to Cologne, the great rail center behind the western front with its all-important bridges over the Rhine. It would undoubtedly have spread from Cologne to the western front, if the signing of the armistice had not stopped the uprisings which, through the destruction of the domineering position of the military caste, aimed at the immediate end of fighting.

✐ Outbreak of Revolution

THE REVOLUTION THAT TOOK PLACE in Munich on November 7, though not linked to the events in Kiel, was equally prompted by the desire for peace. The complete collapse of the Austrian front in Italy during the first days of November made the Bavarian population afraid of an Italian invasion or at least air attacks. Kurt Eisner (1867–1919), an Independent Socialist, gave the signal for an uprising of the Munich workers and the garrison, which consisted largely of peasant soldiers. But as soon as the dynasty had abdicated and the authority of the officers had been broken, the Social Democrats again gained much popular support. The desire for peace rather than radical social change was the prevailing mood of the masses.

The forces actively working for a social revolution were very small. On October 7, the Spartacus League issued a manifesto to the workers and soldiers demanding a socialist revolution leading to the nationalization of banks, heavy industries, and large estates. The revolution was to be carried out by workers' and soldiers' councils, while the parliament as well as the states and dynasties were to be abolished. When Karl Liebknecht was released from prison late in October, the Spartacus League gained a powerful public voice, although Liebknecht's popular appeal lay chiefly in his reputation as the most fearless champion of peace. The leaders of the Independent Socialists did not believe in the possibility of a socialist revolution in Germany, nor did they do much to advance this cause. But among the membership of the party some activists supported the Spartacus League's preparations for the launching of a revolution of the bolshevik type. In Berlin, this activism had been particularly strong in the big factories after the January strikes. The "revolutionary shop stewards," among whom Richard Müller (b. 1880), the head of the Berlin metal workers' union, had become most prominent, were plotting revolution. Emil Barth (b. 1879), another member of this group, obtained some money from the Soviet embassy in order to buy arms. This was a useless action. Even a group of armed workers could not have prevailed against the troops in the city as long as the latter remained loyal to the government. On the other hand, if the regiments would fraternize with the revolutionaries, there was no need for arming the workers.

In meetings held in October by the "revolutionary shop stewards" which Karl Liebknecht and other Spartacists as well as the official leaders of the Independent Socialist party attended, even the "revolutionary shop stewards" were hesitant to call for a socialist revolution that would not only have to defeat the old military order and the German bourgeoisie but also the Social Democrats, who were obviously unwilling to go beyond a democratic reform of the constitution. But November 11 was chosen as the date for inciting a general strike of the workers in Berlin. Yet the spread of the military revolts from Kiel after November 4, the news of the Munich revolution, and the arrest of Ernst Däumig, a well-known radical Independent Socialist writer, on November 8 led, in the morning of November 9, to the call-up of the workers, who left their factories and marched to the governmental districts in the center of Berlin.

✍ *William II's Abdication*

IN THE LAST WEEK OF OCTOBER the leaders of the Majority Socialists had begun to realize that the democratization of the constitution would not halt the rapid drift of the masses toward radical action. The leaders' hope that the announcement of Allied willingness to conclude an armistice might stabilize the situation proved idle. The American note of November 5 that invited the German government to send representatives for the signing of an armistice failed to make a noticeable impression on the angry masses, which continued to see in the monarchical system an obstacle to peace. The Social Democratic leaders were still ready to support the monarchy. They insisted, however, on the abdication of William II in favor of his eldest grandson, who was still a minor and for whom one of the sons of the emperor was to act as regent. Everybody agreed that Crown Prince William (1882–1951), who had acquired the reputation of a profligate and politically inept character, was unfit for the succession. Among the other five sons of William II only two were considered barely acceptable. If William II had abdicated in the last days of October, or even better immediately after Wilson's note of October 14, the German monarchy might conceivably have survived. And although the monarchy would have been shorn of most of its powers, its survival might have made it easier for large sections of the German upper and middle classes to accept a democratic regime. But considering the traditions of the Prussian monarchy and the character of the princes involved, it is more likely that the monarchy would have become the vehicle of counterrevolution without, as in the case of the Italian monarchy, serving as a shield against fascism.

William II, who, as mentioned before, had gone to the headquarters of the Supreme Command, proved impervious to any suggestions of abdication. Prince Max hesitated to bring full pressure on him. Hindenburg and Groener, the new quartermaster general, did not wish the emperor's resignation because they feared the effect it would have on the army, particularly on the officers' corps. The leaders of the Majority Socialists felt that time was running out. On November 6 Ebert demanded from Prince Max the emperor's abdication, setting as a deadline the morning of November 9. But Prince Max, who by now agreed on the necessity of William II's resignation, was unable to prevail on the emperor. At the military headquarters in Spa no decision had been reached in the morning of November 9.

The emperor's proposal that he should lead troops to Berlin and defeat the revolution was called impossible by Hindenburg and Groener, and their judgment was confirmed by the great majority of field commanders who reported that their troops could not be relied upon to fight the revolution at home. Also the peaceful return of the emperor with the army to Germany was declared unfeasible by Groener, since the revolutionary movement was directed against the person of the emperor. And Groener sounded the death knell of the military monarchy of the Hohenzollerns by stating that "the army will march home in good order under its leaders and commanding generals, but not under the command of Your Majesty, for it stands no longer behind Your Majesty!" William II decided to abdicate, but only as German emperor and not as king of Prussia, a senseless decision, since the revolution wanted to see him removed as Prussian "war lord" even more than as German emperor. Moreover, such an announcement would have meant the dissolution of the Empire.

From Berlin all during the morning of November 9 the chancellor had been urging the emperor's abdication. The Majority Socialists had withdrawn Scheidemann and Gustav Bauer from the government and called on their members to leave the factories. Vast columns of workers were converging on the center of the German capital. Some wild shots were fired from both sides, but quickly all the troops fraternized with the demonstrators. Prince Max, who was under the impression that William II's abdication would be momentarily forthcoming, announced it at noontime together with the abdication of the crown prince, the projected regency, and the imminent appointment of Friedrich Ebert as chancellor. A constituent national assembly was to settle Germany's future form of government. It was a desperate last attempt to save the monarchy and, perhaps even more, democracy, which appeared in imminent danger from bolshevism. But shortly thereafter the leaders of the Social Democratic party demanded that they immediately receive the chancellorship as well as the command of the military forces in and around Berlin. Prince Max, with the assent of the members of the imperial cabinet, made Ebert chancellor. Ebert promised to govern constitutionally and agreed to the early convention of a national assembly. He did not commit himself to a regency, although at this moment he still seemed to favor it.

✑ Proclamation of the Republic

BUT EVENTS MOVED FASTER than Ebert had expected. At two o'clock, Scheidemann, speaking to the masses assembled in front of the *Reichstag* building, proclaimed the German republic. This action not only drew the enthusiastic applause of the masses but also was considered a logical event by all the newspapers. But with monarchy gone even democracy was imperiled. Ebert originally had intended to form a government based on a coalition of parliamentary parties. Although he was convinced that the Independent Socialists were needed, even though they demanded a high price, he had also hoped to keep members of the majority parties in the government. But when the Independents insisted that power should be in the hands of the workers' and soldiers' councils and that no decision should be immediately taken on the elections for a constituent assembly, Ebert felt it necessary to accept these demands for the time being. In the evening of November 10 a meeting of all the workers' and soldiers' councils of Berlin elected a council of "people's commissars" as the new government. Richard Müller, the leader of the revolutionary shop stewards, had wished that it could be made a socialist government without the Majority Socialists, but it was obvious that the latter had much greater support than the Independents, particularly among the soldiers' councils.

On the other hand, Ebert realized that the workers' and soldiers' councils had the masses behind them and would not be willing to share their power with any bourgeois party. Moreover the popular movement represented by the councils would not have understood or tolerated a struggle between the Majority and Independent Socialists.

Thus the Independents, including the revolutionary shop stewards, had to resign themselves to a coalition with the Majority Social Democrats. Ebert on his part had to abandon the plan of forming a parliamentary government that would simply add the Independent Socialist party to the government of Prince Max. He accepted the workers' and soldiers' councils as the fountainhead of power and proposed that a council of six people's commissars be elected, of whom three were to be Majority Socialists and three Independents. He even proposed to have Karl Liebknecht join this group. But Liebknecht, who on November 9 had proclaimed the "socialist republic" from the imperial palace, raised so many revolutionary conditions that his inclusion proved impossible. In his place Emil Barth, a rather unimpressive figure, was chosen because he was close to the revolutionary shop stewards. Hugo Haase, the chief of the party, and Wilhelm Dittmann were the other two Independents, while the Social Democrats delegated Ebert, Scheidemann, and Otto Landsberg (b. 1869). Ebert and Haase were to function as chairmen of this council of people's commissars, which took its seat in the federal chancellery and was to be the national executive. But in addition the meeting of the workers' and soldiers' councils of Berlin on November 10 elected from its own ranks a so-called executive council of the Berlin workers' and soldiers' councils that in some not very well-defined fashion was to supervise the operations of the governments of the Empire, Prussia, and the city of Berlin. In this executive council the revolutionary shop stewards gained a very strong position, particularly through Richard Müller's chairmanship.

Thus Ebert was forced to join a revolutionary government, and for the time being it remained doubtful whether he would be able in the end to impose his own democratic policies on the council of people's commissars, and, if so, whether the council would have sufficient authority to carry the country with it. It is true, however, that the party organization that was at Ebert's disposal was much stronger than the Independent Socialist party and Spartacus League. Moreover, the forces to the right of the Social Democrats, though cowed, had not lost all their power and were likely to throw their weight behind Ebert. The people's commissars actually left in office all the federal secretaries of state who had served under Prince Max. In each department one Independent and one Majority Socialist were appointed under-secretaries of state. Quite a few liberals and Centrists, among whom Erzberger was the prominent figure, remained in the government. Of even greater importance was the appeal made by the council of people's commissars to the old civil servants to stay at their posts and cooperate with the new government. And actually, with very few exceptions, all the federal, state, and communal officials kept their jobs, most of them convinced that some intellectual and moral sacrifices on their part were justified in order to stave off bolshevism or chaos.

The military leaders had made a similar decision in the evening of November 9. During the afternoon Hindenburg, Groener, and other high officers had placed before the emperor their opinion that his idea of a peaceful return to Germany as king of Prussia with his troops was bound to lead to civil war and that he could no longer count on the loyalty of the army. They also recommended Holland as the best refuge. William II did not wish to appear as a deserter and not until that night did he give the order that his train should leave at 5 A.M. for Holland.

In the evening of November 10 General Groener, after consultation with Hindenburg, phoned Ebert declaring that the Supreme Command was willing to direct the retreat of the German army and assist in the maintenance of order, provided Ebert would do his best to fight the bolshevik danger by working for the early convention of a constituent assembly. Ebert gave this assurance and welcomed Hindenburg's willingness to remain as supreme commander. No doubt he felt relieved that the complete disintegration of the army could be avoided, but he certainly did not wish to use it for restoring order at home.

Actually, although Ebert may not have realized it and Groener only dimly, the army was no longer a power that could be used to quell the revolution. Groener knew that after the crack second guard division sent from the western front to Berlin had fraternized with the revolutionary garrison of Aachen, it was not possible to put too much trust in any unit of the army. He also realized that all the great rail centers and Rhine bridges on which the supplies of the armies at the front depended were by now in the hands of revolutionaries. How far revolutionary movements would affect troops at the front and undermine the authority of the officers was dubious. Groener, who wanted to save the officers' corps, had valid reasons of his own for establishing good relations between the Supreme Command and the moderate forces of the revolution. At this moment Groener needed Ebert even more than the latter needed the generals.

✑ Signing of Armistice

WHILE ALL OVER GERMANY revolutionary workers' and soldiers' councils were formed and the monarchical state governments were replaced by socialists in bloodless revolutions, armistice negotiations were conducted in the forest of Compiègne. The government of Prince Max had appointed Erzberger as chief delegate, because it was felt that a civilian was more likely to win concessions from the Allies. For political reasons it would have been better if the business had been left to the Supreme Command. For it was the German army and navy rather than the new democratic state that had been defeated. The Supreme Command advised Erzberger that any armistice conditions would have to be accepted if the Allied commanders refused to negotiate. Although formal negotiations were not permitted by Marshal Foch, Erzberger succeeded in gaining some changes. With the authorization of Prince Max, Erzberger signed the armistice at five o'clock in the morning of November 11, 1918. Six hours later the guns all along the lines became silent.

Except for its naval articles, which were of British origin, the armistice was of French making. The Americans had no hand in the drafting of the document but left it to Foch's judgment to decide how Germany could be placed in a military position that would make it impossible for her to resume hostilities. This the armistice achieved by placing the Allied armies on the Rhine and securing the most important bridgeheads over the river. Through the delivery of great numbers of airplanes, guns, mine-throwers, and trucks the fighting capacity of the army was to be crippled. Very little time was allowed for the evacuation of Belgium and the left bank of the Rhine in the obvious expectation that the Germans would thereby be forced to leave much matériel behind. The armistice also demanded the unconditional return of all the Allied prisoners of war. In the east it declared the peace treaties of Brest-Litovsk and Bucarest invalid and demanded the retreat of all the German troops from Turkey, Rumania, and Austria-Hungary. In order to protect the Baltic provinces against bolshevism, however, the Allies reserved the right to set a later date for the evacuation of the German soldiers from that region.

The naval conditions were even stricter. They required the delivery of all German submarines, the surrender of a substantial part of the German battle fleet, and the total disarmament of its remainder. In addition the blockade was to be maintained. As a matter of fact, since the Allied navies now gained access to the Baltic, the blockade became even more stringent than it had been before. The Allies conditionally promised to supply Germany with foodstuffs during the armistice period. But while negotiations on deliveries started only in January 1919, it was largely due to German hesitation to employ German funds and ships in this transaction that food ships did not arrive in German ports before March 25.

✑ Rule of the People's Commissars

ALTHOUGH THE END of fighting was a blessing, Germany was in frightful danger of complete internal collapse. Food remained scarce, and coal became even scarcer, not only leaving the homes without heat but also lowering industrial production. The output of the badly nourished workers was decreasing at an alarming rate. In addition the badly run-down railroads were further incapacitated by the delivery to the Allies of a great quantity of engines and other rolling stock which the armistice demanded. Not only the return of the soldiers but also the whole system of domestic distribution was thereby placed in jeopardy. Against this background the demobilization had to be undertaken and the industries, geared to war production, to be prepared for peacetime uses.

Ebert, Scheidemann, and Landsberg, the Majority Socialists in the council of people's commissars, as well as the Independents, Haase and Dittmann, were fully alert to the perilous state of the German economy and afraid to experiment with it in this condition. Ebert did not believe that the time for nationalization had arrived and Haase, though favoring the nationalization of the coal mines, tended to agree. Ebert insisted that the question of future economic policy should be left to the national assembly. The council of people's commissars confined its legislation almost exclusively to the strengthening of democratic rights and to social policy. The dictatorially promulgated laws were essentially confirmed by the national assembly later on.

In the first proclamation the "state of siege" was lifted, all censorship abolished, and the right of free assembly and association, which was extended even to government workers and officials, made universal. All elections for public bodies were henceforth to be based on equal, secret, direct, and universal voting within a proportional system. All citizens, male and female, over twenty years of age were given the suffrage. An old demand of the Social Democratic party, already raised by the Eisenach program of 1891, was thus realized. Among the social measures was the promise of the almost immediate introduction of the eight-hour day and the abolition of the auxiliary service law of 1916 except for its arbitration committees. The servants' ordinance, which in Prussia had been promulgated in 1810,[4] was declared invalid, and all discriminatory laws against the agricultural workers were struck from the books. Sickness insurance was extended, and relief for the unemployed, to be borne in common by the federal, state, and municipal governments, was introduced. The provisions for labor protection, which had been suspended during the war, were revived again.

Many of these measures had been under discussion in the government

[4] See the author's *A History of Modern Germany, 1648–1840*, p. 409.

offices for some time, and in October 1918 it had been expected that their introduction would buttress the new democratic order. A further attempt to stave off revolutionary developments produced results only after the revolution. By the middle of October even the leaders of German heavy industries realized that in the changed political situation they could not hope to maintain their "master-of-the-house" attitude. The coal mine owners of the Ruhr recognized for the first time the miners' unions as the representatives of the miners. Negotiations were conducted which aimed at the cooperation of the entrepreneurial organizations with the trade unions in all industries during the transition from war to peace. On November 15, 1918, the "central cooperative union" (*Zentralarbeitsgemeinschaft*) was founded, which comprised all the entrepreneurial organizations and German trade unions, the Free (Social Democratic) Trade Union, as well as the Christian and Progressive Unions. The entrepreneurs recognized the trade unions and their unlimited right of association. They accepted them as partners in the projected labor exchanges, and most of all in contract negotiations. Contracts on wages and labor conditions were to be concluded as collective agreements binding whole industries. The entrepreneurs agreed to shop councils which were to watch over the proper execution of the collective agreements, in which provisions were to be made for common arbitration committees. The entrepreneurs also assented to the eight-hour day.

The central cooperative union went far in mapping out a new and systematic labor law. The discussions had originally been conducted with the intention of creating a partnership that would lead to the self-government of industry. The employers did not wish to have the bureaucracy rule over the economy in the transitional period after the war, and the trade unions were equally tired of the governmental direction of the wartime economy. But in the meantime the government had fallen into the hands of labor representatives and was expected to advance the cause of labor. The rank and file of the trade unions, which distrusted the entrepreneurs, did not like the central cooperative union too well. The workers might have taken a greater interest in it if it had given them a share in the economic management of their companies and firms. As it was, the union proved useful during 1918–19 in working out hundreds of collective agreements, but it failed to develop into a partnership that would have administered German social and economic life without government intervention.

The need for a strong government initiative arose chiefly from the urgency and complexity of demobilization, for which a national office, regional commissars, and district offices were created. The national office legally introduced the eight-hour day, though only on a temporary basis. The order was meant to produce more job openings in the period of demobilization. With regard to collective agreements the office assumed the right to impose a new labor contract if entrepreneurs and trade unions failed to reach an agreement. The entrepreneurs were made responsible for taking back every worker and employee returning from war service. Although this was a rather tough method for avoiding mass unemployment, it brought results which no doubt had the effect of moderating the revolution. In February 1919, when 95 per cent of the 6 million soldiers had already been demobilized, only 1.1 million people, almost a quarter of them living in Berlin, drew unemployment relief, and the numbers quickly declined in the following months.

A progressive social policy and democratic representation had formed the major objectives of the Social Democratic party before the war, and these demands were quickly realized by the people's commissars. But the new problems created by the revolution were not clearly faced by them. Socialism had been neither the cause nor the aim of the revolution, which had aimed at the ending of the war. But once the revolution had been successful, it was not surprising that many workers expected decisive progress toward socialism. These demands were loudest among the miners, and most of the socialist leaders and theoretical writers agreed that the mining industry was ripe for nationalization. A substantial segment of the Prussian mines had always been state-owned. The transfer of the other mines to state ownership would have removed the political power that the mine owners had wielded and employed for reactionary and nationalistic purposes. Through the possession of the coal mines the state would also have acquired a strong influence on the iron and steel industry. While it could be questioned whether the nationalization of the coal mines was desirable on objective economic grounds, the Social Democrats did not entertain any such doubts and were bound to lose the faith of many of their followers if they failed to act. Yet only a commission of experts was appointed, which received little political support and whose members resigned in April 1919 complaining of sabotage by the bureaucracy.

✐ *Workers' Councils*

ON ACCOUNT of their old party experience Ebert and Scheidemann were firm believers in parliamentary government and centrally organized trade unions. The workers' councils did not fit into this scheme. Whereas the trade unions represented individual trades on a regional and even national level, the workers' councils represented all the workers of a single locality. The different principles of organization seemed incompatible. In politics the workers' councils appeared as a poor second competitor to parliamentary bodies. Ebert and Scheidemann, like most of the functionaries of the Majority party, wanted the councils, of whose performance they had a very low opinion, to disappear as soon as a national assembly had come into existence. It is extremely difficult to make a fair appraisal of the work of the councils all over Germany. To be sure, there were some councils that were dominated by irresponsible characters, and a good many foolish or even obnoxious acts were committed, which often proved entirely futile. But the great majority managed to fulfill a useful function by infusing more democratic attitudes into the German administration and urging moderation on the part of the people. If only few acts of violence occurred and governmental and economic activity continued, it was largely due to the sober and decent spirit of the members of the German working class on these councils.

A group of the Majority Socialists promoted through its *Socialist Monthly* the eventual transformation of the councils into chambers of labor which were to represent labor the way the chambers of commerce represented the entrepreneurial producer. Much could be said for such a plan in Germany, where democratization had a long way to go. In addition, if the Social Democrats ever achieved socialism, it would be a bureaucratic state socialism without such local democratic bodies. The Independent Socialist leaders took a more positive view of the workers' councils, which they wanted to continue in order to keep the bourgeoisie at bay. But Haase and Dittmann were not opposed to a constituent assembly, though they did not wish it convened too early. The left wing of the Independents, represented by the fierce Georg Ledebour, Ernst Däumig, Richard Müller, and his revolutionary shop stewards, was opposed to all democratic institutions and demanded the building of the socialist republic through the revolutionary councils. The aims of these men made them almost indistinguishable from the Spartacists, at least the reasoning ones. Rosa Luxemburg and Karl Liebknecht, who knew very well that the German working class was not ready to endorse their program and that a long struggle was lying ahead, set out to win the majority of the workers. Since, in contrast to Lenin, they objected to the dictatorship of a party, they did not plan to win power through wild revolutionary coups. But the majority of their followers, most of them the poorest of the poor, were utopian anarchists. Therefore the left Independents hesitated to merge their disciplined workers with the rebellious Spartacus crowd.

The German bourgeoisie naturally wished for the victory of the moderates, but its influence was not great. The old civil servants did their best to collect material demonstrating the damage done by the workers' and soldiers' councils, thus trying to drive a wedge between their Majority and Independent Socialist chiefs. On December 6 a group of young adventurers, among them two aristocratic junior officials of the foreign office, with a handful of soldiers staged the arrest of the executive council of the Berlin workers' and soldiers' councils, and they proclaimed Ebert "president of the republic." This action failed, and its perpetrators had to flee, but it was highly embarrassing for Ebert. In the eyes of the masses the event assumed an even worse appearance, since it had led to bloodshed. Government soldiers called upon to seal off the government section of the city had fired upon a Spartacus demonstration, killing sixteen people. How this shooting developed has never been cleared up. Although it is certain that neither Ebert nor other leaders of the Social Democrats were responsible for the events of December 6, they were accused by the radicals of being hand in glove with counterrevolutionaries while using violence against revolutionaries.

✐ *Conference of States*

THE COUNCIL of people's commissars attempted to strengthen its position beyond Berlin by inviting the new governments of the German states to a conference in Berlin. The Federal Council of the Empire, after losing most of its power to the *Reichstag* in October, had been swept aside by the revolution, and with it the main channel of communication between the national government and the states had disappeared. The council of people's commissars, which in constitutional language could be called a six-headed chancellor, had refused to continue the tie with the Prussian government. The Social Democrats had always described a centralized republic as the ideal form of government, and they would have taken a great step in this direction if the commissars had assumed control of the Prussian government. But they considered their responsibilities too heavy even without it. The Prussian government had then been formed chiefly by the Social Democratic members of the former Prussian parliament. Each ministry received two ministers, one Majority and one Independent Socialist. The cooperation between the council of people's commissars and the Prussian government was quite good. In contrast, it was highly unsatisfactory with regard to the Bavarian government, where Kurt Eisner, the gifted and flamboyant politician who had earlier led the Munich uprising, had made himself full master. He propagated the rule of the soldiers', workers', and peasants' councils, criticized sharply the policies of the people's commissars, and even dabbled in international politics. Eisner introduced considerable heat into the debates of the conference of states that took place in Berlin on November 25. But no common South German front asserted itself there. As a matter of fact the governments of Württemberg, Baden, and Hesse were not only more moderate than Munich but also Berlin.

The conference issued a proclamation in favor of German unity and an early election of a constituent assembly. Until the time of its convention the workers' and soldiers' councils were to represent the will of the people. The relations between the council of people's commissars and the executive committee of the workers' and soldiers' councils of Berlin steadily deteriorated. The latter had expanded its membership by adding some representatives from other German cities. In this process it had not become a national council, but an ever more left-radical body which interfered with the work of the people's commissars and agitated against any plans for elections for a constituent assembly. In order to solve the problem, the council of people's commissars decided to hold a general German congress of workers' and soldiers' councils in Berlin. Representatives were elected by the workers' councils in the industries and by the soldiers' councils of units not yet demobilized.

∽ Congress of Workers' and Soldiers' Councils

THE CONGRESS opened on December 16 amid tumultuous street demonstrations. Of the 450 or so members, by far the largest group were Majority Socialists, and, together with the moderate Independents, the government could count on 350 votes. The government delegation consisted of all the people's commissars except Emil Barth, who openly sided with the opposition. Karl Liebknecht and Rosa Luxemburg had not been elected, and the opposition consisted chiefly of the revolutionary shop stewards and radical members of workers' councils. No significant differences of opinion made themselves felt between Haase and Dittmann on the one side and Ebert, Scheidemann, and Landsberg on the other. The Majority Socialists also applauded the report that Rudolf Hilferding (1877–1940), then editor of the chief Independent press organ, gave on socialization. Still, it was the radical members who ruled the Independent party representation in the congress.

On December 19 the congress voted, with only fifty votes opposed to the proposition, to hold elections for the national constituent assembly on January 19, 1919. This was the earliest technically possible date, in fact four weeks earlier than the government had proposed. The congress also voted that the executive and legislative power should be in the hands of the council of people's commissars until the constituent assembly had convened. A central council, composed of members of workers' and soldiers' councils from all sections of Germany, was to supervise the people's commissars and was empowered to retire or appoint them. Against the advice of the commissars, including Haase and Dittmann, the radicals of the congress wanted to tighten the control of this central council. After their attempt had failed, they gained a majority vote in the Independent party caucus against participation in the central council.

Haase and Dittmann, the official leaders of the Independent Socialist party, would have done well if they had parted company with the radical wing and, even better, had reunited with the Majority Socialists, from whom, as the congress had just shown, they did not differ very much. But they did not wish to split their party, while deciding to continue as people's commissars. Yet ten days later they withdrew from the council.

✍ *Sailors' Revolt in Berlin*

THEIR SEPARATION was caused by the fighting that developed in connection with the mutiny of the people's naval division. This outfit of about 1,000 sailors had come to Berlin after the revolution in order to protect the government. They were quartered in the *Marstall*, the big royal stables, and they also guarded the royal palace, which contained a considerable number of works of art. The discipline of the unit under its elected leaders sadly deteriorated, and very doubtful elements were absorbed. The government decided to dismiss 400 sailors by the end of the year and to discontinue the division's services in the royal palace, from which valuables were disappearing. The sailors declared themselves unwilling to accept these orders unless paid a substantial sum by the government. The latter had no defense against such blackmail, but before the matter had been settled, altercations developed. On December 23 angry sailors held Ebert and Landsberg under arrest for hours in the chancellery and, even worse, mistreated Otto Wels (1873–1939), a prominent leader of the Majority Socialists, now commander of Berlin. They kept him prisoner and threatened his life.

Ebert, who had a direct phone connection to Supreme Headquarters, informed Groener of his predicament and, worried about Wels, called for the help of the army, which still maintained around Berlin about one division of troops from the front who had not yet been demobilized and was glad to be asked for help. But when the troops under General Lequis attacked the palace and stables in the morning of December 24, they showed little liking for the task. They were afraid that they were being used by their officers for sinister political purposes, and some soldiers went over to the sailors. Negotiations had to be opened again, and the government was forced to grant the sailors' demands. The troops withdrew from Berlin, while the government was worse off than before.

✍ *Withdrawal of Independents from Government*

ACTUALLY THE SAILORS cared more about their pay than about politics, but to the radical and, since the events of December 6, suspicious Berlin workers the military action seemed just another proof that the Social Democrats in conjunction with the generals were preparing the counterrevolution. While Emil Barth had sympathized with the sailors, Haase and Dittmann had been absent from Berlin on December 23–24. When they returned, they accepted Barth's one-sided report. They found further evidence for the collusion of the three commissars of the Social Democratic party in their attempt to delay and water down the extreme resolutions which the congress had passed with regard to the authority of the officers in the army and which had aroused Groener's ire. The three Social Democratic leaders had also acceded to the wish of the generals to reduce the army merely to its peacetime strength instead of having it fully demobilized; for they wanted forces for the defense of the German-Polish frontiers and proposed to hold the Baltic countries as a protective wall against bolshevism.

Since the central council essentially sided with Ebert, Scheidemann, and Landsberg, the three Independent commissars resigned on December 29. Their example was followed by all the Independents in the various German state governments except in Bavaria, where Kurt Eisner remained prime minister. The central council elected Gustav Noske, Rudolf Wissel (1869–1962), and Paul Löbe (1875–1967) as the new commissars, but Löbe felt that his place was in his home province, Silesia. In the council of five political unity prevailed, but the question was whether they could maintain themselves in power after they had just had to capitulate to a group of marauding sailors. And it seemed certain that the differences with the revolutionaries on the left would lead to further violence.

✌ Founding of Communist Party

ON DECEMBER 30, 1918, the Spartacus League held a convention and reconstituted itself as the Communist party of Germany. Rosa Luxemburg had drafted the party program, which stated that the party would seize the government with the clear will of the German proletariat and that it would be a long struggle. It was a program that was strictly opposed to blind violence. The delegates adopted it, apparently without giving it much thought. But in opposition to Luxemburg and Liebknecht, who argued that the parliament would be useful for party propaganda, the convention voted 62 to 23 against participation in the elections for the constituent assembly. This vote was not only a demonstration against a bourgeois parliament but also the expression of the utopian belief that power could be won, perhaps even in weeks, by the direct action of a revolutionary minority. Out of a sense of party loyalty Rosa Luxemburg and Karl Liebknecht did not split the party. They were to pay for their loyalty with their lives two weeks later.

One Independent Socialist who refused to relinquish his post after

December 29 was Emil Eichhorn (1863–1925), the president of the Berlin police. Although his office was under the Prussian ministry of interior, he refused to follow its orders. He had built up a security force that was dominated by radical elements and obviously passed arms to radical workers. When the Prussian minister deposed him on January 4, 1919, he declared himself an appointee of the executive council. On the next morning a manifesto of the revolutionary shop stewards, the Independent Socialists, and the Communist party was issued. The action of the Prussian ministry was described as a "new heinous coup against the revolutionary workers of Great-Berlin." With the removal of the "last man trusted by the revolutionary workers" the Ebert-Scheidemann government was said to intend to set up a regime of force. In language insinuating more than was said the workers were called up to mass demonstrations.

✐ *Mass Demonstrations*

The response was impressive; a huge mass of people, among them many with arms, moved through the inner city to Alexander Square, where they were treated to fulminating speeches by Eichhorn, Liebknecht, Pieck, Ledebour, and others. Some groups of fanatic, armed Spartacists occupied the building of the *Vorwärts*, the newspaper of the Majority Social Democrats, as well as the extensive buildings of the three big newspaper combines of Mosse, Ullstein, and Scherl. On the next day other buildings such as the government printing office, where a great amount of money bills was stored, and the important Silesian railroad station fell into the hands of Spartacists. At noon time of this January 6 the workers demonstrated again. The government had not known any other way for its protection than calling out its followers from the factories. When the long procession of radical demonstrators arrived in the government section, they found a living wall of government followers massed on the sidewalks in front of the government buildings. They were unarmed, while many of the radicals carried arms. But no shot was fired. The idea of the brotherhood of workers which the Social Democratic movement had deeply implanted in its members expressed itself for the last time as a positive force.

But another reason for the strange calm of the big masses was the perplexity of their leaders. Only Eichhorn with his security guards, the few hundreds of Spartacist hotheads who occupied the newspaper section of the city, and some other radical workers who followed the harangues of Georg Ledebour were actively fighting. The soldiers still remaining in the city barracks and even the people's naval division declared their neutrality. Richard Müller and Ernst Däumig did not wish to have things develop into a full-blown battle, and their word kept the workers of the big factories from the streets after January 6. Rosa Luxemburg and Karl Liebknecht recognized in the evening of that day the hopelessness of the whole action in which they had participated only in order not to be outdone by the Independents and revolutionary shop stewards. The national leaders of the Independent party disapproved of the decision of the local leaders in Berlin. They offered to mediate between the government and the revolting groups. The government accepted this proposal, though demanding the prior evacuation of the newspaper buildings. But Liebknecht and Luxemburg had lost control over the passionate revolutionaries. However, when fighting started, the two communist leaders supported the uprising against the government.

∾ Ebert's Military Policies

THE TRAGIC MISTAKE that Ebert had made after the revolution was now glaringly exposed. Almost nothing had been done to create armed forces which would protect the new government. In the council of people's commissars Ebert was responsible for military questions, but his major effort had been to cultivate relations with Groener and Hindenburg. Although it was both patriotic and wise to maintain close contacts with the men who were directing the safe return of millions of soldiers, it did not solve the military problems of the socialist government. On December 3 Ebert had proposed the formation of a people's guard (*Volkswehr*), which the council of people's commissars approved nine days later. The 11,000 volunteers organized in eleven companies were supposed to elect their own officers and issue orders on discipline. This no doubt overly democratic system might have worked, provided that the only volunteers accepted were those who firmly believed in democracy and were willing to fight for it. As a matter of fact, the three regiments which did most in the defeat of the Spartacus uprising were composed of Social Democratic workers under republican officers. Another regiment that made a great contribution had been brought together by a lieutenant who succeeded in galvanizing the remaining guard fusiliers. If the attempt had been launched right after November 9 not only in Berlin but in all of the major centers of Germany, it should have been possible to gather a force of 50,000 to 100,000 convinced republicans out of the millions of Social Democrats who had served in the army. And it should also have been possible to find the officers if the search had been extended to the reserve officers, whom the old army quite unjustly had excluded from higher rank and staff appointments. And once they saw that a republican army was becoming a reality, even some talented conservative officers might have been persuaded to conform to the new style.

The difficulties in adopting such a policy were unusually great.

Whereas the Social Democratic party had officially never denied the duty of national defense, its criticism of the militaristic system of the German Empire had instilled in its followers a deep loathing of military service in general, which had turned into a profound hatred of anything military as a consequence of the war. But although the same sentiment prevailed among Austrian workers, Julius Deutsch succeeded in creating a democratic army that proved able to cope with the serious Communist uprising of April and May and was successful in the frontier fighting in Carinthia and the Burgenland. The differences between Austria and Germany lay in the fact that the Austrian Social Democratic party had preserved its unity and Julius Deutsch found understanding helpers, such as Colonel Theodor Körner, the future federal president of the second Austrian Republic.

✑ Noske's Free Corps

ON JANUARY 6, 1919, the council of people's commissars persuaded Gustav Noske, the Social Democratic military expert, to direct the arrangements and operations necessary to free the city from the threat of the Spartacus League. Instead of collecting the democratic forces, Noske turned to the old army. He had gained the impression that very large forces were needed and that the necessary number of men could not be attracted unless they were led by the most competent officers. Thereby he sanctioned a development that had begun in December. Volunteers were hired by officers of various ranks not only from among soldiers still in uniform but also from among civilians with or without former military training. They assumed the obligation of strict obedience to their officers. In the east these so-called free corps (*Freikorps*) sprang up as a protection against Polish insurrections. Around Berlin some free corps were formed in order to have forces ready for internal use. The Supreme Command, now residing in Kassel, made great efforts to stimulate the growth of these free corps, particularly after the disastrous failure of the regular troops in the fighting in Berlin on December 24.

Noske's use of the free corps led to their proliferation in the spring and summer of 1919. Eventually sixty-eight free corps came into existence. They were of different sizes and highly variegated character. Some were commanded by generals, others by captains or lieutenants, while a good many officers and even a few generals served as privates. The commanding officers were nationalists, mostly of a radical rather than conservative type. No doubt the generals and colonels were monarchists at heart, as probably the majority of the other commanding officers still called themselves monarchists, although they were already searching for new political ideals. Among the rank and file of the free corps predominated those who abhorred civilian life that many of them had never tasted, and they rationalized their attitude as service to the nation. Yet particularly among those who entered the corps as temporary volunteers men of higher idealism and moderate political outlook could be found.

Noske himself collected troops in the western suburbs of Berlin. Here, in the residential sections of the bourgeoisie, preparations could be made calmly and the greatest number of temporary volunteers enlisted. On January 11 Noske, at the head of 2,000 men, marched to the government section. He expected to meet resistance, but the city was quiet and most people applauded. The main strong points of the insurgents had already been conquered, most of them by the republican units. Only the *Vorwärts* building had been stormed by a Potsdam regiment, and here the worst cases of mistreatment and shooting of prisoners occurred. The losses during the fighting had been great, but so had been those of the republican forces. From the beginning the free corps displayed ruthlessness, and little was done by the government to counteract it.

The last remaining bulwark of the Spartacists, the police presidium, was taken on January 12 by the guard fusiliers. In the days thereafter the great mass of Noske's troops occupied all of Berlin. In the evening of January 15 Karl Liebknecht and Rosa Luxemburg were murdered by the officers who were charged with delivering them to prison. A military tribunal absolved some of the persons involved and gave others light sentences, while helping their escape. The assassination of the two red leaders filled many workers with deep resentment not only against the soldiery but also against the government that seemed to condone these excesses. Although actually the communists had only a small following among the masses, Liebknecht and Luxemburg were admired for their fearless pacifism during the war. Still, Berlin remained quiet during January. But on March 3 the workers' councils of Berlin proclaimed a general strike as a demonstration for socialization, a final law concerning the future power of the workers' councils, and the dissolution of the free corps. The occasion was used by the Communists for armed uprisings. The majority of the sailors of the people's naval division, fearful that it would be dissolved by the government, joined the insurrectionists. The fighting was both fiercer and bloodier than in January, and over a thousand dead were counted. The revengeful shootings of prisoners and even groups of innocent bystanders were alarming signs of the moral depravity that war and revolution had produced among a substantial section of the younger generation.

Beginning with the second half of January the free corps were used wherever revolts and uprisings occurred. This happened in Bremen, Hamburg, Halle, Leipzig, Thuringia, Brunswick, as well as a few times in the Ruhr district. In all these cases radical elements had tried to impose their rule or used violence in the pursuit of their political or economic demands. Although the restoration of "quiet and order"—the slogan generally used to justify the military actions—was inevitable, it was deplorable that it was done by soldiers who had no regard for democratic forms and obligations. These punitive expeditions against hundreds of thousands of workers, with frequent plundering and numerous innocent people being killed, destroyed the belief that the cause of the workers could be advanced through democracy. Angrily, the people saw everywhere the workers' councils losing their power and disbanding.

✧ Bavarian Revolution

IN BAVARIA the revolution had followed a special course. As has been mentioned before, large groups of the peasantry had joined the Social Democratic workers in the revolutionary movement. Among the Bavarian soldiers, too, the rural population was strongly represented. Kurt Eisner, though an Independent Socialist himself, managed to keep the Majority Socialists behind him even after the elections for a constituent Bavarian assembly on January 12 had shown that the Independent party was by far the smallest among the three revolutionary groups. It received only 3 seats, in contrast to the 16 for the Peasants' Federation and the 61 for the Majority Socialists. Moreover, these 80 seats represented only 44 per cent of the assembly. Still, Eisner felt that the support he received from the congress of Bavarian workers' councils would allow him to stay in power. But the agitation of the bourgeois parties against Eisner intensified, and the right wing of the Majority Socialists did not remain unaffected. On February 21, 1919, while walking to the opening of the Bavarian parliament, Kurt Eisner was killed by a young nationalist, Count Arco, whereupon one of Eisner's fanatic followers shot down the minister of the interior, Auer, and killed two nonsocialist members of the house. The parliament was adjourned. Soldiers and workers demonstrated, and a general strike was called. The two Social Democratic parties and the Peasants' Federation formed a new government, headed by the Majority Socialist Johannes Hoffmann (1867–1930), that relied chiefly on the revolutionary councils.

But the new government proved unable to control the strong emotional tides welling up among the forces composing the councils, who were irked by the existence of the parliament. When in late March Béla Kun turned Hungary into a communist republic and Austria seemed likely to follow suit, the movement to abolish the Bavarian parliament became irresistible. It fell into the hands of a group of humanitarian dreamers, poets, and writers, most of them political anarchists, to whom abolition of parliament was not enough; they wished to abolish private property as well and carry revolutionary propaganda all over Germany. Their attack against private property was bound to repel the peasants, whom Eisner had won for his type of a republic. In addition the tactics and aims of the group now usurping power were bound to split the workers. Whereas the Communists refused to participate in what appeared to them a hopeless adventure, the Independents thought that they ought to follow the masses. On April 7, a communist republic was installed in Munich, and the Hoffmann government went to Bamberg. Northern Bavaria remained quiet.

The regime of the dangerous illusionists lasted only one week, but now the Communists felt it to be their duty to stay with the masses and help them fight it out with the approaching government troops. It was the same sentimental feeling that had moved Karl Liebknecht and Rosa Luxemburg during the January risings in Berlin. Lenin, on the other hand, had never let such sentiments interfere with his political judgment. It is clear that through the continuation of the ill-fated coup the defeat of the left masses inevitably became even greater. But Eugen Leviné-Niessen (1883–1919), who had fought in the Russian revolution of 1905, assumed command and, together with his political friends, prepared the city for resistance.

Prussian and Württemberg troops augmented by Bavarian volunteer forces under General von Epp, who under the monarchy had commanded the elite units of the Bavarian army, marched against Munich, which was conquered on May 1–2. The fighting was heavy, and the wrath of the soldiers rose when it became known that the revolutionaries had shot ten hostages. In return hundreds were shot, among them many who had not even remotely favored the communist republic. When the macabre business was over, the Hoffmann government returned to Munich. With the councils dead, a parliamentary government was formed, backed by the Majority Socialists and parties to their right. Johannes Hoffmann remained prime minister, but the actual power had already slipped from the Social Democrats. Everywhere in Germany the old social and political forces had regained great strength between January and May 1919, but nowhere were the successes of the counterrevolution as great as in Bavaria.

Although civil war went on during the first four months of 1919 and was to break out again thereafter, the defeat of the Spartacus revolts in Berlin in January finally opened the way to the Constituent National Assembly. On January 19 the elections took place without any notable disturbance, and on February 4 the central council of workers' and soldiers' councils formally handed over its authority to the National Assembly.

CHAPTER 10

The Beginnings of the Weimar Republic and the Aftermath of the War

✑ *The Political Parties*

WHILE BETWEEN EARLY NOVEMBER 1918 and early February 1919 the socialists were in command, fighting among themselves over whether and when to adopt democratic institutions, the nonsocialist parties remained on the sidelines. But they were active in adjusting their programs to the conditions created by the inglorious breakdown of the old regime and the potential dangers of bolshevism as well as an oppressive peace treaty. The idea of the sovereignty of the people, which had been regarded by most Germans as an ugly revolutionary notion, had suddenly become a conservative principle that offered the only way of defending a bourgeois order. Even the parties on the right were ready for democratic cooperation and called themselves "people's parties."

✑ *The Center Party*

OF ALL THE PARTIES the Catholic Center party found it easiest to adapt itself to the new situation. Outside of Bavaria the Center did not have close ties with the monarchy and had always been a defender of the rights of parliaments, although few of its leaders had been advocates of parliamentary government. It was the only people's party, if one understands by this term a political party composed of members of all social classes. Used to making compromises between its own component groups, it was able to conduct a relatively flexible policy in parliament, except for church and school questions, since its political program was not rigid. Although committed to private property, the Center, in line with the social teachings of the Catholic Church, was critical of liberal capitalism and favored large-scale social legislation.

Wartime conditions, as we have seen,[1] strengthened the political weight of the workers and peasants within the party. Taking advantage of this trend, Matthias Erzberger, the leader of the left wing of the Centrists, had succeeded in bringing the party into active collaboration with the Progressives and Social Democrats, a collaboration which produced the majority resolution of the *Reichstag* of July 1917.[2] The appointment of the conservative Count Hertling as chancellor stopped further open demonstrations of an antigovernmental nature, but the loss of the war and the revolution put the left wing in the saddle. The list of candidates drawn up by the Center party for the elections to the National Assembly dropped the noblemen and most of the industrialists, while increasing most drastically the number of functionaries of the Christian trade unions. No change, however, occurred in the representation of the middle classes. The Center retained a long line of judges, lawyers, teachers and priests. In order to make sure that the Social Democratic party would not gain a majority, the Center concluded tactical election alliances with the parties to its right.

A few Protestant groups showed willingness to join with the Center party in a superdenominational Christian party. The Center party was ready to accept their support and nominated some Protestant candidates. In some provinces it even campaigned under the name of Christian People's party. But actually very few Protestants were attracted. The Protestants were much too suspicious of Catholic policies to contemplate common action with Catholic fellow citizens. Moreover, the mass of the Protestant ministers and their lay followers were steeped in a monarchist and rightist tradition. Thus the Center remained what it had been in the past, the political representation of the practicing Catholics. The party rallied about 60 per cent of the Catholic voters around its banner. A sizable segment of the rest of the Catholic population voted for parties of the right, but an even larger number for the socialist left.

In 1919 the Center party received a slightly smaller percentage of the popular vote than in the last *Reichstag* elections of 1912. Considering that in 1919 women voted for the first time and the Center profited more than other parties from the women's franchise, the election result indicated that the Center did not stand a chance ever to pass the 20 per cent mark. It might have lost more voters, if the specter of bolshevism had not induced many a Catholic parent to support the Center. In addition, the appointment of the Independent Socialist Adolf Hoffmann (1858–1930), a noisy antireligious propagandist, as Prussian minister of education had spread alarm. Once the threat of bolshevism receded, the Center vote

[1] See p. 474.
[2] See p. 475.

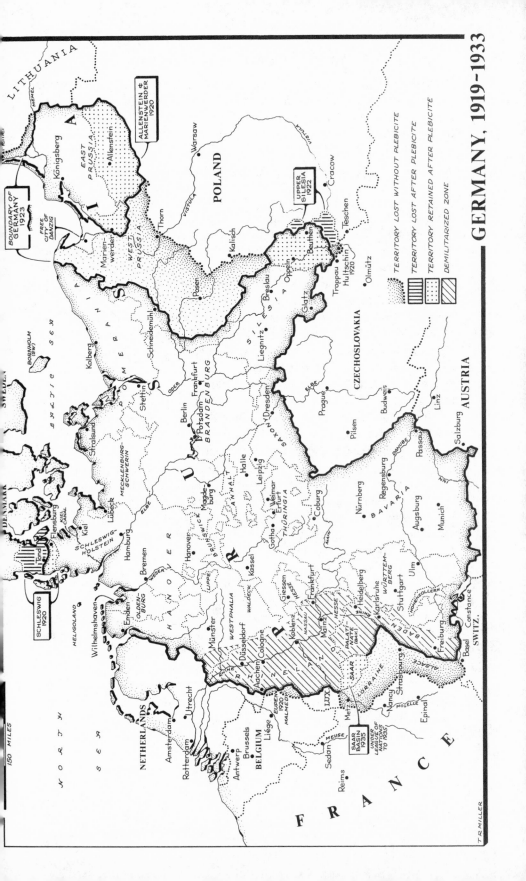

GERMANY, 1919–1933

TERRITORY LOST WITHOUT PLEBICITE
TERRITORY LOST AFTER PLEBICITE
TERRITORY RETAINED AFTER PLEBICITE
DEMILITARIZED ZONE

LITHUANIA

MEMEL

EAST PRUSSIA

Königsberg

Allenstein

ALLENSTEIN & MARIENWERDER 1920

BOUNDARY OF GERMANY 1923

FREE CITY OF DANZIG

WEST PRUSSIA

Marienwerder

Thorn

POLAND

Warsaw

VISTULA

Kalisch

UPPER SILESIA 1922

Cracow

Teschen

Beuthen

Oppeln

Hultschin 1920

Troppau

Olmütz

CZECHOSLOVAKIA

Prague

Pilsen

Budweis

AUSTRIA

Linz

Salzburg

SWEDEN

BORNHOLM (DK.)

BALTIC SEA

Kolberg

Stralsund

POMERANIA

Stettin

ODER

Schneidemühl

Posen

SILESIA

Liegnitz

Breslau

Glatz

MECKLENBURG-SCHWERIN

Lübeck

BRANDENBURG

Berlin

Potsdam

Frankfurt

SAXONY

Dresden

ELBE

DENMARK

Tönder

SCHLESWIG 1920

Flensburg

Kiel

KIEL CANAL

SCHLESWIG-HOLSTEIN

HELIGOLAND

Hamburg

Bremen

WESER

ELBE

ANHALT

Magdeburg

Halle

Leipzig

Weimar

Erfurt

Gotha

THÜRINGIA

Coburg

MAIN

Regensburg

DANUBE

Passau

INN

150 MILES

NORTH SEA

NETHERLANDS

Amsterdam

Rotterdam

Utrecht

BELGIUM

Antwerp

Brussels

Liège

Wilhelmshaven

Emden

OLDENBURG

HANOVER

Hanover

LIPPE

Münster

WESTPHALIA

WALDECK

Kassel

HESSE

Giessen

NASSAU

Frankfurt

Mainz

HESSE

Heidelberg

Karlsruhe

WÜRTTEMBERG

Stuttgart

Ulm

HOHENZOLLERN

BADEN

Freiburg

Basel

Constance

SWITZ.

RHINE

Düsseldorf

Aachen

Cologne

Koblenz

EUPEN 1920

MALMEDY

RHINELAND

SAAR

PALATINATE (BAV.)

SAAR BASIN 1935

LEAGUE OF NATIONS TO 1935

LUX.

Metz

LORRAINE

MOSELLE

Nancy

Strasbourg

ALSACE

Epinal

MEUSE

Sedan

Reims

FRANCE

T. R. MILLER

showed a minor decrease that continued throughout the thirteen years of the Weimar Republic, in which the Center carried the burden of government. But this shrinkage was altogether negligible, and the Center never had to worry about parliamentary elections.

✑ The Bavarian People's Party

WHILE IN 1918–19 the Center proved its solid strength as a Catholic party, the unity of its leadership found its limits in the strong feeling for Bavarian statehood. The Bavarians had enjoyed a good many special privileges. But the central direction of the war and war economy made most of them illusory. The revolution against the king of Bavaria was such an easy success because it could be said that he had failed to protect his subjects against complete domination by Prussia. As early as November 12, 1918, a Bavarian People's party was founded under the guidance of Georg Heim (1865–1938) and Heinrich Held (1868–1938). They proclaimed the principle of "Bavaria for the Bavarians" and declared their utmost opposition to any centralism emanating from Berlin. They argued that with the demise of the old Empire a new one could be founded only by the states through a new act of federation. The future constitution to be ratified by all the state parliaments they said, should abolish the predominance of any single state and create a federal government incapable of interfering with the political life of the individual states.

The Bavarian People's party originally joined the Center party, which had always advocated federal institutions and principles, though in the sense of a federal state and not of a confederation. Outside of Bavaria, however, the members of the Center party had become convinced that the solution to the grave problems facing Germany after the war demanded a strengthening rather than a loosening of the power of the central government. This contrast led in 1920 to the separation of the delegations of the Center and Bavarian parties in the *Reichstag*. Although the two parties continued to vote together most of the time on questions of foreign policy as well as on church, school, and other cultural affairs, their divergence was great in other fields. Owing to Bavaria's less industrialized state, the Bavarian People's party represented chiefly rural and small-town people. Many of its leaders felt great attachment to the Bavarian monarchy, and although no practical attempt was made to bring back the Wittelsbach dynasty, the leaders' wishful thinking made them spurious democrats.

✑ The Democratic Party

ON NOVEMBER 16, 1918, the first proclamation appeared in the press announcing the founding of the Democratic party and asking the support of all the millions who accepted a democratic republic and were opposed to reaction. The new party, while rejecting socialism as a panacea, would aim at a synthesis of individual freedom and social responsibility. Professor Alfred Weber (1868–1958), the brother of Max Weber, and Theodor Wolff (1868–1943), the editor in chief of the *Berliner Tageblatt*, were the moving spirits who had brought together a group of people, most of them intellectuals without narrow party dogmatism, to form the nucleus of the new party. Among others Professor Hugo Preuss (1860–1925) and Albert Einstein signed the proclamation. It was an effort to set new political goals for the middle classes who had been stymied in their political influence by being represented in divided liberal parties immobilized in ruts.

But in order to launch the new party these old parties could not be disregarded. While some of their leaders were needed, others had to be neutralized, and effective campaigning depended on the apparatus of the party organizations in the country. Thus negotiations were undertaken with the Progressives, who accepted the new ideas, and with the National Liberals, whose left wing supported the new party from the beginning. And even the main body of the party was temporarily willing to come in.

✑ The German People's Party

GUSTAV STRESEMANN, the most prominent National Liberal spokesman, was in the eyes of the founders of the Democratic party a liability because of his zealous support of annexationist war aims, and he was told that while he might join, he would have to forgo any party office. Stresemann, who was deeply shaken in his political faith by the collapse of the Empire, originally accepted this verdict. But when he felt that further negotiations were leading to the complete surrender of National Liberal principles and some uneasiness became apparent among the National Liberal rank and file, Stresemann broke loose and began to form a new party after the image of the old National Liberal party and called it the German People's party.

Thus German liberalism remained divided. The Democrats departed from the Progressive party policies most clearly in their determination to close the gulf between the bourgeoisie and the Social Democrats and therefore gave up the belief in an individualistic social order. Friedrich Naumann, who led the Democratic party in the National Assembly, finally was given a practical political role, which, however, was cut short by his sudden death in August 1919. While the People's party accepted parliamentary government, most of its members, though tolerating the republic, preferred the constitutional monarchy. Their attitude toward the Social Democrats remained cold and hostile, and, like the National Liberals before them, they tended to stress the needs of foreign policy over and above domestic issues.

✍ *The German Nationalist People's Party*

THE MONARCHIST PARTIES to the right of the People's party faced the most difficult task. The largest group had formed the German Conservative party; smaller groupings were the Free Conservatives (Reich party) and the Anti-Semites. The Conservatives, who did not believe in democracy, were now forced to fight for their authoritarian aims with the detested means of democracy. Moreover, it was obvious that they were so discredited that unless they cooperated with other parties, they would risk exclusion from all decisions. It is true that the Conservatives, if not by faith at least by practice, had been prepared for democratic methods. In contrast to the hereditary and appointed members of the Prussian House of Lords, the members of the House of Representatives and of the *Reichstag* had always been forced to enter the public arena. Particularly since the early 1890's the Conservatives had stepped up their efforts at gaining mass appeal. Their collaboration with the Federation of Agriculturists and other interest groups deeply entangled the Conservative party in the struggle of plebeian as well as aristocratic materialistic drives.

The Conservatives knew that as Conservatives they would have no chance to build a strong political party. The monarchical idea was not likely at this time to attract many voters unless it was wrapped in nationalism and even a measure of anticapitalism. Therefore, they joined forces with the Christian Socialists and the Free Conservatives to found the German Nationalist People's Party. In the circumstances of 1918–19 the Christian Socialists, the heirs of Stöcker, and the Free Conservatives exercised great influence on the formulation of the platform and also won a very considerable part of the nominations for the election. Two former ministers of the monarchy, both known for their moderation and social-mindedness, Count Posadowski-Wehner (1845–1932) and Clemens von Delbrück (1856–1921), were to play a prominent role in the National Assembly. But the Conservatives refused to accept them as official leaders. A more colorless and less pronounced high official of the Prussian administration, Oskar Hergt (1869–1967) found the approval of all the factions that composed the new German Nationalist People's party.

This new party was very different from the old Conservative party, which had been essentially a Prussian party or, to be exact, at home in agricultural Prussia east of the Elbe. The German Nationalist party managed to cross these frontiers as well as the old social barriers. Since it was able to attract those people who had belonged to the Fatherland party, it gained supporters in western and southern Germany. It won a strong foothold in industry and in the academic world. Alfred Hugenberg (1865–1951) represented both the old and new social strands of the party. As a Prussian official he had played a leading role in the anti-Polish farm settlements in the eastern provinces, had then become a Krupp director, and finally director of a big newspaper combine that also controlled most of the German movie industry. It was mostly due to Hugenberg that not only agricultural but also industrial interests were now represented in the party, although the German People's party, which had no agricultural backing, still retained the largest segment of German industry and trade. In addition, at least in the early years of the republic, the People's party kept the greatest number of higher officials and of professional and academic people, except that the right wing of the old National Liberal party, under the influence of the Pan-German League, turned to the German Nationalists. Another element of the Nationalists' strength lay in the collaboration of some of the large employees' unions, whereas the People's party, in spite of its name, was composed exclusively of people of the middle and upper-middle class.

✐ Elections for National Assembly

THE ELECTIONS for the Constituent National Assembly took place on January 19, 1919, without any disturbances. More than 80 per cent of the electorate, men and women above the age of twenty, went to the polls. The Communists abstained from voting, but they were then a numerically negligible group. An old demand of the Social Democrats was fulfilled by the use of the proportional system. The elections did not produce a socialist majority and showed a surprising weakness of the Independent Socialists. They were handicapped by having gained control of the old party apparatus only in a few places, but obviously the socialist workers looked for the restoration of unity and saw in a vote for the Majority Social Democrats the best means to this end. The Social Democrats received 37.9 per cent of the total popular vote, the Independents 7.6 per cent, the Center 19.7 per cent, the Democratic party 18.6 per cent, the German Nationalist party 10.3 per cent, and the German People's party 4.4 per cent. Considering that Social Democrats, Democrats, and Centrists were committed to building a republic, more than three quarters of the electorate had voted in favor of it.

Since Berlin seemed still too tumultuous to guarantee an undisturbed working of the National Assembly, the government picked Weimar as the meeting place. The small capital could easily be protected by troops and was spacious enough to lodge the national government and parliament. Weimar's name as the glorious center of the greatest cosmopolitan cultural movement in German history was not the motive for its choice, though it was much exploited by the speakers of the assembly. On February 6, 1919, the National Assembly convened in Weimar's national theater and listened to an opening speech of Friedrich Ebert. The council of people's commissars as well as the central council of the German workers' and soldiers' councils of Germany formally handed over their powers to the National Assembly, which at this moment seemed the sole organ of the sovereignty of the people. But this was true only with reservations.

✍ Reich and States

THE NOVEMBER REVOLUTION had not been a centrally directed movement. In each of the member states the people, through the workers' and soldiers' councils, took over the powers of the state governments, and while everywhere the parliaments were swept aside and dissolved, the new socialist governments eagerly defended the rights which the Bismarckian constitution had given the states or, in the case of Bavaria, attempted to add to them. The traditional aim of the Social Democrats had been the creation of a unitary German republic, but the possession of governmental power was tempting, and it could not be denied that there was considerable popular support for state rights. In all, even the smallest, states preparations were made for the elections of a constituent assembly, which took place in Baden as early as January 5 and in Bavaria on Janury 12.

The people's commissars had failed to continue the connection between the national and Prussian governments that Bismarck had created. To be sure, there was no particular friction between the council of people's commissars and the Prussian cabinet, but the question, with which the Frankfurt parliament of 1848–49 had already vainly struggled, of whether it made sense to maintain another central government for two thirds of the nation besides the national government arose again. The new Prussian government, supported by the people's commissars, succeeded in stopping all movements in the provinces aiming at the breakup of the Prussian state into its component provinces or groups of them. A mass meeting of the Rhenish Center party held in Cologne on December 4 called upon all parties of the Rhineland and Westphalia to prepare to establish a West German state within the German Empire, and a committee of all parties was later set up under the chairmanship of the mayor of Cologne, Dr. Konrad Adenauer (1876–1967), who on this occasion stepped into the national limelight for the first time. But the people's commissars, afraid that a West German state might facilitate French designs for the separation of the Rhineland from Germany, demanded that the future of Prussia and the formation of new states be left to the National Assembly. Actually, the states soon indicated that they wished to participate in the making of the new constitution.

On November 25, 1918, a conference of practically all the German state governments had been held in the Berlin chancellery. It was a stormy meeting, particularly because of Kurt Eisner's radical attacks against the policies of the council of people's commissars. Ebert's shrewd direction of the debates saved the day. The conference agreed on the convention of the National Assembly and on common efforts against any separation, but the state governments did not approve of Ebert's thesis that the relationship between the states and the national government would have to be determined by the National Assembly. On December 27 the governments of Bavaria, Württemberg, Baden, and Hesse met in Stuttgart and officially raised the demand that the Empire be reconstituted on a federal basis, and that meant with the cooperation of the states. And when on the day after the elections for the National Assembly the Berlin government published *A Draft for a Future Constitution of the Empire,* the states insisted that the draft to be presented to the National Assembly should have their prior approval. A new conference with the states was held in Berlin on January 25, 1919. It was again a very agitated meeting. Kurt Eisner tried at one point to postpone work on a new constitution. He wanted only a brief law establishing a provisional German government, a law to be approved by a committee of states; any changes made by the National Assembly would have to be sanctioned by the states. Although such extreme aims were defeated, the people's commissars had to make far-reaching concessions to the state governments, among which the Prussian government also became rather vociferous.

A committee of state officials, looking very much like the old Federal Council, was appointed and drafted a law for the creation of a provisional government. It stated that the National Assembly would have the power to draft the future constitution, except that the boundaries of existing German states were not to be changed without the latter's approval. Other laws were not to be presented to the National Assembly without prior debate and approval by the states' committee. If this approval was withheld, the president of the republic could make the law the subject of a plebiscite. The government vetoed the proposal of the states to adopt the voting procedure of the Federal Council for the committee of states. Instead, each state was to have one vote, the larger states one vote per million inhabitants; but no state, and this meant Prussia, was to have more than one third of all votes. Although in theory the full sovereignty of the National Assembly in drafting the constitution was reasserted, the events clearly proved that the states would also exercise an important influence on the making of the constitution in the future. As a matter of fact, the law on the provisional government introducing a president, cabinet, parliament, and committee of states established a pattern that the framers of the final constitution could not easily undo.

⚬ *Hugo Preuss*

As EARLY as November 15, 1918, the people's commissars had appointed Hugo Preuss (1860–1925) as secretary of the interior. He was supposed to prepare the constitution. The candidacy of Max Weber, who had become well known since 1917 by his writings on the reform of the German constitution and was just publishing a series of articles on a future republican order, was discussed by the commissars, but it seems that they knew more about Preuss, who was a left-Progressive member of the Berlin city parliament. Hugo Preuss was professor of constitutional law at the Berlin school of business administration. He was a student of Otto von Gierke, to whose organic theory of state he gave a democratic and activist turn. During the war he published a book, *The German People and Politics*, and in an article written a few days after the revolution he called upon the German liberals to cooperate with the Social Democrats in the establishment of a democratic republic. Preuss was not only a gifted political thinker and scholarly lawyer but also a shrewd political tactician. Yet he suffered from the bane of the expert in politics by having only as much power over the men in actual control as his personal persuasiveness might win.

Preuss invited a group of high officials from all interested ministries and a few professors to conferences in Berlin for a discussion of the future constitution. He wished to revive as much as possible the ideas of 1848–49 without a repetition of what was considered the grave mistake of the Frankfurt Assembly, its long drawn-out debates on the basic rights of the individual citizen, which had kept it from completing the organization of a government in time. In order to provide Germany quickly with a democratic government able to end the chaotic regime of the workers' and soldiers' councils and negotiate a peace treaty, Preuss concentrated entirely on the organizational part of the future constitution. This was the subject of the discussions of the Berlin conferences of December 9–12. The chief questions debated were the degree of centralization, or as the Germans call it "unitarism," the type of governments to be established on the central and state level, and the future of Prussia. Everybody agreed that the republic should become more "unitarian" than the former Empire had been and that Prussia's dominant position was intolerable. But about the measures to be taken to achieve these ends the opinions varied.

Hugo Preuss' idea to dissolve the Prussian state and in its place form a number of states comparable in size to the South German ones was considered politically impractical by a good many people. More unity existed with regard to Preuss' proposal to replace the Federal Council with a "house of states," as the Frankfurt constitution had called such an organ. Whereas the Federal Council consisted of state officials bound by the instructions of their governments, the house of states was to be composed of seventy-five delegates from the state parliaments who would be free in their vote. Max Weber vehemently argued that the central government should not be exclusively based on the parliament, but that there should be a president who was elected by the nation and, apart from the privilege of nominating and dismissing the chancellor, had the right to call for a national plebiscite on a law of which he disapproved in contrast to the parliament. He apparently induced Preuss finally to adopt the institution of a popularly elected president. However, this idea had been on Preuss's mind before and a little later was propagated by Friedrich Meinecke and others independently of Preuss and Weber.

Hugo Preuss completed his draft constitution in the first days of January 1919, and it was debated at a meeting of the council of people's commissars on January 14. The first draft was a clear and logical construction. The power of the states was weakened from above and from below. Municipal self-government was to be freed from much state supervision, while on the other side some important branches of the state administration, such as transportation, were given to the central government, which received potentially unlimited authority to legislate in all fields and the power to intervene directly in the state administration where the state executed national laws. For Preuss the states were no longer states but rather self-administrative regional corporations. In his draft Preuss divided Germany, in which he included German Austria and the German parts of Bohemia, into sixteen regions which were to get the described status. This implied the breaking up of Prussia into a number of lands which would at the same time absorb the small states of North Germany. The highest organs of the republic were to be a parliament elected by all Germans over twenty years of age, a "house of states," and a president elected by the whole people and endowed with the power of initiating a plebiscite on laws he opposed.

In their discussion the people's commissars changed Hugo Preuss' draft chiefly with regard to the relationship between the states and the central government. The reorganization of Germany seemed to them politically unfeasible, and they believed that Germany would have to remain a federal state, even if this meant the survival of Prussia. Although an extension of the legislative and administrative functions of the central government was expected and Ebert wished to see efficient limitations set on

Prussia's influence on the German government, he did not recommend the dissolution of Prussia. The commissars found the house of states a somewhat strange construction, but did not strike it out. The greatest success of Preuss' diplomatic eloquence was the council's acceptance of the provisions made in his draft for a popularly elected president. It was Ebert in particular who criticized what to many Social Democrats looked like a substitute emperor. Ebert found, however, a serious fault in the limitation of the draft to the organizational part of the constitution. Instead, he wanted to give the draft a strong popular note by writing into it the democratic rights which had been made secure by the revolution. And he specified them as freedom of person, freedom of academic teaching, freedom of selecting one's occupation, freedom of the press, of assembly, and association.

In the light of these deliberations Hugo Preuss revised his original draft. It was this revised draft, published together with an explanatory article of the secretary of the interior on January 20, that, as mentioned before, was so severely attacked by the state governments at the Berlin meeting five days later. Although it did not contain the provisions for the immediate breakup of Prussia and the territorial reorganization of the German states, it still included an article that permitted the formation of new states of at least two million inhabitants through plebiscites on popular initiative and flatly stated that "the greatest member state must become smaller and the small member states must grow bigger." These were the aims to which the states objected. On the other hand, they did not oppose the six fundamental rights of citizens which Preuss had appended to his original draft on Ebert's suggestion. To be sure, they looked out of place in a constitutional draft concentrating on the technical organization of government, but they were to develop into the important second part of the Weimar Constitution.

After it had drafted the law for the provisional government of the Empire the committee of states appointed by the Berlin meeting of January 25 turned its attention to the constitution itself. The committee gained in stature when it became a constitutional organ of the Empire with the adoption of the provisional government law by the National Assembly on February 10. The committee of states, composed chiefly of high state officials, the staunchest defenders of state rights, did their utmost to extirpate in the draft constitution all the provisions aimed at the strengthening of the national government at the expense of the states. In the end the national government, though receiving a somewhat broader competence for legislation than in the old Empire, did not get a fully integrated national army or national administration of revenue and of transportation. Even the special rights which Bismarck had granted Bavaria and the South German states in 1871 were to be continued. The people's commissars, trying to avoid a head-on clash with the states, tolerated the practical obliteration of most of Preuss' plans for the new republic. But in the final stage of these discussions with the state representatives they probably expected that the National Assembly would revise the draft in a unitary direction, as actually happened.

✍ *Opening of Weimar Assembly*

ON FEBRUARY 12 the National Assembly elected Friedrich Ebert president. On the following day Philipp Scheidemann (1865–1939) formed a government with seven Social Democratic, four Center, and four Democratic ministers. Count Ulrich von Brockdorff-Rantzau, a professional diplomat without party affiliation who had served as foreign secretary since the middle of December 1918, became foreign minister. Besides Brockdorff-Rantzau, Erzberger, who retained the direction of armistice affairs, Noske, as minister of defense, and Preuss, now minister of interior, were the strongest figures in the cabinet. Prime Minister Scheidemann, though a gifted popular orator and parliamentarian, was not a very strong-willed and independent statesman. However, the government possessed an imposing two-thirds parliamentary majority, provided the cooperation of the parties proved effective, as it surprisingly did.

The two biggest tasks before the National Assembly were the peace treaty and the constitution. But there was a multitude of other laws to be debated and passed. Some of them, such as the tax reform, were of decisive influence on the constitutional practice of the republic. The National Assembly held thirty-eight meetings in Weimar between February 6 and April 15. It met in the University of Berlin on May 12, 1919, to debate the peace treaty which the Allies had handed to a German delegation in Versailles a few days earlier. The National Assembly resumed its session in Weimar between June 22 and August 21. In this period the peace treaty was accepted and the constitution passed. From September 30, 1919, till May 21, 1920, the National Assembly held its meetings in the *Reichstag* building in Berlin.

✍ *Drafting the Constitution*

THE DRAFT OF THE CONSTITUTION as it had emerged from the discussions between the government and committee of states was defended by Hugo Preuss before the National Assembly on February 24 and after a week of general debates was sent unchanged by the house to a committee of twenty-eight members. This constitutional committee held meetings from March 4 till June 2 and engaged in a meticulous review of its work between June 3 and 18. After the signing of the Versailles Treaty the

National Assembly gave the draft constitution its second and third reading on July 2–22. In each of these four stages important changes were made. But the major work was done by the constitutional committee of the National Assembly.

Most of its deliberations were carried on in an objective and cooperative spirit. The membership of the committee contained a very large number of highly competent lawyers who were all willing to contribute constructively to the organization of the republic. Thus the representative of the German Nationalist party, Clemens von Delbrück, the former vice-chancellor under Bethmann-Hollweg, and the representative of the German People's party, Professor Wilhelm Kahl (1849–1932), were active in improving the institutions of the nascent republic. Yet the composition of the constitutional committee excluded the possibility of making the constitution the proclamation of a single philosophy. To many members the democratic constitution was not to serve the realization of progressive political and social ideas but rather to protect the traditional institutions. This applied not only to the two parties of the right but also to the nonsocialist parties forming the government coalition. And while this conflict came into the open most clearly in the formulation of the rights of citizens, it was not missing in the drafting of the structural parts of the constitution.

✍ The Presidency

THE FINAL CONSTITUTION adopted the institution of a Reich president, elected by the people for a seven-year period. The Social Democrats had been the only members to accept such an office reluctantly. Some of them feared that it might become the vehicle of a monarchial restoration as under Napoleon III. In vain did they demand that at least all the members of the formerly reigning dynasties should be declared ineligible. But they succeeded in tying any action of the president to the countersignature of the chancellor. This applied even to the authority that Max Weber and Hugo Preuss had wanted to make the mainstay of presidential power, the right to veto a law passed by parliament and then submit it to a popular plebiscite. Under the constitution the president consequently would have to dismiss the chancellor who disagreed with him and find a new chancellor willing on his part actively to oppose a parliamentary majority. Although not unthinkable, this was not a likely event. As a matter of fact, it never happened in the Weimar Republic. What was overlooked by all the parties in 1919 was the fact that recourse to the popular referendum did not constitute the most promising avenue by which a president might gain the dominant position in the state, but that this end was better served by the emergency powers with which he was endowed by the constitution.

The controversial article 48 of the Weimar Constitution gave the president the right of intervention if a state failed to live up to its duties to the federal constitution and to federal laws. He also received the same right in cases of serious disturbances of public safety and order. To restore order he was empowered temporarily to suspend a number of civil rights. But he had to notify the *Reichstag* of all measures taken by him under article 48, and the *Reichstag* could demand the lifting of any or all such ordinances. All actions of the president thus seemed to be ultimately controlled by the parliament, as clearly all dictatorial powers of the president were given to him as a means of strengthening and protecting democratic government. In the hands of Ebert, the first president of the republic, they were used intentionally only for this purpose, although particularly in the turbulent year of 1923 article 48 was often used for settling by emergency decrees urgent matters on which the parties were slow or unable to agree. Dangerous precedents were thereby set. The political parties were encouraged to believe that they could shun unpleasant legislative responsibilities, because there existed another power capable of sustaining the government. Even worse things were to happen under the presidency of Hindenburg when by the use of the presidential right to appoint and dismiss the chancellor and to dissolve the *Reichstag* parliamentary government was all but abolished. Hitler, as we shall see, was able to lay through article 48 the secure foundation of the Nazi dictatorship before the parliament formally abdicated in April 1933.

The deep-seated distrust of parties induced the nonsocialist parties to adopt the presidential system as a support of the new democratic order. Not only the rightists but also the liberals remained to some extent under the influence of the ideas which had been spread in the past with a view to denouncing the rule of parties and justifying the pseudoconstitutional regime of the monarchy. But it is true that the political parties, after having been forced into a minor role for a long time, were not ideally suited for exercising full governmental responsibility. Max Weber justly pointed out that there could be reasonable doubt whether the German parties even wanted to assume such responsibility. A reorganization and reformation of the German party system was needed that would give the parties a greater willingness to face realities and reach compromises among themselves. As far as they failed to do so, the parties share in the responsibility for the ultimate demise of the Weimar Republic, although the introduction of the presidential system contributed to the flight of the parties from governmental responsibility.

With the introduction of a strong president into German constitutional life the Germans thought they were taking a leaf from the American Constitution. Yet, except for the election by the people, the German president had nothing in common with the American president, who is the powerful chief of the executive, though faced with independent legislative and judiciary branches of government. Moreover, any American president, though quite often a man who has achieved personal eminence outside of a political career, is forced to ally himself with one of the two political parties and is unable to be above parties, let alone oppose party government. In Germany a presidential candidate who was expected to garner a sufficiently large vote was not likely to be a party man but rather an outstanding soldier or bureaucrat who would remain aloof from the parties. The framers of the constitution of 1919 did not sense that under German conditions the presidential system as conceived by them was a doubtful prop of parliamentary government, which the Weimar Constitution, like the October amendments of the former constitution, established as the normal organ of democratic rule.

✌ *The* Reichstag

WHILE THE PRESIDENT APPOINTED the chancellor and, upon the latter's nomination, the ministers, he had to dismiss the chancellor and the ministers against whom the parliament passed a vote of nonconfidence. Thus the *Reichstag*, elected every four years, was established as the chief motor and guardian of democracy. Its independent rights and privileges were meticulously safeguarded. The committee for the protection of the rights of parliament as well as the foreign affairs committee even retained their immune existence after a dissolution of the *Reichstag* till the new *Reichstag* had been organized. Apart from the president's potential recourse to a plebiscite there was only one other possible limitation of the legislative power of the *Reichstag* that was introduced into the constitution by the left. If one third of the *Reichstag* demanded a delay in the final proclamation of a law and one twentieth of the electorate, by an initiative, supported this demand, a referendum had to be held. One tenth of the electorate could launch an initiative for a law, which, if rejected by the *Reichstag*, would be submitted to a referendum. However, the referenda became effective only if at least one half of the electorate participated. It was for the first time that such instruments of direct democracy were adopted by a big state. Past experiences, however, did not justify the expectation of the German Social Democrats that popular initiatives and referenda would be strong forces for progressive policies. In the Weimar Republic referenda, irrespective of whether used by the left or the right, never led to positive results. The radical agitation that usually accompanied these referenda and inevitably was largely directed against the parliament created unrest and further animosity toward the *Reichstag*.

✍ *The* Reichsrat

As THE FOURTH MAJOR ORGAN besides the Reich president, the *Reichstag*, and the Reich government formed by them, a *Reichsrat* was introduced. Ever since the committee of states had been brought into existence it was obvious that the republic would have an organ continuing in some fashion the tradition of the Federal Council of the Bismarckian Reich. But the Federal Council, which had been the modified Federal Diet of the Germanic Confederation and a far more powerful institution in the governance of the German Empire than the *Reichstag*, had been the representation of the federated German princes and was incompatible with the superiority that the *Reichstag* had gained as the embodiment of national sovereignty. In addition the prevailing popular sentiment wanted to deprive the states of everything that suggested the attributes of state sovereignty. Moreover, while the voting arrangements in the Federal Council had protected the South German states against such changes of the constitution as would have detracted from state rights, they had also made Prussian leadership effective.

All states, except Bavaria, were willing to give up some of their prerogatives in favor of the federal government but wished to maintain a body representing the states that could fight any further encroachment of their rights by the national government. Yet they did not wish, and in this the champions of a strong national government concurred, a council dominated by Prussia. However, the idea of dissolving Prussia into a number of states, which alone would have made a healthy federal system possible, was finally rejected not only in view of the strong opposition of the Prussian government, which found substantial popular support in most Prussian provinces, but also because the South German states were afraid that a change of state boundaries once begun might not remain confined to Prussia. All that emerged from the long debates on the reorganization of the internal political map of Germany was an article in the Weimar Constitution that set up procedures for territorial changes of individual states. They required the two-thirds majority needed for laws departing from the constitution. If, however, the state in question approved or the "will of the population" demanded the change, an ordinary law would suffice. The "will of the population" was to be expressed through an initiative of one third of the electorate. In the subsequent plebiscite three fifths of the vote would be decisive, provided they constituted a majority of the registered electorate.

These complicated conditions could hardly be met, the more so since the people were rather indifferent toward territorial reorganization. The only exception was Thuringia, which for centuries had been fragmentized in a ludicrous way for dynastic reasons. Eight Thuringian duchies and principalities formed a single state in 1920. Prussia refused, however, to release her Thuringian districts to complete the political union of the region. In 1922 and 1929 Prussia on her part absorbed the tiny territories of Waldeck-Pyrmont. The only attempt at secession from Prussia failed. In Hanover the Guelf party, which after the revolution called itself the German-Hanoverian party, tried in 1924 to initiate a referendum on the separation of Hanover from Prussia. But the party had only a sectional following, chiefly in the rural areas and small towns of central Hanover, and missed success by a wide margin.

The new organ representing the states, or "lands" (*Länder*) as they were called from now on in order to make them appear as limbs rather than as founding members of the Empire, was again a council of all German governments. Even the midget lands had a vote, the larger ones one vote for every million (in 1921 changed to 700,000) inhabitants. No land was allowed more than two fifths of the votes. This ruling actually applied to Prussia alone, and in order to weaken Prussia's weight still further, only half of the Prussian votes were given to the Prussian government, while the other half was distributed among the Prussian provinces. In 1929 the new *Reichsrat* had sixty-six votes, of which twenty-six altogether belonged to Prussia, eleven to Bavaria, seven to Saxony, four to Württemberg, three to Baden, two each to Thuringia, Hesse, and Hamburg, while all other states had a single vote. As a matter of fact, the Prussian government had only two more votes than Bavaria, and even this proportion was not certain, since some of the Prussian provinces—occasionally as many as eight—might vote against the Prussian government. This situation came close to the disenfranchisement of Prussia. In addition, the membership of delegates elected by the agencies of provincial self-government added an alien element to the *Reichsrat*. Officially the members of the land governments were the chief delegates of their land, but they appointed high officials for the conduct of the routine work of the *Reichsrat*. Ministers as well as their deputies were able to draw on the wide experience that the exercise of the state government, which included the administration of federal laws, gave them. This expert knowledge lent the *Reichsrat* great prestige, but the delegates of the Prussian provinces, which possessed only narrowly circumscribed functions of self-government[3] could not compete with the state officials.

In contrast to the old Federal Council the new *Reichsrat* was no longer

[3] See p. 203.

the organ on which the sovereignty of the Empire rested. It was convened by the national government, and one of that government's members presided over its sessions. Although every law had to be passed by the *Reichsrat*, in case of its rejection the *Reichstag* could override the opposition by a vote of a two-thirds majority. For a law changing the constitution a vote of two thirds of both houses was required. The position of the lands was thus considerably altered. The rights of the national government to enforce the constitutional rule that all the lands had to have a republican constitution, to intervene under certain conditions in the territorial status of the lands, and to preside over their meetings at the *Reichsrat* took away from the lands significant attributes. But more important than such juridical distinctions were the shifts made in the distribution of governmental authority between the Reich and the lands.

✐ Extension of Reich Authority

As in the Bismarckian Empire, three forms of national legislation were recognized. In certain matters the Reich had the exclusive right to legislate, while in others the lands were free to legislate as long as the Reich had not yet made use of its right to legislate, and in a third area the lands would promulgate laws in accordance with norms laid down by the Reich. In all these three categories the Weimar Constitution added substantially to the jurisdiction of the Reich. This was particularly true with regard to the second category. It was also surprising that in the third category the Reich was authorized to issue norms for the land legislation on churches and schools. This showed a fundamental change in the policy of the Center party, which so far had considered churches and schools strictly within the domain of the states. The revolution had demonstrated, however, that some lands, such as Saxony, Brunswick, and possibly even Prussia, might assume a very radical attitude toward religion. The defense of the church and religious education was in this situation conducted best on a national level. It was this experience and decision more than anything else that persuaded the Center party, formerly a staunch champion of state rights, to cooperate in the framing of a constitution more centralistic than the one of 1871.

The administration through Reich agencies was equally extended. Although the administration of external affairs had already been a Reich affair under Bismarck, he had left the states a limited right to appoint and receive diplomatic agents. This right was now abolished. The army formerly had had a common organization and been under the supervision and command of the emperor, but state contingents had remained. Now all the armed forces, including the navy, which had always been a national affair, as well as the administrative military services, were placed under the new Reich defense ministry that was created in August 1919. The Reich administration of postal, telegraph, and telephone service also absorbed those of Bavaria. In addition the Weimar Constitution demanded that the Reich should establish offices of its own for the administration of customs duties and excise levies.

Under the Weimar Constitution the Reich took possession of the state railroads, which from 1920 on were administered through a public corporation. Control of the national government over all communications became complete with the transfer of the waterways to the Reich. In 1927 the Reich established the Reich Institute for Labor Exchange and Unemployment Insurance with subordinate offices on the land and local level. But this proliferation of the legislative powers and direct administration of the Reich, though drastically limiting the activities of the lands, still left to them considerable legislative and administrative authority. Except for extraordinary emergencies all police powers remained with the lands. Within the limits of the old constitution the same was true of the administration of justice, while that of schools and Church relations was little affected by the general norms laid down by the Reich. Actually the lands agreed to the new order, although Bavaria, which in the final vote of the committee of states at Weimar had voted against the constitution, just barely tolerated these changes. The Reich government tried to make it easier for the South German states to give up the special rights which they had retained in 1871 as well as a good many other powers not merely by backing the decisions of the National Assembly but by negotiating with these governments. It is doubtful, however, whether the Weimar government would ever have wrung from the Bavarians these concessions if at the decisive moment the Bavarian government had not been forced to ask for non-Bavarian troops for beating down the communist republic of Munich.

Among the new rights acquired by the Reich the most far-reaching ones were those pertaining to taxation. It will be remembered that as a rule the Bismarckian Reich lived on indirect taxes while the states levied direct taxes and made some annual contributions to cover the expenditures of the Reich.[4] This system had been very unsatisfactory, and although after 1913 the Reich had trespassed a few times into the field of direct taxation, it left its finances in a weak state and extremely ill-prepared for dealing with the problem of war-financing. The Reich had a debt of a little under 5 billion marks in 1914. To this were to be added 161 billion spent on the conduct of the war till 1918. On top of the services of these internal war debts, from now on were piled the internal war burdens, such as veterans' benefits, and last but not least external reparations. It was obvious that henceforth the expenditures of the Reich,

[4] See pp. 269–70.

which prior to 1914 were roughly equal to that of all the states, would tower far above the combined expenditures of all the states and munici-palities. For this reason the Weimar Constitution gave full financial sover-eignty to the Reich, though with the obligation of heeding the financial viability of the lands. It was chiefly the energy and political skill of Matthias Erzberger, who became minister of finance in June 1919, that made the lands accept this fundamental shift. Erzberger not only began at once to tap the new sources of revenue but also took away from the lands the collection of taxes. In order to achieve uniformity, the Reich estab-lished local and regional revenue offices of its own, which before long became the strongest branch of the Reich administration.

The Reich also received from the constitution the right to lay down principles for the levy of taxes by the lands. But after the Reich had taken over the most lucrative direct taxes, such as income, corporation, property, and inheritance taxes, the remaining resources were inadequate for financing land expenditures. As a consequence the Reich returned to the lands a portion of the money collected as income, corporation, and turnover taxes. The Reich also paid from the income of the turnover tax a certain bonus to the financially weak states, a system from which chiefly Bavaria and the tiny states profited. But a safe foundation for the division of revenue between central and land governments was thereby not laid. The fluctuations of economic life and the expansion of governmental activities necessitated continuous adjustments. In addition uncertainties and tensions extended beyond the lands to the over 60,000 disparate com-munities, which had also lost their financial independence and had to rely on subventions from the Reich. The control of all public finance by the Reich increased during the years of the Weimar Republic, and this cold centralization ruined the elements of federalism which were weakly an-chored in the constitution.

The feeling that the Weimar Constitution had failed to create a satis-factory relationship between the Reich and the lands was from the begin-ning rather widespread and soon led to popular demands for *Reichs-reform*, which in 1928 was taken up by the land governments. By that time it had been sufficiently proven that in spite of the discrimination that the constitution practiced against Prussia, she was still too big to conform easily to the policies of the Reich. A large, proud administration, com-manding among other agencies the police forces of two thirds of Ger-many, had many means for delaying or even frustrating the execution of national policies. At the same time the Prussian government declared that it was the champion of a unitarian Reich and ultimately willing to turn over all its powers and administration to the national government, pro-vided the small states would first disappear. But even after the merger of the Prussian and German governments, the Prussian provinces were not to receive all the powers which the South German states possessed under the Weimar Constitution. Thus the thinking about *Reichsreform* veered rather toward further centralization, a trend of which in the end the enemies of democracy in Germany were to take advantage.

✍ Civil Rights

THE CONSTITUTIONAL COMMITTEE of the National Assembly intended to enlarge on the small number of civil rights which on Ebert's insistence had been inserted into the first draft of the constitution. Friedrich Naumann enthusiastically urged turning this part of the constitution into a sort of popular catechism of democratic faith. But the parties wanted something legally precise, the more so since they were greatly at odds about which liberties a democracy should guarantee. There was little divergence on the traditional liberal rights. Equality before the law, equality of political rights for women, freedom of religion, conscience, and opinion, freedom of the press, association, and assembly, academic freedom, freedom of internal migration and emigration, as well as secrecy of postal communication were the chief subjective rights adopted by the constitution. Beyond these a number of institutional guarantees were introduced, in which the differences of the parties clearly emerged. The Social Democrats wanted a secular state, and the constitution accordingly stated that there was no state church and that the churches received full autonomy for the administration of their internal and external affairs. But a real separation of church and state was avoided. The churches remained "corporations of public law" and were supported by taxes collected with the assistance of the state. The contacts between the state and the churches continued to be rather close, and both sides soon felt the need for a clearer definition of their relations, which Bavaria in a concordat and church treaty of 1924 and Prussia in 1929–31 tried to achieve.

But the Center party, supported by the German Nationalist party and, more moderately, by the German People's party, wanted to preserve a maximum of church influence on education. The Social Democratic party and also the Democratic party advocated a state monopoly of youth education. Since the Center party made this issue the crucial test for the coalition with the Social Democrats, the latter agreed to a compromise. They won recognition of the principle that children from all classes would attend the same primary schools, at least for the first four years, before possibly transferring to secondary schools. The admission to secondary education was to depend on the ability of the child rather than the economic and social position of the parents. The schools were supervised exclusively by the state and its organs. But the unity of the schools was broken up by denominational considerations. On the initiative of the parents within the communities denominational schools were to be organized as well as schools cultivating secular philosophies. The latter was a concession to the Social Democrats which was to prove of little consequence, since the ideological interest among the party followers was not great enough to force action. But the churches stood ready to make the best of their opportunities. The constitution provided that the details should be settled by the lands following general rules to be issued by national legislation. The parties, however, failed ever to reach agreement on a general school law, and the denominational grade schools, which had been the norm everywhere except in Baden, simply continued.

The formulation of the fundamental rights concerning churches and schools tended to strengthen conservative institutions and so did most of the other fundamental rights. Of great political significance was the guarantee of the traditional forms and privileges of the German civil service. All the nonsocialist parties agreed from the outset on the preservation of what most Germans deemed to be the finest governmental service of any country. No doubt the German civil servants were as a rule men of high personal integrity and great technical competence. But that they were superior to the French or British civil servants cannot be proven. The vast majority of the German officials lacked political sensitivity and unduly stressed their authority over the people. After all they had been the chief arm of an authoritarian monarchy and, particularly in the political administration, had been selected for their absolute loyalty to the monarch. When William II abdicated, he had released all civil servants from their oath, and with few exceptions they had remained at their posts. Their contribution to the maintenance of public administration in the face of the revolutionary upheavals was of decisive importance for the course of events during the winter of 1918–19. Chaos would have ensued if the food distribution had broken down or if the demobilization of the soldiers had been seriously delayed.

The Majority Socialists knew only too well that they could not have succeeded in leading the way to democracy without the cooperation of the civil service. They were also aware that they did not have among their political followers the personnel necessary to replace at least a good segment of the old civil service. But in consenting to the constitutional guarantee of the privileges of the civil service the Social Democrats overlooked the fact that while the old governmental officials were willing helpers in the fight against bolshevism, it was very doubtful if they could be relied upon as builders of democracy. Provisions for the removal of the hardened antidemocratic officials and safeguards for the loyalty of the civil servants should have been written into the constitution. Instead, the constitution gave the professional government officials practically absolute tenure rights as well as freedom of political activity without careful restrictions.

The sharpest conflict developed over the order of economic life. Old liberal principles, such as freedom of trade, freedom of contract, protection of private property and its hereditary character, were written into the constitution. But at the same time certain socialist rights were embodied in it. They concerned land reform, labor law, and socialization. The entailment of landed estates (*Fideikommisse*)[5] was to be abolished in the future. The creation of homesteads for all Germans was declared the ideal goal, and land needed for providing such housing could be expropriated. Expropriation by the state was also declared to be warranted if the land was needed for farm settlement or the improvement of agriculture. This article, though most useful in the launching of urban building programs, in conjunction with the constitutional provisions on private property proved an inadequate basis for a general land reform such as was carried through in all European countries east of Germany and west of the Soviet Union in the years after World War I.

The constitution no longer spoke about nationalization of industries as a definite or at least desirable aim. The socialization of "suitable" private enterprises against compensation was declared merely permissible. Actually no socialization laws were ever passed. Of greater practical consequence were the articles dealing with the protection of labor. The constitution promised the creation of a comprehensive code of labor law. Although the Weimar Republic did not fulfill this pledge, it issued many special laws, which together covered a widely extended field of social legislation. Liberal reform ideas rather than socialist principles prevailed. Unlimited freedom was given to form unions for the "protection and improvement of working and economic conditions." It was also stated that each German was to have the opportunity of making a living through economic work and that if a job could not be found, the state would provide for his upkeep.

But far-reaching as these social measures were, the direction of all economic enterprise remained the exclusive right of the entrepreneurs. The constitution gave the workers and employees a clear right of participation only in the regulation of wages and working conditions. The factory councils fell far short of the bold expectations which the workers had entertained during the revolution. The regional and Reich labor councils envisaged by the constitution were never organized. But in execution of another proviso, a Reich Economic Council was created on a provisional basis. Draft laws dealing with fundamental problems of social and economic policy were to be presented to this council for review. The

[5] See pp. 107, 469.

distribution of seats in this council among the various economic groups and interests was an insoluble task, and the representation chosen in 1920 from agriculture, industry, commerce and trade, transportation, consumers, and civil service, and in each group from entrepreneurs and workers, seemed rather arbitrary. A final law on the composition of the Reich Economic Council was never passed. Moreover, neither the entrepreneurs nor the trade unions cared much about the council. They felt that they could advance their causes more effectively through the political parties in the *Reichstag.*

✑ *Adoption of Constitution*

THE WEIMAR CONSTITUTION was finally passed by the National Assembly on July 31, 1919, with a 262 to 75 vote. The German Nationalist and the German People's parties, both declaring that they would remain monarchist, voted against the constitution. So did the Independent Socialists, the handful of members of the Bavarian Peasants' Federation, and Dr. Georg Heim as the lonely dissenter of his Bavarian People's party. It was an impressive majority that backed the democratic constitution which went into effect by President Ebert's signature on August 11, 1919. But probably even at this moment the parliamentary vote was not fully representative of the popular sentiment.

There is no way of supporting such an estimate by figures, yet it was obvious that no party took great pride in the new constitution. The Social Democrats, though satisfied that the republic had superseded the monarchy, knew that the constitution had buried the chances for socialization and had not advanced the position of the workers, while riots and strikes kept them acutely aware of the profound disappointment among their followers. The nonsocialist parties, including those that accepted the constitution, were all in some fashion worried that the new state, born out of defeat and revolution, was too radical a break with the tradition of the German past. Even among the Democrats there were more "democrats by intellect" than "democrats by heart," which means that there were few Germans who believed in democracy as an absolute ideal, although many reasoned that after the breakdown of the monarchy democracy had become inevitable. All nonsocialist parties had cooperated to preserve the structure of German society. But they were also inclined to save as much as possible of the traditional political symbols. The new state was not named the German Republic, but the German Reich.

✑ The National Flag

WITH GREAT HEAT the problem of the national flag was debated. The Social Democrats had always denounced Bismarck's black, white, and red tricolor as the flag of the militaristic and authoritarian class state and stuck to their red banner. The revolution had then swept black, white, and red from public view and left only red symbols. It was in Democratic circles that as early as December 1918 the black, red, and gold colors of the liberal and democratic national unity movement of the first half of the nineteenth century were recommended as the symbol on which all Germans except the Communists would be able to agree. The flag of the Frankfurt constitution of 1848–49 was adopted by the constitutional committee of the National Assembly. The expectation in these months that Austria would join Germany gave an additional argument for the change of flags. The Austrians could not be expected to accept the flag of Bismarck's Prusso-German Empire. But in the last plenary debates a majority gave in to the foolish plea of the export interests that the new flag would hurt German trade abroad. Thus alongside the national colors of black, red, and gold, the black, white, and red flag was brought back as the "mercantile flag." Thereby by implication the national colors were declared controversial. This made it easier for the enemies of the Weimar Constitution to heap hateful contempt on the national symbols and, by appropriating black, white, and red to their respective parties, parade as the loyal champions of a great German tradition. The conflict over the flag was to prove one of the worst divisive issues in the Weimar Republic.

✑ Armistice Commission

THE WORK on the constitution had always been under the shadow of international events, as subsequently the Versailles Treaty had the greatest impact on the history of the Weimar Republic. In a note of November 5, 1918, signed by United States Secretary of State Lansing, the way had been opened for the military armistice that was signed at Compiègne on November 11. We have already seen that this armistice was designed to wreck Germany's military capacity for resisting the peace conditions that the Allies might choose to impose.[6] Therefore the armistice had strong political aims, which were further strengthened by its time limitations. The original armistice was specified for a period of thirty-six days. It was extended, each time for a month, on December 13, 1918, and on January 16, 1919, and without terminal date on February 16. The various renegotiations afforded the Allies the chance to impose additional obligations. Thus, for example, they somewhat extended the area of their mili-

[6] See p. 505.

tary occupation along the Rhine and eliminated the threat of warfare between Germans and Poles.

The Germans on their part used the armistice commission to urge favorable revisions of the conditions imposed by the Allies and, though with considerable delay, gained at least one major concession. Chiefly for military reasons the armistice had maintained the naval blockade of Germany. Erzberger had wrested from the Allies only an uncertain promise of food supplies. Once the Allied armies had moved into the Rhineland, this need was soon recognized. But long negotiations ensued over the use of German vessels for transporting these food imports and the use of German gold and securities as payment for them. The French did not wish to have the Germans deplete their gold treasure, which in their eyes was to pay reparations, while the Germans were worried about losing their ships and would have preferred financial credits. Finally, in March 1919 an agreement on food deliveries was reached. Although thereafter the German food situation was eased, this break was late and not dramatic enough to impress the German people. Thus the poisonous assertion that the Allies had starved innumerable Germans to death by continuing the blockade until after the signing of the peace treaty could go unchallenged in Germany.

✑ *Preparations for Peace*

THE LANSING NOTE of November 5 had also prepared the way for the peace conference. The note informed the German government that all the Allied powers had accepted the German demand to make Wilson's Fourteen Points the basis of the peace negotiations, though with two reservations. Point Two, concerned with freedom of the seas, had remained controversial. Reparations, which had been treated in the Fourteen Points in a rather cursory fashion, were now defined as "compensation made by Germany for all damage done to the civilian population of the Allies and their property by the aggression by Germany by land, by sea, and from the air." The consent of the Allies to the Wilsonian peace program had been won by American diplomacy only with great difficulties, and there could be no question that the American interpretation of the Fourteen Points, many of which were broad statements rather than precise rulings, would tend to satisfy as much as possible the wishes of the European Allies. Still, the adoption of the Wilsonian principles gave German diplomacy a bargaining point which it would never have gained without America's intervention. However, since Germany had turned to the Fourteen Points only on the brink of utter defeat, her championship of Wilson's peace program always aroused some suspicion.

The new foreign minister, Count Ulrich von Brockdorff-Rantzau, with his haughty *Junker* manners and appearance, was not the ideal spokesman for a democratic Germany. He had been critical of German wartime policies, to which his own contribution had been the active advocacy of the fomenting of revolution in Russia. He was convinced that the monarchy, both in Russia and Germany, had dug its own grave, and, at least in 1918–19, he often expressed the belief that the future belonged to democracy and socialism. Yet he was running the foreign office in a highly authoritarian way, whereby he expected absolute support from the government. His judgment as a statesman suffered from an inadequate understanding of the spirit of American and English democracy. He predicted, for example, in private that the coming age would witness an increasing power struggle between the United States and Britain.

Although Brockdorff-Rantzau essentially believed that national states are the highest agents of world order, he did not overrate military power and hated soldiers meddling in politics. The rehabilitation of the German economy seemed to him the decisive prerequisite for Germany's revival as a nation, and he was prepared to sacrifice part of the small military force that the Allies conceded to Germany if they would ease her economic burdens. This attitude brought him the spiteful enmity of General Hans von Seeckt (1866–1936), who represented the German army in the peace delegation. Brockdorff-Rantzau prudently avoided all attempts to divide the victorious powers. He clung to the Wilsonian program, hoping to appeal to liberal world opinion. The practical limitations of this diplomatic strategy lay in the weakness of liberalism everywhere. The American elections of November 1918 had deprived Wilson of his Congressional majority, and Theodore Roosevelt (1858–1919), the Republican statesman best known in Europe, decried a little later the Fourteen Points as an undeserved shield for Germany. The British khaki election of December 1918 ended the Liberal supremacy in England and made Lloyd George largely the captive of the nationalist sentiment that was swaying England in the aftermath of the war. In France, too, the nationalists were firmly entrenched.

But the German aim to establish the unadulterated Wilsonian principles as the true criteria of peacemaking was not advanced by the illusory interpretation of the Wilsonian program which the Germans adopted. And in foreign eyes, this interpretation was bound to appear as a trumped-up position. Point Five of the Fourteen Points, for example, stated quite clearly that Alsace-Lorraine would automatically revert to France. When occupying Alsace-Lorraine in November 1918, the French dealt with the country as a liberated French province. Although these may have been high-handed methods, the Germans were ill-advised to argue about a plebiscite, to which the Fourteen Points did not entitle them and which in addition would have resulted in a terrible German defeat.

It was understandable that the Germans put up a strong fight over the cession of eastern territories to the new Poland, since such a transfer might lead to the separation of East Prussia. But Point Thirteen left little room for argument. It read: "An independent Polish state should be erected which should include the territories inhabited by indisputably Polish populations which should be assured a free and secure access to the sea, and whose political and economic independence and territorial integrity should be guaranteed by international covenant." In the German foreign office this was explained as a call for plebiscites only in Poznania (Posen), since only in this province "an area which linguistically is almost solidly Polish can be found." West Prussia was to be excluded because otherwise East Prussia would be severed from the rest of Germany. Poland was to be given "free and secure access to the sea" by the German guarantee of the untrammeled use of the Vistula, railroad lines, and port facilities. Upper Silesia as a major coal resource was simply declared indispensable to Germany; "furthermore union with Poland would not be in the interest of the population."

The inability of the German policy makers to face facts was astounding. The stubbornness with which they fought for their unrealistic reading of the Wilsonian speeches even in Versailles was bound to raise suspicions of bad faith on the Allied side. The comfortable interpretation of Wilson's peace program had a bad effect on German public opinion. The government failed completely to prepare the German people for the great losses which the country inevitably was to suffer. The fact of Germany's military defeat had not been acknowledged by many Germans. That the fighting ended while the German armies were still standing in enemy countries seemed incompatible with defeat. As a matter of fact, everywhere, even by Ebert in Berlin, the homecoming troops were saluted as "unconquered in battle." It was widely believed that Germany had voluntarily laid down her arms when Wilson offered a reasonable settlement of all strife. The American President was given credit in advance for solving the vital German problems with fairness. One South German town greeted the soldiers with streamers bearing the inscription (freely translated): "Welcome, brave soldiers, your work has been done,/God and Wilson will carry it on." A public under such illusions was likely to react even more irrationally to the realities once they were revealed.

Brockdorff-Rantzau early realized that the German government might have to reject a treaty offered by the Allies. However, he hoped that he would be able to demonstrate to the world that the Allies had failed to live up to the promises of the Wilsonian program or might even have discarded it in favor of punitive principles. Germany then would be vindicated as the protagonist of a new just world order and in a position to rally the liberal forces all over the world to her support. In addition, the count suspected that the Allies would substitute the claim of Germany's sole war guilt for the ideas of Wilson. Already in November 1918 the fear of such accusations had led to a German demand for the selection of a committee of eminent neutral persons who were to pass judgment on the origins of the war after the perusal of all relevant diplomatic documents. When in early March the Allies curtly refused a neutral investigation, because Germany's responsibility had long been established, the Germans felt certain that the peace would be built on the assertion of German war guilt and impose unbearable burdens.

The wide discussion of German war guilt in the Allied countries, which in the British elections in particular had assumed a shrill character, had aroused strong feelings among the German public. The latter still believed that, in spite of occasional mistakes, Germany's foreign policy had not contributed more than that of other powers to generating in the years before the war the state of high international tension in which the final catastrophe occurred. Differences of opinion existed as to whether Russian expansionism or British commercial jealousy were chiefly to blame. In any case, the Russian general mobilization of July 30, 1914, was considered ample justification for the German war declarations on Russia and France. About the invasion of Belgium little compunction was felt.

One might have expected the Social Democrats to be critical of Germany's prewar policies, which they had consistently opposed as militaristic. Now after the military collapse and the revolution they might have pointed to their warnings, which had gone unheeded under the monarchy. But the Majority Socialists had accepted the war as a just war of defense and were not willing to raise problems which might show their wartime stand in a dubious light. The only member of the Scheidemann cabinet who at the meetings of the ministers cautioned against pressing the issue of war guilt with the Allies was Eduard David. As undersecretary of foreign affairs in the three months following the revolution he had studied the diplomatic correspondence of July 1914 in the German foreign office.

Here the Independent Socialist Karl Kautsky had been busy at the same time putting these documents in order for publication. Like all Independents who had seceded from the old Social Democratic party largely for reasons of foreign policy, Kautsky was censorious of German policy, although he did not lay all the blame for the outbreak of the war on the German government of 1914. Only Kurt Eisner went all the way by using not only the Bavarian archives but also diplomatic channels to broadcast a confession of guilt, which in his opinion would induce the Allies to grant a lenient peace. But the general removal of the Independents from all governments and Eisner's death set an early end to any meddling of the Independents in foreign affairs. All the other parties were agreed that the Allied charge of Germany's sole responsibility for the war was an intolerable attack on her national honor. This was the first issue after the revolution that brought the parties of the left and right together in a common national sentiment. Brockdorff-Rantzau saw his hand strengthened if at a later date he wanted Germany to resist an Allied dictate. But immediately he wished to use the war guilt question first at the diplomatic conference table. He would have furthered the German cause if he had published the German foreign office documents which Kautsky had collected and speeded up the formation of a parliamentary committee of investigation. Without the presentation of the unpublished material all German statements on the outbreak of the war were likely to appear as subjective judgments continuing German wartime propaganda.

✍ The Allies and the Peace

THERE WAS, indeed, unanimous agreement on Germany's war guilt among the Allied statesmen who assembled in January 1919 in Paris. But on the whole, Woodrow Wilson succeeded in making the Allies adhere to the Lansing note as the legal framework of the treaty. It is true, however, that he bought this result at a heavy price, namely that of stretching his principles to the extent that they covered Allied demands which he himself originally had considered incompatible with his proclaimed ideals. The taking away of all colonies from Germany with the accompanying wholesale condemnation of German colonial administration, the trial of William II, or the adding of war pensions to the reparations bill are examples of this perversion. The belief in the German war guilt in general strengthened the inclination of the peacemakers to give the Fourteen Points the interpretation most favorable to the Allies and the new national states of Europe, as shown particularly by the German-Polish settlement and perhaps even more by the refusal to grant unreserved self-determination to the German elements of the former Habsburg empire, although this course could be defended in formal legal terms.

Yet practically everywhere the drafting of the treaty adhered to the Lansing note. The committee of the peace conference entrusted with the study of war crimes and the "authorship" of the war advised against inserting a war guilt clause in the treaty, and none was written into section VII, called "sanctions," which originated with this committee and the council of the Big Four. But the Germans believed that they had discovered the war guilt charge in article 231, which opened the reparations section VIII.

In the reparations commission of the conference the American representatives were faced with the stormy demand that Germany was to be made responsible for the whole cost of the war she had caused. The Allied statesmen had always promised their peoples that the enemy would have to pay, as the Germans had done on their part. It was clear by now that the total war cost was far beyond Germany's resources, but Clemenceau and Lloyd George believed that their task of making their nations accept less could be eased if the Germans acknowledged their moral responsibility. At the same time the Allied statesmen wanted to get away from the limited German liability for civilian damages resulting from her military action that had been stipulated by the Lansing note. Under these terms England would have received very small money reparations, since her major losses, shipping, could have been made up for by the transfer of German vessels. The members of the Commonwealth would not have gotten anything.

The Americans were chiefly intent on settling the reparation problem in a manner conducive to the speedy recovery of Europe's and the world's economy and therefore eager to have Germany's capacity to pay made the gauge of reparations in the treaty. The young John Foster Dulles (1888–1959) was largely responsible for the general tenor of articles 231–2. The former stated that Germany was responsible for all the damages that the Allies had suffered in the war, which was forced upon them by "the aggression of Germany and her allies." But the following article declared that the Allies recognized that Germany's resources were inadequate for full reparation. However, Germany would be obliged to repair all the damages that the civilian population of the Allied countries had suffered as a consequence of "the aggression on land, on the sea, and from the air."

Article 232 restated the reparation principle of the Lansing note, in which the word "aggression" referred to Germany's military offensives after she had crossed the frontiers of Luxembourg and Belgium. The note did not contain a statement on the origins of the war, nor was it interpreted that way by the Germans. Although it is true that whereas article 232 defined a legal liability, article 231 contained a general moral condemnation, there is not the slightest reason to assume that the word "aggression" here has a different meaning from that in the following article. We have good evidence that the Big Four, when putting articles 231–2 into final shape, did not mention war guilt at all. Rather, they were almost exclusively concerned with the practical application of the reparation principle of the Lansing note. It was on this occasion that Wilson made the concession that war pensions could be considered civilian damages.

Only the Germans' feverish conviction that the treaty was bound to contain a statement on Germany's sole war guilt made them seize upon article 231.

✑ *Presentation of Peace Treaty*

IT WAS ON MAY 7, 1919, that the Allies presented the treaty to the Germans in Versailles. Almost five months had gone by since the Allies had opened their conference in Paris, and to most people this seemed a very long time. But actually the statesmen had never been idle. All these heads of government had not only to give close attention to their own national problems at the most difficult transitory period from war to peace but also to act together as a sort of world government in a politically still-disturbed world and dislocated world economy. During March Wilson and Lloyd George were needed at home, while Clemenceau was laid up as the result of an attempt on his life. Also the Italian Orlando was occupied with the turbulent problems that the aftermath of the war had brought to his country. He played only a minor role in the drafting of the German treaty. The bustle of activities in the drab atmosphere of Paris that for so long had been a city behind the front lines made it hard to separate the crucial problems from the ordinary ones.

Woodrow Wilson was far ahead of the other peacemakers in realizing that World War I had ushered in a new age of history. He recognized that the political isolation of America could not be maintained in the future and that world peace had become indivisible. In order to avoid new destructive wars, new methods of diplomacy had to be adopted and the rule of law to be extended. For its guarantee the democratic nations had to pool their forces. In this vision rested Wilson's greatness. But quite apart from the fact that he eventually failed to persuade the Americans to support his aims, he was unable to select the right means for the realization of his great project. While he was overly optimistic in believing that the spread of democracy as such would silence militant nationalism, he greatly underrated the role of power needed even in the world order visualized by him.

Wilson had an insufficient feeling for still another dimension of change caused by the war. This had been a total war, with the European nations sacrificing their human, social, and economic welfare. The war had also disrupted the world economy, the strongest tie of unity that had come into existence in a world of struggling national states and an absolute prerequisite for a world to be linked closely together. Only a total diplomacy could have straightened out the basic damage caused by the total war. This diplomacy would have provided for the restoration of stable exchange levels, the elimination of trade barriers, and the settlement of international debts. The American announcement that the United States would insist upon the repayment of her loans to the Allies and negotiate individual settlements with each of them served notice to the Allies that the major part of the German reparations would have to be employed for repaying the American war loans. Although Wilson was particularly handicapped in economic matters by the power wielded by the nationalist protectionists in Congress, he himself does not seem to have seen the urgency of a revival of the world economy if the social dislocation in Europe was to be stopped and the new democracies to grow.

The League of Nations, however, was neither strong enough to guarantee the new order created by the Paris treaties nor an effective organ through which peaceful changes could have been achieved. Yet Wilson believed that it was equipped to do both, and this explains his refusal to let any opportunistic thinking or argument regarding balance of power deflect him from the strict application of his principles. While thus the "Polish corridor," which separated East Prussia from the rest of the German Empire, came into being, he was also adamant that the Rhineland should remain German. Lloyd George, on the other hand, was an outright opportunist who did not worry about German power, once the destruction of Germany's navy and the seizure of her colonies had deprived her of the means to importune England. Clemenceau was given more directly to the consideration of power relationships. Although he never made the statement that there were 20 million Germans too many, as attributed to him by German propaganda, he was eager to see a smaller Germany, whereby he realized that France would still remain weaker than her eastern neighbor. While he would have liked to gain permanent military control of the Rhine for France, he was even more concerned about preserving the alliance with England and America.

For this reason Clemenceau eventually accepted the Anglo-American solution of the problems of the Rhineland and French security. The left bank of the Rhine was to be occupied by the Allies only for a period of fifteen years and some sections for even a shorter period. But the territories on the left bank and a strip of land thirty miles wide along the right bank of the Rhine were to be permanently demilitarized. Clemenceau demanded and received an American and British guarantee of these provisions for fifteen years. Thereafter, so Wilson argued, the League of Nations would have grown strong enough to uphold the treaty.

The French also would have liked to annex the part of the Rhineland adjacent to Lorraine. They often called this the restoration of the frontiers of 1814, but actually the Saar district they coveted was a much larger area comprising rich coal mines and industries in many respects complementary to the iron mines of Lorraine. This policy too was opposed by Wilson and Lloyd George. They agreed, however, that in view of the destruction of the coal mines in northern France those of the Saar should be given temporarily to France. The Saar district was separated from Germany and placed under the League of Nations for a period of fifteen years, after which a plebiscite was to settle the future status of the district. No doubt some Frenchmen entertained the hope that within fifteen years an administration of preponderantly French character would be able to win over the Saar population to France.

Closely connected with the Rhineland settlement were the decisions on German disarmament. Compulsory military service was to be abolished; Germany would be allowed to retain a small army of 100,000 men—including 4,000 officers—to consist of volunteers enlisted to serve for long terms. The army was not permitted to possess an air force or tanks and other heavy weapons. Many of the additional measures taken, such as the dissolution of the general staff, were rather naïve because the Allies could not seriously hinder substitute arrangements, as they were unable to suppress the teaching of military science. In this regard the disarmament provisions were not only extravagant, but they also invited violations from the outset. The German navy, which was to retain 15,000 men, was not to have any submarines and only a limited number of relatively small surface vessels. Even the six battleships which Germany was allowed to build were not supposed to exceed 10,000 tons. An Allied military control commission was to be charged with the supervision of both the destruction of the existing German arms and the maintenance of the arms level stipulated by the treaty.

Next to the issues of the Rhineland and of general security it was the reparations problem that caused the strongest division among the Big Four. We have seen before that the British insisted on having war pensions counted as civilian damages for which Germany was liable to pay. Presumably the reparations bill was thereby practically tripled, and as a consequence the receipts were divided differently among the Allies. France, in dire economic and financial straits, raised her demands to astronomic heights. It did not help that even the French could not altogether deny that ultimately Germany's capacity to pay would determine the size of reparations, because the financial experts were deeply split on the estimate of this capacity. The economic liquidation of World War I was for the economists a problem of unprecedented magnitude and complexity.

In the end a proposal to put off the determination of the total German reparations debt as well as of a final payment schedule was adopted. It had been first advanced by the Americans in the hope that at a later date more sober counsels might prevail. The treaty introduced a reparations commission, on which the United States, Britain, France, Italy, Belgium, and Serbia were to be represented and which was supposed to present final solutions to the governments by May 1, 1921. In the meantime, however, Germany had to make preliminary, if big, payments and deliveries. The great disadvantage of this procedure lay in the fact that Germany was forced virtually to sign a blank check, which naturally she resented. Moreover, the expectation that a lapse of two years would calm down wartime passions and lead to a realistic settlement proved in error. The refusal of the United States to ratify the treaty removed the strongest voice of economic sanity from the Allied Reparations Commission, and the reparations problem caused ruinous conflict for many years to come.

John Maynard Keynes in his *Economic Consequences of the Peace*, a book that, together with some brilliant economic analysis, contained a good deal of mistaken political appraisal, criticized Lloyd George and Wilson for their ignorance of the fact that financial and economic rather than political and territorial problems were decisive for a lasting peace and that food, coal, and transportation questions constituted the real dangers of the future. In this form his judgment cannot be accepted. There were frontiers which imperiled a stable order. Still, Europe's lack of economic security with its ensuing crises contributed tremendously to the growth of radical movements ready to fight for the overthrow of the postwar system. In the most virulent case, that of Germany, this situation led to the attack of the frontiers of 1919. It was the continuous interaction of the economic and political factors that determined the critical developments of the postwar period.

While the impact of the reparations—further aggravated by other economic provisions of the treaty, such as the loss of all German property in enemy countries—should not be underrated, the bitterest immediate resentment was aroused by the new frontiers. No offense was taken at the separation of the Danish parts of Schleswig, which Bismarck had promised in the Peace of Prague of 1866 but never executed. In February and March 1920 plebiscites were held in North Schleswig. Although the new boundary still left a Danish minority on the German side and a German minority on the Danish side, the change was beneficial. Although the adjustments in favor of Belgium were made without careful regard to the wishes of the population, they concerned only very small districts and did not provoke much of a German reaction. The same was true of the enforced cession of the Hultschin district to Czechoslovakia. But the loudest and angriest protests were caused by the enforced cession of most of the provinces of Posen and West Prussia as well as of one East Prussian county to Poland, which under the terms of the draft treaty was in addition to receive Upper Silesia outright. The creation of a Polish corridor between East Prussia and Pomerania, which seemed to imperil the easternmost province of Germany, the moving of the Polish frontiers to a distance of only one hundred miles from the German capital, and the loss

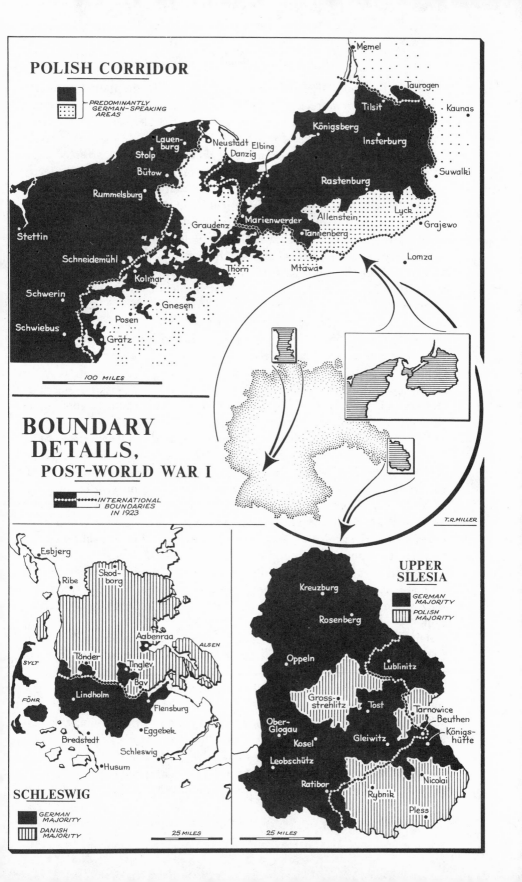

POLISH CORRIDOR

PREDOMINANTLY
GERMAN-SPEAKING
AREAS

Memel
Taurogen
Tilsit
Kaunas
Königsberg
Insterburg
Lauenburg
Neustadt Elbing
Stolp
Danzig
Suwalki
Bütow
Rastenburg
Rummelsburg
Lyck
Graudenz
Marienwerder
Allenstein
Grajewo
Stettin
Tannenberg
Schneidemühl
Thorn
Mtawa
Lomza
Kolmar
Schwerin
Gnesen
Posen
Schwiebus
Grätz

100 MILES

BOUNDARY
DETAILS,
POST-WORLD WAR I

INTERNATIONAL
BOUNDARIES
IN 1923

T.R.MILLER

Esbjerg
Ribe
Skod-borg
Aabenraa
ALSEN
Tønder
Tinglev
SYLT
Bøv
FÖHR
Lindholm
Flensburg
Bredstedt
Eggebek
Schleswig
Husum

SCHLESWIG

GERMAN
MAJORITY

DANISH
MAJORITY

25 MILES

UPPER
SILESIA

GERMAN
MAJORITY

POLISH
MAJORITY

Kreuzburg
Rosenberg
Oppeln
Lublinitz
Gross-strehlitz
Tost
Tarnowice
Ober-Glogau
Beuthen
Kosel
Gleiwitz
Königs-hütte
Leobschütz
Ratibor
Nicolai
Rybnik
Pless

25 MILES

of one of the major breadbaskets as well as one of the most important industrial districts were a stunning blow to the German national consciousness, and it was a foregone conclusion to the Germans that the new Polish state would be a hostile neighbor.

Except for the Upper Silesian case, which was later corrected, the peace conference applied fair criteria in the realization of Point Thirteen, which dealt with the new Poland. It is true that the territories given to Poland contained large groups of Germans and that particularly in West Prussia exclusively German communities existed. But these German districts were surrounded by land settled by Poles. The Allied peacemakers had not accepted the Polish claims for the part of West Prussia east of the Vistula and for the southern section of East Prussia. In these governmental districts of Marienwerder and Allenstein plebiscites were to be held. They resulted in 1920 in votes of 93 per cent and 97 per cent, respectively, in favor of Germany. The German character of the city of Danzig was recognized. The city was not given to Poland in spite of the promise that the new state was to receive "free and secure access to the sea." Danzig was to become a free city, with Poland in charge of its foreign affairs and entitled to the free use of its port. For the supervision of these terms a high commissioner of the League of Nations was to be appointed, although he received only limited powers.

The loss of the German colonies would probably not have caused such wide indignation if it had not been accompanied by the Allied allegation that Germany had proved unfit to administer colonies. Nobody could foresee that thirty years later this loss would prove a blessing in disguise, since noncolonialist Germany found easy acceptance among the independent colored nations. Outside of the American delegation few people believed that the age of colonialism was drawing to its close, although in retrospect it cannot be denied that the weak colonial mandate system that Wilson built into the League of Nations was a significant step toward ultimate decolonization. To the Germans, however, the placement of their colonies under the League appeared as a fraudulent form of annexation.

The Allied demand for the extradition of Germans accused of war crimes, as well as the projected trial of William II, offended the Germans profoundly. We have already seen that few Germans, if any, felt serious responsibility for the war or had knowledge of the outrages committed by German troops. Since the Allied claims were based on principles which were legally ill-defined, the German reaction was passionate in the extreme.

That the Allies prohibited the merger with Germany of Austria and the Sudetenland caused indignation, though at this moment no general protest. The German government early realized that any expansion in the east would have to be paid for by the cession of Rhenish territories to France. It stopped assistance to the Sudeten Germans who attempted to separate from Bohemia. The request of German-Austria to be included in the German republic was treated in a dilatory fashion by the opening of negotiations. From March 1919 on, the Austrian minister was invited to the meetings of the constitutional committee of the Weimar Assembly, and the final Weimar Constitution gave Austria membership in the Federal Council. But this happened after the signing of the Versailles Treaty, and the Allies forced Germany in September 1919 to strike out this provision.

Last but not least the whole procedure of peacemaking that the Allies had chosen greatly irritated the Germans. They had already waxed impatient in the four months which passed before they were invited to the conference. When the German peace delegation had its first meeting with the Allied statesmen at Versailles on May 7, 1919, it learned that this first meeting would also be the last and that Germany would be allowed to make counterproposals in writing only, and within a strictly limited period of time. It is not true, as the Germans soon complained, that in the absence of oral arguments at a round table the Allied policy became dictatorial. Rather, this procedure had been adopted by the Allies in order to safeguard the precarious agreement they had achieved among themselves with such tremendous difficulties. At the same time, there is no question that in subsequent years the reputation of the Paris Conference was impaired by it.

✑ German Peace Strategy

THE GERMAN GOVERNMENT, as mentioned before, had done nothing to prepare the people for the grave losses which the acceptance of the Wilsonian program might entail. When the treaty became known, there was a violent nationalistic reaction, although the masses were rather apathetic. Count Brockdorff-Rantzau's tactics at Versailles were intended to bolster up this nationalistic feeling. They were, however, in the first place aimed at an international audience. The count hoped to activate British liberal opinion as well as the French and Italian socialists against the policies of their governments at the peace conference and to place the blame on these governments if Germany refused to sign the treaty. Then he believed that not only would the common front of the Allies break up but also the internal opposition would compel them to offer a "just" peace, which meant a peace friendly to Germany. The accusation that the Allies had substituted Germany's war guilt for the Wilsonian principles as guaranteed by the Lansing note seemed to him the best way to hold the Allies responsible before the world for the failure of the peace. Therefore in his speech of May 7, with which he replied to Clemenceau's opening remarks, he already started to argue over the war guilt question, and in the following three weeks he dispatched three notes on the subject.

Count Brockdorff-Rantzau badly missed the opportunity for presenting at the Versailles meeting of May 7 the image of a democratic Germany that had given up the attitude of moral superiority. Instead his speech was tactless and aggressive; he was even personally impolite by not apologizing for remaining seated. It was remarkably undiplomatic to speak of the "violent hatred" that the German delegation was facing or to scold the Allies for having made the Germans wait for six weeks for an armistice and for six months for the peace terms and for having killed hundreds of thousands of noncombatants by the continuation of the naval blockade. Small wonder then that the count's speech made a bad impression on the Allied statesmen present and did not win Germany any sympathy abroad.

In Germany, however, the speech set the tone of the passionate protests which were leveled against the draft treaty. The government was appalled. If it declared the treaty unacceptable, the Independents might call the masses to rise; if it took no strong stand against it, the army might revolt. The cabinet decided that the treaty should be called unacceptable in its present form, although there were already then a few ministers who admitted that in the end Germany would be forced to sign any treaty. On May 12 the National Assembly met in Berlin, and Prime Minister Scheidemann denounced the treaty as a means of imprisoning the German people. Carried away by his own rhetoric, as he easily was, he exclaimed: "What hand would not wither that binds itself and us in these fetters?" Speakers of all the parties from the Independents to the German Nationalists condemned the draft treaty.

Counterproposals were worked out both in the foreign office and by the delegation in Versailles. Actually the government wanted to keep the direction of the peace policy in its hands. It also felt that this policy had to be conducted in consultation with the political parties. But Brockdorff-Rantzau, in good authoritarian manner, thought that in this case internal politics might cramp the style of diplomacy. In addition he wanted to draw the Allies into oral negotiations, at least on the level of technical experts, and to broadcast to the world not only how oppressive the treaty was but also that the Germans were better democrats and internationalists than the Allies. Thus, almost at once he began sending off notes on individual topics in quick succession, and not even an order from the cabinet in Berlin to stop this dispatch, particularly of notes on the war guilt question, kept the dogged minister from continuing on his course of action.

On May 29, after an understanding between the cabinet and the delegation had been reached, the comprehensive German counterproposals were transmitted to the Allies. They were accompanied by a note summarizing these propositions and setting forth at length the incompatibility of the Allied draft treaty with the Lansing note. While the counterproposals were unyielding with regard to the Saar and the Polish frontier, they were more conciliatory in disarmament and financial matters. The limitation of the army to 100,000 men was accepted, and there was even readiness expressed to forgo the six battleships if the territorial demands were changed. As reparations the Germans offered the sum of 100 billion gold marks to be paid over an indefinite period of years without interest. While Count Brockdorff-Rantzau was not hopeful that the Allies would easily make concessions, he considered it possible that they might not refuse oral negotiations. If they did, the German counterproposals had demonstrated to liberal world opinion that not Germany but the Allied governments were to blame for blocking the birth of a world order built on law. If on the other hand Germany refused to sign the treaty, the liberal forces would before very long compel their governments to conduct negotiations with Germany on acceptable terms. He believed that he already noticed in the Allied nations signs of growing discontent with the peace policies of their governments.

Yet the German foreign minister misjudged the political world situation. In the United States there was no criticism of the Allied peace terms for Germany. Senator Lodge's fight against Wilson was directed exclusively against the president for trying to entangle the United States in a League of Nations. Some critical voices heard in England did not emanate from the halls of power, and among the mass of the people a virulent hatred of the Germans prevailed. Clemenceau on his part had to guard against Poincaré and the French generals rather than some socialist dissatisfaction. But among the Big Three it was Lloyd George who was willing to modify the peace terms. He was worried that in the case of a breakdown of the existing parliamentary government Germany might turn bolshevik, and he disliked the prospect of a resumption of war and a long occupation of Germany. Wilson was temperamentally opposed to any amendments at this point. Being a man of high principles, he had suffered profoundly from the labors by which the Big Three had arrived at a compromise. But somehow he believed that in the end he had accepted only compromises for which a good case could be made on moral grounds. Therefore he resented the German challenge. Thus Lloyd George won only one major concession to the Germans: The cession of Upper Silesia to Poland was made dependent on a plebiscite. All other changes were insignificant.

The German delegation received the Allied reply to its counterproposals on June 16. The extensive note took up practically all the objections the Germans had raised to the provisions. While in some cases it showed that the Germans had misunderstood these provisions, it maintained throughout that the peace settlement was in agreement with the principles of the Lansing note. But, in addition, the Allies reacted now to the moral indignation that all German notes had displayed, especially those dealing with the war guilt. They emphatically stated that in their judgment the war had been the greatest crime ever committed by a nation against humanity and the freedom of nations. But Lloyd George's private secretary, Philip Kerr, who as Lord Lothian was to step into the limelight of history in the 1930's, went beyond what might still have referred only to Germany's war declarations and subsequent military actions. With the approval of the Big Four he accused imperial Germany of having planned for a long period of time to subjugate Europe and impose Prussian despotism on her. Although this statement did not directly point to article 231, the German interpretation of this article seemed fully confirmed: The word "aggression" not only denoted German military actions but also a politically premeditated war. Brockdorff-Rantzau saw the justification of his belief that the treaty was built on German war guilt and of his diplomatic tactics which had resulted in this Allied admission. He thought it gave him a strong moral basis for Germany's resistance to the treaty.

But, on returning to Weimar, he found the domestic scene, to which he had paid so little attention, completely changed. His obstinate disregard of cabinet decisions had given his enemies in the government the chance to propagate their own policies. Erzberger, who as chief of the armistice delegation had a few contacts with the Allied side, was a bitter foe of the count. And he felt it to be the task of the politician's craft to answer the needs of the day. He knew that in their wretched state the masses wanted no more war and that Germany could not hope to resist an Allied invasion. In that case a peace worse than the one now offered was likely to be concluded, possibly not even with a national government but with a number of German states. While this reasoning was doubtlessly correct, Erzberger was quite wrong in assuming that compliance with the demands of the Allies would induce them to alleviate their peace conditions. But he succeeded with these arguments in winning the support of his party.

✑ Acceptance of Treaty

AMONG THE SOCIAL DEMOCRATS, Eduard David, the minister without portfolio, and Gustav Noske, the defense minister, were the first to face up to the realities of the situation. In addition to the perils of which Erzberger was afraid, they realized that their party would lose millions of voters to the Independents, who might call for strikes or direct political action against a government and parliament that refused to make peace. Economic chaos and civil war were likely to occur, and this in turn would endanger the survival of a national state. A vote taken by the Social Democratic delegation of the National Assembly in the middle of June showed that the members in favor of signing the treaty were in a very strong majority.

A similar vote taken by the Democratic party at the same time, on the other hand, showed an overwhelming majority in strongest opposition to the signing of the peace treaty. To this party belonged the men who had believed that in the circumstances of 1918–19 democracy was the surest way for restoring an ordered society. But they had also been convinced that the Wilsonian program would guarantee a democratic Germany a peace that would minimize her defeat. Understandably, they were saddened by the actual events, but it is characteristic of them that at this moment they were swayed by their nationalist sentiments rather than the firm determination to plant a democratic state in Germany. Some members of the Democratic party may have believed with Brockdorff-Rantzau that after a relatively brief period of tribulations Germany would win a better peace, but for any clear-sighted person there could be no question that the refusal to sign the treaty would make democracy in Germany impossible, at least on a national scale. Actually even on patriotic grounds the treaty had to be accepted, since it was the only way to safeguard the unity of the empire.

The German People's party and the German Nationalists opposed the signing of the treaty. They represented the old ruling classes, whose imprudent policies had led Germany into disaster. The revolution relieved them of governmental responsibility and allowed them a negative attitude now, although an indefinite number of these rightists must have been convinced that the treaty had to be signed, particularly after the high command of the army had explained the hopelessness of the military situation.

Brockdorff-Rantzau gave his report and recommendation to the cabinet on June 18. When the long meeting ended, the final vote showed that the cabinet was evenly split. All its Democratic members expressed themselves in favor of Brockdorff-Rantzau's policy proposal, which had the backing of Prime Minister Scheidemann, whereas the three ministers from the Center party disapproved of it. On their side was also the majority of the Social Democratic ministers. The cabinet resigned, and a government was formed that was ready to move for the acceptance of the treaty in the National Assembly. The new cabinet, which the Democrats did not join, was headed by the Social Democrat Gustav Bauer (1870–1944), with Erzberger as his deputy and minister of finance.

Hermann Müller, the chief expert of the Social Democratic party on foreign relations, replaced Count Brockdorff-Rantzau.

But even the acceptance of the treaty raised the specter of civil war and the division of the Empire. The possibility that the army and the free corps might turn against the government could not be excluded. Still more dangerous was a scheme developed by a sizable group of army officers of all ranks and actively supported by General Walther Reinhardt (1872–1930), like Groener a Württemberg officer, who from January on served as Prussian minister of war. The plan hatched in these circles envisaged the separation from Germany of the eastern provinces of Prussia, where the remaining military forces were to be massed and the war to be continued. It was sad that this least reactionary among the prominent officers should have embraced such ideas. They alienated Groener forever and blocked the cooperation of the two men, which might have changed the political character of the army in the Weimar Republic. Hindenburg had already informed the government that after original gains in Poland military resistance in the west was hopeless. Groener believed that the unity of the Empire together with the preservation of the officers' corps was the principal prerequisite for the rebuilding of Germany as a major power. He did not hesitate to use the full weight of the Supreme Command in order to stop all adventures.

Groener still believed that Germany might be able to sign the peace treaty with some reservations. And this was equally true of the political parties. At least articles 227–30, dealing with the trial of William II and the delivery of German war criminals to Allied courts, and the war guilt article 231 were not to be recognized. This became the program of the government that on June 22, 1919, was approved by the National Assembly with a vote of 237 to 138. The Independents, Social Democrats, Centrists, and a few Democrats formed the majority, while most members of the Democratic party, the German People's party and the German Nationalist party, augmented by a few dissenters from the Center and the Social Democratic parties, constituted the minority. The Allies peremptorily rejected the German reservations and under the threat of ending the armistice demanded the unreserved acceptance of the treaty.

When the chancellor offered to turn the government over to the parties of the right, the People's party under Stresemann began to worry about the consequences of a rejection of the treaty. Both the People's party and the Nationalist party expressed their willingness to make a declaration that they did not question the patriotism of those members of the house who deemed the signing of the treaty necessary. Unhappily this promise was soon to be forgotten, but it was essential for the vote by which the National Assembly, on June 23, authorized the government to accept the treaty. On June 28, 1919, two German ministers, Hermann

Müller and Johannes Bell (1868–1949), affixed their signatures to the peace treaty that had been signed by the representatives of twenty-seven Allied and Associated nations. The ceremony took place in the Hall of Mirrors of the Versailles Palace, where in 1871, with much martial display, William I had been proclaimed German emperor.

The event was viewed by practically all Germans as a deep humiliation. But the main legacy of Bismarck, the unity of Germany, was preserved. If czarist Russia had still existed, the peace might have been infinitely worse. In that case those Frenchmen who wanted to separate the Rhineland from Germany would probably have won out not only in French politics but also at the peace conference. As it was, Wilson and Lloyd George were able to save the Rhineland for Germany, and Clemenceau was realistic and sensible enough to accept this solution. When under the protection of the French army a German state attorney, Dr. Dorten, on June 1, 1919, proclaimed a free Rhenish republic, the French government quickly disavowed the venture.

Thus the German victories in the east during World War I had a distinct influence on the peace of Versailles. And this was true with regard to the whole European peace settlement of Paris. Russia remained pressed back far to the east and deprived of all the territories of Western civilization she had conquered since the days of Peter the Great. The states which had come into being as a result of the Brest-Litovsk Treaty survived. But while imperial Germany had intended to keep them as satellites, the Allied victory not only defeated such German aims but also expanded Poland at Germany's expense. These new states, however, held Russian pressure off Germany's eastern frontiers. On the other hand, they could not hope to defend themselves against a Russia gaining strength unless they allied themselves with Germany, which normally could also offer them more intensive economic exchange than France. The same applied to the successor states of the Habsburg monarchy. For a Germany that would make Europe's peace the exclusive goal of her foreign policy, opportunities for leadership were by no means closed forever by the Versailles Treaty. John Maynard Keynes was utterly mistaken when he called it a "Carthaginian peace."

But the treaty was harsh and bound to make general reconciliation difficult. At the same time, many of its most essential provisions were hard to enforce, particularly if the victorious powers discontinued close cooperation. A true pacification, however, was hindered not only by what was in the treaty but also by what was not in it. Though foreshadowing a most onerous treatment of Germany, the treaty did not solve the problem of reparations, which was not settled for years to come in a fashion that would have stabilized the social and economic conditions of Europe. The struggle about the economic settlement of World War I kept alive and magnified the national hostilities which the political provisions of the peace produced. Moreover, the rejection of the treaty by the Senate of the United States and the American withdrawal from Europe removed just the power that would have mediated many a conflict and might have brought on reasonably early revisions of parts of the treaty.

Nobody in Germany was in the mood to look far into the future, since the present was so oppressive. The signing of the Versailles Treaty whipped up nationalist passions which threatened the government. In reckless ways the large press organs of the rightist parties heaped scorn and ridicule on democracy. Whispering campaigns circulated the worst, as yet considered unprintable, calumnies among the people. The members of the new government were held responsible for the humiliating and disastrous state in which Germany found herself. They had made it impossible for the unvanquished German army to fight on in the fall of 1918 until the basis for a compromise peace had been achieved. The revolution had left Germany impotent to make any show of resistance to the shameful dictate of the Allies in June 1919. Assertions that the homeland had wrecked the front had already been heard at Supreme Headquarters at the time when Ludendorff had compelled the civilian government to sue for an armistice and had then assiduously been spread by the nationalist press. The "stab-in-the-back" legend received general currency through Hindenburg's public testimony in November 1919. It meant injecting poison into the nation.

✍ Popular Unrest

IN THE FALL of 1919 a steep general rise in prices began to play havoc with the livelihood of most groups of the people. To many middle-class people, who in addition were shorn of a considerable part of their income and property by the draconian income tax and capital levy of Erzberger's tax reform, the price rise seemed to hold the threat of pushing them into a proletarian existence. For the workers the price rise meant the loss of the economic gains which they had won during the revolutionary period. In some cases these gains had been excessive considering the profit chances of individual firms and the productivity of the labor force. Therefore, when labor contracts were renegotiated, not only certain iron economic laws but also the revived power of the entrepreneur were encountered.

The workers realized that the revolution had not brought them political gains of any consequence. Nationalization of industry had not occurred, nor was any step taken toward a participation of the workers in the direction of industry. Many took umbrage when the government presented a law on factory councils which, excluding any co-determination of the workers in management, confined their function to the field of human relations between managers and workers. In January 1920, a huge demonstration was held before the *Reichstag*, while the parliament was debating this law. The police, panicky and afraid that the masses would force entrance, opened fire with machine guns. It was another serious grievance of the working class that it was always exposed to the violence of the soldiers and police, who even in the opinion of objective observers were needlessly brutal in their actions. Gustav Noske, the defense minister, and Wolfgang Heine (1861–1944), the Prussian minister of interior, incurred growing criticism among their fellow Social Democrats.

The Bauer cabinet had gained a great parliamentary majority when in October 1919, the Democratic party rejoined the government. But its prestige in the country was waning. The member that in the eyes of the public dominated its policies was Matthias Erzberger, who appeared to enjoy the power he wielded. In spite of his political acumen, he was incautious and quite often tactless in his public statements. Unhappily, he was not too fastidious in his private dealings. Karl Helfferich, vice-chancellor under Bethmann-Hollweg during the war, spearheaded the political attacks against Erzberger. In a series of vitriolic and slanderous articles he held him up to contempt as an irresponsible politician whose activities had harmed the country and whose character was tainted by mixing personal financial gain with politics. The libel suit that followed aroused strong feelings in all political camps. It ended on March 12, 1920, with the court imposing a small financial penalty on Helfferich for libel while finding that the major accusations against Erzberger had been proved correct. Erzberger had to resign from the government, hoping to find justice in a court of appeal. Actually the court action was politically motivated and showed what was to become a grave cancer of the Weimar Republic. The hostility to the republic was strong in the German judiciary, and many judges were eager not only to shield the rightist opponents but also actively to hurt the representatives of the democratic state. During the Helfferich trial a former ensign attempted to assassinate Erzberger. A court attested to the young fanatic's "idealistic motives" and sent him to prison for only one and a half years.

✐ *Kapp* Putsch

ON THE SAME DAY when the court proceedings in the Erzberger *vs.* Helfferich case came to an end, Berlin was on the eve of a counterrevolutionary *coup d'état* that might have ended German democracy altogether. The conflict started in the military realm. The new defense ministry was working hard to organize a new regular army. The decision had already been made that no free corps would become a unit of the future army. The oath that the free-corps members had taken to their leader, who often enough was an officer of junior rank, seemed incompatible with army discipline, and it was clear that the free corps contained elements which the builders of the new army, the *Reichswehr*, considered unruly. Moreover, the numerical limitation of the army demanded by the peace treaty necessitated the gradual disbanding of the free corps. This reduction was opposed by the commander of one of the two army groups into which the army had been divided. General Walther von Lüttwitz (1859–1942), a dyed-in-the-wool Prussian monarchist, was an officer without political experience and judgment but with a burning desire to save the fatherland. For months his staff and in all probability also General von Seeckt, the chief of the office of troops, as the chief of the general staff was now called, had heard him talk about the necessity for the establishment of a strong government based on the army. But Seeckt failed to inform Noske, the defense minister.

On March 10, 1920, Noske ordered that the two marine brigades Ehrhardt and Löwenfeld be withdrawn from the first army group and revert to the command of the navy as the first step in preparation for their dissolution. Lüttwitz protested to President Ebert against any demobilization of existing troop units, particularly the withdrawal of the Ehrhardt brigade from his command. At the same time he raised political demands, such as the replacement of the commander of the army, General Reinhardt, but more than that, the dissolution of the National Assembly, early elections for a *Reichstag*, the popular election of the president, and the appointment of professional civil servants as ministers. Ebert firmly rejected these demands, and on the following day Noske relieved the general of his command, but Lüttwitz refused to leave his post. On March 12 it became clear that Captain Ehrhardt would march his brigade from the suburban army camp to Berlin.

In the evening Noske took counsel with the troop commanders and officers in the defense ministry. While General Reinhardt advocated a fight against the mutiny, all the other generals were doubtful about the attitude of their soldiers. The remarks of General von Seeckt, that fighting between German troops could not be tolerated, were decisive. Noske and Reinhardt failed to find any support, and the troops in Berlin were sent to their barracks. Reinhardt, who felt that his authority with the army had greatly suffered, wanted to be released from service in his post. Seeckt, who did not give the *Putsch* much of a chance of success, cleverly handed in a letter of resignation and went home, where he said he would stay till the government had made a decision with regard to his future.

In the early morning hours of March 13, 1920, the government, except for one minister, left Berlin. Since General Maercker, the military commander of Saxony, proved of dubious loyalty, Ebert and the cabinet went from Dresden to Stuttgart, from where they issued proclamations requesting the noncooperation of all citizens with the illegal government. The free trade unions and the three government parties called a general strike, which soon became effective.

The Ehrhardt brigade, many of its soldiers displaying the swastika on their steel helmets, soon after dawn marched through the Brandenburg Gate and, unopposed, occupied the government section of Berlin. The political wirepuller behind the scene now stepped out into the limelight and made himself both chancellor and Prussian prime minister. He was Wolfgang Kapp, who during the war had become known through his rabid campaign against Chancellor Bethmann-Hollweg and in 1917, together with Tirpitz, had founded the Fatherland party. Lüttwitz became chief of the army, and a retired royalist general became defense minister. Although the self-appointed government issued many public declarations, its chief announced aims were the dissolution of the National Assembly and the Prussian Constituent Assembly. A program of reform was promised for the time when order would have been restored and the way opened for elections. To all those hostile to the republican developments the mere arrival of the Kapp government raised fervent hopes for the return of the beloved political past. In East Prussia the ground swell was so strong as even to engulf the recently appointed Social Democratic high-president, August Winnig (1878–1956). The Löwenfeld brigade moved into Breslau, and although its soldiers committed some disgraceful acts against the population, the army in Silesia joined Lüttwitz and Kapp. The same happened in Pomerania and Schleswig-Holstein. In Mecklenburg the army directly ousted the land government. In Saxony and Thuringia some army units stayed neutral. Here and there, among the rank and file, opposition to the anticonstitutional policies of the officers came into the open. But in practically all cases this could only take the form of complaints. Only in the navy did events occur which were reminiscent of November 1918. The command of Kiel and Wilhelmshaven went over to Kapp. Thereupon the sailors elected commanders of their own, frequently warrant officers.

In southern and western Germany the army refused any cooperation with Kapp. Although none of the commanding officers was a republican, the political climate of these parts warned them to abstain from departing from a constitutional course. In Bavaria, under army pressure, the Social Democratic government was made to resign and replaced by a government that commanded a nonsocialist majority in the Bavarian parliament. But the Bavarians were not in the mood to support a government that seemed to aim at Prussian superiority in Germany. As it was, all troops under the second army group remained loyal to the constitutional government, thus making it possible to isolate the Kapp regime.

Kapp and Lüttwitz had been in contact with a number of politicians of the Nationalist party, and the latter applauded the action of the usurpers. So did the People's party for a moment, but within a day Stresemann recognized his political mistake and beat a hasty retreat. But even open sympathy with the Kapp enterprise failed to induce any prominent member of the Nationalist party to join the government. Kapp and Lüttwitz thus had no chance to form a cabinet. In the first place, however, they were stymied by the refusal of the officials of the ministries to accept any orders from the illegitimate rulers. The only exception was the naval section of the defense ministry, and this was at this moment of negligible help to the usurpers. The strike of the high bureaucracy, which, incidentally, carried on their day-to-day work as much as possible, was frustrating, but the general strike of the workers that everywhere was executed with remarkable solidarity was likely to throw the whole German economy into chaos. Moreover, the radical forces among the masses would inevitably gain in influence. Kapp was the first one to realize the complete failure of his adventurous undertaking. Four days after he had broken into the chancellery, he left by plane for Sweden. It took some prodding by the officers of the defense ministry to make the obtuse General von Lüttwitz disappear from Berlin. The argument that the unity of the army, which rather meant the officers' corps, ought to be quickly restored in view of the rising radicalism of the masses was persuasive. It was this conviction that prompted most officers to close ranks again. For this reason, too, the majority of the officers wanted to have Seeckt appointed the chief of the army, for by his actions on March 12–13 he had blocked the imminent possibility of open fighting between German soldiers.

The general strike demonstrated the tremendous power that the German working class could wield if it was united in action. But it was doubtful whether it was capable of a sustained effort to reconstruct the political order. The Kapp *Putsch* had shown on what weak foundations the Weimar Republic rested. The mere restoration of what had been created in Weimar was therefore insufficient. Carl Legien (1861–1920), the chairman of the general federation of free trade unions, demanded the formation of a government of Social Democrats and Independents to be supported by the socialist, and presumably also the Christian, trade unions. This government was to be charged with carrying forward the nationalization of industries, beginning with coal and potassium, and an active program of social legislation that would give the workers codetermination. In addition, the government was supposed to purge thoroughly all branches of the public administration as well as the armed forces from counterrevolutionary elements.

Since the left wing of the Independent party proved intransigent,

Hermann Müller formed a government of the Weimar coalition, i.e. the Social Democratic party, the Center, and the Democratic party. On its promise that it would fulfill the demands of the trade unions, the latter called off the general strike. But in certain regions the movement of the workers was no longer under the control of the official leadership of the trade unions. In the Ruhr district, radical, largely Communist leaders brought on armed revolution beginning on March 19. The "red army," organized by the insurgents and composed of up to 50,000 men, was the most formidable military force ever created by a revolutionary movement in Germany. In vain did the government send Carl Severing (1875–1952), a courageous and judicious Social Democratic parliamentarian, who promised a full amnesty if the "red army" dissolved voluntarily. The latter kept for a time the whole Ruhr district occupied.

On April 2, 1920, *Reichswehr* troops started the reconquest of the Ruhr. Weeks of bitter and cruel fighting ensued. Among the governmental forces some notorious units of the Ehrhardt brigade were used unblushingly by the generals. Since by military necessity the German troops had trespassed into the demilitarized zone on the eastern bank of the Rhine, the French, on April 6, marched into Frankfurt, Darmstadt, and their surroundings, thereby creating new resentment in Germany. The British protested the unilateral action of the French, who evacuated the cities as early as the middle of May, though only after the German forces had left the zone around Düsseldorf. In still another region, along the state lines of Saxony and Thuringia, a wild Communist revolt erupted and was quelled by the *Reichswehr*. Both sides became guilty of atrocious brutalities. The army now took its revenge for the general strike of the workers, and at the end of a chain of events, motivated by the army and navy officers' hostility to the republic, the army was able to pose as the restorer of quiet and order.

The Kapp *Putsch* brought to an end the cooperation between the army and the Social Democratic party that had been inaugurated by Ebert and Groener and built up by Noske and Reinhardt. It is true that this cooperation was largely based on tactical considerations. The generals who collaborated with Defense Minister Noske knew that for the time being the army could find the necessary political shield only in the dominant political party. Noske, on his part, realized that the republic had to depend on the old officers for organizing the disciplined military forces it needed and for this reason disregarded much in the ideas and manners of these men that must have been extremely distasteful to him. But undoubtedly both Noske and Reinhardt earnestly tried to work toward a firm relationship between the army and the civilian government. The Kapp *Putsch* revealed that this policy was illusory. Reinhardt was shown to be an isolated figure within the officers' corps.

The Communist and radical workers who called Noske a traitor to his class and dubbed the soldiers "Noske bullies" had not been his only critics. The Social Democratic rank and file as well as the party press had been carping, too. They accused the army of cultivating an antidemocratic class spirit and of being extremely wanton in fighting internal disorders. Exception was taken to Noske's serving as a front man for the military camp. The *Putsch* resulted in stormy demands for Noske's removal. And although Ebert attempted to keep him, Noske had become too great a liability for the party. It was unimaginable how he could have worked with an army in which Seeckt represented the moderate wing of the leaders. Prime Minister Hermann Müller was not able to prevail on the Social Democratic leader Otto Wels to become Noske's successor as defense minister. Wels, an intrepid man, as he proved in his entire career, did not feel up to this task. Thus the Social Democratic party gave up the position, which went to a Democrat, Dr. Otto Gessler (1875–1955), who had been a commendable mayor of Nürnberg during the war. But as the son of a noncommissioned officer of the Bavarian army and as a most skeptical republican he was not ideally fitted to inculcate democratic manners upon old-style generals or even to maintain the control of the civilian government over the military establishment.

ᐁ *Seeckt and the* Reichswehr

IN THESE CIRCUMSTANCES it was of even greater significance that General Reinhardt retired as chief of the army. He was aware of the ill feeling of the officers that his demand for an open fight against the Ehrhardt mutineers had caused. Hans von Seeckt was put in his place. Seeckt, who came from a Pomeranian *Junker* and officer family, had distinguished himself during the war as chief of staff of German and Austro-German armies and finally of the Turkish army. He was an officer with a broad education that went far beyond military matters. The lean and sinewy aristocrat, with a monocle in his right eye that made his face look motionless, liked to pose as a sphinx-like character. He was shrewd and tenacious in all his plans and actions, but his rigid thinking was not unaffected by the prejudices of his social class and profession. While he remained a monarchist at heart, he was too astute to believe that the restoration of the monarchy would be possible in the foreseeable future.

But Seeckt was convinced that the army, the foundation on which the Prussian monarchy had rested, had to be preserved. He considered it the guarantor of Germany's eventual revival as a great power and at the same time the organ on which a stable governmental authority could be built. The question of what form such a government ought to take occupied much of Seeckt's thought. Yet when in 1923 he himself might have been able to assume the leadership in a reorganization of the political order, he cautiously abstained from action. He had only contempt for democracy, particularly for parliamentary government. He did not hesitate to let the army develop initiatives in foreign affairs. Seeckt believed in close cooperation with Russia because he saw in it the chance for evading the disarmament clauses of the Versailles Treaty by constructing armament industries in the Soviet Union. But even more important to him was the earliest possible removal of Poland from the map of Europe and the restoration of the German-Russian frontiers of 1815. The German-Russian *rapprochement* was supposed to raise Germany's weight in the balance of power and was likely to make her a desirable ally of England when the latter would fight France, as Seeckt expected in the not too distant future. The world was strangely reflected in his military mind.

Seeckt succeeded in subordinating to himself practically all the offices of the defense ministry. Even the army group commanders, who so far had stood under the defense minister, were placed directly under the "chief of the army command." The Prussian kings, in order to keep control of the army, had always taken care not to centralize all command functions in the hands of a single general, and the fact that since 1917 Hindenburg actually, though not in principle, became the single dominant military figure ushered in the eclipse of the Hohenzollern. For the civilian authorities of the Weimar Republic it was naturally infinitely more difficult to exert influence on the army through this type of organization. Not only the Social Democratic party but also the Democratic and Center parties had no program on how to fit the army into a democratic system, whereas rightist parties wanted to give maximum power to the generals. Although under the constitution the Supreme Command was in the hands of the president and the normal command function with the minister of defense, the rule was adopted that the latter exercised his command authority on the advice of and through the chief of the army. This theory, which Defense Minister Gessler accepted, gave Seeckt practical independence. The only thing that Seeckt wanted the defense minister to do was to act as political cover chiefly in parliament, which the general never entered, while he kept the way to the president and the cabinet open to himself.

The new direction of Seeckt's policy appeared immediately in the purge action taken after the Kapp *Putsch.* Altogether only 172 officers were dismissed, among them twelve generals, but at the same time all the noncommissioned officers and privates who had expressed dissatisfaction with their officers for siding with Kapp were dropped from the service because they had broken discipline. The reduction of numbers to the 100,000-men level that had been imposed by the Versailles Treaty and had to be achieved by January 1, 1921, served as an opportunity for removing from the army all soldiers with republican inclinations. Only soldiers who blindly obeyed superior orders and abstained from politics of their own, even if it concerned matters which the soldiers were sworn to defend, were tolerated in Seeckt's army. Yet it became the rule in the selection of new recruits to employ methods which were politically charged. The local commanders responsible for choosing these recruits were instructed to examine not only the general personal character of the applicants but also their political outlook specifically. And it was quite customary to gather this information from officers of the many patriotic federations and paramilitary organizations, all of them strongly right wing, which, as we shall see, mushroomed all over Germany. The Versailles Treaty, which prohibited the universal draft, was unhesitatingly used for creating an army that, in contrast to the imperial army, did not include any Socialists in its rank and file.

The design to make the army a reliable instrument of its highest commanders led to the exclusion of all politically activist officers. None of the free-corps leaders and few of the junior officers of these units found a place in the new *Reichswehr*. Because of their ardent zeal for the political commitment of the army, they were considered unruly elements. Actually many of them wished for civil war as the preparatory stage for a war of liberation and revenge. Seeckt insisted on a "nonpolitical" army, such as in his opinion the imperial army had been. But in reality the old army had not been unpolitical. It was united by a single faith from which no dissent was allowed. Seeckt in fact acted as a substitute for the king-emperor, and in order to make this more palatable he removed the *Reichswehr* from all contacts with the civilian agencies and the political life of the republic. The army was declared to represent the eternal German state or Reich, whereas the Weimar Republic was only a passing historical form of the German state. This nebulous mystique served to vindicate the aloofness of the army from the existing state and to strengthen its inner coherence under its own chief.

Seeckt succeeded in gaining the respect of the officers in a relatively short time. When at the height of the political crisis of 1923 President Ebert asked him where the *Reichswehr* stood, he gave the characteristic answer: "The *Reichswehr* stands behind me." But this statement was not in line with the vaunted Prussian tradition and showed the weakness of the system that Seeckt implanted. An army that was only loosely connected with the existing state could not hope to mobilize all the energies of the nation for defense, as Seeckt undoubtedly intended. Moreover, while an army that would allow its officers independent political actions and demonstrations would quickly deteriorate into a feuding mob, an army does need officers who possess a general political orientation. The vacuum in which Seeckt tried to keep the officers left them insecure and susceptible to irresponsible political ideas. However, it is not true that the officers had no political beliefs. Already the social composition of the officers' corps was likely to produce predominantly rightist political opinions.

As in the imperial days, the officers were chosen almost exclusively from officers' families and the academically educated bourgeoisie. In the smaller *Reichswehr* practically every second officer was the son of an officer, as compared to every fourth in the imperial army. One fifth of the officers' corps was of noble extraction in 1920 and almost one fourth in 1932. As in the old army, the noblemen were unevenly distributed among the branches of the service and the garrisons. Whereas in the cavalry regiment, which was supposed to cultivate the tradition of the guard, more than 60 per cent of the officers were noblemen and in the parallel infantry regiment almost 50 per cent, few noblemen served in the artillery and in the engineer corps. Half of the generals of the *Reichswehr* were noblemen. To some extent this was the result of the fact that a disproportionally large number of general staff and guard officers were taken into the *Reichswehr*. But no antagonism existed between the noble and bourgeois officers. They were united by the same social manners and political opinions. All of them were critical of the republic, which had been born out of revolution and defeat. The government by political parties was deplored as a continuous cause of national discord and disorder. The Social Democratic party in particular, was despised as the foremost representative of this system and because of its pacifism and internationalism. In the early years of the Weimar Republic the German Nationalist party was determining the political outlook of the average officer. Toward the end of the 1920's the young officers were increasingly attracted by National Socialism.

Moreover, the position of the *Reichswehr* as being above the political parties was constantly compromised by its active collaboration with the rightist patriotic federations. The army favored organizations which cultivated a martial spirit and was not concerned over the fact that this spirit was directed as much against democracy as against foreign enemies. Such paramilitary associations had sprouted all over Germany after 1919. The strongest organization of this type in the first decade of the republic was the *Stahlhelm* (Steel Helmet), founded as early as December 1918 by Franz Seldte (1882–1947) in Magdeburg as an organization of nationally minded war veterans. It grew rapidly during the next years. Its leaders boasted that the *Stahlhelm* at its peak reached a membership of one million in 1927–28, although critical observers consider this figure an exaggeration. The *Stahlhelm* made the preservation of the old soldierly virtues and the comradeship of the trenches its special aims but also espoused trenchant political goals, such as the liberation from "the chains of Versailles" and the replacement of the republic by a stable authoritarian regime. Although the *Stahlhelm* was officially free from close ties with political parties and was originally on friendly terms with the German People's party, it took its political cues mostly, and finally exclusively, from the German Nationalist party. Proclamations, demonstrations, and parades were the chief means of publicizing the program of the *Stahl-helm*. At the same time out of the public eye many activities were carried on to keep its members fit for military service.

There were other paramilitary organizations even more radical than the *Stahlhelm*. Most of them, such as the organizations *Oberland* and *Werwolf*, were the direct descendants of the free corps and continued the tradition of strict loyalty to a single leader. The latter was also true of the storm troopers (SA) of Hitler's National Socialist party (NSDAP), who were strictly subordinate to the party and its sovereign leader. In the early 1920's the SA was confined to Munich and some Bavarian cities. Even by 1930, when its astonishing expansion began, it had not yet reached the 100,000 membership mark.

It was to these militant organizations that the *Reichswehr* looked for assistance in order to overcome the limitations of the Versailles Treaty. When in the spring of 1921 Wojciech Korfanty (1873–1938), the former leader of the Polish members of the German parliament, with the help of armed Polish bands attempted to seize the whole plebiscite area and the Allied occupation forces made no effort to put down this Polish coup, irregular German troops entered the zone. Heavy fighting ensued until the Allies separated the warring parties. The German troops received their weapons and supplies from the *Reichswehr*. The *Reichswehr* also organized a permanent frontier guard along the German-Polish frontier. Groups of irregular soldiers were quartered on the large estates. An officer was attached to each frontier county and charged not only with supervising the active members of the frontier guard but also with keeping the rolls of those men who were to join it in an emergency. These latter were drawn almost exclusively from the patriotic federations.

The frontier guardsmen breathed the spirit of radical nationalism. Since the units were widely scattered and had no legal basis, it was difficult to maintain proper discipline, most of all to keep them from flaunting their contempt of the republic. The secrecy which veiled all these operations emboldened the men to take the law into their own hands. Individuals suspected of betraying secrets of the organizations were declared traitors and killed in cold blood. A wave of such murders occurred from the spring of 1923 on. The *Reichswehr* saw in the frontier guard the reservoir from which it could draw trained reserves in an emergency. At the time of the French invasion of the Ruhr it augmented its cadres by forming special units of temporary volunteers. When the government broke off the passive resistance in the Ruhr in September 1923, these "black *Reichswehr*" troops in the province of Brandenburg staged a revolt that was aimed not only at the government but also at the army command. The attempt to take the fortress of Küstrin was nipped in the bud by the *Reichswehr* commander. But some strong points around Spandau had to be overpowered by regular forces.

Seeckt was greatly dismayed, and orders were issued that the *Reichswehr* troops should avoid getting involved in the political activities of the patriotic federations. But these orders were of no consequence as long as the *Reichswehr* was not prepared to liquidate the whole frontier guard. Its military value was questioned by a good many prominent officers, although they usually defended its existence as necessary for allaying the apprehension felt about its security by the population of the eastern borderlands. But since the *Reichswehr* command never discovered any other source for ready reserves, the frontier guard was kept and later on further strengthened. The *Reichswehr* under Seeckt wanted to be in a position to double its numerical strength in the case of an emergency. Subsequently its sights were even set on tripling its strength.

But with this policy the *Reichswehr* remained tied to the rightist organizations. The county officer, as a rule a pensioned officer of the imperial army, was at the same time an eminent local member of the patriotic organizations, and the same applied to the big landowners who lent their estates for the quartering of frontier guard units. When in 1924 the parties of the Weimar coalition founded their own military federation, the "*Reichsbanner* Black, Red, and Gold," which in a short time enlisted a few million people, it was thought that the frontier guard might use members of this republican organization as well. Yet this hardly ever happened. In the circles which controlled the frontier guard, Social Democrats, who formed the main body of the *Reichsbanner*, were decried as untrustworthy in matters of defense. The continued connection between the *Reichswehr* and the patriotic organizations produced very strained relations between the Social Democratic party and the *Reichswehr*. But if the party was unable to impose some reforms on the army after the defeat of the Kapp *Putsch*, it was beyond its power to achieve any important changes in later years.

It may be mentioned in passing that the navy was even more unscrupulous in its policies. Whole units of the Ehrhardt brigade were incorporated into the navy. It was particularly detrimental that the naval officers' school was filled with Ehrhardt men. Lieutenant Commander von Löwenfeld, whose brigade had occupied Breslau, was kept on the active list and had a most successful naval career. The German naval officers always tried through radical nationalism to make people forget the fact that the revolution of 1918 had begun with mutinies of the German navy.

✐ *Elections, June 1920*

JUST AS THE CABINET of Hermann Müller had proved incapable of carrying through the promised purge of the armed forces, it was unable to achieve the other aims it had promised the trade unions to attack. Neither nationalization of industries nor co-determination of the workers were likely to be passed by the National Assembly, whose dissolution could no longer be delayed. On June 6, 1920, national elections were held for the first *Reichstag* of the Weimar Republic. They revealed the great change of political sentiment that had taken place among the people. The Weimar party coalition, which had commanded a two-thirds majority in the National Assembly, did not even win a simple majority. The losses of the Center and the Bavarian People's parties were very small, but the Social Democratic party received only 21.7 per cent instead of the former 37.9 per cent of the popular vote, while the Independents raised their percentage from 7.6 to 17.8. The Communists voted for the first time and won 2 per cent of the popular vote. The German Democratic party went down from 18.5 to 8.2 per cent. Its losses showed up as gains of the German People's party, which jumped from 4.4 to 13.9 per cent. It almost reached the strength of the German Nationalist party, which, obviously owing to the Kapp *Putsch,* grew from 10.3 to only 15 per cent.

The elections of June 1920 were an event of the first magnitude in the history of the Weimar Republic. The Weimar coalition, though in 1928 it came rather close to it, never won the majority again, and the government from then on always needed the support of forces which were critical of, or even hostile to, the Weimar Constitution. Another lasting effect was the permanent split of the political working class movement into a moderate and a radical camp. Practically every second member of the old Social Democratic party protested by his ballot against the policies of the Majority Social Democrats after January 1919 and not only wished to replace their leaders such as Ebert, Scheidemann, and Noske but also expressed disbelief in a democracy that had failed to give the workers equality in the factory and the state. This was the predominant feeling among those who voted for the Independent party, although among the elected parliamentarians the democratically minded Socialists still constituted a very considerable group.

This disagreement within the Independent party led to full division in October 1920 at the party convention of Halle. The Russian Communist party had sent some of its luminaries to Germany in order to win the party for the Third International. Actually the majority under the leadership of Ernst Däumig (1866–1922), one of the former "revolutionary shop-stewards," in Berlin, decided to join the Third International and merged with the small Communist party, the old Spartacus League. The right wing had its chief spokesmen in Rudolf Hilferding and Wilhelm Dittmann. Like the leaders of the Social Democrats these Independents did not believe that a second revolution could be brought about in the foreseeable future. On the contrary, they were convinced that the growing strength of the counterrevolutionary forces allowed only defensive action. It was logical that the noncommunist leaders of the Independent party tried to establish an understanding with the Social Democrats on common tactics. These contacts led to the successful attempt at reunification, which was consummated at the common party convention in Nürnberg in 1922. Although the union was not beset by further friction, the Independents did not bring very many voters back to the United Social Democratic party.

After the elections of June 1920 the Social Democrats, afraid of losing further strength unless they silenced their critics on the left, made their continuation in government conditional on the participation of the Independents. The latter declined the offer, which was most unrealistic, since neither the Democrats nor the Center would have entered such a cabinet. The Social Democrats preferred to be rid of governmental responsibility altogether and actually never regained the leadership of the national government except in the years of 1928–30, although they were represented in it for eighteen months in 1921–22 and for three months in 1923. Thus, the influence of the Social Democratic party on the national policies of the Weimar Republic remained limited and spotty.

⌒ *Government of Prussia*

YET IN THE LANDS AND CITIES the Social Democratic party held on to power wherever it could. Most important was its position in Prussia. Here Otto Braun (1872–1955), since November 1918 minister of agriculture, had become prime minister after the Kapp *Putsch* and, except for a few months in 1921 and 1925, served in this position until 1932. An agricultural worker in East Prussia, he had risen in the party before World War I to membership in the governing committee. He was no social revolutionary but a determined democratic reformer. Though headstrong, Braun was shrewd and judicious and radiated an authority that enabled him to hold together heterogeneous political forces and make the most of a usually slim parliamentary majority. It was originally a government of the Weimar coalition. When it lost the elections in 1921, the People's party for the first time joined the Weimar parties in a cabinet of what was called "the great coalition," which lasted till 1924. But also in the following years Otto Braun managed to maintain himself in power. It was astonishing that the cooperation between the Center and Social Democratic parties in Prussia did not suffer even in the years when the Center party on the national level was allied with the parties of the right. Braun devoted only a limited amount of his energies to promoting his ideas and aims on the national level. In general he tended to overrate the chances for solving political problems through administrative operations.

Although the Prussian government had lost much of its former political power in 1918–19, it was still the biggest administrative system in Germany and affected the daily lives of the majority of the people. Unquestionably, the Weimar Republic would have perished much earlier if the Prussian government had not been in the hands of democratic statesmen. They had to rule with the aid of civil servants who had been selected by the monarchy, whose demise they deplored. Many of them fought the new regime not only with their ballots but also by trying to sabotage the execution of democratic measures. Few of these officials resigned, and since their tenure rights were guaranteed by the constitution, only a few in high and politically sensitive positions could be removed. The infusion of democratic blood could be achieved only through a long, uphill struggle. And it was never fully successful because the Social Democrats had too few academically trained followers, while the Democrats failed to attract younger people. Only the Center party was able to present a good many candidates and finally abolish the discrimination against Catholics in state service that the old Prussia had practiced.

The government of Otto Braun was most effective where it could make a totally new start. Carl Severing, as minister of the interior, held the key position in the cabinet for many years. This Westphalian Social Democrat was a prudent and imaginative leader of a friendly, if firm, disposition. The creation of a new police force that replaced the authoritarian royal police was his greatest achievement. It was a police that was a reliable and efficient instrument in the hands of a democratic government, democratic also in the sense of considering itself not the lord but the friend of the public. This result was difficult to achieve in circumstances in which the police force was called upon to fight radical revolts on the right and left in which large segments of the population participated. The police force was kept large, since it had to be prepared for civil war. Moreover, in the zones of Germany demilitarized under the terms of the Versailles Treaty the police was the only armed force. Although the majority of the police force of 180,000 men performed only the usual duties of municipal policemen or criminal detectives, 80,000 men were kept in barracks, motorized and armed with rifles and machine guns. As early as the spring of 1921, when a new Communist uprising occurred in the province of Saxony, the Prussian police needed little help from the *Reichswehr* to put down the disturbances and thereafter was never again compelled to require assistance from the army. One of the reasons for the success of the Prussian government in maintaining public order was its forceful suppression of illegal organizations. It was the *Reichswehr* with its unfortunate interest in the paramilitary organizations of the rightist parties which hindered the Prussian government from extirpating the existing centers of civil disobedience altogether.

While the Prussian government was the most active and effective land government in the defense of the new republican institutions, it failed to remodel the Prussian governmental structure along democratic lines. This would have required a strengthening of the weak self-government on the local and provincial level. But the understandable fear that this would give the antirepublican forces new positions of strength, particularly in the eastern provinces, kept the Prussian government of the Weimar coalition from executing any important reform of self-government. The representation of the provincial agencies of self-government in the *Reichsrat* gave an idea of how much friction could be expected. Thus the slightly liberalized bureaucratic-centralistic organization of the Prussian government was essentially preserved in the Weimar Republic.

✑ *Revulsion from Democracy*

THE FEDERAL ELECTIONS of 1920, while shattering the strength of the Social Democratic party, also revealed that the German middle classes were turning away from democracy. After the revolution democracy had appeared to be the best system for defending the social order against the dire threat of bolshevism, and cooperation with the Social Democrats had become acceptable. In addition, democracy seemed to offer the best chance for getting a fair peace. But now it was said that all these expectations had failed. The "dictate of Versailles" had proved Wilsonism a mere pipe dream. Bolshevism had been defeated not by the Social Democrats but by the free corps or, in other terms, the efforts of German middle-class youth in alliance with the old military leaders. These forces could be trusted to act as the strongest shield against similar dangers in the future. The People's party conducted a very noisy and intensive election campaign with the large funds given by Ruhr industrialists. Their foremost slogan, which apparently found a wide response, contained the assurance that the party would liberate the people from "red chains."

To most voters of the People's party this meant not only hostility to communism but also the wish to exclude the Social Democrats from the government. The chief builder of the party, Gustav Stresemann, recognized that it would be a great national loss to drive the Social Democrats into the political wilderness again after they had proved their sense of responsibility during the war and in the revolution. However, Stresemann had great difficulty in making his party follow him in this course. The hard core of resistance came from the Ruhr industrialists, such as Hugo Stinnes (1870–1924), to whom Stresemann had to give parliamentary seats as a reward for their contributions to the party chest. Stresemann had turned to them for financial support only reluctantly. He himself had made his career in the small consumer goods industries and was critical of the politics of the heavy industries. But he had not been able to discover better sources for funds. He succeeded, however, as we have seen, in having his party join the Prussian cabinet of Otto Braun. In 1923 he himself was to become the chancellor of a national government that included the Social Democrats. Yet the election of 1924 showed that this policy was not overly popular with the electorate. The willingness of the People's party to form governmental coalitions with the parties of the left as well as of the right worked to the advantage of the German Nationalist party.

The German Nationalist party emerged from the elections of 1920 not only stronger but also more radical than in 1919. Men like Count Posadowski-Wehner and Clemens von Delbrück, both distinguished civil servants under the monarchy, yet moderate and constructive in their opposition to the new order, were not found in the new parliamentary delegation. Instead, reckless demagoguery prevailed that held the republic responsible for all national misfortunes and incited hatred against its institutions and leaders. At the same time, anti-Semitism was in the ascendancy.

Even within the Center party a shift toward the right was beginning after the elections, although it was still a slow and cautious move. The new chancellor, Konstantin Fehrenbach (1852–1926), was a moderate conservative, but he kept Joseph Wirth (b. 1879), who followed the Erzberger line, as minister of finance. Another Center minister was Heinrich Brauns (1868–1939), a priest and the leading expert of the party on social questions. For the next eight years, under six different chancellors, he headed the ministry of labor and became the architect of the social legislation of the Weimar Republic. A liberal in social politics, he was a conservative in matters of general policies.

In the Fehrenbach government members of the Center party were joined by representatives of the German People's and the Democratic parties. The foreign portfolio was given to Walter Simons (1861–1937), the legal counselor of the foreign office. No parliamentarian was willing to accept the job that in the aftermath of Versailles did not promise any laurels. But it was a serious weakness that until the fall of 1923 this position was not occupied by a man of great imagination who might have commanded attention both at home and abroad. Although Walther Rathenau was a man of large vision and great diplomatic ability, his tenure from February to June 1922 was too short to fill the void. It is understandable that German foreign policy aimed at the revision of the Versailles Treaty, but the problem was whether this should mean merely the restoration of the frontiers of 1914 or the creation of a European order that would overcome the exaggerated sense of national sovereignty that had been a major cause of World War I and, in spite of the League of Nations, had been boosted by the peace settlement of 1919. The old diplomats who gave the official German foreign policy their stamp thought in terms of a merely restorative policy. In addition, they believed that foreign policy should be conducted without reference to domestic needs. To them it did not matter that the nationalist sentiment of the German public was inflamed to a point endangering the republican order.

✎ Reparations and Inflation

THE CHIEF PROBLEM that had remained unsolved in Paris and Versailles was that of reparations. It was to be settled by the Allied Reparations Commission in Paris. Although the fact that the United States had retired from the commission and could no longer urge moderation was a handicap, the experts of the commission were more realistic than the governmental leaders, who did not muster the courage to disappoint the high expectations of their electorates. As it was, the payment of big sums extending over decades could have been made by Germany only in the form of the delivery of goods. This would have required a vast expansion of German industries and exports. But no country was willing to accept imports of a size that would have shifted the production of its own industries. America, which received most of the German reparations in the form of the repayment of loans made to the Allies, sterilized the gold she received and followed protectionist trade practices. Britain and France after 1925 adopted mostly deflationary financial policies that did not create the markets for large additional imports. From 1925 to 1929 France even managed to have an export surplus of one billion marks in the trade with her chief debtor Germany.

Whether Germany was doing all she might have done to introduce more reason into the international debate of reparations may be doubted. Her angry complaints that the German war guilt was being made the basis of reparations and her continuous emphasis on German territorial losses as well as on the inflation of the German currency kept the suspicion alive that Germany wanted to evade all responsibilities. Actually, the reparations were not the cause of inflation, as German politicians asserted and the public readily believed. We have already seen that the German methods of war finance produced a towering governmental debt and an excessive volume of currency held by the public.[7] The reduced produc-

[7] See p. 552.

tion capacity and the depleted stocks of raw materials and goods caused a much steeper price inflation in 1919 than had developed during the war. Government expenditures soared in the period of demobilization, including deliveries under the armistice, unemployment relief, railroad deficits, and the cost of foodstuffs bought for the population. It would not have been possible to stabilize prices and incomes at the level which they had reached during the war even if the budget could have been balanced immediately.

In the second half of 1919 the decline of the mark accelerated. In February 1920 the dollar was traded in Berlin at the rate of 100 marks, in contrast to 4.20 in 1914. After a reaction the rate fluctuated for over a year between 40 and 70. During the first six months of 1921 it was rather stable at about 64 marks. The price level reached at the beginning of 1920 remained little changed until the summer of 1921, and wages slowly advanced to the same level. At this stage the inflationary effects of the currency expansion during the war and immediate postwar period had spent themselves, and a stabilization of the currency would have been possible. But the government proved incapable of balancing the budget and stopping the easy-credit policies of the *Reichsbank.*

The German high bureaucracy showed itself incompetent to diagnose correctly the causes of the inflation. The leading official financial experts saw the cause in the falling rate of exchange, for which they made reparations largely responsible. Therefore they argued that no stabilization could be expected until a final and tolerable settlement had been achieved. This thesis, readily accepted by the German bankers as well, entirely overlooked the fact that the currency inflation had started long before there had been talk about German reparations and that not until the summer of 1921 did Germany make any sizable reparations payments. In the budget year of April 1920 through March 1921 less than one third of the budget deficit could be called expenses under the peace treaty. Only in 1921-22 did three quarters of the deficit come under this category, while in 1922-23 the figure fell to less than one half.

Rudolf Havenstein (1857-1923), the president of the *Reichsbank,* considered it his duty to keep the German economy supplied with the money needed to make payments at the actual price level. Therefore the *Reichsbank* accepted the monthly treasury notes that the government issued to cover the budget deficit. He also granted commercial credit in a most liberal fashion. Thus currency circulation steadily increased. The coverage of the deficits through the note-printing press made the abolition of the deficits in the public budgets even more difficult, since the collection of taxes was lagging behind the depreciation of the currency. This expansion of credits and money circulation was the cause of the German inflation. The depreciation of the international value of the mark merely expressed the understandable expectation of a further decline of its purchasing power, a speculation in which, incidentally, German capitalists freely participated. Thus the decline of the international value of the mark was at times ahead of its purchasing power.

The first large cash payments for reparations were made in the summer of 1921 as the result of political developments which we shall discuss a little later. Since they were financed by a further issuance of money, they seemed to confirm the German view about the impact of reparations on the inflation. In the wake of the Allied decision in October to divide Upper Silesia between Germany and Poland a wave of economic pessimism spread over Germany, and an untrammeled flight of capital from the country began. German purchases of foreign exchange reached high dimensions, while foreigners dumped large holdings of marks on the market. By the end of the year the dollar rate stood at 180, one third of what it had been in May 1921. Until July 1922 several smaller cash payments were made on the reparations account. Thereafter they were stopped. The trade balance was in equilibrium and the only pressure on the international value of the mark was caused by the flight of capital from Germany and by foreign speculation. But the panic of the public, the continued deficit spending of the government, and the simultaneous creation of additional money through note printing drove the mark down further and further.

An international committee of distinguished economists, among them John Maynard Keynes and the Swede Gustav Cassel (1866–1945), was invited by the German government in the fall of 1922 to study the German currency situation. They urged the stabilization of the mark, which they judged to be in the power of the German government. They pointed out that Germany's gold reserve was still not much smaller than in 1914, and in view of the depreciation of the mark constituted twice the value of the total currency circulation. While it was customary to cover only one third of the note circulation with gold, the existing gold reserve was adequate to stabilize the German currency, provided the budget was balanced and the money circulation held within strict limits. But the German authorities stubbornly insisted that the mark could be stabilized only with a foreign loan and only after a moratorium on reparations had been declared.

The French invasion of the Ruhr in January 1923 was met by a call for passive resistance, for which the German government assumed the cost of the mounting subsidies and compensation for the population. The government, still convinced that the depreciation of the mark was the work of the international money market, squandered half of the German gold reserve by large purchases of marks in the belief that these would stop the headlong decline of the exchange rate. But at a time when the *Reichsbank* could not find enough additional printing presses to swell the flood of paper money, it was quixotic to expect that these interventions could result in anything but the mere loss of gold. Whereas between 1920 and 1922 the reduction of the value of the mark to one tenth took two and a half years, thereafter it took only 108 days, and in October 1923, 8 to 11 days. On November 15, 1923, the mark was quoted at a trillionth of its value of 1914. At least from the fall of 1922 on, the mark had ceased to be used as an indicator of prices, which instead merely followed the dollar rate. Ultimately salaries and wages were paid daily, and everybody was in a hurry to get rid of them as quickly as possible. The stores, however, hesitated to sell all their goods for worthless paper money.

Finally, as we shall see, the stabilization of the German currency was accomplished in November 1923 under conditions worse than those of the preceding years and was achieved substantially without foreign help. In retrospect the obstinacy with which the German financial leaders clung to their economic theories seems to have bordered on insanity. But they were actually cool-headed people earnestly trying to give the best of their reasoning. Their views were somewhat hedged in by nationalist pride and ambition. To find the major cause of the German inflation in the reparations demand of Germany's wartime enemies removed the responsibility for this great misfortune from the country. Moreover, if the causal relationship between reparations and inflation was generally recognized, the future burden of reparations would be greatly eased. For this reason the temporary sufferings of the people could be justified.

While the government and its high officials were complacent about the distress of the great mass of the people and the lasting impact that the inflation was bound to have on German society as a whole, there were some social groups that far from suffering from the inflation greatly profited from it. All debtors gained, since all bonds, mortgages, etc., went up the chimney. The chief gain accrued to the landowners and industrial companies who got rid of all their debts. But much greater profits were made by those who received credits or loans from the *Reichsbank* which they were allowed to repay in depreciated marks. For all practical purposes these were lavish free gifts made by the government out of the pockets of the disowned mass of the people. A number of commercial fortunes were amassed this way, but far more important was the tremendous growth of the big industrial enterprises. They were enabled to absorb many smaller firms in their line of production or even to acquire companies in other branches of industry. Hugo Stinnes was the most reckless speculator and acquired a huge industrial empire of the most variegated character around his inherited coal and iron interests. The result of the greatly expanded control of the heavy industries, including the electrical and chemical industries, meant a further concentration of the German economy.

While these select groups made big gains through the inflation or at least did not lose by it, the great mass of the people suffered severe hardships. Since wages and even most salaries did not keep pace with the money devaluation, most workers' families were unable to afford the purchase of adequate food and clothing. Mortality and sickness increased at an alarming rate, particularly among the children of the poor. Small wonder that in these years the Communist party was able to build up a substantial following in spite of the miserable leadership of the party. By 1921 all forces that had endeavored to build a party responsive to German conditions had been crushed, and the party was firmly ruled by mediocre people who were mere pawns of Moscow.

The impoverishment of the greatest part of the middle classes was of even more far-reaching historical consequences. The inflation wiped out practically all their savings. Since the stock exchange was greatly distrusted in Germany, few industrial shares, which maintained their value, were owned by middle-class people. Apart from cash deposits in banks most of their property was held in insurance policies and government bonds, particularly war bonds, which were now hardly worth the paper on which they were printed. The people who had lived on the income of such properties found themselves in dire straits. Many of them became indigent overnight, and especially for the older ones it was too late to take up an occupation. But even those members of the middle classes who were employed were deprived of their smaller or larger private property that had enabled them to plan for their life or that of their families beyond the next day. Economically speaking as mere wage earners they had become proletarians. This, however, was fully true only in the case of the clerical employees, for the many state and public officials of all ranks were at least guaranteed permanent life appointments and this applied also to many other positions. Yet the middle classes were not at all ready, as Karl Marx had predicted, to develop a proletarian consciousness. Quite the contrary, they were determined in the midst of impoverishment to maintain their superior social status, even where, as in the case of the white-collar workers, their status was more symbolic than real.

By most German middle-class people the inflation was considered the result of the hateful policies of the Allies, aggravated and exploited by the speculators of the money markets. Nationalist sentiment was thus further inflamed, but in addition capitalism became suspect and its replacement by some form of socialism was widely demanded. But this socialism, often called German socialism, was the very opposite of Marxism. It did not aim at the abolition of classes but rather at their preservation, without class struggle and the predomination of a single class. A strong authoritarian government seemed ideal to create social peace and provide for the various classes in accordance with their contribution to the common weal. All these obtuse sentiments did not as yet produce a revolutionary attitude. In 1922 the German Racialists (*Deutsch-Völkische*) party broke away from the German Nationalist party and established contacts with the National Socialist party in South Germany. But these two parties that together with a bellicose nationalism brandished ideas of radical social change attracted only a limited number of followers. The great mass of the middle-class people still believed that the restoration of the pre-revolutionary order would satisfy their aims and therefore veered toward the German Nationalist party. Thus the middle-class people, though profoundly harassed by the inflation, gave their confidence to just those forces behind the German Nationalist and German People's parties that, although they had not started the inflation, had profited from it and had therefore been more easily persuaded that an early stabilization was impossible.

The inflation of the German currency was a nightmarish experience to most Germans, and the panic caused by it was likely to recur whenever the economy entered critical days. While it contributed to driving a substantial section of the working class into the Communist camp, it deprived the German middle classes of the material foundation that had given them in the past a sense of relative security. They felt disinherited by the republic, which in their opinion had brought disaster to Germany through the "stab-in-the-back" of the German army, the supine acceptance of disarmament under the terms of the armistice, and the idle trust in Wilson's fraudulent promises. The hostility against the republican institutions, or even more against the forces which were actively supporting the republic, became ever more firmly ingrained.

It is against the background of these fundamental social changes that the political history of the years of 1920–23 must be seen. It was understandable that the German governments concentrated their efforts on foreign affairs, but that they did so while neglecting the deteriorating internal scene proved a grave loss to the infant republic. The Fehrenbach cabinet succeeded in persuading the Allies to forgo the extradition of German officers accused of violations of the Hague Convention on the rules of warfare. The Allies accepted the German proposal to try these cases before German courts and named a group of officers as defendants. Eventually they dropped the matter altogether, after the Leipzig court had blatantly passed light sentences. Moreover, the convicted men soon escaped from prison. However, the bad faith shown by the Germans in this affair was not forgotten and strengthened the determination of the Allies of World War II to deal with German war criminals through international courts.

✍ *London Ultimatum*

THE PROBLEM OF REPARATIONS was discussed by innumerable inter-Allied and international meetings. The Fehrenbach government was unable to convince the Allies that Germany's capacity to pay was severely limited. Probably no German government could have achieved this end at this moment. But more might have been done to disperse the suspicion of the Allies that Germany willfully planned to ruin the sources of reparations. In March 1921 the Allied governments demanded from Germany the acceptance of a reparations settlement that envisaged the payment of forty-two annuities ranging from 2 to 6 billion marks. When the German government rejected this demand, the Allies occupied Düsseldorf, Duisburg, and Ruhrort as sanctions. The sum total of reparations had been set at 132 billion marks. Through the London Ultimatum of May 5, 1921, which contained a threat of Allied occupation of the Ruhr, the Allies then wanted to force the Germans to pay 2 billion marks annually and in addition 25 per cent of the value of German exports.

The German foreign minister, Walter Simons, refused to stoop to meet this ultimatum, and the Fehrenbach cabinet resigned. In its place stepped a government of the Weimar coalition, with Joseph Wirth, the former finance minister, as chancellor. It declared its willingness to try to fulfill the Allied impositions in order to prove their unrealistic character. The terms of the London Ultimatum were approved by the *Reichstag* with the support of the Independents and a few votes of the People's party. Payments were actually started in the summer, but when in July 1922 one billion had been paid, the government requested a moratorium on account of the desolate condition of the German economy. But it did not succeed in convincing the world that Germany was incapable of producing substantial reparations.

✍ *Upper Silesia*

THE WIRTH GOVERNMENT SUFFERED a grave setback in its foreign policy in the Upper Silesian settlement. We have already seen how the Poles by way of insurrection attempted to capture the district whose fate, according to the Versailles Treaty, was to be decided by a plebiscite. National feeling was deeply aroused over the future of the second largest— next to the Ruhr—German industrial district, and the Polish attempts to seize Upper Silesia by force, obviously undertaken with the connivance of the French occupation forces, caused passionate resentment. The defeat of the Polish insurgents by German free-corps troops before and after the plebiscite of March 20, 1921, which resulted in a 60 per cent majority in favor of Germany, seemed in German eyes to insure the full return of the province to Germany. However, this popular assumption that as a result of the plebiscite all of Upper Silesia should remain German was not supported by the Versailles Treaty, which permitted the division of Upper Silesia in accordance with the local results of the plebiscite.

The Allies did not reach an agreement among themselves on the disposition of Upper Silesia and turned the case over to the Council of the League of Nations, which announced its decision on October 20, 1921. About 40 per cent of the district, containing a Polish majority, was assigned to Poland. It was, however, by far the most valuable sector of Upper Silesia in which most of the mines and major industries were located. Moreover, on either side of the dividing line there remained German and Polish minorities of about a quarter of a million people, witnesses to the close integration of the industrial region. In 1922 Germany and Poland concluded a treaty, under League auspices, for the protection of these minorities, which created a better system for the enforcement of minority rights than any of the treaties negotiated at the Paris Peace Conference. But this did not assuage the wrath caused in Germany by the tearing apart of Upper Silesia and the cession of the great industries to Poland. The popular anger was directed not only against Poland and France but also against the League of Nations, which was now decried as an organization of the victorious powers designed to perpetuate the suppression of their former enemies.

✍ Internal Unrest

THE PASSIONS AWAKENED by the distressing economic situation and the discouraging international events led to the most acrimonious attacks against the government and its supporters. They were dubbed by the rightists "politicians of fulfillment" (*Erfüllungspolitiker*), and this became synonymous with "knaves of the victors." In such an atmosphere acts of violence appeared not only excusable but even praiseworthy. The first victim was Matthias Erzberger, who, on August 26, 1921, the eve of his reentry into the political arena, was fatally shot by two former members of the Ehrhardt brigade, who managed to escape. The Reich president, on the basis of article 48 of the constitution, issued an emergency order that allowed the minister of interior to forbid temporarily antirepublican publications, meetings, and organizations. But the agitation continued.

On June 14, 1922, the foreign minister, Walther Rathenau, was murdered in gangster fashion by a group of former Ehrhardt men. Rathenau was the chairman of one of the big German corporations, the German General Electric, founded by his father,[8] and during the war had made a major contribution to German defense by his organization of the supply of strategic raw materials. He was also a social critic aware of the profound changes that war and revolution had forced upon mankind. But the assassins knew next to nothing about Rathenau the patriot and the social thinker but rather wanted to kill the Jew and the director of the policy of fulfillment.

Rathenau's death aroused deep apprehension among the German left at the acute threat which the reckless attacks of the rightists posed to the republic, and even the moderates of the right grew frightened by the spread of lawlessness. The Independents as well as a good many members of the People's party assisted in passing a law "for the protection of the Republic" that Chancellor Wirth presented to the *Reichstag* with a belligerent speech against the antirepublican right. This law made the subversion of the republic by word or action a treasonable crime and established at the *Reichsgericht* in Leipzig a "state court for the protection of the Republic." The law was not as effective in stamping out the radical activities as its authors had hoped. Some state governments impeded the operation of the law, and a biased judiciary blunted its application to rightist violations. In the later years of the Weimar Republic the law was chiefly used against the Communists.

✑ *The Reich and Bavaria*

THE OPPOSITION to a policy of actively suppressing the rightist radicalism was officially backed by the Bavarian government. The seizure of power by Communist elements in Munich in the spring of 1919 had led to a general revulsion from the November revolution and all the changes that had taken place in its wake. The loss of the special state rights which Bavaria had possessed in the old Empire rankled in the Bavarian mind, but there was also felt deep depression over Germany's defenselessness that exposed her to military occupation and foreign demands. For Bavaria's and Germany's deplorable situation, the republican governments in Berlin were made responsible. Since the Kapp *Putsch*, when with the help of the Bavarian army command the Social Democrats had been ousted from the government, Bavaria was ruled increasingly by the reactionary forces in the Bavarian People's party. They deliberately protected all counterrevolutionary elements, without taking into account that for the purebred German nationalists Bavarian state rights did not have any meaning. But the Prussian Ludendorff became an esteemed resident of Munich, and many other radical counterrevolutionaries found a base of operations in

[8] See p. 379.

the Bavarian capital. And although Adolf Hitler (1889–1945) early proved that he was not a man to be easily steered, the benign attitude of the Bavarian governments permitted him to build up the National Socialist party together with its paramilitary storm trooper formations. In contrast, the Prussian government firmly suppressed all National Socialist activities.

Serious friction between the national and Bavarian governments first arose over the dissolution of the citizen guards (*Einwohnerwehren*), on which the Allies insisted in the execution of the disarmament provisions of the Versailles Treaty. A grave conflict developed when the Bavarian prime minister, Gustav von Kahr (1862–1934), refused to apply the emergency order issued to Bavaria by President Ebert after Erzberger's assassination, because Bavaria had its own emergency laws, which, however, were directed exclusively against the left. It was an open challenge of the Weimar Constitution, which very clearly established the superiority of national orders and laws over those of the lands. But Ebert was not willing to force a showdown, while at this moment the majority of the Bavarian People's party hesitated to go to extremes and accepted a compromise. Another compromise was reached when the Bavarian government objected to the introduction of the law for the protection of the republic. But the Bavarian cabinet that Eugen von Knilling (1865–1927) formed in October 1922 again represented the groups most hostile to Berlin.

The authority of the national government was severely tried by these internal disorders. But it suffered even more from the bleak outlook of Germany's future among nations. Lloyd George, recognizing that the problem of German reparations should be treated in conjunction with the international payments and trade situation, had prevailed upon the French to convene a conference in Genoa in April 1922, to which the Soviet Union was also invited. This conference gave Germany the opportunity to assert her relative independence from the West by concluding a treaty with Russia.

↜ Rapallo Treaty

OFFICIAL DIPLOMATIC RELATIONS between Berlin and Moscow had been ruptured since early November 1918, but some contacts continued to exist thereafter, although the Russian leaders did their utmost to foster communist revolution in Germany. It was General von Seeckt who in the first place had favored close relations with Russia. His immediate wish was the strengthening of German military power through the production in Russia of munitions that had been limited by the Versailles Treaty and through the training there of German officers in forbidden services such as tank warfare and aviation. Beyond that Seeckt believed that the Russo-German cooperation in rearmament would eventually lead to a full military alliance which would bring about the restoration of the Russo-German frontier of 1914, and this meant the destruction of the Polish and Baltic states. This alliance in Seeckt's opinion would also allow Germany to free herself in the West. Seeckt persuaded Chancellor Wirth secretly to give him funds for the building of military factories in Russia.

Yet before much was actually done, the foreign office, too, became active in the Russian field. Ago von Maltzan (1875–1927) was the chief proponent of a policy of *rapprochement* with the Soviet Union. In May 1921, two months after a similar Anglo-Russian treaty, a Russo-German trade treaty was concluded. In early 1922 the draft of a general treaty was perfected that settled mutual claims arising from World War I and provided for the resumption of full diplomatic relations. Russian Foreign Minister Chicherin would have liked to sign this treaty while in Berlin on his way to Genoa, but the Germans felt that first the outcome of the conference had to be awaited. At the conference, however, the German delegation felt isolated and became afraid that Britain and France might conclude separate agreements with the Soviet Union, possibly even at Germany's expense, by granting Russia a share in German reparations, a right that was reserved to the victors in the Versailles Treaty. Rathenau, who was still foreign minister at the time, was reluctantly persuaded by Maltzan that the danger could only be banned by the immediate signing of the Russo-German draft treaty.

The treaty, with which the Russians obviously hoped to torpedo the formation of a united front of European powers, was signed at Rapallo in the morning of Easter Sunday, April 16, 1922. The two signatories of the treaty waived all mutual claims for the recompensation of wartime damages. In addition, Germany dropped her demands for indemnities in the case of nationalized German properties in Russia. Both governments promised to boost mutual trade under the most-favored-nation treatment. No secret military and political articles were attached to the treaty, although their existence was often suspected. General von Seeckt felt that Germany could not achieve any gains unless the other powers would discern behind the Rapallo Treaty the ghost of a military alliance. Therefore he severely castigated Count von Brockdorff-Rantzau, who became the first German ambassador to Moscow after the resumption of diplomatic relations and always warned against giving German-Russian relations the character of a military alliance. But even to Brockdorff-Rantzau, the Rapallo policy was a welcome symbol of Germany's determination not to accept the political order of Europe that the Western powers had created in 1919.

Because the Rapallo Treaty was seen as a gesture of defiance, its announcement proved a bombshell at the Genoa Conference, which broke up rather quickly without producing any constructive ideas for the solution of the reparations problem or even improving the atmosphere for its negotiation. On the contrary, the failure of the conference strengthened French doubts about the honesty of German policy and indirectly contributed to Poincaré's decision later in the year to wrest reparations from Germany by force.

∽ Government Crisis, 1922

GERMANY'S INTERNAL AND INTERNATIONAL weakness in 1922 was great. The only development that helped to stabilize the domestic order was the growing willingness of the German People's party under Stresemann's leadership to cooperate with the parties of the Weimar coalition. As mentioned before, the party voted for the law for the protection of the republic. Stresemann also proposed to extend the period of President Ebert's service till July 1925 in order to avoid the additional public unrest that the popular election of a president would entail. A law of extension was passed with the help of the People's party in October 1922. The People's party also worked together with the parties of the Weimar coalition in foreign affairs. Together they approved on November 14, 1922, a note to the Allied powers which asked for a continuation of the moratorium of reparation payments and made some suggestions for the stabilization of the German currency.

It would have been logical to take the People's party into the government, the more so since the party represented the industrial sector of German society, which inevitably was to have an important part in the formulation and execution of reparations policies. Wirth wanted to include the People's party, thus basing his cabinet on the so-called "great coalition," which consisted of the Social Democratic party, the Democratic party, the Bavarian People's party, the Center party, and the German People's party, rather than on the Weimar coalition. But the Social Democrats refused to sit in the same government with the People's party. A new cabinet was formed on November 22, 1922, in which the position of chancellor and some portfolios were taken by men of not clearly identifiable party affiliation, though all of them were right-of-center figures. The chancellor, Wilhelm Cuno (1876–1933), had grown up in the federal bureaucracy to become the head of Germany's biggest shipping line. While he was credited with good contacts in Britain and the United States, this could not make up for his lack of political experience and verve. His foreign minister, Frederic von Rosenberg (1874–1937), a professional diplomat, did not add color to a rather indifferent cabinet.

✑ *Ruhr Invasion*

THIS GOVERNMENT, six weeks after its formation, had to face the deadly threat of the French invasion of the Ruhr district. Poincaré used Germany's failure to fulfill all the deliveries of coal and telegraph poles to have her declared in default of her reparations obligations. And although Britain opposed this policy, Poincaré proceeded to occupy the Ruhr as a "productive pawn." The French control of the Ruhr industries was supposed to guarantee not only the flow of reparations but also the predominance of the French industries in Europe. The coal and iron industries of France and Germany were to a large measure complementary, France being short of coal, while Germany was deficient in iron ore. Prior to 1914 some Ruhr companies had already bought iron mines in France, and French iron firms had acquired individual coal mines in the Ruhr. Hugo Stinnes was busy in 1922 exploring the possibilities of a voluntary Franco-German iron and coal cartel. The Ruhr invasion that began on January 11, 1923, with the arrival of five French and one Belgian divisions was designed to achieve the integration of these key industries under French control. France's desire to win greater national security was a further motive for the Ruhr occupation.

The German delays in their deliveries of reparations in kind were actually very minor infractions played up by the French government. On the other side, it would not have been necessary for the German government to give the French these pretexts for action, particularly since it had received ample warnings about Poincaré's designs. The government now stopped all reparations deliveries and called upon its officials and employees, including the railroad workers, to refuse any cooperation with the occupying forces. The Rhenish people joined in this "passive resistance," which was directed chiefly by the trade unions. All political parties supported this policy. Even the Communist party now found strong nationalist tones in the defense against western "finance capitalism and imperialism." But whereas the Communists wanted to change the nature of the struggle from passive resistance to a general strike, the radicals of the right wished for active instead of passive resistance. Acts of forceful sabotage were committed, and there occurred clashes between the occupation troops and the population which led to bloodshed. But in general the line of passive resistance was maintained, which the French authorities hoped to defeat by the expulsion of the German state officials. Up to 100,000 people, with railroad men and their families constituting the largest group, were driven out from the Rhineland.

For months this passive resistance frustrated any attempts of the occupiers to extract large amounts of coal from the Ruhr. The industries of Lorraine soon felt the pinch. France was also forced to send many engineers and thousands of railroad workers into the Ruhr district. The whole operation grew costly and eventually proved a drag on the French budget that weakened the stability of the French franc. But after the middle of the year the French had the German railroads working and the mines yielding coal. In contrast, the German economy seemed on the brink of disaster. The collapse of the German currency and the separation of the Ruhr district were bound to wreck the whole economic and social fabric. The time was fast approaching when the Berlin government would be unable to pay out the large sums in support of the resistance of the Ruhr population, because there were no presses left to pour forth even more worthless money bills and people were no longer able to buy anything with them.

Germany had no choice but to break off the struggle, although the international and national consequences were unforeseeable. On August 13, 1923, a government of the "great coalition" was formed by Gustav Stresemann. The government was reshuffled on October 6, when Hans Luther (1879–1962) replaced Rudolf Hilferding as minister of finance. On November 2, the Social Democrats withdrew from the government altogether, and the cabinet resigned three weeks later. The hundred days of Stresemann's chancellorship were a period of extraordinary dangers. There loomed the threat of the loss of Germany's richest provinces in the west, of possible further foreign inroads in the east, and the splitting up of the remaining German lands. At the same time the very foundations of the whole social order were gravely imperiled. Although at the end of the hundred days the general conditions were still most precarious, the policies had been developed that were to overcome the crisis of state and society.

The first step was the ending of the German resistance in the Ruhr. Poincaré insisted on unqualified capitulation. After consultation with the heads of the German states and the leaders of the Rhenish industry, Stresemann on September 26, 1923, proclaimed the termination of German resistance in the Ruhr. Simultaneously President Ebert, by authority of article 48, declared a state of emergency and laid the executive power into the hands of the minister of defense, Otto Gessler. But a few hours earlier the Bavarian government had announced a similar state of emergency and appointed Gustav von Kahr "state commissar general." Under the Weimar Constitution any such law of a single land should have been automatically superseded by the national law, and the appointment of the stubborn and zealous Kahr, who believed in the cooperation of the Bavarian autonomists with the rightist national organizations, was a storm signal. He questioned the validity of the federal law and actually gained the support of the Bavarian division of the *Reichswehr*.

◯ *Internal Revolts and Hitler* Putsch

WHEN GESSLER ORDERED the commander of this division, General von Lossow (1868–1938), to close the chief press organ of the National Socialist party, which had published a defamatory article against General von Seeckt and his wife, Lossow refused to obey orders. When Gessler thereupon relieved him of his command, the Bavarian government "as the trustee of the German people" took him and his division into its service. Members of the numerous paramilitary nationalist organizations began to assemble in northern Bavaria, and the call for a "march to Berlin" to establish a nationalist government following the example of the "Fascist march to Rome" of 1922 was freely heard. No doubt north of Bavaria there were many people who would have welcomed such a move. Not only did the German Nationalist party itch to get into the German and Prussian government but also a substantial group of Ruhr industrialists wished for a government of the right that would exclude any representation of labor and abolish the eight-hour day. But such a government had no chance to gain a parliamentary majority, even if Stresemann's party, in which these industrialists were strongly represented, would have joined the German Nationalist and Bavarian People's party. A dictatorial directorate could have been imposed only by force. It seems that General von Seeckt originally toyed with ideas of a dictatorial government.

In October the communists became increasingly active in Saxony and Thuringia. It was the strong radical wing of the Social Democratic party that prevailed in these two lands and led to the formation of "Marxist" governments, which meant socialist-communist coalitions. Under their eyes military centuries were organized, and little was done to stop proletarian acts of violence which erupted against the class enemies. The order of the commanding general in Dresden, to dissolve the red centuries, was answered by acrimonious attacks of the Saxon prime minister against the army. A very serious uprising of the communists in Hamburg on October 22–24, which was suppressed by the police with great difficulties and bloodshed, showed that a policy of waiting was fraught with danger. Therefore, the Saxon government was deposed by military intervention, and a civilian Reich commissar appointed. But on the following day the Saxon parliament managed to elect a Social Democratic government from which the communists remained excluded.

After the intervention in Saxony, which was followed by a similar action in Thuringia, the army was deployed along the northern border of Bavaria. Since this military intervention, which did not lead to any fighting, had restored complete public order in central Germany, the bourgeoisie in this region was no longer tempted to long for the arrival of "forces of order" from Munich. But a military intervention of the

Reichswehr in Bavaria would have been a very different matter. It would have led to heavy fighting, which in turn would have made it impossible to restore an integrated national army. It would also greatly have strengthened the separatistic groups in Bavaria, which so far had little political weight. This might have happened even if the Berlin government had used economic sanctions instead of military force. With the chance that new uprisings from the left or right might start in other parts of Germany, the number of troops available for a sortie into Bavaria was very limited.

This situation explains Gessler's resistance to the demand of the Social Democrats that the Bavarian insurrection should be dealt with in the same manner as the Saxon and Thuringian conflicts. Gessler's and Stresemann's refusal to comply with this demand led to the already mentioned withdrawal of the Social Democrats from the government. If the government chose to remain inactive, this meant that it hoped eventually to be able to negotiate. Kahr, in spite of his obstinacy, hesitated to act, too, and might possibly in the end have been satisfied with substantial concessions to Bavarian autonomy. But he had misjudged his nationalist allies, who were quite unprepared to accept his leadership. When in the evening of November 8, 1923, Kahr and members of the Bavarian government presided over a nationalist demonstration in one of Munich's big beer halls, the National Socialists surrounded the building. Hitler, with a group of his ruffians, entered the hall and fired a shot at the ceiling, shouting that the national revolution had broken out and both the national and Bavarian governments were deposed. Next he forced Kahr, General von Lossow, and Colonel von Seisser, the chief of the state police, who were on the speaker's platform, into an adjacent room, where at gun's point he made them accept his design for the new governments. Together they returned to the hall, where Hermann Göring (1893–1946) had calmed the public and Ludendorff had arrived. Now Hitler proclaimed that General Ludendorff was to form a national army, General von Lossow was to be the "military dictator" and defense minister, Colonel von Seisser the national police minister, while he, Adolf Hitler, would take over the political direction. He "appointed" Kahr "regent of Bavaria" and a National Socialist sympathizer Bavarian prime minister.

While the crowd cheered the beginning of the national revolution and Hitler's bluffing tactics seemed to have made him the master of the Munich scene, he had failed to appraise correctly the character of the persons whom he wanted to coerce into action. Obviously he firmly believed that Kahr and Lossow really intended to march to Berlin and establish a nationalist government. Once the undertaking had been launched, they could be relied upon to cooperate, the more so since the soldiers of the *Reichswehr* would also welcome such an action. In addition he was sufficiently presumptuous to forget that these dignified gentlemen would not so readily hand over their command to an upstart. Nothing had been done to prepare a plan for the occupation of the strategic key positions of the city and, worst of all, Hitler allowed Kahr, Seisser, and Lossow to slip away. They went to the barracks of the Munich infantry regiment from where they rejected their forced participation in Hitler's adventure and called upon the army garrison as well as the state police to put down the uprising. Kahr declared the Nazi party and the allied militant organizations illegal. Before the morning dawned, Hitler knew that his attempt at the seizure of power had miscarried.

It still seemed possible to prove that the army was sympathetic. For this reason a demonstration march of 2,000 to 3,000 Nazis was led by Hitler and Ludendorff into the city. They considered it likely that the soldiers would not shoot at the great commander of World War I. But when the column reached the *Feldherrnhalle*, where the narrow street debouches onto a wide square, it faced a cordon of state police. It is impossible to determine from which side the first stray shots came. Quickly, however, the police fired a salvo that killed sixteen Nazis and threw the demonstrators, among them Hitler, into disorderly flight. Only Ludendorff, his head erect, marched on and reached the square, where he soon had to surrender. The *Putsch* was over, and the Berlin government could have breathed a bit easier if there had not remained so many other fearful problems.

The news of the Munich events of November 8 induced President Ebert on Gessler's suggestion to entrust the full dictatorial power under article 48 to General von Seeckt. Obviously the latter was as anxious as he had been at the time of the Kapp *Putsch* to avoid actual fighting between *Reichswehr* troops. But it is doubtful whether he could have avoided this if Hitler, Ludendorff, and Lossow had marched against Berlin. The quick collapse of Hitler's *Putsch*, due to its own internal contradictions, facilitated Seeckt's task to maintain order in Germany without creating a situation which could have encouraged him to take over the government. Instead, he set his eyes firmly on the presidential succession in 1925 and handed back to Ebert his temporary powers in January 1924.

✍ *Aftermath of Ruhr Invasion*

THE ENDING of the passive resistance in the Ruhr on September 26, 1923, had been undertaken in the expectation that it would lead to negotiations with France on reparations and the evacuation of the Ruhr. Yet the French government refused even after September 26 to negotiate with the Berlin government on the Rhineland, Ruhr, and reparations. It declared that France needed definite guarantees which only commitments

of the local German industrialists could procure. Thus the Ruhr industrialists were to be forced to come to terms with the occupation authorities. The danger that France thereby would gain permanent control of
the industries of the Rhine and Ruhr could hardly be precluded. The big
payments of the government for the Ruhr population continued in October and most of November and with them the mad devaluation of the
mark. The condition of the people grew unbearable.

In these circumstances the Stresemann government gave the Ruhr
industrialists permission to negotiate agreements on industrial production
and reparations deliveries. It promised to reimburse them at a later date
for the special expenditures they would incur with their deliveries, which
they hoped to finance at first by the mobilization of foreign credits.
On November 23 the fundamental agreement was concluded with the
occupation authority. But although this action was an important step
toward ending the financial contributions to the Ruhr for the time being,
what remained to be done to assure the transition to normal working
conditions in the Rhineland as a whole was still a burden that imperiled
the stabilization of the German currency.

✍ *Currency Stabilization*

THE CREATION of a stable mark had been under discussion within the
Stresemann government since its inception as the most urgent task. By
now the *Reichsbank* did not own enough gold and foreign money that
could have served as cover for a new mark currency. Moreover, stability
could be achieved only if the government ceased to have unlimited credit
or, in other words, to pay its way by printing unlimited amounts of paper
money. It was said that in November 1923 actual tax revenue amounted
to only 1 per cent of the federal expenditure. It was therefore necessary
to find the means to operate the government till the budget could be
balanced and taxes regularly collected.

To this end an ingenious solution was found with the establishment of
the *Rentenbank*, which was endowed with the mortgages on all the land
used by agriculture and industries. They replaced gold as security for the
money the bank would issue in strictly limited quantity. The latter would
give the German government 1.2 billion *Rentenmark*, the first quarter of
which was to be used to buy from the *Reichsbank* the treasury bills
which represented the value of the money then in circulation. The remaining three quarters, or as it actually worked out five sixths, were to
serve government operations. 1.2 billion *Rentenmark* were to be given to
the *Reichsbank* in order to enable it to supply the economy with credits.
The construction of the *Rentenmark*, which was to be used only domestically as a means of payment, though somewhat fictitious in the light of

strict financial theory, proved psychologically sound under the unique conditions of the moment. It was appealing to see money appear in denominations similar to those of the happy prewar period and issued in limited quantity by a new bank which did not carry the stigma of the *Reichsbank*. And it seemed plausible to the common man that land would change its value as little as gold. Naturally most important was the stoppage of the printing of the old mark and the subsequent balancing of the budget.

The *Rentenmark* goes back to a plan originally presented by Karl Helfferich, the wartime vice-chancellor and by now a prominent figure in the German Nationalist party, but his ideas were so drastically changed that he could not be called the father of the *Rentenmark*. Finance Minister Hans Luther developed the final arrangements with the assistance of the leading officials of the ministry of finance and with some advice from his predecessor, Rudolf Hilferding, and thereafter conducted the policies necessary for the success of the interim currency. The *Rentenmark* was first issued on November 15, 1923. Five days later the dollar was quoted at 4.2 trillion marks, and the government decided to hold this line, which made one *Rentenmark* equivalent to one trillion marks. On the same day Rudolf Havenstein, the president of the *Reichsbank*, died, making way for the appointment of Dr. Hjalmar Schacht (b. 1877) to succeed him. Luther shortly before had made the astute financier the supervisor of the execution of all currency policies. He was to become the chief architect of a new German currency based on the gold standard and thus freely usable in international trade. This *Reichsmark* superseded the *Rentenmark* a year later.

The *Rentenmark* credit that the government received was small and had to last until sufficient tax money, now levied on a gold basis, would make the balancing of the budget possible. Draconic measures were taken to cut public expenditures, particularly by the removal of officials and workers from the government payroll, which caused a great deal of hardship and resentment. But the gravest question was whether the government would be able to make further contributions to the Ruhr and Rhineland. Although it had cut off the industries from further support, there remained the cost of the considerable unemployment and public services. Between October and December 1923 passionate debates took place within the cabinet and between members of the government and Rhenish leaders on whether these burdens should be continued. At least temporarily the majority of the ministers became convinced that the *Rentenmark* would fail for these purposes. The idea gained ground to turn over to the French the responsibility for the social chaos that the Ruhr invasion had created. But this in all probability would have led to the establishment of a Rhenish state, which, being under French occupation, might have retained few ties with the rest of Germany. Another plan would have further strengthened this trend. Some Cologne bankers never gave the *Rentenmark* a chance because of its financially irregular nature. The president of the Cologne chamber of commerce, Louis Hagen (1855–1932), projected a Rhenish gold currency, which inevitably would have had to lean on the Bank of France.

✍ *Rhenish Separatism*

THE RESISTANCE OF MOST of the Rhineland people and also the firm opposition of some of the Berlin leaders, such as the Prussian prime minister, Otto Braun, induced the federal government finally to continue the payments to the Rhineland and Ruhr and block the founding of a Rhenish bank of issue. Yet the government could do little directly to defeat the open attempts at separating the Rhineland politically from Germany. On the whole, the dregs of the population served as the cohorts of a revolutionary separatism. Under the protection and often enough with the active help of the French and Belgian troops, they proceeded to seize the administrative offices. In the Belgian zone a strong armed band occupied the city hall of Aachen on October 21, 1923, and subsequently similar coups succeeded in München-Gladbach, Duisburg, and Krefeld in spite of strong popular resistance. Beginning on October 22 seizures took place in Koblenz, Bonn, Trier, Mainz, Wiesbaden, and other cities. A Rhenish Republic was proclaimed, and Dr. Dorten, who in 1919 had made the same attempt, tried to set up a government. The farmer Heinz-Orbis, who also had been in evidence in 1919, established a Palatine Republic.

The Rhenish population responded with cold contempt and burning hatred. It disregarded all orders coming from the separatists and made every effort to isolate them completely. Where force came into play, people hit back and sometimes with fearful force. In the middle of November the farmers in the hills of the Siebengebirge slew 180 marauding separatists in what practically amounted to a pitched battle. But planned actions were also undertaken, such as abductions of collaborating German officials to the unoccupied part of Germany, where they could be brought to court. On January 9, 1924, Heinz-Orbis with four of his henchmen was shot, presumably by members of the Black *Reichswehr*. The last wild outburst of popular anger occurred when the citizens of Pirmasens in the Palatinate set fire to their city hall and killed seventeen separatists fleeing from the burning building.

Since the fall of 1923 the British government had become increasingly vocal in its criticism of French policy vis-à-vis Germany. Undoubtedly well informed by its ambassador in Berlin, Lord d'Abernon, called by some wits the lord-protector of Germany, of the disastrous consequences this policy might have in Germany, the London government began to feel that the French were making it impossible for them to receive German reparations. In October the British government inquired whether the American government still stood by the offer which Secretary of State Hughes had made in a speech in New Haven on the eve of the French Ruhr invasion, when he recommended an examination of the reparations problem by experts with American participation. The combined pressure of the United States and Britain compelled France to accept the proposal of a conference of experts, although Poincaré succeeded in protecting the power of the Allied Reparations Commission and in limiting the scope of the recommendations of the conference. The commission agreed on November 30 to convene the experts. The British also protested against the French support of the Rhenish separatists as a unilateral subversion of the Versailles Treaty. France at this time was unpleasantly reminded by the weakening of the French franc of the limits of her strength, which was overtaxed by the lengthening Ruhr struggle, and she was therefore worried about her diplomatic isolation.

∽ *Gustav Stresemann*

WHEN ON NOVEMBER 23, 1923, the doctrinaire attitude of the Social Democrats caused the Stresemann government, from which they had withdrawn early in the month, to fall in the *Reichstag*, optimists believed that they could discern behind the dark clouds hanging over Germany a small silver stripe on the horizon. In any event, by this time, all those policies had been initiated that were to get the German Republic over the grave crisis of 1923. Through an enabling act in September the parliament had given the government the power to issue laws without presenting them first to the legislature. Although the Social Democrats did not join the succeeding government, they willingly renewed this enabling act, without which the necessary steps for balancing the budget and stabilizing the currency could not have been taken promptly.

The new cabinet of the middle parties was led by the head of the Center party, Dr. Wilhelm Marx (1863–1946). A high judge, he was a good republican though somewhat more to the right than Joseph Wirth. With his judicious mind, absolute honesty, and even temper, Marx's strength lay more in keeping a group of differing men together than dominating them. Aside from Hans Luther, who remained minister of finance and completed the restoration of sound public finance, Gustav Stresemann, who retained the foreign ministry, was the foremost member of the Marx government, as he was to be of all the subsequent cabinets of the Weimar Republic till his death in October 1929. Moreover, he was the actual builder of practically all these governments and only as long as he was alive did parliamentary government function, although the nature of the German parties made it even then an insecure system.

It must be deplored that Stresemann was already an ailing man when he reached the summit of his political career. He no longer had the strength to mold the political mind of the younger generation, on which the ultimate fate of his liberalism depended. Stresemann was the only political leader of the Weimar Republic who might have been able to win over the better part of the younger middle-class people for nobler causes than that of blind nationalism. One of the reasons why he might have reached their ears was the fact that he himself had been a nationalist and had never fully extracted himself from nationalist thinking. But his was not an exclusively political nationalism. It was nourished by a genuine enthusiasm for the German cultural heritage, which to him was largely represented by the age of Goethe. This was the basis for his liberal faith not only in cultural freedom but also in the political rights of the individual. In his last years, these convictions helped him to reach out beyond narrow national concepts to more universal aims, such as European union. The son of a Berlin tavern keeper, Stresemann had risen through his own efforts, and he managed to preserve both his optimism and idealism in the face of many enmities which he encountered even after he had arrived at the top. Unless one noticed his fine hands, one might not have suspected him to be a highly sensitive man. His heavy build, the pallor of illness, and his shy demeanor on first contact made him appear rather a mediocre Teuton. But he would suddenly transform himself and grow wings once he had begun to address a gathering, whether it be party caucus, parliament, or popular meeting of any size. Then his ability to give events and necessary decisions an ideal historical meaning enthused his listeners. Though ill-prepared by his earlier life for the diplomatic business, he quickly mastered its techniques and adapted his skill at negotiation as well as his public eloquence to the new tasks with great ease and success.

∽ First and Second Marx Governments

THE FIRST MARX GOVERNMENT still had to fight a steep uphill struggle. Although the parliament had authorized it to issue laws by decree, both the Social Democratic and the German Nationalist parties demanded changes of the laws on taxes, on the small revaluation of the old government bonds, and on labor, where the eight-hour day was no longer enforced but left to bargaining, while the government assumed a strong position in the settlement of labor conflicts. Since elections were due in 1924, the government dissolved the *Reichstag* slightly ahead of time.

The results of the national elections of May 4, 1924, reflected the bitter discontent of wide groups of the people. It was enhanced by the economic events in April. Since February the exchange value of the mark had begun to drop in foreign markets, chiefly due to large imports and the excessive purchase of foreign currency made possible by a rather liberal credit policy of the *Reichsbank*. Its president, Hjalmar Schacht, on April 7, 1924, took the unusual step of ordering a complete credit stop, which forced the holders of foreign money to give it up to the *Reichsbank*, and restored stability before long. Necessary as the adoption of such a measure was for the final stabilization of the German monetary system, it was a harsh cure for the economy, since it led to many business failures and additional unemployment. Few foresaw that job opportunities would grow very fast during the early summer.

The chief losers in the May elections were the Social Democrats, who were reduced from 171 to 100 seats. Conversely, the Communists jumped from 4 to 62 seats. On the other side, the German Nationalists, who incorporated two small groups, gained 106 seats, thereby for once becoming the strongest party in the *Reichstag*. But what was even more alarming was the appearance of a 32-man delegation of a National Socialist Freedom party composed of the German Racialists of northern Germany, who had broken away from the German Nationalist party, and of the National Socialist party of southern Germany. While the Center party maintained its strength rather well, the other middle parties lost heavily: the German People's party close to one third and the Democratic party over one fourth of their seats. The strong move to the right induced the People's party to demand the inclusion of the German Nationalists in the government. But the negotiations between the parties did not lead to an agreement. The Nationalists at first even proposed Admiral von Tirpitz as chancellor, but although this demand was dropped, they did not give any assurance that they would support and continue Stresemann's foreign policy. In these circumstances Ebert reappointed Marx chancellor of a barely modified cabinet.

∽ Dawes Plan

THE GREATEST SINGLE TASK of the two Marx governments, in which they enjoyed the full support of the Social Democratic party, was an agreement with the Allies on reparations which would also lead to the evacuation of the Ruhr district and in the not too distant future, so it was hoped, to the evacuation of the Rhineland as well. The conference of experts which the reparations commission had invited in December 1923 convened in Paris on January 15, 1924. It was the first time after her official withdrawal from Europe that America participated in the solution of a major European problem, and although the American conference members were not official representatives of the United States government, their standing in the financial community was such as to give them a commanding voice in the deliberations of the conference.

It should not be forgotten, however, that the conference was not charged with devising a new reparations settlement but was only asked to define Germany's capacity to pay. The group of experts aimed at taking the reparations out of politics in the sense of making their payment independent of the fluctuations of internal political forces in both the creditor and debtor countries. The reparations were to be made automatic by founding them on economic realities. The extent to which sane economic principles were adopted for the solution of the German reparations would also determine to what degree the world economy would overcome the insecurity created by the war.

It was a distinguished group of experts from four nations that on January 15, 1924, began in Paris its deliberations, in which the Americans, represented by Charles G. Dawes (1865–1951) and Owen D. Young (1874–1962), played leading roles. Quite apart from their economic knowledge, the Americans brought to the conference an optimistic confidence in the future economic development which had a refreshing effect on the discouraged Europeans. The plan that the conference finally presented, commonly called the Dawes Plan because Dawes headed its chief committee, was built on a belief in the strong recuperative strength of Germany and in an expanding world economy, although it contained provisions for revisions if these assumptions were proved wrong.

The Dawes Plan presupposed that Germany would be able to mobilize funds for reparations if she had a stable currency and a balanced budget, two mutually supporting conditions. But it recognized that the internal mobilization of funds was not identical with the actual payment of reparations. The amount that could be transferred to foreign countries without producing the instability of the currency and budget depended on the balance of payments. The Dawes commission estimated that Germany would be capable of raising internally 2.5 billion marks per year, a sum so far considered completely unrealistic in Germany. The commission admitted that the German economy would first have to regain its full productivity. For the first year, therefore, only 200 million marks were to be collected in cash, while 800 million were to come from an international loan. The annual sums were to rise from 1.22 in 1925–26 to 1.5 and 1.75 billion marks in the two years thereafter. Not before 1928–29 was the normal payment of 2.5 billion marks to begin.

The Dawes commission recommended that at the beginning less than a quarter, and eventually half, of the total reparations payments was to be raised through the federal budget, for which the revenue from certain duties and taxes was to serve as guarantee. The other part was to come from a transportation tax and from the payment of dividends to be issued by the industrial corporations and the federal railroads, which were to be organized as private corporations. Actually more than a third of the ultimate reparations annuities was to be collected from the German railroads. The Dawes Plan also demanded an organizational change of the *Reichsbank*. Its control by the government, which had made it the source of unlimited government credit, was to be abolished and an internationally composed general council to be installed over and above the board of directors, which remained German.

Wisely the Dawes commission decided to treat the transfer problem as one demanding special regulation. German obligations were fulfilled by the payment of reparations in German currency to the reparations agent, whose duty it would be to transfer the money to the Allies within the limits of the German balance of international payments. If this did not allow the transfer, the accumulating sums were to be held in Germany. Once they amounted to 5 billion marks, the collection from the transportation tax and the federal budget was to be curtailed. While this transfer protection opened the possibility of revising the plan for the debtor's benefit, it also foresaw some change in favor of the creditor in case Germany reached a certain high level of prosperity, for which the plan established an index. An upward revision of the reparations annuity was then called for.

The Dawes Plan deliberately did not define the total German liability and abstained from political demands except for the evacuation of the Ruhr. The nationalists in Germany denounced the plan as an instrument for the permanent serfdom of the German people. In addition to the lack of a terminal date of reparations the nationalist opposition angrily pointed to the inroads made on German sovereignty by placing the *Reichsbank* and the German railroads under foreign control. The proposed institution of an American reparations agent who was to collect reparations and to be responsible for their transfer was depicted as a further intrusion into the German government. Karl Helfferich, who shortly thereafter died in a railroad accident, set the tone by speaking of a second Versailles.

Actually the Dawes Plan was an enormous step forward to a rational treatment of the economic issues, and no country had more to gain than Germany from the participation of the Americans in the discussion and execution of reparations. It was for reasons quite different from the assertions of the German nationalists that the Dawes Plan eventually proved inadequate for the solution of the reparations problem, but then it had its built-in safety devices, which would have shielded Germany in a financial crisis. The Dawes Plan was accepted by the governments concerned at the London Conference in July and August 1924. Ramsay MacDonald (1866–1937), who presided, and the French representative, Edouard Herriot (1872–1957), were both anxious to have the conference produce positive results. For the Germans the most urgent need was the assurance of the French evacuation of the Ruhr, and although on French insistence this question had been excluded from the conference agenda, Stresemann received from Herriot a promise that he would work for the evacuation within one year. As a matter of fact, the Ruhr district was cleared by July 1925.

But the prospect of getting the *Reichstag* to pass the laws necessary for putting the Dawes Plan into operation seemed hopeless. The laws creating the railroad company under international authority required a two-thirds majority, since it implied a change of the constitution. A qualified majority, however, depended on votes from the German Nationalist party, which appeared adamant and on whom neither concessions nor threats made any visible impression. Both the People's and the Center parties promised the Nationalists admission to the government if they approved the Dawes legislation. On the other side the government made it clear that in case of defeat it would dissolve parliament and appeal to the people. In spite of the large vote it had received the German Nationalist party was anything but monolithic. It contained Pan-Germans whose only aim was to defy the Western powers. The old Conservatives formed a large group within the party that cultivated its memories of the monarchy and refused to contemplate cooperation in the disgraceful Weimar system. Another group of monarchists felt that the chance to renew the monarchy would diminish if the right did not keep its foothold of power in the state. In particular they wanted to maintain their influence on the Prussian administration. The representatives of such mass organizations as the German Employees' Union had equally strong feelings that a mass political party had to win palpable gains for its followers.

The party was particularly sensitive to agricultural and industrial interests. And both the big federation of German industrialists and the federation of agriculturalists called for the acceptance of the Dawes plan as the way for the restoration of the economy. Seeckt, too, was quite active arguing that the Dawes Plan should be adopted. No doubt, to him the removal of foreign troops from the Ruhr and the Rhine was the most important end. All these different pressures brought forth the strange and surprising attitude of the German Nationalist delegation in the *Reichstag*. After all its members had thundered against the Dawes bill for a week, about half of them voted aye at the third reading of the bill, thus providing the two-thirds majority needed for its passage. It was a glaring display of the tensions within this party.

The Dawes Plan went into operation on September 1, 1924, and an American, Parker Gilbert (1892–1938), was named reparations agent. The new *Reichsmark* currency made its appearance, and the social conditions improved. This was mirrored in the results of the new elections of December 7, 1924. It was astonishing that the German Nationalists were able to add 6 more seats, but also the People's party, the Bavarian People's party, the Center party, and the Democratic party each won 3 to 6 additional seats. The greatest gain of 31 seats, however, was made by the Social Democratic party, whereas the Communists lost more than a quarter and the National Socialists more than half of their seats.

In spite of the weakening of the radical wings the formation of a government proved difficult. But finally Hans Luther succeeded in bringing together the bourgeois parties in a cabinet into which each party sent only one political spokesman, whereas all the other ministers, like the chancellor himself, were considered administrators rather than men bound by official party directives. This fictitious interpretation had at least the advantage of making it unnecessary for the German Nationalist members to agree on a common policy among themselves, which they might have found impossible. But the commitment of their party to the government remained weak and might jeopardize it at any moment.

✑ *Ebert's Death and Election of Hindenburg*

THE MOVEMENT to the political right gained new momentum with the death of Friedrich Ebert on February 28, 1925. Ebert had conducted his office with natural dignity and a high sense of responsibility. To his end he remained a good Social Democrat, but democracy rated higher with him than socialism. Therefore he had fought bolshevism during the revolution with the utmost determination and had managed as president to remain above the parties. He did not earn any gratitude. While even many people of his own party cooled toward him, the German bourgeoisie treated him, the "former saddlemaker and innkeeper," with silly, snobbish contempt or worse, hysterical antired hatred. Poisonous calumnies were told about him and even printed, and the judges failed to protect him in the innumerable libel actions he had to bring against his detractors. It was ominous that the mass of the German bourgeoisie did not display a sense of fairness and decency toward a statesman of a differing political faith, even though he had done more than any other single person to protect them against social revolution. This attitude illuminated the gulf that separated the German bourgeoisie from any democratic sentiment.

Ebert had become president through the election by the National Assembly, and his tenure had been extended by the *Reichstag*. Now a president had to be elected by the people in accordance with the constitution. For the first national ballot the German Nationalist and the People's parties had agreed on a single candidate, whereas six other parties were each running one of their own leaders. The voting was abortive, although it indicated that the three Weimar parties together had enough votes to beat the candidate of the parties on the right, Karl Jarres (1874-1951), the mayor of Duisburg. Therefore the right-wing parties went outside the regular circle of political and public figures to a man who in their opinion would have magnetic power beyond the frontiers of the individual parties.

The leader of the German Nationalists, Count Kuno von Westarp (1864-1945), and Admiral von Tirpitz prevailed on the 77-year-old Field Marshal von Hindenburg to become the candidate of the right. It seems that Hindenburg accepted only after getting the permission of his "Imperial lord," William II. In the elections of April 25, 1925, 14.6 million people voted for Hindenburg as against 13.7 million for Wilhelm Marx, the standard bearer of the republican parties, and 1.9 million for the Communist Ernst Thälmann (1886-1944). Since in the second ballot simple plurality was sufficient, Hindenburg was elected. Actually his victory was a close one. It was made possible by the official endorsement of his candidacy by the Bavarian People's party and by the defection of a good number of voters normally favoring the Center party, whose right wing disliked the alliance with the Social Democrats.

About half of the German people thus placed Hindenburg, the hero of the prerepublican order, into the highest office of the republic. They clearly did not feel at home in the republic nor did they have much confidence in the leaders of the political parties. But the popular vote was not simply a vote for monarchy. During the war Hindenburg had already become to many Germans the embodiment of the highest virtues, and they wished to put him in a position of command. They felt humiliated by Versailles and the Ruhr conflict. They had just gone through the frightening experience of hyperinflation, in which the whole structure of society threatened to crumble at any moment. The election of Hindenburg meant to them a guarantee of the traditional social order and an act of defiance of the foreign powers. Although undoubtedly many Hindenburg voters expected him to lead the way toward monarchy, the form of government was of secondary importance to the average voter.

Hindenburg moved with dignity, and his endeavor to conduct his office in accordance with the constitution made him respected by the republicans as well. He must have been aware of the discrepancy between his monarchist faith and his republican position. The memory of his advice to William II to leave for Holland must have bothered him and left him with some gnawing doubts about his own part in the outcome of the war. But he was always anxious to have the public judge him in the light of honest success. Thus he had not hesitated to give currency to the "stab-in-the-back" explanation of the German defeat. He enjoyed the respect of the people and especially wished to retain the affection of the soldiers and ex-soldiers, whose commander he had been in World War I. Even when the leaders of the *Stahlhelm*, the nationalist veterans' organization, heaped abuse on him, he did not relinquish his honorary presidency of this group.

Hindenburg's mind was exceedingly simple, and he needed councillors who would analyze the problems for him and suggest solutions. But he wanted to be convinced of the correctness of a policy in order to be able to justify his decisions before his conscience and his friends. These were no superficial efforts, although in the last years of his life his reactions became increasingly obtuse. And it was just in the years after 1930 that an even greater responsibility devolved upon the old man. As long as parliamentary government functioned in Germany, the role of the *Reichspräsident* in policy making was merely a supporting one. Only with Brüning's formation of a cabinet that was to derive its authority from the president and with the incapacitation of the parliament as a result of the September elections of 1930 did the president become the pivotal political figure in Germany. He was not equal to this task and with progressive senility relied still more heavily on the advice of his personal friends. Since he did not believe in democracy and considered the constitution as nothing but a set of formal rules, he ended by handing over the Weimar Republic to its gravediggers.

In the beginning Hindenburg's cautious acceptance of the policies of the Luther cabinet tended to stabilize the conditions of the Republic. In one field only was a change felt immediately. The function of commander in chief that the constitution gave the president was bound to produce a close relationship between the head of the state and the armed forces. Seeckt, who was bitterly disappointed that he had not been chosen as a candidate for the presidency, saw himself automatically deposed as the first soldier in the state. Moreover, Hindenburg was rather cool toward Seeckt, who had not enjoyed Hindenburg's and Ludendorff's full confidence during World War I. Hindenburg, who valued modesty and simplicity of character and manners, took exception to Seeckt's haughtiness and presumptuousness. In 1926 Seeckt's permission to let Prince William, the eldest son of the crown prince, serve as a "temporary volunteer" at army maneuvers, caused Defense Minister Gessler, who for a long time had suffered from Seeckt's autocratic manners, to request the resignation of the colonel general. Hindenburg raised no objections, and General Heye (1869–1946), who had served on his staff in World War I, was made army chief. Less than a year later Gessler resigned. Twenty million marks had been lost, since an officer of the defense ministry had speculated with some of the hidden military funds. Hindenburg picked General Groener, who had been his chief of staff in 1918–19, as Gessler's successor. He trusted his military as well as his political judgment.

Hindenburg took a special interest in foreign policy. Although he was not on intimate terms with Stresemann, he supported his foreign policy quite consistently. When Hindenburg became president, Stresemann was in the midst of difficult negotiations. The end of the Ruhr struggle had brought back the Allied Military Control Commission, which reported that in many respects Germany had not lived up to the disarmament provisions. Germany was then informed that the first occupation zone, the Cologne-Bonn area, would not be evacuated on January 10, 1925, as would have been possible under the treaty. Stresemann rightly judged that the French would not leave the Rhineland unless they received additional guarantees of their security. They still looked for an arrangement that could take the place of the guarantee pacts negotiated with the United States and Britain at the Paris Peace Conference, pacts which had become defunct when the United States rejected any partnership in Europe.

৵ Locarno Treaties

DURING THE YEAR OF 1924 there had been hope that the security problem would be solved on a universal plane. In early October the League of Nations had proposed to close the gap in its covenant that made war still possible. The Geneva Protocol, drafted for this purpose, planned to make arbitration obligatory and at the same time the test of aggression. A state which refused arbitration or an arbitration award was automatically branded an aggressor against whom all League members were pledged to mutual support. But in England Prime Minister Ramsay MacDonald's Labor cabinet, which had helped to fashion the Protocol, was superseded in November by the Conservative government of Stanley Baldwin (1867–1947). The Conservatives were not willing to make the far-reaching commitments demanded by the Protocol, and they were not unhappy that the opposition of the British dominions to the Protocol gave them grounds to reject it. Since then Britain and France had resumed bilateral conversations on a guarantee pact, which were followed by Berlin with some apprehension as aiming at the revival of the Anglo-French Entente. In February Stresemann offered a German commitment to respect the western frontier as defined by the Versailles Treaty and suggested that the great powers should guarantee the inviolability of the French, Belgian, and German borderlands.

The British foreign secretary, Austen Chamberlain (1863–1937), was originally not attracted by the German proposal and only during the summer was the plan seriously taken up as a substitute for the Anglo-French guarantee pact of 1919 and for the guarantee of Belgian neutrality, which had not been restored in 1919. France demanded that

Germany should renounce revisionist claims in the east as well, but since the British were anxious to avoid any entanglements there, Stresemann was able to confine the German guarantee to the west. Here he accepted not only the frontiers but also the demilitarization of the Rhineland, whereas in the east he consented to no more than the conclusion of arbitration treaties with Poland and Czechoslovakia. Stresemann was willing to accept League membership only on condition that Germany be freed of participation in sanctions which the League might impose under article 16 of its covenant. He wanted to safeguard Germany's relations with Russia by refusing any obligation to fight against her or to have French troops move through Germany. In October 1925 the statesmen of the four big powers as well as of Belgium, Czechoslovakia, and Poland met in Locarno in order to bring the negotiations to a conclusion. Here Stresemann actually succeeded in getting from the members a written statement that in their understanding a League member was expected to participate in sanctions only to the extent compatible with its military conditions and geographical situation. And since Germany had pleaded that in her state of disarmament and considering her central location she was incapable of assuming the risks inherent in sanctions, the declaration practically freed her from any such burdens and thereby allowed her to maintain her special relationship with the Soviet Union that had begun with the Rapallo Treaty.

Britain's desire to keep her commitments to a minimum made these important concessions possible. Sir Austen Chamberlain declared eleven years later that basically the Locarno Treaty had not added to the obligations which England had shouldered before as a member of the League of Nations. Insofar as the nature of any possible future violation and the counteraction to be taken was to be decided upon by the League Council, Chamberlain's statement was essentially correct, although England had at least reaffirmed her strong interest in the Rhine. The treaty made a repetition of the Ruhr invasion or similar French sanction policies impossible. However, France retained the right to take immediate action in case of a "flagrant" violation of the treaty. In order to counter Germany's and Britain's refusal to guarantee the eastern frontiers, France, in addition to the existing alliance with Poland, concluded an alliance with Czechoslovakia.

The Locarno agreements were officially signed in London on December 1, 1925, and were to take effect as soon as Germany would have become a member of the League. But unexpected opposition arose in Geneva not so much to Germany's admission to the League but rather to the changed complexion of the League Council as the result of the creation of an additional permanent seat. Brazil wanted such a seat, and Poland was unhappy to be ranked among the small nations, which were represented on the council for only a year at a time, separated by long intervals. During the summer of 1926 a reform of the League Council was worked out in tedious international negotiations. The representation of the small nations was augmented and reelection after a year no longer excluded. At the fall meeting Germany entered the League as a permanent member of the League Council.

While the delay of Germany's arrival in Geneva enhanced the international applause that greeted her entrance into the League, it aroused suspicion and ill feeling in Germany, where wide circles thought of it as the club of the victors of 1919 for the permanent defense of the international status quo. German public opinion was little impressed by the withdrawal of all Allied troops from the right bank of the Rhine in the summer of 1925, which was followed in December by the military evacuation of the first occupation zone on the left bank, the Cologne-Bonn area. Most Germans believed that Germany had a good right to demand greater revisions.

✑ Berlin Treaty

WITH THE LEAGUE ACTION lagging, the Russo-German negotiations came to fruition ahead of the Locarno Treaty. The Soviet Union had been alarmed by Germany's accommodation to France and Britain. The Soviet government was obsessed with the belief that Britain was building an alliance hostile to Russia. In the eyes of the Soviets the League was the main instrumentality of the imperalist powers for the strangulation of the Soviet Union. Russian Foreign Minister Chicherin came to Berlin on the eve of the departure of the German delegation to the Locarno Conference. The German ambassador to Russia, Count Brockdorff-Rantzau, too, made great efforts to keep Germany from joining the League. Stresemann was prepared to give the Russians full assurance that the Locarno policy was not a break with the Rapallo policy.

A treaty was drafted which stated that the Rapallo Treaty would remain the basis of Russo-German relations and that the two governments would maintain friendly contacts with a view to finding an understanding of all political and economic questions of common interest. It was further stipulated that either power would stay neutral in case of an unprovoked attack of one or more powers on one of them and not participate in an economic boycott in this event. The treaty was accompanied by an exchange of notes in which Germany went rather far in emphasizing that the interpretation of article 16 she had received from the members of the Locarno Conference made it unlikely that she would ever participate in League sanctions. Moreover Germany, as a permanent member of the

League Council, would be in a position to keep it from an unjustifiable denunciation of the Soviet Union as an aggressor.

The treaty was signed by Stresemann and Chicherin in Berlin on April 24, 1926. Stresemann had taken great care that Britain and France were well informed beforehand. Implicitly the two western powers had already recognized the special nature of Germany's relations with Russia in the Locarno agreements. It has often been asserted that through the Treaty of Berlin Germany won an independent position between East and West, but this was not the case. As long as the Rhineland was occupied, even as long as it remained demilitarized and France and Britain determined to maintain this demilitarization, Germany was dependent upon the West. All she had won was some elbowroom in the conduct of her future foreign policy by safeguarding her claims for a revision of the German-Polish frontier. Unlike Seeckt, Stresemann hoped that such a revision might be accomplished, if with some pressure, by peaceful means.

Looking back over the last forty years of German history the critical observer may raise the question whether German foreign policy ought not to have done everything in its power to achieve a reconciliation of the German and Polish peoples. Germany could have offered the Poles great assistance in the building of modern national institutions and industries. Her aim should have been to make the frontiers invisible rather than to revise them. If a strong cooperative relationship between Germany and Poland could have been established, the main achievement of German arms in World War I, the removal of Russia from historic Europe, might not have remained an episode.

But most of the conditions necessary for a genuinely friendly policy did not exist in the Germany of the 1920's. Most Germans were utterly contemptuous of the Poles as a lower breed of men incapable of higher civilization and orderly government. After they had already angrily reacted to the social advancement of the Polish element in the eastern provinces of Prussia before 1918, they responded with hatred to the founding of the new Polish state, which drove numerous Germans from the east, separated Danzig from the Empire, and, through the creation of the corridor, severed East Prussia from Germany. Moreover Poland was the eastern ally with whom France kept Germany encircled. It is only fair to point out that the Poles, on their part, considerably overrating their own strength and proud of having won their national freedom after 150 years of foreign thralldom, were not making it easy for their neighbors to conduct a policy of conciliation. To be sure, no German statesman of that period could have afforded to aim at German-Polish amity, but it was tragic that none even worried about the potential consequences of the bitter hostility between Germans and Poles.

The Locarno Treaties, the Treaty of Berlin, and Germany's entrance into the League were the great successes which gained Stresemann world renown. But the respect which he thus recovered for Germany was not enough for his own people. To his dismay he had not succeeded in getting the Locarno Treaties adopted by the right in parliament. Although the three ministers from the German Nationalist party had given their assent to the treaties in the cabinet meetings, the German Nationalist members of the *Reichstag* were caught by the radical agitation which they had unloosed in the country against the League and any compromise with the former enemies. The party voted against the government. Since the Social Democrats supported Stresemann's foreign policy then and later, this nationalist vote did not affect the fate of the Locarno Treaties. But the government was left in 1926 without a clear majority and, even worse, the German Nationalists were again at liberty to spread their poisonous propaganda against its foreign policy.

ᢍ *Stresemann and Briand*

STRESEMANN HIMSELF was suffering severely from these attacks, because he was not satisfied with the results of his diplomacy. He had hoped that the Locarno Treaties would lead to important concessions from France. As a matter of fact, he established mutually trusting relations with Aristide Briand (1862–1932), the French foreign minister. At the end of the League convention of 1926 the two men had an intimate private meeting at Thoiry and together undertook a political *tour d'horizon* in which the possibility of a settlement of all Franco-German questions of conflict was discussed. Stresemann, who urged the early removal of the occupation forces from the Rhineland and the quick return of the Saar district, gained the impression that Briand was responsive. The latter actually was anxious to further the cause of Franco-German amity but gravely handicapped by the attitude of the French right. At the time of Thoiry, Poincaré was trying to stabilize the French franc, and in this connection the suggestion had been made to mobilize the 16-billion-mark industrial and railroad obligations which Germany had deposited under the Dawes plan. Stresemann was prepared to agree to this proposal if the French would give up the occupation of the Rhineland. But Poincaré managed to stabilize the franc without German assistance, thereby reserving the right to make the disestablishment of the Rhineland occupation dependent on a final general settlement of reparations. Thus, the high hopes which Thoiry had raised proved fallacious.

Briand made a good many concessions in the following years, but none of them was impressive enough to change the sullen attitude of most

Germans toward the French. On the other side the activity and speeches of the belligerent German right added fuel all the time to the resistance in France against a generous policy with regard to Germany. Naturally the lack of appreciation of favors granted to Germany discouraged at times not only the French but also the British. But Stresemann wrested concessions from France and England. At the end of 1926 agreements were reached which abolished all the special ordinances issued in the Rhineland at the time of the Ruhr invasion. An amnesty was declared for past violations and the jurisdiction of military courts strictly limited. In early 1927 the Inter-Allied Disarmament Commission was abolished, later in the year the number of occupation forces in the Rhineland was substantially curtailed, and the French troops in the Saar were withdrawn altogether.

CHAPTER 11

The Weimar Republic, 1926–33

∽ *Parties and Government*

ALTHOUGH TO THE GREAT MAJORITY of the people the revision of the Versailles Treaty moved much too slowly, the Dawes Plan and the Locarno Treaties ushered in years of internal consolidation. After the unrest, violence, and privations of the war and postwar period the years 1926–30 appeared as the golden years of the Weimar Republic. Still, many grave problems remained. The political parties even in these years failed to develop the readiness for compromise sufficient to make energetic and reasonably steady governmental policies possible. The governments were usually formed with interminable delays caused by the horse-trading of the parties, and all of them were of short duration. We mentioned before that the German Nationalists withdrew from the Luther government in November 1925 because their party refused to accept the Locarno Treaties. From January till May 1926 Luther headed a cabinet of the middle parties, which continued in office under Wilhelm Marx when Luther resigned after irritating the republicans quite unnecessarily by issuing an administrative order that seemed to impair black, red, and gold as the official German colors. A man of greater political sensitivity would not have stumbled over such an issue.

Marx ruled with Luther's cabinet to the end of 1926. In parliament the government found the support of the Social Democrats for Stresemann's foreign policy. But in its internal policies it depended more often on the German Nationalists. The greatest public conflict developed over the properties of the former ruling dynasties. For once the Social Democrats joined with the Communists in a popular referendum for a law expropriating the possessions of the princes. The final plebiscite brought 15.5 million people to the polls, 1 million more than had voted for Hindenburg in the year before and 5 million more than had voted for the Social Democratic and Communist parties at the last parliamentary elections. It was a clear sign that monarchistic sentiment was at a low ebb in Germany and also a warning that large groups had not forgotten the losses which they had suffered through the inflation. They revolted against the princely demands for revaluation of those assets that had shrunk or disappeared in the inflation.

In order to base the government on a clear majority, Marx in January 1927 formed his fourth government, which included four German Nationalists as ministers. Their party recognized the "legal validity" of the Weimar Constitution and received in return from its coalition partners the assurance that the past and its symbols should also be respected. The party even supported the renewal of the law for the protection of the republic, a law to be sure that, owing to the attitude of the German jurists, was no longer feared by rightists in 1927.[1] The German Nationalists also accepted Stresemann's direction of foreign policy. The coalition operated, however, chiefly on a parliamentary level. The local and provincial organizations of the German Nationalist party continued their opposition to the republic in no uncertain terms. Worst of all, the many newspapers, the newsreels, and the press service owned by Alfred Hugenberg held up their vitriolic attacks against the leaders of the republic.

The period of the fourth Marx government not only deepened the internal tensions of the German Nationalist party but also threw the Center party into disarray. The political alliance with the German Nationalists chafed the democratic elements in the Center party, some of whom even were members of republican organizations such as the *Reichsbanner* Black, Red, and Gold. The mass following of the Christian trade unions was greatly suspicious of the course the Center leaders steered. Former Chancellor Joseph Wirth angrily left the party, to which he returned, however, a year later. When the finance minister, Heinrich Köhler (1878–1949), introduced legislation raising the salaries of the civil servants, serious verbal clashes occurred within the parliamentary delegation between the strong trade unionist wing and the civil servant group. Even the common bond of the Roman Catholic religion that so far had always integrated the party failed to stop the altercations this time.

✍ School Problem

IT WAS LOGICAL that the leaders tried to emphasize common Catholic aims which in the eyes of all party members might justify the cooperation with the German Nationalists. Naturally, education and state-church relations were the bedrock of such policies. It may be remembered that the Weimar Constitution had authorized the federal legislature to issue laws defining the basic nature of the schools.[2] Under the constitution the

[1] See p. 603.
[2] See p. 552.

school attended by children of all denominations where religious instruction was given separately was the normal type (*Simultanschule*). But parents could also apply for the establishment of schools for single denominations (*Konfessionsschule*) or, as a concession to the Social Democrats, of schools without religious teaching (*weltliche Schule*), provided there were enough pupils.

Attempts to implement the school articles of the constitution had been made in the years after 1919 but failed because the churches on the one side and the liberals on the other could not agree on the influence that the churches might exercise on the schools. The Catholic bishops were discontented with the Center party because it had concluded a compromise on schools with the liberals, which in the opinion of most bishops was extremely dangerous. They were afraid of the Social Democrats who to them were nothing but atheists. As late as 1918 they had admonished Chancellor Hertling and the Prussian deputies of the Center party not to grant universal suffrage in Prussia. About the cooperation between the Center and the Social Democratic parties after 1919 these bishops felt strong misgivings and never went so far as to endorse the Center and the Bavarian People's parties as the exclusive political representation of Catholicism. In the presidential election of 1925 the bishops were anxious not to appear as official supporters of Wilhelm Marx who had to rely so heavily on Social Democratic votes. Once the Center had entered into a coalition with parties on the right, however, it was eager to advance the cause closest to the heart of the bishops and the devout Roman Catholics. Thus a school law to be followed by a concordat became a major aim of the Center party.

The German Nationalists were equally anxious to extend the influence of the churches in education. At least in North Germany and Bavaria the Protestant church governments looked to the German Nationalist party as their champion in the political arena. Likewise, most of the practicing church members gave their vote to this party, which in addition contained a small but vocal and active Catholic group. Both the German People's and the Democratic parties were more solidly Protestant than the German Nationalist party, but, at least outside of Württemberg and apart from a few liberal theologians, most of their members and voters were religiously indifferent and anticlerical.

The school law was prepared by the minister of interior, Walter von Keudell (1884–1953), a German Nationalist. It passed the cabinet in July 1927. Stresemann and Curtius, the two ministers of the German People's party, indicated, however, that they did not commit their party by their vote. A long drawn-out struggle in parliament followed. The law which would have given the denominational school the same status that the interdenominational school possessed under the constitution caused great public commotion. In cultural questions the German People's party was more reliably liberal than in general political decisions. Thus it demanded changes of the draft law within the government, while the Social Democrats and Democrats conducted a strong oppositional campaign in the *Reichstag* and the country. The Center and the Bavarian People's parties, together with the antirepublican German Nationalists, fought over an issue that the Weimar Constitution had settled. It is noteworthy that the ardor for Catholic education could swerve the Center party rather far from a moderate course. By the middle of February 1928 the government coalition was declared broken. Although the Marx government remained in office until July, elections were held on May 20, 1928.

The elections strengthened the left, particularly the Social Democrats, who, with 22 additional members, received 153 seats. The Communists, too, gained by electing 54 deputies. On the other side, the German Nationalists lost 30 seats, about one third of their former strength. Even the National Socialists were reduced from 14 to 12 deputies. But the parties in the middle also suffered losses. The relative strength of the Democratic party declined only a little more than that of the German People's party. This decline was to accelerate in subsequent elections, whereas the Center party later on made up for the rough buffeting it took in 1928. On the same day elections were held for the Prussian parliament. Their results were generally the same with a severe setback for the German Nationalists, the weakening of the middle, and a considerable strengthening of the Social Democratic party. In Prussia, however, the Weimar coalition won a majority which, though small, enabled Otto Braun to continue his republican regime for another four years.

∽ Müller Cabinet, 1928

IN THE NEW *Reichstag* the Weimar parties did not command a majority. Only the "great coalition" that added the German People's party to them afforded a safe basis for a government. But the endless negotiations of the party chiefs were not a good omen for the solidity of such an alliance, although the political conditions were now more favorable than in 1923. None of the parties was overly anxious to assume governmental responsibilities. The Social Democrats felt that their opposition of the last four years had paid off handsomely in the elections and wondered whether it would not be advantageous for the party to remain outside the government. The Center was chagrined by its losses and not attracted by the idea of forming a government with the three parties that had just brought to naught its cherished plan for a school law. The German People's party did not wish to see the Social Democrats in too powerful a position and at first refused to join them in a federal government unless Otto Braun would accept one of their members into his Prussian cabinet. Stresemann in the end practically forced his German People's party to become a partner in the great coalition. The Center party was equally reluctant and originally delegated only a single minister.

The difficulties encountered in the formation of the government of which the leader of the Social Democratic party, Hermann Müller, became chancellor were a warning of how unwieldy the German party system was and how weak in transforming social interests into a common political will. Actually, in the elections of 1928 many votes had gone to organizations which did not even pretend to general political aims beyond the presentation of the economic interests of certain social groups, such as landowners or peasants. The strongest of these organizations, which in 1928 managed to send more deputies into the parliament than the Democratic party, called itself the Economy Party of the German Middle Class. It appealed chiefly to those variegated lower-middle-class people who felt victimized by the inflation. All these organizations, which, though cultivating nationalism, concentrated on materialistic ends, led their followers away from traditional liberalism and conservatism. Soon they were to become the dupes of the radical antiliberal and anticonservative nationalism of the Nazis.

Yet at the moment when the Müller government was installed, few people noticed the clouds at the horizon. Although German agriculture showed some weakness, the overall state of the German economy was still strong, and the election victory of the republican forces indicated at least that the majority of the German people wanted internal and external peace. The government was composed of a number of talented and politically experienced men. The Social Democrats were represented by Carl Severing, who had proven his mettle in Prussia, as minister of interior, by the competent Rudolf Wissel as minister of labor, and by Rudolf Hilferding, the best theoretical mind if not the most successful practical statesman of the party, as minister of finance. Together with Foreign Minister Stresemann the German People's party sent Julius Curtius (1877–1948) as minister of economics in the cabinet. He was the right man for this post and also a most loyal supporter of Stresemann. When after the latter's death he moved into the foreign office, he was less effective. A key figure of the cabinet was General Groener, who stayed on in the ministry of defense, which he had taken over after Gessler's resignation half a year earlier. More than any other man in this government, Groener had the ear and the confidence of President Hindenburg. Although Groener demanded the support of the government even for some projects of the defense department that the Social Democrats greatly disliked, he was, at least in the first year, fully cooperative in strengthening the unity of the cabinet and winning Hindenburg's backing for its policies.

Hindenburg came to like Müller, whom he is reported as having called the best chancellor he had to deal with so far. Hermann Müller was an earnest, diligent, and loyal man, but he lacked lively imagination and was not an inspiring leader. When he died in 1931, the workers of Berlin lined the streets and sadly watched the funeral cortege, sensing that Müller had been their genuine friend to the end. But while he commanded wide popular respect in the party, he was not able to impose his will on its functionaries. He might have struggled harder with them if he had not undergone serious surgery in 1929. The lack of support the Social Democratic party gave its own ministers came into the open almost immediately after the new government had begun its work.

As early as 1927 the defense ministry had prevailed on the Marx government to provide in its draft budget for 1928 the first installment of funds with which to build the first of the six small battleships allowed under the Versailles Treaty. But largely for fiscal reasons the Federal Council had stopped this action. The issue had played a role during the election campaign. While on the one side it was argued that all the possibilities left for German armaments should be fully used, the Social Democrats and Communists on the other clamored that the government was wasting the people's money on battleships instead of spending it for the needed free meals for school children. The Müller cabinet then voted in August before the parliament had been convened to restore the funds. The Social Democratic members concurred in order to stave off the breakup of the government. Yet the party bolted. Eventually it brought in a resolution canceling the appropriation and making a supporting vote mandatory for all party members. It was grotesque to force the chancellor and the ministers to vote against a measure which they had officially endorsed. Moreover battleship "A" was built just the same.

The Müller government was incapable of undertaking any important internal reform, since it would have shaken the precarious balance of social forces on which the coalition rested. It concentrated on foreign policy, which, however, through the reparations question was closely related to public finance. With the approach of the world economic crisis all the unresolved social problems could no longer remain covered up. In 1928 the recovery of the German economy had reached its highest peak both with regard to the number of gainfully employed and to national income. But at the end of the year there were signs of contraction, although nobody could have predicted that this was the beginning of the most catastrophic economic collapse.

✑ Revival of Economy

WITH SURPRISING SPEED economic activity had revived after the currency stabilization and the signing of the Dawes Plan in 1924. The renewal of German industries was largely made possible by the flow of foreign, chiefly American, loans into Germany. Altogether 20 billion marks were lent to Germany between 1924 and 1930, mostly before 1928. Germany on her part had foreign holdings of 5 billion marks. It should not be thought that Germany did not use capital of her own for the rebuilding of her economy. Actually twice as much German capital as the sum total of foreign credits was spent on new investments alone, and almost five times as much for all investments together. But it is clear that the strong momentum of German recovery was produced by the influx of foreign loans.

It has often been said that Germany acted irresponsibly by relying so heavily on the import of foreign capital for its economic modernization. But it was only natural that a country as poor in capital as Germany would borrow from the country that had become the chief creditor nation as a result of the war. What was objectionable was the easygoing manner in which these loans were used. Most of them were short-term credits which were employed by the German recipients for long-term purposes. The chief offenders were the big German banks. Yet cities and other public bodies, which received about one fifth of the foreign funds, used them not only for long-term purposes but also often for financially unproductive projects such as schools, hospitals, or sports fields. The *Reichsbank* created an advisory committee for municipal loans, but otherwise Schacht could only issue occasional warnings which were of no avail.

The revival of business activity had been rapid after July 1924. But prices were overly high after the inflation, and the business structure was not adjusted to the new conditions which a decade of war and inflation had created in Germany and in foreign markets. In the fall of 1925 a serious recession set in. A heavy wave of business failures, among which the most spectacular was the breakup of the empire of Hugo Stinnes, the Ruhr industrialist who had died in 1924, lasted for many months. During the winter of 1925–26 unemployment soared to 2 million, while close to another 2 million worked short hours. Practically one out of two workers was affected by the crisis. The recession purged the economy of many unprofitable enterprises, but it also favored the bigger companies over the smaller and weaker ones. Moreover the big producers got together to eliminate competition and hold the price level. Additional cartels were created and new combines formed. The greatest combines founded in

1926 were the dyestuff trust, *I.G. Farben,* and the steel trust, *Vereinigte Stahlwerke.* New centers of economic and political power were thereby founded.

The depression was overcome by the widespread introduction of modern machines and production methods, learned chiefly from America. The Germans called it the "rationalization" of industries. The efficiency and potential productivity of industries were greatly enhanced, although fewer workers were required and this at a time when the number of people seeking employment greatly increased. By restoring new vitality to the depressed German mining industry, the British coal strike of 1926 contributed to the new upswing of production. The years 1927 and 1928 were prosperous years in Germany. But already in the second half of 1928 the American credits came only haltingly, soon to cease completely. The technical achievements of the German industrialists in the years after 1924 were remarkable. In 1927 national production for the first time reached the level of 1913. Foreign trade, too, approached prewar figures, though nominally rather than according to real value. And until 1929 imports exceeded exports.

Agriculture had its own problems. The revolution of 1918–19 failed to make any structural changes as they took place in the Baltic states, Poland, Czechoslovakia, and Rumania. In Germany itself the republic later bought parcels of land from the big estates and settled farmers on them. The resettlement activities were extensive, and by 1931 about one ninth of the cultivated land was in the hands of new farm settlers. But the result did not decisively change the traditional organization of German agriculture. In particular the big *Junker* estates of eastern Germany survived and, as producers of rye, were especially sensitive to the fluctuations of the world market. In 1925, when Germany had become full master of her foreign economic policies again, the fateful step to impose import duties on agricultural commodities was taken, which constituted a lien on the German standard of living.

The productive capacity of agriculture was greatly enhanced by better management methods, electrification, fuller use of fertilizers, and a beginning mechanization. In 1928 agriculture again achieved the high output of the last years before the war and did even better in the years till 1933. But while agriculture had emerged from the inflation free of debts, in a few years it ran up a large burden of fresh debts and became gravely susceptible to crisis. In the class of the big landowners who still dominated the powerful agrarian professional and pressure organizations, which in 1929 had all been brought together in the "Green Front," the arch enemies of the republic were most numerous. But they did not hesitate to demand unconditional governmental support against all the woes that befell them.

Their public propaganda was prolific, but persuasion was practiced in high places as well. In this connection it became important that, on his eightieth birthday, the industrialists gave Hindenburg the East Prussian estate that had once been owned by the Hindenburg family. It is amazing that the president agreed to having the estate officially listed under the name of his son, thus avoiding the inheritance tax. In any event, Hindenburg now became the immediate neighbor of other *Junkers* and listened to their ideas and complaints.

✎ Social Problems

A GREAT INCREASE OCCURRED in the number of people active in trade. As early as 1907, 334 out of every 10,000 people had been in trade; in 1925, 420; and in 1933, almost 540. Obviously in this sector an unhealthy overcrowding was taking place that was bound to raise the cost of distribution to undesirable heights. The inflation drove a good many *rentiers* into the retail business. Later on numerous employees who had lost their jobs tried to eke out a living as storekeepers. A relatively large social group of economically insecure people still grew to the end of the Weimar Republic, although in the same period modern cost-saving devices of distribution were spreading.

The total civilian work force multiplied from 25 million in 1907 to 32 million in 1925, a clear indication of the losses of the war and inflation as well as of lower incomes. As a result of the war, the employment of women rose very considerably, particularly in industry, which employed 39 per cent of all job holders in 1907 and 42 per cent in 1925. In the area of the new Germany of 1919 the national income, which had been 45 billion marks in 1913, nominally rose to 76.1 in 1929. But with the necessary adjustments for the different purchasing power, the real income of the individual even in the best years, 1928-29, remained 6 per cent less than the prewar income; in 1931 almost 25 per cent; and in 1932 almost 30 per cent.

Normalcy was never quite achieved, and even the period when it appeared close at hand proved only a brief interlude between two disasters. The greatest hardships were suffered by the lower middle classes and the working class. The revolution had brought no improvement of the material conditions of the workers. The greatest change was not the result of the revolution but of the modern machines. While the number of employees increased, skilled labor declined, since its place was frequently taken by labor trained on the job. The wage differences between unskilled and skilled workers became smaller than they had been before the war. A great gain that the revolution had introduced, the eight-hour day, was lost at the close of the inflation. The extension of working hours, which was imposed on poorly nourished and poorly paid workers, leveled off until 1928. The economic depression of 1930 tended to make the forty-eight hour week in practice the maximum time.

The shop councils which the Weimar Assembly had legalized proved a valuable instrument for easing the social relations within the factories. They remained, however, totally ineffective in the ill-defined functions which the law of 1920 gave the council for participation in business policies. Of fundamental importance was the decree issued by the government in 1923 regulating the mediation of labor conflicts. The act recognized as valid all contracts that were the result of the free bargaining between employers and trade unions. Only in difficult cases would a state mediator join the bargaining. If he did not succeed in making the parties agree, he was supposed to propose a contract which would become binding on both parties if one of them accepted the offered contract. The mediator was admonished to act with reason and fairness, but in practice this would mean that the solution he proposed would be in line with the general economic policy of the government. Wages inevitably became political wages, and thereby prices became political prices as well. Considering that the over 2,500 cartels by their agreements removed the price structure far from the free interplay of economic forces, the labor mediation system of the Weimar Republic made this structure even more artificial. Moreover it exposed the republic to attacks from all sides. The trade unions could always blame an unsatisfactory contract on the "reactionary" attitude of the government, while the employers could accuse the government of cutting short prosperity by raising wages too much or, in adversity, of keeping wages on too high a level to allow for the necessary adjustments. While the labor mediation system had been designed to bring employers and workers into peaceful interrelations, its main result was to make the government the master of all labor relations. This inevitably weakened the belief of the members in the practical value of their trade unions.

The most terrifying experience of the German workers was mass unemployment. It had first appeared in 1919 but was quickly overcome and did not reappear until the end of the inflation. During the winter of 1923–24 the number of unemployed rose to 1.5 million but receded in the summer of 1924 to 400,000 and in 1925 to 200,000. Yet in the winter of 1925–26 unemployment jumped to over 2 million and fell in the summer of 1927 to only about .5 million. The winter of 1927–28, with 1.5 million unemployed, was somewhat better than the winter before, but the number declined in the summer of 1928 to only .75 million. The icy winter of 1928–29 saw 2.6 million unemployed, while the low in the following summer was 1.5 million. In the winter of 1929–30 the dreaded figure passed the 3 million mark. It decreased not even by half a million, and this only briefly. Before the summer of 1930 was over, the tide rose disastrously to almost 5 million. In January 1932 and again in January 1933 there were over 6 million unemployed. Even if we consider the history of the years 1923–30 before the big avalanche started, the incidence of unemployment was sufficiently great to keep the workers poignantly reminded of the insecurity of their existence.

It was seen that the case for the unemployed had to be assumed by the state. After the war Germany had used various forms of dole. But the unemployment of 1923–24 induced the minister of labor, Heinrich Brauns, to propose a permanent institution to deal with employment and unemployment. With the exception of the National Socialists and Communists, all parties worked together on the project in rare harmony. The law of July 16, 1927, created a Reich institute for unemployment insurance and labor exchange. The insurance was to provide for the unemployed over the maximum period of half a year. It was to be financed by contributions of workers and employers, both amounting to 3 per cent of the wages. The government was not expected to support the insurance except by loans in times of stress. The regular contributions were designed to build up a fund sufficient to sustain 600,000 unemployed for three months. Yet in the economic depression which soon thereafter enveloped Germany, the unemployment insurance proved hopelessly inadequate. Moreover, since in millions of cases unemployment extended over more than six months, the unemployed soon again depended chiefly on the dole which the municipal welfare agencies distributed.

✍ From Dawes to Young Plan

THUS EVEN THE SEEMINGLY "normal" years showed many dark spots and warning signs. The greatest uncertainty remained the problem of reparations. Technically the Dawes Plan functioned extremely well. While it was operative, Germany, without visible difficulties, paid her indemnities, and the American reparations agent, Parker Gilbert, was able to transfer the German marks into foreign currency and pay the creditors. But in the absence of a favorable trade balance this was possible only because the German balance of payments was favorable, owing to the influx of foreign loans and credits. Actually Germany paid reparations by incurring a growing foreign indebtedness. Although the authors of the Dawes Plan had been aware of the fact that the German economy could not be rebuilt without the import of foreign capital, they had expected that reparations payments would be raised internally through a tax-balanced budget and externally transferred on the strength of a surplus of German exports or foreign services. But the German balance of trade remained passive in the Dawes period and, from 1925 on, the German budget was never fully balanced. Thus Germany's capacity to pay, which the Dawes Plan had been designed to test, was never properly defined.

The Dawes Plan was advantageous for Germany, however. The presence of an American reparations agent in Berlin had encouraged American bankers to lend capital to Germany and probably would have kept them from recalling all the credits in the years after 1930 if the Dawes Plan had not been ended by then. The duty of the agent to stop the transfer of German payments if it endangered the stability of the German currency would also have been of high value in the financial crisis of 1931. On the other hand, the Dawes Plan was only a temporary arrangement and, with the internationalization of the German railroads, the foreign supervision of the *Reichsbank*, and the open critique of German public finance by the reparations agent, introduced foreign controls into the internal life of Germany which to a generation entirely committed to the idea of the independent national state seemed offensive.

Poincaré was not willing to withdraw the French troops from the Rhine until a final reparations settlement had come into existence. It was Stresemann's highest desire to achieve the evacuation of foreign occupation forces. Since in 1927 both he and Curtius believed that Germany was most likely to grow economically stronger, they felt it would be better to have the final reparations debt fixed at an early date. In September 1928 the German government officially raised the demand for a revision of the Dawes Plan. It had been told that Britain would expect reparations as large as her own payments to the United States under the Anglo-American war debt settlement. The French insisted upon receiving in addition to their payments to America a "net indemnity" for the cost of the rebuilding of their war-devastated provinces. They also wanted a substantial part of the German debt made an unconditional obligation since they wished to commercialize their portion of it. With these French and British conditions, of which the German government was aware, little room was left for diplomatic maneuver and financial bargaining. It was clear from the outset that the transfer protection would have to be given up and that the annual German payment would be in the neighborhood of 2 billion marks.

A committee of financial experts was convened in Paris in February 1929. Owen D. Young, who had been a prominent member of the Dawes committee, presided over the long-drawn-out conferences. The president of the *Reichsbank*, Hjalmar Schacht, whose ambition it was to prove that his talent could wrest great concessions from the other side, did not make any notable gains. When he steered closer to the breaking point, the French banks late in April began to recall large amounts of credits from Germany. This move posed a serious threat to German currency and production. The danger was aggravated by the weakness of German public finance, about which more will be heard later. It was under some duress that the German government induced the squirming Schacht to sign the Young Plan on June 7, 1929.

Whereas the Dawes Plan had provided for annual payments rising to 2.5 billion marks for an indefinite time, the Young Plan contained a fifty-nine-year schedule of payments averaging 2.05 billion. The number of years was the same as in the Allied-American war debt settlements. As a matter of fact, the Young Plan envisaged that the German annuities would serve both the Allies and America in the first thirty-seven years and in the last twenty-two years America alone. The plan promised that in case America lowered her claims, the Allies would remit Germany a portion of her reparations debt amounting to two thirds of the sum canceled by the United States. About one third of the German payments were unconditional and could not be deferred. The transfer of the other two thirds could be deferred, though under certain stringent conditions. All German funds would in the future have to come from the general German budget. The foreign control of the German railroad system ceased. In place of the reparations agent the Bank of International Settlements was established. This bank, in which Germany cooperated with the other powers, was supposed to act as the trustee for the German reparations payments.

After the governments had accepted the Young Plan as the basis for discussion, they met at The Hague on August 6–31, 1929. Conflicts between the British and French delayed the deliberations, and in order to reach agreement Germany had to pay part of the price. Although the German concession was not very important, it made a poor impression in Germany, where the Young Plan was under heavy fire from the opposition. But Germany received the pledge that the evacuation of the Allied occupation forces from the Rhineland would begin immediately. The final Hague agreement was not written before January 1930, when a second Hague Conference was held to settle some supplementary matters. The French, understandably alarmed by the reckless agitation against the Young Plan that had broken loose in Germany, came to The Hague with the intention of winning the right of sanctions if a radical German government should renounce the Young Plan. Although the French did not succeed in getting such assurances, Germany again had to make minor economic concessions in order to enable the conference to end with a positive report.

Only after long delay was the Young Plan put into operation. Stresemann, who, though in failing health, had led the German delegation at the first Hague Conference, saw at least the beginning of the Allied evacuation of the Rhineland in September 1929. In the same month he appeared for the last time in Geneva and gave eloquent support to Briand's proposal to enter upon the study of the economic integration of Europe. In the evening of October 2 he wrestled with the delegation of his People's party and persuaded them to continue the government coalition with the Social Democrats. The next morning he died, the last German political leader whose personality reflected the whole spectrum of ideals which German liberalism had cherished since 1848. His death marked the end of a long period of German history, not only the beginning of the end of the Weimar Republic.

✍ *Young Plan Referendum*

AT THE TIME of Stresemann's death the agitation of the radical left and right against the acceptance of the Young Plan had already reached fever pitch. The right was more powerful, because it represented a large section of the socially prominent classes. The German Nationalist party was still the main camp of the dissatisfied opponents of the Weimar Republic. Some of them, however, had felt that their aims could be more easily attained by participation in the government. This course was followed when the party joined the Marx cabinet in 1927. But the party members and sympathizers were dissatisfied with the results of representation in the cabinet. Not only did the radical enemies of the republic in the party grow restive, but also the various interest groups complained. After the elections of May 1928 this led to bitter internal feuding. The losses which the German Nationalists suffered at the polls weakened the position of Count Kuno von Westarp, the conservative leader of the German Nationalist party. Alfred Hugenberg succeeded in grabbing the party chairmanship. He had gained ascendancy through a hold over the local and provincial organizations of the party which the ubiquitous organs of his newspaper chain had given him.

As chairman, Hugenberg began to act as a real boss trying at once to subject to his will the parliamentary delegation, which contained many shades of opinion. Yet he wanted "a bloc and no mush," and this meant that the members of parliament were supposed to adopt his policy of absolute opposition to any dealings with the republic. Although his own political thinking did not place the restoration of monarchy among his primary political aims, he excluded those who had expressed doubts about the monarchy from the party. But more important was the recklessness of his attacks against the government. In July 1929 he, together with the leader of the *Stahlhelm*, Franz Seldte (1882–1947), the chairman of the Pan-German League, Heinrich Class (b. 1868), and Adolf Hitler, formed a national committee that launched a drive for a plebiscite on a law "against the slavery of the German people." The law declared the signing of the Young Plan an act of high treason, for which the chancellor and the ministers, and originally the Reich president as well, were to be sent to prison. The whole text showed the infamous Nazi stamp, and the same foul language dominated the public agitation that the committee unleashed.

A referendum held in September was signed by just over 10 per cent of the voters. This meant that the law had to go to the *Reichstag*, and after it had been rejected there by an overwhelming majority, it became in December the object of a plebiscite, in which 13.8 per cent voted for it. Hugenberg was soundly defeated and had brought the German National-ist party into bad disarray. A fair number of members of parliament had objected to the outrageous article 4 of the law, which threatened the ministers with prison terms. About twenty-one members announced in the *Reichstag* that they would abstain from voting for the article, and a struggle over party discipline ensued. Count Westarp, who was willing to tolerate abstention, found himself in the minority and resigned as floor leader. Ernst Oberfohren (1881–1933), a Hugenberg man, was put in his place. Twelve members withdrew from the party. But they were not a homogeneous group. Some of them formed a Christian-Social group while others went to the Agrarian People's party (*Landvolk*). Gottfried Treviranus (b. 1891), a former naval officer, founded the small "Con-servative People's Union" (*Volkskonservative Vereinigung*), but he was not quite the man to give conservatism a clear and convincing meaning. The secession of the twelve members, followed by similar splits in the land parliaments, thus did not lead to a strong competitive party, particu-larly since the secessionists were lacking the funds and the apparatus for intensive national campaigns. If Count Westarp and his close political friends had gone out of the German Nationalist party together with Treviranus, the secession would have had a wider impact. As it was, he did not leave until six months later.

By then Hugenberg had been able to make the party organization obey his dictates and check the defection of party followers to the moderate right, but he was helplessly watching every second German Nationalist voter turn to the Nazi party. This, however, was his own work. In 1928 the Nazi party had been reduced to a small splinter party, and the Ger-man Nationalist party was the dominant center of opposition to the re-public. Hugenberg's invitation to join him in the referendum against the Young Plan gave Hitler's party, which so far had been considered the lunatic fringe even by antirepublicans, an air of respectability. It also opened important financial sources from among the industrialists. And Hugenberg mistakenly believed that he would profit by vying with the demagoguery of the Nazis. Hitler and his lieutenants could always be shriller, more offensive, and more convincing than the paunchy Hugen-berg in his cutaway coat. The latter thought of Hitler as a useful drummer who would attract the masses while the direction of politics would remain in the hands of those who knew how to rule.

The relatively small official vote for the plebiscite in December 1929 probably gave a wrong picture of the actual shift of political sentiment that was going on in Germany. It was a general movement away from moderation toward a radical emphasis on group interests or, in foreign affairs, a heated nationalism. For a while this change did not find open expression, because many people first wanted to see the evacuation of the Rhineland accomplished, while others wanted to find out to what extent the Young Plan might improve economic conditions.

✑ Discord Within the Government

THE MÜLLER GOVERNMENT proved incapable of formulating a political program that would galvanize the full support of the parties which were represented in the cabinet, let alone have an appeal beyond these parties. The gravest weakness of the "great coalition" lay in the incompatibility of the Social Democratic and the German People's parties. The latter was dominated by the interests of the propertied classes. Half of its parliamentary members were directly or indirectly connected with industry and resentful of the ties with the Social Democrats. As early as 1928 the industrialists of the Rhine and Ruhr tried to win back the freedom to set wage rates by defying the wage settlement that a state mediator had imposed on the industry. Their action led to great suffering among the 250,000 locked-out workers. Carl Severing, the minister of the interior, eventually worked out a compromise.

But the industrialists remained hostile to the labor law that the republic had created and were equally hostile to its social policy. As the economic conditions worsened and disaster finally struck, their pressure on the People's party intensified. Stresemann managed to keep his party from insisting on policies that would have broken up the government. But after his death policies of naked class interest became dominant. On the other side, the members of the Social Democratic party, more than a third of whom were trade union leaders, clung to the defense of workers' rights and benefits, and the growth of mass unemployment enhanced their concentration on these aims.

Tension already rose when Finance Minister Hilferding presented the budget for 1929–30 for the budget year in Germany starting on April 1. It was a budget that successfully strove to abolish the deficits and chiefly used indirect taxes to accomplish this end. Although the proposed budget was approved by the cabinet and the Federal Council, the entrepreneurial organizations (*Arbeitgeberverbände*) agitated against any new taxes and instead demanded drastic cuts of expenditures, particularly those for social purposes. In spite of its representation in the cabinet, the German People's party pressed equally hard for a budget without new taxes. A committee of the parties of the great coalition then began to examine the budget for savings and emerged with spurious estimates which appeared to make only a slight tax raise necessary. For shrinking revenues and the mounting cost of unemployment this budget made no provisions at all. Not even the hope that the Young Plan would mean lesser public expenditures could justify the passing of this budget by the *Reichstag*.

In the summer of 1929 the People's party opened its attacks against further federal contributions to the unemployment insurance program, asserting that it was an ill-conceived institution beset by many abuses. All through the summer the coalition parties struggled hard to find a compromise. While this proved not too difficult between the Social Democratic, the Democratic, and the Center parties, the People's party remained obstinate. The government proposed the abolition of some abuses and the increase of the contributions of workers and employers from 3 to 3.5 per cent. A law correcting certain abuses, which however resulted in only small savings, was before parliament in late September, but even this the People's party would have rejected if Stresemann had not intervened for the last time and persuaded the parliamentary delegation to abstain from voting, thus saving the law and the government.

Yet the federal budget remained in a rickety state. The minister of finance was forced again and again to take up loans, the service of which became an additional lien on the budget. He also laid himself open to the criticism of the *Reichsbank* president, Hjalmar Schacht, who had played a prominent part in drafting the original Young Plan. It was understandable that he felt uneasy about the soundness and practicability of the plan. But he was at the same time an ambitious man who wanted to stay in the limelight of history. Although he kept away from the agitation for the plebiscite against the Young Plan, his vituperative critique of the financial policies of the government was of assistance to Hugenberg and Hitler. On December 6, 1929, he gave the press a memorandum in which he accused the government of having made unnecessary concessions at the Hague Conference. Before the Young Plan could be accepted, he declared, it was imperative to put the public finances in order and make the tax burden bearable for an economy threatened in its productivity.

The government, publicly censured by the head of the national bank, now seemed to act in response to outside pressure when it presented a financial program immediately after Schacht's blast. Although this popular impression was not correct, it is true that the internally-divided government acted too late. The program which it presented to the parliament cut direct taxes and made up for this by raising taxes on consumer goods. But it again proposed raising the contributions to the unemployment insurance program from 3 to 3.5 per cent. The chances for the parliamentary approval of this program would have been more than doubtful if the coalition parties had not wished to get the revision of the Dawes Plan accomplished and to send properly authorized ministers to the forthcoming second Hague Conference. But one third of the members of the German People's party openly voted against the government, while one sixth of the Social Democratic deputies were conspicuous by their absence, and the Bavarian People's party abstained from voting altogether when the government received a final vote of confidence. Only a few practical steps were immediately taken, among them the proposed increase in the contribution to the unemployment insurance program.

But when the finance ministry attempted to get a loan to tide it over the year's end, Schacht refused his cooperation unless the government established at once an amortization fund for the large outstanding loan debt. The government gave in to Schacht's ultimatum. Hilferding, who had never liked to take recourse to borrowing but had not been able to prevail on the People's party to accept his budget proposals, resigned as minister of finance. He had lost support within his own party, many members of which considered him too conciliatory toward the other parties. But more clearly than many of his fellow Social Democrats Hilferding recognized the value of democracy for the defense of workers' rights. Therefore he felt it necessary that the Social Democratic party should make the concessions needed for making democracy work.

Hilferding's place was taken by Professor Paul Moldenhauer (1876–1947), a member of the German People's party. After his return from The Hague he had to give his immediate attention not only to the final passage of the Young Plan by the federal parliament but also to the reform of federal finances. As a matter of fact, the Center party made the latter a prerequisite of the former. Much had changed in the Center party since 1928. The liberal raise of the salaries of government officials that Heinrich Köhler, the Center minister of finance in the last Marx government, had granted had caused internal strife of an intensity never before experienced in the history of the party. In order to restore unity the members of the party elected for the first time a priest, the prelate Dr. Ludwig Kaas (1881–1952), chairman. He had been close to the papal nuncio, Eugenio Pacelli, who in 1930 went from Berlin to Rome to become papal secretary of state. Kaas was a conservative who inevitably laid special emphasis on the realization of the ideal aims of the church, and, as the attempts for a school law had shown again, the Center could hope for allies only on the right. In December 1929 Dr. Heinrich Brüning (b. 1885) became the floor leader of the Center party in parliament, and although he did his best as an intermediary between the parties to hold the "great coalition" together, he hoped for a reform of the German government in which the conservative forces of the right were to be mobilized. Brüning maintained close contacts with Treviranus, the founder of the Conservative People's Union.

In spite of the pressure that the Center party exercised with its insistence on the simultaneous passage of the financial reform and the Young Plan, the negotiations of the government parties went badly. Whereas the Center and the Democratic parties were essentially ready to accept the proposals which the Social Democrats presented to cover the expected budget deficit, the German People's party fought against most of them. With the utmost stubbornness it opposed raising the contributions to the unemployment insurance to 4 per cent. The fact that the cabinet, in which two members of the People's party were holding the crucial portfolios of foreign affairs and finance, agreed on the budget and tax bill on March 5, 1930, did not end the grave party conflicts. The ministers were no longer masters of their own parties. While even the passage of the Young Plan had now become uncertain, Schacht added fuel to the flames. He resigned on March 7 from the *Reichsbank*, publicly castigating once more the irresponsible financial policies of the government. Criticism from such a source strengthened the intransigent attitude of the industrial wing of the People's party. At this moment the Center party made a bold move. On March 11 Brüning was received by Hindenburg, and the communiqué issued stated that the president had concurred in the belief that immediate financial reform was necessary and had assured the leader of the Center party that he would make use "of all constitutional means" to secure the realization of this aim. It was a clear hint that the financial reform would be carried through by article 48 of the Weimar Constitution if the parliament failed to agree.[3]

This stance of the president allowed the Center party to drop its demand for the simultaneous passage of the financial reform and the Young Plan. The latter was actually accepted by the parliament with a good majority on March 12, 1930, and signed by Hindenburg the next day. But immediately thereafter the parties resumed the battle over the tax bill. The conflict between the People's party and the Social Democratic party defied solution. Brüning finally proposed a compromise that left the decision on raising the contributions to the unemployment insurance program to 4 per cent and on additional government grants to a debate on the reform of the Institute of Labor Exchange and Labor Insurance at a later date. The Democratic party accepted the compromise, as did finally the majority of the People's party. The cabinet, too, favored the proposal with only one out of the four Social Democratic members, Minister of Labor Rudolf Wissell (1869–1942), dissenting.

Wissell represented the sentiment of the party better than Hermann

[3] See p. 547.

Müller or Carl Severing. The postponement of the raise of the contributions to the insurance program and the talk about a reform seemed to most Social Democrats only a preparation for the enforced curtailing of the insurance services. The preservation of the social legislation of the republic was one of the main tenets of Social Democratic faith and for the trade union leaders, who held more than one third of the party's seats, it was almost the exclusive political aim. Most members seemed to have given little thought to the fact that a negative vote of the party would mean the end of the "great coalition" with grave consequences for parliamentary government in Germany. As a matter of fact, a good many parliamentary deputies believed that in times of economic crisis, when the Social Democratic party was likely to lose voters to the Communists, it should not participate in a government and accept the responsibility for distasteful legislation.

Yet the situation was more serious than these Social Democrats assumed. The collapse of the Müller government would remove the only parliamentary government that could be formed in the parliament of 1928. After the flight of the largest party from responsibility no party combination existed that commanded a majority. In vain did Hermann Müller, Otto Braun, and Rudolf Hilferding reason that once the parliament had become paralyzed it would be difficult to defend the political and social rights of the working class. But with only a few dissenting votes the Social Democratic party delegation rejected the "Brüning compromise." On March 27, 1930, the Müller cabinet resigned.

✐ *Brüning Cabinet*

ON THE FOLLOWING DAY Hindenburg charged Dr. Heinrich Brüning with the formation of a government, which in view of the parliamentary situation was not to be built on a party coalition. Hindenburg recommended Martin Schiele (1870–1939), a German Nationalist at odds with Hugenberg, as the right man for the ministry of agriculture. Brüning was able to present himself with his cabinet as early as April 1. In addition to all the nonsocialist ministers of the Müller government the cabinet included Schiele and Gottfried Treviranus. The Brüning cabinet emphasized that it was a government above the parties and relied on the confidence of the president. The plans for such a "presidential" or "Hindenburg cabinet" had been hatched in the course of the winter of 1929–30, and it was the defense ministry that had gained Hindenburg's assent.

When Groener had become defense minister, it was clear that he was not the man to continue the humble role that Otto Gessler had played in deference to the chief of the army. After all, General Heye and a good many other leading officers of the defense ministry had been junior officers at Supreme Headquarters when Groener became Ludendorff's successor. Groener was determined to set the rules on the conduct of the army in politics, and he also wanted to be its spokesman in the molding of national policies. Groener's attitude resulted in organizational changes in the defense ministry. A "minister's office" (*Ministeramt*) was established to deal with all political questions, and General Kurt von Schleicher (1882–1934) was made its chief. The chief of the army was thereby largely confined to the technical military field, and General Heye, who disliked to lose his influence on general policy, was replaced in 1930 by General Baron Kurt von Hammerstein-Equord (1878–1943).

Groener was very fond of Schleicher, who had served for some time on his staff during World War I, and he trusted his political acumen. "My cardinal *in politicis*" he called him. Schleicher had been entrusted with many political tasks by Seeckt and had acquired wide personal contacts. Through his former regimental comrade Colonel Oskar von Hindenburg, the son of the president, he had easy access to the latter. Schleicher was a shrewd manipulator, although he never overcame a certain amateurishness in politics. Groener recognized that an army that could not rely on the full support of the people in an emergency would be under a serious handicap. He tried to spread among the officers a better understanding of the political value of the republic and attempted to establish friendlier relations with the Social Democratic party. But he did not achieve great changes. The mass of the party was antimilitaristic in principle, and even such responsible leaders as Otto Braun and Carl Severing remained suspicious because they found sufficient evidence of collusion between the army and antirepublican forces.

It was even more doubtful whether Groener's endeavor to promote good will toward the republic among the officers had any impact. On the contrary, there were signs that the junior officers in particular were rather receptive to Hugenberg's hard-line nationalism and Hitler's militancy. Groener and Schleicher were appalled by Hugenberg's radicalism, which was also resented by Hindenburg. When the Treviranus group seceded from the German Nationalist party, the defense ministry supported the new organization with a financial grant. Groener and Schleicher hoped that the Conservative People's Union was the beginning of that big nationalist, though cooperative, party that was their dream. A coalition of such a party with the parties in the middle would be able to introduce the necessary reforms. For the state needed a stable government capable of conducting long-range policies without the continuous peril of party feuds. The power of the president was to be brought into play. He was to select a man of his personal confidence and let him legislate with emergency decrees under article 48 of the Weimar Constitution. In this way the financial reforms in particular which the adoption of the Young Plan entailed were to be accomplished.

Schleicher seems to have finally decided on such a course of action in December 1929, when the Müller government came close to collapse. Dr. Heinrich Brüning, who was a friend of Treviranus and had called for the "solidarity of the front soldiers of the World War in all parties," was considered the best head of such a "presidential cabinet." Schleicher had known Brüning from meetings of the budget committee, while Groener was greatly impressed when he first took him on a long walk. Hindenburg apparently readily accepted the idea of the "presidential cabinet" that was to be oriented toward the right. When he received Brüning on March 11, 1930, he assured him of presidential support for his financial plans. Brüning himself, as we have seen, did his best to keep the "great coalition" together. As leader of the Center party he observed with keen interest the developments in the German Nationalist party, hoping that many of its members would follow his friend Treviranus and leave Hugenberg. A truly conservative party could then be built with which the Center party would be able to form governments in the future. But he knew that this situation was not yet ripe when Hindenburg made him chancellor.

When Brüning agreed to serve as the chancellor of a "presidential cabinet," he was determined to save democracy in Germany through the establishment of a form of government less dependent on the parties than the governments of the years 1919–30 had been. The attempt to use the power of the head of state for adding to the authority of the government was in a way a turning back to the days of the monarchy, although no members of the Center party could wish to diminish the position of parliament to the part it had played at that time. Brüning hoped that eventually the parliament would be willing to support strong governments, which then could merely keep their special powers under article 48 in reserve. But it was very doubtful whether the men who had made him chancellor would stick to these aims and would loyally back him. As it turned out, Brüning ended parliamentary government, and his successor ended democracy.

✌ *Cultural Life*

BEFORE FOLLOWING THE HISTORY of the Brüning regime, we must briefly review the intellectual and moral climate that had prevailed in the decade before and by now was changing fast. What was true in politics was true in the cultural life as well. All its leaders had gained their basic world view prior to the World War. Although naturally the war modified the outlook of many people, it meant no rupture in the predominant movements of thought. It is characteristic of the civilization of the Weimar

Republic that it lacked unity. There were many schools of thought and art which did not communicate with one another.

The revolution was welcomed by the expressionists, who in the last years before the war had revolted against the existing society and its culture.[4] Their influence on literature, art, the theater, and music was considerable in the early 1920's. Thereafter, when the prewar social structure became stabilized again, expressionism found its supporters only in certain sections of society. The radical right, appealing to all philistines, dubbed it "degenerate art" or "cultural bolshevism." After 1933 the Nazis did their best to drive the expressionist artists out of Germany and even destroyed many of their works.

The ire of the nationalists was equally aroused by modern architecture. Its beginnings, too, went back to the eve of World War I.[5] Peter Behrens and Erich Mendelssohn (1887–1953) were already active at that time, as was Walter Gropius, the man who has done the most to secure the ultimate acceptance of modern architecture. In 1919 he became director of the *Bauhaus* (architects' house) in Weimar, where he brought together an outstanding team of architects and artists who systematically studied the potentialities of modern materials and the best methods of using them in architecture. Gropius wanted to regain in an industrial age the high quality that the artisan had achieved in former centuries. But the ultimate aim of study and training was the building, which had to be designed according to its function. The *Bauhaus* philosophy, because it was of universal application, made those Germans furious who wanted a national German art. In 1925 Gropius had to retreat from Weimar, where the government threatened to withdraw its supports, to Dessau in the tiny state of Anhalt. In 1928 he turned the reins over to Mies van der Rohe (b. 1886). In 1933 the Nazis closed the *Bauhaus*, and it was the United States that gave Gropius, Mies van der Rohe, Mendelssohn, and many other German architects the opportunity for creative achievement which found general acclaim.

Apart from the expressionists, the generation of German writers and artists who had made their appearance in the period between 1890 and 1905 continued their work.[6] In 1923, three years before his death, Rainer Maria Rilke published his *Duino Elegies*, which had occupied him since 1911, and his *Sonnets to Orpheus*, which, too, had engaged him for a number of years. Stefan George proudly continued his way. Through a group of devoted followers, all of them eminent professors, his gospel was carried into scholarship and academic teaching. Hugo von Hofmannsthal's influence reached its height only in the 1920's. In contrast to George he

[4] See p. 413.
[5] See p. 405.
[6] See pp. 401–3.

rejected paganism and stood aside from the Nietzschean trend of German literature.

The most representative writer of the Weimar Republic was Thomas Mann. Just at the end of the war he had issued his *Reflections of a Non-Political Man*, a paean to German culture and an indictment of democratic civilization. Unhappily the book served as an arsenal of antirepublican ideas throughout the Weimar Republic. Its author, however, in 1922 professed his faith in the German Republic. But it was a romanticized republic, which he called on the youth to serve, and he made few converts. With his fictional work he reached an infinitely larger audience, and here he used the artist's right to keep the reader in doubt about the author's personal sympathies. In his great novel of 1924, *The Magic Mountain*, the conversations and experiences of a small group of people in a Swiss tuberculosis sanatorium, remote from the ordinary world, present a symbolic picture of the fundamental cleavages of thought and aspirations which tore the Weimar Republic apart. The struggle between the ideals of the Enlightenment and liberalism with prefascist ideas, as well as the impact of the philosophy of antirationalism, are treated by Thomas Mann with superior critical irony. Although the writer avoids clear-cut decisions of his own, it remains apparent that he is defending the cause of humanity.

Thomas Mann's elder brother, Heinrich, was committed to republicanism and militant literature of the French style. His most important novels were those in which he laid bare the false morals of the bourgeoisie in imperial Germany, such as *Der Untertan*, in which he depicts the German philistine bourgeois who eagerly submits to absolutist rule in order to enjoy social preference, or *Professor Unrat* (known the world over in the movie version as *The Blue Angel*), in which he demonstrates the shaky human existence of another pillar of German authoritarianism, the high school teacher. Heinrich Mann was a writer of high rank, though no Zola, but in spite of the fact that the republic made him president of the academy of poets he did not exercise any influence on the political trends of popular opinion.

There were a good many other writers of deserved repute, many of them Austrians, for in the field of literature and music a close community existed between Germany and Austria. Thus the German-born Richard Strauss became an Austrian, but his music was equally cultivated in both countries.

Whereas the foremost German writers were almost without exception liberals, the German universities differed greatly from the world of contemporary literature. On the whole they remained what they had been before. The republican state governments did not change them institutionally or politically to any considerable degree. A few Social Democrats received professorial chairs, and the prejudice against Catholics eased. But in most universities the conservative professors who were opposed to any reforms retained control. They had even more power than before the revolution, since it was harder for democratic governments to override the wishes of an academic body than it had been for monarchical authorities. Thus nothing was done to enhance the function of the university as an institution for the education of the "whole man" or to change the class complexion of the student body. The often heard slogan, "Free opportunity for the ablest," was not realized by the republic. The universities continued to give their students knowledge chiefly. Owing to the overcrowded conditions, the personal contacts between students and professors became even more tenuous than before. The student corporations[7] still played a major part in forming the minds of the young people. Most of these corporations inculcated in their members a sense of social superiority that did not go well with their professed faith in the community of the German people and after 1919 cultivated a spirit of radical nationalism that was usually coupled with anti-Semitism.

The republican student organizations remained small, as did the number of professors who vainly attempted to fight nationalism actively and to win the students over to an understanding of the republic. They were outnumbered by the nationalistic professors who, often enough using their regular lectures for such purposes, agitated against the republic and for the abrogation of the "shameful dictate of Versailles" and found an enthusiastic response among the great mass of the students. These professors were not necessarily representatives of departments dealing with political subjects, such as history, law, and economics; they also included some eminent scientists, some literary historians, and a good many Protestant theologians.

Still, the majority of the professors, while usually antidemocratic, tried not to let politics interfere too much with their scholarly work, and in the period of the Weimar Republic the German universities continued to reap a rich harvest of high intellectual achievement. But those who had intimately known the German universities before the war judged that the postwar years witnessed a decline. This is noticeable in the humanities and social sciences and may be partly explained by the losses on the battlefields. But the level did not fall off in the sciences. The generation that became productive in the 1920's carried forward research in all fields of science and opened fundamentally new vistas on the universe and nature. The excellence of these German scientists was attested to not only by the Nobel prizes they received but also by the many students whom they attracted from all over the world. Berlin and Göttingen became meccas for the young scientists.

---

[7] See the author's *A History of Modern Germany, 1648–1840*, p. 481.

For the formation of an integrated philosophy of life the stunning development of science was a disturbing phenomenon. In spite of the great technological progress that it produced, basic research always posed new problems and riddles. Not long before his own death Einstein wrote to his friend Max von Laue (1879–1962) that "[we are] much more distant from a deeper understanding of the elementary phenomena than most of our contemporaries believe." At the same time the Newtonian-Kantian concept of science as a system of knowledge based on a single law of causality was shattered. In the nineteenth century this concept had served as the ideal model even for knowledge outside the natural sciences. Yet the new situation was not easily understood by the academicians.

Neo-Kantianism was probably still the most widely represented philosophy in the German universities. Its preoccupation with the theory of knowledge confined its influence largely to the academic scholars. It was important that a philosopher such as Ernst Cassirer (1874–1945) brought sciences and humanities together in his work. His wide-ranging understanding of history and science, art and literature made him a lucid interpreter of the forms of human knowledge and expression. Edmund Husserl's (1859–1938) phenomenological method, through which he freed philosophical logic from Mill's psychology, was also chiefly applied to epistemology. His demand that the philosopher had to proceed from the perception of individual facts to the intuition of the general and essential features, which at the same time are present in man's memory and imagination, opened up a practically limitless field for philosophizing. Max Scheler (1875–1928), one of Husserl's early students, applied the phenomenological method to ethics, sociology, and the analysis of the contemporary world. Scheler came closer than any of the academic philosophers of the period to offering the younger generation a comprehensive world view by which to live. Unhappily his brilliant mind was restless. During the war he published some of the worst pieces of nationalist ideological propaganda only to plunge thereafter into the advocacy of Europeanism. His shift from a religious to a religiously indifferent position confused his audience equally.

The reception of Kierkegaard (1813–55) and Nietzsche led to a new departure in academic philosophy and theology. The new existentialist philosophy proposed to draw logical conclusions from the collapse of the belief that human reason partakes in universal truth. It was this faith that was lost between 1830 and 1840. In its place the following generations adopted the hope that the various natural, social, and humanistic sciences would be capable of creating a satisfactory foundation for thought and life. But in the new century even this belief was called in question. When the conception that reason was more than a mere human capacity broke down, reason became just a technical tool of man but not his bridge to universal truth. In this situation the new philosophy clung to the conception of philosophical existence as the ultimate truth of being. The place of universal ideal truth was taken by the spiritual existence of the individual. The analysis of this individual conciousness became the theme of this existentialist philosophy. Karl Jaspers (b. 1883) of Heidelberg was the first philosopher to take this road. He is a highly disciplined thinker, always conscious of the great cultural philosophical tradition of the West and anxious not to minimize unduly the power of reason. In Martin Heidegger (b. 1889) existentialism found another representative no doubt brilliant but less concerned with the preservation of the cultural heritage. Both philosophers drew large audiences, and Jaspers taught his students probity of mind whereas Heidegger led them into a magic garden of conceptions which transcended sober thought.

The historians, who in the nineteenth century had been among the major intellectual leaders of the nation, had already lost that eminence by the end of the century. In politics, almost without exception, they became self-appointed guardians of the Bismarckian Empire, although they wanted it to grow from a European into a world power. History to them was exclusively the struggle of states, and only political history a legitimate field of academic study. From such a narrow base they had nothing to contribute to the public discussion of the pressing problems of social and political reform. After August 1914 most of them plunged with great passion into the battle for expansionist war aims. During the war even the moderates among them failed to grasp the realities of the German situation, although after the collapse they proved more ready to search for the structural weakness of the monarchical Empire and the political mistakes of its rulers. Still, most German historians went on defending the old regime and fought with great indignation the "war-guilt lie" of Versailles. Friedrich Meinecke, impressed by the disasters of the war, was the only scholar who began to question some of the basic assumptions of German historical thinking. In his *Idea of Raison d'État* of 1924, a study of the conflict of the exercise of power by the statesman and the universal moral commandments starting with Machiavelli, he rejected the Hegelian and Rankean tradition of identifying the actual course of history with the realization of the highest ideas. Although Meinecke did not judge that power was always evil, he recognized its demonic nature and insisted that the absolute validity of universal ethical norms should never be placed in doubt by attempts at an easy harmonization of spirit and life in history.

But such ideas did not exercise a noticeable influence among academic historians and even less among the public at large. On the whole, the professors did not exercise leadership over a wide segment of the people. The ever-increasing specialization and professionalization of scholarship interfered with wide communication. Also, practically all professors had withdrawn from active politics, and their political opinions lacked the critical earmark which one might have expected from men of their calling. As had been the case already during the war, their public political statements as a rule merely vied with those of the popular writers.

In these circumstances people looked elsewhere for a synthesis of a knowledge that would give support to their personal and political beliefs. There was no shortage of self-appointed prophets, sages, preachers, and writers to whom they could turn for this service. The German propaganda had defined the ideological meaning of the war as the battle for the defense and victory of German *Kultur* over and against Russian barbarism and autocracy in the East and the soulless civilization of the West. France, England, and America had no *Kultur* but only a civilization characterized by its exclusive reliance on reason from which they had produced a mechanistic organization of society that forced the individual to conform strictly to its dull egalitarian standards. These theses were endlessly variegated. According to their own lights and tempers the authors described the nature of German *Kultur* differently and displayed lesser or greater contempt toward Western civilization. But the assertion that Germany had nothing in common with Europe and that the acceptance of Western ideas such as rationalism, liberalism, and democracy was a betrayal of Germany's mission was monotonously repeated in the whole war literature.

In the postwar years this peculiar Germanophilism was built up in the most radical fashion. Its basis became an antirationalistic vitalism. Life was the true reality, and it was not dominated by reason but by human instincts and impulses. Therefore it also could not be interpreted logically but only intuitively by internal understanding. The gates of the subjectivism, nay nihilism, which Nietzsche had pushed open were now boldly left behind. In the end the philosopher Ludwig Klages (1872–1956), in his work *The Spirit as the Foe of the Soul* (1929–32), developed these theories into an elaborate system.

Yet the first loud trumpet call was sounded by a relatively young former high school teacher. In the summer of 1918 Oswald Spengler (1880–1936) published the first volume of *The Decline of the West*, which within a year became the most widely studied book in Germany. Spengler proudly announced that he was presenting the key to an understanding not only of the world history of the past but also of the future. History, Spengler said, is the history of cultures which are completely unrelated. Even the affiliation of Western civilization with that of classic antiquity is denied by Spengler. His cultures are enormous plants, which, if one may use the Leibnizian expression, have no windows but repeat the same course of growth and decay following quasi-biological laws. By proceeding to the founding of cities a peasants' civilization reached the state of historical creativity or culture. But with the appearance of big cities the community of productive citizens disintegrated into a milling crowd, and intellectual life deteriorated into a pedantic Alexandrinism. Thus culture became civilization again, until finally men would relapse into the non-historical state of fellahs.

These were the general morphological laws which Spengler assured his readers were operative in the eight historic cultures. These laws enabled him to define the stage that Western culture had reached in this ineluctable cycle. The symptoms of decay, democracy, plutocracy, and technology indicated to him that the age of civilization was superseding that of flowering culture. It would be an iron age of cruel wars in which new Caesars would rise and an elite of steely men, who did not look for personal gain and happiness but for the execution of duties toward the community, would replace the democrats and humanitarians.

Spengler had written his work in the expectation of a German victory and apparently thought of the ensuing German situation as comparable to that of Rome after the Punic wars. As it was, *The Decline of the West* served its concurring readers as an explanation of the defeat. And although the book opened bleak vistas into the distant future, it contained the comforting message that at first the ideals of Western Europe and America would be supplanted by the ideals stemming from the German tradition. In an avidly read pamphlet, *Prussianism and Socialism*, Spengler in 1920 expounded his political tenets for the general public. The socialism which he postulates is nothing but the cooperation of all classes under a strong dictatorial government for the common good. According to this theory, Karl Marx was not a true socialist. His internationalism and insistence on the class struggle marked him as a child of liberalism.

Spengler, who in conversation and correspondence showed no originality or warmth, was an imperious writer. He inaugurated the large literature which is nowadays usually labeled with an expression of Hugo von Hofmannsthal as the "conservative revolution" but might be better called with Ernst Troeltsch the "neoconservative counterrevolution." Arthur Moeller van den Bruck (1876–1925) wrote the probably most representative book of the movement, *The Third Reich* (1923). He had started as an art critic and directed the publication of a German edition of Dostoevsky's works prior to the war. Only the war made him a political writer. In his last book he described the Reich as the most precious possession of the Germans. Through the medieval Empire, the first Reich, they decisively formed Europe. The second, Bismarckian, Reich was only an interim affair, because it partook in the mistakes and sins of liberalism. But it gave the Germans back the Reich, and although it was truncated by the Treaty of Versailles, the Allies did not take it from them. By purging it of liberalism and capitalism the "neoconservatives" would be able to build up the third, and final, Reich in which all the German values would be realized. Moeller van den Bruck gave this "Reich of a thousand years" a mystic quality by letting it appear as the final transcending stage of world history. When the National Socialists took over the term, they removed most of Moeller's basic assumptions, particularly his emphasis on cultural values besides the political ones.

Ernst Jünger (b. 1895) was the greatest prose writer in the group. As a young officer, eager for adventure, who had been highly decorated for heroic deeds, he had found in combat the true existentialist situation of man. The beauty of war was glorified by him in a delirious style. War had brought out in man the elemental wildness and hardness that had been lost in the age of bourgeois liberalism. These warrior men would perform the regeneration of humanity. In Jünger's *The Worker* of 1932 the warrior became the worker. The differences between army and industry disappear in the total mobilization of the nation. Individual freedom is reduced to the mere esthetic experience of the whole, to which the individual in heroic realism owes service and obedience. This worker will replace the decaying bourgeois.

The writers of the "conservative revolution" found a large following among the German middle and upper classes who had been aroused by the intemperate agitation of the war years and shaken in their traditional social beliefs by the war and its aftermath, revolution and inflation. The young people, in particular, who, as members of the youth movement, had lived in protest against bourgeois society and pure rational thought were attracted by the neoconservatives. It may be doubted that the neoconservative ideas were always understood. As a matter of fact, it is questionable whether their authors always knew what exactly they wanted to say. Some of them wanted to startle their readers with bizarre paradoxes, while others considered an opaque mysticism the proof of profundity. Moreover, illogicality was made permissible by the blunt assertion that the time of words and theories was over and that all that mattered from now on were life and deeds.

Naturally this type of thinking contributed nothing to the clarification of muddled minds. On the contrary, it carried their obfuscation to extreme lengths. But this ideology served to maintain the belief in a German society ordered along class lines and in the superiority of the German nation. The neoconservatives showed no capacity, however, for building up a political party. All of them were in principle opposed to political parties, yet even if they visualized the state of the future as a state without them, a party-like organization was needed if they wanted to reach their goals. Moeller van den Bruck, who criticized nineteenth-century conservatism for having been a mere "party conservatism," by which he probably meant a conservatism content with a sectarian role, called upon the believers in the Third Reich to form a "third party." Yet the individualism of the anti-individualistic neoconservatives found its expression only in relatively small fraternal associations (*Bünde*). In the first half of the life of the Weimar Republic the chief impact of the neoconservatives on the party life was to keep the German Nationalist party from becoming simply a reactionary monarchistic party. But although the party stressed nationalism as its common denominator, this did not in the end suffice to dispel the distrust of the young generation in the old leaders. The last years of the republic confronted the neoconservatives with the necessity of choosing their position vis-à-vis the National Socialists.

To the great mass of the antirepublicans no problem existed. To them there was no question but that the Nazi party, which called itself a "movement" rather than a party, was the final rally of the German people against liberalism, democracy, capitalism, and their ruinous consequences. Was not the movement led by former soldiers from the front who were possessed of the true warrior spirit? Did it not espouse an order centering around the leadership principle and demanding obedience and service from its followers? And did it not breathe ardent faith in decision and action as opposed to trust in reason? All these characteristics had for years been propagated by the neoconservatives as the goals of the coming German revolution. Small wonder then that most of those who had been moved by neoconservative ideals flocked to the banners of the Nazi party.

The originators of neoconservatism, however, realized that the Nazis did not live up to their ideals. Moeller van den Bruck, who met with Hitler in 1922, had already been worried over the ideas of the leader of the brown shirts. A group of young and gifted neoconservative writers around Hans Zehrer (1899-1966), who edited the monthly *Die Tat*, made an attempt to establish themselves as the leading brain trust of a future authoritarian state in which the Nazi party would be confined to the organization of popular mass support. Such a state could have received its power only from the army. Although this was a utopian conception, the clever young men of the *Tat*, in their analytical articles, came more closely to grips with the concrete social and political situation than the older neoconservative writers. After Hitler had come to power in 1933, Hans Zehrer refused to accept any political post, although some of his collaborators served the Nazis. Oswald Spengler, though not rejecting every form of cooperation with the Nazis, openly criticized them as early as 1933. He resented their herd character, mass oratory, and lack of *Realpolitik*. Spengler was a Nietzschean in spurning racialism. So was Ernst Jünger, who never became a party member and who in 1939 began to attack the Nazis in a veiled fashion. The neoconservatives prior to 1933 were a major force in mobilizing large groups, particularly the educated

people and the academic youth, against the republican order and, worse
than this, against many of the fundamental values of a humane civilization. But their perversion of German culture still stopped short of the
total barbarization which National Socialism brought to Germany. Even
under the Nazi regime some neoconservatives maintained their dissent,
which a few even turned into active resistance.

✍ Churches

THE CHURCHES SHOWED no capacity for stemming the spread of the raging
nationalistic ideas for the simple reason that their voices reached only
relatively small segments of their members. Moreover the Protestant
churches did not even prove immune to radical nationalism. During the
war they had gone to frightful lengths fostering the war spirit by cater-
ing to the national pride. Germany's collapse did not change the attitude
of most Protestant ministers. They now preached against the "war-guilt
lie" and the shameful dictate of Versailles that was to be undone in the
future. At the same time they were more or less hostile to the republic.
The disappearance of the monarchy had removed the princes as heads of
the churches and with them what the churches considered the chief
guarantee of state support, while they overlooked the fact that the episcopalian position of the princes forced the churches to espouse political
causes which were alien to their religious mission.

The official leaders of the churches and the majority of the Protestant
clergy deplored the end of the unity of throne and altar and looked at the
new state with grave misgivings if not open hostility. They disliked the
great influence that Roman Catholicism exercised in the life of the republic and were afraid of the policies of the "atheistic" Social Democrats.
Actually, although the mass of the latter remained aloof from the
churches, the antireligious propaganda that some party members had
formerly carried on subsided in the years of the Weimar Republic. The
party even tolerated the formation of a group of "religious socialists" in
spite of the fact that this small group of eminent young intellectuals was
most critical of Marxism. For the churches, however, it was most important that the Social Democrats did not insist upon the separation of
church and state. As a matter of fact, state-church relations remained
much the same as before, except that the churches gained much greater
freedom to administer their own affairs.

The Protestant churches failed to make constructive use of these new
opportunities. Traditionalism was too strong among the officials and the
social groups which constituted the main body of the active church membership. The churches continued as *Landeskirchen* along the regional
lines which had been drawn a century before. There were still three

groups of churches—Lutheran, Reformed, and United (Evangelical). Attempts to found a national Protestant Church were unsuccessful, but when the Lutheran archbishop of Sweden called for the convention of a Protestant world council, it was seen that the German Protestants would need a common representation. Chiefly for this purpose the German Evangelical Church Federation was created in 1922. A federal council and an executive committee assumed the conduct of the international relations of the churches and, as far as proved necessary, also their relations with the federal government.

With the monarchy gone it was felt in Protestant circles that with or without the restoration of the monarchy the future of their churches depended on a broadening of their popular base. The church, whether state church or not, was to become a "People's Church." But achieving this by adopting a thoroughly democratic constitution was shunned because, not without good reason, the mass of the laymen were distrusted by the ministers. Progress was made by an intensification of the social work of the churches, but they still remained churches of the pastors rather than of the people. Yet the desire to win contact with a large group of people led the majority of the ministers to look toward the German Nationalists and subsequently even to the National Socialists. In contrast to the "materialistic" Social Democrats these groups were assumed to be "idealists" and therefore closer to religion. Such opinions would not have been so widely held if in modern German Protestantism Lutheranism had not so often been declared to be the national German religion. This assertion could easily degenerate into the conception of a German God.

The Protestant churches did not transcend the class limitations which had bound them in the preceding half-century and did not rise to become an autonomous force of major consequence in German life. But within the churches fresh movements were not altogether missing. We have already mentioned the growing endeavor to meet the social problems. Luther's religion and theology was reinterpreted—and thereby also shown in its relevancy to the problems of the contemporary age—by Karl Holl (1866–1926). Besides the ensuing "Luther renaissance," the so-called dialectical theology became the center of theological debate. Karl Barth's (1886–1968) *Epistle to the Romans* of 1919 was the first major work of this theological existentialism. Its Swiss author taught later at German universities until the Hitler regime forced him out of Germany. The dialectical theology was only one among a number of new theological schools which wanted to restore the absoluteness of Christian religion that in their opinion was not safely anchored in the liberal and historical theology. Probably the majority of the leaders of the church resistance under Hitler came from theologically active groups.

The Roman Catholic Church retained control over a much greater number of its members. While they came from all classes, the majority of its obedient followers was found among the rural and small-town people. Among the upper class as well as among the workers greater independence prevailed. The church gained tremendously by the revolution of 1918. It won full parity with the Protestant churches and did not have to fear the intrusion of the state governments into its internal life. Yet the German Catholics were not overly happy with democracy which they had never wanted before.

Except for the Christian trade unions and the small peasants of southwestern Germany, who formed a deeper attachment to the republic, democracy was generally accepted as an unattractive form of government that had been imposed by the inglorious collapse of the German monarchies. In Bavaria a sizable monarchistic movement survived, while elsewhere small, though influential, groups formed a Catholic wing of the German Nationalist party. Some bishops, such as Cardinal Faulhaber of Munich (1869–1952), were opponents of the republic. In the first place, however, the bishops felt serious misgivings about the continuing coalition with the Social Democrats, as it existed in Prussia and Baden. The old suspicions of them had not died down after the revolution. There was also much uneasiness over this issue within the Center party. Heinrich Brauns, the federal minister of labor, and Adam Stegerwald (1874–1945), the chief leader of the Christian trade unions, under whom Heinrich Brüning was at that time serving his political apprenticeship, were already calling in 1920 for the founding of a social-minded conservative party of Protestants and Catholics which was to form a strong counterweight against the Social Democrats. But under the conditions of the Weimar period such programs, which have been called first attempts in the direction of the Christian Democratic Union of 1946, did not have the slightest chance of realization. Far from aspiring to cooperation with the Catholics, the Protestants wanted to restore their political superiority over them. On the other hand, the Catholic Church, in spite of its criticism of the policies of the Center party, wanted the Center to remain a Catholic party that would work for the achievement of the aims which the church held most urgent in church-state relations.

Although Catholic academic circles carried on lively and interesting debates on the meaning of Christian political and social doctrine, a dominant program of action did not emerge, and the actual policies of the Catholic groups seemed to reflect opportunism rather than faith. In these circumstances it was difficult to hold the party allegiance of the Catholic youth. In addition, the young people were given only a minimal participation in policy making. Although all the old parties were run by old men who had already been in politics before the war, the Center delegation in the *Reichstag*—at least between 1924 and 1930—showed the highest average age of all of the party delegations.

Undoubtedly the relations between the church and the Center party were not so close as they had been before 1918. This might have been all to the good if the Center party had been able to win over important non-Catholic groups and to build up a reasonably strong membership organization. But its electorate was the same as before, and its membership organization never gained great strength. As a result, the party still was greatly dependent on the church and the popular associations under the church's direction.

The German Catholics were conservative nationalists. Bismarck's vilification of the Centrists as "enemies of the Empire" had left them extremely sensitive to any adverse criticism of their patriotism. Most of them suffered greatly from the fact that their participation in the government forced them to assume the responsibility for the Versailles Treaty and the fulfillment of the reparations settlements. The left wing of the Center party stressed the national tone as much as the members more to the right. Adam Stegerwald and a good many other officials of the Christian trade unions were among the most vocal nationalistic speakers. Joseph Wirth, as minister of finance and chancellor, provided the funds for the secret rearmament of the *Reichswehr*. Although the Center party supported Stresemann's foreign policy in parliament, it did so without great conviction.

Neoconservatism had an impact only on those Catholics who had joined the German Nationalists, and even this influence was largely limited to the Reich mystique and the devaluation of liberalism. Against the rising tide of racism and paganism the active Catholics proved mostly immune and National Socialism prior to 1933 was unable to make significant inroads into the active church membership. Social anti-Semitism on religious grounds was rather widespread among German Catholics. But racist philosophies and political anti-Semitism were firmly rejected. Bishops, clergy, and laymen were united in fighting National Socialism during the decisive years 1930–33.

✑ Cultural Crisis

NATIONALISM PERVADED GERMANY to such an extent that even the Communists endeavored to exploit it for their purposes. The Social Democrats, though good patriots, were the most moderate in this respect, yet their influence did not reach beyond the workers' class, and even here they were locked in battle with the Communists. Rainer Maria Rilke wrote in 1923 that Germany had failed in 1918 to reform by returning to her old standards, when humility had been one of the elements of human dignity. But the Germans, who had become "one-sided and willful" and devoted to material aims, had been thinking only of salvation "in a superficial, rash, distrustful, and greedy sense." Germany "wanted to persevere rather than change." The sensitive poet, who saw in the state of the German mind the approaching disaster not only for Germany but for the world, was essentially right. The Germans continued to yearn for national greatness more than for any other good. The intellectuals were entirely unconcerned over the widening gulf between German and Western European–American thought. On the contrary, Germany's isolation appeared to them desirable. This separation was finally carried over to the basic moral principles of Western civilization. It is true that few of the intellectuals went to this length. But by their radical fight against reason they removed themselves from the position of leaders of the popular spirit and conscience, and the half-educated took their place. There were enough of them owing to the shortcomings of the conception or operation of the German school system. Spengler's crude statement that he was on the side of "blood against spirit" was one of the early demonstrations of the eclipse of the German intelligentsia in the moral leadership of the people.

In 1930 it was still difficult to diagnose the full gravity of Germany's cultural crisis. In the arts and sciences creative work was carried forward that did not break away from traditional values and was received with respect also outside of Germany. How tenuous was the hold that liberal artists and scholars had over mass audiences was hard to recognize. Similarly, although the signs of the economic recession were clearly visible in the spring of 1930, nobody could then have foreseen to what depth the economy would plunge.

∽ Brüning's Policies

THUS HEINRICH BRÜNING, at the age of 45 the youngest chancellor Germany had ever had, became the head of the government when intellectually, economically, and politically Germany had reached a most serious impasse. He came from a Catholic upper-middle-class family in Münster and had spent long years before the war studying first languages and history, then economics. He had also traveled abroad. Though not of a strong constitution, he had in 1914 eagerly sought acceptance by the army, in which he served for four years at the western front, finally as the leader of a machine-gun company. He always cherished the memories of these years, which also made him an admirer of the Prussian-German officers' corps. After the war he had become an executive secretary of the federation of Christian trade unions under Adam Stegerwald. In 1924 he was elected to the *Reichstag* where he quickly became known as one of the most diligent and effective members of the budget committee. Four years later he was made the parliamentary floor leader of the Center party with the approval of the new party chairman, Dr. Ludwig Kaas.

Brüning was a man of highest integrity and absolute devotion to duty. His ascetic and prudent personality commanded respect. But the reserved and reticent bachelor did not have the gift of making intimate friends, and he arrived at his decisions after long lonely struggles. Once he had reached these decisions, he stuck to them. He was convinced that even in politics objective solutions to major problems existed which could be found by objective analysis and that their reasonableness would persuade those who were able to rise above party views. There naturally are stubborn facts in political life which defy any partisan approach, but Brüning tended to underrate the necessity which is imposed on the statesman to win the support of people by sentiment rather than by reason.

This tendency already applied to Brüning's relations with Hindenburg, whom he admired but failed to control the way Bismarck had controlled William I. Brüning did not take sufficient care to fight opposing influences in the presidential palace. In his reports to the president he overtaxed the old marshal's mental capacity by his theoretical presentations. Hindenburg always retained some personal reservations about the Westphalian Catholic and academician. This was not serious as long as Hindenburg had full confidence in General Groener, who did yeoman service for the chancellor, but in the fall of 1931 the relations between Hindenburg and Groener grew less intimate. Brüning misjudged Hindenburg, as he often showed little perspicacity in sizing up people.

Although Brüning was not a poor speaker, he did not possess the power of dramatic oratory which might have swayed the masses. His austere appeals for sacrifices for national goals of limited character, goals which in addition were not immediately attainable, did not inspire hope among the millions who found themselves in dire straits or felt deep anxiety about their future. Brüning entirely lacked Roosevelt's or Churchill's gift of communicating to their nations the historic meaning of the crises which engulfed them. He was an old-time conservative nationalist who wanted to restore Germany to the place she had occupied in Europe before 1914. He felt that Stresemann's policies had been too cautious and conciliatory and that German pressure for the revision of the Versailles Treaty had to be increased. As one of its first actions in foreign politics the cabinet helped to kill Briand's plans for a European union. Such a union, it was feared, if comprising strict political commitments, would make a revision of the German frontiers of 1919 forever impossible. Although this had already been Stresemann's fear, he had welcomed economic union. But Brüning and his advisors were opposed to any kind of European institution and, aware of the British objections to Briand's project, declared that a European union without England was unfeasible. Brüning's whole foreign policy suffered from his belief that whereas the European victor states owed much to Germany, Germany owed little or nothing to Europe.

Brüning's first major aim was the abolition of reparations. But he was convinced that Germany should not tackle this problem before she had put her public finances in order. Only then would she be able to state her incapacity to pay reparations and on the other hand be in a position to refuse to submit to any additional political conditions because of financial weakness, as Brüning thought she had done at the time of the negotiations of the Young Plan. That the end of the reparations was not the only aim of a revisionist policy could soon be sensed from the public manifestations of the new cabinet. When the removal of the Allied troops took place on June 30, 1930, the Berlin government issued a proclamation to the Rhenish population that did not even mention the name of Stresemann, whose policies and superhuman exertions should have been credited before those of all others with the achievement of this happy event. Instead, the official proclamation stressed the terrible burdens Germany had assumed in order to free the Rhineland and, beginning with the Saar, hinted at the many other unfulfilled German claims for the revision of the Versailles Treaty. The French and even the British were unpleasantly surprised at not hearing one word of gratitude for the evacuation, which after all took place five years earlier than the Versailles Treaty had stipulated, but instead only shrill nationalistic voices. Quickly such paramilitary organizations as the *Stahlhelm* held open demonstrations in the demilitarized Rhineland.

The Brüning government devoted itself to the balancing of the budget in the spring and early summer of 1930. The first minor measures taken in this direction passed the *Reichstag*, because they were coupled with large grants to the agrarian interests. Although Hugenberg wanted to lead his party immediately into opposition, he had to allow the agrarian wing to help toward the adoption of these measures. But during the debates of the budget for 1930 the German Nationalists under Hugenberg became less tractable. Simultaneously the race with the ever-increasing economic crisis began. The growing unemployment created new budget deficits, which were further enlarged by shrinking production and markets and were reflected in the tapering off of tax revenue. Whereas in April the deficit was given as 400 million marks, at the end of May the minister of finance had to admit that it had risen to 1.1 billion. The government proposed to cover the deficit chiefly by a special tax on government employees. Undoubtedly the pay raise of government workers and officials granted by Finance Minister Köhler in 1927 was highly exaggerated considering German economic conditions. But the imposition of a tax on an individual social group inevitably caused resentment which was made even more galling by the exemption of the army and police from these cuts.

There is no need to go into the details of this legislation, the other side of which was the cutting of the unemployment insurance benefits with the simultaneous increase in the federal contribution to 1 per cent instead of the .5 per cent that the Social Democrats had fought for before the collapse of the Müller cabinet. The parliament was critical of the new budget proposals. The People's party, in which the representatives of heavy industry gained growing control after Stresemann's death, caused its own minister of finance to resign. Under his successor the program was somewhat refashioned in order to make it more acceptable to the parties of the middle and the right. But an offer of the Social Democrats to negotiate a compromise was not taken up by Brüning. Under the influence of Hermann Müller, Otto Braun, and Rudolf Hilferding the Social Democrats wanted to save parliamentary government. But Brüning did not wish to appear to be depending on support from the left. He hoped that he could win sufficient succor on the right and that his chances for such aid might even be improved if he ruled by using the ready symbol of authoritarian government, article 48 of the Weimar Constitution.

✧ Dissolution of Reichstag, 1930

WHEN ON JULY 16, 1930, his government was defeated by a majority of 256 to 193, Brüning issued the entire program as a presidential emergency decree. The whole Communist and Social Democratic parties and most of the German Nationalists as well as the twelve National Socialists voted against him. But after Brüning had taken recourse from the parliament to article 48, more than two dozen German Nationalists under the leadership of Count Westarp gave him their support. The vote by which the *Reichstag* demanded the repeal of the emergency decree was a close one. The chancellor at once dissolved parliament and called for elections on September 14. It was a rather dubious constitutional practice to justify the dissolution with the rejection of the emergency decrees by the *Reichstag*, which had this constitutional authority on the basis of the same article 48. It could also be questioned whether the government should have reissued a week later what was essentially the decree rejected by the *Reichstag*.

The dissolution of the *Reichstag* was an audacious step. There had been feverish public political agitation even after the Young Plan had finally been adopted. Obviously the radical parties gained most in this climate. This was true of the Communists and infinitely more so of the National Socialists, whose propaganda became continuously noisier and clearly more effective. In 1928 the Nazis had been able to garner only 2.8 per cent of the popular vote, but in the state elections in December 1929 they reached as much as 11.3 per cent and in June 1930 14.4 per cent. A national election campaign was bound to provide them with a grand opportunity for further expansion. The government expected the Nazi party to make some gains, but it should be mentioned that not even Hitler and Joseph Goebbels (1897–1945) anticipated the measure of success the Nazis won at the polls. Brüning expected not only that the growth of the Nazi party would not be overly extravagant but also that there would be a large body of German Nationalists who would shed Hugenberg's yoke and form a party that would support the cabinet appointed by Hindenburg. This was an utter miscalculation. The secessionists from the German Nationalist party were without any organizational apparatus and press. It was a complete misunderstanding if Brüning assumed that the radicalization of the voters had not gone too far and that he still would get an obedient parliament for the next four years.

This expectation was completely shattered by the election results. The division in the German Nationalist camp worked in favor of the Nazis. The Conservative People's party, on which Brüning's hopes for an extension of his parliamentary base toward the right were chiefly founded, managed to get only four members elected, and they were elected only on the coattails of one of the agrarian groups that had splintered off from the German Nationalist party. While gaining practically nothing on the right, the government lost its parliamentary strength in the middle. It is true that the Center and Bavarian People's parties did quite well in the election. Both picked up a few additional seats, although their percentage of the popular vote slightly declined owing to the greater voter participation. But the two liberal parties suffered a crushing defeat, from which it could at once be seen that they would be unable to recover.

Many attempts had been made to fuse all the groups outside of the Center party ranging from the German Nationalists to the Social Democrats to form a strong "State party" in support of the president and the chancellor. The merger of the German People's party and the Democratic party into a single "Liberal party" was also much discussed, but neither party was ultimately ready to give up its connections with the right or left respectively. The Democrats then suddenly unified with one of the nationalist federations which abounded in Germany at this time. The Young-German Order, with which they coalesced into the German State party, was one of the more moderate, though less potent, ones. Those leaders of the Democratic party who pulled off this maneuver believed the union would "modernize" the image of the Democratic party and win her the support of many young people. Actually the Democrats and the Young Germans were even less compatible than the

Democrats and the members of the German People's party. The wrangling between the two partners ceased only for a few weeks during the election campaign, and the Young Germans probably marred rather than improved the image of the Democrats in the eyes of the voters, while they themselves could not deliver many votes. The upshot was disastrous. Whereas the Democratic party had still received 25 seats in 1928, it won only 20 in 1930, and the 6 Young Germans on the list seceded from the new party less than four weeks after the election. Thus only 14 Democrats were left, and at that not under their own name. The German People's party did not fare much better. It lost one third of its 45 seats.

The "Marxist" left went down in the popular vote from 42.2 to 38.2 per cent. But relatively few of its regular old voters turned their backs on the Social Democratic party, which with 143 instead of the former 152 deputies remained the strongest party in the *Reichstag*. The Communist party gained 23 in addition to its former 54 seats. As far as these additional votes did not come from disaffected Social Democrats, they derived from those who had not gone to the polls in former elections or from the young voters who voted for the first time. Altogether 2.3 million more citizens voted in 1930 than in 1928.

᭡ Brüning's Course after the Election

BRÜNING'S HOPE OF MOBILIZING the former nonvoters and of winning over the German Nationalists for his moderate nationalist course was proved quixotic by the election results. Although Hugenberg's German Nationalist party lost practically half its seats, his followers largely turned to the radical right, as did hordes of the young voters. Thus the astonishing growth of Hitler's party from 12 to 107 deputies was made possible. Therefore a parliament that had contained a democratic majority, though difficult to unite for constructive policies, and that did not have to be reelected for another two years was replaced by a parliament in which two radically antidemocratic parties had the second and third largest representation. Brüning's wish to build up support for himself on the right was completely defeated. Even if Hugenberg's party had turned around and come to the help of the Brüning government, this would not have given him a parliamentary majority. In this *Reichstag* no parliamentary government was possible without the Social Democrats, the very party against which the National Socialists, the German Nationalists, and the Communists had directed the main force of their reckless campaign and which had also been bitterly attacked by the People's party and the Center party. The Brüning government was vulnerable to the storm that the opponents of the Young Plan had aroused because it had publicly argued that in order to fulfill the plan it was necessary to balance the budget. Thus the opposition could blame the government and the major parties standing behind it for demanding the new sacrifices in order to satisfy the foreign oppressors of the German people. Reparations stemming from the "shameful" Versailles Treaty could be declared the cause of all economic ills and the Young Plan, as predicted by the supporters of the plebiscite against it, as the most diabolic imposition on the German people. The government, as we have already seen, had placed the cancellation of reparations as the chief goal of its foreign policy but could not say so openly since such an announcement in the first year of the plan would have ruined the German credit. For this reason alone it would have been necessary to avoid parliamentary elections till the government was able to announce clearly that it was determined to demand the complete cancellation of reparations.

The election results were proof of how disastrously the strength and character of the Nazi party had been misjudged. Even in republican circles it was widely thought that the party constituted the lunatic fringe of German nationalism that would well up somewhat in a period of great economic strain but die of its own paradoxes once general conditions had improved. Racist movements had risen and ebbed in Germany before in the 1890's and early 1920's. Thus the Nazis were often judged only as a recurrence of these earlier events. And even the tremendous shock that the results of the election of September 1930 caused did not fully open the eyes of the government leaders to the enormous threat that the Nazis posed not only to democracy but also to any government by law as well as to Germany's best cultural traditions. The suppression of the Nazi movement should have become the prime concern of all German policies.

Otto Braun, the Prussian prime minister, proposed an alliance of "all reasonable men" to this end. He suggested that he be made vice-chancellor and that the Prussian and the federal governments be merged. This would have been a historic step. It would finally have abolished the friction between a national and a semi-national government in Berlin, which the Frankfurt Assembly of 1848–49 had already tried to overcome, while the makers of the Weimar Constitution in 1919 had knowingly missed their opportunity. In the years thereafter much public discussion had been carried on over the reform of the constitutional organization of the federal government and the land governments. Since 1928 the federal government had inaugurated a "Reich reform conference" with the land governments, and the majority of its members wished to see Prussia absorbed by the Reich. The union of the federal and the Prussian governments would have had wide appeal and allowed considerable economies.

Yet Otto Braun wanted not only to build up a strong single authority by vesting in it a maximum of executive prerogatives but also to place behind it the support of the majority of the people. The Braun government in Prussia was still a government of the Weimar coalition, and thus Braun's entrance into the Brüning cabinet would practically have restored the "great coalition" of 1928. But after the events of the spring Brüning was skeptical whether any constructive policy could be forged with the Social Democrats. In addition he knew that President Hindenburg did not wish to have them in the government and that the People's party might bolt. Moreover the Social Democrats would place the emphasis on the creation of jobs, which Brüning felt could not be achieved when the business cycle was going down drastically. He thus did not respond to the suggestions on the merger of the federal and the Prussian governments, which Otto Braun on his part apparently did not push too hard.

Brüning also decided not to take the National Socialists and Nationalists into the government, as a few people recommended. They believed that once the Nazis would have to participate in the unpopular measures which the government would be forced to take by the economic crisis, their popularity would quickly wane. This reasoning disregarded the advantages which the Nazis would have gained by moving into governmental and administrative positions. They had already won much more than just parliamentary strength. Thus, for example, the immunity from prosecution that the 107 deputies enjoyed was exploited by making these deputies editors who enabled the sprouting Nazi press organs to conduct their wild and dirty campaign against any government that was not dominated by them. It is entirely improbable that Hitler would have been willing to forgo the great opportunities which waited for the Nazis as an opposition party. Brüning on the other side wanted to exclude the Nazis because they might have forced him to end reparations, or as the Nazis and German Nationalists called them "tributes," by unilateral action rather than by agreement with the victorious powers, as he thought necessary. For this reason he was not altogether sorry about the existence of a strong Nazi party. With a Nazi government looming as the only alternative to his own, Brüning saw his bargaining position with the foreign powers greatly strengthened. The fight against the Nazis at home was therefore not the primary aim of his policy. It was obvious that the Nazi party intended the overthrow of the constitutional order, and there were enough legal grounds to suppress the party. But this could have been done only if the Communists had been banned simultaneously. Yet whereas in 1930 the army supported by the police forces could have held down the radicals of the right and left, in 1932, when Brüning's successor considered such an action, doubts could be raised whether the army still had the power to fight both sides together. In late September 1930 Hitler was allowed to appear before the supreme court at the trial of three young officers who had tried to organize Nazi groups within the army. As witness under oath Hitler declared that his party would seek power in the state by legal methods only, and the Brüning government let the matter rest there.

These were circumstances which kept Brüning from a frontal attack on the Nazis whose threat he himself underrated, while he vastly overrated the impact of the potential successes which he expected to derive from his foreign policy on the internal development. The majority of the Germans wanted much more radical revisions of the Versailles Treaty than Brüning could hope to achieve. Moreover the Germans believed that the victor states owed them these concessions and that it was highly unjust that the Germans should make additional sacrifices in order to receive what was their proper due. The hardships which the great depression imposed were blamed by the people largely, if not exclusively, on the reparations, which in January 1931 even the government began to call "tributes." In these circumstances Brüning's financial policies caused profound popular resentment and resistance.

✑ *Economic Policy*

BRÜNING, PROUD OF BEING SOUNDLY GROUNDED in economics, firmly believed in the necessity for a balanced budget, an active balance of payments, and the stability of the currency in terms of the gold standard. In addition, he was convinced that depressions could not be fought by governments but would have to take their natural course, although once they had spent their ugly force, governments could help in the upswing. Keynesian economics of fighting depressions by deficit spending and credit expansion had not been invented as yet. It should be mentioned however that, even without the new Keynesian economics, the British were more successful than any other country in overcoming the great depression. They did not let it come to the breakdown of their internal credit system but devalued their currency in 1931, cut their budget, and in 1932 introduced a protective tariff. It is not suggested that comparable methods were easily accessible to Germany, but certainly the British leaders were less rigid in their economic theories. In Germany, too, there were at least a few economists who offered sensible advice on battling the depression and unemployment. But with Brüning in command they hardly got a hearing, and a rigid economic orthodoxy prevailed.

Brüning's policies, aimed at proving that Germany was unable to pay reparations, greatly intensified the downturn of business activity, idling factories and throwing millions of workers out on the street. With dwindling production, revenue declined, and balancing the budget continuously called for additional taxes and further cuts of the budget. Expenditures were finally brought down by roughly one third of the 12 billions spent in 1928. Half of this reduction was brought about largely by the cutting of salaries and pensions of all government personnel in three stages. By December 1931 they had been lowered by 19 to 23 per cent. The budget was never exactly balanced, although ten new taxes were introduced in eighteen months. But the deficits were in the end insignificant.

Thus the stabilization of the budget was substantially achieved, although it was a major cause of the fall of production and of the national income to 60 per cent of what it had been in 1928. Only the United States suffered similar losses in the great depression. Germany's vulnerability, however, rested on special causes. Apart from reparations it was produced by the great role that foreign loans and credits had played in the rebuilding and expansion of the German economy after the stabilization of the currency.[8] We have already mentioned that the major part of these loans, to wit, 12 billion marks as of the end of 1930, were in the form of short-term loans, which the debtors, however, largely invested in long-term enterprises. The elections of September 14, 1930, with their chauvinistic landslide results, alarmed the foreign creditors. By September 26, 420 billion marks had been recalled, and the withdrawal of credits continued until February 1931, when a temporary respite was gained. The *Reichsbank* had been able to repay over a billion marks because in 1930 reparation payments had been smaller under the Young Plan than they had been the year before under the Dawes arrangements. In addition the trade balance had become active owing to the falling of consumption and investments, which made imports drop. Perhaps it might have been possible to stabilize the situation after February if nothing had happened to arouse fresh suspicion among Germany's creditors with regard to her economy and policies.

The results of the September elections had at first given rise to general apprehension that Germany would adopt an activist policy of treaty revision. For the foreign creditors, however, the mention of a revision of the Young Plan alone, so shortly after its signing, was sufficiently frightening to make them worry about their loans. Brüning and Curtius, the foreign minister, soon recognized that the revision of the Young Plan would completely wreck German credit abroad. Moreover, the call for the revision of the plan would still not have freed Germany from paying reparations, since a large, protected part of the annual payments had to be made under all circumstances and the rest could only be postponed for a period of two years. Germany was entitled to insist on the convention of an "experts' committee," but what these appointees of the creditor nations would recommend was doubtful.

[8] See p. 636.

✍ *Austro-German Customs Union*

BRÜNING THEREFORE DECIDED TO WAIT with the fight for a revision of the Young Plan in spite of the strong pressures of public opinion and of most political parties. He felt that he would only have a chance of revising, or better still wiping out, reparations if he first laid bare the true situation of the German economy. Thus he went on with his balancing of the budget through cutting expenditures and adding taxes. He was not unaware of the fact that his government needed national successes if it wanted to overcome the radical nationalistic opposition. Therefore he reluctantly agreed to let the German foreign office go ahead with the project of an Austro-German customs union. Discussions of such a plan had been going on between Berlin and Vienna for a long time. But in the opinion of the German foreign office the right moment had now arrived, with Johann Schober (1874–1932) heading the Austrian government and with the worrisome prospect that Austria might turn to Italy if Germany refused to lend the small country assistance in its great economic distress.

The chief negotiations were carried on in great secrecy in the first two months of 1931. When Curtius went to Vienna in early March, basic agreement already existed. It was decided not to create a *fait accompli* but to make an announcement that the two governments intended to conclude a customs union. A mere trade agreement was ruled out, since the two countries were tied by many treaties containing the most-favored-nation clause, which would have necessitated giving the trading advantages of the Austro-German treaty to many other nations. But obviously the German foreign office wished to have the German public understand that the action was an important step in the direction of a future German-Austrian union (*Anschluss*), as the German Customs Union in the nineteenth century had been toward the political unification of Germany.

The dilemma was that, while wishing to create this impression at home, the Germans and Austrians had to deny any political implications of their action in dealing with foreign powers. And more than that, they also had to maintain that the treaty did not compromise Austria's economic and financial independence. For there was not only article 88 of the Peace Treaty of St. Germain, which the Allies had imposed on Austria in 1919, forbidding *Anschluss* as well as "any act" which might "directly or indirectly or by any means whatever" further this end, but also the Geneva Protocol of September 1922. In this latter agreement with the four great European powers, which Austria had to sign in order to receive a loan from the League of Nations, she committed herself not to grant "to any state a special regime or exclusive advantages" of a nature that would threaten Austrian economic independence. By keeping the projected customs union open for other nations to join and by making it possible to end the union through the resignation of one of the two signatories, the Austrian and German governments thought they had overcome the obstacles which the Treaty of St. Germain and the Geneva Protocol had raised against such an action.

Whether the Germans really felt that they had a perfect legal case seems questionable, since it was obvious that their interpretation could be easily challenged. The fact that the German foreign office and foreign service were entirely staffed by lawyers made the directors of German foreign policy always inclined to conceive of international conflicts as mere legal battles. But it was most disingenuous to consider an Austro-German customs union in such a way. Clearly this was a political matter, and the political reaction of the other powers should have been carefully weighed and the action diplomatically well prepared. The belief that the expected displeasure of Czechoslovakia and France could be relatively easily overcome by legal arguments was a serious misjudgment. Moreover, it was unwise to conduct the negotiations under the cloak of complete secrecy, because the plan looked doubly suspicious when it was first revealed by an unfortunate leak in Vienna.

The depth of Czech resentment and French anger that was the response to this disclosure had not been foreseen in Berlin. *Le Temps* published side by side on its front page the treaty on the Prusso-German Customs Union of 1834 and the projected Austro-German treaty, which the French government considered a badly veiled move toward *Anschluss*. Greatly frightened by the feverish chauvinism they saw spreading in Germany after the military evacuation of the Rhineland, the French were afraid that if tolerated this would be only the first event in a series of undertakings designed to shake the foundations of the Paris peace settlement. It was noticed with some apprehension that the rather large German military budget did not greatly suffer from the massive economies made by Brüning. His government even provided funds for the building of a second pocket battleship at a time when the preparatory disarmament conference attempted to draft a general disarmament convention. The Germans were not in need of the battleship, the strategic value of which was nil. Both the British and, naturally more cautiously, the Americans suggested that the building of battleship "B" should be postponed as a German contribution to their policy of making France agree to a meaningful disarmament convention. But here, too, the German government took a merely legalistic attitude, saying that they had disarmed under the Versailles Treaty and were only replacing obsolete ships to the extent allowed by the treaty. It was now up to the victorious powers of 1919 to disarm.

In these circumstances the position of Aristide Briand, who had consistently advocated a policy of reconciliation with Germany, was profoundly endangered by the projected Austro-German customs union. In all probability it was the reason why the French National Assembly did not elect him president of the republic in May 1931. The French government from the outset was determined not to tolerate the execution of the plan. The Italians, after brief hesitation, decided to join the French opposition. The British on their part showed little concern about the customs union, but they were worried that the German move would interfere with the cooperation of the major powers in the urgent tasks of fighting the depression and making progress toward disarmament. Wishing to keep both Briand and Brüning in office, they prevailed on Briand not to use the League Council at its May meeting to compel Austria and Germany to abandon the customs union but first to ask the Hague Court for a legal opinion. While this saved the German government from losing face for the time being, the Austrian position was already crumbling.

The vulnerability of Austria to the pressures by the powers which in 1922 had assisted in restoring her economy was never taken into account by the German foreign office. Nor was the internal weakness of Austria properly gauged. The withdrawal of foreign credits, among which the French were most prominent, weakened the whole credit system. On May 11, 1931, the greatest Austrian bank, the *Creditanstalt*, became insolvent. The bank was estimated to control two thirds of the Austrian industries, and the government had to maintain it in business by guarantees. But this required foreign loans and forced Austria to approach France. The French made the grant of a loan dependent on an Austrian declaration against the customs union and *Anschluss*. In addition they demanded the acceptance of certain direct French controls. The Schober government refused and resigned. At this moment the Bank of England gave Austria the needed loan. The question was how long the bank could afford to leave its loan with Austria.

✑ Bank Crisis and Hoover Moratorium

THE BREAKDOWN of the Austrian *Creditanstalt* made the foreign financiers nervous with regard to all their Central European investments. In May the flight of capital from Germany began. The withdrawal of foreign credits became a dreadful avalanche when it was rumored that the German government intended to declare a moratorium on reparations payments. On June 6, the austere third emergency decree dealing with public finance was published, and the government proclaimed its intention to take steps in order to achieve the liberation from "unbearable reparations." This proclamation was the signal for the largest withdrawal of credits. Between June 8 and 12 the *Reichsbank* lost over 500 million marks in foreign exchange. From June 1 to the middle of July the loss of gold and foreign exchange amounted to 2 billion, making a total of 3.5 to 4 billion in the period since September 14, 1930.

As far back as March Brüning had decided to announce the determination of the government to seek an alleviation of reparations payments. In this case he let reasons of domestic politics direct his actions, for he well knew that the right moment for ending the reparations had not yet arrived. He knew, too, that the announcement of an imminent moratorium of payments under the Young Plan would shake the German credit, although he did not foresee the full impact this might produce on the structure of German finance and economy.

When Brüning and Curtius, on the invitation of the British government, had spent the weekend of June 5–8, 1931, at Chequers in political conversations with Ramsay MacDonald and his foreign secretary, Arthur Henderson, the two British statesmen had persuaded their German guests to delay any action on a moratorium on Young Plan payments until the arrival in Europe of the American secretary of state, Henry L. Stimson, early in July. The British were convinced that because of the close connection with the inter-Allied war debts a revision of reparations could not be achieved without the United States. But when the withdrawals of credits continued during June and the German government was about ready to ask for a postponement of the payments under the Young Plan, President Hoover on June 20, 1931, proposed a moratorium on payments of all intergovernmental debts, which meant in the first place reparations and inter-Allied war debts. The American action, which came as a complete surprise to the Germans, naturally was highly welcomed by them, as it was in England, the only country which had proper advance notice of the plan. Unfortunately the American government failed to prepare the French, the nation most deeply concerned about reparations. Therefore the French were indignant at what they called the presumptuous American methods as well as the proposals themselves. Not without good reason they saw in the latter an attempt to save the private American bank loans which had gone to Germany at the expense of France's sacred rights of reparations. Although on balance the French were not to suffer financial losses during the Hoover moratorium year, they were fearful that once the payment scheme had been set aside and depreciated, it would be difficult, if not impossible, to return to it.

In the negotiations which the Americans, supported by the British, conducted, the French fought stubbornly to retain as much as possible of the Young Plan. After two weeks of meetings in Paris an agreement was reached on July 6. Under it the annual installment of the unconditional reparations debt had to be paid by Germany in 1931–32 but would immediately be given as a loan to the German railroad company by the Bank of International Settlement. Reparations deliveries in kind would have to be made as far as they had already been prepared and would not be a new burden on the German budget.

The Franco-American conflict left in doubt for a good while whether the Hoover moratorium would become operative. The psychological effect of the American initiative was blunted by this delay. A few days after the original announcement the withdrawals of foreign credits from Germany began again in an alarming fashion. Since the fall of the Austrian *Creditanstalt* it should have been clear to everybody in a responsible position that the situation of the German banks was precarious and that the collapse of any of the big German banks might spell disaster for the whole German economy. It was unfortunate that under these conditions the agencies in charge of financial leadership in Germany were weak and divided. After Hjalmar Schacht's resignation Hans Luther had become president of the *Reichsbank*. Yet this stolid man was not really an outstanding financial expert but rather an administrator with strong political ideas of his own, which the newly assumed independence of the bank made him assert against the government. The big German banks, the so-called D-banks (the *Deutsche Bank und Diskonto-Gesellschaft*, the *Dresdner Bank*, the *Darmstädter und Nationalbank*) showed no sense of solidarity, a result not only of their personal discords but also of the inability of most of their directors to diagnose the true character of the developing crisis. The government did not awake early enough to the threatening danger and, once it did, failed to force the big private banks to stand together and to compel the *Reichsbank* to support them to the hilt.

Until early July the credit withdrawn from the banks had been mostly called back by foreign creditors, but after July the banks suffered also from the growing loss of domestic accounts. In view of the close connection between industries and banks it was obvious that bankruptcies of industrial firms might destroy the reserves of the banks. One of the biggest German textile companies, the *Nordwolle* (precisely, the North German Wool Combing Company), became insolvent, and it became known that the *Darmstädter Bank* and the *Dresdner Bank* would suffer big losses. The *Darmstädter Bank* was under the heaviest pressure but was refused help by the other banks and the *Reichsbank*. The former ones still felt that they might survive if only the *Darmstädter Bank* would prove to be insolvent, although they knew that the whole German banking system had never recovered from the inflation and that with the loss of foreign loans and credits their own situation was equally endangered. Only together could they have withstood a general run of the public. In addition it would have required the willingness of the *Reichsbank* to extend to the banks any credit they would need for making payments. President Luther was not prepared to promise such an unrestricted rediscounting. He was afraid that the deviation from the legal minimum gold and foreign exchange coverage of the currency would lead to inflation, a fear unjustified under the conditions existing in 1931. He made desperate last-minute attempts to get large rediscount credits for the *Reichsbank* from London, Paris, and New York. When they failed, he finally refused to change the restrictive policies of the *Reichsbank*.

Since the crash of a single big bank, let alone all the big banks, would have completely ruined the German economy, the government had no choice but to guarantee the deposits of these banks. But the *Deutsche Bank* and the *Dresdner Bank* were still too proud and optimistic to accept government protection. Thus the announcement of this guarantee in the morning of Monday, July 13, was confined to the *Darmstädter Bank*, which alone did not open its doors on that day. But, as might have been expected, this proved to be the signal for a general run of the people on all the banks, including the saving banks. At noon they all had to close. Now all the banks clamored for governmental guarantees and credits, and the government declared two bank holidays. Actually the banks did not resume full payments until August 5, and by that time the German economy had already ceased to be a free economy.

Originally Brüning had tried to get rediscount credits for the *Reichsbank* from the foreign central banks. Together with Curtius he traveled to Paris, where on July 19 he negotiated with Laval, Flandin, and Briand. The French offered credits which thereafter were to be transformed into a loan. But France wanted in exchange renewed direct foreign controls over German public finance and, most of all, a political moratorium. For a five-year period Germany was to abstain from any move toward the revision of the Versailles Treaty. These conditions were completely unacceptable to Brüning. They would have meant the return to a Young Plan made politically less palatable by the reintroduction of controls after the Dawes Plan model and the impossibility of using the disarmament conference for a change of the military provisions of the Versailles Treaty, to mention only the most immediate aims of the German government.

The French and German ministers then proceeded to London, where a conference was held with Ramsay MacDonald and Arthur Henderson, who were joined by Henry L. Stimson and Andrew Mellon. The British by now had made up their minds that the eventual cancellation of debts and reparations was a prerequisite for the revival of international trade and refused to give credits which might have to be used to pay reparations. As a matter of fact the Bank of England would not have been in a position to give credits to the *Reichsbank*. The English bank was under heavy pressure of foreign withdrawals, most, though not all, of them by French creditors. The English and Americans recommended that Germany reach with the foreign holders of the German short-term credits an agreement on a standstill of withdrawals, which was actually concluded a little later. The French together with the two other governments extended a $100 million credit which Germany had received from the central banks for three months and thereafter it was even extended again. But the three conference partners refused to recommend the grant of rediscount credits for the *Reichsbank*.

Thereby the age of international capitalistic cooperation drew to a close. The Germans were now forced to solve their financial crisis by internal means, which necessitated the disregard of legal rights and customs. The bank holidays had in practice served as a complete moratorium on international payments. This was followed by the government control of all foreign exchange transactions. Also a rather unorthodox way was found that made it possible for the *Reichsbank* to supply the banks with sufficient means when they resumed full operations after August 5. These steps might have been taken in early July as well, when they would have prevented the closing of the banks.

The governmental control of foreign exchange, although certain payments under the standstill agreements were exempted from it, actually created two German currencies, one for international, the other for domestic use. Henceforth there was no difficulty in maintaining the international exchange rate. It would have been safe to adopt expansionist policies aiming at raising production and employment. But Brüning did not wish to act before he had gained the cancellation of reparations.

Another possible opportunity for reviving the German economy was not exploited. On September 21, England left the gold standard, and before the year was over seventeen countries had followed the British example. For Germany the devaluation of her currency would have meant a drastic improvement of her competitive position on the world market. Since the devaluation of the pound, one of the two reserve currencies of the world monetary system, made the gold standard very questionable, Germany's departure from it would have been defensible. On the other hand it would have necessitated higher payments on a good many credit contracts which contained a gold clause. What was more important was the fact that the devaluation of the mark would have caused profound opposition by France at a time when a most promising beginning for the eventual abolition of reparations had been made. Another reason for Brüning's decision not to devaluate the mark does not seem convincing in retrospect. It was always said that the inflation of the early twenties had made the Germans overly sensitive to any kind of inflation. But devaluation would not have affected prices in 1931 and therefore would not have been taken by the public as the beginning of a new inflation. And even if the public had panicked and attempted to get rid of its money by purchasing goods, prices would not have been affected, since there was an oversupply of goods.

With the rejection of devaluation only one way was open to Brüning for keeping German exports on a competitive level. Prices had to be brought down, and this implied a lowering of wages. On December 8 the most draconian of all the emergency ordinances was issued. It ordered the cut of all fixed prices by 10 per cent and of free prices by an amount to be determined by a federal price commissioner, the lowering of interest rates and of rents as well as some protection against foreclosures, chiefly in agriculture. Simultaneously it further curtailed the social insurance benefits and cut wages down to the level of January 1927, which amounted to a 10 to 15 per cent cut. Finally, in order to stabilize the budget the ordinance raised taxes, and for the third time in fourteen months the salaries of the government officials and employees were drastically slashed.

✐ End of Reparations

WHEN THIS ORDINANCE, which imposed great sacrifices and could not stop the further growth of unemployment, was promulgated, Brüning believed that the final cancellation of reparations was close at hand and that before long he would be able to replace his deflationary policies with policies aiming at job creation. As it was, the reducation of prices was not even likely to safeguard German exports for long, since everywhere tariffs were going up. The United States had already begun with raising tariffs, Britain went over to protectionism in 1931, Italy also imposed stiff duties, and even a creditor nation such as Switzerland placed severe restrictions on German imports.

But at the same time the belief in the necessity of abolishing German reparations payments had grown immensely. In Britain they were now considered an obstacle to any solution of the world economic crisis. The London Conference had left it to a committee of experts to study the external indebtedness of Germany, the possibility of changing her short-term into long-term credits, and her need for new capital. The committee that convened in August in Basel under the chairmanship of the American banker Albert H. Wiggin was not allowed to make recommendations on the future of reparations. Its report, presented on August 18, was written by the editor of the London *Economist*, Walter Layton. Without specially mentioning reparations, it forcefully pointed out that the granting of new loans to Germany or her holding of long-term credits would be impossible if reparations continued. The report demanded that relations between Germany and the other powers be based on friendly cooperation and mutual confidence and that measures should be taken to prevent Germany's private and public obligations from resulting in a snowballing increase of her external debt or an imbalance between her imports and exports that would threaten the economic prosperity of other countries. The report warned that time was running out.

But the French showed no willingness to accept the recommendations of the Layton Report. In the following weeks they had the satisfaction of seeing the proposed Austro-German customs union come to nothing. As early as the middle of July Austria had been forced to approach the League of Nations with a demand for a new loan, which in the circumstances could only come from Paris. The French brought pressure to bear on Schober to drop the customs union project, and on September 3, 1931 Schober and Curtius had to announce in Geneva that they would not pursue their original plan. The Germans felt deeply humiliated by the French. Brüning, remembering his early resistance to the project, now put all the blame for its failure on Curtius.

Since France still wanted to save the Young Plan, Germany was compelled to use the machinery of the plan for revisions. Consequently she applied for the convention of a special committee at the Bank for International Settlements. Although officially this committee could only deal with a moratorium on the deferrable, and not the protected, part of the annuities, its so-called Beneduce Report boldly indicated that the Young Plan had misjudged future economic developments. In order to avoid a new disaster, it would be necessary without delay to adjust all intergovernmental debts, reparations as well as war debts, to the shattered conditions of the world economy. The British government immediately approached the signatories of the Young Plan, urging the convention of a conference on war debts for January 18, 1932, in Lausanne. But the British soon had to recognize that a compromise with the French was not yet possible. Therefore the conference was delayed and finally convened only in the middle of June 1932, about two weeks before the Hoover moratorium was to come to an end. At that time Brüning was no longer holding office.

✍ *Political Radicalization*

THE DELAY of the Lausanne Conference by almost half a year added to Germany's grave political troubles. All the municipal and state elections after 1930 had shown that the radicalization of the people had increased by leaps and bounds. The Brüning government dismally failed to stem this tide. The plain appeal to cold reason was not enough to satisfy people who were jobless, bankrupt, or just frightened. This applied to industrial workers and employees as well as to the large number of small shopkeepers whose cash registers had never recorded any great income. Especially pitiable was the situation of the youth of all classes. Most of them could not hope to find any remunerative employment or to enter on a career, and even more than their elders they were lured by the revolutionary slogans of the Communists and National Socialists. Thus they sought release for their energies and sentiments in the demonstrations that became the chief expression of German political life in these years. But apart from mass meetings at which the extremist leaders worked up the passions of their followers and from demonstration marches in the streets, an increasing number of bloody fights and battles took place. Most of them were fought between Nazis and Communists, but the Nazis also committed a series of rowdy actions against Jews. Although its powers were extended, the police suffered many casualties.

Government by emergency decrees meant government by the bureaucracy. The parliament ceased having any influence on the legislation and policies of the government. Theoretically the parliament could have repealed the emergency decrees, and the opposition of the right and left never failed to bring in such resolutions. But with the help of the largest—the Social Democratic—party such resolutions were regularly defeated down to May 1932. While to this extent Brüning still relied on parliamentary support, the parties were unable to exercise any influence on the contents and form of legislation. With their decision to tolerate the government, because Brüning's fall would bring on the victory of fascism in Germany, the Social Democratic party had lost all political initiative and the ability to fight for self-chosen aims. It is true that Brüning and his original mentor, Stegerwald, who belonged to the cabinet as minister of labor, were no reactionaries in social questions. On the other hand the federal labor mediators now increasingly decided in favor of the entrepreneurs. Moreover in political matters Brüning had to avoid the appearance of granting special favors to the Social Democrats. He had been called to rule without them and to bring the rightist parties into the government. Now he was accused of leading a veiled "great coalition" and thereby spoiling still another aim of the presidential cabinet, that the chancellor should not pay any attention to the political parties. Although the Social Democrats still derived some power from their leadership in the Prussian administration, the government by emergency decrees lowered the authority and independence of the state governments very considerably. In order to enforce its financial and economic policies the federal government paid less and less attention to the state governments, who in the distressing conditions of these years could not very well afford to fight it. Thus already in the Brüning period the centralization of government, which Hitler was to make absolute beginning in 1933, had made great progress. Still another fundamental transformation was the work of the Brüning government. The policy of lowering prices and wages, the establishment of foreign exchange control, and the guarantee for the banks forced the federal administration to intervene more and more in the operations of the German economy. The bank laws of February 1932 practically gave the government command over the whole banking system, and since the banks controlled the major part of German industries, the foundation for the regimented economy of the Hitler era was laid.

While the Brüning government was protected against parliamentary pressures, it was not secure against the pressures of interest groups, particularly as far as they could exercise their influence through the palace of the president. In the first place there were the agrarians who conducted noisy public propaganda for state assistance and also operated through personal channels. No doubt agriculture needed help in the great economic crisis, but Brüning's program was weighted far beyond a reasonable measure toward the demands of the agriculturists. In view of the great sufferings of the other social groups it could hardly be justified in keeping the prices of agricultural staple products at double and even three times the world market prices. Yet in spite of all these measures the hatred of the agrarian circles for the Brüning government grew steadily. The industrialists also pressed their demands on the government. They wanted maximum freedom for the entrepreneur to conduct his business in times of crisis. They not only wished to see the power of the trade unions restricted but also the interference in business by the government. Essentially they thought that they were the only ones able to master the economic crisis and for that reason expected the government to accept their advice. A group of prominent industrialists succeeded in October 1931 in having Hindenburg publicly suggest to Brüning that he convene a council of economic leaders to work out a program to overcome the crisis. The new economic council did not live up to the expectations of the industrialists. It contained representatives of the trade unions as well and was disbanded after making a report that more or less approved Brüning's economic program. The industrialists had thought of the council rather as a kind of council of state under the auspices of the president that would issue orders and advice to the government. They felt that the Brüning regime still contained too much democracy and wanted a strengthening of the dictatorial element in the government.

Whereas prior to 1930 only a few big industrialists had taken an interest in Hitler and made gifts to his party chest, after his election victory of 1930 Hitler was able to augment his contacts with important figures of German industry. As a consequence the financial contributions of industrialists to the Nazi party increased. Although their official organizations, particularly the powerful Reich Federation of Industry, officially supported Brüning, the dissatisfaction with his policies grew and by the fall of 1931 had reached the critical stage. In a masterful demagogic speech before the tycoons of the Rhenish and Ruhr industries that won large applause, Hitler, on January 27, 1932, had laid to rest their apprehension about the socialist tendencies of his tumultuous movement. He presented himself as the savior from communism and the determined champion of the leadership principle that should be maintained in the economic life of the country as well.

The shift in the political attitude of the German industrialists was also reflected in the changing policies of the German People's party. After Stresemann's death the party was completely under the domination of the big industrialists. It was symptomatic that during the spring and summer of 1931 it participated in a plebiscite that the *Stahlhelm* inaugurated in order to force the dissolution of the Prussian diet and new elections in the largest German state. This plebiscite was to register the strength of the "national opposition," as the enemies of the Brüning government on the right called themselves. Also the Communist party, which saw in the plebiscite a useful means for the further radicalization of the German masses, brought its members to the polls. Thirty-seven per cent of the electorate voted on August 9 in favor of new elections in Prussia. Although these were fewer votes than the parties behind the plebiscite had won in the last federal elections, the result made it clear that the Prussian government, which still relied on the parties of the Weimar coalition, would not survive the next elections to be held in the spring of 1932. On Hugenberg's instigation the "national opposition" put on another show of strength. On October 11, 1931 a big assembly was held in the little spa of Harzburg in Brunswick, which was already ruled by the German Nationalists and Nazis. Here Hugenberg and Hitler, together with the members of their parties in the federal and Prussian parliaments and a good many members of the German People's party and of the Economy party, met with the leaders of the *Stahlhelm*, the great agrarian organizations, and other economic interest groups. In addition the leaders of the Pan-German League and more than a dozen well-known generals of the former imperial army, joined by two sons of William II, appeared. Also General Seeckt was present, and Hjalmar Schacht gave a challenging speech. Both gentlemen were busy making contacts with what they sensed was the wave of the future. There was also a fairly large number of prominent industrialists and bankers who wanted to make their anti-republican sentiments known. However, the assembly agreed only on negative aims, in the first place on a demand for the fall of the Brüning and Braun governments. Hugenberg, who presided over the meeting, apparently was still quite confident that he had more political power than Hitler, but although he was exceedingly conciliatory to Hitler's demands, the latter felt ill at ease in the company of such a mass of reactionary men. He behaved very rudely and, after reviewing the parade of his storm troopers left town without waiting for the parade of the *Stahlhelm*. But the Harzburg meeting impressed the world, in spite of the fact that the conception of the "Harzburg front" did not become practical politics for another year.

The strident opposition of the agrarian and industrial leaders and the steady growth of the Nazi party aroused the concern of the men who had brought Brüning to power. He had been made chancellor to form a coalition of the rightist parties but had failed to do so, and with increasing violence these parties directed their attacks against him. With the immobilization of parliament Brüning became more and more dependent on the army and the president, who were both conscious of their authority with regard to the chancellor. General von Schleicher was apprehensive that the developing civil war situation in Germany would force the army to act and might find it too weak if the situation deteriorated still further. During the summer of 1931 he had already opened negotiations with the Nazi party in order to find out under what conditions it might join the government. His conversations with Captain Ernst Röhm (1887–1934), the chief of Hitler's storm troopers, had led in the fall to a meeting with Hitler, as a result of which Schleicher persuaded Brüning and Hindenburg to see Hitler. But these meetings had led nowhere, and the meeting between Hindenburg and Hitler in particular on the day before the Harzburg gathering was an open failure. Hindenburg found Hitler an odd fellow. He disliked the lengthy monologues with which Hitler tried to impress him. Hindenburg was reported to have said that he would never appoint this "Bohemian corporal" chancellor but at best postmaster general.

On the other hand President Hindenburg demanded from Brüning changes in the composition and character of his government, for which the resignation of Foreign Minister Curtius on October 3 gave an opportunity. Hindenburg asked Brüning to form a government that was "independent" and "without party ties." He also suggested that he invite prominent business leaders to join his cabinet. But they refused to enter the government, and Brüning had to be satisfied with winning a lesser-known representative of the chemical industry as minister of economics, who soon deserted the cabinet. The impression that the members of the Center party had predominated in the Brüning government was deflated by the dropping of two Centrist ministers. Besides the rather insignificant Theodor von Guérard (b. 1863), the minister of transport, Joseph Wirth, the minister of the interior, who since the days of his chancellorship had been particularly hated by the rightist parties, was not reappointed. But no fresh blood was added. Brüning himself took the foreign office, while General Groener was made minister of the interior in addition to his post as minister of defense. The cabinet presented to parliament, which had assembled again after half a year on October 13, was more compact and homogeneous than the first Brüning cabinet had been, but Brüning still intended to rely on the toleration of parliament, and this meant of the Social Democrats in particular, a toleration that made him so suspect in the eyes of the members of the "national opposition." They wanted a dictatorial regime above and, if necessary, against the parties. Schleicher continued his conversations with the Nazi leaders in November and December and informed the president that Hitler was still ready in principle to discuss the participation of the Nazi party in the government. He probably planted in Hindenburg's mind the idea that Brüning was standing in the way of a future national government of the Reich.

✍ Hindenburg's Reelection

BUT FIRST HINDENBURG had to be reelected. In March 1932 presidential elections were due. The parties behind Brüning had no candidates with whom they could hope to defeat a candidacy of Hitler. On the other hand, it seemed unlikely that the eighty-four-year-old president would outlive another seven-year term. Brüning thought at first to have Hindenburg elected regent of the Reich for his lifetime, to be followed after his death by one of the sons of the crown prince, for it was clear to him that, because of their declared sympathies with radical nationalism, the crown prince himself and William II's other sons were unacceptable to the Social Democrats. Hindenburg on his part had always suffered from the memory of his attitude in early November 1918, when he had persuaded the emperor to take refuge in Holland. As president he felt himself like something of a stand-in for the monarch, and he would have liked nothing better than to conclude his public career with the restoration of the monarchy in Germany. But to him this meant the full restoration of the old German-Prussian monarchy. If the rumor current in some circles in Berlin at that time was true, William II did not make Brüning's task any easier. In answer to the question whether he would be willing to return to Germany, William II was reported to have replied that he would be prepared to do so only if all the other ruling dynasties of Germany would be restored. In any event, Brüning dropped his ill-conceived plan of monarchical restoration very quickly. Instead he proposed to have the federal parliament extend Hindenburg's presidency for a period of a year or two, but this also required a two-thirds majority in parliament. It was with some difficulty that Brüning persuaded Hindenburg to let him find out whether he could win the support of the German nationalists and the National Socialists. In the early days of January 1932 Brüning, Groener, and Schleicher held discussions with Hitler, Röhm, and Hugenberg. Brüning suggested the extension of Hindenburg's presidency until the reparations issue had been settled and German equality of the right to arm had been achieved, for which the current discussion at the disarmament conference in Geneva seemed to offer some reasonable hope. Hugenberg's answer was a straight no, and so was Hitler's, except that he tried to drive a wedge between Hindenburg and Brüning by declaring that the Nazi party would support Hindenburg if he replaced Brüning and agreed to new elections in Germany and Prussia. The negotiations showed the weakening of Brüning's position. In order to protect himself against the insinuation that he conducted them in a form that would secure his continuation as chancellor, he repeatedly had to offer Hindenburg his immediate resignation if it was found that his person was in the way of getting the two rightist parties to support the president. In case of his resignation, however, the extension of Hindenburg's presidency would not have helped to achieve Brüning's aims. Before the election Hindenburg wrote to some of his personal friends that with all respect for Brüning's achievements he would have been willing to replace him if the formation of a right-wing government had been possible. Hindenburg's relations with Brüning cooled, since he did not quite forgive him for having brought him into the embarrassing situation of standing as a candidate against many groups which had elected him in 1925 and with which he felt close bonds. It was a bitter blow for him that even the *Stahlhelm*, whose honorary president he was and which he had carefully shielded, turned against him. The German Nationalists chose the deputy chief of the *Stahlhelm*, Colonel Theodor Düsterberg, as their candidate. Hitler hesitated almost a month before he decided to run against Hindenburg. The political risk involved seemed to him very great. He did not even possess German citizenship and could not have gained it by normal legal processes. Instead he had himself appointed a state official at the Brunswick legation in Berlin by the National Socialist minister of the interior in Brunswick and thereby automatically gained German citizenship. On February 22 Goebbels proclaimed Hitler's candidacy.

The campaign was unusually bitter and intense. The Nazis carried their fight into the smallest villages and aroused the most energetic efforts on the part of the middle and the republican parties. Brüning did not pay back the Nazis in their own coin, but his polemics against Hitler and his party were sharper than at any other time of his chancellorship, and he was building up the mythical Hindenburg in adulatory fashion. More soberly Otto Braun called Hindenburg a man of good will and mature judgment on whose word one could rely and who, therefore, deserved preference. To him Hitler was the prototype of the political adventurer who, with his party of desperados, would lead Germany into political suppression and civil war at the risk of ending the Reich.

The elections of March 13, 1932, gave Hindenburg 46.6 per cent of the vote against Hitler's 30.1 per cent. Düsterberg's percentage of 6.8 demonstrated that within the "national opposition" the Nazi party had become the dominant group. The Communist candidate, Ernst Thälmann (1886–1944) received 13.2 per cent, a great disappointment to a party which had hoped that many Social Democrats would give them their vote, because they would reject Hindenburg. Considering that this election witnessed a greater popular participation than any democratic election in Germany before and that it was highest in the cities, the party discipline of the Social Democratic followers was most impressive. The Nazis, whose expectations had been very high, were greatly dejected. But with great speed Hitler declared that he would be a candidate again in the runoff election which had become necessary, since Hindenburg had not gained the majority prescribed by the constitution for the first ballot. Hitler succeeded in infusing his followers with new enthusiasm. Düsterberg withdrew, but not even now was Hugenberg willing to support Hindenburg. He left it to his followers to make their own choice, while the politically inept crown prince tried to lead the monarchists into the Nazi camp by declaring that he would vote for Hitler. The popular participation in the second voting on April 10 was only slightly smaller than on March 13. But this time Hindenburg gained 53 per cent against Hitler's 36.8 per cent which apparently fell far short of the latter's expectations. Captain Röhm, under whose command the storm troopers had grown between January 1, 1931, and April 1932 from 100,000 to 400,000 men, advocated gaining power in the state by revolutionary means, but Hitler remained firmly set on his course of legality and told his followers that the imminent state elections would give them another opportunity to advance the cause of the Nazi party. Actually the Nazis were never to gain a majority in democratic elections, but the 53 per cent who voted for Hindenburg were by no means all supporters of the republic. They included many advocates of a dictatorial system in Germany, as the candidate himself could hardly be counted as a defender of the democratic order.

☞ *Ban of the SA*

THE SUCCESS OF THE PRESIDENTIAL ELECTIONS was followed by the execution of an action that had been prepared for some time. The police authorities of Prussia and other states had been able to collect over a long time proof of the revolutionary plans which were hatched particularly by the paramilitary organizations of the Nazi party. There was ample evidence, for example, that the storm troopers had planned a *coup d'état* in the case of a Hitler victory in the first presidential elections. The Brüning government had always resisted repressive action against the Nazi party.

The army had seen in the storm troopers a useful potential reservoir of manpower once the army could be expanded and had warned against the suppression of these forces until such a time as the international situation would make it possible to use them as a militia subordinate to the army. But now the states demanded a ban of all paramilitary organizations of the Nazi party with a view to the approaching state elections. They even indicated that they would act on their own if the federal government refused to issue a national ban. Generals Groener and von Schleicher, as well as the chief of the army, General von Hammerstein-Equord, agreed that the week after the ultimate reelection of Hindenburg would be the right moment to suppress all the paramilitary organizations of the Nazi party, and even Hindenburg consented to the plan. Schleicher surprisingly changed his mind on April 9, the day before the election. He proposed that Hitler should be warned and requested to fulfill within a certain period a series of concrete measures for the demilitarization of these paramilitary organizations. But he was overruled not only by Groener but also by Hindenburg, and on April 13 the ban on all paramilitary organizations of the Nazi party was issued. There were wild protests on the right, but what mattered more were the intrigues by which Schleicher tried to advance his own policies. He declared that Groener's policy as minister of interior was unbearable for the army. Groener, he said, had been expected to prepare the way for the subordination to the army of all paramilitary organizations and the one-sided anti-Nazi measures were endangering this policy. He persuaded Hindenburg to write an open letter to Groener in which he suggested that similar organizations of other parties should be banned as well, and the appended documentation, which Schleicher had sent behind Groener's back to the president's office, made it clear that Hindenburg was thinking of the *Reichsbanner*, the paramilitary organization of the republican parties. Nothing was said in the letter about the *Stahlhelm*. Simultaneously Schleicher resumed his contacts with the Nazi leaders. His idea of "taming" the Nazi party by bringing it closer to, or possibly even into, the government would be nearer to realization now if he could promise Hitler the repeal of the ban on the paramilitary organizations of the Nazi party.

For the time being, however, all the parties were preoccupied with new elections which took place on April 24 in four fifths of the German states, among them Prussia, Bavaria, Württemberg, and Hamburg. The state elections confirmed the results of the second Hindenburg election. In practice this meant that parliamentary government on the state level came to an end in Germany. The moderate parties lost their majority in all states. On the other hand, with the exception of a few small states, the "national opposition" nowhere gained a majority, and the existing governments continued as caretakers without parliamentary support. This had been true since 1930 in Bavaria. Now it became the case in Württemberg and, most important of all, the Prussia of Otto Braun, where the Weimar coalition was in a minority of 162 to 261. Instead of 8, the Nazi party had elected 162 members of parliament and, with the exception of the Center, had crushed the moderate parties altogether. But the German Nationalists, too, had suffered serious losses, and the "national opposition" could muster only 203 against 220 members. Only if the Center party had joined the Nazis and German Nationalists could a parliamentary government have been formed, but the Nazis were not willing to consider such a coalition at the moment when every attempt was being made to bring down the Brüning government.

✍ End of Brüning Cabinet

AFTER HIS REELECTION Hindenburg had confirmed the Brüning cabinet in office, although he hinted that in the near future he might wish to appoint a government more to the right. The eighty-five-year-old field marshal preferred more and more to take the advice of his immediate circle—his son, the colorless but politically prejudiced Colonel Oskar von Hindenburg, and the chief of the presidential chancery, Otto Meissner (1880–1953), who was an ambitious and unprincipled opportunist. Schleicher was a good friend of Oskar von Hindenburg, with whom he had served as junior officer in the same regiment of the Prussian guards. It was Schleicher's intention to create a presidential government that would be further to the right and find the toleration of the Nazis. A first step in this direction was taken with the removal of General Groener from the defense ministry.

For the last time under the Brüning regime, the *Reichstag* reconvened from May 9 to 13. On May 10 Göring made a sizzling speech attacking Groener, who was a poor speaker and very ineffective in his defense of the ban on the Nazi organizations. His remarks were drowned by noisy interjections of the Nazis. The tumultuous scenes they staged could finally be ended only by the intervention of the police. Schleicher, in cooperation with Hammerstein, told Groener that his resignation was inevitable. Groener, who knew that he had lost Hindenburg's confidence as well, kept Brüning from supporting him with the president, because this would have endangered the whole cabinet. On May 12 he resigned as defense minister but remained minister of the interior. It was ominous that Schleicher refused Brüning's offer to head the ministry of defense.

Actually Schleicher was already constructing a cabinet that would supersede that of Brüning. A shrewd and sensitive man, he was not entirely unaware of the power of social forces, but ultimately he felt that policies were the result of subtle manipulations of persons. He greatly underrated the dynamic force that the Nazi movement represented, while he overrated his capacity for winning over people. The beguiling charm he put on if he wanted to would not turn Nazis into moderates. He even overestimated his ability to influence Hindenburg and the people around him, and his persuasive powers would not suffice to talk them out of ingrained political and social notions.

Schleicher picked as his candidate for chancellor Franz von Papen (b. 1879), a Catholic Westphalian nobleman who had married into the Saar industry. A former cavalry officer, he remained a passionate horseman. He had gone through general staff training and during World War I had become military attaché in Washington, where his sabotage activities induced the American government in 1916 to send him home. After the war Papen took part in politics both in the Westphalian province and the Prussian capital. As a member of the right wing of the Center party he held a seat in the Prussian parliament for ten years. In 1923 he had called for the formation of a dictatorial government and in 1925 supported Hindenburg's election. Essentially he was a reactionary monarchist who wished to see the prewar order of Germany restored and who hated those who in his opinion had destroyed it, which meant in the first place the Social Democrats. Although he owned a substantial part of the shares of *Germania*, the Berlin organ of the Center party, his ideas had not affected the policies of the party. Nobody took this affable and elegant gentleman, who was an attractive partner in social conversation, very seriously politically. With irresponsible lightheartedness Schleicher, who knew Papen, though not intimately, tried to lift him into the chancellorship. Papen seemed sufficiently nationalist to be acceptable to Hugenberg and Hitler, while his membership in the Center party might induce it to tolerate him. Schleicher, who was to become defense minister, put together a cabinet for the future chancellor and again proved his poor political judgment. None of the ten men chosen by him was an eminent or well-known political figure. They were all clearly German nationalists; seven were noblemen, and of the remaining three one was a director of Krupp, another a director of *I.G. Farben*, while the third, Franz Gürtner (1881–1941), as Bavarian minister of justice had played a dubious role in the days of the Hitler *Putsch* of 1923. Five of these men continued as ministers under Hitler.

All this scheming went on while Brüning must have felt relatively safe in the saddle, at least up to the time of the Lausanne Conference, after he had gained an impressive parliamentary victory over the opposition of the left and right on May 12, 1932. In a great speech Brüning defended his policies for the last time. He justified his austere economic policies as necessary for the stability of the German currency and as a means of making the foreign countries recognize Germany's true economic situation. He hoped not only for an end of reparations but also for the grant of equality in armaments for Germany. He warned the Germans not to become weak "at the last hundred meters before the goal." With a majority of 286 to 259 the parliament turned down the resolutions of nonconfidence. But Schleicher and his friends had decided that one could do without parliamentary crutches. Their plan got the approval of Hindenburg, who spent the two weeks between May 12 and 26 on his estate, Neudeck, in Eastern Prussia, where he was exposed to the influence of his agrarian friends and advisors. It is true that within the Brüning cabinet deliberations were carried on which envisaged that such estates as could not be made solvent by the payment of the mortgage debt should be bought by the state and used for farm settlements. This seemed to offer a certain chance for the relief of unemployment. The projects which were still in the working stage were denounced by Hindenburg's friends as "agrarian bolshevism." These conversations strengthened Hindenburg's animosity against Brüning.

After his return to Berlin on May 29, Hindenburg sternly demanded from Brüning a drastic change in the political course of the government. Besides the dropping of the plan for farm settlements in the east, he requested the repeal of the ban on the paramilitary organizations of the Nazi party. He also asked for the dissolution of the present *Reichstag* as being unrepresentative of popular opinion. He indicated he had been informed by a "go-between" that if these things were done the government would be supported by Hugenberg and Hitler. He refused in the future to sign any bill not passed by parliament as long as Brüning would insist on his old policies. On the same day the cabinet voted to tender its resignation. Brüning still had some hope that this step might induce the president to reconsider his political plans, the more so since in the morning of May 30 he received word from Geneva that, after the United States, Great Britain, and Italy, finally even France had indicated that equality in armaments would be granted to Germany. Brüning later accused Hindenburg's entourage of delaying his meeting with the president until a few minutes before Hindenburg had to review the sailors who on the day before the anniversary of the battle of Jutland took over guard service at the presidential palace. Hindenburg was actually already committed to Papen and simply accepted Brüning's resignation.

✍ *Papen Government*

IT WAS A FRIVOLOUS GAME. Papen possessed much less popular and parliamentary support than Brüning, and it was most uncertain that the price for the concessions he was prepared to make would be paid by the "national opposition." The dismissal of Brüning, the repeal of the ban on the paramilitary organizations of the Nazi party, and the dissolution of the *Reichstag* could never secure Papen a broad political base, the lack of which was held against Brüning. With Brüning's resignation democracy in Germany, already debilitated since 1930, was dead. But Brüning was mistaken if he assumed that he was slain only at the last hundred meters before the goal. He had grounded his whole policy on the belief that the gain of important victories in the foreign field would allow him thereafter to recoup the internal situation. Holding out the hope for great national gains in international affairs, he felt that he could remain relatively inactive in the domestic field. But as little as the evacuation of the Rhineland by Allied troops had affected internal German developments in 1930 would the end of reparations and even equality in armaments have solved the grave internal crisis. The favorable result of the Lausanne Conference was to make little impression on the Germans. Those who stormed against the republic wanted to see much bigger victories. Maybe full *Anschluss* or the recovery of the Polish corridor would have made a difference. But already the proposed Austro-German customs union, only a small step in the direction of *Anschluss*, had been defeated by France.

On May 28 Papen had first been informed by Schleicher of what was expected of him. At noontime of May 31 he consulted the chairman of the Center party, Dr. Ludwig Kaas, who told him at once that the party would disapprove of a cabinet led by Papen and that he should give up a candidacy which did not stand a chance in parliament. But when Hindenburg a few hours later appealed to Papen's patriotism, he accepted the office of chancellor. Since everything had been prepared so well by the irresponsible Schleicher and the camarilla around Hindenburg, the cabinet was announced as early as June 1. It called itself the cabinet of "national concentration," while the people called it "the cabinet of the barons." The Center party immediately excluded Papen from membership. The great majority of the party was deeply offended by the treatment that Brüning had received.

The dissolution of the federal parliament was announced, and elections were called for July 31. The new minister of the interior, Baron Wilhelm von Gayl (1879–1950), eased the legal provisions for the maintenance of order and prepared the lifting of the ban on the paramilitary organizations of the Nazi party. It was repealed by a presidential decree of June 16. The delay was caused by the resistance of the land governments. Even after the repeal the South German governments maintained the ban on uniforms, whereupon the Reich cabinet finally issued two ordinances which repealed all special measures of the lands and ordered the general admission of uniforms and public demonstrations. It was a farreaching interference with the rights of the lands in police matters. The return of the storm troopers to the streets, as one might have expected, led to new fights and disorders. Finally, on July 18, Gayl had to proclaim a ban on public demonstrations. While the Nazis happily accepted all the advantages which they received from the Papen government, they failed conspicuously to support it in any respect. In view of the general popular opposition to the "cabinet of the barons" the Nazis did not wish to appear as the allies of reaction. There was a good deal of grumbling within the party about Hitler's contacts with the die-hard conservatives. During the election campaign the Nazis freely attacked the government, and Hitler told Papen and Schleicher that the time to discuss a new government would arrive only after the election.

The reactionary character of the Papen government probably found its clearest expression in social affairs. By further cutting social benefits, particularly in unemployment insurance, and making it possible to interfere with labor contracts, it tried to gain the support of industry. On the other hand, the Papen government broke with Brüning's policy of deflation. It took various measures to create new jobs, partly by public works and the expansion of credit. These measures, however, did not produce immediate results. The unemployment figure in January 1933 was as high as in January 1932. Yet in the summer of 1932 the lowest point of the economic recession had been reached. But an upturn became noticeable only in 1933. While Hitler benefited from the economic policies of the Papen government, Papen could reap the fruits of Brüning's efforts to achieve the end of reparations. At the Conference of Lausanne Papen proved himself a foolhardy dilettante in diplomacy. MacDonald's circumspection and Herriot's reasonableness were responsible for the favorable outcome of the conference. Germany was expected to make a final payment of 3 billion marks. This payment, however, was put off for three years and finally was never made.

↵ *Ouster of Prussian Government*

PAPEN HIMSELF felt that successes in the field of internal affairs would be more important for the future of his government. The reform of the Weimar Constitution with regard to the relationship between the Reich and the lands had been debated a great deal during the late twenties. The relationship between the Prussian and the federal governments had been considered particularly unsatisfactory, and most reform proposals had suggested the merger of the two governments. Even Prussia's Social Democratic prime minister, Otto Braun, had leaned toward such a solution. Now Papen and Gayl took up the idea in order to exclude the last position of power that the Social Democrats occupied. Papen wanted to prove the effectiveness of his government in fighting the "Marxists" by taking over the Prussian government. In addition he probably wanted to keep the Prussian police, the largest armed force after the army, out of the control of the Nazis. On July 17 there had been heavy fatalities in Altona when the Nazis demonstrated in a workers' section. These incidents were taken as an excuse by Papen to inform the Prussian government on July 20 that the federal government felt it necessary to take over governmental powers in Prussia, because its caretaker government had not shown the necessary anticommunist zeal. Carl Severing, the Prussian minister of the interior, who in the absence of Otto Braun was the chief spokesman of the cabinet, protested against this breach of the constitution and declared that he would only give in to force. Thereupon the chancellor proclaimed a state of emergency and placed the commander of the military district of Berlin, General von Rundstedt (1875–1953), in charge of the security of the city, thereby subordinating the police to military command. Actually the Prussian ministers withdrew from their offices in the evening of July 20 when requested by military officers to do so. Severing and the Social Democratic ministers have been much criticized for giving up their positions without a fight. It has been argued that the powerful Prussian police were still at their disposal and that they could have called up the workers for a general strike, as had been done in 1920 after the Kapp *Putsch*. There were indeed many groups of workers ready to fight, and the members of the Iron Front in particular, the paramilitary organization that the Social Democratic party and the trade unions had built up, showed great readiness for action. But at a time when millions of workers were unemployed, a general strike was a doubtful political weapon. Moreover whereas at the time of the Kapp *Putsch* the government officials had denied their services to the Kapp government, in 1932 undoubtedly the vast majority of the Prussian government officials would have accepted the authority of President Hindenburg and the same was true of the Prussian police, which would never have fought the army. It was also questionable whether the caretaker government could have been kept together. It is not likely that the members of the Center party would have approved of open resistance.

Under the conditions of 1932 the Prussian ministers could hardly have chosen to fight. The events revealed the complete loss of power that the Social Democratic party had suffered since it left the Reich government in 1930 and even more since it had been defeated at the polls in Prussia in April 1932. But naturally the easy acceptance of defeat by the Prussian ministers disheartened their followers. It drove many a firebrand into the Communist party and the maturer members into political resignation and inactivity. The Prussian ministers gained little satisfaction from the supreme court. The court refused to issue a temporary order prohibiting the federal government from evicting the Prussian government, and its final judgment, rendered on October 25, did not declare the taking over of the Prussian administration unconstitutional. It ruled, however, that the federal government could not assume the representation of Prussia in the Federal Council, because this would change the federal structure of Germany. Therefore the old cabinet of Otto Braun returned to Berlin, but its function was limited to the instruction of the Prussian vote in the Federal Council. This shadow cabinet was not in a position to interfere with the actions of Papen's commissars who were installed in the Prussian government offices. At once they went to work to "clean" the Prussian government and administration of all its Social Democratic officials and pronounced republican civil servants. Hitler finally dissolved the old cabinet in the first days of his chancellorship. Yet the easy success of Papen's audacious action, though it seemed to give him additional power, did not really solve the problem of his regime. Even a dictatorial regime in the modern world needs some amount of popular acclamation. Although Papen had made it completely clear that he felt nothing but contempt for parliamentary government and for the parties, he still hoped that the federal election of July 31, 1932, would produce a parliament that would cooperate with him. But his hopes were shattered.

✍ *Federal Elections, July 1932*

FROM THE CAMPAIGN, which was fought with the highest passion by all parties, the Nazi party emerged as victor. It more than doubled its vote and membership in the parliament compared to 1930. But it failed to gain a majority. With 37.2 per cent of the popular vote, it had increased its strength only slightly beyond the second presidential election, and it was obvious that it had reached the limits of its potential expansion. Even together with the German Nationalists the Nazis were not able to form a majority government. The Nationalists had lost 4 seats compared with 1930 and together the "national opposition" received only 43.3 per cent of the general vote. The moderate conservative and the liberal parties were practically wiped out and survived only as small splinters. The desertion of the former followers of these parties constituted the chief cause for the swelling ranks of the Nazis. The Social Democratic party, which had hoped to gain additional seats as a consequence of its strong opposition to the Papen regime, actually fell from 24.5 per cent to 21.6 per cent of the popular vote. It lost its position as the strongest political party in parliament, which it had been able to maintain since 1912. The Communists gained by the Social Democratic losses, but their leaders found that even at the height of the economic crisis their gains were rather small. The party won only 14.3 per cent of the popular vote compared to 13.1 per cent in 1930. The Center party and the Bavarian

People's party not only maintained their former strength but even improved their position slightly.

In the new parliament the two totalitarian parties, the Nazi and the Communist parties, held 52.5 per cent of the seats, and even if the German Nationalists had supported a democratic coalition, it would have been in a minority of 289 to 319 seats. On the other hand, a parliamentary majority coalition would have been possible if the Nazis would ever work together with the Center and Bavarian parties. Only the German Nationalists and the remnants of the German People's party could be called supporters of Papen's chancellorship, but together they had gained even less than 7 per cent of the popular vote. Papen himself was unconcerned and stated that he expected both the Center party and the National Socialists to tolerate his presidential cabinet. Schleicher, however, did not think much of Papen's grandiose projects of an authoritarian "new state," which were presented with the whole panoply of the neoconservative ideas of these years, and still considered it possible to "tame" the Nazi party, which had failed to gain a majority. He was willing to make Hitler chancellor and surround him with a cabinet of professional civil servants, while at the same time he would keep the army as a counterweight to any totalitarian plans which Hitler might try to realize. But he underrated Hitler's determination to gain the total power of the state. Hitler knew by now that he could not hope to gain this power through ballots and that he would need the authorization of the President on the basis of article 48. Yet he was not willing to compromise his claim for absolute leadership. On the other hand Hindenburg was by no means inclined at this moment to turn over the power to Hitler. He insisted that a presidential cabinet could not be led by the leader of a political party, particularly one that made claims for totalitarian rule. In an audience which he gave Hitler on August 13, 1932, Hindenburg offered him participation in the government but refused quite sternly to turn over its full power to him. In a sharply worded press communication Hindenburg made his point of view clear to the general public, pointing out that in the conversation with him Hitler had gone back on the promise he had made before the election to support a cabinet installed by the confidence of the president.

At once the Nazi party fell back into rabid agitation against the regime of the aristocratic cavaliers, while the storm troopers committed ever-new acts of provocation and violence against the public order. On August 9, the government established special courts to deal with these excesses and introduced high penalties against violators. During the following night five storm troopers invaded the house of a Communist worker in Upper Silesia and beat him to death in bestial fashion before the eyes of his mother, while seriously wounding a brother. When on August 26 a special court condemned the five murderers to death, the Nazi leaders passionately protested. Hitler dropped his mask and showed his true face. He assured the five condemned men of his unlimited loyalty and published in his newspaper a large proclamation which justified the murder as a step in the struggle of the Nazi party for the "eternal rights of our people" and attacked Papen's "bloody objectivity." The "national Germany" would in the future free the national idea from the limitations of objectivity. Everybody in Germany at this moment could see what a Hitler government held in store for the people. But the sense of law and justice had already been dangerously undermined among the German people, and only very few drew the right conclusions from this incident.

At the same time conversations with a view to the formation of a coalition government in the Reich and in Prussia were conducted by the leaders of the Center and the Nazi parties. It may be admitted that these efforts of the Center party were not merely sparked by the anger felt about Hindenburg's and Schleicher's actions against Brüning but were motivated by a deep concern about the future of Germany. If Kaas believed that the Center party could domesticate the Nazis, this showed an amazing political naïveté and perhaps a lack of concern about democracy. The fate of the coalition between the *popolari* and the Fascist party in Italy should have been a sufficient warning to the Center politicians. On the other side it was doubtful whether the Nazis ever took the negotiations with the Center party seriously. While Gregor Strasser (1892–1934), the powerful chief of the organizational work of the Nazi party, was in favor of a coalition, because he believed that the party could not gain absolute power by itself, Hitler, supported by Goebbels and Röhm, obviously wanted to use the negotiations only as a means of pressure on Papen. No doubt the contacts between the Center and the Nazi parties frightened Papen and warned him that he could not expect to find the support of the new *Reichstag*. But in contrast to Brüning he had succeeded in gaining the full confidence of Hindenburg, who saw in Papen a likable representative of the old order in which the president still lived. Therefore he was willing to let him go ahead with his plans for a "new state," which apparently in his opinion was pretty much the old monarchy, and gave him authority to dissolve the new parliament if it should not support his presidential cabinet.

The new parliament assembled in the first days of September. Hermann Göring was elected president. The first working session took place on September 12, and the government declaration was the only item on the agenda. But before Göring gave Papen the opportunity to deliver his speech, the Communists brought in a motion for a vote of nonconfidence in the government, and Göring had the parliament vote on this motion. The flushed and angry Papen placed the order of dissolution on the president's desk and with his cabinet left the *Reichstag*, which with 512 against 42 votes expressed its disapproval of the government. No German government had ever suffered such a parliamentary defeat before, nor had it ever happened that a government was not allowed to make a declaration or that a parliament was dissolved before it began its debates. The constitution had become a mere football of the warring parties. New elections were set for November 6.

✍ *Elections, November 1932*

FEWER PEOPLE went to the polls than had gone in July. The small losses of the Center and the Bavarian People's parties can be explained entirely by the weaker popular participation in the election. Its most sensational result, however, was the loss suffered by the Nazi party. Whereas in July 37.2 per cent of the voters had supported it, only 33.1 per cent did so in November. It was remarkable that this decline affected all constituencies. Many former Nazi voters had shifted their vote to the conservative rightist parties. Obviously a good many middle-class people had become afraid of the lawlessness of Hitler's storm trooper hordes. They were also frightened by the cooperation of Nazis and Communists in the Berlin transport strike shortly before the election. Papen's antilabor policy and the favor he had shown to the industrialists made some of them return to the German Nationalists. We may assume that the Nazi party received less money from these quarters in the November election than in July. On the other side, some radical followers of the Nazi party who had grown distrustful of Hitler's attitude toward socialism switched their vote to the Communists. The spell of continuous growth of the Nazi party was broken by the election results, which in addition made it definitely clear that the party could never hope to gain a majority in elections.

The chief winner of the decline of the Nazi vote was the German Nationalist party, which from its former 5.9 per cent rose to 8.3 per cent of the vote. Although this brought only a fraction of the voters back whom the party had lost to the Nazis in the September elections of 1930, the party's 51 seats in the parliament put it in a crucial tactical position. While in the new parliament the National Socialists and the German Nationalists fell short of a majority, the Nazi and the Center parties could no longer form a majority by themselves.

The losses of the Social Democratic party reflected the immobility to which it had been condemned by the circumstances. Its vote fell from 21.6 per cent to 20.7 per cent. The party had ceased to attract the first-time young voters, and its left fringe turned to the Communists. For the first time the latter garnered more votes than the Center party. Their percentage of the popular vote rose to 16.9. With 100 Communists and

196 Nazis in a parliament of 584 members the radical parties again had the opportunity to block all legislative work.

Hindenburg wanted a presidential cabinet to continue, but he directed Papen to negotiate with the party leaders in order to find out whether such a cabinet could gain wider popular support than Papen had commanded so far. But Hitler proved as stubborn as before. He demanded the chancellorship of a presidential cabinet. In contrast, Kaas advised the formation of a parliamentary government. Even under the chancellorship of Hitler this would have left the parliament intact, while the army would have remained under the command of a reliable anti-Nazi general. Only Hugenberg recommended the continuation of the Papen regime and the transformation of the government into a dictatorship. To Papen's great annoyance, Schleicher insisted on November 17 that the cabinet offer its resignation to the president in order to give Hindenburg the opportunity to make his influence felt in new conversations with the party chiefs. Schleicher apparently had already made up his mind that Papen would no longer do as chancellor. He himself had brought him into his position because he had hoped that Papen might be able to gain the support of the Center party, but even more because he had expected him to be a man who could be easily directed. Instead Papen had not proved very tractable and had produced plans for constitutional experiments of which Schleicher disapproved.

Hindenburg refused Hitler, with whom he held two meetings, the chancellorship of a presidential cabinet, because he felt it should be above political parties, and he denied him the chance of trying to form a parliamentary government as well. He had come to like the presidential system. In the evening of December 1 Papen and Schleicher discussed the political situation with Hindenburg. Papen argued that Hitler's inflexible attitude had created a real state of emergency for which the Weimar Constitution had not made any provisions. He pleaded for keeping his government in power and having it realize all its projects. He wanted to send the unmanageable parliament home and, beginning with the Communist and the Nazi parties, to suppress all political organizations through the army and police. A new constitution was to be worked out, subsequently to be approved by a plebiscite or a new national assembly.

Schleicher took issue with Papen, warning against such a *coup d'état*, and presented a scheme for which during the last days he had hurriedly tried to lay the foundation. He believed that it would be possible to overcome the hostility of the parties. Finding Hitler immovable, Schleicher had turned to Gregor Strasser, who had a large following within the Nazi party. Among Hitler's chief lieutenants Strasser was the one who had argued for a coalition with other parties. After the November elections he was pessimistic about the future of the party. He noted the defection of many followers and was aware of the party's heavy debts. In his opinion it was bound to shrink still further if the economic experts who said that the worst of the depression had passed were right. How large Strasser's following within the party was is impossible to say, since under the direction of Goebbels the Nazi press displayed only Hitler's views. Schleicher believed that he could split the Nazi party by giving Strasser and some of his friends cabinet posts. He hoped that he could gain the support, or at least the toleration, of the other parties through building up a political front of the free (Social Democratic) and the Christian trade unions that would be supported by other occupational organizations. Papen's rejoinder was that Schleicher's policy would lead to new makeshift arrangements, which his own authoritarian solution would make impossible forever. Hindenburg reappointed Papen to form a government.

But in the preceding weeks Schleicher had already indicated in conversations with most members of the cabinet that Papen's plan would lead to civil war and that the army was not strong enough to cope with such a situation. Moreover, in his opinion, the army should not be used for such a massive political intervention, which might damage its reputation as an integrating power of the nation. In the cabinet meeting of December 2 Schleicher called Papen's projects unrealistic and presented a study prepared by the ministry of defense, presumably influenced by the Berlin transportation strike. In war-game-like operations of three days officers together with other government officials had studied the problem of whether the armed forces would be able to deal with simultaneous terror actions from the left and the right. They had found that in practically all parts of Germany these forces would be inadequate. All the ministers except Papen and Baron von Gayl agreed with Schleicher, who was probably right in his estimate of the military potential. Papen hurried back to Hindenburg, still willing to continue as chancellor if Hindenburg would allow him to appoint a new minister of defense. But the threat of civil war frightened the old man, and he was realistic enough to accept the judgment of the officers on the military potential. He agreed now that Schleicher should try his luck as chancellor. He hated to see Papen give up his office, and in sentimental fashion, which showed his senility, he assured him of his friendship and asked him to stay around as one of his advisors.

∽ Schleicher Government

ALTHOUGH SCHLEICHER indicated that he would not follow a reactionary course in his social policies, the Social Democrats opposed him from the outset. They disliked the authoritarian character of the government and saw no improvement in the replacement of Papen by a general. The majority of the Social Democratic parliamentarians seemed to see in Schleicher a greater danger than in Hitler. The Nazi press voiced opposition to Schleicher, but the Nazis were slow in pressing their attacks against him. Their party, which had suffered another setback in the municipal elections in Thuringia in early December, was now in a serious crisis. Gregor Strasser urged the toleration of the Schleicher cabinet. When parliament assembled on December 6, 1932, for what was to be the last session of the *Reichstag* in the Weimar Republic, the Nazi party put up only sham battles and agreed on December 9 to the temporary adjournment of parliament. On the day before, Gregor Strasser, in a letter to Hitler, had announced his resignation from all his party offices and also had given up his seat in the *Reichstag*. But Strasser failed to follow this step by active attempts to organize his following within the Nazi party. He simply went on leave and thus made it relatively easy for Hitler to assure himself of the loyalty of the upper group of party chiefs and also to bring within the next few weeks the lower echelons into stricter submission again. Schleicher had greatly overrated not only the power that Strasser wielded within the party but also his political cunning. The wily general moved here on a terrain with which he was not sufficiently acquainted. Yet he did not give up his plan to split the Nazi party with Gregor Strasser's help.

Schleicher's first efforts were directed at calming the popular passions and winning friends for the government. He abolished the special courts and moderated other ordinances against political organizations. He repealed the section of Papen's emergency decrees that had undermined the security of wage agreements. He also tried to develop plans for creating work. He held conversations with the free and the Christian trade unions, while at the same time he indicated an understanding of the demands of the industrialists and agrarians. Schleicher attempted to overcome the hostility of the various camps and thus to gather growing support for the government. His ultimate hope was that an improvement in the economic conditions would deflate political radicalism in Germany. Then a declining Nazi party could either be taken into the government and thereby "tamed" or be kept outside the government and left to wither away. In a way this was a return to the political course of Brüning. But in order to win a popular following Schleicher needed in the first place clear political conceptions, which could not be found in his few public statements. What did it mean, for example, if he promised to build an economic system "beyond capitalism and socialism"? His proposals were vague and seemed to stem from considerations of the moment only. He did not gain popular confidence but rather aroused suspicion.

Franz von Papen was smarting under his loss of office. It was some comfort that Hindenburg had asked him to continue at least as an unofficial advisor, but Papen went further in order to regain a political role. Behind the president's and the chancellor's backs he met Hitler in Cologne on January 4, 1933. The meeting took place in the house of a wealthy banker, Baron von Schroeder, who had instigated the encounter. Schroeder was a typical representative of the financial and industrial circles which were alarmed by Schleicher's ideas about cooperation with the trade unions and wished a return to Papen's economic policies. Among the results of the Cologne meeting were large contributions made by industry, which eased the financial situation of the Nazi party. Hitler's willingness to see Papen, whom he disliked, showed the embarrassment of the Nazi leader. Although the Strasser crisis had been largely overcome, he saw himself far from gaining governmental power. If he was kept out much longer, those of his followers who had joined the party out of opportunism would leave, while the mass of his followers might force him off the way of legality into revolution. In the two-hour conversation with Papen, therefore, he agreed to Papen's proposal of joining the German Nationalists, who had supported Papen, with the National Socialists. Papen suggested a duumvirate of Hitler and himself. Hitler left Cologne greatly encouraged that he had found a promising approach to the goal of his dreams. It was now up to Papen to win over Hindenburg for such a plan.

Schleicher had discovered the intrigues of his predecessor. He informed the press about the Papen-Hitler meeting and at the same time launched a strong protest with Hindenburg. But he did not dare bring the matter to a showdown. He felt that his relations with Hindenburg were not strong enough for that. Schleicher did not learn that Hindenburg had actually asked Papen to continue his political probings, nor was he aware that he had lost the friendship of Oskar von Hindenburg on account of a tiff. When on January 11 the National Agrarian League complained bitterly about the agricultural policy of the Schleicher cabinet, Hindenburg rather angrily requested the chancellor to fulfill the demands of the agrarians. Schleicher stood his ground. Two days later he denied Hugenberg the ministry of economics, which the leader of the German Nationalists had wanted to take over, whereupon Hugenberg shifted his support from Schleicher to Papen.

Schleicher was unsuccessful in his negotiations with the trade unions. The chairman of the free trade unions, Theodor Leipart (1867–1947), indicated that he was willing to cooperate. But in a reversal of what happened in March 1930, when the trade unions had compelled the Social Democratic ministers to resign from the government, this time the political chiefs of the party persuaded Leipart to give up any idea of collaborating with Schleicher, since many of them believed that National Socialism could not last very long and a new day for socialism would dawn. They felt that they should withhold any collaboration with Schleicher, who might possibly bring the National Socialists into the government, though actually he was determined not to turn over absolute power to them.

On January 15, 1933, the people of the midget state of Lippe, with 98,000 voters altogether, elected a new parliament. In order to improve the flagging morale of the Nazi party and to impress his opponents Hitler threw all his forces into the election campaign, and the Nazi propaganda was carried into the smallest hamlet. Compared with the federal elections of November 6, 1932, the Nazis gained a few percentage points in the popular vote, and this was now loudly proclaimed to be proof that the Nazi party was on the march again. In reality the event was rather a publicity stunt. The chief losers had been the German Nationalist party and the Communist party, and altogether the election showed a strengthening of the moderate parties. After the Lippe election the negotiations for a Hitler-Papen cabinet were resumed. On January 22, in the house of Joachim von Ribbentrop, Hitler won over Oskar von Hindenburg to the idea of such a cabinet.

On the following day Schleicher reported to the president about the failure of his attempt to split the Nazi party and asked him for authorization to dissolve parliament. Thereafter he wanted to proclaim a state of emergency, postpone new elections, and issue a general ban on the Nazi and Communist parties. Hindenburg reminded him that Schleicher had warned against basing a government exclusively on the support of the army and that these warnings on December 2 had led to the formation of his government. Schleicher replied that he was in a better position than Papen, since he did not have to be afraid of a general strike and could hope for toleration by the Social Democrats, the free trade unions, and the *Reichsbanner*. He added that the friendlier attitude of England as well as France in armaments questions would allow him to strengthen the army by volunteers and thus make it superior to Hitler's storm trooper formations. Hindenburg was afraid of breaking his oath to the constitution, and Meissner had convinced him that the declaration of a state of emergency was unconstitutional. He denied Schleicher the authority for the dissolution of the *Reichstag*, which a few weeks before he had still been ready to give him. The democratic parties did not support Schleicher's cause. When rumors of his proposals to Hindenburg became public, they loudly protested against such a *coup d'état*. In order to maintain the constitution, most of their leaders were now prepared to let Hitler into the government. They lived in the idle expectation that once in the government Hitler would moderate his political aims or that the madness of National Socialism would soon burn itself out.

But although Hindenburg had given up the Schleicher cabinet, he remained entirely undecided about the appointment of Hitler as chancellor. On the other hand, Papen, Hugenberg, and Hitler had not yet reached full agreement about the composition of the cabinet they wished the president to appoint. For quite different reasons both Papen and Hitler wanted to remove Schleicher from the ministry of defense. Both finally accepted General Werner von Blomberg (1878–1946) as successor to Schleicher in a Hitler-Papen cabinet, and Papen succeeded in making Blomberg acceptable to Hindenburg as well. Blomberg had commanded in East Prussia for a number of years. Here the field chaplain on his staff, Ludwig Müller (1883–1945), had first won over the chief of staff, Walther von Reichenau (1884–1942), to National Socialist ideas, and both Reichenau and Müller had persuaded Blomberg that National Socialism was a positive and patriotic force with which the army should cooperate. Blomberg was a restless, emotional person and easily swayed by the men who surrounded him. He explained to Hindenburg that the army would have to collaborate with National Socialism and that Schleicher's political course was thoroughly disliked within the army.

Schleicher was not aware of how far the formation of a Papen-Hitler government had gone. He believed that Hindenburg was likely to appoint a Papen-Hugenberg cabinet and that he himself would retain the ministry of defense. In the last conversation with Hindenburg Schleicher warned against a dictatorial Papen-Hugenberg cabinet that was bound to endanger the position of the president and would get the army into an untenable situation. He urged Hindenburg to appoint a parliamentary government, and not a presidential one under Hitler. This would have necessitated the inclusion of the Center party and thereby have created a certain guarantee of lawful government. Actually the Center party was not only willing but most eager to enter into such a combination. But Papen did not report the readiness of the Center party to the president. The big agrarian and industrialist interest groups urgently pressed Hindenburg for the appointment of a cabinet of the Harzburg front,[9] and so did many of his old friends and neighbors on his East Prussian estates. In the first place, however, the men immediately surrounding him— Papen, Meissner, and Hindenburg's son—declared that a Harzburg cabinet endowed with the presidential powers of article 48 was the only possible solution.

ᴄᴏ *Hitler-Papen Government*

GENERAL VON SCHLEICHER announced his resignation at noontime of January 28. On the same afternoon Hindenburg, surrounded by the triumvi-

[9] See p. 686.

rate, agreed to the formation of a rightist government with the greatest possible guarantees for conservative predominance and commissioned Papen to conduct the necessary negotiations with Hitler and Hugenberg. Hitler demanded the chancellorship for himself and in addition the appointment as Reich commissar for Prussia. Otherwise he declared himself satisfied with the appointment of one of his lieutenants to the federal and another to the Prussian ministry of interior. Papen vainly tried to convince Hitler that Hindenburg would not give him the appointment as Prussian commissar, which the president wished to be in the hands of Papen. On Sunday, January 29, Papen and Hitler had a lengthy discussion. Hitler nominated Hermann Göring as Prussian and Wilhelm Frick as federal minister of the interior. He accepted Papen's appointment as vice-chancellor and Reich commissar for Prussia but now insisted on new federal elections. Papen's entreaties with Hindenburg were successful, and the latter accepted Hitler's assurance that these would be the last elections. Hitler on his part accepted the inclusion of the leader of the *Stahlhelm*, Seldte, into the cabinet, which seemed to endow Hugenberg and Papen with a paramilitary force similar to that possessed by Hitler with his storm troopers. But again Hindenburg seemed to waver.

Only the rumors which spread in the afternoon made Hindenburg overcome his uneasiness. These rumors, originating from a political intriguer, asserted that Schleicher wanted to stall the imminent Nazi government; that the troops of the Potsdam garrison had been alerted and were on their march to Berlin; and that the president was to be brought to East Prussia so that Schleicher and Hammerstein would retain command of the army for the establishment of a military dictatorship. Actually both Schleicher and Hammerstein did not entertain any such ideas. In addition Schleicher believed up to the morning of January 30 that he would retain the ministry of defense.

Blomberg, who was at this moment the German representative at the disarmament conference, was at once recalled from Geneva. When he arrived in Berlin on the morning of January 30, he was met at the railroad station by an aide of General von Schleicher, who wanted to lead him to the ministry of defense, and by Colonel von Hindenburg, who persuaded him to go with him to the presidential palace. At the palace he at once took the oath of office as defense minister before the Hitler-Papen government had been formed.

The new cabinet consisted of three National Socialists and nine conservative bureaucrats or politicians. Hitler had conceded that Papen as vice-chancellor would be present at all his meetings with the president. On the other hand Göring was made deputy commissar for Prussia and received the promise that at a future date a federal ministry of air would be created for him. Hugenberg became minister not only of economics but of agriculture as well and could practically consider himself economic dictator. Seldte received the ministry of labor. The foreign office and the ministries of finance, justice, and transportation remained under the men who had served since the formation of the Papen cabinet in May 1932. Hugenberg and Papen proudly boasted that the basic activities of government were in the hands of the conservatives and that they had Hitler safely fenced in. Yet in order to contain Hitler the conservatives would have had to act in determined unity. But already the first occasion for such common action found the group divided.

Hitler and the members of the cabinet were to take their oath of office at eleven o'clock in Hindenburg's office. They assembled a while before, and when Hitler arrived, he voiced once more his regret that he was not to be appointed Reich commissar for Prussia and emphasized the necessity for new elections by which the German people were to confirm the formation of the new national government. Hugenberg, who apparently had not been informed by Papen about what had happened the day before, at once opposed new elections. He recognized that Hitler hoped with the instruments of government to recoup the losses which the Nazi party had suffered in the November elections and maybe even to gain a full majority. After his experiences with Hitler's "words of honor" Hugenberg remained unimpressed by Hitler's assurance that the results of the new elections would not change the composition of the government. In consternation Papen and the other conservatives implored Hugenberg not to endanger the just accomplished national union. All of them were eager to assist Hitler, but Hugenberg remained stubborn. Yet when at a quarter past eleven Meissner rushed in and admonished the group not to keep President Hindenburg waiting, Hugenberg went along with the others.

Hitler did not become chancellor because the majority of the people wanted to see him in this post. He won the office because the small clique of advisors around Hindenburg persuaded the old man that a Hitler-Papen cabinet was fully compatible with the Weimar Constitution. Although Hitler's appointment as chancellor was perhaps compatible with the letter of the constitution, there can be no question that Hindenburg did not fulfill his duty as president when he appointed the man who had loudly proclaimed that he would destroy the constitution once he had gained governmental power. With the commission to dissolve the parliament and the permission to use the power of article 48 Hindenburg allowed Hitler to lay the foundations of totalitarian rule. This was Hitler's immediate aim, and with the federal and Prussian ministries of the interior he had the chief instruments of executive authority in his hands. The conservative containment of Hitler was illusory. Moreover the most important force for such a containment, the army, was now commanded by General von Blomberg, who was willing to give Hitler the utmost cooperation. Not the conservative German Nationalists but the National Socialists were the victors of January 30. When in the evening and night of that day a seven-hour torch parade of storm troopers and the *Stahlhelm* marched through the Brandenburg Gate and the Wilhelmstrasse, the cheers and *heils* went to the *Führer*.

CHAPTER 12

The Third Empire

I N THE LAST PHASE of the breakdown of the Weimar Republic most
of the momentous decisions were made by very few people. There
can be no doubt that the course of events might have been a different one if another group of people had been in command. It might
have at least become possible to fence Hitler in more securely and
make it much more difficult for him to take over all the organs of government. On the other hand, the people involved were not unrepresentative
of German traditions and social attitudes, and the fact that they were in a
position to settle the fateful issues of the early thirties was due in the first
place to the character of the German political parties.

✌ Sterile Party System

WITH THE EXCEPTION of the Center party none of them contributed to
overcoming the existing social tensions and conflicts. All these parties
represented specific social groups and classes. This social division made
cooperation among the parties extremely difficult, and their conflicts
were heightened by their exclusive ideologies. The nature of the German
parties was a legacy of the Bismarckian era. Bismarck had defeated the
struggle of liberals for parliamentary government in 1866–67 and in the
crisis of 1879 had fragmentized the big National Liberal party. He had
succeeded in defeating parliamentarianism and, apart from the Social
Democratic party, had turned the political parties into pressure groups
rather than organizations anxious to gain governmental control. Only the
Social Democratic party behaved as a party of radical opposition, but
although it declared itself in favor of a republic, even this party might
eventually have accepted a true constitutional monarchy. Still, in the
Weimar Republic the Social Democratic party was the greatest democratic force. Yet during more than half the existence of the Weimar Republic the party was not represented in the government. Too many Social
Democrats were convinced that the party would gain most if it remained
in opposition, as it had done in the Second Empire. Moreover, the party

made no serious effort to win at least a substantial part of the middle-class vote. The program that it had adopted with its pledge to nationalize the key industries and move in the direction of the realization of a socialist state frightened the middle classes. But the old Social Democratic leaders who had risen from the ranks of the party before World War I were afraid that a change of program as well as participation in the government in adverse circumstances would result in growing losses to the Communists.

✍ Political Outlook of the Middle Classes

THE FATE of the Weimar Republic was decided, however, by the middle classes. In 1919 many middle-class people had supported democracy because it promised to be the best shield against bolshevism and at the same time against a harsh peace by the Allied powers. But when by 1920 bolshevism had been put down in Germany, not so much by the Social Democrats as by the army and the free corps, and Wilson had not proved to be a protector against a peace treaty which seemed unbearable to the average German citizen, the middle-class vote went to the right. The preservation of the old social order now became the chief goal of practically all middle-class voters. It was no longer admitted that the old social order had much to do with the loss of the war. Germany's defeat was now ascribed to the "stab in the back" for which the Social Democrats were blamed. Thus they were made responsible simultaneously for the Versailles Treaty and the subsequent sufferings, such as the Rhineland occupation, the Ruhr invasion, the reparations, and inflation. In the critical early 1920's the opposition of the middle classes to the republic had already assumed counterrevolutionary overtones. Stresemann's successful diplomacy and his ability to keep his German People's party from fraternization with the radical right parties introduced the relatively happiest period of the Weimar Republic. But with the appearance of the worldwide economic crisis in 1929 the middle classes became more radical, and some groups were ready for revolutionary action. The hour of National Socialism had arrived.

✍ Early Life of Adolf Hitler

WE HAVE already touched upon the National Socialist party in our outline of the history of the Weimar Republic. But before we turn our attention to the Third Empire, we must look back once more into the party's early history. It is closely connected with Hitler, who made the party great and impressed his stamp upon it. Born in 1889, Adolf Hitler was the son of a minor Austrian state official in Braunau, a little town at the Austro-

Bavarian frontier. Later the family moved to Linz, the small capital of Upper Austria. Hitler seems to have liked Linz, which, after he had become chancellor of Germany, he intended to build up as a big cultural center in competition with Vienna. In *Mein Kampf* and many other autobiographical statements Hitler liked to depict himself as coming from an indigent family, but this is pure fiction. His father received an adequate salary and pension. Even after his father's death his mother received a decent widow's pension, and after her death in 1907 Adolf inherited her savings. His father and mother were in a position to send Adolf to good schools. But he was not a good pupil and left school without a certificate of achievement. Even as a boy he showed certain traits which he never lost. He was moody and willful and always wanted to be the leader when he was in a group.

In 1907 Hitler went to Vienna hoping to be admitted as a student to the Academy of Fine Arts. But he was turned down, since he failed the entrance examination, and when he tried again a year later, he was not even admitted to a new examination. For the next five years Hitler shifted for himself in the imperial capital. For a while he must have got into desperate straits, for at night he had to take refuge in a poor men's asylum. But most of the time Hitler was not penniless. In his early years in Vienna he still received an orphan's allotment, and after that ceased, he came into possession of a small legacy from one of his aunts. From 1910 on he painted postcards and made little sketches, which he sold with the help of a friend. This enterprise gave him a modest livelihood, first in Vienna and later in Munich. At the same time it gave him the freedom to produce no more than he needed for his upkeep and to remain idle on many days. Then he could go to the coffee house and indulge in cake while he read the papers. Apparently he spent some of his time in the public library as well, but he did not read with a critical, open mind in order to broaden his horizon. All he looked for was the confirmation of his own opinions and prejudices.

✍ Hitler's Views on the Working Class

HITLER COMPLAINED in *Mein Kampf* that in Vienna he had to associate with people of a lower type than he had been used to. "Those among whom I passed my younger days belonged to the petit bourgeois class and the ditch which separates that class, which is by no means well off, from the manual laboring class is often deeper than you think. The reason for this attitude, which we may almost call enmity, lies in the fear that dominates a social group which has only just risen above the manual laborer—a fear lest it may fall back into its old condition or at least be classed with the laborers." With this statement he gave away the reason for his contempt for the working class. Although he describes their position in Vienna as miserable and their mores revolting, he scolds them for attempting to improve their circumstances by their own efforts. The masses, he said, will never be able to form political judgments of their own. To the extent that they join the Social Democratic party or trade unions, they only become the dupes of sinister leaders. In contrast to the Social Democrats Hitler admired Karl Lueger (1844–1910) and his Christian Social party, Austria's most powerful political party, which Lueger had organized chiefly from the middle classes, using anti-Semitism as his most powerful weapon. Hitler admired Lueger because as mayor of Vienna he "devoted the greatest part of his political activity to the task of winning over those sections of the population whose existence was in danger." In other words, in Hitler's eyes Lueger laid emphasis upon the social problem in building up a mass party. For this reason Hitler was willing to overlook those aims of Lueger with which he was not in agreement, namely the strengthening of the existing Habsburg Empire. Hitler saw it only as a crumbling structure and the Habsburgs as an anti-German force. In addition he felt that Lueger was wrong in basing his anti-Semitism on religion. Although Hitler thought little of Georg von Schoenerer's (1842–1921) capacity for political leadership, he adopted the racist anti-Semitism of this foremost Austrian champion of pan-Germanism. Thus even in his Viennese days Hitler had a critical eye on political tactics and ideologies.

✍ Racism

In *Mein Kampf* Hitler later wrote: "During these years a view of life and a definite outlook on the world took shape in my mind. These became the granite bases of conduct at that time. Since then I have extended that foundation very little, I have changed nothing in it." In his Austrian years he had already acquired his beliefs in a crude social Darwinism, according to which life is considered an eternal struggle for survival and domination. Hunger and love he called the elemental forces behind this process. Struggle rules supreme within and among peoples. This perverted Darwinism was then linked up with an equally primitive racism. Although he believed that not peoples but races were the primordial forces of history, Hitler admitted that there were no pure races and that the Germans, for example, had mixed with peoples whom they had conquered and with invaders whom they had absorbed. But once the true Germanic elements gained full power over the people, it would be possible to eliminate racially inferior groups and to enhance the breeding of the superior racial stock. Among the races the Nordic or Aryan was the highest, he said, and its chief representative was the German people. Consequently, Germany deserved full satisfaction of all her needs for life and growth. Since agriculture could not raise production beyond the existing level, Germany needed a greater *Lebensraum*, which could be gained only by war and the expulsion, if necessary even annihilation, of other peoples. Even when he was in Austria, Hitler probably looked for that *Lebensraum* in the East, although Eastern expansion became a fixed goal with him only after World War I, when it was connected with the struggle against bolshevism.

Hitler's biological materialism excluded all ethics. In the pursuit of its struggle for power, which is the dictate of the blood, the race-conscious people could use any means. Hitler gloated that his conception of race was the true revolutionary principle of the twentieth century, just as the idea of nation had revolutionized the preceding century. He derided the stupidity of the bourgeoisie and the old upper classes for being hampered by humanitarian scruples. Only people with a fanatic belief in race would be able to fight without being bothered by humanitarian and traditionalist inhibitions. Hitler readily admitted that such people would be barbarians.

Anti-Semitism and Terror

ANTI-SEMITISM WAS THE MAJOR INSTRUMENT in this policy of barbarization. Through vilification, torture, and ultimately the mass murder of the Jews Hitler displayed the ruthlessness he wished to inculcate in his followers. He often described the practical political value of anti-Semitism, particularly in the sense that in order to arouse hatred among people, it was essential to personify the enemy. But it must be emphatically stressed that Hitler himself was a passionate believer in extreme anti-Semitism. The anti-Jewish demonstrations and pogroms of April 1, 1933, and of November 8–9, 1938, were carried on in public, but when in 1942 Hitler ordered the physical extermination of all the European Jews, he knew that this "final solution" of the Jewish problem would frighten most Germans, and therefore it was secretly executed. It was a personal act of Hitler. Yet anti-Semitism was only part of his racism. While the Jews were to him subhuman, there were also such low human races as the Slavs, whom he did not propose to destroy but to deprive of further growth and of their national culture. The use of terror against enemies of the party and the regime was another means of barbarization, but even terror and violence were not merely instruments for acquiring power. Hitler believed in their permanent value. People do not have a natural herd instinct, he said; if left alone, they would rather fight among themselves. Only the fear of an authority commanding and using force can create a community. About the forms in which terror should be used, he probably had not thought too much in Vienna. He learned much about terror from the bolshevik revolution.

Even as a boy Hitler seems to have been convinced that he was destined for great deeds. The frustration of his desire to enter upon a career as an artist did not change his feelings of superiority. The outlook on the world which he acquired in Vienna kept alive his resentment against the old society of property and education in which he, in his own eyes a budding genius, had been deemed a misfit. His conception of "people" or "race" leveled down all social classes and attached no significance to educational differentiation. To his mind, he who would grasp the truth of race and all that went with it was a wiser man than the educated people. Moreover, knowledge of race was at the same time a faith that steeled man for action.

✧ Sources of Hitler's Anti-Semitism

THE PAN-GERMANISM of Schoenerer as well as the Christian Social movement of Vienna's Mayor Karl Lueger gave Hitler his first notions of anti-Semitism and its potential power to move the masses. He derived a theoretical intensification of anti-Semitism from the cheap little Ostara pamphlets, issued by a former monk, who called himself Lanz von Liebenfels (alias Adolf Lanz) and who peddled a racist "theozoology" of his own concoction. These cheap tracts, which were sold at tobacco stands, and probably other similar sheets, together with certain newspapers, provided Hitler's chief literary fare. He no doubt read Richard Wagner's political and anti-Semitic writings and also the book by Richard Wagner's English-born son-in-law Houston Stewart Chamberlain, *Foundations of the Nineteenth Century*, the widely read racist interpretation of world history. He knew of course about Count Arthur de Gobineau's *Inequality of Human Races*, although it is doubtful that he ever did more than dip into it. Nowhere in Hitler's remarks or writings is there a specific reference to Nietzsche. We have, however, a statement by Hitler on the deep impression that Schopenhauer had made on him. But this was probably only repeating Richard Wagner's judgment, and while Wagner had misunderstood Schopenhauer in many respects, nothing in Hitler's thinking showed the slightest imprint of Schopenhauer. It was on the basis of his limited reading in popular and often cranky and murky writings that Hitler formed his initial racist and anti-Semitic ideas.

✑ *Influence of World War I*

WHAT PROMPTED HITLER to move from Vienna to Munich we cannot say with certainty. Probably he felt that only Germany could accomplish pan-German unity. This would explain his reluctance to serve in the Austro-Hungarian army as well as his eagerness to enter the German army after the outbreak of the war of 1914. He was a brave soldier. The wartime was the only period in his life when he willingly accepted orders from superiors and did not get bored by routine. Hitler's political ideas expanded in the army. The Austrian pan-Germans had concentrated on the union of the Germans in Austria and Germany. But the pan-Germans of Germany propagated a program of conquest that would make Germany secure forever as a world power. Under Ludendorff the troops were intensively indoctrinated with such ideas, and the peace treaties of Brest-Litovsk with the Ukraine and Soviet Russia as well as subsequent military and political actions actually created a vast orbit of German satellites and colonies that reached from the White sea to the Black and Caspian seas. These experiences of World War I emboldened Hitler to think in terms of huge German conquests.

No doubt Hitler watched with great interest the attempts to build up a big patriotic mass party, such as Tirpitz and Kapp tried to do with the Fatherland party. But although this party must be considered a fore-runner of the Nazi party, Hitler found fault with this political venture. In his opinion the party addressed itself too exclusively to the bourgeoisie and failed to reach the mass of the people. He also criticized the imperial German government for its mismanagement of internal affairs, particularly its toleration of opposition parties and a critical press. He believed that the nation should be imbued with a single ideology and a single faith.

✑ *Hitler Enters Politics*

IN OCTOBER 1918 Hitler's eyes were affected by a gas attack at the Western front, and he was removed to a military hospital in Pomerania, where he remained throughout the period of the German breakdown, armistice, and revolution. Understandably he was deeply shaken by these events, which to him seemed caused by internal rather than external enemies. At the same time the end of the war posed a personal problem for him. How should he make a livelihood from then on? Should he finally take up a normal civil occupation? But according to his own report he decided at this moment to take up political work. With the old powers and authorities shaken, his sense of political mission broke through. But how would he get into politics? The chance was soon offered to him by the army, which returned him to the home base of his regiment in Munich. It is not clear how he got through the period of the Munich Soviet Republic in April and May 1919. But shortly thereafter he was appointed a political instruction officer by the political department of the army's Munich district command, the department in which Captain Ernst Röhm was active. The instruction officers were supposed to make speeches before the troops in order to keep them in the right political spirit. Hitler's speeches were rather gruesome anti-Semitic affairs, but they seemed to please the men who employed him.

In September he was sent out to investigate a small group, the so-called German Workers' party. This party was founded by a Munich locksmith, Anton Drexler, who earlier during the war had attempted to found an organization that would be both a workers' and a nationalist party. When Hitler went to investigate, he found, in the back room of a beer cellar, a group of twenty to twenty-five people listening to a talk by Gottfried Feder (1883–1941), an engineer and amateur economist. Invited to attend a committee meeting of the party a little later, Hitler saw that it had no strength and was not likely to gain any political importance under its present leadership. But this was an incentive for him to join the party. In any of the old parties he could acquire only an insignificant role, whereas in this struggling party he could hope to assume leadership and to mold it according to his wishes. He joined the committee as its seventh member and at once activated its propaganda and meetings. On February 24, 1920, the first mass meeting took place in the *Hofbräuhaus.* Almost 2,000 people were present when Hitler announced the party's new name, the National Socialist German Workers' party (*Nationalsozialistische Deutsche Arbeiter Partei,* or NSDAP), and proclaimed its twenty-five point program that Gottfried Feder had designed. On April 1, 1920, Hitler left the army and made the organization of the party his full-time business. By quick steps he rose to become its full master.

✎ *Growth of the NSDAP*

CAPTAIN RÖHM was of the greatest assistance in this period. He shared Hitler's conviction that in order to build up a strong nationalist Germany it was necessary to win over the mass of the people to nationalism. Being at home in the army as well as in the free corps he induced many free corps soldiers and ex-service men to join the party. With these men the first fighting bands were established, the nucleus of the storm troopers (*Sturmabteilung,* or SA). In December the party managed to buy a weekly paper, the *Völkische Beobachter,* with secret army funds providing half of the needed money. The other half came from Dietrich Eckart

(1868–1923), a journalist, writer, and poet, to whom Hitler always felt great gratitude, because he taught him a great deal in these years.

Hitler was a genius at mass propaganda. Rhetoric, though the heart, was only part of such propaganda. He was careful to display exciting posters and such impressive symbols as the swastika flag, uniforms, and the Hitler salute. These were the means not only of convincing his followers that they belonged to an irresistible movement but also of shocking his enemies. Another Nazi propaganda device was terror, which became the task of the SA. The storm troopers were supposed not only to protect Nazi meetings from opponents and hecklers by muscle power but also to break up meetings of other parties. In contrast to the old parties the Nazi party was established not merely as an organization for political propaganda but as a fighting force. Since Hitler, through Röhm, enjoyed the protection of the army, he could afford to introduce this violent style into the political life of Munich. As long as the army did not become restless, the Bavarian government was likely to look the other way.

The twenty-five-point party program proclaimed in February 1920 played only a modest part in the propaganda of the party. The program was nationalist, anti-Semitic, and socialist. It demanded the union of all Germans in a greater Germany and the abrogation of the Treaties of Versailles and St. Germain. Jews were to be excluded from citizenship and office. But the program contained more economic than political demands. All war profits were to be confiscated, and all unearned income was to be abolished. The state was to take over all trusts and share in the profits of large industries. The department stores were to be communalized and rented to small shopkeepers. The demands in the agricultural sector were no less far-reaching. Land needed for national purposes should be expropriated without compensation, ground rents abolished, and land speculation suppressed. But while the program expressed the deep convictions of Gottfried Feder, Hitler never felt tied to it. It seemed to him merely a good propagandistic tool in these early years, considering the mood of the lower middle classes and the workers. Once Hitler had reached the stage where he wanted to win over the industrialists or the big agricultural interests, he did not hesitate to reinterpret the program in the most dubious fashion. He was never a socialist. In a speech of 1927 that the Ruhr tycoon Emil Kirdorf (1847–1938) distributed among his fellow industrialists, Hitler said "Highest nationalism is essentially identical with the highest concern about the people, and highest socialism is identical with the highest love of people and fatherland." Socialism and nationalism were for him interchangeable terms, the usage of which depended on the social group he addressed.

✍ Hitler's Imprisonment

WE HAVE ALREADY in another context described the Munich events of November 8–9, 1923[1]. The poor preparation of the *Putsch* and Hitler's ignominious flight from the scene on November 9 should have precluded forever the rise of Hitler's party. But again the Bavarian government helped him by insisting that Hitler should be tried not before the Leipzig Supreme Court but before a Munich court. The Bavarian government was anxious not to let all the circumstances of the *Putsch* be aired, since it had been so deeply involved in a treasonable action against the federal government. Thus Hitler was allowed to prove in his trial that he had acted on high national principles, whereas the members of the government had not been willing to act, although they pretended to represent the same ideals. The court imposed the minimum sentence of five years of imprisonment, but Hitler served only nine months of this sentence and had a rather comfortable sojourn at the fortress of Landsberg. He was free to see visitors and receive newspapers, and he dictated the first volume of *Mein Kampf*.

But while he was in prison the National Socialist movement threatened to fall apart. Gregor Strasser allied it with the older racist parties, and this, in Hitler's opinion, could only dilute its true nature. Moreover, Röhm was building up a substitute SA under a new name, and Hitler had always been suspicious of Röhm's aims. From the beginning Röhm had wanted to keep the SA a separate entity independent of the party in order to combine it with other paramilitary organizations in the national liberation. Hitler, however, considered the SA a force for carrying on party propaganda and street fighting and wanted it firmly subordinated to the leadership of the party. By the time Hitler left Landsberg, the remnants of the former Nazi party and its successors were engaged in endless quarrels among themselves, and Hitler found it relatively easy to reassert his leadership. But before he began the rebuilding of the Nazi party, he first concluded peace with the authorities in power. He drew the lesson from the November events that he could not hope to gain power by a coup but only by legal means. He was to stick to this line with the greatest determination till 1933. It was a policy that aroused the suspicion of a good many of his followers, particularly among the storm troopers, that he had grown soft. Again and again he had to quell attempts of some of his followers who tried to push him toward revolutionary tactics. Actually Hitler did not give up the idea of revolution, but he wanted to realize it only after his accession to power.

---

[1] See pp. 609–11.

✍ *Hitler* vs. *Strasser*

BECAUSE OF THE SHRILL DEMAGOGIC tones of Hitler's first public speech after his release from prison, the Bavarian government forbade him to make public speeches, and other states followed its example. It was not until May 1927 that he was allowed to speak in Bavaria again, while Prussia lifted the ban only after the September elections of 1928. Hitler had to lie low in these early years, because at first he was afraid that the Bavarian authorities might deport him to Austria. The Nazi party seemed in a hopeless situation. In the first election for the presidency in 1925 the party put up Ludendorff as its candidate, but he received no more than 211,000 votes out of a total of about 27 million.

On the other hand, the year 1925 saw the star of Gregor Strasser rise. This bullish Bavarian, a most effective speaker and a capable organizer, carried National Socialism all over northern Germany from the Rhineland to Eastern Prussia. To him socialism meant as much as nationalism, and he proposed the nationalization of heavy industry and of the large estates. For similar reasons he wished to throw the support of the Nazi party behind the Communist referendum for the expropriation of the property of Germany's former princes and rulers. In spite of Hitler's intervention Strasser insisted on his course. In November 1925 a conference of leaders decided in favor of Strasser's policies and adopted a new party program with strong demands for socialism. But Hitler reasserted his authority. At a conference in Bamberg in February 1926 Strasser found himself in the minority and had to see his closest associate, Joseph Goebbels, change sides. In May 1926 Hitler had his sole authority for the appointment and dismissal of party leaders approved by another conference. On this occasion the old twenty-five-point program of February 1920 was declared unalterable.

✍ *The Appeal of Nazism*

BUT THE YEARS between 1925 and 1929 were a difficult period. With the consolidation of the Weimar Republic and with relative prosperity people were not inclined to listen to the voices of doom and hatred. In the absence of visible success Hitler had to do his utmost to maintain the morale of his followers, many of whom expected quick and ample personal rewards. Hitler's confidence, however, knew no bounds. He built up a far larger party organization than was needed in these years, one capable of handling the numbers which he expected eventually to enclose in his party. Germany was divided into *Gaue*, which were more or less identical with the thirty-four federal electoral districts, with a *Gauleiter* appointed by Hitler at their head. The future was not forgotten, and there were seven additional *Gaue* for Danzig, the Saar, Austria, and the Sudetenland. Under the auspices of the party affiliated specialized organizations were created. For the youth the Nazi School Children's League, the Hitler Youth, and the Students' League were launched. There was a Nazi Teachers Association, a Union of Nazi Lawyers and Nazi Physicians as well as an Order of German Women. The central organization of the party was formed along functional lines comparable to various ministries of state.

With the coming of the great depression in 1929 the membership of the Nazi party began to multiply, and the fight for the conquest of total power in the state began in earnest. The party's participation, together with Hugenberg, in the referendum and plebiscite on the Young Plan and in the elections of September 1930 established it as a national party of the first order. The lower middle classes of town and countryside swelled its ranks. These classes, however, combined very heterogeneous groups whose economic demands often were at cross purposes. The farmer wanted high prices for his produce, while the urban consumer wanted to keep his food bill low. The storekeeper wanted to be freed from the competition of department and chain stores, while the bank clerk was glad about their bargain prices. On the other hand, the anticapitalistic and at the same time antiproletarian note in the Nazi program particularly appealed to all the lower middle classes which were threatened by the economic crisis with the loss of their identity. In a vague sense they made free capitalism responsible for the economic cataclysm, while they looked for the appearance of a power that would save them from being swallowed by the proletariat. To be sure, the Nazis offered every social group some advantages, but the strength of the party rested on the transformation of these materialistic interests into a political faith. At home National Socialism promised to abolish parliamentarianism and the multiparty system. In foreign affairs it pressed for revision and expansion. All the commitments from Versailles to the Young Plan were to be thrown off, and Germany was to seek new land abroad. The responsibility for the miserable state of Germany at the time was assigned to the Jews, the devilish foes of the Nordic race. Turning Germany's political fate would solve the material problems of all social classes. By getting himself accepted as the political savior by ever larger groups, Hitler was able to make the discrepancies of the economic and social program appear as negligible.

Although the bulk of its members consisted of people from the lower middle classes, the party drew followers from other classes as well. The representation of workers was relatively small, though not altogether insignificant. Young and unemployed workers in particular joined the Nazi party as storm troopers. Altogether more important, however, was the representation of the higher middle classes. Here again the youthful

elements prevailed. The strong representation of youth in the ranks of the
party made it pose as the wave of the future. Its military and militaristic
character promised action instead of mere talk. The party, which between 1927 and 1929 had grown to 120,000 members, by the summer of
1930 counted 300,000 members and by the beginning of 1932 almost
800,000. The storm troopers (SA) had gathered a force of almost half a
million men by the end of 1932.

✍ Nazi Political Tactics

HITLER HAD WISHED to become the head of a presidential cabinet because
he expected to be able to abolish some of the constitutional safeguards by
the use of article 48. As early as February 4, 1934, the first emergency
decree was issued by which Hitler received discretionary power to limit
the right of assembly and also of the press. This was followed two days
later by another emergency decree that held the government of Otto
Braun responsible for the confusion in the political life of Prussia and
voided the legal powers which the Supreme Court had given it after the
Papen *Putsch*. Now Papen together with the National Socialist president
of the Prussian parliament was able to dissolve that parliament and announce new elections for March 5, simultaneously with the *Reichstag*
elections. It was a thinly veiled breach of law and at the same time a
warning that the Hitler government would not stop short before the
rights of the individual states.

During the election campaign the Hitler party was far superior in
strength to the other parties, in whose activities it could and did actively
interfere. Communist electioneering was virtually suppressed altogether,
although the government had decided not to dissolve the Communist
party yet, because this might have increased the Social Democratic vote.
But the government also interfered drastically in the meetings and press
of the Social Democratic party as well as of the Center party. Since the
German radio network was owned by the state, the Nazis came into its
possession when they entered the government, and during the campaign
the German radio was used almost exclusively by them. These actions of
the government took place under the cover of legality, which the government anxiously tried to preserve. But at the same time the party unleashed
terroristic actions. During February and then again after the election of
March 5 a wave of terror spread over Germany. The storm troopers took
their revenge on their enemies, on whom they inflicted the most heinous
cruelties. Their barracks were not adequate to hold the 100,000 victims of
the SA misdeeds. Thus in the early summer special concentration camps
were opened, and by the end of 1933 there were about fifty of them.
Although the Nazi leaders explained the actions of the storm troopers as

an outbreak of the wrath of the people, it was clear that virtually all these actions were approved, if not directed, by the party. They were designed to arouse fear among the other parties and to demonstrate the monopoly that the party held on the use of violence.

✍ *The* Reichstag *Fire*

IN THE EVENING of February 27, 1933, the *Reichstag* building was discovered in flames, and up to the present day that fire has presented a puzzle. Only one arsonist was apprehended in the building, a young Dutch Communist, or rather ex-Communist, Martinus van der Lubbe, but the Nazis pinned the guilt on the Communists collectively. The *Reichstag* fire, so they asserted, was to serve as the signal for a general revolt of communism in Germany. Yet it is impossible to say what interest the Communist party would have had in the burning of the *Reichstag*. There was only one party that could have gained from the fire, and that was the Nazi party itself. But we do not have sufficient proof to declare the Nazis responsible. One thing, however, is certain: that the Nazis were prepared to take the greatest advantage of the event. It served as a screen for the emergency decree of February 28, 1933, "for the defense against Communist acts of violence endangering the state." Using article 48 the president suspended civil liberties, namely habeas corpus, the right of free expression of opinion, the right of assembly, the right to form associations, and the inviolability of property. Article 48 authorized the president to suspend civil liberties only "temporarily." Therefore the decree of February 28 should have been revoked at the latest after the Supreme Court had found that no connection existed between the *Reichstag* fire and an intended Communist revolution. But it was never revoked. The decree, which abolished all the rights for which the liberal constitutional movement had fought during the nineteenth century, became the chief instrument for establishing the full arbitrary dictatorship of the Hitler government. It left the individual without defense against any governmental intrusion into his private life. The decree of February 28 also permitted the government to take over "temporarily" the governments of the lands. This was to serve as the legal basis for the demolition of the federal structure of the Weimar Republic.

✍ *The Elections of 1933*

FIVE DAYS after the decree of February 28 that transformed Germany into a police state, the election took place. It could hardly have been called a free election. The National Socialists used every means now at their disposal to weaken and cripple the electioneering of the other parties, particularly in the final stage of the campaign when they banned press organs or barred public meetings in order to silence oppositional voices. In the last week before the election practically the whole campaign of the political left through press and meetings was suppressed. Almost all the functionaries of the Communist party were imprisoned by that time, as were a good many leaders and functionaries of the Social Democratic party. Meanwhile the Nazis carried on their gigantic propaganda in a frenzied state. After Hitler had become chancellor, the industrialists had provided election funds for the Nazi party. Goebbels predicted "a very big victory."

The results of the election were astonishing. The Nazis received 43.9 per cent of the popular vote, less than the Social Democrats had gained in the democratic elections of 1919. Compared with the elections of 1932, the increase in the Nazi vote was not the result of a shift from the other parties. Only some Communists may have switched their vote in the March election. The Nazis profited chiefly from the unusually high participation in the elections. Eighty-nine per cent of the electorate went to the polls, and the newly mobilized voters, together with the young first-time voters, gave their votes to the Nazi party. Even those parties that had suffered the greatest terror of the Nazis did not lose much. The Social Democratic party fell from 20.7 per cent to 18.2 per cent, the Communist party from 16.9 per cent to 12.2 per cent, and together these two working-class parties commanded almost one-third of the popular vote. The Center party and the Bavarian People's party held their ground pretty well. The German Nationalist People's party maintained the strength it had gained in the November elections of 1932, but the hope of some German Nationalist leaders that larger groups might rally around the party to strengthen their hands in moderating Nazi policies turned out to be vain. The German Nationalists had conducted a campaign in which here and there they indicated certain reservations with regard to the radicalism of the Nazis, but their campaign speakers had never failed to stress the unity of purpose that existed between the two parties in the government. The Nationalists could point out with some pride that only their 8 per cent gave the Hitler government a bare majority of 52 per cent. Yet what might have given them a crucial position in a parliamentary government was of little consequence with a government that was determined to abolish parliamentarianism and had already taken important steps in that direction. The Nazis simply disregarded the German Nationalists and declared the result of the election of March 5 a grand victory for the Nazi party.

The next few days saw the National Socialist conquest of power in the German lands. The Nazis already ruled a group of smaller lands, such as Thuringia, the two Mecklenburgs, Oldenburg, Brunswick, Anhalt, and

Lippe. But they were not represented in the governments of Bavaria, Württemberg, Baden, Hesse, or Saxony, or in the governments of the three Hanseatic cities. In all these areas the storm troopers fomented unrest and riots, which served as a pretext for declaring that the land governments were not able to restore public security. Reich commissars were appointed to take over the executive functions of the land governments, and by March 10 all the land governments were in the hands of National Socialists.

✍ *The Day of Potsdam*

HITLER MADE a special effort on a number of occasions to demonstrate the close relationship between the German Nationalists and the National Socialists. The presidential directive of March 12 which abolished the black, red, and gold flag and instead demanded the display of the black, white, and red flag of the Bismarckian Empire together with the swastika flag of the Nazi party was a gesture in this direction. But the greatest show was staged in connection with the opening of the new *Reichstag* on March 21, 1933, the anniversary of the opening of the first *Reichstag* under Bismarck. Yet the Nazis wanted to honor at the same time a much older tradition. This state event took place in the garrison church of Potsdam, which had been built by Frederick William I and under whose altar his and his son's remains were buried. Here at noon the members of the new *Reichstag*, except for the Communists and Social Democrats, assembled together with large groups of generals, ministers, and high party officials. One chair, behind which the crown prince and his wife were sitting, was left vacant in order to remind the public that William II was absent. Hindenburg appeared in the uniform of a World War I field marshal, wearing all his wartime decorations, and Hitler for once wore a black tailcoat. Hindenburg read a declaration stating that a clear majority of the people had placed itself behind the government that had come into being through his confidence and that thereby the people had given the government a constitutional basis for its work. Reminding the deputies of the Prussian sense of duty, he appealed to them to support the government in order to solve the grave tasks ahead. Hitler's relatively moderate oration followed the style that had become generally known by that time. Beginning with a review of the glorious early period of the empire, he described the decline in all fields for which the November revolution and the Weimar Republic were responsible. Then he praised the unity of the new national forces and their final victory. Owing to the confidence that Hindenburg had ultimately given them, he said, a union had been created between the symbols of the greatest old and young forces. Thereafter he announced a program of national rebirth that was extremely vague, however, in its details. He asked the *Reichstag* to follow him and ended with a glorification of Hindenburg as the embodiment of the national myth. A parade of the army garrison of Potsdam, the police, the *Stahlhelm*, and the SA ended the demonstration.

It was a well staged and effective show. Many people took it as proof that National Socialism would ultimately be domesticated by a national conservatism. And many bourgeois people concluded that in these circumstances they ought to give their support to Hitler.

✍ *Cabinet and Parliament*

BUT FOR HITLER the "day of Potsdam" was only a screen behind which he could continue to make himself absolute master of the state. The new *Reichstag* was to pass an enabling act which was to give the cabinet the power to legislate even in disregard of the existing constitution. In addition to the *Reichstag* the president was also to be excluded by this act from participating in legislation.

When the cabinet discussed the law, the non-Nazi members again showed little eagerness to limit Hitler's power. By removing the president from the legislative process, they were abandoning the theory of "fencing in" the Nazis. The German Nationalist ministers had also agreed that in order to make the *Reichstag* more manageable the Communist members should not be seated. With the exclusion of the Communists the Nazis by themselves held a majority in the *Reichstag*. But in order to get the enabling act passed a two-thirds majority was needed, and this meant that, in addition to the German Nationalists, the Center party and possibly the surviving smaller parties had to vote in favor of the law. The members of the Center party correctly assumed that if they cast a negative vote they could not keep Hitler from finally achieving his goal. On the other hand, if they approved of the enabling act, the Center party would seem to establish the legality of the Nazi party. Both at home and abroad the Nazi party's prestige would gain by this approval. But a good many members of the Center party argued that the Nazis might dissolve the party or dismiss all Center members from the civil service if they did not vote for the enabling act. The mere survival of the Center party was declared by them to be the chief issue. Other members comforted themselves with the hope that the Nazi regime could not last very long. Brüning, for example, expressed the opinion that the financial and economic policies of the Nazis were bound to ruin them before long.

In conversations with Hitler the Center leaders had gained some promises. Hitler had told Dr. Ludwig Kaas that no measure would be taken against Hindenburg's wishes, that future laws would be discussed by a small working committee, and that equality before the law would remain guaranteed to everybody except the Communists. Government officials belonging to the Center party would not be persecuted. The judiciary would remain independent, and ecclesiastical right would not be touched. Hitler had even agreed to put these reservations into writing. But no such letter was ever received.

✍ *Opening of the New* Reichstag

ON THE AFTERNOON of March 21 the new *Reichstag* was officially opened. It again elected Hermann Göring as president, and he assumed the office with a speech full of calumnies against the fourteen years of the Weimar Republic and adulatory praise of Hitler, who with the "day of Potsdam" had inaugurated a new age. "Now Weimar has been overcome by the return to the spirit of Potsdam." Göring warned, however, that the national revolution was not yet over but was still unfolding. At the first working session of the *Reichstag* two days later, the building in which the meeting took place was surrounded by SA and SS guards. They even entered the meeting hall, where they took position in a threatening formation on the side of the opposition. For the first time Hitler spoke to the parliament. In his customary manner he first gave a grim picture of the fourteen years of the Weimar Republic as a period of decline and corruption. Then he described how the National Socialists had in a few weeks removed the powers which had ruled since 1918 and how the German people had approved of their action in the elections. Now, he said, everything had to be used for rebuilding. All ailments of the life of the people, particularly the Marxist heresy and liberalism, had to be purged. Hitler announced that the Nationalist Socialist aims were to win over the worker for the national state in a real community of the people and to achieve ideological unity. The enabling act, therefore, was also to serve the imposition of ideological uniformity. In addition Hitler proclaimed a radical moral purge. Schools, theaters, movies, literature, the press, and radio were to be purged. Heroism, blood, and race should be the foremost sources of artistic intuition. With regard to the churches he remarked that the national government saw in the two Christian denominations the most important factors for the preservation of German nationhood. The government would respect the rights of the churches but count on their consideration in return. To the dismay of his German Nationalist coalition partners Hitler declared the problem of restoring the monarchy not worth discussing. His assurance that he would preserve the independence of the judiciary was mingled with the threatening exhortation that the judges should recognize the needs and demands of the community. In the economic program that Hitler presented no trace of socialism was found. Instead he promised that, in the future large-scale planning of the economy, private initiative and property should be furthered. In addition he promised that there would be no currency experiments. The "salvation of the German peasant" was an urgent goal, and Hitler promised "a total attack" against unemployment through work creation and labor services.

In his remarks on foreign affairs Hitler was extremely cautious. He praised the German army and also demanded German equality of rights in the disarmament question, but he went far out of his way to impress on the foreign powers the National Socialist desire for peace. Naturally he flattered fascist Italy, but he also showed respect for France. Even with the Soviet Union, Hitler promised to cultivate friendly and mutually useful relations. The fight against communism in Germany was an internal affair, he said, which did not have to interfere with external relations. At the end of his speech he emphasized that the government intended to use the enabling act only insofar as it was necessary for the execution of vitally necessary measures. Neither the existence of the *Reichstag* nor of the *Reichsrat* should thereby be questioned, while the position and the rights of the Reich president were not touched by the enabling act at all. The lands would not be abolished. The enabling act, three times prolongated, served together with the emergency decree of February 28 as the main foundation of all Nazi legislation until 1945.

✍ *The Enabling Act*

AFTER A FEW HOURS of intermission in which the party delegations could deliberate, the meeting was reopened. As the first party representative, Otto Wels (1873–1939), the chairman of the Social Democratic party, courageously defended democracy and the rule by law, thus justifying the rejection of the enabling act by the Social Democrats. After a rude and spiteful rejoinder by Hitler it was the turn of the Center party and of the small middle parties to announce their position. Dr. Ludwig Kaas gave the approval of the Center party, stressing, however, the promises which Hitler had made with regard to the intended use of the enabling act. He did so, although the Center party had not received from Hitler the letter concerning his promises. The other parties followed in quick succession. With a vote of 441 to 94 the government reached its objective. In the same evening the *Reichsrat*, now composed of representatives of the new land governments, passed the law. With this final step Hitler had become independent of Hindenburg and in the future did not have to pay any attention to the German Nationalists in the government. As a matter of fact, he was now the dictatorial ruler of Germany.

The enabling act was perhaps the most important single piece of what was called in Germany at that time political *Gleichschaltung*. The word is hard to translate. What was meant was to make political institutions and agencies, or even individuals, conform to the policies of the Nazi party. The usual translation "coordination" is not very exact. Coordination as practiced by the Nazis was actually subordination of others to the Nazi will.

✑ Centralization of Government

WITH THE ENABLING ACT the Hitler government could legalize the temporary assumption of power in the lands by Reich commissars. On March 31 the government issued the "preliminary law for the coordination of the lands with the Reich." The law also gave the land governments the power to legislate without reference to an emergency decree or to a parliamentary majority. It ordered the dissolution of all land parliaments with the exception of the recently elected Prussian parliament and of all district, city, and village councils. They were not to be reelected but merely to be reorganized on the basis of the result of the federal election of March 5. The "second law for the coordination of the lands with the Reich" of April 7, 1933, introduced Reich governors, whose function it was to see that the directives issued by Hitler were realized. In Prussia, however, Hitler himself assumed this office, while Papen resigned as Reich commissar. Hermann Göring became prime minister of Prussia. With these changes the German lands lost the last attributes of statehood. In January 1934 all land parliaments were abolished and in February, in violation of the enabling act of March 1933, the Federal Council was dissolved and the Reich governors subordinated to the Reich minister of the interior. Thus the lands became mere administrative districts of the empire, and a radical centralism superseded the federal structure of Germany.

Each of these steps not only advanced the authority and power of the central government but also extended the hold of the Nazi party over the state. The law on Reich governors placed the appointment of these governors in the hands of the chancellor, and without exception Hitler appointed Nazis to these posts. Simultaneously the Nazis made every effort to subject the civil service to their will. Although the Nazi leaders were determined to expel many civil servants for political and racial reasons, they realized that they needed the mass of trained government officials to run the government. Even counting the officials who in March had quickly joined the party, there were not enough Nazis to replace the technically trained and experienced government officials. Together with the law on Reich governors, a law was issued "for the restoration of a professional civil service," a title that attempted to give the impression that the Weimar Republic had ruined the much vaunted traditional civil service in Germany. This was by no means the case, nor did the Nazis really intend to restore a traditional German civil service. Instead, they wanted to appoint reliable members of the Nazi party to crucial positions in the government bureaucracy and intimidate the rest of the government officials to obey the orders which they received from the Nazi government. For that reason the law abolished the constitutional rights of the civil service, particularly with regard to tenure. All full-blooded or half-blooded Jews, for whom the Nazis now officially introduced the term "non-Aryans," were to be dismissed at once with the exception of veterans of World War I or those who had lost sons or fathers in that war. This exemption had been inserted on the intervention of Hindenburg. After his death it was disregarded. There was no resistance or open criticism shown by the civil service with regard to the new law. The great majority of the German government officials had disliked the parliamentary regime. They expected that in the future the complete execution of policy would be their responsibility. Many even among those who joined the Nazi party hoped that the rule by the bureaucracy would be able to preserve the tradition of government by law in Germany. As a matter of fact the civil service and the judiciary did a great deal to preserve the legal rights of the individual. But the authority of the civil service rapidly waned. The party with its police methods intervened directly in the executive actions of the state. A person accused of a political offense had little chance of being tried before the ordinary courts. As a rule the political police would send him directly to a concentration camp. The dualism of government service and party which existed in the early years of the Nazi regime steadily disappeared, and the war eliminated the last protection of the individual.

✍ *Trade Unions*

WHILE THE NAZIS quickly conquered the apparatus of the state, they did not forget the great public organizations which had exercised a considerable influence in the Weimar Republic. The largest mass organizations were the trade unions. The Social Democratic free trade unions had four and a half million registered members. The Christian trade unions had a membership of one million, while the liberal trade unions had one of half a million. In addition there existed a number of employee unions. Even now the various unions jealously guarded their independence and remained unable to agree on a common policy. Undoubtedly the fate of the trade union movement in Germany depended on the future of the free trade unions, which had been weakened by the economic depression. On July 20, 1932, when Papen seized the Prussian government, these unions had declined to use the sharpest weapon in their power, because they felt that a general strike at a time of high unemployment would boomerang.

Once again, after Hitler's appointment as chancellor the leaders of the trade unions had not even discussed the possibility of a general strike. Instead, in order to preserve their organizations they had been willing to negotiate with the National Socialists. They went as far as to propose cutting all their ties with the Social Democratic party and confining their activities strictly to social problems. They were even ready to accept the appointment of a Reich commissar for the trade unions. But although there were Nazi leaders who would have liked to retain the existing trade unions and place Nazis in high positions, Hitler wanted to destroy the unions.

A law enacted on April 10 declared May 1 to be "the day of national labor." This day had been used by all parties in the Second International to demonstrate the power of the labor class. But not even the Weimar Republic had recognized May 1 as an official holiday. Its recognition as such by the Nazis could not fail to make an impression on the masses, although the government indicated that the day should not be celebrated as a demonstration of a single class but as a day of national harmony. Not only the workers but also the managers and proprietors were to participate in the demonstrations. The trade unions could hardly afford to protest this action, and actually they called upon their membership to attend the demonstrations planned and organized by the government. Thus on May 1, 1933, in all German cities the factory workers and their directors marched in closed ranks to the meeting places, where they were addressed by Nazi leaders. These were the first mass celebrations for which the Nazis showed a remarkable gift. Hitler himself spoke in the evening to the mass assembled on the Tempelhof field in Berlin. He proclaimed the end of all class differences and the full integration of the working class into the national community. He did not offer any concrete economic or social program but relied on the phraseology of "German socialism." It is doubtful whether Hitler made very many converts with this speech. The most significant result of the magnificent stage show was the confusion it produced among the workers. But, nevertheless, their willingness to give the new regime a chance was undoubtedly strengthened.

This may also explain why the actions of the Nazi party on the morning of May 2 did not meet with stormy protests from the workers. Throughout all of Germany Nazi storm troopers took over the offices, banks, and newspapers of the free trade unions. The old leaders of these trade unions were arrested, often mishandled, and sent to concentration camps. The other trade unions and employee unions voluntarily surrendered to the director of these actions, Robert Ley (1890–1945). The seizure of the trade unions was an action that had no basis in any existing law. It was undertaken by the Nazi party, but no state agency was willing to intervene. As early as May 10 the new German labor front (DAF) held its first national congress. It quickly became clear, however, that the Nazi organization which wanted to represent all workers of "the fist and the brains" was not to assume the functions of a trade union. By a law of May 19 Hitler appointed so-called "labor trustees," named by the land governments to determine wage contracts. The labor front, on the other hand, which finally comprised 20 million people, was left with the task of indoctrinating the workers with the National Socialist spirit. It therefore had to concentrate more on the leisure time of the workers than on the improvement of working conditions and wages. To achieve its objectives, the labor front gained possession of the existing social welfare institutions of the state and the parties. With the large properties of the working class movement and with the considerable income from workers' contributions, it was able to finance its activities. Since the chief goal of its ideological propaganda was to make the workers feel themselves to be the social equals of members of the other classes, the labor front endeavored to convince the workers that they were not excluded from the pleasures enjoyed by the upper classes. Attendance at the theatre and concerts and travel were subsidized for the benefit of members of the labor front by its organization "Strength through Joy."

✍ *Agriculture*

HUGENBERG, as the new minister of economics and agriculture, gave his main attention to agriculture. He quickly succeeded in raising agricultural prices at the expense of the consumer and in freeing the agricultural proprietors of much of their debts at the cost of their credititors. As one might have expected, his policies had a strong bias toward the large estate holders. Meanwhile Hitler's chosen agricultural specialist, Walter Darré (1895–1953), merged the various peasants' organizations under the leadership of the Nazi party. As early as May he succeeded in bringing the leadership of the greatest agrarian organization, the Reich Land League, under Nazi control by falsely accusing its leaders of corruption. When after Hugenberg's resignation, late in June 1933, Darré became the minister of agriculture, it was easy for him to perfect the political organization of the peasantry under local, county, and land peasant leaders and also pass the legislation which laid the control of marketing and pricing policies of all agriculture under the control of the *Reichsnährstand* (Reich food estate). This sounded like the beginning of the corporative organization of economic life. In fact, many enthusiastic Nazis of every rank expected the Third Empire to follow the fascist example and build a corporative order. But Hitler never actually cared about corporatism. He wanted direct government control of all aspects of public life, which he achieved in agriculture behind the nominal front of the *Reichsnährstand*.

The subordination of agriculture to strict government control was further strengthened by ideology. In analogy to May 1, the day of labor, October 3 was proclaimed the day of the peasant, on which the government organized thanksgiving celebrations all over Germany. Central to National Socialist agricultural policy was the law on inherited peasant estates. Darré had already managed to have this law issued in Prussia in May, but in September it became a national law. The peasants, tillers of the German soil, were declared to be the very foundation of popular strength and the progenitors of pure German blood. In order to preserve them as the foundation of national vitality, all farms of 7.5 to 10 hectares (1 hectare-2.4710 acres) were declared indivisible and unsalable. They were to remain the property of the peasant family for all time, even against the will of the peasants themselves. Only the owners of such entailed peasant estates could call themselves peasants in the future. The law on entailed peasant estates applied to about 35 per cent of the units in agricultural production, and it was of doubtful benefit for the farmers who became peasants. Such a farm could neither be sold nor mortgaged, which was advantageous in the depression of 1933 but a grave handicap during the recovery of the following years. Although the National Socialists promised the creation of additional peasant settlements, fewer people were settled under their regime than had been by the Weimar Republic. It was thought, however, that the conquest of Eastern territories by war would provide the opportunity for a large-scale resettlement of German peasants.

Industry, Trade, and Crafts

IN THE REALM OF INDUSTRY, trade, and the crafts, events followed a similar course, yet the "coordination" of big industry was decidedly less radical than that of the other social organizations. A few members of the Reich Federation of German Industry resigned for political or racial reasons, but Krupp remained as president, while the chief representative of the National Socialist party, Wilhelm Keppler (b. 1882), actually represented the interests of the industrialists as much as of the party. During the summer the federation was merged with the Association of German Employers, and the new organization received a corporate name, Reich Estate of German Industry. Industry profited from the law on labor trustees as well, since those appointed to these posts were almost without exception former counsels of the employers' organizations.

The craftsmen, storekeepers, and proprietors of small factories did not fare so well, although these members of the lower middle classes had been the most fervent supporters of the Nazi party. Late in 1932 a militant organization had been founded within the party which was to represent the interests of these groups. Its leader managed to bring together the main organizations of the middle class in a Reich Estate of German Trade and also made himself the leader of a Reich Estate of German Crafts. But when he began to demand the abolition of the department stores and cooperatives so often promised to these groups, he met with Hitler's resistance. Such demands were not compatible with the capitalistic course which Hitler had adopted. He had the whole middle-class organization dissolved through Ley and subordinated to the German labor front.

✑ Destruction of Political Parties

BY BRINGING the whole social life under their heel the Nazis had further undermined the position of the political parties, which had already abdicated as major political forces. Since it was unlikely that the Nazis could tolerate any other party even in a minor position, they pushed on relentlessly to annihilate all the competing parties. Of the Social Democratic leaders, the majority originally believed that they could build up a loyal opposition to the government. They supposed that they could tide over the party organization through the short period in which they assumed the Nazis would rule. For that reason they disapproved of the exodus of some prominent Social Democrats who established a new party center in Prague. They went as far as to approve, with all other parties, Hitler's speech of May 17, in which he painted the Nazis as champions of peace and disarmament. On June 22, 1933, however, the Social Democratic party was outlawed under the pretext that it had not disassociated itself from the treasonable activities of some of its members abroad. On June 28 the State party, the former Democratic party, and on July 4 the German People's party and the Bavarian People's party dissolved by their own initiative. The Center party followed on July 5.

✑ The Center Party and the Roman Catholic Church

SHORTLY AFTER THE PASSAGE of the enabling act Dr. Ludwig Kaas had left the Center party leaderless by going to Rome. He was apparently convinced that no Catholic party could be maintained in Germany and that in these circumstances the Vatican would be the only power capable of safeguarding at least the basic institutions of the Roman Catholic Church in Germany. The Center party was deeply divided. There were those members who felt that it would be impossible to maintain the Center party at all under the new conditions, while others felt that the party might still be able to act as an organization of Catholic Germans working in close cooperation with the Nazi party. Still others just looked for shelter. In the meantime the defections from the Center party steadily increased. Some felt that the National Socialist party with its emphasis on a Christian basis for politics would safeguard Catholic interests and that the best a German Catholic could do would be to join the Nazi party. Early in May the Center party elected Dr. Heinrich Brüning its chairman with far-reaching authority to shake up the party organization and give it a new sense of direction. But Brüning proved incapable of achieving anything. Apparently he tried in two meetings with Hitler to reach some *modus vivendi* for the party, but his efforts were of no avail. In the meantime the negotiations over a concordat conducted in Rome by Papen with the assistance of Kaas were rapidly approaching a successful conclusion. The Center leaders in Germany had to recognize that the Vatican was ready to sacrifice the existence of the Catholic party in Germany for the guarantee of the basic rights of the Roman Catholic Church. On July 5 Brüning dissolved the Center party.

✍ Dissolution of German Nationalist Party

EVEN BEFORE THE CENTER PARTY went out of existence, the German Nationalist party had ended its career. During the elections the party had formed an alliance with the *Stahlhelm*, but this so-called fighting bloc black-white-red did not prove to be well integrated. Franz Seldte, its leader, had readily joined the Hitler cabinet as minister of labor, and soon he made every effort to subordinate the *Stahlhelm* to Hitler. His policies went not unchallenged within the *Stahlhelm*, and the critical voices increased when the SA opened its terrorist activities against the organization. But the efforts to maintain the independence of the *Stahlhelm* in the hope of keeping it ready for the day when Hindenburg and the army would turn against the Nazi party were quite unrealistic. As a first attempt from the right to resist the Nazi onslaught they deserve to be mentioned, and one can find certain connections between this early opposition and the German resistance after 1938. Some of the leading German Nationalists were appalled by the terroristic activities of the SA and the flouting of law and order by the National Socialists. Moreover, they were greatly alarmed by the stolid attitude that Hugenberg displayed. Some of them hoped to organize monarchistic organizations, believing that under the auspices of Hindenburg and with the help of the army they might replace the Nazi regime by a restored monarchy. But these attempts led nowhere. While Hugenberg assured the party that its influence in the government was fully maintained, the Nazis steadily increased their actions against the German Nationalists.

At the same time Hugenberg's position within the cabinet became ever more tenuous. We have already seen how Darré took control of the agricultural organizations and thereby endangered Hugenberg's control of the federal and Prussian ministries of agriculture. But his position in the cabinet became fully untenable when at the World Economic Conference in London he produced a memorandum which demanded the restoration of her former colonies to Germany and placed even the U-kraine within the area of German economic influence. The German delegation at London refused to present this memorandum, whereupon Hugenberg gave it to the press and thereby started a wave of indignation in foreign countries. Apparently he felt that by his extreme nationalistic demands he could outshine the Nazis. But actually he made the German Nationalists appear abroad even worse than the Nazis. On June 27 Hugenberg resigned from the four federal and Prussian ministries of economics and agriculture which had been assigned to him at the time of the formation of the Hitler government. Neither Hindenburg nor the non-Nazi members of the cabinet, Papen, Neurath, Count Lutz Schwerin-Krosigk (1887–1952), Franz Gürtner (1881–1941), or Blomberg, tried to keep him in office. It was the ultimate end of the policy of "fencing-in Hitler," by which Hindenburg had been induced to appoint Hitler as chancellor. On the same June 27 the German Nationalist front dissolved itself. On July 14 the government issued a law that made the National Socialist German Workers' party the only political party in Germany. With the extinction of the political parties, the *Reichstag*, whose continued existence the enabling act had specifically prescribed, lost its last rights. From now on Hitler could even trespass the limits which the enabling act had placed on the authority of the government.

༫ Dualism of Party and State

WITH THE DESTRUCTION of the political parties Hitler had also brought the great organizations of the German economy under his command. Through a combination of terroristic pressure from below and the exploitation of the legal or seemingly legal weapons at the disposal of the government he had achieved these aims. It did not prove, however, a simple matter to direct the activities of the party into the right channels. It was difficult to put brakes on the lawless violence of the SA men or on the interference of zealous party members in the state administration. They all felt themselves now to be the masters of Germany. In July Hitler, not for the first time, tried to tighten the reins: "On the conquest of external power must follow the inner education of man." But Hitler never intended to subordinate the party to the state. "The law for safeguarding the unity of party and state" of December 1, 1933, stated that after the victory of the National Socialist revolution the Nazi party was insolubly tied to the state. This law made the deputy of the leader, Rudolf Hess (b. 1894), and the chief of staff of the SA, Röhm, members of the cabinet in order to guarantee close cooperation of party and state, but the party became a corporation of public law, whose statutes only the leader set. It was endowed with special jurisdiction, with the right to impose prison and arrest penalties. The dualism of state and party was not overcome by this law. Hitler wanted to maintain the independent power of the party as a weapon with which to mold state and people.

✑ Propaganda and Educational Controls

WHILE THE NATIONAL SOCIALISTS were smashing the political parties, the state rights, and the existing power of the social and economic organizations, they were at the same time preparing instruments for controlling the cultural and intellectual life of Germany. Immediately after the election of March 5 Hitler created, with the approval of the cabinet, a new ministry "for popular enlightenment and propaganda" for Joseph Goebbels. The entire press, radio, the movie industry, the theater, and government propaganda were to come under the sway of this new ministry. During the summer and fall of 1933 Goebbels managed to subject the totality of publicly expressed opinions and cultural creations to his orders. He, like Darré, also used an apparently corporative system to establish his control. Only people who were being licensed by the ministry could belong to one of the six chambers, those of literature, the press, radio, the theater, music, and the visual arts, and were allowed to write, publish, and produce art. Moreover, membership in any of these chambers could be revoked for political reasons. In other words, the ministry had the means of forcing the members to toe the National Socialist line laid down by the chambers. The six chambers were finally brought together in the Reich Chamber of Culture, of which Goebbels made himself president.

Also, no time was lost in forcing the educational system into a National Socialist mold. The new civil service law made it possible to purge the educational institutions of all non-Aryan and democratic elements. The universities lost their right of self-government and were reorganized under the leadership principle, with rectors and deans appointed by the minister. Also, the curriculum was changed by the introduction of professors who taught courses on the "science of race" or on National Socialist *Weltanschauung*. The primary and secondary schools were even more drastically reorganized in their educational aims and methods. The nazification of German schools and education was begun by the land ministries of education but was subsequently centralized in a Reich ministry of education. Besides reorganizing the educational and state institutions the National Socialist party created a number of model schools for future Nazi leaders.

In June 1933 Hitler had appointed Baldur von Schirach (b. 1907) "youth leader of the German empire," and all the existing youth organizations were in due course incorporated into the Hitler Youth. Membership in this national organization became more or less obligatory. Here the young people were exposed to virulent Nazi ideology, which they were supposed to carry into the schools and their families. Thus the children were at the same time made unwitting guardians of the political attitude of their parents. The students were brought together in the National Socialist Students Federation, which in a similar manner, through sports, obligatory labor service, and other devices, tried to inculcate the true Nazi spirit. They, too, served quite openly as guardians over the loyalty of the faculties to Nazi principles.

✑ The Protestant Churches

ONLY IN THEIR ATTEMPT to "coordinate" the Christian churches did the Nazis at this time encounter limitations to the relentless extension of their influence over all fields of public and even private life. German Protestantism, still divided into twenty-eight land churches, was particularly open to the National Socialist onslaught. Cleverly the Nazis used the goal of unifying German Protestantism in a national Protestant church, but the deeper cause of the vulnerability of German Protestantism lay in the nationalistic and reactionary spirit that found a home in these churches. As mentioned before,[2] the official leaders of the churches, supported by the great majority of the clergy, had bemoaned the fall of the monarchy and completely failed to define the position of the church in a democratic state which materially maintained them and abstained from intervening in their internal life. The small groups that struggled to meet the new social problems did not gain ascendancy within the churches. As a result, the active church membership did not grow beyond the old conservative upper class and the traditionalist elements of the middle classes in town and country. They helped to glorify the national greatness of the German people under the Empire that had been ruined by evil foreign and internal forces. The same ministers who during World War I had preached that the German military victories were proof that the German cause was favored by heaven now declared that the defeat was only one of the tribulations inflicted by the divine will and that the Germans, if they readopted the heroic qualities of the past, would be able to break the chains that their enemies had imposed and achieve historic greatness. In the early 1920's groups of ministers and laymen appeared who advocated that Christianity be purged of its Judaic heritage. They declared Jesus Christ to have been a Nordic man, the Old Testament to be objectionable, and even the message of the New Testament to have been perverted

[2] See pp. 661-2.

by the teachings of the "rabbi St. Paul." But the official church authorities had fought these groups, which were then considered a crazy fringe. Yet after the National Socialist party had taken the racist Protestants under its wings and in the spring of 1932 had founded the "German Christian Faith Movement," the racist Christian ideas found an amazingly large mass following. In the ecclesiastical elections of 1932 the faith movement managed to win one third of the seats in the synods. The voters were largely church members who had formerly been inactive, and many a minister saw in this sudden popular interest displayed by the Nazis a way opened to the establishment of a true people's church of all classes.

The churches happily welcomed the Hitler government. In contrast to their aloofness from the Weimar Republic they offered their cooperation for the national rebuilding. No doubt the fact that Hindenburg had appointed the new government that contained so many conservative German Nationalists played a role in this first reaction of the churches, but also article 24 of the party program that committed the National Socialists to a "positive Christianity" was much quoted and the reservation overlooked that "the liberty of all religious denominations" could be guaranteed only insofar as they did not jeopardize the existence of the state or violate "the ethical and moral feeling of the Germanic race." But in contrast to the raucous voices of members of the German Christian Faith Movement, Hitler assuaged the church leaders by the staging of his big political show in the Potsdam church and by the declaration about the future of the churches in his speech preceding the adoption of the enabling act by the *Reichstag*. Yet in April the "German Christians" began open warfare against the existing church governments. Their leader declared that "the faithful have the right of revolution" with regard to a church government "which does not unconditionally recognize the national uprising." Hitler named Ludwig Müller (1883–1945), the staff chaplain of the East Prussian army division who had proselytized the chief of staff Colonel von Reichenau and the Commander General von Blomberg, his plenipotentiary in questions concerning the evangelical churches. The church governments accepted the national unification of the German Protestant churches and late in May elected a highly respected conservative as the first Reich bishop. But the German Christians insisted on the election of Ludwig Müller. By the appointment of state commissars and by direct coups the governing bodies of the churches were taken over by Nazis and German Christians. With the use of the new civil service law non-Aryan members and Nazi opponents within the clergy were removed. All the elected bodies of the churches were dissolved and new elections prescribed. With the full support of the Nazi party, with a press by now dominated by the ministry of propaganda, and equally by the coordinated radio, all Protestant Germans were urged to vote in the church elections for the German Christians. In the elections of July 23 the German Christians actually got a two-thirds majority and were now in a position to elect and appoint Nazis to all significant posts of the church government.

∽ Beginnings of Church Opposition

BUT THE DRIVE of the German Christians to introduce a non-Aryan paragraph into the constitution helped to crystallize opposition among the Protestant ministers. Martin Niemöller (b. 1892), minister of the congregation in Berlin-Dahlem, was early active in establishing contacts between the oppositional elements, who received support from some outstanding members of the theological faculties of the universities. Karl Barth, the Swiss Calvinist theologian, who soon was to be suspended from his professorship in Bonn by the Nazis, gave the opposition a deeper theological meaning. So did the young Dietrich Bonhoeffer (1906–1945), a Berlin University docent. The fight of the anti-Nazi theologians led to a renascence of theological thought within Protestantism that survived the Nazi period, at the end of which Bonhoeffer was murdered in cold blood. The new "emergency federation of ministers" made its determination known at the first national synod in Wittenberg, which elected Ludwig Müller Reich bishop. The federation that at that time comprised two thousand ministers distributed on that occasion a protest against the injection of politics and force into the church as well as against the non-Aryan paragraph. On October 20 the emergency federation of ministers elected a central council of brethren with Martin Niemöller as its manager. The activities of the new masters of the official churches became so radical and the propaganda of the German Christians so reckless that resentment among the church membership grew by leaps and bounds. Even the faith movement of the German Christians began to splinter, while by January 1934 the emergency federation of ministers included one third of all the Protestant ministers.

It had become clear that the Protestant churches could not be conquered by the Nazis from within. Hitler, afraid of setting loose a major *Kulturkampf*, decided to shift the church policies of the party. He realized that it was not necessary to win full control of the churches by the Trojan horse of German Christianity but rather that in order to achieve his ultimate goal, namely the destruction of Christian beliefs and their replacement by some sort of racist Germanic philosophy, the party should display open hostility to all churches and keep away from all church parties, including the German Christians. In January 1934 Alfred Rosenberg (1893–1945) was made "plenipotentiary of the leader for the total spiritual and philosophical education of the NSDAP." From now on the party openly favored the Germanic pagan movement of "God-believers." But the harassment of the churches by the imposition of penalties on those opposing paganism or racism continued. The intention was to isolate the churches and undermine their influence on the people's thought and manners. Just what the Nazis ultimately held in store for the churches was demonstrated during the war when a former church commissar, August Jaeger, became *Gauleiter* of the annexed Polish territory of Wartheland.

✍ Nazi Church Control

IN 1933 a Reich church ministry was created under the Nazi Hans Kerrl (1887–1941). It was his task to supervise the churches and suppress any action of the Protestant ministers which in the opinion of the party might have some political impact. Any public discussion of questions of church policy was forbidden. But the church struggle went on in numerous individual actions and acts of suppression. In November 1934 the emergency federation of ministers established a "preliminary" governing body of the German evangelical church, and later on it even set up its own theological school. The active participation in the federation underwent some changes, but about every fourth or fifth Protestant minister took his place in it. Although the federation was the first democratically formed resistance group, its opposition was confined to matters of church policy and religious principle, and its immediate political effect was not great. The ministers, anxious to demonstrate their national loyalty, were often tricked by the Nazis into false compromises. But the existence of this oppositional church strengthened the determination of those Germans who desired to keep free from the ideological and intellectual perversion imposed by nazidom.

✍ Nazis and Roman Catholic Church

IN CONTRAST to the Protestant churches the Roman Catholic Church in Germany had been active in fighting National Socialist teachings. The Catholic Center party, in spite of its internal divisions, had been one of the chief columns of support on which the Weimar Republic had rested. It was therefore not surprising that the Nazis after January 30, 1933, particularly directed their attacks by words and deeds against the Catholic organizations. On the other hand, there were many German Catholics who were attracted by the new authoritarian regime. Impressed by the promises Hitler had given with regard to the future of the churches, by the suppression of communism, and by the enthusiasm with which a good many Catholics had welcomed the arrival of Hitler, the German bishops attempted to establish a basis for the coexistence of church and state. The Fulda conference of German bishops, the most authoritative voice within the German Catholic Church, declared on March 28 that earlier warnings against National Socialism were invalid, although the bishops insisted that certain religious and moral errors would stand condemned.

At the same time the prelate Dr. Ludwig Kaas arrived in Rome. The chairman of the Center party had apparently reached the conclusion that Catholic interests in Germany could no longer be protected by the Center party and that only the universal church could build dams for the protection of the German Catholics. In analogy to the papal concordat with Mussolini of 1929 he recommended the conclusion of a treaty between the Vatican and Hitler. When Vice Chancellor von Papen went to Rome to negotiate a concordat, he offered more than all the governments of the Weimar Republic had been willing to grant. The church cared particularly about the preservation of special Catholic schools. This the German government conceded together with the right of the church to make known papal letters and encyclicals. Freedom of faith and public worship, the protection of the church institutions and of the priests were additional German concessions. On the other hand, the Vatican gave up all the political and social organizations of German Catholicism and recognized the Hitler regime. The negotiations were concluded on July 19, 1933, and the concordat formally signed less than two weeks later.

Hitler forbade any discussion of the concordat. Although every treaty he signed he was willing to break, for the time being the conclusion of the concordat was giving him great advantages. It helped to make his regime respectable among nations and at the same time forced the German Catholics out of politics. Yet Hitler was far from giving up his ultimate goals with regard to the churches. The Nazi government consequently gave the concordat the narrowest interpretation. Conflicts arose continuously, particularly over the provisions about Catholic schools and the Catholic youth organizations. In addition the Catholic Church could not help condemning the paganism and the totalitarian claims of National Socialism, as Cardinal Faulhaber of Munich did first in December 1933 in a number of widely read sermons. The appointment of Alfred Rosenberg as guardian of the cultural activities in Germany induced the Vatican to place his *Myth of the Twentieth Century* on the Index. The struggle between church and state was conducted on a broad front. It reached a dramatic climax with the issue of the papal encyclical *Mit Brennender Sorge* (With deep anxiety) of March 14, 1937, which condemned in strong, clear language the main tenets of National Socialism. Many priests were sent to prison or to concentration camps, and a large number of them became martyrs of their faith. But the opposition of the church was not broken. During the war the Nazi fight against the Christian churches was played down somewhat. Hitler, however, intended to abolish the churches after he would have gained victory in the war.

✑ End of Monarchist Movement

ALTHOUGH THE CHURCH STRUGGLE demonstrated the limitations of "coordination," it did not decisively weaken the Hitler regime. In the second half of 1933 practically all the strategic positions were already in the hands of the Nazi party. The president still retained some powers, yet Hindenburg's health was deteriorating rapidly, and it was not likely that he would take political initiative against Hitler. Only the monarchists hoped that he might help in the restoration of the monarchy, and they propagated the idea that after Hindenburg's death it should be reestablished in Germany. Actually Papen did persuade Hindenburg to express his wish for the restoration of the monarchy. But the president did not make this wish part of the political testament which was published after his death but placed it in the form of a personal letter to Hitler, which the latter refused to publish.

✑ Army Supports Hitler

EVENTS MIGHT HAVE TAKEN a different course if the army had supported a monarchical restoration. But the heads of the German army refused to be drawn into such an adventure. General von Blomberg, the minister of defense, and General von Reichenau, his chief political advisor, felt that with Hitler and his party they could build a stronger army. They must also have believed that monarchistic thinking was no longer strong enough within the officer corps, particularly among the junior grades. The new chief of the army command, General von Fritsch (1880–1939), an officer of the Seeckt school, declared the activities of the monarchists a matter of internal politics in which the army could not intervene. This was still the old formula, that the army was above party politics. But in reality Blomberg and Reichenau had decided to let Hitler build his one-party state. The army had done nothing to stop the terroristic waves which the SA unleashed or the violations of the constitution that the government committed. Hitler had courted the generals from the first days of his chancellorship and had told them that the full rearmament of Germany was his objective. Blomberg and Reichenau trusted Hitler and had taken many steps to bring the armed forces closer to the Nazi party. They did not wish, however, to see the army submerged in the party. On the contrary, they hoped that by their recognition of the political leadership of the party they would retain the monopoly in arms. Strong opposition against this policy of the army, however, arose from Captain Röhm, the chief of the storm troopers.

∽ *SA* vs. *Army*

IN THE FALL OF 1933 the SA comprised about one million men. It is said that with its reserves it reached four and a half million. Captain Röhm saw in the SA the future army of the Third Empire. The existing professional army was in his opinion to serve as the trainer of the SA men. Hitler, on the other hand, had made up his mind that the old professional army would direct the rearmament of Germany, because he felt that he needed the officer corps for this great task. In addition it was doubtful whether the army would not resist with force any attempt to deprive it of its chief function. Moreover, if Hitler turned over military affairs to the SA, he would in the future be completely dependent on Röhm.

Hitler declared the army to be the sole bearer of arms in the nation. To the SA he assigned the function of educating the people in the National Socialist spirit. But for such work the SA was ill fitted, since its leaders were yearning for high military glory. An attempt to bring a limited number of SA men into the frontier guards did not satisfy the leaders, since the army was not willing to give up its control of the frontier guards and was not prepared to accept the SA leaders as officers. Röhm was deeply dissatisfied and angry. Noisy talk was heard in his camp demanding a second revolution which was to separate Hitler from his cooperation with the generals and industrialists. Although by no means certain, it is possible that Röhm might have led a revolt against Hitler. But there is no evidence to prove that he prepared a revolt of the SA in the spring and summer of 1934. For the time being, at least, he apparently intended only to put pressure on Hitler. He seemed confident that the force which he commanded could not in the end be overlooked by Hitler nor by the army if they wanted to rearm Germany. Undoubtedly Hitler was deeply worried about Röhm's attitude. He was equally concerned that the army, which wanted to be freed from the competition of the SA, might still throw its support behind the monarchists, for whom Papen became privately and publicly active. When Hindenburg fell ill and it became clear that not too many days were left to him, Hitler decided to act. For some time material damaging to the SA leaders had been collected, and lists had been drawn up of people who deserved to be purged. Heinrich Himmler, who since April had commanded the police forces of all the German lands, including those of Prussia, and at the same time the SS, which theoretically was still subordinated to Röhm, was to execute the action. The army was in a state of alert and prepared to give support to the police and the SS. In the end the army to its great relief did not have to intervene. Except for providing transportation and some arms to the SS the army could stay out of sight in the events which took place on June 30 and the following two days.

✑ Purge of the SA

IN THE EARLY MORNING OF JUNE 30 Hitler appeared in Munich and ordered the shooting of the high Bavarian SA leaders. He quickly moved on to the little spa of Wiessee, where he found Röhm and his closest friends still asleep. He excoriated them both for their shameless morals and disloyalty. Göring in the meantime was in charge of the purge in other parts of Germany. We do not know how many people were murdered between June 30 and July 2. Hitler in his speech defending his action set the figure at seventy-seven, but we must assume that at least twice that many were actually killed. The victims were chiefly SA leaders, to whom a number of prominent figures of different political complexion were added. Gregor Strasser was shot, and so was General von Schleicher with his wife and Schleicher's closest political associate, General von Bredow. Gustav von Kahr, whom Hitler in his *Putsch* of 1923 had wanted to force under his command, was also killed, although he had been out of all politics for a good many years. Erich Klausener (1885–1934), the leader of the Catholic action in Berlin, was another victim of the blood bath. The fact that nowhere was resistance shown and practically all these people were taken by surprise is another proof that the SA did not prepare a revolt. Hitler's action took place on the eve of the month's leave which Röhm had ordered for the whole SA. The SA leader of Berlin, Karl Ernst, was just about to embark in Bremen for a honeymoon trip, when he was arrested and subsequently shot.

✑ Aftermath of Purge

ON JULY 3 a law was issued that declared all the measures taken between June 30 and July 2 to beat down treasonable attacks legal as having been executed in defense of the state in an emergency. In the speech which Hitler gave on July 13 in order to justify his action he put all the guilt on Röhm but also asserted that Strasser and Schleicher had made plans in common and had even tried to draw France into their sinister schemes. But Strasser, at least at that time, had withdrawn from all political activities and it is unlikely that he made contact with Schleicher. Schleicher's meetings with the French ambassador were of a social character only.

With the fraudulent assertion of such plots and the imminent danger which they had posed, Hitler wanted to justify his killing spree. Circumstances, he asserted, had not made it possible to bring the crimes before the ordinary courts of justice. Instead he had acted as the supreme judge of the German people. With this declaration and the law of July 3, Hitler placed himself above any law. Although the law was confined to the events of June 30 to July 2, 1934, the government was obviously free to pass an indemnity law with regard to any criminal act it might commit in the future.

Blomberg and Reichenau were satisfied with the results of June 30, in which they had been hidden accomplices. It is amazing that none of the generals took exception to the events in spite of the fact that two of the most prominent generals of the army had been murdered and thereby publicly declared infamous traitors. With the removal of the SA as a competing force the army felt that its position was made secure. Blomberg thought that in the future the army, together with the party, would dominate in Germany. The army would be able to check further Nazi "coordination," while devoting itself entirely to the rearmament of Germany. In reality, however, the generals had only helped Hitler more safely into the saddle.

When President von Hindenburg died on the morning of August 2, Hitler assumed the succession on the basis of a law that had been promulgated the day before. He did not accept the Presidential title but took over the functions of head of state and supreme commander of the armed forces. Henceforth he was the "leader and Reich chancellor." Still on the same day the officers and men of the armed forces took "a holy oath" to Hitler. It was an oath not to the constitution, as in the past, or to the country but to the person of Adolf Hitler. It read: "I will render unconditional obedience to the *Führer* of the German Reich and people. . . ." It was his part of the bargain that Blomberg readily paid. But he had no right or authority to impose such an oath on the armed forces. Although it may be assumed that many soldiers took the oath most reluctantly, there is no evidence that anyone refused to take it.

✑ Organization of the SS

THE PREPARATION AND EXECUTION of the blood purge of June 30, 1934, had been in the hands of the SS (*Schutzstaffeln*, security units), which was thereafter built up as the chief instrument of the Nazi power. After his return from prison Hitler had founded the SS as a personal bodyguard. In 1929 he selected Heinrich Himmler (1900–45) as its leader and commissioned him to make the SS a fully reliable élite organization. The SS then consisted of about 290 men, but by 1933 the black-shirted élite corps had grown to about 52,000. Under Himmler it had soon become the force policing the SA and the party membership. For this purpose Himmler had appointed Reinhard Heydrich (1904–42) in 1932 as head of the security service (*Sicherheitsdienst* or SD) of the SS. The shrewd, ruthless, and cynical Heydrich, a navy lieutenant who had been expelled from the service on account of scandals, turned this intelligence and espionage organization into the brain trust of the SS. Heydrich cared little about ideologies but only wanted power, and every means, including the most sinister and repulsive schemes, was used by him.

The General SS (*Allgemeine* SS) was considered a more elegant version of the SA. A good sprinkling of noblemen among the commanders of its military units and a large number of academically trained people, particularly medical doctors, gave the old ruling classes a relatively strong representation. Himmler deliberately cultivated this appearance by appointing many high government officials and industrialists honorary leaders in the SS after 1933. But on the other hand it was made clear that the SS offered rapid advancement to men from all social classes. In the fully activated military groups of the SS there were three organizations: first, Hitler's personal guard regiment (*Leibstandarte*), which by 1933 had been built up to a fully armed division. Second, there were SS troops distributed throughout Germany, which later developed into the Armed SS (*Waffen* SS). Finally the Death's Head Units (*Totenkopfverbände*) were formed as guards for the concentration camps and other special missions. In these latter units many criminal elements could be found, as was true of many of the command posts of the SS.

In the course of the seizure of power by the Nazis in the spring of 1933 Himmler and Heydrich had gained control over all the police forces in the non-Prussian lands, and Heydrich at once had begun to build up a political police office in each of these lands. In Prussia Göring had created the secret state police office (*Gestapo*), which he was forced to turn over to Himmler and Heydrich in April 1934. This was probably done with a view to the impending action against Röhm, and for the same reason the order was issued in June that the SD of the SS should be the only intelligence service in the party. After the blood purge of June 30, 1934, Hitler made the SS independent of the SA. Himmler was successful in transforming the control which the SS had gained over the police into an institutional organization. This process reached its climax in June 1936, when all existing police forces were placed under the Reich government and Himmler, who as chief of the SS was bound only by Hitler's orders, became chief of the German police in the Reich ministry of interior. In these circumstances the influence of the Reich minister of interior, Dr. Wilhelm Frick (1877–1964), became rather negligible, and he was replaced by Himmler in 1943.

♏ *Heinrich Himmler*

WITH COMMAND OVER ALL the instruments of security Himmler became, next to Hitler, the most powerful figure of the Third Empire. The son of a Bavarian high school principal, he had a rather obtuse mind, and he held an obstinate belief in Hitler's racism. The raising and proliferation of a master race for which sufficient living space had to be conquered and, negatively, the annihilation of the Jews as well as the extermination of "worthless sick people" were aims for which he tried to find ruthlessly effective methods. Alongside the Reich security office of the SS that directed the SD, the security police, and the Gestapo, Himmler created the SS race and land settlement main office. It was the function of this office to supervise the selection of SS men according to biological principles which nobody ever succeeded in defining clearly. The office was also to make plans for the land settlement of Aryan people. For each SS man was to become not only an ideal fighter but eventually also an ideal farmer on his own land. Himmler liked to think of the SS as a knights' order comparable to the medieval Teutonic Knights.

The creation of new land settlements could not be achieved in peacetime except on a very limited scale. Only the war seemed to open great opportunities for the realization of such schemes. A few weeks after its beginning Himmler was appointed by Hitler "Reich commissar for the strengthening of the German race," and as such he acquired the right to issue orders to other party or government offices. But during the war relatively little was achieved except for the resettlement of German minorities outside the German boundaries. They were sent to Eastern European regions which the Hitler government intended to annex to Germany. The SS made much bigger plans for the postwar settlement of Germans in these territories, from which the removal of the Poles was being prepared. The German people had to pay dearly for these infamous deeds when the victorious Eastern nations drove the Germans from their homesteads east of the Oder-Neisse rivers in 1945. But even worse crimes had been committed by the SS with the cold-blooded murder of members of the Polish intelligentsia and of millions of Jews.

♏ *Hitler and his Satraps*

ALTHOUGH THE INFLUENCE of the SS permeated the whole of German life, Hitler carefully avoided becoming entirely dependent on Himmler. He let others of his lieutenants stake out their own satrapies. Men like Göring, Goebbels, and Robert Ley as well as some of the *Gauleiters* and Reich governors, such as Fritz Sauckel (1894–1946) in Thuringia, jealously guarded against any interference in the government of their districts. Since the jurisdiction of the individual sectors of administration was ill defined—in many instances overlapped and blurred by the introduction of new special offices—there were continuous conflicts and shuffles going on among Hitler's henchmen. On account of this spreading of decisions among feuding groups it has been said that the Third Empire should not be called a totalitarian state. But we call a governmental system totalitarian when it demands full control over the minds and bodies of its citizens. This claim was certainly true of Hitler's state, and over the twelve years of his rule it was increasingly realized. Hitler obviously liked the absence of fully effective centralized lines of command, because it gave him a chance to play off one subleader against the other. On the other hand he remained loyal to his old comrades from the fighting days of the party. To be sure, whoever opposed him could be certain of the dictator's ruthless vengeance. But if a man merely proved ineffective in his job, Hitler was unlikely to remove him. In general, Hitler cherished faith more than expertness.

✑ Economic Policies

WHEN HITLER BECAME Reich chancellor he was fully aware that, most of all, the people expected him to solve the unemployment problem. And actually nothing contributed so much to the success of his regime with the people as the abolition of unemployment. But for Hitler this aim was subordinate to making the economy serve the rearmament of Germany. At the cabinet meeting of February 8, 1933, Hitler had already rejected projects that would not have been of any use to the armed forces. Yet a period of preparation for drawing blueprints was inevitable before rearmament could be started in earnest. Thus besides the credits which had already been arranged for by the Papen government and which only now were fully employed, a number of other subventions and credits for the creation of jobs was planned. They were mostly smaller projects from which primarily the building industry and the producers of durable consumer goods could profit. In September 1933 a small beginning was made with the building of the *Autobahnen* (highways). These *Autobahnen*, which at the same time were of considerable military value, required the expenditure of 3 billion marks between 1933 and 1938. Only 3 million were spent in 1933, but by 1938 the annual outlay for the *Autobahnen* ran to 916 million. Altogether the special works programs initiated in 1933 amounted to only 1.5 billion marks. But with the growing belief that the depth of the depression had been passed, business optimism revived, and the relatively small sums brought about a considerable lowering of the unemployment figures. By the end of the year there were only four million unemployed left, as compared to the six million in January of the same year, although actual production did not increase at the same pace.

Yet with the big armament program full production was quickly restored in the German economy, and for all practical purposes full employment was reached in 1936. In the speech in which Hitler announced the opening of the Polish war in 1939, he boasted that he had spent 90 billion marks on the rearmament of Germany. Most statesmen and economists at that time accepted this statement as true. In reality, however, Hitler exaggerated in order to frighten his enemies. Altogether Germany spent no more than 60 million marks on armaments between 1933 and 1939. It is true, however, that this was a much larger sum than any government had ever spent on armaments in peacetime.

The economic recovery produced larger tax revenues. All the taxes imposed by Brüning were continued under the Nazi regime, and in 1936 and 1937 the corporation tax was drastically raised. But while the tax revenue tripled between 1933 and 1938, the expenditures of the government in the same period almost quadrupled. As a result, the budget deficit rose from year to year, while an ever-growing segment of the German economy depended upon governmental expenditures. In 1938 more than a third of the total national income came from governmental payments and investments. Thirty-five per cent of the national income relied on government spending, in contrast to 23.8 per cent in Britain and 30 per cent in France, both of which had started to increase their armament expenditures. In the United States government expenditures accounted for only 10.7 per cent of the national income.

It was Hjalmar Schacht whose financial policies enabled the Nazis to start the rearmament program. In March 1933 Hans Luther was eased out of his position as president of the *Reichsbank*. In comformity with the limited lending authority of the *Reichsbank* Luther had offered Hitler only 100 million marks credit for rearmament. Schacht succeeded Luther and in the summer of 1934 was made Reich minister of economics as well. He circumvented the *Reichsbank* statutes and between 1933 and 1938 mobilized 12 billion marks as credits for rearmament. This enormous credit expansion would not have been possible if Germany had not been hermetically sealed against international influences. In this respect Hitler profited from the work of his predecessors, particularly Brüning. The standstill agreements,[3] the Lausanne agreement of 1932 on the end of reparations, and the control of foreign exchange paved the way for an independent national policy aiming at the revival and expansion of the economy. In the summer of 1933 every transfer of interest on foreign debts was forbidden. In the fall of 1934 Schacht's so-called new plan placed all dealings in foreign currency under governmental control. In

[3] See pp. 677–83.

place of multilateral traffic in commodities and capital all foreign commerce was confined to bilateral arrangements, and the volume of imports was strictly limited, with the government setting priorities. Thus it could select those imports that were most needed for rearmament and choose among countries according to strategic considerations. Trade with Western Europe, Britain, and the United States markedly declined, while trade with the southeastern European countries, the Near East, Latin America, and Scandinavia expanded. The low world market prices for raw material favored Germany, while, in order to earn foreign currency, she was often forced to sell industrial goods abroad at dumping prices.

⮑ Raw Materials

THE IDEAL OF THE NAZIS was to achieve full autarchy for Germany. The chief aim of Hitler's war policy was to gain additional land in the East, whereby Germany would become self-sufficient in the production of food and also gain additional sources of raw material. He knew, however, that in order to conduct the war which would produce the ultimate solution of her economic problems, Germany would have to overcome her deficiencies in a number of basic materials, at least on a temporary basis. In spite of a considerable increase in the production of agricultural goods under the Nazi regime, there still remained a 10 per cent gap that had to be closed by imports. Even greater shortages existed in the supply of basic materials needed for industry. For example, Germany had a great steel-making capacity, one that was almost as large as that of France and Britain combined. But in 1929 about 80 per cent of the iron ore supplies had to be imported, with Sweden supplying almost one half of the total imports and an additional quarter originating in Spain, Luxembourg, Norway, and Greece. With the exception of manganese, all the ferro-alloys needed for production of special high-grade steel came from abroad, most of them from overseas. Germany was also weak in the production of aluminum, and there was very little mining of bauxite ore. Moreover, among all the industrial countries, she was far behind in the production of oil. Eight-five per cent of the oil used came from foreign countries, mainly from North and South America. The other 15 per cent was domestic crude oil, or in a very small way synthetic oil. Building up the production of synthetic oil, which was then in an embryonic stage, did not seem attractive, since it cost four to five times as much as natural oil. For rubber, Germany had to rely entirely on foreign imports. The I. G. Farben works had produced a satisfactory synthetic tire rubber by 1930, but this *Buna*, as it was called, was very expensive, because its production required tremendous amounts of electric power.

To overcome all these deficiencies would have required an enormous financial outlay. Schacht moved slowly. He would probably have liked best to solve these problems through the industrialists, and one agreement of this type had in fact been concluded as early as December 1933 between the government and I. G. Farben. The German chemical combine agreed to produce synthetic oil of a defined quality, while the government guaranteed to take this oil at a stated price for a period of ten years. The government had the right to examine the cost calculation and even lay down rules for it. The company thereby was committed to make the necessary investments, but the risk was taken over by the government, and the firm lost its independence from the state. This mixing of the public and the private segments of the economy became rather characteristic of many arrangements which were made under the Nazi regime. But Adolf Hitler was not content with the progress that Schacht made in the raw materials field. He accused him of being obsessed with foreign trade and taking the side of the industrialists instead of that of the state. Finally in 1936 he turned over the whole raw materials program to Göring and made him plenipotentiary of the Four Years' Plan. In a lengthy memorandum Hitler stated that, owing to the shortage of foreign exchange, the deficiencies in raw materials could not be solved by imports. The available foreign exchange had to serve chiefly for food imports, but it was possible to achieve self-sufficiency in a number of strategic raw materials by increasing production at home. He demanded that in all fields where this was possible full self-sufficiency be built up. The full production of fuel in particular should be pushed at greatest speed and be accomplished within eighteen months. The task was to be carried out with the same determination as the conduct of the war, which depended on its fulfillment. He ordered the same build-up for the production of synthetic rubber and also wanted to see an extraordinary increase in the production of iron and light metals, which could serve as substitutes for unavailable metals. He concluded his memorandum with the demand: "First, the German army must be ready for war within four years. Second, the German economy must be prepared for war within four years." It was in this connection that Hitler most clearly expressed his disregard of any special type of economic organization. Said he: "German business will understand the new economic tasks, or it will prove incapable in this modern age, in which a Soviet state erects a gigantic plan, of existing any further. But then it will not be Germany that will perish, but at the utmost some businessmen." And again: "The ministry of economics has only to present the tasks of the national economy, and the private economy will have to fulfill them. If however the private economy believes itself unable to do so, then the National Socialist state will know how to solve these tasks."

✑ *Government Control of Production*

EFFECTIVE PRODUCTION, not ideology, was the criterion that Hitler applied to industry and business. Still, some ideological notions were imposed on German business by the Nazi party. Thus the leadership principle was applied to business as well, and the Nazis preached the return to the personal or family firm away from the anonymous stock companies. They also strengthened the position of the managing directors vis-à-vis the stockholders. But these were relatively minor measures in which Hitler did not seem particularly interested. Although he was not committed in his heart to capitalism, being unsure in economics he thought it most expedient to work with the existing organization and change it only as much as necessary for placing it under complete government control. In theory the Nazis claimed total control of the economy. The government set wages, prices, and the volume of production. It determined credit, the allocation of resources and manpower as well as transportation. But it exercised full control only in the last years of the war. In the years before, the chaotic administration of economic affairs blunted many of these controls. As Hitler needed the generals to run the army, so he needed the representatives of big business to run the economy. And they were able to assert their interests. In 1936 Göring requested the industrialists to expand iron ore production by around ten million tons. With this addition Germany would have produced about half of the needed iron ore. But the industrialists declined. The cost of making pig iron from the low-grade ore would be greater than from Swedish ore, they said. Besides, special new equipment would be required. They also argued that an expansion of ore mining and steel production would be a serious mistake, since once rearmament had been accomplished, the market would be glutted with steel and its price would fall to an intolerable level.

In this situation the government decided to undertake the iron and steel production. It provided most of the capital for a company called Hermann Göring Works. After four years this quasi-socialist enterprise was supposed to produce four million tons of pig iron and the same amount of steel annually, using ore from the Salzgitter district in central Germany. But the targets were never reached. By 1942 the pig iron capacity of the works was only one fourth of the amount which had been planned, and only about one half of the originally contemplated steel production and only 30 per cent of the intended iron ore production had been achieved. The annexation of Austria in 1938 enabled the Göring Works to appropriate the Erzberg mines, which contained iron ore superior to that of the Salzgitter district. Thereafter the expansion of the iron ore and steel production in this district was cut down, while the Austrian resources were to be exploited. But the projected steel mill in Linz was never completed, and the iron ore production did not make considerable progress. Germany did not produce any more steel in 1939 than she had done in 1929, except that the existing Austrian and Czechoslovakian factories added three million tons, and although ore production had doubled since 1929, two thirds of the total ore used by Germany still had to come from foreign countries.

The synthetic rubber production program, on the other hand, was fully successful. As a matter of fact, Germany produced more than she needed for both military purposes and civilian production and could even export a substantial portion. Aluminum production was raised to an adequate level. The mining of bauxite ore from German sources was greatly stimulated, but it sufficed for only about 10 per cent of the German production. For most of the needed bauxite ore Germany had to rely on Hungarian and Yugoslavian sources. Oil production also proved inadequate when war came. Although synthetic oil production had nearly tripled by 1940, this was actually 45 per cent under the projected output. Crude oil mining brought a greater yield in these years than had been anticipated, but the overall production of oil was about 40 per cent below the original plan in 1939 and 20 per cent below it in 1940. Hitler was very conscious of Germany's deficiencies in raw materials, and many of his decisions as commander of the armed forces can be explained as attempts at gaining control of districts where strategic materials could be found.

✍ Rearmament Build-up

THE RESULTS of Göring's Four Years' Plan for raw materials production remained far behind the target that Hitler had set in 1936, partly because of the inefficiency of Nazi administration. This inefficiency was also shown in the management of the rearmament program. No overall plan for rearmament was ever drafted. At least ten governmental agencies were concerned with the program, and their functions were ill-defined. The distribution of resources and the allocation of manpower were entirely inadequate. Moreover, no agency existed that could have coordinated the requirements of the three branches of the armed forces. This unsystematic organization of rearmament made it impossible to divert workers in larger numbers from the civilian economy to war production. The number of workers in the civilian economy was practically unchanged between 1933 and 1939. The manpower needed to build up an army and to supply the necessary munitions had to be drawn from the unemployed, from the young men entering the labor market in the years 1933–39 and from the 400,000 agricultural workers who were turning to the cities.

When delegating power, Hitler never liked to endow a single person with the full authority of decision. As a consequence, he had to act as the ultimate arbiter among the various competing agencies dealing with re-armament. But while he showed an intense interest in the production of weapons and felt sure about his judgment on the technological quality of arms, the problems of the industrial production of munitions were quite alien to him. When he wished that the production of munitions could be larger, he did not wish to create a total war economy, as was suspected of him abroad and as Nazi propaganda seemed to confirm. Hitler refused to cut down civilian consumption and nonwar governmental production. It would have been possible to extend the working hours, which were kept on a relatively low level. With few small exceptions all of German indus-try worked only one shift in all these years, and thus the full capacity of the equipment was not used. It would also have been practical to mobilize more women for work in the war industries, but none of these measures was ever taken. Britain, whose industrial capacity was estimated to have been about 70 per cent of that of Germany, was producing about the same number of planes as Germany at the time of the outbreak of World War II and a larger number of tanks. Naturally, Germany possessed more planes, since she had begun to produce earlier. But once Britain had got started on economic mobilization, she aimed at total mobilization. After Dunkirk in 1940 she began to outproduce Germany, and in 1941 her war output was one third, and in 1942 one half, larger.

Hitler thought that he could avoid a long-drawn-out war in which the industrial potential of the nations would be of great and possibly decisive importance. He believed that he would be able to isolate his victims and in a brief lightning war would conquer one country after another before the democracies of the West could interfere. He also hoped that with each conquest he would expand his raw material re-sources. With Schiller's Wallenstein he believed that "the war itself would feed the war." It was his undoing that he assumed that he could knock out the Soviet Union by a lightning war. The battle of Moscow in December 1941 proved to be a historic turning point. With the simul-taneous entrance of the United States into the war, the German war production was dwarfed. Thereafter the year 1942 saw an expansion of German war production. But when in the summer of 1942 the German armies approached Stalingrad and the Maikop oil fields, it was only with difficulty that the minister of munitions and armaments, Albert Speer (b. 1905), persuaded Hitler not to put brakes on the German war production, as he had done in the late summer of 1941, when he thought that the Russian war had been practically won. The catastrophe of the German army at Stalingrad forced him to admit that a total mobilization was called for. In the winter of 1942 Speer prevailed on Hitler to stop the building of *Autobahnen* as well as of party and government buildings by which the dictator wished to immortalize the Third Reich. Now Speer received orders for an all-out effort. The architect Speer was a genius at organization. Between early 1942 and the summer of 1944 he raised the output of German munitions more than two and a half times. Aircraft production increased from about 15,000 to 25,000 in 1943 and to 40,000 in 1944. The production of armor grew from a total of 6,000 in 1942 to 12,000 in 1943 and to 19,000 in 1944. The peak of German war production was reached by the middle of 1944 at the time of the Normandy invasion. Germany's output of munitions was at that time about 15 to 20 per cent higher than England's war production, but it seems it never reached the level of that of Russia, not to speak of America's war effort. Not even Speer was able to build up a total war economy. He could not overcome the resistance shown by other Nazi bosses, whose full cooperation he would have needed. Speer did exceedingly well, however, in improvising methods by which he raised the German military output. The climax of Germany's war production was achieved at a time when her military defeat was already ineluctable.

The first steps in rearmament had been made possible by Schacht's willingness to help finance the undertaking. But Schacht was a conservative financier. Moreover, although he wanted Germany to have an army to defend herself and to gain stature in world politics, he was averse to wars of conquest. Essentially he wanted a restoration of the German position as of 1914. He placed 12 billion marks in credit bills at Hitler's disposal but insisted that they should be redeemed by the government after five years. Hitler, however, refused to accept such a lien on the German budget after 1938, since it would have necessitated not only a strict limitation of German armaments but also an end to the lavish spending of the government on nonmilitary projects. Schacht's credit bills were only exchanged into government bonds. Thereafter public financing was done by deficit spending. The deposit and savings banks as well as the insurance companies had to invest their incoming monies in government loans. The total debt of the Reich, which had been 11.6 billion marks in 1932 and 47.3 billion in 1939, amounted at the end of the war to 387 billion marks, that is, 95 per cent of the financial wealth of the German people. Thus practically all fortunes and savings of the German people were used for Hitler's war.

∽ Economic Policy and Social Structure

THE ACTUAL economic policy of the Nazis showed little resemblance to their ideological teachings. With the exception of Hitler's refusal to mobilize women for factory work, his policy ran counter to the economic ideals of National Socialism, which considered the work and life of the peasant the ideal state of man and wanted to solve the vital problems of the German future by conquering land for agricultural settlement. The cities, on the other hand, were seen as the source of the degeneracy of the people. Among the urban population the artisans and the small independent businessmen were given preference over the big commercial establishments, such as department or chain stores. But Hitler knew that he could rearm only with big industry, a policy bound to give fresh momentum to the process of industrialization that had been going on for more than half a century. Between 1933 and 1939 the agricultural population of Germany within the boundaries of 1937 declined from 20.8 per cent to 18 per cent of the total population, and workers in agriculture and forestry decreased from 28.9 per cent to 26 per cent. At least 700,000 people migrated from the country to the cities. As a result, practically all the German cities added to their population. In central Germany, where the chemical industries were greatly expanded, cities like Magdeburg, Halle, Halberstadt, Dessau, Bitterfeld, and Bernburg more than doubled their populations between 1933 and 1938. The Nazi government raised and stabilized farm prices. Until 1935 farm income increased, but thereafter stagnated, while the national income continued to rise by 6 to 12 per cent annually. Farm income amounted to 8.7 per cent of the national income in 1933, but only 8.3 per cent in 1937. And in order to make a living the farmer, and particularly the small farmer, had to put in more and more hours of work.

In other sectors of the economy the typical results of the process of industrialization manifested themselves just as clearly. While employment in industry and the crafts remained constant at 41 per cent, it rose in services from 30 to 32 per cent. The proportion of white collar workers and civil servants rose from 18 to 20 per cent between 1933 and 1939, but the number of self-employed fell by 2 per cent from its proportion of 1933. The Nazis deprived labor of all the rights for which it had fought for more than half a century. It lost its right to organize, the right of collective bargaining as well as its freedom of movement and occupational choice. It is very likely, however, that for those whose first experience in economic life had been unemployment these rights meant less than actual employment. Although the Nazi government continued the wage freeze that the Brüning government had introduced, the workers' real income had reached the high level of 1928 by 1937, but this was true only with regard to gross wages and income. Considering the wage tax and the contributions to social insurance, the standard of living in 1937 remained under that of 1928. Wages and salaries amounted to 57 per cent of the national income in 1938 compared to 62 per cent in 1928.

Artisans, shopkeepers, and small businessmen, the social groups which had contributed most to the growth of the Nazi movement in the cities, did not fare well under the Nazi regime. In 1933 a good many measures were taken which seemed initial steps toward the fulfillment of Nazi promises to these groups. But, as mentioned before, the Nazi organizations of crafts and trade were subordinated to the labor front, and thereafter the artisans and small businessmen received few favors from the regime. The department and chain stores were hemmed in by various acts of legislation but continued to exist, although their business shrank. While some cooperatives were inactivated, the majority continued business under the auspices of the labor front. The armament orders went to the big companies, and when the labor shortage began, the squeeze was on small business, the repair trade, and the artisans. Many independent small businessmen were forced to close shop. Those remaining found for a while a certain advantage in lesser competition, but with fixed high prices and the low wages of the consumers their profit margin was cut.

The big industrialists did better. Their profits were large, although the government did much to limit them, particularly by raising taxes on high incomes. Their freedom had largely gone. Only as far as they obeyed the orders from the government could they hope to make money at all. Sardonically, Göring said that businessmen could now apply the free initiative, about which they talked so much, to the Four Years' Plan.

↶ Racist Policies

DELIBERATELY NO ATTEMPT was made to systematize the attitude of the Nazi party with regard to the state. The Weimar Constitution, though debilitated, was officially not superseded by a National Socialist constitution. Likewise, no definitive program of National Socialist economic policy was announced. In politics as in economics expediency proved the sole criterion, and therefore the way to the extension of Nazi controls and Nazi intervention was held open. In contrast, ideology ruled supreme in racist policies. Step by step the anti-Semitic program was realized and ever more exaggerated. The foul propaganda of the party now became the shrill language of the government. Goebbels compared the Jews with vermin that had to be annihilated. The anti–Semitic legislation began with the attempt to exclude Jews from certain occupations. The measures taken went very far and would have gone even further if Hindenburg had not demanded certain limitations. On the other hand, since these measures were still selective and restricted, they could find, if not the approval, at least the toleration of those Germans who were little affected by anti-Semitism. A new stage was reached with the so-called Nürnberg laws announced at the party convention in September 1935. The Reich Citizens Law deprived the Jews of the rights of citizens and declared them to be only subjects (*Staatsangehörige*). Everybody having three Jewish grandparents was to be considered a Jew, though subsequently the Nazi persecution was directed also at people with fewer Jewish ancestors. The Law for the Protection of German Blood and German Honor forbade marriages between Jews and citizens of German or related blood. Extra-marital intercourse between the two races was also forbidden and penalized. Jews were not allowed to employ German women under 45 years of age in their households. In a long list of subsequent orders these principles were made the basis for the full exclusion of Jews from practically all occupations. For a time, however, Jews were not excluded from business life. Schacht warned Hitler again and again not to upset the economic life, and Göring originally supported this position, but after Schacht's resignation the radical forces in the party gained the upper hand. In 1938, by a series of ordinances, the last remaining lines of business were closed to the Jews. They were excluded from the realty business and from attendance at the stock exchange. In April 1938 the government ordered the registration of Jewish commercial businesses and on October 5, 1938, the Jews had to register all their financial possessions that amounted to more than 5,000 marks. There seemed to be uncertainty about how ultimately to dispose of the Jews. At various times certain migration and colonial plans were under discussion. Heydrich, the chief of the secret state police, for a time tried forced deportation. In late October 1938 more than 17,000 Polish Jews who were living in Germany and had become stateless, because the Polish government had canceled their citizenship, were driven over the German-Polish frontier. Since the Polish government did not open the frontier, these helpless people vegetated for a good many days in no-man's land in pitiable condition. Among them were the parents of a young Jew, Herschel Grynspan (b. 1921), who decided as an act of vengeance to shoot the German ambassador in Paris but instead killed one of the secretaries of the embassy, Ernst von Rath (1909–38). For Goebbels this shooting in Paris on November 7, 1938, served as an excuse for moving the anti-Semitic propaganda into high gear. Accordingly, when the party and local leaders from all regions assembled on November 9 for the annual celebration of the *Putsch* of 1923, he urged that stern measures be taken against the Jews. He warned the leaders, however, that this action should not appear to be officially and centrally directed. The SA men were used, but they were ordered not to wear their uniforms. Goebbels apparently thought that by starting the violence against the Jews the SA men might provoke anti-Nazi sentiment among the population. Thus he could demonstrate the indignation of the "seething folk-soul." This was a miscalculation. The population did not join the SA men, and everybody knew at once that the wild acts of the night between November 9 and 10 were ordered and executed by the party. Jewish stores were demolished and robbed, as were the houses and apartments of Jewish families. Many Jews were manhandled, and dozens even murdered. Twenty thousand Jews were arrested and thrown into concentration camps. According to Heydrich's report to Göring 7,500 Jewish stores were demolished and around 250 synagogues were burned. Heydrich estimated that the broken windows alone had a value of 10 million marks. He judged the total damage to have gone into hundreds of millions of marks.

On November 12, 1938, the Jews were ordered to repair the damage of this *Reichskristallnacht* out of their own pockets, since the insurance claims were seized by the government. In addition, they had to pay a penalty of one billion marks. Subsequently all ministers issued additional punitive measures against the Jews. They were practically excluded now from each and every economic activity. No Jews were allowed as students in German schools or universities. They were refused admission to concerts, movies, and theatres. They were also ordered to avoid certain districts and not to appear at certain hours in public. Like a group of lepers, the Jews were excluded from the public, economic, and cultural life of Germany. There were over 500,000 people of Jewish religion in Germany in 1933, or about 0.8 per cent of the total population, about the same percentage as in France and England. With the annexation of Austria 185,000 more were added. Although many had left the country, there were still about 375,000 Jews in Germany in 1938. Many of those remaining would have found it difficult to reestablish themselves in a foreign country. A good many at least sent their children abroad. But it was pathetic to observe how many of them did not leave Germany because they did not consider it possible that Germans would launch pogroms. The deadly danger in which they lived was not realized by the majority of the Jews. Terrible threats could already be heard in the winter of 1938–39, the worst in Hitler's speech of January 30, 1939, when he said: "If the international finance Jewry inside and outside of Europe should succeed in plunging the nations again into a world war, the result will not be the bolshevization of the earth and thus the victory of Jewry but the annihilation of the Jewish race in Europe." It was Hitler, abetted by Goebbels, who two years later was to give the signal for the most monstrous crime committed in Western history, the murder of six million European Jews.

Anti-Semitism was an ideal instrument for achieving Hitler's goals. He used it as the chief means of inculcating in the Germans a consciousness of their master race and of endowing them with a brutal contempt for other races. At the same time anti-Semitism could serve certain temporary tactical purposes. The treatment of the Jews with regard to legal inequality, particularly in economic life, demonstrated the hostility of National Socialism toward liberalism and the realization of socialism. In the early years when, in contrast to his former bellicose propaganda, Hitler had to be cautious in international politics, the enemy at home who could be humbled and persecuted served as a substitute for the foreign enemy.

✍ Foreign Policy

IN *Mein Kampf* HITLER had clearly stated that the National Socialist movement aimed at creating a world power and that this would be done by the conquest of the necessary *Lebensraum* in Eastern Europe. To him this meant the acquisition of land for agricultural settlement that would make Germany independent of foreign trade as well as of land sufficient to make Germany militarily unassailable. He had condemned a mere policy of the revision of Versailles: "The demand for the restitution of the frontiers of the year 1914 is political nonsense of dimensions and consequences which make it appear a crime." He made it unmistakably clear that the land for the expansion of Germany would have to be taken forcibly from Russia and the Eastern European states. The fact that people of influence within and without Germany considered Hitler's statements on National Socialist foreign policy to be negligible campaign rhetoric and took him to be a mere nationalist revisionist was an amazing demonstration of how easily man is swayed by wishful thinking rather than by realistic observation. This was true in Germany as well as abroad. Revisionism was the program of all the German parties, including even the Communists, and one of the achievements of the Weimar Republic was that it undermined the moral validity of the peace settlement of 1919. In England and the United States a considerable number of people were convinced that Germany had been treated unjustly in 1919. Not even France was willing to defend the letter of the Treaty of Versailles.

Hitler's presumed revisionism was comforting insofar as it made it possible to think that war could be avoided. Moreover, peace was the deepest wish of both the English and the French people. The British were very conscious of the irretrievable losses that even a victorious war would cause. In addition the great economic crisis of 1931 had reminded them of the precariousness of their economic condition. Britain was not so strongly affected as other nations, and she made a relatively rapid recovery, but she was doubly anxious not to have political disturbances interfere with her restored balanced economy. France was hit by the economic crisis in 1933, later than all the other nations, and she never recovered her former relative prosperity before World War II. The great wave of industrialization which she had experienced after World War I had created grave social problems that now became incurable and left the Third Republic, which had been able to pass the test of strength successfully during World War I, in a serious internal crisis. Hitler later complained that the foreign countries had not credited him beforehand with the foreign policy that he had conducted, in spite of the fact that he had clearly announced his aims before 1933. Although the latter was true, he forgot that in the early years of his rule he had done his utmost to convince the foreign governments of the peaceful intentions of his foreign policy. To be sure, when on February 3, 1933, Hitler addressed the commanders of the German army, he told them that the true aim of German policy was to be the regaining of political power. For this reason, apart from the extermination of all antimilitary and pacifist thought among the people, Germany's rearmament would be the major objective. Once political power had been won, it could possibly be used for the acquisition of new possibilities for export "but and probably better for the conquest of new *Lebensraum* in the East and its ruthless Germanization." Thus the objectives which he had laid down in *Mein Kampf* were with him from the beginning of his rule. But he feared the intervention of France. As he said before the generals, "the most dangerous time is that of the building of the armed forces. Here it will be shown whether France has statesmen. If so, she will not give us time but will fall upon us, presumably together with her Eastern satellites." Yet in all his public statements he used a different language. He demanded equality for Germany and revisions of those provisions of the Versailles Treaty that had discriminated against her. And he found moving words to condemn war as a means to these ends. His most effective peace speech was the one he gave on May 17, 1933. By this time the popular reaction to the internal events in Germany, particularly the Jewish persecutions, had become so hostile that Hitler felt it necessary to assuage international public opinion. He most emphatically stressed his peaceful intentions and with regard to the disarmament negotiations which were carried on in Geneva declared that the German government was willing to accept any limitation of armaments on the condition that Germany be granted equality. He added that he would agree that the ultimate equality of armaments would be achieved within a transitional period of five years. Hitler was a big liar and a most dramatic actor. He always seemed completely sure of the truthfulness of his declarations, and since he had amazing auto-suggestive power, it is possible that at least temporarily he was convinced that he told the truth. But while he retreated he was already waiting for the moment when he could jump forward again. The French were not prepared to give up their military superiority over Germany at the moment when the Nazis came to power. They were well informed about the steps Germany had already taken to rearm and were understandably worried at the militant hordes of SA men. Therefore they were not willing to grant Germany unconditional equality. Hitler used this French attitude to withdraw from the League of Nations on October 14, 1933. He exploited the opportunity also for internal purposes. The *Reichstag* was dissolved, and new parliamentary elections together with a plebiscite on foreign policy were held. By this time the voters could vote only for or against a single list of candidates that the government had prepared. Over 95 per cent expressed themselves in favor of Hitler's foreign policy and the Nazi party.

✑ Pact with Poland

HITLER DELIBERATELY DODGED France's attempt to draw Germany into a collective security system by adding an East pact to the West pact of Locarno or, as the British wished, by supplementing it with an agreement on air attacks. Instead he insisted that peace would be furthered most successfully by bilateral arrangements. He surprised everybody by signing a pact with Poland in January 1934. The signatories promised to settle all problems between themselves and not to use force for composing their disputes. The pact was concluded for a ten-year period with the proviso that it would remain in force thereafter, although either signatory could then withdraw if he announced his intention six months beforehand. The pact made a profound impression abroad. It showed the power of the Nazi leader that he could dare to shelve the revision of Germany's eastern frontiers, the most ardently desired goal of German nationalism. At the same time Hitler's action seemed to demonstrate that he was earnestly concerned about the peace in Europe. On the other hand, the pact weakened the position of France. The Franco-Polish alliance was a mainstay of the French security system, although after Locarno Franco-Polish relations left much to be desired. France's feeble reaction to the rise of National Socialism persuaded Józef Pilsudski (1867–1935) to seek a direct understanding with Germany. Thus Hitler gained by showing off the fragility of the French security system. The understanding with Poland served him as a valuable protection of his eastern flank when he launched his actions against Austria and Czechoslovakia in 1938.

The Soviet Union was even more disturbed by the pact than France. Originally German-Soviet relations had not seemed too much affected by Hitler's rise to power. Hitler declared that the National Socialist movement did not exclude friendly relations between the two governments. The Soviet government on its part watched with equanimity the extermination of the Communist party in Germany. In the spring of 1933 the two governments renewed the Treaty of Berlin of 1926. In the fall of 1933 Hitler sent a man of pronounced Eastern orientation as ambassador to Russia. But the German officers in the Soviet Union had already been called back in the summer of 1933. Hitler's pact with Poland finally ended a decade of diplomatic understanding between Moscow and Berlin, and the Soviet Union began to improve her relations with the Western powers. In September 1934 she joined the League of Nations. On this basis she could negotiate with France, and on May 2, 1935, agreement was reached about the text of a mutual assistance pact between the Soviet Union and France, followed on May 15 by a pact with Czechoslovakia. Russia's guarantee of Czechoslovakia, however, was to become effective only if France actively came to Czechoslovakia's assistance.

✑ *Austrian Nazi Putsch*

IT WAS THE TIME of Germany's greatest diplomatic isolation. The events in Austria and the announcement of German rearmament contributed heavily to this situation. As everybody knew, the union with Austria (*Anschluss*) was the foremost aim of Hitler's policy, and he originally thought that it could be brought about by internal revolution. The change of government in Germany caused the National Socialist movement in Austria to grow, although, at least before 1938, it never reached the strength of the German party, of which the "land group Austria" was an integral section. The plucky Austrian chancellor, Engelbert Dollfuss (1892–1934), suspended the parliamentary constitution in March 1933 and established an authoritarian regime. In the first days of May the Austrian government forbade National Socialist uniforms and ordered a purge of the officialdom. On May 27 the German government made passport visas to Austria dependent on the payment of 1,000 marks, a step designed to wreck the Austrian tourist trade. In June 1933 the Austrian government banned the Nazi party altogether. The Western powers were alarmed by the terroristic activities of the Austrian Nazis, who obviously received financial support from Germany, as they enjoyed propagandistic assistance from radio Munich. Mussolini (1883–1945) particularly felt antagonized. He joined France and England in February 1934 in a joint declaration on the necessity of preserving Austrian independence and integrity. A month later Mussolini signed the Rome Protocols with Austria and Hungary, which envisaged closer economic relations among the three states as well as common general policies. On June 14–15 the first meeting between Hitler and Mussolini took place in Venice. But it did not lead to an alliance between National Socialist Germany and Fascist Italy, for which Hitler had pleaded in *Mein Kampf*. Mussolini, for whom Hitler felt unfeigned admiration, refused to change his policies with regard to Austria.

On July 25, 1933, the Austrian Nazis struck. They occupied the broadcasting station in Vienna and invaded the chancellery in order to capture the Austrian cabinet, but met and killed only Chancellor Dollfuss. Yet the

Putsch was not successful in Vienna, and after a few days of scattered fighting in Styria and Carinthia it was all over. The leaders of the Austrian Nazi party and a few thousands of their followers had to take refuge in Germany. Hitler denied all knowledge of the plot. He recalled the German minister, who had ostensibly sided with the Nazis, and in his place sent Franz von Papen, who had almost been killed on the day of the Röhm purge but as a conservative Catholic now seemed the right man to make at least temporary peace with the Austrians. The outcome of the Austrian Nazi *Putsch* showed that Hitler could not hope to win by crude revolutionary means. The appearance of Italian troops at the Brenner pass and the Carinthian frontier during the crisis was a grave warning.

The first visible success in the foreign policy of the Nazi regime proved to be the Saar plebiscite of January 13, 1935. It was to be expected that the vote in favor of France would be negligible. More surprising was the fact that the vote for the continuation of the League of Nations' regime was equally insignificant. In a free plebiscite the rather solidly Roman Catholic district voted with an overwhelming majority in favor of the return to Germany. In the eyes of the democratic countries the Nazi government was thereby considerably strengthened.

✍ Western Vacillation

HITLER WAS NOT SLOW in exploiting this advantage. On March 1, 1935, the British government presented a white book to Parliament in which it explained the need for strengthening British armaments in view of Germany's illegal rearmament, which was called a potential danger to peace. The Nazi press hurled horrified recriminations against this British policy. But since by now it had become neither possible nor desirable to keep Germany's rearmament secret any longer, the German government, on March 10, announced its intention of creating a German air force, which actually already existed. It was a trial balloon which was to test the reaction of the Western powers. When the announcement did not seem to arouse the French and British governments, Hitler, on March 16, 1935, proclaimed the revival of compulsory military service in Germany. With this "restoration of German sovereignty in military affairs" Germany unilaterally renounced some major provisions of the Versailles Treaty. The Nazis justified this breach with the failure of the Allies to disarm and the proof of the futility of the League of Nations as well as with the extended arming of other states, including the Soviet Union. Only wordy protests were the answer of the Western powers. The British note of protest already showed clear signs of vacillation. At the end it inquired whether the British foreign secretary, Sir John Simon (1873–1954), who only recently had been snubbed by Hitler, would now be received in

Germany. The visit of Sir John Simon, who was accompanied by Anthony Eden (b. 1897), took place in Berlin on March 25. Hitler refused to be drawn into any collective security arrangement and insisted on building a German army of thirty-six divisions, including one SS division, consisting of 550,000 men altogether. At a conference in Stresa in April, 1935, Britain, France, and Italy reaffirmed their search for collective security in Eastern Europe, an air pact in the West, the independence of Austria, and disarmament. They disapproved of the "method of one-sided cancellation." Britain and Italy reaffirmed all the obligations they had assumed as guarantors of the Locarno Treaty. The League of Nations Council, too, protested against Germany's unilateral action and even threatened sanctions in the case of further breaches of treaties. The League protest was answered by Hitler with a statement which questioned the right of the League Council "to make itself the judge of Germany." But the Stresa front made a deeper impression on Hitler, particularly since it was soon followed by the mutual assistance pacts of the Soviet Union with France and Czechoslovakia. Yet he knew how divided public opinion was in England and France and how strong the desire for peace. Thus on May 21, 1935, he delivered another "peace speech." He criticized the League of Nations and the mania of collective security and railed at the Soviet Union. He denied all German plans of conquest including the annexation of Austria. He offered to sign non-aggression pacts with all the neighbors of Germany and emphasized that she would keep all treaties as far as they had been signed voluntarily. Among these treaties he counted especially the Treaty of Locarno, although he hinted that it might be incompatible with the Franco-Soviet pact.

Hitler did not have to wait long to see the Stresa front completely break up. The British were dissatisfied with the French attitude. The Franco-Soviet Pact seemed to them to bring about the division of Europe into two hostile groups and thus to increase the danger of war. On the other hand, a policy of protestation did not appear to them the right means for limiting Hitler's progress. They thought it better to make concessions to Hitler but not to tolerate any transgression thereafter. Therefore they took up a suggestion that Hitler had made at the time of Sir John Simon's visit in Berlin, namely to hold Anglo-German talks on the limitation of naval armaments. These talks quickly led to an agreement on June 18, 1935. The treaty allowed Germany a navy as large as 35 per cent of the British navy, except that the Germans might build as many as 100 per cent of the number of submarines owned by the British Commonwealth. The conclusion of the naval agreement was an amazingly selfish and at the same time short-sighted act on the part of Britain. Without consulting France and Italy, Britain had declared the military provisions of the Versailles Treaty alterable and by her bilateral deal with Hitler expressed herself against collective action.

The Stresa front was endangered by other circumstances as well. From 1933 on Mussolini had set his eyes on the conquest of Ethiopia. Italo-Ethiopian conflicts had been before the League since early 1935. At the Stresa conference Ethiopia was not mentioned by any partner in order not to upset the formation of a common front against Germany. After a good many conversations with French and British statesmen Mussolini was convinced that due to the seriousness of the German problem neither France nor England would interfere with his peripheral ventures. But he erred with regard to England. Under the heavy pressure of public opinion the British government decided to accuse Italy of aggression and have the League vote in favor of sanctions. This policy was bound to alienate Italy, possibly even to drive her into the arms of Hitler. But the risk would have been tolerable, provided such sanctions had been chosen that would have forced Italy to give up the invasion of Ethiopia. But afraid of open hostilities the British government deliberately avoided having the League take drastic action, such as the cutting off of oil supplies. The Italians were not prevented from conquering Ethiopia, with the result that not only was Italy estranged from France and Britain but also the whole concept of collective security was shown up as futile. Thus Hitler had won a double triumph.

✍ Occupation of the Rhineland

AT FIRST the German dictator had displayed a neutral attitude toward the Ethiopian war. With satisfaction he watched Britain and France getting involved in Mediterranean problems. At the same time he could not fail to notice that Anglo-French relations remained cool. France followed the English lead only very reluctantly and as a consequence was exposed to much vituperation from the other side of the Channel. In this context Hitler was emboldened to take another decisive step toward reversing the military balance of Europe. In the morning of March 7, 1936, units of the German army marched into the Rhineland. Only three battalions, however, crossed the Rhine. It was a flagrant breach of articles 42 and 44 of the Versailles Treaty, which had been reconfirmed by articles 2 and 4 of the Locarno Treaty, and France could have answered the remilitarization of the Rhineland with the partial or full reoccupation of it. All German generals and diplomats had warned Hitler against this action, because they were afraid of the French response and knew that in view of the extremely weak state of the German army, which only a few months earlier had received its first conscripts, effective military resistance was impossible. Hitler had at least agreed that in case of a French military move the troops that had crossed the Rhine would be withdrawn again. But he stuck to his guess that the French would not march.

In order to soften the French and British reaction, Hitler surrounded the remilitarization of the Rhineland with simultaneous peace proposals and assurances. The French ambassador in Berlin, André François-Poncet (b. 1887), probably expressed the situation correctly by saying, "Hitler struck his adversary in the face and as he did so declared: 'I bring you proposals for peace!'" Hitler announced that the Franco-Soviet pact, which the French chamber had ratified eight days before, was incompatible with the Locarno Treaty, but that he was willing to conclude a new pact of nonaggression with France and Belgium for twenty-five years, including also an air pact, as desired by Britain. Demilitarized zones were to be created, this time on both sides of the Franco-Belgian-German frontier, in order to respect German equality. This would have meant even the dismantling of some of the Maginot fortifications. In the east Hitler offered to sign non-aggression pacts with Germany's neighbors analogous to the German-Polish pact of 1934. Once equality had been restored, he said, Germany was prepared to reenter the League of Nations, provided agreement had been reached on the colonial problem and the covenant had been separated from the peace treaties of 1919.

France at this moment had only a caretaker government and although the French ambassador had warned for months that the remilitarization of the Rhineland would be Hitler's answer to the ratification of the Franco-Soviet pact, no plans for this eventuality had been made in Paris. Afterwards the French government consulted with London. The prevailing popular sentiment in England was to condone Hitler's action, which could be called the removal of an unjust imposition on German national sovereignty. Many Englishmen even held France unduly quarrelsome. Without some definite promise of British support the French government felt unable to act, although it received assurances that France's Eastern allies were ready to cooperate. Instead, the French government appealed to the League of Nations Council, which expressed a legal and moral condemnation of Germany's action. But nothing else happened.

It was one of the great turning points in history, of higher significance than what occurred in Munich two years later. Implicitly France admitted that she was incapable of maintaining her Continental leadership through her own power. Moreover once Germany was enabled to fortify her western frontiers, France's eastern alliances were likely to become inoperative. None of these eastern allies, singly or together, was a match for Germany's renewed military power. If the German army managed to keep the French from breaking into Germany and thereby engaging her major force, France's eastern allies could be disposed of. Still, in 1936 France could easily have called Hitler's bluff. Although she would have received little assistance from England, the latter, as the guarantor of the Locarno Treaty, could not have objected to the French action. There was another untoward result of the French passivity. Hitler had acted against the strong advice of the generals and diplomats, and his intuition had been proved right. This gave a tremendous boost to his self-confidence and made him inclined in the future to listen even less to any professional advice. He could also take great satisfaction from the enthusiastic reaction of the German people, whom he called upon again to elect a new parliament.

✍ *Austrian Diplomacy*

WHILE THE OLYMPIC GAMES in Berlin during the summer of 1936 were lavishly arranged by Hitler and Goebbels so as to present to the world the picture of a peaceful Germany, the preparations for war went ahead at the same time. There was also considerable progress in the diplomatic field now. Mussolini, almost immediately drawn into the Spanish imbroglio after completing his conquest of Ethiopia, thought it desirable to soften his opposition to Germany on the Austrian question. Chancellor Kurt von Schuschnigg (b. 1897), Dollfuss' successor, felt compelled to sign an agreement with Germany on July 11, 1936, on the future relationship of Austria and Germany. The German government recognized the sovereignty of Austria and promised not to interfere in her internal affairs. Austria declared that her policy with regard to Germany would always be kept in line with the fact that she was a German state. More important than these general declarations were a number of supplemental secret articles; among them the most important was Austria's assurance that the internal Nazi opposition would receive representation in the government. Schuschnigg saw in this agreement a German promise to abstain from the annexation of Austria, while Hitler took it to mean the entering wedge for the internal "legal" revolution. The Austrian Nazis for their part welcomed the chance for renewed plans for a revolt. None of the interested partners was really satisfied with the agreement, and it was bound to lead to new trouble soon.

✍ *Spanish Civil War*

LESS THAN A WEEK LATER civil war broke out in Spain and created new opportunities for Hitler. The Spanish Civil War did not originate with Hitler, but at the beginning he gave Franco decisive help by transporting a major part of the Spanish troops from Morocco to Spain in planes. Subsequently he lent him measured support. Apart from various supplies and teams of military specialists he sent the Condor Air Legion, a force of 6,750 men. The Spanish war offered a chance to test German matériel and tactics. At the same time it served to supply Germany with costly strategic materials for her rearmament. The German contribution to Franco's cause was not designed to help the Spanish Nationalists win quickly; on the contrary, Hitler showed himself rather interested in seeing the Spanish troubles drag on. They kept Mussolini occupied, and Hitler obviously even hoped that the war might lead to open hostilities between France, England and Italy which would allow him to go on the prowl again.

✎ Anti-Comintern Treaty

ALMOST SIMULTANEOUSLY with the outbreak of the civil war in Spain elections in France had resulted in the formation of a popular front government under Léon Blum (1872–1950). The internal party conflict in France reached a fearful intensity. Voices were heard on the right: "Rather Hitler than Blum!" France was not in a condition to conduct an effective foreign policy supporting one or the other of the Spanish groups, although more than any other nation she was threatened with the formation of a third fascist state at her borders. She accepted the British proposal for establishing a nonintervention committee of the great powers in London, which became a sham to cover up the inactivity of England and France vis-à-vis the Spanish events. Even more than before, Hitler described his policies as directed toward the extermination of Jewish-Asiatic bolshevism, and he called the Third Empire that had been immunized against it the state that would save the heritage of European culture. On November 25, 1936, Germany signed the so-called Anti-Comintern Treaty with Japan. Hitler entered the Far Eastern field with some hesitation. Originally he had thought very little of the Japanese. But their military exploits in the war against China and most of all their anti-League policy had impressed him. Thus the Japanese became to him something like the Aryans of the Far East. The Anti-Comintern Treaty was far from being an alliance, although both signatories were probably not unhappy that others suspected it to be one. In its published part it contained a promise that the two partners would keep each other informed about the activities of the Communist International and would consult on necessary defense measures which they would execute in close cooperation. Third states would be invited to join this common defense. The secret supplementary agreement noted the community of interests between the Soviet Union and the Comintern and committed the signatories to neutrality in case of a conflict of one of them with the Soviet Union. Without mutual agreement the partners also would not conclude political treaties with the Soviet Union that did not agree with the spirit of the present treaty. Although undoubtedly the treaty had an anti-Russian purpose, it was at the same time intended to make an impression on England.

✑ Hitler and Britain

IN *Mein Kampf* Hitler had stated his belief that England was Germany's natural ally. He had criticized the naval rivalry and the struggle for overseas colonies prior to 1914 as grave mistakes of German policy. On the other hand he had stated that with the rise of France as the dominant Continental power England had failed to achieve her true war aims. While trying to keep Germany from the control of the European Continent England had helped to establish France in just that position. Hitler apparently shared the widely held opinion that throughout her history Britain had been against the strongest power on the Continent. Actually this interpretation of British foreign policy is not correct. Britain chose to oppose only those leading powers which she suspected of organizing the Continent for conflict with her. Thus, for example, she accepted without serious opposition the rise of the Bismarckian empire and Germany's predominance under the chancellor. And it was not England that split the Continent into two camps after 1890 but German diplomacy, which, by alienating Russia, brought on the Franco-Russian alliance. It is true that the British government was often unhappy about the French policy in the interwar period and even more that British popular opinion was willing to support the underdog. But it was naïve to believe that the British government would make an alliance with a new Napoleon. Britain could not tolerate France and the Lowlands coming under the shadow of a ruler who sought to control the whole Eurasian hinterland as well. Somehow the dream of German-British cooperation never quite left Hitler. The failure of the British to see their golden opportunity he was inclined to ascribe to Jewish or similar pernicious influences.

✑ Conduct of Diplomacy

HITLER FELT nothing but contempt for the professional diplomats. Since Baron von Neurath had been appointed by Hindenburg, Hitler did not interfere in the beginning much with the organization and normal operations of the German foreign office. Neurath had the reputation of being a strong man of firm opinions. Actually he had few ideas of his own and was too phlegmatic to put up a fight. Hitler sensed correctly, however, that many members of the German foreign service were opposed to his policy and might sabotage its execution. Therefore he preferred to bypass the foreign office and chose to make his foreign policy through Joachim von Ribbentrop (1893–1946). Ribbentrop, an officer's son, and himself an officer in World War I, had become a well-to-do wine merchant. He met Hitler only in 1932 but quickly proved his devotion to him in the behind-the-scenes maneuvers which led to Hitler's appointment as chancellor. The narrow-minded and ambitious Ribbentrop was as servile to Hitler as he was arrogant toward other people. In 1933 with the help of the Nazi party he established a bureau in the *Wilhelmstrasse* from which he began to dabble in foreign affairs. His first great success was the negotiation of the Anglo-German naval agreement of 1935, and this was followed by the Anti-Comintern pact of November 1936. To Ribbentrop's dismay Hitler did not make him foreign minister at once, but sent him as German ambassador to London to work toward an Anglo-German alliance. He soon learned that England would never be willing to support Hitler's grandiose schemes for conquering *Lebensraum* in the East. On the contrary he came to believe that England was Germany's most dangerous enemy and was only playing for time in order to build up her own armaments. He felt, however, that England would not go to war if there were regional changes in Central Europe, particularly if they were to be achieved with lightning speed. This appraisal of British policy as contained in Ribbentrop's last report of January 1938 affected Hitler's major decisions in 1938 and 1939.

In the spring of 1937 Neville Chamberlain (1869–1940) had become prime minister of England in the place of Stanley Baldwin (1867–1947). Chamberlain paid more attention to English arms than his predecessor had done. But he trusted that war could be avoided and Hitler "be appeased" if the Versailles peace settlement were revised by the fulfillment of those claims that Germany might justly raise on the basis of the principle of national self-determination. In November 1937 he sent Lord Halifax (1881–1959), an eminent member of the cabinet, to Germany. On November 19 Halifax met with Hitler in Berchtesgaden and discussed with him means for improving Anglo-German relations. He emphasized that Hitler had done great things not only for Germany but for Europe as well by the annihilation of communism in Germany. He clearly indicated that the Versailles Treaty would have to be revised, and he singled out questions on Danzig, Austria, and Czechoslovakia. He insisted, however, that all changes should be made peacefully. Hitler was not satisfied with these statements because they would not allow him the conquest of a wide *Lebensraum* in the East, which he believed could be achieved only through military action. On the other hand, he could feel rather encouraged since England was obviously prepared to tolerate a revision of Germany's eastern frontiers.

Two weeks earlier Hitler had called together the chiefs of the armed forces and the foreign minister. In a long speech he presented to them his program of foreign policy, which he wanted to have considered his testament in case he should die. His main thesis was again the need for the acquisition of land suitable for large-scale German settlements as well as sources of raw material. He said he was determined to use force to break any resistance to this expansion. The last date for the German attack in the East would be the years 1943–45 because only up to this time would Germany possess superiority in arms. Thereafter her arms might become outdated, and the others might catch up with her rearmament. In addition he himself and the party leaders would grow too old. His first goal was the annexation of Austria and Czechoslovakia. He stated his belief that Italy and France might come to blows over Mediterranean problems or France might be shaken by internal unrest, in which case Germany would have to fall upon Austria and Czechoslovakia as rapidly as possible.

A lively discussion followed Hitler's presentation. Both General von Blomberg and General von Fritsch raised strong objections to Hitler's assumptions. In their opinion France would still have superior power even if she were at war with Italy. The German fortifications in the Rhineland were still entirely inadequate to defeat a French thrust into it. On the other side Czechoslovakian fortifications were too strong to be overcome in a *Blitzkrieg*. Warfare against Czechoslovakia would be protracted and give the Western powers the opportunity to interfere. Yet Hitler remained unmoved by these arguments. He insisted that France would not fight without England, which would not go to war on account of Austria and Czechoslovakia.

✑ Hitler Takes over War Ministry

THE OBJECTIONS raised by the generals and also by Baron von Neurath obviously convinced Hitler that he needed complete control of the army and of German diplomacy if he was to realize the aims of his foreign policy. A chance for getting rid of Blomberg offered itself in early January 1938 when the minister of war and commander in chief of the armed forces had been married in the presence of Hitler and Göring to a lady of low social origin who in the opinion of the officer corps was hardly socially acceptable. Very soon after the wedding, Himmler and Göring discovered a police file which showed that the lady in question had once been registered as a prostitute. The officers now demanded Blomberg's resignation. Hitler, though willing to remove Blomberg, was not prepared to appoint a general who would insist on the relative autonomy of the armed forces. For this reason he did not wish to appoint General von Fritsch, the commander in chief of the army. Himmler and Göring produced at this moment another police record which seemed to reveal General von Fritsch as guilty of homosexuality. These were put-up accusations, which at a later date were shown beyond doubt to be without the slightest foundation.

But as long as there was a shadow over Fritsch, Hitler could get rid of the chief of the army as well. He did not appoint a successor to Blomberg but made himself commander in chief of the armed forces and appointed a new high command under General Wilhelm Keitel (1882–1946). This high command (OKW) became actually nothing but Hitler's personal military staff. As commander in chief of the army Hitler appointed General Walther von Brauchitsch (1891–1948). Brauchitsch, a highly competent officer, was a very sensitive man who found it a great strain to cooperate with Hitler. Moreover, he laid himself open to blackmail by Hitler by having the latter pay the indemnity that his first wife demanded for her consent to a divorce. Hitler's control of the army was now practically complete. At the same time he now replaced Neurath in the foreign office and made Ribbentrop foreign minister. Hjalmar Schacht had already left the ministry of economics, where now the submissive Walter Funk (b. 1890) took over. Thus Hitler excluded the last conservative elements from the government.

⌁ Annexation of Austria

HITLER LATER SAID that he had decided in January 1938 to achieve self-determination for the Austrians during the year "in one way or another," which implied that he was ready to use force or at least the threat of force if necessary. There is no reason to question his words, and the recall of Ambassador von Papen from Vienna looks like a preparatory step in this direction. But Papen still succeeded in persuading the Austrian chancellor to visit Hitler on February 12, 1938, at his mountain retreat. Schuschnigg did not get many words in. A ranting Hitler who had surrounded himself with some generals for the occasion browbeat him into accepting an agreement designed to deliver Austria into Hitler's hands. The Austrians had to promise to conduct their foreign policy in line with German policy. The two armies were to exchange officers, and the Austrian chief of staff, who was disliked by the Nazis, was to be replaced. Most important of all, however, the Nazi party in Austria was to be legalized, imprisoned Nazis were to be freed, and a general amnesty issued for Nazi crimes. Arthur Seyss-Inquart (1892–1946), a Nazi collaborator, was to be made minister of interior and thus would take charge of the internal security forces.

Hitler thought that he had set the stage for the nazification of Austria from the inside. In desperation, however, Schuschnigg suddenly announced on March 9, on four days' notice, the holding of a plebiscite for an independent Austria. The constitutionality of such a move was not beyond doubt. Only people from the age of twenty-four years on were to have a vote, whose secrecy appeared to be uncertain. Since not even all the Nazi sympathizers would have cherished the straight annexation of Austria by Germany, it was most likely that the plebiscite would produce a majority in favor of an independent Austria. On March 10, however, Hitler ordered the army to make preparations for an invasion of Austria. On the following day he informed Mussolini that he was forced to intervene in Austria because of the persecution of the pro-German Austrians and the threat of military cooperation between Austria and Czechoslovakia. This was a very typical Hitlerian lie since there was no military cooperation between Austria and Czechoslovakia whatsoever, and even if there had been, it would not have constituted a threat to big Germany.

On the same March 11 Hitler demanded the postponement of the plebiscite and the dismissal of the Austrian chancellor. Simultaneously the Austrian Nazis were incited to demonstrate against the Schuschnigg government. Schuschnigg announced his resignation in the evening of March 11. But the federal president, Wilhelm Miklas (1872–1956), refused to obey Hitler's command to appoint the minister of interior, Seyss-Inquart, as successor. According to the wishes of Berlin the latter was to request German troops to maintain order in Austria. Yet even Seyss-Inquart was not in favor of German military occupation, since after Schuschnigg's resignation the Austrian National Socialists were able to take over power quickly everywhere. But Hitler, strongly supported by Göring, wanted to have his triumphant military march into Austria. Seyss-Inquart's telegram was therefore dictated from Berlin.

In the early morning of March 12, 1938, German troops moved into Austria. The hastily prepared military operation did not become a model exercise. Many broken-down tanks lined the Austrian roads. But the German troops were received by the population with jubilation and were showered with flowers. Hitler arrived in triumph on the evening of March 12 in Linz. The following day he reached Vienna as the church bells rang and Nazi flags decorated the churches. On March 14 the law was promulgated that declared Austria to be a province of the German Reich. It was probably only the frenetic applause of the Austrian population that induced Hitler to proceed to the full annexation of Austria. Originally he seems to have thought of a looser connection between Germany and Austria. Now, however, he went the whole way, and Austria actually lost her identity and unity. The individual Austrian lands were annexed as *Reichsgaue,* and even the name Austria was suppressed and replaced by the label of East Mark of the German Reich.

Unquestionably in these days the overwhelming mass of Austrians embraced National Socialism out of positive enthusiasm or blind abandon, because the inner tension had been too strong over the years. The ugly side to these events unfortunately was not missing. On March 13 Himmler had already descended with his minions on Vienna, where seventy-six thousand arrests took place during the following weeks. The anti-Semitic excesses and crimes committed by the Austrian mob at Nazi instigation belong to the most heinous misdeeds of National Socialism. The return from Germany of the Austrian legionnaires, who recklessly exploited the opportunities which they gained as members of the ruling party, gave the Nazi regime in Austria a particularly hideous character and soon cooled Austrian sentiment.

This time Mussolini accepted what he thought he had grown incapable of opposing. But with a powerful Germany standing at the gates of the Balkans and only fifty miles from the Adriatic sea, Italy became at best a junior partner of the colossus of the north. England and France, and most sharply the Soviet Union, protested the annexation of Austria, but these were hollow gestures. To the satisfaction of the Germans the League of Nations Council was not even used any more to loose a verbal salvo against Germany.

The achievement of *grossdeutsch* unity raised Hitler to his greatest power. He ordered a plebiscite and the election of a new *grossdeutsch Reichstag*. It was officially reported that 99 per cent voted approval of Hitler's action and in Austria even 99.75 per cent. Publicly the Nazis described the annexation of Austria as the realization of German national self-determination. And the world was inclined to believe their declamations. In reality, however, Hitler looked at the accession of Austria chiefly in terms of the improvements in Germany's strategic position in Central Europe. To Hitler the possession of Austria and Czechoslovakia was necessary before the conquest of Eastern *Lebensraum* was to be launched.

✍ *Czechoslovakia*

WITH THE INCORPORATION OF AUSTRIA, Germany practically encircled the Czechoslovak state. During the days of crisis Hitler had been worried that the Czechs might intervene or at least, by the mobilization of their army, precipitate a major European conflict. Göring had assured the Prague government, when the German troops were about to march into Austria, that *Anschluss* would not affect good German-Czech relations. He gave the Czech minister his "word of honor" that Czechoslovakia would have nothing to fear from Germany. Strangely enough, President Beneš (1884–1948) seems to have been not unimpressed by these blandishments. Yet on April 21, 1938, General Keitel (1882–1946) received orders from Hitler to draft plans for invading Czechoslovakia. Four weeks earlier Konrad Henlein (1898–1945), the leader of the Nazi Sudeten Germans, had already been briefed by Hitler, Ribbentrop, and Hess. He was told to present the Czech government with demands which it could never meet and raise them if the Czechs should appear willing to fulfill them.

This time Hitler planned from the outset to use the army. Within a few days it was supposed to pierce the Czech fortifications and occupy all of Czechoslovakia. The European powers would be stunned and avoid intervening. Thus Hitler would make them respect the new might of Germany. In all probability he might have been stopped if England, France, and the Soviet Union together had declared their strong support of the integrity of Czechoslovakia. Russia proposed such cooperation immediately after the German annexation of Austria but was rebuffed. Russia appeared very weak after Stalin's army purges. Moreover, it was doubtful whether she would ever be able to come to the assistance of Czechoslovakia since neither Poland nor Rumania was likely to allow the passage of Russian troops through their territories. The burden of any war would have fallen on the Western European powers.

But Chamberlain did not wish to take the risk of war. At a conference of British and French ministers late in April the British declared that in the case of a German attack on Czechoslovakia the Western powers could not actively intervene in order to protect Czechoslovakia. France, which under the terms of the Franco-Czech alliance was obliged to come to the help of Czechoslovakia, originally resisted this British policy but soon did not find it too undignified to follow the British course. On the contrary as time went on the French increasingly begged the British to help them escape the embarrassing commitments of the Czech alliance. It was Chamberlain's policy to warn the Germans against the use of naked force but to indicate that the British government was in favor of far-reaching peaceful revisions of the Versailles settlements. The Czechs were told that they could not count on unconditional British support and were under pressure to reach a compromise with the Sudetens.

When about the middle of May the Czech government accused Germany of concentrating troops along the Czech border and on May 20 ordered a partial mobilization of the army, British and French diplomats in Berlin officially warned Hitler that German aggression might lead to a general war. France mentioned her commitments to her ally Czechoslovakia and the Russian obligation toward Czechoslovakia in the case of French intervention. The Germans at once indignantly denied any intentions of crossing the Czech frontiers, and though German troop movements had taken place there was no intention of invading Czechoslovakia at this moment. Hitler was furious when the international press described the events as a humiliation of the German dictator. On May 28 he declared before the leaders of the party and the armed forces that it was "his unchangeable decision . . . to smash Czechoslovakia to pieces"; two days later the army received orders to prepare a military operation to be undertaken after October 1, 1938.

Beginning in July the Nazi press began to work up wild hatred against the Czechs. The Czechs were accused of the reckless suppression of national self-determination. The Western powers conducted an ineffectual policy. While they continued to warn in Berlin against war, they visibly increased their pressure on the Czechs, driving them further and further toward making sweeping concessions. Many Englishmen were easily persuaded that the Czechs had inflicted grave injustices on the Sudetens. But although Czech nationalism after the founding of the state had been overbearing, considerable progress had been made in the cooperation of the Slav and German elements during the 1920's. In any event Hitler, who thought of the Czechs as a low race, was not likely to allow them national self-determination. On September 12, 1938, he made a speech before the Nazi party convention in Nürnberg in which he made the cause of the Sudetens his own and promised them the full support of Germany. He gave his hatred of the Czechoslovak state full rein and uttered foul calumnies against President Beneš. On the next day Henlein broke off the negotiations with the Czech government, and general revolt broke out in many parts of the Sudetenland. The uprisings were quickly put down by the Czechs, and Henlein and some thousand followers of his had to flee to Germany.

✑ *Chamberlain in Berchtesgaden*

CHAMBERLAIN NOW DECIDED to seek a solution by meeting the German dictator personally. In his first plane trip Neville Chamberlain flew on September 15 to Berchtesgaden. Hitler inveighed against the denial of national self-determination to the Sudetens and their sufferings under Czech oppression and threatened to intervene even at the risk of a world war. Chamberlain had to remind him that in these circumstances his visit was a mistake. But instead of supporting autonomy of the Sudetenland within the Czechoslovak state, Chamberlain, to Hitler's surprise, offered to cede the Sudeten territories to Germany. He promised to win the approval of his own cabinet and of the French and Czechoslovak governments. It did not prove difficult to make the British and French governments agree to the prime minister's proposal. Strong nerves, however, were needed to convince the Czech government that it would have to cede the Sudetenland, which contained a substantial part of Bohemian industry and the chain of Maginot-like fortifications protecting the whole state. In exchange the Czechs were promised an international guarantee of their new frontiers.

When Chamberlain flew again to Germany on September 22, Hitler met him at least half way in Godesberg. But as Chamberlain informed him of the French and Czech consent to the cession of the Sudetenland, Hitler told him coldly that this was no longer enough. He demanded now the immediate withdrawal of the Czechs from the Sudetenland and its immediate German military occupation. The exact frontiers could be drawn later, after a plebiscite was held. Chamberlain was profoundly shocked and resisted giving in to Hitler's demands. In the tense, and at times angry, conversation the two men held on the next day, Hitler made the concession that the occupation should not take place before October 1. Chamberlain declared his readiness to pass on Hitler's proposals to the Czech government but without specific British support. Hitler assured the British prime minister that the Czech problem was the last territorial demand which he had to make in Europe. Chamberlain reported to the House of Commons that Hitler made this remark "with great earnestness." This was again one of Hitler's conscious lies, for what he wanted to achieve was the complete destruction of Czechoslovakia. For this purpose he had in the meantime secured Polish and Hungarian assistance. Poland wanted to gain the district of Teschen while Hungary wanted to gain part of Slovakia.

The drift toward war seemed irresistible particularly after Hitler made a frenzied speech on September 26, crammed with the wildest exaggerations of the Sudeten situation and foul aspersions against Beneš. But he did not commit himself definitely to war. He knew that the leaders of the armed forces were against such a gamble. He was also not unconcerned with the military preparations that belatedly started in England and France. Hitler had also noticed with dismay that when a tank division rumbled through the center of Berlin people turned away from the sight. On the other side Chamberlain was still doing his utmost to stave off war. If it had come to war, the British and French would have begun it under the worst possible psychological conditions after having conceded beforehand the substance of what Hitler publicly demanded, thereby alienating the feelings of the Czech people. In addition the Western governments felt largely defenseless against the Nazi air force. Chamberlain finally appealed to Mussolini to arrange a conference which, while giving Hitler what he wanted, would safeguard orderly diplomatic procedures. On Mussolini's bidding, Hitler reluctantly gave in to this demand.

✍ *Munich Treaty*

THE CONFERENCE of the German and Italian dictators and the British and French prime ministers took place in the Brown House in Munich. It began in the early afternoon of September 29 and lasted into the early

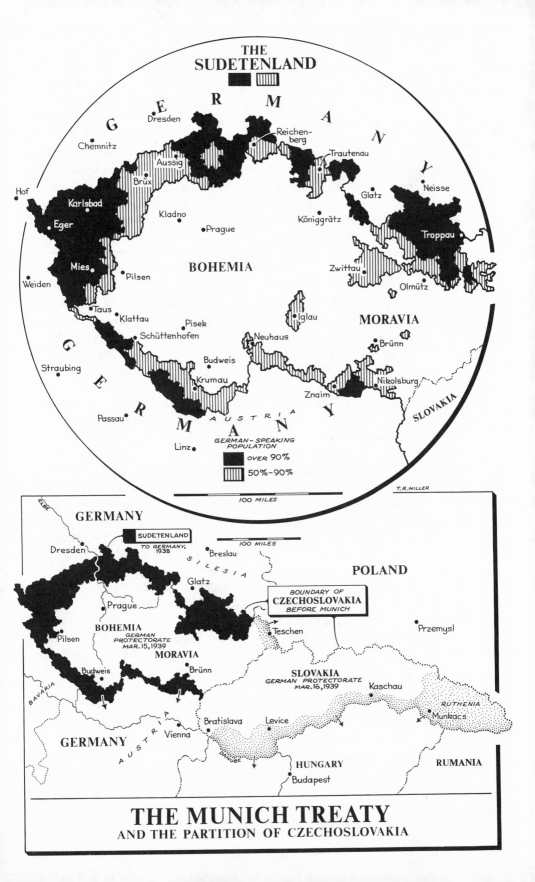

THE SUDETENLAND

GERMANY

Dresden
Chemnitz
Hof
Reichenberg
Trautenau
Glatz
Neisse
Aussig
Brüx
Karlsbad
Eger
Kladno
Königgrätz
Troppau
Prague
Mies
Pilsen
Zwittau
Olmütz
Weiden
BOHEMIA
Taus
Klattau
Pisek
Iglau
Neuhaus
Brünn
Straubing
Schüttenhofen
Budweis
MORAVIA
Krumau
Nikolsburg
Znaim
SLOVAKIA
Passau
AUSTRIA
Linz

GERMAN-SPEAKING POPULATION
■ OVER 90%
▥ 50%–90%

100 MILES

T. R. MILLER

GERMANY

ELBE
Dresden
SUDETENLAND
TO GERMANY, 1938
Breslau
100 MILES
SILESIA
POLAND
Glatz
Prague
BOUNDARY OF
CZECHOSLOVAKIA
BEFORE MUNICH
Pilsen
BOHEMIA
GERMAN PROTECTORATE MAR.15,1939
Teschen
Przemysl
MORAVIA
Budweis
Brünn
SLOVAKIA
GERMAN PROTECTORATE MAR.16,1939
Kaschau
RUTHENIA
BAVARIA
Munkacs
GERMANY
AUSTRIA
Vienna
Bratislava
Levice
DANUBE
HUNGARY
RUMANIA
Budapest

THE MUNICH TREATY
AND THE PARTITION OF CZECHOSLOVAKIA

morning hours of the next day. The British and French were defeated in their attempts to gain admission for the Czechs, and later it was left to them to inform the Czechs of the unhappy outcome of the conference. None of the statesmen present seemed to be bothered by the absence of the Soviet Union. The agreement reached did not make any significant changes in the memorandum that Hitler had presented in Godesberg. Moreover, some of the improvements the Western statesmen had been able to insert in the Munich Treaty were brazenly disregarded by Hitler in the actual execution of the treaty. Thus, for example, the plebiscite envisaged in the treaty was never held, and the Czech boundaries were finally drawn as much on strategic as on demographic grounds. Eight hundred thousand Czechs were living in the territories taken by the Germans whereas a quarter of a million Germans remained in rump Czechoslovakia, where they acted as a fifth column in the ultimate destruction of the Czech state. Nor did Czechoslovakia receive the international guarantees which were promised to her at Munich. On October 10 Czechoslovakia turned over the Teschen district to Poland. On November 2 Ribbentrop and Count Ciano, sitting in the Belvedere palace in Vienna, awarded Hungary sections of Slovakia.

Nazi Germany emerged from the Munich conference as the most powerful state in Europe. Hitler had forced England and France to cut Czechoslovakia into pieces, the state they had created in 1918 and with which France maintained a formal alliance. The British and French governments could not be in doubt that with the ruin of Czechoslovakia German influence would become predominant in all of southeastern Europe. The British government, at least, was fully aware of such a development but expected that after Hitler's declaration that the Sudetenland was his last territorial demand, the German dictator would proceed peacefully and confine German expansion in the foreseeable future to economic penetration. Chamberlain was impressed with the fact that Hitler had signed with him at Munich a common Anglo-German declaration which stated that the Munich Treaty and the Anglo-German naval agreement of 1935 were symbolic of the wish of the two nations "never again to war against each other" and to deal in the future with questions of common concern by "the method of consultation." But although the prime minister believed that he had laid the foundation "for peace in our time" he considered it necessary for Britain to be better armed if she was to maintain her influence for peace. A new arms bill was presented to Parliament which aroused Hitler's ire but was to prove of decisive importance in saving England in the fall of 1940.

∽ Plans of Conquest

HITLER'S REACTION to the British rearmament showed that he was already busy with thoughts of new conquest. It has often been said that Hitler's foreign policy up to the Munich conference was essentially sound as long as it aimed at the realization of national self-determination and that it went off the right path only after Munich, when it became naked imperialism. But this is an entirely unrealistic appraisal of Hitler. It leaves entirely out of consideration how his internal policies from the beginning had aimed at imbuing the Germans with a militaristic spirit that was to enable him to lead them into a war for world power. The inclusion of the Germans of Austria and the Sudetenland was important to him chiefly as a means of increasing the number of legions with which to conduct the final battle. The results of Munich left him deeply dissatisfied. He had wanted to smash Czechoslovakia in order to gain a strategic base for his Eastern conquest. But Chamberlain's and Mussolini's intervention had deprived him of his full prize. On October 21 the armed forces were ordered to prepare for the disposal of rump Czechoslovakia.

∽ Army's Reservations

HITLER WAS, of course, proud of his great victory. He had demonstrated again his genius as a great statesman and proved wrong all those who had warned him against the use of brazen tactics. The generals in particular had been proved again to be pusillanimous and incompetent. He did not know, however, that the generals had not only opposed him in their advice but had been ready to take action against him. In spite of Blomberg's and Reichenau's policy of coordinating the armed forces with National Socialism and in spite of the rearmament, the soldiers had not entirely lost their feeling of reserve with regard to Hitler and even more to the Hitler party. Although the *Luftwaffe*, being an entirely new branch of service built up and commanded by Göring, was a thoroughly nazified force, and the navy, always smarting under the accusation of having been the hotbed of revolution in World War I, was also obsequious, the army, and especially its higher ranks, held the strongest reservations about Hitler. Many officers soon recognized that the idealism of the Nazis was a mere pretense, Göring a pompous windbag, Goebbels an offensive guttersnipe, and the Franconian leader, Julius Streicher (1885–1946), a perverse sadist. For a good while the generals had comforted themselves with the thought that the Nazi revolution would calm down and that the unpleasant elements would then be taken under control. The blood-purge of the SA in June 1934 had particularly raised their hopes. But in place of the SA the SS had risen, and obviously the erosion of government by law continued at a fast pace. Moreover, the SS with its spying seemed to aim at the subordination of the army to the Nazi party. The much-praised old-Prussian virtues, selfless commitment to duty, honesty, and equity appeared endangered by Nazi immorality, and great efforts were made to uphold them. The Nazi attacks on Christian religion alarmed many officers, and no anti-Christian agitation was tolerated, although the army abstained from an open demonstration of its opposition to government policy. The army still wanted to be above party politics, and the chief exponent of this position was General von Fritsch as commander in chief of the army. But it was erroneous to assume that the officer corps could maintain its own ethics against the totalitarian demands of the Nazi regime. The conditions of the Weimar Republic under which General von Seeckt had made the army a state within the state no longer prevailed. The army had chosen to cooperate fully with the Nazi regime in 1933. It could not be expected that Hitler would let the generals mold the character of the army, which in his opinion his will alone had created. The introduction of universal conscription had steadily increased the influx of young Nazis not only into the rank and file of the army but also into the expanding officer corps. The removal of Blomberg and Fritsch in February 1938 was a clear indication of the loss of power that the army had suffered within the state.

The generals had accepted without open objections the murder of Generals von Schleicher and Bredow in June 1934 as well as Hitler's fantastic accusations against them. The infamous manner in which General von Fritsch was removed from his command led again to only a few ineffective protests. The feeling of solidarity among the generals without which decisive action against the regime was not possible was already greatly weakened. Moreover, the eager willingness with which General Keitel was prepared to become Hitler's yes-man in military affairs as well as General von Brauchitsch's easy agreement to serve in Fritsch's place, after accepting a financial gift from Hitler, showed that there were many high leaders of the army who could hardly claim to live up to the vaunted Prussian virtues. An officer beyond reproach, however, was Ludwig Beck (1880–1944), who had been chief of staff of the army since 1933. As such he was not, as in the monarchical age, the highest officer of the army. Since Seeckt had created the office of commander in chief of the army in 1920, the chief of staff could work only through the commander in chief. Beck, an outstanding military thinker, was a man of a fine humanist education, and his intellectual interests and knowledge went far beyond the military field. To many who met him, he seemed a scion of Scharnhorst and those officers of the Prussian reform period who made Pallas Athena their symbol as the goddess who combined education and wisdom with military valor. As a patriot Beck wanted a revision of the

Versailles Treaty and the restoration of Germany as one of the major powers of Europe. But, on the other hand, the domination of Germany over the other great powers of Europe appeared to him incompatible with European history and civilization. Beck had seen in the demise of the Weimar Republic an event that opened new possibilities for a rebirth of Germany as a nation. But his misgivings and apprehensions grew as he watched the moral destruction that the new regime caused. It is impossible to say when he began to realize that the only force left in Germany to stop the pernicious effects of the regime was the army. But it seemed to him contrary to all German military tradition to have the army make revolution. Only when Hitler, disregarding all responsible advice, expressed his intention of starting a war that was likely to end in a national catastrophe did Beck turn to the idea of open military resistance.

✍ Resistance from the Left

In spite of the destruction of party and trade union organizations there had been noticeable opposition to the regime by Social Democratic and Communist workers in the years 1933–35. Incidentally, even then in opposing the totalitarian regime Social Democrats and Communists usually acted separately. The cell formation, the distribution of propaganda, and the sabotage action had been enormously costly, and the Nazi government had easily suppressed revolutionary actions. After 1935 the left resistance fighters succeeded in building up a network of small cells over a major part of Germany, but they were held back by their leaders from open action. Oppositional action was somewhat easier for people with a higher social position. They could cover up their travels or some of their meetings as business and could receive warnings from their friends in government service. Effective opposition against a totalitarian regime that is firmly implanted is possible only in collaboration with people who have their hands at the crucial levers of the governmental apparatus. The most active and effective leader of resistance on this level was Carl Friedrich Goerdeler (1884–1945). This former mayor of Leipzig, who had been price commissar under Papen and for a year under Hitler, resigned from his post in protest against anti-Semitic actions of the Leipzig Nazis, and thereafter devoted himself to building up a front of resistance against Hitler. He was in contact with many former and current high officials. But he also established relations with a number of respected leaders of the Social Democratic party and the trade unions. He maintained connections too with the oppositional elements in the Christian churches. Goerdeler's links reached into the foreign office and equally into the army command. A number of diplomats were actively working against Hitler's foreign policy, which in their opinion could lead only to war. Among the military agencies it was the chief of counterintelligence in particular, Admiral Wilhelm Canaris (1887–1945), and one of his section chiefs, General Hans Oster (1888–1945), who kept the opposition informed and helped its members to get abroad. Yet the opposition could not hope to start a *coup d'état* without the army.

✍ General Ludwig Beck

GENERAL BECK'S DECISION on open military resistance was therefore of the highest significance. He was afraid that war against Czechoslovakia was bound to bring France and England into the conflict. Moreover, he did not share Hitler's opinion that the army could pierce the Czech fortifications and occupy Czechoslovakia in little time. In his opinion the Czech fortifications could hold the advance of the German army for weeks. Since the German West Wall was still in an early stage of construction and could be defended only with a handful of divisions, the French army would not find it difficult to invade Germany in great force. He found Germany lacking in resources for a war of relatively long duration and foresaw a greater military catastrophe than that of 1918.

Beck proposed to Brauchitsch that he inform Hitler that the generals would not be ready to execute his orders for war. A meeting of the commanding generals was held under Brauchitsch's chairmanship, and Beck's military analysis of the situation was approved by the vast majority. But Brauchitsch retreated from his support of a possible strike of the generals, and presented only the strategic memorandum to Hitler, who brushed it off the table. Beck resigned in the middle of August 1938, and Hitler accepted the resignation at once, but stipulated that it should be kept a secret till after the Czech crisis. After long hesitation Beck had become convinced that true patriotism demanded opposition to Hitler. As he told his officers: "The soldiers' obedience has a limit where their knowledge, their conscience, and their responsibility forbid the execution of an order. It is lack of greatness and of recognition of the task if a soldier in a highest position in times like these sees his duties and tasks only within the limited framework of his military assignments without becoming conscious of the highest responsibility to the whole people." Although Beck had felt that in his place he could become active in his opposition only when Hitler made military decisions, he was equally anxious to end the criminal activities of the Nazi regime within Germany. Although without power, Ludwig Beck remained the secret head of all future movements of opposition.

✐ Army Conspiracy

THE NEW CHIEF OF STAFF, General Franz Halder (b. 1884), shared Beck's views about the dangers of a war on Czechoslovakia. He decided to take the necessary steps to arrest Hitler at the moment when he should give the order for the military invasion of Czechoslovakia. The commander of the Berlin-Brandenburg military district, General Erwin von Witzleben (1881–1944), gladly gave him his full support. The Potsdam division under General Count Brockdorff-Ahlefeldt (1887–1943) provided the necessary troops. In Thuringia General Erich Hoepner (1886–1944) was ready with his armored division to block a possible march of Hitler's bodyguard SS division from Munich to Berlin. Through oppositional elements in the foreign office, which included the under-secretary of state, Ernst von Weizsäcker (1882–1951), the British foreign office was informed of the existence of an oppositional group of military and civilian leaders who were ready to overthrow the government if Hitler should go to war. The British were asked to make a strong demonstration of their determination not to tolerate Hitler's destruction of Czechoslovakia, in order to make it clear that a real danger of war existed. But Chamberlain and Halifax still believed that they could achieve peace with Hitler, behind whom, in their opinion, the overwhelming mass of the Germans stood. Chamberlain compared the men of the German opposition with the Jacobites in France in the days of William III. Chamberlain and Halifax had as little imagination as the German bourgeoisie in realizing what Hitler's aims were and what totalitarianism meant.

Halder and Witzleben, and possibly even Brauchitsch, who seems to have been won over at the last moment, were set to launch the operations in the morning of September 29, but when at noontime of September 28 the news arrived that Chamberlain and Daladier had accepted the invitation for a conference at Munich, the plans for action were given up. We do not know whether the coup would have been successful, although it was the best prepared plot ever planned against Hitler. The worst effect of its frustration was the fact that the participants felt thoroughly confounded. Again Hitler had triumphed, and his estimate of the unwillingness of the Western powers to stop him had proved right. That the Western powers might have fought if Hitler had gone to war against Czechoslovakia was now unimportant. Nobody could prove that he had really intended to go to war, and it rather seemed that he had used the threat of war only to gain by diplomacy the German districts of Czechoslovakia. Moreover, not even the generals could deny that the destruction of the Czechoslovak military power which was accomplished with the cession of the Sudetenland was desirable from the point of view of German national interest.

✍ Aftermath of Munich

FROM THE EVENTS OF MUNICH Hitler drew the conclusion that the Western statesmen were unlikely to oppose him, let alone make war on him, if he was going to realize his great design in the East. On December 6, 1938, the German and French foreign ministers signed a treaty in which the two powers promised each other good neighborly relations, the final recognition of the existing frontiers, and consultation on all questions of common interest. The implicit renunciation of a claim for the return of Alsace-Lorraine was to show the goodwill of Germany vis-à-vis its western neighbor. As a *quid pro quo*, Hitler obviously expected a complete *désinteressement* of France in Eastern Europe. But he was not overconfident in this respect, and simultaneous negotiations with Italy between the two general staffs discussed a common war against France.

In the month after Munich, Hitler was still undecided in which direction his next blow for achieving his ultimate aims was to fall. There was no question that he wanted to move soon. Great efforts were made to arouse the German people to a greater militaristic effort. On November 10, 1938, he made a speech before a few hundred German publishers and journalists in which he complained that he had been forced over the years to speak only about peace, because only this had made it possible for him to gain freedom and arms for Germany, but this propaganda for peace might have led to wrong ideas about the aims of his government. He felt that this "pacifist record" should not be played anymore. From now on the only possible way was "quite brutally and recklessly to say the truth." On the night before, the Nazi party had given the German people a demonstration of Nazi brutality in the Jewish pogroms, which we have mentioned before. But in these months he was obviously still considering various possibilities for his next move in foreign affairs.

✍ Negotiations with Poland

IN OCTOBER Ribbentrop started negotiations with the Poles, offering them a "total solution" of all pending questions. Poland was to agree to the return of Danzig and to the building of a German motor road and railroad through the corridor to East Prussia. The German government offered in return a guarantee of the Polish frontiers, a long-term non-aggression pact, and cooperation with regard to political and economic questions of mutual concern. The Germans also suggested that Poland should accede to the anti-Comintern pact. It seems that at this time Hitler thought of making Poland a partner in his Eastern conquest. This would not have excluded actual German domination of Poland. With Danzig in German hands and Poland serving as a military base for operations in the East, she would have become a mere satellite of Germany. But the Poles believed that they were able to defend their independence as long as they avoided an option for either the western or eastern big neighbor. They were convinced that the Soviet Union and Germany could not get together.

The Hitler government avoided all threats against Poland in these negotiations, which ran to the end of January 1939. Good relations with Poland were still profitable as long as the Czech question had not been settled.

✍ March to Prague

To THE SOLUTION OF THE PROBLEM of rump Czechoslovakia Hitler turned his full attention in February. The Slovaks were encouraged and finally pressed to declare their independence from Prague. Unprecedented in diplomatic history was the way Czech President Hácha (1872–1945) and his foreign minister were made by true gangster methods to turn over the government of their country to Hitler. It happened in the night of March 14–15 in the Berlin chancellery when the movement of the German troops had already begun. On March 16, 1939, Hitler proclaimed from the Hradschin in Prague the establishment of a German protectorate, Bohemia and Moravia. With the march to Prague, Hitler admitted that he was not truly interested in national self-determination. Moreover, it was clear that his declarations, like the one made the year before that the Sudetenland was the last territorial acquisition he would demand, were not to be trusted and that he would not hesitate to break treaties if it suited him. During the following week, full pressure was brought to bear on Lithuania, which was forced on March 22 to return the Memel district to Germany. Memel was an opening wedge driven into the Baltic region. Slovakia became a German satellite and had to accept German garrisons. Poland had every reason to fear this German encirclement, but the Polish government had the courage to refuse once more the German offers, which Ribbentrop had presented again on March 21, 1939. Almost immediately thereafter the German press began to play up reports on the mistreatment and persecution of Germans in Poland. Hitler's policy veered in a new direction.

✍ British Diplomacy

AFTER A FEW MOMENTS OF HESITATION even Chamberlain admitted that England had to take a strong stand if it was not to be confronted by a continent brought completely under Hitler's domination. He still clung to his hope for preserving peace, and political steps taken by British diplomacy were intended as acts of deterrence. Chamberlain as late as July 1939 tolerated conversations between British and German officials exploring the possibility of worldwide Anglo-German economic co-operation. The British instigators of these negotiations apparently thought that Hitler could be induced to keep the peace if he were given the means of transforming the German economy, so largely devoted to war purposes, to peaceful production. It was a complete misreading of Hitler's mind and mood. But the deterrents that the British government raised were not sufficiently massive to impress Hitler. It tried to build up an alliance for the defense of Poland and Rumania between the Western powers, the Soviet Union, and the Eastern European states. But these efforts proved of no avail, since Poland and also Rumania refused any cooperation with the Soviet Union. Thus on March 30 the Polish government received a British offer of guarantee, which was accepted at once, and on April 6 a bilateral Anglo-Polish agreement of mutual support was concluded. A week later Britain and France gave similar guarantees to Rumania and Greece, followed later by British and French promises of assistance to Turkey in the case of a Mediterranean conflict. Hitler took these guarantees as gestures rather than as actual threats, although the German press was ordered to inveigh against the British encirclement of Germany. But Rumania, by a far-reaching trade agreement with Germany in March 1939, had practically become dependent on Germany, and it seemed physically difficult for the Western powers to come to the rescue of the Eastern states in case of a war. In any event, Hitler was determined to call what he considered the British bluff. On April 3 the German armed forces received their orders to be ready for a war against Poland by September 1, 1939.

∽ German-Italian "Pact of Steel"

SINCE THE FALL OF 1938 negotiations had been carried on looking toward a military alliance with Japan and Italy. These negotiations were now intensified. But the Japanese proved wary partners and were unwilling at this moment to enter an understanding that was directed against the Western powers rather than the Soviet Union. Hitler and Ribbentrop had therefore to be satisfied with concluding a close alliance with Italy. In order to induce the Italians to sign a far-reaching military alliance, Hitler guaranteed the Brenner frontier and expressed his willingness to remove the Germans from South Tyrol. The signing of the "pact of steel" took place on May 22, 1939, in the Berlin chancellery. The pact envisioned the closest political and economic cooperation. While demanding consultation on all international problems, it placed the two signatories under an almost automatic obligation of mutual assistance in case of war. The provisions of the pact, concluded for a period of ten years, became operative at once. The pact was not, however, as ironclad as its name pretended. Mussolini had warned and continued to warn Hitler that Italy would not be ready for war before 1943. The fact that Hitler did not inform Mussolini during the summer of his immediate plans with regard to Poland gave Mussolini an excuse for not entering the war in September 1939.

Although Hitler assigned great value to the German-Italian alliance, he was still uncertain whether it was an adequate preparation for what was his next aim. In a talk he had these days with the leaders of the armed forces he pointed with pride to what had been achieved so far, but he also stated that no further bloodless territorial acquisitions could be made. With regard to the German-Polish conflict he said that Danzig was not the true objective. Now proper *Lebensraum* had to be won in order to ensure a basis for nutritional autarky. And the old Baltic problem should be tackled. He had decided to attack Poland at the first opportunity that offered itself, for it would always be a state cooperating with Germany's enemies and was a dubious barrier against Russia on account of its internal weakness. The decisive task was to isolate Poland. There should be no simultaneous struggle with the Western powers. But Hitler showed himself in doubt whether this could be avoided. He was also uncertain about the attitudes of Japan and Russia. A remark that it was quite possible that Russia would turn out to be indifferent to the destruction of Poland intimates that Hitler was already meditating on a direct approach to the Soviet Union. His appraisal of the military strength of the Western powers was quite unsettled. While at one moment he would consider a short decisive war possible, at another he would explain that a war between Germany and the democratic states of the West would be a life and death struggle that could last ten to fifteen years. England in his opinion was a tough and brave enemy. It was a Hitler burning for war but still pondering how big a risk he would take and no doubt trying to limit this risk.

Russia and the European Crisis

IT WAS OBVIOUS TO EVERYONE by now that the Soviet Union had acquired a position of crucial importance in the relations of the European powers. Without the Soviet Union, the Western powers could hardly hope to build up an adequate dam against Hitler's imminent drive against Poland. If on the other hand, Germany prevailed on Russia to tolerate the destruction of Poland, all European states east of the Rhine had to be written off by the Western powers, and France and England would face a more serious situation than in 1914. It was not surprising that Stalin would make the most of his tremendous bargaining position. The Russian rulers undoubtedly viewed the old noncommunist world with the greatest suspicion. But between 1934 and 1938 they had seen in the militaristic Nazi Germany a greater threat to Russian security and had been willing to cooperate with the Western powers in the maintenance of peace. The sacrifice of Czechoslovakia, "that far-off country" as Chamberlain had called it, and the exclusion of the Soviet Union from the Munich conference made the Western powers deeply suspect in Russian eyes. Whether the communist rulers really believed, as they asserted, that the Munich Treaty had been concluded in order to divert Hitler's expansionism toward the East cannot be settled on the basis of the available evidence. But unquestionably the actual result of Munich was to facilitate Eastern conquest by Hitler. In the speech before the Eighteenth Party Congress on March 10, 1939, Stalin expressed his disgust at the policy of the Western powers and gloated at the same time that the expected result of Munich, namely a German attack on the Soviet Union, had not materialized. He warned his audience "to be cautious and not to let our country [be] drawn into conflicts by war-mongers who are using other people to pull the chestnuts out of the fire for them." Molotov (b. 1890) echoed these words.

The Russians opened diplomatic conversations with France and England on a mutual assistance pact, while at the same time enticing the Germans into the opening of negotiations on a nonaggression pact. The Moscow rulers insisted that if they were to fight the Germans, their armies should be allowed to move westward beyond the frontiers of 1918. How far they intended to take advantage of the opportunity for a permanent revision of the boundary which had been imposed by the Peace of Brest-Litovsk is difficult to say. They laid themselves open, however, to the suspicion that they desired a reacquisition of their Baltic provinces at least. Neither France nor England could openly sell the Baltic states to Russia, though in a way they had virtually sold Czechoslovakia to Germany. But it was true that the cession of the Sudetenland to Germany had been up to a point a negotiated settlement concluded to stave off unilateral and warlike action by Hitler. With regard to Danzig and the corridor, the British too maintained to the end the attitude that revision of existing treaties should not be excluded. Yet for the Russians, the most immediate problem was to reach agreement on moving the Russian armies into Poland and Rumania in case of German aggression. Both countries refused to the last to give such permission. Without it, however, it was impossible to see how the states could be saved. This dilemma delayed and ultimately frustrated the negotiations between the Western powers and Russia, which were not conducted by the Western powers with great eagerness or shrewdness. This gave Hitler the opportunity for staging the greatest diplomatic coup of his career.

∽ Nazi-Soviet Pact

APPARENTLY A NEW REFUSAL by the Japanese in early August to enter into an anti-Soviet treaty arrangement with Germany and Italy convinced Hitler that if he wanted to immobilize the Soviet Union he would have to make a deal with the Soviet rulers. That the price would be exorbitant Hitler knew, and he authorized Ribbentrop to offer the Russians even more than they eventually demanded. But while the rulers of the Kremlin did not ask for the Turkish straits, they received more than the lion's share in the partition of Eastern Europe, which was contained in the secret supplementary protocol of the nonaggression pact. Finland, Esthonia, and Latvia came into the Russian sphere of interest. In addition, the Soviet Union was free to appropriate Bessarabia. Poland was to be divided along the Narew, Vistula, and San rivers. Hitler had empowered Ribbentrop to grant the Russians control even of the Turkish straits if need be, but the Russians remained silent on the issue. The lavish concessions which Hitler made to the Russians revealed his determination to reach agreement with the Soviet rulers under any conditions. He wanted to make sure that Poland would not receive assistance from the Soviet Union, and more than that he hoped that a pact with the Soviet Union would convince England and France of the hopelessness of supporting Poland. On August 22, while Ribbentrop was on his way to Moscow, Hitler talked to the senior commanders of the German armed forces. He told them that the pact with the Soviet Union was imminent and that the date of the attack on Poland would be the twenty-sixth of August. He explained to them why this was a good moment to start war. Now, he said, Germany possessed a leader behind whom the whole nation was standing, a leader of great political talent. It was better to have war come now while he was only fifty, for it was unforeseeable how long he might live, and he was irreplaceable. The same applied to Mussolini, while on the other side there were no great statesmen. Moreover, the Western powers were inadequately armed and lacked the will to fight. Tension in the Mediterranean and in the Far East was likely to preoccupy Britain. Because he could rely on receiving the necessary raw materials from the East, Germany need not be afraid of a blockade this time. Hitler admonished the soldiers to be pitiless and brutal in order to win for eighty million Germans what was due them.

∽ Outbreak of War

BUT HITLER WAS SURPRISED that the Nazi-Soviet pact of August 23 did not change the British and French attitude. At the last moment the beginning of the invasion of Poland was put off till September 1. The conclusion of an Anglo-Polish military alliance and Mussolini's message that the state of Italian armaments would not allow Italy to come to the active assistance of her ally before 1942 unless she received a tremendous amount of war matériel gave the German dictator pause for thought. He used the next few days for diplomatic maneuvering that was intended if not to keep England and France out of the war at least to place responsibility for the outbreak of the war on the other side. But on September 1 at dawn Hitler started his war. What began as a local war was soon to become a general European war and from 1941 on a global war, one that brought unspeakable misery to the world and was to leave Germany politically crippled and divided.

The Polish campaign was the last one to be designed and executed by the German generals. Hitler was merely a nervous onlooker, though he derived great satisfaction from the fact that he had made the building of the new army possible and created the political setting in which the German army could overwhelm Poland without interference from the outside. The success of the German *Blitzkrieg* emboldened him to believe that it would be possible to defeat the Western powers in the same way. He ordered the attack in the West for November 12. The generals were shocked by Hitler's intention to conduct the war during the winter, but they were chiefly appalled by Hitler's plan to attack at all. They realized that war against France and England was bound to become a struggle for the life or death of Germany, and they objected to taking the offensive while it was possible to stay on the defensive and thus to achieve eventually a compromise peace with the Western powers. The plans for an anti-Hitler coup were resumed largely by the same group that had been ready to act in September 1938. But after Hitler's diplomatic triumph at Munich and the military victory over Poland most generals were averse to opposing Hitler any further. Mutiny and treason seemed doubly damnable in wartime. There was, in addition, the feeling that they were honor-bound by their oath to Hitler. Jakob Burckhardt once called the feeling of honor an "enigmatic compound of conscience and selfishness," and this was no doubt true in the case of most of the generals of Hitler's army. General von Brauchitsch, the commander in chief of the army, in particular proved quite unable to reach clear personal decisions. The generals were eventually satisfied that by a number of accidental events the date of the Western offensive was delayed to the late spring of 1940.

✑ *Western Campaign*

THE PROCRASTINATION OF THE GENERALS with regard to the Western campaign drew Hitler more deeply into the planning of this offensive. The

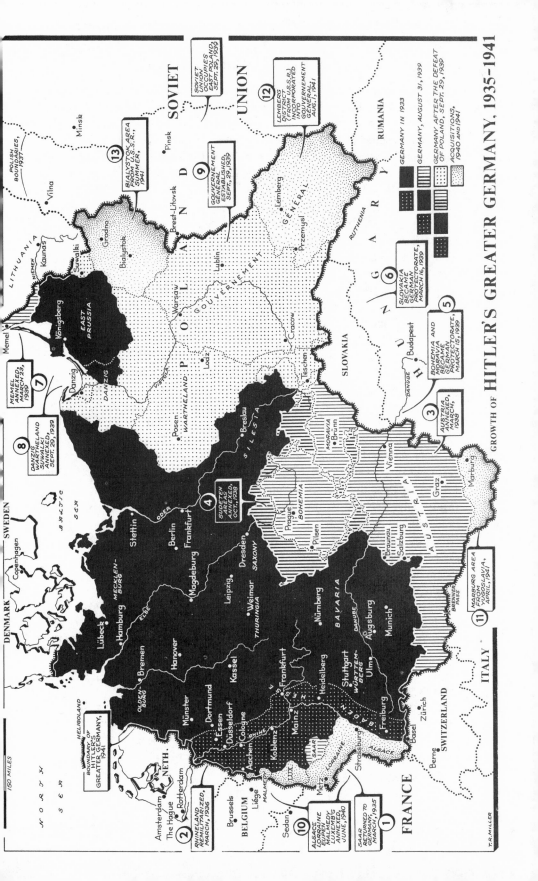

GROWTH OF **HITLER'S GREATER GERMANY, 1935–1941**

150 MILES

N O R T H

S E A

B A L T I C   S E A

SWEDEN

DENMARK
Copenhagen

Minsk

Vilna

LITHUANIA
Kaunas
Memel

NIEMEN

POLISH
BOUNDARIES,
1937

SOVIET

UNION

Pinsk

Grodno

Suwalki

Brest-Litovsk

Bialystok

Lublin

Lodz

Warsaw

Cracow

Lemberg

Przemysl

POLAND

GOUVERNEMENT

GENERAL

WARTHELAND

Posen

Breslau

SILESIA

Teschen

RUTHENIA

RUMANIA

H U N G A R Y

Budapest

SLOVAKIA

DANUBE

Vienna

AUSTRIA

Graz

Marburg

BRENNER
PASS

Salzburg

Braunau

Prague

Pilsen

BOHEMIA

Brünn

MORAVIA

ITALY

SWITZERLAND

Berne

Basel

Zurich

Strassburg

ALSACE

LORRAINE

Metz

Sedan

LUX.

MALMEDY

EUPEN

BELGIUM

Liège

Brussels

NETH.

Rotterdam

Amsterdam
The Hague

HELIGOLAND

Münster

Essen

Dortmund

Düsseldorf

Cologne

Aachen

Koblenz

SAAR

Mainz

RHINE

Frankfurt

Heidelberg

Freiburg

BADEN

Stuttgart

WÜRTTEM-
BERG

Ulm

Augsburg

Munich

BAVARIA

DANUBE

Nürnberg

Dresden

SAXONY

Leipzig

Weimar

THURINGIA

Kassel

Hanover

Magdeburg

Frankfurt

Berlin

Stettin

ODER

ELBE

Bremen

OLDEN-
BURG

Hamburg

Lübeck

MECKLEN-
BURG

Königsberg

EAST
PRUSSIA

Danzig

DANZIG

FRANCE

SAAR
RETURNED TO
GERMANY,
MARCH, 1935 ①

② RHINELAND
REMILITARIZED,
MARCH, 1936

③ AUSTRIA,
MARCH,
1938

④ SUDETEN
AREAS
ANNEXED,
OCT. 1938

⑤ BOHEMIA AND
MORAVIA
BECAME
GERMAN
PROTECTORATE,
MARCH 15, 1939

⑥ SLOVAKIA
BECAME
GERMAN
PROTECTORATE,
MARCH 16, 1939

⑦ MEMEL
ANNEXED,
MARCH 23,
1939

⑧ DANZIG,
WARTHELAND,
SUWALKI
ANNEXED,
SEPT. 29, 1939

⑨ GOUVERNEMENT
GENERAL ESTABLISHED,
SEPT. 29, 1939

⑩ ALSACE
LORRAINE
EUPEN
MALMEDY
LUXEMBG
ANNEXED,
JUNE, 1940

⑪ MARBURG AREA
FROM YUGOSLAVIA,
APRIL, 1941

⑫ LEMBERG
DISTRICT
(FROM U.S.S.R.)
INCORPORATED
INTO
GOUVERNEMENT
GENERAL,
AUG., 1941

⑬ BIALYSTOK AREA
(FROM U.S.S.R.),
SUMMER, 1941

SOVIET
UNION
OCCUPIES
EAST POLAND,
SEPT. 29, 1939

BOUNDARY OF
HITLER'S
GREATER GERMANY,
1941

GERMANY IN 1933

GERMANY, AUGUST 31, 1939

GERMANY AFTER THE DEFEAT
OF POLAND, SEPT. 29, 1939

ACQUISITIONS,
1940 AND 1941

T.R. MILLER

high command of the army wished to adopt a strategy roughly similar to that of the so-called Schlieffen Plan of August 1914. This plan, however, would have lacked the element of surprise. The meadows and canals of the Netherlands and the densely populated industrial area of Belgium would not have provided the greatest opportunity for the employment of tanks. The chief of staff of the central army group, General Erich von Manstein (b. 1887), presented another plan that proposed to use the mass of German motorized power to achieve a breakthrough in the Ardennes and race toward the sea at the Somme estuary. The project had its serious perils. The roads through southern Belgium were few and not ideal. The whole undertaking depended on the most precise preparation and organization. But the plan appealed to Hitler, and he ordered its adoption. It proved the key to the most shattering defeat of the French army. The German armored divisions reached Abbéville on the Somme on May 10 and, wheeling north, occupied Boulogne and Calais in the next few days. But then Hitler, against the advice of Brauchitsch and Halder, but with the assent of the army group commander, Rundstedt, issued the order that halted the armored divisions. Hitler worried about what he considered the exposed position of German armor and wanted to keep the armored divisions intact for the second phase of the battle of France. Moreover, Göring told him that his air force would be capable of disposing of the British army, which was cut off from the south and was coming under the pressure of the German troops which had rapidly occupied the Netherlands and Belgium. But the standstill of the German armor enabled the British to build up defense positions around Dunkirk. Helped by a calm sea, the British managed to remove between May 27 and June 4 three hundred and thirty-eight thousand British and French troops from the beaches of Dunkirk. Hitler's permission to have the German armored forces resume their advance on May 25 came too late. The second phase of the French campaign, which began on June 5, lasted only eleven days. Italy, anxious to participate in the spoils of victory, entered the war on June 10. On July 16 Marshal Pétain formed a new cabinet with Pierre Laval and sued for an armistice.

It was a supreme military victory. Hitler had already been active in planning the operation which preceded the Western offensive. In an extremely bold amphibious operation the Germans had occupied Denmark and Norway in April. But the great success of this risky undertaking was far outdone by the fantastic results of the battle of France, in which Hitler felt that his strategic genius had been the decisive element. From now on he confronted the generals with growing imperiousness till after December 1941 he became the absolute dictator of the army as well.

✧ England Continues War

GREAT AS THE VICTORIES in the West were, they proved inconclusive. Hitler was convinced that with the defeat of the British army and the German occupation of the Atlantic coast from the North cape to the Gulf of Biscay the British would be ready to admit the failure of their European policy. He felt sure that they would be prepared to conclude peace, particularly since he was not to demand from them anything but the return of the German colonies and a free hand for Germany on the Continent. The prospect that Hitler opened to the British was, however, less attractive than he made it out to be by emphasizing that he had no evil intentions against the British empire. Because Hitler could have exploited the resources of the Continent to the full, he could no longer be hindered from building up towering air and naval forces under whose shadow Britain could have led only a most precarious existence. The courageous determination of the British people, rallying around Winston Churchill, to continue the war saved not only the freedom of England but also the chance to rebuild a free civilization in the major part of Europe, including the major part of Germany. Hitler was baffled. Between 1933 and 1938 he had been able to detect the weaknesses of the British ruling classes, but he had no idea of the underlying moral strength which all classes of British society possessed and which in days recognized by all as a time of extreme national crisis produced an unshakable national fortitude.

Immediate plans for the conquest of England did not exist. When plans were drawn, it became clear that the German navy, being small and further weakened by losses suffered in the operations against Norway, would not be able to protect the crossing of what the army command considered the bare minimum of an effective landing force. In any event before landing operations could be undertaken, it was considered necessary to smash the coast defenses of England and to gain control of the air. On August 13, fifteen hundred German planes opened the attack on Britain. But in the following months they failed to subdue British air defenses. The pompous Göring might have done better if he had stuck to the bombing of air bases and port installations instead of trying in addition to destroy industries and break the morale of the civilian population by attacks on London and other cities. In addition, the German *Luftwaffe*, particularly on account of the limited range of its fighters, was not ideally fitted for its mission. Hitler had to recognize that the German air force was not able to create the conditions in which a seaborne invasion of England would be possible. There are signs that he was always somewhat skeptical about Operation Sea Lion, as the project of invasion was called, for he seems to have dropped the plan without a feeling of great disappointment.

Another project for the defeat of Britain that the German navy command championed never fully caught his imagination. The navy urged him to seize Gibraltar, capture North Africa, and open a drive against Suez. This would have excluded Britain from the Mediterranean and given control of the Middle East to Germany. It was a feasible project that would have produced far-reaching consequences. However, Hitler was not interested in North Africa or the Middle East. He negotiated with Franco over the conquest of Gibraltar, and he gave limited support to Mussolini for Italian expansion in North Africa. But to Hitler these were side issues. Through Gibraltar he wanted to lock the Mediterranean to British landings in North Africa and by sending Field Marshal Erwin Rommel (1891–1944) to North Africa he wanted to keep the southern flank of his Italian ally protected.

✍ *Operation Barbarossa*

HIS OWN IDEAS went in another direction. The war in the West had always appeared to him as preparatory to his ultimate design, the war against the Soviet Union. As early as July 1940 he had thought that the English might be left alone and that he should turn against the Russians. In his opinion the British had been decisively defeated, whether they were willing to admit it or not. For a while, however, he was not certain in his mind whether or not additional actions in the West were needed. But the idea of war against the Soviet Union steadily gained in his thinking. As the Operation Sea Lion had to be shelved and the drive against Suez and finally the idea of seizing Gibraltar became infeasible, Operation Barbarossa, the war against Russia, loomed ever larger. When Molotov visited Berlin on November 12–14, 1940, and it proved impossible to deflect the Russians from southeastern Europe and the Balkans toward expansion in the direction of the Persian gulf, Hitler made up his mind to attack Russia in May 1941. Military staffs had been working on war plans since the previous August, and Hitler was convinced that the German army was strong enough to crush Russia in a short war. Political preparations had also been made. Hungary and Rumania had been lined up as satellites of Germany, but there remained the problem of Bulgaria and Yugoslavia.

✍ *The Balkans*

THE BALKAN PROBLEMS had been annoyingly complicated by Italy's aggression on Greece, launched in the last week of October. Pride, jealousy, and pique had induced Mussolini to start this expansionist adventure, which went beyond the strength of Italy and from which he had finally to be saved by German intervention. British landings in Crete and in Greece endangered German war plans in the East, since the Rumanian oil fields came within the range of British bombers. Winning Yugoslavia over to the German side became crucial. Hitler succeeded in making Prince Regent Paul of Yugoslavia an ally, but shortly after, on March 26, a group of Yugoslav officers revolted against the Yugoslav government for taking sides with the Axis and staged a *coup d'état* in favor of the young king, Peter II. Hitler was furious and decided at once on the annihilation of the Yugoslav state. On April 6 German troops crossed the Yugoslav frontiers, while German bombers destroyed Belgrade with a loss of seventeen thousand civilians. At the same time, other troops started to push into Greece. The superiority of German numbers and arms forced the capitulation of the Yugoslav army on April 17 and the Greek army on April 23. In the last days of April all of the Balkan peninsula had been occupied, and a few days later the British were thrown out of Greece and Crete.

✎ *Invasion of Russia*

THE BRIEF BALKAN CAMPAIGN necessitated, however, a rescheduling of the offensive against Russia. Its beginning was now set for June 22, 1941, the same day on which Napoleon's *Grande Armée* had started its ill-fated march toward Moscow a hundred and twenty-nine years earlier. The loss of a full month for warfare in Russia was to prove a contributive cause of the failure of the Germans to capture Moscow. Later in the Russian campaign the German tanks which had been used in the Balkans showed the wear and tear to which they had been exposed. But Hitler disregarded such facts because he vastly underrated Russian military power. Discussing collaboration with the Japanese during the winter, he completely abstained from urging them to fight the Russians in Manchuria. On the contrary, he tried to persuade them to make war against Britain by taking Singapore. If Britain was not ready as yet to admit defeat, this was due, so he calculated, to a hope that either the United States or the Soviet Union might come to her ultimate rescue. Hitler did not think that the United States could effectively intervene to help Britain. Thus, the destruction of Russia would deprive Britain of her last hopes. Simultaneously, the breakdown of the Soviet Union would enable Japan to pin down the United States in the Pacific.

Thus, Hitler thought that the moment was ripe for the accomplishment of what should be the majestic legacy of his genius to the next thousand years of German history, the winning of the *Lebensraum* in the East with which that large Germanic empire could be created that was to rule over all of Europe and, through Europe, over the world. With his incredible gift for making himself believe whatever was useful to his self-interest, he convinced himself that Russia intended to attack Germany. No shadow of proof has been found to support this assertion. Stalin had been quick indeed to take possession of what the Nazi-Soviet agreements had surrendered to him. Within eight months the three Baltic states had disappeared, while Finland, owing to her brave army, survived but with the loss of territory and strategic bases. Rumania was forced to hand over Bessarabia and in addition the Bukovina, which latter had not figured in the Nazi-Soviet pact. But Germany had also not adhered quite strictly to the pact. She had, for example, secured the right of passage for troops through Finland in order to protect the vital iron ore resources in northern Sweden. And she had infiltrated very large military forces into Rumania. Russia, however, had been extremely generous in fulfilling German demands for the delivery of strategic material and to the last moment scrupulously executed these agreements. We may assume that Stalin was disappointed to see France defeated so quickly and completely instead of tying down a major part of Germany's military might in the West. On the other hand, this might have given him additional comfort for not having thrown in his lot with the Western powers in 1939. As a consequence he now looked at Hitler through rose-colored glasses. In spite of the very specific and precise warnings he received from both the British and American governments with regard to the imminent German invasion of the Soviet Union, Stalin trusted that Hitler would keep his pledges. Consequently, the Russian army was taken by surprise on June 22 when Hitler attacked along a front line over a thousand miles long.

Although it soon became clear that the Germans had underestimated the strength of the Russian army and the quality of its arms, the tremendous successes achieved by the German army in the early months of the war seemed to make this ominous fact negligible. Hitler, swollen by the glory of his victory over France, continuously and decisively interfered with the conduct of the war by the army high command. He wanted to conquer everything at once. In the beginning he placed the emphasis on capturing the Baltic region, which was to be capped with the occupation of Leningrad. The central army group was halted east of Smolensk to lend support to the northern group in its drive against Leningrad. But the Germans failed to take the city. Hunger was supposed to bring on the surrender of the city in due course, but in a heroic defense the people fought off all German and Finnish onslaughts till after thirty-two months they were freed. After the northern drive Hitler insisted, against the advice of the generals, on defeating the Russian armies in the Ukraine and taking possession of the riches there. The battles were extremely successful, but they came to an end only by late September. Not until then did the central drive against Moscow begin, which in the opinion of the generals was strategically decisive. But by then transport had become more difficult, and the winter had come earlier than usual. Only a few days after the advance had been resumed on October 2, General Guderian (1888–1954) noticed the first snowflakes. Since Hitler had been sure that the war would end before the winter, the army was not equipped with winter apparel. The troops suffered badly, and with the growing cold and snow progress became slower and threatened to stall. Some small groups got as far as the outskirts of Moscow and saw the flashes of the antiaircraft guns in the Kremlin. But they had to be pulled back. Right at this moment, the Russians, to the complete surprise of the Germans, started a counteroffensive of major proportions. The attack of December 6, 1941, made the German troops reel back, and in the chaotic conditions which prevailed during the next few days the German front was in danger of being ruptured. The danger was overcome, but Moscow was relieved, and the great turning point in the war had been reached. The years of easy conquest and *Blitzkrieg* were over. From now on the war was to become a long-drawn-out test, and Hitler's enemies had gained the time to mobilize their full war potential. Thus, the ultimate defeat of Germany could be foreseen.

ᕫ Japan Enters the War

ON THE DAY AFTER the Russians had opened their counteroffensive, Japanese planes descended on Pearl Harbor. Although Germany was committed to come to the assistance of Japan only in the case of aggression by a third power, Hitler decided at once to ally himself with Japan against the United States. So far, he had always aimed at giving the United States no pretext for entering the war and had even publicly disregarded the high-handed methods which the Roosevelt administration used in its dealings with Germany. On the other hand, Hitler may have felt that the United States with her massive assistance to England was already virtually at war. In any event, not possessing even an elementary knowledge of America, he did not anticipate that the United States would be able to stage a major intervention in the European war in addition to conducting war in the Pacific.

ᕫ Hitler Directs the War

THE MOST IMMEDIATE NEED, however, was to deal with the military crisis that had arisen at the Eastern front. Hitler solved it with his enormous willpower. Sensing that any withdrawal might lead to a rout, he ordered

500 MILES

ARCTIC

Reykjavik

ICELAND

HITLER'S GREAT GERMAN EMPIRE

HITLER'S
GREATER GERMANY
1941 AND 1942

ALLIED
WITH
GERMANY

OCCUPIED
BY
THE AXIS

DENMARK
AND NORWAY
OCCUPIED
APRIL, 1940

Narv

Namsos

Trondheim

Andalsnes

NORWAY

SWED

Oslo

Stavanger

Stockhol

NORTHERN
IRELAND

Edinburgh

NORTH

DENMARK

Göteborg

Copenhagen

EIRE

Dublin

Liverpool

Hull

SEA

BA

Coventry

London

NETH.

Rotterdam

Hamburg

Bremen

Berlin

Magdeburg

Po

Da

Plymouth

Dunkirk

BELG.

Essen

Cologne

GERMANY

Dresden

Breslau

Abbeville
Dieppe

Brest

Rouen

Sedan

LUX.

Frankfurt

Nürnberg

BOHEMIA

Rennes

Paris

Compiègne

Strassburg

MORAVIA

St. Nazaire

LOIRE

Tours

Orléans

FRANCE

Munich

Vienna

FRANCE
CAPITULATES
JUNE 26, 1940

SWITZ.

AUSTRIA

La
Coruña

Bordeaux

Vichy

Lyons

Milan

Verona

Agram

VICHY
FRANCE

Venice

CROATIA

Bilbao

Genoa

YU

PORTUGAL

Madrid

Marseilles

Toulon

Spezia

Florence

CORSICA
(V.FR.)

Rome

Monte
Cassino

Lisbon

SPAIN

Barcelona

Foggia

ITALY

Taranto

Valencia

BALEARIC IS.
(SP)

SARDINIA
(IT.)

Naples
Salerno

Seville

MED

Palermo

GIBRALTAR
(BR)

SP.
MOROCCO

Oran

Algiers

Bougie

Bône

Bizerte

SICILY

Casablanca

FRENCH
MOROCCO
(VICHY FR.)

ALGERIA
(VICHY FR.)

Tunis

TUNISIA
(VICHY FR.)

MALTA
(BR)

T.R. MILLER

NORTH CAPE

OCEAN

Petsamo

Murmansk

Luleå

Tornio

Archangel

FINLAND

LAKE
LADOGA

Vaasa

Turku

Viborg

Leningrad

Helsinki

Reval

ESTONIA

Novgorod

Jaroslavl

SOVIET

Kuibyshev

Riga

LATVIA

Rzhev

Moscow

Memel

LITHUANIA

Vitebsk

Smolensk

Kaunas

*BYELO-
RUSSIA*

KATYN

Tula

EAST
PRUSSIA

Vilna

Mogilev

Bryansk

Orel

Bialystok

Pinsk

Gomel

Kursk

Voronezh

Warsaw

Brest-Litovsk

UNION

Stalingrad

POLAND

Kiev

Kharkov

Cracow

Lemberg

RUSSIAN
FRONT
SPRING, 1944

UKRAINE

Astrakhan

*CASPIAN
SEA*

Kirov

Rostov

Elista

Budapest

Jassy

Odessa

Kerch

Maikop

Piatigorsk

HUNGARY

Kronstadt

CRIMEA

Grozny

RUMANIA

Sevastopol

Yalta

TRANSCAUСASIA

Belgrade

Bucharest

BLACK SEA

Batum

Tiflis

SERBIA

Nish

DANUBE

Varna

Sinop

Trabzon

Kars

MONTE-
NEGRO

BULGARIA

Sofia

IRAN

Skoplje

(TURK.)

Istanbul

ALBANIA

Salonika

Ankara

TURKEY

Mosul

GREECE

Larissa

Izmir

Athens

Adana

Aleppo

Antalya

SYRIA

IRAQ

CRETE

Candia

RHODES

CYPRUS
(BR.)

LEBANON

EUPHRATES

TIGRIS

THE AXIS
1939

FRIENDLY TO
THE AXIS
AUG. 23, 1939 TO
JUNE 22, 1941

DEC., 1941
FARTHEST
AXIS ADVANCE

NOV., 1942

VOLGA

DON

DNIEPER

DNIESTER

BESSARABIA

all troops to fight where they stood. The order was ruthlessly enforced. The German losses were heavy, but by the spring of 1942 the lines were not only standing but had been reinforced by replacements and new weapons. Heated arguments had flown between Hitler and his generals about the best way to meet the crisis. He considered the generals cowards, lacking in the National Socialist faith that made the impossible possible. Accepting Brauchitsch's resignation, he made himself commander in chief of the army on December 19. The direction of military operations, he declared, was an easy affair. What mattered was to instill in the army the National Socialist spirit. From then on, there were two German high commands. One was the high command of the army (OKH), which was in charge of the war in Russia, but not including Finland. There was in addition the high command of the armed forces (OKW) that had been created in 1938 and that was now declared responsible for all the other fronts.

Hitler was ill equipped for the role of warlord. He had never commanded even a small military unit. And he was quite unable to translate general strategic conceptions into concrete operational orders. He had read widely in military history, but the general conclusions he had drawn from it on the nature of modern war were rather commonplace. He had acquired a great knowledge of military technology and engineering, but information about ordnance and interest in technology are minor attributes of commandership. On the other hand, his ignorance of basic science and his dislike of intellectuals made him disregard the results that might derive from scientific research. The development of atomic energy for military purposes was thereby blocked. But Hitler had strategic ideas that were more than lucky hunches. He loved to plan operations which involved stealth and surprise like the Norwegian landings. He was willing to take great risks by adopting novel ideas like the Manstein plan for the operations in France. Moreover, he had a keener psychological sense than the generals when he decided in December 1941 on a policy of no retreat. He also saw the foreign policy implications of German strategy more clearly than the professionals. Hitler's strategy, however, could be a lien on the conduct of war if it led to ultimately hopeless ventures. A German army was left behind on the Crimea, because its withdrawal, Hitler argued, would affect the political attitude of Turkey adversely, and later on a whole army group cut off by the Russians was left in the Baltic in order to demonstrate to the Swedes that Germany had not lost control of the Baltic, but the ultimate loss of these troops probably was more damaging than a timely withdrawal would have been. It was his weakness that he was running the war as he had run the party, with an eye to the propagandistic effect. Closely connected with his propagandistic habits was his inability to face and appraise facts objectively. Wishful thinking made him underestimate the enemy's strength in general, while at the same time he felt that German inferiority in numbers or arms could be made up for by National Socialist fanaticism. But the fault did not lie with the German soldiers, who fought with the utmost bravery and skill in the Russian war. Hitler, however, distrusted the conservative officers, whose superior airs he suspected to be hostile to himself. He began to build up the armed SS. The SS divisions, of which there were ultimately thirty-nine, received the best people and the most modern weapons. He intended them to become the future active peacetime army of the Third Empire. Thus the idea of Röhm for which he had paid with his life was ultimately accepted by Hitler. But the SS divisions did not turn the tide of the war.

✑ The Turning Point of the Russian War

THE OPERATIONS PLANNED FOR 1942 again aimed at achieving too much at once. The drive toward the Volga, the jugular vein of Russia, would have been very promising if it had been supported by sufficient armor. But the motorized divisions were sent to the support of the army group that was to advance from Rostov to the Caucasus, where it was to capture the big oil fields to the south. Actually, the German troops reached the Caucasus, and the swastika flag was hoisted on its highest mountain, the Elrus. But the troops fell short of occupying the big oil fields to the south. Meanwhile the German sixth army under General Paulus (1890–1957) had reached Stalingrad, but in that city the Russians fought the invaders with desperate determination. Moreover, they managed to pierce the rather weakly defended flanks of the long wedge driven toward Stalingrad and to encircle the German sixth army in that city. There was a good chance that it might have broken out to the rear, but Hitler ordered the army to fight it out in Stalingrad. Göring, as usual, boasted that his air force would be able to keep the army provisioned. Meanwhile the German troops in the Caucasus, their lines of retreat threatened, had to be pulled out of that region in a hurry. After ghastly fighting in Stalingrad during the pitiless Russian winter, the starved remnants of an army of three hundred thousand men fell on January 30, 1943, into Russian captivity. The German army had thereby lost its capacity for launching major offensive operations.

Hitler tried once more on July 5, 1943, at Kursk to force a breakthrough in the Russian front. The best troops and the best weapons were brought together for this operation. But the Russians had received early warnings, and the last German reserves were used up in vain. After eight days the offensive had to be broken off because at the central front the Russians succeeded in cutting the German lines and taking Orel. From then on, the long retreat began that ended in the battle of Berlin in April

1945. Hitler was not able to pull any strategic surprises. His continuous orders to defend every position and every town and city proved immensely costly. His experiences as a private in World War I, when for years the armies had fought over every foot of ground, dominated his thinking. These experiences were quite inappropriate to the spacious Russian theater of war in which no continuous front line existed. Impervious to any advice, he did not listen to the generals who would have conducted a more flexible defense. They might have saved many lives, although none of them could have won the war.

✑ Allied Gains

BY 1942 THE ALLIES had already gained a major victory by overcoming the submarine danger. The Allied shipping losses were very serious in the beginning, but by the end of the year more ships were being built than the German submarines sank. After the end of 1942 Allied losses dropped sharply, and in 1943 the number of German submarines lost tripled. America was able, essentially unhindered, to transport food, raw materials, arms, and soldiers to Europe. The year 1942 had also brought the war to the German civilian population. At the end of March 1942 the Royal Air Force had begun its offensive against Germany. Lübeck, Rostock, Cologne, and Essen were the first German cities to suffer large-scale bombing attacks. In January 1943 the American air force began its daytime attacks on German cities with hundreds, and up to a thousand, planes. Since the German air force had been used from 1941 on largely in the Russian and African theaters of war, the fighter planes had to be brought back to Germany, but they proved unable to protect the air over the country. If Germany had concentrated on the production of fighter planes exclusively, the Allied air offensive might have been halted. But Hitler did not want to give up the simultaneous production of bombing planes, and because of Göring's bungling, a number of the fighter planes that were produced were badly constructed. The invention of the jet plane came too late to have a marked impact on the war in the air. Moreover, one of the most important results of Allied air warfare was that these attacks delayed the development and production of the new rocket weapons. When the Germans finally did begin to employ them against England, they caused, understandably, some apprehension. But because these so-called V-weapons could not be relied upon to reach their targets with any certainty, they were merely a great nuisance, and their use ended with the Allied occupation of the Atlantic coast of Europe.

The naval and aerial superiority of the Western powers enabled them to launch amphibious operations and finally to invade the European continent. The stage had been set for this by Allied landings in North Africa in November 1942. This North African campaign ended on May 13, 1943, with the surrender of a quarter of a million German and Italian troops. Then on July 10 the Anglo-American armies landed in Sicily, which they occupied within a week against ineffectual Italian resistance. The impending invasion of the Italian mainland led to the fall of Mussolini, and the government of Pietro Badoglio (1871–1956), which succeeded him, accepted an armistice. The Germans, however, still managed to hold the major part of the Italian peninsula, and they even made Mussolini the head of an Italian republic. But the Italian collapse forced them to bring additional troops to Italy and southeastern Europe, and the fall of Mussolini and his subsequent sad fate as Hitler's puppet strengthened the energies and hopes of the national resistance movements everywhere in Europe.

Hitler in Defeat

WHILE THE RUSSIANS CONTINUED to grind down the major part of the German army, the Allies launched their big invasion of the Continent on June 6, 1944. The success of the landing and the quick reconquest of all of France and Belgium spelled total disaster for the Nazi empire, and there are many signs that Hitler had been fully aware of the impending doom. As a matter of fact there are quite a few observers who believed that he had become conscious of the possibility of invasion as early as 1942, and it is at least probable that he had known of it since 1943. But he was not concerned with the future of the German people. As a completely self-centered megalomaniac he cared only about his own glory. Fighting to the last moment and dying on the ruins of Germany, he would leave a glowing memory as the greatest leader in German history, and he was active in the last months of his life building up such an image of himself. He asserted that he had never planned a war, that the war was the work of world Jewry and the politicians in its service. He had never intended to conduct a war against England and America, and the war against Russia had become necessary because Stalin had intended to strike. The war was lost by the generals, and treason had raised its head against the leader. He did not feel sorry, nor remorseful, about the losses he had caused Germany, let alone the countries beyond. He accused the Germans as having proved themselves weak. Therefore, he said, the future belongs to the stronger Eastern nation. Besides, the survivors of the war are of little value, for the good men have fallen. For this reason he wanted the fighting to go on to the bitter end and to adopt a scorched earth policy, irrespective of the future needs of the people.

But almost to the last week of his life there was some hope left in Hitler. As late as December 1944 he thought he would still have a chance to reverse the fortunes of war. The offensive in the Ardennes was a last desperate gamble on his part. The last German reserves were lost in this attempt, while the thinning of the Eastern front by the transfer of German troops to the West enabled the Russians in their January offensive to advance to the Oder and cut off East Prussia. Another wishful thought welling up in him was his expectation that the war alliance between the Soviet Union and the Western powers would rupture and that Germany would thereby gain a bargaining position. But whatever frictions existed in this wartime alliance, there was complete unity in the determination to annihilate Hitler and National Socialism. This goal was unalterable because the policy of the Allied governments was enthusiastically supported by the peoples.

Nazi Crimes

ALTHOUGH NOT EVEN OUTSIDE of the Axis countries was the full measure of the crimes of National Socialism known, sufficient information existed to make the Nazis appear as the most nefarious enemies of humanity and all humane feelings. The Nazi policies in the occupied countries of Western Europe were conducted with undue harshness, and when the resistance became active, the most barbarous reprisals were taken. The regular army adhered in general to the rules of international law, as it did in combat, and Field Marshal Rommel even managed to give the fighting in North Africa a chivalrous touch. But in Eastern Europe the situation was different from the outset. In the East, Hitler wanted to find the great *Lebensraum* in which millions of Germans were to be settled and many more millions to be raised. This meant the extermination of all national cultures by the extermination of their political and cultural leadership, the expulsion of many millions from their land and domicile to Siberia, and the killing of other millions by starvation or direct murder. The first drastic steps in this direction were taken in Poland after September 1939. Not only were the provinces of Western Prussia and Posen, which had been ceded in 1919, immediately annexed by the Third Empire but also a large section of Central Poland. From these territories, now named Gau Wartheland, many Poles were driven out, and Germans, chiefly from the Baltic region, were settled in them. The rest of Poland was placed under a Nazi governor of the so-called general-gouvernement Poland. Here every effort was made to begin the transformation of the Polish nation into a people of laboring helots. All higher schools and universities were closed, and many Polish professors and other leaders were killed. Hitler approved a directive written by Himmler for the Nazi governor which said that there should be no higher school than a four-grade primary school for the non-German population of the East. The goal of this primary school had to be merely, "simple arithmetic up to five hundred at the highest, writing of one's name, the inculcation of the doctrine that it was a divine commandment to obey the Germans and to be honest, diligent and good." Reading was not necessary.

The crimes committed by the SS in Poland in 1939–40 led to protests by the army chief, General von Blaskowitz (1883–1948), but were of no avail. With the invasion of Russia the plans to lay the basis for a future German empire in the East that was to reach to the Urals were pushed on a larger scale and with much greater intensity. Hitler called the war a struggle of ideologies and racial conflicts and admonished the generals that it had to be conducted with unprecedented mercilessness. But he did not believe that the conservative generals would free themselves of their obsolete moral concepts. He issued the order that all the political commissars captured with the Russian troops should be shot out of hand, an order that the army commanders largely sabotaged. Hitler excluded the army from the actual government of the conquered areas, turning it over instead to party bosses. A Reich ministry for the occupied Eastern areas was created under Alfred Rosenberg, but the ministry did not succeed in exercising effective control over the governors appointed by Hitler. They in turn were overridden by the operations of the SS, which were under the direct command of Himmler. There were still other agencies of the German government that exercised a direct influence on occupation policies. The chaotic conditions of the German government, however, did not improve the lot of the subjected people. In June 1942 Himmler officially approved the so-called "general plan East," which represented the thinking of Hitler as well. This plan envisaged the expulsion of 80 to 85 per cent of the Poles in the general-gouvernement, 65 per cent of the Ukrainians, 75 per cent of the White Russians, and 50 per cent of the Czechs. Those elements of the Slav population that showed Aryan influence were to be assimilated. A wide network of German settlements, connected by military roads and protected by the armed SS, was to be laid out first. Then, over the years the total area was to be covered by German villages and towns.

The war was a welcome opportunity to the Nazis to make at least a beginning with the depopulation of the Eastern regions. The occupied territories were recklessly exploited, and everything of possible use for the German war effort requisitioned, including food, even though this might cause famine. Of the five million prisoners of war, two million died in German captivity, while another million is unaccounted for. Under the influence of the military reverses of 1943 Hitler forbade further postwar planning. But the occupation policies went on unabated. The growing lack of manpower in Germany made the occupied countries sources of slave labor. Close to five million foreign workers were recruited, a little less than two million in Russia, more than three quarters of a million in Poland, just under three quarters of a million in France, and around a quarter of a million each in the Netherlands, Yugoslavia, and Italy. Fritz Sauckel (1894–1946), who was placed in charge of this slave traffic, admitted that at best two hundred thousand out of the five million foreign workers had come voluntarily. The pitiable victims, men, women, and children, were collected by force from their homes or from the streets and transported, mostly under horrible conditions, to Germany. There these foreign workers, particularly those placed in industrial jobs, were underfed, overworked, and lived under unhygienic conditions. Their mortality rate was very high. Toward the end of the war, however, when labor became ever scarcer, the Germans tried to take somewhat greater care of them. But in the winter of 1944–45 food shortages became general in Germany.

ᴐ The "Final Solution"

APPALLING AS THE BEASTLY crimes of the Nazis against the people in the occupied countries were, they were even outdone by the nefarious murder of European Jewry. It was the greatest mass killing in history, and the atrocious cruelty with which it was systematically executed will remain a horrible warning to what an abysmal state of depravity man may sink under the influence of blind beliefs and savage urges. The mass killings of Jews started after the end of the Polish campaign and were continued in the Ukraine after the German army had broken into southern Russia. Special task force units of the SS (*Einsatz Kommandos*) were driving together hundreds of Jews under horrible conditions and shooting them, but this process seemed too slow. In July 1941 Heydrich was commissioned to work out a plan for the "final solution" of the Jewish problem. It was Hitler's will to annihilate all of the Jews, and it was originally Goebbels more than Himmler who recommended to the dictator the most radical course of action, but the SS undertook to realize the plan. On January 1942 Heydrich held a conference in Wannsee, a suburb of Berlin, where agreement was reached on the final program. Moving from the West to the East, the Jews of Europe were first to be collected in ghettos and finally brought to death in extermination camps in Poland. As a new method of killing, extermination camps with gas ovens had already been built in 1941. The largest one of them was to become Auschwitz. Altogether six million Jews were murdered. They suffered death not because they had committed any crime but only because they were members of a group on which Hitler had decided to pin all the blame for the evils of this world.

There were signs that biological destruction might have found in the end much wider application. Even the master race itself might not have been fully excepted. In October 1939 a select group of Nazi doctors was permitted, or rather ordered, to put to death persons suffering incurable illness. It is remarkable that the questionnaire sent to the doctors covered not only health questions but also questions about race and actual working capacity. By the fall of 1941 about seventy thousand people had become victims of this so-called euthanasia program. The secret could not be kept, however, and many people were shocked. Bishop Wurm (1868–1953) of Württemberg and Bishop Count Galen (1878–1946) of Münster raised their voices publicly against the practice, and the operation was largely stopped thereafter. It is the only major case in which public indignation stopped Nazi practices.

⁓ Causes for Hitler's Rise

IF HITLER HAD WON the war that he had started in 1939 and expanded in 1940 and 1941, his victory would have brought the darkest fate to Europe and Russia. Even the conditions of the German people would have been unenviable. In April 1942 Hitler had the *Reichstag* pass a law that gave him the official authority to punish everyone, officer and soldier, government official and judge, party official, entrepreneur and worker, irrespective of existing legal regulations, for any neglect of his duty to the nation. Hitler acquired thereby the powers of an oriental despot. There is no doubt that he would have used them in victory as well. As we know from recorded dinner conversations at his headquarters, he would have continued the barrack state and fully extirpated the Christian and humanist traditions of German civilization. Only the defeat of Nazi Germany has made it possible for the Germans to recover their roots in their national past and renew the ties that over a millennium linked German culture with the rest of Europe. A good many sensitive Germans felt that the Nazi regime was like a military occupation of Germany by a foreign gangster group. There were indeed traits in the Nazi system quite foreign to anything Germany had seen before. Yet this is not to assert that Hitler's conquest of power in Germany was a fortuitous event. We may recall once more that the German bourgeoisie had never fought for or aspired to democratic government. The liberals of 1848–49 primarily wanted the abolition of feudal privilege, equality before the law, and, in general, government by law. But once granted these aims, they were willing to compromise on the authoritarian character of government. They felt that the national unification of Germany, which they desired, could only be established together with the existing state governments. It was true that the German liberals of the mid-nineteenth century wanted national unification not only because they wanted to see Germany influential among nations but also because they expected that the limitation of the power of the small states in Germany would have a liberalizing effect on German life. Yet this did not mean democracy, which the German liberals suspected of offering little support to the social position of the bourgeoisie itself. A true fight for a democratic order would have required that the liberals champion some of the basic social ideals of the lower classes also. This they proved unwilling to do.

Bismarck is always accused of having stymied the liberal development of Germany. This is true, but it should not be forgotten that German liberalism was a relatively willing victim. The majority of the liberals rejoiced in receiving German national unification from the military and authoritarian monarchy, as they gladly accepted the support of their economic interest by this government. The German industrialists were finally even ready, in exchange for the government support of their own economic interests, to approve the protection of the economic and political power of the surviving feudal class. Nationalism became the common denominator between the old ruling classes and the new domineering elements of German industrialization, with the latter proving to be the more dynamic force in transforming German nationalism into an aggressive imperialism. Colonialism and navalism found their strongest support in the leading groups of the new German industrialism. But even in that section of German liberalism that had refused to compromise with Bismarck, a substantial group felt that internal democratic reforms would have to go hand in hand with an activist foreign, and that meant imperialist, policy. During World War I the nationalism of the upper and middle classes reached its first climax under the leadership of the army. The achievement of world power had an attraction all of its own, but the social forces that dominated German nationalism in World War I at the same time saw in conquest a means of maintaining the existing political and social order of the Empire with its class privileges. The Allied victory, internal revolution, the specter of bolshevism, and the hope for a Wilsonian peace temporarily induced the German bourgeoisie in 1918–19 to adopt democracy and even to display some willingness to come to an understanding with the Social Democratic working class movement. Yet this was only a brief interlude. Since the Germans did not receive the easy peace they had hoped for and since it soon appeared possible to suppress communism without the Social Democrats, the German upper and middle classes went back to the defense of the old social order. With the stab-in-the-back theory the responsibility for Germany's defeat was shifted from the imperial regime to the Social Democrats, while Wilson was accused of having tricked Germany into surrender with his democratic promises. Nationalism thus reappeared, and in an even more dangerous form, since the external and internal enemies were more directly linked than in World War I. Over the years of the Weimar Republic German nationalism was not always equally radical, but the general pattern was always present. The Great Depression could not fail to heat up the nationalist passions to fever pitch. The old upper classes would probably have preferred an authoritarian regime in the hands of the army and the high bureaucracy, but it became clear that only a government with wide mass support could hope to defeat democracy. Preferably, it had to be a government that would pose as the representative of all social classes. This was the major reason why a Hitler government was accepted by the Germans in 1933.

But it would be one-sided to look at the rise and the subsequent support of the Nazi party exclusively in terms of social conflict. The actual decline of German education goes far to explain not only why so many Germans voted the Nazis into power but also why they were willing to condone so many of their subsequent crimes. German education hardly dealt with "the whole man"; it chiefly produced men proficient in special skills or special knowledge but lacking not only in the most primitive preparation for civic responsibility but also in a canon of absolute ethical commitments. Although the churches provided this for a good many people, and to a greater extent within the Roman Catholic Church than within the Protestant churches, the number of Germans who looked to the church for guidance was limited. The higher philosophy and the humanities of the period were largely formalistic or relativistic and did not produce a firm faith. In these circumstances it was inevitable that so many people fell for cheap and simple interpretations of life and history, as offered by the racists. To young people in particular this proved an irresistible temptation.

It has often and quite correctly been pointed out that never more than a good one third of the German voters voted for the Nazi party in free elections. But in some respects the fact should not be stressed too much. Although the true conservatives among the German nationalists kept strong reservations about the Nazis, many of the followers of Hugenberg had no strong objections to Nazi aims and considered the alliance between National Socialism and the German Nationalist party to be a happy amalgamation.

Moreover, nationalism had an appeal beyond the two parties of the right and served after January 30, 1933, as the strongest motive for conversion to the new regime. On the other hand, strong as nationalism and the contempt for democratic institutions were, many, and perhaps even most, of those who voted for Hitler in 1933 did not wish to see government by law buried. But little of this sentiment was clearly expressed, although in the beginning it might possibly have had a moderating influence on Nazi policy and at the very minimum acted as a temporary brake on the building up of the totalitarian system. It was shameful to see how easily even those who recognized the increasing subversion of law and justice comforted their own consciences. Many said that this was just the work of the party functionaries and that if Hitler knew what happened he would remedy the situation. Others just refused to take cognizance of the events. Still others argued that these excesses were the price to be paid for the renewal of a strong national state capable of giving its citizens a decent livelihood. The achievement of full employment, together with Hitler's successes in the international field, were the major reasons for the restraint of those who held, at least in the back of their minds, mental reservations about this or that aspect of Nazi policy or who even departed in one direction or another from the straight rules of Nazi conduct. Hitler's bloodless victories, the rearmament of Germany, the remilitarization of the Rhineland, the annexation of Austria and the Sudetenland were received with admiration for his political genius. There was no war enthusiasm among the German people when Hitler opened hostilities against Poland, but then the defeat of Poland as well as the subsequent triumph over France swelled the national pride. But even when the losses began to pile up after the battle of Moscow and the opening of the full air war on Germany, the great majority of the German people obeyed orders and fought on in dour determination.

✑ *Demand for Unconditional Surrender*

IT HAS OFTEN BEEN SAID that the declaration of unconditional surrender as an Allied war aim at the Casablanca Conference in 1943 was an important element in strengthening the fighting spirit of the German soldiers. It should not be forgotten, however, that this declaration was largely motivated by the wish to hold the Russo-Western alliance closely together. It was an assurance of the Western powers to Russia that, in spite of the delay in building up a second front in Western Europe immediately, the Western powers were resolved to fight with the Soviet Union to achieve the full annihilation of Nazism. With regard to Germany the insistence on unconditional surrender meant that there would not be as in 1918 a grant of principles that would allow future German rulers to say that Germany had been betrayed into ending the war. It signified in addition that the Allies would never deal with the Nazi government or with a government that came out of the Third Empire without democratic legitimation. Although it was realized that probably only a government led by the military could supersede Hitler, the military were regarded with supreme suspicion. In the eyes of the Allies the generals were largely to blame for the revival of German nationalism and the destruction of the Weimar Republic. Moreover, and understandably, no sharp distinction was drawn in the Allied countries between the Nazi party and the German armed forces. If the Nazis could carry out their crimes all over the Continent from the North Cape to the Mediterranean and from the Channel to the Baltic and the Black seas, this was due to the victories of the German army. Just the same, it is possible that if the revolt of July 1944 had led to the establishment of a government under General Beck, the Allies might have accepted it, like the Badoglio government in Italy working under Allied orders.

Whether the declaration of unconditional surrender made much difference in the German will to fight on is more than doubtful. What might have brought on a great shift would have been a declaration by the Western allies that they were willing to make peace with a non-Nazi government and were prepared to assist such a government in further resistance to the Soviet Union. But then revolution in Germany would have been very difficult, and such an offer might rather have given Hitler the chance of reaching a separate peace with Russia. The unintended publication of the Morgenthau Plan that proposed to wreck all heavy German industry also did not have as strong an effect on the will of the Germans to fight on as is usually asserted. By this time, the attempt on Hitler's life on July 20, 1944, had failed, and the internal terror had vastly increased. The Morgenthau Plan was exploited by Goebbels as a warning of what defeat would mean. But even in the official Nazi view a German victory would be possible only by employing the forthcoming new miracle weapons or by dividing the anti-German alliance. The Morgenthau Plan, however, was no indication of a split in the alliance. A more general sentiment kept most Germans fighting. The individual member of the armed forces or party was afraid that he would lose his last hold on organized life in the growing chaos if he placed himself outside the last remnants of order.

∽ Opposition to the Nazi Regime

OPPONENTS OF THE REGIME did exist. We have already heard about the continuation of resistance within the labor organizations and the opposition in the churches. There was, in addition, a large group of silent opponents. They liked to call themselves "internal emigrants," because they did not want to sacrifice their ideals to Nazism. This was not easy to avoid, and most of them were forced to make some compromises, particularly if they had to hold on to a job. On the other hand, incautious remarks often made them victims of Nazi persecution. The number of people executed on the basis of court judgments increased enormously in the Nazi period. It is safe to assume that this proliferation was due almost entirely to the high incidence of what the Nazis called political crimes.

But the number of opponents of the regime who were illegally killed was infinitely greater. Most of them were murdered in the concentration camps. About a million people had passed through these camps by the time war broke out. Many of the camp prisoners had been brought there because of their political activities prior to 1933, and many for racial reasons. But the institution of these camps was an indication of the acute apprehension felt by the Nazi leaders about the internal opposition, the more so since these leaders obviously felt that the cruelties and crimes committed in the camps would seem repulsive even to their own mass following. Thus they tried to silence all reports about what happened in these camps and made even greater efforts to suppress any information about the extermination camps. It is certainly true that many millions of Germans did not know what happened in the camps, although many of them could have learned about it easily enough if they had not assiduously tried to take no notice of the outrages of National Socialism. Greatly as the Germans were infected with anti-Semitism of various degrees, the mass extermination of the Jews would not have found support outside a very small minority. This does not free the Germans from their co-responsibility, since they tolerated and even backed earlier stringent anti-Semitic measures, which were then used by Hitler for perpetrating the final mass murder.

Apart from defeat in war, the overthrow of a modern totalitarian government can result either from struggles among the leaders of the ruling party or from action by the armed forces, provided they can count on some popular support once the government has been deposed. In 1938–39 the situation had been relatively propitious for such an attempt. Thereafter the victories in Poland and France made such action appear utterly foolhardy. But Carl Goerdeler continued his conspiratorial activities. Another center of Nazi opposition developed at Kreisau, the Silesian estate of Count von Moltke. A great-grandson of the military leader of the wars for German unification, Helmuth James von Moltke (1907–45), became the head of a circle of convinced anti-Nazis from all parties. Originally, the group devoted itself only to making plans for the constitution and organization of a Germany to follow Nazi defeat. It was an important step forward that these men from various political parties began to converse together, but the plans drafted were, though by no means reactionary, rather conservative. They underrated the importance of the mass factor in modern politics, but events might have rectified this weakness by themselves. The Kreisau group finally moved closer to active opposition. But the generals refused to cooperate with them. The only exception was Field Marshal Rommel, who was prepared to give his full support after the success of the Allied invasion in France, but he was wounded and thereby put out of action. General Ludwig Beck remained

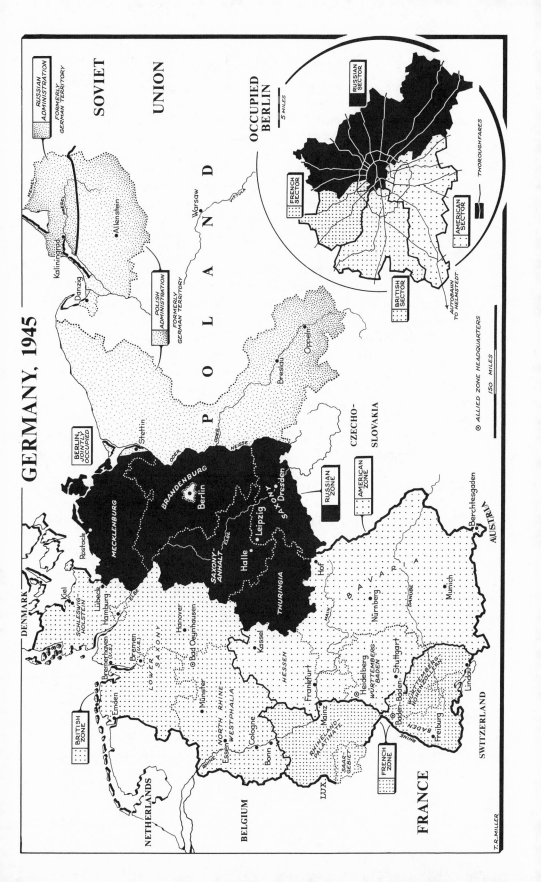

GERMANY, 1945

DENMARK

NETHERLANDS

BELGIUM

LUX.

FRANCE

SWITZERLAND

SOVIET UNION

POLAND

CZECHO-SLOVAKIA

AUSTRIA

BRITISH ZONE

FRENCH ZONE

RUSSIAN ZONE

AMERICAN ZONE

BERLIN JOINTLY OCCUPIED

POLISH ADMINISTRATION FORMERLY GERMAN TERRITORY

RUSSIAN ADMINISTRATION FORMERLY GERMAN TERRITORY

⊙ ALLIED ZONE HEADQUARTERS

150 MILES

OCCUPIED BERLIN

FRENCH SECTOR

BRITISH SECTOR

RUSSIAN SECTOR

AMERICAN SECTOR

THOROUGHFARES

AUTOBAHN TO HELMSTEDT

5 MILES

Kiel
Lübeck
Rostock
Stettin
Kaliningrad
Danzig
MEMEL
Allenstein
Warsaw
VISTULA
Breslau
Oppeln
ODER
NEISSE
Berlin
BRANDENBURG
MECKLENBURG
SAXONY-ANHALT
Halle
Leipzig
Dresden
SAXONY
THURINGIA
ELBE
ELBE
Hof
Nürnberg
Munich
Berchtesgaden
BAVARIA
DANUBE
MAIN
Stuttgart
WÜRTTEMBERG-BADEN
WÜRTTEMBERG-HOHENZOLLERN
BADEN
Baden-Baden
Freiburg
Lindau
RHINE
Heidelberg
Mainz
RHINELAND PALATINATE
SAAR GEBIET
Frankfurt
HESSEN
Kassel
Bonn
Cologne
Essen
NORTH RHINE-WESTPHALIA
RHINE (WESR)
Münster
Bad Oeynhausen ⊙
Hanover
LOWER SAXONY
Bremen
Bremerhaven
Emden
Hamburg
SCHLESWIG-HOLSTEIN

T.R.MILLER

the recognized leader of the opposition. But although General von Witz-leben was also willing to serve and General Oster and others were active in the cause, not all of them were holding an active command of troops.

Younger men brought new energy and ideas to the task. First among them was Count Claus Stauffenberg (1907–1944). This young colonel, a highly educated man who had been close to Stefan George, was a great patriot, and as such he had welcomed the formation of the Hitler gov-ernment in 1933. But at the same time he possessed a sensitive conscience and had soon passionately turned against Hitler. Stauffenberg, who had lost in North Africa his right hand, two fingers of his left one, and an eye, also had unbending courage. He came to believe that the only way to win over the army and the state officials was by assassinating Hitler. This would cut the tie with which the officers felt bound by their oath to him. Stauffenberg, who had occasional access to the conferences which Hitler held with his military staff, declared his readiness to plant a bomb that would kill Hitler and to assume direction of a *coup d'état* in Berlin thereafter. On July 20, 1944, this attempt was made but failed, owing to a number of unlucky incidents and mistakes. Hitler took a terrible ven-geance on all members of the opposition. The plot of July 20, 1944, has been rightly called the revolt of conscience. The men who participated in it were desirous of saving their country not only from further destruc-tion through the war but also from the annihilation of its moral fiber by a heinous regime. Many of them did not even fully care whether they would succeed in their action. They felt the point had been reached where it was necessary that some Germans should demonstrate by the sacrifice of their lives before the world and history that the sense of obligation to humane values had not perished in Germany. With their deed they laid a foundation stone for a new beginning of German history in a world totally changed by the events which Hitler had brought on.

Great were the sacrifices all the belligerents had to make after July 1944, although there could no longer be any doubt about the outcome of the war. But Hitler was incapable of admitting defeat until the last re-sources of Germany had been spent. If he had had his will, a scorched earth policy would have been adopted for all of Germany. The future of the German people was of no concern to him, and all he left was a last hoarse rallying cry to his shallow anti-Semitism. On April 30 he com-mitted suicide in his bunker under the ruins of the Reich Chancellery. To the German people his escape into death was announced as a heroic soldier's end.

When Hitler's one-thousand-year empire collapsed, he had reduced Germany to the geographic area she had occupied one thousand years before.

Index

The text of this book was set on the Linotype in Janson, a recutting made direct from type cast from matrices long thought to have been made by the Dutchman Anton Janson, who was a practicing type founder in Leipzig during the years 1668–87. However, it has been conclusively demonstrated that these types are actually the work of Nicholas Kis (1650–1702), a Hungarian, who most probably learned his trade from the master Dutch type founder Dirk Voskens. The type is an excellent example of the influential and sturdy Dutch types that prevailed in England up to the time William Caslon developed his own incomparable designs from these Dutch faces.